# MEKHILTA
## DE-RABBI SHIMON BAR YOḤAI

EDWARD E. ELSON CLASSIC

# MEKHILTA

## DE-RABBI SHIMON BAR YOHAI

Translated into English, with
Critical Introduction and Annotation

W. DAVID NELSON

2006 • 5767
The Jewish Publication Society
Philadelphia

Introductory material by W. David Nelson originally appeared in the *Encyclopaedia of Midrash. Vol. I: Biblical Interpretation in Formative Judaism,* edited by Jacob Neusner and Alan J. Avery Peck. Leiden: Brill Academic Publishers, 2005.

The Jewish Publication Society
2100 Arch Street
Philadelphia, PA 19103
www.jewishpub.org

Composition and design by Desperate Hours Productions, Philadelphia

Manufactured in the United States of America

06 07 08 09 10  11 12 13  10 9 8 7 6 5 4 3 2 1


Library of Congress Cataloging-in-Publication Data

Mekhilta de-Rabbi Simeon ben Yohai. English & Hebrew.
   Mekhilta de-Rabbi Shimon bar Yohai / translated into English with critical introduction and annotation [by] W. David Nelson.
   p. cm.
   Includes bibliographical references and index.
   ISBN 13: 978-0-8276-0799-6
   ISBN 10: 0-8276-0799-7
   1. Bible. O.T. Exodus–Commentaries.  I. Nelson, W. David. II. Title.

BM517.M45E5 2006
 296.1'4–dc22

                                2006043714

For my father and my mother, the truest blessing of them all:

ת״ר: שלשה שותפין הן באדם: הקב״ה, ואביו, ואמו

תלמוד בבלי, קידושין דף ל עמוד ב

Our rabbis taught: Three are partnered in the formation of a man—the Holy One, blessed be He, his father, and his mother.

Babylonian Talmud, Tractate Kiddushin 30b

# Contents

# Acknowledgments

This publication is not only the realization of my efforts, but also the result of the interest, dedication, and investment of many people. Given the range of resources and level of commitment required to produce a publication of this complexity, this project could not have come to fruition without such support. I will not be able to acknowledge by name everyone who contributed to this publication, so I begin by expressing my deep indebtedness and gratitude for the assistance of so many, whose care and concern was a wellspring from which I drew the strength and sustenance necessary to complete this endeavor.

Over a period of many years, I have benefited from the expertise, energy, and mentoring of teachers who embody the best ideals of the professional guild I have recently joined. This project has been particularly shaped by the contributions of three such individuals. Professor Martin S. Jaffee generously volunteered his intellectual interest, effort and time to this project, particularly at its earliest stage of development. For this I am deeply grateful, as well as for his willingness to shape and influence my professional development in many ways over a span of more than twenty years. Over the past three years, Professor Avigdor Shinan lent his critical eye, vast knowledge, and keen advice to this project. In addition to his scholarly assistance, I have benefited from his joyful countenance, generosity of spirit, and love of learning—a greater model of supportive mentoring and positive collegiality cannot be found.

Finally, to my mentor, Professor Richard Sarason I express the appreciation of a student, the admiration of a colleague, and the emotion of a friend. This project has been influenced by his intellect, wisdom, and exhaustive efforts in ways simply too numerous to delineate. The work of a mentor is never complete; the gratitude of a student has no limits. All should have the fortune to be blessed with a teacher such as he.

I thank the Yad Hanadiv/Beracha Foundation for granting me a Visiting Research Fellowship in Jewish Studies at The Hebrew University in Jerusalem for the 2004–2005 academic year. Under the sponsorship of this generous fellowship, I was afforded the opportunity to devote a year of uninterrupted attention to this publication in an unparalleled scholarly environment dedicated to the study of Judaism. I extend appreciation to Brite Divinity School and Texas Christian University for granting me both a semester research leave and a semester leave of absence, which facilitated my ability to accept this fellowship opportunity.

I have had the good fortune of working with The Jewish Publication Society on this project. I know of no other publisher in the United States devoted to Jewish scholarship that can marshal the resources required for a publication such as this, and I am honored that JPS designated this book to be the initial publication in its new Elson Classics Series. I thank Dr. Ellen Frankel for her steadfast devotion to this project, and to both Carol Hupping and Janet Liss for their extensive production expertise and assistance. I also extend my deep appreciation to Michele Alperin for the tremendous skill, keen eye, and meticulous concern she brought to this publication as its primary proofreader.

Finally, words cannot express my gratitude for the love, encouragement, and support I have received from the members of my family over the many years of work I have devoted to this endeavor. My reverence for the past, passion for the present, and hope for the future stems from all they have brought into the world. They are the truest blessing of them all.

W. David Nelson
Fort Worth, Texas
29 Chesvan 5766

# Introduction

The *Mekhilta de-Rabbi Shimon b. Yoḥai*[1] is an anthology of early Rabbinic traditions of interpretation (midrash) of the biblical Book of Exodus. The majority of the traditions it preserves were created during the tannaitic period of early Rabbinic Judaism (approximately 70–200 C.E.), although a portion of its material dates to the beginning of the subsequent amoraic period (approximately 200–500 C.E.). The date of editorial redaction of these traditions into anthological form is uncertain; however, the scholarly consensus is that the text was edited sometime during the amoraic period. The interpretive materials are editorially organized as a running commentary on the biblical Book of Exodus, but the entirety of the Book of Exodus is not commented upon in the manuscript traditions of the text that have been identified to date.

The origin of the name of the text is uncertain and of unknown provenance. Classical Rabbinic sources from antiquity do not allude to the text either by name or as an independent entity. Its authorship, and thus its title, is attributed erroneously to Rabbi Shimon b. Yoḥai, a second-century C.E. disciple of Rabbi Akiva. This association is most likely due to the fact that the text begins with a quotation in his name. In addition to its current name, the text is referred to in medieval Jewish sources as the *Mekhilta de-Rabbi Akiva, Sifre d'Vei Rav,* and *Mekhilta d'Sanya* (Mekhilta of the Burning Bush[2]).

The *Mekhilta de-Rabbi Shimon b. Yoḥai* belongs to the corpus of Rabbinic texts routinely designated as either the halakhic or tannaitic midrashim. The exegetical material it contains is presented as a sequentially structured commentary on the verses of the biblical Book of Exodus. The text often focuses its interpretation on a single word, phrase, or element within a given biblical verse, although the connection between the subject of the biblical verse and the text's interpretive comment is frequently difficult, if not impossible, to discern. The thematic nature of the text's interpretation is most often motivated by the biblical text upon which the text is commenting. That is, if the biblical text discusses a matter of religious praxis, then the interpretation associated with that verse, word, or phrase is most often legalistic (halakhic) in nature; otherwise, the interpretation is most often thematically oriented toward rabbinic homily or lore (aggadic). However, it is important to stress that this is not an absolute phenomenon; legal biblical texts are often interpreted in aggadic fashion and vice versa. Thus, the overall thematic nature of the interpretation in the *Mekhilta de-Rabbi Shimon b. Yoḥai* is variegated, and it is inappropriate to label the text as primarily aggadic or halakhic.

The exegetical content in the *Mekhilta de-Rabbi Shimon b. Yoḥai* displays all of the general characteristics common to the texts of the halakhic/tannaitic midrashic corpus. The text is structured as an ongoing commentary on the verses of a biblical book. It is composed almost exclusively in Rabbinic Hebrew, augmented by a small, but considerable, amount of Western/Palestinian Aramaic and Greek loanwords. The vast majority of the named sages date to the tannaitic period, although the majority of the interpretive content of the text is presented anonymously. The text often incorporates interpolations from the Mishnah and Tosefta into its interpretive endeavors. The types of hermeneutical methods employed in the *Mekhilta de-Rabbi Shimon b. Yoḥai* are consistent with those attested in the other halakhic midrashim; and the specific, technical terminology it uses, either to signify hermeneutical assumptions or to introduce specific exegetical ploys, is consistent with the terminology that is employed in other tannaitic, midrashic texts.

As mentioned above, the *Mekhilta de-Rabbi Shimon b. Yoḥai* belongs to the corpus of Rabbinic texts routinely designated as either the halakhic or tannaitic midrashim. Scholarly interpretation of the mass of evidence for this corpus has resulted in the long-standing and widely held hypothesis that for each of the first five books of the Hebrew Bible, excluding the book of *Genesis*, there once existed at least two such tannaitic, Rabbinic anthological collections of midrashic traditions. Thus, the *Mekhilta de-Rabbi Shimon b. Yoḥai* is commonly considered to be the halakhic/tannaitic midrashic parallel counterpart in this corpus to the substantially more well-known and well-studied *Mekhilta de-Rabbi Ishmael* to the Book of Exodus. The fact that the *Mekhilta de-Rabbi Shimon b. Yoḥai* has received considerably less scholarly consideration than its counterpart is due primarily to the text's complicated reconstructive history, fragmented manuscript attestation, and intriguing history of transmission.

# Reclamation and Reconstruction of the *Mekhilta de-Rabbi Shimon b. Yoḥai*

At some point in the medieval period, the *Mekhilta de-Rabbi Shimon b. Yoḥai* ceased to exist as a discrete textual entity. That is, the transmission of the independent manuscript tradition of the text essentially came to an end, and gradually, over time, the scholarly realm of Rabbinic Judaism allowed the text to slip from its active consciousness. The disappearance of the text was undoubtedly assisted in the sixteenth century by the advent of printed Jewish texts in western Europe. Because, the *Mekhilta de-Rabbi Shimon b. Yoḥai* was never printed, it gradually faded away. It was eventually superseded entirely by its parallel tannaitic counterpart, the *Mekhilta de-Rabbi Ishmael,* whose manuscript traditions were available to early Jewish book printers. That text was transferred to printed format, and was actively both transmitted and studied in the subsequent history of Judaism.

However, active interest in the *Mekhilta de-Rabbi Shimon b. Yoḥai* was rekindled in the second half of the nineteenth century, with the efforts of a small group of German Wissenschaft scholars. Although by then the text had been lost for centuries, scholars had been aware for some time of the prior existence of another collection of tannaitic, midrashic traditions for the Book of Exodus in addition to the *Mekhilta de-Rabbi Ishmael.* This was due primarily to the numerous references to this collection by medieval rabbinic authorities.[3] To cite but one example, Rabbi Moses ben Naḥman (1194–1270) stated in his commentary to Exodus 22:12:[4]

> Thus I have seen in the *Mekhilta de-Rabbi Shimon b. Yoḥai:* Abba Shaul says: He should bring evidence of it, as it says in Scripture: "Thus said the Lord: As a shepherd rescues from the lion's jaws two shank bones, etc." (Amos 3:12).[5]

What was unique about the efforts of the nineteenth-century German scholars was the fact that their notice of the lost text ultimately led to an attempt by one of their ranks to reconstruct it from a variety of disparate sources. It was David Zvi Hoffmann (1843–1921) who undertook the effort to reconstruct the *Mekhilta de-Rabbi Shimon b. Yoḥai;* however, it is important to note that in doing so he built considerably upon the previous efforts of two of his contemporaries, Meir Friedmann (Ish Shalom, 1831–1908) and Israel Levy (1841–1917).

In his introduction to his edition of the *Mekhilta de-Rabbi Ishmael,* published in 1870, Meir Friedmann reminded the scholarly world that there once had existed another collection of tannaitic, midrashic materials for the biblical Book of Exodus. Friedmann cited various medieval references to the *Mekhilta de-Rabbi Shimon b. Yoḥai* and commented:

> From these quotations two things can be proven: That this *Mekhilta* is not a collection of mystical topics, but rather a collection of *aggadah* (=lore) and midrash like the other midrashic anthologies. According to these selected quotations, it [also] appears that it comprises the Book of Exodus ... and that in all instances, the early rabbinic authorities had two *Mekhiltot*....[6]

Friedmann was not content, however, merely to cite the many medieval references to the *Mekhilta de-Rabbi Shimon b. Yoḥai*. Rather, in an appendix to his edition of the *Mekhilta de-Rabbi Ishmael* he outlined his intention to gather together these known references, in order to reconstruct partially the *Mekhilta de-Rabbi Shimon b. Yoḥai*:

> Herein I have added a few traditions I have located that [originally] stemmed from the *Mekhilta de-Rabbi Ishmael* but were removed. In many instances I highlighted traditions I found that are stated as stemming from the *Mekhilta [de-Rabbi Ishmael]*, or I suggested traditions that appeared to me to stem from the *Mekhilta [de-Rabbi Ishmael]*, but they are not now in our possession. ... I also have selected and gathered here an appendix of excerpted traditions I located that are stated as stemming from the unspecified *Mekhilta* or from the *Mekhilta de-Rabbi Shimon b. Yoḥai*, but they are not now in our possession. I don't claim to have completed exhaustively this task, because it is very possible that additional quotations that stem from [either] *Mekhilta* that have eluded me will be located.[7]

Friedmann concluded this appendix by gathering together the texts of the excerpts that he believed came from the *Mekhilta de-Rabbi Shimon b. Yoḥai*, and despite the fact that his efforts resulted in only a small sample of excerpts, they distinguished him as the first modern scholar to attempt to reconstruct portions of this text.

Whereas Friedmann cited and collected the excerpts from the *Mekhilta de-Rabbi Shimon b. Yoḥai* known in his day, it was Israel Levy who first conjectured, and subsequently proved, that these excerpts could actually lead to the discovery of a wealth of new ones. At the end of the nineteenth century, *Midrash ha-Gadol*, a thirteenth-century Yemenite anthology of midrashic traditions, was just beginning to attract the attention of European Jewish scholars, and Levy suspected that within this valuable anthology were many more portions of the missing *Mekhilta de-Rabbi Shimon b. Yoḥai.* His research led Levy to posit in 1889 that major portions of the lost *Mekhilta de-Rabbi Shimon b. Yoḥai* were interspersed throughout *Midrash ha-Gadol.*[8]

In order to support his hypothesis, Levy compared the excerpts from the *Mekhilta de-Rabbi Shimon b. Yoḥai* cited by Friedmann with parallel traditions from *Midrash ha-Gadol* and, if available, with parallels from the *Mekhilta de-Rabbi Ishmael* as well. As a result of this comparison, Levy noted that there were parallels in *Midrash ha-Gadol* to the majority of the excerpts from the *Mekhilta de-Rabbi Shimon b. Yoḥai*; however, parallels to these excerpts often were not found in the *Mekhilta de-Rabbi Ishmael.* Moreover, Levy also noticed that when there were parallel traditions in both *Midrash ha-Gadol* and the *Mekhilta de-Rabbi Ishmael* to the excerpts from the *Mekhilta de-Rabbi Shimon b. Yoḥai,* there often were strong similarities in the wording of the excerpt and its parallel in *Midrash ha-Gadol* that did not exist between the excerpt and its parallel in the *Mekhilta de-Rabbi Ishmael.*

In Levy's opinion, these characteristics led to the conclusion that the author of *Midrash ha-Gadol* incorporated materials directly from the *Mekhilta de-Rabbi Shimon b. Yoḥai* as he compiled and created his anthology of midrashic materials.[9] Equally important was what this conclusion implied: that *Midrash ha-Gadol* potentially could serve as a viable source for the reconstruction of the lost *Mekhilta de-Rabbi Shimon b. Yoḥai.* It was Friedmann and Levy, therefore, who blazed the trail that David Zvi Hoffmann would subsequently follow, in order to reconstruct on a grand scale the *Mekhilta de-Rabbi Shimon b. Yoḥai* for the first time.

Hoffmann published his monumental reconstruction of the text in 1905, the first major addition to the corpus of tannaitic midrashim in the history of modern midrashic study.[10] Hoffmann's text comprised almost entirely material gleaned from *Midrash ha-Gadol,* with notable exceptions being three sets (= seven pages) of manuscript fragments he incorporated from manuscripts from the Cairo Genizah[11] and a small group of fragments from the *Mekhilta de-Rabbi Shimon b. Yoḥai,* referred to as the *Notes of Rav Abraham ha-Laḥmi.*[12] Indeed, Hoffman's employment of the source materials at his disposal was eclectic, marked by unsystematic, arbitrary, and unarticulated guidelines of incorporation and interpolation. For example, he often emended or altered traditions gleaned from *Midrash ha-Gadol* on the basis of their attestation in other Rabbinic texts, such as the Babylonian and Palestinian Talmuds and various medieval and early modern anthologies and rabbinic legal texts. In his defense, Hoffmann was merely following the editorial zeitgeist of his time as he labored to reproduce the *Mekhilta de-Rabbi Shimon b. Yoḥai,* and his efforts, even a century later, are worthy of praise and admiration.

In 1955, Jacob Nahum Epstein (1878–1952) and his student Ezra Zion Melamed (1903–1994) published an updated, critical edition of the *Mekhilta de-Rabbi Shimon b. Yoḥai.*[13] At the time of its publication, half a decade had passed since the publication of Hoffmann's edition of the text. In this 50-year interim, an immense amount of medieval manuscript evidence of the text had emerged around the world, in libraries in cities such as Leningrad, Oxford, Cambridge, New York, and Paris, and the massive discoveries of the Cairo Genizah were beginning to receive organized, systematic examination.[14] Epstein himself was responsible for the discovery of the largest single manuscript (50 pages) of the text, which he located and identified in 1928 among facsimile photographs of the Firkovich manuscript collections in Leningrad.[15] Altogether, 13 sources eventually emerged, yielding a total of 95 pages or fragments of manuscript text, an amount that ultimately constituted approximately 75 percent of the reconstructed edition. Obviously, such a relative abundance of manuscript evidence for the *Mekhilta de-Rabbi Shimon b. Yoḥai* created the imperative to supplant Hoffmann's edition with one that took into consideration all of this new evidence, and it was Epstein who set out to accomplish this.

Ultimately, however, Epstein's greatest contribution to this project was simply to gather together all of the manuscript evidence that had become available only in a piecemeal fashion throughout the first half of the 20th century. As a result, Epstein found himself constantly anticipating a future manuscript discovery, and fighting the urge to begin piecing the text together with what he had. He did not begin the arduous process of evaluating and arranging all of the evidence until 1950, and at the time of his death in 1952 he had managed to prepare for publication only four pages of his edition, along with an abbreviated introduction. The project then fell into the hands of Melamed, who managed over the next few years to arrange and edit all of the original manuscript materials, in addition to the supplementary excerpts from *Midrash ha-Gadol,* that were to be incorporated into the text. Melamed also developed for the text the standard apparatus found in many of the critical editions of Rabbinic texts, including a delineation of textual variants found in the various manuscripts and in *Midrash ha-Gadol,* a list of parallel traditions located in other Rabbinic texts, and his and Epstein's personal notations for the text.

Perhaps one of the most valuable purposes served by the Epstein/Melamed edition of the *Mekhilta de-Rabbi Shimon b. Yoḥai* was the validation it provided for the initial research on this text conducted decades earlier by Friedmann, Levy, and Hoffmann. Although these three men were the first modern scholars to address the prior existence of this lost text and to promote the possibility of its reconstruction and reclamation, the fruit of their labor was the edition of the text published by Hoffmann, an edition reconstructed almost entirely from materials gleaned from *Midrash ha-Gadol*. Despite Levy's limited examination of excerpts from the *Mekhilta de-Rabbi Shimon b. Yohai* and their parallels in *Midrash ha-Gadol,* the overall correlation between these two texts remained, at best, obscure. Because of its reliance upon *Midrash ha-Gadol* for its textual content, Hoffmann's edition was blemished by uncertainties about its reliability and, ultimately, its usefulness for scholarly purposes. That is, Hoffmann's text was almost entirely unsubstantiated by any direct manuscript evidence, and as such it could not be adduced as a reliable reconstruction of the text as presumably it once existed. Thus, the endeavor to identify and reclaim the *Mekhilta de-Rabbi Shimon b. Yohai* remained marred by scholarly suspicion and uncertainty.

But with the publication of the Epstein/Melamed edition of the *Mekhilta de-Rabbi Shimon b. Yohai,* based as it was to such a great extent upon direct manuscript evidence of the text, many of these doubts were laid to rest. For even the most cursory comparison between the Epstein/Melamed and Hoffmann versions of the text revealed a remarkably close correlation between their textual content. Moreover, a careful comparison of the two editions shows the accuracy with which Hoffmann often was able to identify and cull the appropriate traditions belonging to the *Mekhilta de-Rabbi Shimon b. Yohai* from *Midrash ha-Gadol*.[16] Finally, the critical edition published by Epstein and Melamed demonstrated the overall high degree of precision with which the excerpts from the *Mekhilta de-Rabbi Shimon b. Yohai* were preserved in *Midrash ha-Gadol*. The irony of the situation is obvious; as the Epstein/Melamed critical edition of the text bestowed Hoffmann's edition with the validity it sorely needed, it also supplanted it as the one most suitable for scholarly usage and immediately rendered it obsolete.

## Evidence of the Text

There currently are 140 manuscript fragments (excluding *Midrash ha-Gadol*) of various size and in various condition that have been identified for the *Mekhilta de-Rabbi Shimon b. Yohai*.[17] This manuscript material accounts for approximately 75 percent of the Epstein/Melamed critical version of the text, with the additional material gleaned almost exclusively from *Midrash ha-Gadol*. The manuscript evidence for the *Mekhilta* de-Rabbi Shimon b. Yoḥai is dispersed among libraries around the world: New York (Jewish Theological Seminary Adler Collection); Cambridge, England (Cambridge University Library Taylor-Schechter Genizah Collection); Saint Petersburg, Russia (Antonin and Firkovich Collections); Oxford, England (Bodlein); Manchester, England (John Rylands Gaster Collection); and Paris (Alliance Collection). As expected, the diffusion of this material evidence only complicates a fully informed assessment of the interrelationship of the material evidence and the scope and nature of the entire text.

Menahem Kahana has examined the entirety of this evidence, and it is his judgment that the manuscript evidence comprises eight separate, direct textual codices of the Mekhilta de-Rabbi Shimon b. Yoḥai, as well as four separate, indirect textual witnesses.[18] No single source or codex is a comprehensive witness for the text, and it is commonly believed that the entirety of the text has yet to be identified or reconstructed, even if one includes the interpolations from Midrash ha-Gadol. In the Epstein/Melamed critical edition of the text, the following verses of the biblical Book of Exodus receive exegetical commentary: 3:2, 3:7, 3:8, 6:2, 12:1–24:10,[19] 30:20–21, 30:26, 30:32, 31:12, 31:15, 34:12, 34:14, 34:18–24, 34:26, and 35:2.

The Epstein/Melamed critical edition of the text remains the overall best edition of the Mekhilta de-Rabbi Shimon b. Yoḥai available for scholarly purposes, in so far as it incorporates most of the direct manuscript evidence currently available. Nonetheless, additional direct manuscript evidence for the text has become available since the publication of the Epstein/Melamed edition, as well as new indirect textual witnesses other than Midrash ha-Gadol.[20] Particularly significant are materials from Yalkut Temani, the 15th-century anthology of midrashim arranged in relation to the Jewish festivals of Hanukkah and Purim, and the fast day of Tisha b'Av. From within the manuscript collection for this anthology, housed at the Jewish Theological Seminary in New York, Menahem Kahana has identified the entire midrashic treatment of parashat Amalek (Exodus 17:8–15) from the Mekhilta de-Rabbi Shimon b. Yoḥai.[21] None of this material was utilized to fashion the Epstein/Melamed edition of the text, although it now represents the most reliable attestation of this portion of the text.

Moreover, the material gleaned from Midrash ha-Gadol that is incorporated into the Epstein/Melamed edition is not representative of all the available manuscript evidence for Midrash ha-Gadol, and was incorporated unsystematically.[22] The editors utilized only four manuscripts of Midrash ha-Gadol as source material for their reconstruction of the text. From the beginning of the text until parashat Yitro, they made use of only the Berlin #148 manuscript, presumably only on the basis of the fact that this was the manuscript used by Hoffmann in his edition of the *Mekhilta de-Rabbi Shimon b. Yoḥai.* There is no rationale other than this, however, for this reliance, and this is particularly problematic when one considers that Hoffmann emended this manuscript in his edition of the text on the basis of three other manuscripts. None of these emendations is clearly demarcated or noted in the Epstein/Melamed edition of the text, which only complicates additionally the informed utilization of the text. From parashat Yitro until the end of the text, Epstein and Melamed utilized a manuscript owned privately by Mordecai Margulies, again offering no rationale for this particular decision.

Thus, the appropriate utilization and incorporation of *Midrash ha-Gadol* as a source for the *Mekhilta de-Rabbi Shimon b. Yoḥai* demands considerable additional research and consideration. The most complete critical edition of *Midrash ha-Gadol* to the biblical Book of Exodus, published by Mordecai Margulies in 1956,[23] illustrates clearly this need. Margulies utilized 14 manuscript sources in fashioning his edition of *Midrash ha-Gadol* to the Book of Exodus, in contrast, as stated above, to the four utilized by Epstein and Melamed. Moreover, Margulies selected the Mahlman manuscript as the source for the base text of his edition, deeming it to be the most reliable and best source of *Midrash ha-Gadol* for the Book of Exodus. This manuscript was available to Epstein and Melamed; however, they used it only as a source to emend their base text.

The section of material at the beginning of the *Mekhilta de-Rabbi Shimon b. Yoḥai,* incorporated from a manuscript source attributed to R. Abraham Ha-Lahmi, also requires additional scrutiny. This material constitutes a small but significant collection of aggadic interpretations of Exodus 3:2ff. and Exodus 6:2ff.—Moses' encounter and subsequent interaction with God at the burning bush. These traditions are particularly interesting and intriguing because they are entirely absent from this text's tannaitic counterpart, the *Mekhilta de-Rabbi Ishmael,* which begins instead with materials associated with Exodus 12:1. Equally intriguing, however, is the fact that these traditions of interpretation are virtually absent from the entire corpus of classical Rabbinic literature, from the earliest tannaitic stratum through the Babylonian Talmud, but are well attested in subsequent, medieval collections of Rabbinic interpretation.[24] This fact alone provides sufficient reason to pause and consider whether the provenance of these traditions is, indeed, the *Mekhilta de-Rabbi Shimon b. Yoḥai.*

These traditions appear in print for the first time in the 1844 Vilna edition of the *Mekhilta de-Rabbi Ishmael.*[25] They were appended at the end of the text under the title *Mekhilta Parashat Shemot Va'Era* by the editor of the text, R. Isaac Landa. In his introduction to the text, Landa describes how he came to possess this collection of traditions, claiming to have viewed briefly a manuscript copy of these traditions attributed to R. Abraham ha-Lahmi among the papers of the Vilna Gaon, which were in the possession of the Gaon's grandson. Subsequently, Rabbi S. A. Wertheimer claimed to have viewed and copied these materials for inclusion in his 1913 collection of manuscripts entitled *Sefer 'Oṣar Midrashim Kitvei Yad*.[26] The Wertheimer manuscript now resides among the holdings of the library at the Jewish Theological Seminary in New York City.[27] Finally, additional fragmentary manuscript evidence for some of these traditions exists among the manuscripts from the Cairo Genizah held at Cambridge University.[28]

Epstein and Melamed utilized these source materials in a variety of ways as they reconstructed the beginning of their edition of the *Mekhilta de-Rabbi Shimon b. Yoḥai*. In some instances they incorporated portions of the text directly from the 1844 Vilna edition of the *Mekhilta de-Rabbi Ishmael*. In other instances they chose to incorporate portions of the text directly from the Cairo Genizah materials, in place of the Vilna materials. Finally, they routinely utilized either the Wertheimer manuscript as attested in *Sefer 'Oṣar Midrashim Kitvei Yad* or *Midrash ha-Gadol* to amend these textual materials, without any overt notation. The result is a highly eclectic, unsystematically reconstructed unit of materials of uncertain provenance which clearly warrants additional research.

An updated critical edition of the *Mekhilta de-Rabbi Shimon b. Yoḥai* is also clearly warranted. For his recent monograph, *The Two Mekhiltot on the Amalek Portion*, Menahem Kahana devised new critical editions of tractate Amalek for both the *Mekhilta de-Rabbi Shimon b. Yoḥai* and the *Mekhilta de-Rabbi Ishmael*, both of which he utilized to compare the tractate in the two texts.[29] This excellent effort reveals both the need for, and the potential scholarly benefit that would be provided by, an updated, systematic critical edition of the text.

## History of Scholarship on the *Mekhilta de-Rabbi Shimon b. Yoḥai*

The history of modern scholarship on the *Mekhilta de-Rabbi Shimon b. Yoḥai* has been greatly influenced by the complicated reconstructive nature of the text. The text's piecemeal composition, diverse body of manuscript evidence, and lack of a single, comprehensive base text clearly has been a source of concern and distrust for scholars over the past two centuries, as evidenced by the relatively small amount of scholarship it has generated when compared to its parallel counterpart, the *Mekhilta de-Rabbi Ishmael*. As a result, the majority of the scholarship produced on the *Mekhilta de-Rabbi Shimon b. Yoḥai* has been primarily concerned with identifying new evidence for the text, as well as issues relating to the process of reconstructing the text.

The *Mekhilta de-Rabbi Shimon b. Yoḥai* factored prominently, but not exclusively, in the sizeable body of scholarly research produced during the 19th and 20th centuries devoted to constructing an overall conceptualization of, or rationale for, the entire corpus of tannaitic midrashim. The genesis of this interest is found in the work of David Z. Hoffmann, who, as discussed above, first reconstructed the *Mekhilta de-Rabbi Shimon b. Yoḥai* in 1905. Hoffmann's reclamation of this text was by no means an isolated academic foray into the corpus of the tannaitic midrashim. Rather, his desire to reconstruct the work was, in part, motivated by his ideas concerning the proper conceptualization of the entire tannaitic midrashic corpus, ideas that he had begun developing nearly two decades before he published the text. By reconstructing the *Mekhilta de-Rabbi Shimon b. Yoḥai*, Hoffmann hoped not only to reclaim a text once lost, but also to buttress the claims he had made about all of the tannaitic midrashim.

In 1886, Hoffmann published his *Zur Einleitung in die halachischen Midraschim*,[30] a prodigious work that reached monumental status in rabbinic scholarly circles in its own time, and has retained such renown to this very day, despite having received over a century of sound criticism. At the time of its publication only four documents of the tannaitic midrashic corpus were available, one for each of the final four books of the Pentateuch: 1. *Mekhilta de-Rabbi Ishmael* (Exodus); 2. *Sifra* (Leviticus); 3. *Sifre* (Numbers); and 4. *Sifre* (Deuteronomy). In his work, Hoffmann closely examined and compared these documents, and concluded that the tannaitic midrashim extant at that time rightfully should be divided into two groups, one that stemmed from the tannaitic "School of Rabbi Ishmael b. Elisha" (comprising the *Mekhilta de-Rabbi Ishmael* and *Sifre Numbers*), and one that stemmed from the contemporaneous "School of Rabbi Akiva" (comprising *Sifra* and *Sifre Deuteronomy*). The midrashic output of these two putative schools, in Hoffmann's view, was differentiated by the following criteria:[31]

1) Two of the midrashim (*Mekhilta* and *Sifre Numbers*) contain a significant majority of statements attributed to sages known or presumed to be students of Rabbi Ishmael b. Elisha, whereas the other two midrashim (*Sifra* and *Sifre Deuteronomy*) contain a

majority of statements attributed to sages known or presumed to be students of Rabbi Akiva.

2) Moreover, the *Mekhilta* and *Sifre Numbers* only infrequently cite statements made by students of Akiva, and likewise, the *Sifra* and *Sifre Deuteronomy* only infrequently cite statements made by students of Ishmael.

3) In the midrashim attributed to the School of Ishmael are found many anonymous tannaitic statements *(baraitot)* that are also cited elsewhere, primarily in the two Talmuds, "in the name of the School of Ishmael" *(tanna de-vei Rabbi Ishmael).*

4) In the midrashim attributed to the School of Ishmael one finds a preference for utilizing exegetical techniques and hermeneutic principles assumed to be favored by Rabbi Ishmael. Likewise, in the midrashim attributed to the School of Akiva there is a predilection for the interpretive style assumed to be favored by Rabbi Akiva.

5) Each of the two groups of midrashim utilize different systems of redactional/technical terminology.

At the core of Hoffmann's schematization of the tannaitic midrashic corpus was a distinction he believed existed between the exegetical preferences of Ishmael and Akiva. Ishmael, along with his disciples, understood the Torah to speak in plain human language, meaning that the Torah could be understood correctly within the boundaries of rational linguistic conventions. Believing the Torah to communicate along standard linguistic lines, Ishmael and his disciples preferred to employ "straightforward" exegetical techniques to draw meaning from the biblical text. In opposition to Ishmael and his disciples were Akiva and the members of his "school." According to these tannaitic ages, the Torah did not speak in human language; rather, it communicated its messages in a divine, transrational language, one that transcended the limits of disciplined human thinking and was unique to the Torah itself. Therefore, in order to determine the proper understanding of the Torah, Akiva employed drastic, "complex" exegetical techniques.[32] Having perceived a distinction in the exegetical preferences of Ishmael and Akiva, Hoffmann then extended this distinction to the entire corpus of the tannaitic midrashim known at that time, arguing that the differences in these sages' interpretive techniques eventually led each of them to produce his own "set" of midrashim to the books of the Pentateuch mentioned above. In Hoffmann's opinion, therefore, acknowledging the distinctions in the interpretive preferences of Ishmael and Akiva served as the key to understanding and evaluating the overall distinctions that demarcated the individual texts of the tannaitic midrashic corpus.

As noted above, when Hoffmann published his conceptual framework of these midrashim only four texts of the corpus were available—two that stemmed from the purported "Ishmaelean" school and two from the purported "Akivan" school. Operating under the assumption that each school produced "complete sets" of tannaitic midrashim, Hoffmann reasoned that four texts from the tannaitic midrashic corpus had been lost over the passage of time. By reconstructing the lost text of the *Mekhilta de-Rabbi Shimon b. Yoḥai*, Hoffmann intended to fill in one of the "gaps" of his framework by reproducing the Akivan counterpart to the Ishmaelean *Mekhilta de-Rabbi Ishmael*.[33] Indeed, as he reproduced the missing text, Hoffmann analyzed closely its constituent traditions, in order to reveal the traits that allowed him to place it among the texts he claimed stemmed from the Akivan school, such as the usage of Akivan technical terminology and the frequent citation of Akivan sages. Finally, Hoffmann noted that the halakhic pronouncements in the *Mekhilta de-Rabbi Shimon b. Yoḥai* often stood in opposition to counterparts located in the *Mekhilta de-Rabbi Ishmael.* The reconstruction of the *Mekhilta de-Rabbi Shimon b. Yoḥai* played a fundamental role, therefore, in both the construction and maintenance of Hoffmann's theoretical division of the entire tannaitic midrashic corpus.

It is virtually impossible to overestimate the influence that Hoffmann's ideas about the tannaitic midrashim have had on subsequent scholarship. As M. D. Herr wrote in his entry in the *Encyclopedia Judaica:*

> The division laid down by Hoffmann became one of the cornerstones
> of the research into the literature of the sages, and his interpretation
> also (that is, the identification of type A as *de-Vei* R. Ishmael and
> type B as *de-Vei* R. Akiva) has been accepted since his time until the
> present time by almost all scholars.[34]

In spite of its widespread scholarly acceptance, the notion that there were exegetical "schools" of Ishmael and Akiva that disagreed over accepted exegetical norms and techniques has been revealed to be erroneous.[35] Rather, it was the anonymous redactors of the subsequent Palestinian and Babylonian Talmuds who created the concept of these two exegetical schools of thought, in order to facilitate their systematization of the tannaitic tradition they had inherited from their Rabbinic predecessors. Moreover, of the five criteria delineated above that differentiate the corpora in Hoffmann's theory, only the criterion of technical terminology is absolute (#5); the other four criteria are, at best, relative.

Although gradually discredited throughout the 20th century, Hoffmann's theoretical division of the tannaitic midrashic corpus continued to serve as the basis for the work of a number of subsequent scholars. Its influence is most prominently seen, for example, in the work of Hanoch Albeck (1890–1972),[36] Jacob Epstein (1878–1952),[37] and Ezra Melamed (1903–1994).[38] All of these scholars essentially took Hoffmann's theory and made conceptual adjustments to it, in the attempt to continue to provide a rationale for perceiving a purposeful division of the texts within the corpus. As a result, much of the scholarship during the 20th century on the *Mekhilta de-Rabbi Shimon b. Yohai* has been subsumed into these larger, programmatic inquiries into the relationship among all the texts of the tannaitic midrashic corpus, as well as the relationship among the tannaitic midrashim and other Rabbinic texts that either immediately pre-date or post-date them. For the most part, this scholarship has had as its goal the creation of a working conceptualization that encompasses all the tannaitic midrashim, and has been motivated by the desire to understand and account for the existence of parallel recensions of these early midrashic texts. In general, this scholarship has been historical in orientation, believing that a comparison of the constituent texts of the tannaitic midrashic corpus can reveal specific historical developments and ideological differences within the nascent Rabbinic movement.

The extensive work of Menahem Kahana on the *Mekhilta de-Rabbi Shimon b. Yohai* produced recently merits particular recognition. Kahana has personally examined most, if not all, of the manuscript evidence currently available for the text, allowing him to make informed conjectures about the interrelationship of the fragmented, dispersed evidence. His knowledge of the current state of the evidence for the entire tannaitic midrashic corpus resulted in his recent publication of *The Two Mekhiltot on the Amalek Portion,* also referenced above, which contains two new critical editions of tractate Amalek in both the *Mekhilta de-Rabbi Shimon b. Yohai* and the *Mekhilta de-Rabbi Ishmael.* Kahana's effort in this work includes, as well, a detailed comparison of these tractates in accordance with a number of criteria, including: differences in hermeneutical methods, prooftext employment, technical and redactional terminology usage; variances and parallelisms between the two tractates, named Sages, halakhic differences, and the relationship of the tractates to other Rabbinic texts. Based upon this exhaustively detailed comparison of these two tractates from the texts, Kahana argues for the primacy or originality of the *Mekhilta de-Rabbi Ishmael* over the *Mekhilta de-Rabbi Shimon b. Yoḥai.* In Kahana's opinion, the *Mekhilta de-Rabbi Shimon b. Yoḥai* is a secondary redaction by early Rabbinic editors attempting not only to develop a more lofty literary style for the midrashic traditions, but also to loosen the strict reliance of the text's interpretation on the wording of Scripture.

There remains, however, much research to be conducted on the *Mekhilta de-Rabbi Shimon b. Yoḥai,* in order to understand more clearly the scope of its contents, its relationship to the other texts in the early Rabbinic corpus, and its full significance as one of the earliest collections of Rabbinic tradition. Potential subject areas for future scholarship include a comparison of its halakhic material with parallel halakhic material in the *Mekhilta de-Rabbi Ishmael;* a full evaluation of its relationship to *Midrash ha-Gadol* and other indirect textual witnesses; and a systematic analysis of its documentary and editorial characteristics.

## Explanation of Translation

This translation—the first comprehensive translation of the *Mekhilta de-Rabbi Shimon b. Yoḥai* into any language—is based almost exclusively on the base text of the Epstein/Melamed critical edition, which has been reproduced here in its entirety. Given the source-critical complexities of the text, the extent of its reconstruction, and its variegated manuscript basis, an attempt to determine or devise another base text for the purposes of this translation would have served only to complicate to a prohibitive degree the nature of this challenging endeavor. Thus, in spite of the problematic aspects of this edition discussed above, in very few instances did I deviate from translating this base text in order to ground the translation on the basis of alternative attestations in other sources. In each instance, I noted and explained my decision to do so.

As is often the case with translations of hermeneutical texts from the period of classical antiquity, I have endeavored to achieve a balance between the concern for idiom and the obligation to render faithfully the language of the original text. When such a compromise proved elusive, my tendency was to favor a less idiomatic rendering of the text in favor of one that more closely represents its original language, however stilted or artificial the result. This decision supports, in particular, the needs of those who will turn to this translation for assistance with both translating and comprehending the complicated hermeneutical content of the text in its original language. In order to render into English the repetitive style, rhetoric, and modes of expression of the text, I have translated its technical terminology, recurring phrases, and repeated idiomatic expressions the same way, as much as possible. In instances when I felt the need to augment the translation beyond the original language of the text, I demarcated such words and phrases by placing them within brackets [ ]. These should be differentiated from the brackets surrounding numbers that appear in the left margin of the English translation, which refer to the corresponding page in the Epstein/Melamed critical edition of the text.

A primary goal of this translation was to organize the content of the text in such a way as to facilitate the ability to reference with precision any specific location within it. Toward this purpose, I have divided the English translation into chapters, sections, units of traditions, and sub-units. The following example illustrates the relationship between this method of division and its corresponding reference system: XII:II:2.A–E corresponds to chapter 12:section 2:unit 2.sub-units A through E. To facilitate quick cross-referencing between the divisions of the English translation and the Hebrew text, the reader has been provided in the right margin of the Hebrew text with the corresponding English translation references. A diamond symbol (♦) has been placed within the Hebrew text, in order to mark each location of a progression in the English reference system.

In its entirety, the translation of the text is also divided into 10 named tractates, following the traditional division of the tannaitic counterpart to this text, the *Mekhilta de-Rabbi Ishmael*.[40] Although I endeavored to divide the translation on the basis of what I perceived to be inherent editorial/redactional or thematic transitions in the text, I do not claim these decisions to be absolute or immune from alternative proposition.

My commentary and annotation of the text are designed to accomplish a number of goals. First and foremost, I have used the commentary to provide explanations of the interpretive content of the text, elucidations on its hermeneutics, pertinent background information, and clarifications about the relationship between either the tradition of interpretation or the translation and the text's original language. In addition, I have made use of the notations to highlight and cross-reference traditions or material in other texts of the classical Rabbinic corpus that are parallel to the material in the *Mekhilta de-Rabbi Shimon b. Yoḥai*. If the parallel is from a text that is organized traditionally in such a way that facilitates specific textual location referencing, I have simply provided the textual reference (e.g., Mishnah Rosh Hashanah 1:1, Tosefta

Makkot 3:5), and no other. In these instances, the reader will have no difficulties locating the parallel reference in both the original text and its translations. However, when referencing parallel material in a text that is not organized as such, thus making it difficult to render the textual location with precision, I have chosen to provide the traditional textual reference as well as a reference to a translation of the text that facilitates a more precise textual identification. The following is a list of the textual editions and translations I used for these references:

*Mekhilta de-Rabbi Ishmael:*
H. Horovitz and I. Rabin, *Mechilta D'Rabbi Ishmael,* (Jerusalem: Wahrmann Books, 1970).
Jacob Z. Lauterbach, *Mekilta de-Rabbi Ishmael,* 3 vol., (Philadelphia: Jewish Publication Society of America, 1933).
Jacob Neusner, *Mekhilta According to Rabbi Ishmael: An Analytical Translation,* 2 vol., (Atlanta: Scholars Press, 1988).

*Sifra:*
Jacob Neusner, *Sifra: An Analytical Translation,* 3 vol., (Atlanta: Scholars Press, 1988).

*Sifre Numbers:*
Jacob Neusner, *Sifre To Numbers: An American Translation and Explanation,* 2 vol., (Atlanta: Scholar Press, 1986).

*Sifre Deuteronomy:*
Reuven Hammer, *Sifre to Deuteronomy* (New Haven: Yale University Press, 1986).
Jacob Neusner, *Sifre to Deuteronomy: An Analytical Translation,* 2 vol., (Atlanta: Scholars Press, 1987).

*Genesis Rabbah:*
Jacob Neusner, *Genesis Rabbah: The Judaic Commentary to the Book of Genesis: A New American Translation,* 3 vol., (Atlanta: Scholars Press, 1985).

*Leviticus Rabbah:*
Jacob Neusner, *Judaism and Scripture: The Evidence of Leviticus Rabbah* (Chicago and London: University of Chicago Press, 1986).

*Palestinian Talmud:*
Jacob Neusner, *The Talmud of the Land of Israel: A Preliminary Translation and Explanation,* 35 vol., (Chicago, University of Chicago Press, 1982).

*Babylonian Talmud:*

Jacob Neusner, ed., *The Talmud of Babylonia: An America Translation,* 36
   vol. (Atlanta: Scholars Press, 1984).

To conclude, in recent decades there has been a remarkable and commendable increase in scholarly interest in early Rabbinic Judaism and Rabbinic biblical interpretation. The vast potential held by Rabbinic literature and Rabbinic hermeneutics to research in the humanities is now acknowledged among an ever-broadening range of scholars of multiple disciplines. It is my hope, therefore, that this translation and commentary will render accessible the *Mekhilta de-Rabbi Shimon b. Yoḥai* to a wider audience of scholars and, as such, will facilitate and engender additional, needed attention on this invaluable source of early midrash.

# Notes

[1] Hebrew/Aramaic title: מכילתא דרבי שמעון בר יוחאי (Mekhilta d'Rabbi Shimon bar Yoḥai).

[2] Due to the fact that the text begins with traditions of interpretation associated with the burning bush narrative at Exod. 3:1. See note 12 below.

[3] For extensive listings of the medieval references to the *Mekhilta de-Rabbi Shimon b. Yoḥai,* see D. Z. Hoffmann, introduction to *Mechilta de-Rabbi Simon b. Jochai: Ein halachischer und haggadischer Midrasch zu Exodus* (Frankfurt am Main: J. Kauffmann, 1905), 3–8; J. N. Epstein and E. Z. Melamed, introduction to *Mekhilta d'Rabbi Šim'on b. Jochai: Fragmenta in Geniza Cairensi reperta digessit apparatu critico, notis, praefatione instruxit* (Jerusalem: Mekitze Nirdamim, 1955), 13–15; and J. Z. Lauterbach, "The Two Mekiltas," *Proceedings of the American Academy for Jewish Research* 4 (1933), 124–29.

[4] Exod. 22:12: "If it [i.e., a borrowed animal] was torn by beasts, he [i.e., the borrower] shall bring it as evidence. He need not replace what has been torn by beasts."

[5] See translation LXXIII:III:2.A–C.

[6] M. Friedmann, introduction to *Mechilta de-Rabbi Ismäel* (Vienna: J. Holzwarth, 1870), 53–54. Translated from the original Hebrew.

[7] Ibid., 119.

[8] See Israel Levy, "Ein Wort über die 'Mechilta des R. Simon,'" in *Jahresbericht des jüdisch-theologischen Seminars* (Breslau: S. Schottlaender, 1889), 2–3, where he proposes: "In den folgenden Zeilen möge zunächst der Nachweis geführt werden, dass diese Mechilta zum grossen Theil im Sammelwerke Midrasch Haggadol enthalten ist, wodurch uns eine neue Quelle für ein besseres Verständniss des talmudischen Schriftenthums erschlossen wird, so dann eine Vermuthung über die Schule, aus der sie stammte, aufgestellt und Einzelnes bemerkt werden."

[9] It should be emphasized that, unlike many medieval midrashic anthologies, *Midrash ha-Gadol* does not identify the original source texts from which its materials are taken. It presents these materials as a running commentary on Scripture.

[10] Hoffmann, *Mechilta de-Rabbi Simon b. Jochai.*

[11] See Hoffmann, *Mechilta de-Rabbi Simon b. Jochai,* 12–14, 118–22, and 137–45 and the corresponding footnotes. It is interesting to note that Hoffmann did not incorporate these materials into his base text, choosing instead simply to note their existence in his critical apparatus.

[12] Original Hebrew title: הגהות רב אברהם הלחמי. These interesting fragments are midrashic traditions about Exodus chapters 3 and 6. Because these *Hagahot* fragments interpret the burning bush narrative (Exod. 3:1–4:17), they draw a connection between the *Mekhilta de-Rabbi Shimon b. Yoḥai* and the text מכילתא דסניא (Mekhilta of the Burning Bush) mentioned by several medieval rabbinic authorities. For more information, see Epstein and Melamed, introduction to *Mekhilta D'Rabbi Simon b. Jochai,* 14.

[13] Epstein and Melamed, *Mekhilta D'Rabbi Simon b. Jochai.* Reprinted in 1979 with handwritten emendations and additional notations by Melamed.

[14] For a most engaging, thorough presentation of the history of the acquisition of the Cambridge Genizah Collection, along with a survey of many of the valuable insights its contents have provided for a variety of scholarly interests, see Stefan C. Reif, *A Jewish Archive from Old Cairo: The History of Cambridge University's Genizah Collection* (Richmond, Surrey: Curzon Press, 2000).

[15] These two collections of ancient Hebrew manuscripts in Leningrad, among the largest collections of Hebrew manuscripts in the world, were first assembled by the Polish Karaite Abraham Firkovich (1786–1874). In his zeal to defend the Karaites against the Rabbanites, Firkovich traveled extensively, collecting ancient manuscripts and books, hoping to discover proof of ancient roots for the Karaite movement. It is likely that on one such journey to Palestine in 1830, Firkovich acquired manuscripts from the Cairo Genizah, including this manuscript of the *Mekhilta de-Rabbi Shimon b. Yoḥai.* For more on Firkovich, see Z. Ankori, *Karaites in Byzantium* (New York: Columbia University Press, 1959) and H. L. Strack, *Abraham Firkowitsch und seine Entdeckungen* (Leipzig: J.C. Hinrichs, 1876).

[16] For a detailed examination and evaluation of the interpolation of material from *Midrash ha-Gadol* in tractate Pisḥa of both the Hoffmann and Epstein/Melamed versions of the *Mekhilta de-Rabbi Shimon b. Yoḥai,* see W. David Nelson, "The Reconstruction of the *Mekhilta of Rabbi Shimon b. Yoḥai:* A Reexamination," *Hebrew Union College Annual, 70–71* (Cincinnati: Hebrew Union College Press, 2001), 261–302.

[17] An invaluable source of information on the manuscript evidence for not only the *Mekhilta de-Rabbi Shimon b. Yoḥai*, but also the entire halakhic/tannaitic midrashic corpus, is *Menahem Kahana, Manuscripts of the Halakhic Midrashim: An Annotated Catalogue* (Jerusalem: The Israel Academy of Sciences and Humanities and Yad Izhak Ben-Zvi, 1995).

[18] Ibid., 50–59.

[19] However, there are biblical verses in this large, continuous section that do not have midrashic traditions associated with them. They are few in number, and there is no reason to surmise from the manuscript evidence available that midrashic traditions associated with these verses are missing.

[20] For a delineation of Cairo Genizah fragments of the text that are not incorporated into the Epstein/Melamed edition, see H. L. Strack and G. Stemberger, *Introduction to the Talmud and Midrash* (Minneapolis: Fortress Press, 1996), 258.

[21] For a description of these manuscripts, see Menahem I. Kahana, *The Two Mekhiltot on the Amalek Portion: The Originality of the Version of the Mekhilta d'Rabbi Ishma'el with Respect to the Mekhilta of Rabbi Shim'on ben Yohay* (Heb.) (Jerusalem: The Magnes Press, 1999), 121–33.

[22] For a description of the incorporation of materials from Midrash ha-Gadol into the Epstein/Melamed edition of the *Mekhilta de-Rabbi Shimon b. Yoḥai*, see Epstein and Melamed, introduction to *Mekhilta D'Rabbi Simon b. Jochai*, 46–58.

[23] Mordecai Margulies, *Midrash Haggadol on the Pentateuch: Exodus* (Jerusalem: Mosad Harav Kook, 1956).

[24] E.g., *Exodus Rabbah* 2:5 and corresponding material in *Midrash ha-Gadol*.

[25] *Mekhilta* (Vilna:1844) with introduction and running textual commentary authored by R. Isaac E. Landa (Hebrew: לנדא).

[26] S. A. Wertheimer, *Sefer 'Oṣar Midrashim Kitvei Yad* (Jerusalem: Achim Lipschitz, 1913), 9–10; 58–63.

[27] JTS Rab. 2404, foll. 1–2.

[28] T–S C 4a.4.

[29] See note 21.

[30] D. Z. Hoffmann, *Zur Einleitung in die halachischen Midraschim* (Berlin: M. Driesner, 1886–87).

[31] Ibid., particularly 5–20.

[32] For additional information about the purported exegetical preferences of Ishmael and Akiva, see Hoffmann, *Zur Einleitung*, 5–12; J. N. Epstein, *Mevo'ot le-Sifrut ha-Tannaim* (Jerusalem: Magnes Press, 1957), 521–35; E. Z. Melamed, *Pirkei Mavo le-Sifrut ha-Talmud* (Jerusalem: Galor, 1973), 170–80; and M. D. Herr, "Hermeneutics," *Encyclopedia Judaica* (Jerusalem: Keter Publishing House, 1972), 8:366–72.

[33] In fact, Hoffmann's theoretical framework of the tannaitic midrashic corpus generated many efforts to reconstruct other missing components from fragmentary manuscript evidence and medieval midrashic compilations, in order to fill in the other three "gaps." Hoffmann himself published *Midrasch Tannaim zum Deuteronomium* (Berlin: H. Itzkowski, 1908/9), which he believed to be a partial reconstruction of the lost Ishmaelean counterpart to *Sifrei Deuteronomy*. This work was preceded by Solomon Schechter's publication of several fragments from this text from the findings in the Cairo Genizah, all of which were incorporated by Hoffmann in his publication. See S. Schechter, "Genizah Fragments," *Jewish Quarterly Review* 16 (1904), 446–52, and "The Mekhilta to Deuteronomy," *Jewish Quarterly Review* 16 (1904), 695–99. Additional fragmentary evidence was identified and published throughout the 20th century by a variety of scholars, including J. N. Epstein, L. Finkelstein, H. Fox, and M. Kahana. For a full delineation, see Strack and Stemberger, *Talmud und Midrash*, 273–75. Most recently, Menahem Kahana has published *Sifre Zuta on Deuteronomy: Citations from a New Tannaitic Midrash* (Jerusalem: Magnes Press, 2002).

In 1894 Schechter identified and published a fragment from the Cairo Genizah that he believed stemmed from *Sifrei Zuta*, the lost Akivan counterpart to *Sifrei Numbers*. See *Jewish Quarterly Review* 6 (1894), 656–63. In 1917, H. Horovitz published a critical edition of *Sifrei Zuta*, based upon all the known manuscript evidence, along with excerpts from medieval compilations that he conjectured were taken from this text: *Sifrei al Sefer ba-Midbar ve-Sifrei Zuta* (Leipzig: Gustav Fock, 1917). S. Lieberman published a comprehensive study of this text: *Sifre Zutta: The Midrash of Lydda* (New York: JTS Publications, 1968). As with *Midrash Tannaim*, various scholars throughout the 20th century identified and published additional fragmentary evidence belonging to this text, including J.N. Epstein and S. Lieberman. See Strack and Stemberger, *Talmud and Midrash*, 268–70.

[34] M. D. Herr, "Midreshei Halakha," *Encyclopedia Judaica*, 11:1523. Recent scholarly interest in the hermeneutical distinctions between the purportedly "Ishmaelean" and "Akivan" corpora of the halakhic midrashim is evidenced by the publication of Azzan Yadin, *Scripture as Logos: Rabbi Ishmael and the Origins of Midrash* (Philadelphia: University of Pennsylvania Press, 2004).

[35] See Jay Harris, *How Do We Know This? Midrash and the Fragmentation of Modern Judaism* (Albany: State University of New York Press, 1995), 25–72.

[36] Hanoch Albeck, *Untersuchungen über die halakischen Midraschim* (Berlin: Akademie-Verlag, 1927); and Hanoch Albeck, *Mavo la-Talmudim* (Tel Aviv: Dvir, 1969).

[37] Epstein, *Mevo'ot le-Sifrut ha-Tannaim*.

[38] Melamed, *Pirkei Mavo le-Sifrut ha-Talmud*; E. Z. Melamed, *Midreshei Halakhah shel ha-Tanna'im be-Talmud Bavli* (Jerusalem: Magnes Press, 1943); and E. Z. Melamed, *Ha-Yahas she-Bein Midreshei Halakhah la-Mishnah ve-la-Tosefta* (Jerusalem: Da'at, 1966).

[40] I employed the same names for the tractates here as used in the *Mekhilta de-Rabbi Ishmael*; however, because the *Mekhilta de-Rabbi Shimon b. Yoḥai* includes initial material that has no parallel in the *Mekhilta de-Rabbi Ishmael*, I was compelled to create a name for that tractate—"Sanya." See notes 2 and 12 above.

# Abbreviations

| | |
|---|---|
| H/R | Horovitz-Rabin critical edition of the *Mekhilta de-Rabbi Ishmael* |
| Laut. | Lauterbach edition/translation of the *Mekhilta de-Rabbi Ishmael* |
| Neus. | Neusner |
| Sifre Num. | Sifre Numbers |
| Sifre Deut. | Sifre Deuteronomy |
| b. | Babylonian Talmud |
| t. | Tosefta |
| m. | Mishnah |
| y. | Jerusalem/Palestinian Talmud |
| Ref. | Refer to |
| Ms. | Manuscript |
| JTS. Rab. | Manuscript Catalogue Reference Information—Jewish Theological Seminary of New York Library Manuscript Collection |

# Tractate Sanya

*Chapter One*

(Textual Source: JTS Rab. 2404, folios 1–2 and Notes of Rav Abraham Ha-Laḥmi—
הגהות רב אברהם הלחמי)

I:I

1.

A. "Now Moses was tending (the flock of his father-in-law Jethro), etc. An angel of the Lord appeared to him (in a blazing fire out of a bush), etc." (Exod. 3:1–2):[1]

B. R. Shimon b. Yoḥai says, "Why did the Holy One, blessed be He, appear from the highest heavens and speak with Moses from within the bush? Because just as this bush was the thorniest of all the trees in the world, in that any bird that entered into it could not manage to exit without tearing itself limb from limb, likewise was the slavery of Israel in Egypt the most oppressive slavery in the world.

C. "[Moreover, so oppressive was Egypt that] no male or female slave ever left Egypt a free person, except for Hagar. As it says in Scripture, 'And Pharaoh put men in charge of him, (and they sent him off with his wife and all that he possessed)' (Gen. 12:20).[2]

D. "And how does one know from Scripture that the slavery of Israel was more oppressive than any slavery in the world? As it says in Scripture, 'And the Lord said, "I have *marked well*[3] the plight of my people (in Egypt, and have heeded their outcry on account of their taskmasters)"' (Exod. 3:7).

E. "And why does Scripture state 'I have seen' twice?[4] Because after [the Egyptian taskmasters] drowned their[5] sons in water, they would then embed them [into the walls of a] building.

---

[1] It is intriguing that the *Mekhilta de-Rabbi Shimon b. Yoḥai* begins with this series of interpretations associated with Exodus 3, particularly when compared to its tannaitic counterpart, the *Mekhilta de-Rabbi Ishmael*, which is commonly assumed (based upon its manuscript evidence) to begin with an interpretation of Exodus 12. The fact that the *Mekhilta de-Rabbi Shimon b. Yoḥai* begins with earlier chapters of the Book of Exodus compels the scholarly community to consider two possibilities: either that the early "canonization" of these texts in antiquity was not as stable or as absolute as the later medieval manuscript and printed evidence for these texts suggests or that our evidence for the *Mekhilta de-Rabbi Ishmael* might not attest the text accurately or completely.

[2] 1.C is clearly disjunctive to the interpretive progression of this unit between 1.B and 1.D, which compels one to view it as an editorial interpolation and augmentation. Nonetheless, it is attested in all the available sources for this unit of tradition. The gist of the interpretation is clear: Gen. 12:20 indicates that Abraham departed Egypt with his wife *and all that he possessed*—which included his future concubine, the Egyptian maidservant Hagar.

[3] Emphasis added. Utilizing a routine, midrashic hermeneutic ploy, the text is focusing its attention on the scriptural employment of the infinitive absolute—ראה ראיתי (I have *marked well*)—in Exod. 3:7, assuming that the apparent doubled form of the verb requires interpretive explication. The text, therefore, determines that the doubled verb indicates a doubled form of oppression by the Egyptian taskmasters.

[4] See note 3.

[5] I.e., the sons of the Israelites.

# מסכתא דסניא

◆ ומשה היה רועה וכו׳ וירא מלאך ה׳ אליו וכו׳.    A   1

ר׳ שמעון בן יוחאי אומר מפני מה נגלה הקב״ה משמי    B
מרום והיה מדבר עם משה מתוך הסנה. אלא מה הסנה
‹הזה› קשה מכל אילנות שבעולם שכל צפור שנכנסת
לתוכה אינה יוצאת מתוכו בשלום עד שמתתכת
איברים אברים. כך היה שיעבודן של ישראל במצרים
קשה מכל שיעבוד שבעולם. ◆ ומעולם לא יצא ממצרים    C
‹לא› עבד ולא שפחה בן חורין אלא הגר בלבד שנא׳
ויצו עליו פרעה וגו׳ (בר׳ יב כ). ◆

ומנין שהיה שיעבודן של ישראל קשה מכל שיעבוד    D
שבעולם שנא׳ ויאמר ה׳ ראה ראיתי את עני עמי וגו׳.
◆ ומה ת״ל ראה ראיתי שני פעמים. מאחר שהיו משקיעין    E
את בניהן במים היו חוזרי׳ וכובשים אותם בבנין. ◆

F.   "They told a parable: To what is the matter alike? It is like one who took a staff and struck two people with it, such that the two of them received a wound from the blow of the staff. Likewise was the slavery of Israel in Egypt the most oppressive slavery in the world. And this was abundantly clear to God. Thus it is stated in Scripture, 'Yes I am mindful of their sufferings' (Exod. 3:7)."[6]

I:II

1.   A.   R. Eliezer says, "Why did the Holy One, blessed be He, appear from the highest heavens and speak with him from within the bush? Because just as this bush is the lowliest of all the trees in the world, likewise had Israel descended to the lowest level. And the Holy One, blessed be He, descended with them and redeemed them. As it says in Scripture, 'I have *come down*[7] to rescue them from the Egyptians' (Exod. 3:8)."

2.   A.   R. Joshua says, "Why did the Holy One, blessed be He, appear from the highest heavens and speak with Moses from within the bush? Because when Israel went down to Egypt, God's presence went down with them. As it says in Scripture, 'I Myself will go down with you (to Egypt) ...' (Gen. 46:4).[8]

"When they left [Egypt], God's presence was revealed[9] with them. As it says in Scripture, '... and I Myself will also bring you back' (Gen. 46:4).

"[When] they went down to the [Reed] Sea, God's presence was with them. As it says in Scripture, 'The Angel of God (which had been going ahead of the Israelite army) moved (and went behind them)' (Exod. 14:19).

"[When] they came to the wilderness [of Sinai], God's presence was with them. As it says in Scripture, '... and in the wilderness, where you saw (how the Lord your God carried you) ...' (Deut. 1:31)."

3.   A.   R. Ḥiyya and R. Judah say, "Come and observe the love of He who spoke and the world
[2]        came into being! In that whenever Israel is situated in suffering, there is [also] anguish before Him, as if it were possible. As it says in Scripture, 'In all their afflictions, He did not afflict' (Isa. 63:9).[10]

B.   "From this I only know [that God suffered along with] the suffering of the [entire] community. How does one know from Scripture [that the same holds true for] the suffering of the individual? The verse states, 'He shall call to me, and I will answer him. I will be with him in trouble' (Ps. 91:15). And thus Scripture states, 'Whoever touches you (touches the pupil of his eye)' (Zech. 2:12)."

C.   R. Judah says, "The verse does not employ a *vav* [at the end of the word 'eye' in the Zechariah 2:12 above, which would render its meaning as 'his eye'], rather a *yud* [which

---

[6] The implication of this parable is that the physical cruelty of the Egyptian taskmasters to the Israelites was felt by God as well. The parable, therefore, builds on the "double" theme established in 1.E, while simultaneously leading the theme in a different direction. This is motivated by the text's understanding of an interpretive relationship between the two clauses in Exod. 3:7. The "doubled" infinitive absolute in the first half of the verse is interpreted as referring to the twofold cruelty of the Egyptians as explained in 1.E. The employment of the parable in this fashion, however, carries the theme forward and applies it subtly as well to the second part of the verse ("I am mindful of their sufferings"), which is understood to indicate that two sufferers—both the Israelites and God—feel the corporeal pain.

[7] Emphasis added.

[8] Compare 2.A–3.C with *Mekhilta de-Rabbi Ishmael,* Pisḥa (H/R, 51:9—52:8; Laut. vol. 1, 113:85–115:112; Neus., XIV:II:5.A–T).

[9] I.e., went out.

[10] In the manuscript tradition of the Hebrew Bible, Isa. 63:9 has variant attestations. The verse as it is cited in the text of the *Mekhilta de-Rabbi Shimon b. Yoḥai* employs the Hebrew word of negation לא. However, the text's interpretation clearly assumes the traditional, Jewish rendering of this word, which is the prepositional ל with the third person, masculine pronominal suffix—לו—"to Him." This variation renders the meaning of the verse: "In all their afflictions, He [i.e., God] was (also) afflicted." This midrashic tradition is widely attested throughout the corpus of early Rabbinic literature. See, e.g., *Mekhilta de-Rabbi Ishmael,* Pisḥa (H/R, 51:9–15; Laut., vol. 1, 113:85–90; Neus., XIV:II:5.A–H); and *Sifre Num.,* Piska 84 (Neus., LXXIV:IV:1.FF–JJ). Also compare with parallel below at XVI:IV:4.A–E.

משלו משל למה הדבר דומה לאחד שנטל את המקל
והכה בו שני בני אדם ונמצאו שניהם מקבלין את
הפציעה מתחת יד המקל כך היה שיעבוד[ן] של ישראל
במצרים קשה מכל שיעבוד שבעולם וגלוי וידוע לפני
המקום לכך נאמר כי ידעתי את מכאוביו. ◆

I:II

ר׳ אליעזר אומ׳ מפני מה נגלה הקב״ה משמי מרום
והיה מדבר עמו מהסנה. אלא מה הסנה הזה שפל מכל
אילנות שבעולם כך ירדו ישראל למדרגה התחתונה
והקב״ה ירד עמהם וגאלם שנאמ׳ וארד להצילו מיד
מצרים. ◆

ר׳ יהושע אומ׳ מפני מה נגלה הקב״ה משמי מרום
והיה מדבר עם משה מהסנה אלא כשירדו ישראל
למצרים שכינה ירדה עמהם שנאמ׳ אנכי ארד עמך
וגו׳ (בר׳ מו ד) ‹כשיצאו› נגלה שכינה עמהם ‹שנאמר
ואנכי אעלך גם עלה (שם) ירדו לים שכינה עמהם שנא׳
ויסע מלאך האלקים (שמ׳ יד יט) באו למדבר שכינה
עמהם› שנא׳ ובמדבר אשר ראית וגו׳ (דב׳ א׳ לא).  ◆
ר׳ חייא ור׳ יהודה אומרי׳ בוא וראה רחמיו של מי שאמר
והיה העולם שכל זמן שישראל נתוני׳ בצער צרה
‹כביכול› לפניו שנא׳ בכל צרתם לא צר (יש׳ סג ט).  ◆
אין ליא לא צרת צבור צרת יחיד מנין ת״ל יקראני ואענהו
עמו אנכי בצרה (תה׳ צא טו) וכן הוא אומר כי [כל] הנוגע
בכם וגו׳ (זכ׳ ב יב).  ◆ ר׳ יהודה אומר אין ת״ל ו׳׳ו
אלא יו׳׳ד מלמד שכל מי שמזיק לאדם מישראל כאילו
מזיק לפני מי שאמר והיה העולם. וכל זמן שישראל

F
A 1
A 2
A 3
B
C

renders its meaning as 'my eye'].[11] This teaches that whosoever harms a person from Israel, it is as if he does harm before He who spoke and the world came into being. And whenever Israel dwells at ease, the Holy One, blessed be He, dwells at ease with them in joy. And thus Scripture states, '... that I might see the prosperity of your chosen ones' (Ps. 106:5)."

## I:III

1.  A. R. Yosi ha-Galili says, "Why did the Holy One, blessed be He, appear from the highest heavens and speak with Moses from within the bush? Because it is pure, in that the nations of the world do not use it as an idol."

## I:IV

1.  A. R. Eliezer ben Arach says, "Why did the Holy One, blessed be He, appear from the highest heavens and speak with Moses from within the bush? Shouldn't He appear[12] from the heights of the world, from the cedars of Lebanon and from the tops of mountains and from the tops of hills?

    B. "Rather, the Holy One, blessed be He, humbled His presence, and made His request normally, lest the nations of the world should say incorrectly, '[Only] because He is God and the master of His world did he[13] obey His illogical request!'

    C. "Therefore, the Holy One, blessed be He, pressed Moses [about it at the bush] for six days, and on the seventh he said to Him, 'Make someone else Your agent!' (Exod. 4:13). As it says in Scripture, 'But Moses said to the Lord, "Please, Lord, I am not a man (of words)"' (Exod. 4:10).

    D. "They told a parable: To what is the matter alike? It is like a king who had a servant whom he loved completely. The king sought to make him his administrator overseeing the maintenance of the members of the king's palace. What did the king do? He took the slave by his hand, and brought him into his treasury, and showed him his silver vessels, golden vessels, fine stones and gems, and all that he possessed within his treasury. After this, he brought him outside and showed him [his] trees, gardens, parks, enclosed areas, and all that was his in the fields.

    "Afterward, the slave closed his hand and said, 'I am unable to be the administrator overseeing the maintenance of the members of the king's palace.' The king said to him, 'Since [you knew] that you could not be the administrator, why did you put me through all this trouble?' And the king was angry with him, and decreed that he should never enter his palace.

    E. "Likewise, the Holy One, blessed be He, pressed Moses [at the bush] for six days, and on the seventh [Moses] said to him, 'Make someone else Your agent!' [At that moment,] the Holy One, blessed be He, swore that he would never enter the Land of Israel. As it says in Scripture, '(Because you did not trust Me enough to affirm my sanctity in the sight of the Israelite people), therefore you shall not lead (this congregation into the land that I have given them)' (Num. 20:12)."

---

[11] Compare 3.C with *Mekhilta de-Rabbi Ishmael,* Shirata (H/R, 135:1–3; Laut., vol. 2, 43:10–12; Neus., XXXI:I:3.A–C).

[12] This introductory interrogative in 1.A, as reconstructed in the Epstein/Melamed text, is a confusing combination by the editors of a variant of the phrase that appears in *Midrash Ha-Gadol* with a variant phrase attested in the *Notes of Rav Abraham ha-Laḥmi.* The combination of the different introductory clauses from the two versions is neither clear nor particularly easy to render into idiomatic English. I have chosen to translate the introductory clause as it appears in the JTS manuscript for this portion of the text (JTS Rab. 2404, folios 1–2).

[13] I.e., Moses.

שרויים ברווחה הקב״ה שרוי ברווח׳ עמהם ובשמחה. וכן הוא אומ׳ לראות בטובת בחירך וגו׳ (תה׳ קו ה).

I:III

A 1 ר׳ יוסי הגלילי אומ׳ מפני מה נגלה הקב״ה משמי מרום והיה מדבר עם משה מהסנה מפני שהוא טהור שאין אומות העולם עושין אותו ע״ז.

I:IV

A 1 ר׳ אל(י)עזר בן ערך אומר וכי מפני מה נגלה הקב״ה משמי מרום והיה מדבר עם משה בסנה והלא היה לך <יכול המקום שידבר מגבהי עולם> מארזי הלבנון ומראשי ההרים ומראשי הגבעות

B אלא השפיל הקב״ה את שכינתו ועשה דברו כדרך ארץ שלא יהיו אומות העולם אומרי׳ מפני שהוא אלוה ובעל עולמו עשה דברו שלא כדין.

C לפיכך כבש הקב״ה את משה ששה ימים ובשביעי אמר לו שלח נא ביד תשלח (שמ׳ ד יג) שנא׳ ויאמר משה אל ה׳ בי ה׳ לא איש וגו׳ (שם י).

D משלו משל למה הדבר דומה למלך שהיה לו עבד והיה אוהבו אהבה גמורה (ו)בקש המלך לעשותו אפטרופוס שלו להיות מפרנס בני פלטין של מלך מה עשה (אותו) המלך תפס את העבד בידו והכניסו לבית גנזיו והראהו כלי כסף וכלי זהב אבני׳ טובות ומרגליות וכל מה שיש לו בבית גנזיו ומאחר כן הוציאו והראהו אילנות גנים ופרדסים וקרפיפות וכל מה שיש לו בשדות. לאחר כן כבש העבד את ידו ואמר איני יכול לעשות אפטרופוס להיות מפרנס בני פלטין של מלך. אמ׳ לו המלך הואיל ולא היית יכול לעשות אפטרופוס למה הטרחתני כל הטורח הזה וכעס עליו המלך וגזר עליו שלא יכנס לפלטין שלו.

E כך כבש הקב״ה למשה ששה ימים ובשביעי אמר לו שלח נא ביד תשלח. נשבע לו הקב״ה שלא יכנס לארץ ישראל שנא׳ לכן לא תביאו וגו׳ (במ׳ כ יב).

(Textual Source: Ms. T-S Cambridge C 4a.4)[14]

2.  
[3]

A. The Holy One said, "Moses, it is absolutely clear to Me that you shall shepherd my people Israel!"[15] Moses responded before God, "I am unable—'Make someone else Your agent!'" (Exod. 4:13). The Holy One said to him, "You say, 'Make someone else Your agent!' Behold, Joshua your disciple and attendant, raised by your hand—he will bring Israel into the land. As for you, you will not enter with them!"

B. Moses responded before God saying, "Master of the World, you say to me, 'Go down to Egypt and bring out My people, the Children of Israel!' Certainly I am an agent and I ... [manuscript lacuna] ... Rather, this commission on which you are sending me actually contains two tasks! My Master ... [manuscript lacuna] ... A commission is better [when undertaken by] two people, and not [just] one! In accordance with what is said in Scripture, 'Two are better than one' (Eccles. 4:9). Likewise [it says in Scripture], '(A case can only be valid) on the testimony of two witnesses (or more)' (Deut. 19:15)."

C. The Holy One, blessed be He, said, "Moses, it is absolutely clear to Me that you are standing [here] beseeching favor for Aaron your brother, that he should accept it upon himself to go out [with you] on My commission! Already the Holy Spirit dwells upon him, and he has gone out and is waiting for you on the road to Egypt. And when he sees you, he will be happy. In accordance with what is said in Scripture, 'There is Aaron your brother the Levite ... (Even now he is setting out to meet you, and he will be happy to see you)' (Exod. 4:14)."

D. And the Holy One, blessed be He, said additionally to Moses, "When I appeared to you in the bush, you hid your face so [you] would not see My presence. In accordance with what is said in Scripture, 'And Moses hid (his face)' (Exod. 3:6).

"And now, who has given you the right and permission to speak before Me like a mortal slave who has permission to speak [in such a manner] before his master? Moses, you talk too much!

[4]

"Do I not possess [heavenly] messengers, do I not possess troops, do I not possess *seraphim,* do I not possess angels and [heavenly] beasts and *ofanim* and the wheels of the chariot that I could send to Egypt so that I might bring out My people? But you say, 'Make someone else Your agent!' Certainly you are deserving of immediate drowning! But what am I to do with you, for I am so very loving and faithful?"

*Chapter Two*

(Textual Source: Ms. T-S Cambridge C 4a.4)

II:I

1.

A. "God spoke (to Moses and said to him, 'I am the Lord')" (Exod. 6:2):

B. R. Eliezer says, "... [manuscript lacuna] ... to afflict him, for if He reversed the divine attribute of justice to that of mercy ...[16]

[14] The Cambridge manuscript incorporated here into the text is significantly fragmented. The editors appear to have reconstructed it primarily from the Hoffmann version of the text, which itself is based upon a single manuscript of *Midrash ha-Gadol.* There are, however, minor inconsistencies in this reconstructive pattern.

[15] Noteworthy is the parallelism between the language used by God here with Moses ("You shall shepherd my people Israel") and the language used by God with King David in 2 Sam. 5:2 ("... and the Lord said to you: 'You shall shepherd My people Israel; you shall be ruler of Israel'"). There is a broadly developed aggadic interest in drawing comparisons between David and Moses. For an interesting discussion and delineation of examples, see Sandra R. Shimoff, *Rabbinic Legends of Saul, Solomon, and David: Political and Social Implications of Aggada* (St. Mary's Seminary and University Ecumenical Institute Dissertation, 1981), particularly pp. 193–97.

[16] As is evident here, the Cambridge manuscript is fragmented at this point, and ends abruptly in the middle of this tradition. Worth noting, however, are the apparent affinities between the text as it appears here and the following tradition found at *Exodus Rabbah* 6:1:

על דבר זה בקשה מדת הדין לפגוע במשה הה״ד וידבר אלהים אל משה ולפי שנסתכל הקב״ה שבשביל צער ישראל דבר כן חזר
ונהג בו במדת רחמים הה״ד ויאמר אליו אני יי

| | |
|---:|:---:|
| [א"ל הק' משה] גלוי וידוע לפני שאתה תרע[ה] את | A 2 |

עמי יש'. אמר משה [וה]שיב לפני המק' איני יכ' שלח

נא ביד תשלח (שמ' ד יג) אמר לו [הק' אתה או' שלח נא]

[ב]יד תשלח הרי יהושע תלמידך ומשרתך וגידול ידך הוא

| | |
|---:|:---:|
| יכניס את יש' לארץ אתה] [א]ין אתה נכנס עמהן • השיב | B |

משה לפני המק' ואמר [רבונו של עולם אתה או' לי]

רד למצרים והוציא את עמי בני ישראל בודיי אני שליח

ואני [...] [אל]א שזו השליחות שאתה שולח אותי יש בה

שתי שליחות ר[בוני...] [יפה] שליחות בשני בני אדם ולא

באחד כענין (זה) שנ' טובים הש[נ]ים מן האחד] (קה' ד ט)

| | |
|---:|:---:|
| [...] כך על פי שנים עדים וג' (דב' יט טו) • אמר לו הקב"ה | C |

משה גלוי וידוע לפני ש[אתה עומד] [ו]מבקש רחמים על

אהרן אחיך שיק[בל] עליו ויל[ך בשליחותי כב]ר שרת

עליו] רוח הקשה והוא יוצא) ומשמר לך בשבילי מצרים

וכשהוא ר[ואה אותך הוא] שמח כענין שנ' הלא אהרן אחיך

| | |
|---:|:---:|
| הלוי וג' (שמ' ד יד) • ועוד אמ[ר לו הקב"ה למשה] | D |

[כ]שנגליתי עליך בסנה היית(י) מסתיר את פניך שלא

לראות שכינ[תי כענין שנ' ויסתר] [מ]שה וג' (שמ' ג ו)

ועכשו מי נת[ן לך] פתחון פה ורשות לדבר לפני [כעבד

בשר ודם שיש לו רשות] לדבר לפני רבו מש[ה] דברן את

אין] ל[י שלוחין אין לי גדודין אין לי שרפים אין] [לי]

מלאכים וחיות ואופנ[י]ם וגלגלי מרכבה שאשלחם למצרים

ואוציא את בני] [שא]תה או' שלח נא ביד תשלח [בודיי אתה

ראוי לשטיפה מיד] [אב]ל מה אעשה לך שבעל הרחמי[ם

אני בע]ל אמונה [אני וידבר] [אלקים א]ל משה וג' פס' •

| | |
|---:|:---:|
| | II:I |

| | |
|---:|:---:|
| (ב) וידבר א[לקים וג' • ר' אלעזר [או'] [...לפ]גוע] | B/A 1 |

בו שאם הוא

English: Because of this, [God's] divine attribute of justice sought to strike Moses. Thus it is written in Scripture, "God spoke to Moses …" (Exod. 6:2). But when the Holy One, blessed be He, reflected that Moses spoke like this because of Israel's grief, He switched and behaved toward him [under the influence of God's] divine attribute of mercy. Thus it is written in Scripture, "… and said to him, 'I am the Lord' (Exod. 6:2)."

(Textual Source: JTS Rab. 2404, folios 1–2 and Notes of Rav Abraham Ha-Laḥmi—
הגהות רב אברהם הלחמי)

II:II

1.    A.   "And God spoke to Moses (and said to him, 'I am the Lord')" (Exod. 6:2):

       B.   R. Yosi said, "The Holy One, blessed be He, said to Moses, 'I am He who spoke and the world came into being. As it says in Scripture, "God, the Lord God spoke and summoned the world" (Ps. 50:1). And Scripture says, "From Zion, perfect in beauty" (Ps. 50:2). I am He who spoke to Abraham between the parts [of the split heifer, goat, ram, turtledove, and bird, saying]: "Know that your offspring shall be strangers" (Gen. 15:13).

       C.   "'But now, as the [obligation to fulfill] the oath [that I swore to your forefathers] to bring the Children of Israel out from Egypt is incumbent upon me,[17] and I am requesting [of you] to bring them out—you say to me, "Make someone else Your agent!"'"

2.    A.   R. Joshua says, "'And God spoke to Moses' (Exod. 6:2):

       B.   "The Holy One, blessed be He, said to Moses, 'I am trustworthy to pay the reward [for the devoted action of] Isaac son of Abraham, from whom departed a fourth [of a *log*] of blood on top of the altar.[18] And I said to him, "Because of your great strength, those condemned to death will be retrieved" (Ps. 79:11).[19]

       C.   "'But now, as the [obligation to fulfill] the oath [that I swore to your forefathers] to bring the Children of Israel out from Egypt is incumbent upon me,[20] and I am requesting [of you] to bring them out—you say to me, "Make someone else Your agent!"'"

3.    A.   R. Shimon (ben Yoḥai) says, "'And God spoke to Moses ...' (Exod. 6:2):

       B.   "The Holy One, blessed be He, said to Moses, 'I am He who said to Jacob, "Your offspring shall be like the dust

(Textual Source: Ms. T-S Cambridge C 4a.4)[21]

of the earth" (Gen. 28:14).

       C.   "'But now, as the [obligation to fulfill] the oath [that I swore to your forefathers] to bring the Children of Israel out from Egypt is incumbent upon me,[22] you say to me, "Make someone (else Your agent)!"'"

---

[17] Epstein and Melamed interpolated here into the Hebrew text the verb "and you have come," based upon its attestation in the Hoffmann edition of the text. Hoffmann gleaned this material from the Berlin manuscript of *Midrash ha-Gadol*. The word, however, renders the sentence both awkward and difficult, and I have chosen to translate the text without reference to it.

[18] According to the text, and in contradiction to the biblical text in Genesis 22, Abraham actually slightly punctured Isaac with the slaughtering knife upon the altar, drawing from him a fourth of a *log* of blood. This amount of drawn blood rendered Isaac a suitable sacrificial offering, according to Rabbinic law, and ultimately facilitated Abraham's fulfillment of the divine decree, while simultaneously sparing Isaac's life. Moreover, as a result of Abraham's obedience and faithful performance of God's decree to sacrifice his beloved son, Isaac, Rabbinic tradition holds that he accrued merit on behalf of the subsequent generations of Jews, from which they could benefit and receive forgiveness for future transgressions and protection in times of trouble or danger. This Rabbinic theological concept is typically referred to as "Merit of the Forefathers" (זכות אבות).

[19] This prooftext is missing in the Cambridge manuscript, and has been interpolated based upon its attestation in the Berlin manuscript of *Midrash ha-Gadol*. The text's method of employing Ps. 79:11 as a prooftext is intriguing. In its biblical context, the verse is in reference to God. Moreover, the word "great" in the biblical text is prefixed with a כ (כגדל), as opposed to here, where it is prefixed with a ב. According to its biblical context, therefore, it is translated, "*As befits* Your great strength, those condemned to death will be retrieved." In our text, however, God quotes this verse to Abraham, and does so in reference to Abraham, with the different prefix perhaps serving both to accommodate and emphasize this transferal: "*Because of* your [i.e., Abraham's] great strength [of character], those [future generations of Jews] condemned to death will be retrieved."

[20] See note 17.

[21] The Cambridge manuscript incorporated here into the text is significantly fragmented. The editors appear to have reconstructed it primarily from the Hoffmann version of the text, which itself is based upon a single manuscript of *Midrash ha-Gadol*. There are, however, even minor inconsistencies in this reconstructive pattern.

[22] See note 17. In this instance, however, the verb is actually attested in the Cambridge manuscript, and not interpolated by the authors.

| | | |
|---|---:|---:|
| <הופך> מדת הדין למדת [הרחמים] ◆ וידבר אלקים אל משה. | B/A | 1 |
| א״ר יוסי אמ׳ לו הקב״ה אני הוא שאמרתי והיה העולם שנא׳ | | |
| אל אלקים ה׳ דבר ויקרא ארץ (תה׳ נ א) ואומר מציון מכלל | | |
| יופי (שם ב) אני הוא שאמרתי לאברהם בין הבתרים ידוע | | |
| תדע <כי גר יהיה זרעך> (בר׳ טו יג) ◆ ועכשיו הרי שבועה | C | |
| מבוהלת <ובאת> לפני להוציא את בני ישראל ממצרים ואני | | |
| מבקש להוציאם ואתה אומר לי שלח נא ביד תשלח. ◆ ר׳ | A | 2 |
| יהושע אומ׳ וידבר אלקים אל משה ◆ א״ל <הקב״ה ל>משה | B | |
| נאמן אני לשלם שכר יצחק בן אברהם שיצא ממנו רביעית | | |
| דם על גבי המזבח ואמרתי לו בגודל זרועך הותר בני תמותה | | |
| (תה׳ עט יא) ◆ ועכשיו הרי השבועה מבוהלת <ובאת> לפני | C | |
| של׳א כדרך ארץ להוציא את בני ישראל ממצרים ואני מבקש | | |
| להוציאם ואתה אומר לי שלח נא ביד תשלח. ◆ ר׳ שמעון | A | 3 |
| (בן יוחאי) אומר וידבר אלקים אל משה (וגו׳) ◆ א״ל הקב״ה | B | |
| <למשה> אני הוא שאמרתי ליעקב והיה זרעך [כעפר] [הארץ] | | |
| (בר׳ כח יד) ◆ עכשיו] הרי שבועה מבוהלת ובאת [לפני | C | |
| להוציא את] [בני ישראל ממצרים ואת]ה אומ׳ שלח נא. ◆ | | |

4.  A.  R. Judah says, "'And God spoke (to Moses)' (Exod. 6:2):

    B.  "The Holy One, blessed be He, said to Moses, 'I judge truthfully, I am full of love, I am trustworthy to pay a reward, and Israel is enslaved at the hand of those who are uncircumcised and impure. And I am seeking to bring them out from beneath their hand, but you say to me, "Make someone (else Your agent)!"'"

[5]

5.  A.  R. Nehemiah says, "The Holy One, blessed be He, said to Moses, 'The suffering of Israel in Egypt is abundantly clear to me ... [manuscript lacuna] ... a severe suffering. As it says in Scripture, "God looked at the children of Israel, (and God took note)" (Exod. 2:25).

    B.  "'They live in anguish and you live in ease, and I have lovingly remembered to bring them out from Egypt. But you say to me, "Make someone (else Your agent)!"'"

6.  A.  R. Yosi ha-Galili says, "'And God spoke (to Moses)' (Exod. 6:2):

    B.  "The Holy One, blessed be He, said to Moses, 'In Egypt, Israel became worthy of destruction [when they impurified themselves] with Egyptian idols. [As it says in Scripture,] "And I said to them, 'Cast away, every one of you, the detestable things that you are drawn to and (do not defile yourselves) with the fetishes of Egypt ... But they defied me and refused to listen to Me ...'" (Ezek. 20:7–8).

    C.  "'But on account of My great name, and for the sake of the Merit of the Forefathers[23] [I refrained from such a punishment]. As it says in Scripture, "God heard their moaning (and God remembered His covenant with Abraham and Isaac and Jacob)" (Exod. 2:24). [I also refrained] in order that My name not be degraded by them. For thus Scripture says, "But I acted for the sake of My name, (that it might not be profaned in the sight of the nations of the world among whom they were. For it was before their eyes) that I had made Myself known to Israel to bring them out of the Land of Egypt" (Ezek. 20:9).'"

7.  A.  R. Tarfon says, "The Holy One, blessed be He, said, 'It is abundantly clear to me that Israel deserves to leave Egypt and be handed over to Ammon, Moab, and Amalek. However, because of the oath that I swore to fight their war, I shall rescue them. As it says in Scripture, "Hand upon the throne of the Lord! (The Lord will be at war with Amalek throughout the ages) ..." (Exod. 17:16). And Scripture says, "But I acted for the sake of My name that it might not be profaned" (Ezek. 20:9).

    B.  "'And behold I am seeking to bring them out from Egypt, but you say to me, "Make (someone else Your agent)!"'"

8.  A.  R. Joshua b. Korḥa says, "'And God spoke (to Moses)' (Exod. 6:2):

    B.  "The Holy One, blessed be He, said, 'Israel did not deserve to be given manna in the wilderness, but rather [they deserved to wander about] in hunger and thirst, naked and uncovered. But I paid them the reward of Abraham their forefather, who arose and served before the ministering angels. As it says in Scripture, "He took curds and milk ..." (Gen. 18:8).

    C.  "'And behold I am seeking to bring them out from Egypt, but you say to me, "Make someone else Your agent!"'"

---

[23] See note 18.

| | | |
|---|---|---|
| ר' יוהדה או' וידבר אלקים ♦ אמ' הקב"ה [למשה אני דן | B/A | 4 |
| ב]אמת אני מלא רחמים אני נאמן לשלם שכר וישראל | | |
| [משועבדין ביד ער]לים וטמאים ואני מבקש להוציאם מתחת | | |
| ידם ואתה א[ו' [שלח נא ♦ ר' נחמי]ה או' אמ' הקב"ה | A | 5 |
| למשה גלוי וידוע לפני צער ישראל במצרי[ם] [...צע]ר | | |
| קשה שנ' וירא אלקים א' בנ' ישראל וג' (שמ' ב' כה) ♦ הם | B | |
| שרויים בצרה [ואתה שרוי ברווח] ואני כבר פקדתי אותם | | |
| ברחמ' להוציאם ממצרים ואתה א[ו' [שלח נא ♦ ר' יוסי] | A | 6 |
| הג' או' וידב' אלקים ♦ אמ' [הקב"ה] למשה כלייה נתחייבו | B | |
| ישראל במצ' [...שנטמאו] בגלולי מצרים [...שנ'] ואומר | | |
| אליהם איש שקוצי עיניו [השליכו ובגלולי מצ' וג' וים]רו | | |
| בי ול' אבו לש' אלי וג' (יחז' כ ז - ח) ♦ אלא בעבור שמי הגדול | C | |
| ולמען זכות אבות [שנ' וישמע אלקים א]ת נאקתם וג' (שמ' | | |
| ב כד) ולמען שלא יתחלל שמי בהם שכן הו' או' ואעש [למען | | |
| שמי וג' אשר] נודעתי אליהם לאמר להוציאם מארץ מצ' | | |
| וג' (יחז' כ ט) ♦ ר' טרפ[ון] [או' אמר הקב"ה גל]וי וידוע לפני | A | 7 |
| שישראל ראו[ים] ל[צא]ת ממצרים ולהנ[תן] [ביד עמון | | |
| ומואב ועמלק אלא בשבועה נשבעתי ללחום] מלחמתם | | |
| ואוש[יע] [אותם שנ' כי יד על כס יה וג' (שמ' יז טז) ואו' | | |
| ואעש ל[מען שמי לבלתי הח[ל'ל] (יחז' כ ט) ♦ [והריני מבקש | B | |
| להוציאם ממצ' ואתה או' לי שלח וג'. ♦ ר' יהו]שע בן קרחה | A | 8 |
| או' וידבר אלקים ♦ [אמ' הקב"ה לא היו] ישראל [ראויין ל]יתן | B | |
| להם מן במדבר אלא ברע[ב] [וצמא ערום ועריה א]בל | | |
| מש[לים אני להם] שכר אברהם אב[יהם] שעמ[ד ועשה] | | |
| ♦ לפני מלאכי] השרת שנ' [ויקח] חמאה וחלב [וג' (בר' יח ח) ♦ | | |
| והריני מבקש [להוציאם ממצרים ואתה או' לי שלח נא | C | |
| ביד תשלח] ♦ | | |

(Textual Source: JTS Rab. 2404, folios 1–2 and Notes of Rav Abraham Ha-Laḥmi—
הגהות רב אברהם הלחמי)

II:III

1.
[6]

A.   R. Akiva says, "The Holy One, blessed be He, said to Moses, 'I have sworn by means of oath, decree, and proclamation that you shall not enter into the Land of Israel!

B.   "'For thus Scripture says, "*Therefore* you shall not lead this congregation" (Num. 20:12). And [scriptural usage of the word] "therefore" only means "oath." As it says in Scripture, "Therefore I swear against the House of Eli" (1 Sam. 3:14).'"

C.   R. Akiva said [additionally], "And why all this anger [on God's behalf]? Because [Moses] said [to God], 'Ever since I came to Pharaoh to speak in Your name, (he has dealt worse with this people, and still you have not delivered Your people)' (Exod. 5:23)."

2.

A.   R. Eliezer the Modiite says, "Forbid that that righteous one[24] should ever have spoken in such a manner as this! Rather, this was what he said before Him, 'Master of the World, isn't a redeemer one who rescues? Master of the World, I know that You will bring Your children out from Egypt. Is it possible that You will bring them out by the hand of another, because have I not merited that they leave by my hand?'

B.   "The Holy One, blessed be He, replied to Moses, 'Moses, you have so merited, and by your hand I will bring them out from Egypt!'

C.   "And you know that this was so, for you learn this from the response that He gave him.[25] As it says in Scripture, 'Then the Lord said to Moses, "You shall soon see (what I will do to Pharaoh)"' (Exod. 6:1)."

II:IV

1.

A.   And the Sages say, "The Holy One, blessed be He, said to Moses, 'Moses, the merit of Amram your father has stood up for you.'

B.   "For he arose and did a great thing for Israel, and his opinion was aligned with the opinion of God. For when Egypt imposed heavy labor upon Israel and drowned them in the Nile, [Israel] said, 'What are we accomplishing? We take wives and give birth to sons and weary ourselves, and then they drown our sons in water and then hide them in the [walls of] a building!'

C.   "So [Amram] arose and did a great thing for Israel. What did he do? He divorced his wife when she was three months pregnant, and she went to her father's house. All of Israel followed, divorcing their wives [when they were three months pregnant]. After three months, [Amram] once again married his wife, upholding what is said in Scripture, 'A certain man of the house of Levi went and married a Levite woman, etc.' (Exod. 2:1). And there were [even] ministering angels rejoicing before her like grooms and brides, upholding what is said in Scripture, '(He sets the childless woman among her household) as a happy mother of children. Hallelujah' (Ps. 113:9). And as Egypt was counting [on her to take] nine months [to give birth], she gave birth [at what they thought to be] six months!

D.   "Now, why was the account [of Amram taking a wife in Exod. 2:1] needed? To delineate if Amram took a wife or not? Rather, [it was needed] to inform all the earth's inhabitants of the merit of Amram the Righteous!"

---

[24] I.e., Moses.
[25] I.e., the response of God to Moses' comments in Exod. 5:23.

A 1   ר' עקיבא אומ' אמ' הקב"ה למשה בשבועה בגזירה

B באמירה נשבעתי שלא תכנס לארץ (ישראל) ◆ ‹וכן הוא אומר לכן לא תביאו את הקהל הזה (במ' כ יב) ואין לכן אלא שבועה שנא' ולכן נשבעתי לבית עלי (ש"א ג יד)› ◆ אמר ר'

C עקיבא וכל כעס זה למה זה בשביל שאמר ומאז באתי אל פרעה לדבר בשמך (שמ' ה כג). ◆ א'ר אליעזר המודעי חלילה

A 2 לאותו צדיק שיאמר כלשון הזה אלא כך אמר לפניו רבון העולמים לא מי שגואל הוא מציל הוא. רבון העולמים יודע אני שאתה עתיד להוציא את בניך ממצרים שמא על יד אחר אתה עתיד להוציאם ואני לא זכיתי שיצאו על ידי. ◆

B השיב הקב"ה ואמ' למשה אתה זכית ועל ידך אני מוציאם ממצרים ◆ תדע לך שכן שמתוך תשובה שאמר לו

C אתה למד שנא' ויאמר ה' אל משה עתה תראה וגו'. ◆

II:IV

A 1   וחכמי' אומרי' ‹א"ל הקב"ה למשה משה› זכות עמרם

B אביך עמדה לך ◆ שעמד ועשה דבר גדול בישראל והסכימה דעתו לדעתו של מקום ‹שכשהכבידו מצרים עבודה קשה על ישראל והיו מטבעין אותן ביאור› אמרו מה אנו מועילים נושאי' נשים ומולידי' בנים ומייגעין עצמינו ומאחר שמשקעין את בנינו במים חוזרים וכובשים אותם בבנין ◆ ועמד

C ועשה דבר גדול בישראל. מה עשה גרש את אשתו בתוך שלשה חדשים מעוברת שהיתה והלכה לבית אביה ועמדו כל ישראל וגרשו את נשותיהן. לאחר שלשה חדשים חזר ועשה בה קדושין לקיים מה שנאמר וילך איש מבית לוי ויקח את בת לוי וגו'. והיו מלאכי השרת משחקין לפניה כחתנים וככלות לקיים מה שנאמר אם הבנים שמחה הללויה (תה' קיג ט). ומצרים מנו לה תשעה חדשים והיא ילדה בתוך ששה

D חדשים. ◆ וכי למה הוצרך הדבר ‹לומר› אם לקח עמרם אשה אם לא לקח אלא להודיע לכל באי העולם זכותו של עמרם הצדיק. חסלת פרשתא ◆

(Textual Source: Midrash ha-Gadol)

II:V

1.    A.    Moses responded before the Holy One, blessed be He, "Master of the World! [If] I, a prophet the son of a prophet, have accepted *your* command with great doubts, [then] how will Pharaoh, an evil one the son of an evil one, as well as [all of] Egypt, rebellious ones the sons of rebellious ones, accept *my* command?"

      B.    He [i.e., God] said, "You will speak the holy language[26] like an angel, and Aaron your brother will speak [it in] Egyptian. As it says in Scripture, 'See, I have placed you as God over Pharaoh, and Aaron your brother shall be your prophet' (Exod. 7:1)."

(Textual Source: JTS Rab. 2404, folios 1–2 and Notes of Rav Abraham Ha-Laḥmi—
רב הגהות אברהם הלחמי)

      C.    Moses responded before the Holy One, blessed be He, "Master of all the world! You have said to me, 'Go down to Egypt and bring the children of Israel out of Egypt!' But I am afraid of the people from whom I fled!"

      D.    He [i.e., God] said, "Don't be afraid of them, for all of them have died! As it says in Scripture, '... for all the men who sought (to kill you) are dead' (Exod. 4:19)."

[7]   E.    The Holy One, blessed be He, responded [further] to Moses, "Who rendered the men Pharaoh sent to catch you mute, deaf, and blind? Was it not I? As it says in Scripture, 'Who gives man speech? (Who makes him dumb or deaf, seeing or blind? Is it not I, the Lord?)' (Exod. 4:11)."

2.    A.    R. Eliezer b. Judah ish Bartotha says, "Moses replied before the Holy One, blessed be He, saying, 'You are saying to me, "Go and bring 600,000 people out from under the Egyptian burden and servitude!" If you were saying this to me for only 100 or 200 people, the command would still be very hard for me! If I had been preparing them for this for a year or two before the command, then the command would already have been completed!

            "'However, since they have enslaved them for 210 years, Pharaoh will now say to me, "He who has enslaved a slave for 10 years with no one protesting against it, [should allow] another to come along and take him out from under his control?" Or, "He who has served the plantation for 10 years with no one protesting against it [should allow] another to come along and take him out from under his control?"

      B.    "'Master of the World! These things which you are saying to me are both very difficult and honorable. [As it says in Scripture,] "For I am slow of speech and slow of tongue" (Exod. 4:10).'"[27]

---

[26] I.e., Hebrew.

[27] Moses' response here is based upon the text's emphasis on his words in Exod. 4:10. In that verse, Moses claims to be "slow" (Hebrew: *k'vad*, כבד) *both* of speech and tongue. The text is intrigued with the double employment of the word "slow" in the biblical verse, and is suggesting that this indicates that Moses is declaring to God that the things God requests of him are both "very difficult" (Hebrew: *k'vadim*, כבדים) and "honorable" (Hebrew: *m'chubadim*, מכובדים).

II:V

A 1 ⟨השיב משה ואמ׳ לפני הקב״ה רבש״ע אני נביא בן נביא
מספק ספיקות נכנסתי לדבריך פרעה רשע בן רשע ומצרים
מרודים בני מרודים היאך יכנסו לדברי. ◆

B א״ל אתה דבר בלשון
הקודש כמלאך ואהרן אחיך ידבר בלשון מצרי שנא׳ ראה
נתתיך אלהים לפרעה ואהרן אחיך יהיה נביאך (שמ׳ ז א)⟩.

C השיב משה ואמ׳ לפני הקב״ה רבון כל העולמים אתה אמרת
לי רד למצרים והוצא את בני ישראל ממצרים מתיירא אני
מבני אדם שברחתי מהם. ◆

D אמר לו אל תירא מהם שכולם מתו
שנאמ׳ כי מתו כל האנשים המבקשים וגו׳ (שמ׳ ד יט). ◆

E השיב
הקב״ה ואמ׳ למשה בני אדם ששלח פרעה לתפשך מי עשאם
אלמים חרשים סומים לא אני שנאמ׳ ויאמר א׳ אל משה מי
שם פה (שמ׳ ד יא). ◆

A 2 ⟨ר׳ אלעזר בן יהודה איש ברתותא אומר⟩
השיב משה ואמר לפני הקב״ה אתה אומר לי לך הוציא ששים
רבוא בני אדם מתחת סבלות מצרים ומתחת שיעבודן של
מצרים אלו על ק׳ על ק׳ בני אדם או על ק״ק בלבד אתה אומר לי
הדבר עדיין קשה לי מאד אלו חתרתי בהם שנה או שתים
לפני הדבר כבר היה הדבר עשוי אלא מאחר ששיעבדו בהן
מאתים ועשר שנים עכשיו יאמר לי פרעה ⟨מי שעבדו עבד
עשר שנים ולא מיחה בו כל בריה יבוא אחר ויוציאו מתחת
ידו או מי שעבד הכרם עשר שנים ולא מיחה בו כל בריה
יבוא אחר ויוציאו מתחת ידו⟩. ◆

B רבש״ע כבדים ומכובדים
דברים הללו שאתה אומר לי כי כבד פה וכבד לשון אנכי⟩. ◆

# Tractate Pisḥa

*Chapter Three*

(Textual Source: Midrash ha-Gadol)

III:I

1.    A.  "The Lord said to Moses and Aaron in the Land of Egypt" (Exod. 12:1):

      B.  This teaches that before the Land of Israel was consecrated [as the exclusive location for divine speech] all lands were suitable for divine speech. But once the Land of Israel was so consecrated, there was no divine speech with the prophets anywhere [outside of the Land of Israel], except next to water.[1]

      C.  As it teaches in Scripture, "The word of the Lord came to the priest Ezekiel son of Buzi, by the Chebar Canal in the Land of the Chaldeans" (Ezek. 1:3). And Scripture says, "And I was by the Ulai river" (Dan. 8:2). And Scripture says, "... when I was on the bank of the great river, the Tigris" (Dan. 10:4).

      D.  And likewise with Jonah, [God] only spoke with him next to water.

      E.  R. Judah says, "Even at first [God] only spoke with the prophets next to water.[2] As it says in Scripture, 'The word of the Lord came [היה היה] (to the priest Ezekiel son of Buzi)' (Ezek. 1:3)."[3]

      F.  R. Nehemiah says, "[Rather, it is the case that] even at first [God] spoke with the prophets anywhere. What [therefore] does the verse 'The word of the Lord came to Ezekiel' come to teach? This teaches that the Holy Spirit was not frequently upon him."

2.    A.  "(The Lord said to Moses and Aaron) in the Land of Egypt" (Exod. 12:1):

      B.  One might think [that God spoke] within the [boundaries of] the city. Scripture states, [however,] "... in the *Land* (of Egypt)." [God] did not speak with him [even within] a field [within the city.[4] Rather,] He spoke with him outside of the city.

      C.  And so did Moses say to Pharaoh, "As I go out of the city (I shall spread out my hands to the Lord)" (Exod. 9:29). And just as with prayer [as indicated in Exod. 9:29], which is less significant, [it is the case that Moses] would not pray within the city, then is it not all the

---

[1] Only next to water, presumably, because of its purificatory capabilities.

[2] I.e., it was the case even before the consecration of the Land of Israel that God only spoke outside the Land of Israel next to places of water.

[3] The seemingly doubled scriptural infinitive absolute is understood to indicate a twofold nature of the divine speech, i.e., the divine speech that occurred *before* the consecration of the Land of Israel was like the speech that Ezekiel received *after* the consecration, in that it was received next to water.

[4] Note m. Arakhin 9:5: "Whatever is within the city wall is considered 'a dwelling house in a walled city' (ref. Lev. 25:29), except for the fields. R. Meir says, 'Even fields.'"

# מסכתא דפסחא

III:I

1 B/A     ויאמר ה׳ אל משה ואל אהרן בארץ מצרים. ◆ מלמד
שהיו כל הארצות כשרות לדיבור עד שלא נתקדשה
ארץ ישראל אבל משנתקדשה ארץ ישראל לא היה

C     דבור עם הנביאים בכל מקום אלא על המים ◆ שנ׳ היה
היה דבר ה׳ אל יחזקאל בן בוזי הכהן בארץ כשדים
על נהר כבר (יחז׳ א ג) ואומר ואני הייתי על אובל אולי
(דנ׳ ח ב) ואומ׳ ואני הייתי על <יד> הנהר הגדול הוא

D     חדקל (דני׳ י ד) ◆ וכן יונה לא היה מדבר עמו אלא על

E     המים. ◆ ר׳ יהודה אומ׳ אף כתחלה לא היה דיבר עם
הנביאים אלא על המים שנ׳ היה היה. ◆ ר׳ נחמיה אומר

F     כתחלה היה דיבר עם הנביאים בכל מקום מה ת״ל
היה היה דבר ה׳ אל יחזקאל אלא מלמד שלא היתה
רוח הקדש תדירה עליו. ◆

2 B/A     בארץ מצרים ◆ יכול בכרך ת״ל בארץ בשדה לא היה

C     מידבר עמו מידבר היה עמו מחוץ לכרך ◆ וכן משה אומר
לפרעה כצאתי את העיר (שמ׳ ט כט) ומה תפלה קלה
לא נתפלל בתוך הכרך דבר חמור לא כ״ש. ומפני מה
לא דבר עמו בתוך הכרך מפני שהיא מלאה גלולים.
◆

more so [the case with regard to] the more significant divine speech? And why would He not speak with him inside the city? Because it was full of idols.

D. But still I might say, "He spoke with Moses outside of the city, but when Moses spoke [the divine message] to Aaron, he would not speak to him outside the city." Scripture states, [however,] "The Lord said to Moses and Aaron in the Land of Egypt" (Exod. 12:1). This equates the divine speech [to] Aaron to the divine speech [to] Moses. Just as Moses' was outside the city, likewise Aaron's was outside the city.

[8]

E. Just as Moses [would relate the divine command to Pharaoh beginning with] "Thus said …," likewise Aaron [would begin with] "Thus said …" Just as Moses was a judge over Pharaoh, speaking without fear, likewise Aaron was a judge over Pharaoh, speaking without fear. Just as Moses was manager for the Red Heifer, the light, the anointing oil, and the incense of spices,[5] likewise was Aaron manager for the Red Heifer, the light, the anointing oil, and the incense of spices. Scripture states, "The Lord said to Moses and Aaron" (Exod. 12:1). This equates the greatness of Aaron with the greatness of Moses.[6]

III:II[7]

1.  A. "(The Lord said to Moses and Aaron in the Land of Egypt,) saying" (Exod. 12:1):

B. R. Eliezer says, "How do we know from Scripture that the order [of transmission] of the divine speech in the wilderness was just like the order [of transmission] of divine speech [as it occurred] in the Land of Egypt? [Perhaps] you don't need [scriptural proof, because it can be deduced by means of ] (logical) analogy:

C. "The word 'spoke' is said here,[8] and the word 'spoke' is said in the wilderness.[9] Just as with 'spoke' said in the wilderness, Aaron heard it first and repeated it [back to Moses] first, likewise with 'spoke' mentioned here, Aaron heard it first and repeated it first.

D. "However, I might retort that when Aaron preceded the[10] sons [in receiving divine speech] in the wilderness he had been anointed with the anointing oil. Shall [we assume] that Aaron preceded the sons here,[11] when he had not [yet] been anointed with the anointing oil?[12]

E. "Scripture states, 'And the Lord said to Moses and to Aaron …' (Exod. 12:1). This teaches that Aaron preceded the sons.

F. "And how do we know from Scripture that the sons preceded the elders? [Perhaps] you don't need [scriptural proof, because it can be deduced by means of] analogy: The word 'spoke' is said here, and the word 'spoke' is said in the wilderness. Just as with 'spoke' said in the wilderness, the sons preceded the elders, likewise with 'spoke' mentioned here, the sons preceded the elders.

G. "However, I might retort that the sons preceded the elders in the wilderness, when they likewise preceded them in ascending Mount [Sinai].[13] Shall [we assume] here that the sons

---

[5] See Lev. 6:9ff. and Num. 19:1ff.

[6] Exod. 12:1 mentions three things: (1) God spoke, (2) God spoke to Moses and Aaron, and (3) God spoke to Moses and Aaron in the Land of Egypt. III:I:1.A–F addresses particularities concerning points #1 and #2—there was divine speech, and it was delivered in Egypt. III:I:2.A–E then addresses points #2 and then #3—where in Egypt the divine speech occurred, and to whom it was delivered, Moses and/or Aaron. Our text, therefore, has interpreted the verse in typical, atomized fashion, and by doing so has created a new reading of the verse that magnificently incorporates all three of its clauses.

[7] Compare III:II:1.A–K with b. Eruvin 54b, which discusses the order in which Moses transmitted *mishnah* (as opposed to divine speech here), stating that Moses heard it first from God, and then repeated it to Aaron, who in turn repeated it back to him, and so on to the sons, elders, and common Israelites.

[8] I.e., to Moses in the Land of Egypt.

[9] See Lev. 11:1.

[10] I.e., his.

[11] I.e., in the Land of Egypt.

[12] Thus, the logic of 1.C will not prove the point stated in 1.B, and one must indeed rely upon Scripture for proof of this point.

[13] See Exod. 24:1.

ועדיין אני אומ' דיבר היה עם משה חוץ לכרך אבל     D

כשהיה משה מדבר עם אהרן לא היה מדבר עמו

חוץ לכרך ת״ל ויאמר ה' אל משה ואל אהרן (בארץ

מצרים) מקיש דברות אהרן לדברות משה מה משה חוץ

לכרך אף אהרן חוץ לכרך. ◆ מה משה בכה אמר אף     E

אהרן בכה מה משה אלהים לפרעה אמר דבר ולא

ירא אף אהרן אלהים לפרעה אמר דבר ולא ירא מה

משה גזבר על הפרה ועל המאור ועל שמן המשחה ועל

קטרת הסמים אף אהרן גזבר על הפרה ועל המאור

ועל שמן המשחה ועל קטרת הסמים. ת״ל ויאמר ה'

אל משה ואל אהרן מקיש גדולתו שלאהרן לגדולתו

שלמשה. ◆

    III:II

לאמר ◆ ר' אליעזר אומ' מנין שכסדר דיברות שהיו     B/A   1

במדבר כך היו בארץ מצרים אין צריך דין הוא ◆ נאמר כאן     C

דיבר ונאמר דיבר במדבר (ויק' יא א) מה דיבר האמור

במדבר אהרן שמע תחלה ושנה תחלה אף דיבר

האמור כאן אהרן שמע תחלה ושנה תחלה ◆ מה לי קדם     D

אהרן את הבנים במדבר שכן נמשח בשמן המשחה

יקדום אהרן את הבנים כאן שהרי לא נמשח בשמן

המשחה ◆ ת״ל ויאמר ה' אל משה ואל אהרן מלמד     E

שאהרן קדם את הבנים. ◆ ומניין שהבנים קודמין את     F

הזקנים אין צריך דין הוא נאמר כאן דיבר ונאמר דיבר

במדבר מה דיבר האמור במדבר בנים קדמו את הזקנים

אף דיבר האמור כאן בנים קדמו את הזקנים. ◆ מה     G

לי בנים קדמו את הזקנים במדבר שכן קדמו לעלות

preceded the elders, when they had not [yet] preceded [them] in ascending the mountain?

H.   "Scripture states, '… and he spoke to his sons …' (ref. Lev. 21:24). This teaches that the sons preceded the elders.

I.   "And how do we know from Scripture that the elders preceded Israel? [Perhaps] you don't need [scriptural proof, because it can be deduced by means of] analogy: The word 'spoke' is said here, and the word 'spoke' is said in the wilderness. Just as with 'spoke' said in the wilderness, the elders preceded Israel, likewise with 'spoke' mentioned here, the elders preceded Israel.

J.   "However, I might retort that when the elders preceded Israel in the wilderness, they likewise were sanctified with the Holy Spirit. Shall [we assume] here that the elders preceded Israel, when they had not yet been sanctified with the Holy Spirit?

K.   "Scripture states, 'And Moses called to all the elders of Israel …' (Exod. 12:21). This teaches that the elders preceded Israel."

*Chapter Four*

(Textual Source: Midrash ha-Gadol)[14]

IV:I

1.   A.   "(The Lord said to Moses and Aaron in the Land of Egypt,) saying" (Exod. 12:1):

B.   "Saying" [means exclusively] to Israel.[15]

2.   A.   "*This* month (shall mark) for you (the beginning of months; it shall be the first of the months of the year for you)" (Exod. 12:2):

B.   This teaches that the Holy One, blessed be He, showed Moses with his finger the image of the moon and said, "Look for it [to appear] like this[16] and [then] sanctify the beginning of months for yourselves."[17]

(Textual Source: Midrash ha-Gadol)

3.   A.   "This month (shall mark) for *you*" (Exod. 12:2):

B.   [Which means that] the earliest forefathers did not calculate by it.[18]

[9]   C.   One might think that the earliest forefathers did not calculate by it, because the Torah had not yet been given in their time. However, once the Torah was given and thereafter, [all] people should calculate by it.

D.   Scripture states, [however,] "… for *you*" (Exod. 12:2). [This means,] you calculate by it, and [other] people do not calculate by it.[19]

---

[14] The editors indicate that they interpolated section IV:I:1.A–2.B based upon its attestation in a number of disparate sources, including as an appendix to the end of the Adler manuscript for *Midrash ha-Gadol* (Exodus).

[15] The text assumes that the infinitive "saying" (Hebrew: לאמר) in the verse is redundant and unnecessary. As such, it interprets it as indicating that God's command in Exod. 12:1–2 is directed exclusively at Israel.

[16] The text is overemphasizing the demonstrative pronoun "this" in Exod. 12:2, interpreting it as indicating that God, literally, pointed to an image of the new moon for demonstrative purposes.

[17] The text interprets the fact that Exod. 12:2 twice states "for you" (Hebrew: לכם) as empowering Israel to declare and sanctify new months *for themselves*. In effect, this places the power of determining the annual calendar, and the holy times therein, in the hands of Israel. Also, it is interesting to note how, in 2.B, the text's interpretation addresses every element of Exod. 12:2—the emphasis of the demonstrative pronoun ("This month"), the exclusivity of the calendar for Israel ("for you"), and the "beginning of months." This is a common midrashic method of interpretation—fashioning an interpretive reading of a verse that incorporates cohesively every atomized element within that verse. Compare 1.A–2.B with *Mekhilta de-Rabbi Ishmael*, Pisḥa (H/R, 6:11–12; Laut., vol. 1, 15:167–69; Neus., II:I:1.A–B).

[18] Again, interpreting "for you" in Exod. 12:2 literally and specifically, i.e., the calculation of the Jewish calendar began only with the Israelites who departed from Egypt.

בהר יקדמו בנים את הזקנים כאן שהרי לא קדמו

לעלות בהר ◆ ת״ל ואל בניו דבר מלמד שהבנים קודמין    H

לזקנים. ◆ ומניין שהזקנים קודמין את ישראל אין צריך    I

דין הוא נאמר כאן דבר ונאמר במדבר דבר מה דבר

האמור במדבר זקנים קודמין את ישראל אף דבר

האמור כאן זקנים קודמין את ישראל ◆ מה לי קדמו    J

זקנים את ישראל במדבר שכן נתקדשו ברוח הקודש

יקדמו זקנים את ישראל כאן שהרי לא נתקדשו ברוח

הקודש ◆ ת״ל ויקרא משה לכל זקני ישראל (שמ׳ יב    K

כא) מלמד שהזקנים קודמין את ישראל. ◆

                                                    IV:I

[לאמר ◆ לאמר לישראל. ◆ החדש הזה לכם ◆ מלמד    B/A 2    B/A 1

שהראה לו הקב״ה למשה באצבע דמות לבנה ואמר כזה

ראה וקדש לכם ראש חדשים] ◆

החדש הזה לכם ◆ לא מנו בו אבות הראשונים, ◆ יכול    C/B/A    3

לא מנו בו אבות הראשונים שהרי לא ניתנה תורה

בימיהם אבל משניתנה תורה ואילך יהו באי בראשית

מונין בו ◆ תלמוד לומר לכם אתם מונין בו ואין באי    D

בראשית מונין בו. ◆

---

[19] An ongoing common theme in this text—the exclusivity of Israel—is again stressed here. Also, compare 3.A–D with *Mekhilta de-Rabbi Ishmael,* Pisḥa (H/R, 7:11–14; Laut., vol. 1, 18:35–40; Neus., II:III:1.A–G).

**IV:II[20]**

1.     A.     "(This month shall mark for you) the beginning (of months)" (Exod. 12:2):

       B.     One might think [that this month also marks] the beginning of years, sabbatical years, and jubilee years.[21]

       C.     Scripture states, [however,] "... the beginning of months" (Exod. 12:2), [which means that] it is the beginning of months, and it is not the beginning of years, sabbatical years, and jubilee years.

2.     A.     "It shall be the first of the months of the year for you" (Exod. 12:2):

       B.     And not [the first month for calculating of the annual cycles of] tithe of cattle or fruit trees.

       C.     And for what is it the first [month]? For [calculating the reign] of kings, [the dates of the] festivals, for the heave offering of the *shekels,* and for the rent of houses.

**IV:III[22]**

1.     A.     "It shall be the first (of the months of the year for you)" (Exod. 12:2):

       B.     Since it says in Scripture "Keep the *month* of Abib (and offer a passover sacrifice to the Lord your God)" (Deut. 16:1), [one must ask] how do you "keep" it?[23]

       C.     You add days to it.

       D.     One might think that if it was a year shortened [by the discrepancy between the lunar and solar calendars] 10 or 20 days, one should intercalate[24] accordingly.

       E.     Scripture states, [however,] "(Keep the) *month* (of Abib)" (Deut. 16:1). [This means that] one does not intercalate less than [a total of days equaling one] month.

       F.     One might think that if it was a year shortened by 40 or 50 days, one should intercalate accordingly.

       G.     Scripture states, [however,] "(Keep the) *month* (of Abib)" (Deut. 16:1). [This means that] one does not intercalate more than [a total of days equaling one] month.

2.     A.     One might think that one should intercalate [by adding a second month of] Nisan.

       B.     Scripture states, [however,] "It shall be the *first* of the months of the year for you" (Exod. 12:2). [This means that] you shall make one Nisan, and you shall not make two Nisans.

       C.     One might think that one should intercalate [by adding a second month of] Tishrei.

       D.     Scripture states, [however,] "Keep the month of Abib" (Deut. 16:1). [This means that you must] "keep"[25] the month that is next to [the month of] Abib.[26] And which is this? Adar.

3.     A.     One might think that just as if the year is shortened, one adds days to it, likewise if the year is lengthened, one subtracts days from it.

       B.     Scriptures states, [however,] "You shall keep this institution at its set time from year

---

[20] Compare IV:II:1.A–2.C with m. Rosh Hashanah 1:1; t. Rosh Hashanah 1:1; *Mekhilta de-Rabbi Ishmael,* Pisḥa (H/R, 6:18–7:11; Laut., vol. 1, 16:13–18:34; Neus., II:II:1.A–4.C).

[21] I.e., one might think that the month of Nisan is the first of the ordered months of the calendrical year, as well as the first month of the annual calendar employed for the reckoning of sabbatical and jubilee years.

[22] Compare IV:III:1.A–3.B with *Mekhilta de-Rabbi Ishmael,* Pisḥa (H/R, 8:1–9:5; Laut. vol. 1, 19:51–22:86; Neus., II:IV:1.A–9.C).

[23] The text reads literally the word "keep" (Hebrew: שמור) in Deut. 16:1, i.e., "guard." Thus, the text inquires as to how one guards/ensures that Passover falls in the spring season.

[24] I.e., add days.

[25] I.e., intercalate a second month.

[26] The month of "Abib" (spring) in Deut. 16:1 is presumed to be the month of Nisan.

IV:II

| | | |
|---|---|---|
| B/A | 1 | ראש ◆ יכול ראש לשנים ולשמטים וליובלות ◆ |
| C | | ת״ל ראש חדשים לחדשים הוא ראש ואינו |
| A | 2 | ראש לא לשנים ולא לשמטים ולא ליובלות. ◆ (ראשון |
| C/B | | הוא לכם ◆ ולא למעשר בהמה ולא לפירות ◆ למה הוא |
| | | ראשון למלכים ולרגלים לתרומת שקלים ולשכר בתים). |
| | | ◆ |

IV:III

| | | |
|---|---|---|
| B/A | 1 | ראשון הוא ◆ מכלל שנ׳ שמור את חדש האביב (דב׳ |
| D/C | | טז א) היאך אתה משמרו ◆ הוסיף לו ימים. ◆ יכול אם |
| | | היתה שנה חסרה עשרה ימים או עשרים יום יעבר כן |
| F/E | | ת״ל חדש אין פחות מחדש. ◆ יכול אם היתה שנה חסרה |
| G | | ארבעים יום או חמשים יום יעבר כן ◆ ת״ל חדש אין |
| B/A | 2 | יתר על חדש. ◆ יכול יעבר ניסן ◆ ת״ל ראשון הוא לכם |
| C | | ניסן אחד אתה עושה ואי אתה עושה שני ניסן. ◆ יכול |
| D | | יעבר תשרי ◆ ת״ל שמר את חדש האביב שמור את |
| A | 3 | החדש הסמוך לאביב ואיזה זה אדר. ◆ יכול כשם שאם |
| | | היתה שנה אפילה יוסיף לה ימים כך אם היתה שנה |
| B | | בכירה יבצור ממנה ימים ◆ ת״ל ושמרת את החקה הזאת |

to year" (Exod. 13:10). [This means that your calendar year should have] no less than 12 months.

## Chapter Five

### (Textual Source: Midrash ha-Gadol)

V:I[27]

1.    A.    "Speak to the *whole* community of Israel (and say that on the tenth of this month each of them shall take a lamb to a family, a lamb to a household)" (Exod. 12:3):

       B.    This teaches that this scriptural section was spoken aloud to the entire assembled congregation.

V:II[28]

1.    A.    R. Judah says, "[This verse serves] to give a negative commandment[29] for each positive commandment[30] stated in the scriptural section.

       B.    "'… on the tenth of this month each of them shall take' (Exod. 12:3)—this teaches that the paschal sacrifice of Egypt[31] was taken [aside][32] on the tenth.[33]

       C.    "One might think that even the paschal sacrifice of the [subsequent] generations was also to be taken [aside] on the tenth.

       D.    "Scripture states, [however,] '… *this* (month)' (Exod. 12:3), [which means that] the paschal sacrifice of Egypt was taken [aside] on the tenth, but the paschal sacrifice of the generations was not taken [aside] on the tenth.[34]

       E.    "[Perhaps] I should exclude the first paschal sacrifice [from this obligation to take it aside on the tenth], but not exclude the second paschal sacrifice.[35]

       F.    "Scripture states, [however,] 'You shall keep watch over it until the fourteenth day of *this month*' (Exod. 12:6), [which means that the lamb for] the first paschal sacrifice is taken [aside] on the tenth, but [the lamb for] the second paschal sacrifice is not taken [aside] on the tenth."[36]

---

[27] V:I:1.A–B is a brief and relatively simple unit of midrashic tradition; the text interprets literally the word "whole" in Exod. 12:3. However, in its brevity this unit of tradition expresses clearly the essential theological concern that serves as the basis for the substantially convoluted halakhic exegesis in this chapter, namely, that the redemption of the Exodus, both actuated and represented by the paschal offering, was experienced collectively by all of the enslaved community of Israel. Moreover, the Exodus from Egypt served as a prelude to the subsequent giving of Torah at Sinai, the historical event that formed the Jewish people, a nation united by the obligation to observe the divinely ordained *halakhah* as dictated in Torah. For the early Rabbinic community, for whom the paschal sacrifice was no longer a performed reality, God commands that all Jews must experience alike the ongoing redemptive experience of the paschal sacrifice, as actualized by the transformative Passover seder meal.

[28] Compare V:II:1.A–F with t. Pesaḥim 9:5; *Mekhilta de-Rabbi Ishmael,* Pisha (H/R, 10:13–11:1; Laut., vol. 1, 24:35–25:44; Neus., III:III:1. A–2.D); b. Pesaḥim 96a (Neus., IV.E:Pesaḥim:9:5:I.2.A–X).

[29] I.e., a commandment that proscribes an action.

[30] I.e., a commandment that prescribes an action.

[31] I.e., the paschal sacrifice offered in Egypt by the Israelites at the time of the Exodus, as opposed to the paschal sacrifice that was offered by the subsequent generations after the Exodus.

[32] I.e., acquired, designated, and set aside specifically as the lamb for the paschal offering, and consecrated only for such holy use.

[33] This is the positive commandment referred to by R. Judah in 1.A.

[34] This is the negative commandment referred to by R. Judah in 1.A. R. Judah is interpreting the word "this" in Exod. 12:3 specifically and in exclusionary fashion.

[35] See Num. 9:1–14. The second paschal sacrifice was offered one month later, on the 14th of Iyar, by those who were unable to offer the first paschal sacrifice at its appointed time in the month of Nisan.

[36] R. Judah resolves the apparent redundancy of Exod. 12:3 and Exod. 12:6, both of which appear to require that the paschal lamb be set aside (Exod. 12:3) or watched over (Exod. 12:6) from the 10th to the 14th of Nisan. Exod. 12:3 clarifies the difference between the paschal sacrifice of Egypt and that of the subsequent generations, whereas Exod. 12:6 clarifies the difference between the first paschal sacrifice of the month of Nisan and the second of the month of Iyar.

למועדה מימים ימימה (שמ' יג י) אין פחות משנים עשר חדש. ◆

B/A 1 דברו אל כל עדת בני ישראל ◆ מלמד שפרשה זו נאמרה בהקהל. ◆

A 1 ר' יהודה אומ' ליתן לא תעשה על כל עשה

B האמור בפרשה. ◆ בעשור לחדש הזה ויקחו להם

C מלמד שפסח מצרים מקחו מבעשור. ◆ יכול אף פסח

D דורות יהא מקחו מבעשור ◆ ת"ל הזה פסח מצרים מקחו

E מבעשור ואין פסח דורות מקחו מבעשור. ◆ אוציא

F פסח ראשון ולא אוציא פסח שני ◆ ת"ל והיה לכם למשמרת עד ארבעה עשר יום לחדש הזה (שמ' יב ו) פסח ראשון מקחו מבעשור ואין פסח שני מקחו מבעשור. ◆

**V:III**

1.  A.  "... (each of them) shall take" (Exod. 12:3):[37]

    B.  This teaches that each and every one takes [aside a lamb] for himself.

2.  A.  "... each man shall take for himself" (Exod. 12:3):

    B.  Based on this they said that one does not take [a lamb aside] for a minor.[38]

3.  A.  "... a lamb to a father's house, (a lamb to a household)" (Exod. 12:3):

    B.  One might think that a paschal sacrifice of Egypt was only sacrificed for fathers' houses. How does one know from Scripture that [a lamb should be sacrificed] even for families?

    C.  Scripture states, "Go, pick out lambs for your families" (Exod. 12:21).

    D.  How does one know from Scripture [that a lamb should be sacrificed] even for households?

    E.  Scripture states, "... a lamb to a household" (Exod. 12:3).[39]

**V:IV**

1.  A.  "'But if the household is too small (for a lamb, then a man and his neighbor next to his house shall take in proportion to the number of persons; according to what each can eat you shall make your count for the lamb)' (Exod. 12:4):

    B.  "This teaches that they may continue to reduce [the number of people holding shares in a paschal lamb] as long as there remains one from the first group [that owned the lamb]."—The words of R. Judah.

    C.  R. Yosi says, "[It does not matter if the people maintaining a share in the lamb come from] the original group or a subsequent group. [What matters is] only that they not leave the paschal lamb as is."[40]

2.  A.  "(But if the household is too small) for a lamb" (Exod. 12:4):[41]

    B.  [They may enroll[42] others in their offering if they are too small[43] to afford to acquire the associated things necessary to prepare the paschal lamb] for eating,[44] but not [simply in order to raise funds for] other [general] purchases.

    C.  Rabbi says, "Even [to raise funds for] other [general] purchases. So if he did not have [enough funds to acquire them], he may enroll others on his portion, and the proceeds will be *hullin*.[45] For on this condition did they take [aside their lambs] from the very beginning."

3.  A.  "'(But if the household is too small for a lamb, then a man and his neighbor next to his house) shall take' (Exod. 12:4):

    [10]  B.  "This teaches that each and every group [of people in joint ownership] acquires [a lamb] for itself.

---

[37] Compare 1.A–B with *Mekhilta de-Rabbi Ishmael*, Pisha (H/R, 11:2–3; Laut., vol. 1, 25:45–47; Neus., III:IV:1.A–D), where the parallel material is, however, in halakhic opposition.

[38] Interpreting "man" in Exod. 12:3 (translated idiomatically simply as "each") specifically and in exclusionary fashion. Compare with m. Pesahim 8:7 and b. Pesahim 91b (Neus., IV.D: Pesahim:8:7:I.3.A–I.6.B).

[39] By emphasizing that a lamb should be offered (presumably, if feasible) for a series of family units, each smaller than the prior (i.e., fathers' houses, families, and households), the text emphasizes the desirability that the liberating experience of the paschal sacrifice be experienced at the most local and heightened level of intimacy possible. Compare with *Mekhilta de-Rabbi Ishmael*, Pisha (H/R, 11:4–7; Laut., vol. 1, 26:50–53; Neus., III:IV:3.A–E).

[40] I.e., ownerless. Compare with t. Pisha 7:7 and y. Pesahim 8:36a (Bokser, 8:4:II:B.2).

[41] Compare 2.A.–C with b. Pesahim 90a (Neus., IV.D:Pesahim:8:4:I.8.A–O).

[42] I.e., sell partial ownership in the paschal lamb to others.

[43] I.e., poor.

[44] E.g., to acquire the wood for the roasting fire or the appropriate slaughtering knife to sacrifice the offering.

[45] I.e., the proceeds may be used for all types of purchases, and not only for purchases of a holy or consecrated nature.

| | | |
|---|---|---|
| ויקחו • מלמד שכל אחד ואחד לוקח לעצמו. • ויקחו | A 2 | B/A 1 |
| להם איש • מיכאן אמרו אין מקח לקטן. • שה לבית אבות | A 3 | B |
| יכול לא יהא פסח מצרים נשחט אלא לבתי אבות ומניין | | B |
| אף למשפחות • ת״ל משכו וקחו להם צאן למשפחותיכם • | | C |
| (שמ׳ יב כא). מניין אף לבתים • ת״ל שה לבית. • | | E/D |

| | | |
|---|---|---|
| ואם ימעט הבית • מלמד שמתמעטין והולכין ובלבד | B/A | 1 |
| שישתייר שם אחד מחבורה ראשונה דברי ר׳ יהודה. • | | |
| ר׳ יוסי אומר בין מחבורה ראשונה ובין מחבורה | C | |
| אחרונה ובלבד שלא יניחו את הפסח כמות שהוא. • מהיות | A | 2 |
| משה • מכדי אכילה ולא מכדי מקח. • רבי אומר אף מכדי | C/B | |
| מקח שאם אין לו ממנה אחרים על חלקו ומעות | | |
| חולין שמתחלה לא לקחו אלא על מנת כן. • ולקח | A | 3 |
| הוא • מלמד שכל חבורה וחבורה לוקחת לעצמה • | B | |

C. "Based on this they said: You do not slaughter a paschal lamb in the first place for a single person.[46] As it says in Scripture, 'You shall not slaughter the paschal sacrifice *in any one ...*' (Deut. 16:5)."[47]—The words of R. Judah.

D. R. Yosi says, "Sometimes there is [only] one [person], and you slaughter it for him, and sometimes there are 10, and you do not slaughter it for them.

E. "How is this so? [When you have] one [person] who is able to eat it [all], you slaughter it for him, [and when you have] 10 who are not able to eat it [all], you do not slaughter it for them, so that they will not cause the [leftover portions of the] paschal offering to become spoiled."[48]

4. A. "(But if the household is too small for a lamb, then a man) and his neighbor (next to his house)" (Exod. 12:4):[49]

B. Ben Bag Bag says, "I might assume [this includes] his neighbor [who lives nearby] in a field. How does one know from Scripture [that this includes only] his neighbor at home?

C. "Scripture states, 'next' (Exod. 12:4), [meaning the one] who dwells next to his house—door to door."

D. Rabbi says, "Three [types of neighbors]

(Textual Source: Manuscript Antonin 236.1)

are mentioned [here in Scripture]: 'his neighbor'—this [refers to] his neighbor in the field; 'his neighbor'—this [also refers to] his neighbor at home; 'who dwells near'—this [refers to] he who dwells near his house, close to [his] door.

E. "[But only for] the paschal sacrifice of Egypt [does] 'his neighbor' [mean] he who dwells near his house, whereas [for] the paschal sacrifice of the [subsequent] generations 'his neighbor' does not [mean] he who dwells near his house."[50]

F. Rabbi Shimon says, "'His neighbor' [means] he who dwells near his house even for the paschal sacrifice of the [subsequent] generations.

G. "For above all, the Torah only speaks with peaceful intentions [as illustrated here where the Torah's intention is] that one should not leave his beloved, his neighbors, acquaintances, close ones, or one of his town's citizens and go off and perform the paschal sacrifice with others. As it says in Scripture, 'A close neighbor is better than a distant brother' (Prov. 27:10)."

5. A. "(But if the household is too small for a lamb, then a man and his neighbor next to his house shall take) in proportion to the number of (persons)" (Exod. 12:4):[51]

B. "In proportion to the number of"[52] means only (according to the) number. For thus Scriptures states, "... from which the Lord's number[53] was thirty-two" (Num. 31:40).

6. A. One might think that it is a commandment to slaughter it only for those enrolled on it. But if one slaughtered for those not enrolled on it, he transgressed a commandment, but it is [nonetheless a] valid [offering].

B. Scripture states, [however,] "... proportion to the *number* ... you shall make your *count*" (Exod. 12:4).

---

[46] Compare with m. Pesaḥim 8:7.

[47] The phrase "in any one" is understood here by R. Judah as "for any one person."

[48] Compare with *Sifre Deut.*, Piska 132 (Hammer, 175; Neus., CXXXII:I:2.A–D).

[49] Compare 4.A–G with *Mekhilta de-Rabbi Ishmael*, Pisḥa (H/R, 11:14–16; Laut., vol. 1, 27:65–67; Neus., III:IV:7.A–F).

[50] Compare 4.E–G with t. Pisḥa 8:12–13.

[51] Compare 5.A–7.D with *Mekhilta de-Rabbi Ishmael*, Pisḥa (H/R, 12:1–6; Laut., vol. 1, 27:68–28:77; Neus., III:V:1.A–2.H).

[52] Hebrew: במכסת. The text attempts here to clarify the meaning of this term.

מיכאן אמרו אין שוחטין פסח לכתחלה על היחיד שנאמר
לא תוכל לזבוח את הפסח באחד (דב' טז ה) דברי ר'
יהודה. ◆ ר' יוסי אומ' פעמים שהוא אחד ושוחטין אותו

עליו פעמים שהן עשרה ואין שוחטין אותו עליהן. ◆ הא
כאיזה צד אחד ויכול לאכלו שוחטין אותו עליו עשרה
ואין יכולין לאכלו אין שוחטין אותו עליהן שלא
יביאו את הפסח לידי פסול. ◆ ושכנו ◆ בן בגבג אומ' שומע

אני שכינו שבשדות שכינו שבגגות ◆ מניין ת"ל הקרוב
הקרוב אל ביתו פתח אל פתח. ◆

רבי אומר שלשתן נאמרו שכינו(ת) זה שכינו שבשדות
שכינו זה שכינו שבגגות הקרוב זה הקרוב אל ביתו סמוך
לפתח פסח ◆ מצ' שכינו קרוב לביתו ואין פסח דורות שכינו
קרוב לביתו ◆ ר' שמע' או' אף פסח דורות שכינו קרוב
לביתו ◆ וכל כך לא דברה תורה אלא מפני דרכי שלום שלא
יהא אדם מניח אהבו ושכניו מכיריו ומיודעיו ואחד מבני
עירו והולך ועושה פסח אצל אחרים שנ' טוב שכן קרוב
מאח רחוק (מש' כז י) ◆ במכסת ◆ אין במכסת אלא במנין
וכן הוא או' ומכסם[53] לייי שנים ושלשים נפש (במ' לא מ) ◆

יכול מצוה לשחטו למנויו ואם שחטו שלא למנויו
עבר על מצוה והוא כשר ◆ תל' לו' מכסת תכוסו ◆

| | C |
| | D |
| | E |
| B/A | 4 |
| | C |
| | D |
| | E |
| | F |
| | G |
| B/A | 5 |
| A | 6 |
| B | |

53 Hebrew: ומכסם.

C.   Scripture repeats it[54] [in order to emphasize that this sacrifice would be] invalid.

7.   A.   Because it says in Scripture "man" (Exod. 12:4), I only know [that the commandment of the paschal sacrifice is directed to a] man. How does one know from Scripture to include the woman and child?

B.   Scripture states, "... (in proportion to the number of) *persons*" (Exod. 12:4).

C.   If so, then why does it say [earlier in the verse] "man"? [Because] just as a man is able to eat an olive's amount,[55] likewise [must] the child be able to eat an olive's amount.[56]

D.   R. Judah says, "Just as a man knows how to distinguish [something] edible [from something inedible], likewise [must] the child know how to distinguish [something] edible [from something inedible]. And what is [behavior indicating the ability] to distinguish edible [from inedible]? Anyone who, when given a stone, tosses it away, [but when given a] nut, keeps it."[57]

### (Textual Source: Midrash ha-Gadol)

8.   A.   "... in proportion to the number ... you shall make your count" (Exod. 12:4):

B.   This teaches [both] that one may be enrolled [for a share in a paschal offering] and [that one may] enroll [others].

C.   Based on this they said: The members of a group [in joint ownership of a paschal lamb] who enrolled others [as joint members] of their portion, the right [to do so] is theirs. [If] they wanted to withdraw [from ownership] and to enroll others over their portion, the right is theirs. An individual from a group who enrolled another over his portion, the right is his. [If] he wanted to withdraw and to enroll others over his portion, the right is his.[58]

[11]

9.   A.   "... according to what each can eat" (Exod. 12:4):

B.   This excludes the sick, uncircumcised, and impure who are not able to eat it.

10.   A.   "... (according to what each can eat you shall make your count) for the lamb" (Exod. 12:4):[59]

B.   Ben Bag Bag says, "I might assume [this refers to either] a living lamb or a slaughtered one.

C.   "[But] you [must] logically reason: "Lamb" is stated here in Scripture and "lamb" is stated above in Scripture.[60] Just as "lamb" stated above [requires] a live lamb, and not a slaughtered lamb, likewise "lamb" stated here [requires] a live lamb, and not a slaughtered lamb."

D.   Based on this they said: Under all circumstances, people may be enrolled [as joint members] of a paschal sacrifice, and they may withdraw from it until it is slaughtered.[61]

*Chapter Six*

### (Textual Source: Midrash ha-Gadol)

VI:I

1.   A.   "(You shall have) a lamb (without blemish, a yearling male. You may take it from the sheep or from the goats)" (Exod. 12:5):

B.   Why does Scripture state "without blemish"?

---

[54] I.e., Scripture states both "number" and "count."
[55] I.e., the amount that must be eaten in order to fulfill the commandment.
[56] The child must be old enough to eat this amount in order to be obligated to fulfill the commandment.
[57] Compare 7.D with t. Hagigah 1:2.

| | | |
|---|---|---|
| C | A 7 | שנה עליו הכתוב לפסול ◆ לתוך שנ' איש אין לי אלא |
| | B | איש מנ' לרבות את האשה ואת הקטן ◆ תל' לו' נפשות ◆ |
| | C | אם כן למה נאמר איש מה איש שיכול לאכל כזית אף |
| | D | קטן שיכל לאכל כזית ◆ ר' יהודה או' מה איש שיודע |
| | | הפרש אכילה אף קטן היודע הפרש אכילה <איזו היא |
| | | הפרשת אכילה> כל שנותנין לו אבן וזורקו אגוז ונוטלו ◆ |
| 8 | C/B/A | במכסת תכסו ◆ מלמד שנמנין וממנין ◆ מיכן אמרו |
| | | בני חבורה שהמנו אחרים על חלקם הרשות בידם רצו |
| | | להמשך ולהמנות אחרים על חלקם הרשות בידם אחד |
| | | מבני חבורה שהמנה אחר על חלקו הרשות בידו |
| | | רצה להמשך ולהמנות אחרים על חלקו הרשות בידו. ◆ |
| 9 | B/A | לפי אכלו ◆ פרט לחולה [ו]לערל ולטמא שאין יכולין |
| 10 | B/A | לאכלו. ◆ על השה ◆ בן בגבג אום' שומע אני שה חי או שה |
| | C | שחוט ◆ הרי אתה דן נאמר כאן שה ונאמר להלן שה מה |
| | | שה האמור להלן שה חי ולא שה שחוט אף שה |
| | D | האמור כאן שה חי ולא שה שחוט ◆ מיכן אמרו לעולם |
| | | נמנין על הפסח ומושכין ידיהן ממנו עד שישחט. ◆ |
| VI:I | | |
| 1 | B/A | שה ◆ מה ת'ל תמים ◆ ר' עקיבא אום' צריך לאמרו |

[58] Compare 8.C with t. Pisḥa 7:7.
[59] Compare 10.A–C with y. Pesaḥim 8:36a (Bokser, 8:3:III:D).
[60] Exod. 12:3.
[61] Compare 10.D with m. Pesaḥim 8:3.

C. R. Akiva says, "It needs to say it, for up to now [the subject of] perfection has not been mentioned. For every time Scripture says 'lamb' it includes [lambs both] perfect and blemished. One might think this is also [the case] here.

D. "Scripture states, [however,] 'without blemish' (Exod. 12:5), [which means] perfect and not blemished.

E. "Every time Scripture says 'lamb' it includes [both] adult and young. One might think this is also [the case] here.

F. "Scripture states, [however,] 'a yearling' (Exod. 12:5).

G. "I only know that at the time of its slaughter it must be perfect and a year old. How does one know from Scripture that this includes the collecting of its blood and the sprinkling of its blood?[62]

H. "Scripture states, 'You shall have (a lamb without blemish, a yearling)' (Exod. 12:5), [meaning that] as long as it is yours[63] it must be perfect and a year old."

VI:II

1. A. "(You may take it) from the sheep or from the goats" (Exod. 12:5):

B. Which excludes crossbreeds.

C. Sheep and goats are the (specific) decree of the (divine) king.

2. A. "(You may take it) from the sheep or from the goats" (Exod. 12:5):

B. [Scripture states this] to exclude shorn cattle, and to exclude an animal that actively or passively had sexual relations with a human being.

C. I only have [as options] the [specific animals] stated here.

3. A. "You may take it (from the sheep or from the goats)" (Exod. 12:5):

B. [Scripture states this] to include the 14th [of Nisan as a day upon which] it is not proper to take [the lamb aside].

C. But isn't it[64] a matter of logical reasoning?

D. If the 10th [of Nisan], which is not proper for the slaughter [of the paschal lamb], is proper for taking [it aside], [then] is it not logical that the 14th, which is proper for the slaughter, should [also] be proper for taking [it aside]?

E. [No! Because] Scripture states, "You may take it" (Exod. 12:5). Which includes the 14th [of Nisan as a day upon which] it is not proper to take [the lamb aside].[65]

*Chapter Seven*

(Textual Source: Midrash ha-Gadol)

VII:I

1. A. "You shall keep watch over it (until the fourteenth day of this month, and all the assembled congregation of the Israelites shall slaughter it at twilight)" (Exod. 12:6):

---

[62] I.e., the lamb must be perfect and have not reached the age of two at the time that its blood is collected and sprinkled.

[63] I.e., in your possession.

[64] I.e., the opposite conclusion—the 14th of Nisan is an acceptable day for taking aside the paschal lamb.

[65] It is difficult to discern clearly how the text understands the clause "You may take it" in Exod. 12:5 as a delimiter in this fashion, i.e., to mean that the lamb cannot be set aside on the 14th of Nisan. The text appears to be reading the clause as "you *must* take it," and views Exod. 12:5 in continuity with the verses immediately prior to it, in which it is commanded that the lamb be taken aside on the 10th of Nisan, as well as in distinction from Exod. 12:6, which commands the slaughtering of the lamb on the 14th day of the month.

שלא נאמרה תמות אלא (עד) עכשיו שכל מקום שנ' שה | C

תופס תמימין ובעלי מומין יכול אף זה כן • ת"ל תמים | D

תם ולא בעל מום • בכל מקום שנ' שה תופס גדולים | E

וקטנים יכול אף זה כן • ת"ל בן שנה. • אין לא אלא | G/F

בשעת שחיטתו שיהא [תם ו]בן שנה מניין לרבות קיבול

דמו וזריקת דמו • ת"ל יהיה לכם כל זמן שהוא לכם | H

יהא תם ובן שנה. •

VI:II

מן הכבשים ומן העזים • פרט לכלאים. • כבשים | C/B/A | 1

ועזים גזירת מלך. • מן הכבשים ומן העזים • להוציא את | B/A | 2

החלוק ש[ב]בן הבקר ולהוציא את הרובע ואת הנרבע •

אין לי אלא דברים האמורים כאן בלבד. • תקחו • להביא | B/A 3 | C

את יום ארבעה עשר שאין כשר למקח • והלא דין הוא • | C

ומה עשירי שאין כשר לשחיטה כשר למקח ארבעה | D

עשר שכשר בשחיטה אינו דין שיהא כשר במקח • ת"ל | E

תקחו להביא את יום ארבעה עשר שאין כשר למקח. •

VII:I

והיה לכם למשמרת • ר' עקיבה אומ' נאמר כאן | B/A | 1

B. R. Akiva says, "The word 'watch' is said here in Scripture, and the word 'watch' is said there in Scripture.[66] Just as 'watch' said here [means] that they should inspect it for perfection over and over again [beginning] three days before the slaughter, likewise 'watch' said there [means] that they should inspect it for perfection over and over again [beginning] three days before the slaughter.

C. "Based on this they said: There should be no less than three inspected lambs in the Chamber of Lambs, sufficient for a *Shabbat* and the two festival days of the New Year."[67]

2.  A. "(You shall keep watch over it) until the fourteenth day of this month" (Exod. 12:6):

[12]  B. This [is in agreement with] what they said: The second paschal sacrifice is not taken [aside] on the tenth.[68]

3.  A. "(And all the assembled congregation of the Israelites) shall slaughter *it* (at twilight)" (Exod. 12:6):

B. [The emphasis on "it" indicates] that they should not slaughter with it ordinary animals, and that they should not slaughter with it the festival offering.

4.  A. "And all the assembled congregation of the Israelites (shall slaughter it at twilight)" (Exod. 12:6):

B. This teaches that the paschal sacrifice of Egypt was slaughtered in three groups: in "assembly," "congregation," and "Israel."[69]

(Textual Source: Manuscript Antonin 236.1)

VII:II[70]

1.  A. "(And all the assembled congregation of the Israelites shall slaughter it) at twilight" (Exod. 12:6):

B. One might think [this means] once it becomes night. Scripture states, [however,] "(until the fourteenth) *day*" (Exod. 12:6).[71]

C. Or [perhaps if it means] "day" [then it means anytime] from the second hour [of daylight and on]. Scripture states, [however,] "at twilight" (Exod. 12:6).[72]

D. How is it? From the sixth hour [of daylight][73] and forward. For Beit Shammai says, "'At evening' only means when the day begins to turn toward evening."

E. Hananyah ben Hachinai says, "'At twilight' [could mean] between two evenings,[74] [meaning] between the beginning of the 14th and the beginning of the 15th, with night and day in the middle.

F. "[However] since Scripture says '(fourteenth) *day*' (Exod. 12:6), [then] the night is excluded.

G. "One might think, [however, that it would still be correct to include within this range the entire] morning. Scripture states, [however,] 'at twilight' (Exod. 12:6). Just as 'at twilight' [means] when the day turns to evening, so too when Scripture says 'day' [it doesn't mean the morning, but rather] when the day begins to depart toward evening—from the sixth hour and forward.

H. "And thus Scripture states, 'Alas for us! For the day is departing!' (Jer. 6:4)."

---

[66] I.e., Num. 28:2.

[67] m. Arakhin 2:5.

[68] Compare with m. Pesahim 9:5 and with V:II:1.A–F above.

[69] The text interprets separately the words "assembled," "congregation," and "Israelites" in Exod. 12:6. Compare with m. Pesahim 5:5 and *Mekhilta de-Rabbi Ishmael*, Pisha (H/R, 17:12–13; Laut., vol. 1, 42:110–12; Neus., V:III:4.A.–C.).

[70] Compare VII:II:1.A–I with substantially similar parallel material in y. Pesahim 31:4 (Bokser, 5:1:I:A–I), and with substantially different parallel material in *Mekhilta de-Rabbi Ishmael*, Pisha (H/R, 17:13–18:3; Laut., vol. 1, 45:29–46:43; Neus.,V:III:5.A–9.A).

| | | |
|---|---|---|
| שמירה ונאמר להלן שמירה (במ' כח ב) מה שמירה | B | |
| שנאמרה כאן שיהיו מבוקרין ועומדין קודם שחיטה | | |
| שלשה ימים אף שמירה האמ' להלן שיהיו מבוקרין | | |
| ועומדין קודם שחיטה שלשה ימים ◆ מיכן אמרו אין | C | |
| פוחתין משישה טלאים המבוקרין בלשכת טלאים כדי | | |
| לשבת ולשני ימים טובים שלראש השנה. ◆ עד ארבעה | A | 2 |
| עשר יום לחדש הזה ◆ זה הוא שאמרו פסח שני אין | B | |
| מקחו מבעשור. ◆ ושחטו אותו ◆ שלא ישחט עמו חולין | B/A | 3 |
| ושלא ישחט עמו חגיגה. ◆ כל קהל עדת ישראל ◆ מלמד | B/A | 4 |
| שפסח מצרים נשחט בשלש כתות בקהל ועדה וישראל. ◆ | | |
| | VII:II | |
| בין הערבים ◆ יכול משתחשך תל' לו' יום ◆ או יום | C/B/A | 1 |
| יכול' משתי שעות תל' לו' בין הערבים ◆ הכאיזה צד משש | D | |
| שעות ולמעלה שבית שמאי או' אין בערב אלא משפנה | | |
| יום ◆ חנניה בן <ח>כינאי או' בין הערבים בין שתי הערבים | E | |
| בין אור ארבעה עשר לאור (יה) ויום ולילה באמצע ◆ | | |
| כשהוא או' <יום> כבר יצא לילה ◆ יכול שחרית תל' לו' | G/F | |
| בית הערבים מה בין הערבים משנפנה יום אף כשאמר יום | | |
| <משפנה יום> משש שעות ולמעלה ◆ וכן הוא או' אוי לנו | H | |
| כי פנה היום (ירמי' ו ד). ◆ | | |

---

[71] Thus, connoting to some degree that the sacrifice should take place during the daytime.

[72] Hebrew: בין הערבים—connoting to some degree that the sacrifice should take place during the evening (ערב).

[73] I.e., noon.

[74] He reads בין הערבים in Exod. 12:6 as "between the two evenings."

*Chapter Eight*

(Textual Source: Midrash ha-Gadol)

VIII:I

1.    A.    "They shall take some of the blood (and put it on the two doorposts and the lintel of the houses in which they are to eat it)" (Exod. 12:7):

       B.    [This means] there must be [enough] blood to constitute a "taking."

2.    A.    "(They shall take) some of the blood" (Exod. 12:7):[75]

       B.    Some of the lifeblood, and not some of the blood of the flesh, and not some of the blood of the skin, and not some of the blood that is drained out last.

3.    A.    "(They shall take some of the blood) and put it on the two doorposts and the lintel" (Exod. 12:7):

       B.    One might think that he should put it [also] on the lintel and posts of windows.

       C.    Scripture states, [however,] "of the houses" (Exod. 12:7). [This means] he puts it on the lintel and doorposts of houses,[76] but he does not put it on the lintel and posts of windows.

4.    A.    One might think [that if there were] 10 houses, one within the next, with the group eating in the innermost, they need to place [the blood] upon [the doorposts and lintels of] all of them.

       B.    Scripture states, [however,] "... of the houses in which they are to eat it" (Exod. 12:7).

5.    A.    How can you say from Scripture that [if] a group was eating in one house that had five doorways, they must place some of the blood on each and every lintel, [and] some of the blood on each and every doorpost?

       B.    Scripture states, "... and put it on the two doorposts and the lintel" (Exod. 12:7). [This means they place] some of the blood upon each and every lintel and some of the blood on each and every doorpost.

       C.    How can you say from Scripture that [if] five groups were eating in one house that had five doorways, they must place some of the blood [of each group's offering] upon each and every lintel, and some of the blood [of each group's offering] upon each and every doorpost?

       D.    Scripture states, "... and put it on the two doorposts and the lintel" (Exod. 12:7). [This means they place] some of the blood [of each group's offering] upon the lintel and some of the blood [of each group's offering] upon the doorpost.[77]

VIII:II

1.    A.    "... of the houses in which they are to eat it" (Exod. 12:7):

       B.    Since it says in Scripture, "It shall be eaten in one house" (Exod. 12:46), this teaches that the paschal sacrifice of Egypt was eaten only in one house. How does one know from Scripture [that it was eaten] even in two houses?

       C.    Scripture states, "... of the *houses* in which they are to eat it" (Exod. 12:7).

---

[75] Compare 2.A–B with *Sifra*, Diburah Deḥobah 3:7 (Neus. XXXIX:III:1.4.A–C).

[76] I.e., on the doors.

[77] Although not stated explicitly, the implied conclusion in 5.D is that some of the blood from each and every group should be placed on each and every doorpost and lintel. It is unclear exactly how the text interprets or understands the clause in Exod. 12:7 in order to justify these conclusions in 5.A–D.

| | | |
|---|---|---|
| B/A | 1 | ♦ ולקחו מן הדם ♦ שיהא בדם כדי לקיחה. |
| B/A | 2 | מן הדם ♦ מדם הנפש ולא מדם הבשר ולא מדם העור ולא |
| A | 3 | מדם התמצית. ♦ ונתנו על שתי המזוזות ועל המשקוף ♦ |
| C/B | | יכול יתן על משקוף ומזוזות שלחלונות ♦ ת״ל על הבתים |
| | | על משקוף ומזוזות שלבתים הוא נותן ואינו נותן על |
| A | 4 | משקוף ומזוזות שלחלונות. ♦ יכול עשרה בתים זה לפנים |
| | | מזה לפנים מזה וחבורה אוכלת בפנימי יכול יהא צריך |
| B | | ליתן על כולם ♦ ת״ל על הבתים אשר יאכלו אתו בהם. ♦ |
| A | 5 | מנין אתה אומר חבורה אוכלת בבית אחד ולו חמשה |
| | | פתחים צריך ליתן מדם על כל משקוף ומשקוף מדם |
| B | | על כל מזוזה ומזוזה ♦ ת״ל ונתנו על שתי המזוזות ועל |
| | | המשקוף מדם על כל משקוף ומשקוף ומדם על כל |
| C | | מזוזה ומזוזה. ♦ מנין אתה אומ׳ חמש חבורות אוכלות |
| | | בבית אחד ולו חמשה פתחים שיהו צריכין ליתן מכל |
| | | דם ודם על כל משקוף ומשקוף ומכל דם ודם על כל |
| D | | מזוזה ומזוזה ♦ ת״ל על שתי המזוזות ועל המשקוף מכל |
| | | דם ודם על המשקוף ומכל דם ודם על המזוזה. ♦ |

| | | |
|---|---|---|
| B/A | 1 | על הבתים אשר יאכלו אותו בהם ♦ מכלל שנ׳ בבית |
| | | אחד יאכל (שמ׳ יב מו) מלמד שאין פסח מצרים נאכל |
| C | | אלא בבית אחד. מניין אף בשני מקומות ♦ ת״ל על הבתים |

D. Thus you learn that the paschal sacrifice of Egypt was eaten in two places. However, one may only eat it in one place.[78]

2. A. "... (in which) they are to eat *it*" (Exod. 12:7):

B. [This teaches that] they should not eat with it ordinary animal [offerings] and the festival offering.

C. "... in which (they are to eat it)" (Exod. 12:7):

D. The verse speaks about [things] intrinsic to the paschal offering.[79]

## VIII:III

1. A. "They shall eat (the flesh that same night. They shall eat it roasted over the fire, with unleavened bread and with bitter herbs)" (Exod. 12:8):

B. An "eating" [is not ritually valid if the amount eaten] is less than [an amount equal to] an olive.[80]

2. A. "(They shall eat) the flesh" (Exod. 12:8):

B. And not from the bones, and not from the sinews or horns, and not from the hooves, rather anything that may be eaten of an adult ox [may likewise be eaten of a lamb]: Just as with the adult ox the tips of the shoulderblades and the grisly parts may be eaten, [13] likewise here [with the lamb] the tips of the shoulderblades and the grisly parts [may be eaten].[81]

3. A. "(They shall eat the flesh) that same night" (Exod. 12:8):

B. For one might think that it may be eaten as [other] holy offerings—during the day.

C. Scripture states, [however,] "... that same night" (Exod. 12:8).

4. A. R. Eliezer ben Azariah says, "[The phrase] 'that same night' is said here, and it is said subsequently, 'For that same night I will go through the Land of Egypt' (Exod. 12:12).[82]

B. "Just as 'that same night' stated subsequently [means] until midnight, likewise 'that same night' stated here [means] until midnight."

C. R. Akiva said to him, "Why do I need [Scripture to state 'that same night']? For has it not already been said, '... and you shall eat it hurriedly' (Exod. 12:11), [which means] at the time of the hurrying?[83]

D. "Why does the Scripture state 'that same night' (Exod. 12:8)? Because one might think that it may be eaten like [other] holy offerings—during the day.

E. "[So] Scripture states, 'that same night' [to emphasize that] it is eaten at night, and it is not eaten like [other] holy offerings during the day."

5. A. "(They shall eat it) roasted over the fire" (Exod. 12:8):

B. And not roasted [additionally by the heat absorbed through] a spit, and not roasted [additionally by the heat absorbed through] a grate, and not roasted [by] any other thing.[84]

---

[78] I.e., portions from one sacrifice can be eaten in more than one house; however, a person must eat his individual portion in one house only.

[79] Compare with b. Pesaḥim 95a (Neus., IV.E:Pesaḥim:9:3:I.1.A–2.C).

[80] Compare with *Sifra*, Tsav 10:10 (Neus. XCIII:III:6.C).

[81] Compare with m. Pesaḥim 7:11.

[82] Compare 4.A–E with *Mekhilta de-Rabbi Ishmael*, Pisḥa (H/R, 19:7–8; Laut., vol. 1, 46:40–43; Neus., VI:I:8.A–C); and b. Berakhot 9a (Neus., I:Tractate Berakhot:LXXXI:H–K).

[83] I.e., the time when the Israelites hurried to leave Egypt—the middle of the night.

אשר יאכלו אותו בהם ◆ הא למדת שפסח מצרים נאכל     D

בשתי מקומות אבל האוכלו אין אוכלו אלא במקום

אחד. ◆ יאכלו אותו ◆ שלא יאכלו עמו חולין ושלא יאכלו     B/A    2

עמו חגיגה. ◆ בהם ◆ בגופו שלפסח הכתוב מדבר. ◆     D/C

                                                 VIII:III

ואכלו ◆ אין אכילה פחותה מכזית. ◆ את הבשר ◆     A/B/A    2/1

ולא מן העצמות ולא מן הגידים ולא מן הקרנים ולא מן     B

הטלפים אלא כל הנאכל בשור הגדול מה הנאכל בשור

הגדול ראשי כנפים והסחוסין אף כן ראשי כנפים

והסחוסין. ◆ בלילה הזה ◆ [שיכול יהא נאכל כקדשים ביום ◆     B/A    3

ת"ל בלילה הזה] ◆ אמ' ר' אלעזר בן עזריה נאמר כאן     A   4     C

בלילה הזה ונאמר למטה ועברתי בארץ מצרים בלילה הזה

(פי"ב) ◆ מה לילה הזה הנאמר למטה עד חצות אף לילה     B

הזה הנאמר כאן עד חצות. ◆ אמ' לו ר' עקיבה מה אני צריך     C

והלא כבר נאמר ואכלתם אותו בחפזון (פי"א) בשעת חפזון ◆

מה ת"ל בלילה הזה שיכול יהא נאכל כקדשים ביום ◆ ת"ל     E/D

בלילה הזה בלילה הוא נאכל ואין נאכל כקדשים ביום. ◆ צלי     A    5

אש ◆ ולא צלי שפוד ולא צלי אסכלה ולא צלי דבר אחר. ◆     B

---

[84] I.e., the paschal sacrifice must be roasted only by the heat of the fire, and not at all by heat absorbed from the fire through a spit or something else used to hold the meat over the fire. Compare with *Mekhilta de-Rabbi Ishmael*, Pisḥa (H/R, 19:9; Laut., vol. 1, 46:44–45; Neus., VI:I:9.A–B).

C.   R. Judah says, "Just as a wood [spit] does not burn [the meat from within], likewise a metal [spit] does not heat [the meat from within]."

D.   [But] they said to him, "It is not alike. [With a spit] of wood, you can heat part of it, without heating all of it. [However, with a spit] of metal, [if] you heat part of it, you heat all of it."[85]

6.   A.   "(They shall eat it) roasted over the fire" (Exod. 12:8):[86]

B.   Since it says, "... but roasted—head, legs, and entrails—over the fire" (Exod. 12:9), [you might think] it is commanded to roast all of it at once.

C.   How does one know from Scripture [that if] one wants he may tear off part and place it limb by limb on top of coals?

D.   Scripture states, "roasted over the fire" (Exod. 12:8), [which means] in any manner.

7.   A.   "(They shall eat it roasted over the fire,) with unleavened bread and with bitter herbs" (Exod. 12:8):[87]

B.   [Scripture] includes here many herbs: lettuce, endive, chervil, ivy, and maror.

C.   R. Judah says, "Even thorns and wild lettuce."

D.   R. Ilai says in the name of R. Eliezer, "Even palm ivy. But I searched all his students, requesting a partner for myself, but I did not find [one]."[88]

8.   A.   "(They shall eat it roasted over the fire,) with unleavened bread and with bitter herbs" (Exod. 12:8):

B.   It is commanded that all of it be eaten at once.

C.   Hillel the Elder used to wrap one up in the other and eat them.

D.   One might think that omission of any of them invalidates it.

E.   Scripture states, [however,] "They shall eat *it*" (Exod. 12:8), [which means that] even one of them [suffices].

(Textual Source: Manuscript Antonin 236.1)

VIII:IV

1.   A.   "Do not eat any of it raw [Hebrew: נא], (or cooked in any way with water, but roasted—head, legs and entrails—over the fire)" (Exod. 12:9):[89]

B.   The word "raw" [נא] only means insufficiently cooked.[90]

C.   One might think that it would be permissible to eat it [entirely] raw.

D.   Scripture states, [however,] "roasted over fire" (Exod. 12:8), [which means that] roasted is permissible, and all other [manners] are prohibited.

(Textual Source: Midrash ha-Gadol)

E.   Then let Scripture state, "Do not eat any of it unless it is roasted over fire!" If that was the case, then I might say that it is permissible to eat it [roasted over fire, but still] insufficiently cooked [נא]!

---

[85] I.e., part of the wood spit that is not covered by the meat will absorb heat, but not the part of the wood spit that is covered by the meat. The metal spit, however, will absorb heat through its exposed portion and transfer the heat to the portion covered by the meat. Compare with b. Pesaḥim 74a (Neus., IV.D:Pesaḥim:7:2:I.1.A–2.C).

[86] Compare 6.A–D with b. Pesaḥim 75a (Neus., IV.D:Pesaḥim:7:2:III.3.A–J).

[87] Compare 7.A–D with b. Pesaḥim 39a (Neus., IV.B:Pesaḥim:2:6:I.3.A–4.A).

[88] I.e., none of R. Eliezer's disciples would agree to eat the offering in this manner with R. Ilai.

| | |
|---|---|
| C | ר' יהודה אומ' כשם ◆ ששלעץ אין נשרף של מתכת |
| D | אין מרתיח. ◆ אמרו לו אין דומה של עץ חם ומקצתו |
| A | לא חם כולו ושל מתכת חם מקצתו חם כולו. ◆ צלי |
| B | אש ◆ מכלל שנ' כי אם צלי אש ראשו על כרעיו ועל |
| C | קרבו מצוה לצלותו כולו כאחד ◆ מנין רצה מנתחו ומטילו |
| D | איבר איבר על גבי גחלים ◆ ת"ל צלי אש מכל מקום. ◆ |
| B/A | על מצות ומרורים ◆ ריבה (כאן) מרורים הרבה החזרת |
| C | והעלשין ו[ה]תמכה ו[ה]חרחבינה ו[ה]מרור. ◆ ר' יהודה |
| D | אומ' אף חורולין וחזרת גלין. ◆ ר' אלעאי אומ' משום ר' |
| | אליעזר אף העירקבילין וחיזרתי על כל תלמידיו ובקשתי |
| | לי חבר ולא מצאתי. ◆ על מצות ומרורים יאכלוהו ◆ מצוה |
| B/A | לאכול כולן כאחת. ◆ הלל הזקן היה כורכן זה בזה |
| C | ואוכלן. ◆ יכול יהו מעכבין זה את זה ◆ ת"ל יאכלוהו |
| E/D | אפילו אחד מהן. ◆ |

6

7

8

VIII:IV

| | |
|---|---|
| B/A | אל תאכלו ממנו נא ◆ אין נא אלא שלא בישל כל |
| D/C | צורכו ◆ יכול יהא מותר לאכל ממנו חי ◆ תל' לו' צלי אש |
| E | צלי מותר לך ושאר הכל אסור לך ◆ [יאמר אל תאכלו |
| | ממנו כי אם צלי אש אילו כן הייתי אומר יכול יהא מותר |

1

[89] Compare 1.A–J with y. Pesaḥim 7:34b (Bokser, 7:2:II:A.1–C.2).
[90] I.e., partially cooked and inedible.

F. Scripture states, [however,] "Do not eat any of it raw [נא]" (Exod. 12:9).

G. Thus, if one eats it insufficiently cooked, he gets the 40 lashes!

H. One might think that just as it is prohibited to eat it insufficiently cooked, likewise should it be prohibited if it is sufficiently cooked.

I. Scripture states, [however,] "(Do not eat any of it raw, or cooked in any way) with water" (Exod. 12:9).

J. [Cooked] with water is prohibited, but if it is sufficiently cooked it is not prohibited.

(Textual Source: Manuscript Antonin 236.1)

2.   A. [If] one boiled it and afterward roasted it, or roasted it and afterward boiled it, it is prohibited.

B. As it says in Scripture, "or cooked in any way with water" (Exod. 12:9).

3.   A. One might think if he ate it partially cooked while it was not dark,[91] he would[92] be guilty [of the prohibition of eating it partially cooked].

B. [Because] one might logically reason:

C. Just as at the time when he is [under the obligation to] "get up and eat [it] roasted"[93] he is [prohibited from] eating it partially cooked, [likewise] during the time when he is not [under the obligation to] "get up and eat [it] roasted"[94] isn't it logical that he would [also] be [prohibited from] eating it partially cooked?

[14]  D. How does one know from Scripture [that, indeed, if one eats it partially cooked] while it is still [the] day [of the 14th of Nisan he would be guilty of the prohibition of eating it partially cooked]?

E. Scripture states, "Do not eat any of it raw or cooked in any other way (but roasted)" (Exod. 12:9), [in order to emphasize] that he is guilty [for eating it partially cooked] on the day [of the 14th].

4.   A. "'... but roasted (—head, legs, and entrails—) over the fire' (Exod. 12:9):

B. "One would place its head and its legs and its entrails inside of it."[95]—The words of R. Yosi ha-Galili.

C. R. Akiva said to him, "Even those that were [normally] cooked inside were to be parched, so they hung them outside of it."

D. R. Ishmael called it a "lamb with a helmet" [because the legs and entrails were piled on top of the head]. R. Tarfon called it *"tochbar,"*[96] because its inside[97] was like its outside.[98]

## VIII:V

1.   A. "'You shall not leave any of it over until morning. (If any of it is left until morning, you shall burn it)' (Exod. 12:10):

B. "One might think that if

(Textual Source: Manuscript Oxford Heb. E 55.1)

one leaves any of it over until morning he gets the 40 lashes.

---

[91] I.e., on the 14th of Nisan.

[92] Epstein and Melamed correctly note that the word "not" [Hebrew: "לא"] that appears here in the manuscript must be erroneous, because it contradicts the logic of the unit in 4.C. However, the overall argumentation of this unit is flawed and rhetorically inconsistent, particularly in comparison to its parallels elsewhere, e.g., b. Pesaḥim 41b and *Midrash ha-Gadol,* where the argumentation is coherent.

[93] I.e., on the 15th of Nisan.

[94] I.e., on the 14th of Nisan.

| | | |
|---|---|---|
| לאכול ממנו נא ◆ ת״ל אל תאכלו ממנו נא ◆ הא אם | G/F | |
| אכל ממנו נא הרי זה לוקה את הארבעים. ◆ יכול כשם | H | |
| שאסור לאכול ממנו נא כך אם בשל כל צרכו יהא אסור ◆ | | |
| ת״ל במים ◆ במים אסור לך הא אם בשל כל צרכו | J/I | |
| אינו אסור לך]. ◆ בשלו ואחר כך צלאו צלאו ואחר כך | A | 2 |
| בשלו אסור ◆ שנ׳ ובשל מבושל במים ◆ יכול אם אכל ממנו | A 3 | B |
| נא עד שלא חשכה (לא) יהא חיב ◆ דין הוא ◆ ומה אם | C/B | |
| בשעה שהוא בעמוד אכל צלי הרי ‹הוא› בבל תאכל נא | | |
| בשעה שאין בעמוד אכל צלי (צלי) אינו דין שיהא בבל | | |
| תאכל נא ◆ מבעוד יום מנ׳ ◆ תל׳ לו׳ אל תאכלו ממנו נא | E/D | |
| ובשל לחיב עליו מבעוד יום ◆ כי אם צלי אש ג׳ ◆ היה | B/A | 4 |
| נותן את ראשו ואת כרעיו ואת בני מעיו לתוכו דברי | | |
| ר׳ יוסי הגלילי ◆ אמר לו ר׳ עקיבא אף הן הנחמרין | C | |
| המתבשלין בתוכו אלא תולן חוצה לו ◆ ר׳ ישמעאל קורא | D | |
| אתו גדי מקולס ר׳ טרפון קורא אתו תוכבר שתוכו כברו. ◆ | | |
| | VIII:V | |
| ולא תותירו ממנו עד בקר ◆ יכול אם הותיר ממנו | B/A | 1 |

---

95 I.e., inside the body cavity.
96 Hebrew: תוכבר.
97 Hebrew: tokho—תוכו.
98 Hebrew: baro—ברו.

C.    "Scripture states, [however,] 'If any of it is left until morning, you shall burn it' (Exod. 12:10).

D.    "Scripture comes to give a positive commandment[99] for each negative command-ment."[100]—The words of R. Judah.

E.    R. Jacob said to him, "It's not like that. Rather he shouldn't do it at all!"[101]

2.    A.    "If any of it is left until morning, you shall burn it" (Exod. 12:10):

B.    One might think that he should burn it on the day of the festival.

C.    Scripture states, [however,] "You shall not leave any of it over until morning. If any of it is left until morning ..." (Exod. 12:10).

D.    [The verse includes] two "mornings" [corresponding to] the morning of the 15th [of Nisan] and the morning of the 16th.

E.    This teaches you that the [commandment of] burning [the remnants] of holy offerings does not supersede [the prohibition from burning] on festival days. And [certainly] there is no need to state this for the [more stringent] *Shabbat!*

## Chapter Nine

### (Textual Source: Ms. Oxford Heb. E 55.1)

IX:I

1.    A.    "This is how you shall eat it: (your loins girded, your sandals on your feet, and your staff in your hand;) and you shall eat it hurriedly: (it is a passover offering to the Lord)" (Exod. 12:11): [102]

B.    With haste [like] those going out on a journey.

C.    I only know [from this verse] that its eating must be in haste. How does one know from Scripture to include [in haste] the collecting of its blood and the sprinkling of its blood?[103]

D.    Scripture states, "This" (Exod. 12:11).[104]

2.    A.    "This" (Exod. 12:11):

B.    One might think that I should include [in haste] its roasting and the rinsing of its entrails.

C.    Scripture states, [however,] "This" (Exod. 12:11), [which means] this [and nothing else].

3.    A.    "... (and you shall eat) *it* (hurriedly)" (Exod. 12:11):[105]

B.    It is [done] in haste, but the paschal sacrifice of the [subsequent] generations[106] is not [done] in haste.

---

[99] I.e., a commandment that proscribes an action.

[100] I.e., a commandment that prescribes an action.

[101] I.e., one should not leave some over until morning.

[102] Compare 1.A–B with *Mekhilta de-Rabbi Ishmael*, Pisha (H/R, 22:10–12; Laut., vol. 1, 51:1–4; Neus., VII:I:1.A–D).

[103] Compare 1.C with *Sifre Deut.*, Piska 128 (Hammer, p. 172–3; Neus., CXXVIII:I:1.D–F).

[104] Hebrew: וככה. It is unclear how the text gleans this interpretation, although it appears to be based upon its understanding that the morphology of the word וככה in Exod. 12:11 is unusual.

[105] Compare 3.A–D with b. Pesahim 96a (Neus., IV.E:Pesahim:9:5:II.1.A–III.1.D).

[106] I.e., the paschal sacrifice offered by the subsequent generations of Israelites after the Exodus, as opposed to the paschal sacrifice in Egypt by the Israelites at the time of the Exodus.

| | | |
|---|---|---|
| עד בקר יהא לוקה את הארבעים ◆ תל' לו' והנותר ממנו | C | |
| עד בקר באש תשרפו. ◆ בא כת' ליתן עשה על לא תעשה. | D | |
| דב' ר' יהודה ◆ אמ' לו ר' יעקב לא מפני כך אלא שלא | E | |
| עשה זה כלום. ◆ והנותר ממ' עד בק' בא' תש'. ◆ יכול יהא | B/A | 2 |
| שורפו (ביום) ביום טוב ◆ תל' לו' ולא תותירו ממ' ע' בק' | C | |
| והנ' ממ' ע' בקר ◆ שני בקרים כן בקר חמשה עשר ובקר | D | |
| ששה עשר ◆ ללמדך שאין שריפת קדשים דוחה את | E | |
| יום טוב ואין צורך לומר את השבת: פסו' ◆ | | |
| | | IX:I |
| וככה תאכלו אתו וג' ואכלתם אותו בחפזון ◆ בבהילות | B/A | 1 |
| יוצאי ◆ דרכים אין לי אלא אכילתו שהיא בחפזון מנ' | C | |
| לרבות קיבול דמו וזריקת דמו ◆ תל' לו' ◆ וככה ◆ ככה ◆ | A 2 | D |
| יכול שאני מרבה צלייתו והדחת קרביו ◆ תל' לו' ככה | C/B | |
| ככה ◆ אתו ◆ אתו בחפזון ואין פסח דורות בחפזון ◆ | B/A | 3 |

C.   Another interpretation:

D.   It is [done] in haste, but [the commandment to eat] unleavened bread and bitter herbs is not [done] in haste.

## IX:II

1.

A.   "(It is a) passover offering (to the Lord)" (Exod. 12:11):[107]

B.   In that all its rites are [to be done] for the sake of the paschal offering.

C.   "*It* (is a passover offering to the Lord)" (Exod. 12:11):

D.   Which excludes [the lamb] whose slaughter [was not conducted specifically] for His name.

E.   "(It is a passover offering) to the Lord [YHWH]" (Exod. 12:11):

F.   [That is,] for the special name.[108]

## IX:III

1.

A.   "For that night I will go through the Land of Egypt (and strike down every first-born in the Land of Egypt, both man and beast: and I will mete out punishments to all the gods of Egypt, I the Lord)" (Exod. 12:12):[109]

B.   Like a king who goes from place to place.

2.

A.   Another interpretation:

B.   It says here "go through" and it says below, "For when the Lord goes through to smite" (Exod. 12:23).

[15]

C.   Just as "go through" stated there [refers to] a plague, likewise "go through" stated here [refers to] a plague.

D.   And thus Scripture states, "For there shall be lamenting in every vineyard, etc." (Amos 5:17).

3.

A.   "For that night" (Exod. 12:12):

B.   This is what R. Eliezer ben Azariah said:

C.   "[The phrase] 'that night' is said here, and it says above 'that night' (Exod. 12:8).

D.   "Just as 'that night' stated here [means] until midnight, likewise 'that night' stated above [means] until midnight."

4.

A.   "... and I will strike down every first-born" (Exod. 12:12):[110]

B.   I only know from this [that this refers to] Egyptian first-born that are in Egypt. How does one know from Scripture [that this also refers to] other first-born that are in Egypt?

C.   Scripture states, "... *every* first-born" (Exod. 12:12).

D.   How does one know from Scripture [that this also refers to] Egyptian first-born who are in another place?

E.   Scripture states, "... every first-born" (Exod. 12:12).

---

[107] Compare 1.A–B with *Mekhilta de-Rabbi Ishmael*, Pisḥa (H/R, 23:2–3; Laut., vol. 1, 53:21; Neus., VII:II:1.A–B).
[108] I.e., the tetragrammaton (YHWH—יהוה).
[109] Compare 1.A–B with *Mekhilta de-Rabbi Ishmael*, Pisḥa (H/R, 23:4; Laut., vol. 1, 52:22–23; Neus., VII:II:2.A–B).
[110] Compare 4.A–H with *Mekhilta de-Rabbi Ishmael*, Pisḥa (H/R, 23:10–14; Laut., vol. 1, 53:31–54:35; Neus., VII:II:5.A–F).

| | | |
|---|---|---|
| D/C | | דב' אח' ◆ אתו בחפזון ואין מצות ומררים בחפזון. ◆ |

| | | |
|---|---|---|
| D/C/B/A | 1 | פסח ◆ שיהיו ‹כל› מעשיו לשם פסח: ◆ הוא ◆ פרט |
| F/E | | לששחטו שלא לשמו ◆ לייי ◆ לשם המיוחד: פסו' ◆ |

| | | |
|---|---|---|
| B/A | 1 | ועברתי בארץ מצ' ◆ כמלך שעובר ממקום למק' ◆ |
| B/A | 2 | ד' א' ◆ נא' כן עבירה ונא' למטה ועבר ייי לנגף (פכ"ג) ◆ |
| C | | מה עבירה האמ' להלן מגפה אף עב' האמ' כן מגפה ◆ |
| A 3 | D | וכן הוא או' ובכל כרמים מספד וג' (עמ' ה יז) ◆ בלילה |
| C/B | | הזה ◆ זה שאמ' ר' אלעזר בן עזריה ◆ נא' כן בלילה |
| D | | הזה ונ' למעלה בלילה הזה ◆ מה בל' הזה האמ' כן |
| A 4 | | עד חצ' אף בלילה הז' האמ' למעלה עד חצות. ◆ והכיתי |
| B | | כל בכור ◆ אין לי אלא בכור מצריים שבמצרים |
| C | | בכורות אחרים שבמצ' מנ' ◆ תל' [לו'] כל בכור. ◆ |
| E/D | | בכורות מצ' שבמק' אח' מנ' ◆ תל' לו' כל בכור ◆ |

F. How does one know from Scripture [that this refers to] the first-born of Ham, Cush, Egypt, Put, and Canaan?

G. Scripture states, "... *every* first-born" (Exod. 12:12).

H. And thus Scripture states, "[The Lord] struck down all the first-born in Egypt" (Ps. 78:51).

5. A. "... both man and beast" (Exod. 12:12):

B. I only know from this that the first-born of domesticated beasts were smitten. How does one know from Scripture [that this refers as well to] wild beasts?

C. Scripture states, "... both man and beast" (Exod. 12:12).[111]

D. It is never the case that a man is smitten without his servants smitten with him!

6. A. "... (and I will mete out punishments) to all the gods of Egypt" (Exod. 12:12):

B. I only know from this [that it refers to] Egyptians' gods that are in Egypt. How does one know from Scripture [that it refers as well to] other gods that are in Egypt?

C. Scripture states, "... to *all* the gods of Egypt" (Exod. 12:12).

D. How does one know from Scripture [that it refers as well to] Egyptian gods that are in other places?

E. Scripture states, "... to *all* the gods of Egypt" (Exod. 12:12).

F. How does one know from Scripture [that this refers to] the gods of Ham, Cush, Egypt, Put, and Canaan?

G. Scripture states, "... to *all* the gods of Egypt" (Exod. 12:12).

H. And Scripture says, "I give Egypt as a ransom for you, (Cush and Saba in exchange for you)" (Isa. 43:3).

7. A. "... and I will mete out punishments (to all the gods of Egypt, I the Lord)" (Exod. 12:12):[112]

B. [Punishments] differing one from the other. [Idols] of wood decayed, and [idols] of stone burned, and [idols] of metal rotted.

8. A. "... (and I will mete out punishments to all the gods of Egypt), I the Lord" (Exod. 12:12):

B. I who punished the generation of the flood, and the people of the generation of the Tower of Babel, and the people of Sodom. And in the future, I will punish *Gog* and *Magog* and all its hosts. And if you do not believe concerning [the time] to come, believe it from the past!

9. A. Another interpretation:

B. "... I the Lord" (Exod. 12:12):

C. [This indicates God's] kingship. Any instance that recalls the shame of idolatry, [also] recalls the praise of God.

D. And thus Scripture states, "(It is a piece of wood,) silver beaten flat, that is brought from Tarshish" (Jer. 10:9). And what does Scripture state [next]? "Thus shall you say to them: (Let the gods, who did not make heaven and earth, perish from the earth and from under these heavens)" (Jer. 10:11).

E. And Scripture says, "But the Lord is truly God ... He made the earth by His might ..." (Jer. 10:10,12). And Scripture says, "(Their idols are silver and gold, the work of men's hands)"

[16]

---

[111] It is unclear what the basis is for this interpretation. Perhaps the *vav* in the word ועד in Exod. 12:12 is viewed by the text as grammatically extraneous and, therefore, indicative of this extension of meaning.

[112] Compare 7.A–B with *Mekhilta de-Rabbi Ishmael*, Pisḥa (H/R, 24:11; Laut., vol. 1, 56:64–65; Neus., VII:III:5.A–C).

| | | |
|---|---|---|
| בכור[ות חם] וכוש ומצ׳ ופוט וכנען מנ׳ • תל׳ לו׳ | G/F | |
| כל בכור • וכן הוא או׳ ויך כל בכ[ור] במצ׳ • מאדם | A 5 | H |
| <ו>עד בהמה • אין לי אלא בכו׳ בהמ׳ שלקו בכו׳ | B | |
| חיה מן[נ׳] • תל׳ לו׳ מאדם <ו>עד בהמה • אן <לך> אדם | D/C | |
| שלוקה שאין שמשיו לוקין עמו • ובכל אלהי מצ׳ • | A | 6 |
| אין לי אלא אלהי מצ׳ שבמצ׳ אלהי אחר[י]ם שבמצ׳ | B | |
| מנ׳ • תל׳ לו׳ ובכל אלהי. • אלהי מצ׳ שבמקומות אחרים | D/C | |
| מנ׳ • תל׳ לו׳ ובכל אלהי • <אלהי> חם וכוש ומצ׳ ופ׳ | F/E | |
| וכנען מנ׳ • תל׳ [לו׳ ובכל אלהי] • ואו׳ נתתי כפרך מצרים וג׳ | H/G | |
| (ישע׳ מג ג) • אעשה שפטים • משונ[י]ם זה מזה] שלעץ | B/A | 7 |
| נימוק (ו)שלאבן נשרף שלמתכת הרקיב • אני [יי׳ • אני] | B/A | 8 |
| שפרעתי מדור המבול. ומאנשי דור הפלגה ומאנשי | | |
| סדום. ואני עתיד ליפרע מגוג ומאגוג ומאגפיו ואם <אין> | | |
| אתם מאמינים לבא האמינו לשעבר. • ד׳ א׳ • אני יי׳ • מלכות | C/B/A | 9 |
| כל מקום שמזכיר גניאה שלעב׳ זר׳ שם הוא מזכיר | | |
| שבחו שלמק׳ • וכן הו׳ או׳ כסף מרוקע מתרשיש יובא | D | |
| וג׳ (ירמ׳ י ט) (ו)מהוא או׳ בסוף כדנה תאמרון להום וג׳ • | | |
| ואו׳ ויי׳ אי[ם אמת וג׳ עשה ארץ בכחו וג׳ (שם יא, | E | |
| י, יב) ואומ׳ פה להם ולא ידברו וג׳ (תה׳ קטו ה) ואו׳ | | |

They have mouths, but cannot speak ..." (Ps. 115:5). And Scripture says, "(Let the nations not say, 'Where, now, is their God?') when our God is in heaven (and all that He wills He accomplishes)" (Ps. 115:3).

10.     A.     "... (and I will mete out punishments) to all the gods of Egypt" (Exod. 12:12):

       B.     You only find that [when] each and every nation is smitten, its gods are smitten with it.

       C.     And thus Scripture states, "(Babylon is captured) ... Bel is shamed, Merodach is dismayed. (Her idols are shamed/Her fetishes are dismayed)" (Jer. 50: 2). And thus Scripture states, "Fallen, fallen is Babylon, (and all the images of her gods have crashed to the ground)" (Isa. 21:9). And thus Scripture states concerning our ancestors, "... and I will heap your carcasses upon your lifeless fetishes" (Lev. 26:30).

       D.     And afterward, in the future, when all the nations of the world are destroyed, their gods will be destroyed with them.

       E.     As it states in Scripture concerning them, "As for idols, they shall vanish completely" (Isa. 2:18).

## IX:IV

1.     A.     "And the blood shall be (a sign) *for you* (on the houses where you are staying. When I see the blood I will pass over you, so that no plague will destroy you when I strike the Land of Egypt)" (Exod. 12:13):[113]

       B.     [A sign] for you and not for strangers.

       C.     For you and not for women.

       D.     This teaches that they did not make them[114] into groups [owning their own lamb] in Egypt.[115]

2.     A.     "(And the blood shall be) a sign (for you) on the houses where you are staying" (Exod. 12:13):

       B.     One might think that he should place [the blood upon the doorposts and lintels of] the place [where he] sleeps [that night].

       C.     Scripture states, [however,] "... on the houses in which they are to eat it" (Exod. 12:7).

       D.     One might think that he should only place [it] upon [the doorposts and lintels of] the place [where he] eats [the sacrifice].

       E.     Scripture states, [however,] "... on the houses where you are staying."

       F.     One might think [therefore] that he should place [it] on both [places].

       G.     Scripture states, [however,] "a sign" (Exod. 12:13).

       H.     "Signs" is not stated. Consequently [we learn] that the place of eating [the sacrifice] was also the place of sleeping [that night].[116]

3.     A.     "When I see the blood I will pass over (you, so that no plague will destroy you when I strike the Land of Egypt)" (Exod. 12:13):[117]

       B.     Why do I need [Scripture to state], "When I see"? Isn't everything revealed before Him?

       C.     Rather, [it states this] so one will only place [the blood] on a location that is visible to all who pass by.

---

[113] Compare 1.A–C with *Mekhilta de-Rabbi Ishmael*, Pisha (H/R, 22:10–12; Laut., vol. 1, 51:1–4; Neus., VII:I:1.A–D).

[114] I.e., strangers or women.

[115] Compare with m. Pesaḥim 8:7.

[116] Compare with t. Pisḥa 8:17 and *Mekhilta de-Rabbi Ishmael*, Pisha (H/R, 24:12–14; Laut., vol. 1, 56:66–69; Neus., VII:III:6.A–F).

[117] Compare 3.A–C with *Mekhilta de-Rabbi Ishmael*, Pisha (H/R, 24:15–18; Laut., vol. 1, 56:70–77; Neus., VII:III:7.A–F).

| | | |
|---|---|---|
| 10 | B/A | ואלקינו בשמים וג׳ (שם ג) ◆ ובכל אי׳ מצ׳ ◆ אין לך כל אומה ואומה שלוקה ‹אלא› שאלהי שלה לוקים עמה. ◆ |
| | C | וכן הוא או׳ הוביש בל חת מרודך וג׳ (ירמ׳ נ ב) וכן הוא או׳ נפלה נפ׳ בבל וג׳ (ישע׳ כא ט) וכן הוא אומ׳ באבתינו ונתתי את פגריכם ע׳ פג׳ גלוליכם וג׳ (ויק׳ כו ל) ◆ |
| | D | ואחר כך לעתיד לבוא כשיאבדו כל אומות העולם |
| | E | יאבדו אלהיהם עמהם ◆ לפי שנ׳ בהם והאלילם כליל יחלף (ישע׳ ב יח): פסוק. ◆ |

IX:IV

| | | |
|---|---|---|
| 1 | C/B/A | והיה הדם לכם ◆ לכ׳ ולא לגרים ◆ לכ׳ ולא לנשים ◆ |
| 2 D | A | מלמ׳ שלא עשאוהו חבורות במצ׳. ◆ לאות על הבתים אש׳ |
| | C/B | אתם שם ◆ יכ׳ יתן על מקום לינה ◆ תל׳ לו׳. ע׳ הב׳ אש׳ |
| | E/D | יאכ׳ אתו בהם: ◆ יכ׳ לא יתן אלא על מקום אכילה. ◆ תל׳ לו׳ |
| | G/F | על הבתים אש׳ את׳ שם. ◆ יכ׳ יתן כן וכן ◆ תל׳ לו׳ לאות. ◆ |
| | H | ולא לאותת אמור מעתה מק׳ אכילה שם היתה לינה. ◆ |
| 3 | B/A | ורא׳ את הדם ופסח׳ ◆ מה אני צריך וראיתי והלא הכל |
| | C | גלוי לפניו ◆ אלא שלא יתן אלא על מקום הניראה לכל |

4.    A.    "'... I will pass over you' (Exod. 12:13):

      B.    "If the notion was not written, it would be impossible to state it! '... I will pass over'—like a father who serves the son!"—The words of R. Eliezer.

      C.    But the Sages say, "Like a king who pushes the pace with his own feet."

5.    A.    "... so that no plague (will destroy you)" (Exod. 12:13):[118]

      B.    This teaches that there was a plague in Egypt.

      C.    "... (so that no plague) will destroy (you)" (Exod. 12:13).

      D.    This teaches that there was destruction in Egypt.

      E.    "... (so that no plague will destroy you) when I strike (the Land of Egypt)" (Exod. 12:13).

      F.    This teaches that there was a striking in Egypt.

      G.    This teaches that the Egyptians were smitten that night with three types of divine punishments: With plague, destruction, and striking.

## IX:V

1.    A.    "This day shall be to you one of remembrance. You shall celebrate it (as a festival to the Lord throughout the ages. You shall celebrate it as an institution for all time)" (Exod. 12:14):[119]

      B.    You celebrate the [precise] day that is a memorial for you. And which is this? The festival [that celebrates] your leaving Egypt.

      C.    But still the matter is unclear.[120]

      D.    Scripture states, "(They set out from Ramses in the first month, on the fifteenth day of the first month.) It was on the morrow of the passover offering (that the Israelites started out) ..." (Num. 33:3).

      E.    And when did they eat the passover offering? On the night of the holiday.[121] Thus, they could only have left [Egypt] the very day of the holiday.

2.    A.    "You shall celebrate it" (Exod. 12:14):

      B.    "Celebrate" is stated here, and "celebrate" is stated in the wilderness.[122]

[17]    C.    Just as "celebrate" stated in the wilderness requires a burnt offering and offerings of well-being, likewise "celebrate" stated here requires a burnt offering and offerings of well-being.

      D.    [However, is this indeed the case?] The "celebrate" stated in the wilderness requires a burnt offering and offerings of well-being, [and] it also requires [specifically] bulls. Should "celebrate" stated here [likewise require] a burnt offering and offerings of well-being, since it does not require bulls?

      E.    Scripture states "to the Lord" [here and] "to the Lord" [at Exod. 24:5].

### (Textual Source: Midrash ha-Gadol)

      F.    [Which provides the opportunity to interpret this using a] *gezerah shaveh*:[123]

      G.    Just as "to the Lord" stated in the wilderness requires a burnt offering and offerings of well-being, likewise "to the Lord" stated here requires a burnt offering and offerings of well-being.

---

[118] Compare 5.A–G with *Mekhilta de-Rabbi Ishmael*, Pisḥa (H/R, 24:6–9; Laut., vol. 1, 55:51–58; Neus., VII:III:2.A–B).

[119] Compare 1.A–E with *Mekhilta de-Rabbi Ishmael*, Pisḥa (H/R, 25:11–16; Laut., vol. 1, 58:96–104; Neus., VII:IV:1.A–F).

[120] I.e., the precise time when the Israelites left Egypt is still unclear.

[121] I.e., the night of the 15th of Nisan.

עובר. ◆ ופסחתי עליכם ◆ לולי דבר כת' לא היה איפשר | B/A | 4

לאומרו ופסחתי כאב שמביא לבן: דב' ר' [אלי]עזר ◆

וחכמ' אומ' כמלך שדוחק פסיעותיו ברגליו. ◆ ולא יהיה | A 5 | C

[ב]כם נגף ◆ מלמ' שבמצ' היתה מגפה. ◆ למשחית ◆ מלמ' | D/C/B

שבמצ' היתה [..תה] השחתה. ◆ בהכותי ◆ מלמ' שבמצ' | F/E

היתה מכה. ◆ מלמ' שלקו [ה]מצריים באותו לילה בשלשה | G

מיני פורעניות: במגפה ובהשחתה ובמכה. פסו' ◆

IX:V

והיה היום הזה לכם לזכרון וחגתם אתו ◆ יום | B/A | 1

שהיה לכם לזכרון אתה חוגג ואי זה זה מועד צאתך

ממצרים. ◆ ועד אין דבר תלוי בדלא תלי ◆ תל' לו' ממחרת | D/C

הפסח וג' ◆ אימתי אכלו [את הפסח ב]לילי יום טוב | E

ואף לא יצאו אלא ביום טוב ◆ וחגתם אתו ◆ נא' כן חגיגה | B/A | 2

ונא' [חגיגה במד]בר ◆ מה חגיגה האמ' במדבר טעונה | C

עולה ושלמים אף חגיגה האמורה [כן טעונה עולה]

ושלמ'. ◆ מה לחג' האמ' במדבר טעונה עלה ושלמ' שכן | D

היא טעונ' [פרים] תיטען חגיגה האמ' כן עלה ושלמ'

שכן אינה טעונה פרים ◆ תל' לו' לשם לשם (שמ' כד ה) ◆ | E

לגזירה שוה ◆ מה לשם האמור במדבר טעונה עולה | G/F

ושלמים אף לשם האמור כאן טעונה עולה ושלמים.

◆

---

[122] Exod. 5:1 and 24:5.
[123] I.e., the employment of the same word in separate scriptural contexts, thus facilitating the application of the meaning of the word in one context to the other.

3.  A.  One might think that a festival offering is required all seven [days].[124]

    B.  Scripture states, [however,] "You shall celebrate *it*" (Exod. 12:14), [which means you offer a festival offering on] only one day.

    C.  If so, then why does Scripture state, "Seven days (you shall eat unleavened bread)"? (Exod. 12:15).

    D.  [In order to teach that one makes] payments all seven [days].

4.  A.  How does one know from Scripture that if one did not offer up the festival offering [during the first] six [days of the festival] he should offer it on the seventh?

    B.  Scripture states, "(You shall observe it as a festival of the Lord *for seven days* in the year) … You shall observe it in the seventh month …" (Lev. 23:41).

5.  A.  One might think if he did not celebrate during the festival, he should celebrate after the festival.

    B.  Scripture states, [however,] "(You shall celebrate) *it*" (Exod. 12:14), [meaning that] you celebrate it, and you do not celebrate outside of the festival.

6.  A.  One might think that he has not satisfied the requirement [for the paschal offering] until the eating of the meat.

    B.  Scripture states, [however,] "(You shall celebrate) *it*" (Exod. 12:14), and later Scripture says, "He shall sprinkle it"[125] (Lev. 16:15).

    C.  Just as [the sacrifice] stated later [is fulfilled through the sprinkling of] the blood, and not [the eating of the] meat, this one stated here [is fulfilled through] the blood, and not the meat.

7.  A.  "… throughout the ages … as an institution for all time" (Exod. 12:14):[126]

    B.  This practice is [to be conducted] by [all] generations.

## Chapter Eight

### (Textual Source: Ms. Antonin 236)

X:I

1.  A.  "Seven days you shall eat unleavened bread. (On the very first day you shall remove leaven from your houses, for whoever eats leavened bread from the first day to the seventh day, that person shall be cut off from Israel)" (Exod. 12:15):[127]

    B.  A person fulfills his obligation [to eat unleavened bread all seven days] of Passover with unleavened bread [made with the intention that it] be eaten all seven [days].

    C.  Excluded (as unleavened bread with which to fulfill this commandment) are the loaves of the thanksgiving offering and the wafers of the *Nazir* offering,[128] which are not (made with the intention that they) be eaten all seven (days).

2.  A.  "… you shall remove leaven from your houses" (Exod. 12:15):

    B.  One might think that he may burn it during the festival.

    C.  Scripture states, [however,] "… the *very* (first day you shall remove leaven from your houses)" (Exod. 12:15).

---

[124] Compare 3.A–D with b. Ḥagigah 9a (Neus., XII:Ḥagigah:1:7:I.2.A.).

[125] I.e., the blood of the sin offering upon the cover of the Ark.

[126] Compare 7.A–B with *Mekhilta de-Rabbi Ishmael*, Pisḥa (H/R, 26:12–13; Laut., vol. 1, 60:127–29; Neus., VII:IV:3.A–D) and *Sifre Numbers*, Piska 109 (Neus., CVIX:I:3.A–B).

[127] Compare 1.A–C with *Sifra*, Emor 11:4 (Neus., CCXXX:I:4.A–F); and b. Pesaḥim 38b (Neus., IV:B:Pesaḥim:2:5:IX.1.A–2.E).

[128] Ref. Num. 6:1ff.

| | | |
|---|---|---|
| יכול תיטען חגיגה כל שבעה ◆ ת״ל אותו יום אחד בלבד ◆ | B/A | 3 |
| אם כן למה נאמר שבעת ימים ◆ תשלומין כל שבעה. ◆ | D/C | |
| מניין לא חג כל ששה יחוג כל שבעה ◆ ת״ל בחדש השביעי | B/A | 4 |
| תחגו אותו (ויק׳ כג מא). ◆ יכול לא חג ברגל יחוג אחר | A | 5 |
| הרגל ◆ ת״ל אותו אותו אתה חוגג ואי אתה חוגג חוץ | B | |
| הרגל. ◆ יכול יהא מעוכב עד אכילת בשר ◆ ת״ל אותו ולהלן | B/A | 6 |
| הוא אומר והזה אותו (ויק׳ טז טו) ◆ מה אותו האמור | C | |
| להלן דם ולא בשר אף אותו האמור כאן דם ולא בשר. ◆ | | |
| לדורותיכם חקת עולם ◆ שינהוג הדבר לדורות. ◆ | B/A | 7 |
| | | X:I |
| שבעת ימים מצות תא]כל ◆ מצה] הנאכלת כל שבעה | B/A | 1 |
| אדם יוצא בה ידי חובתו בפסח ◆ יצאו חלות תודה | C | |
| ורקיקי נזיר שאין נאכלין כל שבעה ◆ תשביתו שאר | A | 2 |
| מבתיכם ◆ יכול יהא שורפו ביום טוב ◆ תל׳ לו׳ אך ◆ | C/B | |

D. This teaches that one does not burn it during the festival, and there is no need to say [that this is also the case] on *Shabbat!*[129]

3.
A. "... you shall remove leaven (from your houses)" (Exod. 12:15):[130]

B. On the day before the first day of the festival. Or one might think on the first day of the festival.

C. Scripture states, [however,] "No work at all shall be done on them" (Exod. 12:16).

D. And wasn't burning a type of work? What does the Scripture [mean when it] teaches, "(On the very first day) you shall remove leaven from your houses" (Exod. 12:15)?

E. [It means] on the day before the first day of the festival.

4.
A. "... you shall remove leaven from your houses" (Exod. 12:15):[131]

B. By burning [it].

C. [If] the [end of] the time of burning [the leaven] arrived, and one had not procured fire for himself with which to burn it, he should crumble it up and scatter it in the wind, or throw it in the sea to the fish.[132]

D. R. Judah says, "He should wait until he reaches civilization[133] and [then] burn it."

E. For R. Judah says, "The commandment of removing it [is fulfilled] only by burning.[134]

F. "For here is the logic:

G. "If the leftovers of a sacrifice, which are not subject to the scriptural prohibitions 'It shall not be seen'[135] and 'It shall not be found,'[136] require burning, then isn't it logical that leaven, which is subject to the scriptural prohibitions 'It shall not be seen' and 'It shall not be found,' must [also] require burning?"

H. They replied to him, "The logic that you employ is intended to be stringent, but its outcome is [actually] lenient. [For according to your argument] isn't it logical that if one has not procured fire for himself to burn it, he might wait and keep it [until he is able to procure fire], and [as a result] might transgress with it the prohibitions of 'It shall not be seen' and 'It shall not be found'? For the Torah states, '... (on the very first day) you shall remove leaven from your houses' (Exod. 12:15), [which means] you [should] remove it in any manner."

[18]

I. R. Judah reasoned in another manner: "Eating the leftovers of a sacrifice is prohibited, and eating leaven is prohibited. Just as the leftovers require burning, likewise leaven requires burning."

J. They said to him, "The carcass of an animal that died without proper slaughtering will prove [our point against you], because eating [it] is prohibited, but it does not require burning."

K. He [R. Judah] said to them, "There is a difference [between the leftovers of a sacrifice and the carcass that invalidates your argument. That is, deriving] benefit from leftovers of a sacrifice is prohibited, and [deriving] benefit from leaven is prohibited. But do not prove [your point using the example of the] carcass, from which [deriving] benefit is permissible!"

---

[129] The text understands the word meaning "the very" [Hebrew: אך] in Exod. 12:15 to be indicative of this interpretation.

[130] Compare 3.A–E with *Mekhilta de-Rabbi Ishmael,* Pisḥa (H/R, 27:13–28:6; Laut., vol. 1, 63:38–64:47; Neus., VIII:II:1.A–K).

[131] Compare 4.A–P with *Mekhilta de-Rabbi Ishmael,* Pisḥa (H/R, 28:6–29:3; Laut., vol. 1, 64:47–66:86; Neus., VIII:II:2.A–4.B); and b. Pesaḥim 27b (Neus., IV:B:Pesaḥim:2:1:VII.1.A–P).

[132] Compare 4.C with m. Pesaḥim 2:1.

[133] I.e., until he is in a place where he can procure fire.

[134] Compare 4.E with m. Pesaḥim 2:1.

[135] Exod. 13:7—"Throughout the seven days ... no unleavened bread shall be seen with you and no leaven shall be seen in all your territory."

[136] Exod. 12:19—"No leaven shall be found in your houses for seven days."

מלמד שאין שורפין אתו ביום טוב ואין צריך לומר בשבת ◆ | D |

תשביתו שאר ◆ (מערב) מערב יום טוב או יכול ביום טוב ◆ | B/A | 3

תל׳ לו׳ כל מלאכה לא יעשה בהם ◆ והלא שריפה מעין | D/C |

מלאכה היתה מה תל׳ לו׳ תשביתו שאר מבתיכם ◆

מערב יום טוב ◆ תשביתו שאר מבתיכם ◆ בשריפה ◆ הגיעה | C/B/A 4 | E

שעת ביעור ולא ניתמנה לו האור שישרפנו מפרר

וזורה לרוח או מטיל לים לדגים ◆ ר׳ יהודה או׳ ממתין | D |

עד שיגיע לישוב וישרפנו ◆ שהיה ר׳ יהודה או׳ אין מצות | E |

השבתתו אלא שריפה. ◆ והרי דין ◆ ומה נותר שאין כתוב | G/F |

עליו בל יראה ובל ימצא טעון שריפה חמץ שכתוב

עליו בל יראה ובל ימצא אין דין שיטען שריפה ◆ אמרו | H |

לו לר׳ יהודה כל דין שאתה דן תחילתו להחמיר וסופו

להקל אינו דין הרי מי שלא ניתמנה לו אור לשורפו יהא

יושב ומשמרו ויהיה עובר עליו משום בל יראה ובל ימצא

והתורה אמרה תשביתו שאר מבתיכם משביתו אתה בכל

דבר ◆ היה ר׳ יהודה [דנו] (דינו) דין אחר (ה)נותר אסור | I |

באכילה וחמץ אסור באכילה מה נותר טעון שריפה אף

חמץ טעון שריפה ◆ אמרו לו נבלה תוכיח שאסורה באכילה | J |

ואינה טעונה שריפה ◆ אמר להם הפרש נותר אסור בהניה | K |

וחמץ אסור בהניה ואל תוכח נבלה שמותרת בהנייה ◆

L.   They said to him, "The stoned ox[137] will prove [our point], because [deriving] benefit from it is prohibited, but it does not require burning!"

M.   He said to them, "There is a difference. [Transgressing the prohibition of] leftovers is punishable by excommunication, and [transgressing the prohibition of] leaven is punishable by excommunication. Do not prove [your point using] the stoned ox, [the transgression] of which is not punishable by excommunication!"

N.   They said to him, "The milk of the stoned ox will prove [our point], because it is not punishable by excommunication, and it does not require burning!"

O.   He said to them, "There is a difference. Regarding leftovers, one becomes culpable [for transgression of the specific prohibition of] 'Let none remain over,'[138] and regarding leaven, one becomes culpable [for transgression of the specific prohibition of] 'Let none remain over.'[139] Do not prove [your point using] the milk of the stoned ox, for which one does not become culpable [for the prohibition of] 'Let none remain over'!"

P.   They said to him, "The guilt offering for when one is in doubt as to whether or not he transgressed will prove [our point] according to your logic, because one becomes culpable with it [for transgression of] 'Let none remain over,' but it does not require burning! And the Torah stated, '... you shall remove leaven from your houses' (Exod. 12:15), [which means] you remove it any manner!"

(Textual Source: Midrash ha-Gadol)

X:II

1.   A.   "... for whoever eats leavened bread" (Exod. 12:15):[140]

B.   Since it says in Scripture, "For whoever eats what is leavened" (Exod. 12:19), I only know that [the prohibition applies to that] which leavened on its own.[141] How do I know from Scripture [that the prohibition applies as well to] that which leavened through something else?

C.   Scripture states, "... for whoever eats leavened bread" (Exod. 12:15).

2.   A.   "... that person shall be cut off" (Exod. 12:15):

B.   And not the [entire] community.

3.   A.   "... that (person shall be cut off)" (Exod. 12:15):

B.   Not the one forced to transgress, and not the one who transgressed unwittingly, and not the one who was misled and transgressed under false premises.

4.   A.   "... (that person shall be cut off) from Israel" (Exod. 12:15):

B.   But Israel is in peace.

5.   A.   "... from the first day to the seventh day" (Exod. 12:15):

B.   One might think that the first day and the seventh day are not included in the rule, just as the head and feet are not included in the rule it states in Scripture regarding the leper, "(If the eruption spreads out over the skin so that it covers all the skin of the affected person) from head to foot ..." (Lev. 13:12).

---

[137] Exod. 21:28ff.

[138] Lev. 22:29–30: "When you sacrifice a thanksgiving offering to the Lord ... it shall be eaten on the same day. You shall not leave any of it until morning."

[139] Exod. 12:10: "Let none of it remain over until morning. If any of it is left until morning, you shall burn it."

[140] Compare 1.A–C with b. Pesaḥim 43a (Neus., IV:B:Pesaḥim:3:1:X.1.A–PP).

[141] I.e., without a leavening agent.

| | |
|---|---|
| אמרו לו שור הנסקל יוכיח שאסור בהנייה ואינו | L |
| טעון שריפה ◆ אמר להם הפרש נותר חייבין עליו כרת | M |
| וחמץ חייבין עליו כרת ואל יוכיח שור הנסקל שאין חייבין | |
| עליו כרת ◆ אמרו לו חלב שור הנסקל יוכיח (שאין חייבין) | N |
| [שחייבין] עליו כרת ואין טעון (עלי) שריפה ◆ אמר להם | O |
| הפרש נותר חייבין עליו בבל תותיר(ו) וחמץ חייבין עליו | |
| בבל תותיר ואל יוכיח חלב שור הנסקל שאין חייבין עליו | |
| בבל תותיר ◆ אמרו לו אשם תלוי כדבריך <יוכיח ש>חייבין | P |
| עליו משום בל תותר ואין(ם) טעון שריפה והתורה | |
| אמרה תשביתו שאר מבתיכם משביתו אתה בכל דבר | |
| ◆ | |

| | |
|---|---|
| | X:II |

| | | |
|---|---|---|
| כי כל אכל חמץ ◆ מכלל שנ׳ כי כל אכל מחמצת (פי״ט) | B/A | 1 |
| אין לי אלא שנתחמץ מאליו שנתחמץ מידי אחרים מניין ◆ | | |
| ת״ל כי כל אכל חמץ. ◆ ונכרתה הנפש ◆ ולא הצבור. | B/A 2 | C |
| ההוא ◆ לא אנוס ולא שוגג ולא מוטעה. ◆ מישראל ◆ וישראל | B/A 4 | B/A 3 |
| בשלום. ◆ מיום הראשון עד יום השביעי ◆ יכול אין יום | B/A | 5 |
| הראשון ויום השביעי בכלל כשם שנ׳ במצורע מראשו | | |
| ועד רגליו (ויק׳ יג יב) ואין הראש והרגלים בכלל ◆ | | |

C. Scripture states, [however,] "... (you shall eat unleavened bread) until the twenty-first day of the month at evening" (Exod. 12:18).

D. R. Judah says, "This is proven in this place—'... from the first day to the seventh day' (Exod. 12:15)."[142]

*Chapter Eleven*

(Textual Source: Ms. Antonin 236)

XI:I

1.    A. "(You shall celebrate) a sacred occasion on the first day, (and a sacred occasion on the seventh day. No work at all shall be done on them; only what every person is to eat, that alone may be prepared for you)" (Exod. 12:16):[143]

B. With what do you sanctify it? Sanctify it with food, sanctify it with drink, sanctify it with clean clothes!

2.    A. "(You shall celebrate) a sacred occasion on the first day, and a sacred occasion on the seventh day" (Exod. 12:16):[144]

B. I only know from this that work is prohibited on the first and last day of the festival. How does one know from Scripture [that work is also prohibited on] the intervening days of the festival?

C. You could argue: If work is prohibited on the first and last day of the festival, neither of which are preceded and followed by holidays, then is it not logical that work be prohibited on the intervening days of the festival, which are preceded and followed by holidays?

D. Behold, the six days of the week will prove [the opposite], because they are preceded and followed by holidays,[145] but work is not prohibited on them!

[19]   E. No! If you argue using the six days of the week, for which there is not a *Musaf* sacrifice,[146] can you say [the same is the case] for the intervening days of the festival, which do have a *Musaf* sacrifice?

F. Behold, the new month days will prove [the opposite of 2.C above], for they have a *Musaf* sacrifice, but work is not prohibited on them!

G. No! If you argue using the new month days, which are not called [in Scripture] "sacred occasion," can you say [the same is the case] for these [days] that are called "sacred occasion"? And since they are called "sacred occasion," it is logical that work be prohibited [also] on them!

3.    A. "No work at all shall be done on them" (Exod. 12:16):

B. One might think he should not clean a vegetable, rinse the dishes, or make the beds!

C. However, you should reason: "Work" is stated here [in Scripture] and "work" is stated later [in reference to the building of the] Tabernacle. Just as "work" stated in reference to the Tabernacle is work that involved forethought,[147] likewise the [prohibited] "work" stated here is work that involves forethought.

D. Or [you should reason]: Just as the work [stated in reference] to the Tabernacle is completed work, likewise I know only that completed work [is prohibited here], in that

---

[142] I.e, this point is made in Exod. 12:15, and there is no reason to bring proof from elsewhere in Scripture.

[143] Compare 1.A–B with *Sifra*, Emor 12:4 (Neus. CCXXXVI:I:4.A–D); and *Mekhilta de-Rabbi Ishmael*, Pisḥa (H/R, 30:1–4; Laut., vol. 1, 68:1–6; Neus., IX:I:1.A–B).

[144] Compare 2.A–G with *Mekhilta de-Rabbi Ishmael*, Pisḥa (H/R, 30:5–18; Laut., vol. 1, 68:7–70:33; Neus., IX:I:3.A–N).

[145] I.e., *Shabbat*.

ת״ל עד יום האחד ועשרים לחדש בערב (פי״ח). ◆ ר׳ אומר     D/C

ממקומו מוכרע מיום הראשון עד יום השביעי. ◆

       XI:I

ביום הראשון מקרא קודש ◆ במה אתה מקדשהו     B/A    1

‹קדשהו› במאכל קדשהו במשתה קדשהו בכסות

נקייה ◆ ביום הראשון מק׳ קו׳ וביום השביעי מק׳ קו׳ ◆     A    2

אין לי אלא יום טוב ראשון ואחרון שאסורין במלאכה     B

חולו שלמועד מנ׳ ◆ אמרת ומה יום טוב ראשון ואחרון     C

שאין לפניהם (שאין) ואחריהן מקודשין ‹אסורין

במלאכה› חולו שלמועד שלפניהם ואחריהן מקודשין

אינו דין שיהו אסורין במלאכה ◆ הרי ששת ימי     D

בראשית יוכיח‹ו› שלפניהם ואחריהן מק׳ מקודשין

ואינן אסורין במלאכה ◆ לא אם אמרת בששת ימי     E

בראשית שאין עמהן קרבן מוסף תאמר בחולו של

מועד שיש עמהן קרבן מוסף ◆ הרי ראשי חדשים יוכיחו     F

שיש עמהן קרבן מוסף ואינן אסורין במלאכה ◆ לא     G

אם אמרת בראשי חדשים שאין קרוין מקרא קודש

תאמר באילו שקרוין מקרא קודש הואיל וקרוין מקרא

קודש דין הוא שיהו אסורין במלאכה ◆ כל מלאכה     A    3

לא יעשה בהם ◆ יכול לא יקנב את הירק ולא ידיח את     B

הכלים ולא יציע את המיטות ◆ הרי אתה דן נא׳ כן     C

מלאכה ונ׳ להלן מלאכה במשכן מה מלאכה ‹ה›אמורה

במשכן מלאכה שיש עמה שאובה אף מלאכה

האמורה כן מלאכה שיש עמה שאובה ◆ או ‹מה›     D

מלאכה הא׳ במשכן מלאכה גמורה אף אין לי אלא

מלאכה גמורה שלא יכתב כל הספר ושלא יארג כל

---

[146] I.e., an additional sacrifice, added to the routine daily and afternoon sacrifices, marking the special nature of the festival day.

[147] The word that appears here in ms. Antonin is actually שאובה and this word is attested elsewhere in parallels to this portion of the text. Nonetheless, it makes absolutely no sense contextually. I have chosen, therefore, to translate here the word במחשבה, which itself is attested in *Midrash ha-Gadol* and elsewhere as well. For more on these parallel attestations, see Epstein & Melamed, *Mekhilta D'Rabbi Shimon b. Jochai*, p. 19, textual variants for line 8.

one should not write an entire document, or weave an entire piece of clothing, or sift the entirety of the sifter.

E.    How does one know from Scripture that one should not [even] write two letters, or weave two threads, or make two meshes [toward the construction of] baskets and hampers, sifters and sieves?

F.    Scripture states, "work" (Exod. 12:16), [meaning,] all [kinds of] work.

G.    I know only [that the work prohibited is work that is] optional. How does one know from Scripture [that the prohibition extends as well to work that is] holy,[148] so that one should not write two letters in holy documents, phylacteries, and doorpost inscriptions, or weave two stitches in the priestly undercoat, undergarments, or cloak?

H.    Scripture states, "work" (Exod. 12:16), [meaning,] all [kinds of] work.

I.    I know only [that the work prohibited is work] for which one becomes liable for a sin offering. How does one know from Scripture [that the prohibition applies as well] to work for which one is not liable for a sin offering, so that one should not write [even] one letter, or weave one stitch, make one mesh [toward the construction of] baskets and hampers, sifters and sieves?

J.    Scripture states, "work" (Exod. 12:16), [meaning,] all [kinds of] work.

K.    I only know that [the logic displayed in 3.I is true for work that is] optional. How does one know from Scripture [that the prohibition extends as well to work that is] holy, so that one should not write one letter in phylacteries and doorpost inscriptions, or weave one stitch in the priestly undercoat, undergarments, or cloak?

L.    Scripture states, "work" (Exod. 12:16), [meaning,] all [kinds of] work.

[20]    M.    I know only [that the work prohibited is work] for which one becomes liable for a sin offering. How does one know from Scripture [that the prohibition applies as well] to work for which one is not liable for a sin offering, so that one should not climb a tree, ride a beast, swim in water, clap hands, dance, or slap one's thigh?[149]

N.    Scripture states, "work at all" (Exod. 12:16).

O.    I only know that [the logic displayed in 3.M is true for work that is] mundane. How does one know from Scripture [that the prohibition extends as well to work that is] holy, so that one should not dedicate [things to God], make vows of valuation or vows of devotion, or set aside *terumah* offerings and tithes?[150]

P.    Scripture states, "(Tomorrow is) a day of rest, a holy Sabbath (of the Lord)" (Exod. 16:23).

4.    A.    "If [Scripture only] said, '(No work) shall be done on them which every person is to eat,' I might say that [preparation] of food should not be done on them, and [preparation] of [things] that are not food should not be done on them.

B.    "Scripture states, [however,] '(No work shall be done on them;) only[151] (what every person is to eat)' (Exod. 12:16).

C.    "This divides the matter [between what may and may not be done]."—The words of R. Yosi ha-Galili.

---

[148] Literally: "commanded."
[149] Compare 3.M with m. Betzah 5:2.
[150] Compare 3.O with m. Betzah 5:2.
[151] Hebrew: אַךְ.

E

הבגד ושלא יעשה כל הנפה • ומנ׳ לא יכתב שתי אותות

ולא יארג שני חוטין ולא יעשה שני בתי ניריּן בסלים

G/F

ובסוגין בנפה ובכברה תל׳ לו׳ מלאכה כל מלאכה • אין

לי <אלא> ברשות במצוה מנ׳ לא יכתב שתי אותות

בספרים ובתפילים ובמזוזות ולא יארג שני חוטין

H

בכתנת במכנסים ובמעיל • תל׳ לו׳ מלאכה כל מלאכה •

I

אין לי אלא מלאכה שחייבין עליה חטאת מלאכה

שאין חייבין <עליה> חטאת מנ׳ לא יכתב אות אחת ולא

יארג חוט אחד ולא יעשה בית אחד בסלין ובסוגין

K/J

בנפה ובכברה תל׳ לו׳ מלאכה כל מלאכה • אין לי

אלא ברשות <ב>מצוה מנ׳ לא יכתב אות אחת (בחמ)

בתפילין ובמזוזות ולא יארג חוט אחד בכותנת ובמכנסים

M/L

ובמעיל • תל׳ לו׳ מלאכה כל מלאכה • אין לי אלא

מלאכה שחייבין על מינה חטאת מלאכה שאין חייבין

על מינה חטאת מנ׳ לא עולין באילן ולא רוכבין על

גבי בהמה לא שטין על פני המים לא מספקין לא

O/N

מרקדין ולא מטפחין • תל׳ לו׳ כל מלאכה • אין לי אלא

ברשות במצוה מנ׳ אין מקדישין אין מעריכין ואין

P

מגביהין ואין מתרימין תרומה ומעשרות • תל׳ לו׳ שבתון

A 4

שבת קדש (שמ׳ טז כג) • אילו אמר לא יעשה בהם

אשר יאכל לכל נפש הייתי אומר את שהוא אוכל נפש

<לא> יעשה בהם ואת שאינו אוכל נפש (לא) יעשה

C/B

בהם • תל׳ לו׳ אך • הפסיק העינין דברי ר׳ יוסי הגלילי •

5.    A.    "Similarly you say: 'There was nothing inside the Ark but the two tablets of stone' (1 Kings 8:9).

       B.    "One might think that the two tablets of stone were not in it.

       C.    "Scripture states, [however,] 'but'[152] (1 Kings 8:9).

       D.    "This divides the matter [between what was and was not in the Ark]."—The words of R. Yosi ha-Galili.

6.    A.    "Similarly you say: '(The king said to him, "How many times must I adjure you) to tell me nothing but the truth in the name of the Lord?"' (1 Kings 22:16).

       B.    "One might think that he [i.e., the king of Israel] said to him, 'Don't tell me the truth!'

       C.    "Scripture states, [however,] 'but'[153] (1 Kings 22:16).

       D.    "This divides the matter [between what he should and should not say]."—The words of R. Yosi ha-Galili.

7.    A.    "Similarly you say: 'For David had done what was pleasing to the Lord and never turned throughout his life from all that He had commanded him, (except in the matter of Uriah the Hittite)' (1 Kings 15:5).

       B.    "One might think that he did not turn [aside from the Lord's commandment] in the matter of Uriah the Hittite, but in other matters he did turn aside.

       C.    "Scripture states, [however,] 'but'[154] (1 Kings 15:5).

       D.    "This divides the matter [between those matters in which he did and did not turn aside]."—The words of R. Yosi ha-Galili.

8.    A.    "Similarly you say: 'No Anakites remained in the land of the Israelites, (but some remained in Gaza, Gath, and Ashdod)' (Josh. 11:22).

       B.    "One might think that none remained in Gaza, Gath, and Ashdod, but some remained in all other places.

       C.    "Scripture states, [however,] 'but'[155] (1 Kings 15:5).

       D.    "This divides the matter [between where they did and did not remain]."—The words of R. Yosi ha-Galili.

       E.    R. Akiva said to him, "Why do I need [Scripture to state that no Anakites remained in the land of the Israelites in the first place?] For didn't they remain [elsewhere, in Gaza, Gath, and Ashdod, as stated in that same verse]? Rather, this teaches that a great curse overcame them,[156] and [thereafter] they dwindled in number over time."

9.    A.    If Scripture [merely] stated, "(No work at all) shall be done on them; only what every person is to eat (may be prepared for you)," I might have stated that [any work toward the preparation] of food may be done on them, and [any work not toward the preparation] of food may not be done on them.

       B.    Scripture states, [however,] "(No work at all shall be done on them; only what every person is to eat,) that alone (may be prepared for you)" (Exod. 12:16).

---

[152] Hebrew: רק.
[153] Hebrew: רק.
[154] Hebrew: רק.
[155] Hebrew: רק.
[156] I.e., the Anakites who remained.

| | | |
|---|---|---|
| A | 5 | כיוצא בו אתה או׳ אין בארון רק שני לוחות האבנים |
| C/B | | (מ״א ח ט) ‹יכול שלא היו בו שני לוחות אבנים› • תל׳ |
| A 6 | D | לו׳ רק הפסיק העינין דברי ר׳ יוסי הגלילי • כיוצא בו |
| | | אתה או׳ אשר לא תדבר אלי רק אמת בשם יי (מ״א כב |
| D/C/B | | טז) • יכול שאמר לו אל תדבר לי אמת • תל׳ לו׳ רק • הפסיק |
| A | 7 | העינין דברי ר׳ יוסי הגלילי • כיוצא בו אתה או׳ אשר |
| | | עשה דור הישר בעיני יי ‹ו›לא סר מכל אשר צוהו ג׳ |
| B | | (מ״א טו ה) • יכול בדבר אוריה החתי לא סר אבל סר |
| D/C | | בדברים אחרים • תל׳ לו׳ ‹רק› • הפסיק העינין דברי ר׳ |
| A | 8 | יוסי הגלילי • כיוצא בו אתה או׳ לא נותר ענקים בארץ |
| B | | בני יש׳ (יהו׳ יא כב) • יכול בעזה בגת ובאשדוד לא נותר |
| D/C | | אבל נותר בשאר מקומות • תל׳ לו׳ רק • הפסיק העינין |
| E | | דברי ר׳ יוסי הגלילי • אמר לו ר׳ עקיבא מה אני צריך |
| | | והלא כבר נותרו אלא מלמד שנכנסה בהם מאירה והיו |
| A | 9 | מיתמעטין והולכין. • אילו אומר לא יעשה בהם אך אשר |
| | | יאכל לכל נפש הייתי או׳ את שהוא אוכל נפש יעשה |
| B | | בהם ואת שאינו אוכל נפש לא יעשה בהם • תל׳ לו׳ לבדו • |

[21]    C.    [Which serves to emphasize that] you do not sift, grind, or sift [in the preparation of food].

10.    A.    How does one know from Scripture that one may make a fire and warm himself before it; and heat water for himself; and wash his face, hands, and feet in it; and bathe the baby in it?[157]

       B.    Scripture states, "… (may be prepared) *for you*."

       C.    [You may do] anything for your needs.

11.    A.    One might think that [food] may be prepared for the [first or seventh] day as well as for the next day.

       B.    Scripture states, [however,] "… what every person is to eat … may be prepared for you" (Exod. 12:16).

       C.    That which is eaten on them may be prepared, and that which is not eaten on them may not be prepared.

12.    A.    "… only what every person[158] is to eat" (Exod. 12:16):[159]

       B.    I might assume [that one may] even [prepare food] for cattle, for it is called *"nefesh."*

       C.    In accordance with what is said in Scripture, "One who kills a beast[160] shall make restitution for it" (Lev. 24:18).

13.    A.    One might think they may scatter nuts for the chickens and make cakes for the dogs.[161]

       B.    Scripture states, [however,] "… for you" (Exod. 12:16), [meaning,] for you, and not for gentiles—for you, and not for dogs.

       C.    It once occurred that Simon of Teman did not come to the schoolhouse on the night of the festival. R. Judah ben Baba found him the next morning. He said to him, "Why didn't you come last night to the schoolhouse?"

       D.    He said to him, "I happened upon the opportunity to fulfill a religious duty, and I performed it. A troop[162] of gentiles came into the city, and we were afraid that they would be hostile to the citizens. So we slaughtered a calf for them, and fed them food and drink, and sheltered them so that they would not be hostile to the citizens."

       E.    He said to him, "I'd be surprised if your reward [for this deed] was not lost in the injury you [caused]! For behold they said, 'They do not prepare food on festival days for gentiles or dogs.'"

14.    A.    R. Akiva says, "'… only what every person is to eat' (Exod. 12:16):[163]

       B.    "[Scripture employs the term *"nefesh"*] to include [preparing food for] cattle.

       C.    "Perhaps it includes other people as well as cattle!

       D.    "Scripture states, [however,] '… (may be prepared) *for you*.'

       E.    "And what is the reason for this division? Because you are required [to feed] the cattle, but you are not required [to feed] the other people."

---

[157] Compare 10.A with m. Betzah 2:5. Compare 10.A–C with b. Betzah 28:2.

[158] Hebrew: *nefesh*—נפש.

[159] Compare 12.A–C with *Mekhilta de-Rabbi Ishmael*, Pisḥa (H/R, 32:4–10; Laut., vol. 1, 73:68–78; Neus., IX:II:2.A–J).

[160] Hebrew: *nefesh b'heimah*—נפש בהמה.

[161] Compare 13.A–E with t. Betzah 2:6.

[162] The word that actually appears here in the manuscript is ברשות. This word makes no contextual sense, and its appearance is certainly the result of an error in transmission of the word בלשת that appears in the parallels to this tradition found in *Midrash ha-Gadol* and t. Yom Tov 2:6. This is the word I translate here.

[163] Compare 14.A–E with *Mekhilta de-Rabbi Ishmael*, Pisḥa (H/R, 32:7–10; Laut., vol. 1, 73:74–78; Neus., IX:II:2.G–J); and b. Betzah 28b (Neus., VII:Tractate Besah:3:7a:VI:A–R).

| | | |
|---|---|---|
| C | A 10 | שאין בוררין ואין טוחנין ואין מרקידין ◆ מנ׳ לעושה |
| | | מדורה ומתחמם כנגדה ומחמין לו חמין ומרחץ בהם |
| B | | פניו ידיו ורגליו ומרחץ בהם את התינוק ◆ תל׳ לו׳ לכם ◆ |
| C | B/A 11 | לכל שהו צורככם ◆ יכול יעשה מן היום למחר ◆ תל׳ לו׳ |
| C | | אשר יאכל לכל נפש יעשה לכם ◆ את שנאכל בהם יעשה |
| A | 12 | ואת שאין יאכל בהם לא יעשה ◆ אך אשר יאכל לכל |
| B | | נפש ◆ שומע אני אף נפשות בהמה שהיא קרויה נפש ◆ |
| C | A 13 | כעינין שנ׳ ומכה נפש בהמה ישלמנה (ויק׳ כד יח) ◆ יכול |
| | | יהו מהלקטין תורמסין לתרנוגלים ועושין לימודים |
| B | | לכלבים ◆ תל׳ לו׳ לכם ‹לכם› ולא לגוים לכם ולא לכלבים. ◆ |
| C | | מעשה בשמעון התימני שלא בא בלילי יום טוב |
| | | לבית המדרש לשחרית מצאו ר׳ יהודה בן באבא אמר לו |
| D | | מפני מה לא באתה אמש לבית המדרש ◆ אמר לו מצוה |
| | | אחת אירע לידי ועשיתי‹ה› ברשות שלגוים נכנס(נ)ו |
| | | לעיר והינו מתיראין שמא יצהיבו את בני העיר שחטנו |
| | | להם עגל אחד והאכלנום והשקינום וסכנום שלא |
| E | | יצהיבו את בני העיר ◆ אמר לו תמיה אני עליך שלא |
| | | יצא שכרך בהפסדך שהרי אמרו אין עושין ביום טוב לא |
| A | 14 | לאכילת גוים ולא לאכילת כלבים ◆ ר׳ עקיבא או׳ אך |
| B | | אשר יאכל לכל נפש ◆ להב‹י›א את נפשות בהמה |
| C | | במשמע ◆ משמע מביא את נפש בהמות ואת נפשות |
| D | | אחרים ◆ תל׳ לו׳ לכם ◆ מה ראית לחלוק שאתה |
| E | | מוזהר על הבהמה ואין אתה מוזהר על אחרים ◆ |

15.   A.   "... (only what every person is to eat, that alone may be prepared) for you" (Exod. 12:16):[164]

      B.   [Food may be prepared] for you, but not for heaven.[165]

[22]  C.   Abba Saul would reason differently: "If at the time when human stoves are not open,[166] the heavenly stoves are open,[167] then at the time when human stoves are open,[168] is it not logical that the heavenly stoves be open?"

(Textual Source: Midrash ha-Gadol)

XI:II

1.    A.   "You shall observe the Feast of Unleavened Bread, (for on this very day I brought your ranks out of the Land of Egypt. You shall observe this day throughout the ages as an institution for all time)" (Exod. 12:17):

      B.   R. Judah says, "You shall repeat the precepts of *matzah*.[169]

      C.   "[Thus] it teaches: 'Three women may knead at three kneading troughs one after the other.' But the Sages say three women may [simultaneously] work on one dough, one kneading, one rolling, and one baking. R. Akiva says that all women, all wood, and all ovens are not alike. This is the general rule: If it[170] swells, she should sprinkle it with water.'"[171]

2.    A.   R. Shimon says, "'You shall observe the Feast of Unleavened Bread' (Exod. 12:17):

      B.   "Unleavened bread that is fit to be guarded.[172]

      C.   "Excluded are the priestly doughs, which are not fit to be guarded."

3.    A.   "(You shall observe the Feast of Unleavened Bread,) for on this very day I brought your ranks out (of the Land of Egypt)" (Exod. 12:17):

      B.   This teaches that God's ranks are called [the same thing] as Israel's ranks, and Israel's ranks are called [the same thing] as God's ranks.[173]

4.    A.   "You shall observe this day" (Exod. 12:17):

      B.   You observe it early, from the night of the 14th (of Nisan).

      C.   Based on this they said, "On the night of the 14th they search for leaven by the light of a candle, and they do not search by the light of the sun, or the light of the moon, or the light of a torch, but only by the light of a candle."[174]

      D.   And even though there is not [direct scriptural] proof of this matter, there is a hint [of proof in Scripture] of this matter: "At that time I will search Jerusalem with candles" (Zeph. 1:12).

5.    A.   "(You shall observe this day throughout the ages) as an institution for all time" (Exod. 12:17):

      B.   It should be practiced for generations.

---

[164] Compare 15.A–C with t. Ḥagigah 2:10 and b. Betzah 20b (Neus., VII:Tractate Besah:2:4:IX:A–C).

[165] I.e., sacrifices to God should not be conducted.

[166] I.e., *Shabbat,* when cooking is not allowed.

[167] I.e., sacrifices are conducted on *Shabbat.*

[168] I.e., festival days, when cooking is allowed.

[169] R. Judah understands the biblical imperative "You shall observe" to mandate a review of the rules concerning unleavened bread.

[170] I.e., the dough.

[171] Compare 1.C with m. Pesaḥim 3:4.

[172] R. Shimon understands Exod. 12:17 to read, "You shall *guard* the unleavened bread."

[173] See Exod. 12:41.

[174] Compare 4.C with t. Pisḥa 1:1.

| | | |
|---|---|---|
| C/B/A | 15 | לכם ‹לכם› ולא לגבוה ◆ היה אבא שאול דנו דין אחד ומה |
| | | אם בשעה שלא נפתחו כירי הדיוט נפתחו כירי שמים |
| | | בשעה שנפתח‹ו› כירי הדיוט אינו דין שיפתחו כירי שמים ◆ |

| | | |
|---|---|---|
| B/A | 1 | ושמרתם את המצות ◆ ר׳ יהודה אומר שנו בדקדוקי |
| C | | מצו(ו)ת ◆ מלמד ששלש נשים לשות בשלש עריבות זו |
| | | אחר זו. וחכמים אומרים שלש נשים עסיקות בבצק |
| | | אחת לשה ואחת אורכת ואחת אופה. ר׳ עקיבה אומר |
| | | לא כל הנשים ולא כל העצים ולא כל התנורים שוין |
| A | 2 | זה הכלל תפוח ותלטוש בצונן. ◆ ר׳ שמעון אומר |
| C/B | | ושמרתם את המצות ◆ מצה הראויה להשתמר ◆ יצא חלוט |
| A | 3 | שאין ראוי להשתמר. ◆ כי בעצם היום הזה הוצאתי |
| B | | את צבאותיכם ◆ מלמד שצבאות מקום (נקראו) צבאות |
| | | ישראל וצבאות ישראל (נקראו) צבאות מקום. ◆ |
| B/A | 4 | ושמרתם את היום הזה ◆ שמריהו מלפניו ‹מאור ארבעה |
| C | | עשר› ◆ מכאן אמרו אור ארבעה עשר בודקין את |
| | | החמץ לאור הנר ואין בודקין לא לאור חמה ולא לאור |
| D | | לבנה ‹ולא לאור האבוקה› אלא לאור הנר ◆ ואעפ״י |
| | | שאין ראיה לדבר זכר לדבר בעת ההיא אחפש את |
| A | 5 | ירושלים בנרות (צפ׳ א יב). ◆ לדורותיכם חקת עולם ◆ |
| B | | שינהוג [ה]דבר לדורות. ◆ |

*Chapter Twelve*

(Textual Source: Midrash ha-Gadol)

XII:I

1.  A.  "In the first month, (from the fourteenth day of the month at evening, you shall eat unleavened bread until the twenty-first day of the month at evening)" (Exod. 12:18):[175]

    B.  One might think the entirety (of the month). Scripture states, [however,] "… from the fourteenth" (Exod. 12:18).

    C.  Or, if from the fourteenth, one might think [beginning] once it becomes night. Scripture states, [however,] "… (fourteenth) *day*" (Exod. 12:18).[176]

    D.  Or, if from the day, one might think from two hours [of daylight and on]. Scripture states, [however,] "… at evening" (Exod. 12:18).[177]

    E.  Just as "at evening" [means] when the day begins to turn toward evening, likewise when "day" is said [it means] when the day begins to turn toward evening—from the sixth hour [of daylight][178] and forward.

2.  A.  One might think you are obligated [to eat] unleavened bread on the fourteenth.

    B.  Scripture states, [however,] "(You shall slaughter the passover sacrifice … For seven days you shall eat unleavened bread) *with it*" (Deut. 16:2–3), [meaning,] with it you are obligated [to eat] unleavened bread, and you are not obligated [to eat] unleavened bread on the fourteenth.

    C.  If so, why is "fourteenth day" said, if not for the matter of unleavened bread? It is taught regarding the matter of removal of leaven.

(Textual Source: Ms. Antonin 236)

3.  A.  "… until the twenty-first day of the month at evening" (Exod. 12:18):

    B.  One might think that you are obligated [to eat] unleavened bread all seven [days].

    C.  Scripture states, [however,] "… with it" (Deut. 16:3), [meaning,] with it[179] you are obligated for unleavened bread, and you are not obligated [to eat] unleavened bread all seven [days].

    D.  If so, why is "until the twenty-first day of the month at evening" said?

    E.  For I might think that I only know [from 3.C] that at the time when you have[180] the paschal sacrifice [you are obligated to eat unleavened bread].

    F.  How does one know from Scripture [that you must eat unleavened bread even] at the time when you do not have the paschal sacrifice?

    G.  Scripture states, "… (for seven days) *thereafter*" (Deut. 16:3).

4.  A.  "… you shall eat unleavened bread" (Exod. 12:18):[181]

    B.  Scripture fixes this as an obligation.

    C.  I only know [from this verse that this commandment was in effect] when the Temple existed. How does one know from Scripture [that it is in effect even] when the Temple does not exist?

---

[175] Compare 1.A–E with parallel material above VII:II:1.A–I and with *Sifra*, Emor 11:1 (Neus., CCXXX:I:1.A–G).

[176] Thus, connoting to some degree that the obligation begins during the daytime.

[177] Thus, connoting to some degree that the obligation begins during the evening.

[178] I.e., noon.

[179] I.e., with the paschal sacrifice.

XII:I

| | | |
|---|---|---|
| או • בארבעה עשר ת"ל בכולו יכול • בראשון | C/B/A | 1 |
| יכול יום או • יום ת"ל משתחשך יכול בארבעה עשר | D | |
| אף היום משפנה בערב מה • בערב ת"ל שעות משתי | E | |
| יכול • ולמעלה. שעות משש יום משפנה יום כשאמור | A | 2 |
| (דב' טז ג) עליו ת"ל • עשר בארבעה מצה חייב את | B | |
| בארבעה מצה חייב אתה ואין חייב אתה עליו | | |
| אינו אם עשר בארבעה נאמר למה כן אם • עשר | C | |
| יום עד • חמץ. לביעור עניין תניהו מצה לאכילת עניין | A | 3 |
| כל במצה חיב את יכול • בערב לחודש ועשר[ים]ן האחד | B | |
| חיב אתה וא' במצה חייב אתה עליו עליו לו' תל' • שבעה | C | |
| ועשרים האחד יום עד נא' למה כן אם • שבעה כל מצה | D | |
| שיש בשעה אלא לי אין שיכול • בערב לחודש | E | |
| • (עליו) לו' תל' • מנ' פסח לך שאין בשעה • פסח לך | G/F | |
| בזמן אלא לי אין • חובה הכתוב קבעו מצות תאכלו | C/B/A | 4 |
| • מנ' קים המקדש בית שאין >בזמן<ב קים המקדש שבית | | |

---

[180] I.e., when you offer up and eat the paschal sacrifice.
[181] Compare 4.A–D with b. Pesaḥim 28b (Neus., IV:B:Pesaḥim:2:2:I.3.C–E).

D.    Scripture states, "... at evening" (Exod. 12:18).

5.      A.    "... you shall eat unleavened bread" (Exod. 12:18):

B.    I only know [from this verse that this commandment was in effect] in the land [of Israel]. How does one know from Scripture [that it is in effect even] outside the land?

C.    Scripture states, "... in all your settlements you shall eat unleavened bread" (Exod. 12:20).

D.    If our goal is to broaden [the application of the commandment] "... you shall eat unleavened bread" [by using the verse] "... in all your settlements you shall eat unleavened bread," then why does Scripture state, "... until the twenty-first day of the month at evening"?

E.    If it does not [concern] the matter immediately before it [in Scripture], it is taught [concerning] the matter immediately after it.

(Textual Source: Ms. Firkovich II A 268)

**XII:II**

1.      A.    "(No leaven shall be found in your houses for) seven days. (For whoever eats what is
[23]         leavened, that person shall be cut off from the community of Israel, whether he is a stranger or a citizen of the country)" (Exod. 12:19):[182]

B.    I only know that [this applies to] days. How does one know from Scripture [that it applies as well to] nights?

C.    Scripture states, "... until the twenty-first day of the month (at evening) ..." (Exod. 12:18).

2.      A.    "No leaven shall be found in your houses" (Exod. 12:19):[183]

B.    Since it says in Scripture, "... no leaven shall be seen with you" (Exod. 13:7), one might think he may hide [his leaven out of sight] or receive [the leaven of others] as a deposit.

C.    Scripture states, [however,] "No leaven shall be found in your houses" (Exod. 12:19).

D    Or [perhaps because Scripture says], "... (no leaven) shall be found" (Exod. 12:19), one might think that he should not see [even leaven belonging] to others.

E.    Scripture states, [however,] "... (no leavened bread shall be seen) with you" (Exod. 13:7), [meaning,] you should not see yours, [but] you may see that belonging to others.

F.    One might think that Scripture spoke only of the non-Jew whom you have not defeated. How does one know from Scripture, however, [that this includes] the non-Jew whom you have defeated, and to whom you leased your house, and he dwelt with you in your courtyard?

G.    Scripture states, "No leaven shall be found in *your* houses" (Exod. 12:19).

H.    But still I might say that [your leaven] is prohibited in [your] house under [the prohibitions] that it "not be seen"[184] and "not be found,"[185] while that of others is permitted. [But] it is permitted to hide [your leaven] that is in the fields or receive [leaven as] a deposit, however, this is prohibited [for the leaven belonging] to others!

I.    Scripture states, [however,] "leaven" (Exod. 12:19) and "leaven" (Exod. 13:7) [in order to provide the opportunity] for a *gezerah shaveh*:[186]

[182] Compare 1.A–C with *Mekhilta de-Rabbi Ishmael,* Pisha (H/R, 33:15–17; Laut., vol. 1, 76:3–6; Neus., X:I:2.A–E).

[183] Compare 2.A–M with *Mekhilta de-Rabbi Ishmael,* Pisha (H/R, 33:18–34:8; Laut., vol. 1, 76:7–77:24; Neus., X:I:3.A–4.N); and b. Pesahim 5b (Neus., IV:A:Pesahim:1:1:I.24.A–26.H).

[184] Exod. 13:7—"Throughout the seven days ... no unleavened bread shall be seen with you and no leaven shall be seen in all your territory."

[185] Exod. 12:19—"No leaven shall be found in your houses for seven days."

| | | |
|---|---|---|
| D | B/A 5 | תל' לו' בערב ◆ תאכלו מצות ◆ אין לי אלא בארץ |
| C | | בחוצה לארץ מנ' ◆ תל' לו' בכל משבתיכם תאכלו מצות ◆ |
| D | | אם סופנו לרבות עליו תאכלו מצות בכל משבתיכם תאכלו |
| E | | מצות מה תל' לו' עד יום האחד ⟨ועשרים לחדש⟩ ◆ אם |
| | | אינו ענין לשלפניו תנהו ענין לשלאחריו. סל' פסו' ◆ |

XII:II

| | | |
|---|---|---|
| 1 | C/B/A | שבעת ימים. ◆ אין לי אלא ימים לילות מנין ◆ ת״ל עד |
| 2 | B/A | יום האחד ועשרים. וגו' ◆ שאר לא ימצא בבתיכם ◆ מכלל |
| | | שנא' לא יראה לך שאר (שמ' יג ז) ⟨יכול יטמין ויקבל |
| D/C | | פקדון ◆ ת״ל שאר לא ימצא בבתיכם ◆ או לא ימצא⟩ יכול |
| E | | אי אתה רואה לאחרים ◆ ת״ל לך לך אי את רואה רואה |
| F | | אתה לאחרים (ת״ל לך) ◆ יכול לא דבר הכת' אלא בגוי |
| | | שלא כיבשתו אבל גוי שכיבשתו והשכרתה לו ביתך ושרוי |
| G | | עמך בחצר שלך מנין ◆ ת״ל לו' שאר לא ימצא בבתיכם ◆ |
| H | | ועדיין אני אומ' שבבית אסור בבל יראה ובבל ימצא |
| | | ושל אחרים מותר שבשדות מותר להטמין ולקבל פקדון |
| I | | ושל אחרים יהא אסור ◆ ת״ל שאר שאר לגזירה שוה |

---

[186] I.e., the employment of the same word in separate scriptural contexts, thus facilitating the application of the meaning of the word in one context to the other.

J. Just as "leaven" stated there (Exod. 13:7) [applies to] your [leaven] and not others', likewise "leaven" stated here [applies] to yours and not others'. Just as "leaven" stated there is included in the general prohibited category that it "not be seen" and "not be found," likewise "leaven" stated here is included in the general prohibited category that it "not be seen" and "not be found."

K. Rabban Shimon ben Gamliel says, "But wasn't [the prohibition that] it 'not be found' [presumed] in [the prohibition that] it 'not be seen'? So why does Scripture state, '(No leaven) shall be found'?

L. "[To teach that] you are obligated to destroy [that leaven] which is accessible to you. That which is not accessible to you, you are not required to destroy.

M. "Based on this they said: 'Leaven upon which debris has fallen, or that fell into a pit or into a cistern or into a cask—if the dogs and swine are able to search for it and bring it to you, you are bound and obligated to destroy it. But if [the dogs and swine] are not [able], you are not obligated to destroy it.'"[187]

3. A. [If] a non-Jew entered into the house of a Jew with leaven in his hand, he is not obligated [to destroy it]. [But if the non-Jew] placed him in charge of it, he is obligated to destroy it.[188]

B. As it says in Scripture, "... no leaven shall be seen with you" (Exod. 13:7).

C. But if he[189] designated a house for it, and placed it within it, he is not obligated.

4. A. One might think that for figs and dates that leavened on their own[190] one would be culpable [for possessing or eating them during the proscribed period of days].

B. For it is a matter of logic:

C. Just as one is culpable for that which leavened [on account] of something else,[191] is it not logical that one would be culpable for these that leavened on their own?

D. Scripture states, [however,] "... (for whoever eats) leavened bread [ḥametz]" (Exod. 12:15).

E. Ḥametz is unique in that it is a type of grain. [Thus,] these that are not a type of grain are excluded [from the prohibition].

5. A. R. Shimon says, "Since we have not learned [in Exod. 12:19] that one is culpable for excommunication [as well] because of leaven, Scripture states, '... no leavened bread shall
[24]     be found with you, and no leaven shall be seen with you' (Exod. 13:7).[192]

B. "[Meaning,] just as one is culpable for excommunication for [the scriptural injunction of] 'no leavened bread shall be seen with you,' likewise is one culpable for excommunication for [the scriptural injunction of] 'no leaven shall be seen with you.'"

6. A. "For whoever eats what is leavened" (Exod. 12:19):[193]

B. Since it says [in Scripture], "For whoever eats leavened bread [ḥametz]" (Exod. 12:15), I only know [the prohibition applies to something] that leavened [on account] of something else.

C. How does one know from Scripture [also prohibited is something] that leavened on its own?

---

[187] Compare 2.M with m. Pesaḥim 2:3.
[188] Compare 3.A–C with t. Pisḥa 2:11.
[189] I.e., the Jew in the scenario at 3.A.
[190] I.e., without the aid of a leavening agent.
[191] I.e., with the aid of a leavening agent.
[192] Compare 5.A–B with b. Betzah 7b (Neus., VII:Tractate Besah:XXXIII:A–Q).
[193] Compare 6.A–D with XII:II:4.A–E and X:II:1.A–C above.

מה שאר האמור להלן לך ולא לאחרים אף שאר J

האמ' כאן לך ולא לאחרים ומה שאר האמור להלן הרי

הוא בכלל בל יראה ובל ימצא אף שאר האמור

כן הרי הוא בכלל בל יראה ובל ימצא • רבן שמע' K

בן גמליאל אומ' והלא בכלל בל יראה (ו)בל ימצא

היה מה ת״ל לא ימצא • את שמצוי לך את זקוק L

לבערו את שאין מצוי לך אי(ן) אתה זקוק לבערו • מיכן M

אתה אומ' חמץ שנפלה עליו מפולת או שנפלה לתוך

הבור או לתוך הדות או לתוך הפיטוס אם יכולין

(ה)כלבים וחזירין לחפש אחריו ולהוציאו אתה חייב

וזקוק לבער אותו ואם לאו אי אתה זקוק לבערו •

נכרי שבא לביתו של יש' וחמץ בידו אין זקוק לו הפקידו A 3

לו חייב לבערו • שנא' לא יראה לך שאר • ייחד לו בית C/B

ונתנו בתוכו אין זקוק לו • יכול תאנים ותמרים שנתחמצו A 4

מאיליהן יהא חייב עליהן • דין הוא • או מה אם זה C/B

שחימוצו מאחרים חייבין עליו אלו שהחמיצו מאיליהן

אינו דין שיהא חייב עליהן • ת״ל חמץ (שם יב א) • מה E/D

חמץ מיוחד שהוא מין דגן יצאו אלו שאינן מין דגן • ר' A 5

שמע' אומ' לפי שלא למדנו לשאור שחייבין עליו כרת

ת״ל לא יראה לך חמץ ולא יראה לך שאר (שם יג ז) •

מה לא יראה לך (שאר מה ל[א ירא]ה לך) חמץ חייבין B

עליו כרת אף לא יראה [לך] שאר חייבין עליו כר[ת • כי A 6

כל] אוכל מחמצת • מכלל [שנא' כי כל אוכל] חמץ (שם B

יב טו) אין לי אלא ש[נתחמץ מא]חרין • נתחמץ [מ]איליו C

D.    Scripture states, "For whoever eats what is leavened" (Exod. 12:19).

7.    A.    "... (that) *person* shall be cut off" (Exod. 12:19):[194]

     B.    And not the [entire] community.

8.    A.    "... *that* (person shall be cut off from the community of Israel)" (Exod. 12:19):

     B.    Not the one forced to transgress, and not the one who transgressed unwittingly, and not the one who transgressed under false premises.

9.    A.    "... (that person shall be cut off) from the community of Israel" (Exod. 12:19):

     B.    But Israel [is in] peace.

10.    A.    "... whether he is a stranger" (Exod. 12:19):

     B.    This is the [male] stranger.

11.    A.    "... a citizen" (Exod. 12:19):

     B.    This is the [male] citizen.

12.    A.    "... of the country" (Exod. 12:19):

     B.    [Scripture states this] to extend [the prohibition of leaven to include all] unowned leaven.

### XII:III

1.    A.    "You shall eat nothing leavened. (In all your settlements you shall eat unleavened bread)" (Exod. 12:20):[195]

     B.    This includes Babylonian porridge, Median beer, Edomite vinegar, and Egyptian barley beer.[196]

     C.    One might think that one would be culpable [of the prohibition in Exod. 12:20] on their account.

     D.    Scripture states, [however,] "... leaven [*hametz*]" (Exod. 12:15).

     E.    Because *hametz* is particular in that it is a pure species, these, which are not pure species, are excluded.[197]

     F.    Why [then] did they come [forward as examples in 1.B]?

     G.    In order [to provide the opportunity for Scripture] to give [in opposition to] them a prohibitive commandment.[198]

2.    A.    One might think that a person could fulfill his obligation [to eat unleavened bread if it is prepared] with dough made from rice.

     B.    Scripture states, [however,] "... (you shall eat unleavened) *bread*" (Exod. 12:20).

     C.    Just as "bread" mentioned later[199] [is to be made only from] the five species of cereals,[200] likewise is "bread" mentioned here [to be made only from] the five species of cereals.

3.    A.    Another interpretation:[201]

---

[194] Compare 7.A–9.B with X:II:2.A–4.B above.

[195] Compare 1.A–G with b. Pesahim 43a (Neus., IV:B:Pesahim:3:1:X.1.M–Y).

[196] Compare 1.B with m. Pesahim 3:1.

[197] I.e., these items have *hametz* blended into them, but they are not composed exclusively of *hametz*. As such, they are prohibited as leaven; however, if one transgresses through them, he will not incur the punishment of excommunication.

[198] I.e., a commandment that proscribes an action.

[199] I.e., Num. 15:19.

[200] I.e., wheat, barley, rye, oat, and spelt.

[201] Compare 3.A–D with b. Pesahim 35a (Neus., IV:B:Pesahim:2:5:I.1.A–2.B).

| | | |
|---|---|---|
| מנין • ת״ל כי כל אכל מחמצת • ונכרתה הנפש • ולא | B/A 7 | D |
| הציבור • הה[ן]א • ולא אנוס ולא שוגג ולא מוטעה. • | B/A | 8 |
| מעדת ישראל. • יש׳ שלום. • בגר • זה הגר. • | B/A 10 | B/A 9 |
| ובאזרח • זה אזרח • הארץ • לרבות שאר הפקיר. סל׳ | B/A 12 | B/A 11 |
| פסו׳ • | | |

XII:III

| | | |
|---|---|---|
| כל מחמצת לא תאכלו. • לרבות כותח הבבלי | B/A | 1 |
| ושכר המדי וחומץ האדומי וזיתס המצרי • יכול יהא חייב | C | |
| עליהן • ת״ל חמץ • מה חמץ מיוחד שהוא מין גמור יצאו | E/D | |
| אלו שאינן מין גמור • למה באו • ליתן עליהן לא תעס • | G/F | |
| יכול יהא אדם יוצא ידי חובתו בעיסת אורז • ת״ל לחם | B/A | 2 |
| (דב׳ טז ג) • מה לחם האמ׳ להלן (במ׳ טו יט) מחמשת | C | |
| מינין אף לחם האמ׳ כאן מחמשת (ה)מינין. • ד״א • | A | 3 |

B. "(And they baked the dough that they had taken out of Egypt,) unleavened cakes, for it was not yet leavened" (Exod. 12:39):

C. [This teaches that] *matzah* comes [only from that which ] could become both unleavened and leavened.

D. Excluded is dough made from rice, which could not become both unleavened and leavened.

4. A. "One might think that a person could fulfill his obligation [to eat unleavened bread] with [produce designated as] first fruits.[202]

B. "Scripture states, [however,] 'In all your settlements you shall eat unleavened bread' (Exod. 12:20).

C. "Excluded are first fruits, which are not eaten in all your settlements."—The words of R. Yosi ha-Galili.

D. R. Akiva says, "'They shall eat it with unleavened bread and bitter herbs' (Num. 9:11).

E. "Just as bitter herbs [is something] whose species is not [subject] to the offering of first fruits, likewise unleavened bread [must be made of something] whose species is not [subject] to the offering of first fruits.

F. "Or [I might reason that] just as bitter herbs does not serve as the first-fruits offering, likewise unleavened bread does not serve as the first-fruits offering."

5. A. One might think that a person could fulfill his obligation [to eat unleavened bread] with untithed produce that has not been fixed,[203] or with first tithe from which the priestly tithe has not been taken, or with second tithe or dedicated produce that have not been redeemed.[204]

B. Scripture states, [however,] "... leaven [*hametz*]" (Exod. 12:15).

C. [Thus,] because *hametz* is particular, in that its prohibition is on its own account,[205] these are excluded because their prohibition is due to another matter.[206]

6. A. And how does one know from Scripture that the priests fulfill their obligation [to eat unleavened bread even] with *terumah* [consumed] outside the Temple, and [the rest of Israel] with second tithe [brought to and consumed] in Jerusalem?

B. Scripture states [twice], "*matzot, matzot*" (Exod. 12:15 and Exod. 12:18). Scripture [repeats this in order to] broaden [the scope of what is permissible].

C. R. Yosi ha-Galili says, "A person does not fulfill his obligation [to eat unleavened bread] with second tithe [brought to and consumed] in Jerusalem.

D. "As it says in Scripture, '... (you shall eat unleavened bread), bread of distress' (Deut. 17:3).

E. "The second tithe is [thus] excluded, for it eaten only in joy."

F. But the Sages say, "A person does fulfill his obligation with second tithe [brought to and consumed] in Jerusalem.

G. "As it says in Scripture, '*matzot, matzot*' (Exod. 12:15 and Exod. 12:18). Scripture [repeats this in order to] broaden [the scope of what is permissible].

[25] H. "If so, then why does it state in Scripture, 'bread of distress'?

---

[202] Compare 4.A–6.I with *Mekhilta de-Rabbi Ishmael*, Pisha (H/R, 35:7–36:2; Laut., vol. 1, 80:55–81:76; Neus., X:I:11.A–V); and b. Pesahim 36a (Neus., IV:B:Pesahim:2:5:VIII.9.A–K).

[203] I.e., tithed.

[204] Compare 5.A with m. Pesahim 2:5. Compare 5.A–C with b. Pesahim 35b (Neus., IV:B:Pesahim:2:5:VIII.2.A–D).

[205] I.e., because Scripture prohibits specifically the eating of *hametz*.

[206] I.e., they are not prohibited specifically in and of themselves because of their intrinsic nature. Rather their prohibition is due to negligent tithing.

| | | |
|---|---|---|
| עוגות מצות כי לא חמץ (שמ׳ יב לט) ◆ מצה הבאה לידי מצה | C/B | |
| וחימוץ ◆ יצאת עיסת אורז שאינה באה לידי מצה וחימוץ ◆ | D | |
| יכול יצא אדם ידי חובתו בבכורים ◆ ת״ל בכל מושבו׳ | B/A | 4 |
| תאכלו מצות ◆ יצאו בכורים שאין נאכלין בכל מושבו׳ | C | |
| דברי ר׳ יוסי הגלילי ◆ ר׳ עקיבא אומ׳ על מצות ומרורים | D | |
| יאכלוהו (במ׳ ט יא) ◆ מה מרורים שאין במינן בכורים | E | |
| אף מצה שאין במינה (באה) בכורים ◆ או מה מרורים | F | |
| שאין באים בכורים אף מצה שאין באה בכורים ◆ יכול | A | 5 |
| יהא אדם יוצא ידי חובתו בטבל שלא ניתקן ובמעשר | | |
| ראשון שלא נתרם ובמעשר שני והקדש שלא נפדו ◆ | | |
| תל׳ לו׳ חמץ ◆ מה חמץ מיוחד שאיסורו מאליו יצאו אלו | C/B | |
| שאיסורן מידי דבר אחר. ◆ ומנין (שהכנים) שהכהנים | A | 6 |
| יוצאין ידי חובתן בתרומה בגבולין ויש׳ במעשר שני | | |
| בירוש׳ ◆ ת״ל מצות מצות ריבה הכת׳ ◆ ר׳ יוסי הגלילי | C/B | |
| אומ׳ אין אדם יוצא ידי חובתו במעשר שני בירושלם ◆ | | |
| שנא׳ לחם עני ◆ יצא מעשר שני שאין נאכל אלא | E/D | |
| בשמחה ◆ וחכ׳ מ׳ אומ׳ יוצא אדם ידי חובתו במעשר שני | F | |
| בירושלם ◆ שנא׳ מצות מצות ריבה הכת׳ ◆ אם כן למה | H/G | |

     I.     "To exclude [making] unleavened bread with three [things in the dough]: with wine, with oil, and with honey."[207]

## Chapter Thirteen

### (Textual Source: Ms. Firkovich II A 268)

**XIII:I**

1.    A.     "Then Moses called out to all the elders of Israel (and said to them, 'Draw forth and take for yourselves a lamb for your families, and slaughter the passover offering')" (Exod. 12:21):[208]

       B.     This teaches that Moses showed honor to the elders.

       C.     This teaches that the elders preceded all of Israel.

       D.     This teaches that Moses served the elders of his generation.

2.    A.     R. Yosi ha-Galili says, "Great is maturity: If they [who possess it] are old, then their maturity is great because thus they are beloved in Scripture. If they [who possess it] are young, then their maturity is great because their youth is of secondary importance."[209]

3.    A.     "... and said to them" (Exod. 12:21):

       B.     This teaches that he fixed his eyes upon them from the moment he spoke to them.

4.    A.     "... 'Draw forth (and take for yourselves a lamb for your families)'" (Exod. 12:21):[210]

       B.     R. Eliezer says, "He said to them, 'Draw back your hands from idolatry!'

       C.     "In accordance with what is said in Scripture, [beginning with] 'I also said to them: (Cast away) every one of you, the detestable things of his eyes (and do not defile yourselves with the fetishes of Egypt),' and up until 'But I acted for the sake of My name ...' (Ezek. 20:7–9)."

5.    A.     R. Akiva says, "'... Draw forth ...'—he who has [a lamb].

       B.     "'... and take ...'—he who does not.[211]

       C.     "'... for yourselves ...'—[Scripture states this] to include he who gives [a lamb as] a gift.

       D.     "'... a lamb ...'—every time Scripture states 'lamb' it includes sheep and goats."

6.    A.     Another interpretation:

       B.     "... 'Draw forth and take for yourselves a lamb for your families'" (Exod. 12:21):

       C.     Consequently, we learn that small cattle are acquired through drawing [them toward you].[212]

7.    A.     R. Ishmael says, "One might think that the passover offering of the subsequent generations would only be suitable if it was bought. And don't be astonished [by this idea], because it is suitable to bring the thanksgiving offering from that bought with tithe money, but it is not suitable to bring [it] from the tithe [itself]!

       B.     "Scripture states, [however,] '... Draw forth ...'—he who has [a lamb]; '... and take ...'—he who does not."

8.    A.     "... and slaughter the passover offering" (Exod. 12:21):

---

[207] I.e., unleavened bread made with these succulent items can no longer be considered "bread of distress."

[208] Compare 1.A–D with *Mekhilta de-Rabbi Ishmael,* Pisḥa (H/R, 36:3–10; Laut., vol. 1, 81:77–82:12; Neus., XI:I:1.A–2.I).

[209] This tradition, as it appears in ms. Firkovich, is difficult to render not only because of a lacuna in the manuscript, but also because the overall tradition is corrupt due to faulty transmission. Parallels to this tradition that are more concise and coherent can be found elsewhere. See *Exodus Rabbah* 5:12, *Leviticus Rabbah* 11:8, *Midrash ha-Gadol* (Exodus 12:21), and *Tanḥuma* Exodus 29.

[210] Compare 4.A–6.B with *Mekhilta de-Rabbi Ishmael,* Pisḥa (H/R, 36:11–14; Laut., vol. 1, 82:14–83:19; Neus., XI:I:4.A–D).

[211] I.e., purchase a lamb.

[212] Compare 6.C with m. Kiddushin 1:4.

| | | |
|---|---|---|
| I | | נאמ' לחם עוני • פרט למצה שלשה (בין) בין בשמן ובדבש. סל' פסו' • |

| 1 | B/A | ויק[רא] משה לכל זקני יש' • מלמד שנהג משה |
| | D/C | כבוד לזקנים • מלמד ש[הזקנים קוד]מין לכל יש' • מלמד |
| 2 | A | [שנ]שתמש משה בזקנים שבדורו • ר' [יוסי הגל'] |
| | | אומ' גדולה זקנה א[ם ...ג]דולים הם גדולה זקנה שכך |
| | | חיבבה הכת' אם ילדים הם גדולה זקנה שכך ניטפלה |
| 3 | B/A | ילדות • ויאמר אלהם • מלמד שנתן עיניו בהם משעה |
| 4 | B/A | שאמר להן • משכו • ר' אליעזר אומ' אמ' להן משכו |
| | C | ידיכם מעבודה זרה • כענין שנא' ואומר אלהם איש (את) |
| | | שקוצי עיניו וגו' ועד ואעשה למען שמי וגו' (יחז' כ ז - ט) • |
| 5 | B/A | ר' עקיבה אומ' משכו מי שיש לו • וקחו מי שאין לו • |
| | D/C | לכם לרבות את הנותן מתנה • צאן בכל מקום שנא' |
| 6 | B/A | צאן תופס כבשים ועזים. • ד"א • משכו וקחו לכם צאן למש' • |
| | A / C | נמצינו למדין לבהמה דקה שנקנית במשיכה • ר' ישמעאל |
| | | אומ' יכול לא יהא פסח דורות כשר אלא אם כן |
| | | היה לקוח אל תתמה שהרי תודה כשרה להביא מן |
| B | | הנלקח בכסף מעשר ולא כשרה להביא מן המעשר • ת"ל |
| 8 | A | משכו מי שיש לו וקחו מי שאין לו • ושחטו הפסח • |

B.   Its commandment [is fulfilled] only upon its [proper] slaughter.

C.   For it is a matter of logic:

D.   If the burnt offering, for which [Scripture] did not fix a set time for slaughter, the commandment [is fulfilled] only upon its slaughter, then concerning the passover offering, for which [Scripture] did fix a set time for slaughter, is it not logical that its commandment [should be fulfilled] only upon its slaughter?

E.   No! If you reason using the burnt offering, for which [Scripture] fixed a set place of slaughter, can you then say [the same applies] to the passover offering, for which [Scripture] did not fix a set place of slaughter? And since [Scripture] did not fix a set place of slaughter [for the passover offering, one would assume] that its commandment [would not be fulfilled only] upon its slaughter.

F.   Scripture states, [however,] "... and slaughter the passover offering" (Exod. 12:21), [meaning that] its commandment [is fulfilled] only upon its [proper] slaughter.

9.   A.   "Take (a bunch of hyssop, dip it in the blood that is in the basin, and apply some of the blood that is in the basin to the lintel and to the two doorposts. None of you shall go outside the door of his house until morning)" (Exod. 12:22):[213]

B.   R. Judah says, "'Take' is said here [in Scripture], and 'take' is said concerning the Red Heifer,[214] and 'take' is said concerning the *lulav*,[215] and 'take' is said concerning the leper.[216]

C.   "Just as 'take' said here [requires] a bunch [of hyssop], likewise 'take' said there [requires] a bunch."

D.   But the Sages say, "Concerning this [hyssop for the dipping of the blood of the passover offering], if it is not a bunch, it is invalid. Concerning those [other instances requiring hyssop], even if it is not a bunch, it is valid."

10.  A.   "... hyssop" (Exod. 12:22):[217]

B.   Not Greek hyssop, not Roman hyssop, not *Kohalit* hyssop, not desert hyssop, nor any hyssop that has an epithet.[218]

11.  A.   "... and dip it in the blood" (Exod. 12:22):[219]

B.   There must be enough blood for dipping.

12.  A.   "(Take a bunch of hyssop, dip it in the blood) that is in the basin [*saf*]" (Exod. 12:22):[220]

B.   I might think *saf* [means] vessel or that *saf* [means a hole next to the] doorpost, because [in Scripture] a vessel is called a *saf* and a doorpost is called a *saf*.

[26]   C.   And how does one know from Scripture that a vessel is called a *saf*? As it says in Scripture, "... the vessels [*sipot*] and the snuffers" (1 Kings 7:50). And how does one know from Scripture that a doorpost is called a *saf*? As it says in Scripture, "When they placed their threshold [*sipam*] next to My threshold and their doorposts next to My doorposts" (Ezek. 43:8).

D.   Scripture states, [however,] "... and apply some of the blood ... to the lintel and to the two doorposts" (Exod. 12:22).

---

[213] Compare 9.A–D with *Mekhilta de-Rabbi Ishmael,* Pisḥa (H/R, 37:1–3; Laut., vol. 1, 83:26–30; Neus., XI:I:6.A–F).

[214] Num. 19:6.

[215] Lev. 23:40.

[216] Lev. 14:6.

[217] Compare 10.A–B with *Mekhilta de-Rabbi Ishmael,* Pisḥa (H/R, 37:3–4; Laut., vol. 1, 83:31–33; Neus., XI:I:7.A–B).

[218] Compare 10.B with m. Parah 11:7.

[219] Compare 11.A–B with *Mekhilta de-Rabbi Ishmael,* Pisḥa (H/R, 37:5; Laut., vol. 1, 84:34–35; Neus., XI:I:8.A–B).

[220] Compare 12.A–G with *Mekhilta de-Rabbi Ishmael,* Pisḥa (H/R, 37:5–8; Laut., vol. 1, 84:35–39; Neus., XI:I:9.A–E).

| | |
|---|---|
| אין מצותו אלא בשחיטה ◆ שהיה בדין ◆ ומה עולה שלא קבע | D/C/B |
| לה זמן שחיטה אין מצותה אלא בשחיטה פסח שקבע | |
| לו זמן שחיטה אינו דין שלא תהא מצותו אלא | |
| בשחיטה ◆ לא אם אמרת בעולה שקבע לה מקום שחיטה | E |
| תאמר בפסח שלא קבע לו מקום שחיטה הואיל | |
| ולא קבע לו מקום שחיטה לא תהא מצותו בשחיטה ◆ | |
| ת״ל ושחטו הפסח אין מצותו אלא בשחיטה ◆ | F |
| ולקחתם ◆ ר׳ יהודה אומ׳ נאמ׳ כאן לקיחה | B/A 9 |
| <ונאמרה לקיחה> בפרה ונאמ׳ לקיחה בלולב ונאמ׳ לקיחה | |
| במצורע ◆ מה לקיחה האמ׳ כאן אגודה אף לקיחה האמורה | C |
| להלן אגודה ◆ וחכמ׳ אומ׳ זה [א]ם אין אגוד פסול | D |
| והלז אף על פי ש[אין אגוד כ]שר ◆ אזוב ◆ לא איזוביון | B/A 10 |
| [לא א]זוב רומי ולא איז׳ כוחלית ולא [אזוב מדברית ולא | |
| כ]ל אזוב שיש [לו שם לווי]. ◆ וטבלתם בדם ◆ שיהא [בדם | B/A 11 |
| כדי טבילה ◆ אשר בסף ◆ שומע אני בסף] כלי או בסף מזוזה | B/A 12 |
| מפני [שהכלי קרוי סף ומזוזה קרויה סף ◆ ומנין שהכ]לי | C |
| קרוי סף שנא׳ והספו׳ [והמזמרות (מ״א ז נ) ומנין שהמזוזה | |
| קרויה סף שנ]א׳ בתתם סיפם את [ספי ומזוזתם אצל מז׳ | |
| (יחז׳ מג ח) ◆ ת״ל והגעתם אל המש׳ ואל שתי] המזוזות ◆ | D |

E.    A vessel that can reach [both] is stated.[221] With a *saf* that is a vessel, and not a *saf* that is [a hole next to the] doorpost.

F.    R. Akiva says, "Since the verse [mentions the *saf*] twice, one should place [the blood] in [both] a *saf* that is a vessel and a *saf* that is [a hole next to the] doorpost, and he should pour what remains of the blood over the threshold."

13.   A.    "(None of) *you* (shall go outside the door of his house until morning)" (Exod. 12:22):

      B.    I only know [that this refers to] you.[222] How does one know from Scripture [that this refers as well to] converts, women, and slaves?

      C.    Scripture states, "(None of) *you* shall go outside" (Exod. 12:22).[223]

## XIII:II

1.    A.    "For when the Lord *goes through* to smite the Egyptians, (He will see the blood on the lintel and the two doorposts, and the Lord will pass over the door and not let the Destroyer enter and smite your home)" (Exod. 12:23):[224]

      B.    It says here, "go through," and it says there, "go through."[225]

      C.    Just as "go through" stated there [refers to] a plague, likewise "go through" stated here [refers to] a plague.

      D.    And thus it states, "For there shall be lamenting in every vineyard, etc." (Amos 5:17).

2.    A.    "(For when the Lord *goes through* to smite the Egyptians,) He will see the blood on the lintel and the two doorposts" (Exod. 12:23):

      B.    Which excludes a house that does not have lintel or doorpost.

3.    A.    "... and the Lord will pass over the door" (Exod. 12:23):

      B.    Behold, this is a warning!

4.    A.    "... and not let the Destroyer enter and smite your home" (Exod. 12:23):

      B.    This teaches that once permission is given to agents to injure, in the end they will complete their missions, but they do not return [back to report the completion] to the holy place.[226]

5.    A.    "You shall observe this (as an institution for all time, for you and for your descendants)" (Exod. 12:24):

      B.    Observe the commandment stated in this matter[227] [for all times].

      C.    One might think [this imperative for all times includes] even [the command to use] a bunch of hyssop [to sprinkle the blood on] the lintel and two doorposts.

      D.    Scripture states, [however,] "(You shall observe) *this* as an institution for all time, for you and for your descendants" (Exod. 12:24), [meaning] that the matter should be observed for generations.

---

[221] I.e., a vessel that can be moved.

[222] I.e., adult Jewish males.

[223] It is unclear upon what basis the text establishes this interpretation. Perhaps the text notices that Exod. 12:22 includes the second person, masculine, plural personal pronoun (Hebrew: ואתם) in this imperative clause, even though it is not grammatically required. Thus, the text understands the added "emphasis" by the biblical text on "you" to establish a larger range of people included in the prohibition.

[224] Compare 1.A–D with parallel above in IX:III:2.A–D.

[225] Exod. 12:12.

[226] I.e., to God.

[227] I.e., the passover offering.

| | | |
|---|---|---|
| E | | בסף שיכול ליגע אמור מעתה בסף כלי ולא בסף |
| F | | מזוזה ◆ ר' עקיבה אומ' הואיל ושני כתובים קיימין |
| | | יהא נותן בסף כלי ובסף מזוזה שירי הדם היה |
| 13 | B/A | שופך על יסוד האסקופה. ◆ אתם ◆ אין לי אלא אתם |
| | C | גרים נשים ועבדים מנין ת"ל ואתם לא תצאו וגו' ◆ |

XIII:II

| | | |
|---|---|---|
| 1 | B/A | ועבר יוי לנגף את מצ' וגו' ◆ נאמ' כאן עברה ונא' |
| | C | להלן עברה ◆ מה עברה האמ' להלן מגפה אף עברה האמ' |
| | D | כאן מגפה ◆ וכן הוא אומ' ובכל כרמים מספד וגו' (עמ' |
| 2 | B/A | ה יז). ◆ וראה את הדם על המש' ועל שתי המזוזות ◆ פרט |
| 3 | A | לבית שאין לו שקף ואין לו מזוזה. ◆ ופסח יוי על הפתח ◆ |
| 4 B | A | הרי זו אזהרה. ◆ ולא יתן המשחית לבא אל בתיכם |
| | B | לנגף. ◆ מלמד שכיון שניתנה רשות לשלוחין לחבל סופן |
| | | לעשות שליחותן אבל אין חוזרי למקום הקדש. ◆ |
| 5 | B/A | ושמרתם את הדבר הזה ◆ שמור מצוה האמורה |
| | D/C | בענין ◆ יכול אף אגודת אזוב ומשקוף ושתי המזוזות ת"ל |
| | | הזה לחק לך ולבניך עד עולם שינהוג הדבר לדורות. |
| | | סל' פסו' ◆ |

*Chapter Fourteen*

(Textual Source: Ms. Firkovich II A 268)

XIV:I

1.  A.  "And when you enter the land (that the Lord will give you, as He has promised, you shall observe this rite)" (Exod. 12:25):

    B.  This [corresponds to the] seven nations [that the Israelites conquered in the Land of Canaan].[228]

    C.  "... that the Lord will give you" (Exod. 12:25):

    D.  This [corresponds to the] three lands [that God promised, in addition to the seven above, to Abraham at Gen. 15:19, but were not conquered].[229]

2.  A.  "(And when you enter the land) ... you shall observe this rite" (Exod. 12:25):

    B.  It was quite clear to God[230] that once Israel entered into the land, they would thereafter conduct the passover offering.

    C.  And thus Scripture states, "Encamped at Gilgal (in the steppes of Jericho, the Israelites offered the passover sacrifice on the fourteenth of the month, toward evening)" (Joshua 5:10).

3.  A.  "And when your children ask you, ('What do you mean by this rite?' you shall say, 'It is the passover sacrifice to the Lord, because He passed over the houses of the Israelites in Egypt when He smote the Egyptians, but saved our houses. The people then bowed low in homage ')" (Exod. 12:26–7):[231]

    B.  They[232] will ask you, "What is [the meaning of] this rite to you?"

    C.  This is the wicked son, who [by phrasing the question "to you"] removed himself from the community.

    D.  Thus, [in your reply] you too remove him from the community and say to him, "'It is because of what the Lord did for *me* (when I went free from Egypt)' (Exod. 13:8).

    E.  "'... for me ...' He acted, but for you He did not act."

4.  A.  "You shall say, 'It is the (passover) *sacrifice*'" (Exod. 12:27):[233]

    B.  In that all its rites are [to be done] for the sake of the sacrifice.

    C.  "'(It is the) passover (sacrifice)'" (Exod. 12:27):

    D.  In that all its rites are [to be done] for the sake of the paschal offering.

    E.  "'*It* (is the passover sacrifice)'" (Exod. 12:27):

    F.  Which excludes [the lamb] whose slaughter [was not conducted specifically] for His name.

    G.  "(It is the passover sacrifice) to the Lord [YHWH]" (Exod. 12:27).

    H.  [That is,] for the special Name.[234]

5.  A.  "... because He passed over the houses of the Israelites in Egypt" (Exod. 12:27):

    [27]  B.  "Passing over" [is stated] three [times] in this [scriptural] section: "... because He passed" (Exod. 12:27); "... and the Lord will pass over" (Exod. 12:23); "... I will pass over you" (Exod. 12:13).

---

[228] The Hittites, Perizzites, Rephaim, Amorites, Canaanites, Girgashites, and Jebusites.

[229] The Kenites, the Kenizzites, and the Kadmonites. According to Rabbinic tradition, these three will be inherited in the messianic period. See *Sifre Deut.*, Piska 164 (Hammer, p. 195; Neus., CLXIV:I:1.A–D).

[230] Literally: He who spoke, and the world came into being.

[231] Compare 3.A–E with *Mekhilta de-Rabbi Ishmael*, Pisḥa (H/R, 66:8–13; Laut., vol. 1, 149:100–105; Neus., XVII:I:14.A–G).

XIV:I

| | | |
|---|---|---|
| C/B/A | 1 | והיה כי תבוא אל הארץ • זו ארץ שבעה • אשר |
| A 2 | D | יתן ייי לכם • זו ארץ שלשה. • ושמרתם את העבדה הזאת • |
| B | | גלוי וידוע לפני מי שאמר והיה העולם שכשיש' נכנסין |
| C | | לארץ עתידין לעשות את הפסח • וכן הוא אומ' ויחנו |
| | | בני ישר' בגלגל וגו' (יהו' ה י) סל' פסו' • |
| B/A | 3 | והיה כי יאמרו אליכם בניכם. • עתידין לומר לכם |
| C | | מה העבודה הזאת לכם • זה בן רשע שהוציא את עצמו |
| D | | מן הכלל • אף אתה הוציאו מן הכלל ואמור לו בעבור זה |
| E | | עשה ייי לי (שמ' יג ח) • לי עשה ולא לך עשה. • |
| B/A | 4 | ואמרתם זבח (פסח) • שיה]יו כל מ]עשיו לשום |
| F/E/D/C | | זבח. • פ]סח • שיהיו כ]ל מעשיו לשו]ם פ]סח ה]וא • פרט |
| A 5 | H/G | לשש]חטו שלא לש]מו • לייי • לש]ם] המיוחד • [אשר] פסח |
| B | | [על בתי בני יש' במצ' • שלוש פסיחות נאמרו] בפרשה |

---

232 I.e., the children.
233 Compare 4.A–F with parallel above in IX:II:1.A–F.
234 I.e., the tetragrammaton (YHWH—יהוה).

C. How does one know from Scripture that if you had a courtyard entirely [full] of Israelites, the "passing over" was only over the houses?

D. As it says in Scripture, "... because He passed over the *houses* of the Israelites" (Exod. 12:27).

E. [How does one know from Scripture that] if Egyptians and Israelites dwelled [together] in a courtyard, the "passing over" was only over the doors?

F. As it says in Scripture, "... and the Lord will pass over the *door*" (Exod. 12:23).

G. [How does one know from Scripture that] if Egyptians and Israelites were situated in [the same] bed, the "passing over" was only over the Israelites?

H. As it says in Scripture, "... I will pass over *you*" (Exod. 12:13).

I. And thus Scripture states, "Like the birds that fly, even so will the Lord of Hosts shield (Jerusalem) ..." (Isa. 31:5). If the matter was not written, it would be impossible to state it: like an animal that lowers itself over its child and nurses it!

J. And thus Scripture states, "And in the wilderness, where you saw how (the Lord your God) carried you, (as a man carries his son)" (Deut. 1:31). And Scripture says, "A thousand may fall (at your left side, ten thousand at your right, but it shall not reach you)" (Ps. 91:7). And Scripture says, "The Lord is your guardian ... now and forever" (Ps. 121:5–8).

6.  A. "... because He passed over the houses of the Israelites in Egypt" (Exod. 12:27):[235]

B. I only know [that God passed over] the houses of the Israelites. How does one know from Scripture [that God also passed over] the houses of converts, women, and slaves?

C. Scripture states, "... but saved *our* houses" (Exod. 12:27).

7.  A. "The people then bowed low in homage" (Exod. 12:27):

B. This teaches that they rejoiced over the good news as if it had already occurred.

## XIV:II

1.  A. "And the Israelites went and did so. (Just as the Lord had commanded Moses and Aaron, so they did)" (Exod. 12:28):[236]

B. [This teaches] that a reward was given to them for setting out [to do God's command], just like a reward [was given] for doing [God's command].

2.  A. "Just as the Lord had commanded Moses" (Exod. 12:28):

B. We find that in the first [part of the] scriptural portion[237] God spoke to Moses, but in the second [part] he[238] related them[239] to the Israelites, who then rejoiced. How does one know from Scripture that he[240] heard the two of them[241] from the mouth of God, and then returned and taught them to the Israelites?

C. Scripture states, "Just as the Lord had commanded Moses" (Exod. 12:28).

D. I only know, [however,] that the scriptural portion was assigned to Moses. How does one know from Scripture that Aaron was also with him?

---

[235] Compare 6.A–C with parallel above in XIII:I:13.A–C.
[236] Compare 1.A–B with *Mekhilta de-Rabbi Ishmael,* Pisḥa (H/R, 42:9–10; Laut., vol. 1, 96:89–92; Neus., XII:II:6.A–7.C).
[237] I.e, Exod. 12:1–21.
[238] I.e., Moses.
[239] I.e., God's words.
[240] I.e., Moses.
[241] I.e., both scriptural portions.

| | | |
|---|---|---|
| אשר פסח [ופסח יי ופסחתי עליכם • מנין אתה או' חצר] | C | |
| שכולה יש' לא היתה [פסיחה אלא על הבתים • שנא' | D | |
| אשר פסח] על בתי בני יש'. • מצ' ויש' [שרוים בחצר | E | |
| לא היתה פסיחה אלא על] הפתחים • שנא' ופסח יי על | F | |
| הפתח (שמ' יב כג). • מצ' ויש' נתונין במטה לא היתה | G | |
| פסיחה אלא על יש' • שנא' ופסחתי עליכם (שם יג) • וכן | I/H | |
| הוא אומ' כצפרים עפות כן יגן ייי צבא' וג' (ישע' לא | | |
| ה) אלמלא דבר כת' אי אפשר לאמרו כחיה ששוחה על | | |
| בנה ומניקתו • וכן הוא אומ' ובמדבר אשר ראית אשר | J | |
| נשאך וג' (דב' א לא) ואומ' יפל מצדך אלף וג' (תה' | | |
| צא ז) ואומ' ייי שומרך וג' עד מעתה ועד עולם (שם | | |
| קכא ח). • אשר פסח על בתי בני יש' במצ' • אין לי אלא | B/A | 6 |
| בתי יש' בתי גרים נשים ועבדים מנין • ת"ל לו ואת | C | |
| בתינו הציל • ויקד העם וישתחו • מלמד ששמחו על | B/A | 7 |
| הבשורה כמעשה. סל' פסו' • | | |

| | | |
|---|---|---|
| וילכו ויעשו בני יש' • ליתן להן שכר הליכה כשכר | B/A | 1 |
| עשייה • כאשר צוה ייי את משה • לפי שמצינו שפרשה | B/A | 2 |
| ראשונה אמ' לו המקום למשה ושנייה ואמ' להן ליש' | | |
| ושמחו ומנין שאף שתיהן שמע מפי הק' וחזר ושנאן | | |
| להן ליש' • ת"ל כאשר צוה ייי את משה • אין לי אלא | D/C | |
| משה שהפרשה תלויה בו מנין שאף אהרן היה עמו • | | |

E.    Scripture states, "Just as the Lord had commanded Moses and Aaron" (Exod. 12:50).

F.    One might think that [because] Moses and Aaron were [so] engaged [in God's] command [to bring the Israelites out from Egypt], they did not have a passover offering themselves![242]

G.    Scripture states, [however,] "(Just as the Lord had commanded Moses and Aaron,) so they did" (Exod. 12:28,50).

H.    And how does one know from Scripture that, even though they were not commanded to be ready [to leave Egypt], they were ready, and [even though they were not commanded] to hurry, they hurried?

I.    Scripture states, "... so they did" (Exod. 12:28,50).

J.    So they did, [and] they did so with intention.

## Chapter Fifteen

### (Textual Source: Ms. Firkovich II A 268)

XV:I

1.    A.    "In the middle of the night (the Lord struck down all the first-born in the Land of Egypt, from the first-born of Pharaoh who sat on the throne to the first-born of the captive who was in the dungeon-house, and all the first-born of the cattle)" (Exod. 12:29):

B.    Moses said to the Israelites, "For that night I will go through the Land of Egypt" (Exod. 12:12) without establishing precisely the time for them, so that they would not sit around and entertain evil notions, saying, "The time has already arrived, but we [still] have not been redeemed!"

[28]    C.    But when Moses spoke to Pharaoh, what did he say? "Thus says the Lord: 'At midnight (I will go forth among the Egyptians ...'" (Exod. 11:4).

D.    He said to him, "The moment [will occur] precisely at midnight, [and not] a hair's breadth earlier or a hair's breadth later, [because God] is sitting on the [heavenly] sundial, and He determines [the time] with hairsbreadth precision. For a kingdom will not strike its neighbor even a thread's breadth [earlier or later than God determines]. Rather, if the time arrives for a kingdom to fall during the day, then it falls in the day; if at night, then it falls at night!"[243]

E.    And thus it states in Scripture, "... and Noph [shall face] adversaries in broad daylight ..." (Ezek. 30:16). And Scripture says, "In Tehaphenehes daylight shall be darkened (when I break there the power of Egypt)" (Ezek. 30:18). And Scripture says, "That very night, (Belshazzar, the Chaldean king,) was killed ..." (Dan. 5:30).

F.    And likewise, when the time arrived for our forefathers to fall, what is stated about them in Scripture? "Alas for us, for day is declining ..." (Jer. 6:4).

2.    A.    "... the Lord struck down all the first-born in the Land of Egypt" (Exod. 12:29):[244]

B.    [And He] did not [strike] through an agent.

3.    A.    "... from the first-born of Pharaoh" (Exod. 12:29):[245]

B.    I might think [that this refers to] his son.[246]

[242] Compare 2.F–J with *Mekhilta de-Rabbi Ishmael*, Pisḥa (H/R, 42:11–12; Laut., vol. 1, 96:93–96; Neus., XII:II:8.A–9.C).

[243] Compare 1.D–E with parallel below at XVI:V:2.D–E.

[244] Compare 2.A–B with *Mekhilta de-Rabbi Ishmael*, Pisḥa (H/R, 43:2–3; Laut., vol. 1, 97:9–11; Neus., XIII:II:1.A–D).

[245] Compare 3.A–I with *Mekhilta de-Rabbi Ishmael*, Pisḥa (H/R, 43:6–12; Laut., vol. 1, 97:18–98:27; Neus., XIII:II:3.A–4.E).

[246] I.e., the first clause in the verse indicates that Pharaoh's son was the first-born.

| | |
|---|---|
| F/E | ת״ל כאשר צוה ייי את משה ואת אהרן ✦ יכול משה ואהרן |
| G | שהיו עסוקין במצוה לא היה להם פסח ✦ ת״ל כן עשו ✦ |
| H | ומנין שאף על פי שלא נאמ׳ להן עתידין היו ומעותדין |
| J/I | היו זריזין היו ומזורזין היו ✦ ת״ל כן עשו ✦ <כן עשו> וכן |
| | היה בלבם לעשות. סל׳ פסו׳. ✦ |

| | | |
|---|---|---|
| B/A | 1 | ויהי בחצי הלילה ✦ משה אמ׳ להן ליש׳ ועברתי |
| | | בארץ מצ׳ בלילה הזה (יב יב) ולא קבע להן זמן שלא יהו |
| | | יושבין ומהרהרין הרהורין רעים ואומר<ים> כבר הגיעה |
| | | שעה ולא נגאל<נ<ו ✦ אבל כשאמ׳ לו משה לפרעה |
| C | | מה הוא אומ׳ כה אמר [ייי כח]צות הלילה וגו׳ (שמ׳ |
| D | | יא ד) ✦ אמ׳ [לו הד]בר שקול לכשיחצה הלילה [אם כחוט |
| | | הש[ע]ר]ה ולמעלה אם [כחוט ה]שע]ר]ה ו[למטה] יושב |
| | | על [אבן שעו]ת ומכוין את השעה כח[וט השערה] |
| | | שאין [מלכות] נוגעת [בחברת]ה אפילו כמלא נימא |
| | | אלא [הגיע זמנה ש]ל מלכות ליפול ביום [נופלת ביום |
| E | | בליל]ה נופ[לת בלילה ✦ וכן הוא או]מ׳ <ו>נוף צרי יומם |
| | | וגו׳) (יחז׳ ל טז) ואו׳ [ובתחפנחיס חשך היום (שם יח) |
| F | | ואו׳ ביה בלי]ליא קטיל וגומ׳ (דנ׳ ה ל). ✦ ואף כשהגיע |
| | | זמנן של אבותינו ליפול מה נאמ׳ בהן אוי לנו כי פנה |
| A | 2 | היום וגו׳ (ירמ׳ ו ד). ✦ וייי הכה כל בכור בארץ מצר׳ ✦ |
| B/A 3 | B | ולא ביד שליח ✦ מבכור פרעה ✦ שומע אני זה בנו ✦ |

C.   But when Scripture [then] says, "… who sat on the throne" (Exod. 12:29), his son is already [in this clause, and thus the first clause does not refer to Pharaoh's son]!

D.   Then why does Scripture state, "… from the first-born of Pharaoh" (Exod. 12:29)? This teaches that the evil Pharaoh [himself] was a first-born.[247]

E.   But the punishment [of God] did not touch him! Why? In order to mislead the hearts of the Egyptians, so that they would say, "Pharaoh is so strong that the punishment did not touch him!"

F.   And about him Scripture states, "He exalts nations, then destroys them" (Job 12:23). And likewise Scripture states, "… and I will mete out punishments to all the gods of Egypt, (I the Lord)" (Exod. 12:12).

G.   And wasn't Baal-Zephon among the Egyptian gods? Why didn't the punishment touch him? In order to mislead the hearts of the Egyptians, so that they would say, "Baal-Zephon is so strong that the punishment did not touch him!"

H.   And about him Scripture states, "He exalts nations (then destroys them)" (Job 12:23). And in the end, what does Scripture say? "Water covered their adversaries; (not one of them was left)" (Ps. 106:11).

I.   This teaches that even Baal-Zephon was crushed.

4.   A.   Scripture says here, "… to the first-born of the captive" (Exod. 12:29), but above Scripture says, "… to the first-born of the slave girl" (Exod. 11:5).

B.   This teaches that through this punishment [the two] of them were enslaved by Israel.

5.   A.   "… the first-born of the *captive*" (Exod. 12:29)—this is the one placed in the arbitration room.[248]

B.   "… who was in the … *house* …" (Exod. 12:29)—this is the one imprisoned in the prison-house.[249]

C.   "… (who was in the) *dungeon* …" (Exod. 12:29)—this is the one placed in the deep pit.[250]

D.   Why were they struck with them?[251] Because they were saying, "Our gods will free us from the Egyptians who enslave us!"[252]

E.   R. Eliezer the son of R. Yosi ha-Galili says, "Why were [the captives] struck with them? Because they were saying, 'It's our wish that we be in our servitude and Israel be in their servitude!'"

6.   A.   "… to the first-born of the captive" (Exod. 12:29)—this teaches that they captured them.

[29]   B.   "… to the first-born of the slave girl" (Exod. 11:5)—this teaches that Egypt conquered them as slaves and handmaidens.

C.   "… who is behind the millstones" (Exod. 11:5)—this teaches that they were crushing them [with labor].

---

[247] The text reads the first clause in Exod. 12:29 (מבכר פרעה) as "from the first-born Pharaoh."

[248] Hebrew: דייטי; Greek: δίαιτα.

[249] In 5.B–C the text interprets separately both of the nouns in the construct noun בבית־הבור.

[250] Hebrew: דייפנטא; Greek: διαφάτνη.

[251] I.e., why were the captives struck along with the Egyptians?

[252] Compare 5.D–E with *Mekhilta de-Rabbi Ishmael*, Pisḥa (H/R, 43:12–44:1; Laut., vol. 1, 98:28–99:38; Neus., XIII:II:5.A–6.D).

| | | |
|---:|---:|---:|
| כשהוא אומ׳ היושב על כסאו כבר בנו אמור ✦ מה ת״ל | D/C | |
| מבכור פרעה מלמד שפרעה הרשע בכור היה ✦ ולא נגעה | E | |
| בו פורענות וכל כך למה כדי לפתות ליבן של מצריים | | |
| שיהו אומ׳ קשה פרעה שלא נגעה בו פורענות ✦ ועליו הוא | F | |
| או׳ משגיא לגוים ויאבדם וג׳ (איוב יב כג) וכן הוא אומ׳ | | |
| ובכל אלהי מצ׳ אעשה שפטים אני ייי (שמ׳ יב יב) ✦ | | |
| והלא בעל צפון בכלל אלהי מצ׳ היה מפני מה לא | G | |
| נגעה בו פורענות כדי לפתות לבן של מצ׳ שיהוא אומ׳ | | |
| קשה בעל צפון שלא נגעה בו פורענות ✦ ועליו הוא אומ׳ | H | |
| משגה לגוים וגו׳ אבל (באחרונה) באחרונה מה הוא | | |
| אומ׳ ויכסו מים צריהם וגו׳ (תה׳ קו יא) ✦ מלמד אף בעל | I | |
| צפון נתכתת. ✦ כאן הוא אומ׳ בכור השבי ולהלן הוא | A | 4 |
| אומ׳ בכור השפחה (שמ׳ יא ה) ✦ מלמד שבמדה הזאת | B | |
| נשתעבדו בהן ביש׳ ✦ בכור השבי זה שנתון בדייטי. ✦ אשר | B/A | 5 |
| בבית זה שחבוש בבית האסורין ✦ הבור זה שנתון | C | |
| בדייפנטא ✦ מפני מה לקו עמהן מפני שהיו אומ׳ אלהינו | D | |
| יפרע לנו מן המצ׳ שמשעבדין אותנו ✦ ר׳ אליעזר בנו | E | |
| של ר׳ יוסי הגלילי אומ׳ מפני מה לקו עמהן מפני שהיו | | |
| אומ׳ רצוננו נהיה בשעבודנו ויש׳ יהיו בשעבודן ✦ עד | A | 6 |
| בכור השבי מלמד ששבו אותן ✦ עד בכור השפחה מלמד | B | |
| שכיבשו אותן מצ׳ לעבדים ולשפחות ✦ אשר אחר הרחים | C | |
| מלמד שהיו מפריכין בהן. סל׳ פסו׳. ✦ | | |

## XV:II

1.   A.   "And Pharaoh arose in the night, (with all his slaves and all the Egyptians, because there was a loud cry in Egypt, for there was no house where there was not someone dead)" (Exod. 12:30):[253]

     B.   He did not arise in the usual manner that kings arose—with music. He did not arise in the usual manner that kings arose—at the third hour [of the day]—and they [normally] go to sleep at the second hour [of the evening].

2.   A.   "... with all his slaves and all the Egyptians" (Exod. 12:30):

     B.   Just as no one would awaken him,[254] likewise no one would awaken his slaves, and likewise neither one of these[255] would awaken the Egyptians!

3.   A.   "... because there was a loud cry in Egypt" (Exod. 12:30):

     B.   This teaches that they saw their gods split and falling before them.

     C.   And even though this matter is not explicitly stated here, it is explained [in Scripture] later: "Then the earth rocked and quaked ... Smoke went up from His nostrils ..." (2 Sam. 22:9).

4.   A.   "... for there was no house where there was not someone dead" (Exod. 12:30):[256]

     B.   R. Nathan says, "Was there no house that did not have a first-born in it?

     C.   "Rather, when one of them had a first-born son who died, he would make a statue of him. And on that day[257] they were ground, crushed, and scattered before them, and it was hard on them like the very day they buried them."

     D.   Another interpretation:

     E.   Because the Egyptians used to bury in their houses, and [on Passover] the dogs entered through the sewers, dug, and brought out the first-born from their graves, and sported with them. And it was hard on them like the very day they buried them.

## XV:III

1.   A.   "He summoned Moses and Aaron in the night (and said, 'Up, depart from among my people, both you and the Israelites with you! Go, worship the Lord as you said!')" (Exod. 12:31):[258]

     B.   One might think that they[259] went outside to [talk with] him.

     C.   But wasn't it already stated in Scripture, "None of you shall go outside the door of his house until morning" (Exod. 12:22)?

     D.   Rather, this teaches they peeked out at him from the balcony and said to him, "We aren't leaving at night. We're leaving at dawn!"

2.   A.   "... 'Up, depart from among my people'" (Exod. 12:31):

     B.   One might think [he intended for them] to tarry.

     C.   Scripture states, [however,] "'Up!'" (Exod. 12:31).

3.   A.   "'... you (and the Israelites with you)'" (Exod. 12:31):

---

[253] Compare 1.A-B with *Mekhilta de-Rabbi Ishmael*, Pisḥa (H/R, 44:5–6; Laut., vol. 1, 99:43–48; Neus., XIII:II:8.A–G).

[254] I.e., Pharaoh.

[255] I.e., neither Pharaoh nor his slaves.

[256] Compare 4.A–E with *Mekhilta de-Rabbi Ishmael*, Pisḥa (H/R, 44:9–14; Laut., vol. 1, 99:51–100:60; Neus., XIII:II:10.A–F).

[257] I.e., Passover.

[258] Compare 1.A–D with *Mekhilta de-Rabbi Ishmael*, Pisḥa (H/R, 44:16–45:2; Laut., vol. 1, 100:64–66; Neus., XIII:II:12.A–B).

XV:II

B/A 1 ויקם פרע[ה] ליל[ה] ◆ לא עמד כדרכן [שהמ]לכים
עומדין ב[זמ]ר לא[ עמ]ד] כ[דרך שה]מלכים עומדין

A 2 [בשלש שעות] [וי]שנים [בשתי ש]עות] ◆ [הוא וכל
B ע[בדיו וכל מצ׳ ◆ מה הוא ש[לא העמידו] אדם אף עבדיו
שלא [העמידן א]ד[ם ואף מצ׳ שלא העמיד]ו זה] את
B/A 3 זה. ◆ ותהי צעק[ה] גדולה במצרים ◆ מ[ל[מד] שהי[נ]ו רואין
C אלהיהם מתבקעין] ונופלים לפניהם ◆ ואף על [פי שהדברים
סתומים כאן מפורשים להל[ן] ותגעש ותרעשה
A 4 הארץ וגו׳ עלה עשן באפו וגו׳ (ש״ב כב ט) ◆ כי אין
B בית אשר אין שם מת. ◆ ר׳ נתן אומ׳ וכי לא היה שם בית
C שלא היה בו בכור ◆ אלא כיון שנולד בן בכור לאחד
מהן ומת היה עושה לו דיוקני והיו אותו היום נידקות
ונשחקות ונזרות לפניהם והיה קשה להן כאילו אותו
היום קברום. ◆ ד״א ◆ לפי שהמצ׳ היו קבורים בבתיהם
E/D והכלבים נכנסין דרך ביבין ומחטטין ומוציאין בכורות
מקבריהן ומתעתעין בהן והיה קשה להן כאילו אותו
היום קברום. סל׳ פסו׳. ◆

XV:III

C/B/A 1 ויקרא למשה ולאהרן לילה ◆ יכול באו אצלו ◆ והלא
כבר נאמר ואתם לא תצאו איש מפתח ביתו עד בקר
D (שמ׳ יב כב) ◆ אלא מלמד שהצציצו מתוך גזוצטרא ואמ׳
A 2 לו בלילה אין אנו יוצאין אנו יוצאין בחצי היום. ◆ צאו
A 3 C/B מתוך עמי ◆ יכול (מתוך עמי יכול) שהות ◆ ת״ל קומו ◆ אתם ◆

B.    I only know "you." How does one know from Scripture [that this included] converts and slaves?

C.    Scripture states, "'... *both* you ...'" (Exod. 12:31).

4.    A.    "'... and the Israelites with you'" (Exod. 12:31):

B.    Which includes women and children.

5.    A.    "'Go, worship the Lord as you said!'" (Exod. 12:31):

B.    "Your [prediction] has been fulfilled!"

C.    [As it says in Scripture,] "Moses said, '(We will all go,) young and old ...'" (Exod. 10:9).

## XV:IV

1.    A.    "'(Take also) your flocks (and your herds, as you said, and be gone! And may you bring a blessing upon me also!)'" (Exod. 12:32):

B.    "Your flocks [come] also from mine!"

C.    "'... (and) your herds'" (Exod. 12:32):

D.    "Your herds [come] also from those of the princes!"

2.    A.    "'Take ... as you said, and be gone!'" (Exod. 12:32):

B.    "Your [prediction] has been fulfilled!"

C.    [As it says in Scripture,] "And Moses said, 'You yourself must provide us with sacrifices and burnt offerings'" (Exod. 10:25).

3.    A.    "'And may you bring a blessing upon me *also!*'" (Exod. 12:32):

[30]    B.    "Also my wives and my children!"

4.    A.    Another interpretation: "'And may you bring a blessing upon me also!'" (Exod. 12:32):

B.    From here you say that Pharaoh knew that he was lacking in prayer, and God does not forgive someone until he has persuaded his neighbor [to forgive him as well].[260]

C.    What reward did he take for this?—"In that day, there shall be an altar to the Lord (inside the Land of Egypt and a pillar to the Lord at its border)" (Isa. 19:19).

D.    The mouth that said, "'Who is the Lord that I should heed Him (and let go)?'" (Exod. 5:2) is [also] the mouth that said, "'The Lord is right, and I and my people are in the wrong'" (Exod. 9:27).

E.    What reward did he take for this?—"You shall not abhor an Egyptian, (for you were a stranger in his land)" (Exod. 23:8).

F.    The mouth that said, "'I will pursue, I will overtake, I will divide the spoil'" (Exod. 15:9) is [also] the mouth that said, "'Let us flee from the Israelites'" (Exod. 14:25).

G.    What reward did he take for this?—"You put out your right hand, (the earth swallowed them)" (Exod. 15:12). They merited being buried, so that the wildlife and birds would not eat them.

---

[260] Compare 4.B with m. Baba Kamma 8:7.

| | | |
|---|---|---|
| אין לי אלא אתם גרים ועבדים מנין ✦ ת״ל גם אתם ✦ גם | A 4 | C/B |
| בני יש׳ ✦ לרבות נשים וטפלין. ✦ ולכו עבדו את ייי כדברכם ✦ | A 5 | B |
| עמדה שלכם ✦ | | B |
| | | |
| ויאמר משה בנער<י>נו ובזקנינו וגו׳ (שם י ט) ✦ | | C |

XV:IV

| | | |
|---|---|---|
| צאנכם ✦ גם צאנכם משלי ✦ בקרכם ✦ גם בקרכם משל שרים ✦ | D/C/B/A | 1 |
| קחו כאשר דברתם ולכו ✦ עמדה שלכן ✦ ויאמר משה גם | C/B/A | 2 |
| אתה תתן בידינו זבחים ועולות (שם כה). ✦ וברכתם | A | 3 |
| אתי ✦ גם אתי אף לנשי ולטפלי. ✦ ד״א וברכתם גם אותי ✦ | A 4 | B |
| מיכן אתה אומ׳ שהיה פרעה יודע שהוא מחוסר תפלה | | B |
| ואין המק׳ מוחל לו לאדם עד שיפיס את חבירו ✦ [מה] | | C |
| שכר נטלו על כך ביום ההוא [יהיה מזבח לייי] וגו׳ | | |
| (ישע׳ יט יט) ✦ הפה שאמ׳ מ<י>י ייי א[שר אשר [אשמ]ע | | D |
| בקולו (שמ׳ ה ב) הוא [הפה שאמ׳] ייי הצדיק ואני ועמי | | |
| [הרשעים] (שם ט כז) ✦ מה ש[כר נט]ל<ו> על [כך] [לא | | E |
| תת]עב מצרי וגו׳ (דב׳ כג ח) ✦ הפה שאמ׳ [ארדף] אשיג | | F |
| א[חל]ק שלל (שמ׳ טו ט) הוא הפה [שאמ׳ אנוסה] מפני | | |
| יש׳ (שם יד כה) ✦ מה ש[כר נטלו על כך נטי]ת ימינך | | G |
| וגו׳ (שם טו יב) זכו [ליקבר שלא יאכלו אותן חיה | | |
| ועופות. סל׳ פס]ו׳. ✦ | | |

## XV:V

1.   A.   "The Egyptians urged the people (to hurry, to have them leave the country, for they said, 'We shall all be dead')" (Exod. 12:33):

     B.   This teaches that terror seized Pharaoh, and they [i.e., the Egyptians] were preparing their dead and their slain, and they were placing them [i.e., the Israelites] on coaches and wagons [to leave].

2.   A.   "... to hurry, to have them leave the country" (Exod. 12:33):

     B.   But not [to go] to the Land of Canaan.

     C.   Thus it says, "We must go a distance of three days into the wilderness ..." (Exod. 8:23).

3.   A.   "... for they said, 'We shall all be dead'" (Exod. 12:33):

     B.   They said, "Moses said to us that first-borns would die, but we see that those who have died are first-borns and are not first-borns!"

     C.   But they did not know that they were all steeped in promiscuity. One man had sexual intercourse with 10 women, and 10 sons were born to him, all of whom were first-borns to the women. [Or] 10 men had sexual intercourse with one woman, and she gave birth to 10 sons, all of whom were first-borns to the men.

     D.   Thus did they say, "'We shall all be dead'" (Exod. 12:33).

## XV:VI

1.   A.   "So the people took their dough before it was leavened, (their kneading bowls wrapped in their cloaks upon their shoulders)" (Exod. 12:34):[261]

     B.   This teaches that it was close to becoming leavened.

2.   A.   "... their kneading bowls wrapped (in their cloaks upon their shoulders)" (Exod. 12:34):[262]

     B.   What remained of the unleavened bread and what remained of the bitter herbs.[263]

3.   A.   Another interpretation: "... their kneading bowls wrapped ..." (Exod. 12:34):

     B.   Is it really the case that they hadn't prepared what to take and what not to take? And doesn't Scripture at the end of the story praise them for being wealthy?

     C.   Rather, this teaches that they only carried out a small amount [of dough] into which a blessing entered, and they ate from it for 31 days, and it was as pleasing to them as the manna.[264]

## XV:VII

1.   A.   "The Israelites had done Moses' bidding (and borrowed from the Egyptians objects of silver and gold, and clothing)" (Exod. 12:35):

     B.   He said to them, "Don't go walking from neighbor to neighbor, so that you won't look like people up to no good!"

---

[261] Compare 1.A–B with *Mekhilta de-Rabbi Ishmael*, Pisḥa (H/R, 46:5–7; Laut., vol. 1, 103:108–12; Neus., XIII:III:3.A–C).

[262] Compare 2.A–B with *Mekhilta de-Rabbi Ishmael*, Pisḥa (H/R, 46:8–10; Laut., vol. 1, 104:113–17; Neus., XIII:II:4.A–F).

[263] The text presumes that the Hebrew word for "their kneading bowls" (משארותם) is related to the Hebrew root meaning "to remain over" (שאר).

[264] Compare 3.C with *Mekhilta de-Rabbi Ishmael*, Pisḥa (H/R, 49:7–9; Laut., vol. 1, 110:42–45; Neus., XIV:I:10.A–D) and with parallel material below at XXXVIII:II:3.A–H.

XV:V

| | | |
|---|---|---|
| B/A | 1 | ותחזק מצ׳ על העם ♦ מלמ[ד] שנפלה לו ותרא |

לפרעה והיו] מניחין את מיתיהן ואת חלליהן והיו משקעין
אותן בקרונות ובעגלות. ♦ למהר לשלחם מן הארץ ♦ ולא

| | | |
|---|---|---|
| B/A | 2 | |
| C | | לארץ כנען ♦ כן הוא אומ׳ דרך שלשת ימים נלך במדבר |

(שמ׳ ח כג). ♦ כי אמרו כולנו מתים.

| | | |
|---|---|---|
| B/A | 3 | ♦ אמרו משה אמ׳ |

לנו בכורות מתים ואנו רואין שמתין בכורות ושאינן
בכורות ♦ והן אינן יודעין שכולם שטופין בזמה אחד בא

| | | |
|---|---|---|
| C | | |

על עשר נשים וילדו לו עשר<ה> בנין נמצאו כולן
בכורי נשים עשרה אנשים באו על אשה אחת וילדה
לה עשרה בנים נמצאו כולן בכורי אנשים

| | | |
|---|---|---|
| D | | ♦ לכך אמרו |

כולנו מתים. סל׳ פסו׳ ♦

XV:VI

| | | |
|---|---|---|
| B/A | 1 | וישא העם את בצקו טרם יחמץ ♦ מלמד שקרב |

להחמיץ. ♦ משארותם צרורות וגו׳ ♦ מה ששיירו מן המצה

| | | |
|---|---|---|
| B/A | 2 | |
| A | 3 | ומה ששיירו מן המרור. ♦ ד״א משארותם צרורות וגו׳ ♦ |
| B | | וכי לא היה בידם מה ליטול ומה לא ליטול והלא לסוף |
| C | | העניין הכת׳ משבחן שהיו בני אדם עשירים ♦ אלא מלמד |

שלא נטלו בידם אלא דבר מועט ונכנסה בו ברכה
ואכלו ממנו שלשים ואחד יום שהיה יפה להן כמן.
סל׳ פסו׳ ♦

XV:VII

| | | |
|---|---|---|
| B/A | 1 | ובני יש׳ עשו כדבר משה ♦ אמ׳ להן לא תהו מהלכין |

משכונה לשכונה שלא תהו נראין כבני אדם תרמאין. ♦

2.      A.   "... and borrowed from the Egyptians objects of silver and gold, and clothing"
[31]           (Exod. 12:35):[265]

        B.   Let he who is worthy of silver objects, borrow silver objects, [and he who is worthy of gold objects,] borrow gold objects!

        C.   The last [of the three stated] was the most valuable: "... and clothing" (Exod. 12:35).

        D.   How does one know from Scripture that the clothing was the most valuable of all?

        E.   Scripture states, "... objects of silver and gold and clothing" (Exod. 12:35).

        F.   The most valuable is the last [one stated].

## XV:VIII

1.      A.   "And the Lord had disposed the Egyptians favorably toward the people, (and they let them have their request. Thus they stripped the Egyptians)" (Exod. 12:36):[266]

        B.   What was the nature of this predisposition: "And the Lord had *disposed* the Egyptians favorably toward the people"?

        C.   This teaches that during the three days that the Egyptians lived in darkness, the Israelites walked freely in their houses without even one of them being suspected, not even [of stealing] a pin!

        D.   [Therefore,] the Egyptians reasoned logically to themselves, saying, "When would be the best time for these [people] to take [our things and not return them]? When we live in light or when we lived in darkness? When they [could have] taken for themselves, or when we give to them?"

2.      A.   Another interpretation: "... disposed ... toward the people" (Exod. 12:36):

        B.   This teaches that the Holy Spirit dwelled upon them.[267]

        C.   And thus Scripture says, "But I will fill the House of David and the inhabitants of Jerusalem (with a spirit of pity and compassion. And they shall lament to Me about those who are slain, wailing over them as over a favorite son and showing bitter grief as over a first-born)" (Zech. 12:10).

        D.   [Because] it is not the same when one says to another, "Lend me a piece of clothing!" and he replies, "I don't have it!" [or] "Lend me a tray!" and he replies, "I don't have it!" [as it is when] one says to another, "Lend me the piece of clothing in such and such a place, lend me the tray in such and such a place!"[268]

3.      A.   "... and they let them have their request" (Exod. 12:36):

        B.   Rabbi says, "When the Israelites were in Egypt, what was said in Scripture about them?—'Each woman shall borrow from her neighbor and the lodger in her house' (Exod. 3:22). This teaches that they lived with them.

        C.   "Once they had voided the slavery, what was said in Scripture about them?—'(Tell the people) to borrow, each man from his *neighbor* (and each woman from hers)' (Exod. 11:2). This teaches that they were neighbors to them.

        D.   "Once they had been redeemed from the slavery, what was said in Scripture about them?—'... and they let them have their request' (Exod. 12:36). [However,] they[269] did

---

[265] Compare 2.A–F with *Mekhilta de-Rabbi Ishmael,* Pisha (H/R, 46:14–16; Laut., vol. 1, 105:126–28; Neus., XIII:III:7.A–B).

[266] Compare 1.A–2.D with *Mekhilta de-Rabbi Ishmael,* Pisha (H/R, 46:17–47:7; Laut., vol. 1, 105:129–106:141; Neus., XIII:III:8.A–9.C).

[267] I.e., upon the Israelites.

| | |
|---|---|
| וישאלו ממצרי' כלי כסף וכלי זהב וש' ◆ הראוי לישאל כלי | B/A 2 |
| כסף ישאל כלי כסף כלי זהב ישאל כלי זהב ◆ חביב | C |
| האחרון ושמלות ◆ מנין שהשמלות חביבות מן הכל ◆ ת"ל | E/D |
| כלי ז[הב ו]שמלות ◆ חביב האחרון ◆ שמלות. סל' פסו'! ◆ | F |

XV:VIII

| | |
|---|---|
| וייי [נתן א]ת חן העם [בעי]ני מצ' ◆ מה הוא [החן | B/A 1 |
| הזה וייי] [נתן את חן הע]ם ב[עיני מצ' ◆ מל]מד ששלשת | C |
| ימים הי[ו מצריים] שרויין באפל[ה וי]שראל [מקרקר]ין | |
| בבתיהם ולא נחשד [אחד] מהן אפילו על הצינ[ורה | D |
| והיו מצ'ין דנ[ין קל וחומר [בעצמן ואומרין] אמתי ראויין | |
| אלו ליט[ו]ל כשאנו שרויין באורה או כשהיינו] | |
| שרויין באפילה כשנטלו [לעצמן או כשאנו נותנין להן] ◆ | A 2 |
| ד"א את חן העם ◆ מלמד ששרת עליהן רוח הק' ◆ וכאן | C/B |
| הוא אומ' ושפכתי על בית דויד ועל יושבי ירושלם וג' | |
| (זכ' יב י) ◆ אין דומה האמור לו השאילני נוניא והוא | D |
| אומ' אין לי השאילני סקולת סקוטלא והוא אומ' אין | |
| לי לאומר לו השאילני נוניא שבמקום פלוני השאילני | |
| סקוטלא שבמקום פלוני. ◆ וישאילום ◆ ר' אומ' כשהיו ישר' | B/A 3 |
| במצ' מה נאמ' בהן ושאלה אשה משכנתה ומגרת ביתה | |
| (שמ' ג כב) מלמד שהיו גרין עמהן ◆ כשבטלו מן השעבוד מה | C |
| נאמ' בהן וישאלו איש מאת רעה<ו> (שם יא ב) מלמד | |
| שהיו רעים להם ◆ כשנגאלו מן השיעבוד מה נאמ' בהן | D |
| וישאילום מה שהשאילום לא הגיעום והיו משאילין אותן בעל | |

---

268 The implication here being that because the Israelites were under the influence of the Holy Spirit, they were able to ask for specific items that they knew were in specific places, thus preventing the Egyptians from claiming that they did not possess such items to lend.

269 I.e., the Israelites.

not [at first] accept that which they lent them, so they lent it to them against their will, which teaches that they[270] feared them as humans fear their Creator!

E.   "[And another reason the Egyptians let the Israelites have their request] was because they were saying, 'Tomorrow the nations of the world will see them in the wilderness and say, "Look how wealthy [even] the slaves of Egypt are!"'

F.   "And from where in Scripture can you say that each and every person from Israel [was so rich] that he [himself] could erect the Tent of Meeting, with all its vessels, all its golden hooks, boards, wooden bars, columns, and pedestals?

G.   "Scripture states, '(Tell the Israelite people to bring Me gifts. You shall accept gifts for Me) from *every person* whose heart so moves him' (Exod. 25:2).

H.   "[God said,] 'Each and every person from Israel can [himself] do all that I am commanding you [concerning the building of the Tabernacle].'"

4.   A.   One might think that one of them did not take [items borrowed from the Egyptians].

[32]   B.   Scripture states, [however,] "He led them out with silver and gold. (None among their tribes faltered)" (Ps. 105:37)

C.   And which feeble one was like David?

D.   As it says in Scripture, "... and the feeblest of them shall be in that day like David ..." (Zech. 12:8)

5.   A.   One might think that [because] Moses and Aaron were [so] engaged [in God's] command [to bring the Israelites out from Egypt], they did not take from the spoils of Egypt.[271]

B.   Scripture states, [however,] "(And I will dispose the Egyptians favorably toward this people,) so that when *you* go, *you* will not go away empty-handed" (Exod. 3:21).

6.   A.   One might think that Moses and Aaron were transgressing both positive and negative commandments![272]

B.   Scripture states, [however,] "Moreover, Moses himself (was much esteemed in the Land of Egypt) ..." (Exod. 11:3).

7.   A.   "Thus they stripped the Egyptians" (Exod. 12:36):

B.   They turned it[273] into something like a fishpond without any fish in it.[274]

C.   Another interpretation:

D.   They turned it into something like a fort without any provisions.[275]

8.   A.   Why does Scripture praise the plunder at the Red Sea more than the plunder of Egypt? Because in Egypt they took what was in the houses, but at the sea they took what was in the treasuries. For such was the manner of kings—when they went out to war they took all their silver and gold with them, in order to keep others [from coveting their riches in their absence and, thus,] rebelling behind them.[276]

B.   And thus Scripture states, "... there are wings of a dove sheathed in silver, (its pinions in fine gold)" (Ps. 68:14). "... in silver" [refers to] the plunder of Egypt. "... its pinions in fine gold" [refers to] the plunder at the sea.

---

[270] I.e., the Egyptians feared the Israelites.

[271] Compare 5.A–B with parallel material above in XIV:II:2.F–J.

[272] I.e., commandments that prescribe or proscribe activity.

[273] I.e., Egypt.

[274] This interpretation is based upon an imputed connection between the Hebraic roots for the scriptural phrase "thus they stripped" (וינצלו) and the word "fishpond" (מצולה).

כורחן מלמד שהיו יראין מהן כבני אדם שיריאין מן קוניהן ✦

ומפני שהיו אום' למחר יהו אום' העו' הער' רואין אותן במדבר ויאמרו E

ראו כמה עשירים הן עבדיהם של מצ' ✦ ומנין אתה אומר שלא F

היה כל אחד ואחד מיש' שלא היה יכול להעמיד אהל מועד

וכל כליו וכל קרסיו קרשיו בריחיו עמודיו ואדניו ✦

ת"ל מאת כל איש אשר ידבנו לבו (שמ' כה ב) ✦ אין H/G

לך כל אחד ואחד מיש' שאין יכול לעשות כל מה

שאמרתי לך ✦ יכול (לא) היה בהן אחד שלא נטל ✦ ת"ל B/A 4

וייציאם בכסף וזהב וג' (תה' קה לז) ✦ ואי זה הוא כושל C

כדוד ✦ שנא' והיה הנכשל בהם וג' (זכ' יב ח) ✦ יכול משה A 5 D

ואהרן <ש>היו עסוקין במצוה לא נטלו מביזת מצ' ✦

ת"ל לו והיה כי תלכון לא תלכו ריקם (שמ' ג כא). ✦ B

איפשר משה ואהרן שהיו עוברין על מצות עשה ועל A 6

מצות לא תעשה ✦ ת"ל גם [ה]איש משה וג' (שם יא ג) ✦ B

וינצלו את מצר' ✦ ע[שאוה כמצול]ה זו שאין בה דגים ✦ B/A 7

[ד"א] ✦ עשאוה כמצודה זו שאין בה [דגן ✦ למה] משביח A 8 D/C

הכת' ביזת ים [יותר מביזת] מצ' [אלא מה] שבבת]ים

[נטלו ב]מצ' ומה שהיה בתיסוורא[ות נטלו] על הי[ם

שכך דרכם] [של מלכ]ים בשעה שיוצאין למלח[מה]מה

מוציאין כל כ[ספן וזהבן עמהן [כדי שלא להמריד

אחרים תחתיהן ✦ וכן הוא] אום' כנפי יונה נחפה [בכסף זו B

ביזת מצרים ואברותיה בירקרק] חרוץ זו ביזת הים. ✦

275 The same connection is being made here as above with the word for "fort" (מצודה).
276 Compare 8.A–E with Mekhilta de-Rabbi Ishmael, Pisḥa (H/R, 47:7–11; Laut., vol. 1, 106:142–49; Neus., XIII:III:10.A 13.C).

C.   [Similarly,] "We will add wreaths of gold for you ..." (Song 1:11) [refers to] the plunder at the sea. "... in addition to your spangles of silver" (Song 1:11) [refers to] the plunder of Egypt.

D.   [Similarly,] "... and you continued to grow up ..." (Ezek. 16:7) [refers to] the plunder of Egypt. "... until you attained to womanhood ..." (Ezek. 16:7) [refers to] the plunder at the sea.

E.   The spoil that they plundered at the sea was many times [greater than that in Egypt].

## Chapter Sixteen

### (Textual Source: Ms. Firkovich IIA 268)

XVI:I

1.   A.   "The Israelites journeyed from Raamses to Succoth, (about six hundred thousand men on foot, aside from children)" (Exod. 12:37):[277]

B.   [The distance] from Raamses to Succoth was 120 miles.

C.   The voice of Moses traveled [the distance] of a 40-day journey![278]

D.   And you should not be surprised, for it has already been stated in Scripture, "Then the Lord said to Moses and Aaron, 'Each of you take handfuls (of soot from the kiln, and let Moses throw it toward the sky in the sight of Pharaoh. It shall become a fine dust all over the Land of Egypt) ...'" (Exod. 9:8–9).

[33]   E.   And, behold, it can be so reasoned: If the dust, whose nature was not to move about, traveled a distance of 40 days, then how much the more [we can assume this was the case with] the voice [of Moses], whose nature was to move about!

2.   A.   "... to Succoth" (Exod. 12:37):[279]

B.   R. Akiva says, "They made actual booths for themselves in Succoth!"

C.   R. Eliezer says, "Booths [constructed of] clouds of glory came, and they encamped [in them] upon the rooftops at Raamses!"

D.   They related a parable to what the matter is alike:

E.   Concerning a groom who brought a palanquin to the door of the bride's house, so that she could enter it immediately.

3.   A.   R. Nehemiah says, "'... to Succoth ...' (Exod. 12:37).[280]

B.   "Whenever you need to place a *lamed* at the beginning [of the word], place [instead] a *heh* at its end!"[281]

4.   A.   "... about six hundred thousand" (Exod. 12:37):

B.   [Scripture here] approximates, [and the number could have been] a bit lower or higher. But, specifically, what does Scripture state?

C.   "... 603,550" (Num. 1:46).

5.   A.   Rabbi says, "Behold Scripture states, 'The men of Ai killed (about thirty-six of them)' (Josh. 7:5):

---

[277] Compare 1.A–E with *Mekhilta de-Rabbi Ishmael*, Pisḥa (H/R, 47:12–48:4; Laut., vol. 1, 107:1–10; Neus., XIV:I:1.A–F).

[278] According to Rabbinic tradition, Egypt was 400 parasangs in length and width, and the typical day's journey was 10 parasangs. Therefore, to travel the length or width of Egypt would take 40 days. Assuming that the Israelites were located all over the country, the call by Moses to congregate at Raamses traveled the distance of a 40-day journey. See b. Pesaḥim 93a (Neus., IV:E:Pesaḥim:9:2: I.1.A–2.C).

[279] Compare 2.A–E with *Mekhilta de-Rabbi Ishmael*, Pisḥa (H/R, 48:5–10; Laut., vol. 1, 108:11–21; Neus., XIV:I:3.A–I); and *Sifra*, Emor 17:11 (Neus., CCXXXIX:II:6.A–7.B).

[280] Compare 3.A–B with *Mekhilta de-Rabbi Ishmael*, Pisḥa (H/R, 48:11; Laut., vol. 1, 108:21–22; Neus., XIV:I:4.A–B).

[281] R. Nehemiah here explains the locative, ה, of Biblical Hebrew.

| | | |
|---|---|---|
| C | תורי זהב נעשה לך (שה"ש א יא) זו ביזת ים עם נקדות | |
| D | הכסף זו ביזת מצ' • ותרבי ותגדלי (יחז' טז ז) זו ביזת | |
| E | מצ' ותבואי בעדי עדים <זו בזת הים> • כפולה ומכופלת | |
| | בזה שבזזו על הים. סל' פסו' • | |

| 1 | B/A | ויסעו בני ישר' מרעמסס סכותה. • מרעמסס לסוכות |
| | C | מאה ועשרים מיל • והיה קולו של משה הולך מהלך |
| | D | ארבעים יום • ואל תתמה שהרי כבר נאמר ויאמר ייי |
| | | אל משה ואל אהרן קחו לכם מלא חפניכם וגו' (שמ' ט |
| | E | ח) • והרי דברים קל וחומר ומה אבק שאין דרכו להלך |
| | | <הרי הוא הולך מהלך ארבעים יום קול שדרכו |
| | | להלך> על אחת כמה וכמה. • סוכותה • ר' עקיבה אומ' |
| 2 | B/A | סוכות ממש עשו להן בסוכות • ר' אליעזר אומ' סוכות |
| | Ç | ענני כבוד באו וחנו על גגי רעמסס • מושלו משל למה הדבר |
| | D | דומה • לחתן שהביא אפריון לפתח ביתה של כלה כדי שתכנס |
| | E | לו מיד. • ר' נחמיה אומ' סוכותה • שכל מקום שצריך ליתן |
| 3 | B/A | לו למד בתחילתו תן לו הי בסופו • כשש מאות אלף • |
| 4 | A | אומיד הין חסיר הין יתר אבל בפרט מה הוא אומ' • שש מאות |
| | C/B | אלף ושלשת אלפים וחמש מאות וחמשים (במ' א מו) • |
| 5 | A | ר' אומ' הרי הוא אומ' ויכו מהם אנשי העי וגומ' (יהו' ז ה) • |

B. "How many were there? If there were 37 of them, let it state it! If there were 35 of them, let it state it!

C. "Why does Scripture state, '... *about* thirty-six' (Josh. 7:5)?

D. "This teaches that they were [chosen] in proportion to all of Israel.

E. "Similarly you state [from Scripture], 'Then He brought me into the inner court of the House of the Lord, (and there, at the entrance to the Temple of the Lord ... were about twenty-five men)' (Ezek. 8:16):

F. "How many were there? If there were 24 of them, let it state it! If there were 26 of them, let it state it!

G. "Why does Scripture state, '... *about* twenty-five' (Ezek. 8:16)?

H. "This teaches that they were [chosen] in proportion to all of Israel."

6. A. "... on foot" (Exod. 12:37):

B. Who wage war.

7. A. "... men" (Exod. 12:37):

B. Excluding women.

8. A. "... aside from children" (Exod. 12:37):

B. This teaches that [also] those less than 20 years of age went up with them.[282]

## XVI:II

1. A. "[Moreover,] a *mixed* [multitude] went up with them."

"[Moreover,] a mixed *multitude* went up with them."

"*Moreover*, a mixed multitude went up with them" (Exod. 12:38):

B. This [threefold emphasis] teaches that converts and slaves [also] went up with them, three [times as many] as they.

2. A. "... both flocks and herds" (Exod. 12:38):

B. I only know from this [that] flocks and herds [went up with them]. How does one know from Scripture to include camels, donkeys, and horses?

C. Scripture states, "... very much livestock" (Exod. 12:38).

3. A. Similar to this, you say [from Scripture], "... their kneading bowls wrapped in their cloaks upon their shoulders" (Exod. 12:34).

B. Is it really the case that they hadn't prepared what to take and what not to take? Rather, this teaches that they cherished the commandment.

4. A. Similar to this you say [from Scripture], "... for you have been whining before the Lord and saying, ('If only we had meat to eat')" (Num. 11:18).

B. Is it really the case that they hadn't prepared what to eat and what not to eat? Rather, this teaches that they requested food for free.

5. A. Similar to this you say [from Scripture], "The Reubenites and the Gadites owned cattle in very great numbers" (Num. 32:1).

---

[282] I translate here the word that appears here in *Midrash ha-Gadol*: עלו—"went up," and not the word found here in the Firkovich manuscript: עשו—"they made."

| | |
|---|---|
| B | שמה מה היו אם שלשים ושבעה היה להן |
| C | ליאמר אם שלשים וחמשה היה להן ליאמר • מה |
| D | ת״ל כשלשים וששה • מלמד שהיו שקולין כנגד כל |
| E | ישראל. • כיוצא בו אתה אומ׳ ויבא אתי אל חצר בית |
| F | ייי הפנימית אל פתח היכל ייי וגו׳ (יחז׳ ח טז) • שמה |
| | מה היו אם עשרים וארבעה היה לה ליאמרן אם |
| G | עשרים וש[ש]ה היה להן ליאמר • מה ת״ל כעשרים |
| H        B/A 6 | וחמשה • מלמד שהיו שקו[לין כנ]גד כל יש׳. • רגלי • עו[ש]ה |
| B/A 7        B/A 8 | מלחמה.] • [גב]רים • חו[ן]ץ מנשי[ם • לב]ד מטף • מל[מ]ד |
| | שעשו עמהן פ[חות מבן] [עשרים שנה]. סל׳ פ[סו׳] • |

XVI:II

| | |
|---|---|
| A    1 | ערב עלה אתם ערב [רב עלה] אתם וגם ערב |
| B | [רב עלה אתם • מלמד] שעלו מהן גרים ועבדים [שלשה] |
| B/A 2 | כיוצא בהן. • צאן ובקר • א[י]ן לי אלא צאן ובקר מנין |
| C | לרבות גמלים וחמורים] וסוסים • ת״ל מקנה כבד מ[א]ד • |
| A    3 | כיוצא בו אתה או׳ משארותם] צרורות בשמלותם על |
| B | שכמם (שמ׳ יב לד). • וכי לא היה בידן מה ליטול ‹ומה |
| A    4 | לא ליטול› אלא מלמד שהיו מחבבין את המצוה. • כיוצא |
| | בו אתה אומ׳ כי בכיתם באזני ייי לאמר (במ׳ יא יח) • |
| B | וכי לא היה בידם מה לוכל ומה לא לוכל אלא מלמד |
| A    5 | שבקשו אוכל של חנם. • כיוצא בו אתה אומ׳ ומקנה |
| | רב היה לבני יש׳ ראובן ולבני גד (שם לב א) • |

B.   One might think that there were [cattle] for these, but for the other tribes there were not.

C.   Rather, this teaches that these [tribes] were engaged in it.[283]

## XVI:III

1.   A.   "And they baked unleavened cakes [ugot] of the dough that they had taken out of Egypt, (for it was not leavened, since they had been driven out of Egypt and could not delay, nor had they prepared any provisions for themselves)" (Exod. 12:39):

    B.   [The word] "ugah" can only mean cakes cooked over coals.

    C.   In accordance with what is said in Scripture, "Knead and make cakes [ugot]!" (Gen. 18:6).

2.   A.   "... for it was not leavened" (Exod. 12:39):[284]

    B.   This teaches that unleavened bread is made only from species [that can become] leavened.

3.   A.   "... since they had been driven out of Egypt ..." (Exod. 12:39):

[34]   B.   Just as they were driven out of Egypt, a miracle was performed on their behalf, [in that it] was not allowed to become leavened.[285]

4.   A.   "... and could not delay" (Exod. 12:39):

    B.   This teaches that they were not able to tarry.

5.   A.   "... nor had they prepared any provisions for themselves" (Exod. 12:39):

    B.   This teaches that they did not take provisions for the way.

6.   A.   "... nor had they prepared any provisions for themselves" (Exod. 12:39):

    B.   This teaches that they did not take even grain or nuts for the children for the way.

## XVI:IV

1.   A.   "The length of time (that the Israelites lived in Egypt was four hundred and thirty years. At the end of the four hundred and thirtieth year, to the very day, all the ranks of the Lord departed from the Land of Egypt)" (Exod. 12:40–41):[286]

    B.   Did they really live in Egypt for 430 years? Weren't they only in Egypt for 210 years?

    C.   But did Israel really live in Egypt for 210 years?

    D.   For wasn't Kohath among those who went down into Egypt? As it says in Scripture, "The span of Kohath's life was 133 years" (Exod. 6:18). And it also says in Scripture, "The span of Amram's life was 137 years" (Exod. 6:20).

    E.   [Add to this] the 80 years Moses [lived in Egypt], and, behold, [you have] 350 years [that the Israelites dwelled in Egypt]!

    F.   Why does Scripture state, "The length of time (that the Israelites lived in Egypt was four hundred and thirty years)" (Exod. 12:40)?

    G.   They lived [through many periods of foreign] dwelling:

    H.   Abraham lived in the land of the Philistines (see Gen. 20:1). Isaac lived in the Land of Canaan (see Gen. 25:11). Jacob lived in the land where his father had lived (see Gen. 37:1).

---

[283] I.e., cattle farming.

[284] Compare 2.A–B with parallel above in XII:III:2.A–C and with b. Pesaḥim 35a (Neus., IV:B:Pesaḥim:2:5:I.1.A–2.B).

[285] The Israelites had not yet been instructed by Moses about the prohibition of leaven during the holiday (such instruction occurs at Exod. 13:3). Thus, the miracle here was that God timed the expulsion of the Israelites from Egypt to occur before their cakes had the opportunity to leaven, which prevented them from committing a transgression unwittingly.

[286] Compare 1.A–P with *Mekhilta de-Rabbi Ishmael*, Pisḥa (H/R, 50:4–9; Laut., vol. 1, 111:54–63; Neus., XIV:II:1.A–D).

| | | |
|---|---|---|
| B | | יכול לאלו היה ולשאר שבטים לא היה • אלא מלמד |
| C | | שאילו פשטו ידיהן בו. סל' פסו' • |

XVI:III

| 1 | A | ויאפו את הבצק אשר הוציאו ממצ' עוגות מצות • |
| | C/B | אין עוגה אלא חררה • כענין שנא' לושי ועשי עוגות (בר' |
| B/A 2 | A 3 | יח ו). • כי לא חמץ • מלמד שממין חמץ הבא מצה • כי |
| | B | גורשו ממצ' • מה שגרשו ממצ' נעשה להן בו נס שלא |
| 4 | B/A | להחמיץ • ולא יכלו להתמהמה • מלמד שלא יכלו לה |
| 5 | B/A | להשתהות. • צדה לא עשו להם • מלמד שלא נטלו בידם |
| 6 | B/A | זוודין לדרך. • וגם צדה לא עשו להם • מלמד שאף קליות |
| | | ואגוזים לא נטלו בידם לתינוקות לדרך. סל' פסו' • |

XVI:IV

| 1 | B/A | ומושב בני ישר' וגו' • וכי שלשים שנה וארבע |
| | | מאות שנה ישבו במצ' והלא לא היו במצ' אלא מאתים |
| | C | ועשר שנים • וכי מאתים ועשר שנים ישבו שנא' יש' במצ' • |
| | D | והלא קהת מיורדי מצ' היה <שנא'> ושני חיי קהת |
| | | שלש ושלשים ומאת שנה (שמ' ו יח). ונאמ' ושני חיי |
| | E | עמרם שבע ושלשים ומאת שנה (שמ' ו כ) • ושמנים של |
| | F | משה הרי שלש מאות וחמשים שנה • מה ת"ל ומושב בני |
| | H/G | יש' וגו' • ישיבות הרבה ישבו. • ישיבת אברהם בארץ |
| | | פלשתים (בר' כ א) ישיבת יצחק בארץ כנען (שם כה |
| | | יא) ישיבת יעקב בארץ מגורי אביו (שם לז א) • |

I.   [If] you gather them [together], you end up with 400 years.

J.   And how does one know from Scripture that they [were in Egypt] 400 years?

K.   Behold it was said to Abraham [at the covenant] between the parts, "Know well [that your offspring shall be like strangers in a land not theirs, and they shall be enslaved and oppressed four hundred years]" (Gen. 15:13).

L.   And regarding Isaac it states, "(Then his brother emerged, holding on to the heel of Esau. So they named him Jacob.) Isaac was sixty years old (when they were born)" (Gen. 25:26).

M.   Likewise, Jacob said to Pharaoh, "The years of my sojourn [on earth] are one hundred and thirty" (Gen. 47:9).

N.   Behold, [you have] 190 years! And they remained there [another] 210 years [thus totaling 400].

O.   And a hint about this [period of time is found scripturally] in the years of Job. When Israel went down to Egypt, Job was born. And when they left, he died.

P.   As it says in Scripture, "... and the Lord gave Job twice what he had before" (Job 42:10). And Scripture says, "Afterward, Job lived (one hundred and forty years) ..." (Job 42:15).

2.   A.   ["... at the end of the four hundred and thirtieth year, to the very day ..." (Exod. 12:41):][287]

B.   At midnight God spoke with Abraham our forefather [at the covenant] between the parts,[288] and at midnight Isaac was born, and at midnight the Egyptian first-borns were smitten.

C.   As it says in Scripture, "... at the *end* (of the four hundred and thirtieth year, to the very day)" (Exod. 12:41).

D.   There was one end for all of them.

3.   A.   "... four hundred and thirtieth year" (Exod. 12:41):[289]

B.   [How does one] account for these 30 years?

C.   From the day that God spoke with Abraham our forefather [at the covenant] between the parts until Isaac was born [equals] 30 years. And from the death of Isaac until they left Egypt was 400 years.

4.   A.   "... to the very day, (all the ranks of the Lord departed from the Land of Egypt)" (Exod. 12:41):[290]

B.   This teaches that even God's ranks were in pain with Israel.

C.   As it says in Scripture, "In all their troubles, He was troubled" (Isa. 63:9).[291]

D.   And Scripture says, "When he calls on Me, I will answer him. I will be with him in distress" (Ps. 91:15).

E.   And Scripture says, "... from before Your people, whom You redeemed for Yourself from Egypt, a nation and its god" (2 Sam. 7:23).

---

[287] Compare 2.A–D with *Mekhilta de-Rabbi Ishmael,* Pisḥa (H/R, 51:5–9; Laut., vol. 1, 112:78–113:84; Neus., XIV:II:4.A–H).

[288] See Gen. 15:10ff.

[289] Compare 3.A–C with *Mekhilta de-Rabbi Ishmael,* Pisḥa (H/R, 50:4–9; Laut., vol. 1, 111:54–63; Neus., XIV:II:1.A–D).

[290] Compare 4.A–E with *Mekhilta de-Rabbi Ishmael,* Pisḥa (H/R, 51:9–15; Laut., vol. 1, 113:85–114:95; Neus., XIV:II:5.A–J).

[291] In the manuscript tradition of the Hebrew Bible, Isa. 63:9 has variant attestations. The verse as it is cited in the text of the *Mekhilta de-Rabbi Shimon b. Yoḥai* employs the Hebrew word of negation לא. However, the text's interpretation clearly assumes the traditional Jewish rendering of this word, which is the prepositional ל with the third person, masculine pronominal suffix—לו—"to Him." This variation renders the meaning of the verse: "In all their afflictions, He [i.e., God] was (also) afflicted." This midrashic tradition is widely attested throughout the corpus of early Rabbinic literature. See, e.g., *Mekhilta de-Rabbi Ishmael,* Pisḥa (H/R, 51:9–15; Laut., vol. 1, 113:85–90; Neus., XIV:II:5.A–H) and *Sifre Num.,* Piska 84 (Neus., LXXIV:IV:1.FF–JJ). Also, compare with parallel above at I:II:3.A–C.

| | | |
|---|---|---|
| ה[רי] את מלקטן ועושה אותן ארבע מאות [שנה ◆ ומ[נין | J/I | |
| שארבע מאות [שנה] היו ◆ הרי נאמ' לאברהם בין [הבתרים | K | |
| יד[וע תדע וגומ' (בר' טו יג) ◆ ביצחק הוא אומ' ויצח[ק | L | |
| בן ששים שנה וגומ' (שם כה כו) ◆ [וכן י]עקב אמ' | M | |
| לפרעה ימי שני מגורי שלשים [ומא[ת שנ]ה (שם מז | | |
| ט) ◆ הרי] [מאה ו]תשעים שנה נשתייר<ו> שם מאתים | N | |
| ועש[ר שנים ◆ וסימן לדבר [שנותינו של איוב כשירדו יש' | O | |
| למצ' נולד איוב ו]כשעלו מת ◆ שנא' ויוסף [ייי את כל | P | |
| אשר לאיוב למשנה (איוב מב י) ואו' ויחי' איוב אחרי | | |
| זאת וגומ' (שם טז) בחצי ◆ בחצי ◆ הלילה נדבר עם אבינו | B/A | 2 |
| אברהם בין הבתרים ובחצי הלילה הלילה נולד יצחק | | |
| ובחצי הלילה לקו בכורות מצ' ◆ שנ' ויהי מקץ ◆ קץ אחד | D/C | |
| לכולן ◆ שלשים שנה וארבע מאות שנה ◆ שלשים שנה | B/A | 3 |
| אלו מה טיבן ◆ מיום שנידבר עם אבינו אברהם בין | C | |
| הבתרים ועד שנולד יצחק ל' שנה ומשנולד יצחק ועד | | |
| שיצאו יש' ממצ' ארבע מאות שנה. ◆ | | |
| | | |
| ויהי בעצם היום הזה וגו' ◆ מלמד שאף צבאות | B/A | 4 |
| מקום היו עם יש' בצער ◆ שנא' בכל צרתם לא צר וגומ' | C | |
| (ישע' סג ט) ◆ ואומ' יקראני ואעננו עמו אנכי בצרה | D | |
| וגומ' (תה' צא טו) ◆ ואומ' מפני עמך אשר פדית <לך> | E | |
| ממצ' גוים ואלהיו (ש"ב ז כג). סל' פסו' ◆ | | |

## XVI:V

1.　A.　"That was for the Lord a night of vigil (to bring them out of the Land of Egypt. That same night is the Lord's, one of vigil for all the children of Israel throughout the ages)" (Exod. 12:42):

[35]　B.　This teaches that this first redemption was designated for them [by God to occur precisely] after [a certain number of] generations, jubilees, sabbatical years, years, months, *Shabbatot,* days, hours, minutes, and seconds.

2.　A.　"'... that same night is the Lord's, one of vigil (for all the children of Israel throughout the ages)' (Exod. 12:42):

　　B.　"This redemption occurred in this season. The second redemption [in the Messianic Era] will occur in a different season.

　　C.　"And thus Scripture states, 'And like a lion he called out: "On my Lord's lookout (I stand ever by day)"' (Isa. 21:8). And Scripture says, 'The Dumah Pronouncement: A call comes to me from Seir: "Watchman, what of the night? Watchman, what of the night?"' (Isa. 21:8–11).

　　D.　"Why [does Scripture here refer to a] watchman? [Because] a watchman [ensures that] a nation not conquer another nation, or one kingdom another kingdom, even a hairsbreadth [before the determined time]. Rather, if a kingdom's time to fall arrives in the day, it falls in the day. If at night, then it falls at night.[292]

　　E.　"And thus Scripture states, '... and Noph shall face adversaries in broad daylight' (Ezek. 30:16). And Scripture says, 'In Tehaphnehes' day, light shall be withheld ...' (Ezek. 30:18). And Scripture says, 'That very night, (Belshazzar the Chaldean King) was killed (and Darius the Mede received the kingdom) ...' (Dan. 5:30).

　　F.　"And who is the watchman?[293] It is the Holy One, blessed be He, who is called a watchman [in Scripture]: 'See the watchman of Israel neither slumbers nor sleeps!' (Ps. 121:4)."—The words of R. Eliezer.

　　G.　R. Joshua says, "They were redeemed in Nisan, and in the future they will be redeemed in Nisan![294]

　　H.　"As it says in Scripture, '... one of vigil for all the children of Israel throughout the ages' (Exod. 12:42)."

3.　A.　("*That* was for the Lord a night of vigil") (Exod. 12:42):

　　B.　Scripture does not state "That ... night" [in reference to the children of Israel at the end of the verse, but rather only states it in reference to God at the beginning of the verse].

　　C.　Why does Scripture state, "*That* (was for the Lord a night of vigil)" (Exod. 12:42)?

　　D.　[To indicate that] He knows it [i.e., the precise moment of the Exodus], but the forefathers did not know it.

　　E.　As it says in Scripture, "For a day of vengeance (I planned) to myself ..." (Isa. 63:4).

---

[292] Compare 2.D–E with parallel above at XV:I:D–E.
[293] I.e., the watchman referred to in Isa. 21:8–11.
[294] Compare 2.G–H with *Mekhilta de-Rabbi Ishmael,* Pisḥa (H/R, 52:9–13; Laut., vol. 1, 115:113–116:121; Neus., XIV:II:6.A–H).

XVI:V

| | |
|---|---|
| B/A | 1 |

ליל שמורים הוא לייי ◆ מלמד שנשתמרה להן
גאולה ראשונה לדורות וליובלות ולשמטים ולשנים
ולחדשים ולשבתות ולימים ולשעות ולעיתים ולעונות. ◆

| | |
|---|---|
| B/A | 2 |

הוא הלילה הזה לייי שמורים ◆ גאולה זו נגאלין בפרק

C

זה שנייה נגאלין בפרק אחר ◆ וכן הוא אומ׳ ויק׳ אריה
על מצפה ייי וגו׳ (ישע׳ כא ח) ואומ׳ משא דומה אלי

D

קורא מש׳ וגו׳ ואומ׳ אמ׳ שומר וגו׳ (שם יא) ◆ מה משמר
משמר שלא תיכנס אומה באומה מלכות במלכות
אפילו כחוט השערה אלא הגיע זמנה של מלכות ליפול

E

ביום נופלת ביום בלילה נופלת בלילה ◆ וכן הוא אומ׳
נוף צרי יומם (יחז׳ ל טז) ואומ׳ ובתחפנחס חשך היום

F

וגו׳ (שם יח) ואומ׳ ביה בליליא קטיל וגו׳ (דנ׳ ה ל) ◆ מה
הוא שומר זה הקב״ה שנקרא שומר הנה לא ינום ולא

G

יישן וגו׳ (תה׳ קכא ד) דברי ר׳ אליעזר ◆ [ר׳] יהושע אומ׳

H

בניסן נגאלו ובניסן עתידין ליגאל ◆ שנא׳ שימורים [לכל]

| | |
|---|---|
| D/C/B/A | 3 |

בני יש׳ לדורותם ◆ [שאין ת״ל] הוא ◆ [מה ת״ל הוא ◆ הוא

E

י]דע בו ולא יד[עו] בו אבות הראשונים ◆ [שנא׳ כי יום]
נק[ם בלבי] וגומ׳ (ישע׳ סג ד). [סל׳ פסו׳]

*Chapter Seventeen*

(Textual Source: Ms. Firkovich IIA 268)

XVII:I

1.     A.   "(The Lord said to Moses and Aaron: This is the *law* of the passover offering.) No uncircumcised person may eat of it. No foreigner shall eat of it" (Exod. 12:43,48):[295]

        B.   Why does Scripture state "law"?

        C.   To stress the applicability to the paschal sacrifice of the subsequent generations[296] that which is stipulated for the paschal sacrifice of Egypt,[297] as well as [the applicability] to the paschal sacrifice of Egypt that which is stipulated for the paschal sacrifice of the subsequent generations, except for the things that Scripture specifically eliminates.

        D.   One might think [that] even the bunch of hyssop, lintel, and two doorposts [prescribed in Exod. 12:22 are also applicable to the paschal sacrifice of the subsequent generations].

        E.   Scripture states, [however,] "*This* (is the law of the passover offering)" (Exod. 12:43).

(Textual Source: Midrash ha-Gadol)

2.     A.   "No foreigner shall eat of it" (Exod. 12:43):[298]

        B.   Why do I need [Scripture to state this]? For hasn't it already been stated, "No uncircumcised person may eat of it" (Exod. 12:48)?

        C.   Why does Scripture state, "No foreigner shall eat of it" (Exod. 12:43)? This [is in reference to] the heretical Israelite who practiced idolatry.

        D.   I only know that [this refers to the] male [heretic]. How does one know from Scripture [that this includes] the female [heretic]?

        E.   Scripture states, "No foreigner[299] shall eat of it" (Exod. 12:43).

3.     A.   One might think that he[300] would invalidate the [entire] group [offering the sacrifice] with him.

        B.   Scripture states, [however,] "... This (is the law of the passover offering)" (Exod. 12:43).

        C.   He does not invalidate the group [offering] with him.[301]

4.     A.   "No (foreigner) shall eat of it" (Exod. 12:43):

        B.   He does not eat it, but he does eat unleavened bread and bitter herbs.

XVII:II

1.     A.   "But any slave a man (has bought may eat of it) once he has been circumcised" (Exod. 12:44):

        B.   This teaches that one circumcises [gentile] slaves against their will.[302]

        C.   One might think that one circumcises [all gentile] men against their will.

        D.   Scripture states, [however,] "... slave a man *(has bought)*" (Exod. 12:44), [meaning that] you

---

[295] The second sentence ("No uncircumcised person may eat of it") is from Exod. 12:48, and is placed here in the manuscript for no apparent reason.

[296] I.e., the paschal sacrifice offered by the subsequent generations after the Exodus.

[297] I.e., the paschal sacrifice offered in Egypt by the Israelites at the time of the Exodus.

[298] Compare 2.A–E with *Mekhilta de-Rabbi Ishmael,* Pisḥa (H/R, 53:5–6; Laut., vol. 1, 118:19–22; Neus., XV:I:3.A–C).

[299] Literally: No *child* of a foreigner.

[300] I.e., the foreigner referred to in Exod. 12:43.

[301] The text's basis for this interpretation is ambiguous.

[302] Circumcision here is synonymous with conversion to Judaism.

XVII:I

| | | |
|---|---|---|
| 1 | A | כל ערל לא יאכל בו וכל בן נכר לא יאכל [בו ◆ |
| | C/B | מה] ת״ל חוקה ◆ ליתן א[ת] הא[מ]ור בפסח מ[צ]' בפסח |
| | | דורות ואת הא[מור בפסח] דורות בפסח מצ' חוץ מ[ן]דברים |
| | D | שמיעט בו הכת' ◆ יכול אף אגודת אזוב] ומשקוף |
| E | 2 B/A | ושתי מזוזות ◆ ת״ל זא[ת...] ◆ כל בן נכר לא יאכל בו ◆ מה |
| | | אני צריך והלא כבר נאמר וכל ערל לא יאכל בו (פמ״ח) ◆ |
| | C | מה ת״ל כל בן נכר לא יאכל בו זה ישראל משומד שעבד |
| | E/D | ע״ז. ◆ אין לי אלא איש אשה מנין ◆ ת״ל כל בן נכר לא |
| | 3 B/A | יאכל בו. ◆ יכול יפסול את החבורה הבאה עמו ◆ ת״ל זאת ◆ |
| C | 4 B/A | אין פוסל את החבורה הבאה עמו. ◆ לא יאכל בו ◆ בו |
| | | אינו אוכל אבל אוכל הוא במצה ובמרור. ◆ |

XVII:II

| | | |
|---|---|---|
| 1 | B/A | עבד איש ומלתה אותו ◆ מלמד שאדם מוהל עבדי |
| | C | איש על כרחו ◆ יכול יהא אדם מוהל בני איש על כרחו ◆ |
| | D | ת״ל עבד איש עבדי איש מוהל על כרחו ואין מוהל בני |

circumcise a person's slave against his will, but you do not circumcise [all] men against their will.[303]

E.    I only know this applies to male slaves. How does one know from Scripture [it applies as well] to female slaves?[304]

F.    Scripture states, "... *any* slave a man" (Exod. 12:44).

2.    A.    "... may eat of it once he has been circumcised" (Exod. 12:44):[305]

B.    If Scripture is speaking [here about the uncircumcised slave], then, behold, it has already been stated, "No uncircumcised person may eat of it" (Exod. 12:48).

C.    Why does Scripture state, "... may eat of it once he has been circumcised" (Exod. 12:44)?

D.    This [is in reference] to [the uncircumcised slave's] master, for if one has male slaves, but does not circumcise them, or female slaves, but does not immerse them [in the ritual conversion bath], then they prevent him from eating the paschal offering.[306]

3.    A.    "But any slave" (Exod. 12:44):[307]

[36]    B.    From here you state: If a convert dies who owns (non-Jewish) slaves, both adult and young, how does one know from Scripture if they then must declare themselves freemen [and circumcise themselves and offer a paschal offering like all Israelites]?

C.    Scripture states, "But any slave a man (has bought may eat of it once he has been circumcised)" (Exod. 12:44).

D.    [This applies] to the slave over whom his master has dominion. Excluded is the slave over whom his master no longer has dominion.

4.    A.    "(But any) slave a man" (Exod. 12:44):[308]

B.    I only know [this applies] to the slaves of a man. How does one know from Scripture [that it applies as well] to the slaves of a woman?

C.    Scripture states, "... has bought" (Exod. 12:44).

D.    I only know [this applies to the slave who is purchased]. How does one know from Scripture [that it applies as well to the slave] who is inherited or given to one as a gift?

E.    Scripture states, "But any slave" (Exod. 12:44).

F.    If this is the case, then why does Scripture state "... has bought ..."?

G.    This teaches that slaves are acquired by means of money.

5.    A.    One might think that even [uncircumcised] slaves of a minor would prevent him[309] from eating the paschal offering.

B.    Scripture states, [however,] "(But any) slave a *man* (has bought) ..." (Exod. 12:44).

C.    [Uncircumcised] slaves of adult men prevent them from eating the paschal offering, but [uncircumcised] slaves of minors do not prevent them from eating the paschal offering.

---

[303] Compare 1.D with y. Yebamot 8d (Neus., 8:1:VI.A–VII.A) and b. Yebamot 48a (Neus, XIII.B:Tractate Yebamot:4:12:I.45.F–L).

[304] I.e., that only female gentile slaves are converted against their will, and not all gentile women.

[305] Compare 2.A–D with *Mekhilta de-Rabbi Ishmael,* Pisḥa (H/R, 53:7–54:1; Laut., vol. 1, 119:25–120:41; Neus., XV:I:5.A–O); and b. Yebamot 70b (Neus., XIII.C:Tractate Yebamot:8:2A–E:I.2.M–X).

[306] The text here reads Exod. 12:44 in the following manner: "Once you have circumcised any slave a man has bought, then he [i.e., the owner of the slave] may eat of it."

[307] Compare 3.A–D with b. Yebamot 48a (Neus., XIII.B:Tractate Yebamot:4:12:I.45.F–L).

[308] Compare 4.A–C with *Mekhilta de-Rabbi Ishmael,* Pisḥa (H/R, 53:6–7; Laut., vol. 1, 118:23–24; Neus., XV:I:3.4.A–D).

[309] I.e., the minor owner of the slaves.

| | | |
|---|---|---|
| איש על כרחו. ◆ אין לי אלא עבדים שפחות מנין ◆ ת״ל | F/E | |
| וכל עבד איש. ◆ ומלתה אותו אז יאכל בו ◆ אם בו הכתוב | B/A | 2 |
| מדבר הרי כבר נאמר וכל ערל לא יאכל בו (פמ״ח) ◆ | | |
| מה ת״ל ומלתה אותו אז יאכל בו ◆ זה רבו שאם היו | D/C | |
| לו עבדים שלא מלו ושפחות שלא טבלו מעכבין אותו | | |
| לאכול פסח. ◆ וכל עבד ◆ מיכאן אתה אומר גר שמת והיו | B/A | 3 |
| לו עבדים גדולים וקטנים וקראו עצמן בני חורין מנין ◆ | | |
| ת״ל וכל עבד ◆ עבד שרשות רבו עליו יצא זה שאין רשות | D/C | |
| רבו עליו. ◆ עבד איש ◆ אין לי אלא עבדי איש עבדי אשה | B/A | 4 |
| מנין ◆ ת״ל מקנת כסף ◆ אין לי אלא שלקח ירש וניתן | D/C | |
| לו במתנה מנין ◆ ת״ל וכל עבד ◆ אם כן למה נאמר מקנת | F/E | |
| כסף ◆ מלמד שעבדים נקנין בכסף. ◆ יכול אף עבדי קטן יהוא | A 5 | G |
| מעכבין אותו לאכול פסח ◆ ת״ל עבד איש ◆ עבדי איש מעכבין | C/B | |
| אותו לאכול פסח ואין עבדי קטן מעכבין אותו לאכול פסח. ◆ | | |

6.　A.　One might think that one would be prohibited from eating [the paschal offering if he did not circumcise his male slaves], but he would be allowed to slaughter and sprinkle [its blood].[310]

　　B.　Scripture states, [however,] "... (may eat of it) once[311] he has been circumcised" (Exod. 12:44), and below Scripture says, "(If a stranger who dwells with you would offer the passover to the Lord, all his males must be circumcised.) Then[312] he shall be admitted to offer it" (Exod. 12:48).

　　C.　[Scripture states twice] "*az, az*" [in order to provide the opportunity] for a *gezerah shaveh*:[313]

　　D.　Just as "*az*" stated here[314] [means he is] prohibited from eating, likewise "*az*" stated there[315] [means he is] prohibited from eating. And just as "*az*" stated there [means he is] prohibited from [any of the] work [involved with the paschal offering, i.e., slaughtering and sprinkling], likewise "*az*" stated here [means he is] prohibited from [any of the] work.

7.　A.　I only know [this applies] to the paschal offering of Egypt. How does one know from Scripture [that it applies as well] to the paschal offering of the subsequent generations?[316]

　　B.　Scripture states, "(This is) the law (of the passover offering)" (Exod. 12:43).

## XVII:III

1.　A.　["No bound or hired laborer shall eat of it" (Exod. 12:45):][317]

　　B.　"Bound" is the [slave] acquired forever,[318] and "hired" is the [slave] acquired for [a number of] years.

　　C.　Then let it[319] speak [only of the] "bound" [slave]! Why do I need it to speak of the "hired"? If the one acquired forever is prohibited from eating the paschal offering, then is it not logical that the one acquired for [only a number of] years would be prohibited from eating the paschal offering?

　　D.　If this were so, [however, and Scripture spoke only of the "bound" slave,] I might say that [the] "bound" [slave] is the [slave] acquired for [a number of] years.

　　E.　[Thus] when Scripture says [also] "hired," I know that "hired" comes to teach about the "bound" that it is [a slave] acquired forever.

2.　A.　R. Ishmael says, "How does one know from Scripture that an uncircumcised person is prohibited from eating *terumah*?[320]

　　B.　"It is a matter of logic:

　　C.　"Just as the paschal offering, which is permitted to laymen,[321] is prohibited for eating to the uncircumcised person, then is it not logical that *terumah*, which is prohibited to laymen, be prohibited for eating to the uncircumcised person?

---

[310] Compare 6.A–D with b. Yebamot 71a (Neus., XIII.C:Tractate Yebamot:8:2A–E:I.7.A–R).

[311] Hebrew: *az*—אז.

[312] Hebrew: *az*—אז.

[313] I.e., the employment of the same word in separate scriptural contexts, thus facilitating the application of the meaning of the word in one context to the other.

[314] I.e., Exod. 12:44.

[315] I.e., Exod. 12:48.

[316] Compare 7.A–B with t. Pisha 8:18.

[317] Compare 1.A–E with *Sifra*, Emor 4:17–18 (Neus., CCXVIII:II:4.A–6.D); and b.Yebamot 70a (Neus., XIII.C:Tractate Yebamot:8:E:I.2.A–M).

[318] See Gen. 21:1–6.

[319] I.e., Scripture in Exod. 12:45.

[320] Compare 2.A–F with *Mekhilta de-Rabbi Ishmael*, Pisha (H/R, 54:5–14; Laut., vol. 1, 121:46–122:63; Neus., XV:I:7.A–9.D); and b.Yebamot 70a (Neus., XIII.C:Tractate Yebamot:8:2A–E:I.2.A–M).

| | |
|---:|:---:|
| יכול יהא אסור לאכול אבל יהא מותר לשחוט ולזרוק ♦ ת״ל אז | 6 B/A |
| יאכל בו ולהלן נאמר ואז יקרב לעשותו (פמ״ח) ♦ אז אז | C |
| לגזירה שוה ♦ מה אז האמור כאן אסור באכילה אף | D |
| זה האמור להלן אסור באכילה מה אז האמור להלן | |
| אסור במלאכה אף אז האמור כאן אסור במלאכה. ♦ אין לי אלא | 7 A |
| פסח מצרים פסח דורות מניין ♦ ת״ל חקה. ♦ | B |

XVII:III

| | |
|---:|:---:|
| תושב זה קנוי קנין עולם ושכיר זה קנוי קנין שנים. ♦ | 1 B/A |
| יאמר תושב מה אני צריך לומר שכיר אם קנוי קנין | C |
| עולם אסור לאכול פסח קנוי קנין שנים אינו דין שיהא | |
| אסור לאכול פסח. ♦ אילו כן הייתי אומר תושב זה | D |
| קנוי קנין שנים ♦ כשהוא אומר ושכיר בא שכיר ולימד | E |
| על התושב שקנוי קנין עולם. ♦ ר׳ ישמעאל אומר מניין | 2 A |
| לערל שאסור לאכול בתרומה ♦ דין הוא ♦ ומה פסח שמותר | C/B |
| לזרים ערל אסור לאכול ממנו תרומה שאסורה | |
| לזרים אינו דין שיהא ערל אסור לאכול ממנה ♦ | |

[321] I.e., Jewish nonpriests.

D. "No! If you speak of the paschal offering, for which one may become culpable on its account through inappropriately intentioned action, or [improper treatment of the] leftover, or through impurification, then can you say [the same applies to] *terumah*, for which one does not become culpable on its account through inappropriately intentioned action, or [improper treatment of the] leftover, or through impurification?

E. "[Thus] Scripture states [here] 'bound' and 'hired' (Exod. 12:44) [and it teaches elsewhere] 'bound' and 'hired' (Lev. 22:10) [in order to provide the opportunity] for a *gezerah shaveh*:[322]

F. "Just as 'bound' and 'hired' stated in regard to the paschal offering [mean that] the uncircumcised person is prohibited from eating it, likewise 'bound' and 'hired' stated in regard to *terumah* [mean that] the uncircumcised person is prohibited from eating it."

3. A. ["No (bound or hired laborer) shall eat of *it*" (Exod. 12:45) :][323]

B. Of it he shall not eat, but he may eat unleavened bread and bitter herbs.

## XVII:IV

1. A. "(It shall be eaten) in one house. (You shall not take any of the flesh outside from the house. You shall not break a bone of it) (Exod. 12:46):[324]

B. I only know [that this includes the] house. How does one know from Scripture to include the courtyard, garden, and sukkah?

C. Scripture states, "It shall be eaten in one" (Exod. 12:45).

D. If so, then why does Scripture state, "It shall be eaten in one *house*"?

E. [To emphasize that it must be eaten] among one group.

2. A. "You shall not take ... from the house ..." (Exod. 12:46):[325]

B. I only know [it is prohibited to take it] from one house to the next. How does one know from Scripture [that also it is prohibited to take it] from one group to the next?

C. Scripture states, "... outside" (Exod. 12:46), [meaning,] outside its eating place.

3. A. "It shall be eaten (in one house). You shall not take any of the flesh from the house outside" (Exod. 12:46):

B. At its [ceremonial] hour of eating one becomes culpable, but one does not become culpable when it is not its [ceremonial] hour of eating.

4. A. "It shall be eaten (in one house). You shall not take (any of the flesh) from the house" (Exod. 12:46):

B. One becomes culpable over [the amount] that constitutes an "eating," but one does not become culpable over [an amount] less than an olive.

5. A. "It shall be eaten (in one house). You shall not take (any of the flesh) from the house" (Exod. 12:46):

B. One becomes culpable over [a sacrifice] that is suitable, but one does not become culpable over [a sacrifice] that is disqualified.

6. A. I only know this regarding the paschal sacrifice of Egypt.[326] How does one know

---

[322] See note 310.

[323] Compare 3.A–B with b. Pesaḥim 28b (Neus., IV:B:Pesaḥim:2.2:I.3.G).

[324] Compare 1.A–E with t. Pisha 6:11; and *Mekhilta de-Rabbi Ishmael*, Pisha (H/R, 54:15–55:3; Laut., vol. 1, 121:46–122:63; Neus., XV:I:.10.A–M).

[325] Compare 2.A–C with *Mekhilta de-Rabbi Ishmael*, Pisha (H/R, 55:3–8; Laut., vol. 1, 123:76–82; Neus., XV:I:11.A–I); y. Pesaḥim 35b (Bokser, 7:13:I:A–D); and b. Pesaḥim 85b (Neus., IV:D:Pesaḥim:7:11:I.8.A–E).

[326] I.e., the paschal sacrifice offered in Egypt by the Israelites at the time of the Exodus.

D ל לא אם אמרת בפסח שחייבין עליו משום פגול ונותר וטמא

תאמר בתרומה שאין חייבין עליה משום פגול ונותר

E וטמא ◆ ת״ל תושב ושכיר תושב ושכיר (ויק׳ כב י) לגזירה

F שוה ◆ מה תושב ושכיר האמור בפסח ערל אסור לאכול

ממנו אף תושב ושכיר האמור בתרומה ערל אסור

3 B/A לאכול ממנה. ◆ לא יאכל בו ◆ בו אינו אוכל אוכל הוא

במצה ובמרור. ◆

XVII:IV

1 B/A בבית אחד ◆ אין לי אלא בית מנין לרבות חצר גנה

D/C וסוכה ◆ ת״ל באחד יאכל ◆ אם כן למה נאמר בבית אחד

E 2 B/A יאכל ◆ בחבורה אחת. ◆ לא תוציא מן הבית ◆ אין לי <אלא>

C מבית לבית מחבורה לחבורה מנין ◆ ת״ל חוצה חוץ

A למקום אכילתו. ◆ יאכל לא תוציא מן הבית מן הבשר ◆

B בשעת אכילה הוא חייב ואינו חייב שלא בשעת אכילה. ◆

4 B/A יאכל לא תוציא מן הבית ◆ על כדי אכילה הוא חייב ואינו

5 B/A חייב על פחות מכזית. ◆ יאכל לא תוציא מן הבית ◆ על

6 A הכשר הוא חייב ואינו חייב על הפסול. ◆ אין לי אלא

from Scripture [that it was also the case for] the paschal sacrifice of the subsequent generations?[327]

B.   Scripture states, "(This is) the law (of the passover offering)" (Exod. 12:43).

7    A.   "It shall be eaten ... You shall not break a bone of it" (Exod. 12:46):

B.   One becomes culpable over [the amount] that constitutes an "eating," but one does not become culpable over [an amount] less than an olive.

8.   A.   "You shall not break a bone of it" (Exod. 12:46):

B.   When it is pure. Not when it is impure.[328]

9.   A.   You shall not break a bone *of it*" (Exod. 12:46):

B.   Of it you shall not break. You may break [a bone] of the festival sacrifice that comes with it.

C.   Because it has [characteristics that are] not in the [other] holy sacrifices, and in the [other] holy sacrifices there are [characteristics that are] not in it, you are not able to judge from one to the next.

## XVII:V

1.   A.   "The whole community of Israel shall offer it" (Exod. 12:47):[329]

B.   Since it says, "... and all the assembled congregation of the Israelites shall slaughter it" (Exod. 12:6), this teaches that the paschal sacrifice was slaughtered in three groups: in "assembly," "congregation," and "Israel."

C.   One might think that it would be disqualified, if they [all] slaughtered it at the same moment.

[37]  D.   Scripture states, [however,] "The whole community of Israel shall offer it" (Exod. 12:47).

2.   A.   "(The whole community of Israel shall offer) it" (Exod. 12:47):

B.   And even on *Shabbat*.

3.   A.   "(The whole community of Israel shall offer) it" (Exod. 12:47):

B.   And even in a state of impurity.

## XVII:VI

1.   A.   "(If a stranger who dwells with you would offer the passover to the Lord,) all his males must be circumcised. (Then he shall be admitted to offer it. He shall then be as a citizen of the country. But no uncircumcised person may eat of it)" (Exod. 12:48):

B.   I only know [he must circumcise the person who was] completely uncircumcised.[330] How does one know from Scripture [he must circumcise the person] who was circumcised but not immersed, or was immersed but not circumcised, or if [he was circumcised] but there were shreds [of foreskin remaining] that would prevent him from eating the paschal offering and the *terumah*?

C.   Scripture states, "... all his males must be circumcised" (Exod. 12:48), [meaning that] shreds [of foreskin remaining] prevent him from eating the paschal offering and the *terumah*.

2.   A.   "Then[331] he shall be admitted to offer it" (Exod. 12:48):

[327] I.e., the paschal sacrifice offered by the subsequent generations of Israelites after the Exodus.

[328] Compare 8.B with m. Pesaḥim 6:11.

[329] Compare 1.A–B with m. Pesaḥim 5:5; and *Mekhilta de-Rabbi Ishmael,* Pisḥa (H/R, 17:12–13; Laut., vol. 1, 42:110–12; Neus., V:III:4. A–C).

[330] Circumcised here is synonymous with converted to Judaism, and, conversely, uncircumcised is synonymous with unconverted. The

|  | | |
|---|---|---|
| פסח מצרים פסח דורות מנין ♦ ת״ל חקה. ♦ יאכל ועצם לא | A 7 | B |
| תשברו בו ♦ על כדי אכילה הוא חייב ואינו חייב על | | B |
| פחות מכזית. ♦ ועצם לא תשברו בו ♦ בטהור לא בטמא. ♦ ועצם | A 9 | B/A 8 |
| לא תשברו בו ♦ בו אי אתה שובר שובר אתה בחגיגה | | B |
| הבאה עמו ♦ הא מפני שיש בו מה שאין בקדשים | | C |
| ובקדשים מה שאין בו אי אתה יכול לדונן זה מזה. ♦ | | |

XVII:V

|  | | |
|---|---|---|
| כל עדת ישראל יעשו אותו ♦ מכלל שנאמר ושחטו | B/A | 1 |
| אותו כל קהל עדת ישראל (שמ׳ יב ו) מלמד שפסח | | |
| נשחט בשלש כתות בקהל ועדה וישראל ♦ יכול אם | | C |
| שחטו בבת אחת יהא פסול ♦ ת״ל כל עדת ישראל יעשו | | D |
| אותו. ♦ אותו ♦ ואפילו בשבת. ♦ אותו. ♦ ואפילו בטומאה. ♦ | B/A 3 | B/A 2 |

XVII:VI

|  | | |
|---|---|---|
| המול לו כל זכר ♦ אין לי אלא ערל גמור מנין מל | B/A | 1 |
| ולא טבל טבל ולא מל או שהיו בו ציצין (ה)מעכבין | | |
| אותו לאכול בפסח מעכבין אותו לאכול בתרומה ♦ ת״ל | | C |
| המול לו כל זכר הציצין מעכבין אותו לאכול בפסח | | |
| ומעכבין אותו לאכול בתרומה. ♦ ואז יקרב לעשותו ♦ | A | 2 |

conversion ceremony requires both circumcision and immersion in a ritual bath.

B. Behold this is explained nicely!

C. *"Az"* is stated here and *"az"* is stated above.[332] Just as *"az"* stated above is "... then[333] he may eat of it," likewise is *"az"* stated here [in order to mean] that then he may eat of it. And just as *"az"* stated here is "Then he shall be admitted to offer it," likewise is *"az"* stated there [in order to mean] that then he shall be admitted to offer it.

3. A. "He shall then be as a citizen of the country" (Exod. 12:48):[334]

B. Just as the citizen only enters into the covenant by three things—by circumcision, immersion, and [offering] an acceptable sacrifice, likewise the convert only enters into the covenant by three things—by circumcision, immersion, and an acceptable sacrifice.

4. A. "But no uncircumcised person may eat of it" (Exod. 12:48):

B. I only know [that this refers to the person who was] completely uncircumcised. How does one know from Scripture [that this refers as well to the person] who was circumcised without having the inner lining torn or [the person who was circumcised] but there were shreds [of foreskin remaining] that would prevent him from eating the paschal offering and the *terumah?*

C. Scripture states, "But no uncircumcised person may eat of it," [meaning that] shreds [of skin remaining] prevent him from eating the paschal offering and the *terumah.*

5. A. "But no uncircumcised person may eat of it" (Exod. 12:48):

B. Since we have already found that the public may perform the paschal offering in impurity in the instance when the majority of them are impure, then one might think that a single person could be the deciding factor in [the similar case when half are circumcised and half are] uncircumcised.

C. Scripture states, [however,] "But no uncircumcised person may eat of it" (Exod. 12:48).

6. A. "(But no uncircumcised person) may eat of it" (Exod. 12:48):[335]

B. Of it he may not eat, but he may eat unleavened bread and bitter herbs.

## XVII:VII

1. A. "There shall be one law for the citizen (and for the stranger[336] who dwells among you)" (Exod. 12:49):

B. Just as the citizen accepted upon himself all the words of the Torah, likewise [for] the convert[337] who accepted upon himself all the words of the Torah.

C. From here they stated: If a convert accepted upon himself all the words of the Torah except for one, they do not accept him. R. Yosi in the name of R. Judah says, "Even one word from the precepts of the scholars."[338]

2. A. "... for the stranger"[339] (Exod. 12:49):

B. This is the convert.

C. "... who dwells" (Exod. 12:49):

[331] Hebrew: *az*—אָז.
[332] I.e., Exod. 12:44.
[333] Hebrew: *az*—אָז.
[334] Compare 3.A–B with *Sifre Num*, Piska 108 (Neus., CVIII:I:2.H).
[335] Compare 6.A–B with parallel above at XVII:I:4.A–B.
[336] Hebrew: *ger*—גֵּר.
[337] Hebrew: *ger*—גֵּר.
[338] Compare 1.C with t. Demai 2:5, y. Demai 22d, and b. Bekhorot 30b (Neus., XXXI.A:Tractate Bekhorot:4:10:V.3.A–C).

| | |
|---|---|
| C/B | הרי זה מפורש יפה ◆ נאמר כאן אז ונאמר להלן אז מה אז האמור להלן אז יאכל בו אף אז האמור כאן אז יאכל בו ◆ ומה אז האמור כאן אז יקרב לעשותו אף אז האמור להלן אז יקרב לעשותו. |
| B/A   3 | ◆ והיה כאזרח הארץ ◆ מה אזרח אין נכנס לברית אלא בשלשה דברים במילה ובטבילה ובהרצאת קרבן אף גר אין נכנס לברית אלא בשלשה דברים במילה ובטבילה ובהרצאת קרבן. ◆ |
| B/A   4 | וכל ערל לא יאכל בו ◆ אין לי אלא ערל גמור מנין מל ולא פרע את המילה או שהיו בו ציצין מעכבין אותו לאכול בפסח מעכבין אותו לאכול בתרומה |
| C | ת״ל וכל ערל לא יאכל בו הציצין מעכבין אותו לאכול בפסח ומעכבין אותו לאכול בתרומה. |
| A   5 | ◆ וכל ערל לא יאכל בו ◆ |
| B | לפי שמצינו שהצבור עושין פסח בטומאה בזמן שרובן טמאים יכול יהא יחיד מכריע את הערלה |
| C | ◆ ת״ל וכל |
| B/A   6 | ערל לא יאכל בו. ◆ לא יאכל בו ◆ בו אינו אוכל אוכל הוא במצה ובמרור. ◆ |

<br>

XVII:VII

| | |
|---|---|
| B/A   1 | תורה אחת יהיה לאזרח ◆ מה אזרח שקיבל עליו |
| C | כל דברי תורה אף הגר שקיבל עליו כל דברי תורה ◆ |
| | מיכאן אמרו גר שקיבל עליו כל דברי תורה חוץ מדבר אחד אין מקבלין אותו ר׳ יוסי ביר׳ יהודה אומר |
| C/B/A   2 | אפילו דבר אחד מדקדוקי סופרים. ◆ לגר ◆ זה הגר. ◆ הגר ◆ |

D. This includes women converts.

E. "... among you" (Exod. 12:49):

F. This includes women and freed slaves.

3. A. "And the Israelites did so. (As the Lord had commanded Moses and Aaron, so they did)" (Exod. 12:50):

B. [Scripture states twice that they "did so" in order] to give them a reward for "going" [to perform God's commandments that was] equal to the reward for [actually] "doing" [them].

C. As it is written above, "And the Israelites went and did so" up to "So they did, they did so with intention."[340]

4. A. "That very day[341] (the Lord freed the Israelites from the Land of Egypt, troop by troop)" (Exod. 12:51):

B. "That very day" can only mean at the height of the day.

5. A. "... the Lord freed the Israelites from the Land of Egypt, troop by troop" (Exod. 12:51):

B. This teaches that they did not leave in a commotion, rather organized.

## Chapter Eighteen

### (Textual Source: Midrash ha-Gadol)

XVIII:I

1. A. "The Lord spoke further to Moses, saying: 'Consecrate to Me (every first-born; man and beast, the first issue of every womb among the Israelites is Mine)'" (Exod. 13:1–2):

B. "Consecrate to Me" means only "Dedicate to Me!"

2. A. One might think that if you dedicate [a first-born], then it is consecrated, but if not, then it is not consecrated.[342]

B. Scripture states, [however,] "... is Mine" (Exod. 13:2).

C. Whether you dedicate it or not.

3. A. "... the first issue of (every) womb" (Exod. 13:2):

B. Which excludes that which comes out by means of caesarean section.

4. A. "... among the Israelites" (Exod. 13:2):

B. I only know [this applies] to [the children of] Israel. How does one know from Scripture that this includes converts and freed slaves?

C. Scripture states, "... (every) first-born" (Exod. 13:2).

5. A. "... every first-born" (Exod. 13:2):[343]

[38] B. Based on this you say: [In the case of] a female convert who became pregnant before she converted,[344] but gave birth after she converted, the [child is considered] a first-born [concerning] inheritance, but is not a first-born [concerning the rights of] the priest.

---

[339] Hebrew: *ger*—גר.

[340] See above XIV:II:1.A–2.J.

[341] Hebrew: *b'etzem*—בעצם.

[342] Compare 2.A–C with *Mekhilta de-Rabbi Ishmael*, Pisḥa (H/R, 58:11–12; Laut., vol. 1, 130:34–131:38; Neus., XVI:I:5.A–G).

[343] Compare 5.A–E with m. Bekhorot 8:1.

| | | |
|---|---|---|
| F/E/D | | לרבות נשי גרים. ◆ בתוככם ◆ לרבות את הנשים ואת העבדים המשוחררין. ◆ |
| 3 | B/A | ויעשו כל בני ישראל ◆ ליתן להם שכר הליכה כשכר |
| | C | עשייה ◆ כי דכתיב לעיל וילכו ויעשו בני ישראל כול' עד וכן היה בלבם לעשות. ◆ |
| 4 | B/A | ויהי בעצם היום הזה ◆ אין עצם אלא תוקפו שליום. ◆ |
| 5 | A | הוציא ה' את בני ישראל מארץ מצרים על צבאותם ◆ |
| | B | מלמד שלא יצאו מהומה אלא מטורקסין. ◆ |

XVIII:I

| | | |
|---|---|---|
| 1 | B/A | וידבר ה' אל משה לאמר קדש לי ◆ אין קדש לי |
| 2 | A | אלא הפר(י)ש לי ◆ יכול אם מפרישו אתה הרי הוא |
| | C/B | מקודש ואם לאו אינו מקודש ◆ ת"ל לי הוא ◆ בין שאתה |
| 3 | B/A | מפרישו ובין שאין אתה מפרישו. ◆ פטר רחם ◆ פרט |
| 4 | B/A | ליוצא דופן. ◆ בבני ישראל ◆ אין לי אלא ישראל מנין |
| 5 C | A | לרבות גרים ועבדים משוחררין ◆ ת"ל בכור ◆ כל בכור ◆ |
| | B | מכאן אתה אומר הגיורת שהיתה הורתה שלא בקדושה ולידתה בקדושה בכור לנחלה ואין בכור לכהן ◆ |

C.    R. Yosi ha-Galili says, "[It is considered] a first-born [concerning] inheritance and [the rights of] the priest.

D.    "As it says in Scripture, '... the first issue of every womb among the Israelites' (Exod. 13:2).

E.    "[Meaning,] as long as it is the first issue of the womb of an Israelite."

6.    A.    "... man and beast" (Exod. 13:2):[345]

B.    Those who are subject [to the law of first-born redemption for] human [first-borns are also] subject [to the law of first-born redemption for] beasts. The Levites are excluded, because they are not subject [to the law for] humans, [and thus] are not subject [to the law for] beasts.

7.    A.    "... is Mine" (Exod. 13:2):

B.    [When it is] certain, but not [when there is] doubt.

8.    A.    "... is Mine" (Exod. 13:2):

B.    Whether you dedicate it or not.

9.    A.    "... is Mine" (Exod. 13:2):

B.    Only one first-born [receives] the inheritance.[346]

10.    A.    "... is Mine" (Exod. 13:2):

B.    It[347] is offered, and a substitute is not offered.

## XVIII:II

1.    A.    "And Moses said to the people, 'Remember this day, (on which you went free from Egypt, the house of bondage, how the Lord freed you from it with a mighty hand. No leavened bread shall be eaten)'" (Exod. 13:3):

B.    Since it says in Scripture, "And when, in time to come, your son asks you saying, ('What does this mean?')" (Exod. 13:14), one might think that if he asks you, then you tell him, but if not, then you do not tell him.

C.    Scripture states, [however,] "And you shall explain to your son (on that day)" (Exod. 13:8), [meaning,] even though he did not ask you.

D.    I only know [that one should explain the significance of the passover offering] when he has a son. How does one know from Scripture [that if one does not have a son, he should explain it] to himself or to someone else?[348]

E.    Scripture states, "And Moses said to the people, 'Remember this day, on which you went free from Egypt'" (Exod. 13:3).

2.    A.    "'... the house of bondage'" (Exod. 13:3):[349]

B.    R. Judah says, "One might think that we were slaves to slaves.

C.    "Scripture states, [however,] '... from the house of bondage, from the hand of Pharaoh, king of Egypt' (Deut. 7:8). We were slaves to the king, and not slaves to slaves.

D.    "And Scripture says, '(I the Lord am your God who brought you out from the land of the

---

[344] Literally: "before in holiness."

[345] Compare 6.A–B with *Mekhilta de-Rabbi Ishmael,* Pisha (H/R, 58:1–2; Laut., vol. 1, 129:18–130:20; Neus., XVI:I:2.A–C).

[346] I.e., twins will not divide an inheritance.

[347] I.e., the first-born.

[348] Compare 1.D with t. Pisha 10:11.

| | |
|---|---|
| D/C | ר′ יוסי הגלילי אומר בכור לנחלה ולכהן • שנאמר |
| E | פטר כל רחם בבני ישראל • עד שיפטרו רחם מישראל. • |
| B/A    6 | באדם ובבהמה • את שיש לך בו באדם יש לך בו |
| | בבהמה יצאו לוים שאין לך בהם באדם לא יהא לך |
| B/A 8    B/A 7 | בהם בבהמה. • לי הוא • ודאי ולא הספק. • לי הוא • בין |
| B/A    9 | שאתה מפרישו ובין שאי אתה מפרישו. • לי הוא • אין |
| B/A    10 | בכור לנחלה אלא אחד. • לי הוא • הוא קרב ואין |
| | תמורתו קריבה. • |

| | |
|---|---|
| XVIII:II | |
| B/A    1 | ויאמר משה אל העם זכור את היום הזה • מכלל |
| | שנאמר והיה כי ישאלך בנך מחר לאמר יכול אם |
| C | [י]שאלך אתה מגיד לו ואם לאו אי אתה מגיד לו • ת″ל |
| D | והגדת לבנך אע″פ שאינו שואלך. • אין לי אלא בזמן |
| E | שיש לו בן בינו לבין עצמו בינו לבין אחרים מנין • ת″ל |
| | ויאמר משה אל העם זכור את היום הזה (אשר |
| B/A    2 | יצאתם ממצרים). • מבית עבדים • ר′ יהודה אומר יכול |
| C | שהיינו עבדים לעבדים • ת″ל מבית עבדים ‹מיד פרעה |
| | מלך מצרים (דב′ ז ח) עבדים למלכים היינו ולא |
| D | עבדים לעבדים • ואומר מהיות להם עבדים (ויקר′ כו |

---

³⁴⁹ Compare 2.A–Г with *Mekhilta de-Rabbi Ishmael*, Pisḥa (H/R, 222:10–11; Laut., vol. 2., 237:102–8; Neus., LI:I:14.A–D); and *Sifra*, Beḥuqotai 3:5 (Neus., CCLXIII:I:7.A–E).

Egyptians) to be *their* slaves no more' (Lev. 26:13). We were *their* slaves, but we were not slaves to slaves."

E.    R. Nehemiah says, "Would it really be disgraceful to us if we were slaves to the Egyptians' slaves? Wouldn't it be quite a step up (going from the slaves of slaves to redemption by God)?

F.    "Rather, this teaches that they were doing housework, fieldwork, men's work, and women's work."

3.    A.    "'... how the Lord freed you ... with a mighty hand'" (Exod. 13:3):

B.    This is in reference to the Ten Plagues.

C.    "'... *from it* (with a mighty hand) ...'" (Exod. 13:3):

D.    This teaches that the slaying of the first-born was equal to all of them.

4.    A.    "'... No leavened bread shall be eaten'" (Exod. 13:3):[350]

B.    And [no leavened bread should be fed] even to the dogs.

C.    This [verse] comes to prohibit [taking] any benefit from it.

5.    A.    R. Yosi ha-Galili says, "How does one know from Scripture that leaven was prohibited for only one day in Egypt?[351]

B.    "Scripture states, '... No leavened bread shall be eaten' [and then begins the next verse immediately with the word] 'Today' (Exod. 13:3–4)."

## XVIII:III

1.    A.    "'Today you go free, in the month of Abib'" (Exod. 13:4):[352]

B.    In a month that is suitable,[353] not hot and not cold.

C.    And thus Scripture states, "God restores the lonely to their homes, sets free the imprisoned, safe and sound"[354] (Ps. 68:7).

2.    A.    Another opinion: "... safe and sound"[355] (Ps. 68:7): [meaning,] "on account of their upright deeds," [and this is in reference to] Abraham, Isaac, and Jacob.

B.    Another opinion: [This is in reference to] Moses, Aaron, and Miriam.

3.    A.    Another opinion: "... safe and sound"[357] (Ps. 68:7): [meaning,]: "they sang songs,"[358] [and this means that at the time of the Exodus] there were those who sang and those who wept.

B.    And thus Scripture states, "In vain do you rise early and stay up late, you who toil for the bread you eat. He provides as much for His loved ones while they sleep" (Ps. 127:2).

---

[350] Compare 4.A–C with y. Pesaḥim 28c (Bokser, 2:1:II:A–H).

[351] Compare 5.A–B with y. Pesaḥim 28d (Bokser, 2:2:IV:H–I) and b. Pesaḥim 28b (Neus., IV:B:Pesaḥim:2:2:I.2.D).

[352] Compare 1.A–3.B with *Mekhilta de-Rabbi Ishmael*, Pisḥa (H/R, 62:3–10; Laut., vol. 1, 139:154–140:165; Neus., XVI:III:3.A–I).

[353] Hebrew: כשר.

[354] Hebrew: כושרות.

[355] Compare 1.A–C with *Sifre Deut.*, Piska 128 (Hammer, p. 172; Neus., CXXVIII:III:1.A–C).

[356] Hebrew: כושרות.

[357] Hebrew: כושרות.

[358] Hebrew: בכו שירות.

יג)> לׁהם הׁיינו עבדים ולא היינו עבדים לעבדים. ◆ ר'          E

נחמיה אומר וכי גנאי הוא לנו שהיינו עבדים
לעבדיהם שלמצרים והלא מעלה גדולה היא ◆ אלא          F
מלמד שהיו עושין מלאכת בית ומלאכת שדה
מלאכת אנשים ומלאכת נשים. ◆ כי בחזק יד הוציא ה'          Λ          3
אתכם ◆ אלו עשר מכות. ◆ מזה ◆ מלמד שמכת בכורות          D/C/B
שקולה כנגד כולן. ◆ ולא יאכל חמץ היום ◆ ואפילו          B/A          4
לכלבים ◆ הרי זה בא לאסרו בהנאה. ◆ ר' יוסי הגלילי          A 5          C
אומר מנין לחמץ במצרים שלא נאסר אלא יום אחד ◆
ת"ל ולא יאכל חמץ היום.          B

XVIII:III

היום אתם יוצאים בחדש האביב ◆ בחדש שהוא          B/A          1
כשר לא חם ולא צונן ◆ וכן הוא אומר אלקים מושיב          C
יחידים ביתה מוציא אסירים בכושרות (תה' סח ז) ◆
[ד"א] בכושרות במעשה כשרים שבהן אלו אברהם          A          2
יצחק ויעקב. ◆ ד"א זה משה אהרן ומרים. ◆ ד"א          A 3          B
בכושרות בכו שירות אלו בוכים ואלו משוררים ◆ וכן          B
הוא אומר שוא לכם משכימי קום מאחרי שבת אוכלי
לחם העצבים כן יתן לידידו שנא (תה' קכז ב). ◆

XVIII:IV

1.  A.  "'So,[359] (when the Lord has brought you into the land of the Canaanites, the Hittites, the Amorites, the Hivites, and the Jebusites, which He swore to your fathers to give you, a land flowing with milk and honey, you shall observe in this month the following practice)'" (Exod. 13:5):[360]

    B.  [The word] "so"[361] only means immediately.

2.  A.  "'... when (the Lord) has brought you (into the land)'" (Exod. 13:5):

    B.  Do the commandment stated [in the following verses],[362] for it is because of its reward that you will enter the land.

3.  A.  "'... which He swore to your fathers'" (Exod. 13:5):[363]

    B.  Everything is on account of the merit of your fathers.

4.  A.  "'... to give you'" (Exod. 13:5):

    B.  So that it won't seem to you as if it is an inheritance of your fathers, but as if it is now given to you as a gift.

5.  A.  "'... a land flowing with milk and honey'" (Exod. 13:5):

    B.  R. Eliezer says, "'Milk' [refers to] the fruit, and 'honey' [refers to] the dates."

    C.  R. Akiva says, "'Milk' [refers to] actual milk. For Scripture states, 'And in that day, the mountains shall drip with wine, the hills shall flow with milk' (Joel 4:18). And 'honey' [refers to] the honey of the forests. For thus Scripture states, 'When the people came to the forest and found a flow of honey there' (1 Sam. 14:26)."

6.  A.  Another opinion: Scripture says here "flowing with milk and honey"

(Textual Source: Ms. Firkovich IIA 268)

[39]    and Scripture says later "flowing with milk and honey" (Deut. 26:9).

    B.  Just as [the reference] there [is to] the land of the five [Canaanite] nations [west of the Jordan river], likewise here [the reference is to] the five nations.

    C.  Based on this R. Yosi ha-Galili used to say, "They do not bring first fruits from beyond the Jordan, for it is not a land flowing with milk and honey."[364]

7.  A.  "'... you shall observe in this month the following practice'" (Exod. 13:5):[365]

    B.  Since it states in Scripture, "You shall slaughter the passover sacrifice for the Lord your God, from the flock and the herd" (Deut. 16:2), one might think that the paschal sacrifice of the subsequent generations[366] could come from either the flock or the herd.

    C.  Scripture states, [however,] "'... you shall observe in this month the following practice'" (Exod. 13:5).

    D.  Just as the paschal sacrifice of Egypt[367] came only from the sheep and goats, likewise the paschal sacrifice of the subsequent generations came only from the sheep and goats.

---

[359] Hebrew: והיה.

[360] Compare 1.A–2.B with *Sifre Deut.*, Piska 55 (Hammer, pp. 112–13; Neus., LV:I:1.A–2.B); and Piska 297 (Hammer, p. 287; Neus., CCXCVII: I:1.A–2.B); and with parallel material below at XIX:I:1.A–2.B.

[361] Hebrew: והיה.

[362] I.e., in Exod. 13:6ff.

[363] Compare 3.A–B with *Sifre Deut.*, Piska 184 (Hammer, p. 206; Neus., CLXXXIV:I:2.A–B).

[364] Compare 6.C with m. Bikkurim 1:10.

[365] Compare 7.A–D with *Mekhilta de-Rabbi Ishmael*, Pisḥa (H/R, 64:4–5; Laut., vol. 1, 144:25–26; Neus., XVII:I:4.A–B).

| | | |
|---|---|---|
| B/A 2 | B/A 1 | והיה • אין והיה אלא מיד. • כי יביאך • עשה מצוה |
| A | 3 | האמורה בענין שבשכרה תכנס לארץ. • אשר נשבע |
| B/A 4 | B | לאבתיך • הכל בזכות אבותיך. • לתת לך • שלא תהא |
| | | בעיניך כאלו היא ירושת אבותיך אלא כאלו עכשיו |
| B/A | 5 | ניתנה לך במתנה. • ארץ זבת חלב ודבש • ר' אליעזר |
| C | | אומר חלב זה חלב הפירות דבש זה דבש תמרים. • ר' |
| | | עקיבה אומר חלב זה חלב ודאי וכן הוא אומר והיה |
| | | ביום ההוא יטיפו ההרים עסיס והגבעות תלכנה חלב |
| | | (יואל ד יח) דבש זה דבש היערות וכן הוא אומר ויבא |
| A | 6 | העם אל היער והנה הלך דבש (ש"א יד כו). • ד"א נאמר |
| | | כאן זבת חלב ודבש [ונאמר להלן זבת חלב ודבש (דב' |
| B | | כו ט) • מה להלן] ארץ חמשת עממין אף [כאן ארץ |
| C | | חמשת עממים • מיכן היה ר' יוס[י הגלילי אומ' אין |
| | | מביאין [בכורים מעבר לירדן שאינה ארץ זבת חלב |
| B/A | 7 | ודבש]. • ועבדת את העבודה [הזאת בחדש הזה • מכלל |
| | | שנא' וזבחת פ[סח לייי אלהיך צאן ובקר (דב' טז ב) |
| C | | [יכול יה]א פסח דורות בא מן הצאן ומן הבקר • |
| D | | ת"ל ועבדת את העבוד' הזאת בחדש הזה • מה |
| | | פסח מצ' לא בא אלא מן הכבשים ומן העזים אף |
| | | פסח דורות אינו בא אלא מן הכבשים ומן העזים • |

---

[366] I.e., the paschal sacrifice offered by the subsequent generations of Israelites after the Exodus.
[367] I.e., the paschal sacrifice offered in Egypt by the Israelites at the time of the Exodus.

8.     A.    R. Eliezer says, "Scripture states to bring a paschal offering in Egypt and to bring a paschal sacrifice in the subsequent generations.[368]

        B.    "Just as the paschal sacrifice of Egypt did not come from the tithe, likewise the paschal sacrifice of the subsequent generations did not come from the tithe."

        C.    R. Akiva said to him, "My master, you infer [the rule for] a possible [situation] from an impossible [one]! For they didn't have tithes while in Egypt!"

        D.    R. Eliezer said to him, "Even though it's an impossibility, it's still strong proof!"

        E.    [Thus,] R. Akiva went and changed the logical reasoning: Scripture states to bring a paschal offering in Egypt and to bring a paschal sacrifice in the subsequent generations.

        F.    Just as the paschal sacrifice of Egypt came only from the nonconsecrated food, likewise the paschal sacrifice of the subsequent generations came only from the nonconsecrated food.

9.     A.    Another opinion:

        B.    Wasn't the paschal offering in the general category [of sacrifices]? Why [did Scripture] single it out?

        C.    [In order] to draw an analogy from it:

        D.    Just as the paschal offering, which comes as an obligatory, vowed, and freewill [offering], came only from the nonconsecrated food, likewise anything that comes as an obligatory, vowed, or freewill [offering] comes only from the nonconsecrated food.

10.    A.    Since it says in Scripture concerning the paschal offering of the subsequent generations, "You shall cook and eat it" (Deut. 16:7), I might think that one could cook it in water and eat it.

        B.    Scripture states, [however,] "'... you shall observe in this month the following practice'" (Exod. 13:5).

        C.    Just as the paschal sacrifice of Egypt could only be eaten roasted, likewise the paschal sacrifice of the subsequent generations could only be eaten roasted.

## XVIII:V

1.     A.    "Seven days you shall eat unleavened bread, (and on the seventh day there shall be a festival to the Lord)" (Exod. 13:6):[369]

        B.    How can one state from Scripture that if the [first] six days [of the festival] passed and one had not offered up the festival offering, then it is [nonetheless] required all seven days?

        C.    Scripture states, "Seven days you shall eat unleavened bread, and *on the seventh day there shall be a festival to the Lord*" (Exod. 13:6).

2.     A.    "Throughout[370] the seven days unleavened bread shall be eaten. (No leavened bread shall be found with you, and no leaven shall be found with you in all your territory)" (Exod. 13:7):

        B.    When Scripture states *"et,"* [it does so] to include the 14th day [of Nisan as one on which]

---

[368] Compare 8.A–F with b. Menahot 82a (Neus., XXIX.C:Tractate Menahot:8:6:I.1.A–G).

[369] Compare 1.A–C with *Mekhilta de-Rabbi Ishmael*, Pisha (H/R, 64:20–65:8; Laut., vol. 1, 146:53–147:72; Neus., XVII:I:9.A–K).

[370] Hebrew: *et*—את.

| | | |
|---|---|---|
| ר' אליעזר אומ' נאמ' הביא פסח במצ' ו<נאמ'> הביא | A | 8 |
| פסח דורות ◆ מה פסח מצ' אינו בא מן המעשר אמ' לו ר' | B | |
| עק' אף פסח דורות אינו בא מן המעשר ◆ אמ' לו ר' עקיבה | C | |
| ר' דנין איפשר משאי איפשר וכי מעשר היה להן במצ' ◆ | | |
| אמ' לו ר' אליעזר אף שאי אפשר ראיה גדולה היא ◆ חזר ר' | E/D | |
| עקיבה והחליף את הדין נאמ' הביא פסח במצ' ונאמ' | | |
| הביא פסח דורות ◆ מה פסח מצ' אינו בא אלא פסח מן | F | |
| החולין אף פסח דורות אינו בא אלא מן החולין. ◆ ד"א ◆ | A | 9 |
| והלא פסח בכלל היה מה יצא ◆ להקיש אליו ◆ מה פסח | D/C/B | |
| שהוא בא חובה ובא בנדר ובנדבה ואינו בא אלא מן | | |
| החולין כך כל דבר שהוא בא חובה ובא בנדר ונדבה | | |
| אינו בא אלא מן החולין ◆ לתוך שנא' בפסח דורות (סל' | A | 10 |
| פסו') ובשלת ואכלת (דב' טז ז) <יכול> יהא מבשלו | | |
| ואוכ[ל]ו ◆ ת"ל ◆ ועבדת את העבדה הזאת בחדש הזה ◆ | B | |
| מה פסח מצ' אין נאכל אלא צלי אף פסח דורות אין | C | |
| נאכל אלא צלי. ◆ | | |

| | | |
|---|---|---|
| | | XVIII:V |
| שבעת ימים תאכל מצות ◆ <מנין> אתה אומ' שאם | B/A | 1 |
| עברו ששת ימי החג ולא חג שטעון חגיגה כל שבעה ◆ | | |
| ת"ל שבעת ימים תאכל מצות וגומ' | C | |

| | | |
|---|---|---|
| מצות יאכל את שבעת הימים ◆ כשהוא אומ' את | B/Λ | 2 |

one is obligated [to eat unleavened bread].[371]

3. A. "No leavened bread shall be found with you" (Exod. 13:7):[372]

B. [But] you may see others'.[373]

C. "No leavened bread shall be found with you" (Exod. 13:7):

D. [But] you may see [that belonging] to the Most High.[374]

E. "No leavened bread shall be found with you" (Exod. 13:7):

F. [But] you may see [that belonging] to the baker.

4. A. Another opinion: "No leavened bread shall be found with you" (Exod. 13:7):

B. Nullify it in your heart.[375]

C. Based on this they said: If a man was on the way to slaughter his passover offering, (or to circumcise his son, or to eat the betrothal meal at his father-in-law's house, and he remembered that he had left ḥametz in his house, if he has time to go back and remove it and return to fulfill his religious duty, he should go back and remove it. But if not, he may annul it in his heart.)[376]

5. A. "No leavened bread shall be found with you, and no leaven shall be found with you in all
[40] your territory" (Exod. 13:7):[377]

B. This was a dispute between the School of Shammai and the School of Hillel.

C. For the School of Shammai says: [Prohibited is] leaven in the amount of an olive, and leavened bread in the amount of a date. But the School of Hillel says: For both it is the amount of an olive.

## XVIII:VI

1. A. "And you shall explain to your son (on that day, 'It is because of this that the Lord did for me when I went free from Egypt')" (Exod. 13:8):[378]

B. [You explain to him] even if he did not ask you.

C. I only know [that one should explain the significance of the passover offering] when he has a son. How does one know from Scripture [that if one does not have a son, he should explain it] to himself or to another's son?

D. Scripture states, "And you shall explain it to your son" (Exod. 13:8).

2. A. "'... It is because of this, that the Lord did for me'" (Exod. 13:8):[379]

B. [Thus, a father explains this to his son] all the time that the pieces of the paschal offering are there.

3. A. "'... that the Lord did for me'" (Exod. 13:8):

B. One might think that the merit of all of them had to be combined, for if this had not been the case, then they would not have deserved [being taken out of Egypt].

---

[371] The text does not indicate here what commandment in Exod. 13:7 is obligatory also on the 14th day of the month. I presume that the indication is that the commandment to eat unleavened bread is intended here, because the text focuses on the particle *et* in the first sentence of Exod. 13:7, which discusses this obligation. However, one could also conclude that the text indicates here that the commandment in the second sentence of this verse—which prohibits the possession of leavened bread—should also apply to the 14th day of the month. This is the indication in the parallel material in *Mekhilta de-Rabbi Ishmael* at Pisḥa (H/R, 65:9–12; Laut., vol. 1, 147:73–80; Neus., XVII:I:10.A–F).

[372] Compare 3.A–F with *Sifre Deut.*, Piska 131 (Hammer, p. 175; Neus., CXXXI:I:1.A–3.B).

[373] I.e., that belonging to a non-Jew.

[374] I.e., leaven dedicated to God.

| | | |
|---|---|---|
| A | 3 | להביא את יום ארבעה עשר שחייב במצ(ו)ה • ולא |
| C/B | | יראה לך חמץ • רואה אתה לאחרים • ולא יראה לך חמץ • |
| F/E/D | | רואה אתה לגבוה • ולא יראה לך חמץ • רואה אתה |
| C/B/A | 4 | לפלטיר. • ד״א ולא יראה לך חמץ • בטל בלבבך • [מכאן |
| | | אתה אומר ההולך לשחוט את פסחו] וכולה מתניתא. • |
| B/A | 5 | ולא יר[אה לך חמץ ולא יראה לך שאור • זה הוא] |
| C | | חילוק שבין בית שמאי לבי[ת הילל • שבית שמאי אומ׳ |
| | | שאור כזית] וחמץ ככותבת ובית הילל א[ומ׳ זה וזה |
| | | כזית. סל׳ פסו׳ |

| | | |
|---|---|---|
| | XVIII:VI | |
| C/B/A | 1 | והגדת] לבנך • אף על פי שלא (י)שאלך • אין |
| | | לי אלא בזמן שיש לו בן בינו ל[בין] עצמו ובינו לבין |
| A 2 | D | אחרים מנין • ת״ל והגדת לבנך. • בעבור זה עשה יי׳ לי |
| B/A 3 | B | כל זמן שגופו של פסח קיים • עשה יי׳ לי • יכול |
| | | עד שנצטרפה זכות כולן אילו כן לא היו כדיי בדבר • |

---

[375] Compare 4.B with b. Pesaḥim 4b (Neus., IV:A:Pesaḥim:1:1:I.16.J).
[376] Compare 4.C with m. Pesaḥim 3:7 and t. Pisḥa 3:12.
[377] Compare 5.A–C with *Sifre Deut.,* Piska 131 (Hammer, p. 175; Neus., CXXXI:I:5.A–D).
[378] Compare 1.A–D with parallel above at XVIII:II:1.C–E (particularly 1.D here with 1.E above).
[379] Compare 2.A–B with *Mekhilta de-Rabbi Ishmael,* Pisḥa (H/R, 66:9–10; Laut., vol. 1, 149:96–99; Neus., XVII:I:13.A–F).

C.     Scripture states, [however,] "'... It is because of this, (that the Lord did *for me*)'" (Exod. 13:8). This teaches that each and every person among Israel merited miracles being performed on his behalf.

## XVIII:VII

1.   A.     "'(And this shall serve) *you* (as a sign on your hand and as a reminder between your eyes, in order that the Teaching of the Lord may be in your mouth, that with a mighty hand the Lord freed you from Egypt)'" (Exod. 13:9):

    B.     [This shall serve as a sign for you,] but not others.

2.   A.     Since Scripture says, "'... on your hand ... between your eyes'" (Exod. 13:9), one might think he may place it on the outside of his undergarment.

    B.     Scripture states, [however,] "'... And this shall serve *you*'" (Exod. 13:9), [meaning, you] but not others.[380]

3.   A.     "'... on your hand and ... between your eyes'" (Exod. 13:9):[381]

    B.     [One might think that] just as the one on the head has the four [scriptural sections on four separate parchments], likewise the one on the hand should have the four [scriptural sections on four separate parchments].

    C.     Scripture states, [however,] "'... as a [single] sign (on your hand)'" (Exod. 13:9), [meaning, one,] and not four. "As a [single] sign," [one,] and not three. "As a [single] sign," [one,] and not two.

    D.     R. Judah says, "Just as [on the] outside it is one sign, likewise inside it is one sign."[382]

    E.     R. Yosi says, "R. Judah changed his mind about it, and agreed [with me that in the case of] one who has two head-phylacteries, but not one for the hand, he may cover one of them with a skin, and make one for the hand."[383]

4.   A.     One might think that he may wear it on the palm of his hand.[384]

    B.     Scripture states, [however,] "'... on your hand and ... between your eyes'" (Exod. 13:9).

    C.     Just as [the one] between your eyes [is placed] on the upper part of the head, likewise [the one] on your hand [is placed] on the upper [part of] the arm.

    D.     But [still] one doesn't know upon which [arm] he should place it—upon the right or left!

    E.     Scripture states, "... and you shall bind them ... and you shall write them" (Deut. 6:8–9), [meaning,] just as writing is with the right hand, likewise binding [of the phylacteries is done] with the right hand. And since binding is [done] with the right hand, it is placed on the left arm.

    F.     And thus Scripture states, "... even there Your hand will be guiding me, (Your right hand will be holding me fast)" (Ps. 139:10). And Scripture says, "Her [left] hand reached for the

---

[380] The gist of this interpretation is not entirely clear. The implication of the prooftext is that the phylactery is a sign for the Jew who wears it, and not for others. Thus, the text here seems to stress either that the phylactery for the hand must be placed directly on the arm of the person who wears it, because it serves in this fashion as a direct sign for him, or that the phylactery need not be placed on the outside of an undergarment, in order that it be seen by other people. Compare with *Mekhilta de-Rabbi Ishmael*, Pisḥa (H/R, 67:1–3; Laut., vol. 1, 151:121–24; Neus., XVII:I:17.A–C); and b. Menaḥot 37b (Neus., XXIX.A:Tractate Menaḥot:3:7:III.37.A–38.C).

[381] Compare 3.A–E with *Mekhilta de-Rabbi Ishmael*, Pisḥa (H/R, 66:14–20; Laut., vol. 1, 150:106–17; Neus., XVII:I:15.A–J); *Sifre Deut.*, Piska 35 (Hammer, p. 65; Neus., XXXV:II:1.A–3.B); and b. Menaḥot 34b (Neus., XXIX.A:Tractate Menaḥot:3:7:III.2.A– 5.J).

[382] According to a parallel tradition found at b. Menaḥot 34b the issue here is whether the scriptural portions for the hand-phylactery may be written on four separate parchments, then tied together to form "one," as required.

[383] Since the head-phylactery has its scriptural portions written on four separate parchments, R. Yosi claims that this scenario represents a concession by R. Judah.

[384] Compare 4.A–G with *Mekhilta de-Rabbi Ishmael*, Pisḥa (H/R, 66:20–67:11; Laut., vol. 1, 151:118–152:139; Neus., XVII:I:16.A–21.D); *Sifre Deut.*, Piska 35 (Hammer, p. 65; Neus., XXXV:II:4.A–6.C); and b. Menaḥot 37b (Neus., XXIX.A:Tractate Menaḥot:3:7:III.37.A–H).

| | | |
|---|---|---|
| ת״ל בעבור זה מלמד שכל אחד מיש׳ היה כדי שיעשו נסין על ידיו. סל׳ פסו׳ ◆ | C | |
| | | XVIII:VII |
| והיה לך ◆ ולא לאחרין ◆ מכלל שנא׳ על ידך ובין | A 2 | B/A 1 |
| עיניך יכול יתן על בית יד אונקלי שלו מבחוץ ◆ ת״ל | B | |
| והיה לך ולא לאחרין ◆ על ידך ובין עיניך ◆ מה בין עיניך | B/A | 3 |
| ארבע אף על ידך ארבע ◆ ת״ל לאות ולא ארבע לאות | C | |
| ולא שלש לאות ולא שתים ◆ ר׳ יהודה אומ׳ כשם שאות | D | |
| אחת מבפנים כך אות אחת מבחוץ ◆ אמ׳ ר׳ יוסי חזר בו | E | |
| ר׳ יהודה ומודה ר׳ יהודה במי שיש לו שתי תפילין | | |
| שלראש ואין לו שליד שמביא את העור וחופה את | | |
| אחת מהן ועושה אותה שליד ◆ יכול יתן על פס ידו ◆ ת״ל | B/A | 4 |
| על ידך ובין עיניך ◆ מה בין עיניך בגבוה שבראש אף על | C | |
| ידך בגבוה שביד ◆ אבל אי אתה יודע באי זה מקום | D | |
| הוא נותן אם בימין אם בשמאל ◆ ת״ל וקשרתם | E | |
| וכתבתם (דב׳ ו ח - ט) מה כתיבה בימין אף קשירה | | |
| בימין ומכלל שקשירה בימין (ו)נתינה בשמאל ◆ וכן | F | |
| הוא אומ׳ גם שם ידך תנחני וגו׳ (תה׳ קלט י) ואומ׳ | | |

tent pin, (her right for the workmen's hammer)" (Judg. 5:26).

G.  Thus, whenever Scripture states "hand," you assume it is the left, unless Scripture specifies for you the right.

5.    A.  Since it states in Scripture, "'… on your hand and … between your eyes'" (Exod. 13:9), [one might think that] just as "on your hand" [the phylactery has only] one parchment, likewise "between your eyes" [it should have only one parchment].[385]

B.  Scripture states, [however,] "frontlet, frontlet, frontlet, frontlet" (Exod. 13:16, Deut. 6:8, Deut. 11:18).[386]

C.  Thus, four frontlets are mentioned [meaning that the phylactery for the head should have four separate rolls of parchment].

D.  One might think, [therefore,] that he should put [these four parchment rolls] in four [separate] places.[387]

E.  Scripture states, [however,] "'… as a reminder between your eyes'" (Exod. 13:9).

[41]    F.  This teaches that you put them in one place.

6.    A.  Rabbi says, "In two places [in Scripture the word "frontlets"] is written *totafot,* but in one place it is written *totefet.*"

B.  "This teaches that you place them in one place."

7.    A.  One might think he should place it[388] upon his forehead.[389]

B.  Scripture states, [however,] "'… on your hand and … between your eyes'" (Exod. 13:9).

C.  Just as "on your hand" [means] on the highest [point] on the hand, likewise "between your eyes" [means] on the highest point of the head.

8.    A.  R. Eliezer b. Jacob says, "[The term 'between your eyes'] is [contextually] superfluous. [Thus, it is included in Scripture in order that it be used] to draw an analogy and to reason a *gezerah shaveh:*[390]

B.  "It states here in Scripture 'between your eyes,' and it states later in Scripture 'You shall not gash or shave the *front of your heads* [literally, "*between your eyes*"] …' (Deut. 14:1).

C.  "Just as 'between your eyes' there [means] a place where there is hair, likewise 'between your eyes' [here means] a place where there is hair."

9.    A.  "'… in order that the Teaching of the Lord may be in your mouth'" (Exod. 13:9):

B.  This [commandment] includes converts and freed slaves.

10.   A.  Another interpretation:[391]

B   "'… in order that the Teaching of the Lord may be in your mouth'" (Exod. 13:9).

C.  This [serves] to exclude women [from the commandment].

---

[385] Compare 5.A–6.B with *Mekhilta de-Rabbi Ishmael,* Pisḥa (H/R, 66:14–20; Laut., vol. 1, 150:106–17; Neus., XVII:I:15.A–J); and *Sifre Deut.,* Pisḳa 35 (Hammer, p. 65; Neus., XXXV:II:2.A–3.B).

[386] The first two articulations in Scripture of "frontlets" (Exod. 13:16 and Deut. 6:8) are read here in the singular, with the third articulation at Deut. 11:18 read in the plural (i.e., as "two frontlets"). In the eyes of our text, this creates a total of four scriptural articulations of the word "frontlets."

[387] I.e., in four separate containers.

[388] I.e., the phylactery "between your eyes".

[389] Compare 7.A–C with *Sifre Deut.,* Pisḳa 35 (Hammer, p. 65; Neus., XXXV:II:4.A–6.C).

[390] I.e., the employment of the same word in separate scriptural contexts, thus facilitating the application of the meaning of the word in one context to the other.

[391] Compare 10.A–D with *Mekhilta de-Rabbi Ishmael,* Pisḥa (H/R, 68:1–6; Laut., vol. 1, 153:154–154:164; Neus., XVII:I:24.A–L).

| | | |
|---|---|---|
| ידה ליתד תשלחנה וגומ' (שופ' ה כו) ◆ הא כל מקום | G | |
| שנ' יד אתה תופס את השמאל עד שיפרוט לך הכת' | | |
| ימין ◆ מכלל שנא' על ידך ובין עיניך מה על ידך אות | A | 5 |
| אחת אף בין עיניך אות אחת ◆ ת"ל טוטפות טוט' טוט' | B | |
| טוט' ◆ הרי ארבע טוטפות אמורות ◆ יכול יתן | D/C | |
| בארבע‹ה› מקומות ◆ ת"ל ולזכרון בין עיניך ◆ [מלמד | F/E | |
| שנותנם במקום אחד. ◆ רבי אומ' בשני] מקומות כת' | A | 6 |
| טוטפות [במקום אחד כת' טטפת] ◆ מלמד שנותנין | B | |
| במקום אחד ◆ יכול יתנם [על גבי מצחו ◆ ת"ל על יד]ך | B/A | 7 |
| ובין עיניך ◆ מה על ידך בגבוה שביד [אף בין עיניך | C | |
| בגבו]ה שבראש ◆ ר' אליעזר בן יעקב אומ' מופנה | A | 8 |
| [להקיש ו] לדון גזרה שוה ◆ נאמ' כאן בין עיניך ונאמר | B | |
| להלן לא תתגודדו וגו' (דב' יד א) ◆ מה בין עיניך האמ' | C | |
| להלן מקום שער אף עיניך האמ' כאן מקום שער ◆ למען | A | 9 |
| תהיה תורת ייי בפיך ◆ לרבות גרים ועבדים משוחררין. ◆ | B | |
| ד"א ◆ למען תהיה תורת ייי בפיך ◆ להוציא את הנשים ◆ | C/B/A | 10 |

D.  Just as women are exempt [from the commandment to wear] phylacteries, [which is] a particular positive, time-bound commandment,[392] likewise are women exempt from all positive, time-bound commandments.

11.  A.  "'... the Teaching of the Lord may be in your mouth'" (Exod. 13:9):[393]

B.  [Phylacteries are to be made only] from that which you may eat with your mouth.[394]

C.  Based on this they said: They only write [the scriptural portions] upon the skin of a pure beast.

12.  A.  "'You shall keep this institution at its set time (from year to year)'" (Exod. 13:10):[395]

B.  Since it states in Scripture, "'(And this shall serve) you (as a sign on your hand)'" (Exod. 13:9), I might think that even minors (are included in the command to wear phylacteries).

C.  Scripture states, [however,] "'You (shall keep this institution)'" (Exod. 13:10).

D.  I[396] am only speaking to he who knows how to keep them.[397]

E.  Based on this they said: If a minor knows how to take care of his phylacteries, he is obligated [to fulfill the commandment to wear] phylacteries.[398]

13.  A.  Another interpretation:

B.  "'You shall keep this institution'" (Exod. 13:10).

C.  R. Eliezer says, "This [refers to] the law of the paschal offering."

D.  R. Akiva says, "This [refers to] the law of phylacteries."

14.  A.  ["'You shall keep this institution at its set time from year to year'" (Exod. 13:10):][399]

B.  One might think [that the commandment to wear] phylacteries may be observed at night as during the day.

C.  For it is a matter of logic:

D.  If [the commandment of the] mezuzah, which is not observed by overnight travelers or travelers through the desert,[400] is nonetheless observed at night as in the day, then is it not logical that [the commandment of] phylacteries, which is observed by overnight travelers or travelers through the desert, should be observed at night as in the day?

E.  Scripture states, [however,] "'... from year to year'"[401] (Exod. 13:10), which excludes nights.

15.  A.  ["'You shall keep this institution at its set time from year to year'" (Exod. 13:10):][402]

B.  One might think [that the commandment to wear] phylacteries may be observed on festivals and *Shabbatot*.

C.  For it is a matter of logic:

D.  If [the commandment of the] mezuzah, which is not observed by overnight travelers or

---

[392] I.e., a commandment that prescribes a specific religious action to be conducted within a set period of time.

[393] Compare 11.A–C with y. Megillah 71d (Neus., 1:9:XII.W–GG), and b. *Shabbat* 108a (Neus., II.D:*Shabbat*:13:2:IV.3.A–C).

[394] I.e., the parchment upon which the scriptural portions of the phylacteries are written must come from an animal that is suitable for consumption by a Jew.

[395] Compare 12.A–E with *Mekhilta de-Rabbi Ishmael*, Pisha (H/R, 68:9–13; Laut., vol. 1, 154:169–77; Neus., XVII:I:26.A–I).

[396] I.e., God.

[397] I.e., to take care of them.

[398] Compare with t. Ḥagigah 1:2.

[399] Compare 14.A–16.E with *Mekhilta de-Rabbi Ishmael*, Pisha (H/R, 68:15–69:10; Laut., vol. 1, 155:181–157:209; Neus., XVII:I:2.A–32.D).

[400] The commandment requires that one place a mezuzah only upon the doorpost of one's permanent dwelling.

[401] Literally: "from *days* to *days*."

[402] See note 391.

| | | |
|---|---|---|
| D | | מה (ה)תפילין מיוחדת מצות עשה שהזמן גרמה |
| | | נשים פטורות כך כל מצות עשה שהזמן גרמה |
| B/A | 11 | נשים פטורות ♦ תורת ייי בפיך ♦ ממה שאתה אוכל בפיך ♦ |
| C | | מיכן אמרו אין כותבין תפילין אלא על עור בהמה |
| | | טהורה. סל' פסו' ♦ |

| | | |
|---|---|---|
| B/A | 12 | ושמרת את החוקה הזאת למועדה ♦ מכלל שנא' |
| C | | והיה לך לאות על ידך שומע אני אף קטנים במשמע ♦ ת"ל |
| D | | ושמרת ♦ לא אמרתי אלא למי שיש בו דעת לשמר ♦ |
| E | | מיכן אמרו תינוק שיודע לשמר את תפיליו חייב |
| C/B/A | 13 | בתפילין. ♦ ד"א ♦ ושמרת את החוקה. ♦ ר' אליעזר אומ' |
| D | | זאת חוקת הפסח ♦ ר' עקיבה אומ' זו חוקת תפילין ♦ |
| D/C/B/A | 14 | יכול יהו תפילין נוהגות בלילות כימים ♦ דין הוא ♦ ומה |
| | | מזוזה שאין נוהגת בהולכי ימים ובהולכי מדברות הרי |
| | | היא נוהגת בלילות כימים תפילין שנוהגות בהולכי |
| | | ימים והולכי מדברות אינו דין שיהו נוהגות בלילות |
| E | | כימים ♦ ת"ל מימים פרט ללילות ♦ יכול יהו תפילין |
| B/A 15 | | נוהגות בימים טובים ובשבתות ♦ דין הוא ♦ ומה מזוזה |
| D/C | | שאין נוהגת לא בהולכי ימים ולא הולכי מדברות הרי |

travelers through the desert,[403] is nonetheless observed on festivals and *Shabbatot,* then is it not logical that [the commandment of] phylacteries, which is observed by overnight travelers or travelers through the desert, should be observed on festivals and *Shabbatot?*

E.   Scripture states, [however,] "'... from year to year'"[404] (Exod. 13:10), [meaning, most days] but not *all* days.

16.   A.   ["'You shall keep this institution at its set time from year to year'" (Exod. 13:10):][405]

B.   R. Akiva says, "One might think [that the commandment to wear] phylacteries may be observed on festivals and *Shabbatot.*

C.   "For it is a matter of logic:

[42]   D.   "If [the commandment of the] mezuzah, which is not observed by overnight travelers or travelers through the desert,[406] is nonetheless observed on festivals and *Shabbatot,* then is it not logical that [the commandment of] phylacteries, which is observed by overnight travelers or travelers through the desert, should be observed on festivals and *Shabbatot?*

E.   "Scripture states, [however,] "'... as a sign on your hand'" (Exod. 13:9), [meaning that] *Shabbatot* and festivals are excluded, for they themselves are a sign!

17.   A.   "'... at its set time'" (Exod. 13:10):

B.   This teaches that you intercalate the year only in the period next to the festival.[407]

C.   And how does one know from Scripture that you intercalate the month only during the day, as well as sanctify the new month only during the day?

D.   Scripture states, [however,] "'... from year to year'"[408] (Exod. 13:10).

*Chapter Nineteen*

(Textual Source: Ms. Firkovich IIA 268)

XIX:I

1.   A.   "'And when (the Lord has brought you into the land of the Canaanites, as He swore to you and to your fathers, and has given it to you)'" (Exod. 13:11):[409]

B.   "And when"[410] only means immediately.

2.   A.   "'... (the Lord) has brought you'" (Exod. 13:11):

B.   Do the commandment stated [above],[411] for it is because of its reward that you will enter the land.

3.   A.   "'... into the land of the Canaanites'" (Exod. 13:11):

B.   Was it really [only] the land of the Canaanites? Wasn't it [actually] the land of the five nations [west of the Jordan river]?

C.   Rather, this teaches that Canaan was the forefather of them all.

D.   And thus Scripture states, "Canaan begot Sidon ... (and the Jebusites, the Amorites, the Girgashites, the Hivites)" (Gen. 10:15).

---

[403] See note 383 above.
[404] Literally: "from *days* to *days.*"
[405] See note 391.
[406] Ibid.
[407] I.e, the preceding month of Adar.
[408] Literally: "from *days* to *days.*"

| | | |
|---|---|---|
| היא נוהגת בימים טובים ובשבתות תפילין שנוהגות | | |
| בהולכי ימים ובהולכי מדברות אינו דין שיהוא | | |
| נוהג<ות> בימים טובים ובשבתות • ת״ל מימים ולא כל | E | |
| ימים • ר׳ עקיבה אומ׳ יכול יהו תפילין נוהגות בימים | B/A | 16 |
| טובים [ובשבתות • דין הוא • ומה מזוזה שאין נוהגת] | D/C | |
| בהולכי ימים והולכי מדברות הרי היא [נוהגת בימים | | |
| טובים] ובשבתות תפילין שנוהגות בהולכי ימים | | |
| [והולכי מדברות] אינו דין שיהו נוהגות בימים טובים | | |
| ובשב[תות] ת״ל לאות על ידך] יצאו שבתות וימים | E | |
| טובים שכולם אות. • למועדה • [מלמד שאין] מעברין | B/A | 17 |
| את השנה אלא בפרק <ה>סמוך למועד • ומנין שאין | C | |
| מעברין את החדש אלא ביום ואין מקדשין את החדש | | |
| אלא ביום • ת״ל מימים ימינה. סל׳ פסו׳ | D | |
| | | XIX:I |
| והיה • אין והיה אלא מיד • כי יביאך • עשה | B/A 2 | B/A 1 |
| מצוה האמורה בענין שבשכרה תיכנס לארץ • אל | A | 3 |
| ארץ הכנעני • וכי ארץ כנעני היית והלא היא ארץ | B | |
| חמשת עממין • אלא מלמד שכנען היה אביהן שלכולן • | C | |
| וכן הוא אומ׳ וכנען ילד את צידון וגו׳ (בר׳ י טו) • | D | |

---

[409] Compare 1.A–B with parallel above at XVIII:IV:1.A–B.
[410] Hebrew: והיה.
[411] I.e., the commandments stipulated in Exod. 13:6ff.

4.    A.    "'... as He swore to you and to your fathers'" (Exod. 13:11):[412]

        B.    Everything [is due] to your merit and the merit of your forefathers.

5.    A.    "'... and has given it to you'" (Exod. 13:11):[413]

        B.    It should not seem to you [that it is] an inheritance of the forefathers. Rather, [it should be] as if it is now given to you as a gift.

## XIX:II

1.    A.    "'... you shall set apart for the Lord every first issue of the womb. (Every male firstling that your cattle drop shall be the Lord's)'" (Exod. 13:12):[414]

        B.    Sanctification of the male first-borns [is mentioned in Scripture at] three places: in the Land of Egypt, in the wilderness, and upon their entrance into the land [of the Canaanites].

        C.    In the Land of Egypt: "'Consecrate to Me every first-born'" (Exod. 13:2).

        D.    In the wilderness: "'For every first-born is mine'" (Num. 3:13).

        E.    Upon their entrance into the land: "'... you shall set apart for the Lord every first issue of the womb'" (Exod. 13:12).

2.    A.    One might think that only normal offspring [constitute the] "first issue of the womb" for cattle. How does one know from Scripture [that these also constitute the "first issue of the womb"]: The sign of offspring in small cattle, [which is] a discharge [from the womb], and for large cattle, [which is] the afterbirth, and for women, [which is] the fetus-sack and the afterbirth?[415]

        B.    Scripture states, "'... that your cattle drop,'" (Exod. 13:12), [meaning,] anything that the cattle drop [constitutes the "first issue of the womb"].

3.    A.    "'... you shall set apart for the Lord every first issue of the womb'" (Exod. 13:12):

        B.    Which excludes [the first offspring of a] male animal.[416]

4.    A.    ["'... you shall set apart for the Lord every first issue of the womb'" (Exod. 13:12):][417]

        B.    Which excludes that which comes out by means of caesarean section.

5.    A.    "'(Every male firstling) that your (cattle drop shall be the Lord's)'" (Exod. 13:12):

        B.    Which excludes female (first-born offspring).

6.    A.    R. Yosi b. Kippar says, "Three (types of first-born male offspring) are mentioned: the first-born of humans, the first-born of cattle, and the first issue of the womb, along with the tithe [that is given] with them."[418]

7.    A.    "'... you shall set apart for the Lord every first issue of the womb'" (Exod. 13:12):

        B.    Which excludes that which comes out by means of caesarean section.[419]

8.    A.    "'(Every) male (firstling that your cattle drop shall be the Lord's)'" (Exod. 13:12):

---

[412] Compare 4.A–B with parallel above at XVIII:IV:3.A–B.

[413] Compare 5.A–B with parallel above at XVIII:IV:4.A–B and with *Mekhilta de-Rabbi Ishmael*, Pisḥa (H/R, 70:8; Laut., vol. 1, 159:18–19; Neus., XVIII:I:5.A–B).

[414] Compare 1.A–E with b. Bekhorot 4b (Neus., XXXI.A:Tractate Bekhorot:1:1F–H:I.1.P).

[415] Compare 2.A with t. Bekhorot 2:12 and m. Bekhorot 3:1.

[416] I.e., the first male offspring of *female* animals are set aside, and not necessarily the first male offspring of male animals.

[417] Compare 4.A–B with parallel above at XVIII:I:3.A–B.

[418] See Lev. 27:32.

[419] See note 416.

| | | |
|---|---|---|
| אשר נשבע לך ולאבותיך ◆ הכל בזכותך ובזכות אבותיך ◆ | B/A | 4 |
| ונתנה לך ◆ לא תהא בעיניך כירושת אבות אלא כאילו | B/A | 5 |
| עכשיו נתנה לך במתנה. סל׳ פסו׳ ◆ | | |

XIX:II

| | | |
|---|---|---|
| והעברת כל פטר רחם לייי ◆ בשלשה מקומות | B/A | 1 |
| נתקדשו בכורות בארץ מצר׳ ובמדבר ובכניסתן לארץ ◆ | | |
| בארץ מצ׳ קדש לי כל בכור (שמ׳ יג ב) ◆ במדבר כי לי | D/C | |
| כל בכור (במ׳ ג יג) ◆ ובכניסתן לארץ והעברת כל פטר | E | |
| רחם לייי ◆ יכול אין לי פטר בבהמה אלא ולד גמור | A | 2 |
| מנין סימן לולד בבהמה דקה טינוף ובגסה שיליא | | |
| ובאשה שפיר ושיליא ◆ ת״ל שגר בהמה כל שהבהמה | B | |
| שוגרת ◆ והעברת כל פטר רחם לייי ◆ פרט לחיה זכר ◆ | B/A | 3 |
| פרט לייי ליוצא דופן. ◆ אשר יהיה לך ◆ פרט לנקבה ◆ | B/A 5 \| B/A 4 | |
| ר׳ יוסי בן כיפר אומ׳ שלשתן נאמרו בכור אדם ובכור | A | 6 |
| בהמה ובכור פטר חמור ומעשר עמהן. ◆ והעברת | A | 7 |
| כל פטר רחם לייי ◆ פרט ליוצא דופן ◆ זכר ◆ | A 8/ \| B | |

B.  Which excludes [the offspring] whose sex is unknown or the hermaphrodite.

9.  A.  "'(Every male firstling) that *your* (cattle drop shall be the Lord's)'" (Exod. 13:12):

B.  Which excludes [the offspring of cattle] that are jointly owned.

C.  One might think that Scripture excludes [the case] of brothers who acquired [animals] from [their father's] estate, and then divided [them up].

D.  Scripture states, [however,] "'... that *your*'" (Exod. 13:12).

10. A.  Ben Azzai says, "It says here 'set apart,'[420] and it says 'passes'[421] in regard to the tithed [cattle discussed at Lev. 27:32].[422]

[43]  B.  "Just as with 'passes' stated in regard to the tithed [cattle at Lev. 27:32], it is established [in Scripture] that consecration takes effect upon [both] it[423] and the blemished [offspring], likewise with 'set apart' stated here, it is established that consecration takes effect upon [both] it and the blemished [offspring]."

11. A.  R. Shimon says, "An immature animal[424] can enter the shed [to be tithed], for it is like [the case of] the first-born:[425]

B.  "Just as we have found that a first-born is sanctified before its [due] time,[426] even though it may only be sacrificed at its [due] time, likewise this [tithed animal] may be sanctified before its [due] time, even though it may only be sacrificed at its [due] time."

12. A.  R. Joshua b. Korha says, "'Every first issue of the womb is Mine, (from all your livestock that drop a male as firstling, whether cattle or sheep)' (Exod. 34:19).

B.  "This is a general statement (in Scripture). One might think [this includes offspring belonging to] others.

C.  "Scripture states, [however,] '... your livestock' (Exod. 34:19).

D.  "One might think even female [offspring].

E.  "Scripture states, [however,] '... a male' (Exod. 34:19).

F.  "One might think even [the offspring] of wild beasts.

G.  "Scripture states, [however,] '... firstling, whether cattle (or sheep)' (Exod. 34:19).

H.  "This is a general statement (in Scripture) that needs its specification."

## XIX:III

1.  A.  "'But every firstling *ass* (you shall redeem with a sheep. If you do not redeem it, you must break its neck. And you must redeem every first-born male among your children)'" (Exod. 13:13):[427]

B.  But not a firstling camel, and not a firstling horse.

C.  Based on this you say: If his ass, which had not yet given birth, gave birth to a species of a horse, and likewise his camel, which had not yet given birth, gave birth to a species of camel or a species of ass, they are exempt from [the law of] firstlings.

---

[420] Hebrew: והעברת.

[421] Hebrew: יעבר.

[422] Compare 10.A–B with *Mekhilta de-Rabbi Ishmael*, Pisha (H/R, 70:9–20; Laut., vol. 1, 159:20–160:40; Neus., XVIII:I:6.A–7.N).

[423] I.e., the normal male offspring.

[424] I.e., less than seven days old.

[425] Compare 11.A–B with t. Bekhorot 7:6 and b. Bekhorot 21b (Neus., XXXI.A:Tractate Bekhorot:3:1A–R:I.5.H).

[426] I.e., the time when it emerges from the womb.

[427] Compare 1.A–E with m. Bekhorot 1:2.

| | | |
|---|---|---|
| פרט לטומטום ואנדרגינס ◆ אשר יהיה לך ◆ פרט לשלשותפין ◆ | B/A 9 | B |
| יכול שני מוציא את האחין שקנו מתפוסת הבית ואחרכך | | C |
| חלקו ◆ ת״ל יהיה לך ◆ בן עזאי אומ׳ נאמ׳ נאם׳ כאן העברה | A 10 | D |
| [ונאמ׳ העברה במעשר] ◆ מה [העב]רה האמורה במעשר | | B |
| ⟨קדושה חלה עליו ועל בעל מום קבוע אף העברה | | |
| האמורה כאן⟩ [קדושה חלה עליו ועל] בעל מום | | |
| קבוע ◆ ר׳ שמעון אומ׳ מחוסר זמן [נכנס לדיר והרי הוא | A 11 | |
| כבכור] ◆ מה מצינו בבכור שקדש לפני זמנו אף על [פי | | B |
| שאינו קרב אלא בז]מנו אף זה יקדש לפני זמנו אף על | | |
| פי שאינו קרב אלא בזמנו ◆ ר׳ יהושע בן קרחה אומ׳ כל | A 12 | |
| פטר רחם לי (שמ׳ לד יט) ◆ הרי זה כלל יכול אף | | B |
| שלאחרים ◆ ת״ל מקנך ◆ יכול אף של נקבה ◆ ת״ל תזכר ◆ | E/D/C | |
| יכול אף של חיה ◆ ת״ל ופטר שור ◆ זה הוא כלל שצריך | H/G/F | |
| לפרטו ◆ | | |
| | XIX:III | |
| ופטר חמור ◆ ולא פטר גמל ולא פטר סוס ◆ מיכן אתה | C/B/A | 1 |
| אומ׳ חמורו שלא ביכרה וילדה כמין סוס וכן גמלו שלא | | |
| ביכירה וילדה כמין גמל או כמין חמור פטור מן הבכורה | | |
| ◆ | | |

D. Scripture states two times: "The firstling of an ass" (Exod. 13:13) [and] "the firstling of an ass" (Exod. 34:20).

E. Only if [both] the mother and the offspring are asses.

2. A. R. Meir says, "Behold Scripture states, 'But[428] the firstling of an ox, (the firstling of a sheep or the firstling of a goat may not be redeemed. They are consecrated)' (Num. 18:17):[429]

B. "This is the general principle: [Included in the law of] the firstling [are only instances in which both the animal giving birth] is an ox and the offspring is an ox.

C. "'... the firstling of a sheep' (Num. 18:17): [This means that included in the law of the firstling are only instances in which the animal giving birth is a sheep] and the offspring is a sheep.

D. "'... the firstling of a goat' (Num. 18:17): [This means that included in the law of the firstling are only instances in which the animal giving birth is a goat] and the offspring is a goat.

E. "One might think that [the law of the firstling applies] even if it[430] possesses [only] partial traits of its mother's [species].

F. "Scripture states, [however,] 'But'[431] (Num. 18:17)."[432]

3. A. "'... you shall redeem ... you must redeem'" (Exod. 13:13):[433]

B. [Scripture states this twice to indicate that you shall redeem it] immediately, [and that] you shall redeem it with whatever [value].

C. R. Yosi b. Judah says, "Not with less than a *shekel*."

4. A. "'... (you shall redeem) with a sheep'" (Exod. 13:13):[434]

B. I might assume [this means] a live sheep or a slaughtered sheep.

C. [However,] you should reason:

D. "Sheep" is said here [in Scripture], and "sheep" is said above [in Scripture] (Exod. 12:3). Just as "sheep" stated above [means] a live sheep and not a slaughtered sheep, likewise "sheep" stated here [means] a live sheep and not a slaughtered sheep.

5. A. "'... you shall redeem'" (Exod. 13:13):[435]

B. Not with a calf, not with a wild beast, not with a slaughtered animal, not with a diseased animal, not with a mixed breed, and not with a *koy*.[436]

6. A. One might think that if one redeemed it while [still] in its mother's womb, then it is [suitably] redeemed.

B. Scripture states, [however,] "'If you do not redeem it, you must break its neck'" (Exod. 13:13), [meaning,] that which can have its neck broken is that which can be redeemed. That which cannot have its neck broken is that which cannot be redeemed.

---

[428] Hebrew: אַך.

[429] Compare 2.A–F with t. Bekhorot 1:5 and b. Bekhorot 17a (Neus., XXXI.A:Tractate Bekhorot:2:5:III.1.C–H).

[430] I.e., the offspring.

[431] Hebrew: אַך.

[432] The text assumes the word Hebrew word אַך serves as a delimiter in this manner.

[433] Although it appears in ms. Firkovich that an infinitive absolute clause is being interpreted here (Hebrew: פדה תפדה—You shall surely redeem), I have chosen to follow the parallels to this tradition, which indicate that of interest here is the repetition in Exod. 13:13 "You shall redeem ... you must redeem." See b. Bekhorot 10b (Neus., XXXI.A:Tractate Bekhorot:1:4:II.2.QQ) and t. Bekhorot 1:15.

[434] Compare 4.A–D with b. Bekhorot 12a (Neus., XXXI.A:Tractate Bekhorot:1:5:I.1.A–F).

[435] Compare 5.A–B with m. Bekhorot 1:5; and *Mekhilta de-Rabbi Ishmael*, Pisḥa (H/R, 71:7–8; Laut., vol. 1, 161:54–56; Neus., XVIII:I:11.A–B).

[436] I.e., an animal about which it cannot be determined if it is wild or domestic.

| | | |
|---|---|---|
| ת״ל ופטר חמור פטר חמור שני פעמים • עד שיהא | E/D | |
| היולד והולד חמור • ר׳ מאיר אומ׳ הרי הוא אומ׳ | A | 2 |
| אך בכור שור (במ׳ יח יז) • כלל בכור שור הנולד שור • | B | |
| בכור כשב הנולד כשב • בכור עז הנולד מין עז • יכול | E/D/C | |
| אף על פי שיש בו מקצת סימנין דומה לאמו • ת״ל | F | |
| אך • פדה תפדה • מיד תפדה בכל שהוא • ר׳ יוסי בר׳ | C/B/A | 3 |
| יהודה אומ׳ אין פחות משקל • בשה • שומע אני שה חי | B/A | 4 |
| או שה שחוט • הרי אתה דן • נאמ׳ כאן שה ונאמן להלן | D/C | |
| שה (שמ׳ יב ג) מה שה האמ׳ להלן שה חי ולא שה | | |
| שחוט אף שה האמ׳ כאן שה חי ולא שה שחוט • תפדה • | A | 5 |
| לא בעגל ולא בחיה ולא בשחוטה ולא בטריפה ולא | B | |
| בכלאים ולא בכוי • יכול אם פדאו במעי עמו יהא פדוי • | A | 6 |
| ת״ל ואם לא תפדה וערפתו את שבא לכלל עריפה בא | B | |
| לכלל פדייה את שלא בא לכלל עריפה לא בא לכלל פדייה • | | |

7.    A.    One might think that if one redeemed it after [its] death, then it is [suitably] redeemed.

    B.    Scripture states, [however,] "'If you do not redeem it, you must break its neck'" (Exod. 13:13), [meaning,] that which can be redeemed is that which can have its neck broken. That which cannot be redeemed is that which cannot have its neck broken.

8.    A.    "'... you must break its neck'" (Exod. 13:13):[437]

    B.    It says in Scripture here "break" (Hebrew: עריפה) and it says ahead "break" (Deut. 21:4).

    C.    Just as "break" stated ahead [means that you] break [its neck by] grabbing it [and using] a hatchet from the back side [of the neck] and then burying it, and it is prohibited to benefit [from it[438]], likewise "break" stated here [means that you] break [its neck by] grabbing it [and using] a hatchet from the back side [of the neck] and then burying it, and it is prohibited to benefit [from it].

9.    A.    "'And you must redeem every first-born male among your children'" (Exod. 13:13):

    B.    Why do I need [Scripture to state this]? For has it not already been said in Scripture "'... I redeem every first-born among my sons'" (Exod. 13:15)?

[44]    C.    [It needs to state this to prove that if] one must redeem both himself and his son,[439] then he comes before his son.[440]

    D.    [But] R. Judah says, "His son comes before him."

10.    A.    "'And you must redeem every first-born male among your children'" (Exod. 13:13):[441]

    B.    This teaches that a son is required to redeem himself [if his father did not redeem him].

    C.    [Scripture states,] "'... I redeem every first-born among my sons'" (Exod. 13:15).

    D.    Even after death.

## XIX:IV

1.    A.    "'And when your son asks you, (in time to come, saying, "What does this mean?" you shall say to him, "It was with a mighty hand that the Lord brought us out from Egypt, the house of bondage)"'" (Exod. 13:14):

    B.    From his question and his speech you know [the extent] of his knowledge.

2.    A.    "'... you shall say to him'" (Exod. 13:14):

    B.    For you should not be embarrassed to say to him (that we were slaves in Egypt). Rather, begin with the matter about which you are embarrassed!

3.    A.    "'When Pharaoh stubbornly refused to let us go, (the Lord slew every first-born in the Land of Egypt. Therefore I sacrifice to the Lord every first male issue of the womb, but I redeem every first-born among my sons)'" (Exod. 13:15):

    B.    How does one know from Scripture that as the Egyptians became afraid, Pharaoh became stubborn?

    C.    Scripture states, "'But I will harden Pharaoh's heart'" (Exod. 7:3).

---

[437] Compare 8.A–C with *Mekhilta de-Rabbi Ishmael*, Pisḥa (H/R, 71:15–72:1; Laut., vol. 1, 162:68–163:73; Neus., XVIII:I:14.A–15.C); y. Qiddushin 63a (Neus., 2:8:I.Z–EE); and b. Bekhorot 10b (Neus., XXXI.A:Tractate Bekhorot:1:4:II.2.CC).

[438] I.e., to benefit from the corpse of the animal.

[439] I.e., a man who is a first-born son has a first-born son, while simultaneously learning that he, himself, was never redeemed by his father.

[440] The text reads Exod. 13:13 (וכל בכור אדם בבניך תפדה) literally: "You shall redeem any first-born person [along] with your sons," i.e., even the unredeemed, first-born father. Exod. 13:15 only stipulates that one redeems "every first-born *among*" one's sons. How this proves that the unredeemed father must first redeem himself is, nonetheless, unclear. See parallels at m. Bekhorot 8:6 and b. Kiddushin 29a (XIX.A:Qiddushin:1:7:I.5.A–C).

[441] Compare 10.A–D with *Mekhilta de-Rabbi Ishmael*, Pisḥa (H/R, 72:9–73:7; Laut., vol. 1, 164:89–166:113; Neus., XVIII:I:18.A–19.T).

| | | |
|---|---|---|
| יכול פדאו לאחר מיתה יהא פדוי • ת״ל ואם לא | B/A | 7 |
| תפדה וערפתו את שבא לכלל פדייה בא לכלל עריפה | | |
| ואת שלא בא לכלל פדייה לא בא לכלל עריפה • | | |
| וערפתו • נאמ' כאן עריפה ונאמ' להלן עריפה (דב' כא | B/A | 8 |
| ד) • מה עריפה האמ' להלן עריפה בקמיצה בקופין | C | |
| מאחריו וקוברו ואסור בהנאה אף עריפה האמ' כאן | | |
| עריפה [ב]קמ[י]צה ובק[ו]פיץ מאחריו וקוברו] ואסור | | |
| בהנאה. • וכל בכור אדם בבניך ת[פדה • מה אני צריך] | B/A | 9 |
| והלא כבר נאמ' וכול בכור בני אפדה (שמ' יג טו) • הוא | C | |
| ל[פדות ובנו לפדות] הוא קודם את בנו • ר' יהודה אומ' | D | |
| בנו קודמו • [וכל בכור אדם בבניך] תפדה • מלמד שהבן | B/A | 10 |
| חייב לפדות את עצמו • וכל בכ[ור] בני אפדה • אפילו | D/C | |
| לאחר מיתה. סל' פסו' • | | |
| | | |
| | XIX:IV | |
| | | |
| והיה כי ישאלך בנך • משאלתו ומדיבורו אתה יודע | B/A | 1 |
| מדעתו • ואמרת אליו • שלא תתבייש מלומר לו אלא | B/A | 2 |
| מילתא די את בהית בה הקדם אמרה. סל' פסו' • | | |
| | | |
| ויהי כי הקשה פרעה לשלחנו • מנין אתה אומ' כשמצ' | B/A | 3 |
| מתרככין פרעה מתקשה • ת״ל ואני אקשה את לב פרעה | C | |

D. [And how does one know from Scripture] that as Pharaoh became afraid, the Egyptians became stubborn?

E. Scripture states, "'And I will stiffen the hearts of the Egyptians'" (Exod. 14:17).

F. [And how does one know from Scripture] that as both of them became afraid, the Lord caused [them both] to become stubborn?

G. Scripture states, "'... For I have hardened his heart (and the hearts of his courtiers)'" (Exod. 10:1).

4.  A. "'Therefore I sacrifice to the Lord every first male issue of the womb ...'" (Exod. 13:15):[442]

B. Because [it states] this, why does Scripture [then] state, "'... but I redeem every first-born among my sons'" (Exod. 13:15)?

C. [Because] how can you state from Scripture that if [one man] married five virgins, and they gave birth to five sons, then he is obligated to redeem all of them?

D. Scripture states, "'... but I redeem every first-born among my sons'" (Exod. 13:15).

5.  A. "'And so it shall be as a sign upon your hand (and as a symbol on your forehead that with a mighty hand the Lord freed us from Egypt)'" (Exod. 13:16):

B. Based on this they said: Phylacteries of the head do not impair [the suitability] of [phylacteries] of the hand, and [phylacteries] of the hand do not impair [the suitability] of [phylacteries] of the head. And if one has only one [of the two], he should don [it alone].[443]

6.  A. And how does one know from Scripture that when donning the phylacteries, one should don only the [phylactery] of the hand first?[444]

B. Scripture states, "'And so it shall be as a sign upon your hand'" (Exod. 13:16).

C. And how does one know from Scripture that when taking them off, one should take off only the [phylactery] of the head first?

D. Scripture states, "'... and as a symbol on your forehead'" (Exod. 13:16).

E. As long as [the phylacteries] are between your eyes, both shall be there.

7.  A. "'... that with a mighty hand the Lord freed us from Egypt'" (Exod. 13:16):

B. This teaches that the phylacteries are mentioned [in Scripture] as a remembrance of the Egyptian Exodus.

[442] Compare 4.A–D with *Mekhilta de-Rabbi Ishmael,* Pisha (H/R, 72:8–9; Laut., vol. 1, 164:85–88; Neus., XVIII:I:17.A–C); and b. Kiddushin 29b (XIX.A:Qiddushin:1:7:I.7.A–E).

[443] Compare with m. Menahot 4:1 and t. Menahot 6:12.

[444] Compare 6.A–E with *Mekhilta de-Rabbi Ishmael,* Pisha (H/R, 67:11–14; Laut., vol. 1, 152:140–44; Neus., XVII:I:22.A–E); *Sifre Deut.,* Piska 35 (Hammer, p. 65; Neus., XXXV:IV:1.A–E); and b. Menahot 36a (Neus., XXIX.A:Tractate Menahot:3:7:III.27.A–E).

| | |
|---|---|
| E/D | (שם ז ג) • וכשפרעה מתרכך מצ' מתקשין • ת"ל |
| F | ואני הנני מחזק את לב מצ' (שם יד יז) • וכשאלו |
| G | ואלו מתרככין המקום מחזק • ת"ל כי אני הכבדתי את |
| B/A 4 | לבו וגומ' (שם י א) • על כן אני זובח לייי וגו' • מפני כך |
| C | וכל בכור בני אפדה מה ת"ל • מנין אתה אומ' שאם |
| | נשא חמש נשים בתולות וילדו לו חמשה בנים שחייב |
| D | לפדות את כולן • ת"ל וכל בכור בני אפדה. סל' פסו' • |
| | |
| B/A 5 | והיה לאות על ידכה • מיכן אמרו תפילין של ראש |
| | אין מעכבות של יד ושל יד אין מעכבות של ראש ואם |
| A 6 | אין לו אלא אחת יתן • ומנין בנותן את התפילין לא |
| B | יהא נותן אלא של יד ‹תחלה› • ת"ל והיה לאות על |
| C | ידכה • ומנין כשחולץ אין חולץ אלא של ראש ‹תחלה› |
| E/D | ת"ל ולטוטפות בין עיניך • כל זמן שהן בין עיניך יהיו |
| B/A 7 | שתים • כי בחוזק יד הוציאנו ייי ממצר' • מלמד שנאמרו |
| | תפילין זכר ליציאת מצ' סליק פרש' • |

# Tractate Beshallaḥ

*Chapter Twenty*

(Textual Source: Midrash ha-Gadol)

XX:I

1.    A.    "Now when Pharaoh let (the people) go" (Exod. 13:17):

[45]    B.    R. Nehorai[1] says, "Pharoah had clemency [from God, in that] if he did not pursue them,[2] God would have regarded him as if he had sent them away [without being forced by God]. However, because he did pursue them, God compounded upon him the first [punishment] to the last.

    C.    "In accordance with what is said in Scripture, '... to the utter ruin of moist and dry alike' (Deut. 29:18)."

2.    A.    "... (God did not lead them) by way of the land of the Philistines, although it was nearer" (Exod. 13:17):

    B.    Near was the day of the giving of the Torah, on which Israel would stand before Mount Sinai.

3.    A.    Another interpretation:

    B.    "... although it was nearer" (Exod. 13:17):

    C.    Near was [the time for] the divine punishment of Egypt and of Pharaoh to come upon them.

4.    A.    "... for God said, 'The people may have a change of heart (when they see war, and return to Egypt)'" (Exod. 13:17):[3]

    B.    The Holy One, blessed be He, said, "If I bring them now into [the Land of Israel] by the straight route, they will [immediately begin] seizing the fields and vineyards, and they will neglect the Torah. Rather, I will make them go around in the wilderness for 40 years, and they will eat the manna and drink the water of the well, and the Torah will [have time to] take root in their bodies."

    C.    Based on this would R. Shimon ben Yoḥai say, "The Torah was given to be expounded only by those who eat manna. Like them[4] are those who eat [the priestly] heave offering."[5]

---

[1] This name appears here in the text spelled unusually as נוהראי. I have translated it in accordance with its more usual spelling—נהוראי.

[2] I.e., the Israelites.

[3] Compare 4.A–C with *Mekhilta de-Rabbi Ishmael*, Beshallaḥ (H/R, 76:5–9; Laut., vol. 1, 171:27–34; Neus., XIX:I:9.A–E).

[4] The word here in the text is שניים, which makes little or no contextual sense. I have chosen to translate here, instead, the word that appears in the parallel to this unit of tradition in the *Mekhilta de-Rabbi Ishmael*—ושוין.

# מסכתא דבשלח

| | | |
|---|---|---|
| ויהי בשלח פרעה ◆ ר' נהוראי אומר רתיון היתה | B/A | 1 |
| לפרעה שאילו לא רדף אחריהם העלה עליו המקום | | |
| כאילו שלחם אלא מתוך שרדף אחריהם גלגל עליו | | |
| המקום ראשונות ואחרונות ◆ כענין שנאמר למען ספות | C | |
| הרוה את הצמאה (דב' כט יח). ◆ דרך ארץ פלשתים כי | A | 2 |
| קרוב הוא ◆ קרוב יום מתן תורה שיעמדו בו ישראל | B | |
| לפני הר סיני. ◆ ד"א ◆ כי קרוב הוא ◆ קרובה היא פורענותן | C/B/A | 3 |
| של מצרים ושל פרעה לבא עליהן. ◆ כי אמר אלקים פן | A | 4 |
| ינחם העם ◆ אמר הקב"ה אם אני מכניסן דרך פשוטה | B | |
| עכשיו הן מחזיקין בשדות ובכרמים ובטילין מן | | |
| התורה אלא הריני מקיפן למדבר ארבעים שנה | | |
| ויאכלו את המן וישתו מי באר והתורה מתישבת | | |
| בגופן. ◆ מכאן היה ר' שמעון בן יוחאי אומר לא ניתנה | C | |
| תורה לדרוש אלא לאוכלי מן שנים להן אוכלי תרומה. ◆ | | |

---

[5] That is, those who study Torah should have their sustenance provided for them, just as the temple Priests were provided with the heave offering as a source of food.

5.    A.    Another interpretation:[6]

    B.    When the Canaanites heard that Israel was entering the land, they immediately burned the crops, cut down the trees, tore down the buildings, and stopped up the water sources.

    C.    The Holy One, blessed be He, said, "I did not promise their forefathers that I would bring them into a ruined land! Rather, this is what they were promised:

    D.    "'(When the Lord your God brings you into the land that He swore to your fathers, Abraham, Isaac, and Jacob, to assign to you—great and flourishing cities that you did not build,) houses full of all good things that you did not fill' (Deut. 6:11).

    E.    "Behold, I will detain them in the wilderness until the Canaanites repair that which they have ruined!"

6.    A.    "... (for God said, 'The people may have a change of heart) when they see war, (and return to Egypt')" (Exod. 13:17):[7]

    B.    This is the Amalekite war.

    C.    As it says in Scripture, "And the Amalekites (and the Canaanites) who dwelt in that hill country came down (and dealt them a shattering blow at Hormah)" (Num. 14:45).

7.    A.    Another interpretation:[8]

    B.    This is the war of the Ephraimites, who left before the end [of the period of Egyptian slavery].

    C.    "... (and return to Egypt)" (Exod. 13:17):

    D.    [The Israelites] might return [to Egypt], in order not to see the bones of their Ephraimite brothers.[9]

## XX:II

1.    A.    "So God led the people (roundabout, by way of the wilderness at the Sea of Reeds)" (Exod. 13:18):

    B.    He placed them in dire straits [in the wilderness], so that they were unable to return [to Egypt] either forward or backward.

2.    A.    "(The Israelites went up) armed[10] (out of the Land of Egypt)" (Exod. 13:18):[11]

    B.    [The word] "ḥamushim" only means "armed," as it says in Scripture, "The Reubenites, the Gadites, and the half-tribe of Manasseh went across armed before their brothers" (Josh. 4:12).[12]

    C.    This teaches that they went up equipped with five[13] types of armament: bow, lance, shield, spear, and sword.

3.    A.    Another interpretation:

    B.    "... armed"[14] (Exod. 14:18):

---

[6] Compare 5.A–E with *Mekhilta de-Rabbi Ishmael*, Beshallaḥ (H/R, 76:9–14; Laut., vol. 1, 171:34–172:42; Neus., XIX:I:10.A–E).

[7] Compare 6.A–C with *Mekhilta de-Rabbi Ishmael*, Beshallaḥ (H/R, 76:14–15; Laut., vol. 1, 172:43–45; Neus., XIX:I:11.A–C).

[8] Compare 7.A–D with *Mekhilta de-Rabbi Ishmael*, Beshallaḥ (H/R, 76:16–77:2; Laut., vol. 1, 172:45–173:53; Neus., XIX:I:12.A–13.B).

[9] According to Rabbinic tradition, the tribe of Ephraim miscalculated the termination of the period of Egyptian slavery, and left the country 30 years before the date designated by God for redemption of the Israelites. On their way to Canaan, the Philistines waged war against the Ephraimites, and killed 300,000 of them. The bones of the dead were piled and strewn along the road. Thus, God did not lead the Israelites to the Land of Israel by the most direct route, lest they see these bones, become frightened, and return to Egypt.

[10] Hebrew: ḥamushim—חמושים. The original meaning of this word is uncertain.

[11] Compare 2.A–C with *Mekhilta de-Rabbi Ishmael*, Beshallaḥ (H/R, 77:14–16; Laut., vol. 1, 174:70–175:74; Neus., XIX:I:17.A–18.B); and y. *Shabbat* 8b (Neus., 6:3:I.A–E).

[12] The text here actually lists the Gadites before the Reubenites in this verse, in contrast to the biblical text.

| | | |
|---|---|---|
| ד״א ◆ כיון ששמעו כנעניים שישראל נכנסין | B/A | 5 |
| לארץ עמדו ושרפו את הזרעים וקצצו את הנטיעות | | |
| וסתרו הבניינות וסיתמו המעיינות ◆ אמר הקב״ה אני | C | |
| הבטחתים לאבותיהם שאני מכניסן לארץ חריבה | | |
| אלא כך הן מובטחים ◆ ובתים מלאים כל טוב אשר לא | D | |
| מלאת (דב׳ ו יא) ◆ הריני מעכבן במדבר עד שיעמדו | E | |
| כנעניים ויתקנו מה שקלקלו. ◆ בראתם מלחמה ◆ זו | B/A | 6 |
| מלחמת העמלקי ◆ שנא׳ וירד העמלקי הישב בהר | C | |
| ההוא (במ׳ יד מה) ◆ ד״א ◆ זו מלחמת בני אפרים שיצאו | B/A | 7 |
| קודם לקץ. ◆ ושבו מצרימה ◆ שלא יראו עצמות אחיהם | D/C | |
| בני אפרים ויחזרו. ◆ | | |

XX:II

| | | |
|---|---|---|
| ויסב אלקים את העם ◆ הניחם במספק ולא היו | B/A | 1 |
| יכולין לחזור לא לפניהם ולא לאחריהם. ◆ וחמושים ◆ | A | 2 |
| אין חמושים אלא מזויינין שנא׳ ויעברו בני גד ובני | B | |
| ראובן וחצי שבט מנשה חמושים עברו לפני אחיהם | | |
| (יהו׳ ד יב) ◆ מלמד שעלו מטוקסין בחמשה מיני זיין | C | |
| קשת ואלה ותריס ורומח וחרב. ◆ ד״א ◆ וחמושים ◆ | B/A | 3 |

---

[13] Hebrew: ḥamisha—חמשה.
[14] See note 10.

C. There were some of them who went up with four generations [of family] and there were some of them who went up with five[15] generations.

4. A. Another interpretation:[16]

B. "... went up armed"[17] (Exod. 14:18):

C. This teaches that converts and slaves [also] went up with them, five[18] [times as many] as they.

5. A. Another interpretation:[19]

B. "... went up armed"[20] (Exod. 14:18):

C. In that one out of five[21] did not go up with them. And there are those who say one out of fifty. And there are those who say one out of five hundred.

D. R. Nehorai[22] says, "By the temple service [I promise]—not even one out of five thousand! And thus Scripture states, 'I let you grow like the plants of the field (and you continued to grow)' (Ezek. 16:7)."

E. And when did [those who did not go up] die? During the [three] days of [the plague of] darkness. While Egypt was living in darkness, Israel was burying its dead. And they gave thanks and praised God, because their enemies did not see [this] and rejoice in their loss.

## XX:III

1. A. "And Moses took with him the bones of Joseph (who had exacted an oath from the Children of Israel, saying, 'God will be sure to take notice of you: then you shall carry up my bones from here with you)'" (Exod. 13:19):[23]

B. Come and see how cherished the commandments were to Moses, in that when all of Israel was busy with the looting of Egypt, Moses was busy [fulfilling] a commandment.

[46]

C. And concerning him Scripture states, "He whose heart is wise accepts commands" (Prov. 10:8).

D. And how[24] would Moses, our master, have known where Joseph was buried?

E. They said: Seraḥ the daughter of Asher survived from that[25] generation. Moses went to her, and said to her, "Where is Joseph buried?" She said to him, "The Egyptians made a casket of metal for him, and they sunk it in the Nile river, so that its waters would be blessed."

Moses went and stood on the bank of the Nile and said, "Joseph, Joseph! The hour has arrived that the Holy One, blessed be He, swore to redeem Israel, and [the time to fulfill] the oath that you adjured on Israel [to remove and take your bones to the Land of Israel[26]] has arrived. Now, God's presence and Israel are detained because of you! If you would reveal yourself, it would be good, but if not, then we are released from your oath!"

Immediately, Joseph's casket surfaced.

---

[15] Hebrew: ḥamisha—חמשה.

[16] Compare 4.A–C with XVI:II:1.A–B above.

[17] Ibid.

[18] See note 13.

[19] Compare 5.A–E with Mekhilta de-Rabbi Ishmael, Beshallaḥ (H/R, 77:16–78:5; Laut., vol. 1, 175:74–85; Neus., XIX:I:19.A–K).

[20] See note 10.

[21] See note 13.

[22] See note 1.

[23] Compare 1.A–E with Mekhilta de-Rabbi Ishmael, Beshallaḥ (H/R, 78:6–16; Laut., vol. 1, 176:86–177:102; Neus., XIX:I:20.A–K); and b. Sotah 13a (Neus., XVII.Tractate Sotah:1:9:LXXV.A–X).

[24] The text here uses the interrogative technical term "ומנין," which typically is employed to ask "how does one know from Scripture?" However, in this instance the term is not used in this manner.

[25] I.e., Joseph's.

| | |
|---|---|
| C | יש מהן שעלה בארבעה דורות ויש מהן שעלה בחמשה |
| C/B/A    4 | דורות. ◆ ד״א ◆ וחמושים עלו ◆ מלמד שעלו עמהם גרים |
| C/B/A    5 | ועבדים חמשה כיוצא בהם. ◆ ד״א ◆ וחמושים עלו ◆ שלא |
| | עלו עמהם אחד מחמשה ויש אומרים אחד מחמשים |
| | ויש אומרים אחד מחמש מאות. ◆ ר׳ נהוראי אומר |
| D | העבודה ולא אחד מחמשת אלפים וכן הוא אומר |
| | רבבה כצמח השדה נתתיך (יחז׳ טז ז) ◆ ואימתי מתו |
| E | בימי האפילה שהיו מצרים שרויין בחשך וישראל |
| | מקברין מיתיהן והודו ושיבחו לשם שלא ראו |
| | שונאיהן ושמחו בפורענותן. ◆ |

XX:III

| | |
|---|---|
| B/A    1 | ויקח משה את עצמות יוסף עמו ◆ בוא וראה כמה |
| | חביבות מצות על משה רבינו שכל ישראל עסיקין |
| | בבזה שלמצרים ומשה עסוק במצוה ◆ ועליו הוא אומר |
| C | חכם לב יקח מצות (מש׳ י ח) ◆ ומנין היה יודע משה |
| D | רבינו היכן יוסף קבור ◆ אמרו שרח בת אשר נשתיירה |
| E | מאותו הדור הלך משה אצלה ואמר לה היכן יוסף קבור |
| | אמרה לו ארון שלמתכת עשו לו מצריים וקבעוהו בנילוס |
| | נהר כדי שיתברכו מימיו. הלך משה ועמד על שפת |
| | נילוס אמר יוסף יוסף הגיעה שעה שנשבע הקב״ה |
| | לישראל לגאלן והגיעה שבועה שהשבעת את ישראל עכשו |
| | שכינה וישראל מעוכבין לך אם אתה מגלה עצמך הרי מוטב |
| | ואם לאו נקים אנחנו משבועתך מיד צף ארונו שליוסף. ◆ |

[26] See Gen. 50:25.

2.    A.    R. Nathan says, "Joseph was buried in a labyrinth of [buried] kings. Moses went and stood in the labyrinth of kings, and said, 'Joseph, Joseph!' Immediately, Joseph's casket shook, and Moses went and took it and brought it with him.[27]

      B.    "Thus it is stated in Scripture, 'And Moses took with him the bones of Joseph' (Exod. 14:19)."

3.    A.    For all the 40 years that Israel was walking in the wilderness, the ark of God's presence and the casket of Joseph went side by side. And those passing by would say, "What's the purpose for these two boxes?" And they would say to them, "One is for God's presence, and one is for a dead person." They would say [in response], "Is it possible[28] for a dead person to walk with God's presence!" [Israel would respond,] "This [dead person is worthy of this because] he upheld that which was written by the other:[29]

      B.    "On the tablets of the Ten Commandments it is written, 'I am the Lord your God!' (Exod. 20:2), and concerning Joseph it is written in Scripture, '[And Joseph said] … am I a substitute for God?' (Gen. 50:19).

      C.    "On [the tablets also] is it written, 'You shall have no (other gods besides Me)!' (Exod. 20:2), and concerning Joseph it is written in Scripture, 'For I am a God-fearing man' (Gen. 42:18).

      D.    "On [the tablets also] is it written, 'You shall not take (the name of the Lord your God in vain)' (Exod. 20:7), and concerning Joseph it is written in Scripture, '… by Pharaoh, you shall not depart from this place!' (Gen. 42:15).

      E.    "On [the tablets also] is it written, 'Remember the Sabbath day' (Exod. 20:8), and concerning Joseph it is written in Scripture, '(When Joseph saw Benjamin with them, he said to his house steward, "Take the men into the house) and slaughter and prepare (an animal)"' (Gen. 43:16). And the word 'prepare' refers only to the needs of *Shabbat*!

      F.    "On [the tablets also] is it written, 'Honor your father' (Exod. 20:12), and concerning Joseph it is written in Scripture, 'Joseph sustained his father' (Gen. 47:12).

      G.    "On [the tablets also] is it written, 'You shall not murder' (Exod. 20:13), and concerning Joseph it is written in Scripture, 'How then could I do this most wicked thing, and sin before God?' (Gen. 39:9). He said to her,[30] 'It's not enough [for you] that I would be counted among the adulterers, but also among the murderers!'[31]

      H.    "On [the tablets also] is it written, 'You shall not commit adultery' (Exod. 20:13), and concerning Joseph it is written in Scripture, '… he did not yield to her request to lie beside her, to be with her' (Gen. 39:10).

      I.    "On [the tablets also] is it written, 'You shall not steal' (Exod. 20:13), and concerning Joseph it is written in Scripture, 'Joseph gathered in all the money (that was to be found in the Land of Egypt and in the Land of Canaan, as payment for the rations that were being procured), and Joseph brought the money into Pharaoh's palace' (Gen. 47:14).

      J.    "On [the tablets also] is it written, 'You shall not bear (false witness against your neighbor)' (Exod. 20:13), and concerning Joseph it is written in Scripture, 'And Joseph brought bad reports of them (to their father)' (Gen. 37:2). 'And Joseph *produced* (bad reports)' is not written, but rather, 'And [Joseph] *brought*.'

---

[27] Compare 2.A–B with *Mekhilta de-Rabbi Ishmael,* Beshallah (H/R, 78:16–17; Laut., vol. 1, 177:102–9; Neus., XIX:I:20.K–P).

[28] I.e., proper.

[29] I.e., written by God. Compare 3.A–K with *Mekhilta de-Rabbi Ishmael,* Beshallah (H/R, 79:9–80:6; Laut., vol. 1, 178:122–181:151; Neus., XIX:I:22.A–T); b. Sotah 13a; and y. Berakhot 4c (Neus., 2:2:III.I–M).

[30] I.e., to Potiphar.

[31] Contrary to the biblical narrative, the text here assumes that Potiphar's wife not only asked Joseph to lie with her, but also asked him to murder her husband.

ר' נתן אומר יוסף בקברניטן שלמלכים היה קבור הלך 2 A
משה ועמד על קברניטן שלמלכים ואמר יוסף מיד
נזדעזע ארונו שלמשה הלך משה ונטלו והביאו עמו ◆
לכך נאמר ויקח משה את עצמו יוסף עמו. ◆ כל אותן B A 3
ארבעים שנה שהיו ישראל מהלכין במדבר היה ארון
השכינה וארונו שליוסף מהלכין זה בזה זה והיו
העוברים והשבים אומרין מה טיבן שלשני ארונות
הללו אמרו להן אחד שלשכינה ואחד שלמת. וכי
אפשר למת להלך עם השכינה אמרו קיים זה מה
שכת' בזה. ◆ בלוחות כת' אנכי ה' אלקיך (שמ' כ ב) B
וביוסף כת' כי התחת אלקים אני (בר' נ יט). ◆ בזה כת' C
לא יהיה לך (שמ' כ ב) וביוסף כת' את האלקים אני
ירא (בר' מב יח). ◆ בזה כת' לא תשא (שמ' כ ז) ורייחף D
כת' חי פרעה אם תצאו מזה (בר' מב טו). ◆ בזה כת' E
זכור את יום השבת (שמ' כ ח) וביוסף כת' וטבוח טבח
והכן (בר' מג טז) ואין והכן אלא לצורך השבת. ◆ בזה F
כת' כבד את אביך (שמ' כ יא) וביוסף כת' ויכלכל יוסף
את אביו (בר' מז יב). ◆ בזה כת' לא תרצח (כ יג) וביוסף G
כת' ואיך אעשה הרעה הגדולה הזאת וחטאת
לאלקים (בר' לט ט) אמר לה לא די שאמנה עם
המנאפים אלא אף עם הרצחנין. ◆ בזה כת' לא תנאף H
(שמ' כ יג) וביוסף כת' ולא שמע אליה לשכב אצלה
להיות עמה (בר' לט י). ◆ בזה כת' לא תגנוב (שמ' כ יג) I
וביוסף כת' וילקט יוסף את כל הכסף [וגו'] ויבא
יוסף את הכסף ביתה פרעה (בר' מז יד). ◆ בזה כת' J
לא תענה (שמ' כ יג) וביוסף כת' ויבא יוסף את דבתם
רעה (בר' לז ב). ◆ ויוציא יוסף אין כת' אלא ויבא. ◆

K. "On [the tablets also] is it written, 'You shall not covet' (Exod. 20:14), and concerning Joseph it is written in Scripture, 'But he refused, and said to his master's wife' (Gen. 39:8)."

4. A. "(And Moses took with him the bones of Joseph,) who had exacted an oath from the Children of Israel" (Exod. 13:19):[32]

B. R. Nathan says, "Why did he impose an oath on his brothers, but not impose an oath upon his sons?

C. "He said, 'If I impose an oath on my sons, the Egyptians will not allow them to bring me up.[33] They[34] will say, "Our father brought up his father," but they will respond to them, "Your father was a king."'

D. "Therefore, he did not impose an oath on his sons."

5. A. "... who had exacted an oath" (Exod. 13:19):

B. He imposed an oath on them that they would impose an oath upon their children, and their children [would impose an oath] on their children.[35]

6. A. "... (who had exacted an oath saying), 'God will be sure to take notice of you'" (Exod. 13:19):[36]

B. He took notice of you in Egypt, [and] He will take notice of you at the sea. He took notice of you at the sea, [and] He will take notice of you in the wilderness. He took notice of you in the wilderness, [and] He will take notice of you at the rivers of Arnon. He took notice of you in this world, [and] He will take notice of you in the world to come.[37]

7. A. "'(God will be sure to take notice of you:) then you shall carry up my bones (from here with you)'" (Exod. 13:19):

B. He said to them, "When I was king I brought my father up (to be buried) when he was [still a] complete [corpse]. But you should bring me up (whenever possible), even (if only my) bones! And when you bring me up, bury me in any place that you desire! It is acceptable to me that only the three Patriarchs and three Matriarchs enter[38] the grave of the forefathers.

[47] C. "As it says in Scripture, 'There were buried Abraham (and his wife Sarah; there were buried Isaac and his wife Rebekah; and there I buried Leah)' (Gen. 49:31). And Scripture says, '(My father made me swear, saying, "I am about to die. Be sure to bury me) in the grave which I made ready for myself (in the Land of Canaan)"' (Gen. 50:5)."

8. A. "'... then you shall carry up my bones (from here with you)'" (Exod. 13:19):

B. I might assume this means immediately.

C. Scripture states, [however,] "'... (then you shall carry up my bones from here) *with you*'" (Exod. 13:19).[39]

D. R. Shimon b. Eliezer says, "How does one know from Scripture that the bones of all the tribes [i.e., bones of the tribal progenitors] went up with him?

E. "Scripture states, '... then you shall carry up my bones (from here with you)'" (Exod. 13:19).[40]

---

[32] Compare 4.A–D with *Mekhilta de-Rabbi Ishmael,* Beshallaḥ (H/R, 80:6–13; Laut., vol. 1, 181:152–62; Neus., XIX:I:23.A–24.D).

[33] I.e., bring his bones to the Land of Israel for burial.

[34] I.e., Joseph's sons.

[35] The text understands the apparent doubling of the infinitive absolute in Exod. 14:19 (השבע השביע) to facilitate this interpretation.

[36] Compare 6.A–B with *Mekhilta de-Rabbi Ishmael,* Beshallaḥ (H/R, 80:13–16; Laut., vol. 1, 182:163–67; Neus., XIX:I:25.A–E).

[37] The text understands the apparent doubling of the infinitive absolute in Exod. 14:19 (פקד יפקד) to facilitate this interpretation.

| | | |
|---|---|---|
| בזה כת' לא תחמד (שמ' כ יד) וביוסף כת' וימאן ויאמר אל | K | |
| אשת אדוניו (בר' לט ח). ◆ כי השבע השביע את בני ישראל ◆ | A | 4 |
| ר' נתן אומר מפני מה השביע אחיו ולא השביע את בניו. ◆ | B | |
| אמר אם אני משביע את בני אין מצרים מניחין אותן | C | |
| להעלות אותי. הן אומ' אבינו העלה את אביו ואומרין | | |
| להן אביכם מלך היה ◆ לפיכך לא השביע בניו. ◆ השבע | A 5 | D |
| השביע ◆ השביען <שישביעו> לבניהם ובניהם לבניהם. ◆ | B | |
| פקד יפקד ◆ פקד במצ' יפקד על הים. פקד על הים | B/A | 6 |
| יפקד במדבר. פקד במדבר יפקד בנחלי ארנון. פקד | | |
| בעולם הזה יפקד בעולם הבא. ◆ והעליתם את עצמותי ◆ | A | 7 |
| אמר להם אני שאני מלך העליתי את אבא כשהוא | B | |
| שלם אבל אתם העלו אותי ואפילו עצמות <וכשאתם | | |
| מעלין אותי קברו אותי בכל מקום שתרצו מקובל אני | | |
| שאין נכנס לקבר אבות אלא שלשה אבות ושלש | | |
| אמהות ◆ שנא' שמה קברו את אברהם וגו' (בר' מט לא) | C | |
| ואומר בקברי אשר כריתי לי (בר' נ ה) כי הוא פוסק> ◆ | | |
| והעליתם את עצמותי ◆ שומע אני מיד ◆ ת"ל אתכם. ◆ ר' | D/C/B/A | 8 |
| שמעון בן אלעזר אומר מנין שכל עצמות שבטים | | |
| עלו עמו ◆ ת"ל והעליתם את עצמותי מזה אתכם. | F | |
| ◆ | | |

[38] I.e., be buried in.

[39] According to the parallel attestation of this tradition in the *Mekhilta de-Rabbi Ishmael,* Beshallaḥ (H/R, 80:16–17; Laut., vol. 1, 182:168–71; Neus., XIX:I:26:A–E), the biblical verse emphasizes that Joseph's bones should be brought up "with you," meaning whenever the Children of Israel are emancipated and go up to the Land of Israel, i.e., not immediately after his death.

[40] The basis for this interpretation is unclear.

9.    A.    One might think that if Moses had not attended to it, then Israel would not have attended to it.[41]

    B.    Scripture states, [however,] "The bones of Joseph, which the Israelites had brought up from Egypt, were buried at Shechem" (Josh. 24:32).

    C.    This teaches that they intended to bring him up, but when Israel saw that Moses was attending to it, they said, "His honor should be served by the eminent instead of the lowly!"

10.    A.    One might think that if Moses and Israel had not attended to it, then his sons would not have attended to it.

    B.    Scripture states, [however,] "(The bones of Joseph, which the Israelites had brought up from Egypt) ... had become an inheritance of Joseph's sons"(Josh. 24:32).

    C.    Rather, when his sons saw that Moses and [all of] Israel were attending to it, they said, "His honor should be served by the many rather than the few!"

### XX:IV

1.    A.    "They set out from Succoth, (and encamped at Etham, at the edge of the wilderness)" (Exod. 13:20):[42]

    B.    R. Akiva says, "Succoth only means clouds of glory.

    C.    "As it says in Scripture, '... because over every glory is a canopy' (Isa. 4:5).

    D.    "And likewise in the time to come, 'which shall serve as a pavilion[43] for shade from heat by day' (Isa. 4:6)."

2.    A.    Another opinion:

    B.    "They set out from Succoth, etc." (Exod. 13:20):

    C.    Israel marched on three journeys before they arrived at the (Reed) Sea.

### XX:V

1.    A.    "The Lord went before them in a pillar of cloud by day, (to guide them along the way, and in a pillar of fire by night, to give them light, that they might travel day and night)" (Exod. 13:21):[44]

    B.    This teaches that seven clouds of glory were with Israel:

    C.    "... in a pillar of cloud by day" (Exod. 13:21)—this is one.

    D.    "... when Your cloud rests over them" (Num. 14:14)—this is two.

    E.    "... and when You go before them in a pillar of cloud by day" (Num. 14:14)—this is three.

    F.    "When the cloud lingered (over the Tabernacle many days)" (Num. 9:19)—this is four.

    G.    "When the cloud lifted (from the Tabernacle)" (Exod. 40:36)—this is five.

    H.    "But if the cloud did not lift" (Exod. 40:37)—this is six.

    I.    "For over the Tabernacle a cloud of the Lord rested by day" (Exod. 40:38)—this is seven.

    J.    Four (clouds were with them) in (each of) the four directions, with one (also) above and one below. And one preceded them, preparing the way for them by raising the lowland and lowering the highland for them, (thus) making a level road for them.

---

[41] Compare 9.A–10.C with b. Sotah 13b (Neus., XVII.Tractate Sotah:1:9:LXXV:S–X).

[42] Compare 1.A–D with *Mekhilta de-Rabbi Ishmael,* Beshallaḥ (H/R, 80:18–21; Laut., vol. 1, 182:172–77; Neus., XIX:I:27:A–E).

[43] Hebrew: *sukkah*—הכס.

[44] Compare 1.A–L with *Mekhilta de-Rabbi Ishmael,* Beshallaḥ (H/R, 81:1–9; Laut., vol. 1, 183:178–92; Neus., XIX:I:28:A–L).

| | |
|---|---|
| יכול אלו לא היה משה מתעסק בו לא היו ישראל מתעסקין | A 9 |
| בו • ת״ל ואת עצמות יוסף אשר העלו בני ישראל | B |
| ממצרים קברו בשכם (יהו׳ כד לב) • מלמד שהיה בלבם | C |
| להעלותו אלא כיון שראו ישראל שהיה משה מתעסק | |
| בו אמרו הניחו לו כבודו בגדולים יתר מן הקטנים. | |
| • | |
| יכול אלו לא היה משה וישראל מתעסקין בו ולא היו | A 10 |
| בניו מתעסקין בו • ת״ל ויהיו לבני יוסף לנחלה • אלא | C/B |
| כיון שראו בניו שהיה משה וישראל מתעסקין בו | |
| אמרו הניחו לו כבודו במרובין יתר ממועטין. • | |

XX:IV

| | |
|---|---|
| ויסעו מסכות • ר׳ עקיבה אומ׳ אין סוכות אלא ענני | B/A 1 |
| כבוד • שנא׳ כי על כל כבוד חפה (ישע׳ ד ה) • וכן לעתיד | D/C |
| לבוא וסכה תהיה לצל יומם מחורב (שם ו). • ד״א • | A 2 |
| ויסעו מסכות וכו׳ • שלש מסעות נסעו ישראל עד שלא | C/B |
| הגיעו לים. • | |

XX:V

| | |
|---|---|
| וה׳ הולך לפניהם יומם בעמוד ענן • מלמד | B/A 1 |
| ששבעה ענני כבוד היו עם ישראל • יומם בעמוד ענן | C |
| הרי אחד. • ועננך עומד עליהם (במ׳ יד יד) הרי שנים. • | D |
| ובעמוד ענן אתה הולך לפניהם יומם (שם) הרי | E |
| שלש‹ה›. • ובהאריך הענן (במ׳ ט יט) הרי ארבע‹ה›. • | F |
| ובהעלות הענן (שמ׳ מ לו) הרי חמש‹ה›. • ואם לא | H/G |
| יעלה הענן (שם לז) הרי שש‹ה›. • כי ענן ה׳ על המשכן | I |
| יומם (שם לח) הרי שבעה. • ארבעה מארבע רוחות | J |
| ואחד מלמעלה ואחד מלמטה ואחד שמקדים לפניהם מתקן | |
| להם את הדרכים מגביה להם את השפל ומשפיל | |
| להם את הגבוה ועושה להם דרך סרט ומישור • | |

K. In accordance with what is said in Scripture, "Let every valley be raised, every hill and mount made low. Let the rugged ground become level and the ridges become a plain" (Isa. 40:4). And Scripture says, "Thus there shall be a highway for the other part of His people out of Assyria, such as there was for Israel when it left the Land of Egypt" (Isa. 11:16).

L. Behold, this [verse in Isaiah 40:4] came to teach [one thing], and consequently taught what would be in the future! "Let every valley be raised, every hill and mount be made low"—this is what it was like for them as they left the Land of Egypt!

2.  A. Another interpretation:

B. "The Lord went before them (in a pillar of cloud) by day" (Exod. 13:21):

C. R. Yosi ha-Galili says, "Were it not written in Scripture, it would be impossible to say it! It was like a father carrying a torch before his son or a ploughman carrying a torch before his servant!"

3.  A. "... by day to guide ... and by night" (Exod. 13:21):

B. [Scripture] equates their travel by days with their travel by nights.

C. Just as they were not wanting for light (during) their travels by days, likewise were they not wanting for light (during) their travels by nights.

D. Just as (during) their travels by night—"They shall not hunger or thirst, hot wind and sun shall not strike them" (Isa. 49:10), likewise (during) their travels by day—"They shall not hunger or thirst, hot wind and sun shall not strike them" (Isa. 49:10).

## XX:VI

1.  A. "The pillar of cloud by day and the pillar of fire by night did not depart (from before the people)" (Exod. 13:22):[45]

B. Scripture tells that when the pillar of cloud was there, the pillar of fire grew brighter, and when the pillar of fire was there, the pillar of cloud shined.

2.  A. Another interpretation:

B. "The pillar of cloud by day ... did not depart"(Exod. 13:22)—the light of the sun did not interfere with it.

C. "... and the pillar of fire by night" (Exod. 13:22)—the light of the moon did not interfere with it.

3.  A. Another interpretation:

B. "... did not depart" (Exod. 13:22)—even though they[46] aggrieved, and even though they angered, and even though they insulted.

4.  A. Another interpretation:

B. "... did not depart" (Exod. 13:22)—even though they moved back [their encampment] 12 miles.

5.  A. Another interpretation:

[48]  B. "... did not depart" (Exod. 13:22)—who really needed a pillar of cloud and who really needed a pillar of fire?

---

[45] Compare 1.A–B with *Mekhilta de-Rabbi Ishmael*, Beshallaḥ (H/R, 82:16–17; Laut., vol. 1, 187:234–35; Neus., XIX:I:31:A–B).
[46] I.e., the Israelites.

| | |
|---|---|
| K | כעניין שנא׳ כל גיא ינשא וכל הר וגבעה ישפלו |
| | והיה העקב למישור והרכסים לבקעה (ישע׳ מ ד) ואומ׳ |
| | והיתה מסלה לשאר אשר ישאר מאשור כאשר |
| | היתה לישראל ביום עלותו מארץ מצרים (ישע׳ |
| L | יא טז). ◆ הרי זה בא כמלמד ונמצא למד מה לעתיד |
| | לבוא כל גיא ינשא וכל הר וגבעה ישפלו כך היה להן |
| | בעלייתן מארץ מצרים. ◆ ד״א ◆ וה׳ הלך לפניהם יומם ◆ ר׳ |
| C/B/A   2 | |
| | יוסי הגלילי אומר אלמלא מקרא כתוב אי אפשר |
| | לאמרו כאב שנוטל פונס לפני בנו וכרב שנוטל פונס |
| | לפני עבדו. ◆ ללכת יומם ולילה ◆ מקיש נסיעתן בימים |
| B/A   3 | |
| C | לנסיעתן בלילות ◆ מה נסיעתן בימים לא היו מחוסרין |
| D | אורה אף נסיעתן בלילות לא היו מחוסרין אורה. ◆ מה |
| | נסיעתן בלילות לא ירעבו ולא יצמאו ולא יכם שרב |
| | ושמש (ישע׳ מט י) אף נסיעתן בימים לא ירעבו ולא |
| | יצמאו ולא יכם שרב ושמש. ◆ |

| | | |
|---|---|---|
| A | 1 | לא ימיש עמוד הענן יומם ועמוד האש לילה ◆ |
| B | | מגיד הכת׳ שכשעמוד הענן קיים היה עמוד האש |
| B/A | 2 | צומח כשעמוד האש קיים עמוד הענן זורח. ◆ ד״א ◆ לא |
| C | | ימיש עמוד הענן יומם אין אור חמה מבטלו ◆ ועמוד |
| B/A | 3 | האש לילה אין אור הלבנה מבטלו. ◆ ד״א ◆ לא ימיש |
| B/A | 4 | אע״פ ממרים ואע״פ מכעיסין ואע״פ מנאצין, ◆ ד״א ◆ לא |
| A | 5 | ימיש אע״פ שנרתעין לאחוריהם שנים עשר מיל. ◆ ד״א ◆ |
| B | | לא ימיש וכי מי נצרך לעמוד ענן ומי נצרך לעמוד אש ◆ |

C. Rather (the pillars were necessary) to make a division between the male and female impure from a flux, and the women who were menstrually impure, and the women who were impure from (recent) childbirth who were among them.

6.    A. R. Meir says, "Behold Scripture states, '... and he waited on them under the tree as they ate' (Gen. 18:8).

B. "Therefore, the Holy One, blessed be He, preceded them with seven clouds of glory."[47]

*Chapter Twenty-One*

(Textual Source: Midrash ha-Gadol)

XXI:I

1.    A. "(The Lord said to Moses, 'Tell the Israelites) to turn back and encamp before Pi-Hahiroth, (between Migdol and the sea, before Baal-zephon. You shall encamp facing it, by the sea)'" (Exod. 14:1–2):[48]

B. Moses said to them, "Retreat!"

C. When they sounded the horn to retreat, those among them who lacked faith began to tear their hair and rip their clothes.

D. Moses said to them, "From the mouth of the Holy (One, blessed be He,) was it said to me that you are free people!"

2.    A. "... between Migdol and the sea" (Exod. 14:2):[49]

B. There was the greatness of Egypt, and there was their glory, and to there Joseph gathered all the money.

C. In accordance with what is said in Scripture, "And Joseph brought the money into Pharaoh's palace" (Gen. 47:14).

3.    A. "... before Baal-zephon" (Exod. 14:2):[50]

B. Baal-zephon remained for them,[51] of all the [Egyptian idolatrous] gods,[52] in order to entice the hearts of the Egyptians.

C. And concerning it Scripture states, "He exalts nations, then destroys them" (Job 12:23).

4.    A. "'You shall encamp facing it, by the sea'" (Exod. 14:2):

B. Scripture tells that there were [Egyptian] troops in Migdol corresponding to all those [Israelites] leaving Egypt.

5.    A. Another interpretation:

B. "'You shall encamp facing it, by the sea'" (Exod. 14:2):

C. In order to entice the hearts of the Egyptians.

---

[47] In and of itself, this tradition is unclear. However, a more detailed parallel tradition to this is found at *Mekhilta de-Rabbi Ishmael,* Beshallaḥ (H/R, 81:9–19; Laut., vol. 1, 184:193–185:208; Neus., XIX:I:2:A–H). Emphasizing the theme that people are treated in accordance with how they treat others, that parallel tradition connects various types of hospitality provided by Abraham to the divine messengers in Genesis 18 with various types of protection and shelter provided by God to the Israelites in both Egypt and the wilderness. 6.A–B appears to be an extremely truncated or shorthand version of this tradition.

[48] Compare 1.A–D with *Mekhilta de-Rabbi Ishmael,* Beshallaḥ (H/R, 83:11–84:8; Laut., vol. 1, 188:20–190:36; Neus., XX:I:4:A–K). Also, see note 57 below.

[49] Compare 2.A–C with *Mekhilta de-Rabbi Ishmael,* Beshallaḥ (H/R, 84:8–10; Laut., vol. 1, 190:37–40; Neus., XX:I:5:A–C).

[50] Compare 3.A–C with *Mekhilta de-Rabbi Ishmael,* Beshallaḥ (H/R, 84:10–12; Laut., vol. 1, 190:41–43; Neus., XX:I:6:A–C).

[51] I.e., for the Egyptians.

[52] The word that appears here in the text makes no contextual sense. Thus, I translate the word that appears in the parallel to this tradition in the *Mekhilta de-Rabbi Ishmael* (הייראות).

| | | |
|---|---|---|
| אלא ליתן הפרש לזבים ולזבות לנדות ולייולדות שהיו | C | |
| ביניהן. ◆ ר' מאיר אומר הרי הוא אומ' והוא עומד | A | 6 |
| עליהם תחת העץ ויאכלו (בר' יח ח) ◆ לפיכך הקדים | B | |
| להם הקב"ה שבעה ענני כבוד. ◆ | | |

| | | |
|---|---|---|
| וישובו ויחנו לפני פי החירות ◆ אמר להן משה חזרו | B/A | 1 |
| לאחוריכם ◆ כיון שתקעו קרן לחזור התחילו מחוסרי | C | |
| אמנה שבהן מתלשין בשערן ומקרעין בכסותן ◆ אמר | D | |
| להם משה מפי הקודש נאמר לי שאתם בני חורין. ◆ בין | A | 2 |
| מגדול ובין הים ◆ שם היתה גדולתן שלמצרים ושם | B | |
| היתה תפארת שלהם ולשם כינס יוסף את כל הכסף ◆ | | |
| כענין שנאמר ויבא יוסף את הכסף ביתה פרעה (בר' | C | |
| מז יד). ◆ לפני בעל צפון. ◆ בעל צפון נשתייר להם | B/A | 3 |
| מחיראות כדי לפתות את ליבן שלמצרים ◆ ועליו הוא | C | |
| אומר משגיא לגוים ויאבדם (איוב יב כג). ◆ נכחו תחנו | A | 4 |
| על הים ◆ מגיד הכתוב שהיו במגדול אכלוסין כנגד כל | B | |
| יוצאי מצרים. ◆ ד"א ◆ נכחו תחנו על הים ◆ כדי לפתות | C/B/A | 5 |
| לבם שלמצרים. ◆ | | |

## XXI:II

1.    A.   "'(Pharaoh will say of the Israelites, "They are astray in the land,) the wilderness has closed in on them"'" (Exod. 14:3):

       B.   Pharaoh said, "Baal-zephon gathered evil beasts unto them, who would not let them cross."

       C.   And thus it was.

2.    A.   When Israel saw the closed sea and the enemy pursuing, they lifted up their eyes to the wilderness. The Holy One, blessed by He, gathered evil beasts unto them who would not let them cross.[53]

       B.   As it says in Scripture, "'... the wilderness has closed in[54] on them'" (Exod. 14:3).

       C.   "Closed in" only means "evil beast."

       D.   In accordance with what is said in Scripture, "My God sent His angel, who shut[55] the mouths of the lions" (Dan. 6:23).

## XXI:III[56]

1.    A.   "'(Then I will stiffen Pharaoh's heart and he will pursue them), that I may gain glory through Pharaoh (and all his host. And the Egyptians shall know that I am the Lord. And they did so)'" (Exod. 14:4):

       B.   When the Holy One, blessed be He, punishes the wicked, His name is glorified in the world.

       C.   And thus Scripture states, "'I will set a sign among them, and send from the survivors to the nations: to Tarshish, Pul, and Lud—that draw the bow—to Tubal, Javan, and the distant coasts, that have never heard My fame nor beheld My glory'" (Isa. 66:19).

       D.   What [else] does Scripture state?

       E.   "'... They shall declare My glory among these nations'" (Isa. 66:19).

2.    A.   Similar to this, you say: "'I will punish him with pestilence and with bloodshed, and I will pour torrential rain'" (Ezek. 38:22).

       B.   What [else] does Scripture state?

       C.   "'Thus will I manifest My greatness and My holiness, and make Myself known in the sight of many nations'" (Ezek. 38:23).

3.    A.   Similar to this, you say: "'O Lord, my strength and my stronghold, my refuge in a day of trouble'" (Jer. 16:19).

       B.   What [else] does Scripture state?

       C.   "'To You nations shall come from the ends of the earth and say: "Our fathers inherited utter delusions, things that are futile and worthless"'" (Jer. 16:19).

4.    A.   Similar to this, you say: "Thus said the Lord: 'Egypt's wealth and Nubia's gains and Sabaites, long of limb, shall pass over to you and be yours, pass over and follow you in fetters, bow low to you and reverently address you'" (Isa. 45:14).

       B.   What [else] does Scripture state?

---

[53] Compare 2.A–D with *Mekhilta de-Rabbi Ishmael*, Beshallaḥ (H/R, 85:3–7; Laut., vol. 1, 191:57–62; Neus., XX:I:12:A–E).

[54] Hebrew: סגר.

[55] Aramaic: סגר. Dan. 6:23 associates this verb with lions (= wild beasts).

[56] Compare XXI.III.1.A–5.H with *Mekhilta de-Rabbi Ishmael*, Beshallaḥ (H/R, 85:14–86:5; Laut., vol. 1, 192:75–193:89; Neus., XX:I:15:A–I).

| | | |
|---|---|---|
| B/A | 1 | סגר עליהם המדבר • אמר פרעה בעל צפון כינס |
| C | | עליהן חיות רעות ואין מניחות אותן לעבור • וכן היה. • |
| A | 2 | כיון שראו ישראל ים סוגר ושונא רודף נשאו עיניהם |
| | | למדבר כינס עליהן הקב"ה חיות רעות ולא היו |
| C/B | | מניחות אותן לעבור • שנא' סגר עליהם המדבר • אין |
| D | | סגירה אלא חיה רעה • כענין שנא' אלהי שלח מלאכיה |
| | | וסגר פום אריותא (דני' ו כג). • |

| | | | |
|---|---|---|---|
| B/A | 1 | | ואכבדה בפרעה • כשהקב"ה נפרע מן הרשעים שמו |
| C | | | מתגדל בעולם • וכן הוא אומר ושמתי בהם אות |
| | | | ושלחתי מהם פליטים אל הגוים תרשיש פול ולוד |
| | | | מושכי קשת תובל ויון האיים הרחוקים אשר לא |
| D | | | שמעו את שמעי ולא ראו את כבודי • מהוא אומר • |
| A | 2 | E | והגידו את כבודי בגוים (ישע' סו יט). • כיוצא בו אתה |
| B | | | אומר ונשפטתי אתו בדבר ובדם וגשם שוטף • מהוא |
| C | | | אום' • והתגדלתי והתקדשתי ונודעתי לעיני גוים רבים |
| A | 3 | | (יחז' לח כב - כג). • כיוצא בו אתה אומר ה' עזי ומעזי |
| C/B | | | ומנוסי ביום צרה • מהוא אומר • אליך גוים יבואו מאפסי |
| | | | ארץ ויאמרו אך שקר נחלו אבותינו הבל ואין בם מועיל |
| A | 4 | | (ירמ' טז יט). • כיוצא בו אתה אומר כה אמר ה' יגיע מצרים |
| | | | וסחר כוש וסבאים אנשי מדה עליך יעבורו ולך יהיו אחריך |
| B | | | ילכו ובזקים יעבורו ואליך ישתחוו אליך יתפללו • מהוא אומר • |

C. "'... Only among you is God, there is no other god at all!'" (Isa. 45:14).

5.    A.    Similar to this, you say: "'For liberators shall march up on Mount Zion to wreak judgment on Mount Esau'" (Obad. 1:21).

     B.    What [else] does Scripture state?

     C.    "'... and dominion shall be the Lord's'" (Obad. 1:21).

     D.    And Scripture says: "The Lord is king for ever and ever. The nations will perish from His land" (Ps. 10:16).

     E.    And Scripture says: "May sinners disappear from the earth, and the wicked be no more. Bless the Lord, O my soul. Hallelujah!" (Ps. 104:35).

     F.    And Scripture says: "The Lord watches over the stranger. He gives courage to the orphan and widow, but makes the path of the wicked tortuous" (Ps. 146:9).

     G.    What [else] does Scripture state?

     H.    "The Lord shall reign forever, your God, O Zion, for all generations. Hallelujah!" (Ps. 146:10).

## XXI:IV

1.    A.    "When the king of Egypt was told (that the people had fled, Pharaoh and his courtiers
[49]      had a change of heart about the people and said, 'What is this we have done, releasing Israel from our service?')" (Exod. 14:5):[57]

     B.    The Children of Israel traveled from Raamses to Succoth, and from Succoth to Etham, and from Etham to Pi-hahiroth.

     C.    [They traveled on] Friday, *Shabbat,* and Sunday, which were the 15th, 16th, and 17th [days of the month of Nisan].

     D.    On Monday—which was the fourth [day] of their journey [and] which was the 18th day [of Nisan]—Israel was readying their cattle and preparing their equipment to leave.

     E.    The commanders said to them, "Your appointed time has arrived to return to Egypt! In accordance with what is said in Scripture: 'So we must go a distance of three days into the wilderness' (Exod. 8:23)."

     F.    They said to them, "When we left [Egypt], we left with Pharaoh's permission."

     G.    They said to them, "No matter what you want, you will end up returning and upholding the orders of the kingdom!"

     H.    Israel rose up against them and struck some of them, wounded some of them, and killed some of them. So they went and told Pharaoh.

     I.    Thus it is said, "When the king of Egypt was told" (Exod. 14:5).

     J.    Who told him? The commanders who were with them. And there are those who say he had guards [who told him]. And there are those who say Amalek told him.

2.    A.    "... that the people had fled" (Exod. 14:5):[58]

     B.    Were they really fleeing?

---

[57] Compare 1.A–J with *Mekhilta de-Rabbi Ishmael,* Beshallaḥ (H/R, 83:11–84:8; Laut., vol. 1, 188:20–190:36; Neus., XX:I:4:A–K). This comparison indicates that this tradition of interpretation is fragmented in the *Mekhilta de-Rabbi Shimon b. Yoḥai* (see XXI:I:1.A–D above), whereas it is associated entirely with Exod. 14:2 in the *Mekhilta de-Rabbi Ishmael.* This fragmentation obfuscates to a degree the overall meaning and context of this tradition in the *Mekhilta de-Rabbi Shimon b. Yoḥai.* However, also noteworthy is the fact that the last two lines of the tradition here (1.I–J) are associated instead with Exod. 14:5 in the *Mekhilta de-Rabbi Ishmael.*

[58] Compare 2.A–E with *Mekhilta de-Rabbi Ishmael,* Beshallaḥ (H/R, 86:8–12; Laut., vol. 1, 194:97–103; Neus., XX:II:2.A–E).

אך בך אל ואין עוד אפס אלהים (ישע׳ מה יד). ◆    C

כיוצא בו אתה אומר ועלו מושיעים בהר ציון לשפוט את    A   5

הר עשו ◆ מהוא אומר ◆ והיתה לה׳ המלוכה (עוב׳ כא) ◆ ואומר    D/C/B

ה׳ מלך עולם ועד אבדו גוים מארצו (תה׳ י טז) ◆ ואומר    E

יתמו חטאים מן הארץ ורשעים עוד אינם ברכי נפשי את ה׳

הללויה (תה׳ קד לה). ◆ ואומר ה׳ שומר את גרים יתום ואלמנה    F

יעודד ודרך רשעים יעות ◆ מהוא אומר ◆ ימלוך ה׳ לעולם    H/G

אלקיך ציון לדור ודור הללויה (תה׳ קמו י). ◆

       XXI:IV

ויגד למלך מצרים ◆ נסעו בני ישראל מרעמסס    B/A   1

לסכות ומסכות לאיתם ומאיתם לפי החירות ◆ ערב    C

שבת ושבת ואחד בשבת שהן חמשה עשר וששה עשר

ושבעה עשר, ◆ בשני בשבת ‹שהוא רביעי› לנסיעתן    D

שהוא יום שמנה עשר היו ישראל מציעין בהמתן

ומתקינין כליהן לצאת ◆ אמרו להן קטרין הגיע    E

פרתזזמיא שלכם לחזור למצרים כעניין שנא׳ דרך

שלשת ימים נלך במדבר (שמ׳ ח כג) ◆ אמרו להן כיון    F

שיצאנו ממצרים יצאנו מרשות פרעה. ◆ אמרו להם    G

רוצים ולא רוצים סופכם לחזור ולקיים דברי מלכות ◆

עמדו עליהן ישראל והכו מהן ופצעו מהן והרגו מהן והלכו    H

והגידו לפרעה ◆ לכך נאמר ויגד למלך מצרים ◆ מי הגידו    J/I

לו קטרין שהיו עמהן. ויש אומרין דידכאות היו לו ויש

אומרין עמלק הגיד לו. ◆ כי ברח העם ◆ וכי בורחים היו    B/A   2

C.    Has it not been said, "As the Israelites were departing defiantly" (Exod. 14:8)?

D.    Rather, because they killed the commanders, they[59] went and said to Pharaoh, "They struck some of us, and wounded some of us, and they do not [even] have a ruler or chief!"

E.    In accordance with what is said in Scripture, "The locusts have no king, yet they all march forth in formation" (Prov. 30:27).

3.  A.    "... Pharaoh and his courtiers had a change of heart about the people" (Exod. 14:5):[60]

B.    [Just] yesterday [it was]: "Pharaoh's courtiers said to him, 'How long shall this one be a snare to us? Let the men go!'" (Exod. 10:7).

C    And [now] today: "... Pharaoh and his courtiers had a change of heart about the people" (Exod. 14:5).

D.    They said, "'What is this we have done, releasing?'" (Exod. 14:5):

E.    They said, "If we had released [them] but not been smitten, it would have been enough. However, we released [them] and were smitten!

F.    "If we were smitten but did not release [them], it would have been enough. However, we were smitten and we released [them]!

G.    "If we had released [them] and were smitten, but did not give [them] our property. However, we released [them], and were smitten, and gave [them] our property!"

H.    They told a parable: To what is the matter alike?

I.    It is like a human king who said to his servant, "Bring me a fish from the market!" He went and brought him a rotten fish. He[61] said, "I decree that you will either eat the fish or receive 100 stripes or pay 100 *maneh*."[62] He said, "Well, I will eat the fish!" He had not managed to finish [eating it] when he fell ill, so he said, "Well, I will take 100 stripes!" He had received [only] 60 or 70, collapsed,

(Textual Source: Ms. Firkovich IIA, 268)

and said, "Well, I will pay 100 *maneh*!" Consequently, he ate the fish, received 100 stripes and paid 100 *maneh*!

J.    Likewise did it occur with Egypt—they were smitten, and they released [them], and they gave [them] their property!

K.    Thus it is said, "'What is this we have done, releasing Israel from our service?'" (Exod. 14:5).

4.  A.    Another interpretation:[63]

B.    "'What is this we have done'" (Exod. 14:5):

C.    Scripture tells that when Israel went out from Egypt, the monarchy of Egypt ended.

5.  A.    "'... from our service'" (Exod. 14:5):[64]

B.    [Scripture here actually reads,] "Who are our servants?"[65]

C.    [They said,] "Now all the nations of the world will be chiming against us like a bell, saying, 'These [people] were in their possession, but they released them and they left them!'

D.    "Now, how can we send to Aram Soba[66] and to Aram Neharim[67] for our tax collection and

---

[59] I.e., the remaining Egyptian guards.
[60] Compare 3.A–K with *Mekhilta de-Rabbi Ishmael*, Beshallaḥ (H/R, 86:12–20; Laut., vol. 1, 195:104–18; Neus., XX:II:3.A–4.J).
[61] I.e., the king.
[62] A *maneh* is a weight of precious metal, commonly gold or silver, equal in value to 50 sacred *shekels* or 100 common *shekels*.
[63] Compare 4.A–C with *Mekhilta de-Rabbi Ishmael*, Beshallaḥ (H/R, 86:20–87:2; Laut., vol. 1, 196:119–20; Neus., XX:II:5.A–C).

| | |
|---|---|
| והלא כבר נאמר ובני ישראל יוצאים ביד רמה (פ״ח) ✦ | C |
| אלא מתוך שהרגו את הקטרין הלכו ואמרו לפרעה | D |
| הכו ממנו ופצעו ממנו ואין להם לא מושל ולא | |
| שר ✦ כענין שנא׳ מלך אין לארבה ויצא חוצץ כולו | E |
| (מש׳ ל כז). ✦ ויהפך לבב פרעה ועבדיו אל העם ✦ | A 3 |
| אתמול ויאמרו עבדי פרעה אליו עד מתי יהיה זה לנו | B |
| למוקש שלח את האנשים (שמ׳ י ז) ✦ והיום ויהפך לבב | C |
| פרעה ועבדיו אל העם. ✦ ויאמרו מה זאת עשינו כי | D |
| שלחנו ✦ אמרו אלו שלחנו ולא לקינו כדאי היה אלא | E |
| שילחנו ולקינו. ✦ אלו לקינו ולא שילחנו כדאי היה אלא | F |
| לקינו ושילחנו. ✦ אלו שילחנו ולקינו ולא ניטל ממונינו | G |
| כדאי היה אלא שילחנו ולקינו וניטל ממונינו. ✦ מושלו | H |
| משל למה הדבר דומה ✦ למלך בשר ודם שאמר לעבדו | I |
| הבא לי דג מן השוק הלך והביא לו דג מבאיש אמר | |
| גזירה או אוכל אתה את הדג או לוקה מאה מכות או | |
| נותן מאה מנה. אמר הריני אוכל את הדג לא הספיק | |
| לגמור נפשו קניטה עליו אמר הריני לוקה מאה מכות | |
| לקה ששים או שבעים נתקלקל אמ׳ הריני נותן מאה | |
| מנא נמצא אכל את הדג ולקה מא[ה מכות] ונתן מאה | |
| מנא ✦ כך נעשה להן למצ׳ לקו ושילחו [וניטל ממונם] ✦ | J |
| לכך נאמ׳ מה זאת עשינו כי שלחנו את יש׳ מעב[דנו ✦ | K |
| ד״א ✦ ויאמרו] מה זאת עשינו ✦ מגיד הכת׳ שכיון שיצאו | C/B/A 4 |
| [יש׳ ממצרים בטלה מלכו]תן של מצ׳: ✦ מעבדינו ✦ מי | B/A 5 |
| עובדינו ✦ עכשיו יהיו [כל אומות העולם מקי]שות עלינו | C |
| בזוג ואומ׳ ומה אלו שהיו ברש[ו]תם הניחום והלכו | |
| להן] ✦ עכשיו היאך אנו שולחין לארם צו[ב]ה ולארם | D |

[64] Compare 5.A–N with *Mekhilta de-Rabbi Ishmael*, Beshallaḥ (H/R, 87:2–19; Laut., vol. 1, 196:120–197:142; Neus., XX:II:6.A–7.G).

[65] Our text here reads מעבדינו (from our service) in Exod. 14:5 as מי עבדינו (Who are our servants?).

[66] Assyria in the region of the Tigris and Euphrates Rivers.

[67] Allepo.

to send us male and females slaves!"

E.   This teaches you that Pharaoh was ruler from one end of the world to the other, and he had governors from one end of the world to the other.

[50]   F.   [And this was actually] for Israel's honor.[68]

G.   And concerning him[69] Scripture states, "The king sent to have him freed; (the ruler of nations released him)" (Ps. 105:20).

H.   Concerning the kingdom of Babylon, Scripture states, "'The nation or kingdom that does not serve him (—King Nebuchadnezzar of Babylon—and does not put its neck under the yoke of the king of Babylon, that nation I will visit, declares the Lord, with sword, famine, and pestilence)'" (Jer. 27:8).

I.   Concerning the kingdom of Media, Scripture states, "Then King Darius wrote to all peoples (and nations of every language that inhabit the earth)" (Dan. 6:26).

J.   And Scripture says, "King Ahasuerus imposed tribute (on the mainland)" (Esther 10:1).

K.   Concerning the kingdom of Greece, Scripture states, "'... the beast had four heads ...'" (Dan. 7:6).

L.   Concerning the fourth kingdom,[70] Scripture states, "... it will devour the whole earth, tread it down, and crush it" (Dan. 7:23).

M.   Thus, every nation and kingdom under which Israel was subjugated ruled from one end of the world to the other, for the [sake of] Israel's honor.

N.   Thus it says in Scripture, "... and said, 'What is this we have done, (releasing Israel from our service)?'" (Exod. 14:5).

6.   A.   Another interpretation:[71]

B.   "... and said, 'What is this we have done, releasing Israel from our service?'" (Exod. 14:5):

C.   They said, "Hasn't it gone well for us because of them?"

D.   R. Yosi would say, "They told a parable: To what is the matter alike?

E.   "It is like someone who had a field the size of a *kor,* and sold it for a small amount. The one who purchased [it] went and opened water springs and planted gardens and orchards. The seller began to choke!

F.   "Likewise, [when] Egypt released [them], they did not know just what they had released!

G.   "And thus Scripture states, 'Your limbs are an orchard of pomegranates' (Song 4:13)."

7.   A.   R. Shimon says, "They told a parable: To what is the matter alike?

B.   "It is like someone who received a residence overseas as an inheritance, and sold it for a small amount. The one who purchased [it] went and discovered in it stores of silver, gold, and precious stones and gems. The seller began to choke!

C.   "Likewise did it occur with Egypt—they were smitten, and they released [the Israelites], and they gave [them] their property!

D.   "Thus it says in Scripture, 'What is this we have done, (releasing Israel from our service)?' (Exod. 14:5)."

---

[68] That is, Israel should only be subjugated by a mighty, worldwide power.
[69] I.e., Pharaoh.
[70] I.e., Rome.
[71] Compare 6.A–7.D with *Mekhilta de-Rabbi Ishmael,* Beshallaḥ (H/R, 87:19–88:7; Laut., vol. 1, 197:142–198:155; Neus., XX:II:8.A–9.E).

נהרים להעלות] לנו מיסים ולשלח לנו עבדים

E ושפ[חות • ללמדך שהיה פרע]ה שליט מסוף העולם

ועד סופו ושן[לטונות היו לו מסוף העו]לם ועד סופו •

G/F מפני כבודן של יש' • ועל]יו הוא אומ' שלח מלך

H ויתירהו] וגומ' (תה' קה כ) • במלכות בבל הוא אומ'

I והיה ה[גוי והממלכה אשר וגו]מ' (ירמ' כז ח) • במלכות

מדי הוא אומר באדין דריוש מלכא כ[תב לכל עממיא

J ר]גו' (דנ' ו כו) • ואומ' וישם המלך אחשורוש מס וגומ'

K (אס' י א) • במלכות יון הוא אומ' וארבעה רישין

L לחיותא וגו' (דנ' ז ו) • במלכות רביעית ‹הוא אומר›

M ותאכול כל ארעא ותדוש‹ינה› ותדק' (שם כג). • הא

אין לך כל אומה ומלכות ששלטה בהן ביש' ולא

שלטה מסוף העולם ועד סופו מפני כבודן של יש' •

N 6 B/A לכן נאמ' ויאמרו מה זאת עשינו וגו' • ד"א • ויאמרו מה

D/C זאת עשינו. • אמרו והלא בשבילן טובה באה עלינו • היה

E ר' יוסי אומ' מושלו משל למה הדבר דומה • לאחד

שהיה לו בית כור ומכרו בדבר מועט והלך אותו לוקח

ופתח בו מעיינות ונטע בו גנות ופרדסים התחיל

G/F המוכר נחנק • כך מצ' שילחו ולא ידעו מה שילחו • וכן

A 7 הוא אומ' שלחיך פרדס וגומ' (שה"ש ד יג) • ר' שמע'

B אומ' מושלו משל למה הדבר דומה • לאחד שנפלה לו

פלטירה בירושה במדינת הים ומכרה בדבר מועט

הלך אותו לוקח ומצא בה בה אוצרות של כסף וזהב

C ואבנים טובות ומרגליות התחיל המוכר נחנק • כך

D נעשה להן למצ' לקו [ושילחו ו]ניטל ממונן • לכן נאמ'

ויאמרו מה זאת עשינו וגומ' [סל' פסו']. •

XXI:V

1. A. "He hitched his chariot (and took his men with him)" (Exod. 14:6):[72]

   B. He hitched it himself. Normally kings will stand around while others arrange [things] for them. But here he hitched it. When the [other] heads of state saw that he hitched himself, each and everyone arose and hitched for themselves.

2. A. Four [people] hitched [their own animals] gladly.

   B. Abraham our father hitched gladly. As it says in Scripture, "Abraham arose early in the morning (and saddled his ass)" (Gen. 22:3).

   C. Joseph hitched gladly. As it says in Scripture, "Joseph hitched his chariot, etc." (Gen. 46:29).

   D. Pharaoh hitched gladly. As it says in Scripture, "He hitched his chariot, etc." (Gen. 22:3).

   E. Balaam hitched gladly. As it says in Scripture, "When Balaam arose in the morning (he saddled his ass), etc." (Num 22:21).

[51] F. R. Shimon b. Yoḥai says, "Let [the one] act of saddling come and offset [the other act] of saddling!

   G. "Let the act of saddling that Abraham did, [in order] to go and do the will of his father in heaven offset the act of saddling that Balaam did, [in order] to go and curse Israel!

   H. "Let [the one] hitching come and offset [the other] hitching!

   I. "Let the hitching done by Joseph to greet Israel his father suspend the hitching done by Pharaoh to pursue Israel!

   J. "Let the [one] sword held in hand come and offset [the other] sword held in hand.

   K. "Let the sword held in hand [by Abraham on Mount Moriah]—'And Abraham stretched out his hand, etc.' (Gen. 22:10)—offset the sword held in hand [by Pharaoh], as Pharaoh said, 'The foe said, ("I will pursue, I will overtake, I will divide the spoil ... I will bare my sword ...")' (Exod. 15:9).

   L. "[And let the sword held in hand by Abraham] suspend the sword held in hand by Pharaoh, who said, '"I will bare my sword, my hand shall subdue them"'" (Exod. 15:9).[73]

3. A. "... and took his men with him" (Exod. 14:6):[74]

   B. He took them with him by means of persuasion.

   C. [He said,] "Normally, kings will walk at the rear [of the troops], while their troops are at the front. However, I shall walk before you at the front! Normally, kings will plunder for themselves and take the portion first. However, I shall share the plunder with you! And not only this, but I shall also open up storehouses for you, and I shall distribute among you silver, gold, and precious stones and gems!"

   D. In accordance with what is said in Scripture, "'... I will divide the spoil ...'" (Exod. 15:9).

   E. Thus it says in Scripture, "... and took his men with him" (Exod. 14:6).

   F. He took them with him by means of persuasion.

XXI:VI

1. A. "He took six hundred of his picked chariots, (and the rest of the chariots of Egypt, with third officers in all of them)" (Exod. 14:7):[75]

---

[72] Compare 1.A–2.L with *Mekhilta de-Rabbi Ishmael*, Beshallaḥ (H/R, 88:8–20; Laut., vol. 1, 198:156–200:176; Neus., XX:II:10.A–12.B).
[73] 2.L appears to be redundant.

| | | |
|---|---|---|
| ויאסור את רכבו ◆ הוא בידו אסרו דרך [מלכים | B/A | 1 |
| להיות] עומדין ואחרים מציעין להן אבל כאן הוא | | |
| [אסרו כיון שראו גדו]לי מלכות שהציע הוא לעצמו | | |
| עמד כל א[חד ואחד והציע] לעצמו. ◆ ארבעה אסרו | Λ | 2 |
| בשמחה ◆ אברה[ם אבינו אסר בש]מחה ‹שנא'› וישכם | B | |
| אברהם בבוקר וגומ' (בר' כב ג). ◆ יוסף [אסר בשמחה | C | |
| שנא' ויאס]ור יוסף מרכבתו וגומ' (שם מו כט) ◆ פרעה | D | |
| אסר [בשמחה שנא' ויאסור את] רכבו וגו' ◆ בלעם אסר | E | |
| בשמחה שנא' ויקם [בלעם בבוקר וגו'] (במ' כב כא) ◆ ר' | F | |
| שמע' בן יוחי אומ' תבוא חבישה תעמוד [על חבישה | | |
| תבוא חב]ישה שחבש אברהם לילך ולעשות ר[צון | G | |
| אביו שבשמי]ם תעמוד על חבישה שחבש בלעם לילך | | |
| לקל[ל את] יש' ◆ תבוא אסירה ותעמוד על אסירה | H | |
| תבוא אסירה שאסר יוסף לקראת יש' אביו ותעלה | I | |
| על אסירה שאסר פרעה לרדוף אחרי יש' ◆ תבוא חרב | J | |
| יד ותעמוד על חרב יד ◆ תבוא חרב יד וישלח אברהם | K | |
| את ידו וגומ' (בר' כב י) ותעמוד (על חרב יד שאמ' | | |
| פרעה אמר אויב ◆ ותעלה) על חרב יד של פרעה שאמ' | L | |
| אריק חרבי תורישמו ידי (שמ' טו ט) ◆ ואת עמו לקח | A | 3 |
| עמו ◆ לקחן עמו בדברים ◆ דרך מלכים להיות מהלכין | C/B | |
| בסוף וחיילותם תחלה אבל אני הריני מהלך לפניכן | | |
| תחלה דרך מלכים להיות בוזזין לעצמן ונוטלין חלק | | |
| בראש אבל אני אשוה לכן בביזה ולא עוד אלא שאני | | |
| פותח לכן תיסוורואות ומחלק אני לכם כסף וזהב וכל | | |
| אבנים טובות ומרגליות ◆ כענין שנא' אחלק שלל ◆ ‹לכן | E/D | |
| נאמר› ואת עמו לקח עמו ◆ לקחן עמו בדברים. סל' פסו' | F | |

| | | |
|---|---|---|
| ויקח שש מאות רכב בחור ◆ משלמי היו ◆ אם תאמר | C/B/A | 1 |

[74] Compare 3.A–F with *Mekhilta de-Rabbi Ishmael*, Beshallaḥ (H/R, 88:20–89:3; Laut., vol. 1, 200:177–85; Neus., XX:II:13.A–F).
[75] Compare 1.A–I with *Mekhilta de-Rabbi Ishmael*, Beshallaḥ (H/R, 89:4–10; Laut., vol. 1, 201:186–96; Neus., XX:II:14.A–I).

B.   Whose were they?[76]

C.   If you say they were Pharaoh's, has it not been said in Scripture, "'(For if you refuse to let them go, and continue to hold them,) then the hand of the Lord will strike (your livestock in the fields—the horses, the asses, the camels, the cattle, and the sheep—with a very severe pestilence)'" (Exod. 9:3)?

D.   And if you say they were the Egyptians', has it not been said in Scripture, "... all the livestock of the Egyptians died" (Exod. 9:6)?

E.   And if you say they were the Israelites', has it not been said in Scripture, "'Our own livestock, too, (shall go along with us—not a hoof shall remain behind)'" (Exod. 10:26)?

F.   Whose were they?

G.   Behold Scripture states, "(Those among Pharaoh's courtiers) who feared the Lord's word (brought their slaves and livestock indoors to safety)" (Exod. 9:20).

H.   As a result we learn that [even] those among Pharaoh's courtiers who feared the Lord's word were a snare for Israel!

I.   Based on this they would say, "[Even] the worthy among the gentiles, kill! The best of the snakes, crush its brains!"

2.   A.   R. Shimon b. Gamliel says, "Come and see the wealth and magnitude of this kingdom![77]

B.   "In that it did not have [even] one troop division unoccupied. Rather, all of them were running day and night!

C.   "And thus Scripture states, 'He took six hundred of his picked chariots' (Exod. 14:7).

D.   "Compared to those of Egypt, all of theirs[78] are standing idle!"[79]

3.   A.   "... with third officers in all of them" (Exod. 14:7):[80]

[52]   B.   [The word] "third officer" only refers to warriors.

C.   In accordance with what is said in Scripture, "... third officers, all of them riding on horseback" (Ezek.23:23).

4.   A.   Another interpretation:

B.   "... with *third* officers" (Exod. 14:7):

C.   In that they were armed in three ways.

5.   A.   Another interpretation:

B.   "... with third officers" (Exod. 14:7):

C.   R. Shimon ben Gamliel says, "This [refers to] the third man on the chariot.

D.   "Because at first there were only two. Pharaoh came and added another one, in order to hasten the pursuit of Israel."

E.   There are those who say [that] Antoninus added [the third].

6.   A.   Another interpretation:

B.   "... with third officers" (Exod. 14:7):

---

[76] I.e., the animals for the chariots.
[77] I.e., Rome.
[78] I.e., Rome's troops.
[79] Compare 2.A–D with *Mekhilta de-Rabbi Ishmael,* Beshallaḥ (H/R, 89:10–12; Laut., vol. 1, 201:196–99; Neus., XX:II:15.A–C).
[80] Compare 3.A–7.G with *Mekhilta de-Rabbi Ishmael,* Beshallaḥ (H/R, 89:12–90:4; Laut., vol. 1, 202:200–203:218; Neus., XX:II:16.A–20.F).

משל פרעה היו הרי כבר נאמ' הנה יד ייי הויה וגו'

D (שמ' ט ג) ◆ ואם תאמר משל מ[צ' היו] הרי כבר נאמ'

E וימת כל מקנה מצ' ◆ ואם <תאמר> משל יש' [היו הרי

F כבר] נאמ' וגם מקנינו וגומ' (שם י כו) ◆ מ[ש]למי היו ◆

G הרי הוא א[ומ' הירא את דבר] ייי מעבדי פרעה וגומ'

H (שם ט כ) ◆ נמצינו למדין [הירא את דבר ייי] מעבדי

I פרעה הן היו תקלה ליש' ◆ מיכ]ן אמרו הכשר שבגוים]

A    2 הרוג יפה שבנחשים רצץ [את] מוח]ו. ◆ רבן שמע' בן

גמליאל אומ'] בוא וראה עשרה וגדולתה של מלכות

B [זו ◆ שאין לה נו]מרין אחת בטלה אלא כולן רצות ביום

C ובלילה ◆ [וכן הוא או]מ' ויקח שש מאות רכב בחור ◆

B/A    3 כנגדן של מצ' כולן עומדות בטלות. ◆ ושלישים על כולו: ◆

A 4    C אין שלישים אלא גבורים ◆ כעניין שנא' שלישים וקרואים

D/C/B רוכבי סוסים כולם (יחז' כג כג). ◆ ד"א ◆ ושלישים

C/B/A    5 שהיו משולשין בזיין. ◆ ד"א ◆ ושלישים ◆ רבן שמע'

D בן גמליאל אומ' זו שלישו של מרכבה ◆ שמתחלה לא היו

אלא שנים בא פרעה והוסיף עוד אחת למהר ולרדוף אחרי

B/A 6    E יש' ◆ ויש' אומ' אנטונינוס הוסיפה. ◆ ד"א ◆ ושלישים ◆

C. Three [Egyptian horsemen] for every one [Israelite].

D. There are those who say 30 for every one.

E. There are those who say 300 for every one.

F. R. Shimon ben Eliezer says, "How would Pharaoh know how many [people] died during the three days of darkness!

G. "Rather, he brought out their census lists, and according to the lists he placed troops against them."

7.    A. Another interpretation:

B. "... with third officers in all of them" (Exod. 14:7):

C. In order to destroy [them].

D. "I[81] said [in the past], 'Every boy that is born (you shall throw into the Nile)' (Exod. 1:22).

E. "And now: '... with third officers in all of them' (Exod. 14:7).

F. "In order to destroy them!

G. ""'I will bare my sword, my hand shall subdue them'" (Exod. 15:9)."

XXI:VII[82]

1.    A. "The Lord stiffened the heart of Pharaoh king of Egypt" (Exod. 14:8):

B. In that his heart was divided as to whether or not to pursue them.

2.    A. "... and he gave chase to the Israelites" (Exod. 14:8):

B. Scripture tells that if it had been another nation, he would not have pursued them.

3.    A. "The Israelites were leaving with a raised hand" (Exod. 14:8):

B. Scripture tells that while the Egyptians were pursuing Israel, they were insulting, blaspheming, and reviling.

C. But Israel [was] glorifying, exalting, praising, heralding, hailing, and offering songs and great praise and exultation and glory and victory and majesty to He who spoke, and the world came into being—for war is His!

D. In accordance with what is said in Scripture, "... with paeans to God in their throats, etc." (Ps. 149:6). And Scripture says, "Exalt God over the heavens, etc." (Ps. 57:6). And Scripture says, "O Lord, You are my God. I will extol You, etc." (Isa. 25:1).

4.    A. Another interpretation:

B. "... with a raised hand" (Exod. 14:8):

C. With an uncovered head.

5.    A. Another interpretation:

B. "... with a raised hand" (Exod. 14:8):

C. In that their hand was raised against Egypt.

---

[81] I.e., Pharaoh.

[82] Compare XXI:VII.1.A–5.C with *Mekhilta de-Rabbi Ishmael*, Beshallaḥ (H/R, 90:5–13; Laut., vol. 1, 203:219–204:232; Neus., XX:II:21.A–25.B).

| | |
|---|---|
| שלשה לכל אחד ואחד • ויש אומ' שלשים | D/C |
| לכל אחד ואחד. • ויש אומ' שלש מאות לכל אחד | E |
| ואחד. • ר' שמע' בן אלעזר אומ' וכי <מ>אין היה פרעה | F |
| יודע כמה מתו בשלשת ימי אפילה • אלא הוציא | G |
| טימוסין שלהן ולפי טימוסין נתן עליהן חיילות. • ד"א • | A 7 |
| ושלישים על כלו • על מנת לכלות • אני אמרתי כל הבן | D/C/B |
| הילוד וגו' (שמ' א כב) • עכשיו ושלישים על כולו • על | F/E |
| מנת לכלות • אריק חרבי תורישמו ידי (שם טו ט). סל' פסו' • | G |

<br>

| | |
|---|---|
| | XXI:VII |
| ויחזק ייי את לב פרעה מלך מצ' • שהיה לבו חלוק | B/A 1 |
| אם לרדוף ואם לא לרדוף • וירדף אחרי בני יש' • מגיד | B/A 2 |
| הכת' שאם היתה אומה אחרת לא היה רודף אחריה. • | |
| ובני ישר' יצאים ביד רמה • מגיד הכת' שכשהיו מצריים | B/A 3 |
| רודפין אחרי ישראל היו מנאצין ומחרפין ומגדפין • | |
| ויש' מפארין ומרוממין ומשבחין [ומקלסין] ומהללין | C |
| ונותנין שיר ושבח גדולה ותהלה ותפארת ונצח [והוד | |
| למי ש[אמר והיה העולם ש[המ]לחמה שלו • כעניין | D |
| שנאמ' [רוממות אל בגרונם] וגו' (תה' קמט ו) ואומ' | |
| רומה [על ה] שמים אלקים וגומ' (שם נז ו) ואומ' [ייי | |
| אלקי אתה ארוממך] וגו' (ישע' כה א). • ד"א • ביד רמה • | B/A 4 |
| בראש גלוי. • <ד"א> • ביד רמה • [שהיתה ידן רמה] על | C/B/A 5 C |
| מצ'. סל' פסו' • | |

*Chapter Twenty-Two*

(Textual Source: Ms. Firkovich IIA, 268)

XXII:I

1.    A.    "The Egyptians pursued them (and all the chariot horses of Pharaoh, his horsemen, and his warriors overtook them encamped by the sea, near Pi-hahiroth, before Baal-zephon)" (Exod. 14:9):[83]

      B.    Scripture tells that not one of them stumbled, so that they would not consider it a bad omen and turn back.

      C.    Thus we find that gentiles believe in bad omens.

[53]       D.    As it says in Scripture, "Those nations that you (are about to dispossess do indeed resort to soothsayers and augurs)" (Deut. 18:14). And Scripture states, "The elders of Moab and the elders of Midian, (versed in divination, set out)" (Num. 22:7). [And Scripture states,] "... Balaam, son of Beor, the auger, etc." (Josh. 13:22).

      E.    But here, not one of them stumbled, so that they would not consider it a bad omen and turn back.

2.    A.    "... overtook them encamped by the sea ... (before Baal-Zephon. As Pharaoh drew near) ..." (Exod. 14:9–10):[84]

      B.    When Pharaoh saw Baal-zephon, he rejoiced, saying, "Baal-zephon agrees with my decree. I said to drown them in water, [and] Baal-zephon agrees with my decree to drown them in water!"

      C.    He began[85] [to prepare] an altar and incense before his idol.

      D.    As it says in Scripture, "... before Baal-Zephon. As Pharaoh drew near ..." (Exod. 14:9–10).[86]

3.    A.    Another interpretation:[87]

      B.    "As Pharaoh drew near" (Exod. 14:10):

      C.    In that he drew near [to him] the divine punishment about to come upon him.

4.    A.    Another interpretation:[88]

      B.    "As Pharaoh drew near" (Exod. 14:10):

      C.    The [distance] that Israel walked in three days the [Egyptian] commanders walked in a day and a half. And the [distance] that the commanders walked in a day and a half Pharaoh walked in one day.

5.    A.    "... The Israelites caught sight (of Egypt advancing upon them)" (Exod. 14:10):[89]

      B.    Because they had beaten up the commanders, they knew that in the end they would pursue them.

6.    A.    ["... of Egypt advancing upon them" (Exod. 14:10):][90]

      B.    [The plural participle] "advancing upon them" is not written here, but rather [the singular participle] "advancing upon them."

---

[83] Compare 1.A–E with *Mekhilta de-Rabbi Ishmael*, Beshallaḥ (H/R, 91:1–5; Laut., vol. 1, 204:1–7; Neus., XXI:I:1.A–E).

[84] Compare 2.A–D with *Mekhilta de-Rabbi Ishmael*, Beshallaḥ (H/R, 91:6–9; Laut., vol. 1, 205:10–15; Neus., XXI:I:3.A–E).

[85] The text includes here the word "says," which makes no contextual sense. I have inserted "to prepare" in its place.

[86] This interpretation is based on the fact that the verb in Exod. 14:20 "drew near" (Hebrew: הקריב) also means "to offer a sacrifice."

[87] Compare 3.A–C with *Mekhilta de-Rabbi Ishmael*, Beshallaḥ (H/R, 91:6; Laut., vol. 1, 205:8–10; Neus., XXI:I:2.A–B).

[88] Compare 4.A–C with *Mekhilta de-Rabbi Ishmael*, Beshallaḥ (H/R, 91:9–11; Laut., vol. 1, 205:15–18; Neus., XXI:I:4.A–D).

| | | |
|---|---|---|
| ויִרְדְּפוּ מצרים אחריהם ◆ מִ[גִּיד הכת׳ שלא נכש]ל | B/A | 1 |
| [אָחָ]ד מהן כדי שלא ינחשו ויחזרו לאחוריהן ◆ [וכן | C | |
| מצינו שהגוי]ם מנחשין ◆ שנא׳ כי הגוים האלה אשר | D | |
| אתה וגו׳ (דב׳ יח יד) [ואומ׳ וילכו] זקני מואב וזקני | | |
| מדין וגומ׳ (במ׳ כב ז). ואת בלעם בן בעור הקוסם וגו׳ | | |
| (יהו׳ יג כב) ◆ אבל כאן לא נכשל אחד מהן כדי | E | |
| שינחש<ו> ויחזרו לאחוריהן. ◆ וישיגו אותם חונים על | A | 2 |
| הים וגו׳ ◆ כיון שראה פרעה את בעל צפון שמח אמ׳ | B | |
| הסכים בעל צפון לגזירתי אני אמרתי לטבעם במים | | |
| הסכים בעל צפון לגזירתי לטבען במים ◆ התחיל אומ׳ | C | |
| ומזבח ומקטר לפני עבודה זרה שלו ◆ שנא׳ לפני בעל צפון: | D | |

| | | |
|---|---|---|
| ופרעה הקריב. ◆ ד״א ◆ ופרעה הקריב ◆ שהקריב | C/B/A | 3 |
| הפורענות לבוא עליו. ◆ ד״א ◆ ופרעה הקריב ◆ מה שהלכו | C/B/A | 4 |
| יש׳ בשלשה ימים הלכו קטרין ביום ומחצה ומה | | |
| שהילכו קטרים ביום ובמחצה הילכו פרעה ביום אחד ◆ | | |
| וישאו בני יש׳ את עיניהם ◆ מתוך שהכו מן הקטרין היו | B/A | 5 |
| יודעין שסופן לרדף אחריהם. ◆ והנה מצ׳ נסעים | B/A | 6 |
| אחריהם אין כת׳ כן אלא נוסע אחריהם ◆ | | |

---

[89] Compare 5.A–B with *Mekhilta de-Rabbi Ishmael*, Beshallaḥ (H/R, 91:12–13; Laut., vol. 1, 205:19–21; Neus., XXI:I:5.A–B).

[90] Compare 6.A–D with *Mekhilta de-Rabbi Ishmael*, Beshallaḥ (H/R, 91:13–15; Laut., vol. 1, 206:22–25; Neus., XXI:I:6.A–D).

C. Scripture tells that all of them were formed into various squadrons [each advancing] like a single person.

D. And from them this kingdom[91] learned to lead [its troops] in various squadrons.

7. A. "(Greatly frightened), the Israelites cried out to the Lord" (Exod. 14:10):[92]

B. They seized the devices [for divine assistance] of their forefathers—the devices of Abraham, Isaac, and Jacob.

C. Concerning Abraham, Scripture states, "... with Bethel on the west" (Gen. 12:8). What is stated next? "And he built there an altar (to the Lord and invoked the Lord by name)" (Gen. 12:8).

D. Concerning Isaac, Scripture states, "And Isaac went out to meditate in the field ..." (Gen. 24:63). And "meditate"[93] only means prayer. In accordance with what is said in Scripture, "I pour out my complaint[94] before Him, etc." (Ps. 142:3). And Scripture says, "May my prayer[95] be pleasing to Him, etc." (Ps. 104:34). And Scripture says, "Evening, morning, and noon, (I complain[96] and moan and He hears my voice)" (Ps. 55:18). And Scripture says, "A prayer of the lowly man when he is faint (and pours forth his plea[97] before the Lord)" (Ps. 102:1).

E. Concerning Jacob, Scripture states, "He happened upon a certain place" (Gen. 28:11). And "happen upon"[98] only means prayer. As it says in Scripture, "As for you, do not pray for this people ... (do not plead[99] with me), etc." (Jer. 7:16).

F. And Scripture says, "Fear not, O worm Jacob, etc." (Isa. 41:14). Just as this worm only bites the tree with its mouth, likewise Israel only has prayer.

G. And Scripture states, "(And now, I assign to you one portion more than to your brothers) which I wrested from the Amorites with my sword and bow" (Gen. 48:22).

H. Did [God] really seize with His sword and bow? Has it not already been said, "I do not trust in my bow, (it is not my sword that gives me victory)" (Ps. 44:7)?

I. Thus, why does Scripture state, "... which I wrested from the Amorites, etc." (Gen. 48:22)? This is prayer. And "my sword"[100]—this is prayer.[101] And thus Scripture states, "Blessed is he who trusts in the Lord, etc." (Jer. 17:7). And Scripture states, "Cursed is he who trusts in man, etc." (Jer. 17:5). This is prayer.

[54]

J. Concerning Judah, Scripture states, "And this he[102] said of Judah" (Deut. 33:7). What does he say? "Hear, O Lord the voice of Judah, etc." (Deut. 33:7).

K. Concerning David, Scripture states, "(David replied to the Philistine), 'You come against me with sword and spear and javelin, (but I come against you in the name of the Lord of Hosts, the God of the ranks of Israel), etc.'" (1 Sam. 17:45). And Scripture states, "They [call] on chariots, they [call] on horses, (but we call on the name of the Lord our God), etc." (Ps. 20:8). And Scripture states, "They collapse and lie fallen (but we rally and gather strength), etc." (Ps. 20:9).

---

[91] I.e., Rome.

[92] Compare 7.A–O with *Mekhilta de-Rabbi Ishmael*, Beshallaḥ (H/R, 91:15–93:11; Laut., vol. 1, 206:26–209:65; Neus., XXI:I:7.A–P).

[93] Hebrew: *siḥah*—שיחה.

[94] Hebrew: *siḥi*—שיחי.

[95] Hebrew: *siḥi*—שיחי.

[96] Hebrew: *asiḥah*—אשיחה.

[97] Hebrew: *siḥo*—שיחו.

[98] Hebrew: *pegiah*—פגיעה.

[99] Hebrew: *tifgah*—תפגע.

[100] Hebrew: *b'kashti*—בקשתי.

[101] Hebrew: *bakasha*—בקשה.

[102] I.e., Moses.

מגיד ‹הכת'› שנעשו כולן טורמאות טורמאות כאיש    C

אחד ◆ ומהן למדה מלכות זו להיות נוהגין טורמאות    D

טורמאות. ◆ ויצעקו בני יש' אל ייי ◆ תפסו בידן אומנות    B/A   7

אביהן אומנות אברהם יצחק ויעקב ◆ באברהם הוא    C

אום' בית אל: מים וגו' מה נאמר שם ויבן שם מזבח

וגו' (בר' יב ח) ◆ ביצחק הוא אום' ויצא יצחק לשוח    D

בשדה וגו' (שם כד סג) ואין שיחה אלא תפלה כענין

שנא' אשפוך לפניו שיחי וגו' (תה' קמב ג) ואומ' יערב

עליו שיחי וגו' (שם קד לד) ואומ' ערב ובקר וצהרים

וגו' (שם נה יח) ואומ' תפלה לעני כי יעטוף וגו' (שם

קב א) ◆ ביעקב הוא אום' ויפגע במקום (בר' כח יא)    E

ואין פגיעה אלא תפלה שנא' ואתה אל תתפלל בעד

העם הזה וגו' (ירמ' ז טז) ◆ ואומ' אל תיראי תולעת    F

יעקב וגו' (ישע' מא יד) מה תועלת זו אין מכה לארז

אלא בפיה כך אין ליש' אלא תפלה ◆ ואומ' אשר    G

לקחתי מיד האמורי בחרבי ובקשתי (בר' מח כב) ◆ וכי    H

בחרבו ובקשתו לקח והלא כבר נאמר כי לא בקשתי

אבטח וגו' (תה' מד ז) ◆ הא מה ת"ל אשר לקחתי מיד    I

האמורי וגו' זו תפלה ובקשתי זו בקשה וכן הוא אום'

ברוך הגבר אשר יבטח בייי וגומ' (ירמ' יז ז) ואומ' ארור

הגבר אשר יבטח באדם וגו' (שם ה) זו תפלה ◆ ביהודה    J

הוא אום' וזאת ליהודה ויאמר מה הוא אום' שמע ייי קול

יהודה וגומ' (דב' לג ז) ◆ בדויד הוא אום' אתה בא אלי    K

בחרב ובחנית ובכידון וגו' (ש"א יז מה) ואומ' אלה ברכב ואלה

בסוסים וגו' (תה' כ ח) ואומ' [המה] כרעו ונפלו וגו'

◆

L. Concerning Asa, what does Scripture state?—"Asa called to the Lord his God, etc." (1 Chron. 14:10). And Scripture states, "(Help us) O Lord our God ... Let no mortal hinder You!" (1 Chron. 14:10).

M. Concerning Moses, Scripture states, "From Kadesh, Moses sent messengers to the king (of Edom: 'Thus says your brother Israel: You know all the hardships that have befallen us), that our ancestors went down (to Egypt) ... We cried to the Lord and He heard'" (Num. 20:14–16).

They[103] said to him, "You are proud about what your forefather bequeathed to you, [as it says in Scripture,] 'The voice is the voice of Jacob, etc.' (Gen. 27:22), [and it says in Scripture,] 'And the Lord heard our voice' (Deut. 26:7). And we are proud about what our forefather bequeathed to us, [as it says in Scripture,] '... but the hands are the hands of Esau' (Gen. 27:22), [and it says in Scripture,] 'Yet by your sword you shall live' (Gen. 27:40)."

What does Scripture state?—"But Edom answered him, 'You shall not pass through us (else we will go out against you with the sword), etc.'" (Num. 20:18).

N. Here too you say, "... the Israelites cried out to the Lord" (Exod. 14:10).

O. They seized the devices [for divine assistance] of their forefathers—the devices of Abraham, Isaac, and Jacob.

## XXII:II

1. A. "And they said to Moses, 'Was it for want of graves in Egypt that you brought us to die in the wilderness? (What have you done taking us out of Egypt?)'" (Exod. 14:11):[104]

B. Once they had put leaven in the dough,[105] they went to Moses and said to Moses, "Is this not the very thing we told in Egypt?" (Exod. 14:12).

C. What did they say to Moses in Egypt? Behold Scripture states, "(As they left Pharaoh's presence,) they came upon Moses and Aaron standing in their path" (Exod. 5:20).

D. They said to him, "We were upset about our enslavement in Egypt. [However,] our death in the wilderness is more difficult for us than our enslavement in Egypt. We were distressed about the death of our brothers in the darkness. [However,] the death which we are dying in the wilderness is more difficult for us than the death of our brothers in the darkness, for our brothers were eulogized and buried, but as for us, our corpses will be strewn to wither during the day and to freeze at night."

2. A. "But Moses said to the people, 'Have no fear! (Stand by, and witness the deliverance which the Lord will work for you today!)'" (Exod. 14:13):[106]

B. To inform you of the wisdom of Moses, who would stand and pacify all those thousands, and all those tens of thousands!

C. About him it is explained in tradition, "Wisdom is more of a stronghold to a wise man (than ten magnates that a city may contain)" (Eccles. 7:19).

3. A. "'Stand by, and witness (the deliverance which the Lord will work for you today)!'" (Exod. 14:13):[107]

B. "Standing by" in every instance only means the Holy Spirit.

---

[103] I.e., the Edomites.
[104] Compare 1.A–D with *Mekhilta de-Rabbi Ishmael*, Beshallaḥ (H/R, 93:12–18; Laut., vol. 1, 209:66–210:76; Neus., XXI:I:8.A–F).
[105] I.e., once they had incited discontent.
[106] Compare 2.A–C with *Mekhilta de-Rabbi Ishmael*, Beshallaḥ (H/R, 93:19–94:2; Laut., vol. 1, 210:77–80; Neus., XXI:I:9.A–E).
[107] Compare 3.A–C with *Mekhilta de-Rabbi Ishmael*, Beshallaḥ (H/R, 94:2–8; Laut., vol. 1, 210:81–211:86; Neus., XXI:I:10.A–D).

באסא מה הוא אומ׳ ויקרא אסא אל ייי אלקיו וגו׳ ואומ׳ ייי    L

אלקינו אתה אל יעצר עמך אנוש (דה״ב יד י). ◆ במשה הוא    M

אומ׳ וישלח משה מלאכים מקדש אל מלך וגו׳ וירדו אבותינו

וגומ׳ ונצעק אל ייי וישמע ייי (במ׳ כ יד - טז) אמ׳ לו אתם

מתגאין במה שהוריש אתכם אביכן הקול קול יעקב

(וגומ׳) (בר׳ כז כב) וישמע קולינו (במ׳ כ טז) <ו>אנו

מתגאין במה שהוריש לנו אבא והידים ידי עשיו ועל

חרבך תחיה (בר׳ כז מ). מה הוא אומ׳ ויאמר אליו

אדום לא תעבור בי וגו׳ (במ׳ כ יח) ◆ אף כן אתה אומ׳    N

ויצעקו בני יש׳ אל ייי ◆ תפסו בידן אומנות אבותיהן    O

אומנות אברהם יצ׳ ויעקב. סל׳ פסו׳ ◆

                                         XXII:II

ויאמרו אל משה המבלי אין קברים במצ׳    A    1

לקחתנו למות במדבר ◆ משנתנו שאר בעיסה הלכו להן    B

אצל משה אמ׳ לו למשה הלא זה הדבר אשר דברנו

אליך במצ׳ (חדל) ◆ מה אמרו לו למשה במצ׳ הרי הוא    C

אומ׳ ויפגעו את משה ואת אהרן נצבים לקראתם

(שמ׳ ה כ) ◆ אמרו לו היינו מצטערין על שיעבודינו במצ׳    D

מיתתנו במדבר קשה לנו יתיר משיעבודנו במצ׳ היינו

מצטערין על מיתת אחינו באפילה <מיתה> שאנחנו

מתים במדבר קשה לנו יתר ממידת אחינו באפילה

שאחינו נספדין ונקברין אבל אנו תהא נבלתינו

מושלכת לחורב ביום ולקרח בלילה. סל׳ פסו׳ ◆

ויאמר משה אל העם אל תיראו ◆ להודיע חכמתו של    B/A    2

משה שהיה עתוד ועומד ומפייס כל אותן אלפים וכל אותן

רבבות ◆ ועליו מפרש בקבלה (ו)החכמה תעז לחכם וגו׳ (קה׳    C

ז יט) ◆ התיצבו וראו ◆ אין יצבה בכל מקום אלא רוח הקודש    B/A    3

◆

[55]     C.     In accordance with what is said in Scripture, "Call Joshua and stand by (in the Tent of Meeting that I may instruct him)" (Deut. 31:14). And Scripture says, "The Lord came, and stood there, (and He called as before: 'Samuel! Samuel!')" (1 Sam. 3:10). And Scripture says, "... and take them to the Tent of Meeting and let them stand there, etc." (Num. 11:17). And Scripture says, "And the Lord was standing beside him" (Gen. 28:13). And Scripture says, "I saw my Lord standing (by the altar, and He said)" (Amos 9:1).

4.     A.     What was Israel like at that moment? Like a dove that was fleeing a hawk, and entered in a cave into the cleft of a rock where there was a nested snake before it. It couldn't enter forward [into the cleft] because of the snake. It couldn't go back out, because of the hawk. So it was crying and clapping its wings, so that the dovecote's owner would hear and come.[108]

    B.     Likewise, when Israel saw a closed-up sea [before them] and the enemy pursuing them [from behind], they lifted up their eyes in prayer.

    C.     About them it is explained in tradition, "O my dove, in the cranny of the rocks, etc." (Song 2:14). [And Scripture continues,] "For your voice is sweet" (Song 2:14), [meaning, sweet] in prayer. [And Scripture continues,] "And your face is comely" (Song 2:14), [meaning, comely] in deeds.

5.     A.     Another interpretation:[109]

    B.     "'Stand by, and *witness* the deliverance which the Lord ...'" (Exod. 14:13):

    C.     They said to him,[110] "When?" He said to them, "Today." They said to him, "We don't have enough strength to make it!"

    D.     At that moment Moses prayed, and God showed them squadrons of ministering angels passing before them.

    E.     In accordance with what is said in Scripture, "When the attendant of the man of God rose early (and went outside, he saw a force, with horses and chariots, surrounding the town. 'Alas, master, what shall we do?' his servant asked him. 'Have no fear,' he replied. 'There are more on our side than on theirs.') Then Elisha prayed: ('Lord, open his eyes and let him see.') And the Lord opened the servant's eyes, etc." (2 Kings 6:15–17).

    F.     Likewise, Moses prayed, and God showed them squadrons of ministering angels passing before them.

    G.     And thus Scripture states, "Out of the brilliance before Him, (hail and fiery coals pierced His clouds. Then the Lord thundered from heaven, the Most High gave forth His voice—hail and fiery coals. He let fly His shafts and scattered them. He discharged lightning and routed them)" (Ps. 18:13–15).

    H.     "His clouds" corresponds with their squadrons.

    I.     "Hail" corresponds with their catapults.

    J.     "Fiery coals" corresponds with their exploding arrows.

    K.     "Then the Lord thundered from heaven" corresponds with the noise caused by fastening their shields.

    L.     "The Most High gave forth His voice" corresponds with their crying.

---

[108] Compare 4.A–C with *Mekhilta de-Rabbi Ishmael*, Beshallaḥ (H/R, 94:8–13; Laut., vol. 1, 211:86–94; Neus., XXI:I:11.A–12.C).

[109] Compare 5.A–N with *Mekhilta de-Rabbi Ishmael*, Beshallaḥ (H/R, 94:13–95:7; Laut., vol. 1, 211:95–213:113; Neus., XXI:I:13.A–14.I).

[110] I.e., to Moses.

| | |
|---|---|
| כענין שנא' קרא את יהושע והתיצבו וגומ' (דב' לא יד) ואומ' | C |
| ויבא יייי ויתיצב וגו' (ש"א ג י) ואומ' (ולקחת) [והקהלת] | |
| אתם אל אוהל מועד והתיצבו שם וגומ' (במ' יא טז) | |
| ואומ' והנה יייי נצב עליו (בר' כח יג) ואומ' ראיתי את יייי | |
| נצב (עמ' ט א) ◆ למה היו יש' דומין באותה השעה | A  4 |
| ליונה שפרחה מפני בן הנץ נכנסה לה למערה לנקיק | |
| הסלע ונחש מכונן לפנים ממנה ליכנס לפנים אינה יכולה | |
| מפני הנחש לצאת לחוץ אין יכולה מפני בן הנץ והיתה | |
| צווחת ומטפחת בגפיה כדי שישמע בעל השובך ויבא ◆ | |
| כך כיון שראו יש' ים סוגר ושונא רודף נשאו עיניהם | B |
| בתפלה ◆ ועליהן מפרש בקבלה יונתי בחגוי הסלע וגו' | C |
| (שה"ש ב יד) כי קולך ערב בתפלה ומראך נאוה | |
| במעשים. ◆ ד"א ◆ התיצבו וראו את ישועת יייי ◆ אמרו לו | C/B/A  5 |
| אמתי אמ' להן היום אמ' לו אין בנו כח לסבול ◆ נתפלל | D |
| משה באותה שעה והראן המק' טורמאות של מלאכי | |
| שרת עוברין לפניהן ◆ כענין שנא' וישכם משרת איש | E |
| האלקים וגו' ויתפלל אלישע (אל יייי) ויאמר וגו' ויפקח | |
| אלקים את עיני הנער וגו' (מ"ב י טו - יז) ◆ אף כך התפלל | F |
| משה והראן המקום טורמאות של מלאכים שהן עוברין | |
| לפניהם ◆ וכן הוא אומ' מנוגה נגדו וגו' (תה' יח יג) ◆ | G |
| עביו כנגד טורמאות שלהן ◆ ברד כנגד אבני בלסטא שלהן ◆ | I/H |
| גחלי אש כנגד נפט שלהן. ◆ וירעם בשמים יייי כנגד הגפת | K/J |
| תריסין שלהן ◆ ועליון יתן קולו כנגד צווחות שלהן. ◆ | L |

M. "He let fly His shafts and scattered them" corresponds with their arrows.

N. "He discharged lightning and routed them" corresponds with the glistening of their armament.

6. A. Another interpretation:[111]

B. "He let fly His shafts and scattered them. (He discharged lightning and routed them)" (Ps. 18:15):

C. The arrows scattered them and the lightning brought them together.

D. "... and routed them" (Ps. 18:15):

E. He confounded and confused them, and took their standards, and they didn't know what they were doing.

7. A. Another interpretation:[112]

[56] B. "... and routed them" (Ps. 18:15):

C. "Routing" only means "sudden death."

D. In accordance with what is said in Scripture, "... routing them into utter panic, (until they are wiped out,) etc." (Deut. 7:23).

8. A. God cautioned Israel against returning to Egypt in three places:[113]

B. "'... for the Egyptians whom you see today (you will never see again)'" (Exod. 14:13). And Scripture says, "... since the Lord has warned you, 'You must not go back that way again, etc.'" (Deut. 17:16). And Scripture says, "... by a route which I told you you should not see again" (Deut. 28:68).

C. By those three they [nonetheless] went back and by those three they fell:

D. First, in the days of Sennacherib: "Woe to those who go down to Egypt for help, etc." (Isa. 31:1). What is said about them in Scripture?—"For the Egyptians are man, not God, etc." (Isa. 31:3).

E. Second, in the days of Yoḥanan ben Keraḥ: "We will go to the Land of Egypt ... The sword that you fear (shall overtake you there)" (Jer. 42:14–16).

F. Third, in the days of Trajan.

G. By those three they went back, and by those three they fell.

9. A. Israel stood by the sea in four groups. One said, "Let's fall into the sea!" And one said, "Let's return to Egypt!" And one said, "Let's wage war!" And one said, "Let's cry out against them!"[114]

B. Concerning the one that said, "Let's fall into the sea!"—"'Stand by, and witness the deliverance which the Lord ...'" (Exod. 14:13).

C. Concerning the one that said, "Let's return to Egypt!"—"'... for the Egyptians whom you see (today you will never see again)'" (Exod. 14:13).

D. Concerning the one that said, "Let's wage war!"—"'The Lord will battle for you'" (Exod. 14:14).

E. Concerning the one that said, "Let's cry out against them!"—"'... You hold your peace!'" (Exod. 14:14).

[111] Compare 6.A–E with *Mekhilta de-Rabbi Ishmael*, Beshallaḥ (H/R, 95:7–8; Laut., vol. 1, 213:113–15; Neus., XXI:I:15.A–D).

[112] Compare 7.A–D with *Mekhilta de-Rabbi Ishmael*, Beshallaḥ (H/R, 95:9; Laut., vol. 1, 213:116–17; Neus., XXI:I:16.A–C).

[113] Compare 8.A–G with *Mekhilta de-Rabbi Ishmael*, Beshallaḥ (H/R, 95:10–96:1; Laut., vol. 1, 213:118–214:128; Neus., XXI:I:17.A–J); and y. Sukkah 55b (Neus., 5:1:VI.A–H).

M ◆ וישלח חציו ויפיצם וגומ' שהן חצים כנגד חיצים שלהן ◆

N　B/A 6 וברקים רב ויהמם כנגד צחצוח זיין שלהן. ◆ ד"א ◆ וישלח חציו

C ויפיצם וגו' ◆ שהן חצים מפזרין אותן וברקים מכנסין אותן.

E/D ויהומם ◆ המן עירבבן ניטל סגניים שלהן ולא היו יודעין

7　C/B/A מה הן עושין. ◆ ד"א ◆ ויהומם ◆ אין מהומה אלא מגפה ◆

D　A 8 כעניין שנא' והמם מהומה גדולה וגו' (דב' ז כג) ◆ בשלשה

B מקומות הזהיר המקו' את יש' שלא לחזור למצ' ◆ כי

כאשר ראיתם את מצ' היום וגו' ואומ' וייי אמר לכם

לא תוסיפון וגומ' (דב' יז טז). ואומ' בדרך אשר

אמרתי <לך> לא תוס' עוד לראותה (שם כח סח). ◆

D/C בשלשתן חזרו ובשלשתן נפלו. ◆ ראשונה בימי סנחריב

הוי היורדים מצרים לעזרה וגו' (ישע' לא א) מה נאמ'

E בהן ומצרים אדם ולא אל וגומ' (שם ג) ◆ שנייה בימי

יוחנן בן קרח לא כי ארץ נלך וגו' והיתה החרב אשר

F אתם יראים ממנה (ירמ' מב יד, טז). ◆ שלישית בימי

G טרוגינוס ◆ בשלשתן חזרו ובשלשתן נפלו. ◆

A 9 בארבע כיתות עמדו יש' על הים אחת אומרת

ניפול לים ואחת אומ' נחזור למצ' ואחת אומרת נעשה

B מלחמה ואחת אומ' נצווח כנגדן ◆ זו שאמרה ניפול לים

C התיצבו וראו את ישועת ייי ◆ זו שאמ' נחזור למצ' כי

D כאשר ראיתם את מצ' וגומ' ◆ זו שאמ' נעשה עמהן מלחמה

E ייי ילחם לכם. ◆ זו שאמרה נצווח כנגדן ואתם תחרישון. ◆

[114] Compare 9.A–E with *Mekhilta de-Rabbi Ishmael,* Beshallaḥ (H/R, 96:1–6; Laut., vol. 1, 214:128–36; Neus., XXI:I:18.A–I); and y. Taanit 65d (Neus., 2:5:I.A–I).

10.　　A.　Another interpretation:[115]

　　　　B.　"'The Lord will battle for you'" (Exod. 14:14):

　　　　C.　Not just now, but forever "'the Lord will battle for you'" (Exod. 14:14).

11.　　A.　R. Meir says: "'The Lord will battle for you'" (Exod. 14:14):

　　　　B.　"When you are standing quietly, God fights your war for you and performs miracles and great deeds for you. How much the more so when you say praise before him!"

12.　　A.　Rabbi says, "'"The Lord will battle for you'" (Exod. 14:14):

　　　　B.　"For you God performs miracles and great deeds, while you stand silently!

　　　　C.　"They[116] said to him,[117] 'What should we do?' He said to them, 'You should exalt, acclaim, herald, glorify, and give praise, song, glory, and cheer to He to whom war belongs!'

[57]　　D.　"In accordance with what is said in Scripture, '... with paeans to God in their throats, etc.' (Ps. 149:6). And Scripture says, 'Exalt Yourself over the heavens, O God' (Ps. 57:6). And Scripture says, 'O Lord, You are my God. I will extol You, etc.' (Isa. 25:1).

　　　　E.　"At that moment, Israel opened its mouth and sang a song: 'I will sing to the Lord, for He has triumphed gloriously, etc.' (Exod. 15:1)."

*Chapter Twenty-Three*

(Textual Source: Ms. Firkovich IIA, 268)

XXIII:I[118]

1.　　A.　"Then the Lord said to Moses, 'Why do you cry out to me? (Tell the Israelites to go forward)'" (Exod. 14:15):

　　　　B.　R. Joshua says, "Israel only [had the option of] marching forward."

2.　　A.　R. Eliezer says, "The Holy One, blessed be He, said to Moses, 'My children are in distress, with a closed-up sea [before them] and the enemy pursuing them [from behind]. But you stand and multiply prayer before me! Why do you cry out to me? Tell the Israelites to go forward!'" (Exod. 14:15).

　　　　B.　For he[119] would say, "There is a time to cut [prayer] short, and there is a time to lengthen [prayer].

　　　　C.　"'O God, pray heal her!' (Num. 12:13)—behold, [this is an example of] cutting short.

　　　　D.　"'I stayed on the mountain forty days and forty nights' (Deut. 9:9)—behold, [this is an example of] lengthening."

3.　　A.　R. Meir says, "He[120] said to him, 'If for a single man I turned the sea into dry land—in accordance with what is said in Scripture, "... let the water be gathered" (Gen. 1:9)—[then likewise] for this holy congregation, I will turn the sea into dry land!'

　　　　B.　"Thus Scripture states, 'As to the holy and mighty ones that are in the land, etc.' (Ps. 16:3)."

4.　　A.　R. Ishmael says, "He said to him, 'For the merit of Jerusalem will I split the sea for them!'

---

[115] Compare 10.A–12.E with *Mekhilta de-Rabbi Ishmael*, Beshallaḥ (H/R, 96:7–15; Laut., vol. 1, 215:137–49; Neus., XXI:I:19.A–21.F).

[116] I.e., the Israelites.

[117] I.e., to Moses.

[118] XXIII:I is a unit comprised entirely of short interpretive treatments of Exod. 14:15, all of which attempt to give additional substance to the nature and tone of the conversation that took place between God and Moses in that verse. Compare XXIII:I:1.A–27.C with *Mekhilta de-Rabbi Ishmael*, Beshallaḥ (H/R, 97:1–100:9; Laut., vol. 1, 216:1–223:97; Neus., XXII:I:1.A–24.E).

| | | |
|---|---|---|
| C/B/A | 10 | ד״א ♦ ייי ילחם לכם וגו׳ ♦ לא לשעה אלא לעולם |
| B/A | 11 | ייי ילחם לכם. ♦ ר׳ מאיר אומ׳ ייי ילחם לכם ♦ אם |
| | | כשאתם עומדין ושותקין המקום עושה לכן מלחמה |
| | | ועושה לכם נסים וגבורות קל וחומר כשאתם אומ׳ |
| B/A | 12 | לפניו שבח. ♦ ר׳ אומ׳ ייי ילחם לכם ♦ המקום עושה לכם |
| C | | נסים וגבורות ואתם עומדין ושותקין ♦ אמרו לו מה |
| | | עלינו לעשות אמ׳ להן היו מפארין ומרוממין |
| | | ומשבחין ומקלסין ומהדרין ונותנין שבח וגדולה |
| | | ותהלה ותפארת והדר ונצח למי שהמלחמה שלו ♦ |
| D | | כעניין שנא׳ רוממות אל בגרונם וגומ׳ (תה׳ קמט ו) |
| | | ואומ׳ רומה על שמים אלקים (שם נז יב) ואומ׳ ייי |
| E | | אלקי אתה ארוממך וגו׳ (ישע׳ כה א) ♦ באותה שעה |
| | | פתחו יש׳ פיהם ואמ׳ שירה אשירה לייי כי גאה גאה |
| | | וגו׳ (שמ׳ טו א). סל׳ פסקא. ♦ |

XXIII:I

| | | |
|---|---|---|
| B/A | 1 | ויאמר ייי אל משה מה תצעק אלי וגומ׳ ♦ ר׳ יהושע |
| A | 2 | אומ׳ אין ליש׳ אלא ניסוע בלבד ♦ ר׳ אליעזר אומ׳ אמ׳ |
| | | לו הקב״ה למשה בני שרויין בצרה וים סוגר ושונא |
| | | רודף ואתה עומד ומרבה בתפלה לפני מה תצעק אלי |
| B | | דבר אל בני יש׳ ויסעו ♦ שהיה אומ׳ יש שעה לקצר ויש |
| C | | שעה להאריך ♦ אל נא רפא נא לה (במ׳ יב יג) הרי |
| D | | לקצר: ♦ ואשב בהר ארבעים יום וארבעים לילה (דב׳ ט |
| A | 3 | ט) הרי להאריך ♦ ר׳ מאיר אומ׳ אמ׳ לו אם לאדם יחידי |
| | | עשיתי <ים> יבשה כעניין שנא׳ יקוו המים (בר׳ א ט) |
| B | | לקהל קדשים אלו איני עושה <ים> יבשה ♦ כן הוא |
| A | 4 | אומ׳ לקדושים אשר בארץ המה וגומ׳ (תה׳ טז ג) ♦ ר׳ |
| | | ישמעאל אומ׳ אמ׳ לו בזכות ירוש׳ אני קורע להן את הים ♦ |

B.  "As it says in Scripture, 'Awake, awake, clothe yourself with splendor. O arm (of the Lord!) ... It was you that dried up the sea, etc.'" (Isa. 51:9–10).

5.  A.  Another interpretation:

B.  [God said,] "I already made a promise to Jacob their forefather—'... but God will be with you and bring you back (to the land of your fathers), etc.'" (Gen. 48:21).

6.  A.  R. Akiva says, "[God said,] 'For the merit of Jacob will I split the sea for them. For I said to him, "Your descendants shall be as the dust of the earth. You shall spread out to the west"' (Gen. 28:14)."

7.  A.  R. Judah ben Beteira says, "[God said,] 'I already promised the forefathers of these [people]— "But the Israelites had marched through the sea on dry ground" (Exod. 14:29).'"

8.  A.  R. Banyah says, "[God said,] 'For the merit of the commandment that Abraham did will I split the sea for them—"And he split the wood" (Gen. 22:3).'

B.  "What does Scripture say?—'The waters were split' (Exod. 14:21)."

9.  A.  R. Shimon b. Yoḥai says, "Already the sun and moon and stars and planets were beseeching mercy on their behalf!

B.  "As it says in Scripture, 'Thus said the Lord, who established the sun for light by day (the laws of moon and stars for light by night, who stirs up the sea into roaring waves), etc.' (Jer. 31:35)."

10.  A.  Shimon the Yemenite says, "[God said,] 'For the merit of circumcision[121] will I split the sea for them.'
[58]

B.  "As it says in Scripture, 'Thus said the Lord, "As surely as I have established my covenant[122] with day and night, etc."' (Jer. 33:25).

C.  "Which covenant is it that applies day and night? You only find circumcision.

D.  "Behold Scripture states, 'Who split the Sea of Reeds into parts' (Ps. 136:13)."[123]

11.  A.  R. Avtilas the Elder [says], "They told a parable: To what is the matter alike?

B.  "To a human king who was angry at his son. A certain administrator would appeal before him. He said to him, 'You are only appealing to me on behalf of my son. I've already reconciled with him!'

C.  "Likewise, the Holy One, blessed be He, said to Moses, 'You are only appealing to me on behalf of my children. I've already reconciled with them!'

D.  "'Then the Lord said to Moses, "Why do you cry out to me? (Tell the Israelites to go forward), etc."' (Exod. 14:15)."

12.  A.  Rabbi says, "He[124] said to him, 'Yesterday you said to me, "Ever since I came to Pharaoh (to speak in Your name, he has dealt worse with this people, and still you have not delivered your people)" (Exod. 5:23).

B.  "'But on this day you multiply prayer before me!'"

13.  A.  And the Sages say, "For the sake of His name did he deal with them.

B.  "As it says in Scripture, 'For My sake, My own sake, do I act, etc.' (Isa. 48:11). And Scripture

---

[121] Hebrew: *brit*—ברית.
[122] Hebrew: *brit*—ברית.
[123] 10.D is difficult to understand; however, its meaning becomes clearer when supplied with the sentence that follows in the parallel to this tradition in Midrash ha-Gadol: "Don't read it as 'into parts,' but rather, as 'for those circumcised.'" [אל תקרא לגזרים אלא לגזורים].
[124] I.e., God.

| | | |
|---|---|---|
| B | שנא׳ <...> עורי עורי לבשי עז זרוע וגומ׳ הלא את | |
| B/A | היא המחרבת ים וגו׳ (ישע׳ נא ט - י). ◆ ד״א ◆ כבר עשיתי | 5 |
| A | הבטחה שהבטיחן יעקב אביהן והיה אלקים עמכם | |
| A | והשיב אתכם וגו׳ (בר׳ מח כא) ◆ ר׳ עקי׳ אומ׳ בזכות | 6 |
| | יעקב אני קורע להן את הים שאמרתי לו והיה זרעך | |
| A | כעפר הארץ ופרצת ימה (שם כח יד). ◆ ר׳ יהודה בן | 7 |
| | בתירא אומ׳ כבר הבטחתי אבותיהן של אלו. ובני יש׳ | |
| A | הלכו ביבשה בתוך הים (שמ׳ יד כט) ◆ ר׳ בניה אומ׳ | 8 |
| | בזכות מצוה שעשה אברהם אני קורע להן את הים | |
| B | ויבקע עצי עלה (בר׳ כב ג) ◆ מה הוא אומ׳ ויבקעו | |
| A | המים ◆ ר׳ שמע׳ בן יוחי אומ׳ כבר חמה ולבנה כוכבים | 9 |
| B | ומזלות יבקשו עליהן רחמים ◆ שנא׳ כה אמר ייי נותן | |
| A | שמש לאור יומם וגו׳ (ירמ׳ לא לה). ◆ שמעון התימני | 10 |
| B | אומ׳ בזכות מילה אני קורע להן את הים ◆ שנא׳ כה | |
| | אמר ייי אם לא בריתי יומם ולילה וגומ׳ (ירמ׳ לג כה) ◆ | |
| C | אי זו היא ברית שנוהגת ביום ובלילה אי אתה מוצא | |
| D | אלא מילה ◆ מה האו אומ׳ לגוזר ים סוף לגזרים (תה׳ | |
| A | קלו יג). ◆ ר׳ אבטילס הזקן מושלו משל למה הדבר | 11 |
| B | דומה ◆ למלך בשר ודם שכעס על בנו והיה אפטרופוס | |
| | ההוא מבקש מלפניו ואמ׳ לו כלום אתה מבקש | |
| C | מלפני אלא בשביל בני כבר נתרציתי לו ◆ כך אמ׳ לו | |
| A 12 D | הקב״ה למשה כלום אתה מבקש מלפני אלא בשביל | |
| | בני כבר נתרציתי להן ◆ מה תצעק אלי וגו׳ ◆ ר׳ או׳ אמ׳ לו | |
| A 13 B | אמש אמרתי לי ומאז באתי אל פרעה וגו׳ (שמ׳ ה כג) ◆ | |
| B | היום הזה אתה מרבה בתפלה לפני ◆ וחכמ׳ אומ׳ למען | |
| | שמו עשה עמהן ◆ שנא׳ למעני למעני אעשה וגו׳ (ישע׳ | |

says, '… who divided the waters before them, etc.' (Isa. 63:12)."

14.  A.  Rabbi says, "He[125] said to him, 'Yesterday they were saying, "… Was it for want of graves in Egypt" (Exod. 14:11).

     B.  "'Now you multiply prayer before me!—"Why do you cry out to me? (Tell the Israelites to go forward), etc." (Exod. 14:15).'

     C.  "He got them to stop thinking about it!"

15.  A.  R. Meir says, "He[126] said to him, 'The faith with which Israel believed in Me in Egypt merits that I split the sea for them.'

     B.  "For they didn't say to Moses, 'How can we turn back behind us [as commanded in Exod. 14:1] without frightening the children who are with us?'

     C.  "Rather, they believed and followed Moses!"

16.  A.  R. Eliezer ben Azariah says, "[God said,] 'For the merit of my servant Abraham will I split the sea for them.'

     B.  "As it says in Scripture, 'Mindful of His sacred promise (to His servant Abraham), He led His people out in gladness, etc.' (Ps. 105:43)."

17.  A.  R. Eliezer ben Judah ish Bartotha says, "[God said,] 'For the merit of the tribes will I split the sea for them.'

     B.  "As it says in Scripture, 'You will crack his skull with Your bludgeon' (Hab. 3:14)."

18.  A.  Shamaya says, "[God said,] 'The faith with which Abraham believed in Me merits that I split the sea for them.'

     B.  "[As it says in Scripture,] 'He put his trust in the Lord, etc.' (Gen. 15:6)."

19.  A.  Avtalion says, "[God said,] 'For the faith with which Israel believed [in Me] in Egypt will I split the sea for them.'

     B.  "As it says in Scripture, 'The people believed' (Exod. 4:31)."

20.  A.  Shimon Ish Kitron says, "[God said,] 'For the merit of [transporting home] the bones of Joseph will I split the sea for them.'

     B.  "As it says in Scripture, 'And he left his garment in her hand (and *fled*), etc.' (Gen. 39:12). What does Scripture [also] state?—'The sea saw them and *fled*, etc.' (Ps. 114:3)."

21.  A.  R. Nathan says in the name of R. Yosi ha-Mahozi, "The Holy One, blessed be He, said to Moses, 'I have already had it written concerning you, "He is trusted throughout" (Num. 12:7).

     B.  "'You are under My control, and the sea is under My control. I have already made you commander over it!'"

22.  A.  R. Hananiah ben Nekhusa says, "[God said,] 'I have already had it written, "A brother is
[59]     born to share adversity" (Prov. 17:17).

     B.  "'[Meaning,] I am a brother to Israel in their time of distress!'

     C.  "And [the word] 'brothers' [in Scripture] refers only to Israel.

     D.  "As it says in Scripture, 'For the sake of my brothers and friends, etc.' (Ps. 122:8)."

23.  A.  R. Eliezer the Modiite says, "The Holy One, blessed be He, said to Moses, 'You are

---

[125] I.e., God.
[126] I.e., God.

| | | |
|---|---|---|
| A | 14 | מח יא) ואומ' בוקע מים מפניהם וגו' (שם סג יב) ◆ ר' |
| | | אומ' אמ' לו אמש היו אומ' המבלי אין קברים במצ' |
| B | | (שמ' יד יא) ◆ עכשיו אתה מרבה בתפלה לפני מה |
| A 15 | C | תצעק אלי וגו' ◆ הסיע דברים מלבן. ◆ ר' מאיר אומ' אמ' |
| | | לו כדי אמנה שהאמינו בי יש' במצ' אני קורע להן את |
| B | | הים ◆ שלא אמרו לו למשה היאך נחזור לאחורינו שלא |
| C | | נשבור לב טף שעמנו ◆ אלא האמינו והלכו אחרי משה. ◆ |
| A | 16 | ר' אלעזר בן עזריה אומ' בזכות אברהם עבדי אני |
| B | | קורע להן את הים ◆ שנא' כי זכר את דבר קדשו וגומ' |
| A | 17 | ויוציא עמו בששון וגו' (תה' קה מג) ◆ ר' אלעזר בן |
| | | יהודה איש ברתותא אומ' בזכות שבטים אני קורע |
| B | | להן את הים ◆ שנא' נקבת במטיו ראש פרזיו (חב' ג יד) |
| A | 18 | וגו' ◆ שמעיה אומ' כדי אמונה שהאמין בי אברהם אני |
| B | | קורע להן את הים ◆ והאמין בייי וגומ' (בר' טו ו). ◆ |
| A | 19 | אבטליון אומ' כדי אמונה שהאמין יש' במצ' אני קורע |
| A 20 | B | להן את הים ◆ שנא' ויאמן העם (שמ' ד לא). ◆ שמעון |
| | | איש קטרון אומ' בזכות עצמות יוסף אני קורע להן |
| B | | את הים ◆ שנא' ויעזוב בגדו אצלה וגו' (בר' לט יב) מה |
| A | 21 | אמ' הים ראה וינס וגומ' (תה' קיד ג) ◆ ר' נתן אומ' |
| | | משום ר' יוסי המחוזי אמ' לו הקב"ה למשה כבר |
| B | | הכתבתי עליך בכל ביתי נאמן הוא (במ' יב ז) ◆ אתה |
| A | 22 | ברשותי והים ברשותי כבר עשיתיך גיזבר עליו. ◆ ר' |
| | | חנניה בן נכוסא אומ' כבר הכתבתי ואח לצרה יולד |
| C/B | | (מש' יז יז) ◆ אח אני ליש' בשעת צרתן ◆ אין אחים אלא |
| A 23 | D | יש' ◆ שנאמ' למען אחי ורעי וגומ' (תה' קכב ח) ◆ ר' |
| | | אלעזר המודעי אומ' אמ' לו המקום למשה על בני |

commanding Me concerning My children.

B.   "'As it says in Scripture, "Will you instruct Me about the works of My hands?" (Isa. 45:11).

C.   "'I don't need a command! I have been mindful of them since the six days of Creation!

D.   "'As it says in Scripture, "Thus said the Lord: If the heavens above could be measured, etc." (Jer. 31:37).'"

24.   A.   R. Aha says, "The Holy One, blessed be He, said to Moses, 'Moses! Why do you cry out to me!'

B.   "He [also] said to him, 'Were it not for your crying, I would have already destroyed them from the world!'

C.   "As it says in Scripture, '(He would have destroyed them) had not Moses His chosen one (confronted Him in the breach to avert His destructive wrath)' (Ps. 106:23)."

25.   A.   R. Shimon ben Eliezer ish Kefar Akkum says, "[God said,] 'Why do you cry out to me? Their cry has already preceded your cry: "Greatly frightened, the Israelites cried out to the Lord" (Exod. 14:10).'"

26.   A.   Others say, "[God said,] 'The faith with which the Israelites believed in Me in Egypt merits that I split the sea for them.

B.   "'Because they didn't say to Moses: "We are going out into the wilderness in vain! This is all chaos, for there's nothing to it! We don't [even] have provisions for the way!"

C.   "'Rather, they went out on faith [alone].'

D.   "And about them it is explained in tradition, 'Go proclaim to Jerusalem: Thus said the Lord: I accounted, etc.' (Jer. 2:2).

E.   "What reward did they take for this?—'Israel was holy to the Lord, etc.' (Jer. 2:3)."

27.   A.   R. Yosi ha-Galili says, "[When the Israelites went into the sea,] He[127] said to him, 'Already Moriah was uprooted from its place, with Isaac's altar built upon its back, as if the wood was arranged on it, and as if Isaac was bound and placed on the altar, and as if Abraham held in his hand the knife to slaughter his son.'

B.   "He[128] said before Him, 'Master of the World! What am I to do!'

C.   "He said, 'You should glorify, exalt, etc.!'"

*Chapter Twenty-Four*

(Textual Source: Ms. Firkovich IIA, 268)

XXIV:I[129]

1.   A.   "And you lift up your rod (and hold out your arm over the sea and split it, so that the Israelites may march into the sea on dry ground)" (Exod. 14:16):

B.   Ten miracles were performed for Israel at the sea:

C.   The sea was split and turned into a kind of vault. As it says in Scripture, "You will crack [his] skill with Your bludgeon, etc." (Hab. 3:14).[130]

D.   It was divided into two. As it says in Scripture, "And you lift up your rod, etc." (Exod. 14:16).

---

[127] I.e., God.

[128] I.e., Moses.

[129] Compare XXIV:I:1.A–IV:5.D with *Mekhilta de-Rabbi Ishmael*, Beshallah (H/R, 100:10–104:12; Laut., vol. 1, 223:1–232:119; Neus., XXIII: I:1.A–12.C).

[130] The text reads this verse as: "You pierced it [i.e., the waters] because of [or: with] his tribes." That is, God pierced the waters of the sea on behalf of Israel, and the pierced waters formed a kind of vault.

| | | |
|---|---|---|
| אתה מצויני ♦ שנא׳ על בני ועל בפועל ידי תצווני (ישע׳ | B | |
| מה יא) ♦ איני צריך ציווי כבר מוזכרין הן לפני משת | C | |
| ימי בראשית ♦ שנא׳ כה אמר יי אם ימדו שמים וגומ׳ | D | |
| (ירמ׳ לא לז). ♦ ר׳ אחא אומ׳ אמ׳ לו הקב״ה למשה משה | A | 24 |
| מה תצעק אלי ♦ אמ׳ לו אילולי צעקתך כבר | B | |
| איבדת<י>ם מן העולם ♦ שנא׳ לולי משה בחירו וגומ׳ | C | |
| (תה׳ קו כג). ♦ ר׳ שמע׳ בן אלעזר איש כפר עיכום או׳ | A | 25 |
| מה תצעק אלי כבר קדמה צעקתם לצעקתך וייראו | | |
| מאד ויצעקו בני יש׳ אל יי (שמ׳ יד י) ♦ אחרים אומ׳ | A | 26 |
| כדיי אמנה שהאמינו ב(נ)י יש׳ במצ׳ קורע אני להן את | | |
| הים ♦ שלא אמ׳ לו למשה לאין אנו יוצאין למדבר תהו | B | |
| הזה שאין בו כלום ואין בידינו מחיה לדרך ♦ אלא יצאו | C | |
| על אמונה ♦ ועליהן מפרש בקבלה הלוך וקראת באזני | D | |
| ירושלם לאמר כה אמר יי זכרתי לך וגו׳ (ירמ׳ ב ב) ♦ | | |
| מה שכר נטלו על כך קדש יש׳ ליי וגומ׳ (שם) ♦ ר׳ יוסי | A 27 | E |
| הגלילי אומ׳ אמ׳ לו כבר המוריה נעקר ממקומו | | |
| ומזבחו של יצחק בנו על גביו ומערכתו כאילו ערוכה | | |
| עליו ויצחק כאילו עקוב ונתון על גבי המזבח ואברהם | | |
| כאילו בידו מאכלת לשחוט את בנו ♦ אמ׳ לפניו רבונו | B | |
| שלעולם אני מה עלי לעשות ♦ אמ׳ הוי מפאר ומרומם | C | |
| וכול׳ עניינא. סל׳ פסו׳ ♦ | | |

| | | |
|---|---|---|
| | | XXIV:I |
| ואתה הרם את מטך וגו׳ ♦ עשרה נסים נעשו להן ליש׳ | B/A | 1 |
| על הים ♦ נבקע ים ונעשה כמין כיפה שנא׳ נקבת במטיו וגו׳ | C | |
| (חב׳ ג יד) ♦ נחלק לשנים שנא׳ ואתה הרם את מטך וגומ׳ ♦ | D | |

E.    It was turned into clay. As it says in Scripture, "You will make Your steeds tread the sea, etc." (Hab. 3:15).

F.    It was made dry. [As it says in Scripture,] "But the Israelites had marched through the sea on dry ground, etc." (Exod. 14:29).

G.    It was split into pieces. As it says in Scripture, "... who split apart the Sea of Reeds ..." (Ps. 136:13).

[60]   H.    It was turned into rocks. As it says in Scripture, "You shattered the heads of the monsters (upon the water), etc." (Ps. 74:13).

I.    It was turned into crumbs. As it says in Scripture, "You broke the sea into pieces with Your power, etc." (Ps. 74:13).

J.    It was piled in heaps. As it says in Scripture, "At the blast of Your nostrils the waters piled up, etc." (Exod. 15:8).

K.    He brought out sweet water from the salty water.

L.    He congealed the water into two parts, making it into a kind of glass ball. As it says in Scripture, "The deeps froze in the heart of the sea" (Exod. 15:8).

## XXIV:II

1.    A.    "The angel of God, (who had been going ahead of the Israelite army,) now moved (and followed behind them. The pillar of cloud shifted from in front of them and took up a place behind them)" (Exod. 14:19):

     B.    R. Judah says, "Behold, this verse of Scripture is rich in many ways!

     C.    "They told a parable: To what is the matter alike?

     D.    "To a human king who would walk along the way in the wilderness with his son with him. [If] robbers approached in front of him to abduct him,[131] he would take him and place him behind him. If a wolf [approached] from behind him, he would take him and carry him on his shoulders. In accordance with what is said in Scripture, '... and in the wilderness, where you saw how the Lord your God carried you, etc.' (Deut. 1:31).

     E.    "If he began to be distressed, he would take him in his arms. In accordance with what is said in Scripture, 'I have pampered Ephraim, etc.' (Hos. 11:3).

     F.    "If he began to be distressed because of the sun, he would spread his clothes over him. As it says in Scripture, 'He spread a cloud for cover, etc.' (Ps. 106:39).

     G.    "If he hungered, he fed him bread. In accordance with what is said in Scripture, 'I will rain down bread for you, etc.' (Exod. 16:4).

     H.    "If he was thirsty, he gave him water to drink. As it says in Scripture, 'He brought forth streams from a rock' (Ps. 78:16).

     I.    "'Streams' means only 'living water,' as it says in Scripture, 'A garden spring, (a well of fresh water,) etc.' (Song 4:15). And Scripture says, 'Drink water from your own cistern, running water, etc.' (Prov. 5:15)."

2.    A.    R. Nathan asked R. Shimon b. Yoḥai, "Why in every instance is it written in Scripture 'angel of the Lord' but here it is written 'angel of God'?"

     B.    He said to him [in response], "[The word] 'God' in every instance means only 'judge.'

---

[131] I.e., the son.

ונעשה טיט שנא' דרכת בים וגומ' (שם טו). ◆    E

נעשה יבשה ובני יש' הלכו ביבשה וגומ' (שמ' יד כט) ◆    F

נעשה גזרים שנא' לגוזר ים סוף לגזרים וגו' (תה'    G

קלו יג) ◆ נעשה סלעים שנא' שברת ראשי תנינים וגו'    H

(תה' עד יג) ◆ נעשה פירורין שנא' פוררת בעזך ים וגו'    I

(שם) ◆ נעשה ערמות שנא' וברוח אפך נערמו מים וגומ'    J

(שמ' טו ח) ◆ יצאו להן <זכרי> מים מתוקים מתוך מים    K

מלוחים ◆ קפא הים על שני חלקים נעשה כמן בולס    L

של זכוכית שנא' קפאו תהומות בלב ים (שמ' טו ח).

סל' פסו' ◆

                                  XXIV:II

ויסע מלאך האלהים וגו' ◆ ר' יהודה אומ' הרי זה    B/A    1

מקרא עשיר במקומות הרבה ◆ מושלו משל למה הדבר    C

דומה ◆ למלך בשר ודם שהיה מהלך בדרך ובנו עמו    D

במדבר באו ליסטין לשבותו מלפניו נטלו ונתנו

לאחוריו בא זאב ליטלו מאחוריו נטלו ונתנו לפניו

ליסטים מלפניו וזאב מאחוריו נטלו והרכיבו על

כתיפו כעניין שנ' ובמדבר אשר ראית אשר נשאך יי'

וגו' (דב' א לא) ◆ התחיל מצטער לקחו על זרועותיו    E

כעניין שנא' אנכי תרגלתי לאפרים וגו' (הושע יא ג) ◆

התחיל מצטער מפני חמה פרס עליו בגדיו שנא' פרס    F

ענן למסך וגומ' (תה' קה לט) ◆ הרעיב האכילו לחם    G

כעניין שנא' הנני ממטיר לכם וגומ' (שמ' טז ד) ◆ צמא    H

השקהו מים שנא' ויוציא נוזלים מסלע (תה' עח טז) ◆

אין נוזלים אל /אלא/ מים חיים שנא' מעין גנים וגו'    I

(שה"ש ד טו) ואומ' שתה מים מבורך ונוז' וגומ' (מש'

ה טו) ◆ שאל ר' נתן את ר' שמע' בן יוחי מפני מה בכל    A    2

מקום כת' מלאך יי' וכאן כת' מלאך האלקים ◆ אמ' לו    B

אין אלקים בכל מקום אלא דין שהיו יש' באותה

For at that moment the Israelites were [being judged] whether they would win or lose to the Egyptians."

## XXIV:III

1.    A.   "And it came between the army of the Egyptians and the army of Israel. (Thus there was the cloud with the darkness, and it cast a spell upon the night, so that the one could not come near the other all through the night)" (Exod. 14:20):

       B.   It drove a wedge between the army of the Egyptians and the army of Israel.

2.    A.   "Thus there was a cloud with the darkness" (Exod. 14:20):

       B.   The cloud was for Israel and the darkness was for Egypt.

       C.   You find that whoever is placed in darkness sees he who is located in light. And Egypt was located in darkness, and Israel was located in light. In accordance with what is said in Scripture, "People could not see one another ... (but all the Israelites enjoyed light in their dwellings), etc." (Exod. 10:23).

       D.   From this you learn about the time to come: "Arise, shine, for your light has come ... Because, behold, darkness shall cover the earth, etc." (Isa. 60:1–2).

       E.   Not only this, but also that the Egyptians were located in darkness and could see Israel, located in light, eating and drinking and rejoicing. They shot arrows and catapult stones at them, but the angel and cloud caught them. In accordance with what is said in Scripture, "Fear not, Abram, I am a shield to you, etc." (Gen. 15:1). And Scripture says, "God is my rock, I take shelter in Him, etc." (2 Sam. 22:3). And Scripture says, "The word of the Lord is pure, (He is a shield to all who take refuge in Him,) etc." (2 Sam 22:31).

[61]

3.    A.   "... so that the one could not come near the other all through the night" (Exod. 14:20):

       B.   The Egyptian who was standing was unable to sit, and the one sitting was unable to stand. The one who was loaded [with supplies] was unable to unload, and the one who was unloaded was unable to load up.

       C.   He was [actually] touching the darkness! As it says in Scripture, "... a darkness that can be touched" (Exod. 10:21).

4.    A.   Another interpretation:

       B.   "... so that the one could not come near the other all through the night" (Exod. 14:20):

       C.   In that the army of the Egyptians did not draw near the army of the Israelites, and the army of the Israelites did not draw near the army of the Egyptians.

## XXIV:IV

1.    A.   "Then Moses held out his arm over the sea (and the Lord drove back the sea with a strong east wind all that night, and turned the sea into dry ground. The waters were split)" (Exod. 14:21):

       B.   The sea began to stand against Moses.

       C.   They told a parable: To what is the matter alike?

       D.   To a human king who had two gardens, one within the other. He sold the inner one, but left the outer one alone. When the purchaser came to enter [the inner garden], the guard would not let him. He[132] spoke up in the name of the king, but he [still] wouldn't receive him. He showed him [the king's] seal, but he wouldn't receive him. He brought the king,

---

[132] I.e., the purchaser.

השעה אם להינצל אם לאבד מן המצריים. סל׳ פסו׳ ◆

| | | |
|---|---|---|
| ויבוא בין מחנה מצ׳ ובין מחנה יש׳ ◆ חצץ בין מחנה | B/A | 1 |
| מצ׳ ובין מחנה יש׳ <...> ◆ ויהי הענן והחושך ◆ ענן ליש[ר]׳ | B/A | 2 |
| וחושך למצ׳ ◆ את מוצא שכל מי שנתון באפילה רואה | C | |

מי ששרוי באורה והיו מצ׳ שרויין באפילה ויש[ר]׳
שרויין באורה כעניין שנא׳ לא ראו איש את אחיו וגומ׳

| | | |
|---|---|---|
| (שמ׳ י כג) ◆ מיכן את מוצא לעתיד לבוא אומ׳ קומי | D | |

אורי כי בא אורך וגומ׳ ואומ׳ כי הנה החושך וגומ׳

| | | |
|---|---|---|
| (ישע׳ ס ב). ◆ ולא עוד אלא שהיו המצריים שרויין | E | |

באפילה ורואין את יש׳ שהן שרויין באורה ואוכלין
ושותין ושמחין והיו מזרקין בהן חצים ואבני בלסטא
והיה מלאך וענן מקבלן כעניין שנא׳ אל תירא אברם
אנכי מגן לך וגומ׳ (בר׳ טו א) ואומ׳ אלקי צורי אחסה
בו וגומ׳ (ש״ב כב ג) ואומ׳ כל אמרת אלוה צרופה

| | | |
|---|---|---|
| וגומ׳ (שם לא) ◆ ולא קרב זה אל זה כל הלילה. ◆ היה | B/A | 3 |

מצרי עומד אין יכול לישב יושב אין יכול לעמוד טעון
אין יכול לפרוק פרוק אין יכול לטעון ◆ והיה ממשש

| | | |
|---|---|---|
| באפילה שנא׳ וימש חושך (שמ׳ י כא). ◆ ד״א ◆ ולא קרב | C | |
| | B/A | 4 |

זה אל זה כל הלילה ◆ שלא קרב מחנה מצ׳ לתוך מחנה

| | | |
|---|---|---|
| יש׳ ולא מחנה יש׳ למחנה מצ׳. סל׳ פסו׳. ◆ | C | |

| | | |
|---|---|---|
| ויט משה את ידו על הים ◆ התחיל הים עומד כנגד | B/A | 1 |
| משה ◆ מושלו משל למה הדבר דומה ◆ למלך בשר ודם | D/C | |

שהיו לו שתי גנות זו לפנים מזו מכר את הפנימית
והניח את החיצונה בא לוקח להכנס ולא הניחו שומר
אמ׳ לו בשם המלך ולא קבל עליו הראהו טבעת ולא
קיבל עליו נהג המלך ובא כיון שראה שומר את המלך

who came. When the guard saw the king, he began to flee. He[133] said to him, "What are you fleeing?" He said to him, "I'm not fleeing from before you, rather I'm fleeing from before the king."

E. Likewise, when Moses came and stood before the sea, he spoke to it in the name of the Holy One, but it wouldn't receive him. He showed him the staff, but it wouldn't receive him. When the Holy One, blessed be He, appeared, "the sea saw and began to flee" (Ps. 114:3).

Moses said to it, "I was speaking to you in the name of the Holy One, but you wouldn't accept it. I showed you the staff, but you wouldn't accept it. Now 'what alarmed you, O sea, that you fled?' (Ps. 114:5)."

It said to him, "Not from before you, son of Amran, rather, 'Tremble from before the Lord!' (Ps. 114:7)."

2.　A. "... and the Lord drove back the sea with a strong east wind all that night" (Exod. 14:21):

B. With the strongest of the winds. And which is this? This is the east wind.

C. And thus you find that the people of the Flood and the people of Sodom were punished only with an east wind. As it says in Scripture, "They perish by a blast from God" (Job 4:9)—this is the generation of the Flood. "... are gone at the breath of His nostrils" (Job 4:9)—these are the people of Sodom.

D. And thus you find that the people of the Tower of Babel were punished only with an east wind. As it says in Scripture, "Thus the Lord scattered them, etc." (Gen. 11:8).

E. "Scattering" refers only to the east wind. As it says in Scripture, "Like the east wind, I will scatter them, etc." (Jer. 18:17).

F. And thus you find that Egypt was punished only with an east wind. As it says in Scripture, "The Lord drove an east wind, etc." (Exod. 10:13).

G. And thus you find that the 10 tribes were punished only with an east wind. As it says in Scripture, "For though he flourish among reeds, a blast, a wind of the Lord, etc." (Hos. 13:15).

[62]　H. And thus you find that the tribes of Benjamin and Judah were punished only with an east wind. As it says in Scripture, "Like the east wind, I will scatter them before, etc." (Jer. 18:17).

I. And thus you find that Tyre was punished only with an east wind. As it says in Scripture, "Say to Tyre ... the tempest wrecked you, etc." (Ezek. 27:3,26).

J. And thus you find that this wanton kingdom[134] will only be punished by an east wind. As it says in Scripture, "... was wrecked in an easterly gale, etc." (Ps. 48:8).

K. And thus you find that God will only punish the wicked in Gehenna with an east wind.

---

[133] I.e., the purchaser.
[134] I.e., Rome.

התחיל בורח אמ' לו מה לך בורח אמ' לו לא מלפניך

אני בורח אלא מלפני המלך אני בורח ◆ כך כשבא משה

ועמד על הים אמ' לו בשם הקדש ולא קיבל עליו

הראהו המטה ולא קיבל עליו כיון שנגלה עליו

הקב''ה הים ראה וינס אמ' לו משה הייתי אומ' לך

בשם הק' ולא הי<י>תה מקבל עליך הראיתיך את

המטה ולא קיבלת עליך עכשיו מה לך הים כי תנס

(תה' קיד ה) אמ' לו לא מלפניך בן עמרם אלא מלפני

אדון חולי ארץ (שם ז). ◆ ויולך ייי את הים ברוח קדים

עזה כל הלילה ◆ בעזה שברוחות ואי זו זו רוח הקדים ◆

וכן אתה מוצא באנשי מבול ובאנשי סדום שלא נפרע

מהן אלא ברוח קדים שנא' מנשמת אלוה יאבדו

(איוב ד מ) זה דור המבול. ומרוח אפו יכלו (שם) אלו

אנשי סדם ◆ וכן את מוצא באנשי מגדל שלא נפרע מהן

אלא ברוח קדים שנא' ויפץ ייי אתם (ברוח) וגומ' (בר'

יא ח) ◆ אין הפצה אלא ברוח הקדים שנא ברוח קדים

אפיצים וגומ' (ירמ' יח יז) ◆ וכן אתה מוצא במצ' שלא

נפרע מהן אלא ברוח קדים שנא' וייי נהג רוח קדים

וגו' (שמ' י יג) ◆ וכן את מוצא בעשרה שבטים שלא

נפרע מהן אלא ברוח קדים שנא' כי הוא בין אחים

יפריא יב' ק' וגומ' (הושע יג טו): ◆ וכן את מוצא בשבט

בנימן ויהודה שלא נפרע מהן אלא ברוח קדים שנא'

ברוח קדים אפיצם לפני וגומ' (ירמ' יח יז) ◆ וכן את

מוצא בצור שלא נפרע ממנה אלא ברוח קדים שנא'

צור את אמרת וגומ' (יחז' כז ג) ברוח הקדים שב[ר]ך

וגומ' (שם כו). ◆ וכן את מוצא במלכות עליזה זו שאין

(שאין) נפרעין ממנה אלא ברוח קדים שנא' ברוח

קדים תשבר וגומ' (תה' מח ח). ◆ וכן את מוצא

כשהמקום עתיד ליפרע מן הרשעים בגיהנם אין נפרע

מהן אלא ברוח קדים שנא' כי ערוך מאתמול תפתה

Column markers (right margin, top to bottom): E, A 2, B, C, D, E, F, G, H, I, J, K

As it says in Scripture, "The Topheth has long been ready for him, etc." (Isa. 30:33). What does it [also] say?—"His pitiless blast bore them off, etc." (Isa. 27:8).

L.   Also here you say, "... with a strong east wind" (Exod. 14:21). With the strongest of the winds. And which is this? This is the east wind.

3.   A.   "... and turned the sea into dry ground" (Exod. 14:21):

B.   He made it like a desolate waste.

4.   A.   "The waters were split" (Exod. 14:21).

B.   All the water in the world was split.

C.   How would you say from Scripture that [even] water in a well, ditch, cave, pit, pitcher, cup, and flask [was also split]?

D.   "The sea was split" is not written here, rather, "The waters were split" (Exod. 14:21), [meaning,] all the water in the world was split.

E.   And thus Scripture states, "Clouds streamed water, etc." (Ps. 77:18).

F.   It states here "deep" (Ps. 77:17) and it states earlier "deep"—"... where deep calls to deep in the roar of Your cataracts" (Ps. 42:8).[135]

5.   A.   R. Nathan says, "How does one know from Scripture that the waters above and below were split?

B.   "As it says in Scripture, 'The waters saw You, O God' (Ps. 77:17)—these are the upper waters. 'The waters saw You and were convulsed' (Ps. 77:17)—these are the lower waters. And Scripture says, 'The mountains rock at the sight of You, etc.' (Hab. 3:10).

C.   "And when [the waters of the sea] returned, all the water in the world returned.

D.   "'The water turned back' is not written here in Scripture, rather, 'The waters turned back' (Exod. 14:28), [meaning,] all the water in the world returned."

*Chapter Twenty-Five*

(Textual Source: Ms. Firkovich IIA, 268)

XXV:I[136]

1.   A.   "The Israelites went into the sea on dry ground, (the waters forming a wall for them on their right and on their left)" (Exod. 14:22):[137]

B.   R. Meir says it one way, and R. Judah says it another way.

C.   R. Meir says, "When the tribes came and stood by the sea, this one said, 'I'll go down [first],' and that one said, 'I'll go down [first].' While they were bickering with each other, the tribe of Benjamin jumped and fell into the waves of the sea.

D.   "As it says in Scripture, 'There is little Benjamin who rules them' (Ps. 68:28).

E.   "Don't read 'rules them,'[138] rather 'went down into the sea!'[139]

---

[135] 4.F is confusing here. A comparison with the parallel to this material in the *Mekhilta de-Rabbi Ishmael* reveals that it most likely belongs with the unit of tradition immediately following in 5.A–D. See *Mekhilta de-Rabbi Ishmael,* Beshallaḥ (H/R, 104:5–10; Laut., vol. 1, 231:111–232:117; Neus., XXIII:I:11.A–F).

[136] Compare XXV:I:1.A–III:5.I with *Mekhilta de-Rabbi Ishmael,* Beshallaḥ (H/R, 104:13–109:16; Laut., vol. 1, 232:1–243:159; Neus., XXIV: I:1.A–17.G).

[137] Compare 1.A–2.K with t. Berachot 4:18 and b. Sotah 36b (Neus., XVII.Tractate Sotah:7:5:XX.A–X).

[138] Hebrew: *rodem*—רודם.

[139] Hebrew: *rad yam*—רד ים.

 וגומ' (ישע' ל לג) מה הוא אומ' הגה ברוחו הקשה

 וגומ' (שם כז ח) ◆ אף כן אתה אומר ברוח קדים עזה    L

בעזה שברוחות ואי זו זו זו רוח קדים ◆ וישם את הים    A   3

לחרבה ◆ עשאו כחרבה. ◆ ויבקעו המים ◆ כל מים שבעולם    B/A 4   B

נחלקו ◆ מנין אתה אומ' מים שבבאר ושבשיח ושבמער'    C

ושבבור ושבחבית ושבכוס ושבצלוחית ◆ ת"ל ויבקע    D

הים אין כת' כן אלא ויבקעו המים כל מים שבעולם

נחלקו ◆ וכן הוא אומר זורמו מים עבות וגומ' (תה' עז    E

יח) ◆ נאמ' כאן תהום ונא' להלן תהום אל תהום קורא    F

לקול צנוריך (שם מב ח) ◆ ר' נתן אומ' מנין שהמים    A   5

העליונים והתחתונים נחלקו ◆ שנ' ראוך מים אלקים    B

(שם עז יז) אלו מים העליונים. ראוך מים יחילו (שם)

אילו מים התחתונים. ואומ' ראוך יחילו הרים וגו' (חב'

ג י) ◆ וכשחזרו כלמים שבעולם חזרו ◆ שנא' וישב הים    D/C

אין כתיב כאן אלא וישובו המים (שמ' יד כו) כל מים

שבעולם חזרו. סל' פסו' ◆

   XXV:I

ויבואו בני יש' בתוך הים ביבשה. ◆ ר' מאיר אומרו    B/A   1

דבר אחד ור' יהודה אומרו ד"א ◆ ר' מאיר אומרו    C

משבאו שבטים ועמדו על הים זה אומ' אני ארד וזה

אומ' אני ארד מתוך שצוח<ב>ין זה עם זה קפץ שבט

בנימן ונפל לו לתוך גלי הים ◆ שנא' שם בנימן צעיר    D

רודם (תה' סח כח) ◆ אל תקרא רודם אלא רד ים ◆    E

F. "The princes of [the tribe of] Judah began to throw stones at them.

G. "As it says in Scripture, 'The princes of Judah who command[140] them' (Ps. 68:28).

H. "They told a parable: To what is that matter alike?

I. "It is like a human king who had two sons, one old and one young. He said to the old one, 'Wake me at the third hour [of sunlight]!' He said to the young one, 'Wake me at dawn!'

J. "The young one came to wake him at dawn, but the old one would not allow him, saying to him, 'Didn't he say to me the third hour!' He[141] said to him, 'Didn't he say to me at dawn!'

[63]    K. "While they were bickering with each other, their father awoke and said to them, 'I know that the two of you were only trying [to preserve] my honor. Thus, I won't hold back your reward!'

L. "What reward did the tribe of Benjamin receive? God's presence dwelt in its territory.

M. "As it says in Scripture, 'He dwells amid His slopes' (Deut. 33:12).

N. "What reward did the tribe of Judah receive? It received the monarchy.

O. "As it says in Scripture, '... the princes of Judah who command them' (Ps. 68:28).

P. "The word 'command' only means monarchy.

Q. "In accordance with what is said in Scripture, 'Then, at Belshazzar's command, they clothed (Daniel in purple ... that he should rule as one of three in the kingdom), etc.' (Dan. 5:29).

R. "'... the princes of Zebulun and Naphtali' (Ps. 68:28).

S. "Scripture tells that just as miracles were performed at the sea for Israel on behalf of the tribes of Judah and Benjamin, likewise were miracles performed for Israel on behalf of the tribe of Zebulun and the tribe of Naphtali in the days of Deborah and Barak.

T. "Thus Scripture states, 'She summoned Barak, etc.' (Judg. 4:6). And Scripture says, 'Zebulun is a people that mocked, etc.' (Judg. 5:18)."

2.    A. R. Judah says, "When the tribes came and stood by the sea, this one said, 'I'll go down [first],' and that one said, 'I'll go down [first].'

B. "As it says in Scripture, 'Ephraim surrounds Me with deceit, etc.' (Hos. 12:1).

C. "Naḥshon ben Aminadav jumped and fell into the sea and its waves.

D. "As it says in Scripture, '... but Judah stands firm with God, etc.' (Hos. 12:1).

E. "Don't read it 'stand firm,'[142] rather 'went down into the sea'![143]

F. "And concerning him it is explained in tradition, 'Deliver me, O God, for the waters have reached (my neck). I am sinking into the slimy deep, etc.' (Ps. 69:2–3) [and] '... (Let the floodwaters) not sweep me away, etc.' (Ps. 69:16).

G. "The Holy One, blessed be He, said to Moses, 'My beloved one is drowning in the sea, and

---

[140] The Hebrew word in Psalm 68:28 for "command them" (*rigmatam*—רגמתם) is read as the verb "to stone" (*ragam*—רגם).

[141] I.e., the young one.

[142] Hebrew: *rad im*—רד עם.

[143] Hebrew: *rad yam*—רד ים.

| | |
|---|---|
| התחילו ש[נ]רי יה[ו]דה] לרגם אותן באבנים ◆ שנא׳ שרי | G/F |
| יהודה רגמתם (שם) ◆ מוש[לו משל] למה הדבר דומה ◆ | H |
| למלך בשר ודם שהיו לו שני בנים [אחד] גדול ואחד | I |
| קטן אמ׳ לגדול הנראה שתעמידני לשלש שעות אמ׳ | |
| לקטן הנראה שתעמידני עם הנץ החמה ◆ בא קטן | J |
| והעמידו עם הנץ החמה ולא הניחו גדול אמ׳ לו אני | |
| לא אמר לי אלא עד שלש שעות אמ׳ לו אני לא אמר | |
| לי אלא עם הנץ החמה ◆ מפני שצוחבין זה עם זה נעור | K |
| אביהן (אביהן) אמ׳ להן יודע אני ששניכם לא | |
| נתכונתם אלא לכבודי אף אני אינ[י] מקפיח שכרכם ◆ | |
| מה שכר נטלו שבט בנימן שרת שכינה בחלקו ◆ שנא׳ | M/L |
| ובין כתפיו שכן (דב׳ לג יב) ◆ מה שכר נטלו שבטו של | N |
| יהודה נטל מלכות ◆ שנא׳ שרי יהודה רגמתם (תה׳ סח | O |
| כח) ◆ אין רגימה אלא מלכות ◆ כענין שנא׳ באדין אמר | Q/P |
| בלשאצר והלבישו וגומ׳ (דנ׳ ה כט) ◆ שרי זבולון (ו)שרי | R |
| נפתלי (תה׳ סח כח) ◆ מגיד הכת׳ שכשם שנעשו נסים | S |
| ליש׳ על ידי שבט יהודה ובנימן על הים כך נעשו נסים | |
| ליש׳ על ידי שבט זבולן ושבט נפתלי בימי דבורה | |
| וברק ◆ כן הוא אומ׳ ותשלח ותקרא לברק וגומ׳ (שופ׳ ד | T |
| ו) ואומ׳ זבולן עם חרף נפשו וגומ׳ (שם ה יח) ◆ ר׳ יהודה | A |
| אומ׳ כשבאו שבטים ועמדו על הים זה אומ׳ אני ארד | |
| זה אומ׳ אני ארד ◆ שנא׳ סבבוני בכחש אפרים וגומ׳ | B |
| (הושע יב א) ◆ קפץ נחשון בן עמינדב ונפל לו לתוך הים | C |
| וגליו ◆ שנא׳ ויהודה עוד רד עם אל (וגומ׳) (שם) ◆ אל | E/D |
| תקרא רד <עם> אלא רד ים ◆ ועליו מפרש בקבלה | F |
| הושיעני אלקים כי באו מים וגומ׳ טבעתי ביון מצולה | |
| וגומ׳ (תה׳ סט ג) אל תשטפני וגו׳ (שם טז) ◆ אמ׳ לו | G |
| הקב״ה למשה ידידי משוקע בים ואתה עומד ומרבה | |

you stand and multiply prayer before Me! "Why do you cry out to Me ... and you lift up your rod, etc." (Exod. 14:15–16).'

H.   "What did the tribes say at the sea?—'... the sanctuary, O Lord, which Your hands established, (the Lord will reign for ever and ever!)' (Exod. 15:17).

I.   "At that moment, the Holy One, blessed by He, said to Moses, 'He who sanctifies My name by the sea shall rule over Israel!

J.   "'As it says in Scripture, "When Israel went forth from Egypt ... (Judah became His holy one), etc." (Ps. 114:1–2).'

K.   "Judah, who sanctified My name by the sea, shall rule over Israel!"

3.   A.   R. Tarfon and his disciples were sitting in a vineyard in Yavneh. R. Tarfon said to his disciples, "I'm going to ask you a question." They said to him, "Teach us!"

B.   [R. Tarfon said,] "What blessing does one say who drinks water to quench his thirst? I say: '... who creates souls and their needs.'"

C.   They said to him, "Teach us [more], our Master!"

D.   He said to them, "Behold Scripture states, 'Then they sat down to a meal. (Looking up, they saw a caravan of Ishmaelites coming from Gilead, their camels bearing gum, balm, and ladanum), etc.' (Gen 37:25).

[64]   E.   "This is to inform you of how far the merit of the righteous extends. For if Joseph, that dear one, had gone down to Egypt with the Arabs, wouldn't they have killed him with their bad stench! Rather, on account of the stench of the Arabs, the Holy One, blessed be He, arranged for him sacks full of spices through which the wind would blow."

F.   He said to them, "On account of what merit did Judah receive the monarchy?

G.   "If [it was] because of what is said in Scripture—'... she is more in the right than I' (Gen. 38:26)—[then the fact that the] confession atones for sleeping [with Tamar] should be enough!

H.   "If [it was] because of what is said in Scripture—'... what do we gain by killing our brother?' (Gen. 37:26)—[then the fact that the] saving of the life atones for the selling [of Joseph into slavery] should be enough!

I.   "If [it was] because he said, 'Now your servant has pledged himself for the boy, etc.' (Gen. 44:32) [then] in every instance one who pledges [against a loan] must make payment!"

J.   They said to him, "Teach us [the answer already]!"

K.   He said to them, "When the tribes came and stood by the sea, this one said, 'I'll go down [first],' and that one said, 'I'll go down [first].' Nahshon ben Aminadav jumped and fell into the sea."

L.   As it is written above,[144] and he shall rule over Israel.

4.   A.   "... the waters forming a wall for them ..." (Exod. 14:22):

B.   He turned them into a kind of wall.

5.   A.   "... on their right and on their left ..." (Exod. 14:22):

B.   "... on their right ..." by the merit of Torah; "... and on their left ..." by the merit of phylacteries.

C.   And why on the right for Torah? Because it was given from the right.

D.   As it says in Scripture, "... lightning flashing at them from His right" (Deut. 33:2).

---

[144] See above XXV:I:2.A–K.

בתפלה לפני מה תצעק אלי וגומ' ואתה הרם את

מטך וגומ' (שמ' יד טז) ♦ מה אמרו שבטים על הים    H

מקדש ייי כוננו ידיך (שם טו יז) ♦ באותה שעה [אמ' לו]    I

הקב"ה למשה מי ש[ק]ידש שמ[י]ן על הים הוא מושל

[על יש'] ♦ שנא' ב[צ]את יש' ממצ' וגומ' (תה' קיד א) ♦    J

יהודה שקידש את שמי על [הים] ימשול על יש' ♦ וכבר    A 3    K

היה ר' טרפון ותלמידיו יושבין בכרם [ביב]נה אמ'

להן ר' טרפון לתלמידיו אשאל לפניכן שאלה אמ' לו

[יל]מדנו ♦ השותה מים לצמאו מה הוא מברך שאני    B

אומ' בורא נפשות וחסרונן ♦ אמ' לו למדתנו רבינו ♦    C

<אמר להן> הרי הוא אומ' וישבו לאכל לחם וגומ'    D

(בר' לז כה) ♦ להודיע זכותן שלצדיקים עד היכן היא    E

מקדמת שאילו ירד יוסף למצ' חביב הוא עם הערביין

לא היו הורגין אותו בריח רע שלהן אלא זימן לו

הקב"ה שקים מלאים בשמים והרוח מנשבת בהן

מפני ריחן שלערביים ♦ אמ' להן באי זה זכות נטל    F

יהודה את המלכות ♦ אם משום שנא' צדקה ממני (שם    G

לח כו) דיה להודאה שתכפר על הביאה ♦ אם מש' שנ'    H

מה בצע כי נהרג את אחינו (שם לז כו) דייה להצלה

שמכפרת על המכירה ♦ אם משום שאמר כי [ע]בדך    I

ערב את הנער וגומ' (שם מד לב) והלא ערב הוא ובכל

מקום ערב משלם ♦ אמ' לו למדינו ♦ אמ' להן שכשבאו    K/J

שבטים ועמדו על הים זה אומ' אני יורד וזה אומ' אני

יו[ר]ד קפץ נחשון בן עמינדב ונפל לו לתוך הים ♦

כדכת' לע[י]ל. והוא ימשל על יש'. ♦ והמים להם    A 4    L

חומה ♦ עשאן כמין חומה ♦ מימינם ומשמאלם ♦    A 5    B

מימינם בזכות תורה ומשמאלם בזכות תפילין ♦    B

ולמה מימינם בשביל תורה שניתנה מימין ♦ שנא' מימינו    D/C

6.    A.    Another interpretation:

      B.    "... on their right ..."—this is the mezuzah; "... and on their left ..."—this is prayer.

## XXV:II

1.    A.    "At the morning watch, (the Lord looked down upon the Egyptian army from a pillar of fire and cloud, and threw the Egyptian army into panic)" (Exod. 14:24):

      B.    He[145] brought forward on their behalf [the merit of]:

      C.    Abraham's morning—"And Abraham arose early in the morning, etc." (Gen. 22:3);

      D.    Isaac's morning—"... the two of them walked off together" (Gen. 22:6);

      E.    Jacob's morning—"And Jacob arose early in the morning" (Gen. 28:18);

      F.    Moses' morning—"And Moses arose early in the morning" (Exod. 34:14);

      G.    And [the morning] of Joshua—"And Joshua arose early in the morning" (Josh. 3:1);

      H.    Samuel's morning—"And Samuel arose early in the morning" (1 Sam. 15:12).

      I.    How does one know from Scripture [also] the morning of the prophets who will arise over them in the future?—"... they are renewed every morning, etc." (Lam. 3:23).

      J.    How does one know from Scripture [also] the morning of the world to come?—"Hear my voice, O Lord, at daybreak, etc." (Ps. 5:4).

      K.    Thus you find that when God punishes the wicked, He punishes them only in the morning.

      L.    As it says in Scripture, "Each morning I will destroy, etc." (Ps. 101:8).

2.    A.    Another interpretation:

      B.    "At the morning watch" (Exod. 14:24):

      C.    "Who has roused victory from the east, etc." (Isa. 41:2).

3.    A.    "... the Lord looked down upon the Egyptian army" (Exod. 14:24):

      B.    In that God's punishment is not like human punishment.

      C.    A human does not heal with what he wounds. Rather, He wounds with a knife and heals with a compress.

[65]    D.    But the Holy One, blessed be He, heals with what he wounds.

      E.    And thus you find that when God wounded Job, He wounded him only with a whirlwind. As it says in Scripture, "For He crushes me with a whirlwind, etc." (Job 9:17). But when He healed him, He healed him only with a whirlwind. As it says in Scripture, "Then the Lord replied to Job out of the whirlwind and said ..." (Job 38:1).

      F.    And when the Holy One, blessed be He, exiled Israel, He exiled them only like doves. As it says in Scripture, "And if any survive, (they shall take to the mountains. They shall be like doves of the valley,) etc." (Ezek. 7:16). But when He brings them back in, He brings them back in only like doves. As it says in Scripture, "... like doves to their cotes" (Isa. 60:8).

      G.    And when God scattered Israel, He scattered them only like clouds. As it says in Scripture, "Alas! The Lord in His wrath has covered with a cloud[146] (Fair Zion), etc." (Lam. 2:1). But

---

[145] I.e., God.
[146] The text here translates the verb יעיב in Lam. 2:1 as "covered with a cloud."

אש דת למו (דב' לג ב). • ד"א • מימינם • זו מזוזה •     B/A   6

ומשמאלם • זו תפלה. סל' פסו' •

XXV:II

ויהיא באשמורת הבקר • כבר הקדים להן • בוקרו     C/B/A   1

של אבינו אברהם וישכם אברהם בבקר וגומ' (בר' כב

ג) • בוקרו של יצחק וילכו שניהם יחדו (שם ו) • בוקרו     E/D

של יעקב וישכם יעקב בבקר (שם כח יח) • בוקרו של     F

משה וישכם משה בבקר (שמ' לד ד). • בוקרו של     G

יהושע וישכם יהושע בבקר (יהו' ג א). • בוקרו של     H

שמואל וישכם שמואל בבוקר (ש"א טו יב) • בוק[ר]ן     I

של נביא[י]ם] שעתידין לעמד על[י]הן מני[ן חדשים

לבקרים וגומ' (איכה ג כג) • בוקרו של עולם הבא מנין     J

ייי בקר תשמע קולי וגומ' (תה' ה ד) • וכן את מוצא     K

<כ>שהמקום נפרע מרשע[י]ם] אין נפרע מהן אלא

בבוקר • שנא' לבקרים אצמית וגומ' (שם קא ח). • ד"א •     A 2    L

ויהי באשמורת הבוקר. • מי העיר ממזרח צדק וגומ'     C/B

(ישע' מא ב) • וישקף ייי על מחנה מצ' • שלא כמדת בשר     B/A   3

ודם מדת המקום • בשר ודם במה שמכה בו אין מרפא     C

אלא מכה באוזמיל ומרפא ברט[י]ה • אבל הק' במה     D

שמכה הוא מרפא • וכן את מוצא כשהכה המקום את     E

איוב לא הכהו אלא בסערה שנא' אשר בסערה

ישופני וגומ' (איוב ט יז) וכשרפאו לא רפאו אלא

בסערה שנא' ויען ייי את איוב מן הסערה ויאמר (שם

לח א) • וכשהגלה הקב"ה את יש' לא הגלם אלא כיונים     F

שנא' וכיונים ופלטו פליטיהם וגומ' (יחז' ז טז)

וכשהוא מכנסן אין מכנסן אלא כיונים שנא' וכיונים

אל ארבותיהם (ישע' ס ח). • וכשפיזר המקום את ישר'     G

לא פיזרן אלא בעבים שנא' איכה יעיב באפו וגומ'

when He brings them back in, He brings them back in only like clouds. As it says in Scripture, "Who are these that float like a cloud, etc." (Isa. 60:8).

H.     And when God blessed Israel, He blessed them only by looking down. As it says in Scripture, "Look down from your holy abode, etc." (Deut. 26:15). And when He punished Egypt, He only punished by looking down. As it says in Scripture, "... the Lord looked down upon the Egyptian army, etc." (Exod. 14:24).

4.     A.     "... from a pillar of fire and cloud ..." (Exod. 14:24):

B.     The cloud turned the sea into mud and the pillar of fire heated it into tar. And the horses' heels were destroyed—[both] its upper node and its lower socket. And thus Scripture states, "Then the horses' hoofs pounded, etc." (Judg. 5:22).

5.     A.     "... and threw the Egyptian army into panic" (Exod. 14:24):

B.     He confounded them and confused them, taking their standards, so they did not know what they were doing.

6.     A.     Another interpretation:[147]

B.     "... and threw (the Egyptian army) into panic" (Exod. 14:24):

C.     The term "throw into panic" only means "sudden death."

D.     In accordance with what is said in Scripture, "... throwing them into utter panic (until they are wiped out)" (Deut. 7:23).

## XXV:III

1.     A.     "He locked [or: removed] the wheels of their chariots (so that they moved forward heavily. And the Egyptians said, 'Let us flee from the Israelites, for the Lord is fighting for them against Egypt!')" (Exod. 14:25):

B.     R. Judah says, "Because of fire from above, the wheels down below were burned. But the yokes and chariots ran on, and entered [the sea] against their [drivers'] will.

C.     "Because they were loaded with silver, gold,

### (Textual Source: JTS ENA 1180.44)

and precious stones and gems, so that Israel would receive the spoil."

2.     A.     R. Nehemiah says, "Because of thunder from above, the pins [in the wheels of the Egyptian chariots] flew off down below.

B.     "As it says in Scripture, 'The thunder of Your rumbling was on the wheels, etc.' (Ps. 77:19).

C.     "But the yokes and chariots ran on, and entered [the sea] against their [drivers'] will.

D.     "Because they were loaded with silver, gold, and precious stones and gems, so that Israel would receive the spoil."

3.     A.     "... so that they moved forward heavily" (Exod. 14:25):

B.     By the measure with which they meted out did You measure them.

C.     They said, "Let heavier work (be laid upon the men)" (Exod. 5:9).

D.     Likewise, by that measure did You measure them: "... so that they moved forward heavily" (Exod. 14:25).

---

[147] Compare 6.A–D with parallel above at XXII:II:7.A–D.

|   |   |
|---|---|
| H | (איכה ב א) וכשהוא מכנסן אין מכנסן אלא בעבים שנא' מי אלה כעב תעופינה וגומ' (ישע' ס ח). ◆ וכשבירך המקום את יש' לא בן[יר]כן אלא בהשקפה שנא' השקיפה ממעון קדשך וגומ' (דב' כו טו) [ו]כשנפרע מן המצ' לא נפרע אלא בהשקפה שנא' וישקף יי אל |
| B/A 4 | מחנה מצרים וגומ' ◆ בעמוד אש וענן ◆ ענן עושה את הים טיט ועמוד אש מרתיחו כזפת והיו טלפי סוסים נשמטין זכר מלמעלה ונקבה מלמטה וכן הוא אומ' |
| A 5 | אז הלמו עקבי סוס וגומ' (שופ' ה כב) ◆ ויהם את מחנה |
| B | מצ' ◆ הממן עירבבן נטל סגנין שלהן ולא היו יודעין מה |
| C/B/A 6 | הן עושין. ◆ ד"א ◆ ויהם ◆ אין ויהם מהומה אלא מגפה ◆ |
| D | כענין שנא' והמם מהומה גדולה (דב' ז כג). סל' פסו' |

|   |   |
|---|---|
| XXV:III | |
| B/A 1 | ויסר את אופן מרכבות' ◆ ר' יהודה אומ' מחמת |
| C | אש של מעלה נשרפו גלגלים מלמטה והיו מוטות מרכבות רצות ונכנסות על כרחן ◆ שהיו טעונות כסף וזהב [ואב]נים טובות ומרגליות [כדי שיטלו יש' את הביז]ה. |
| A 2 | ◆ ר' נחמיה [אומ' מחמת רעם שלמעלה ניתזו |
| B | צנורות] מלמטה ◆ שנא' קול רעמך בגלגל וגומ' (תה' עז |
| C | יט) ◆ והיו מו[טות] מרכ[בות רצ]ות [ונכנסו]ת על כרחן ◆ |
| D | שהיו טעונות כסף וזהב ואבנים טובות ומרגליות כדי |
| B/A 3 | שיטלו יש' את הביזה. ◆ וינהגהו בכבדות ◆ במדה שמדדו |
| C | בה מדדת להן ◆ הם אמרו תכבד העבודה (שמ' ה ט) ◆ |
| D | אף אתה באותה מדה מדדתה להן וינהגהו בכבדות ◆ |

E.    In the past, mules pulled the chariot. Now the chariot pulled the mules!

4.    A.    "And the Egyptians said, 'Let us flee from the Israelites'" (Exod. 14:25):

[66]    B.    The stupid among them said, "We are fleeing because of these sad and afflicted ones!"

C.    The wise among them said, "He who fought for them in Egypt, He will perform miracles for them any time!"

5.    A.    R. Yosi says, "How does one know from Scripture that these [people] at the sea were struck with the same plagues that these [people] in Egypt were struck with, and that they saw each other?

B.    "Scripture states, '... for the Lord is fighting for them against Egypt!' (Exod. 14:25).

C.    "And not only against Egypt, but against anyone who troubles them in all generations.

D.    "And thus Scripture states, 'He beat back His foes, etc.' (Ps. 78:66). [And Scripture says,] '... my foes and my enemies, etc.' (Ps. 27:2). [And Scripture says,] '... (then I would subdue) their enemies at once, etc.' (Ps. 81:15). [And Scripture says,] '... the 10 sons of Haman, etc.' (Esther 9:10). And Scripture says, 'Then Ephraim's envy shall cease (and Judah's) harassment (shall end), etc.' (Isa. 11:13). And Scripture says, 'To break Assyria, etc.' (Isa. 14:25).

E.    "This measure [of punishment] extends through all the generations.

F.    "As it says in Scripture, 'That is the plan that is planned, etc.' (Isa. 14:26).

G.    "Why?—'Because the Lord of Hosts has planned. Who then can foil it?' (Isa. 14:27).

H.    "Thus, not only against Egypt, but against anyone who troubles them in all generations.

I.    "Thus it is said, '... for the Lord is fighting for them against Egypt!' (Exod. 14:25)."

## Chapter Twenty-Six

### (Textual Source: JTS ENA 1180.44)

XXVI:I[148]

1.    A.    "Then the Lord said to Moses, 'Hold out your arm over the sea, (that the waters may come back upon the Egyptians and upon their chariots and upon their horsemen)'" (Exod. 14:26):

B.    The sea will not stand against you.

2.    A.    "'... that the waters may come back upon the Egyptians, etc.'" (Exod. 14:26):

B.    He[149] changed their fortune by returning their own sin upon them, [by saying,] "I shall judge them by means of the plan that they devised.

C.    "They devised to destroy My sons in water. Thus, I shall only destroy them in water!"

D.    And thus Scriptures states, "He has dug a pit and deepened it, etc." (Ps. 7:16). And Scripture says, "He who digs a pit will fall in it, etc." (Prov. 26:27). And Scripture says, "He who digs a pit will fall in it ... He who quarries stones, etc." (Eccles. 10:8–9). And Scripture says, "His mischief will recoil upon his skull, etc." (Ps. 7:17).

E.    And thus Solomon says, "A man (gets his fill of good from) the fruit of his speech, etc." (Prov. 12:14).

---

[148] Compare XXVI:I:1.A—VI:8.R with *Mekhilta de-Rabbi Ishmael,* Beshallaḥ (H/R, 110:1–115:15; Laut., vol. 1, 243:1–255:164; Neus., XXV: I:1.A–30.F).

[149] I.e., God.

לשעבר פרדות מושכות את המרכבה עכשיו מרכבה E

מושכת את הפרדות. ◆ ויאמר מצ' אנוסה מפני יש' ◆ A 4

טפשים שבהן אמרו מפני דוים וסיגופן שלאלו אנו B

בורחין ◆ [פקחים] שבהן אמרו מי שנלחם להן במצ' C

הוא יעשה להן נסין בכל זמן ◆ ר' יוסי אומ' מניין A 5

שבמכה שאילו שבמצ' לוקין אלו שעל הים [לו]קין

והיו רואין זה את זה ◆ ת"ל כי ייי נלחם להם במצ' ◆ ולא C/B

במצרים בלבד אלא בכל המצירין להן על פני כל

הדורות ◆ וכן הוא אומ' ויך צריו אחור וגומ' (תה' עח D

סו) צרי ואויבי וגומ' (שם כז ב) כמעט אויביהם וגומ'

(שם פא טו) עשרת בני [המן וגומ'] (אס' ט י) ואומ'

וסרה קנאת אפרים וצוררי וגומ' (ישע' יא יג) ואומ'

לשבר אשור [וגומ'] (שם יד כה) ◆ מידה זו נוהגת על פני E

כל הדורות ◆ שנא' זאת העצה היעוצה וגומ' (שם כו) ◆ F

מפני מה כי ייי צבא' יעץ ומי יפר וגומ' (שם כז) ◆ הא לא H/G

במצ' בלבד אלא בכל המצירין להן על פני כל הדורות ◆

לכך נאמ' כי ייי נלחם להם במצ'. סל' פסקא ◆ I

XXVI:I

ויאמר ייי אל משה נטה את ידך על הים ◆ אין הים B/A 1

עומד כנגדך. ◆ וישובו המים על מצ' וגומ' ◆ החזיר עליהן B/A 2

את הגלגל שיחזור עליהן זדונן ש<ב>מחש' שח[ישבו]

בה אני דנם ◆ הם חישבו לאבד בני במים אף אני איני C

מאבדן אלא במים ◆ וכן הוא אומ' בור כרה ויחפרהו D

וגומ' (תה' ז טז) [ואומ' כורה] שחת בה יפול(ו) וגומ'

(מש' כו כז) חופר גומץ בו יפל וגומ' מסיע אבנים וגומ'

(קה' י ח - ט) ואומ' ישוב עמלו בראשו וגומ' (תה' ז יז) ◆ E

F. And thus Isaiah says, "According to their desserts, so shall He repay, etc." (Isa. 59:18).

G. And thus Jeremiah says, "... wondrous in purpose and mighty in deed, etc." (Jer. 32:19).

H. And thus Elijah says, "Wickedness be far from God ... For He pays a man according to his actions, etc." (Job 34:10–11).

I. And thus Jethro says, "Now I know that the Lord is greater (than all gods), etc." (Exod. 18:11).

J. I knew in the past His [greatness, and now] even more, in that by means of the plan that Egypt devised to destroy Israel, God judged them.

K. [As it says in Scripture,] "... yes, by the result of their very schemes against [the people]" (Exod. 18:11).

L. Based on this they said, "With what measure a man metes it shall be measured to him again."[150]

XXVI:II

1.
[67]

A. "Moses held his arm out over the sea, (and at daybreak the sea returned to its normal state, and the Egyptians fled at its approach. But the Lord hurled the Egyptians into the sea)" (Exod. 14:27):

B. The sea did not stand against Moses.

2.

A. "... and at daybreak the sea returned to its normal state" (Exod. 14:27):

B. "Its normal state"[151] only means "its strength."

C. As it says in Scripture, "... though your abode be strong"[152] (Num. 24:21).

D. R. Nathan says, "'Normal state' only means 'powerful.'

E. "As it says in Scripture, 'It is a powerful[153] nation, etc.' (Jer. 5:15)."

3.

A. "... and the Egyptians fled at its approach" (Exod. 14:27):

B. How do you say from Scripture that anywhere Egypt ran, the sea would precede it there?

C. Scripture states, "... and the Egyptians fled at its approach."

D. They told a parable: To what is the matter alike?

E. To a dove who fled from a hawk and entered into the king's dining room. The king opened the eastern window, and it left. The hawk entered [the dining room] after it, and the king closed all the windows and began shooting arrows at it.

F. Likewise, when the last of the Israelites arose from the sea, Egypt went down after them. The sea closed up on them from the four directions, in order to destroy them, and the ministering angels threw ice-stones and hailstones at them.

G. In accordance with what is said in Scripture, "I will punish him with pestilence and with bloodshed, (and I will pour torrential rain, hailstones, and sulfurous fire upon him,) etc." (Ezek. 38:22).

4.

A. "But the Lord hurled the Egyptians into the sea" (Exod. 14:27):

B. Like a person stirs a pot, in that what is at the bottom comes to the top, and what is at the top goes down to the bottom.

---

[150] Compare 2.L with m. Sotah 1:7 and t. Sotah 3:1–2 and 4:1.
[151] Hebrew: eitano—איתנו.

| | | |
|---|---|---|
| ◆ וכן שלמה אומ׳ מפרי פי איש וגומ׳ (מש׳ יב יד) ◆ | F | |
| ◆ וכן ישעיה אומ׳ כעל גמולות כעל וגומ׳ (ישע׳ נט יח) ◆ | G | |
| וכן ירמיה אומ׳ גדול העצה ורב העליליה וגומ׳ (ירמי׳ לב | H | |
| יט) ◆ וכן אליהו[א] אומ׳ חלילה לאל מר]שע וגומ׳ כי | I | |
| פועל אדם ישלם לו וגומ׳ (איוב לד י - יא) ◆ וכן [יתרו] | J | |
| אומ׳ עתה ידעתי כי גדול יי וגומ׳ (שמ׳ יח יא) ◆ מכירו | K | |
| הייתי לשעבר וביותר שבמחשבה שחשבו מצ׳ לאבד | | |
| את יש׳ בה דנם המקום ◆ כי בדבר אשר זדו עליהם ◆ | L | |
| מיכן אמרו במדה שאדם מודד בה מודדין לו. סל׳ פסו׳ ◆ | | |

| | | XXVI:II |
|---|---|---|

| | | |
|---|---|---|
| ויט משה את ידו על הים ◆ אין הים עומד כנגד | B/A | 1 |
| משה ◆ וישב הים לפנות בוקר לאיתנו ◆ אין איתנו אלא | B/A | 2 |
| תקפו ◆ שנא׳ איתן מושביך (במ׳ כד כא) ◆ ר׳ נתן אומ׳ אין | D/C | |
| איתן אלא לשון קשה ◆ שנא׳ גוי איתן הוא וגומ׳ (ירמ׳ | E | |
| ה טו) ◆ ומצרים נסים לקראתם ◆ מנין אתה אומ׳ שבכל | B/A | 3 |
| מקום שהיה מצ׳ רץ שם היה הים מקדמו ◆ ת״ל ומצר׳ | C | |
| נסים לקראתם. ◆ מושלו משל למה הדבר דומה ◆ ליונה | E/D | |
| שברחה מבן הנץ ונכנסה לה לטרקלין שלמלך פתח | | |
| המלך חלון מזרחית ויצאת והלכה לה נכנס בן הנץ | | |
| אחריה נעל המלך כל אותן חלונות והתחיל יורה בו | | |
| חצים ◆ כך כיון שעלה האחרון שביש׳ מן הים ירדו מצ׳ | F | |
| אחריהם סתם עליהם הים] מארבע רוחותיו כדי | | |
| לאבדן והיו מלאכי שרת מזרקין בהן אבני ברד ואבני | | |
| אלגביש ◆ כענין שנא׳ ונשפטתי אתו בדבר ובדם וגומ׳ | G | |
| (יחז׳ לח כב) ◆ וינער יי את מצ׳ בתוך הים ◆ כאדם שמנער | B/A | 4 |
| את הקדרה שתחתון עולה למעלה ועליון יורד למטה. | | |
| ◆ | | |

[152] Hebrew: *eitan*—איתן.
[153] Hebrew: *eitan*—איתן.

5.　　A.　Another interpretation:

　　　B.　"But the Lord hurled[154] the Egyptians into the sea" (Exod. 14:27):

　　　C.　He[155] gave them the strength of youth,[156] in order that they be able to accept punishment.

6.　　A.　Another interpretation:

　　　B.　"But the Lord hurled[157] the Egyptians into the sea" (Exod. 14:27):

　　　C.　He handed them over to young[158] angels and to merciless angels, in order that they would steal their souls.

　　　D.　In accordance with what is said in Scripture, "A ruthless messenger will be sent against him" (Prov. 17:11). And Scripture says, "They die in their youth, etc." (Job 36:14).

## XXVI:III

1.　　A.　"The waters turned back (and covered the chariots and horsemen—Pharaoh's entire army that followed them into the sea. Not one of them remained)" (Exod. 14:28):[159]

　　　B.　All the water in the world returned.

2.　　A.　"'... and covered the chariots and horsemen, etc.' (Exod. 14:28):

　　　B.　"Even Pharaoh. As it says in Scripture, 'Who hurled Pharaoh and his army into the Sea of Reeds, etc.' (Ps. 136:15)."—The words of R. Judah.

### (Textual Source: Ms. Paris, Alliance Collection)

　　　C.　R. Nehemiah says, "Except for Pharaoh. As it says in Scripture, 'Nevertheless, (I have spared you) for this purpose, etc.' (Exod. 9:16)."

　　　D.　There are those who say, in the end he went and drowned. As it says in Scripture, "For the horses of Pharaoh, etc." (Exod. 15:19).

## XXVI:IV

1.　　A.　"But the Israelites had marched through the sea on dry ground, (the waters forming a wall for them on their right and on their left)" (Exod. 14:29):

　　　B.　The ministering angels were surprised, saying, "Can human beings who served idols cross through the sea on dry land?"

2.　　A.　Even the sea was filled with anger[160] against them and sought to destroy them.

[68]　B.　Above[161] Scripture says "wall,"[162] and here[163] Scripture says "wrath."[164]

3.　　A.　Who caused them to be victorious?

　　　B.　"... on their right and on their left" (Exod. 14:29):

　　　C.　On their right—by the merit of Torah, which they would receive from the right.

　　　D.　As it says in Scripture, "... lightning flashing at them from His right" (Deut. 33:2).

　　　E.　And on their left—by the merit of phylacteries [which are worn on the left arm].

---

[154] Hebrew: *va-y'n'aer*—וינער.
[155] I.e., God.
[156] Hebrew: *ne'arut*—נערות.
[157] Hebrew: *va-y'na'er*—וינער.
[158] Hebrew: *ne'arim*—נערים.
[159] Compare 1.A–B with parallel above at XXIV:IV:5.A–D.

| | | |
|---|---|---|
| ד״א • וינער יייי את מצ׳ בתוך הים • נתן בהן כח | C/B/A | 5 |
| נערות כדי שיהו יכולין לקבל פורענות. • ד״א • וינער יייי | B/A | 6 |
| את מצ׳ בתוך הים • מסרן למלאכים נערים למלאכים | C | |
| אכזרין כדי שישמטו את נפשותן • כענין שנא׳ ומלאך | D | |
| אכזרי ישלח בו (מש׳ יז יא) ואומ׳ תמות בנוער נפשם | | |
| וגומ׳ (איוב לו יד). סל׳ פסו׳ • • | | |

XXVI:III

| | | |
|---|---|---|
| וישובו המים • כל מים שבעולם חזרו • ויכסו את | A/B/A | 2/1 |
| הרכב ואת הפרשים וגומ׳ • אפילו פרעה שנא׳ ונער | B | |
| פרעה וחילו בים סוף וגומ׳ (תה׳ קלו טו) דברי ר׳ | | |
| יהודה • ר׳ נחמיה אומ׳ חוץ מפרעה שנא׳ ואולם בעבור | C | |
| זאת וגו׳ (שמ׳ ט טז) • ויש אומ׳ באחרונה בא וטבע | D | |
| שנא׳ כי בא סוס פרעה וגו׳ (שם טו יט). סל׳ פסו׳ • | | |

XXVI:IV

| | | |
|---|---|---|
| ובני ישראל הלכו ביבשה בתוך הים • היו מלאכי | B/A | 1 |
| שרת מתמיהין לומ׳ בני אדם שעבדו עבודה זרה | | |
| יעברו ביבשה בתוך הים • אף הים נתמלא עליהן חמה | A | 2 |
| ובקש לאבדן • שלמעלה הוא אומ׳ חומה וכאן הוא | B | |
| אומ׳ חמה • מי גרם להן להינצל • מימינם ומשמאלם. • | B/A | 3 |
| מימינם בזכות תורה שעתידין לקבל בימין • שנא׳ מימינו | D/C | |
| אשדת למו (דב׳ לג ב) • ומשמאל<ם> בזכות תפילין, • | E | |

---

[160] Hebrew: ḥeimah—חמה.
[161] I.e., Exod. 14:22.
[162] Hebrew: ḥomah—חומה.
[163] I.e., Exod. 14:29.
[164] By revocalizing the Hebrew to read ḥeimah—חמה.

4.  A.  Another interpretation:

    B.  On their right—by the merit of [the] mezuzah.

    C.  And on their left—by the merit of phylacteries.

5.  A.  R. Pappias interpreted [the following verse]: "He is one; who can dissuade Him?" (Job 23:13).

    B.  "He, alone, judges all the creatures of the world, and there is no refuting His word."

    C.  R. Akiva said to him, "Enough from you, Pappias!"

    D.  [R. Pappias responded to him,] "How do you interpret [the verse] 'He is one; who can dissuade Him'?"

    E.  [R. Akiva said,] "There is no refuting the word of He who spoke, and the world came into being. For everything is [according to His] judgment and everything [is according to His] estimation."

6.  A.  R. Pappias interpreted [the following verse]: "Now that the man has become like one of us" (Gen. 3:22).

    B.  "Like one of the ministering angels."

    C.  R. Akiva said to him, "Enough from you, Pappias!"

    D.  [R. Pappias responded to him,] "How do you interpret [the verse] 'Now that the man has become like one (of us)'?"

    E.  [R. Akiva said,] "This teaches that the Holy One, blessed be He, placed before him two paths—the path of life and the path of death, and he chose the path of death."

7.  A.  R. Pappias interpreted [the following verse]: "They exchanged their glory for the image of a bull that feeds on grass" (Ps. 106:20).

    B.  "I might [erroneously] assume [this refers to] a heavenly ox.

    C.  "Scripture states, [however,] '... feeds on grass' (Ps. 106:20)."

    D.  R. Akiva said to him, "Enough from you, Pappias!"

    E.  [R. Pappias responded to him,] "How do you interpret [the verse] '... for the image of a bull that feeds on grass'?"

    F.  [R. Akiva said,] "I might [erroneously] assume [this refers to] any ox.

    G.  "Scripture states, [however,] '... feeds on grass.'

    H.  "There is nothing more repulsive and abominable that an ox when it is eating grass!"

8.  A.  R. Pappias interpreted [the following verse]: "... to a mare in Pharaoh's chariots, etc." (Song 1:9).

    B.  "Pharaoh rode on a male horse. As if it were possible, the Holy One, blessed be He, appeared to him on a male horse. [As it says in Scripture,] 'He mounted a cherub and flew, etc.' (Ps. 18:11).

    C.  "He[165] switched and rode on a female horse. As if it were possible, the Holy One, blessed be He, appeared to him on a female horse. [As it says in Scripture,] '... to a mare in Pharaoh's chariots' (Song 1:9)."

    D.  R. Akiva said to him, "Enough from you, Pappias!"

---

[165] I.e., Pharaoh.

| | | |
|---|---|---|
| ד"א • מימינם בזכות מזוזה • ומשמאלם בזכות | C/B/A | 4 |
| תפילין: • דרש ר' פפיוס והוא באחד ומי ישיבנו (איוב | A | 5 |
| כג יג) • ישיבנו [הוא דן י]חידי את כל באי העולם ואין | B | |
| להשיב על דבריו • אמ' לו ר' עקיבה דייך פפיוס • הא מה | D/C | |
| אתה מקיים והוא באחד [ומי ישיבנו • שלא] להשיב על | E | |
| דבריו של מי שאמר והיה העולם [שהכל בדין והכל | | |
| באומד. • דרש ר' פפיוס הן האדם היה כאחד [ממנו | A | 6 |
| (בר' ג' כב) • כאחד ממלאכי השרת • אמ' לו ר' עקיבה | C/B | |
| דייך פפיוס • מה] [אתה מקיים הן האדם היה כאחד • | D | |
| מלמד שנתן הקב"ה] [לפניו שני] דרכים דרך חיים | E | |
| ודרך מות ובחר ה[וא לו] דרך [המות] • דרש ר' פפיוס | A | 7 |
| וימירו את כבודם בתבנית שור אוכל [עשב (תה' קו כ) • | | |
| ש]ומע אני שור שלמעלה • ת"ל אוכל עשר • אמ' [לו] ר' | D/C/B | |
| עקיבה [דייך פ]פיוס • מה אתה מקיים בתבנית שור | E | |
| אוכל עשב • שומע [אני בשו]ר שבשאר ימות השנה • ת"ל | G/F | |
| אוכל עשב • אין מנוול ומשוקץ [משור ב]שעה שהוא | H | |
| אוכל עשב. • דרש ר' פפיוס לסוסתי [ברכבי] פרעה | A | 8 |
| וגומ' (שה"ש א ט) • רכב פרעה על סוס זכר כויכול | B | |
| נגלה לו [הקב"ה] על סוס זכר וירכב על כרוב ויעף | | |
| וגומ' (תה' יח יא) • חזר ורכב על [סוס נק]בה | C | |
| כויכול נגלה לו הקב"ה על סוס נקבה לסוסתי | | |
| [ברכבי] פרעה • אמ' לו ר' עקיבה דייך פפיוס • | D | |

E.  [R. Pappias responded to him,] "How do you interpret [the verse] '... to a mare[166] in Pharaoh's chariots'?"

F.  [R. Akiva said,] "What [is actually] written [in the verse is] '... to my joy.'[167]

G.  "[God said,] 'Just as I rejoiced in destroying Egypt, so too I rejoiced in destroying Israel.'"

9.    A.  Who caused them to be victorious?

B.  "... on their right and on their left" (Exod. 14:29).

C.  "On their right"—by the merit of Torah. And all [the rest] as written above.

## XXVI:V

1.    A.  "Thus the Lord delivered (Israel) on that day (from the hand of the Egyptians. Israel saw the Egyptians dead on the shore of the sea)" (Exod. 14:30):

B.  [Israel was] like a bird placed in the hand of a person. If the person should close his hand on it and squeeze it, behold, he would kill it.

C.  And thus Scripture states, "We are like a bird escaped (from the fowler's trap), etc." (Ps. 124:7) [and] "Blessed is the Lord, who did not let us be ripped apart, etc." (Ps. 124:6).

[69]  D.  And there are those who say [that God in Exod. 14:30] is like a person who delivers a newborn from the womb of its mother.

E.  And thus Scripture states, "... but you the Lord took (and brought out of Egypt), etc." (Deut. 4:20).

2.    A.  "Israel saw the Egyptians dead on the shore of the sea" (Exod. 14:30):

B.  What is only written here is [actually] "... *dying* on the shore of the sea."

C.  They were dying, but not yet dead.

D.  Similar to this, you say: "But as she breathed her last—for she was dying" (Gen. 35:18).

E.  Was she actually dead?

F.  Rather, just as above, she was dying, but not yet dead, so too here [with the Egyptians], they were dying, but not yet dead.

3.    A.  Another interpretation:

B.  "Israel saw the Egyptians dead" (Exod. 14:30):

C.  For four reasons:

D.  So that Israel would not say, "Just as we came up [out of the sea] on this side, so too did they come up on the other side."

E.  Another interpretation: So that the Egyptians would not say, "Just as we perished in the water, so too did they perish in the water."

F.  Another interpretation: So that [the Israelites would notice] the yokes and chariots that were loaded with silver, gold, and precious stones and gems, so that Israel would take the spoil.

G.  Another interpretation: So that they would set their eyes upon them and reprove them. And thus Scripture states, "... so I censure you and confront you with charges" (Ps. 50:21). And Scripture says, "When my enemy sees it, she shall be covered with shame, etc." (Mic. 7:10).

---

[166] Hebrew: *le-susati*—לסוסתי.

| | | |
|---|---|---|
| G/F/E | | מה אתה מקים לסוסתי ברכבי פרעה ◆ <לססתי כת'> ◆ כשם |
| A | 9 | ששתי על מצ' לאבדן כך ששתי על יש' לאבדן ◆ מי |
| C/B | | גרם להן להינצל ◆ מימינם ומשמאלם ◆ מימינם בזכות |
| | | תורה וכל כדכתיב לעיל. סל' פסו' ◆ |

<br>

| | | |
|---|---|---|
| | XXVI:V | |
| B/A | 1 | ויושע ייי ביום ההוא ◆ כצפור שנתונה ביד אדם |
| | | שאם מכביש אדם ידו עליה קימעה הרי הוא הורגה ◆ |
| C | | וכן הוא אומ' נפשינו כצפור נמלטה וגומ' (תה' קכד ז). |
| D | | ברוך ייי שלא נת<נ>נו טרף וגומ' (שם ו) ◆ ויש אומ' |
| E | | כאדם ששומט עובר ממעי אמו ◆ וכן הוא אומ' ואתכם |
| A | 2 | לקח ייי וגומ' (דב' ד כ) ◆ וירא יש' את מצרים מתים על |
| C/B | | שפת הים ◆ אין כתיב כן אלא מת על שפת הים ◆ מתין |
| D | | ואינן מתין. ◆ כיוצא בו אתה אומ' ויהי בצאת נפשה כי |
| F/E | | מתה (בר' לה יח) ◆ וכי מתה היית ◆ אלא מה לה[ן] מתה] |
| B/A | 3 | ואינה מתה אף כאן מתין ואינן מתין. ◆ ד"א ◆ וירא יש' |
| D/C | | את מצ' <מת> ◆ מפני ארבעה דברים ◆ שלא יהו יש' אומ' |
| E | | כשם [שעלינו מצד זה] [כך הן עלו מצד אחר. ◆ ד"א |
| | | שלא יהו מצריים אומ' כשם] [שאבדנו במים כך הן |
| F | | אבדו במים. ◆ ד"א בשביל מוטות] [ומרכבות שהיו |
| | | טעונות כסף וזהב ואבנים טובות ומרגליות] כדי |
| G | | [שיטלו ישראל] את הבזה. ◆ ד"א כדי שיהו נות[נין |
| | | עיניהן] בהן ומוכיחין אותן וכן הוא אום' אוכיחך |
| | | ואערכה לע[י]ניך (תה' נ כא) ואומ'] ותרא אויבתי |
| | | ותכסה בושה וגומ' (מיכה ז י) סל' פסו' ◆ |

167 Hebrew: le-sasti—לססתי.

XXVI:VI

1.  A.   "And when Israel saw the wondrous power (which the Lord had wielded against the Egyptians, the people feared the Lord. They had faith in the Lord and His servant Moses)" (Exod. 14:31):

    B.   [They saw] severe plagues and different plagues, and different deaths and severe deaths.

2.  A.   R. Yosi ha-Galili says, "How can you say from Scripture that in Egypt the Egyptians were struck with 10 plagues, but at the sea they were struck with 50 plagues?

    B.   "While in Egypt, Scripture says, '... and the magicians said to Pharaoh: ("This is the *finger* of God!")' (Exod. 8:15). While at the sea, Scripture says, 'And when Israel saw the wondrous power,[168] etc.' (Exod. 14:31).

    C.   "With how many [plagues] were they struck with one finger? Ten plagues!

    D.   "So you must say now that in Egypt they were struck with 10 plagues and at the sea they were struck with 50 plagues!"

    E.   R. Eliezer says, "How does one know from Scripture that each and every plague that God, blessed be He, brought upon the Egyptians was actually four plagues?

    F.   "As it says in Scripture, 'He inflicted His burning anger upon them, (wrath, indignation, trouble, a band of deadly messengers,) etc.' (Ps. 78:49).

    G.   "'Wrath'—one. 'Indignation'—two. 'Trouble'—three. And 'a band of deadly messengers'—four.

    H.   "So you must now say that in Egypt they were struck with 40 plagues, and at the sea they were struck with 200 plagues!"

    I.   R. Akiva says, "How does one know from Scripture that each and every plague that God, blessed be He, brought upon the Egyptians was actually five plagues?

    J.   "As it says in Scripture, 'He inflicted His burning anger upon them, (wrath, indignation, trouble, a band of deadly messengers), etc.' (Ps. 78:49).

    K.   "Behold [His burning anger] is one, etc.

    L.   "So you must now say that in Egypt they were struck with 50 plagues, and at the sea they were struck with 250 plagues!"

4.  A.   "... the people feared the Lord" (Exod. 14:31):

    B.   In the past they did not fear the Lord.

[70] C.   Now: "... the people feared the Lord" (Exod. 14:31).

5.  A.   "They had faith in the Lord and His servant Moses" (Exod. 14:31):

    B.   If they had faith in Moses, how much the more so in God!

    C.   This teaches you that [for] anyone who has faith in the shepherd of Israel, it's as if he believed in He who spoke, and the world came into being.

6.  A.   Similar to this you say: "... and the people spoke against God and against Moses" (Num. 21:5).

    B.   If against God they spoke, how much the more so against Moses!

    C.   Rather, this teaches you that [for] anyone who speaks against the shepherd of Israel, it's as if he speaks against He who spoke, and the world came into being.

7.  A.   Another interpretation:

---

[168] Hebrew, literally: the great hand.

| | | |
|---|---|---|
| B/A | 1 | וַיַּרְ[א יִשְׂרָאֵל] אֶת הַיָּד הַגְּדֹולָה. ◆ מַכּוֹת חֲמוּרוֹת |
| | | וּמַכּוֹת מְשׁוּנּוֹת זוֹ [מִזּוֹ וּמִיתוֹת] מְשׁוּנּוֹת וּמִיתוֹת |
| A | 2 | חֲמוּרוֹת זוֹ מִזּוֹ ◆ ר׳ יוֹסֵי הַגְּלִילִי אוֹמ׳ מִ[נַּיִן אַתָּה] אוֹמ׳ |
| | | שֶׁלָּקוּ מִצְ׳ בְּמִצְ׳ עֶשֶׂר מַכּוֹת וְעַל הַיָּם לָקוּ חֲמִישׁ[ים |
| B | | מַכּוֹת] ◆ שֶׁבְּמִצְ׳ הוּא אוֹמ׳ וַיֹּאמְרוּ הַחַרְטֻמִּים אֶל פַּרְעֹה |
| | | וְגוֹ׳ (שמ׳ ח טו) [וְעַל הַיָּם] הוּא אוֹמ׳ וַיַּרְא יִשְׂ׳ אֶת הַיָּד |
| D/C | | הַגְּדֹלָה וְגוֹ׳ ◆ כַּמָּה לָקוּ בְּ[אֶצְבַּע עֶשֶׂר] מַכּוֹת ◆ אֱמוֹר |
| | | מֵעַתָּה בְּמִצְ׳ לָקוּ עֶשֶׂר מַכּוֹת וְעַל הַיָּם [לָקוּ] חֲמִשִּׁים |
| E | | מַכּוֹת ◆ ר׳ אֱלִיעֶזֶר אוֹמ׳ מִנַּיִן שֶׁכָּל מַכָּה וּמַכָּה שֶׁ[הֵבִיא] |
| F | | הַמָּקוֹם בָּ׳׳ה עַל הַמִּצְ׳ הָיְתָה שֶׁל אַרְבַּע מַכּוֹת ◆ שֶׁנֶּ׳ |
| G | | וִישַׁלַּח בָּם חֲרוֹן אַפּוֹ וְגוֹמ׳ (תה׳ עח מט) עֶבְרָה ◆ אַחַת |
| | | וָזַעַם שְׁתַּיִם וְצָרָה שָׁלֹשׁ. וּמִשְׁלַ׳ מַלְאֲכֵי רָעִים אַרְבַּע. ◆ |
| H | | אֱמוֹר מֵעַתָּה בְּמִצְרַיִם לָקוּ אַרְבָּעִים מַכּוֹת וְעַל הַיָּם |
| I | | לָקוּ מָאתַיִם מַכּוֹת. ◆ ר׳ עֲקִיבָ׳ אוֹמ׳ מִנַּיִן שֶׁכָּל מַכָּה |
| | | וּמַכָּה שֶׁהֵבִיא הַמָּקוֹם בָּ׳׳ה עַל הַמִּצְ׳ הָיְתָה שֶׁל חָמֵשׁ |
| K/J | | מַכּוֹת ◆ שֶׁנֶּ׳ יְשַׁלַּח בָּם חֲרוֹן אַפּוֹ וְגוֹמ׳ ◆ הֲרֵי אַחַת וְכוּל ◆ |
| L | | אֱמוֹר מֵעַתָּה בְּמִצְ׳ לָקוּ חֲמִשִּׁים מַכּוֹת וְעַל הַיָּם לָקוּ |
| B/A | 4 | חֲמִשִּׁים וּמָאתֵ׳ מַכּוֹת. ◆ וַיִּירְאוּ הָעָם אֶת יְיָ ◆ לְשֶׁעָבַר לֹא |
| A 5 | C | הָיוּ יְרֵאִין אֶת יְיָ ◆ עַכְשָׁיו וַיִּירְאוּ הָעָם אֶת יְיָ. ◆ וַיַּאֲמִינוּ |
| B | | בַּיְיָ וּבְמֹשֶׁה עַבְדּוֹ ◆ אִם בְּמֹשֶׁה הֶאֱמִינוּ קַל וָחֹמֶר |
| C | | בַּמָּקוֹם ◆ לְלַמֶּדְךָ שֶׁכָּל הַמַּאֲמִין בְּרוֹעֶה יֵשׁ׳ כְּאִלּוּ |
| A | 6 | הֶאֱמִין בְּמִי שֶׁאָמַר וְהָיָה הָעוֹלָם. כַּיּוֹצֵא ◆ בּוֹ אַתָּה אוֹמ׳ |
| B | | וַיְדַבֵּר הָעָם בֵּאלֹקִים וּבְמֹשֶׁה (במ׳ כא ה) ◆ אִם בֵּאלֹקִים |
| C | | דִּבְּרוּ קַל וָחֹמֶ[ר] [בְּמֹשֶׁה] ◆ אֶלָּא לְלַמֶּדְךָ שֶׁכָּל הַמְדַבֵּר |
| A | 7 | בְּרוֹעֶה יֵשׁ׳ כְּאִלּוּ מְדַבֵּר [בְּמִי שֶׁאָמַר וְהָיָה הָעוֹלָם. ◆ ד׳׳א ◆ |

B. "They had faith in the Lord and His servant Moses" (Exod. 14:31):

C. So great is faith before He who spoke, and the world came into being that as a reward for the faith with which they believed, they merited that the Holy Spirit dwell upon them, and they sang the Song at the Sea.

D. As it says in Scripture, "They had faith in the Lord and His servant Moses. Then Moses and the Israelites sang" (Exod. 14:31; 15:1).

8.  A. R. Nehemiah says, "How does one know from Scripture that anyone who performs a divine commandment on faith before He who spoke, and the world came into being is worthy of having the Holy Spirit dwell upon him and of [then] singing a [divinely inspired] song?

B. "For thus we find with the forefathers that as a reward for the faith with which they believed, they merited that the Holy Spirit dwell upon them, and they sang a song.

C. "As it says in Scripture, 'They had faith in the Lord and His servant Moses. Then Moses and the Israelites sang' (Exod. 14:31, 15:1).

D. "And thus you find that Abraham only inherited this world and the world to come as a reward for faith.

E. "As it says in Scripture, '... and he believed in the Lord' (Gen. 15:6).

F. "And thus you find that Israel was redeemed from Egypt only as a reward for faith.

G. "As it says in Scripture, '... and the people believed, etc.' (Exod. 4:31). And Scripture says, '... the Lord guards the loyal, etc.' (Ps. 31:24).

H. "He recalls the faith of the forefathers.

I. "And Scripture says, '... thus his hands remained steady,[169] etc.' (Exod. 17:12). And Scripture says, 'Open the gates (and let a righteous nation enter, [a nation] that keeps faith)' (Isa. 26:2).

J. "Through this gate the most faithful enter.

K. "And thus Scripture says, 'It is good to praise the Lord ... to proclaim at daybreak ... You have gladdened me, O Lord, etc.' (Ps. 92:2–3,5).

L. "What caused us to rejoice? The faith with which [the forefathers] believed in this world, which is entirely darkness.

M. "And thus Jehoshaphat says, '... trust firmly in the Lord your God, etc.' (2 Chron. 20:20).

N. "And thus you find that the exiled will only be gathered by faith.

O. "As it says in Scripture, '... from Lebanon, my bride, with me!' (Song 4:8). And Scripture says, 'And I will espouse you forever with faithfulness, etc.' (Hos. 2:22). And Scripture says, '... but the righteous man is rewarded with life for his faithfulness, etc.' (Hab. 2:4). And Scripture says, 'O Lord, Your eyes look for faith, etc.' (Jer. 5:3).

P. "Thus, so great is faith before He who spoke, and the world came into being that as a reward for the faith with which they believed, the Holy Spirit dwelled upon them, and they sang the Song at the Sea.

Q. "As it says in Scripture, 'They had faith in the Lord and His servant Moses. Then Moses and the Israelites sang' (Exod. 14:31, 15:1).

R. "And further on Scripture says, 'Then they believed His promise, and sang (His praises), etc.' (Ps. 106:12)."

---

[169] More literally: faithful.

ויאמינו בייי ובמשה עבדו] ◆ [גדולה אמנה לפני מי     C/B

שאמר והיה העולם שבשכר אמנה] [שהאמינו] זכו

ששרת עליהן רוח הק' ואמרו שירה ◆ שנאמר [ויאמינו]     D

בייי ובמשה עבדו. אז ישיר משה ובני יש' ◆ ר' נחמיה     A    8

[אומ' מני]ן שכל העושה מצוה אחת באמונה לפני מי

שאמ' והיה [העולם] כדיי הוא שתשרה עליו רוח

הקודש ויאמר שירה ◆ [שכן מצינו] באבותינו שבשכר     B

אמנה שהאמינו זכו ששרת [עליהן ר]וח הקודש

ואמרו שירה ◆ שנא' ויאמינו בייי ובמשה [עבדו] אז     C

ישיר משה ובני יש' ◆ וכן את מוצא באברהם שלא ירש     D

[העולם] הזה והעולם הבא אלא בשכר אמנה ◆ שנא'     E

והאמין בייי (בר' טו ו) ◆ [וכן א]ת מוצא שלא נגאלו יש'     F

ממצ' אלא בשכר אמונה ◆ שנא' ויאמן [העם] וגו' ואומ'     G

אמונים נוצר ייי (תה' לא כד) ◆ מזכיר אמונת אבות. ◆     H

ואומר ויהי ידיו אמונה וגומ' (שמ' יז יב) ואומ' פתחו     I

שערים (ישע' כו ב) ◆ בשער זה בעלי אמונים נכנסין ◆ וכן     K/J

הוא אומ' טוב להודות לייי וגומ' להגיד בבקר וגומ' כי

שמחתני ייי וגומ' (תה' צב ב - ג, ה) ◆ מי גרם לנו לשמוח     L

בשמחה הזאת אמנה שהאמינו בעולם שכולו לילות ◆

וכן יהושפט אומ' האמינו בייי אלקיכם וגומ' (דה"ב כ     M

כ) ◆ וכן את מוצא שאין גליות מתכנסות אלא באמונה ◆     N

שנא' אתי מלבנון כלה וגומ' (שה"ש ד ח) ואומ'     O

וארשתיך לי באמונה וגומ' (הושע ב כב) ואומ' וצדיק

באמונתו יחיה וגומ' (חב' ב ד) ואומ' ייי עיניך הלא

לאמונה וגומ' (ירמ' ה ג) ואומ' ייי אלקי ארוממך וגו'

(ישע' כה א) ◆ הא גדולה אמונה לפני מי שאמ' והיה     P

העולם שבשכר אמנה שהאמינו שרת עליהן רוח הק'

ואמרו שירה ◆ שנא' ויאמינו בייי ובמשה עבדו. אז ישיר     Q

משה ◆ ולהלן הוא אום' ויאמינו בדבריו ישירו וגומ' (תה'     R

קו יב) סל' פסו' ◆

# Tractate Shirata

*Chapter Twenty-Seven*

(Textual Source: Ms. Paris, Alliance Collection)

XXVII:I[1]

1. A. "Then Moses and the Israelites sang (this song to the Lord)" (Exod. 15:1):

   B. There [are times when the word] "then" [refers] to the past and there [are times when] "then" [refers] to the future to come.

   [71]

   C. "It was then that men began to invoke the Lord by name" (Gen. 4:26); "... then she added, 'A bridegroom of blood because of the circumcision'" (Exod. 4:26); "Then Joshua built an altar" (Josh. 8:30); "Then David said" (1 Chron. 15:2); "Then Solomon said" (1 Kings 8:12)—[these instances refer] to the past.

   D. "Then you will see that you will glow" (Isa. 60:5); "Then the lame shall leap like a deer" (Isa. 35:6); "Then (the eyes of the blind) shall be opened" (Isa. 35:5); "... then our mouths shall be filled with laughter" (Ps. 126:2); "Then they shall say among the nations" (Ps. 126:3)—[these instances refer] to the future to come.

2. A. Rabbi says, "'Then Moses and the Israelites sang' is not [actually] written here; rather, 'Then Moses will sing.'

   B. "As a result we learn about the resurrection of the dead from the Torah."

3. A. Another interpretation:

   B. "... Moses and the Israelites" (Exod. 15:1):

   C. Scripture tells that Moses was equal to Israel, and Israel was equal to Moses, at the moment when they sang the song.

4. A. Another interpretation:

   B. "... Moses and the Israelites" (Exod. 15:1):

   C. This teaches that Moses sang the song in front of all Israel.

5. A. "... this song" (Exod. 15:1):

   B. Is it really one song? Isn't it 10 songs?

   C. First was [the song] sung in Egypt: "For you there shall be singing, as on a night, etc." (Isa. 30:29).

---

[1] Compare XXVII:I:1.A–VI:15.C with *Mekhilta de-Rabbi Ishmael*, Shirata (H/R, 116:1–121:5; Laut., vol. 2, 1:1–12:153; Neus., XXVI:I:1.A–17.H).

# מסכתא דשירתא

| | | |
|---|---|---|
| B/A | 1 | [אז ישיר משה ובני יש׳ • אז] לשעבר [ויש |
| C | | אז] לעתיד [לבוא • אז הוחל לקרוא בשם ייי |
| | | (בר׳ ד כו) אז אמרה חתן [דמים למולות (שמ׳ ד |
| | | כו) אז יבנה יהושע מזבח (יהו׳ ח ל) אז אמר] [דויד |
| | | (דהי״א טו ב) אז אמר שלמה (מ״א ח יב) לשעבר • |
| D | | אז תראי ונהרת (ישע׳ ס ה)] א[ז יד]ל[ג כ]איל פסח |
| | | (ישע׳ לה ו). אז תפקחנה (שם ה). אז ימלא שחוק |
| | | פ[ינו (תה׳ קכו ב). אז יאמרו] בגוים הגדיל ייי (שם ג |
| A | 2 | ‹לעתיד לבוא› • ר׳ אומ׳ אז שר משה ובני יש׳ אין כת׳ |
| B | | כ]ן אלא] אז ישיר משה • נמצינו למדין לתחית המתים |
| C/B/A | 3 | מן התו[רה. • ד״א] • משה ובני ישר׳ • מגיד הכת׳ שהיה |
| | | משה שקול כנגד יש׳ [ויש]ר׳] שקולין כנגד משה בשעה |
| C/B/A | 4 | שאמ׳ את השירה. • ד״א • [משה] ובני יש׳ • מלמד שאמר |
| B/A | 5 | משה שירה כנגד כל יש׳ • את [השירה] הזאת • וכי שירה |
| C | | אחת היא והלא עשר שירות הן • ר[אשונה] שנאמרה |
| | | במצ׳ השיר יהיה לכם כליל וגומ׳ (ישע׳ ל כט). • |

D. Second was [the song] sung by the sea: "This is my God and I will glorify Him, etc." (Exod. 15:2).

E. Third was [the song] sung by the well: "Then Israel sang this song, etc." (Num. 21:17).

F. Fourth was [the song that Moses] sang: "Then Moses recited the words in the hearing of the entire congregation, etc." (Deut. 31:30).

G. Fifth was [the song that] Joshua sang: "Then Joshua addressed the Lord, etc." (Josh. 10:12).

H. Sixth was [the song that] Deborah sang: "And Deborah sang, etc." (Judg. 5:1).

I. Seventh was [the song that] David sang to the Lord: "David addressed (the words of this song) to the Lord, etc." (2 Sam. 22:1).

J. Eighth was [the song that] Solomon sang: "(A psalm of David:) A song for the dedication (of the House), etc." (Ps. 30:1).

6. A. Did David build it? Didn't Solomon build it?

B. As it says in Scripture, "When Solomon had completed the construction of the House for the Lord, etc." (1 Kings 6:14).

C. Rather, because David offered his life for it, it is called by his name.

D. And where did David offer his life for the House?

E. As it says in Scripture, "O Lord, remember in David's favor" (Ps. 132:1), and all [the rest] of the matter.

F. What is said about him?—"Now look to your own House, O David!" (1 Kings 12:16).

G. Thus, each and every thing for which a person offers his life is called by his name!

7. A. Moses offered his life for three things that are called by his name:

B. He offered his life for the Torah, and it is called by his name.

C. As it says in Scripture, "Be mindful of the Teaching of My servant Moses, etc." (Mal. 3:22).

D. Is it really Moses' Torah? Isn't it the Lord's Torah?

E. As it says in Scripture, "The Torah of the Lord is perfect" (Ps. 19:8).

F. Rather, because he offered his life for it, it is called by his name.

G. And where did Moses offer his life for the Torah?

H. [As it says in Scripture,] "And he was there with the Lord (forty days and forty nights. He ate no bread and drank no water), etc." (Exod. 34:28). And Scripture says, "I stayed on the mountain, etc." (Deut. 9:9).

I. He offered his life for Israel and they are called by his name.

J. As it says in Scripture, "Hurry down, for your people have acted basely" (Exod. 32:7).

[72] K. And are they really Moses' people? Aren't they the Lord's people?

L. As it says in Scripture, "Yet they are Your very own people" (Deut. 9:29). And Scripture says, "... in that it was said of them, 'These are the people of the Lord, etc.'" (Ezek. 36:20).

M. Rather, because Moses offered his life for Israel, they are called by his name.

N. And where did Moses offer his life for Israel?

| | | |
|---|---|---|
| D | שנייה ש[נאמרה] על הים זה אלי ואנוהו וגומ׳ (שמ׳ טו ב) ✦ | |
| E | שלישית שנאמ׳ על הבאר אז [ישיר] יש׳ וגומ׳ (במ׳ כא | |
| F | יז) ✦ רביעית שאמ׳ וידבר משה באזני כל קהל יש׳ וגומ׳ | |
| G | (דב׳ לא ל) ✦ [.] חמישית שאמ׳ יהושע אז ידבר יהושע | |
| H | ליי׳ וגומ׳ (יהו׳ י יב) ✦ ששית שאמ׳ דבורה ותשר דבורה | |
| I | וגומ׳ (שופט׳ ה א) ✦ שביעית שאמר דוד (ליי׳) וידבר | |
| J | דוד ליי׳ [וגו׳] (ש׳׳ב כב א) ✦ שמינית שאמ׳ שלמה מזמור | |
| A | שיר חנוכת וגומ׳ (תה׳ ל א) ✦ וכי דויד בנאו והלא שלמה | 6 |
| B | בנאו ✦ שנא׳ ויבנה שלמה את הבית ליי׳ וגומ׳ (מ׳׳א ו יד) ✦ | |
| D/C | אלא שנתן דויד נפשו עליו נקרא על שמו ✦ והיכן נתן | |
| E | דויד נפשו על הבית ✦ שנא׳ זכור יי׳ לדויד (תה׳ קלב א) | |
| F | וכול ענינא. ✦ מה נאמ׳ לו עתה ראה ביתך דויד (מ׳׳א יב | |
| G | טז). ✦ הא כל דבר ודבר שאדם נותן נפשו עליו נקרא | |
| A | על שמו. ✦ שלשה דברים נתן משה נפשו עליהן ונקראו | 7 |
| C/B | על שמו ✦ נתן נפשו על התורה ונקראת על שמו ✦ שנא׳ | |
| D | זכרו תורת משה עבדי וגומ׳ (מלאכי ג כב) ✦ וכי תורת | |
| E | משה היא והלא תורת יי׳ ✦ שנא׳ תורת יי׳ תמימה (תה׳ | |
| F | יט ח) ✦ אלא לפי שנתן נפשו עליה [נקראת על שמו ✦ | |
| H/G | והיכן נתן משה נפשו על התורה ✦ ויהי שם] [עם ה׳ | |
| | וגומ׳ (שמ׳ לד כח) ואומ׳ ואשב בהר וגומ׳ (דב׳ ט ט). ✦ | |
| J/I | נתן נפשו] [על יש׳] ונקראו על שמו ✦ שנא׳ לך רד כי שחת | |
| K | עמך (שמ׳ לב ז) ✦ וכי] [עמו של משה הן והלא עם ה׳ הם ✦ | |
| L | שנא׳ והם עמך ונחלתך (דב׳ ט כט)] [ואומ׳ בא]מור להן עם | |
| M | יי׳ אלה וגומ׳ (יחז׳ לו כ). ✦ אלא לפי שנתן משה נפשו | |
| N | [על יש׳] נקראו על שמן ✦ והיכן נתן משה נפשו על יש׳ ✦ | |

O. [As it says in Scripture,] "Some time after that, when Moses had grown up ... He turned this way and that, etc." (Exod. 2:12).

P. He offered his life for the laws, and they are called by his name.

Q. As it says in Scripture, "You shall appoint magistrates and officials, etc." (Deut. 17:18).

R. Were they really Moses'?

S. Has it not already been said, "... for judgment is God's" (Deut. 1:17). And Scripture says, "God stands in the divine assembly, (among the divine beings He pronounces judgment,) etc." (Ps. 82:1).

T. Rather, because he surrendered his life for them, they are called by his name.

U. And where did he surrender his life for the laws?

V. Behold, Scripture states, "Who made you ... When Pharaoh learned of the matter (he sought to kill Moses), etc." (Exod. 2:14–15). And Scripture says, "He executed the Lord's judgments, etc." (Deut. 33:21). From laws he fled, and to laws he returned!

W. Thus, each and every thing for which a person offers his life is called by his name!

8.    A. Ninth was [the song that] Jehoshaphat sang: "After taking counsel with the people, he stationed singers to the Lord" (2 Chron. 20:21).[2]

B. And what differentiated this song of thanksgiving from all the songs of thanksgiving in the Torah?

C. Because "Praise the Lord, because He is good, because His mercy lasts forever" is not stated.

D. As if it were possible, there is no joy before God over the destruction of the wicked. How much the more so over the destruction of that righteous one, who was equal to all!

E. As it says in Scripture, "... but the righteous is an everlasting foundation" (Prov. 10:25).

F. Tenth [is the song to be sung] in the time to come.

G. As it says in Scripture, "Sing to the Lord a new song, etc." (Isa. 42:10). And Scripture says, "Sing to the Lord a new song, His praises in the congregation of the faithful" (Ps. 149:1).

9.    A. All songs of salvation in the past were called by a feminine name.

B. Just as the female gives birth, likewise songs of salvation in the past were followed by subjugation.

C. But the song of salvation in the time to come is called by a masculine name.

D. Just as the man does not give birth, in accordance with what is said in Scripture, "Ask and see: Surely males do not give birth!" (Jer. 30:6) likewise the song of salvation in the time to come will not be followed by subjugation. As it says in Scripture, "But Israel has won through the Lord triumph everlasting. You shall not be shamed or disgraced in all the ages to come!" (Isa. 45:17).

10.   A. "... to the Lord" (Exod. 15:1):

B. To the Lord they sang it, and not to a human being.

C. Not in accordance with what is said in Scripture [here], "... the women of all the towns of Israel came ... The women sang as they danced, and they chanted: (Saul has slain his thousands, David, his tens of thousands), etc." (1 Sam. 18:6–7).

---

[2] Compare 8.A–E with b. Megillah 10b.

| | |
|---|---|
| ויהי בימים [ההם וי]גדל משה וגומ' ויפן כה וכה | O |
| וגומ' (שמ' ב יב) ◆ נתן נפשו על הדינין [ונקראו | P |
| על שמו ◆ שנא' שפטים ושוטרים תתן לך וגומ' (דב' | Q |
| טז יח) ◆ וכי של [משה הן] ◆ והלא כבר נאמ' כי | S/R |
| המשפט לאלקים הוא (שם א יז). ואומ' כי אלקי | |
| [משפט] ייי וגומ' (ישע' ל יח) ואומ' אלקים נצב בעדת | |
| אל וגומ' (תה' פב א) ◆ אלא לפי שמסר [נפשו ע]ליהן | T |
| נקראו על שמו ◆ והיכן מסר נפשו על הדינין ◆ הרי [הוא | V/U |
| א]ומר מי שמך וגומ' וישמע פרעה את הדבר הזה | |
| וגומ' (שמ' ב יד - טו) [ואומ'] צדקת ייי עשה וגומ' (דב' | |
| לג כא) מדינין הלך לדינין חזר. ◆ הא כל [דבר] ודבר | W |
| שאדם נותן נפשו עליו נקרא על שמו. ◆ תשיעית שאמ' | A | 8 |
| יהושפט ויועץ אל העם ויעמד משוררים לייי (דה"ב כ | |
| כא) ◆ וכי מה נשתנית הודאה זו מכל הודאות שבתורה ◆ | B |
| שלא נאמ' בה הודו לייי כי טוב כי לעולם חסדו (שם). ◆ | C |
| כביכול אין שמחה לפני המקום באבדן שלרשעים קל | D |
| וחומר באבדן שלצדיק ההוא שהיה שקול כנגד הכל ◆ | |
| שנא' וצדיק יסוד עולם (מש' י כה). ◆ עשירית לעתיד | F/E |
| לבוא ◆ שנא' שירו לייי שיר חדש וגו' (ישע' מב י) ואומ' | G |
| הל' שירו לייי שיר חדש תהלתו בקהל חסידים (תה' | |
| קמט א) ◆ כל תשועות שעברו נקראו על שם נקבה ◆ | A | 9 |
| כשם שהנקבה יולדת כך תשועות שעברו יש אחריהן | B |
| שעבוד ◆ אבל תשועה הבאה לעתיד לבוא נקראת על | C |
| שם זכר ◆ כשם שאין זכר יולד כענין שנא' שאלו נא | D |
| וראו אם יולד זכר וגומ' (ירמ' ל ו) כך תשועה העתידה | |
| ל[בוא אין אחריה שעבוד] שנא' יש' נושע בייי [תשועת | |
| עו]למ]ים [לא תבושו ולא תכלמו עד עולמי עד (ישע' | |
| מה יז). ◆ לייי ◆ לייי אמרוה ולא לבשר] [ודם ◆ לא כענין | C/B/A | 10 |
| שנא' ותצאנה הנשים מכל ערי ישראל וגומ' ותעניה | |
| הנשים] ה[משחקות ותאמרנה וגומ' (ש"א יח ו - ז) | |
| ◆ | |

D.   But here, they sang it to the Lord, and not to a human being.

11.   A.   "They said" (Exod. 15:1):[3]

B.   R. Nehemiah says, "The Holy Spirit dwelled on Israel, and they sang the song like people reciting the *Shema*."

C.   R. Akiva says, "Moses opened up singing, 'I will sing to the Lord,' and Israel answered after him and finished with him like those reciting the Hallel in the synagogue."

D.   Eliezer ben Taddai says, "Moses opened up singing, 'I will sing to the Lord,' and Israel answered after him and finished with him, 'Horse and driver He has hurled into the sea.'

[73]   E.   "Moses opened up singing, 'The Lord is my strength and might,' and Israel answered after him and finished with him, 'This is my God and I will glorify Him.'

F.   "Moses opened up singing, 'The Lord, the Warrior,' and Israel answered after him and finished with him, 'The Lord is His name.'"

12.   A.   Greatness befits the Lord. Might befits the Lord—splendor, triumph, and majesty.

B.   And thus David says, "Yours, Lord, are greatness, (might, splendor, triumph, and majesty,) etc." (1 Chron. 29:11).

C.   They told a parable: To what is the matter alike?

D.   To a human king who entered a city. And they were praising him as a mighty warrior, when he was nothing but weak, [and praising him] as a wise man, when he was nothing but stupid, [and praising him] as a rich man, when he was nothing but poor, [and praising him] as a merciful man, when he was nothing but merciless, [praising him] as a judge and faithful man, when he had none of these qualities—they were flattering him.

E.   However, this is not the case with He who spoke, and the world came into being.

F.   Rather, "I will sing to the Lord" (Exod. 15:1), because He is a mighty warrior.

G.   As it says in Scripture, "... the great, the mighty, the awesome God, etc." (Deut. 10:17). And Scripture says, "... the Lord, mighty and valiant, etc." (Ps. 24:8). And Scripture says, "The Lord goes forth like a warrior, etc." (Isa. 42:13). [And Scripture says,] "For You are great and perform wonders, etc." (Ps. 86:10). [And Scripture says,] "You are great and great (is Your name), etc." (Jer. 10:6).

H.   [Rather,] "I will sing to the Lord" (Exod. 15:1), because He is wise.

I.   As it says in Scripture, "The Lord founded the earth by wisdom ... By His knowledge, etc." (Prov. 3:19–20). [And Scripture says,] "For the Lord grants wisdom, etc." (Prov. 2:6). [And Scripture says,] "With Him are wisdom and courage, etc." (Job 12:13). [And Scripture says,] "Who would not revere You, O King of the nations?" (Jer. 10:7).

J.   [Rather,] they sang to the Lord, because He is rich.

K.   As it says in Scripture, "Lo, the heavens belong to the Lord, your God, etc." (Deut. 10:14). [And Scripture says,] "His is the sea, He made it, etc." (Ps. 95:5). [And Scripture says,] "Silver is mine, etc." (Hag. 2:8). [And Scripture says,] "Consider, all lives are Mine, etc." (Ezek. 18:4).

L.   [Rather,] "I will sing to the Lord" (Exod. 15:1), because He is merciful.

M.   As it says in Scripture, "The Lord, the Lord—a God compassionate, etc." (Exod. 34:6). [And Scripture says,] "For the Lord (your God) is a compassionate God, etc." (Deut. 4:31). And

---

[3] Compare 11.A–F with t. Sotah 6:2–4.

| | | |
|---|---|---|
| אבל כאן לייי אמרוה ולא לבשר [ודם. ◆ ויאמרו | A 11 | D |
| לאמר. ◆ ר' נחמיה אומ' רוח הקודש שרת על יש' ואמ' | B | |
| [שירה] כבני אדם שקוראין את שמע ◆ ר' עקיבה אומ' | C | |
| משה פ[תח] ואמ' אשירה לייי ויש' עונין אחריו | | |
| וגומרין עמו כקור[אין את] ההלל בבית הכנסת. ◆ | | |
| אלעזר בן תדאי אומ' משה פותח [ואומ'] אשירה לייי | D | |
| ויש' עונין אחריו וגומרין עמו. סוס ורו[כבו רמה] בים. ◆ | | |
| מושה פותח ואומ' עזי וזמרת יה ויש' עונין אחר]יו | E | |
| וגומרין] עמו זה אלי ואנוהו (וגומ') ◆ משה פותח ואומ' | F | |
| יייי איש מלחמ[ה ויש'] עונין אחריו וגומרין עמו יייי | | |
| שמו. ◆ לייי נאה הגדולה לייי [נאה] גבורה לו תפארת | A | 12 |
| נצח והוד ◆ וכן דוד אומ' לך ייי הגדולה [וגומ'] (דה"א | B | |
| כט יא) ◆ משלו משל למה הדבר דומה ◆ למלך בשר ודם | D/C | |
| שנ[כנס] למדינה והיו מקלסין לפניו שהוא גבור ואינו | | |
| אלא חלש שהוא חכם ואינו אלא טיפש שהוא עשיר | | |
| ואינו אלא עני שהוא רחמן ואינו אלא אכזרי שהוא | | |
| דיין והוא נאמן ואין בו אחת מכל אלו המדות אלא | | |
| שמחניפין לו. ◆ אבל מי שאמ' והיה העולם אינו כן ◆ אלא | F/E | |
| אשירה לייי שהוא גבור ◆ שנא' האל הגדול הגבור | G | |
| והנורא (דב' י יז) ואומ' ייי עזוז וגבור וגומ' (תה' כד ח) | | |
| ואומ' ייי כגבור יצא וגומ' (ישע' מב יג) כי גדול אתה | | |
| ועושה נפלאות וגומ' (תה' פו י) גדול אתה וגד' וגומ' | | |
| (ירמי' י ו) ◆ אשירה לייי שהוא חכם ◆ שנא' ייי בחכמה | I/H | |
| יסד אר[ץ וגומ' בדעתו וגומ' (מש' ג יט - כ) כי ייי נתן | | |
| חכמה וגומ' (מש' ב ו) עמו חכמה וגבורה וגומ' (איוב | | |
| יב יג) מי לא ייראך מלך הגוים וגומ' (ירמ' י ז) ◆ שירו | J | |
| לייי שהוא עשיר (וגומ') ◆ שנא' הן לייי אלקיך השמים | K | |
| וגומ' (דב' י יד) אשר לו הים והוא עש' וגומ' (תה' צה | | |
| ה) לי הכסף וגומ' (חגי ב ח) הן כל הנפשות לי הנה | | |
| וגומ' (יחז' יח ד) ◆ אשירה לייי שהוא רחמן ◆ שנא' ייי ייי | M/L | |

Scripture says, "The Lord is gracious and compassionate" (Ps. 145:8). And Scripture says, "O Lord, be mindful of Your compassion" (Ps. 25:6).

N.    [Rather,] "I will sing to the Lord" (Exod. 15:1), because He is a judge.

O.    As it says in Scripture, "… for judgment is God's" (Deut. 1:17). And Scripture says, "… for the Lord is a God of justice" (Isa. 30:18). And Scripture says, "God stands in the divine assembly, among the divine beings He pronounces judgment" (Ps. 82:1).

P.    [Rather,] "I will sing to the Lord" (Exod. 15:1), because He is faithful.

Q.    As it says in Scripture, "… the faithful God, etc." (Deut. 7:9). [And Scripture says,] "The Rock! His deeds are perfect, etc." (Deut. 32:4).

R.    [Rather,] "I will sing to the Lord" (Exod. 15:1), because He is deserving, splendid, and praiseworthy.

S.    As it says in Scripture, "For who in the skies (can equal the Lord), etc." (Ps. 89:7). [And Scripture says,] "O Lord, God of hosts, who is like You, etc." (Ps. 89:9)—You are emblematic of Your host! [And Scripture says,] "Who is like You among the gods, O Lord" (Exod. 15:11). [And Scripture says,] "My beloved is clear-skinned and ruddy" (Song 5:10), and all [the rest] of the matter.

13.   A.    R. Yosi ha-Galili says, "Behold Scripture says, '… from the mouths of infants and
[74]        sucklings, etc.' (Ps. 8:3):[4]

B.    "'Infants'—these are those who are in their mother's womb.

C.    "As it says in Scripture, 'Or why was I not like a buried stillbirth, (like babies who never saw the light?)' (Job 3:16).

D.    "And 'sucklings' only means those who are on their mother's breast.

E.    "Both of these opened their mouths in song, and sang the song: 'I will sing to the Lord, etc.' (Exod. 15:1)."

F.    Rabbi says, "'Infants'—these are those who are outside.

G.    "As it says in Scripture, '… to cut off babes from the streets, etc.' (Jer. 9:20). And Scripture says, 'Little children beg for bread, etc.' (Lam. 4:4).

H.    "And 'sucklings'—these are those who are on their mother's breast.

I.    "Both of these opened their mouths in song, and sang the song: 'I will sing to the Lord' (Exod. 15:1)."

15.   A.    And not Israel alone sang the song: "Sing to the Lord, for He is highly exalted."

B.    Rather, [also] the ministering angels.

C.    As it says in Scripture, "O Lord, our Lord, how majestic is Your name, etc." (Ps. 8:2).

*Chapter Twenty-Eight*

(Textual Source: Ms. Paris, Alliance Collection)

XXVIII:I[5]

1.   A.    "… for He is highly exalted" (Exod. 15:1):

B.    He exalted me, and I exalted Him.[6]

---

[4] Compare 13.A–I with t. Sotah 6:4–5 and y. Sotah 20c (Neus., 5:4:I.A–II.G).

[5] Compare XXVIII:I:1.A–II:8.C with *Mekhilta de-Rabbi Ishmael,* Shirata (H/R, 121:6–125:16; Laut., vol. 2, 12:1–22:139; Neus., XXVII:I:1.A–II:8.E).

[6] The text interprets here the seemingly doubled verbal nature of the infinitive absolute "highly exalted" (Hebrew: גאה גאה).

אל רחום וגומ׳ (שמ׳ לד ו) [כי אל רחום ייי (דב׳ ד לא)

ואומ׳ חנון ורחום ייי (תה׳ קמה ח) ואומ׳ זכור רחמיך

ייי (תה׳ כה ו)] ◆ [אשירה לייי שהוא דיין ◆ שנא׳ כי | O/N

המשפט לאלקים (דב׳ א יז) ואומ׳ כי אלקי משפט ייי

(ישע׳ ל יח)] [ואומ׳ אלקים נצב בעדת אל בקרב

אלהים ישפוט (תה׳ פב א)( [אשירה] לייי שהוא נאמן ◆ | P

שנא׳ האל הנאמן וגומ׳ (דב׳ ז ט) הצור תמים פעלו | Q

[וגומ׳ (שם לב ד) א[שירה לייי שהוא נאה שהוא הדור | R

שהוא משובח ◆ שנא׳ [כי מי ב]שחק וגומ׳ (תה׳ פט ז) ייי | S

אלקי צבא׳ מי כמוך וגומ׳ (שם ט) אתה בתוך צבא

[שלך מי] כמוך באלים ייי (שמ׳ טו יא) דודי צח ואדום

וגומ׳ (שה״ש ה י) וכל עניינא. הא [לייי נא]ה הגדולה

וכול כדכת׳ לעיל. ◆ ר׳ יוסי הגלילי אומ׳ הרי הוא [אומ׳ | A | 13

מ[פי עוללים ויונקים וגומ׳ (תה׳ ח ג) ◆ עוללים אלו | B

שבמעי אימן ◆ שנא׳ או [כנפל טמ]ון לא אהיה וגומ׳ | C

(איוב ג טז) ◆ ואין יונקים אלא שעל שדי אימן ◆ אלו ואלו | E/D

פת[חו פיהן ואמרו שירה אשירה לייי וגומ׳ ◆ ר׳ אומ׳ | F

עוללים [אלו שב]חוץ ◆ שנא׳ להכרית עולל מחוץ וגו׳ | G

(ירמ׳ ט כ) ואומ׳ עוללים שאלו לחם [וגומ׳] (איכה ד

ד) ◆ ויונקים אלו שעל שדי אימן ◆ אלו ואלו פתחו פיהן | I/H

ואמרו שירה אשירה לייי ◆ ולא יש׳ בלבד אמרו שירה | A | 15

שירו לייי כי גאה גאה ◆ אלא מלאכי שרת ◆ שנא׳ ייי | C/B

אדונינו מה אדיר שמך וגומ׳ (תה׳ ח ב) ◆

XXVIII:I

◆ | כי גאה גאה ◆ הגאני והגאיתיו | B/A | 1

C. He exalted me in Egypt, [as it says in Scripture,] "Then you shall say to Pharaoh, 'Thus says the Lord, etc.'" (Exod. 4:22).

D. Thus, I exalted Him, and sang before Him the song. [As it says in Scripture,] "For you, there shall be singing, etc." (Isa. 30:29).

2. A. "... for He is highly exalted" (Exod. 15:1):

B. He exalted me, and I exalted Him.

C. He exalted me by the sea, [as it says in Scripture,] "The angel of God ..." (Exod. 14:19).

D. And, thus, I exalted Him, and I sang before Him the song: "This is my God, and I will exalt Him" (Exod. 15:2).

3. A. Another interpretation:

B. "... for He is highly exalted" (Exod. 15:1):

C. And He will be exalted in the future.

D. As it says in Scripture, "For the Lord of Hosts has ready a day against all, etc." (Isa. 2:12), and all [the rest] of the matter.

4. A. Another interpretation:

B. "... for He is highly exalted" (Exod. 15:1):

C. He is exalted above all who are exalted.

D. By the [very] means that the nations of the world exalt themselves before Him, He exacts punishment from them!

E. For thus we find with the men of the Tower, that by the [very] means that they exalted themselves before Him, He exacted punishment from them.

F. And concerning Sodom, Scripture says, "As I live—declares the Lord God—(your sister Sodom and her daughters did not) do, etc." (Ezek. 16:48).

G. And Rabban Gamliel already ... [manuscript lacunae].

5. A. For thus you find with Egypt, that by the [very] means that it exalted itself before Him, He exacted punishment from it.

B. As it says in Scripture, "... he took six hundred of his picked chariots" (Exod. 14:7).

C. What [else] does Scripture say?—"Pharaoh's chariots ... (He has cast into the sea), etc." (Exod. 15:4).

6. A. For thus you find with Sisera, that by the [very] means that he exalted himself before Him, He exacted punishment from him.

B. As it says in Scripture, "So Sisera ordered all his chariots, etc." (Judg. 4:13).

C. What [else] does Scripture say?—"The stars fought from heaven, etc." (Judg. 5:20).

7. A. For thus you find with Samson, that by the [very] means that he exalted himself before Him, He exacted punishment from him.

B. As it says in Scripture, "His father and mother said to him ... Get me that one, etc!" (Judg. 14:3).

C. What [else] does Scripture say?—"The Philistines seized him and gouged (out his eyes), etc." (Judg. 16:21).

|  | | |
|---|---|---|
| הגאני במצ' ואמרת אל פרעה כה אמר ייי | C | |
| וגומ' (שמ' ד כב) ♦ אף אני הגאיתיו ואמרתי לפניו | D | |
| שירה השיר יהיה לכם וגומ' (ישע' ל כט) ♦ כי גאה | A | 2 |
| גאה ♦ הגאני והגאיתיו ♦ הגאני על הים ויסע מלאך | C/B | |
| האלקים (שמ' יד יט) ♦ ואף אני הגאיתיו ואמרתי לפניו | D | |
| שירה זה אלי ואנוהו. ♦ ד"א ♦ כי גאה גאה ♦ ועתיד | C/B/A | 3 |
| להתגאות ♦ שנא' כי יום לייי צבא' על כל וגומ' (ישע' ב | D | |
| יב) וכול עניינא. ♦ ד"א ♦ כי גאה גאה ♦ מתגאה הוא על כל | C/B/A | 4 |
| הגאים ♦ במה שאומ' העו' מתגאין לפניו בו נפרע מהן ♦ | D | |
| וכן מצינו באנשי מגדל שבמה שנתגאו לפניו בו נפרע | E | |
| מהן וכול ♦ ובסדום הוא אומ' חי אני נאם ייי אם עשתה | F | |
| וגומ' (יחז' טז מח) ♦ וכבר היה רבן גמליאל [...] ♦ [וכן את | A 5 G | |
| מוצא במצ' שבמה שנתגאו לפניו בו נפרע מהם ♦ שנא'] | B | |
| [ויקח שש מאות רכב בחור (שמ' יד ז) ♦ מה הוא אומ' | C | |
| מרכבות פרעה וגומ'] ♦ [וכן את מוצא בסיסרא שבמה | A | 6 |
| שנתגאה] לפניו בו [נפרע] ממנו ♦ שנא' ויזעק סיסרא | B | |
| את כל רכבו וגומ' (שופ' ד יג) ♦ מה הו[א אומ' מן] | C | |
| שמים נלחמו וגומ' (שם ה כ). ♦ וכן את מוצא בשמשון | A | 7 |
| במה [שנתגאה] לפניו בו נפרע ממנו ♦ שנא' ויאמר | B | |
| שמשון אל אביו אתה ק[ח לי] וגומ' (שופ' יד ג) ♦ מה | C | |
| הוא אומ' ויאחזוהו פלשתים וינקרו וגומ' (שופ' טז כא) | | |
| ♦ | | |

D.    Rabbi says, "The beginning of his corruption was in Gaza. Therefore He punished him only in Gaza."

8.   A.    For thus you find with Absalom, that by the [very] means that he exalted himself before
[75]         Him, He exacted punishment from him.

B.    As it says in Scripture, "No one (in all of Israel) was so admired for his beauty as Absalom ... When he cut his hair, etc." (2 Sam. 14:25–26).

C.    What [else] does Scripture say?—"Absalom encountered some of David's followers, etc." (2 Sam. 18:9).

D.    R. Judah the Patriarch says, "He would cut his hair every 12 months.

E.    "As it says in Scripture, 'After a period of forty years, Absalom said to the king, etc.' (2 Sam. 15:7)."

F.    R. Yosi says, "He would cut his hair every 30 days.

G.    "As it says in Scripture, '... he had to have it cut from days to days, etc.' (2 Sam. 14:26)."

H.    Rabbi says, "He would cut his hair every Friday, for thus is common practice, for kings to cut their hair from Friday to Friday."

9.   A.    For thus you find with Sennacherib, that by the [very] means that he exalted himself before Him, He exacted punishment from him.

B.    As it says in Scripture, "Through your envoys you have blasphemed my Lord ... It is I who has drawn and drunk strange waters, etc." (2 Kings 19:23–24).

C.    What [else] does Scripture say?—"... an angel of the Lord went out and struck down (one hundred and eighty-five thousand) in the Assyrian camp, etc." (2 Kings 19:35).

D.    They said, "The greatest among them was appointed over 185,000. The least among them no less than 2,000.

E.    "As it says in Scripture, 'So how could you refuse anything (even to the deputy of one of my master's lesser servants), etc.' (2 Kings 18:24). [And Scripture says,] '... I'll give you two thousand horses, etc.' (2 Kings 18:23).

F.    "What [else] does Scripture say?—'This is the word that the Lord has spoken concerning him: (Fair maiden Zion) despises you ... Whom have you blasphemed and reviled, etc.?' (2 Kings 19:21)."

10.   A.    For thus you find with Nebuchadnezzar, that by the [very] means that he exalted himself before Him, He exacted punishment from him.

B.    As it says in Scripture, "Once you thought in your heart, 'I will climb to the sky, etc.'" (Isa. 14:13).

C.    What [else] does Scripture say?—"Instead you are brought down to Sheol, etc." (Isa. 14:15).

11.   A.    And thus you find with the prince of Tyre, that by the [very] means that he exalted himself before Him, He exacted punishment from him.

B.    As it says in Scripture, "O mortal, say to the prince of Tyre ... Because you have been so haughty, etc." (Ezek. 28:2).

C.    What [else] does Scripture say?—"The death of the uncircumcised, etc." (Ezek. 28:10).

12.   A.    Thus, by the [very] means that the nations of the world exalt themselves before Him, He exacts punishment from them!

| | | |
|---|---|---|
| ר' א[ומ'] תחלת קלקלתו בעזה לפיכך לא היה | D | |
| עונשו אלא בע[זה] • וכן] את מוצא באבשלום שבמה | A | 8 |
| שנתגאה לפניו בו נפ' מ[מנו] • שנא' וכאבשלום לא היה | B | |
| איש יפה וגומ' ובגלחו את [ראשו] וגומ' (ש"ב יד כו) • | | |
| מה הוא אומ' ויקרא אבשלום לפני עבדי דוד וג[ומ' | C | |
| (ש"ב יח ט) • ר'] יהודה הנשיא אומ' כל שנים עשר חדש | D | |
| היה מגלח שנא' [ויהי] מקצה ארבעים שנה ויאמר | E | |
| אבשלום אל המלך וגומ' (ש"ב טו ז) • ר' יונ[סי] אומ' כל | F | |
| שלשים יום היה מגלח • שנא' והיה מקץ ימים לימים | G | |
| אשר יגלח וגומ' (ש"ב יד כו) • ר' אומ' כל ערב שבת היה | H | |
| מגלח שכן דרך מלאכים להיות מגלחין מערב שבת | | |
| לערב שבת. • וכן את מוצא בסנחריב שבמה שנתגאה | A | 9 |
| לפניו בו לקה • שנא' ביד מלאכיך חרפת יי וגומ' אני | B | |
| קרתי ושתיתי וגומ' (מ"ב יט כג - כד) • מה הוא אומ' | C | |
| ויצא מלאך יי ויכה במחנה אשור וגומ' (שם לה) • | | |
| אמרו גדול שבהן הוא ממונה על מאה ושמונים | D | |
| וחמשה אלף. קטן שבהן אין פחות משני אלפים (וגו') • | | |
| שנ' איך תשיב פני פחת אחת וגומ' (מ"ב יח כד) אתן | E | |
| לך (אלף) אלפים סוס (שם יח כג) • מה הוא אומ' וזה | F | |
| הדבר אשר דבר יי עליו בזה לך וגומ' את מי חרפת | | |
| וגדפת וגומ' (שם יט כא) • וכן את מוצא בנבוכד[נצר] | A | 10 |
| שבמה שנתגאה לפניו בו נפרע ממנו • שנא' ואתה | B | |
| [אמרת בלבב]ך השמים אעלה וגומ' (ישע' יד יג) • מה | C | |
| הוא אומ' אך אל שאול [תורד וגומ' (ישע' יד טו). • וכן | A | 11 |
| את מוצא בנגיד צור שבמה שנתגאה לפניו בו] [נפרע | | |
| ממנו • שנ' בן אדם אמור לנגיד צור וגומ' יען גבה לבך | B | |
| וגומ' • מה] [הוא אומ'] מותי ערלים וגומ' (יחז' כח י). • | C | |
| הא במה שהאומות מתגאין לפניו [בו נפרע מהן • | A | 12 |

B.    Thus it is said, "... for He is highly exalted" (Exod. 15:1).

## XXVIII:II

1.    A.    "Horse and driver (He has hurled into the sea)" (Exod. 15:1):

B.    Were there really only one horse and one driver?

C.    Has it not already been said, "... he took six hundred of his picked chariots" (Exod. 14:7)?

D.    Rather, this teaches that before God they were only like one horse and one rider!

2.    A.    Similar to this, you say, "When you go out to war ... (and see horse and rider), etc." (Deut. 20:1).

B.    Were there really only one horse and one rider?

[76]    C.    Rather, when Israel does the will of God, [then] before them their enemies are only like one horse and one rider!

3.    A.    Another interpretation:

B.    "Horse and driver" (Exod. 15:1):

C.    This teaches that the horse was attached to its rider, and its rider was attached to the horse.

4.    A.    "... He has hurled" (Exod. 15:1):

B.    One verse says, "He has hurled (into the sea)," and another verse[7] says, "He has cast (into the sea)."

C.    How do you harmonize the two verses?

D.    "He has hurled"—in that they ascended to the heights; "He has cast"—in that they descended to the depths.

E.    And they were not separated from each other!

F.    Normally, [when] a person throws two dishes into the air [at the same time], eventually one separates from the other.

G.    But here—"He has hurled" and "He has cast."

H.    "He has hurled"—in that they ascended to the heights; "He has cast"—in that they descended to the depths.

I.    And they were not separated from each other!

5.    A.    Another interpretation:

B.    "... He has hurled" (Exod. 15:1):

C.    When Israel saw that the guardian angel of Egypt had fallen, they began to give praise before Him.

D.    Thus it is said, "... He has hurled (into the sea)" (Exod. 15:1).

E.    And thus you find that God does not exact punishment from kingdoms until their guardian angels first fall.

F.    As it says in Scripture, "In that day, the Lord will punish the host of heaven in heaven, etc." and after this Scripture says, "and the kings of earth, etc." (Isa. 24:21).

---

[7] I.e., Exod. 15:4.

| | | |
|---|---|---|
| B | לכך נאמר כי גאה גאה. ◆ | |
| XXVIII:II | | |
| B/A 1 | סוס ורכבו וכי ◆ סוס אחד ◆ [ורכב אחד היה ◆ | |
| C | והלא כבר נאמר ויקח שש מ[אות רכב בחור | |
| D | (שמ׳ יד ז) ◆ [אלא מלמד שלא היו לפני המקום אלא | |
| A 2 | כסוס] אחד וכרכב אחד. ◆ [כיוצ]א בו אתה אומ׳ כי | |
| B | ת[צא למ]לחמה וגומ׳ (דב׳ כ א) ◆ [וכי] סוס אחד ורכב | |
| C | [אח]ד ◆ אלא כשיש׳ עו[שין] רצונו שלמקום אין | |
| A 3 | אויביהן לפניהן [אלא כס]וס אחד ורוכב [אחד] ◆ ד״א ◆ | |
| C/B | סוס ורכבו ◆ מלמד שהיה [סוס קשור ברוכבו ורוכבו | |
| B/A 4 | קשור ב]סוס. ◆ רמה ◆ כת׳ אחד או׳ רמה [וכת׳ אחר או׳ | |
| D/C | ירה ◆ כאיזה צד יתקיימו] שני כתובים ◆ רמה שהיו עולין | |
| E | [למרו]ם ירה שהיו יורדין לתהום ◆ ‹ולא היו נפרדין זה | |
| F | מזה ◆ בנוהג שבעולם אדם זורק שני כלים לאויר› | |
| G | לסוף אחד מהן ליפרד מחברו ◆ [אבל] כאן רמה וירה ◆ | |
| H | רמה כשהיו עולין למעלה מרום ירה שהיו יורדין | |
| C/B/A 5 I | לתהום ◆ ולא היו נפרדין זה מזה. ◆ ד״א ◆ רמה ◆ כיון שראו | |
| E/D | יש׳ שרה של מצ׳ שנפל התחילו נותנין לפניו את השבח ◆ לכך נאמ׳ רמה ◆ וכן את מוצא שאין המקום | |
| F | נפרע מן המלכיות עד שמפיל את שריהן תחלה ◆ שנא׳ ביום ההוא יפקד ייי על צבא המקום במ׳ (וגומ׳) ואחר כך על מלכי האדמה וגומ׳ (ישע׳ כד כא). ◆ | |

G.     [And Scripture says,] "How are you fallen from heaven, O Shining One, son of Dawn," and after this Scripture says, "How are you felled to earth, O vanquisher of nations!" (Isa. 14:12).

H.     [And Scripture says,] "For My sword shall be seen in the sky," and after this Scripture says, "Lo, it shall come down upon Edom, etc." (Isa. 34:5).

6.     A.     Another interpretation:

B.     "Horse and rider ..." (Exod. 15:1).

C.     The Holy One, blessed be He, would bring the horse and its rider, and stand them in judgment.

D.     He would say to the horse, "Why did you run after My children?" It would say to him, "The Egyptian made me run against my will!"

E.     As it says in Scripture, "The Egyptians pursued" (Exod. 14:23).

F.     And He would say to the Egyptian, "Why did you run after My children?" He would say to Him, "The horse made me run against my will!"

G.     As it says in Scripture, "For the horses of Pharaoh went" (Exod. 15:19).

H.     So the Holy One, blessed be He, would bring the horse and its rider and judge them as one.

7.     A.     Antoninus asked this of Rabbi, saying to him, "After a person dies, and his body is entirely destroyed, does the Holy One, blessed be He, bring him to justice?"

B.     He said to him, "You have asked me about the body, [which] is impure. Ask me about the soul, which is pure!"

C.     They told a parable: To what is the matter alike?

D.     It is like a human king who had an orchard, and in it were appealing first fruits. He placed in it two guards, one lame and one blind. The lame one said to the blind one, "I am looking at appealing first fruits!" The blind one, "As if I can see!" The lame one said to him, "As if I can walk!"

[77]     [So] the lame one rode on the back of the blind one, and they took the first fruits. After a few days, the king came and sat in judgment over them. He said to them, "Where are the first fruits?" The blind one said to him, "As if I can see!" The lame one said to him, "As if I can walk!"

The king was clever. What did he do? He made the one ride on the back of the other, so they were walking about. The king said to them, "This is what you did, and you ate them!"

E.     Likewise, the Holy One, blessed be He, brings the body and the soul, and stands in judgment over them. He says to the body, "Why did you sin before Me?" It says before Him, "Master of the World, from the day that the soul departed from me, I've been cast to the ground like a stone!" He says to the soul, "Why did you sin before Me?" It says before Him, "Master of the World, is it I who sinned? It is the body that has sinned! From the day that I departed it, haven't I been pure before You?"

The Holy One, blessed be He, brought the soul and placed it inside the body, and judged them both as one.

F.     As it says in Scripture, "He summoned the heavens above" (Ps. 50:4)—[meaning,] to bring the soul. And afterward, "... and the earth, (for the trial of the people)" (Ps. 50:4)—

איך נפלת משמים הילל בן שחר ואחר כך נגדעת לארץ    G

חולש על גוים (שם יד יב) ♦ כי רותה בשמים חרבי ואחר כך    H

הנה על אדום תרד וגומ' (שם לד ה). ♦ ד"א ♦ סוס ורוכבו ♦    B/A    6

היה הקב"ה מביא סוס ורוכבו ומעמידן בדין ♦ אומ'    D/C

לסוס מפני מה רצתה אחרי בני [אומ'] לו מצרי היה

מריצני על כרחי ♦ שנא' וירדפו מצ' (שמ' יד כג) ♦ ואומ'    F/E

למצרי מפני מה רצתה אחרי בני אמ' לו סוס היה

מריצני על [כרחי] ♦ שנא' כי בא סוס פרעה (שם טו יט) ♦    G

והיה הקב"ה מביא סוס ורוכבו [ודנן כאחד] ♦ [זו שאל    A 7    H

אנטנינוס את רבי אמ' לו ומאחר שאדם זה] [מת וגוף

כולה כלום הקב"ה מביאו לדין ♦ אמ' לו עד שאתה]    B

[שואלני על גוף טמא שאליני על נשמה שהיא טהורה ♦

מושלו] [משל למה הדבר דומה ♦ למלך בשר ודם    D/C

שהיה לו פרדס] והיה בו בכורות נא[ות והושיב בו שני

שומרים אחד חיגר ואחד] סומא אמ' לו חיגר [לסומא

בכורות נא[ו]ת אני רוא[ה]ה אמ' לו] <סומא> וכי רואה

אני אמ' לו חיגר וכי יכו[ל אני ל]הלך רכב חיגר [על

גבי] סומא והלכו ונטלו את הבכורות [לימי]ם בא

המלך ויש[ב עליהן] בדין אמ' להן היכן הן בכורות

אמ' [לו] סומה וכי רואה [אני אמ'] לו חיגר וכי יכול

אני להלך המל[ך פקח היה מה עשה] הרכיב זה על

גבי זה והיו מהלכין אמ' להן המלך כך [עשיתם]

ואכלתם ♦ כך הקב"ה מביא גוף ונשמה ומעמידן בדין    E

אומ' [לגוף] מפני מה חטאת לפני אומ' לפניו רבונו של

עולם מיום ש[יצאת] ממני נשמה אני מושלך כאבן.

אומ' לנשמה מפני מה חטאת לפני אם' לפניו רבונו

של עולם אני שחטאתי גוף חטא מיום שיצאתי ממנו

לא טהורה אני לפניך הקב"ה מביא נשמה ומכניסה

בגוף ודנן כאחד ♦ שנא' יקרא אל השמים מעל (תה' נ ד)    F

להביא נשמה ואל הארץ להביא את הגוף ואחר כך

[meaning,] to bring the body, and afterward to judge the one with the other.

8.    A.    Isi ben Shammai says, "Scripture says here[8] only 'horse' (Exod. 15:1) [without delineating the punishment]. But later Scripture says, 'In that day, declares the Lord, I will strike every horse with *panic* and its rider with *madness* ... (while I strike every horse of the peoples with *blindness*), etc.' (Zech. 12:4), [and] 'This will be the *plague* with which the Lord will smite (those people that warred against Jerusalem), etc.' (Zech. 14:12). And Scripture says, 'The same *plague* will strike the horses, etc.' (Zech. 14:15).

      B.    "That which is delineated comes and teaches about what is not delineated!

      C.    "Just as five plagues are delineated, so too that which is not delineated [will consist] of five plagues!"

*Chapter Twenty-Nine*

(Textual Source: Ms. Paris, Alliance Collection)

XXIX:I[9]

1.    A.    "(The Lord is) my strength and song" (Exod. 15:2):

      B.    "My strength" means only my stronghold.

      C.    As it says in Scripture, "O Lord, my strength and my stronghold, etc." (Jer. 16:19). And Scripture says, "The Lord is my strength and my shield, etc." (Ps. 28:7).

2.    A.    Another interpretation:

      B.    "... my strength" (Exod. 15:2):

      C.    "My strength" means only Torah.

      D.    As it says in Scripture, "The Lord will give strength to His people, etc." (Ps. 29:11). And Scripture says, "The king of justice loves strength, etc." (Ps. 99:4).

3.    A.    Another interpretation:

      B.    "... my strength" (Exod. 15:2):

      C.    "My strength" means only monarchy.

      D.    As it says in Scripture, "O Lord, the king rejoices in Your strength" (Ps. 21:2). And Scripture says, "The Lord is strength to His people, etc." (Ps. 28:8).

4.    A.    Another interpretation:

      B.    "... my strength" (Exod. 15:2):

      C.    You help and support everyone in the world, but me especially!

5.    A.    "The Lord (is my strength) and my song" (Exod. 15:2):

      B.    You are a song to everyone in

(Textual Source: Add. to 1180 Ms. New York)

the world, but me especially!

[78]    C.    For, behold, the nations of the world sing the pleasure and praise of He who spoke, and the world came into being. But mine are pleasing before Him.

        D.    As it says in Scripture, "The favorite of the songs of Israel, etc." (2 Sam. 23:1).

---

[8] The Hebrew text here is נאמן (it is believed), instead of נאמר (as I have translated).

[9] Compare XXIX:I:1.A–14.C with *Mekhilta de-Rabbi Ishmael*, Shirata (H/R, 126:1–129:2; Laut., vol. 2, 22:1–29:101; Neus., XXVIII:I:1.A– II:11.C).

| | |
|---|---|
| A 8 | לדין עמו ‹מידיין עמו›. ◆ איסי בן שמי אומ' נאמן כאן |
| | סוס סתום ונאמ' להלן ביום ההוא נאם ייי (צבאות) |
| | אכה כל סוס בשגעון ורכבו בתמהון וגומ' (זכ' יב ד) |
| | וזאת תהיה המגפה אשר יגוף ייי וגומ' (זכ' יד יב) |
| B | ואומ' וכן תהיה מגפת הסוס וגומ' (שם טו) ◆ בא |
| C | מפורש ולמד על הסתום ◆ מה ‹מ›פורש בחמש מכות |
| | אף סתום [בחמש מכו]ת. סל' פסו' ◆ |

XXIX:I

| | |
|---|---|
| C/B/A 1 | עזי וזמרת. ◆ אין עוזי אלא תוקפי ◆ [שנא' ייי עוזי |
| | ו]מעוזי ומנוסי וגומ' (ירמ' טז יט) ואומ' ייי עזי ומגיני |
| D/C/B/A 2 | וגומ' (תה' כח ז). ◆ ד"א ◆ [עזי ◆ אין עזי אלא] תורה ◆ שנא' ייי |
| | עז לעמו יתן (וגומ') (תה' כט יא) ואומ' ועז מלך |
| C/B/A 3 | [משפט אהב (תה' צט ד). ◆ ד"א ◆ עזי ◆ אין עזי אלא מלכות ◆ |
| D | שנא' ייי בעזך ישמח] [מלך (תה' כא ב) ואומ' ייי עוז |
| C/B/A 4 | למו וגומ' (תה' כח ח). ◆ ד"א ◆ עזי ◆ עוזר וסומך אתה] |
| B/A 5 | [לכל באי האולם ולי ביותר. ◆ וזמרת יה ◆ זמרה אתה |
| C | לכל באי] [העולם ולי ביותר ◆ שהרי אומות העולם |
| | אומרים ניאותו ושבחו] [שלמי שאמר והיה העולם |
| D | אבל שלי נעים לפניו ◆ שנא' ונעים] [זמירו]ת יש' ◆ |

E.   He made me special, and I also made Him special.

F.   He made me special: "And the Lord has affirmed (this day that you are ... His treasured people" (Deut. 26:18).

G.   And I also made Him special: "You have affirmed this day (that the Lord is your God)" (Deut. 26:17).

H.   Israel says, "Who is like You, O Lord, among the mighty" (Exod. 15:11).

I.   And the Holy Spirit brings good tidings to them, saying, "O happy Israel! (Who is like you,) etc." (Deut. 33:29).

J.   Israel says, "Who ... is like the Lord our God when we call upon Him" (Deut. 4:7).

K.   And the Holy Spirit brings good tidings to them, saying, "Or what great nation (has laws and rules as perfect as all this Teaching that I set before you this day), etc." (Deut. 4:8).

L.   Israel says, "Hear, O Israel! The Lord is our God, (the Lord alone,) etc." (Deut. 6:4).

M.   And the Holy Spirit brings good tidings to them, saying, "And who is like Your people, Israel, etc." (1 Chron. 17:21).

N.   Israel says, "Like an apple tree among trees of the forest, so is my beloved, etc." (Song 2:3).

O.   And the Holy Spirit brings good tidings to them, saying, "Like a lily among (thorns), etc." (Song 2:2).

P.   Israel says, "This is my God (and I will glorify Him), etc." (Exod. 15:2).

Q.   And the Holy Spirit brings good tidings to them, saying, "The people I formed for Myself, etc." (Isa. 43:21).

R.   Israel says, "For You are their strength in which they glory" (Isa. 89:18).

S.   And the Holy Spirit brings good tidings to them, saying, "Israel in whom I glory" (Isa. 49:3).

6.   A.   "He has become my salvation" (Exod. 15:2):

B.   You are salvation for everyone in the world, but me especially!

7.   A.   "He has become" (Exod. 15:2):

B.   He was, and He will be [my salvation].[10]

C.   He was—in the past. He will be—in the time to come.

D.   [As it says in Scripture,] "But Israel has won through the Lord triumph everlasting" (Isa. 45:17).

8.   A.   "This is my God and I will glorify Him" (Exod. 15:2):

B.   R. Eliezer says, "How does one know from Scripture that a female slave by the sea saw what Isaiah and Ezekiel did not see?

C.   "As it says in Scripture, '... and spoke parables through the prophets' (Hos. 12:11). And Scripture says, '... the heavens opened and I saw visions of God' (Ezek. 1:1).

D.   "They told a parable: To what is the matter alike?

E.   "It is like a human king who entered a city with a circle of guards surrounding him, and soldiers before him and after him, and warriors on his right and on his left. Everyone needed to ask about him, to know which was him,[11] because he was human like [the rest] of them.

[10] The text here reads ויהי in Exod. 15:2 as both "He has become" and "He will become."
[11] I.e., the king.

| | | |
|---|---|---|
| הוא עשאנ[י] [אמרה] ואף א[נ]י עשיתי[ו אמ]רה]. ◆ הוא | F/E | |
| [עשאני] אמרה וייי האמירך היום (דב׳ כו יח) ◆ ואף אני | G | |
| עשיתיו אמרה את [ייי] האמרת היום (שם יז). ◆ יש׳ אומ׳ | H | |
| מי כמוך באלים ייי (שמ׳ טו יא) ◆ ורוח [הקודש] מבשרת | I | |
| על ידיהן ואומ׳ אשריך יש׳ וגומ׳ (דב׳ לג כט) ◆ יש׳ אומ׳ | J | |
| מי [כייי אלקינו] בכל קראינו אליו (דב׳ ד ז) ◆ ורוח | K | |
| הקודש מבשרת על ידן ואומ׳ [ומי גוי גדול וגומ׳] (שם | | |
| ח) ◆ יש׳ אומ׳ שמע יש׳ ייי אלקינו וגומ׳ (דב׳ ו ד) ◆ ורוח | M/L | |
| הקודש [מבשרת על י]דן ואומ׳ ומי כעמך יש׳ וגומ׳ | | |
| (דה״א יז כא) ◆ ישר׳ אומ׳ כתפוח בעצי היער [כן דודי | N | |
| וגומ׳] (שה״ש ב ג) ◆ ורוח הק׳ מבשרת על ידן ואומ׳ | O | |
| כשושנה בין וגומ׳ (שם ב). ◆ יש׳ אומ׳ זה אלי ואנוהו | P | |
| (וגומ׳) ◆ ורוח הק׳ מבשרת על ידן ואומ׳ עם זו יצרתי לי | Q | |
| וגומ׳ (ישע׳ מג כא) ◆ יש׳ אומ׳ כי תפארת עוזמו אתה | R | |
| (תה׳ פט יח) ◆ ורוח הק׳ מבשרת על ידן ואומ׳ יש׳ אשר | S | |
| בך אתפאר (ישע׳ מט ג). ◆ ויהי לי לישועה. ◆ ישועה אתה | B/A | 6 |
| לכל באי <ה>עולם ולי ביותר ◆ ויהי לי ◆ <היה לי> והווה | B/A | 7 |
| לי ◆ היה לי <ל>שעבר והווה לי לעתיד לבא. ◆ יש׳ נושע | D/C | |
| בייי תשועת עולמים (ישע׳ מה יז). ◆ זה אלי ואנוהו. ◆ ר׳ | B/A | 8 |
| אלעזר אומ׳ מנין שראתה שפחה על הים מה שלא | | |
| ראהו ישיעהו /ישעיהו/ יחזקאל ◆ שנא׳ וביד | C | |
| הנביא<ים> אדמה (הושע יב יא). ואומ׳ נפתחו | | |
| השמים ואראה מראות אלקים (יחז׳ א א) ◆ מושלו משל | D | |
| למה הדבר דומה ◆ למלך בשר ודם שנכנס למדינה | E | |
| ואילת צפירה מקפתו וחיילות מלפניו ומאחריו | | |
| וגבורים מימינו ומשמ[אלו הכל צריכין] לשאול עליו | | |
| ולידע איזה הוא מפני שהוא בשר וד[ם כיוצא בהן] ◆ | | |

F.   "However, when the Holy One, blessed be He, appeared by the sea, not one of them had to ask. Rather, all of them recognized Him, and all of them opened their mouths in song and sang, 'This is my God' (Exod. 15:2)."

9.   A.   "... and I will glorify Him" (Exod. 15:2):[12]

B.   R. Ishmael says, "And how is it really possible for a man to praise his Creator?

C.   "Rather, he praises Him [by performing His] religious commandment.

[79] D.   "He prepares for Him a pleasing sukkah, a pleasing *lulav,* pleasing prayers, and pleasing garment-fringes."

E.   Abba Shaul says, "He imitates Him. Just as He is gracious and merciful, you too should be gracious and merciful!"

F.   R. Yosi the Damascene says, "I shall make a spectacular temple for Him, as it says in Scripture, '... Your holy abode' (Exod. 15:13).

G.   "The world 'abode'[13] means only the Temple, as it says in Scripture, '... and have laid desolate his homesteads'[14] (Jer. 10:25 and Ps. 79:7). And Scripture says, 'When you gaze upon Zion, our city of assembly, (your eyes shall behold Jerusalem as a secure homestead)' (Isa. 33:20)."

H.   R. Yosi ha-Galili says, "He speaks the pleasure and praises of He who spoke, and the world came into being."

I.   R. Akiva says, "He speaks before the nations of the world the pleasure and praises of He who spoke, and the world came into being.

J.   "For, behold, the nations of the world ask Israel, saying to them: 'How is your beloved better than any other?' (Song 5:9). For you are put to death and killed for Him!

K.   "In accordance with what is said in Scripture, '... Therefore do maidens love you' (Song 1:3), [and] 'For Your sake we shall be killed all day long, etc.' (Ps. 44:23).

L.   "[Israel responds to them,] 'Let a bit of His praise be said to you, because you don't recognize Him!—"My beloved is clear-skinned and ruddy ... His head is finest gold, etc." (Song 5:11) up to "Such is my darling, O maidens of Jerusalem!" (Song 5:16).'

M.   "When the nations of the world hear the pleasures and praises of He who spoke, and the world came into being, they say to Israel, 'Let us come with you!'

N.   "As it says in Scripture, 'Whither has your beloved gone, etc.' (Song 6:1).

O.   "But Israel responds to them, 'You have no share in Him! Rather, "I am my beloved's, and my beloved is mine, etc." (Song 6:3).'"

P.   And the Sages say, "We will accompany Him until we come with you to His Temple!"

Q.   "They told a parable: To what is the matter alike?

R.   "It is like a human king who entered a city. They said to him, 'Your son is in such-and-such city.' He left after him, and attended to him. He entered another[15] city, and they said to him, 'Your son is in such-and-such city.' He left after him, and attended to him.

S.   "Likewise, when Israel descended to Egypt, God's presence was with them. As it says in Scripture, 'I Myself will go down with you to Egypt' (Gen. 46:4). When they left, God's

---

[12] Compare 9.A–E with y. Peah 15b (Neus., 1:1:X.R) and b. *Shabbat* 133b (Neus., II.E:*Shabbat*:19:2:I.2.A–I).

[13] Hebrew: *naveh*—נוה.

[14] Hebrew: *navehu*—נוהו.

[15] I translate here the word אחרת in the place of the word אחת (one) that appears here in this manuscript.

אבל כשנגלה המקום על הים לא נצרך אחד [מהן   F

לשאול אלא] [הכירו כולם ופתחו כולם פיהם ואמרו

זה אלי. ❖ ואנוהו • ר' [ישמעאל אומ' וכי היאך אפשר לו   B/A   9

לאדם לנאות את קונו] • [אלא היה נאה לפניו במצוה ❖   C

עשה לו סוכה נאה לולב נאה] [תפלין נאות ציצית   D

נאה. ❖ אבא שאול אומ' הדמה לו מה הוא] [חנון ורחום   E

אף אתה היה חנון ורחום. ❖ ר' יוסי בן [דרמ]סקית   F

אומ' אעשה לו ב[ית מקדש] נאה [שנא'] נוה קדשך

(שמ' טו יג) ❖ אין נ[וה אלא] בית המקדש שנא' ואת   G

נוהו השמו (ירמ' י כה, תה' עט ז). ואומ' חזה ציון

[קרית] מועדינו וגומ' (ישע' לג כ). ❖ ר' יוסי הגלילי אומ'   H

דיבר בניאותו ושב[חו שלמי] שאמר והיה העולם. ❖ ר'   I

עקיבה אומ' דיבר ניאותו [ושבחו] שלמי שאמר והיה

העולם ❖ לפני אומ' העו' שהרי [אומ' העו' שואלין] את   J

יש' ואומ' להן מה דודך מדוד (שה"ש ה ט) שכך אתם

מומתין [עליו] וכך אתם נהרגין עליו ❖ כעניין שנא' על כן   K

עלמות אהבוך (שה"ש א ג). ואומ' [כי] עליך הורגנו כל

היום וגומ' (תה' מד כג) ❖ נאמ' לכן מקצת שבחו אי   L

אתם מכירין אותו דודי צח ואדום וגומ' ראשו כתם

פז וגומ' (שה"ש ה יא) עד זה דודי וזה רעי בנות

ירושלם (שם טז) ❖ כיון ששמעו אומ' העולם ניאות   M

שבחו שלמי שאם' והיה העולם אמ' להן ליש' <נבוא

עמכם> ❖ שנא' אנה הלך דודך וגומ' (שם ו א) ❖ ויש' אומ'   O/N

להן אין לכם חלק בו אלא אני לדודי ודודי לי וגומ'

(שם ג) ❖ וחכמ' אומ' נילאינו עד שנבוא עמכם לבית   P

מקדשו. ❖ מושלו משל למה הדבר דומה ❖ למלך בשר   R/Q

ודם שנכנס למדינה ואמ' לו הרי בנ(י)ך במדינת פלו'

יצא אחריו ועמד עליו נכנס למדינה אחת אמ' לו הרי

בנ(י)ך במדינת פלוני יצא אחריו ועמד עליו ❖ כך   S

כשירדו יש' למצ' שכינה עמהן שנא' אנכי ארד עמך

presence was with them. [As it says in Scripture,] '... and I Myself will also bring you back' (Gen. 46:4). When they went down to the sea, God's presence was with them. As it says in Scripture, 'The angel of God moved, etc.' (Exod. 14:19). They came to the wilderness, [and] God's presence was with them. [As it says in Scripture,] '... and in the wilderness where you saw how the Lord your God carried you, etc.' (Deut. 1:31).

[80]

T. "Until they came to the Temple. As it says in Scripture, "... [manuscript lacunae] ... Scarcely had I passed them when I found the one I love ... (till I brought him ... to the chamber of her who conceived me[16]) ..." (Song 3:4).

U. This [refers to] the Tent of Meeting, for from there Israel was held accountable for the Law![17]

10. A. "... the God of my father" (Exod. 15:2):

B. With me He behaves with a merciful quality. But with my father(s) He behaved with a judgmental quality.

11. A. "... my God" (Exod. 15:2):

B. The word "my God" means only a merciful quality.

C. And thus Scripture states, "My God, my God, why have You abandoned me, etc." (Ps. 22:2). [And Scripture says,] "O God, pray heal her" (Num. 12:13). [And Scripture says,] "The Lord is God. He has given us light" (Ps. 118:27).

12. A. Another interpretation:

B. "... the God of my father and I will exalt Him" (Exod. 15:2):

C. I am the beloved daughter of the beloved, the queen daughter of kings, the pure one daughter of pure ones, the holy one daughter of holy ones.

D. They told a parable: To what is the matter alike?

E. It is like a human king who marries a woman. Sometimes he is embarrassed by her. Sometimes he is embarrassed by her family. Sometimes he is embarrassed by her father.

F. But I am the beloved daughter of the beloved, the queen daughter of kings, the pure one daughter of pure ones.

13. A. R. Shimon ben Eliezer says, "When Israel does the will of God, His name is made great in the world.

B. "As it says in Scripture, 'When all the kings of the Amorites heard, etc.' (Josh. 5:1), [and Scripture says,] 'When we heard about it, we lost heart, etc.' (Josh. 2:11).

C. "But when Israel does not do the will of God, His name is profaned in the world.

D. "As it says in Scripture, 'But when they came to those nations (they caused My holy name to be profaned) ... Say to the House of Israel: Thus said the Lord God: Not for your sake (will I act) ... I will sanctify My great name, etc.' (Ezek. 36:20–23)."

14. A. "... the God of my father and I will exalt Him" (Exod. 15:2):

B. It's not for the miracles that He did for me that I give praise before Him. Rather, it's for the miracles that He did with my forefathers, and that He will do in the future with me.

C. Thus it is said, "... the God of my father and I will exalt Him" (Exod. 15:2).

---

[16] Hebrew: *horati*—הורתי.
[17] Hebrew: *hora'ah*—הוראה.

מצ׳ (בר׳ מו ד) עלו שכינה עמהן [ואנכי] אעלך גם

עלה (שם). ירדו לים שכינה עמהן שנ׳ ויסע מלאך

[האלקי]ם וגומ׳ (שמ׳ יד יט) באו למדבר שכינה

עימהן ובמדבר אשר [ראית אשר נשא]ך ייי אלקיך

וגומ׳ (דב׳ א לא) ◆ עד שבאו לבית המקדש שנא׳ [...    T

כמעט שעברתי מהם [עד שמצאתי א]ת שאהבה

נפשי וגומ׳ (שה״ש ג ד) ◆ זה אהל מועד שמשם נתחייבו    U

[יש׳ בהוראה]. ◆ אלקי אבי ◆ [עמי נוהג במידת רח]מים    B/A    10

ועם אבותי [נוהג] במידת הדין. ◆ אלי ◆ אין אלי אלא    B/A    11

מידת רחמים ◆ וכן הוא אומ׳ [אלי אלי למ]ה עזבתני    C

וגומ׳ (תה׳ כב ב) אל נא רפא נא לה (במ׳ יב יג). אל ייי

ויאר לנו (תה׳ קיח כז). ד״א ◆ [אלקי אבי וא]רומ׳ ◆ אני    C/B/A    12

אהובה בת אהובין מלכה בת מלכים טהורה [בת

טה]ורים קדושה בת קדושים. ◆ מושלו משל למה    D

[הדבר] דומה ◆ למלך בשר ודם שנשא אשה פעמים    E

בוש בה [פעמים] בוש במשפחתה פעמים בוש

באבותיה. ◆ אבל אני אהובה [בת א]הובים מלכה בת    F

מלכים [טהורה בת] טהורין קדושה בת קדושים. ◆ ר׳    A    13

שמעון בן אלעזר אומ׳ כשישראל עושין רצונו

שלמקום שמו מתגדל בעולם ◆ שנא׳ ויהי כשמע כל    B

מלכי האמורי וגומ׳ (יהו׳ ה א) ונשמע וימס לבבנו

וגומ׳ (יהו׳ ב יא) ◆ וכשאין יש׳ עושין רצונו שלמקום    C

שמו מחולל בעולם ◆ שנא׳ ויבא אל הגוים אשר באו    D

שמה וגומ׳ לכן אמור לבני ישר׳ כה אמר ייי אלקים

לא למענכם וגומ׳ וקדשתי את שמי הגדול וגומ׳ (יחז׳

לו כ - כג) ◆ אלקי אבי וארומ׳ ◆ לא על נסים שעשה עמי    B/A    14

אני נותנת לפניו את השבח אלא על נסים שעשה עם

אבותי ועתיד הוא לעש׳ ◆ עמי לכך נאמ׳ אלקי אבי    C

וגומ׳. סל׳ פסו׳

◆

*Chapter Thirty*

(Textual Source: Add. to 1180 Ms. New York)

XXX:I[18]

1.  A.  "The Lord is a man of war. Lord is His name!" (Exod. 15:3):

    B.  R. Judah says, "Behold, this verse of Scripture is rich in many ways!

    C.  "It tells that He appeared to them in all types of armor.

    D.  "He appeared to them in a coat of mail and a helmet. As it says in Scripture, 'He donned victory like a coat of mail, (with a helmet of triumph on His head,) etc.' (Isa. 59:17).

    E.  "He appeared to them like a mighty warrior.

[81]  F.  "As it says in Scripture, 'Gird your sword upon your thigh, O hero, etc.' (Ps. 45:4).

    G.  "He appeared to them like a horseman.

    H.  "As it says in Scripture, 'He mounted a cherub, etc.' (Ps. 18:11).

    I.  "He appeared to them with a bow."

    J.  "As it says in Scripture, 'All bared and ready is Your bow, etc.' (Hab. 3:9).

    K.  "He appeared to them with a shield.

    L.  "As it says in Scripture, 'His fidelity is an encircling shield' (Ps. 91:4). And Scripture says, '... take up shield and buckler, etc.' (Ps. 35:2).

    M.  "He appeared to them with a spear.

    N.  "As it says in Scripture, '... Your flashing spear in brilliance, etc.' (Hab. 3:11). And Scripture says, '... ready the spear and javelin, etc.' (Ps. 35:3).

    O.  "I might assume that He needs all these measures.

    P.  "Scripture states, [however,] 'The Lord is a man of war. Lord is His name!' (Exod. 15:3).

    Q.  "He fights with His name, and He does not need all these measures.

    R.  "If so, why did Scripture need to delineate all these proof-verses?

    S.  "To inform that if Israel needs one of them, behold, He will do it for them!

    T.  "Woe unto the nations of the world, for what their ears are hearing! For He who spoke, and the world came into being is going to go to war with them!"

2.  A.  Another interpretation:

    B.  "The Lord is a man of war. Lord is His name!" (Exod. 15:3):

    C.  [This verse is stated] because when the Holy One, blessed be He, appeared by the sea, He looked to them like a young man waging war.

    D.  [As it says in Scripture,] "(The Lord is a man of war.) Lord is His name!" (Exod. 15:3).

    E.  [However,] He looked to them at Sinai like an old man full of mercy.

    F.  [As it says in Scripture,] "As I looked on ... (the Ancient of Days took His seat), etc." (Dan. 7:9).

    G.  [Thus, this verse is stated] so as to deny the opportunity for the nations of the world to say [that] there are two powers in the heavens.

---

[18] Compare XXX:I:1.A–11.M with *Mekhilta de-Rabbi Ishmael*, Shirata (H/R, 129:4–132:9; Laut., vol. 2, 30:1–37:101; Neus., XXIX:I:1.A–II:5.H).

| | | |
|---|---|---|
| יי' איש מלחמה יי' שמו • ר' יהודה אומ' הרי זה | B/A | 1 |
| מקרא עשיר במקומות הרבה • מגיד שנגלה להן בכל | C | |
| כלי זיין • נראה להן בשריון וכובע שנא' וילבש צדקה | D | |
| כשריין וגומ' (ישע' נט יז) • נראה להן כגבור • שנא' חגור | F/E | |
| חרבך על ירך גבור וגומ' (תה' מה ד) • נראה להן כפרש | G | |
| שנא' וירכב על כרוב וגומ' (שם יח יא) • נראה להן | I/H | |
| בקשת • שנא' ער[יה] תעור קשתך וגומ' (חב' ג ט) • נראה | K/J | |
| להן בצנה ומגן • שנא' צנה וס[חרה] אמתו (תה' צא ד) | L | |
| [ואומ' החזק מגן וצנה וגומ' (שם לה ב) • נראה להן | M | |
| בחנית • שנא' לנגה ברק] חנית[ך] וגומ' (חב' ג יא) ואומ' | N | |
| והרק ח[נ]ית [וסגור וגומ' (תה' לה ג) • שומע אני שצריך] | O | |
| כל המדות הללו • ת[''] ל ח' איש מלחמה ה' שנ[ו] • ב[שמו] | Q/P | |
| הוא נלחם ואין צריך לכל המדות הללו • אם כן למה | R | |
| צרך הכת' לפרט כל המקראות הללו> • לומר שאם | S | |
| יצטרכו יש' לאח[ד מהן הרי הוא] ע[ושה להן • אוי להן | T | |
| לאומות העולם ממה ששומעות אזניהם] [שמי שאמ'] | | |
| והיה ה[עולם עתיד הוא להלחם בהם. • ד''א] • יי' איש | B/A | 2 |
| מלחמה יי' איש שמו • לפי שכשנגלה ה[קב''ה על הים] | C | |
| נראה להן כבחור עושה מלחמה • יי' שמו • נגל[ה עליהן | E/D | |
| בסיני] כזקן מלא רחמים • חזה הוית וגומ' (דנ' ז ט) • | F | |
| שלא ליתן פתחון פ[ה] לומר שתי רשויות יש בשמים • | G | |

H.   Rather, "the Lord is a man of war. (Lord is His name!)" (Exod. 15:3).[19]

I.   "The Lord is a man of war"—[it was] He who fought in Egypt!

J.   "Lord is His name!"—[it was also] He who fought by the sea!

K.   [And it was] He at the Jordan and He at the wadis of Arnon. [It was] He in this world and [will be] He in the world to come! [It was] He in the past and [will be] He in the time to come!

L.   As it says in Scripture, "See, then, that I, I am He, etc." (Deut. 32:39); [and] "Thus said the Lord, the King of Israel, etc." (Isa. 44:6); [and] "I, the Lord, who was first, etc." (Isa. 41:4); [and] "I am He—I am the first, and I am the last, etc." (Isa. 48:12).

3.   A.   Another interpretation:

B.   "The Lord is a man of war. Lord is His name!" (Exod. 15:3):

C.   There is a mighty warrior who stands in battle, whose strength at the age of 40 is not the same at the age of 60 or the age of 70. Because all the while he ages, his strength is diminished.

D.   However, it is not so with He who spoke, and the world came into being.

[82]   E.   "The Lord is a man of war"—[it was] He who fought in Egypt.

F.   "Lord is His name"—[it was] He in the past [and it will be] He in the time to come!

G.   And thus Scripture states, "For I am the Lord—I have not changed, etc." (Mal. 3:6).

4.   A.   Another interpretation:

B.   "The Lord is a man of war. Lord is His name!" (Exod. 15:3):

C.   There is a mighty warrior who stands in battle wearing [all types of] armor. But he doesn't have strength or might, and doesn't know the methods of warfare.

D.   However, it is not so with He who spoke, and the world came into being. Rather, He has strength and might, [and knows] the methods of warfare.

E.   And thus David says, "For the battle is the Lord's, and He will deliver you into our hands" (1 Sam. 17:47). And Scripture says, "Blessed is the Lord, my rock, (who trains my hands for battle,) etc." (Ps. 144:1).

5.   A.   Another interpretation:

B.   There is a mighty warrior who stands in battle, and once the arrow has left his hand, he is unable to make it come back.

C.   However, it is not so with He who spoke, and the world came into being. Rather, whenever Israel does not do the will of God, a decree [of punishment] leaves from before Him.

D.   As it says in Scripture, "When I whet My flashing blade, etc." (Deut. 32:41).

E.   [But if] they repent, He retracts [the decree].

F.   As it says in Scripture, "... and My hand lays hold on judgment" (Deut. 32:41).

G.   I might assume that He retracts it empty.

H.   Scripture states, [however,] "Vengeance will I wreak on My foes" (Deut. 32:41).

I.   [God says,] "I will retract it [and then send it] on the nations of the world!"

---

[19] I have chosen not to translate the phrase "Another interpretation" inserted here by the editors of the text.

אלא ייי איש מלחמה ◆ [ד״א] ייי איש מלחמה הוא          I/H

נלחם במצ׳ ◆ ייי שמו הוא [נלחם על] הים ◆ והוא על          K/J

הירדן והוא על נחלי ארנון הוא בעולם הזה והוא

לעולם הבא הוא לשעבר <ו>הוא לעתיד לבוא ◆ שנא׳          L

ראו עתה כי אני אני הוא וגומ׳ (דב׳ לב לט) כה אמ׳ ייי

מלך יש׳ וגומ׳ (ישע׳ מד ו) אני ייי ראשון וגומ׳ (שם מא

ד) אני הוא אני ראשון אף אני אחרון (שם מח יב). ◆ ד״א ◆          A          3

ייי איש מלחמה ייי שמו ◆ יש גבור עומד במלחמה וכחו          C/B

עליו כבן ארבעים שנה אבל אין דומה לבן ששים או

לבן שבעים שכל זמן שהוא הולך כוחו מתמעט ◆ אבל          D

מי שאמר והיה העולם אינו כן ◆ ייי איש מלחמה          E

הנלחם במצ׳ ◆ ייי שמו הוא לשעבר הוא לעתיד לבוא ◆          F

וכן הוא אומ׳ כי אני ייי לא שניתי וגומ׳ (מלאכי ג ו) ◆          G

ד״א ◆ ייי איש מלחמה ייי שמו. ◆ יש גבור עומד במלחמה          C/B/A          4

ועליו כלי זיין אבל אינו יודע לא כח ולא גבורה ולא

טכסיסי מלחמה ◆ <אבל מי שאמר והיה העולם אינו          D

כן אלא יש לו כח וגבורה וטכסיסי מלחמה> ◆ וכן דוד          E

אומ׳ כי לייי המלחמה ונתן אתכם בידינו (ש״א יז מז)

ואומ׳ ברוך ייי צורי וגומ׳ (תה׳ קמד א). ◆ ד״א ◆ יש גבור          B/A          5

עומד במלחמה ומשהחץ יוצא מידו אינו יכול להחזירו ◆

אבל מי שאמר והיה העולם אינו כן אלא כשאין יש׳ עושין          C

רצונו שלמקום גזירה יוצא מלפניו ◆ [שנא׳ אם שנו]תי          D

ברק חרבי וגומ׳ (דב׳ לב מא) ◆ עשו תשובה הוא מחזירה ◆          E

שנא׳ [ותאחז במשפ]ט ידי (שם) ◆ שומע אני שמחזירה ריקם ◆          G/F

ת״ל אשיב נקם (שם) ◆ [לצרי אני מחזירה על אומות העולם.          I/H
◆

6.     A.     Another interpretation:

        B.     There is a mighty warrior who stands in battle, who when engulfed with jealous anger and might will strike in anger without discernment, even his father, even his mother, and even his relatives!

        C.     However, it is not so with He who spoke, and the world came into being. Rather, "The Lord is a man of war" (Exod. 15:3). He wages war.

        D.     And nonetheless, "Lord is His name" (Exod. 15:3). He is merciful upon all His creation.

        E.     What is His name?—"Lord, a God compassionate and gracious, etc." (Deut. 34:6).

7.     A.     Another interpretation:

        B.     "The Lord is a man of war. Lord is His name!" (Exod. 15:3):

        C.     There is a mighty warrior in battle. The nearby cities come to him to inquire before him about their needs. They[20] say to them, "He is preoccupied with the battle. He will go out, and once he has won and returned, [then] you should ask for your needs before him, and he will do [them]!"

        D.     However, it is not so with He who spoke, and the world came into being. Rather, even [though] all the world's creatures cry out before Him, He hears the cry of all of them.

        E.     As it says in Scripture, "You who hear prayer, etc." (Ps. 65:3).

8.     A.     Another interpretation:

        B.     "The Lord is a man of war" (Exod. 15:3):

        C.     There is a mighty warrior who stands in battle. He is unable to feed his troops or to supply their provisions.

        D.     However, it is not so with He who spoke, and the world came into being. Rather, He feeds and provides for all the world's creatures and for all the works of His hands that He created in His world.

        E.     As it says in Scripture, "Who gives food to all flesh, His steadfast love is eternal" (Ps. 136:25). And Scripture says, "... who gives the beasts their food, etc." (Ps. 147:9). [And Scripture says,] "The Lord is good to all, and His mercy, etc." (Ps. 145:9).

9.     A.     "The Lord is a man of war" (Exod. 15:3):

        B.     Is it [really] possible to say this?

        C.     Has it not already been said, "And one would call to the other" (Isa. 6:3); [and] "And there, coming from the east, was the Presence of the God of Israel" (Ezek. 43:2)?

        D.     Rather, because of My love for you, and because of your holiness, in that you sanctified My name through you.

        E.     And thus David says, "They [call] on chariots, they [call] on horses ... They collapse and lie fallen ... O Lord, grant victory, etc." (Ps. 20:8–10).

        F.     In that I shall sanctify My name through you!

10.     A.     Another interpretation:

        B.     "The Lord is a man of war" (Exod. 15:3):

---

[20] I.e., the residents of the warrior's city.

| | | |
|---|---|---|
| 6 | B/A | ד״א ♦ יש גבור עומד במלחמה [ומשקנאה וגבורה] לובשתו |
| | | [א]פי' [אביו וא]פי' אמו וא[פי'] קרו[ב]יו [אינו מבחין אלא |
| C | | מכה והולך בחמה ♦ אבל מי שאמר והיה העולם אינ]ו [כן |
| D | | אלא יייי איש מלחמה הוא עושה מלחמה ♦ ואע״פ כן יייי |
| E | | שמו ר]חמן הוא [על כל בריו]תיו ♦ מה שמו יייי יייי אל |
| 7 | B/A | רחום וחנון וגומ' (שמ' לד ו). ♦ ד״א ♦ יייי איש [מלחמה] יייי |
| C | | שמו ♦ יש גבור במלחמה מדינות קרובות באות [אצלו |
| | | ל]תבוע צרכיהן מלפניו אמ' להן זועף הוא למלחמה |
| | | הוא [יוצא] כשינצח ויחזור אתם משאלין צרככן |
| D | | מלפניו והוא עושה ♦ [אבל] מי שאמר והיה העולם אינו |
| | | כן אלא אפילו כל באי העולם [צוע]קין לפניו שומע |
| E | | צעקת כולם ♦ שנא' שומע תפלה וגומ' (תה' סה ג). ♦ ד״א ♦ |
| 8 A | E | יייי איש מלחמה ♦ יש גבור עומד במלחמה אין יכול לזון |
| C/B | | חיילותיו ולספק אספסוטאות שלהן ♦ אבל מי שאמ' |
| D | | והיה העולם אינו כן אלא זן ומפרנס את כל באי |
| | | העולם ואת כל מעשה ידיו שברא בעולמו ♦ שנא' נותן |
| E | | לחם לכל בשר כי לעולם חסדו (תה' קלו כה) ואומ' |
| | | נתן לבהמה לחמה וגומ' (שם קמז ט) טוב יייי לכל |
| 9 | B/A | ורחמיו וגומ' (שם קמה ט). ♦ יייי איש מלחמה ♦ אפשר |
| C | | לומר כן ♦ והלא כבר נאמ' וקרא זה אל זה ואמ' (ישע' ו |
| | | ג) והנה כבוד אלקי יש' בא מדרך הקדים (יחז' מג ב) ♦ |
| D | | אלא מפני חיבתכן ומפני קדושתכן שקדשו את שמי |
| E | | על ידיכין ♦ וכן דוד אומ' אלה ברכב ואלה בסוסים |
| | | וגומ' המה כרעו ונפלו וגומ' יייי הושיעה וגו[מ' (תה' כ י) ♦ |
| 10 B/A | F | ש]אקדש את שמי על ידיכן. ♦ ד״א ♦ יייי איש מלחמה יייי שמו ♦ |

[83]    C.    [As it says in Scripture,] "Pharaoh's chariots and his army He has cast into the sea" (Exod. 15:4).

11.     A.    "Pharaoh's chariots and his army He has cast into the sea" (Exod. 15:4):

        B.    With what measure a man metes, You shall measure him again![21]

        C.    Scripture says, "(But Pharaoh said,) 'Who is the Lord that I should heed Him?'" (Exod. 5:2).

        D.    Likewise, You showed them the fear and dread of You by the sea!—"Pharaoh's chariots, etc." (Exod. 15:4).

        E.    Pharaoh said, "Every boy that is born (you shall throw into the Nile), etc." (Exod. 1:22).

        F.    Likewise with You, by that very same measure You measured them!—"Pharaoh's chariots (... He has cast into the sea), etc." (Exod. 15:4).

        G.    Scripture says, "... he took six hundred of his picked chariots" (Exod. 14:7).

        H.    Likewise with You, by that very same measure You measured them!—"Pharaoh's chariots (... He has cast into the sea), etc." (Exod. 15:4).

        I.    Scripture says, "... with third officers in all of them" (Exod. 15:7).

        J.    Likewise with You, by that very same measure You measured them!—"... and the pick of his officers (are drowned in the Sea of Reeds)" (Exod. 15:4).

        K.    He[22] worked the Children of Israel ruthlessly.

        L.    Likewise with You, You hardened the water into mud over them, and they sank in it.

        M.    [Because] drowning only occurs in mud, as it says in Scripture, "... and Jeremiah sank into the mud" (Jer. 38:6). And Scripture says, "I am sinking into the slimy (deep), etc." (Ps. 69:3). [And Scripture says,] "Let the floodwaters not sweep me away, etc." (Ps. 69:16).

*Chapter Thirty-One*

(Textual Source: Add. to 1180 Ms. New York)

XXXI:I[23]

1.      A.    "The deeps covered them" (Exod. 15:5):

        B.    Were there really [multiple] depths there?

        C.    Rather, this teaches that the lowest depth arose [from the sea] and struck the firmament above them and darkened the heavenly luminaries over them.

        D.    And thus Scripture says, "All the lights that shine in the sky I will darken (above you) ... I will vex the hearts of many peoples, etc." (Ezek. 32:9–10). And Scripture says, "The stars and constellations of heaven (shall not give off their light), etc." (Isa. 13:10). Why?—"And I will requite the world (its evil), etc." (Isa. 13:11). [And Scripture says,] "In Tehaphnehes daylight shall be withheld, etc." (Ezek. 30:18). Why?—Because, behold, "... the cloud shall cover it, and its daughter towns shall go into captivity, etc." (Ezek. 30:18).

2.      A.    Another interpretation:

        B.    "The deeps covered them" (Exod. 15:5):

---

[21] Compare 11.B with m. Sotah 1:7.
[22] I.e., Pharaoh.
[23] Compare XXXI:I:1.A–II:6.D with parallel material (in partially different editorial order, however,) in *Mekhilta de-Rabbi Ishmael,* Shirata (H/R, 132:10–134:15; Laut., vol. 2, 37:1–42:73; Neus., XXX:I:1.A–18.B).

| | | |
|---|---|---|
| C | מרכב' פרעה וחילו ירה בים. סל' פסו' ✦ |
| B/A | 11 | מרכבות פרעה וחילו ירה בים ✦ במדה שאדם מודד |
| C | בה מדדתה לו ✦ הוא אמ' מי ייי אשר אשמע בקולו |
| D | (שמ' ה ב) ✦ אף אתה הראתה להן י[ראתך ואימתך] על |
| E | הים. מרכבות פרעה וגומ' פרעה א[מ' כל הבן] הילוד |
| F | וגומ' (שמ' א כב) ✦ [אף אתה באותה מדה] מדדתה ל[הן |
| G | מרכבות] [פרעה וגומ'] ✦ הוא אמ' ויקח שש מאות רכב ✦ |
| H | אף אתה באותה מדה] [מדדתה להן מרכבות פרעה |
| J/I | וגומ' ✦ הוא אמ' ושלישים על כלו ✦ אף אתה] [באותה |
| K | מד]ה מדדתה לה[ן ומבחר] שלישי[ו ✦ הוא העביד את |
| L | בני יש' בפרך ✦ אף אתה] הק[שית עלי]הן מים כטיט |
| M | והיו משתקעין בו ✦ אין [טביעה] אלא בטיט שנא' |
| | ויטבע ירמיה‹ו› בטיט (ירמ' לח ו) ואומ' טבעתי |
| | [ביון] וגומ' (תה' סט ג) אל תשטפני שבולת וגומ' (שם |
| | טז) סל' פסו' ✦ |

| | XXXI:I |

| | | |
|---|---|---|
| C/B/A | 1 | תהומות [יכסיומו] ✦ וכי תהומות שם ✦ אלא מלמד |
| | שעלה תהום התחתון ו[היכה] עליהן את הרקיע והקדיר |
| D | עליהן את המאורות ✦ וכן ה[וא אומ'] כל מאורי אור |
| | בשמים אקדירם וגומ' והכעסתי לב [עמים] רבים וגומ' (יחז' |
| | לב ט) ואומ' כי כוכבי השמים וכסיליהם וגומ' (ישע' יג י) |
| | מפני [מה] ופקדתי על תבל וגומ' (שם) ובתחפנחס חשך |
| | היום וגומ' (יחז' ל יח) מפני מ[ה] כי הנה הענן יכסה |
| B/A | 2 | ובנתיה בשבי תלכנה וגומ' (שם) ✦ ד'א ✦ תהומות יכסיומו ✦ |

C.   Were there really [holes in the bottom of the sea, creating] depths there? Wasn't it level ground?

D.   Rather, this teaches

(Textual Source: Ms. JTS ENA (Adler) 1179)

that the lowest depth [of waters] and the highest [height of waters] arose in war against Egypt with all types of punishments.

3.   A.   Jonah descended one depth. As it says in Scripture, "The deep engulfed me" (Jon. 2:6).

[84]   B.   They[24] descended two depths. As it says in Scripture, "The deeps covered them. They went down into the depths like a stone" (Exod. 15:5).

C.   And were there really depths there? Wasn't it level ground?

D.   Rather, this teaches that the great sea burst from within, and waged war with them with all kinds of punishments.

4.   A.   Jonah descended one depth. As it says in Scripture, "You cast me into the deep, into the heart of the sea" (Jon. 2:4).

B.   But they descended two depths. As it says in Scripture, "They went down into the depths like a stone" (Exod. 15:5).

5.   A.   Another interpretation:

B.   "They went down into the depths like a stone" (Exod. 15:5):

C.   This verse [refers to the] average among them.[25]

D.   The more worthy among them were tossed about like straw, the average like a stone, and the evil sank like cement in mighty waters.

6.   A.   Scripture says, "(When you deliver the Hebrew women,) look at the birth stone" (Exod. 1:16).

B.   Likewise, You hardened the water into stones on them, and it struck them on the place of their stones.[26]

7.   A.   Another interpretation:

B.   Why [does Scripture state in Exod. 15:5 that they sank] like a stone?

C.   Because He hardened their hearts like stones.

D.   But as for us, [You acted] out of Your love and Your goodness and Your manifold mercy, and with Your right hand that is extended to all the creatures of the world!

E.   As it says in Scripture, "... but Your right hand, Your arm, and Your goodwill, etc." (Ps. 44:4). [And Scripture says,] "By Myself have I sworn, from My mouth has issued (truth), a world that shall not turn back. To Me every knee shall bend, etc." (Isa. 45:23).

XXXI:II

1.   A.   "Your right hand, O Lord, glorious in power. (Your right hand, O Lord, shatters the foe!)" (Exod. 15:6):

B.   You are [both] alluring and distinguished in power.[27]

---

[24] I.e., the Egyptians at the sea.

[25] I.e., the average evil Egyptians.

[26] I.e., their genitals.

[27] The text here reads the word "glorious" (Hebrew: נאדרי) in Exod. 15:6 as two words: "becoming" (Hebrew: נאה) and "distinguished" (Hebrew: אדיר).

| | | |
|---:|:---:|---:|
| | D/C | וכי יש תהומות שם והלא שנית היא ◆ אלא מלמד |
| | | מלמד שעלה תהום התחתון והעליון והיו נלחמין במצ' בכל |
| 3 | A | מיני [פורעניות ◆ יונה ירד לתהו]ם אחד שנא' תהום יסובבני |
| | B | (יונה ב ו) ◆ והן ירדו [לשתי תהומות שנא' תהומ]ות יכסיומו |
| | C | ירדו במצולות כמו אבן ◆ וכי [יש מצולות שם והל]א שנית |
| | D | היא ◆ אלא מלמד שנפרץ הים הגדול [לתוכו והיה |
| 4 | A | נלחם] בהן בכל מיני פורעניות. ◆ יונה ירד למצולה |
| | B | [אחת שנא' ות]שליכני מצולה בלבב ימי' (שם ד) ◆ והם |
| | | ירדו לשתי מצולות [שנא' ירדו במצולות כמ]ו אבן. ◆ |
| 5 | C/B/A | ד''א ◆ ירדו במצולות כמו אבן. ◆ זו כת בינונית שבהן ◆ |
| | D | כשרים שבהן מיטרפין כקש בינוניים כאבן רשעים |
| 6 | A | [צללו כעופר]ת במ[י]ם א[ד]ירים ◆ הוא אומ' וראיתן על |
| | B | האבנים (שמ' א טז) ◆ [אף אתה הקשית] להן מים |
| 7 | A | כאבנים והיו מכין אותן על מקום האבנים [שלהן ◆ ד''א ◆ |
| | D/C/B | למ]ה כמו אבן ◆ לפי שהקשו את ליבן כאבנים. ◆ אבל |
| | | אנו בחסדך [ובטובך וברח]מיך הרבים ובימינך שפשוטה |
| | E | לכל באי העולם ◆ שנא' כי [ימינך וזרועך] ואור פניך |
| | | וגומ' (תה' מד ד). בי נשבעתי יצא מפי דבר לא ישוב כי |
| | | לי תכרע [כל ברך וגומ'] (ישע' מה כג) סל' פסו' ◆ |

| | | |
|---:|:---:|---:|
| 1 | B/A | ימינך ייי נאדרי בכח ◆ נאה אתה ואדיר בכח ◆ |

C. Because You provided the people of the Flood with an extension of time, so that they might repent. But they didn't.

D. As it says in Scripture, "The Lord said, 'My breath shall not abide in man, etc.'" (Gen. 6:3).

E. But You didn't finish their destruction until they had completed their wickedness before You.

F. And thus we find that You provided the people of the Tower with an extension of time, so that they might repent. But they didn't.

G. As it says in Scripture, "... and the Lord said, 'If, as one people ... (then[28] nothing that they may propose to do will be out of their reach), etc.'" (Gen. 11:6).

H. The word "then" means only repentance, as it is said in Scripture, "And now,[29] O Israel, what does the Lord your God (demand of you), etc." (Deut. 10:12).

I. But You didn't finish their destruction until they had completed their wickedness before You.

J. And thus we find that You provided the people of Sodom with an extension of time, so that they might repent. But they didn't.

K. As it says in Scripture, "... the Lord rained upon Sodom (and Gomorrah sulfurous fire), etc." (Gen. 19:24).

L. "Rain" is stated here [in this verse], and "sulfurous fire" is stated here, [meaning,] if they repent, behold—rain! But if not—sulfurous fire!

M. You brought Ten Plagues unto the Egyptians in Egypt, but You didn't finish their destruction until they had completed their wickedness before You!

2.  A. Another interpretation:

B. "Your right hand, O Lord, glorious in power" (Exod. 15:6):

C. When the Israelites do the will of God, they turn the left into the right.

D. As it says in Scripture, "Your right hand, O Lord ... Your right hand, O Lord" (Exod. 15:6).[30]

E. But when Israel doesn't do the will of God, they turn the right into the left.

F. As it says in Scripture, "He has withdrawn His right hand in the presence of the enemy, etc." (Lam. 2:3).

3.  A. Another interpretation:

B. When Israel does the will of God, there is no anger before Him.

C. As it says in Scripture, "There is no anger in Me" (Isa. 27:4).

D. But when Israel does not do the will of God, He is filled with hatred of Israel.

E. As it says in Scripture, "For the Lord's anger will flare up against you, etc." (Deut. 11:17).

4.  A. Another interpretation:

[85] B. When Israel does the will of God, He wages war on their behalf.

C. As it says in Scripture, "The Lord will battle for you" (Exod. 14:14).

D. But when Israel does not do the will of God, as if it were possible, He wages war against them.

---

[28] Hebrew: ועתה.
[29] Hebrew: ועתה.
[30] I.e., two right hands—one replacing God's left hand.

| | | |
|---|---|---|
| ◆ שנתתה ארכה לדור המבול כדי שיעשו תשובה ולא עשו | C | |
| ◆ שנא' ויאמר [ייי לא ידון רוחי באדם] וגומ' (בר' ו ג). ◆ | D | |
| ◆ ולא גמרת עליהן כלאה עד שהשלימו [רשען לפניך]. ◆ | E | |
| וכן] מצינו באנשי מגדל שנתתה להן ארכא שמא יעשו | F | |
| תשובה [ולא עשו ◆ שנ]א' ויאמר ייי הן עם אחד וגומ' | G | |
| (שם יא ו) ◆ אין עתה אלא תשובה [שנא' ועתה יש' מה] | H | |
| ייי אלהיך וגומ' (דב' י יב) ◆ ולא גמרתה עליהן כלאה | I | |
| עד שהשלימו [רשען לפניך]. ◆ וכן מצינו באנשי סדום | J | |
| שנתתה להן [ארכא לעשות] תשובה [ולא] עשו ◆ שנא' | K | |
| וייי המטיר על סדם וגומ' (בר' יט כד) ◆ נאמ' כאן מטר | L | |
| ונאמר [גפרית ואש אם עשו] תשובה הרי מטר ואם | |
| לא גפרית ואש ◆ [עשר מכות] [הבאת על המצ' במ]צ' | M | |
| ולא גמרתה עליהן כלאה עד שהשלימו רשען לפניך. ◆ | |
| [ד"א] ◆ ימינך ייי נאדרי בכח ◆ כשישראל עושין רצונו | C/B/A | 2 |
| שלמקום עושין [את] השמאל ימין ◆ שנא' ימינך ייי | D |
| ימינך ייי ◆ וכשאין יש' עושין רצונו של מקום עושין את | E |
| הימין שמאל ◆ שנא' השיב [אחור ימינו מפני אויב וגו]מ' | F |
| (איכה ב ג) ◆ ד"א ◆ <כשיש' עושין רצונו של מקום אין | B/A | 3 |
| חמה לפניו ◆ שנא' חמה אין לי (ישע' כז ד) ◆ ו<וכשאין | D/C |
| יש' עושין רצונו שלמקום [הוא מתמלא על שונאיהם | |
| שליש'] חמה ◆ שנא' וחרה אף ייי בכם וגומ' (דב' יא יז). ◆ | E |
| ד"א ◆ כש[ישראל עושין רצונו] שלמקום הוא נלחם | B/A | 4 |
| להן ◆ שנא' ייי ילחם לכם (שמ' יד יד) ◆ וכשאין | D/C |
| יש' עושין רצונו שלמקום כויכול הוא נלחם בהן ◆ | |

E. As it says in Scripture, "Then He became their enemy, and Himself made war against them" (Isa. 63:10).

F. Not only this, but also they make the Merciful One merciless!

G. In accordance with what is said in Scripture, "The Lord has acted like a foe, etc." (Lam. 2:5).

5. A. "... shatters the foe" (Exod. 15:6):

B. This [refers to] Pharaoh.

C. As it says in Scripture, "The foe said ..." (Exod. 15:9).

D. There are those who say this [refers to] Esau.

E. As it says in Scripture, "Because the enemy gloated (over you) ..." (Ezek. 36:2).

6. A. ["... shatters the foe" (Exod. 15:6):]

B. "Shattered the foe" is not written here. Rather, "will shatter the foe."

C. [Meaning—] in the time to come.

D. And thus Scripture states, "You tread the earth in rage, etc." (Hab. 3:12).

*Chapter Thirty-Two*

(Textual Source: Ms. JTS ENA (Adler) 1179)

XXXII:I[31]

1. A. "In Your great triumph You break Your opponents. (You send forth Your fury, it consumes them like straw)" (Exod. 15:7):

B. You have been made greatly proud over those who rose up against You!

C. And who are they who rose up against You? They who rose up against Your beloved.

D. [As it says in Scripture,] "Amraphel, King of Shinar, Arioch, King of Ellasar, etc." (Gen. 14:1).

E. What does Scripture say [concerning them]?—"At night, (he and his servants) deployed against them (and defeated them), etc." (Gen. 14:15).

F. And about Him it is explained in tradition, "Who has roused (a victor) from the east ... He pursues them, he goes on unscathed, etc." (Isa. 41:2–3). And Scripture says, "The Lord said to my lord, 'Sit at My right hand'... The Lord will stretch forth, etc." (Ps. 110:1–2) until "... a rightful king by My decree" (Ps. 110:4). And Scripture says, "Fear not, Abram, I am a shield for you, etc." (Gen. 15:1). And Scripture says, "O God, the rock, wherein I take shelter" (2 Sam. 22:3). And Scripture says, every "word of the Lord is pure, etc." (2 Sam. 22:31, Ps. 18:31).

2. A. Another interpretation:

B. "In Your great triumph You break Your opponents" (Exod. 15:7):

C. You have been made greatly proud over those who rose up against You!

D. And who are they who rose up against You? They who rose up against Your sons.

E. And who are they who rose up? Pharaoh and all his army.

F. As it says in Scripture, "... he took six hundred of his picked chariots, etc." (Exod. 14:7).

---

[31] Compare XXXII:I:1.A–3.E with *Mekhilta de-Rabbi Ishmael*, Shirata (H/R, 135:16–136:17; Laut., vol. 2, 45:33–47:63; Neus., XXXI:I:16.A–20.H).

שנא' ויהפך להם [לאויב הוא נלחם] בם (ישע' סג י) ◆ ולא עוד     F/E

אלא שעושין את הרחמן אכזרי ◆ כע[נין שנא' היה ייי] כאויב     G

וגומ' (איכה ב ה) <...> ◆ תרעץ אויב ◆ זה פרעה ◆ שנא' אמר     C/B/A    5

אויב (שמ' טו ט) ◆ ויש [אומ' זה עשו ◆ שנא'] יען כי אמר     E/D

האויב וגומ' (יחז' לו ב) ◆ רעצתה אויב אין כת' כאן אלא     B/A    6

תרעץ אויב ◆ לעתיד לבוא ◆ וכן הוא אומ' בזעם תצעד     D/C

ארץ וגומ' (חב' ג יב) סל' פסו' ◆

                                               XXXII:I

וברוב גאונך תהרוס קמיך. ◆ הרביתה להתגאות     B/A    1

[כנגד מי שק[מ]ו] נגדך ◆ ומי הן שקמו כנגדך מי שקמו     C

כנגד ידידיך ◆ אמרפל מלך שנער אריוך מלך אלסר     D

וגומ' ◆ מה הוא אומ' ויחלק [עליהם לילה] וגומ' (בר' יד     E

טו) ◆ ועליו מפרש בקבלה מי העיר ממזרח וגומ' ירדפם     F

יעבור שלום וגומ' (ישע' מא ג) ואומ' נאם ייי לאדוני

שב לימני וגומ' מטה עזך יש[לח] ייי וגומ' (תה' קי ב)

עד על דברתי מלכי צדק (שם ד) ואומ' אל תירא אברם

אנכי מגן לך וגומ' (בר' טו א) ואומ' אלקי צורי אחסה

בו (ש"ב כב ג). ואומ' כל א[מרת ייי צרופה] וגומ' (שם

לא), (תה' יח לא). ◆ ד"א ◆ וברוב גאונך תהרוס קמיך ◆     B/A    2

הרבית [להתגאות כנגד] כל מי שקמו כנגדך ◆ ומי הן שקמו     D/C

כנגדך מי ש[קמו כנגד בניך] ◆ ומי הם שקמו פרעה וכל חילו ◆     E

שנא' ויקח שש מא[ו]ת רכב בחור וגו]מ' (שמ' יד ז) ◆     F

G. What does Scripture say [about them]?—"Pharaoh's chariots and his army, etc." (Exod. 15:4).

H. [Also] Sisera and all his chariots.

I. As it says in Scripture, "So Sisera ordered all his chariots, etc." (Judg. 4:13).

J. What does Scripture say?—"(The stars) fought from heaven, etc." (Judg. 5:20).

K. [Also] Sennacherib and all his army.

L. As it says in Scripture, "Through your envoys you have blasphemed ... I have dried up with the soles of my feet, etc." (2 Kings 19:23).

M. What does Scripture say?—"The Lord sent an angel who annihilated every mighty warrior, etc." (2 Chron. 32:21). And Scripture says, "This same day at Nob he shall stand, etc." (Isa. 10:32). And Scripture says, "This is the word that the Lord has spoken concerning him, etc." (2 Kings 19:21).

3.   A. Nebuchadnezzar and all his army said, "It's [not] possible to dwell with [other] human

### (Textual Source: Mekhilta de-R. Ishmael)

beings! I'll make a small cloud for myself, and I shall dwell within it.

B. "As it says in Scripture, 'I will mount the back of a cloud, etc.' (Isa. 14:14)."

C. The Holy One, blessed be He, said, "You wanted to separate yourself from humanity. The end will be that humanity will be separated from you!

D. "As it says in Scripture, 'Twelve months later ... the king exclaimed ... The words were still on the king's lips ... There and then the sentence was carried out upon Nebuchadnezzar the king' (Dan. 4:25–30). [And Scripture says,] 'King Belshazzar gave a great banquet ... Belshazzar said, under the influence of wine ... The golden vessels that had been taken ... They drank wine ... Just then, the fingers of a human hand appeared ... The king's face darkened, etc.' (Dan. 5:1–6).

[86]

E. "And concerning him, Scripture says, 'Ah, you who make others drink to intoxication' (Hab. 2:15). And Scripture says, 'You shall be sated with shame, rather than glory' (Hab. 2:16). And Scripture says, 'On that night, Belshazzar was slain' (Dan. 5:30)."

## XXXII:II[32]

1.   A. "You have broken Your opponents" is not written here! Rather, "You will break Your opponents" (Exod. 15:7).

B. In the time to come.

C. And thus Scripture states, "Do not ignore the shout of Your foes, the din of Your adversaries that ascends all the time" (Ps. 74:23). [And Scripture says,] "Surely, Your enemies, O Lord" (Ps. 92:10). [And Scripture says,] "Those who keep far from You perish. You annihilate all who are untrue to You" (Ps. 73:27).

2.   A. Another interpretation:

B. "You have broken Your opponents" is not written here! Rather, "You will break Your opponents" (Exod. 15:7).

C. In the time to come.

D. And thus Scripture states, "O God, smash their teeth in their mouth, shatter the fangs of lions, O Lord" (Ps. 58:7).

---

[32] Compare XXXII:II:1.A–6.G with *Mekhilta de-Rabbi Ishmael*, Shirata (H/R, 136:17–137:15; Laut., vol. 2, 47:64–50:99; Neus., XXXI:I:21.A–II:4.G).

| | |
|---|---|
| מה הוא [אומ' מרכ]בות פרעה וחילו וגומ' (שם | G |
| טו ד) • סיסרא [וכל רכבו • ש]נא' ויזעק סיסרא | I/H |
| את כל רכבו וגומ' (שופ' ד יג) • מה הוא אומ' מן | J |
| שמים [נלח]מו וגומ' (שם ה כ) • סנחריב וכל אגפיו • | K |
| שנא' ביד מלאכיך חרפת [וגומ' ואחריב] בכף פעמי | L |
| וגומ' (מ"ב יט כג) • מה הוא אומ' וישלח ייי מלאך | M |

ויכ]חד כל גבו]ר חיל וגומ' (דה"ב לב כא). עוד היום
בנוב לע]מד וגומ' (ישע' י לב) ואומ'] וזה הדבר אשר

| | |
|---|---|
| דבר ייי בזה לך וגומ' (מ"ב יט כא) • נבוכדנצר וכל חילו | A 3 |
| אמ' איפשר לדור עם בני [אדם אעשה לי עב קטנה | |
| ואדור בתוכה • שנא' אעלה על במתי עב וגו' (ישע' יד | B |
| יד). • אמר הקב"ה אתה רצית לפרוש עצמך מבני אדם | C |
| סוף בני אדם נפרשין ממך • שנא' לקצת ירחין תרי | D |

עשר וגו' ענה מלכא ואמר וגו' עוד מלתא בפום מלכא
וגו' בה שעתא מלתא ספת על נבוכדנצר וגו' מהו
אומר כולא מטא על נבוכדנצר מלכא (דני' ד כה - ל).
בלשאצר מלכא עבד לחם רב בלשאצר אמר בטע' חמרא
באדין הייתיו מאני דהבא וגו' אשתיו חמרא בה שעתא
נפקת אצבען די יד אינש וגו' אדיין מלכא זיוהי שנוהי

| | |
|---|---|
| וגו' (דני' ה א - ו) • ועליו הוא אומר הוי משקה רעהו | E |

מספח חמתך ואף שכר (חבק' ב טו) ואומר שבעת קלון
מכבוד (שם טז) ואומר ביה בליליא קטיל בלשאצר]. •

| | |
|---|---|
| הרסת קמיך אין כת' כן אלא תהרוס קמיך • לעתיד | B/A 1 |
| לבוא • וכן הוא אומר אל תשכח קול צורריך שאון | C |

קמיך עולה תמיד (תה' עד כג) כי הנה אויביך יאבדו
(תה' צב י) כי הנה רחיקיך יאבדו הצמתה כל זונה

| | |
|---|---|
| ממך (תה' עג כז). • ד"א • הרסת קמיך אין כת' כן אלא | B/A 2 |
| תהרס קמיך • לעתיד לבוא • וכן הוא אומר אלקים הרס | D/C |

שנימו בפימו מלתעות כפירים נתץ ה' (תה' נח ז) •

E.  Why? "For they do not consider the Lord's deeds, the work of His hands. May He tear them down, never to rebuild them" (Ps. 28:5).

3.  A.  "You send forth Your fury" is not written here. Rather, "You will send forth Your fury" (Exod. 15:7).

    B.  And thus Scripture states, "Pour out Your wrath on them, may Your blazing anger overtake them" (Ps. 69:25). [And Scripture says,] "Pour out Your fury on the nations that do not know You" (Ps. 79:6).

4.  A.  "It consumed them like straw" is not written here. Rather, "It will consume them like straw) (Exod. 15:7).

    B.  And thus Scripture states, "The House of Jacob shall be fire, and the House of Joseph flame, and the House of Esau shall be straw. They shall burn it and devour it" (Obad. 1:18). And Scripture says, "In that day, I will make the clans of Judah like a flaming brazier among sticks and like a flaming torch among sheaves. They shall devour all the besieging peoples right and left, and Jerusalem shall continue on its site, in Jerusalem" (Zech. 12:6).

5.  A.  "... like straw" (Exod. 15:7):

    B.  When all [types of] wood burn, they don't make a sound. But when straw burns, its sound travels.

    C.  Likewise, the voices of the Egyptians traveled because of the punishments that were coming upon them.

    D.  When all [types of] wood burn, they have some substance. But when straw burns, it has no substance.

### (Textual Source: Ms. T-S Cambridge Misc. 36.132)

    E.  Likewise, the Egyptians did not have substance because of the punishment.

    F.  Because Scripture says, "... he took six hundred of his picked chariots" (Exod. 14:7), I might assume they had some substance!

    G.  Scripture states, [however,] "... it consumes them like straw" (Exod. 15:7).

    H.  Just as straw has no substance, likewise the Egyptians had no substance because of the punishment.

    I.  And thus Scripture states, "They lay down to rise no more, they were extinguished, quenched like a wick" (Isa. 43:17).

6.  A.  And thus you find that there was no kingdom lower than the Egyptians. But they held power for the moment, because of Israel's honor.

    B.  When Scripture speaks metaphorically about kingdoms, it compares them to gold and silver. [As it says in Scripture,] "The head of that statue was of fine gold. Its breast and arms were of silver. Its belly and thighs, of bronze. Its legs were of iron, and its feet part iron and part clay" (Dan. 2:32–33).

    C.  [But] when Scripture speaks metaphorically about Egypt, it compares them to lead. [As it says in Scripture,] "They sank like lead" (Exod. 15:10).

    D.  When Scripture speaks metaphorically about kingdoms, it compares them to beasts. [As it says in Scripture,] "Four mighty beasts different from each other emerged from the sea. The first was like a lion ... the second ... like a bear ..." The third "... as I looked on, there was another, like a leopard ... there was a fourth beast—fearsome, dreadful, and very powerful ..." (Dan. 7:3–7).

מפני מה כי לא יבינו אל פעולות ה' ואל E

מעשה ידיו יהרסם ולא יבנם (תה' כח ה). ◆ שלחת A 3

חרונך אין כת' כן אלא תשלח חרנך ◆ וכן הוא אומר B

שפך עליהם זעמך וחרון אפך ישיגם (תה' סט כה)

שפך חמתך על הגוים אשר לא ידעוך (תה' עט ו). ◆

אכלמו כקש אין כת' כן אלא יאכלמו כקש ◆ וכן הוא B/A 4

אומר והיה בית יעקב אש ובית יוסף להבה ובית עשו

לקש ודלקו בהם ואכלום (עוב' יח). ואומר והיה ביום

ההוא אשים את אלופי יהודה ככיור אש בעצים

וכלפיד אש בעמיר ואכלה על ימין ועל שמאל את

העמים סביב וישבה ירושלם עוד תחתיה בירושלם

(זכ' יב ו). ◆ כקש ◆ כל העצים כשהן דולקין אין להן קול B/A 5

אבל קש כשהוא דולק קולו הולך ◆ כך היו המצריים C

קולן הולך מפני פורעניות שהיו באות עליהן. ◆ כל D

‹ה›עצים כשהן דולקין יש בהן ממש אבל קש

כשהוא דולק אין בו ממש. ◆ כך מצריים לא היה בהן E

ממש מפני פורעניות. ◆ לפי שהוא אומ' ויקח שש מאות F

רכב בחור (שמ' יד ז) שומיע אני יש בהן ממש ◆ ת"ל G

יאכלמו כקש ◆ מה קש אין בו ממ[ש אף] מצ' לא היה H

בהן ממש מפני פורענות ◆ וכן הוא או' יחדו ישכבו בל I

יקומו ד(ו)עכו כפשתה כבו (ישע' מג יז) ◆ וכן את מוצא A 6

שאין מלכות ירודה יתיר מן המצ' אלא שנטלה מלכות

לשעה מפני כבודן של יש' ◆ כשהוא מושל מלכויות מושלן B

בכסף וזהב הוא צלמא די דהב טב חדוהי ודרעוהי

דכסף מעוהי וירכתיה די נחש [שקוה]י די פרזל רגלוהי

מנהון די פרזל ומנהון דין חסף (דני' ב לב - לג) ◆ כשהוא C

מושל מצ' מ‹ו›שלן בעו[פרת צל']לו כעופרת ◆ כשהוא מושל D

מלכוי[ות מוש]לן בחיות וארבע חיון רברבן סלקן מן ימא שנין

דא [מן] דא קדמיתא כאריה תניית[א כד] תליתיתא וארו

אחרי כנמר רביעתא דחילא ואמתני ותקיפא יתירא (דני' ז ג - ז)

◆

E.    But when Scripture speaks metaphorically about Egypt, it compares them to foxes. [As it says in Scripture,] "Catch us the foxes, the little foxes that ruin the vineyards. For our vineyard is in blossom" (Song 2:15).

[87]

F.    And when Scripture speaks metaphorically about kingdoms, it compares them to cedars. [As it says in Scripture,] "Assyria was a cedar in Lebanon with beautiful branches and shady thickets, of lofty stature, with its top among leafy trees" (Ezek. 31:2). [And Scripture says,] "The tree that you saw grow and become mighty, whose top reached heaven, which was visible throughout the earth" (Dan. 4:17). [And Scripture says,] "Yet I destroyed the Amorite before them, (whose stature was like the cedar's)" (Amos 2:9).

G.    But when Scripture speaks metaphorically about Egypt, it compares them to straw. [As it says in Scripture,] "... it consumes them like straw" (Exod. 15:7).

## XXXII:III[33]

1.    A.    "At the blast of Your nostrils the waters piled up" (Exod. 15:8):

B.    With what measure they meted out, You measured them!

C.    They said, "Let us deal shrewdly with them" (Exod. 1:10).

D.    Thus, You placed wisdom[34] in the water.

E.    [As it says in Scripture,] "At the blast of Your nostrils the waters became wise"[35] (Exod. 15:8).

2.    A.    "The floods stood straight like a leather bottle" (Exod. 15:8):

B.    Just as a leather bottle is wrapped up tightly, likewise the Egyptians were wrapped up tightly, and they were overcome by the odor of the sea.

C.    In accordance with what is said in Scripture, "He makes the depths seethe like a cauldron" (Job 41:23).

D.    But for the Israelites [the sea smelled like] all types of spices.

E.    As it says in Scripture, "He makes the sea like an ointment pot" (Job 41:23). And Scripture says, "Awake, O north wind! Come, O south wind! Blow upon my garden, that its perfume may spread. Let my beloved come to his garden, and enjoy its luscious fruits!" (Song 4:16).

3.    A.    Another interpretation:

B.    "(The floods) stood straight like a leather bottle" (Exod. 15:8):

C.    Just as

### (Textual Source: Ms. Firkovich II A 268)

a leather bottle is wrapped up tightly, so too were the souls of the Egyptians wrapped up tightly, and they couldn't put anything in [their bodies] or let anything out.

D.    But Israel was eating and drinking, and was rejoicing. And channels of sweet water went out for them from the salty water.

E.    In accordance with what is said in Scripture, "He brought forth streams from a rock" (Ps. 78:16).

F.    And "streams" only means fresh water.

---

[33] Compare XXXII:III:1.A–5.I with parallel material (in partially different editorial order, however,) in *Mekhilta de-Rabbi Ishmael*, Shirata (H/R, 137:20–139:3; Laut., vol. 2, 50:106–53:147; Neus., XXXI:II:6.A–13.I).

[34] Hebrew: *armimut*—ערמימות.

[35] Hebrew: *ne'ermu*—נערמו.

‹וכש›[הוא] מ‹ו›של מצ' מ‹ו›שלן בשועלין אחזו לנו שועלים E

שועלים קטנים מחבלים כרמים וכרמנו ס[מדר] (שה"ש ב

טו) ◆ וכשהוא מושל מלכיות מ‹ו›שלן בארזין הנה אשור F

ארז בלבנון יפה ענף וחר[ש מצל וג]בה קומה ובין

עבותים היתה צמרתו (יחז' לא ג) אילנא די חזיתא די

רבא ותקיף ורומיה ימ[טא ל]שמיא וחזותיה לסוף

ארעא (דני' ד ח) ואנכי השמדתי את האמרי מפניכם (עמ'

ב ט) ◆ וכשהוא מושל מצ' [מושלן] בקש יאכלמו כקש. ◆ G

XXXII:III

וברוח אפך נערמו מים ◆ במידה שמדדו בה  B/A 1

מדדתה להן ◆ הן אמ' הבה נתחכמה לו ◆ אף אתה נתתה  D/C

ערמימות למים ◆ וברוח אפיך ‹נערמו מים› ◆ נצבו כמו  A 2 E

נד נוזלים ◆ מה נד צרור ועמוד כך מצריין צרורין  B

ועומדין והיו מתעלפין מריח הים ◆ [כען]ין שנ' ירתיח  C

כסיר מצולה (איוב מא כג) ◆ אבל ליש' לכל מיני  D

בשמים ◆ שנ' ים ישים כמרקחה (שם כג) וא' עורי צפון  E

ובאי תימן הפיחי גני ויזלו בשמיו יבוא דודי לגנו

ויאכל פרי מגדיו (שה"ש ד טז) ◆ ד"א ◆ נצבו כמו נד ◆ מה  C/B/A 3

נד צרור ועומד כך היתה נפשם של מצ' צרורה

ועומדת ואינן לא מוכנסין ולא מוצאין ◆ וישראל  D

אוכלין ושותין ושמחין ויצא להן זכרון מים מתוקין

מתוך מים מלוחין ◆ כענין שנא' ויוצא נוזלים מסלע  E

(תה' עח טז) ◆ אין נוזלים אלא מים חיים ◆  F

G.   As it says in Scripture, "A garden spring, (a well of fresh water, a stream of Lebanon,) etc." (Song 4:15).

4.    A.   "The deeps froze in the heart of the sea" (Exod. 15:8):

B.   Where is the human heart located? Two-thirds [of the way up the body].

C.   Likewise, the water of the sea froze on them from two-thirds of the way on up, in order to destroy them.

5.    A.   A sea does not have a heart, but a heart was given to it. As it says in Scripture, "The deeps froze in the heart of the sea" (Exod. 15:8).

B.   A terebinth does not have a heart, but a heart was given to it. As it says in Scripture, "... in the heart of the terebinth" (2 Sam. 18:14).

C.   The heavens do not have a heart, but a heart was given to them. As it says in Scripture, "... to the heart of the heavens" (Deut. 4:11).

D.   Let the sea, which does not have a heart but was given a heart, come and exact punishment from the Egyptians, who were waging war against Israel with all kinds of punishments!

[88]   E.   Let the terebinth, which does not have a heart but was given a heart, come and exact punishment from Absalom, who stole three hearts—the heart of his father, the heart of the court, and the heart of the men of Israel.

F.   Let the heavens, which do not have a heart but were given a heart, come and bring down manna for Israel, who accepted the Torah, which was given on the heart.

G.   [As it says in Scripture,] "And these words (which I command you this day shall be upon your heart)" (Deut. 6:6).

H.   And not only the heavens rejoiced over the redemption of Israel, but also the mountains and all the hills.

I.   As it says in Scripture, "Shout, O heavens, for the Lord has acted ..." (Isa. 44:23). And Scripture says, "Shout, O heavens, and rejoice, O earth, etc." (Isa. 49:13).

*Chapter Thirty-Three*

(Textual Source: Ms. Firkovich II A 268)

XXXIII:I[36]

1.    A.   "The enemy said, ('I will pursue, I will overtake, I will divide the spoil. My desire shall have its fill of them. I will bare my sword. My hand shall subdue them')" (Exod. 15:9):

B.   This was [once] the beginning of the scriptural portion. However, there is no [concern for what comes] first and last in the Torah!

2.    A.   Similar to this, you say: "On the eighth day" (Lev. 9:1):

B.   This was [once] the beginning of the scroll. However, there is no [concern for what comes] first and last in the Torah!

3.    A.   Similar to this, you say: "In the year that King Uzziah died" (Isa. 6:1):

B.   This was [once] the beginning of the scroll. However, there is no [concern for what comes] first and last in the Torah!

4.    A.   Similar to this, you say: "Go proclaim to Jerusalem" (Jer. 2:2):

---

[36] Compare XXXIII:I:1.A–16.G with parallel material (in partially different editorial order, however,) in *Mekhilta de-Rabbi Ishmael*, Shirata (H/R, 139:5–141:14; Laut., vol. 2, 54:1–59:78; Neus., XXXII:I:1.A–15.G).

| | | |
|---|---|---|
| G | A 4 | שנא' מעין גנים וגומ' (שה"ש ד טו) ◆ קפאו תהומות בלב |
| | C/B | ים. ◆ היכן לבו של אדם נתון על שני חלקים ◆ כך קפאו עליהם |
| 5 | A | מי ים משני חלקים <ו>למעלה כדי לאבדן ◆ ים לא היה לו |
| | B | לב ונתן לו לב שנא' קפאו תהומות בלב ים. ◆ אלא לא |
| | | היה לה לב וניתן לה לב שנא' בלב האלה (ש"ב יח יד). ◆ |
| | C | שמים לא היה להן לב וניתן להן לב שנא' עד לב |
| | D | השמים (דב' ד יא). ◆ <יבא> ים שלא היה לו לב וניתן |
| | | לו לב ויפרע מן המצ' שהיו נלחמין בהן ביש' בכל מיני |
| | E | [פור]עניות ◆ תבוא אלה שלא היה לה לב וניתן לה לב |
| | | ותיפרע מן אבשלום שגנב שלשה לבבות לב אביו ולב |
| | F | [בי]ת ד[י]ן ולב אנשי יש' ◆ יבואו שמים שלא היה להן |
| | | לב וניתן להן לב ויורידו מן ליש' שקבלו את התו' |
| | H/G | שניתנה על לב ◆ והיו הדברים האלה וגומ' (שם ו ו) ◆ ולא |
| | | שמים בלבד היו שמחין בגאולתן של יש' אלא [אף |
| | I | ההרים וכל] הגבעות ◆ שנא' רנו שמים כי עשה ייי [וגומ' |
| | | (ישע' מד כג) ואומ' רנו שמים וגילי] ארץ וגומ' (שם |
| | | מט יג). סל' פסו' ◆ |

| | | |
|---|---|---|
| 1 | B/A | אמר א[י]וב ◆ זה היה תחלת הפרשה אלא] שאין |
| 2 | A | מוקדם ומאוחר בתורה ◆ כיוצא [בו אתה אומ' ויהי |
| | B | ביום השמיני] (ויק' ט א) ◆ זה היה [תחלת] הספר אלא |
| 3 | A | שאין מוקדים [ומאו]חר בת[ורה] ◆ <כיוצא בו אתה |
| | B | אומ' בשנת מות המלך עזיהו (ישע' ו א) ◆ זה היה תחלת |
| 4 | A | הספר אלא שאין מוקדם ומאוחר בתורה> ◆ כיוצא בו |
| | | אתה אומ' הלך וקראת באזני ירו[של'] (ירמ' ב ב) ◆ |

B. This was [once] the beginning of the scroll. However ... [insert] all the rest [of the expression: "There is no concern for what comes first and last in the Torah"].

5.    A. Similar to this, you say: "O mortal, stand up on your feet, etc." (Ezek. 2:1):

B. And there are those who say: "... propound a riddle and relate an allegory to the House of Israel" (Ezek. 17:2):

C. This was [once] the beginning of the scroll. However, there is no ... [insert] all the rest [of the expression: "... concern for what comes first and last in the Torah"].

6.    A. Similar to this, you say: "Israel is a ravaged vine, etc." (Hos. 10:1):

B. This was [once] the beginning of the scroll. [Insert] all the rest [of the expression: "There is no concern for what comes first and last in the Torah"].

7.    A. Similar to this, you say: "I, Koheleth, was king" (Eccles. 1:12):

B. This was [once] the beginning of the scroll. However, there is no [concern for what comes] first and last in the Torah!

8.    A. Another interpretation:

B. "The enemy said" (Exod. 15:9):

C. And just how did Israel know what Pharaoh thought about them in Egypt?

D. Rather, the Holy Spirit dwelled upon them, and they knew what Pharaoh thought about them in Egypt.

E. What did Pharaoh say to his troops? He said to them, "We wouldn't pursue Israel, except for the silver and gold that we have lost, which is worth it to us!"

[89]    F. When the part of the people who had lost [only] a small amount of wealth heard, they said, "For this small amount[37] we're not going to pursue Israel!"

9.    A. Another interpretation:

B. He[38] said to them, "We are all equal in the booty! And not only this, but I'll also open treasuries for you, and I'll distribute silver, and gold, and precious stones and gems to you!"

C. As it says in Scripture, "I will divide the spoil" (Exod. 15:9).

10.    A. Another interpretation:

B. Pharaoh said, but didn't know what he was saying, "A man may arrange his thoughts, (but what he says depends on the Lord,) etc." (Prov. 16:1).

C. He didn't say [in Exod. 15:9] "We will pursue, we will overtake" but rather "I will pursue, I will overtake."

D. [Meaning,] he will be pursued by them, and he will be seized by them!

E. "I will deliver their spoil" is not written here [in Exod. 15:9], but rather, "I will deliver the spoil."

F. [Meaning,] the spoil will be divided among them!

G. "My desire shall have its fill of them" is not written here [in Exod. 15:9], but rather, "My desire shall have its fill of him."

---

[37] The meaning of this word (אתירא) is difficult to determine.

[38] I.e., Pharaoh.

| | | |
|---|---|---|
| זה היה תחלת הספר אלא וכול' ◆ כיוצא בו אתה אומ' בן | A 5 | B |
| אדם עמו[ד ע]ל רגליך וגומ' (יחז' ב א) ◆ ויש אומ' חוד | B | |
| חידה ומשול משל על בית י[ש'] (שם יז ב) ◆ זה היה | C | |
| תחלת הספר אלא שאין וכול' ◆ כיוצא בו אתה אומ' | A 6 | |
| [גפן] בוק[ק] יש' וגומ' (הושע י א) ◆ זה היה תחלת | B | |
| הספר וכול. ◆ כיוצא בו אתה אומ' [אני] קהלת הייתי | A 7 | |
| מלך (קה' א יב) ◆ זה היה תחלת הס[פר] אלא שאין | B | |
| מוקדם ומאוחר בתורה. ◆ ד"א ◆ אמ' אויב ◆ וכי מאין יש' | C/B/A 8 | |
| יודעין מה פרעה מחשב עליהן במצ' ◆ אלא שרת רוח | D | |
| הק' עליהן והיו יודעין מה פרעה מחשב עליהן במצ' ◆ | | |
| מה אמ' פרעה לחייילותיו אמ' להן אפילו אם אין אנו | E | |
| רודפין אחרי יש' אלא בשביל הכסף והזהב שאיבדו | | |
| ממנו כדי הוא לנו ◆ כיון ששמעו מקצת העם שאיבדו | F | |
| ממון מועט אמ[ר]ו הא אתירא לא <נרדוף> אחרי יש'. ◆ | | |
| ד"א ◆ אמ' להן כולנו שוין בביזה ולא עוד אלא שאני | B/A 9 | |
| פותח לכם תיסווראות ומחלק אני לכן כסף וזהב | | |
| ואבנים טובות ומרגליות ◆ שנאמר אחלק שלל. ◆ ד"א ◆ | A 10 | C |
| אמ' פרעה ולא ידע מה אמר לאדם מערכי לב וגומ' | B | |
| (מש' טז א) ◆ נרדף נשיג לא אמ' כן אלא ארדוף אשיג | C | |
| נרדף הוא להם ונתפש הוא בידן. ◆ אחלק שללהן אין | E/D | |
| כת' כן אלא (תמלאם) אחלק שלל ◆ מתחלק הוא שלל | F | |
| להן ◆ תמלא[ם] נפשי אין כת' כן אלא תמלאמו נפשי ◆ | G | |

H.   [Meaning,] their desire shall have its fill of him![39]

I.   "My hand shall subdue them" is not written here [in Exod. 15:9], but rather, "My hands shall cause it to be inherited."

J.   [Meaning,] I shall cause them to inherit my riches and my glory!

11.  A.   [In Exod. 15:9, Pharaoh was saying,] "In the past you would plunder their property, and I would absolve you, because of the law of the kingdom. [However,] now 'I will divide the spoil' (Exod. 15:9)!

B.   "In the past, you would kill them, and I would absolve you, because of the law of the kingdom. [However,] now, 'my desire shall have its fill of them. (I will bare my sword!)' (Exod. 15:9).

C.   "In the past, you would try to rape their sons and daughters, and I would absolve you, because of the law of the kingdom. [However,] now, 'I will bare my sword. My hand shall subdue them!' (Exod. 15:9)"

12.  A.   Egypt attacked Israel in three units.

B.   One said, "Let's take their wealth, but not kill them!" And one said, "Let's kill them, but not take their wealth!" And one said, "Let's kill them, and take their wealth!"

C.   [In reference to] the one that said, "Let's take their wealth, but not kill them!" [Scripture states,] "I will divide the spoil" (Exod. 15:9). [In reference to] the one that said, "Let's kill them, but not take their wealth!" [Scripture states,] "My desire shall have its fill of them" (Exod. 15:9). [In reference to] the one that said, "Let's kill them and take their wealth!" [Scripture states,] "I will bare my sword. My hand shall subdue them" (Exod. 15:9)

13.  A.   And there are those who say they even wanted to sodomize their[40] males.

B.   In accordance with what is said in Scripture [in Ezek. 28:1ff.] concerning the Prince of Tyre: "They shall give their swords against your prized shrewdness" is not written here [in Ezek. 28:7]. Rather [Scripture states], "They shall unsheath their swords against your prized shrewdness."

C.   Because he was haughty and proud, God likewise humiliated him, and the nations of the world insulted him.

14.  A.   Pharaoh threatened [the Israelites] in five ways in Egypt: "The foe said, ['I will pursue.
[90]      I will overtake. I will divide the spoil. My desire shall have its fill of them. I will bare my sword']" (Exod. 15:9).

B.   In correspondence with them, the Holy Spirit mocked them [in five ways]: "You made Your wind blow, etc." (Exod. 15:10).

15.  A.   They told a parable: To what is the matter alike?

B.   It is like a band of thieves that would stand behind the king's palace and [individually would] say, "I'm going to find the king's son and kill him! I'm going to hang him! I'm going burn him! I'll kill him in many bad ways!"

C.   When the king heard, he was filled with anger at them.

D.   Likewise, Pharaoh threatened in Egypt, [as it says in Scripture,] "The foe said, ['I will pursue. I will overtake. I will divide the spoil. My desire shall have its fill of them. I will bare my sword']" (Exod. 15:9).

---

[39] I.e., their fill of Pharaoh.
[40] I.e., Israel's.

| | | |
|---|---|---|
| ממלאין הן נפשן הימנו ◆ תורישם ידי אין כת' כן אלא | I/H | |
| תורישמו ידי ◆ מולשני עשרי וכבודי להן ◆ לשעבר הייתם | A 11 | J |
| בוזזין נכסיהן והייתי ממחה בידכן מפני נימוס | | |
| [מלכות עכשיו אחלק שלל] ◆ לשעבר הייתם הורגין | B | |
| בהן והייתי [ממחה בידכם מפני נימוס] מלכות עכשיו | | |
| תמלאמו נפשי ◆ [לשעבר הייתם מ]בקשין [לאנוס] | C | |
| בניהן ובנותיהן והייתי ממ[ח]ה בידכ]ם מ[פ]ני נימוס | | |
| מלכות עכשיו אריק חרבי תורישמו ידי. ◆ בש[ן]לש] | A | 12 |
| כיתות באו מצ' על יש' ◆ אחת אומ' ניטול ממונם ולא | B | |
| נהר[גם] ואחת אומ' נהרוג ולא ניטול ממונם ואחת | | |
| אומר' נהרגם וניטול ממונם ◆ זו שאמרה ניטול ממונם | C | |
| ולא נהרגם אחלק שלל. וזו שאמ' נהרגם ולא ניטול | | |
| ממונם תמלאמו נפשי ו[זו ש]אמ' נהרגם וניטול | | |
| ממונם אריק חרבי תורישמו ידי. ◆ ויש אומ' אף לבעול | A | 13 |
| את זכוריהן ◆ כענין שנא' בנגיד צר נתנו חרבותם (יחז' | B | |
| כח ז) ביופי חכמ' אין כת' כן אלא והריקו חרבותם על | | |
| יפי חכמתך ◆ לפי שנתגאה וגבה לבו כך השפילו | C | |
| המקום ובזזו אותו אומות העולם. ◆ | | |
| חמשה דברים היה פרעה עומד ומנאץ במצ' אמ' | A | 14 |
| אויב וגומ' ◆ וכנגדן הייתה רוח הקדש מלעגת עליהן | B | |
| נשפת ברוחך כסמו ים וגומ'. ◆ מושלו משל למה הדבר | A | 15 |
| דומה ◆ לערבי ליסטים שהיה עומד אחר פלטירו של מלך | B | |
| אמ' מוצא אני בנו של מלך והורגו אני וצולבו אני ושורפו | | |
| אני מ<י>תות רעות אני ממיתו ◆ שמע המלך נתמלא עליו | C | |
| חמה ◆ כך היה פרעה עומד ומנאץ במצ' אמ' אויב וגומ' ◆ | D | |

E.  In correspondence with them, the Holy Spirit mocked them: "You made Your wind blow, (the sea) covered them, etc." (Exod. 15:10).

F.  And thus you will find in the time to come: "Why do nations assemble ... (kings of the earth) take their stand ... Let us break ... He who is enthroned in heaven (Ps. 2:1–4). And Scripture says, "They rave with their mouths ... But You, O Lord, laugh at them, etc." (Ps. 59:8–9). And thus Scripture says, "Sheba and Dedan, and the merchants of Tarshish, etc." (Ezek. 38:13). And Scripture says, "On that day, when *Gog* sets foot on the soil of Israel ..." until "... and every wall shall crumble to the ground" (Ezek. 38:18–20).

16.  A.  "They sank like lead in the majestic waters" (Exod. 15:10):[41]

B.  The Holy One, blessed be He, is called majestic, as it says in Scripture, "... is the Lord, majestic on high" (Ps. 93:4).

C.  Israel is called majestic, as it says in Scripture, "... the majestic ones in whom is my whole desire" (Ps. 16:3).

D.  Egypt is called majestic, as it says in Scripture, "They sank like lead (in majestic waters)" (Exod. 15:10).

E.  Water is called majestic, as it says in Scripture, "Above the thunder of the mighty waters, (more majestic than the breakers of the sea)" (Ps. 93:4).

F.  The Holy One, blessed be He, who is called majestic, is revealed through Israel, who is called majestic, and exacts punishment from the Egyptians, who are called majestic, with water, which is called majestic!

G.  As it says in Scripture, "They sank like lead in majestic waters" (Exod. 15:10).

*Chapter Thirty-Four*

(Textual Source: Ms. Firkovich II A 268)

XXXIV:I[42]

1.  A.  "Who is like You among the gods, O Lord, (who is like You, majestic in holiness, awesome in splendor, working wonders)!" (Exod. 15:11):

B.  When they saw that Pharaoh and his army were destroyed in the sea, and that the kingdom of Egypt was destroyed, and the judgments that were made against their idolatry, all of them opened their mouths and declared the majesty of God, saying, "Who is like You among the gods, O Lord" (Exod. 15:11).

[91]  C.  And not only Israel, but also when the nations of the world saw what happened to Egypt and their idolatry, they all repented for their idolatry and declared the majesty of God, saying, "Who is like You among the gods, O Lord" (Exod. 15:11).

D.  And thus you find with the time to come: The nations of the world will atone for their idolatry, as it says in Scripture, "On that day, men shall fling away the idols of silver ... And they shall enter the clefts in the rocks, and the crevices in the cliffs, etc." (Isa. 2:20–21). What [else] does Scripture state? "As for idols, they shall vanish completely" (Isa. 2:18).

2.  A.  Another interpretation:

B.  "Who is like You among the gods" (Exod. 15:11):

C.  Who is like You in the world, and who is like You with the miracles and might that You performed for us by the sea.

---

[41] Compare 16.A–G with b. Menaḥot 53a (Neus., XXIX.B:Tractate Menaḥot:5:1:I.3.H–BB).

[42] Compare XXXIV:I:1.A–5.G with *Mekhilta de-Rabbi Ishmael*, Shirata (H/R, 141:15–143:2; Laut., vol. 2, 59:1–61:33; Neus., XXXIII:I:1.A–4.F).

| | | |
|---|---|---|
| וכנגדן היתה רוח הקדש מלעגת <עליו> נשפת | E. | |
| ברוחך כסמו ים וגומ' ◆ וכן את מוצא לעתיד | F | |
| לבוא למה רגשו גוים וגומ' יתיצבו וגו' ננתקה | | |
| וגומ' יושב בשמים וגומ' (תה' ב א - ב) ואומ' הנה | | |
| יביעון בפיהם וגומ' ואומ' ואתה ייי תשחק ל[מ]ו וגומ' | | |
| (שם נט ח - ט) וכן הוא אומ' שבא ודדן סחרי תרשיש | | |
| וגומ' (יחז' לח יג) ואומ' ביום ההוא ביום בוא גוג על | | |
| אדמת יש' וגומ' עד וכל וחומה לארץ תפול (שם יח - | | |
| כ). ◆ צללו כעופרת במים אדירים ◆ (אמ') הקב"ה נקרא | B/A | 16 |
| אדיר שנא' אדיר במרום ייי (תה' צג ד) ◆ יש' נקראו | C | |
| אדירים שנא' ואדירי כל חפצי בם (שם טז ג) ◆ [מצ'] | D | |
| נקראו אדירים שנא' צללו כעופרת וגומ'. ◆ מ[ים נקראו | E | |
| אדירים] שנא' מקולות מים רבים אדי' (שם צג ד) ◆ | | |
| נגלה הקב"ה שנ[קרא אדיר] על ידי יש' שנקראו | F | |
| אדירים ויפרע מן המצ' שנקר[או אדירים] במים שנקראו | | |
| אדירים ◆ שנא' צללו כעופרת במים א[די]רים סל' פסו' | G | |
| | XXXIV:I | |
| | | |
| מי כמוכה באלים ייי ◆ כיון שראו שאבד פרעה | B/A | 1 |
| וחילו בים ואבדו מלכות מצ' ושפט<י>ם שנעשו בעבו' | | |
| זרה שלהן פתחו כולן פיהן והודו למקום ואמרו מי | | |
| כמוך באלים ייי ◆ <ולא ישראל בלבד אלא אף אומות | C | |
| העולם כיון שראו מה שאירע למצרים ועבו' זרה שלהן | | |
| כפרו כולן בעבו' זרה שלהן והודו במקום ואמרו מי | | |
| כמכה באילים ייי> ◆ וכן את מוצא לעתיד לבוא שעתידין | D | |
| אומות העולם לכפור בעבו' זרה שלהן שנא' ביום ההוא | | |
| ישליכו איש אלילי כספו וגו' לבוא בנקרות הצור ובס' | | |
| הס' וגומ' (ישע' ב כ - כא) מה הוא אומ' והאלילים כליל | | |
| יחלף (שם יח). ◆ ד"א ◆ מי כמכה באילים ◆ מי כמוך | C/B/A | 2 |
| בעולם ומי כמוך בנסים וגבו' שעשיתה לנו על הים | | |
| ◆ | | |

D. And thus Scripture says, "... awesome deeds at the Sea of Reeds" (Ps. 106:22). And Scripture says, "He sent His blast against the Sea of Reeds, etc." (Ps. 106:9).

3.  A. Another interpretation:

B. "Who is like You among the gods" (Exod. 15:11):

C. Who is like You, who sees the humiliation of His children, and keeps quiet?

D. And thus Scripture says, "I have kept silent far too long, etc." (Isa. 42:14).

E. [God said,] "I kept quiet in the past, but from this point forward 'I will scream like a woman in labor, I will pant and gasp'" and [continuing with] the rest of the passage until "... without fail" (Isa. 42:14–17).

4.  A. Another interpretation:

B. "Who is like You among the gods" (Exod. 15:11):

C. [Who is like You] among those who stand before You on high?

D. And thus Scripture says, "For who in the skies can equal the Lord ..." [continuing] until "... Your faithfulness surrounds You, etc." (Ps. 89:7–9).

E. Among His host—"There is none like You among the gods, O Lord, and there are no deeds like Yours" (Ps. 86:8). [And Scripture says,] "My beloved is clear-skinned and ruddy ..." [continuing] until "... is delightful" (Song 5:10–16).

5.  A. Another interpretation:

B. "Who is like You among the gods" (Exod. 15:11):

C. [Who is like You] among these who call themselves gods?

D. Pharaoh called himself god, as it says in Scripture, "... who said my Nile is my own. I made it for myself" (Ezek. 29:3). Thus Scripture states, "I will deal with you and your Nile" (Ezek. 29:10).

E. Sennacherib called himself god, as it says in Scripture, "Which among all the gods of [those] countries saved their countries, etc." (2 Kings 18:35). What [else] does Scripture state?—"... an angel of the Lord went out, etc." (2 Kings 19:35).

[92]  F. Nebuchadnezzar called himself god, as it says in Scripture, "Once you thought in your heart, etc." (Isa. 14:13). What [else] does Scripture state?—"Instead, you are brought down to Sheol, etc." (Isa. 14:15).

G. Hiram called himself god, as it says in Scripture, "O mortal, say to the prince of Tyre, etc." (Ezek. 28:2). What [else] does Scripture state?—"By the hands of strangers you shall die, etc." (Ezek. 28:10).

## XXXIV:II[43]

1.  A. Another interpretation:

B. "Who is like You among the gods" (Exod. 15:11):

C. [Who is like You] among these whom others call gods?

D. What is their[44] nature?—"They have mouths, but cannot speak" (Ps. 115:5).

E. However, it is not so with He who spoke, and the world came into being.

---

[43] Compare XXXIV:II:1.A–11.D with parallel material (in different editorial order, however,) in *Mekhilta de-Rabbi Ishmael*, Shirata (H/R, 143:2–144:13; Laut., vol. 2, 62:34–65:89; Neus., XXXIII:I:5.A–15.C).

[44] I.e., idols.

| | | |
|---|---|---|
| וכן הוא אומ' נוראות על ים סוף (תה' קו כב) | D | |
| ואומ' ויגער ביום סוף וגומ' (שם ט). ◆ ד"א ◆ | A | 3 |
| מי כמכה באלים <ייי> ◆ מי כמוך שרואה בעלבון בניו | C/B | |
| ושותק ◆ וכן הוא אומ' החשיתי מעולם וגומ' (ישע' מב | D | |
| יד) ◆ שת(י)קתי לשעבר מיכן ואילך כיולדה אפעה | E | |
| אשום [וא]שאף יחד וכל ענינא עד ולא עזבתים (שם | | |
| טז). ◆ ד"א ◆ מי כמוכה באלים ייי ◆ בשעומדין לפניך | C/B/A | 4 |
| במרום ◆ וכן הוא אומ' כי מי בשחק יערוך לייי וגומ' עד | D | |
| ואמונתך סביבותיך וגומ' (תה' פט ז - י) ◆ אתא [ב]תוך | E | |
| צבא שלו אין כמוך באלים ייי ואין כמעשיך (תה' פו | | |
| ח) דודי צח ואדום וגומ' עד [מחמד]ים (שה"ש ה י - | | |
| טז) ◆ ד"א ◆ מי כמוכה באלים ייי ◆ באלו שקראו עצמן | C/B/A | 5 |
| [אל]הות ◆ פרעה קרא עצמו אלוה שנא' יען אשר אמר | D | |
| לי יאורי ואני עש' (יחז' כט ג) כן הוא אומ' הנני אליך | | |
| ואל יאוריך (שם י). ◆ סנחריב קרא <עצמו> אלוה שנא' | E | |
| מי בכל אלהי הארצות אשר הציל את ארצו וגומ' | | |
| (מ"ב יח לה) מה הוא אומ' ויצא מלאך ייי וגומ' (שם | | |
| יט לה) ◆ נבוכדנצר קרא עצמו אלוה שנא' [ואתה | F | |
| אמרת] בלבבך וגומ' (ישע' יד יג) מה הוא אומ' אך אל | | |
| שאול תורד וגומ' (שם טו) ◆ [חירם קרא] עצמו אלוה | G | |
| שנא' בן אדם אמור לנגיד צור וגומ' (יחז' כח ב) [מה | | |
| הוא אומ' מו]תי ערלים תמות ביד זרים וגומ' (שם י). ◆ | | |

XXXIV:II

| | | |
|---|---|---|
| ד"א ◆ מי כמכה [באלים ייי] ◆ באלו שאחרים קוראין | C/B/A | 1 |
| אותן אל(ו)הות ◆ מה טיבן פה להם ולא [יד]ברו (תה' | D | |
| קטו ה) ◆ אבל מי שאמ' והיה העולם אינו כ(א)ן ◆ | E | |

F. Rather, He spoke [all] the Ten Commandments at once, as it says in Scripture, "God spoke all these words, saying, etc." (Exod. 20:1). And Scripture says, "Behold, My word is like fire, etc." (Jer. 23:29).

G. "They have eyes, but cannot see" (Ps. 115:5):

H. However, it is not so with He who spoke, and the world came into being.

I. [As it says in Scripture,] "For (the eyes) of the Lord range (over the entire earth), etc." (2 Chron. 16:9). And Scripture says, "... the eyes of the Lord, ranging over (the whole earth), etc." (Zech. 4:10). And Scripture says, "The eyes of the Lord are everywhere, etc." (Prov. 15:3).

J. "They have ears, but cannot hear" (Ps. 115:6):

K. However, it is not so with He who spoke, and the world came into being.

L. Rather, "You who hear prayer, all mankind comes to You" (Ps. 65:3). And Scripture says, "You will listen to the entreaty of the lowly, O Lord, etc." (Ps. 10:17). And Scripture says, "O you who linger in the garden, a lover (is listening), etc." (Song 8:13). And Scripture says, "Then those who fear God will speak, etc." (Mal. 3:16). And Scripture says, "Before they pray (I will answer), etc." (Isa. 65:24).

M. "They have noses, but cannot smell" (Ps. 115:6):

N. However, it is not so with He who spoke, and the world came into being.

O. Rather, "... an offering by fire of pleasing odor to the Lord" (Lev. 1:10). [And Scripture says,] "The Lord smelled the pleasing odor" (Gen. 8:21).

P. "They have hands, but cannot touch" (Ps. 115:7):

Q. However, it is not so with He who spoke, and the world came into being.

R. Rather, "My own hand founded the earth, etc." (Isa. 48:13). [And Scripture says,] "My own hands stretched out the heavens, etc." (Isa. 45:12). [And Scripture says,] "Who measured the waters with the hollow of His hand, etc." (Isa. 40:12).

S. "They have feet, but cannot walk" (Ps. 115:7):

T. However, it is not so with He who spoke, and the world came into being.

U. Rather, "Then the Lord will come forth and make war on those nations, etc." (Zech. 14:3). And Scripture says, "The Lord goes forth like a warrior, etc." (Isa. 42:13). And Scripture says, "On that day, He will set his feet, etc." (Zech. 14:4).

V. "They can make no sound in their throats" (Ps. 115:7):

W. However, it is not so with He who spoke, and the world came into being.

X. Rather, "His mouth is delicious, etc." (Song 5:16). And Scripture says, "... to the sound that comes out of His mouth" (Job 37:2).

2.    A. "Who is like You among the gods, O Lord, who is like You, majestic in holiness" (Exod. 15:11):

[93]   B. You are suited to and mighty in holiness.

C. For the way of God is not like the way of a human being. A human being cannot say two things at once.

D. However, it is not so with He who spoke, and the world came into being.

E. Rather, He spoke [all] the Ten Commandments at once. In accordance with what is said in Scripture, "God spoke ..." (Exod. 20:1) [continuing] as written above [at 1.F].

F אלא אמ' עשר דברות בדיבור אחד שנא' וידבר אלקים
את כל הדברים האלה וגומ' (שמ' כ א) ואומ' הלא כה

G דברי כאש וגומ' (ירמ' כג כט) ◆ עינים להם ולא יראו

I/H (תה' קטו ה). ◆ אבל מי שאמ' והיה העולם אינו כן ◆ אלא
כי יייי משטט וגומ' (דה"ב טז ט) ואומ' עיני <יייי> המה
משוטטים וגומ' (זכ' ד י) ואומר בכל מקום עיני יייי
וגומ' (מש' טו ג). ◆ אזנים להם ולא ישמעו (תה' קטו ו) ◆

J
L/K אבל מי שאמר והיה העולם אינו כן ◆ אלא שומע תפלה
עדיך כל בשר יבואו (תה' סה ג). ואומ' תאות ענוים
שמעת יייי וגומ' (שם י יז) ואומ' היושבת בגנים חברים
וגומ' (שה"ש ח יג) ואומ' אז נדברו יראי וגומ' (מלאכי ג
טז) ואומ' והיה טרם יקראו וגומ' (ישע' סה כד). ◆ אף

M לחן ולא יריחון (תה' קטו ו). ◆ אבל מי שאמ' והיה

N העולם אינו כן ◆ אלא אשה ריח ניחוח לייי (ויקר' א ט).

O וירח יייי את ריח הניחוח (בר' ח כא). ◆ ידיהם ולא

P ימישון (תה' קטו ז). ◆ אבל מי שאמר והיה העולם אינו

Q כן ◆ אלא אף ידי יסדה ארץ וגומ' (ישע' מח יג) ואף אני

R ידי נטו שמים וגומ' (שם מה יב) ואומ' מי מדד בשעלו
מים וגומ' (שם מ יב). ◆ רגליהם ולא יהלכו (תה' קטו ז) ◆

S אבל מי שאמר והיה העולם אינו כן ◆ אלא ויצא יייי

U/T ונלחם בגוים וגומ' (זכ' יד ג) ואומ' יייי כגבור יצא וגומ'
(ישע' מב יג) ואומ' ועמדו רגליו ביום ההוא וגומ' (זכ'
יד ד) ◆ לא יהגו בגרונם (תה' קטו ז). ◆ אבל מי שאמ'

W/V
X והיה העולם אינו כן ◆ אלא וחכו ממתקים וגומ' (שה"ש
ה טז) ואומ' והגה מפיו יצא (איוב לז ב). ◆ מי כמוכה

A 2
B באלים יייי מי כמוך נאדר בקודש ◆ נאה (ו)אתה ואדיר

C בקודש ◆ שלא כמדת בשר ודם מדת המק' בשר ודם

D אין יכול לדבר שני דברים כאחד ◆ אבל מי שאמר והיה

E העולם אינו כן ◆ אלא אמ' עשר דברות בדיבור אחד
כענין שנא' וידבר אלקים (שמ' כ א) כדכת' לעיל.
◆.

3.     A.    Another interpretation:

        B.     For the way of God is not like the way of a human being. A human being cannot hear two people as one.

        C.     However, it is not so with He who spoke, and the world came into being.

        D.     Rather, "(all mankind comes to You,) You who hear prayer, etc." (Ps. 65:3).

4.     A.     Another interpretation:

        B.     For the way of God is not like the way of a human being. A worker does the work along with the owner of the house, sowing with him, ploughing with him, weeding with him, [and] he pays him [only] one coin!

        C.     However, it is not so with He who spoke, and the world came into being.

        D.     Rather, [if] someone wants children, He gives him children. As it says in Scripture, "Sons are the provision of the Lord, etc." (Ps. 127:3). [If] someone wants wisdom, He gives him wisdom. As it says in Scripture, "For the Lord grants wisdom, etc." (Prov. 2:6). [If] someone wants property, He gives him property. As it says in Scripture, "Riches and honors are Yours to dispense, etc." (1 Chron. 29:12).

5.     A.     "Awesome in splendor" (Exod. 15:11):

        B.     For the way of God is not like the way of a human being. The fear of a human being is greater for those at a distance than for those close by.

        C.     However, it is not so with He who spoke, and the world came into being.

        D.     Rather, the fear of Him is greater for those close by than for those at a distance. As it says in Scripture, "... it stormed fiercely around Him" (Ps. 50:3). And Scripture says, "... a God greatly dreaded in the council of holy beings, etc." (Ps. 89:8). And Scripture says, "Dominion and dread are with Him, etc." (Job 25:2). And Scripture says, "Through those near to Me, I show Myself holy" (Lev. 10:3).

6.     A.     "... working wonders" (Exod. 15:11):

        B.     For the way of God is not like the way of a human being. A human being builds the bottom [of a building] first, and afterward the top.

        C.     However, it is not so with He who spoke, and the world came into being.

        D.     Rather, He builds the top first, and afterward he builds the bottom. As it says in Scripture, "In the beginning, God created (the heavens and the earth), etc." (Gen. 1:1).

7.     A.     Another interpretation:

        B.     "... working wonders" (Exod. 15:11):

        C.     For the way of God is not like the way of a human being. When a human being lays roofing beams, he lays beams with wood, stones, and mortar.

        D.     However, it is not so with He who spoke, and the world came into being. Rather, when He laid the beams of His world, He only laid beams with water. As it says in Scripture, "He set the rafters of His lofts in the waters, etc." (Ps. 104:3).

8.     A.     Another interpretation:

        B.     "... working wonders" (Exod. 15:11):

        C.     For the way of God is not like the way of a human being. A human being cannot fashion a creature from water.

| | |
|---|---|
| B/A 3 | ד״א ♦ שלא כמדת ‹בשר ודם מדת המקום› בשר ודם אין |
| C | יכול לשמוע משני בני אדם כאחד ♦ אבל מי שאמר |
| D | והיה העולם אינו כן ♦ אלא שומע תפלה וגומ׳ (תה׳ סה |
| B/A 4 | ג). ♦ ד״א ♦ שלא כמדת בשר ודם מדת המק׳ פועל עושה |
| | מלאכה אצל בעל הבית זורע עמו וחורש עמו מנכש |
| C | מטבע אחד נותן לו ♦ אבל מי שאמר והיה העולם אינו |
| D | כן ♦ אלא תאוב לבנים בנים נותן לו שנא׳ הנה נחלת ייי |
| | בנים וגומ׳ (תה׳ קכז ג) תאוב לחכמה חכמה נותן לו |
| | שנא׳ כי ייי יתן חכמה וגומ׳ (מש׳ ב ו). תאוב לנכסים |
| | נכסים נותן לו שנא׳ והעושר והכבוד מלפניך וגומ׳ |
| B/A 5 | (דה״א כט יב) ♦ נורא תהלות ♦ שלא כמדת בשר ודם |
| | מדת המקום בשר ודם מוראו על הרחוקים יתר מן |
| D/C | הקרובים ♦ אבל מי שאמר והיה העולם אינו כן ♦ אלא |
| | מוראו ‹על› הקרובים יתר מן הרחוקים שנא׳ |
| | וסביביו נשערה מאד (תה׳ נ ג) ואומ׳ אל נערץ בסוד |
| | קדושים רבה וגומ׳ (שם פט ח) ואומ׳ המשל ופחד |
| | עמו וגומ׳ (איוב כה ב) ואו׳ בקרובי אקדש (ויק׳ י ג) ♦ |
| B/A 6 | עושה פלא ♦ שלא כמדת בשר ודם מדת המקום בשר |
| | ודם בונה תחתון ואחר כך בונה עליון. ♦ אבל מי שאמר |
| C | והיה העולם אינו כן ♦ אלא בונה עליון ואחר כך בונה |
| D | תחתון שנאמ׳ בראשית ברא אלהים וגומ׳ (בר׳ א א). ♦ |
| C/B/A 7 | ד״א ♦ עושה פלא ♦ שלא כמדת בשר ודם מדת המק׳ |
| D | בשר ודם כשהוא מקרה מקרה בעצים ובאבנים ובעפר. ♦ אבל |
| | מי שאמר והיה העולם אינו כן אלא כשהוא מקרה עולמו |
| | אין מקרה אלא במים שנא׳ המקרה במים עליותיו וגומ׳ |
| C/B/A 8 | (תה׳ קד ג). ♦ ד״א ♦ עושה פלא ♦ שלא כמדת בשר |
| | ודם מדת המק׳ בשר ודם אין יכול לצור צורה במים ♦ |

        D.     However, it is not so with He who spoke, and the world came into being. Rather, He fashioned a creature from water. As it says in Scripture, "God said, 'Let the waters bring forth swarms (of living creatures), etc.'" (Gen. 1:20).

9.       A.     Another interpretation:

        B.     "... working wonders" (Exod. 15:11):

        C.     For the way of God is not like the way of a human being. A human being cannot fashion a creature in darkness.

        D.     However, it is not so with God. Rather, He fashioned a creature in darkness. As it says in Scripture, "... when I was shaped in a hidden place, knit together in the recesses of the earth" (Ps. 139:15).

10.      A.     Another interpretation:

        B.     "... working wonders" (Exod. 15:11):

[94]    C.     For the way of God is not like the way of a human being. When a human being fashions a form, he begins from its head, or its feet, or from one of its limbs.

        D.     However, it is not so with God. Rather, when He fashions a form, He fashions it [all] at once. As it says in Scripture, "Because He forms it all" (Jer. 10:16). And Scripture says, "There is no rock[45] like our God" (1 Sam. 2:2), [meaning,] there is no fashioner[46] like our God.

11.      A.     Another interpretation:

        B.     "... working wonders" (Exod. 15:11):

        C.     For the way of God is not like the way of a human being. A human being goes to a sculptor [and] says to him, "Make me a bust of [my] father!" He says to him, "Bring me your father and stand him in front of me, or bring me his likeness, and I'll make it for you according to its likeness!"

        D.     However, it is not so with He who spoke, and the world came into being. Rather, from [only one] drop of semen, He gives someone a son who looks like the image of his father!

## XXXIV:III[47]

1.       A.     Another interpretation:

        B.     "... working wonders" (Exod. 15:11):

        C.     He did [wonders] for [the] forefathers, and He does [wonders] for us in each and every generation.

        D.     And thus Scripture states, "I praise You, for I am awesomely, wondrously made, etc." (Ps. 139:14). And Scripture says, "You, O Lord my God, have done many things, etc." (Ps. 40:6).

2.       A.     Another interpretation:

        B.     "... working wonders" (Exod. 15:11):

        C.     "He worked wonders" is not written here. Rather, "He [is] working wonders."

        D.     [Including] the time to come.

        E.     And thus Scripture states, "Assuredly, a time is coming—declares the Lord—when it shall no more be said, 'As the Lord lives (who brought the Israelites out of the Land of Egypt,'

---

[45] Hebrew: *tzur*—צור.

[46] Hebrew: *tzayyar*—צייר.

[47] Compare XXXIV:III:1.A–3.F with parallel material (in different editorial order, however,) in *Mekhilta de-Rabbi Ishmael*, Shirata (H/R, 144:13–22; Laut., vol. 2, 66:90–67:106; Neus., XXXIII:I:.16.A–18.E).

| | | |
|---|---|---|
| אבל מי שאמר והיה העולם אינו כן אלא | D | |
| צר צורה במים שנא׳ ויאמר אלקים ישרצו המים | | |
| וגומ׳ (בר׳ א כ). ♦ ד״א ♦ עושה פלא ♦ שלא | C/B/A | 9 |
| כמדת בשר ודם מדת המק׳ בשר ודם אין יכול לצור | | |
| צורה באפילה ♦ אבל המקום אינו כן אלא יצר צורה | D | |
| באפילה שנא׳ אשר עושיתי בסתר רקמתי בתחתיות | | |
| ארץ (תה׳ קלט טו). ♦ ד״א ♦ עושה פלא ♦ שלא כמדת בשר | C/B/A | 10 |
| ודם מדת המקום בשר ודם כשהוא צר צורה מתחיל | | |
| מראשה או מרגלה או מאחד מאבריה ♦ אבל המקום | D | |
| ב״ה אינו כן אלא כשהוא צר צורה צר הכל כאחד | | |
| שנא׳ כי יוצר הכל הוא (ירמ׳ י טז) ואומ׳ ואין צור | | |
| כאלקינו (ש״א ב ב) אין צייר כאלקים. ♦ ד״א ♦ עושה פלא ♦ | B/A | 11 |
| שלא כמדת בשר ודם מדת המקום בשר ודם הולך | C | |
| אצל עושה צלמין אומ׳ לו עשה לי צורתו שלאבה | | |
| אומ׳ לו הבא לי אביך והעמידו לפני או הביא לי | | |
| דיוקנו ואעשה לך כצורתה. ♦ אבל מי שאמר והיה | D | |
| העולם אינו כן אלא נותן לאדם זה בן מטיפה של | | |
| מים דומה לצורתו של אביו. ♦ | | |

XXXIV:III

| | | |
|---|---|---|
| ד״א ♦ עושה פלא ♦ עשה עם אבות ועושה | C/B/A | 1 |
| עמנו בכל דור ודור ♦ וכן הוא <או׳> אודך על כי | D | |
| נוראות נפלאתי וגומ׳ (תה׳ קלט יד) ואומ׳ רבות עשית | | |
| אתה ייי אלקי וגומ׳ (שם מ ו). ♦ ד״א ♦ ע(ו)שה פלא ♦ | B/A | 2 |
| אין כת׳ כן אלא עושה פלא ♦ לעתיד לבוא ♦ וכן הוא אמ׳ | E/D/C | |
| לכן הנה ימים באים נאם ייי לא יאמר עוד חי ייי וגומ׳ | | |

but rather, 'As the Lord lives who brought the Israelites out of the northland, and out of all the lands to which He had banished them), etc.'" (Jer. 16:14).

F.   They told a parable: To what is the matter alike?

G.   It is like one who had wanted sons. A daughter was born to him, and he began swearing by the life of the daughter. Afterward, a son was born to him. He ceased [swearing by the] daughter and began swearing by the life of the son.

H.   And they told another parable: To what is the matter alike?[48]

I.   To one who was walking along the way, and encountered a wolf and was saved from it. He would recount the miracles that were done for him with the wolf. Afterward, he encountered a lion, and was saved from it. And he would recount the miracles that were done for him with the lion. Afterward, he encountered a snake and was rescued from it. He would recount the miracles that were done for him with the snake.

J.   Thus, it is said, "Assuredly, a time is coming—declares the Lord—when it shall no more be said, etc." (Jer. 16:14).

3.   A.   Another interpretation:

B.   "... working wonders" (Exod. 15:11):

C.   He did [wonders] for [the] forefathers, and He will do [wonders] with the children.

D.   And thus Scripture states, "I will show him wondrous deeds, as in the days when you left from the Land of Egypt" (Mic. 7:15).

E.   [Meaning,] I will show you what I did not show the ancestors. Wonders with which I did not amaze the forefathers. For [the miracles] that I will perform with the children are not like the miracles and mighty acts that I performed for the forefathers. Rather, [wonders with which] I did not amaze the forefathers.

[95]   F.   And thus Scripture states, "Who works great marvels" (Ps. 136:4). Wonders that He did not perform for the forefathers. As it says in Scripture, "Who works great marvels alone" (Ps. 136:4). And Scripture says, "Blessed is the Lord God, God of Israel (who does wondrous things alone)" (Ps. 72:18).

*Chapter Thirty-Five*

(Textual Source: Ms. Firkovich II A 268)

XXXV:I[49]

1.   A.   "You put out Your right hand, the earth swallowed them" (Exod. 15:12):

B.   Scripture tells that all souls are in the palm of He who spoke, and the world came into being.

C.   As it says in Scripture, "In His hand is every living soul, etc." (Job. 12:10).

2.   A.   Upon what merit was a burial given to them?

B.   Because he[50] said, "The Lord is in the right, and I and my people are in the wrong" (Exod. 9:27).

C.   The Holy One, blessed be He, said to them, "You righteously [accepted] the judgment upon yourselves. [Therefore,] I shall give you a burial!"

---

[48] Compare 2.H–I with t. Berachot 1:11, y. Berachot 4a (Neus., 1:5:VIII.G–I), and b. Berachot 13a (I:Tractate Berakhot:1:5:I).
[49] Compare XXXV:I:1.A–V:7.K with *Mekhilta de-Rabbi Ishmael*, Shirata (H/R, 145:1–149:3; Laut., vol. 2, 67:1–76:126; Neus., XXXIV:I:1.A–27.G).
[50] I.e., Pharaoh.

| | | |
|---|---|---|
| (ירמ׳ טז יד) ◆ מושלו משל למה הדבר דומה ◆ לאחד | G/F | |

שהיה תאוב לבנים נולדה לו בת התחיל נודר בחיי
הבת ואחר כך נולד לו בן הניח הבת ואתחיל נודר
בחיי הבן. ◆ ועוד מושלו משל למה הדבר דומה ◆ לאחד

| | I/H |
|---|---|

שהיה מהלך בדרך ופגע בו זאב וניצל ממנו והיה
מתנא בנסים שנעשו [שעשה לו בזאב ואחר כך פגע
בו ארי וניצל ממנו והיה מתנא בנסים שנעשו] לו
בארי ואחר כך פגע בו נחש והוצל מידו והיה מתנא

| | | |
|---|---|---|
| בנסים שנעשו לו בנחש ◆ לכך נאמר הנה ימים באים | J | |
| נאם ייי ולא יאמר עוד וגומ׳ (שם). ◆ ד״א ◆ עושה פלא ◆ | B/A | 3 |
| עשה עם אבות ועתיד לעשות עם הבנים ◆ וכן הוא אומ׳ | D/C | |

כימי צאתך מארץ מצ׳ אראנו נפלאות (מיכה ז טו). ◆

| | | |
|---|---|---|
| אראך מה שלא הראיתי לאבות נפלאות מה שלא | E | |

הפלאתי לאבות שלא כנסין וגבורות שעשיתי לאבות
עתיד אני לעשות עם בנים אלא מה שלא הפלאתי

| | |
|---|---|
| לאבות ◆ וכן הוא אומ׳ לעשה נפלאות ונפלאי נפלאים | F |

מה שלא עש׳ לאבות שנא׳ לעושה נפלאות גדולות
לבדו (תה׳ קלו ד) ואומ׳ ברוך ייי אלקים אלקי יש׳
(שם עב יח). סל׳ פסו׳ ◆

| | |
|---|---|
| | XXXV:I |

| | | |
|---|---|---|
| נטית ימינך תבלעמו ארץ ◆ מגיד הכת׳ שכל הנפשות | B/A | 1 |
| בכף מי שאמר והיה העולם ◆ אשר בידו נפש כל חי | C | |
| וגומ׳ (איוב יב י) ◆ בזכות מה ניתן להן קבורה ◆ שאמ׳ | B/A | 2 |
| ייי הצדיק ואני ועמי הרשעים (שמ׳ ט כז). ◆ אמ׳ להן | C | |

הקב״ה אתם צדקתם עליכם את הדין אני אתן לכן קבורה ◆

D. As it says in Scripture, "You put out Your right hand. The earth swallowed them" (Exod. 15:12).

3.    A. Because the sea threw them to the dry land, and the dry land threw them to the sea, the sea said to the dry land, "Take your troops!" and the dry land said to the sea, "Take your troops!"

B. The dry land said to it, "If, at the time when I only accepted the blood of Abel—a single person—it was said concerning him: 'Therefore you shall be more cursed (than the ground), etc.' (Gen. 4:11), [then] now how can I accept the blood of this entire multitude?"

C. [This could not happen] until the Holy One, blessed be He, swore to it: "I won't place you in judgment!"

D. As it says in Scripture, "You put out Your right hand, etc." (Exod. 15:12).

E. "Right hand" only means an oath. As it says in Scripture, "The Lord has sworn by His right hand, etc." (Isa. 62:8).

4.    A. Another interpretation:

B. "You put out Your right hand" (Exod. 15:12):

C. Scripture tells that when the Holy One, blessed be He, stretches out His hand, the wicked flee from the world.

D. It is written, "And He will stretch out His arm against the north and destroy Assyria, etc." (Zeph. 2:13). And Scripture says, "I will stretch out My hand against the Philistines, etc." (Ezek. 25:16). And Scripture says, "I will stretch out My hand against Judah, etc." (Zeph. 1:4).

E. They told a parable: To what is the matter alike?

F. It is like eggs placed in a person's hand. If he stretches open his hand on them, immediately they fall and are broken.

G. Likewise, when God stretches out His hand, "... the helper shall trip, and the helped one shall fall, and both shall perish together" (Isa. 31:3).

## XXXV:II

1.    A. "In Your love You led (the people You redeemed)" (Exod. 15:13):

B. An act of love You performed for us, [even though] we had no [meritorious] deeds!

C. In accordance with what is said in Scripture, "I will recount the kind acts of the Lord, the praises of the Lord, etc." (Isa. 63:7). And Scripture says, "I will sing of the Lord's steadfast love forever, etc." (Ps. 89:2). And Scripture says, "Your steadfast love, O Lord, fills the earth, etc." (Ps. 119:64). And Scripture says, "But the Lord's steadfast love is for all eternity, etc." (Ps. 103:17). And Scripture says, "I declare: Your steadfast, etc." (Ps. 89:3).

2.    A. "... the people" (Exod. 15:13):

B. Even though the entire world is Yours, You have no people other than Israel!

C. As it says in Scripture, "The people I formed for Myself" (Isa. 43:21).

3.    A. Rabbi sat and interpreted that [each] Israelite woman gave birth to 600,000 at a time!

[96]   B. His disciples responded to him at that moment saying, "Who is greater—a righteous man or all mankind?"

C. He said to them, "A righteous man."

| | | |
|---|---|---|
| D | A 3 | שנ' נטית ימינך תבלעמו ארץ ◆ לפי שהיה |
| | | הים זורקן ליבשה ויבשה זורקתן לים הים אום' |
| | | ליבשה קבלי אוכלוסיך ויבשה אום' לים קבל |
| B | | אוכלוסיך ◆ אמ' לו יבשה ומה אם בשעה שלא קבלתי |
| | | אלא דם הבל יחידי נאמ' בו ועתה ארור אתה וגומ' |
| | | (בר' ד יא) עכשיו היאך אני יכולה לקבל דם כל |
| C | | ההמון הזה ◆ עד שנשבע לה הקב"ה שאין אני מעמידך |
| E/D | | בדין ◆ שנא' נטית ימינך וגומ' ◆ אין ימין אלא שבועה |
| B/A | 4 | שנא' נשבע ייי בימינו וגומ' (ישע' סב ח). ◆ ד"א ◆ נטית |
| C | | ימינך ◆ מגיד הכת' שכשהק' מטה את ידו הרשעים |
| D | | פונין מן העולם ◆ כת' ויט ידו על צפון ויאבד את אשור |
| | | וגומ' (צפ' ב יג) ואומ' ונטיתי ידי <על> פלשתים וגומ' |
| | | (יחז' כה טז) ואומ' הנני נוטה ידי על יהודה וגומ' (צפ' |
| F/E | | א ד). ◆ מושלו משל למה הדבר דומה ◆ לבצים שנתונות |
| | | ביד אדם שאם מטה ידו מהם מיד נופלות |
| G | | ומשתברות ◆ כך כשהמקום מטה ידו כשל עוזר ונפל |
| | | עזור יחדו כלם יכליון (ישע' לא ג). סל' פסו' ◆ |

XXXV:II

| | | |
|---|---|---|
| B/A | 1 | נחית בחסדך. ◆ חסד שעשית עמנו לא היה בידנו |
| C | | מעשים ◆ כעניין שנא' חסד<י> ייי אזכיר תהלות ייי וגומ' |
| | | (שם סג ז) ואומ' חסדי ייי עולם אשירה וגומ' (תה' פט ב) |
| | | ואמ' חסדך ייי מלאה הארץ וגומ' (שם קיט סד) ואומ' |
| | | וחסד ייי מעולם עד עולם וגומ' (שם קג יז) ואומ' כי אמרתי |
| B/A | 2 | עולם חסד וגומ' (שם פט ג). ◆ עם זו ◆ אף על פי שכל |
| C | | העולם כולו שלך הוא אין לך עם אלא יש' ◆ שנא' עם זו |
| A | 3 | יצרתי לי (ישע' מג כא) ◆ וכבר היה ר' יושב ודורש שילדה אשה |
| B | | מיש' רבוא ששים בכרס אחת ◆ ונענו תלמידיו באותה |
| C | | השעה ואמרו מי גדול צדיק או כל אדם ◆ אמ' להן צדיק ◆ |

D.  They said to him, "How?"

E.  He said to them, "We find that when Jochebed, the mother of Moses, gave birth to Moses, he was equal to all of Israel!

F.  "And thus we find that Moses was equal to all of Israel at the moment when they sang the song. As it says in Scripture, 'Then Moses and the Israelites sang' (Exod. 15:1).

G.  "[And Scripture says,] 'And there never again arose a prophet in Israel like Moses, etc.' (Deut. 34:10). And Scripture says, 'Just as the Lord had commanded His servant Moses, etc.' (Josh. 11:15). And Scripture says, 'There are sixty queens, etc.,' and it says, '... only one is my dove, my perfect one, etc.' (Song 6:8–9)."

4.  A.  "In Your strength You guide them (to Your holy abode)" (Exod. 15:13):

B.  You guide us with power, [because] "strength" means only power.

C.  As it says in Scripture, "O Lord, my power and my stronghold, etc." (Jer. 16:19). [And Scripture says,] "The Lord is my power and my shield, etc." (Ps. 28:7).

5.  A.  Another interpretation:

B.  "In Your strength You guide them" (Exod. 15:13):

C.  [You guide them] by the merit of Torah, which they were about to receive!

D.  As it says in Scripture, "The Lord will grant strength to His people, etc." (Ps. 29:11). And Scripture says, "The strength of a king who loves justice, etc." (Ps. 99:4).

6.  A.  Another interpretation:

B.  "In Your strength You guide them" (Exod. 15:13):

C.  [You guide them] by the merit of the House of David, which would receive the monarchy.

D.  As it says in Scripture, "O Lord, (the king) rejoices in Your strength, etc." (Ps. 21:2). And Scripture says, "The Lord is their strength; (He is a stronghold for the deliverance of His anointed,) etc." (Ps. 28:8). And Scripture says, "He will give strength to His king, etc." (1 Sam. 2:10).

7.  A.  "... to Your holy abode" (Exod. 15:13):

B.  [You guide them] by the merit of the Temple, which they would build.

C.  As it says in Scripture, "... to Your holy abode" (Exod. 15:13). And Scripture says, "... and desolated His home" (Ps. 79:7). And Scripture says, "When you gaze upon Zion, etc." (Isa. 33:20).

## XXXV:III

1.  A.  "The people hear, they tremble" (Exod. 15:14):

B.  When they heard that Pharaoh and his army were destroyed in the sea, and that the kingdom of Egypt was destroyed, and [heard] the judgments that were made against their idolatry, they began to tremble.

2.  A.  Another interpretation:

B.  When they heard that the Holy One, blessed be He, raised the horn of Israel, they began to get angry.

C.  God said to them, "How many kings arose from you without My children becoming angry? As it says in Scripture, 'These are the kings who reigned in the land of Edom, etc.' (Gen. 36:31). How many rulers arose from you without My children becoming angry? [As it says in Scripture,] 'The clans Lotan, Shobal, etc.' (Gen. 36:29).

| | |
|---|---|
| E/D | אמרו לו במה • אמ' להן מצינו שילדה יוכבד אמו של |
| F | משה את משה ששקול כנגד כל יש' • וכין מצינו שהיה משה |
| | שקול ככל יש' בשעה שאמ' שירה שנא' אז ישיר משה |
| G | ובני יש' (שמ' טו א). • ולא קם נביא עוד ביישר' כמשה וגומ' |
| | (דב' לד י) ואומ' ככל אשר צוה יי את משה עבדו וגומ' |
| | (יהו' יא טו) ואומ' ששים המה מלכות וגו' ואומ' אחת |
| A  4 | היא יונתי תמתי וגומ' (שה"ש ו ח - ט). • נהלת בעזך. • |
| C/B | נהלתנו בתוקף אין עזי אלא תוקף • שנא' ייי עזי ומעזי |
| | וגומ' (ירמ' טז יט) ואומ' ייי עזי ומגני וגומ' (תה' כח ז) • |
| D/C/B/A  5 | ד"א • נהלת בעזך • בזכות תורה שעתידין לקבל • שנא' ייי |
| | עוז יתן וגומ' (שם כט יא) ואומ' ועוז מלך משפט וגומ' |
| C/B/A  6 | (תה' צט ד). • ד"א • נהלת בעזך • בזכות בית דוד שעתידין |
| D | לקבל את המלכות (וגומ') • שנא' ייי בעזך וגומ' (שם כא |
| | ב) ואומ' ייי עז למו וגו' (שם כח ח) ואומ' ויתן עוז |
| B/A  7 | לעמו וגומ' (ש"א ב י) • אל נוה קדשך • בזכות בית |
| C | המקדש] שעתידין לבנות • שנא' אל נוה קדשך. ואומ' |
| | ואת נוהו השמו (תה' עט ז) ואו' חזה ציון וגומ' (ישע' |
| | לג כ). סל' פסו' • |

XXXV:III

| | |
|---|---|
| B/A  1 | שמעו עמים ירגזון • כיון ששמעו שאבד פרעה |
| | וחילו בים ואבדה מלכות מצ' ושפטים שנעשו |
| B/A  2 | בעבודה זרה שלהם <התחילו מתרגזין. • ד"א • כיון |
| | ששמעו שהקב"ה מגביה קרנם שליש> התחילו |
| C | כועסין • אמ' להן המקום כמה מלכים עמדו מכם ולא |
| | רגזו בני ואלה המלכים אשר מלכו בארץ אדום וגומ' |
| | (בר' לו לא) כמה שלטונות עמדו מכם ולא כעסו |
| | בני אלוף לוטן אלוף שובל וגומ' (שם כט) • |

[97]    D.    "Now you are becoming angry? I'll show you anger, for which there is no conciliation with the Lord!—'The Lord is king, people tremble, etc.' (Ps. 99:1)."

3.    A.    "Agony grips the dwellers in Philistia" (Exod. 15:14):

    B.    They[51] said, "Now they are coming to take the vengeance of Ephraim, their forefathers!"

    C.    As it says in Scripture, "Like the Ephraimite bowmen, etc." (Ps. 78:9).

4.    A.    Another interpretation:

    B.    "Agony grips the dwellers in Philistia" (Exod. 15:14):

    C.    They said, "They have no other way [to go] except over us! Now they are coming and will seize our property and destroy our land!"

## XXXV:IV

1.    A.    "Now the clans of Edom are dismayed" (Exod. 15:15):

    B.    If you say [they were dismayed] because [they thought] they were coming to inherit their land, behold it has already been said in Scripture, "And charge the people as follows ... Do not provoke them (because I will not give you of their land), etc." (Deut. 2:4–5).

    C.    Rather, [it was] because of taxes [they thought the Israelites might impose].

2.    A.    [Another interpretation:]

    B.    They said, "Now they are coming to incite hatred between our father and their father!"

    C.    As it says in Scripture, "Now Esau harbored a grudge against Jacob, etc." (Gen. 27:41).

3.    A.    "The tribes of Moab, (trembling grips them)" (Exod. 15:15):

    B.    If you say [they trembled] because [they thought] they were coming to inherit their land, behold it has already been said in Scripture, "Do not harass the Moabites" (Deut. 2:9).

    C.    Rather, [it was] because of taxes [they thought the Israelites might impose].

4.    A.    Another interpretation:

    B.    They said, "Now they are coming to incite hatred between our father and their father!"

    C.    [As it says in Scripture,] "And there was quarreling between the herdsmen of Abram (and those of Lot's cattle), etc." (Gen. 13:7).

5.    A.    "All the dwellers of Canaan are aghast" (Exod. 15:15):

    B.    When they heard that the Holy One, blessed be He, said to Moses, "In the towns of the latter peoples, however, (which the Lord your God is giving you as a heritage, you shall not let a soul remain alive,) etc." (Deut. 20:16), they began to be aghast.

    C.    They[52] said [nonetheless boastfully] to each other, "We are not afraid." But, on account of their wealth and their property, they began to behave.

    D.    [But the dwellers of Canaan said,] "However, they are only coming to us, in order to destroy us!" So they began to be aghast.

    E.    And "aghast"[53] means only "melting away," as it says in Scripture, "Earth and all its inhabitants dissolve,[54] etc." (Ps. 75:4). And Scripture says, "Thus hearts shall melt[55] and many shall fall" (Ezek. 21:20).

---

[51] I.e., the dwellers in Philistia.

[52] I.e., Edom and Moab.

[53] Hebrew: namogu—נמגו.

| | | |
|---|---|---|
| D | | עכשיו אתם כועסין אני נותן לכם כעס שאין בו רצון ייי מלך |
| 3 | A | ירגזו עמים וגומ' (תה' צט א). ◆ חיל אחז ישבי פלשת ◆ |
| | C/B | אמרו עכשיו הן באין לגבות עיוורותן של אפרים אביהם ◆ שנ' |
| 4 | A | בני אפרים נושקי רומי קשת וגומ' (שם עח ט). ◆ ד"א ◆ |
| | C/B | חיל אחז ישבי פלשת ◆ אמרו אין להן דרך אלא עלינו |

(אמ') עכשיו הן באין ובוזזין את נכסינו ומחריבין את
ארצינו. סל' פסו' ◆

XXXV:IV

| | | |
|---|---|---|
| 1 | B/A | אז נבהלו אלופי אדום ◆ אם תאמר שהן באין |
| | | לירש את ארצם הרי כבר נאמ' ואת העם צו לאמר |
| | C | וגומ'. אל תתגרו בם וגומ' (דב' ב ד - ה) ◆ אלא מפני |
| 2 | B/A | ארונינאות ◆ אמרו עכשיו הן באין לגבות שנאה שבין |
| | C | אבינו לאביהן ◆ וישטם עשו את יעקב וגומ' (בר' כז |
| 3 | B/A | מא). ◆ אילי מואב ◆ אם תאמר שהן באין לירש את |
| | | ארצם הרי כבר נאמר אל תצר את מואב (דב' ב ט) ◆ |
| C | B/A 4 | אלא מפני ארונונאות. ◆ ד"א ◆ אמרו עכשיו הן באין לגבות |
| | C | מריבה שבין אבינו לאביהן ◆ ויהי ריב בין רועה מקנה |
| 5 | B/A | אברם וגומ' (בר' יג ז). ◆ נמוגו כל יושבי כנען ◆ כיון |
| | | ששמעו שאמ' לו הקב"ה למשה רק מערי העמים |
| | C | האלה וגומ' (דב' כ טז) התחילו נמוגים ◆ אמרו אלו |
| | | לאלו אין אנו מתיראין אלא מפני ההמון ומפני |
| | D | נכסיהן התחילו נמוסין ◆ אבל אין באין [עלינו אלא] |
| | E | לכלותינו התחילו נמוגים ◆ ואין נמיגה אלא המסאה |

שנא' נמוגים ארץ וכל יושביה וגומ' (תה' עה ד)
ואומ' למען למוג לב והרבה המכש' (יחז' כא כ)
◆

---

[54] Hebrew: *nemogim*—נמוגים.
[55] Hebrew: *lamug*—למוג.

F.    Thus [Scripture says], "All the dwellers of Canaan are aghast" (Exod. 15:15).

XXXV:V

1.    A.    "Terror and dread descend upon them" (Exod. 15:16):

B.    Terror on those near, and dread on those far away.

C.    And thus Scripture says, "When all the kings of the Amorites heard, etc." (Josh. 5:1).

2.    A.    "Through the might of Your arm they are still as stone" (Exod. 15:16):

[98]    B.    When Israel crossed the sea, Amalek and all the nations of the world gathered to wage war with them. At that moment, Moses prayed and they all were struck dumb like a stone.

C.    As it says in Scripture, "Through the might of Your arm, they are still as stone" (Exod. 15:16).

3.    A.    Another interpretation:

B.    "Through the might of Your arm" (Exod. 15:16):

C.    When the spies of Israel entered the land, anyone who might have wanted to say, "These are the spies of Israel," was struck dumb like a stone.

D.    Thus it is said, "Through the might of Your arm they are still as stone" (Exod. 15:16).

4.    A.    Another interpretation:

B.    "Through the might of Your arm" (Exod. 15:16):

C.    When Israel crossed the Jordan, all the kings of Canaan were gathered to wage war with them.

D.    As it says in Scripture, "When the news reached King Jabin of Hazor, etc." (Josh. 11:1), [continuing] until "... together at the Waters of Merom to give battle to Israel" (Josh. 11:5).

E.    At that moment, Joshua prayed and they all were struck dumb like a stone.

F.    Thus it is said, "Through the might of Your arm they are still as stone" (Exod. 15:16).

5.    A.    "Until Your people cross over, O Lord" (Exod. 15:16):

B.    Until they cross the sea. Until they cross the Jordan. Until they cross the wadis of Arnon.

6.    A.    "(Until) this people whom You have ransomed (cross over)" (Exod. 15:16):

B.    [As it says in Scripture,] "The people I formed for Myself" (Isa. 43:21).

7.    A.    "... You have ransomed"[56] (Exod. 15:16):

B.    The Land of Israel is called an acquisition.

C.    As it says in Scripture, "Who acquires heaven and earth" (Gen. 14:19).

D.    The Torah is called an acquisition.

E.    As it says in Scripture, "The Lord acquired me at the beginning of His way, etc." (Prov. 8:22).

F.    Israel is called an acquisition.

G.    As it says in Scripture, "The people I acquired for Myself, etc." (Isa. 43:21).

H.    The Temple is called an acquisition.

---

[56] Or: "have acquired."

<לכך> נמוגו כל יושבי כנען. סל' פסוק' ◆    F

XXXV:V

תפול עליהם אימתה ופחד ◆ אימתה על הקרובים.    B/A    1

ופחד על הרחוקים ◆ וכן הוא אומ' ויהי כשמוע כל    C

מלכי האמורי וגומ' (יהו' ה א). ◆ בגדול זרועך ידמו    A    2

כאבן ◆ כיון שעברו יש' את הים כינס עליהן עמלך (ו)וכל    B

מלכי אומות העולם לבוא להלחם עמהן נתפלל משה

באותה שעה ודממו כולן כאבן ◆ שנא' בגדל זרועך ידמו    C

כאבן. ◆ ד"א ◆ בגדול זרועך ◆ כיון שנכנסו מרגלי יש' לארץ    C/B/A    3

כל מי שרוצה לאמר אלו מרגלי יש' היו דומין כאבן ◆

לכך נאמר בגדול זרועך ידמו כאבן. ◆ ד"א ◆ בגדל זרועך    B/A    4    D

כיון שעברו יש' את הירדן נתכנסו עליהם מלכי כנען    C

לבוא להלחם עמהן ◆ שנא' ויהי כשמע יבין מלך חצור    D

וגומ' (יהו' יא א) עד יחדו על מי מרום להלחם עם יש'

(שם ה). ◆ נתפלל יהושע באותה השעה ודממו כולן    E

כאבן ◆ לכך נאמר: בגדול זרועך ידמו כאבן. ◆ עד יעבור    A    5    F

עמך ייי. ◆ עד יעבור את הים עד יעבור את הירדן עד יעבור    B

את נחל ארנון. ◆ עם זו ◆ עם זו יצרתי לי (ישע' מג כא) ◆    B/A    6

קנית ◆ ארץ ישראל נקראת קנין ◆ שנא' קונה שמים וארץ (בר'    C/B/A    7

יד יט) ◆ תורה נקראת קנין ◆ שנא' ייי קנני ראשית דרכו    E/D

וגומ' (מש' ח כב) ◆ ישראל נקראו קנין ◆ שנא' עם זו    G/F

יצרתי לי וגומ' (ישע' מג כא) ◆ בית המקדש נקרא קנין ◆    H

I. As it says in Scripture, "He brought them to His holy hill, etc." (Ps. 78:54).

J. Let Israel, who is called an acquisition, enter the Land of Israel, which is called an acquisition, and build the Temple, which is called an acquisition, by the merit of Torah, which is called an acquisition.

K. Thus is it said, "... this people whom You have ransomed" (Exod. 15:16).

*Chapter Thirty-Six*

(Textual Source: Ms. Firkovich II A 268)

XXXVI:I[57]

1. A. "You will bring them and plant them (in Your own mountain)" (Exod. 15:17):

B. The forefathers prophesied, but did not know what they prophesied!

C. "You will bring us and plant us" is not written here. Rather, "You will bring them and plant them."

D. [Meaning,] the children will enter, but the parents will not.

E. And thus Scripture states, "If you do not know, O fairest of women, (go follow the tracks of the sheep, and graze your kids,) etc." (Song 1:8).

F. [Meaning,] the kids enter, but the goats do not enter.

2. A. Another interpretation:

B. "You will bring them and plant them" (Exod. 15:17):

C. Like[58] a vineyard, which is planted row by row.

D. And thus Scripture states, "... from the eastern border to the western border: Dan—one [tribe], etc." (Ezek. 48:1).

3. A. "You will bring them and plant them" (Exod. 15:17):

B. There will be no uprooting.

C. And thus Scripture states, "I will build them and not overthrow them, etc." (Jer. 24:6). [And Scripture says,] "And I will plant them upon their soil, etc." (Amos 9:15).

4. A. "... in Your own mountain" (Exod. 15:17):

B. In the mountain about which You promised us.

C. And thus Scripture states, "For only on My holy mountain, on the lofty mount of Israel, etc." (Ezek. 20:40).

5. A. Another interpretation:

[99] B. "... in Your own mountain" (Exod. 15:17).[59]

C. Torah is called an inheritance, [as it says in Scripture,] "... and from Mattanah to Nahaliel, etc." (Num. 21:19).[60]

D. Israel is called an inheritance, [as it says in Scripture,] "Yet they are Your people and Your inheritance, etc." (Deut. 9:29).

---

[57] Compare XXXVI:I:1.A–III:4.C with *Mekhilta de-Rabbi Ishmael*, Shirata (H/R, 149:5–152:2; Laut., vol. 2, 76:1–83:91; Neus., XXXV:I:1.A–II:10.B).

[58] Instead of the prepositional prefix "in," I translate here the prepositional prefix "like" as attested in *Midrash ha-Gadol*.

[59] Literally: "in the mountain of Your inheritance."

[60] A fuller explication of 5.C is found at b. Eruvin 54a (Neus., III.C:Erubin:5:1:I.35.F–36.E). The gist is that Torah (i.e., wisdom and learning) will be given as a "gift" (Hebrew: *mattanah*—מתנה) to whoever conducts himself with humility, and as such, it represents an "inheritance from God" (Hebrew: *nahal el*—נחל אל).

| | |
|---|---|
| I | שנא' ויביאם אל גבול קדשו וגומ' (תה' עח נד) ◆ |
| J | יבואו יש' שנקראו קנין לארץ <ישראל> שנקראת |
| | קנין ויבנו בית המקדש שנקרא קנין בזכות תורה |
| K | שנקראת קנין ◆ לכך נאמ' עם זו קנית. סל' פסו' ◆ |

| | | |
|---|---|---|
| | | XXXVI:I |
| 1 | B/A | תביאמו ותטעמו ◆ נתנבאו אבות ולא ידעו מה |
| | C | נתנבאו ◆ תביאנו ותטעינו אין כת' כן אלא תביאנו |
| | E/D | ותטעמו ◆ בנים נכנסין ואין אבות נכנסין ◆ וכן הוא אומ' |
| | | אם לא תדעי לך היפה בנשים וגומ' (שה"ש א ח) ◆ |
| F | 2 B/A | גדיים נכנסין ואין התיישים נכנסין. ◆ ד"א ◆ תביאמו |
| | D/C | ותטעמו ◆ בכרם שהוא נטוע שורות שורות ◆ וכן הוא |
| | | אומ' מפאת קדים ועד פאת ים דן אחד וגומ' (יחז' מח |
| 3 | C/B/A | א) ◆ ותטעימו ◆ נטיעה שאין לה נתישה ◆ וכן הוא אומ' |
| | | ובניתים ולא אהרוס וגומ' (ירמ' כד ו) ונטעתים על |
| 4 | B/A | אדמ' וגומ' (עמ' ט טו). ◆ בהר נחלתך ◆ בהר שהבטחתנו |
| | C | בו ◆ וכן הוא אומ' כי בהר קדשי בהר מרום יש' וגומ' |
| 5 | C/B/A | (יחז' כ מ). ◆ ד"א ◆ בהר נחלתך ◆ תורה נקראת נחלה |
| | D | וממתנה נחליאל וגומ' (במ' כא יט) ◆ יש' נקראו |
| | | נחלה והם עמך ונחלתך וגומ' (דב' ט כט) ◆ |

E. The Land of Israel is called an inheritance, [as it says in Scripture,] "When you enter the land (that the Lord your God is giving you as an inheritance), etc." (Deut. 26:1).

F. The Temple is called an inheritance, [as it says in Scripture,] "... in the mountain of Your inheritance" (Exod. 15:17).

G. Let Israel, who is called an inheritance, enter the Land of Israel, which is called an inheritance, and build the Temple, which is called an inheritance, by the merit of Torah, which is called an inheritance.

H. Thus it is said, "... in the mountain of Your inheritance" (Exod. 15:17).

6. A. "The place You made to dwell in, O Lord" (Exod. 15:17):

B. This is one of the places where the earthly throne corresponds precisely with the heavenly throne.

C. As it says in Scripture, "Thus said the Lord: The heaven is My throne, etc." (Isa. 66:1). And Scripture says, "O mortal, this is the place of My throne and the place for the soles of My feet, etc." (Ezek. 43:7). And Scripture says, "The Lord is in His holy palace; the Lord—His throne is in heaven, etc." (Ps. 11:4). [And Scripture says,] "I have now built for You a stately House, etc." (1 Kings 8:13).

7. A. So beloved is the Temple before He who spoke, and the world came into being, that the entire world was created only by the word of the Holy One, blessed be He.

B. As it says in Scripture, "By the word of the Lord the heavens were made, etc." (Ps. 33:6).

C. However, when He built the Temple, as if it were possible, it [required actual] work from Him!

D. [As it says in Scripture,] "The place You made to dwell in" (Exod. 15:17).

E. Woe to the nations of the world for what their ears are hearing! Because the Temple is called work before He who spoke, and the world came into being, and they destroyed it!

F. [As it says in Scripture,] "... how they cried, 'Strip her, strip her to her very foundations'" (Ps. 137:7).

G. What [else] does Scripture state?—"Prophesy all those things to them, and then say to them: The Lord roars from on high. He makes His voice heard from His holy dwelling ... Tumult has reached the ends of the earth, for the Lord has a case against (the nations), etc." (Jer. 25:30–31).

8. A. "The sanctuary, O Lord, which Your hands established" (Exod. 15:17):

B. So beloved is the Temple before He who spoke, and the world came into being, that the entire world was created only with one of His hands.

C. As it says in Scripture, "My own hand founded the earth, etc." (Isa. 48:13).

D. But when he built the Temple, He built it with His two hands.

E. As it says in Scripture, "The sanctuary, O Lord, which Your hands established" (Exod. 15:17).

## XXXVI:II

1. A. ["The Lord will reign for ever and ever" (Exod. 15:18):]

[100] B. When? When You build it with Your two hands!

C. [As it says in Scripture,] "The Lord rebuilds Jerusalem. He gathers in the exiles of Israel" (Ps. 147:2).

ארץ יש׳ נקראת נחלה והיה כי תבוא אל הארץ וגומ׳ (שם     E

כו א) ♦ בית המקדש נק׳ נחלה בהר נחלתך. ♦ יבואו יש׳     G/F

שנקראו נחלה לארץ ישראל שנקראת נחלה ויבנו בית

המקדש שנקרא נחלה בזכות תורה שנקרא‹ת› נחלה ♦ לכך     H

נאמר בהר נחלתך. ♦ מכון לשבתך פעלת יי♦י ♦ זה אחד מן     B/A    6

המקומות שכסא שלמטה מכוון כנגד כסא שלמעלה ♦

שנא׳ כה אמ׳ ייי השמים כסאי וגומ׳ (ישע׳ סו א) ואומ׳     C

בן אדם את מקום כסאי ואת מקום כפות רגלי וגומ׳

(יחז׳ מג ז) ייי בהיכל קדשו ייי בשמים כסאו וגומ׳

(תה׳ יא ד) ואומ׳ בנה בניתי בית זבול וגומ׳ (מ׳׳א ח יג)

♦ חביב בית המקדש לפני מי שאמר והיה העולם שכל     A    7

העולם כולו לא נברא אלא במאמרו של הקב׳׳ה ♦ שנא׳     B

בדבר ייי שמים נעשו וגומ׳ (תה׳ לג ו) ♦ אבל כשבנה בית     C

המקדש כיכול פעולה היא לפניו ♦ מכון לשבתך פעלת ♦     D

אוי להן לאומות העולם כמה ששומע‹ו›ת אזניהם     E

שבית המקדש קרוי פעולה לפני מי שאמר והיה

העולם והחריבו אותו ♦ האומרים ערו ערו עד היסוד     F

בה (שם קלז ז) ♦ מה הוא אומ׳ הנבא אליהם את     G

הדברים האלה ואמרת אלהם ייי ממרום ישאג

וממעון קדשו יתן קולו שאג ישאג וגומ׳ ואומ׳ בא

שאון עד קצה הארץ כי ריב לייי וגומ׳ (ירמ׳ כה ל -

לא). ♦ מקדש ייי כוננו ידיך ♦ חביב בית המקדש לפני מי     B/A    8

שאמר והיה העולם שכל העולם כולו לא נברא אלא

בידו אחת ♦ שנא׳ אף ידי יסדה ארץ וגומ׳ (ישע׳ מח יג) ♦     C

אבל כשבנה בית המקד׳ לא בנאו אלא בשתי ידיו ♦     D

שנא׳ מקדש ייי כוננו ידיך. ♦     E

    XXXVI:II

אמתי כשתבננו בשתי ידיך ♦ בונה     C/B/A    1

ירושלים ייי נדחי יש׳ יכנס (תה׳ קמז ב). ♦

D. They told a parable: To what is the matter alike?

E. It is like thieves who entered the king's palace, and seized some of his servants; they killed some of them, crucified some of them, burned some of them, and laid waste to the palace. After some time, the king came and sat in judgment over them. He seized some of them, killed some of them, crucified some of them, burned some of them, dwelled [once again] in his palace, and his kingship was acknowledged in the world.

2.    A. R. Yosi says, "If Israel had said [at the sea], 'The Lord is king for ever and ever' (Ps. 10:16), no nation or kingdom would have ruled over them.

B. "Rather [they said], 'The Lord will reign for ever and ever' (Exod. 15:18), [meaning,] in the time to come.

C. "Why?

D. "'Because the horses of Pharaoh ...' [continuing] until '... the waters of the sea' (Exod. 15:19).

E. "But we are with You, and are Your inheritance, the flock of Your pasture, the children of Abraham Your beloved, the offspring of Isaac Your favorite, the family of Jacob Your first-born. The vine that You removed from Egypt, and the nest that Your right hand planted.

F. "[As it says in Scripture,] '... but the Israelites marched on dry ground in the midst of the sea' (Exod. 15:19)."

## XXXVI:III

1.    A. "Then Miriam the prophetess, Aaron's sister, took (a timbrel in her hand)" (Exod. 15:20):

B. Where [do we learn] that Miriam prophesied?

C. Behold Scripture states, "The woman conceived and bore a son. And when she saw, etc." (Exod. 2:1).

D. She said to her father, "You will ultimately have a son who will redeem Israel from Egypt!"

E. Her father [eventually] answered her, saying, "[So, just] where is your prophecy?"

F. But, still, she stood by her prophecy, as it says in Scripture, "And his sister stood herself from a distance (to learn what would befall him)" (Exod. 2:4).

G. In every instance, "standing oneself" only means the Holy Spirit.

H. As it says in Scripture, "Call Joshua (and stand yourselves in the Tent of Meeting), etc." (Deut. 31:14). And Scripture says, "The Lord came, and stood there, etc." (1 Sam. 3:10). [And Scripture says,] "And the Lord was standing beside him, etc." (Gen. 28:13). [And Scripture says,] "I saw my Lord standing by the altar, etc." (Amos 9:1).

I. "... (stood herself) from a distance" (Exod. 2:4):

J. "From a distance" only means the Holy Spirit.

K. As it says in Scripture, "The Lord revealed Himself to me from a distance, etc." (Jer. 31:3).

L. "... to learn" (Exod. 2:4):

M. "To learn" means only the Holy Spirit.

N. As it says in Scripture, "For the land shall be filled with learning of the Lord, etc." (Isa. 11:9).

מושלו משל למה הדבר דומה ◆ ללסטין שנכנסו לתוך | E/D

פל(י)טין של מלך תפסו מעבדיו והרגו מהן וצלבו

מהן ושרפו מהן והחריבו פלטין שלו לאחר זמן בא

המלך וישב עליהן בדין תפס מהן והרג מהן וצלב

מהן ושרף מהן וישב פלטין שלו ונודע‹ה› מלכותו בעולם. ◆

ר׳ יוסי אומ׳ אילו אמרו יש׳ יײ מלך עולם ועד | A | 2

(תה׳ י טז) לא שלטה בהם אומה ומלכות ◆ אלא יײ | B

ימלוך לעולם ועד לעתיד לבוא. ◆ מפני מה ◆ כי בא סוס | D/C

פרעה וגומ׳ עד מי הים ‹...› ◆ אבל אנו עמך ונחלתך | E

וצאן מרעיתיך בני אברהם אוהבך זרע יצחק יחידיך

משפחת יעקב בכורך גפן שהסעתם ממצ׳ וכנה שנטעה

ימינך ◆ ובני ישראל הלכו ביבשה בתוך הים. סל׳ פסק׳ ◆ | F

XXXVI:III

ותקח מרים הנביאה אחות אהרן ◆ היכן נתנבאה | B/A | 1

מרים ◆ הרי הוא אומ׳ ותהר האשה ותלד בן ותרא אותו

וגומ׳ (שמ׳ ב ב) ◆ אמרה לו לאביה סופך להוליד בן | D

שעתיד לגאל את יש׳ ממצ׳ ◆ ענה אביה ואמ׳ לה היכן | E

היא נבואתך ◆ ועדיין היא בנבואתה עומדת [שנא׳] | F

ותתצב אחותו מרחוק (שם ב ד) ◆ אין כל יציבה בכל | G

מקום אלא רוח הקודש ◆ שנא׳ קרא את יהושע וגומ׳ | H

(דב׳ לא יד) ואומ׳ ויבא יײ ויתיצב וגומ׳ (ש״א ג י) והנה

יײ נצב עליו וגו׳ (בר׳ כח יג) ראיתי את יײ נצב על

המזבח וגומ׳ (עמ׳ ט א) ◆ מרחוק (שמ׳ ב ד) ◆ אין מרחוק | J/I

אלא רוח הקדש ◆ שנא׳ מרחוק יײ נראה לי וגומ׳ (ירמ׳ | K

לא ב) ◆ לדעה (שמ׳ ב ד) ◆ אין לדעה אלא רוח הקדש ◆ | M/L

שנא׳ כי מלאה הארץ דעה את יײ וגומ׳ (ישע׳ יא ט). ◆ | N

2.　A.　"(Then Miriam the prophetess,) Aaron's sister, (took a timbrel in her hand)" (Exod. 15:20):

　　B.　Was she really [only] Aaron's sister? Wasn't she the sister of both of them?

　　C.　Rather, because he gave his life for her, she is called in reference to his name.

　　D.　Similar to this, you say: "(Simeon and Levi,) the two sons of Jacob (and the brothers of Dinah), took, etc." (Gen. 34:25).

　　E.　Was she [only] the sister to the two of them?

(Textual Source: Ms. JTS ENA 3308.5)

[101]　　Wasn't she the sister of all the (12) sons of Jacob?

　　F.　Rather, because they gave their lives for her, she is called in reference to their names.

　　G.　Similar to this, you say: "... of their sister, (Cozbi,) daughter of the Midianite chieftain" (Num. 25:18).

　　H.　Was she really their sister? Wasn't she the [chief's] daughter of their [entire] nation?[61]

　　I.　Rather, because she gave her life for it, it is called in reference to her.

3.　A.　"... a timbrel in her hand" (Exod. 15:20):

　　B.　Just where did they get timbrels by the sea?

　　C.　Rather, because the righteous [among them] were certain when they left Egypt that God would perform miracles and mighty acts for them, thus they took timbrels and flutes!

4.　A.　"And Miriam chanted for them: (Sing to the Lord, for He has triumphed gloriously)" (Exod. 15:21):

　　B.　Scripture tells that just as Moses sang the song to the men, likewise his sister sang the song to the women.

　　C.　[As it says in Scripture,] "Sing to the Lord, for He has triumphed gloriously" (Exod. 15:21).

---

[61] The text at 2.H appears to be corrupt in this manuscript. I have translated here in accordance with its parallel attestation and variants in *Mekhilta de-Rabbi Ishmael*.

| | |
|---|---|
| אחות אהרן ♦ וכי אחות אהרן היתה והלא אחות | B/A 2 |
| שניהם ♦ אלא לפי שנתן נפשו עליה נקראת על שמו. ♦ | C |
| כיוצא בו אתה אומ' ויקחו שני בני יעקב וגומ' (בר' לד | D |
| כה) ♦ וכי אחות שניהם היתה והלא אחות כל השבטים | E |
| היתה ♦ א[לא לפי שנתנו] נפשם עליה נקראת על | F |
| שמם. ♦ כיוצא בו אתה אומ' בת נשיא מדין אחותם | G |
| (במ' כה יח) ♦ וכי אחותם [בת אומתם] היתה ♦ אלא לפי | I/H |
| שנתנה אומתה נפש' עליה נק' על שמה. ♦ את התף | A 3 |
| בידה. ♦ וכי מאין להם ‹ליש'› תופים על הים ♦ אלא לפי | C/B |
| שהצדיקים מובטחין עם יציאתן ממצ' שהמק' עושה | |
| להן ניסין וגבורות לפיכך נטלו טופין ומחולות בידם. | |
| ♦ סל' פסו' | |
| | |
| ותען להן מרים ♦ מגיד הכת' שכשם שאמ' משה | B/A 4 |
| שירה לאנשים כך אחותו אמרה שירה לנשים ♦ שירו | C |
| לייי כי גאה גאה. סל' פסו' ♦ | |

# Tractate Vayassa

*Chapter Thirty-Seven*

Textual Source: Ms. JTS ENA 3308.5

XXXVII:I[1]

1. A. "Then Moses caused Israel to set out from the Sea of Reeds" (Exod. 15:22):

   B. R. Joshua says, "Israel undertook this journey because of Moses. Even though they undertook all [other] journeys because of God, this journey they only undertook because of Moses.

   C. "Thus it is said, 'Then Moses caused (Israel) to set out' (Exod. 15:22)."

   D. R. Eliezer the Modiite says, "They journeyed because of God, because we find two or three [instances] in Scripture where they journeyed only because of God.

   E. "As it says in Scripture, 'On a sign from the Lord they made a camp and on a sign from God they broke camp' (Num. 9:23).

   F. "Also this one they journeyed because of God. If so, why does Scripture state, 'Then Moses caused (Israel) to set out' (Exod. 15:22)?

   G. "To inform you of the praiseworthiness of Israel! Because they didn't say to Moses, 'Where are we going? To the wilderness? This is all chaos, for there's nothing to it! We don't [even] have provisions for the way!'

   H. "Rather, they went out on faith [alone].

   I. "And about them it is explained in tradition, 'Go proclaim to Jerusalem, etc.' (Jer. 2:2).

   J. "And thus we find that they retreated three stations. As it says in Scripture, 'They set out from Pi-hahiroth ... They set out from Marah and came to Elim ... They set out from Elim and encamped by the Sea of Reeds' (Num. 33:8–10).

   K. "And thus we find that they retreated eight stations, because of the honor of Aaron, in order to bury him. As it says in Scripture, 'The Israelites marched from Beeroth-bene-jaakan to Moserah. (Aaron died there), etc.' (Deut. 10:6).

   L. "Did he really die in Moserah? Didn't he die on Mount Hor? Rather, they retreated eight stations, because of the honor of Aaron, in order to bury him. As it says in Scripture, 'They set out from Moserah ... They set out from Kadesh and encamped at Mount Hor, etc.' (Num. 33:31,37)."

---

[1] Compare XXXVII:I:1.A–5.B with *Mekhilta de-Rabbi Ishmael,* Vayassa (H/R, 152:6–154:7; Laut., vol. 2, 84:1–89:63; Neus., XXXVI:I:1.A–II:2.E).

# מסכתא דויסע

| | | |
|---|---|---|
| B/A | 1 | ויסע משה את יש' מים סוף. ◆ ר' יהושע אומ' |
| | | זו נסיעה נסעו יש' על פי משה לפי שכל מסעות |
| | | כולן לא נסעו אלא על פי הגבורה אבל נסיעה זו |
| C | | לא נסעו אלא על פי משה ◆ לכך נאמ' ויסע משה ◆ |
| D | | ר' אליעזר המודעי אומ' על פי הגבורה נסעו לפי |
| | | שמצינו מקום שנים ושלשה שלא נסעו אלא על פי |
| E | | הגבורה ◆ שנא' על פי יייי יחנו ועל פי יייי יסעו (במ' ט כג) |
| F | | <...> ◆ אף זו על פי הגבורה נסעו אם כן מה הוא אומ' |
| G | | ויסע משה ◆ [להודיע שבחם של יש' שלא אמרו לו |
| | | למשה לאין] אנו יוצאין למד[בר תהו הזה שאין בו |
| H | | כלום ואין בידינו מחיה] ◆ אלא [יצאו על אמונה ◆ |
| I | | ועליהם מפורש בקבלה הלוך וקראת] באזני ירושלם |
| J | | וגומ' (ירמ' ב ב) ◆ [וכן מצינו שחזרו לאחוריהן שלשה |
| | | מסעות] [שנא' ויסעו מפני החירות ויסעו ממרה |
| | | ויבואו אילימה ויסעו מאילים] וגומ' [ויחנו] על [ים |
| K | | סוף (במ' לג ח - י) ◆ וכן מצינו שחזרו לכבודו של אהרן |
| | | לקבורת]ו שמונה מסעות שנא' ובני יש' נסעו מבארות |
| L | | בני יעקן] מסרה [וגומ' (דב' י ו) ◆ וכי במוסירה מת |
| | | והלא בהר ההר מת אלא שחזרו] לכ[בודו של אהרן |
| | | לקבורתו שמונה מסעות שנא' ויסעו ממוסרות [וגומ' |
| | | ויסעו מקדש ויחנו בהר] ההר [וגומ' (במ' לג לא, לז) ◆ |

2.     A.    R. Eliezer says, "Because of God they journeyed.

[102]    B.    "Why does Scripture say, 'Then Moses caused (Israel) to set out' (Exod. 15:22)?

       C.    "Because he made them journey against their will. Because when they saw the corpses of the people who had enslaved them 'with mortar and bricks and with all sorts of tasks in the field' (Exod. 1:14), they said, 'It appears that there is no one left in Egypt! Let's make an idol to go down to Egypt in front of us!'

       D.    "As it says in Scripture, 'Let us make a captain and return to Egypt' (Num. 14:4).

       E.    "One might think that they said it, but didn't do it. Scripture states, [however,] 'Refusing to obey, unmindful of Your wonders that You did for them ... Even though they made themselves a molten calf and said: "This is your God, etc."' (Neh. 9:17–18)."

3.     A.    R. Judah b. Ilai said, "Israel had an idol, and Moses removed it at that moment.

       B.    "As it says in Scripture, '(Then Moses caused Israel to set out) from the Sea of Reeds' (Exod. 15:22).

       C.    "[He caused them to set out] from the thing in their possession! And what was this? This was an idol!

       D.    "What does Scripture say?—'And they rebelled at the sea, the Sea of Reeds' (Ps. 106:7)."

4.     A.    "They went on into the wilderness of Shur" (Exod. 15:22):

       B.    This is the wilderness of Kuv.

       C.    They said about the wilderness of Kuv that it was 800 parasangs by 800 parasangs, with all of it full of snakes and scorpions.

       D.    As it says in Scripture, "... who led you through the wilderness, etc." (Deut. 8:15). And Scripture says, "The 'Beasts of the Negev' Pronouncement: Through a land of distress ... of viper, etc." (Isa. 30:6).

       E.    And "viper" means only snake.

       F.    They said of this snake: When it would look at the shadow of a bird flying in the air, the bird would crumble and fall apart

### Textual Source: Midrash ha-Gadol

limb by limb!

       G.    And thus Scripture states, "They never ask themselves: Where is the Lord who brought us up from the Land of Egypt, who led us through a land of deserts and pits, a land of drought and darkness ...?"[2] (Jer. 2:6).

       H.    [That is,] a place of shadow and death.[3]

5.     A.    R. Abba said, "Our great Rabbi told me this matter:

       B.    "There was a man in the Land of Israel whose name was Baldy. And why did they call him Baldy? Because he was once walking to gather wood on the mountain, when he saw a snake sleeping, but the snake didn't see him. All his hair fell out and didn't grow to the day of his death. And they would call him Baldy."

---

[2] Hebrew: tzalmavet—צלמות.

[3] Hebrew: tzal imo mavet—צל עמו מות. The gist of this wordplay interpretation is that even though the wilderness of Kuv was a place of shadow and death, i.e., a place where vipers would merely look at the shadows of flying birds and they would self-destruct, the Israelites nonetheless marched through it undaunted.

ר' אלי[עז]ר או[מ' על פי הגבורה [נסעו ✦ מהו אומ' ויסע   B/A   2

משה ✦ שהסיען] בעל כורחם כיון שראו פגרי בני [אדם]   C

שהיו מעבידין בהן בחומר ובלבנים ובכל עבודה

בשדה (שמ' א יד) [אמרו] דומה שלא נשתייר אדם

במצ' נעשה עבודה זרה שתרד בראשנו ✦ למצ' נתנה   D

ראש ונשובה מצ' (שמ' יד ד) ✦ יכול שאמרו ולא עשו   E

ת"ל וימאנו לשמע ולא זכרו נפלאותיך אשר עשיתה

עמהם ואומ' ואף כשעשו להן (!) עגל מסכה ויאמרו

זה אלהיך וגומ' (נחמ' ט יח) ✦ אמ' ר' יהודה ב"ר אלעאי   A   3

עבודה זרה היתה בידן של יש' והיסיעה משה באותה

שעה ✦ שנא' מים סוף ✦ מדבר שבידן ואיזה זה זה עבו'   C/B

זרה ✦ מה הוא אומ' וימרו על ים בים סוף (תה' קו ז). ✦   D

ויצאו אל מדבר שור ✦ זה מדבר כוב ✦ אמרו עליו על   C/B/A   4

מדבר כוב שהיה שמונה מאות פרסה על שמונה

מאות פרסה וכולו מלא נחשים ו[עק'] ✦ שנא' המוליכך   D

במדבר וגומ' (דב' ח טו) ואומ' משא בהמות נגב

ב[ארץ צרה] [וצוקה] וגומ' ואפעה (ישע' ל ו) ✦ אין   E

אפעה אלא איכעוס ✦ אמרו איכעוס [זה] בשעה שהוא   F

רואה צל עוף ה[פורח באויר מתאכל אותו העוף

ונושר] איברים איברים ✦ וכן הוא אומר ולא אמרו איה   G

ה' המעלה אותנו מארץ מצרים המוליך אותנו בארץ

ערבה ושוחה בארץ ציה וצלמות (ירמ' ב ו) ✦ מקום   H

שהצל עמו מות. ✦ אמר ר' אבא דבר זה שח לי רבינו   A   5

הגדול ✦ אדם אחד היה בארץ ישראל ושמו מריטה   B

ולמה קורין אותו מריטה שפעם אחת הלך ללקט

עצים מן ההר וראה את הנחש ישן והנחש לא ראהו

ונשר כל שערו ולא צמח בו שער עד יום מותו והיו

קורין אותו מריטה. ✦

XXXVII:II[4]

1.　A.　"They traveled three days in the wilderness and found no water" (Exod. 15:22):

　　B.　R. Joshua says, "In order to fatigue them."

　　C.　R. Eliezer the Modiite says, "Wasn't there water beneath the feet of Israel? For the land overlays only water!

　　D.　"As it says in Scripture, 'Who spread the earth over the water' (Ps. 136:6).

　　E.　"Why does Scripture state, '... and found no water' (Exod. 15:22)? In order to test them."

### Textual Source: Ms. JTS ENA 3308.5

　　F.　Others say, "They had used up the water that they took from between the clefts.

　　G.　"As it says in Scripture, '... and found no water' (Exod. 15:22).

　　H.　"And they didn't find water even in their utensils.

[103]　I.　"In accordance with what is said in Scripture, 'Their nobles sent ... They came to the cisterns, they found no water. They returned, their vessels empty' (Jer. 14:3)."

### Textual Source: Midrash ha-Gadol

　　J.　Those who interpret metaphorically say, "These are the words of Torah, which are compared to water.

　　K.　"As it says in Scripture, 'Ho, all who are thirsty, come for water' (Isa. 55:1).

　　L.　"Because they had been separated from the words of Torah for three days, they rebelled. Thus, the prophets among them declared that they should read

### Textual Source: Ms. JTS ENA 1180.47

the Torah on *Shabbat,* Monday, and Thursday. How? They read on *Shabbat,* skip Sunday, read on Monday, skip Tuesday and Wednesday, and read on Thursday, and skip Friday."

2.　A.　"They came to Marah, but they could not drink the water of Marah" (Exod. 15:23):

　　B.　R. Joshua says, "Israel came to three places that day. As it says in Scripture, 'They came to Marah, etc.' (Exod. 15:23)."

　　C.　R. Eliezer the Modiite says, "They only came to one place."

3.　A.　"And the people grumbled (against Moses, saying: What shall we drink?), etc." (Exod. 15:24):

　　B.　R. Joshua says, "Israel should have asked the advice of the greatest one among them, saying, 'What will we drink?' Instead, they arose and murmured against Moses!"

　　C.　R. Eliezer the Modiite says, "Israel was accustomed to standing and murmuring about Moses. And not Moses alone, but also about the Almighty. Thus it is said, 'What shall we drink?' (Exod. 15:26)."

4.　A.　"So he cried out to the Lord" (Exod. 15:25):

　　B.　From this we learn that the righteous are not difficult to complain to. And along the way, we learn that the prayer of the righteous is brief.

---

[4] Compare XXXVII:II:1.A–12.C with *Mekhilta de-Rabbi Ishmael,* Vayassa (H/R, 154:7–157:3; Laut., vol. 2, 89:64–94:147; Neus., XXXVI:II: 3.A–XXXVIII:2.F).

| | |
|---|---|
| A | 1 |

וילכו שלשת ימים במדבר ולא מצאו מים ◆

ר' יהושע אומר כדי ליגען. ◆ ר' אלעזר המודעי

C/B

אומר והלא מים תחת רגליהן שלישראל הם הארץ

אין צפה אלא על פני המים ◆ שנא' לרוקע הארץ

D

על המים (תה' קלו ו) ◆ מה ת"ל ולא מצאו מים כדי

E

לנסותם. ◆ [אחרים אומ' מים שנטלו מבין הגזורים

F

של]מ[ן]ו באותו מקום ◆ שנא' ולא מצאו מים] ◆ [ואף

H/G

בכליהם] לא מ[צאו ◆ כענין שנא' ואדיריהם שלחו וגומ'

I

באו על גבים] לא מצאו מים שבו כליהם ריקם וגומ'

(ירמ' יד ג). ◆ דורשי רשומות אומ' אלו דברי תורה

J

שנמשלו במים ◆ שנ' הוי כל צמא לכו למים (ישע' נה א) ◆

K

לפי שפירשו מדברי תורה שלשת ימים לכך מרדו

L

לפיכך התקינו להם נביאים שביניהם שיהיו קוראין

בתורה [בשבת] בשני ובחמישי [הא כיצד] קוראין

בשבת ומפסיקין באחד בשבת וקוראין בשני

ומפסיקין בשלישי וברביעי וקוראין בחמישי

ומפסיקין בערב שבת. סל' פסו' ◆

| | |
|---|---|
| A | 2 |

ויבואו מרתה ולא יכלו לשתות מים ממרה וגומ' ◆

ר' יהושע אומ' לשלשה מקומות באו יש' באותו היום

B

שנא' ויבאו מרתה וגומ' ◆ ר' אלעזר המודעי אומ' לא

C

באו אלא למקום אחד. ◆

וילונו העם וגומ' ◆ ר' יהושע אומ' היה להן ליש'

B/A  3

לימלך בגדול שביניהן לומר מה נשתה אלא שעמדו

ואמרו דברי תרעומת על משה. ◆ ר' אלעזר המודעי

C

אומ' למודין הן יש' להיות עומדין ואומ' דברי

תרעומת על משה ולא על משה בלבד אלא אף על

הגבורה לכך נאמר מה נשתה. סל' פסו'. ◆

ויצעק אל יְיָ ◆ מיכן את למד שאין צדיקים קשין

B/A  4

לקבל ולפי דרכינו למדנו שתפלת צדיקים קצרה ◆

5.   A.   It once occurred that someone passed before R. Eliezer (to lead prayer), and extended his benedictions. His disciples said to him, "Master! Do you see that so-and-so is extending his benedictions?" So they said about him, "He's the Blesser!"[5]

      B.   He[6] said to them, "He didn't extend more than Moses! As it says in Scripture, 'I threw myself down before the Lord, etc.' (Deut. 9:18). And Scripture says, 'I stayed on the mountain, etc.' (Deut. 9:9)."

      C.   Again it occurred that someone passed before R. Eliezer and abbreviated his benedictions. His disciples said to him, "Master! Do you see that so-and-so is abbreviating his benedictions?" So they said about him, "He's a disciple of the Sages!"

      D.   He said to them, "He didn't abbreviate more than Moses, who said, 'O God, pray heal her!' (Num. 12:13)."

      E.   He used to say: "There is a time to abbreviate and a time to extend! 'O God, pray heal her!' (Num. 12:13)—behold [this is a time] to abbreviate! 'I stayed on the mountain forty days and forty nights' (Deut. 9:9)—behold [this is a time] to extend!"[6]

6.   A.   "… and the Lord showed him a piece of wood" (Exod. 15:25):

      B.   R. Joshua says, "This is willow wood."

      C.   R. Eliezer the Modiite says, "This is olive wood.

### Textual Source: Midrash ha-Gadol

You don't have wood more bitter than olive!"

      D.   R. Nathan ben Joseph says, "This is cedar wood."

[104]   E.   And there are those who say even the roots of a fig tree or the roots of a pomegranate tree.

      F.   Those who interpret metaphorically say, "He showed him the words of Torah, which are compared to wood.

      G.   "As it says in Scripture, 'She is a tree of life to those who grasp her' (Prov. 3:18)."

7.   A.   R. Ishmael b. R. Yoḥanan ben Berukah says, "Come

### Textual Source: Ms. JTS ENA 1180.47

and see how different the ways of human beings are from the ways of God! [For] a human, something sweet improves something bitter. But it is not so [for] He who spoke, and the world came into being. Rather, something bitter improves something bitter. How so? He put something worn[7] into something spent[8] to do the miracle!

      B.   "Similar to this, you say: '… he went to the spring, and threw a little salt in it, and he said, "Thus said the Lord: (I heal this water), etc."' (2 Kings 2:21).

      C.   "Isn't it the case with drinking water that when you place salt in it, it goes bad? How so [with God]? He puts something that ruins into something ruined to do the miracle!

      D.   "Similar to this, you say: 'When Isaiah said, "Let them take a cake of figs (and apply it to the rash, and he will recover), etc."' (Isa. 38:21).

      E.   "Isn't it the case for human beings, when they place a cake of figs (on bad skin), it immediately goes bad? Rather, He puts something that ruins on something ruined to do the miracle!"

---

[5] Compare 5.A–E with b. Berachot 34a (Neus., I:Tractate Berakhot:5:4:V.A–H).
[6] I.e., R. Eliezer.
[7] I.e., a piece of wood.
[8] I.e., the bitter water.

ומעשה באחד שעבר לפני ר' אל>י<עזר והאריך 5 A

בברכותיו אמ' לו תלמידיו רבינו ראיתה פלו' שהאריך

בברכותיו כדי שיאמרו מברכן הוא ◆ אמ' להן לא B

האריך יתר ממשה שנא' ואתנפל לפני ייי וגומ' (דב' ט

יח) ואומ' ואשב בהר וגומ' (שם ט) ◆ ושוב מעשה באחד C

שעבר לפני ר' אל>י<עזר וקיצר בברכותיו אמרו לו

תלמידיו ר' ראיתה פלוני שקיצר בברכותיו כדי

שיאמרו תלמ' חכמ' הוא ◆ אמ' להן לא [קיצר יתר D

ממשה שאמ' אל נא רפא] נא לה (במ' יב יג) ◆ שהיה E

אומ' יש שעה [לקצר ויש שעה להאריך אל נא רפא]

נא לה הרי לקצר ואשב בהר [ארבעים יום וארבעים

לילה הרי] להאריך. ◆ ויורהו ייי עץ ◆ ר' [יהושע אומ' זה B/A 6

עץ של ערבה ◆ ר' אלעזר] המודעי אומ' זה עץ שלזית C

אין לך מר יותר מזית ◆ ר' נתן בן יוסף אומר זה עץ D

שלקדרוס ◆ ויש אומרין אף עיקרי תאנה ועיקרי רמון. E

דורשי רשומות אומרין הורהו דברי תורה שמשולין F

בעץ ◆ שנא' עץ חיים היא למחזיקים בה (מש' ג יח). ◆ ר' A 7 G

ישמעאל ביר' יוחנן בן ברוקה אומ' בוא וראה כמה

פורשין דרכי בשר ודם מדרכי מקום בשר ודם מתוק

מרפא את המר אבל מי שאמר והיה העולם אינו כן

אלא מר מרפא את המר הא כיצד נותן דבר

המתאכיל לדבר המתאכיל כדי לעשות נס. ◆ כיוצא בו B

אתה אומ' ויצא אל >מוצא< המים וישלך שם (מעט)

מלח ויא' כה אמר ייי וגו' (מ"ב ב כא) ◆ והלא מים יפין C

כיון שנותנין לתוכן מלח מיד הן מבאישין הא כיצד

נותן דבר המתכיל לדבר המתאכיל כדי לעשות נס. ◆

כיוצא בו אתה אומר ויאמר ישע' ויקחו [ישאו] דבילת D

תאנים וגומ' (ישע' לח כא) ◆ והלא בשר ודם כיון E

שנותנין עליו דבלי תאינה מיד מתאכל אלא נותן

דבר המתכיל לדבר המתאכיל כדי לעשות נס. ◆

8.    A.    "... he threw it into the water" (Exod. 15:25):

      B.    At that moment, the Israelites were petulant and angering their father in heaven, like a son who is petulant with his father and a disciple who angers his master.

      C.    They said before Him, "We have sinned by murmuring about the water!"

9.    A.    "'... and the water became sweet' (Exod. 15:25):

      B.    "The water [had become bitter⁹] for the time being, and then became sweet."— The words of R. Joshua.

      C.    But R. Eliezer the Modiite says, "They were bitter from their very beginning. As it says in Scripture, 'The water, the water' (Exod. 15:23–25)—two times."

10.   A.    "'There He made for them rule and law' (Exod. 15:25):

      B.    "'Rule'—this is *Shabbat*. 'And law'—this is honoring [one's] father and mother."—Thus are the words of R. Joshua.

      C.    R. Eliezer the Modiite says, "'Rule'—these are the laws against sexual impropriety. As it says in Scripture, 'You shall keep My charge not to, etc.' (Lev. 18:30). 'And law'—these are the laws of robbery, the laws of damages, and the laws of fines."

11.   A.    "'... and there He put them to the test'¹⁰ (Exod. 15:25):

      B.    "[Which really means:] There He raised them [in greatness]. In accordance with what is said in Scripture, '... King Evil-merodach raised ...'¹¹ (2 Kings 25:27)."—Thus are the words of R. Joshua.

[105] C.    R. Eliezer the Modiite said to him, "You [can only write the Hebrew verb] '[to raise] in greatness' with [the Hebrew letter] *sin*. But here, it is only [the letter] *samekh*.

      D.    "Why does Scripture state,

Textual Source: Midrash ha-Gadol
'... and there He put them to the test' (Exod. 15:25)?

      E.    "[It means] there God tested Israel."

12.   A.    Another interpretation:

      B.    "... and there He put them to the test" (Exod. 15:25).

      C.    There our forefathers tested God.

## XXXVII:III¹²

1.    A.    "'He said: If you will heed diligently (the voice of the Lord your God)' (Exod. 15:26):

      B.    "[If] a person heeds one commandment, he is given many commandments to heed.

      C.    "As it says in Scripture, 'If you hearken, you will hearken'¹³ (Exod. 15:26).

      D.    "[If] a person forgets one commandment, he will be caused to forget many commandments.

---

⁹ These words are attested in the parallels to this tradition in both *Midrash ha-Gadol* and *Mekhilta de-Rabbi Ishmael*.

¹⁰ Hebrew: *nisahu*—נסהו.

¹¹ Hebrew: *nasah*—נשא.

¹² Compare XXXVII:III:1.A–3.C with *Mekhilta de-Rabbi Ishmael*, Vayassa (H/R, 157:4–158:15; Laut., vol. 2, 95:148–97:185; Neus., XXXVIII: 3.A–9.B).

¹³ I translate here the seemingly doubled verbal form of the infinitive absolute (שמע תשמע), upon which the text bases this interpretation.

|  |  |
|---|---|
| B/A 8 | וישלך אל המים ◆ באותה שעה היו יש׳ מתחטין ומתגרין |
|  | לפני אביהם שבשמים כבן שמתחטא לאביו וכתלמיד |
| C | שמתגרה לפני רבו ◆ אמרו לפניו חטאנו שמה |
| B/A 9 | שנתרעמנו על המים. ◆ וימתקו המים ◆ לפי שעה הומתקו |
| C | דברי ר׳ יהושע ◆ ור׳ אלעזר ‹המודעי› אומ׳ מדין הן |
| A 10 | מתחילתן שנא׳ מים מים שני פעמים. ◆ שם שם לו חק |
| B | ומשפט. ◆ חוק זו שבת ומשפט זה כיבוד אב ואם כך |
| C | דברי ר׳ יהושע ◆ ור׳ אלעזר המודעי אומ׳ חוק אלו |
|  | עריות שנא׳ [ושמרתם] את משמרתי לבלתי וגומ׳ (ויק׳ |
|  | יח ל) משפט אלו דיני אונסין ודיני חבלות ודיני |
| B/A 11 | קנסות] ◆ ושם נסהו ◆ ושם נעשה לו[הם נסאון לישראל |
|  | כענין שנא׳ נשא אויל] מרודך וגומ׳ (מ״ב כה כז) כך |
| C | דברי ר׳ יהושע ◆ אמר לו ר׳ אלעזר המודעי והלא] אין |
|  | גדולה בכל מקום אלא ב[שין וכאן אינו אלא סמך ◆ |
| E/D | A 12 | מה ת״ל] ושם נסהו ◆ שם נסה המקום את ישראל. ◆ ד״א ◆ |
| C/B | ושם נסהו ◆ שם ניסו אבותינו את המקום. ◆ |

XXXVII:III

|  |  |
|---|---|
| B/A 1 | ויאמר אם שמע תשמע ◆ שמע אדם מצוה אחת |
| C | משמיעין אותו מצות הרבה ◆ שנא׳ אם שמע תשמע. ◆ |
| D | שכח אדם מצוה אחת משכחין אותו מצות הרבה ◆ |

E.  "As it says in Scripture, 'If you forget, you will forget'[14] (Deut. 8:19).

F.  "'... the voice of the Lord your God' (Exod. 15:26):

G.  "This teaches that whoever heeds the Almighty, Scripture attributes it to him as if he served before the Eternal One, blessed be He.

H.  "'... doing what is upright is His sight' (Exod. 15:26):

I.  "This [refers to] business dealings. For anyone who conducts business faithfully, and people are at ease with him, Scripture attributes him with upholding the entirety of the Torah.

J.  "'... giving ear to His commandments' (Exod. 15:26):

K.  "These are halakhot.[15]

L.  "'... keeping all His laws' (Exod. 15:26):

M.  "These are Rabbinic prohibitions.

N.  "'... then I will not bring upon you any of the diseases that I brought upon the Egyptians' (Exod. 15:26):

O.  "But if I do bring them, then—'... I the Lord am your healer' (Exod. 15:26)."—Thus are the words of R. Joshua.

P.  R. Eliezer the Modiite says, "'(If) you will heed' (Exod. 15:26):

Q.  "One might think it is optional.

R.  "Scripture states, [however,] '... diligently' (Exod. 15:26).

S.  "Scripture fixed it as obligatory."

2.  A.  Another interpretation:

B.  "... you will heed" (Exod. 15:26):

C.  This is the principle in which the entire Torah is encompassed!

D.  "... to the voice of the Lord your God" (Exod. 15:26):

E.  These are the Ten Commandments that were said on Mount Sinai.

F.  "... doing what is upright in His sight" (Exod. 15:26):

G.  These are the praiseworthy aggadot[16] that are heard in the ears of everyone.

H.  "... giving ear to His commandments" (Exod. 15:26):

I.  These are Rabbinic prohibitions.

J.  "... keeping all His laws" (Exod. 15:26):

K.  These are the laws against sexual impropriety.

L.  If you do this—"... then I will not bring upon you any of the diseases that I brought upon the Egyptians" (Exod. 15:26).

M.  Why does Scripture state, "... for I the Lord am your healer" (Exod. 15:26)?

N.  The Holy One, blessed be He, said to Moses: "The words of Torah that I am giving to you are life for you [and] healing for you. As it says in Scripture, 'They are life to him who finds them, healing for his whole body'" (Prov. 4:22).

[14] As above, I translate the seemingly doubled verbal form of the infinitive absolute (שכח תשכח).
[15] I.e., commandments pertaining to legal praxis.

| | | |
|---|---|---|
| ◆ שנא' אם שכח תשכח (דב' ח יט). ◆ לקול ה' אלקיך ◆ | F/E | |
| מלמד שכל השומע בקול גבורה מעלה עליו <הכת'> | G | |
| כאלו שימש לפני חי העולמים ב"ה. ◆ והישר בעיניו | H | |
| תעשה ◆ זה משא ומתן שכל הנושא ונותן באמונה ורוח | I | |
| הבריות נוחה הימנו מעלה עליו הכת' כאלו קיים כל | | |
| התורה כולה. ◆ והאזנת למצותיו ◆ אלו הלכות. ◆ ושמרת | L/K/J | |
| כל חקיו ◆ אלו גזירות. ◆ כל המחלה אשר שמתי במצרים | N/M | |
| לא אשים עליך ◆ ואם אשים כי אני ה' רפאך כך דברי | O | |
| ר' יהושע. ◆ ר' אלעזר המודעי אומ' שמוע ◆ יכול רשות ◆ | Q/P | |
| ת"ל תשמע ◆ קבעו הכת' חובה. ◆ ד"א ◆ תשמע ◆ זה הכלל | C/B/A 2 | S/R |
| שכל התורה כולה כלולה בו. ◆ לקול ה' אלקיך ◆ אלו | E/D | |
| עשר דברות שנאמרו על הר סיני. ◆ והישר בעיניו תעשה ◆ | F | |
| אלו אגדות משובחות הנשמעות באזני כל אדם. ◆ | G | |
| והאזנת למצותיו ◆ אלו גזירות. ◆ ושמרת כל חקיו ◆ אלו | K/J/I/H | |
| עריות. ◆ אם עשית כן כל המחלה אשר שמתי במצרים | L | |
| לא אשים עליך ◆ מה ת"ל כי אני ה' רפאך ◆ אמר לו הקב"ה | N/M | |
| למשה דברי תורה שנתתי לך חיים הן לך רפואה הן לך | | |
| שנ' כי חיים הם למוצאיהם ולכל בשרו מרפא (מש' ד כב). ◆ | | |

---

16 I.e., Rabbinic nonlegal traditions.

3.    A.    "... for I the Lord am your healer" (Exod. 15:26):

      B.    R. Isaac says, "If there is no disease in them, why do they need healing?

      C.    "Say this: 'I will not bring upon you' (Exod. 15:26)—in this world. '... for I the Lord am your healer' (Exod. 15:26)—in the world to come."

## Chapter Thirty-Eight

### Textual Source: Midrash ha-Gadol

### XXXVIII:I[17]

1.    A.    "And they came to Elim, where there were twelve springs and seventy palm trees" (Exod. 15:27):

      B.    Scripture tells that that place had more spoiled water than any place. For there were 12 springs there, but they only sustained 70 palm trees. But when Israel came, 600,000 people encamped, and they sustained them with water, and they spent a second and third night there!

2.    A.    "'And they encamped there beside the water' (Exod. 15:27):

      B.    "Scripture teaches that Israel would only dwell beside water."—Thus are the words of R. Joshua.

      C.    R. Eliezer the Modiite says, "From the day the Holy One, blessed be He, created the world, He created there 12 springs corresponding to the 12 tribes and 70 palm trees corresponding to the 70 elders."

3.    A.    "And they encamped there beside the water" (Exod. 15:27):

      B.    Scripture teaches that they were sitting and occupied with the words of Torah that were given to them at Marah.

### XXXVIII:II[18]

1.    A.    "They set out from Elim. The whole Israelite community came to the wilderness of Sin, (which is between Elim and Sinai,) on the fifteenth day (of the second month after their departure from the Land of Egypt)" (Exod. 16:1):

      B.    Why is [the word] "day" said [here] in Scripture?

      C.    To inform as to which day [of the month] coincided with *Shabbat*. Because from the day the Holy One, blessed be He, created the world until it[19] was given to them, [*Shabbat*] was fixed [to fall] on the 22nd of [the month of] Iyar.

2.    A.    Another interpretation:

      B.    "... on the fifteenth" (Exod. 16:1):

      C.    Why is "day" said [here] in Scripture?

      D.    To inform on which day the Torah was given to Israel.

3.    A.    Another interpretation:

      B.    Why is "day" said [here] in Scripture?

---

[17] Compare XXXVIII:I:1.A–3.B with *Mekhilta de-Rabbi Ishmael*, Vayassa (H/R, 158:16–159:5; Laut., vol. 2, 98:1–12; Neus., XXXVII:I:1.A–2.E).
[18] Compare XXXVIII:II:1.A–3.H with *Mekhilta de-Rabbi Ishmael*, Vayassa (H/R, 159:6–16; Laut., vol. 2, 98:13–100:32; Neus., XXXVII:I:3.A–5.G).
[19] I.e., the Torah.

ד״א כי אני ה׳ רפאך • ר׳ יצחק אומ׳ אם אין בהם מחלה    B/A   3

למה הן צריכין רפואה • אלא אמור מעתה לא אשים    C

עליך בעולם הזה כי אני ה׳ רפאך לעולם הבא. •

XXXVIII:I

ויבאו אלימה ושם שתים עשרה עינת מים    A   1

ושבעים תמרים • מגיד שהיה אותו מקום מקולקל    B

במים יתר מכל המקומות שהרי היו שנים עשר

מבועים ולא סיפקו אלא שבעים דקלים. וכשבאו

ישראל חנו ששים רבוא בני אדם וסיפקו להן מים

ולנו ושנו ושילשו. • ויחנו שם על המים • מלמד שלא היו    B/A   2

ישראל שרויין אלא על המים כך דברי ר׳ יהושע. • ר׳    C

אלעזר המודעי אומר מיום שברא הקב״ה את העולם

ברא שם שנים עשר מבועין כנגד שנים עשר שבטים.

ושבעים דקלים כנגד שבעים זקנים. • ויחנו שם על    A   3

המים • מלמד שהיו יושבין ועוסקין בדברי תורה    B

שניתנו להן במרה. •

XXXVIII:II

ויסעו מאלים ויבאו כל עדת בני ישראל אל מדבר    A   1

סין בחמשה עשר יום • למה נאמר יום • לידע איזה יום    C/B

שאירעה שבת להיות. שסדורה ובאה מיום שברא

הקב״ה את העולם ועד שניתנה להם בעשרים ושנים

באייר. • ד״א • ⟨בחמשה עשר⟩ • למה נאמר יום • לידע יום    D/C/B/A   2

שניתנה בו תורה לישראל. • ד״א • למה נאמר יום •    B/A   3

C. To inform as to which day manna was [initially] given to Israel.

D. They ate the cakes that they brought from Egypt for 31 days.

E. And thus Scripture states, "And they baked unleavened cakes of the dough that they had taken out of Egypt" (Exod. 12:39).

F. And here [Scripture states], "… on the fifteenth day of the second month" (Exod. 16:1).

G. And next to it Scripture says, "I will rain down bread for you" (Exod. 16:4).[20]

[106]   H. R. Shila says, "They were sustained by it for 61 meals."[21]

## XXXVIII:III[22]

1.   A. "The whole Israelite community grumbled against Moses and Aaron in the wilderness" (Exod. 16:2):

B. R. Joshua says, "Israel should have asked the advice of the greatest one among them, saying, 'What will we eat?' Instead, they arose and murmured against Moses!"

C. R. Eliezer the Modiite says, "Israel was accustomed to standing and murmuring against Moses. And not Moses alone, but also against the Almighty. Thus it is said, 'The whole Israelite community grumbled' (Exod. 16:2)."

2.   A. "The Israelites said to them: If only we had died by the hand of the Lord" (Exod. 16:3):

B. They said, "If only we had died during the three days of darkness in Egypt!"

3.   A. "… when we sat by the fleshpots" (Exod. 16:3):

B. R. Joshua says, "Did all of them really have an appetite? Rather, they made it up and spoke.

C. "'… when we ate our fill of bread' (Exod. 16:3):

D. "Did all of them really have an appetite? Rather, they made it up and spoke."

E. R. Eliezer the Modiite says, "Israel were royal slaves in Egypt, and they would go out to the market and take bread, meat, fish, and anything, and no one would stop them from doing so. And they would go out to the field and take figs, grapes, and anything, and no one would stop them from doing so."

4.   A. "For you have brought us out into this wilderness" (Exod. 16:3):

B. They said, "You have brought us to this desolate wilderness that has nothing!"

5.   A. "… to starve this whole congregation to death" (Exod. 16:3):

B. R. Joshua says, "You don't have anything more difficult than famine. As it says in Scripture, 'Better off were the slain of the sword than those slain by famine' (Lam. 4:9)."

C. R. Eliezer the Modiite says, "[The meaning in Scripture here of] 'to starve' is that famine after famine comes upon us."

D. Another interpretation: Darkness after darkness.

---

[20] Exod. 16:1–4 establishes that God promised the manna on the 15th day of the second month after the departure, i.e., the 15th of Iyar. Exod. 16:13 establishes that the manna fell the next morning after the day it was promised, i.e., on the 16th of Iyar. Since the Israelites departed Egypt on the 15th of Nisan, this means that the cakes they brought out with them lasted for the 31 days between the departure and the first day of the manna.

[21] Given that there were two meals a day, one would think that the cakes would have provided 62 meals during the 31 days they were used. However, it appears that R. Shila has noted in Exod. 16:13 that God provided the quail on the evening of the 15th of Iyar, thus eliminating one meal on the 31st day.

[22] Compare XXXVIII:III:1.A–5.D with *Mekhilta de-Rabbi Ishmael*, Vayassa (H/R, 159:16–160:9; Laut., vol. 2, 100:33–101:57; Neus., XXXVII: I:6.A–10.C).

| | |
|---:|:---|
| D/C | לידע יום שניתן בו מן לישראל. ◆ חררה שהוציאו ממצרים |
| E | אכלו ממנו אחד ושלשים יום ◆ וכן הוא אומר ויאפו את |
| F | הבצק אשר הוציאו ממצרים (שמ' יב לט) ◆ וכאן |
| G | בחמשה עשר יום לחדש השני ◆ בצדו הוא אומ' הנני |
| H | ממטיר לכם לחם. ◆ ר' שילא אומ' נסתפקו הימנה |
| | ששים ואחת סעודה. ◆ |

XXXVIII:III

| | | |
|---:|---:|:---|
| 1 | B/A | וילונו כל עדת בני ישראל ◆ ר' יהושע אומ' היה להן |
| | | לישראל לימלך בגדול שבהן לומר מה נאכל אלא |
| | C | שעמדו ואמרו דברי תרעומת על משה. ◆ ר' אלעזר |
| | | המודעי אומ' למודין הן ישראל להיות עומדין |
| | | ואומרין דברי תרעומת על משה ולא על משה בלבד |
| | | אלא אף על הגבורה לכך נאמר וילונו כל עדת בני ישראל. ◆ |
| 2 | A | ויאמרו אליהם בני ישראל מי יתן מותינו ביד ה' ◆ |
| | B | אמרו לואי מתנו בשלשת ימי החשך במצרים. ◆ |
| 3 | B/A | בשבתינו על סיר הבשר ◆ ר' יהושע אומ' והלא תאובין |
| | D/C | הן לכל אלא שבידו ואמרו. ◆ באכלנו לחם לשבע ◆ והלא |
| | E | תאובין הן לכל אלא שבידו ואמרו. ◆ ר' אלעזר המודעי |
| | | אומר עבדים היו ישראל במלכות מצרים והיו יוצאין |
| | | לשוק ונוטלין פת ובשר ודגים וכל דבר ואין כל בריה |
| | | ממחה על ידן. והיו יוצאין לשדה ונוטלין תינין וענבים |
| | | ורמונים וכל דבר ואין כל בריה ממחה על ידן. ◆ כי |
| 4 | A | הוצאתם אותנו אל המדבר הזה. ◆ אמרו הוצאתם |
| | B | אותנו למדבר תותו הזה שאין בו כלום. ◆ להמית את |
| 5 | A | כל הקהל הזה ברעב ◆ ר' יהושע אומר אין לך קשה יתר |
| | B | מן הרעב שנא' טובים היו חללי חרב מחללי רעב |
| | | (איכה ד ט). ◆ ר' אלעזר המודעי אומ' ברעב בא רעב בא |
| | C | עלינו רעב אחר רעב. ◆ דבר אחר דבר חשך אחר חשך. |
| | D | ◆ |

*Chapter Thirty-Nine*

Textual Source: Midrash ha-Gadol

XXXIX:I[23]

1.   A.   "And the Lord said to Moses: Behold, I will rain down (bread) for you" (Exod. 16:4):

     B.   R. Joshua says, "The Holy One, blessed be He, said to Moses, 'Behold, I shall appear immediately and I won't hold back!'"

     C.   R. Eliezer the Modiite says, "Scripture only says 'behold' in reference to the Patriarchs."

2.   A.   "... will rain down (bread) for you" (Exod. 16:4):

     B.   R. Joshua says, "[God said,] 'Certainly you don't deserve it!'"

     C.   R. Eliezer the Modiite says, "Scripture only says 'for you' because of the merit of your Patriarchs."

3.   A.   "... from the heavens" (Exod. 16:4):

     B.   From the storehouse of good that is in the heavens.

     C.   In accordance with what is said in Scripture, "The Lord will open for you His bounteous store, the heavens" (Deut. 28:12).

4.   A.   Rabban Shimon ben Gamliel says, "Come and see how beloved Israel is before their father in heaven. Because they are so beloved, the act of Creation was mixed up for them! The upper region was lowered and the lower region was raised.

     B.   "At first, bread would rise up from the earth, as it says in Scripture, 'In a land of grain and wine' (Deut. 33:28).

     C.   "And the dew would come down from heaven, as it says in Scripture, '... under heavens dripping dew' (Deut. 33:28).

     D.   "But now, things are mixed up.

     E.   "The bread began to fall from the heavens, as it says in Scripture, '... bread (for you) from the heavens' (Exod. 16:4).

     F.   "And the dew rose up from the earth, as it says in Scripture, 'When the fallen dew arose' (Exod. 16:14)."

5.   A.   "... and the people shall go out and gather" (Exod. 16:4):

     B.   R. Joshua says, "[This means] that you should not [just] go out to your courtyard and gather [it]. Rather, you should go out to the wilderness and gather [it]."

6.   A.   "... each day that day's portion" (Exod. 16:4):

     B.   R. Joshua says, "[This means] that one should gather on one day for the next, and thus, on the eve of *Shabbat* for *Shabbat*."

     C.   R. Eliezer says, "[This means] that one should not gather on one day for the next."

     D.   And thus would R. Eliezer say, "He who has what he will eat today, but says, 'What will I eat tomorrow?'—behold, this is one lacking faith!

     E.   "As it says in Scripture, '... each day that day's portion' (Exod. 16:4).

     F.   "He who created [the] day, created [also] its provision!"

[23] Compare XXXIX:I:1.A–21.C with *Mekhilta de-Rabbi Ishmael*, Vayassa (H/R, 160:11–163:8; Laut., vol. 2, 102:1–107:84; Neus., XXXVIII:I: 1.A–21.F).

| | | |
|---|---|---|
| ויאמר ה' אל משה הנני ממטיר לכם ◆ ר' יהושע | B/A | 1 |
| אומ' אמ' לו הקב"ה למשה הריני נגלה מיד ואיני | | |
| מעכב. ◆ ר' אלעזר המודעי אומ' אינו אומ' הנני אלא | C | |
| לאבות. ◆ ממטיר לכם ◆ ר' יהושע אומ' בודאי אין ראוי | B/A | 2 |
| לכם. ◆ ר' אלעזר המודעי אומר אינו אומר לכם אלא | C | |
| בזכות אבותיכם. ◆ מן השמים ◆ מאוצר טוב שבשמים ◆ | B/A | 3 |
| כענין שנ' יפתח ה' לך את אוצרו הטוב את השמים | C | |
| (דב' כח יב). ◆ רבן שמעון בן גמליאל אומר בוא וראה | A | 4 |
| כמה חביבין ישראל לפני אביהן שבשמים ולפי שהן | | |
| חביבין נתחלפו להן מעשה בראשית נעשו עליונים | | |
| תחתונים ותחתונים עליונים ◆ שמתחלה היה הלחם | B | |
| עולה מן הארץ שנא' אל ארץ דגן ותירוש (דב' לג כח) ◆ | | |
| והטל היה יורד מן השמים שנא' אף שמיו יערפו טל | C | |
| (שם) ◆ עכשיו נתחלפו הדברים ◆ התחיל הלחם יורד מן | E/D | |
| השמים שנ' לחם מן השמים ◆ והטל עולה מן הארץ שנ' | F | |
| ותעל שכבת הטל (שמ' טז יד). ◆ ויצא העם ולקטו ◆ (ר' | B/A | 5 |
| יהושע אומר) שלא תהיו יוצאין לחצרותיכם ומלקטין | | |
| אלא שתהיו יוצאין למדברות ומלקטין. ◆ דבר יום ביומו ◆ | A | 6 |
| ר' יהושע אומר שילקט אדם מן היום למחר וכן מערב | B | |
| שבת לשבת. ◆ ר' אליעזר אומר שלא ילקט אדם מן היום | C | |
| למחר. ◆ וכן היה ר' אליעזר אומר מי שיש לו מה שיאכל | D | |
| היום ויאמר מה אני אוכל למחר הרי זה ממחוסרי אמנה | | |
| שנ' דבר יום ביומו. ◆ מי שברא יום ברא פרנסתו. ◆ | F/E | |

7.  A.  Another interpretation:

    B.  "... each day that day's portion" (Exod. 16:4):

    C.  R. Shimon says, "Because of the love for Israel, they were given each day that day's portion!

    D.  "They told a parable: To what is the matter alike?

    E.  "It is like a human king who was angry at his son, and said, 'He shouldn't show his face—except for the beginning of the year, let him come and take his allowance!' He would be sustained the whole year, but would anticipate [the next visit, saying], 'Oh that I could show my face to dad [now], but [then] I wouldn't be sustained!' When he was reconciled with him, he[24] said, 'Let him come every day and take his allowance!' That son said, 'It's good that I get to see the king every day!'

[107]

    F.  "Likewise [with] Israel—because of their affection, they were given provisions daily, in order that they would grieve and receive the face of God's presence every day!"

8.  A.  "... that I may thus test them, to see whether they will follow My instructions or not" (Exod. 16:4):

    B.  It was an opportunity to exalt them in front of all the creatures of the world.

    C.  For God provides in any situation one's needs to whoever devotes his entire heart to serve Him.

9.  A.  R. Joshua says, "If a person learns[25] two laws in the morning and two laws in the evening, and [otherwise] works all day, it is attributed to him as if he upheld the entire Torah."

    B.  R. Eliezer says, "The Torah was given for interpretation only to those who eat manna.[26]

    C.  "How else could a person sit and learn, and not know how he will eat and drink, or how he will be clothed and covered!

    D.  "Thus, the Torah was given for interpretation only to those who eat manna. And like them[27] are those who eat the terumah."[28]

10. A.  "But on the sixth day, when they apportion (what they have brought in)" (Exod. 16:5):

    B.  Based on this [you learn] that one should gather on the eve of Shabbat for Shabbat.

11. A.  "... it shall prove to be double"[29] (Exod. 16:5):

    B.  [It shall prove to be] different.[30]

    C.  You say bread that is different. Isn't it, instead, bread that is doubled?

    D.  When Scripture says, "... they gathered double the amount of bread" (Exod. 16:22), bread that is doubled is mentioned.

    E.  So why does Scripture state, "... it shall prove to be double" (Exod. 16:5)?

    F.  [To emphasize that it also was] different!

    G.  Every day one omer [of manna] would fall, but on Shabbat, two omers. Every day its fragrance would spread about,

---

[24] I.e., the king.

[25] Or: recites.

[26] I.e., to those who do not work for a living.

[27] The word that actually appears here in the text is שנייה, which makes little or no contextual sense. I have translated instead the word שוין, which appears in the parallel to this tradition in the Mekhilta de-Rabbi Ishmael.

[28] I.e., priests who eat the priestly tithe.

[29] Hebrew: mishneh—משנה.

| | |
|---|---|
| 7 | ד"א ◆ דבר יום ביומו ◆ ר' שמעון אומר מפני |
| | חיבתן שלישראל ניתן להם דבר יום ביומו ◆ |
| E/D | מושלו משל למה הדבר דומה ◆ למלך בשר ודם שכעס |
| | על בנו ואמר אל יראה פני אלא מתחלת השנה יבוא |
| | ויטול פרנסתו. היה מתפרנס כל השנה והוא |
| | מתבלקט הלווי אראה פני אבה ולא אתפרנס כיון |
| | שנתרצה לו אמר יבוא בכל יום ויטול פרנסתו. אמר |
| | אותו הבן כדאי אם אין בידי אלא ראיית המלך בכל |
| F | יום כדאי הוא. ◆ כך ישראל מפני חיבתן ניתן להן |
| | פרנסת יום יום כדי שיהיו מחלין ומקבילין פני שכינה |
| | בכל יום. ◆ למען אנסנו הילך בתורתי אם לא ◆ נסוי הוא |
| 8 | B/A |
| C | להן לכל באי העולם. ◆ (שכל מי שמלאו לבו לעבוד את |
| 9 | A |
| | השם בכל לבו הוא ממציא לו ספקו מכל מקום). ◆ ר' |
| | יהושע אומר שנה אדם שתי הלכות בשחרית ושתי |
| | הלכות בערבית ועשה מלאכה כל היום מעלה עליו |
| B | כאלו קיים כל התורה כולה. ◆ ר' אליעזר אומר לא |
| C | ניתנה תורה לדרוש אלא לאוכלי המן. ◆ הא כאיזה צד |
| | היה אדם יושב ושונה ואינו יודע מאין יאכל וישתה |
| D | ומאין ילבש ויתכסה ◆ הא לא ניתנה תורה לדרוש אלא |
| | לאוכלי המן שנייה להן לאוכלי תרומה. ◆ |
| 10 | B/A |
| | והיה ביום הששי והכינו ◆ מכאן שילקט אדם מערב |
| 11 | C/B/A |
| D | אומר לחם שמשונה או אינו אלא לחם כפול ◆ כשהוא |
| | אומר לקטו לחם משנה (פכ"ב) הרי לחם משנה אמור ◆ |
| G/F/E | הא מה ת"ל והיה לחם משנה ◆ לחם שהוא משונה. ◆ בכל יום |
| | היה יורד עומר אחד ובשבת שני עמרים בכל יום היה |

---

30 Hebrew: *meshuneh*—משונה.

Textual Source: Ms. Firkovich II A 268

but on *Shabbat,* even more so. Every day it would glow like gold, but on *Shabbat* even more so.

12.  A.  "So Moses and Aaron said to all the Israelites: 'By evening you shall know (it was the Lord who brought you out from the Land of Egypt)'" (Exod. 16:6):

     B.  They said to them, "While you are sleeping in your beds, God will provide sustenance for you."

13.  A.  "... it was the Lord who brought, etc." (Exod. 16:6):

     B.  Based on this you say that the Exodus from Egypt was equal before God to all the miracles and mighty acts that God performed for Israel.

14.  A.  "... and in the morning you shall see the glory of the Lord, because He has heard your grumblings against the Lord" (Exod. 16:7):

     B.  Based on this you learn that the manna was given to Israel with a shining countenance. The manna, which they requested [properly] in regard to religious law, was given to them with a shining countenance.

     C.  But the meat, which they requested inappropriately, was given to them with a dark countenance.

15.  A.  "For who are we (that you should grumble against us)?" (Exod. 16:7):

     B.  He said to them, "What is our distinction that you stand and murmur against us?"

16.  A.  "Moses said: 'Since it is the Lord who will give you flesh to eat in the evening'" (Exod. 16:8):

[108]  B.  Based on this you learn that at night the meat was given to Israel.

     C.  The manna, which they requested [properly] in regard to religious law, was given to them with a shining countenance.

     D.  The meat, which they requested inappropriately, was given to them with a dark countenance.

17.  A.  "But as for us—(your grumbling) is not against us, (but against the Lord,) etc." (Exod. 16:8):

     B.  They said to them, "If it was against us that you were murmuring, we wouldn't be troubled. However, since you are murmuring against the Eternal One, blessed be He ...!"

18.  A.  "Then Moses said to Aaron: 'Say to the whole Israelite community: Draw near the Lord, etc.'" (Exod. 16:9):

     B.  R. Joshua says, "Scripture only says 'draw near' in order to give judgment."

     C.  R. Eliezer the Modiite says, "Scripture only says 'draw near the Lord' when God's presence is revealed."

19.  A.  "And it came to pass as Aaron spoke (to the whole Israelite community, they turned toward the wilderness, and there, in a cloud, appeared the Presence of the Lord)" (Exod. 16:10):

     B.  Why does Scripture state ["As it came to pass"[31]]?

     C.  This teaches that as God decreed, so it was.

20.  A.  "... they turned toward the wilderness" (Exod. 16:10):

     B.  R. Joshua says, "Scripture only says 'they turned' in order to give judgment."

---

[31] This clause—the subject of this interrogative—is absent in the text here, but present in the parallel to this tradition in the *Mekhilta de-Rabbi Ishmael.*

ריחו נודף ובשבת ביותר בכל יום ויום מצהיב כזהב
ובשבת ביותר. סל׳ פסו ◆

| | | |
|---|---|---|
| ◆ ויאמר משה ואהרן אל כל בני יש׳ ערב וידעתם. | A | 12 |
| אמרו להם עד שאתם ישינין על מיטותיכם המקום | B | |
| מפרנס אתכם ◆ כי ייי הוציא וגומ׳ ◆ מיכן אתה אומ׳ | B/A | 13 |
| ששקולה יציאת מצ׳ לפני המקום כנגד כל נסים | | |
| וגבורות שעשה המקום ליש׳. סל׳ פסו׳ ◆ | | |
| ובוקר וראיתם את כבוד ייי בשמעו את תלונותיכם | A | 14 |
| על ייי. ◆ מיכן את למד שבפנים מאירות ניתן לה[ן] מן | B | |
| ליש׳ מן ששא[לו] אותו כהלכה ניתן להן בפנים | | |
| מאירות ◆ ובשר ששאלו אותו שלא כעני[י]ן ניתן להן | C | |
| בפנים חשכות ◆ ונחנו מה ◆ אמ׳ ◆ <להן> אנו מה אנו | B/A | 15 |
| ספונין שאתם עומדין ומתרעמין עלינו. סל׳ פסו׳ ◆ | | |
| ויאמר משה בתת ייי לכם בערב בשר לאכול ◆ מיכן | B/A | 16 |
| את למד שבפנים חשוכות ניתן להן בשר ליש׳ ◆ מן | C | |
| ששאלו אתו כהלכה נתן להן בפנים מאירות ◆ בשר | D | |
| ששאלו אתו שלא כענין ניתן להן בפנים חשוכות ◆ | | |
| ונחנו מה לא עלינו וגומ׳ ◆ אמרו להן אילו עלינו הייתם | B/A | 17 |
| עומדין ומתרעמין לא היינו מצטערין אלא שאתם | | |
| מתרעמין לפני קיים עולמ׳ בר׳ ה׳ [.] סל׳ פסו׳ ◆ | | |
| ויאמר משה אל אהרן אמור אל כל עדת בני יש׳ | A | 18 |
| קרבו לפני ייי וגומ׳ ◆ [ר׳ יהושע אומ׳] אינו אומ׳ קרבו | B | |
| אלא ליתן את הדין ◆ ר׳ [אלעזר המודעי אומ׳ אינו אומ׳ | C | |
| קר]בו לפני ייי אלא כשנתגלתה השכינה ◆ | | |
| [ויהי כדבר אהרן ◆ מה ת״ל ◆ מלמד שכשם ש]גזר | C/B/A | 19 |
| המק׳ היה. ◆ ויפנו אל [המדבר ◆ ר׳ יהושע אומ׳ אינו] אומ׳ | B/A | 20 |

C.    R. Eliezer the Modiite says, "Scripture only says 'they turned' in reference to the Patriarchs.

D.    "As it says in Scripture, 'toward the wilderness' (Exod. 16:10).

E.    "Just as the wilderness has no sin or punishment, likewise the Patriarchs had no sin or punishment."

21.    A.    "... and there, in a cloud, appeared the Presence of the Lord" (Exod. 16:10):

B.    R. Yosi b. R. Shimon says, "Whenever Israel wanted to stone Moses and Aaron, God appeared in a cloud.

C.    "God said, 'It's better that a pillar of cloud be smitten, but let them not stone Moses and Aaron!'"

## Chapter Forty

### Textual Source: Ms. Firkovich II A 268

XL:I[32]

1.    A.    "The Lord spoke to Moses: 'I have heard the grumbling of the Israelites'" (Exod. 16:11–12):

B.    R. Joshua says, "The Holy One, blessed be He, said to Moses, 'It's extremely clear to Me what Israel has been saying and what they will say before Me.'"

2.    A.    "'Speak to them and say'" (Exod. 16:12):

[109]

B.    Say to them, "You have been standing between two things. You asked for manna from Me, because it's impossible for a person to be without bread. I gave [it] to you. You came back and asked for meat inappropriately. Behold, I'll give [it] to you. Why do I give it to you? So that you won't think to say, 'He's not able to give us meat!' Rather, behold I give [it] to you, but in the end I will exact punishment from you!

C.    "[Thus Scripture states] '... because I am the Lord, your God' (Exod. 16:12). [Meaning]—I am a judge who exacts punishment."

3.    A.    "In the evening (quail arose and covered the camp)" (Exod. 16:13):

B.    From here you learn that meat was given to Israel with a dark countenance.

C.    Manna, which they requested [properly] in regard to religious law, was given to them with a shining countenance.

D.    Meat, which they requested inappropriately, was given to them with a dark countenance

4.    A.    "... quail arose and covered the camp" (Exod. 16:13):

B.    I don't know how much.

C.    Behold Scripture states, "... some two cubits deep on the ground" (Num. 11:31).

D.    It was two cubits high off the ground, so that one could stand and take some at the level of his heart with no trouble. From one's heart and down is two cubits, and from one's heart and up is one cubit.

E.    And thus Scripture states, "... some two cubits deep on the ground" (Num. 11:31). And later on Scripture says, "(He rained meat on them like dust) ... making them come down inside His camp, etc." (Ps. 78:28).

---

[32] Compare XL:I:1.A–4.E with *Mekhilta de-Rabbi Ishmael*, Vayassa (H/R, 163:10–164:1; Laut., vol. 2, 107:1–108:20; Neus., XXXIX:I:1.A–4.D).

| | |
|---|---|
| C | ויפנו אלא ליתן את הדין ◆ ר׳ אלעזר [המודעי אומ׳ אינו |
| E/D | אומ׳ ויפנו אל]א לאבות הראש׳ ◆ שנא׳ אל המדבר ◆ מה |
| | [מדבר אין בו חטא ועון] כך אבות הראשונים אין בהן |
| B/A 21 | חטא ועון ◆ [והנה כבוד ייי נראה] בענן ◆ ר׳ יוסי בר׳ |
| | שמעון אומ׳ כל זמן שיש׳ מבקשין [לסקול למ]שה |
| C | ולאהרן המקום נגלה בענן ◆ אמ׳ המקום מוטב ילקה |
| | עמוד ענן ואל יסקלו משה ואהרן. סל׳ פסקא ◆ |

XL:I

| | |
|---|---|
| A 1 | וידבר ייי אל משה לאמר. שמעתי את תלונות |
| B | בני יש׳ ◆ ר׳ יהושע אומ׳ אמ׳ לו [הקב״ה ל]משה |
| | גלוי וידוע לפני מה שהיו יש׳ אומ׳ ומה עתידין |
| B/A 2 | [לומר ל]פני ◆ דבר אלהם לאמר ◆ אמור להן בין |
| | שני הדברים הייתם [עומדי]ן שאלתם ממני מן לפי |
| | שאי איפשר לו לאדם להיות (לו) [בלא לחם] נתתי |
| | לכם חזרתם ושאלתם בשר שלא כענין הריני נותן |
| | [לכם] מפני מה אני נותן לכם כדי שלא תהיו |
| | סבורין לומר אין ספק בידו ליתן לנו בשר אלא הריני |
| | נותן לכם ולבסוף אני נפרע מכם. ◆ כי אני ייי אלקיכם |
| C | אני דיין ליפרע. [סל׳ פסו׳] ◆ |
| B/A 3 | ויהי בערב ◆ מיכן את למד שבפנים חשיכות נתן |
| C | להן בשר ליש׳ ◆ מן ששאלו אותו כהלכה ניתן להן |
| D | בפנים מאירות ◆ בשר ששאלו אותו שלא כענין ניתן |
| B/A 4 | להן בפנים חש׳. ◆ ותעל השלו ותכס את המחנה ◆ איני |
| C | יודע כמה ◆ הרי הוא אומ׳ וכאמתים על פני הארץ (במ׳ |
| D | יא לא) ◆ שתי אמות היה גבוה מן הארץ שיהיה אדם |
| | עומד כנגד לבו ונוטל מדבר שאין בו צער מן לבו |
| E | ולמטה שתי אמות מלבו ולמעלה אמה אחת ◆ וכן הוא |
| | אומ׳ וכאמתים על פני הארץ. ולהלן הוא אומ׳ ויפל |
| | בקרב מחנהו וגומ׳ (תה׳ עח כח) ◆ |

XL:II[33]

1.    A.    R. Yosi says, "'(A wind from the Lord started up, swept quail from the sea) and strewed them over the camp, about a day's journey on this side and about a day's journey on that side' (Num. 11:31):

      B.    "[The quail covered an area] three parasangs in each direction. Thus Scripture states, '... some two cubits deep on the ground' (Num. 11:31), and thus Scripture states, '... making them come down inside His camp, etc.' (Ps. 78:28)."

      C.    R. Josiah says, "'... and strewed them over the camp, about a day's journey on this side and about a day's journey on that side' (Num. 11:31).

      D.    "Why does Scripture state [a second time], 'and about a day's journey on that side' (Num. 11:31)? [It means] three by three [parasangs], which is nine. Nine by nine [parasangs], which is 81.

      E.    "Thus Scripture states, '... some two cubits deep on the ground' (Num. 11:31). And later on Scripture says, '... making them come down, etc.' (Ps. 78:28)."

      F.    Others say, "'... and strewed them over the camp, about a day's journey on this side and about a day's journey ...' (Num. 11:31).

      G.    "'... about' [refers to] an average day's walk—10 parasangs. '... a day's' (Num. 11:31)—[makes] 20 [parasangs]. '... on this side' (Num. 11:31)—[makes] 40 [parasangs].

      H.    "Why does Scripture state again, '... and about a day's journey on that side' (Num. 11:31)? Behold, this [makes] 80 [parasangs] toward heaven.

      I.    "And thus Scripture states, 'You spread a table for me, etc.' (Ps. 23:5)."

2.    A.    One might think that the roads were ruined [by the quail].

      B.    Scripture states, [however,] "... some two cubits deep on the[34] ground" (Num. 11:31).

      C.    [Meaning it fell] on the unused[35] areas on the ground.

      D.    And later on Scripture says, "... making them come down inside His camp (around His dwelling place), etc." (Ps. 78:28).

      E.    In that the manna was placed two cubits [deep] on the ground around the dwelling places.

3.    A.    R. Eliezer the son of R. Yosi ha-Galili says, "The Israelites only ate manna from the top.

      B.    "How did the manna fall for Israel? A north wind went out and cleaned off the wilderness, and rain fell and leveled the ground. Dew fell on top of it and wind blew over it, turning it into something like tables of gold. And the manna would fall down on it, and from it the Israelites would gather and eat.

      C.    "Behold, it can be so reasoned: If God spared those who transgressed His will in this world, how much the more so will He pay a good reward for the righteous in the time to come!"

4.    A.    And thus Scripture states, "The meat was still between their teeth, etc." (Num. 11:33).

[110]   B.    They said, "The wicked among them ate and it passed [through them] immediately. [However,] it lasted 31 days for the suitable among them!"

---

[33] Compare XL:II:1.A–7.B with *Mekhilta de-Rabbi Ishmael*, Vayassa (H/R, 164:1–165:11; Laut., vol. 2, 108:20–111:51; Neus., XXXIX:I:5.A–11.C).

[34] Hebrew: *al p'nei*—עַל פְּנֵי.

[35] Hebrew: *panui*—פָּנוּי.

XL:II

| | |
|---|---|
| A | 1 |

ר' יוסי אומ' ויטש על המחנה כדרך
יום כה וכדרך יום כה (במ' יא לא) ◆

| B | |

שלשה פרסאות לכל רוח ורוח כן הוא אומ' וכאמתים

| C | |

על פני הארץ וכן הוא אומ' ויפל בקרב מחנהו וגומ' ◆ ר'
יאשיה אומ' ויטש על המחנה כדרך יום כה וכדרך יום

| D | |

כה ◆ מה ת״ל וכדרך יום כה שלש על שלש הרי תשע

| E | |

תשע על תשע הרי שמנים ואחד ◆ כן הוא אומ'
וכאמתים על פני הארץ. ולהלן הוא אומ' ויפל בקרב
וגומ' ◆ אחרים אומ' ויטש על המחנה כדרך יום כה

| F | |

כדרך ◆ הילוך [בינונית] עשרה פרסאות יום עשרים כה

| G | |

ארבעים ◆ מה ת״ל שוב וכדרך יום כה הרי שמנים כלפי

| H | |

למעלה ◆ וכן הוא אומ' תערך לפני שלחן וגומ' (תה' כג

| I | |

ה) ◆ יכול שהיו אסטרטיאות ומקולקלות ◆ ת״ל וכאמתים

| B/A | 2 |

על פני הארץ ◆ על הפנוי שבארץ ◆ ולהלן הוא אומ' ויפל

| D/C | |

בקרב מחנהו וגומ' ◆ שהיה מסובב למשכנות שתי

| E | |

אמות היתה נטולה מן הארץ ◆ ר' אלעזר בנו של ר' יוסי

| A | 3 |

הגלילי אומ' אף מן לא אכלו אותו יש' אלא מן הגבוה ◆
כיצד יורד המן ליש' ויצתה הרוח צפונית וכברה את

| B | |

המדבר וירד מטה וכבש את הארץ וירד עליו הטל
והרוח מנשבת בו ונעשה כמין שולחנות של זהב והמן
היה יורד עליו וממנו יש' מלקטין ואוכלין ◆ והרי דברים

| C | |

קל וחומר אם חס המקום על עוברי רצונו בעולם הזה
על אחת כמה וכמה שישלם שכר טוב לצדיקים
לעתיד לבוא ◆ וכן הוא אומ' הבשר עודנו בין שניהם

| A | 4 |

וגומ' (במ' יא לג) ◆ אמרו רשעים שביניהם אכלו ונותנו

| B | |

מיד ◆ כשל שביניהם ניתרו אחד לשלשים יום ◆

5.     A.   "... when the anger of the Lord blazed forth against the people (and the Lord struck the people with a very severe plague)" (Num. 11:33):

        B.   This teaches that God had not brought upon them a plague as severe as this since the day they had left Egypt.

6.     A.   "That place was named Kibroth-hattaavah (because the people who had the craving were buried there)" (Num. 11:34):

        B.   One might think this was its name of old.

        C.   Scripture states, [however,] "... because the people who had the craving were buried there" (Num. 11:34).

        D.   It was named for that for which they were scolded, and this was not its name of old.

7.     A.   "(Then the people set out) from Kibroth-hattaavah, etc." (Num. 11:35):

        B.   This teaches that they retreated one encampment.

## XL:III[36]

1.     A.   "In the morning there was a fall of dew about the camp" (Exod. 16:13):

        B.   [This is to be understood] in accordance with what we have [already] said [above].

2.     A.   "When the fall of dew lifted, (there, over the surface of the wilderness, lay a fine and flaky substance, as fine as frost on the ground)" (Exod. 16:14):

        B.   Scripture comes to teach you how manna fell down for the Israelites.

        C.   A north wind went out and cleaned off the wilderness ... and the rest as it is written above.

3.     A.   "'... there, over the surface of the wilderness' (Exod. 16:14):

        B.   "But not over the entire wilderness. Rather, over a part of it.

        C.   "'... a fine' (Exod. 16:14):

        D.   "This teaches that it was fine.

        E.   "'... and flaky' (Exod. 16:14):

        F.   "This teaches that it was flaky.

        G.   "'... as fine as frost on the ground' (Exod. 16:14):

        H.   "This teaches that it fell like a covering of ice on the ground."—Thus are the words of R. Joshua.

        I.   R. Eliezer the Modiite says, "'When the fall of dew lifted' (Exod. 16:14):

        J.   "As if it were possible, the Holy One, blessed be He, stretched out His hand and received the prayers of the forefathers, of those who dwelled in dust, and He brought down the manna like dew for Israel!

        K.   "'... there, over the surface of the wilderness' (Exod. 16:14):

        L.   "But not over the entire wilderness. Rather, over a part of it.

        M.   "'... a fine' (Exod. 16:14):

        N.   "This teaches that it fell from the heavens. As it says in Scripture, 'Who spread out the

---

[36] Compare XL:III:1.A–10.E with *Mekhilta de-Rabbi Ishmael,* Vayassa (H/R, 165:12–167:5; Laut., vol. 2, 111:52–115:107; Neus., XXXIX:II: 1.A–10.D).

| | | |
|---|---|---|
| 5 | B/A | ואף ייי חרה בעם (שם) ◆ מלמד שלא הביא עליהן המקום |
| 6 | A | מכה קשה כיוצא בזו מיום שיצאו ממצ׳ ◆ ויקרא שם המקום |
| | B | ההוא קברות [התאו]ה (שם לד) ◆ יכול כן היה שמו |
| | D/C | מקדם ◆ ת״ל כי שם קברו את העם המתאוים (שם) ◆ על |
| 7 | A | מה שערערו נקרא ולא כן היה שמו מקדם. ◆ מקברות |
| | B | התאוה וגומ׳ (שם לה) ◆ מלמד שחזרו חנייה אחת לאחוריהן. ◆ |

XL:III

| | | |
|---|---|---|
| 1 | B/A | ובבוקר היתה שכבת הטל סביב למחנה ◆ לענין |
| | | שאמרנו. סל׳ פסו׳ ◆ |
| 2 | B/A | ותעל שכבת הטל. ◆ בא כת׳ ללמדך היאך ה[י]ה מן |
| | C | יורד] להן ליש׳ ◆ יצתה רוח צפונית וכיברה את המדבר |
| 3 | B/A | וכול׳ כדכת׳ לעיל. ◆ והנה על פני המדבר ◆ ולא על |
| | D/C | המדבר כולו א[לא] על מקצתו. ◆ דק ◆ מלמד שהוא דק ◆ |
| | G/F/E | מחספס ◆ מלמד שהוא מחספס ◆ דק ככפור על הארץ ◆ |
| | H | מלמד שהיה יורד כגליד על הארץ כך דברי ר׳ יהושע ◆ |
| | J/I | ר׳ אלעזר המודעי אומ׳ ותעל שכבת הטל ◆ כוייכול |
| | | פשט המקום את ידו ומקבל תפלתן של אבות של |
| | K | שכני עפר והוריד המן כטל ליש׳ ◆ <ו>הנה על פני |
| | M/L | המדבר ◆ ולא על המדבר כולו אלא <על> מקצתו ◆ דק ◆ |
| | N | מלמד שהיה יורד מן השמים שנא׳ הנוטה כדק שמים |

skies like *fine* gauze, etc' (Isa. 40:22).

O. "Because it fell from the heavens, how does one know from Scripture that it did not fall cold?[37]

P. "The verse teaches, 'warm.'[38]

Q. "Because it fell from above to below, one might think it fell loudly. How does one know from Scripture that it only fell quietly?

R. "The verse teaches, 'silently.'[39]

S. "Because it fell on the ground, how does one know from Scripture that it only fell on the utensils?

T. "The verse teaches, 'bowl.'"[40]

U. R. Tarfon says, "It only fell upon those gathering [it]."

4. A. "… as frost"[41] (Exod. 16:14):

B. As if it were possible, the Holy One, blessed be He, stretched out His hand and received the prayers of the forefathers, of those who dwelled in dust, and brought down the manna like dew for Israel!

C. In accordance with what is said in Scripture, "I have found his ransom"[42] (Job 33:24).

5.
[111]

A. R. Tarfon and his disciples were sitting [studying] with R. Eliezer the Modiite sitting among them. R. Eliezer the Modiite said to them, "The height of the manna that fell for Israel was 60 cubits."

B. They said to him, "Eliezer, our brother, how do you know?"[43]

C. He said to them, "I'm interpreting a verse from the Torah! Which quality is more abundant— the quality of good or the quality of bad? Certainly you will say the quality of good!

D. "Concerning the quality of punishment[44] Scripture says, '(The *windows* of the sky broke open) … Fifteen cubits high (did the waters swell), etc.' (Gen. 7:11,20).

E. "There you have it—15 cubits in the river, 15 cubits on the mountain, and 15 cubits on the valley!

F. "But concerning the quality of good, Scripture says, 'So He commanded the skies above, (He opened the *doors* of heaven) and rained down manna upon them (for food), etc.' (Ps. 78:23–24).

G. "The minimal number of doors is two. How many windows in a door? Four. Four and four are eight! Eight and eight are sixteen!

H. "So go and compute that the height of the manna that fell for Israel was 60 cubits!"[45]

---

[37] The interpretations in 3.O–T are all based on words spelled with letters from the word in Exod. 16:14 for "flaky" (Hebrew: מחספס).

[38] Hebrew: *mah*—מה.

[39] Hebrew: *ḥas*—חס.

[40] Hebrew: *saf*—סף.

[41] Hebrew: *kefor*—כפור.

[42] Hebrew: *kofer*—כופר.

[43] Literally: "Eliezer, our brother, how long will you gather up words and bring them upon us?"

[44] I.e., bad.

[45] The parallel to this tradition in the *Mekhilta de-Rabbi Ishmael* does not include the final doubling of the number of windows from eight to sixteen, as our text does at 5.G. This is a problematic inclusion in our text, because it impairs the apparent logic of Eliezer's interpretation, which is as follows: In 5.D, Gen. 7:11–20 establishes that the opening of the (presumably two) windows in the heavens resulted in 15 cubits of water. Ps. 78:23–24 in 5.F establishes that the doors of heaven opened to rain down the manna, and 5.G establishes a total of eight windows between the two doors of heaven. Therefore, if the opening of the two heavenly windows in Gen. 7:11–20

וגומ' (ישע' מ כב) ◆ או לפי שהיה יורד מן השמים מנין    O

שלא היה יורד צונן ◆ ת"ל מח. ◆ או לפי שהיה יורד    Q/P

<מלמעלה למטה יכול היה יורד> בקול מנין שלא

היה יורד אלא בשתיקה ◆ ת"ל חס ◆ או לפי שהיה יורד    S/R

על הקרקע מנין שלא היה יורד אלא על הכלים ◆ ת"ל    T

סף ◆ ר' טרפון אומ' לא היה יורד אלא על העוסמפים ◆    U

ככפור ◆ כוייכול פשט המקום את ידו וקבל תפלתן    B/A    4

שלאבות של שכ' עפר והוריד המן כטל ליש' ◆ כעניין    C

שנא' מצאתי כפר (איוב לג כד). ◆ וכבר היה ר' טרפון    A    5

ותלמידיו יושבין ור' אלעזר המודעי יושב ביניהן אמ'

להן ר' אלעזר המודעי ששים אמה היה גבהו שלמן

שהיה יורד להן ליש' ◆ אמ' לו אלעזר אחינו עד מתי    B

אתה מגבב ומביא עלינו ◆ אמ' להן מקרא מן התורה    C

אני דורש וכי אי זו מדה מרובה מדת הטוב או מדת

הרע הוי אומ' מדת הטוב ◆ במדת פורענות הוא אומר    D

חמש עשרה אמה מלמעלה [וגו]מ' (בר' ז כ) ◆ מה נפשך    E

וחמש עשרה אמה בתוך הנחל חמש עשרה אמה על

פני ההר חמש עשרה אמה על פני הבקעה ◆ ובמדת    F

הטוב הוא אומ' ויצו שחקים ממעל וגומ' וימטר

עליהם מן וגומ' (תה' עח כד) ◆ מעוט דלתות שתים    G

כמה ארובות בדלת ארבע ארבע על ארבע הרי [שמנה

שמנה] על שמנה הרי ששה עשר ◆ הא צא וחשב    H

ששים אמה היה גבהו של מן שהיה יורד להן ליש'. ◆

resulted in a depth of 15 cubits of water, then the opening of the eight windows for the manna would have resulted in a depth of manna four times as deep, i.e., 60 cubits.

6.    A.    Isi ben Akiva says, "How does one know from Scripture that manna fell for Israel until all the nations saw it?

      B.    "Scripture states, 'You spread a table for me (in full view of my enemies), etc.' (Ps. 23:5)."

7.    A.    "When the Israelites saw it, they said one (to another, 'What is it?' For they did not know what it was. And Moses said to them, 'That is the bread which the Lord has given you to eat ')" (Exod. 16:15):

      B.    Like a man says to his fellow, "What is it?"

      C.    Likewise, the Israelites said, "What is it?" (Exod. 16:15).

8.    A.    "'And Moses said to them, etc.' (Exod. 16:15):

      B.    "Moses spoke to the elders, and the elders spoke to the Israelites."—Thus are the words of R. Joshua.

      C.    R. Eliezer the Modiite says, "Moses spoke to the elders, and he [also] spoke to the Israelites."

9.    A.    "'That is the bread which, etc.'" (Exod. 16:15):

      B.    R. Yosi ben Shimon says, "The Israelites were like horses fattened up.

      C.    "It says here 'to eat' (Exod. 16:15), and it says farther on 'Each man ate the bread of strong'[46] (Ps. 78:25).

      D.    "He[47] said to them, 'This bread that you are eating will stick to your limbs!'"[48]

10.   A.    Another interpretation:

      B.    "Each man ate the bread of strong horses, (He sent them provisions in plenty)" (Ps. 78:25):

      C.    R. Joshua says, "In that manna fell down [in a volume] corresponding to all of Israel."

      D.    And there are those who say, "It would fall upon [their] limbs, and one would gather and eat it from his limbs.

      E.    "Thus it is said, '... the bread of limbs, etc.' (Ps. 78:25)."[49]

## Chapter Forty-One

### Textual Source: Ms. Firkovich II A 268

XLI:I[50]

1.    A.    "This is what the Lord has commanded: Gather of it (as much as each of you requires to eat, an *omer* to a person for as many of you as there are. Each of you shall fetch for those in his tent)" (Exod. 16:16):

[112] B.    They said, "When Naḥson ben Aminadav and the members of his household would go out to gather, they would gather a large amount, but the poor among Israel would gather [only] a little.

      C.    "But when they came with a measure [to see how much each had, it ended up, nonetheless], '... an *omer* to a person for as many of you as there are, etc.' (Exod. 16:16)."[51]

2.    A.    They said, "He who ate this amount[52] was healthy and blessed. Less than this—sick to his stomach. More than this—behold this was a glutton!"

---

[46] Hebrew: *abirim*—אבירים.
[47] I.e., Moses.
[48] Hebrew: *avarim*—אברים.
[49] See 9.A–D above with corresponding notes.

| | | |
|---|---|---|
| 6 | A | איסי בן עקביה אום' מנין שירד להן מן ליש' עד |
| | B | שראו אותו כל האומות ◆ ת"ל תערך לפני שלחן וגומ' |
| | | (תה' כג ה). סל' פס'. ◆ |
| 7 | B/A | ויראו בני יש' ויאמרו איש וגומ' ◆ כאדם שאומ' |
| 8 | C | לחבירו מה הוא ◆ כך אמרו יש' מן הוא ◆ ויאמר משה |
| | B | אלהם וגומ' ◆ משה אמ' להן לזקנים וזקנים אמרו להן |
| | C | ליש' כך דברי ר' יהושע ◆ ר' אלעזר המודעי אומ' אמ' |
| 9 | A | להן משה לזקנים והוא אמ' לכל יש' ◆ הוא הלחם אשר. ◆ |
| | C/B | ר' יוסי בן שמע' אום' כסוסים ניתפטמו ישר' ◆ נאמ' |
| | | כאן לאכלה ונאמ' להלן לחם אבירים אכל איש (תה' |
| | D | עח כה) ◆ אמ' להן לחם זה שאתם אוכלין ניטוח הוא |
| 10 | C/B/A | באברים. ◆ ד"א ◆ לחם אבירים אכל איש ⟨זה⟩ ◆ ⟨ר'⟩ |
| | D | יהושע (אום') שהיה יורד ⟨לו⟩ מן כנגד כל יש'. ◆ ויש |
| | | אום' על איברים היה (היה) יורד ומאבריו היה מלקט |
| | E | ואוכל ◆ לכך נ⟨אמ' ל⟩חם אב⟨י⟩רים וגומ' סל' פס'. ◆ |

XLI:I

| | | |
|---|---|---|
| 1 | B/A | זה הדבר אשר צוה ייי לקטו ממנו ◆ אמרו כשהיה |
| | | יוצא נחשון בן עמינדב ללקט הוא ובני ביתו היו |
| | C | מלקטין הרבה ועני שביש' היה מלקט קימאה ◆ וכשהן |
| 2 | A | באין במדה עמר לגלגלת מספר וגומ' ◆ אמרו האוכל |
| | | כשיעור הזה בריא ומבורך פחות מיכן מקולל במעיו |
| | | יתר על כן הרי זה רעבתן. סל' פס'. ◆ |

---

[50] Compare XLI:I:1.A–21.B with *Mekhilta de-Rabbi Ishmael*, Vayassa (H/R, 167:7–169:16; Laut., vol. 2, 115:1–120:84; Neus., XLI:I:1.A–XL:II:10.B).
[51] See also Exod. 16:18.
[52] I.e., an *omer*.

3.  A.   "The Israelites did so, (some gathering much, some little)" (Exod. 16:17):

    B.   They did what they were commanded, and did not transgress decrees.

4.  A.   "And Moses said to them, '(Let no one leave any of it over until morning,) but they paid no attention to Moses, etc.'" (Exod. 16:19–20):

    B.   These were those among them lacking in faith.

5.  A.   "Some of them left of it (until morning)" (Exod. 16:20):

    B.   (Good)[53] people didn't leave it; other people left it.

6.  A.   "... it became infested with maggots and stank" (Exod. 16:20):

    B.   Is it possible that [only] after it brings forth worms, it [then] stinks? Rather, it [first] stinks and afterward brings forth worms.

    C.   In accordance with what is said later in Scripture, "... it did not stink (and there were no maggots in it), etc." (Exod. 16:24).

7.  A.   "And Moses was angry with them" (Exod. 16:20):

    B.   Moses was mad at them, and said to them, "Why have you done this?"

8.  A.   "So they gathered it every morning, (each as much as he needed to eat. For when the sun grew hot, it would melt)" (Exod. 16:21):

    B.   Every dawn, each according to [the amount] he could eat.

    C.   Those who interpret Scripture metaphorically say, "From this [we learn] about the manna, 'by the sweat of your brow shall you get bread to eat' (Gen. 3:19)."

9.  A.   "... for when the sun grew hot" (Exod. 16:21):[54]

    B.   At the fourth hour [of daylight].

    C.   You say at the fourth hour. Isn't it, instead, at the sixth hour?

    D.   When Scripture says, "... as the day grew hot" (Gen. 18:1), the sixth hour is spoken of!

    E.   Thus, how can I understand "... for when the sun grew hot" (Exod. 16:21)?

    F.   At the fourth hour.

10. A.   "... it would melt" (Exod. 16:21):

    B.   When the sun shone upon it, it would melt, and streamlets would form out of it and run down to the Great Sea. Then harts and gazelles would come and drink from it, and the nations of the world would come and hunt them, and taste in them the taste of manna that God gave to Israel.

11. A.   "On the sixth day they gathered double the amount of food, etc." (Exod. 16:22):

    B.   Based upon this [we learn] that one should prepare his *eruv* for each and every *Shabbat*.[55]

---

[53] The adjective "good" is not present in this manuscript. I have included it based upon the parallel to this tradition in the *Mekhilta de-Rabbi Ishmael*.

[54] Compare 9.A–F with y. Berakhot 7b (Neus., 4:1:V.A–O) and b. Berakhot 27a (Neus., I:Berakhot:4:1:IX.A–M).

[55] *Eruv* ("mixing") refers to halakhic/legal ways to enable actions that, otherwise, are forbidden on *Shabbat* and/or Jewish festivals. Referenced here is the prohibition on *Shabbat* to walk more than 2,000 cubits from one's village or residence. However, by establishing an *eruv teḥumim* ("boundary *eruv*") one, in effect, "mixes" forbidden areas with permitted areas, and is, thus, able to extend the distance one may walk. In order to do this, one places food for two meals within 2,000 cubits of one's residence, effectively establishing another residence from which one may walk an additional 2,000 cubits (see, e.g., m. Erubin, chapters 3–7). Our text's interpretation stresses that one must establish anew an *eruv* such as this for each and every *Shabbat*, and not simply reuse an *eruv* previously established.

| | | |
|---|---|---|
| ויעשו כן בני יש׳ וגומ׳ ◆ עשו מה שנתפקדו ולא | B/A | 3 |
| ‹עברו› על גזירות. ◆ | | |
| ◆ ויאמר משה אלהם וגומ׳ ולא שמעו אל משה ◆ | A | 4 |
| אלו מחוסרי אמנה שבהן ◆ ויותירו אנשים ◆ אנשים | B/A 5 | B |
| לא הותירו שאר אנשים הותירו. ◆ וירם תולעים | A | 6 |
| ויבאש. ◆ איפשר מאחר שמרחיש יבאש אלא מבאיש | B | |
| ואחר כך מרחיש ◆ כענין שנ׳ להלן ולא הבאיש וגומ׳ | C | |
| (שמ׳ טז כד) ◆ ויקצף עליהם משה ◆ כעס עליהן משה | B/A | 7 |
| ואמר להם מפני מה עשיתם כך. סל׳ פסו׳ | | |
| וילקטו אתו בבקר בבקר ◆ משחרית לשחרית איש | B/A | 8 |
| לפי אכלו ◆ דורשי רשומות אומ׳ מיכן שהיה בו במן | C | |
| בזעת אפך תאכל לחם (בר׳ ג יט). ◆ וחם השמש ◆ בארבע | B/A | 9 |
| שעות ◆ אתה אומ׳ בארבע שעות או אינו אלא בשש | C | |
| שעות ◆ כשהוא אומ׳ כחום היום (שם יח א) הרי שש | D | |
| שעות אמור ◆ הא מה אני מקיים וחם השמש ◆ בארבע | F/E | |
| שעות ◆ ונמס ◆ כיון שזורחת עליו חמה היה פושר ויורד | B/A | 10 |
| ונחלים מושכין ממנו והולכין (ממנו) לים הגדול | | |
| ואיילות וצביים באין ושותין מהן ואומות העולם | | |
| באין וצדין מהן וטועמים מהן טעם מן שנתן המקום | | |
| ליש׳ סל׳ פסו׳. ◆ | | |
| ◆ ויהי ביום הששי לקטו לחם משנה וגומ׳ ◆ | A | 11 |
| ◆ מיכן שיערב אדם מערב שבת לערב שבת. ◆ | B | |

12.  A.  "And all the chieftains of the community came and told Moses" (Exod. 16:22):

 B.  They said to him, "Master Moses! What differentiates this day from other days?"

[113]  C.  He said to them, "'This is what the Lord meant: It is a day of rest, a holy Sabbath of the Lord'" (Exod. 16:23).

 D.  They said to him, "When?"

 E.  He said to them, "'Tomorrow'" (Exod. 16:23).

13.  A.  "Bake what you would bake and boil what you would boil" (Exod. 16:23):

 B.  They baked that which is baked and boiled that which is boiled.

 C.  R. Joshua says, "It tasted baked for he who wanted to bake, and it tasted boiled for he who wanted to boil."

 D.  R. Eliezer the Modiite says, "'Bake what you would bake, etc.' (Exod. 16:23):

 E.  "For he who wanted to taste something baked it tasted like all the baked things in the world. [For he who wanted to taste] something boiled it tasted like all the boiled things in the world."

14.  A.  R. Eliezer says, "'Bake what you would bake, etc.' (Exod. 16:23):[56]

 B.  "They baked that which is baked and boiled that which is boiled.

 C.  "How so? If a festival falls on the day before *Shabbat,* how can you say from Scripture that one is permitted to bake or boil [food on the holy day for the subsequent *Shabbat*] only if he ceremoniously mixes?[57]

 D.  "Scripture states, 'Bake what you would bake, etc.' (Exod. 16:23).

 E.  "[Which means that] you may bake that which is [already] baked and you may boil that which is [already] boiled."

15.  A.  "... and all that is left (put aside until morning) ... So they put it aside until morning, etc." (Exod. 16:23):

 B.  [This is to be understood] in accordance with what we have already said.

16.  A.  "Then Moses said: Eat it today, (for today is a Sabbath of the Lord)" (Exod. 16:25):

 B.  Based on this R. Jeremiah would say, "There are three meals on *Shabbat.*"

17.  A.  "Because the Israelites were used to going out at dawn, they said to him [on the day of *Shabbat*], 'Master Moses! Let's go out at dawn!'

 B.  "He said to them, 'Eat it today!' (Exod. 16:25).

 C.  "They said to him, 'Because we didn't go out at dawn, let's go out at dusk.'

 D.  "He said to them, '... for today is a Sabbath of the Lord' (Exod. 16:25).

 E.  "At that moment, the hearts of the Israelites sunk. They said to him, 'Master Moses! Since we did not find it today, perhaps we will not find it tomorrow!'

---

[56] Compare 14.A–E with y. Betzah 61a (Neus., 2:1:I.A–E) and b. Betzah 15b (Neus., VII:Tractate Besah:2:1:III.A–C).

[57] I.e., the *halakhah* of *eruv tavshilin* ("mixed cooking"). During a festival, one is allowed to cook food only to be consumed during the period of the festival. During *Shabbat,* one is not allowed to begin cooking food anew. In order to prepare food for *Shabbat,* therefore, one must begin the preparation of a cooked dish before *Shabbat,* and then continue its cooking during *Shabbat.* Thus, in order to cook food for *Shabbat* on a festival day that immediately precedes *Shabbat,* one must place aside some cooked food and bread for *Shabbat* before the beginning of the festival day. This cooking, which began before the festival, may thus be continued on the festival for the needs of both the festival and the subsequent *Shabbat.*

| | | |
|---|---|---|
| 12 | B/A | ויבואו כל נשיאי העדה ויגידו למשה • אמרו לו רבינו |
| | | משה מה נשתנה יום זה משאר ימים • |
| | C | אמ' להן הוא אשר דבר ייי שבתון שבת קדש לייי • |
| E/D | A 13 | אמרו לו • אימתי אמ' להן • מחר את אשר תאפו אפו |
| | B | ואת אשר תבשלו בשלו • על האפוי אפו ועל המבושל |
| | C | בשלו • ר' יהושע אומ' הרוצה לאפות מתאפה לו |
| | D | והרוצה לבשל מתבשל לו • ר' אלעזר המודעי אומ' את |
| | E | אשר תאפו אפו וגומ' • הרוצה (לידע) לטעום דבר |
| | | האפוי טועם בו <טעם> כל אפויין שבעולם דבר |
| 14 | A | בשול טועם בו טעם כל בישולין שבעולם • ר' |
| | B | אל<י>עזר אומ' את אשר תאפו אפו וגומ' • על האפוי |
| | C | אפו ועל הבישול בשלו • כיצד יום טוב שחל להיות |
| | | בערב שבת מנין אתה אומ' שא<ין> רשאין לופות ולבשל |
| | E/D | אלא אם כן עירבו • ת"ל את אשר תאפו אפו וגומ' • על |
| | | האפוי אפו ועל המבושל בשלו ואת כל העודף וגומ' • |
| 15 | B/A | ויניחו אותו עד הבקר וגומ' • לענין שאמרנו. סל' פסו' • |
| 16 | B/A | ויאמר משה אכלוהו היום • מיכן שהיה ר' ירמיה |
| 17 | A | אומ' שלש סעודות בשבת • לפי שהיו יש' רגילין לצאת |
| | B | בשחרית אמ' לו רבינו משה נצא בשחרית • אמ' להן |
| | C | אכלוהו היום • אמרו לו הואיל (וליצאנו) [ולא יצאנו] |
| | D | בשחרית נצא בין הער[בים] • אמ' להן כי שבת היום לייי |
| | E | לפי שקבע לבן של יש' באותה שעה אמרו לו [ר]ב[י]נו משה |
| | | הואיל ולא מצאנוהו היום שמא לא נמצאהו למחר • |

F.  "He said to them, '… (you will not find it) today' (Exod. 16:25), [which means] today you won't find it, [but] you will find it tomorrow."—The words of R. Joshua.

G.  R. Eliezer Ḥisma says, "In this world you will not find it, [but] you will find it in the world to come."

18.  A.  R. Joshua says, "Moses said to Israel, 'If you gain merit by observing *Shabbat,* you will be saved from three divine punishments: from the day of *Gog;* from the day of the Messiah; and from the days of the great Rabbinic court, blessed be it!'"

B.  R. Eliezer the Modiite says, "Moses said to Israel, 'If you gain merit by observing *Shabbat,* God is going to give you the Land of Israel, and the world to come, and a new world, the monarchy of the House of David, the priesthood, and the levitical offices!'"

C.  R. Eliezer says, "Moses said to Israel, 'If you gain merit by observing *Shabbat,* God is going to give you three festivals: the festival of Nisan, the festival of Atzeret, and the festival of Tishrei.'"

19.  A.  "Six days you shall gather it. (On the seventh day, the Sabbath, there will be none)" (Exod. 16:26):

[114]  B.  R. Joshua says, "We have learned that it did not fall on *Shabbat.* How does one know from Scripture [that this was also the case] on a festival?

C.  "Scripture states, '… there will be none' (Exod. 16:26)."

20.  A.  R. Eliezer the Modiite says, "'Six day you shall gather it' (Exod. 16:26):

B.  "We have learned that it did not fall on *Shabbat.* How does one know from Scripture [that was also the case] on a festival?

C.  "Scripture states, '… there will be (none)' (Exod. 16:26).

D.  "How does one know from Scripture [that this was also the case] on the Day of Atonement?

E.  "Scripture states, '… there will be (none)' (Exod. 16:26)."

21.  A.  "On the seventh day (some of the people went out to gather), etc." (Exod. 16:27):

B.  These were those lacking faith among them.

*Chapter Forty-Two*

## Textual Source: Ms. Firkovich II A 268

XLII:I[58]

1.  A.  "And the Lord said to Moses: 'How long will you refuse (to obey My commandments and My teachings)?'" (Exod. 16:28):

B.  The Holy One, blessed be He, said to Moses, "Say to the Israelites: I brought you out from Egypt, and I split the sea for you, and I brought down the manna for you, and I stirred up the quail for you, and I performed miracles and mighty acts for you! For how long will you refuse to keep My commandments and My Torah?

C.  "Perhaps you will say that I have placed too many commandments upon you! I gave you [only] this *Shabbat* in Marah to observe it, but you haven't observed it!

D.  "Perhaps you will say: What reward is there in observing *Shabbat?*

E.  "Scripture states, '(Happy is the man) … who keeps the Sabbath and does not profane it, etc.' (Isa. 56:2).

---

[58] Compare XLII:I:1.A–16.E with *Mekhilta de-Rabbi Ishmael,* Vayassa (H/R, 169:18–173:10; Laut., vol. 2, 121:1–128:118; Neus., XLI:I:1.A–II:12.G).

| | |
|---|---|
| אמ' להן היום היום אי אתם מוצאין אותו | F |
| מוצאין אתם אותו למחר דברי ר' יהושע ◆ ר' | G |
| אלעזר חסמא אומ' בעולם הזה אי אתם מוצאין אותו | |
| מוצאין [את]ם אותו לעולם הבא ◆ ר' יהושע אומ' אמ' | A 18 |
| להן משה ליש' אם תזכו לשמר שבת תנצלו משלש | |
| פורעניות מיומו של גוג ומיומו של משיח ומימי בית | |
| דין הגדול בר' הוא ◆ ר' אלע[זר] המודעי אומ' אמ' להן | B |
| משה ליש' אם תזכו לשמר שבת עתיד המקום ליתן | |
| לכן ארץ יש' ◆ ועולם הבא ועולם חדש ומלכות בית | |
| דויד וכהונה ולויה. ◆ ר' אל<י>עזר אומ' אמ' להן משה | C |
| ליש' אם תזכו לשמר שבת עתיד המק' ליתן לכן | |
| שלשה מועדות חג של ניסן וחג של עצרת וחג של | |
| תשרי סל' פסו' ◆ | |
| שׁשׁת ימים תלקטוהו. ◆ ר' יהושע אומ' למדנו שלא | B/A 19 |
| היה יורד בשבת ביום טוב מנין ◆ ת"ל לא יהיה בו ◆ ר' | A 20 C |
| אלעזר המודעי אומ' ששׁת ימים תלקטוהו ◆ למדנו | B |
| שלא היה יורד בשבת ביום טוב מנין ◆ ת"ל לא יהיה ◆ | C |
| ביום הכפו' מנין ◆ ת"ל לא יהיה בו. ◆ | E/D |
| ויהי ביום השביעי וגומ' ◆ אלו מחוסרי אמנה שבהן. | B/A 21 |
| סל' פסקא ◆ | |

XLII:I

| | |
|---|---|
| ויאמר ייי אל משה עד אנה מאנתם וגומ' ◆ אמ' לו | B/A 1 |
| הקב"ה למשה אמ' להן ליש' הוצאתי אתכם ממצ' | |
| וקרעתי לכם את הים והורדתי לכם את המן והיגזתי | |
| לכם את השליו ועשיתי לכם נסים וגבורות עד מתי | |
| אתם ממאנים לשמור מצותי ותורתי ◆ שמא תאמרו | C |
| מצות הרבה היטלתי עליכם שבת זו שנתתי לכם במרה | |
| לשמרה ולא שמרתן אותה ◆ שמא תאמרו שומר שבת | D |
| מה שכר נוטל ◆ ת"ל שומ' שבת מחללו וגומ' (ישע' נו ב) | E |
| ◆ | |

  F. "Thus you learn that he who observes *Shabbat* is distanced from transgression!"

2. A. "Mark that the Lord has given you the Sabbath. (Therefore He gives you two days' food on the sixth day. Let everyone remain where he is. Let no one leave his place on the seventh day)" (Exod. 16:29):

  B. He[59] said to them, "Be careful! Because it is God who gave you *Shabbat!*"

3. A. "Therefore He gives you two day's food on the sixth day" (Exod. 16:29):

  B. Based on this R. Josiah would say, "Doubled bread—two *omers* for each person."

4. A. "Let everyone remain where he is" (Exod. 16:29):

  B. One should not go out [more than] four cubits from his place![60]

  C. "... (let no one leave his place) on the seventh day" (Exod. 16:29):

  D. [One should not go out more than] 2,000 cubits.

  E. When they heard this matter, they accepted it upon themselves and rested: "So the people remained inactive on the seventh day" (Exod. 16:30).

5. A. "So the people remained inactive on the seventh day" (Exod. 16:30):

  B. R. Joshua, R. Eliezer, and R. Eliezer the Modiite say, "Moses said to Israel," [continuing] as written above for "He said to them, 'Eat it today!' (Exod. 16:25).[61]

  C. "When they heard this matter, they accepted it upon themselves and rested: 'So the people remained inactive, etc.' (Exod. 16:30)."

6. A. "The house of Israel named it manna. (It was like coriander seed, white, and it tasted like wafers in honey)" (Exod. 16:31):

  B. Those who interpret the Torah metaphorically say, "Israel named it manna."

7. A. "It was like coriander seed" (Exod. 16:31):

  B. You don't know what [it was like].

  C. R. Joshua says, "Say it was like the seed of flax! You [might] say: Just as the seed of flax is red, so too this was red. Scripture states, [however,] 'white' (Exod. 16:31)."

  D. R. Eliezer the Modiite says, "What was it like? Like a word of *aggadah* that tugs at a man's heart."[62]

  E. R. Yosi says, "It speaks for itself that it was manna! Because it did not fall on *Shabbatot*, and not on festivals, and not on the Days of Atonement!"

[115]

  F. Others say, "Just as a prophet tells the Israelites about [their private] rooms and secrets, so too would the manna tell the Israelites about [their private] rooms and secrets![63]

  G. "How so? A wife offends her husband. She says, 'He is acting offensively to me!' and he says, 'She is acting offensively to me!' They come to Moses for a judgment, and he says to them, 'There will be a verdict in the morning.'

---

[59] I.e., Moses.

[60] The distance beyond one's city that one is allowed to walk on *Shabbat* is 2,000 cubits. Once one realizes that he has walked beyond that distance on *Shabbat*, he is only allowed to move an additional four cubits. See m. Eruvin, chapter 4, and parallels to 4.A–E at y. Eruvin 21d (Neus., 4:1:II.A–I) and b. Eruvin 51a (Neus., III.B:Erubin:4:9:III.1.A–K).

[61] See above XLI:I:18.A–C.

[62] *Aggadah* connotes Rabbinic traditions of lore, homily, and legend, in distinction to *halakhah*, which connotes Rabbinic legal traditions. This interpretation is a play on the similarity between the word for coriander seed, *zerah gad*—זרע גד, and the term *aggadah*.

[63] Compare 7.F–J with b. Yoma 75a (Neus., V.C:Yoma:8:2:I.17.A–C).

| | | |
|---|---|---|
| הא למדתה שכל המשמר שבת מרוחק הוא מן | F | |
| העבירה. סל׳ פסו׳ ◆ | | |
| ראו כי יייי נתן לכם השבת. ◆ אמ׳ להן הזהרו | B/A | 2 |
| שהמקום נתן לכן את השבת ◆ עלכן הוא נותן לכם | A | 3 |
| ביום השש׳ לחם יומים ◆ מיכן היה ר׳ יאשיה אומ׳ לחם | B | |
| כפול שני העומר לאחד ◆ שבו איש תחתיו ◆ ארבע אמות | B/A | 4 |
| ארבע אמות אל יצא איש ממקומו ◆ ביום הש׳ ◆ אלפים | D/C | |
| אמה ◆ כיון ששמעו את הדבר הזה [קיבלו] עליהן | E | |
| ושבתו וישבתו העם ביום הש׳. ◆ | | |
| וישבתו העם ביום הש׳ ◆ ר׳ יהושע ור׳ אל<י>עזר ור׳ | B/A | 5 |
| אלעזר המודעי אומ׳ אמ׳ להן משה לישר׳ כדכת׳ לעיל | | |
| ויאמר משה אכלוהו היום ◆ כיון ששמעו את [ה]דבר | C | |
| הזה קיבלו עליהן ושבתו וישבתו העם וגומ׳. סל׳ פסו׳ | | |
| ◆ | | |
| ויקראו בית יש׳ את שמו מן ◆ דורשי רשומות אומ׳ | B/A | 6 |
| יש׳ קראו אותו מן ◆ והוא כזרע גד. ◆ אי אתה יודע של | B/A | 7 |
| מה ◆ ר׳ יהושע אומ׳ <הוי> אומ׳ של זרע פשתן או אתה | C | |
| אומ׳ מה זרע פשתן אדום אף זה אדום ת״ל לבן ◆ ר׳ | D | |
| אלעזר המודעי אומ׳ למה הוא דומה לדבר אגדה | | |
| שהוא מושך את לב האדם ◆ ר׳ יוסי אומ׳ הוא מגיד על | E | |
| עצמו שהוא מן לפי שאינו יורד לא בשבתות ולא | | |
| בימים טובים ולא ביום הכיפורים ◆ אחרים אומ׳ כשם | F | |
| שהנביא מגיד להן חדרים וסתרים ליש׳ כך היה המן | | |
| מגיד ליש׳ חדרים וסתרים ◆ הא כיצד אשה סורחת על | G | |
| בעלה היא אומ׳ הוא סורח עלי והוא אומ׳ היא סורחת | | |
| עלי באין אצל משה לדין אמ׳ להן לבקר משפט | | |
| ◆ | | |

H. "At dawn, if manna was found in her husband's house, then certainly she was acting offensively toward her husband. But if it was found in her father's house, then certainly he was acting offensively toward her.

I. "Likewise with one who sells a slave to his friend, with the one saying, 'I bought him' and the other saying, 'I didn't sell him!' They come to Moses for a judgment, and he says to them, 'There will be a verdict in the morning.'

J. "At dawn, if manna was found in the house of his[64] first master, than certainly he didn't sell [him]. But if it is found in the house of his next master, then certainly he [legitimately] bought [him]."

8. A. "... and it tasted like wafers in honey" (Exod. 16:31):

B. R. Joshua says, "Like a dumpling stew."

C. R. Eliezer the Modiite says, "Like sifted flour that floats on top of a sieve and is kneaded with honey and butter."

9. A. If I should say, "(Moses said), 'This is what (the Lord has commanded: Let one *omer* of it be kept throughout the ages)'" (Exod. 16:32), one might think He did not authorize [it], and Aaron did not put it away until the 40th year.

B. Scripture states, [however,] "As the Lord had commanded Moses, Aaron placed it (before the Pact to be kept)" (Exod. 16:34).

C. When was the Ark made? In the second year.

D. And this is one of the things that were created on the eve of *Shabbat* at twilight. And these are they: the rainbow; the manna; the well; letters; writing; the tablets; the mouth of [Balaam's] ass; the mouth of the earth; Moses' grave; the cave in which Moses and Elijah stood; and Aaron's staff with its almonds and flowers.[65]

E. And there are those who say: Even the clothes of the first man.

F. And there are those who say: Also the priestly garment and the demons.

G. R. Josiah says in the name of his father, "Also the ram and the *shamir*."[66]

H. R. Nehemiah says, "Also the fire and the female mule."

I. R. Judah says, "Also the pair of tongs." He used to say, "Tongs are made with tongs.[67] [Thus,] how did the first pair of tongs come into existence? Were they not created?"

10. A. Seven things are hidden from human beings. And these are they: the day of [one's] death; the day of consolation; the extent of [God's] judgment; a person doesn't know in what way he might profit; a person doesn't know what his fellow is thinking; [the time of the messianic restoration of] the monarchy of the House of David; and [the time of the destruction of] the evil monarchy.[68]

[116]

11. A. "And Moses said to Aaron: 'Take a jar, (put one *omer* of manna in it, and place it before the Lord, to be kept throughout the ages)'" (Exod. 16:33):

B. I don't know what this jar [is made of]—of gold, of silver, of copper, of iron, of tin, or of lead!

---

[64] I.e., the slave's.

[65] Compare 9.D–I with *Sifre Deut.*, Piska 355 (Hammer, p. 372; Neus., CCCLV:IV:2.A–H); and b. Pesaḥim 54a (Neus., IV.C:Pesahim:4:4C–E: I.5.A–I.7.D).

[66] The worm that, according to legend, cut the stones used to build the Temple. These were used in place of the iron instruments that were prohibited because they were objects of warfare.

[67] That is, tongs cannot be fashioned without using a set of tongs.

[68] Compare 10.A with b. Pesaḥim 54b (Neus., IV.C:Pesahim:4:4C–E:I.8.A–B).

| | | |
|---|---|---|
| לשחרית אם נמצא מן בבית בעלה בידוע שהיא | H | |
| סורחת על בעלה ואם נמצא בבית אביה בידוע שהוא | | |
| סורח עליה ◆ וכן המוכר עבד לחבירו זה אומ' לקחתי | I | |
| וזה אומ' לא מכרתי באין אצל משה לדין אמ' להן | | |
| לבקר משפט ◆ לשחרית אם נמצא מן בבית רבו רא[שון | J | |
| בידו]ע שאינו מוכר ואם נמצא בבית רבו אחרון בידוע | | |
| שהוא לוקח. ◆ וטעמו כצפיחית בדבש ◆ ר' יהושע אומ' | B/A | 8 |
| כאידפס האיסקריטין ◆ ר' אלעזר המודעי אומ' כסלת | C | |
| זו שצפה על גבי נפה ול[ושה בדבש וחמאה ◆ | | |
| אם אומ'] אני זה הדבר יכול (לא המחה ולא) | A | 9 |
| [לא] [הניחו אהרן אלא בשנת] הארבעים ◆ ת"ל כאשר | B | |
| דבר ייי אל משה (שמ' טז לד) [ויניחהו אהרן וגו]מ' ◆ | | |
| אמתי נעשה [ה]ארון בשנה שניה ◆ וזה אחד מן | D/C | |
| הדבר[ים שנבראו בין] השמשות בערב שבת ואילו הן | | |
| קשת ומן ובא[ר והכתב והמכתב] והלוחות ופי האתון | | |
| ופי הארץ וקבורתו שלמשה ומערה שעמד בה משה | | |
| ואליהו ומקלו של אהרן שקדיה ופרחיה ◆ ויש אומ' אף | E | |
| בגדו שלאדם הראשון ◆ ויש אומ' [אף הכתונות] | F | |
| והמ[זיקים] ◆ ר' יאשיה אומ' משום אביו אף האיל | G | |
| והשמ[יר]. ◆ ר' נחמיה אומ' אף האור והפרדה ◆ ר' יהודה | I/H | |
| אומ' אף הצבת הוא היה אומ' צבתא בצבתא | | |
| מתעבדא צבתא קדמיתא מה הות הא לאו בריריה | | |
| הות. ◆ שבעה דברים מכוסין מבני אדם ואילו הן יום | A | 10 |
| מיתה ויום נחמה ועמק הדין ואין אדם יודע במה | | |
| משתכר ואין אדם יודע מה בלבו שלחברו ומלכות | | |
| בית דויד ומלכות חייבת. סל' פסו' ◆ | | |
| ויאמר משה אל אהרן קח צנצנת אחת ◆ צנצנת זו | B/A | 11 |
| איני יודע שלמה היא אם שלזהב אם שלכסף אם | | |
| של[נח]שת ואם שלברזל אם שלבדיל ואם שלעופרת | | |
| ◆ | | |

C. Scripture states, [however,] "a jar"[69] (Exod. 16:33).

D. I can only say this is a utensil that keeps thing cooler[70] than others. You must say it was a clay jar!

12. A. "... put one *omer* of manna in it, and place it before the Lord (to be kept throughout the ages)" (Exod. 16:33):

B. R. Joshua says, "For the Patriarchs."

C. R. Eliezer the Modiite says, "For the generations."

D. R. Yosi says, "For the days of Jeremiah. Because Jeremiah would say to the Israelites, 'Busy yourselves with Torah!' [The Israelites would respond,] 'If we busy ourselves with Torah, how are we going to sustain ourselves?' He would bring out the jar of manna and say to them, 'Look at that with which your forefathers, who busied themselves with Torah, sustained themselves! The same with you! If you busy yourselves with Torah, God will ultimately sustain you!'"

13. A. And this is one of three signs that Elijah will reveal to Israel. And these are they: the jar of manna;

### Textual Source: Midrash ha-Gadol

the jar of water; and the jar of anointing oil.

14. A. "And the Israelites ate manna forty years (until they came to a settled land. They ate the manna until they came to the border of the land of Canaan)" (Exod. 16:35):

B. R. Joshua says, "Israel ate manna for 40 days after the death of Moses. Moses died on the 7th of Adar, and they ate it for the [remaining] 24 [days] of Adar and for 16 [days] of Nisan.

C. "And thus Scripture states, '(On the day after the passover offering, on that very day, they ate of the produce of the country) ... On the day after, when they ate of the produce of the land, the manna ceased' (Josh. 5:11–12)."

D. R. Eliezer the Modiite says, "Israel ate manna for 70 days after the death of Moses. Moses died on the 7th of Adar, and they ate it for the [remaining] 24 [days] of Adar, and for the 30 [days] of the second [leap month] Adar, for it was an intercalated year, and for 16 [days] of Nisan.

E. "And thus Scripture states, 'On the day after ... the manna ceased' (Josh. 5:12)."

F. R. Eliezer says, "Israel ate the manna for 70 [days] after the death of

### Textual Source: Ms. Firkovich II A 268

Moses. Moses died on the 7th of Shevat, and they ate it for the [remaining] 24 [days] of Shevat, and for the 30 [days] of Adar, and that was not an intercalated year. But they ate it for 16 [days] of Nisan.

G. "And thus Scripture states, '... the manna ceased, etc.' (Josh. 5:12)."

H. Others say, "Israel ate manna for 54 years—for the 40 years of Moses' life and for 14 years after the death of Moses—7 during which they conquered [the land of Canaan] and 7 during which they divided [it].

I. "As it says in Scripture, 'And the Israelites ate manna 40 years (until they came to a settled land. They ate the manna until they came to the border of the land of Canaan)' (Exod. 16:35).

---

[69] Hebrew: *tzinzenet*—צנצנת.
[70] Hebrew: *m'tzayen*—מציין.

| | | |
|---|---|---|
| D/C | | ת״ל [צנצנת] אחת ◆ לא אמרתי אלא כלי שמציין יתר |
| A | 12 | מח[נברו אמר כ]לי חרש ◆ ותן שמה מלא העומר מן בה. |
| C/B | | והנח [אותו לפני יי׳ ◆ ר׳] יהושע אומ׳ לאבות ◆ ר׳ אלעזר |
| D | | המודעי אומ׳ לדורות ◆ ר׳ יוסי אומ׳ לימות ירמיה לפי |

שהיה ירמיה אומ׳ להן ליש׳ ה<ת>עסקו בתורה אם
נתעסק בתורה מאין אנו מתפרנסין [הו]ציא להן
צנצנת המן אמ׳ להן אבותי[כם] שנתעסקו בתורה
ראו במה [נתפרנסו אף אתם אם נתעסקתם] בתורה

| A | 13 | לסוף שהמ[ן]ק׳ מפרנס אתכם ◆ וזו אחת משלש אותות] |

שעתיד אליהו לגל[ו]ת להן לישראל ואלו הן צלוחית
שלמן] [וצלוחית שלמים וצלוחית שלשמן המשחה.
סל׳ פסו׳ ◆

| B/A | 14 | ובני יש׳ אכלו את המן ארבעים שנה ◆ ר׳ יהושע |

אומ׳ ארבעים יום אכלו יש׳ את המן אחר מיתתו
שלמשה מת משה בשבעה באדר ואכלו ממנו עשרים
וארבעה שלאדר וששה עשר שלניסן ◆ וכן הוא אומ׳

| C | | וישבת המן ממחרת באכלם מעבור הארץ (יהו׳ ה יב) ◆ |
| D | | ר׳ אלעזר המודעי אומ׳ שבעים יום אכלו יש׳ את המן |

אחר מיתתו שלמשה מת משה בשעה באדר אכלו
ממנו עשרים וארבעה שלאדר ושלשים שלאדר שני
שהיא היתה שנה מעוברת ואכלו ממנו ששה עשר

| F/E | | בניסן ◆ וכן הוא אומ׳ וישבת המן ממחרת]. ◆ [ר׳ אליעזר |

אומ׳ שבעים יום אכלו יש׳ את המן אחר מיתתו]
שלמשה מת משה בשבעה בשבט ואכלו ממנו כ״ד
שלשבט ול׳ שלאדר ועיבור לא היתה לשנה באותה

| G | | שנה ואכלו ממנו בי״ו בניסן ◆ וכן הוא אומ׳ וישבת המן |
| H | | וגומ׳ (יהו׳ ה יב). ◆ אחרים אומ׳ חמשים וארבע שנה |

אכלו יש׳ את המן ארבעים בחייו שלמשה וארבע
עשרה לאחר מיתתו שלמשה שבע שכיבשו ושבע

| I | | שחילקו ◆ שנא׳ ובני יש׳ אכלו את המן ארבעים שנה ◆ |

J.   "For Scripture doesn't need to say 'until they came to a settled land.' Why does Scripture state 'a settled land'?

[117]       K.   "This teaches that Israel ate manna for 14 years after the death of Moses—7 during which they conquered the land and 7 during which they divided [it]."

15.   A.   Miriam died—the well ceased to exist, but it returned.

B.   Aaron died—the pillar of cloud ceased to exist, but it returned.

C.   Moses died—the three of them[71] ceased to exist, and they did not return.

16.   A.   "The *omer* (is a tenth of an *ephah*)" (Exod. 16:36):

B.   I don't know how much [an *omer* is].

C.   Scripture states, [however,] "… a tenth of an *ephah*" (Exod. 16:36).

D.   One tenth of three *seahs*, which is seven quarters of a *kab* and a bit more.

E.   And a bit more is one-fifth of a quarter of a *kab*.

*Chapter Forty-Three*

Textual Source: Ms. Firkovich II A 268

XLIII:I[72]

1.   A.   "The whole Israelite community continued from the wilderness of Sin (by stages as the Lord would command. They encamped at Rephidim, and there was no water for the people to drink)" (Exod. 17:1):

B.   Along the way we learn that the enemy only comes because of sin and transgression.

2.   A.   "The people quarreled with Moses. (They said, 'Give us water to drink.' Moses replied to them, 'Why do you quarrel with me? Why do you try the Lord?')" (Exod. 17:2):

B.   They crossed the line of the law.

3.   A.   "Moses replied to them, 'Why do you quarrel, etc.'" (Exod. 17:2):

B.   He said to them, "The whole time you quarrel with me, behold, you are trying God!"

4.   A.   Another interpretation:

B.   He said to them, "The whole time you quarrel with me, behold, God is performing miracles and mighty acts for you, and His name is glorified in the world!"

5.   A.   "But (the people) thirsted there (for water. And the people grumbled against Moses and said, 'Why did you bring us up from Egypt, to kill us and our children and livestock with thirst?')" (Exod. 17:3):

B.   This teaches that thirst afflicted them.

C.   Above Scripture says, "They came to Marah, (but they could not drink the water,) etc." (Exod. 15:23):

Textual Source: Midrash ha-Gadol

D.   [At Marah] thirst did not afflict them, but here thirst afflicted them.

6.   A.   "… and said, 'Why did you bring us up from Egypt'" (Exod. 17:3):

---

[71] I.e., the well, pillar of cloud, and manna.
[72] Compare XLIII:I:1.A–17.G with *Mekhilta de-Rabbi Ishmael*, Vayassa (H/R, 173:12–175:16; Laut., vol. 2, 129:1–134:77; Neus., XLII:I:1.A–16.D).

שאין ת״ל עד בואם אל ארץ [נושבת מה] ת״ל אל | J

[ארץ] נושבת • מלמד שארבע עשרה שנה אכל]ו יש׳ | K

את המן א[חר מיתתו שלמשה שבע שכיבשו את

הארץ [ושבע ש]חילקו • מתה מרים בטלה הבאר | A | 15

וחזרה • מת אהרן בטל עמוד ענן וחזר • מת משה בטלו | C/B

שלשתן ולא חזרו. סל׳ פסו׳ •

והעומר • איני יודע <כ>מה • ת״ל עשירית האיפה • | C/B/A | 16

אחד מעשרה בשלש [סאין ש]הן שבעת רבעים ועוד • | D

[ועוד זה אחד מחמשה ברובע סל׳ פס]קא • | E

XLIII:I

ויסעו כל עדת בני [יש׳ ממדבר סין • לפי דרכינו | B/A | 1

למדנו שאין] השנאה באה [אלא על החטא ועל העבירה. •

וירב העם ע[ל משה וגו׳ • שעברו [על שורת הדין • | B/A | 2

ויאמר אליהם משה מה תריבון] וגומ׳ • אמ׳ [להם כל | B/A | 3

זמן שאתם מידינין כנגדי הרי א[תם מנסין את

המקום • [ד״א • אמ׳ להם כל זמן שאתם מידיינין כנגדי | B/A | 4

ה[רי המק[ום] עושה [לכם נסים וגבורות ושמו

מתגדל בעולם. ס]ל׳ פסו׳ •

ויצמ]א ש]ם [וגומ׳ מלמד • שנגע בהם צמאון • ולהלן | C/B/A | 5

הוא אומ׳ ויב]או ומרתה [וגומ׳ (שמ׳ טו כג) • לא נגע בהן | D

צמאון אבל כאן נגע בהן צמאון • ויאמר למה זה העליתנו ממצ׳ | A | 6

B. He said to them, "Normally, [when] someone becomes angry within his house, he only directs it toward someone unimportant. But here, they have directed it toward someone important!"

7. A. "'... to kill us and our children and livestock'" (Exod. 17:3):

B. Based on this, R. Josiah would say, "When the house falls, woe [also] unto the windows!"

8. A. Another interpretation:

B. "'... to kill us and our children and livestock'" (Exod. 17:3):

C. They said,

### Textual Source: Ms. Firkovich II A 268

"A person's livestock is his life!"

D. How so? The person who goes out along the way without his cattle with him suffers.

9. A. "Moses cried out to the Lord, saying, ('What shall I do with this people? Before long they will be stoning me!')" (Exod. 17:4):

B. [This] informs you of the praiseworthiness of Moses! For he didn't say, "Because they are quarreling against me, I'm not going to ask [God] for mercy on them!"

C. Rather, he said, "What shall I do with this people?" (Exod. 17:4).

D. He said before Him, "Master of the World! Between You and them, behold, I'm dead! For you said to me, 'Don't get angry with them!' [As it says in Scripture,] '... that You should say to me: Carry them in your bosom, etc.' (Num. 11:12)."

10. A. In this instance, God assuages [a situation] while Moses heightens [the anger]. But in the incident of the Golden Calf, God heightens while Moses assuages.

11. A. "Then the Lord said to Moses, 'Pass before the people. (Take with you some of the elders of Israel, and take along the rod with which you struck the Nile, and set out)'" (Exod. 17:5):

B. [Meaning]—pass over their words!

[118] C. R. Judah says, "Pass over their sins!"

D. R. Nehemiah says, "Pass before the people, and let he who is troubled speak out!"

12. A. Another interpretation:

B. "'Pass before the people'" (Exod. 17:5):

C. [Meaning]—bring them water!

D. "'Take with you some of the elders of Israel'" (Exod. 17:5)—for testimony, so that they won't say that there were springs there.

13. A. "'... the rod with which you struck the Nile, etc.'" (Exod. 17:5):

B. This is one of the three instances when Israel was rebellious, saying that something was [only] for punishment.

C. And these are they: the rod, the Ark, and the incense.

D. They said that the incense was [only] for punishment [because] it killed Nadab and Abihu. In the end, they knew that it was actually a blessing. [As it says in Scripture,] "He put on the incense and made expiation for the people" (Num. 17:12).

| | | |
|---|---:|---|
| אמ' להן דרך ארץ אדם כועס בתוך ביתו אין | B | |
| נותן פניו אלא בקטן אבל כאן נתנו פניהם בגדול. ◆ | | |
| להמית אתי ואת בני ואת מקני ◆ מיכאן היה ר' | B/A | 7 |
| יאשיה אומ' נפל ביתא חבל לכותא ◆ ד"א ◆ להמית אתי | B/A | 8 |
| ואת בני ואת מקני] אמרו שלאדם אינו אלא | C | |
| חייו ◆ הא כיצד אדם יוצא לדרך ואין בהמתו עמו | D | |
| מסתגיף הוא. סל' פסו' ◆ | | |
| ויצעק משה אל ייי לאמר. ◆ להודיע שבחו שלמשה | B/A | 9 |
| שלא אמ' הואיל והן מדינין כניגדי אף אני איני מבקש | | |
| ‹עליהן› רחמ' ◆ אלא אמ' מה אעשה לעם הזה ◆ אמ' | D/C | |
| לפניו רבונו שלעולם בינך לבינם הריני הרוג שאמרת | | |
| לי אל תקפיד כנגדן כי תאמר אלי שאהו בחיקך וגומ' | | |
| (במ' יא יב) ◆ כאן מקום ממיך ומשה מגביה אבל | A | 10 |
| במעשה העגל המקום מגביה ומשה ממיך סל' פסו' ◆ | | |
| ויאמר ייי אל משה עבור לפני העם ◆ עבר על | B/A | 11 |
| דבריהם ◆ ר' יהודה אומ' עבור על חטא שלהן ◆ ר' נחמיה | D/C | |
| אומ' עבור לפני העם ודרגשא ליה ‹י›מליל. ◆ ד"א ◆ | A | 12 |
| עבור לפני העם ◆ הוציא להן מים ◆ וקח אתך מזקני יש' | D/C/B | |
| לעדות שלא יאמרו מעינות היו שם. ◆ | A | 13 |
| ומטך אשר הכית | | |
| בו את היאור וגומ' ◆ זה אחד משלשה דברים שהיו יש' | B | |
| מתרעמין ואומ' של פורענות הוא ◆ ואילו הן מטה | C | |
| וארון וק[טורת ◆ קטורת זו אמרו של פורענות הי]א | D | |
| היא הרגה את נדב וא[ביהוא לסוף ידעו שהיא של | | |
| ברכה ויתן את] הקטורת ויכפר על [העם (במ' יז יב) | | |
| ◆ | | |

E. They said that the Ark was [only] for punishment [because] it killed Uzza, the Philistines, and Beit Shemesh. In the end, they knew that it was actually a blessing. [As it says in Scripture,] "The Ark of the Lord remained in the house of Obed … and the Lord blessed Obed-edom" (2 Sam. 6:11).

F. They said that the rod was [only] for punishment [because] it brought the Ten Plagues upon the Egyptians in Egypt. In the end, they knew it was actually a blessing. [As it says in Scripture,] "'… the rod with which you struck the Nile'" (Exod. 17:5).

## Textual Source: Midrash ha-Gadol

14. A. "'I will be standing there before you on the rock at Horeb. (Strike the rock and water will issue from it, and the people will drink)'" (Exod. 17:6):

B. He[73] said to him, "Anywhere you see human footprints—in accordance with what is said in Scripture, '… there was the semblance of a human form' (Ezek. 1:26)—there I am standing before you."

15. A. "'Strike the rock'" (Exod. 17:6):

B. Based on this, R. Yosi ben Zimra says, "This rod was made of sapphire.

C. "'Strike the rock' is not written here; rather, 'Strike with the rock.'"

16. A. "He named (the place Massah and Meribah, because the Israelites quarreled and because they tried the Lord, saying, 'Is the Lord present among us or not?')" (Exod. 17:7):

B. R. Joshua says, "Moses named it Massah and Meribah."

C. R. Eliezer the Modiite says, "God named it Massah and Meribah. As it says in Scripture, 'He named the place' (Exod. 17:7).

D. "Based upon this [we know] that the High Court, blessed be it, is called 'The Divine Place.'"

## Textual Source: Ms. Firkovich II A 268

17. A. "… because the Israelites quarreled, etc." (Exod. 17:7):

B. R. Joshua says, "[The Israelites said,] 'If He is [really] the Master of all Creation, blessed be He, if indeed He is over us, then we shall know. If not, we shall not know.'"

C. R. Eliezer the Modiite says, "[The Israelites said,] 'If He supplies our needs in the wilderness, we shall worship Him. But if not, we shall not worship Him.'"

D. R. Josiah and R. Eliezer Hisma say, "This verse is interpreted and explained by Job: 'Can papyrus thrive without marsh? (Can rushes grow without water?)' (Job 8:11).

E. "Now is it really possible for papyrus to exist without marshes and woods? And is it possible for rushes to exist without water?

[119] F. "Likewise, it is impossible for Israel to separate from the words of Torah. Because the Israelites separated from the words of Torah for three days, therefore the enemy came upon them. For the enemy only comes because of sin and transgression.

G. "As it says in Scripture, '… because the Israelites quarreled, etc.' (Exod. 17:7)."

---

[73] I.e., God.

ארון זה אמרו שלפורענות הוא הוא הרג] את עזא E

ואת פלש[תי]ם ואת בית שמש לסוף שהוא ידעו של

ברכה וישב] [ארון ייי] בית ע[ובד וגומ' ויברך ייי את

בית עבד אדום (ש"ב ו יא) • מטה] [זה אמרו של F

פורענות הוא הוא הביא עשר מכות על המצריים]

[במצ' לסוף ידעו שהוא של ברכה ומטך אשר הכית

בו את היאר] •

[הנני עמד לפניך שם על הצור בחרב • אמ' לו כל B/A 14

מקום שאתה מוצא רושם רגלי אדם כעניין שנ' דמות

כמראה אדם (יחז' א כו) שם אני עומד לפניך • והכית A 15

בצור • מיכאן ר' יוסי בן זימרה אומר מקל זה B

שלסמפיר הוא • והכית על הצור אין כת' כן אלא C

והכית בצור. ⟨סל' פסוק⟩ •

ויקרא שם המקום וגומ' • ר' יהושע אומ' משה קראו B/A 16

מסה ומריבה. • ר' אלעזר המודעי אומ' המקום קראו C

מסה ומריבה שנא' ויקרא שם המקום • מיכן לב"ד D

הגדול ב"ה שנקרא מקום]. • על ריב בני יש' וגומ'. • ר' B/A 17

יהושע אומ' אם ישנו רבון כל המעשים ברוך הוא אם

ישנו עלינו נדע ואם לאו לא נדע. • ר' אלעזר המודעי C

אומ' אם סיפק צרכינו במדבר נעבדנו ואם לאו לא

נעבדנו. • ר' יאשיהו ור' אלעזר חסמא אומ' מקרא זה D

רשום ומפורש על ידי איוב היגאה גמא בלא בצה

וגומ' (איוב ח יא) • וכי איפשר לגמא זה להיות שלא E

בצים ושלא עצים ואיפשר אחו זה להיות שלא מים •

כך אי איפשר להן ליש' לפרוש מדבר[י] תורה לפי F

שפרשו יש' מדברי תורה שלשת ימים לפיכך בא

עליהן שונא שאין שונא בא אלא על החטא ועל

העברה • שנא' על ריב בני יש' וגומ' סל' פסקא • G

# Tractate Amalek

## Chapter Forty-Four

(Textual Source: Ms. Firkovich II A 268)

XLIV:I[1]

1. A. "Amalek came (and fought with Israel at Rephidim)" (Exod. 17:8):

   B. R. Joshua says, "He would enter beneath the clouds of glory, and steal people from Israel and kill them.

   C. "As it says in Scripture, '(Remember what Amalek did to you on your journey ... he surprised you on the march), when you were famished and weary, etc.' (Deut. 25:18)."

   D. Others say, "'... he did not fear God' (Deut. 25:18)—this [actually refers] to Israel!"

2. A. R. Eliezer says, "He attacked with impudence.

   B. "All the [other] attacks that he made were only done in secrecy.

   C. "As it says in Scripture, '... he surprised you on the march, etc.' (Deut. 25:18).

   D. "But he made this attack with impudence."

3. A. R. Yosi ben Ḥalafta says, "'Amalek came' (Exod. 17:8):

   B. "He came under counsel. Because he went and gathered thousands and tens of thousands, in order to receive punishment.

   (Textual Source: Midrash ha-Gadol)

   C. "They said to him,[2] 'How will we be able to stand up to them? Pharaoh stood up to them, and God drowned him in the sea. How will we be able to stand up to them?'

   D. "He said to them, 'I'll give you counsel as to what you should do. If they beat me—flee! But if not, come and help me with them!'"

4. A. R. Nathan ben Joseph says, "Amalek passed through five nations and came and waged war with Israel.

   B. "As it says in Scripture, 'Amalekites dwell in the Negeb region. Hittites, Jebusites, and Amorites inhabit the hill country. And Canaanites (dwell by the Sea and along the Jordan)' (Num. 13:29).

   C. "He was inside all of them."

---

[1] Compare XLIV:I:1.A–10.C with *Mekhilta de-Rabbi Ishmael*, Amalek (H/R, 176:1–178:7; Laut., vol. 2, 135:1–140:67; Neus., XLIII:I:1.A–11.D).
[2] I.e., to Amalek.

# מסכתא דעמלק

| | | |
|---|---|---|
| ויבא עמלק ◆ ר׳ יהושע אומ׳ שהיה נכנס תחת ענני | B/A | 1 |
| כבוד וגונב נפשות מישר׳ והורגן ◆ שנא׳ ואתה עיף ויגע | C | |
| וגומ׳ (דב׳ כה יח) ◆ אחרים אומ׳ ולא ירא אלקים (שם) | D | |
| זה [ישר׳] ◆ ר׳ אליעזר אומ׳ [שב]א עליך בגלוי פנים ◆ לפי | B/A | 2 |
| שכל ביאות כולן [שבא לא בא אלא במטמוניות ◆ שנ׳ | C | |
| אשר קרך] בדרך וגומ׳ (שם) ◆ אבל ביאה זו בא בגלוי | D | |
| פנים ◆ ר׳ יוסי בן חלפתא אומ׳ ויבא עמ]לק ◆ שבא בעצה | B/A | 3 |
| לפי [שהלך וכינס כל אותן אלפים וכל אותן רבבות] | | |
| בשביל לקבל פורענות ◆ [אמ׳ לו היאך אנו יכולים | C | |
| לעמוד כנגדן פרעה שעמד כנגדם טיבעו המקום בים | | |
| היאך אנו יכולים לעמוד כנגדן ◆ אמ׳ להן אני אתן לכם | D | |
| עצה מה תעשו. אם ינצחוני ברחו ואם לאו בואו | | |
| וסייעונו עליהן. ◆ ר׳ נתן בן יוסף אומ׳ חמשת עממים | A | 4 |
| פסע ובא עמלק ועשה מלחמה עם ישר׳ ◆ שנ׳ עמלק | B | |
| יושב בארץ הנגב והחתי והיבוסי והאמורי יושב בהר | | |
| והכנעני וגומ׳ (במ׳ יג כט) ◆ הוא היה לפנים מכולם | C | |
| ◆ | | |

D.  Rabbi says, "He came only from the mountains of Seir. Amalek passed through 400 parasangs and came and waged war with Israel."

5.  A.  Others says, "Let thankless Amalek come and exact punishment from a thankless people!

### (Textual Source: *Mekhilta de-Rabbi Ishmael*)

B.  "Similar to this: 'These were the men who conspired against him: Zabad son of Shimeath the Ammonitess, etc.' (2 Chron. 24:26).

C.  "Let these [thankless ones] come and exact punishment from thankless Joash!

D.  "As it says in Scripture, 'King Joash disregarded the loyalty that his father Jehoiada had shown to him, and killed his son. As he was dying, he said: "May the Lord see and requite it!"' (2 Chron. 24:22).

E.  "What was his punishment in the matter?—'At the turn of the year, the army of Aram marched against him ... They inflicted punishment on Joash' (2 Chron. 24:23–24).

F.  "Don't read [the word in the verse as] 'punishment'[3] but [read it as] 'sodomy'[4]!

G.  "And what sort of sodomy did they do with him? They said that they appointed over him cruel guards who had not know a woman in their lives, and they violated him with sodomy.

H.  "In accordance with what is said in Scripture, 'Israel's pride shall be humbled, etc.' (Hos. 5:5). [And Scripture says], 'When they withdrew, having left him with many wounds, his courtiers plotted against him because of the murder of the sons of Jehoiada the priest, and they killed him in bed and he died' (2 Chron. 24:25)."

### (Textual Source: Midrash ha-Gadol)

6.  A.  "... at Rephidim" (Exod. 17:8):[5]

[120]  B.  R. Ḥananiah said, "We inquired of R. Eliezer about this matter when he was holding court in the Great School, [saying,] 'What [is the meaning of] Rephidim?'

C.  "He said to us, '[Understand it] according to its literal meaning!'"

7.  A.  R. Ḥananiah also said, "We inquired of R. Eliezer about this matter when he was holding court in the Great School, [saying,] 'Why does Israel redeem the first-born of donkeys, but does not redeem the first-born of camels and the first-born of horses?'

B.  "He said to us, 'It is a decree of the King, King of kings, blessed be He!'"

8.  A.  Another interpretation:

B.  [You redeem the first-born of donkeys] because they helped Israel when they left Egypt, in that each and every one had 70 donkeys before him, which were loaded with gold, silver, precious stones, and gems.

### (Textual Source: Ms. Firkovich II, 268)

9.  A.  Those who interpret the Torah metaphorically say, "[The verse] doesn't [say] 'Rephidim' but 'weakening of the hands.'[6]

B.  "Because Israel weakened their hands from the words of Torah, thus the enemy came upon them.

C.  "Because the enemy only comes because of sin and transgression.

---

[3] Hebrew: *sh'fatim*—שפטים.
[4] Hebrew: *shiputim*—שפוטים.
[5] Compare 6.A–9.F with b. Bekhorot 5b (Neus., XXXI.A:Tractate Bekhorot:1:1F–H:I.6.A–O).
[6] Hebrew: *rifyon yadayim*—ריפיון ידיים.

ר' אומ' לא בא אלא מהררי שעיר ארבע מאות פרסה D

פסע ובא עמלק ועשה מלחמה עם ישר'. ◆ אחרים אומ' A 5

יבוא עמלק כפוי טובה ויפרע מעם כפויי טובה] ◆

[כיוצא בו ואלה המתקשרים עליו זבד בן שמעת B

העמונית וגומ' (דה"ב כד כו) ◆ יבואו אלו כפויי טובה C

ויפרעו מן יואש כפוי טובה] ◆ [שנא' ולא זכר יואש D

המלך החסד אשר עשה יהוידע אביו ויהרג את בנו

ובמותו אמר ירא אלקים וידרוש (שם כב) ◆ מה ענשו E

של דבר ויהי לתקופת השנה עלה עליו חיל ארם וגומ'

ואת יואש עשו שפטים ◆ אל תקרי שפטים אלא F

שפוטים ◆ ומה שפוטים עשו בו אמרו העמידו עליו G

בריונות קשים אשר לא ידעו אשה מימיהם וענו אותו

במשכב זכור ◆ כענין שנ' וענה גאון ישראל וגומ' (הושע H

ה ה) ובלכתם ממנו כי עזבו אותו במחלואים רבים

התקשרו עליו עבדיו בדמי בני יהוידע הכהן ויהרגוהו

על מטתו וימת (דה"ב כד כה)]. ◆ [ברפידים ◆ אמר ר' B/A 6

חנניה דבר זה שאלנו את ר' אליעזר כשהוא יושב

במותבא רבא רפידים מהוא ◆ אמר לנו כמשמעו. ◆ ועוד A 7 C

אמר ר' חנניה דבר זה שאלנו את ר' אליעזר כשהוא

יושב במותבא רבא מפני מה פדו ישראל פטרי

חמורים ולא פדו פטרי גמלים ופטרי סוסים ◆ אמר לנו B

גזירת מלך מלכי המלכים ב"ה. ◆ ד"א ◆ לפי שסייעו את B/A 8

ישראל ביציאתן ממצרים שאין לך כל אחד ואחד

שלא היו לו שבעים חמורים לפניו שהיו טעונים כסף

וזהב ואבנים טובות ומרגליות] ◆ דורשי רשומות A 9

אומרים אין רפידים אלא ריפיון ידיים ◆ לפי שריפו יש' B

ידיהם מדברי תורה [לפיכ]ך בא עליהם שונא ◆ לפי C

שאין השונא בא אלא על החטא [ועל העביר]ה ◆

D. "As it says in Scripture, 'When the kingship of Rehoboam was firmly established, and he grew strong, he abandoned (the Torah of the Lord, he and all Israel with him), etc.' (2 Chron. 12:1).

E. "And what is said concerning him in Scripture?—'There were also male prostitutes in the land, etc.' (1 Kings 14:24).

F. "And what was his punishment in the matter? As it is written, 'In the fifth year of King Rehoboam, King Shishak of Egypt marched against Jerusalem and carried off the treasures of the House of the Lord and the treasures of the royal palace. He carried off everything. He even carried off all the golden shields that Solomon had made' (1 Kings 14:24–25)."

10. A. And this is one of the things that returned to their [original] place.

B. The exile returned to its place, as it says in Scripture, "In olden times, your forefathers lived beyond the Euphrates" (Josh. 24:2). What [else] does Scripture state?—"… and exiled the people to Babylon" (Ezra 5:12).

C. Heavenly writing returned to its place, as it says in Scripture, "You yourselves saw that I spoke to you from the very heavens" (Exod. 20:19). What [else] does Scripture state?— "You see it, then it is gone" (Prov. 23:5).

## XLIV:II[7]

1. A. "Moses said to Joshua, 'Pick some men for us, (and go out and do battle with Amalek)'" (Exod. 17:9):

B. Based on this [we learn] that the honor of one's disciple should be as dear to him as the honor of his fellow.

C. For the entire world should learn from Moses, who didn't say to Joshua, "Pick some men for me." Rather, [he said,] "Pick some men for us" (Exod. 19:9).

D. He treated him like himself.

E. And how does one know from Scripture that the honor of one's fellow should be as dear to him as the honor of his master?

F. For thus we find with Aaron, who said to Moses, "Oh, my lord" (Num. 12:11).

G. And wasn't he his younger brother? But he treated him like his master.

H. And how does one know from Scripture that the honor of one's master should be as dear to him as the honor of heaven?

I. For thus we find with Joshua, who said to Moses, "My lord, Moses, restrain them!" (Num. 11:28).

J. He said to them, "Just as the Holy One, blessed be He, restrains, so too should you restrain!"

K. And thus Scripture states, "(He said to Gehazi,) 'Tie up your skirts, take my staff in your hand, etc.'" (2 Kings 4:29).

L. They said to Gehazi, "Where are you going?" He said to them, "To raise the dead." They said to him, "Is it man who kills and resurrects? Isn't it the Holy One, blessed be He, who kills and resurrects?" He said to them, "My master also kills and resurrects!"

---

[7] Compare XLIV:II:1.A–6.G with *Mekhilta de-Rabbi Ishmael*, Amalek (H/R, 178:9–179:15; Laut., vol. 2, 140:68–143:113; Neus., XLIII:II: 1.A–8.H).

| | | |
|---|---|---|
| שנ' ויהי כהכין מלכ' רחבעם וכחזקתו עזב את ג' (דה״ב יב | D | |
| א) ◆ ומה [נא' בו וגם] קדש היה בארץ ג' (מ״א יד כד) ◆ | E | |
| ומה עונשו שלדבר דכ' ויהי בשנה [החמישית] למלך | F | |
| רחבעם עלה [שישק] [מלך מ]צרים ויקח את אוצרות | | |
| בית ייי ואת אוצרות בית המלך הכל לקח ויקח את | | |
| מגיני הזהב אשר עשה שלמה (מ״א יד כו) ◆ וזה אחד מן | A | 10 |
| הדברים שחזרו למקומן ◆ גלות חזרה למקומה שנא' | B | |
| בעבר הנהר ישבו אבותיכם מעולם ת (יהו' כד ב) | | |
| מהוא או' ועמה הגלי לבבל (עז' ה יב) ◆ כתב שמים חזר | C | |
| למקומו שנ' אתם ראיתם כי מן השמים דברתי עמכם | | |
| (שמ' כ יח) מהוא או' התעיף עינך בו ואיננו (מש' כג ה) ◆ | | |

XLIV:11

| | | |
|---|---|---|
| ויאמר משה אל יהושע בחר לנו אנשים ◆ מיכן | B/A | 1 |
| שיהא כבוד תלמידו של אדם חביב עליו ככבוד חבירו ◆ | | |
| וילמוד כל העולם ממשה שלא אמר לו ליהושע בחר | C | |
| לי אנשים אלא בחר לנו אנ' ◆ עשאו כמותו ◆ ומנין שיהא | E/D | |
| כבוד חברו של אדם חביב עליו ככבוד רבו ◆ שכין | F | |
| מצאנו באהרן שא' למשה בי אדוני (במ' יב יא) ◆ והלוא | G | |
| אחיו קטן הוא <...> אלא עשאו רבו ◆ ומנין שיהא כבוד | H | |
| רבו של אדם חביב עליו ככבוד שמים ◆ שכין מצאנו | I | |
| ביהושע שא' למשה אדני משה כלאם (במ' יא כח) ◆ א' | J | |
| לו כשם שהק' מכלה כך אתה כלי ◆ וכין הוא או' חגור | K | |
| מתנך וקח משענתי בידך וג' (מ״ב ד כט) ◆ אמרו לו | L | |
| לגחזי להיכן אתה הולך א' להן להחיות מתים אמ' לו | | |
| וכי אדם ממית ומחיה והלוא הק' ממית ומחיה אמ' | | |
| להן אף רבי ממית ומחיה ◆ | | |

(Textual Source: Midrash ha-Gadol)

2.      A.      "'... some men'" (Exod. 17:9):

        B.      Mighty warrior men. Men who fear sin.

3.      A.      "'... and go out and do battle with Amalek'" (Exod. 17:9):

[121]   B.      R. Joshua says, "Moses said to Joshua, 'Go out from beneath the wings of the Cloud and do battle with Amalek!'"

        C.      R. Eliezer the Modiite says, "The Holy One, blessed be He, said to Moses, 'Say to Joshua: "This head of yours—why are you guarding it? Isn't it for the crown? Go out and do battle with Amalek!"'"

4.      A.      "'"Tomorrow I will station myself on top of the hill, with the rod of God in my hand"'" (Exod. 17:9):

        B.      "Tomorrow we will be ready and standing on top of the hill.

        C.      "'"... with the rod'" (Exod. 17:9):

        D.      "Which the Holy One, blessed be He, said should be in your hand, will be in my hand forever."—Thus are the words of R. Joshua.

        E.      R. Eliezer the Modiite says, "Tomorrow we'll declare a fast, and we will be ready and depending upon the acts of the forefathers.

        F.      "'Top' (Exod. 17:9)— these are the acts of the Patriarchs. 'Of the hill' (Exod. 17:9)—these are the acts of the Matriarchs."

5.      A.      "'... with the rod of God in my hand'" (Exod. 17:9):

        B.      Moses said before God, "With this rod You brought them out from Egypt, and split the sea for them, and brought down the manna for them, and stirred up the quail for them, and performed miracles and mighty acts for them. With this rod, You will perform miracles and mighty acts at this moment!"

6.      A.      Isi ben Judah says, "There are five words in the Torah for which it's unclear how they relate syntactically with the word next to them: lifting up; cursed; tomorrow; like almond blossoms; and get up.[8]

        B.      "How does one know from Scripture [about] 'lifting up'?—'Surely if you do right, there is lifting up' (Gen. 4:7) [can also be read] 'there is lifting up, even if you do not do right' (Gen. 4:7).

        C.      "[How does one know from Scripture about 'cursed'?]—'Cursed be their anger so fierce' (Gen. 49:7) [can also be read] 'For when they are angry, they slay men, and when pleased, they maim cursed oxen' (Gen. 49:6–7).

        D.      "[How does one know from Scripture about 'tomorrow'?]—'Tomorrow I will station myself on top of the hill' (Exod. 17:9) [can also be read] 'Go out and do battle with Amalek tomorrow' (Exod. 17:9).

        E.      "[How does one know from Scripture about 'almond blossoms'?]—'Almond blossoms with calyx and petals' (Exod. 25:34) [can also be read] 'and on the lampstand there shall be four cups shaped like almond blossoms' (Exod. 25:34).

        F.      "[How does one know from Scripture about 'get up'?]—'This people will get up and go astray' (Deut. 31:16) [can also be read] 'You are soon to lie with your fathers and get up' (Deut. 31:16).

---

[8] Compare 6.A–G with b. Yoma 52b (Neus., V.B:Yoma:5:1F–I:I.3.D–G).

| | |
|---|---|
| אנשים אנשים ♦ גבורים אנשים יראי חטא. ♦ וצא הלחם | A/B/A 3/2 |
| בעמלק ♦ ר' יהושע אומר אמר לו משה ליהושע צא | B |
| מתחת כנפי הענן והלחם בעמלק. ♦ ר' אלעזר המודעי | C |
| אומר אמר לו הקב"ה למשה אמור ליהושע ראשך זה | |
| למה אתה משמרו לא לכתר צא והלחם בעמלק. ♦ מחר | A 4 |
| אנכי נצב על ראש הגבעה ומטה האלקים בידי ♦ מחר | B |
| נהיה מעותדין ועומדין על ראש הגבעה ♦ ומטה ♦ שאמר | D/C |
| הקב"ה תהא בידך תהא בידי לעולם כך דברי ר' | |
| יהושע ♦ ור' אלעזר המודעי אום' מחר נגזור תענית ונהא | E |
| מעותדין ועומדין על <מעשה אבות> ♦ ראש אלו מעשה | F |
| אבות הגבעה אלו מעשה אמהות. ♦ ומטה האלקים | A 5 |
| בידי ♦ אמר משה לפני המקום במטך זה הוצאתם | B |
| ממצרים וקרעת להם את הים והורדת להן את המן | |
| והגזת להן את השלו ועשית להם נסים וגבורות | |
| במטה זה אתה תעשה להן נסים וגבורות בשעה זו. ♦ | |
| איסי בן יהודה אומר חמשה דברים יש שאין להם | A 6 |
| בתורה הכרע שאת ארור מחר משוקדים וקם ♦ שאת מנין | B |
| הלא אם תיטיב שאת או שאת ואם לא תיטיב (בר' ד ז) ♦ | |
| ארור אפם כי עז או כי באפם הרגו איש וברצונם עקרו שור | C |
| ארור (בר' מט ו) ♦ מחר אנכי נצב על ראש הגבעה או צא | D |
| הלחם בעמלק מחר. ♦ משוקדים כפתוריה ופרחיה או במנורה | E |
| ארבעה גביעים משוקדים (שמ' כה לד) ♦ וקם העם הזה | F |
| וזנה או הנך שוכב עם אבותיך וקם (דב' לא טז) ♦ | |

G. "These are the five words in the Torah for which it's unclear how they relate syntactically with the word next to them."

XLIV:III[9]

1. A. "Joshua did as Moses told him (and fought with Amalek, while Moses, Aaron, and Hur went up to the top of the hill)" (Exod. 17:10):

   B. He did what he was commanded, and did not transgress Moses' decree.

2. A. "... while Moses, Aaron, and Hur went up to the top of the hill" (Exod. 17:10):

   B. [This is to be understood] in accordance with what we have already said.

### (Textual Source: Ms. Firkovich II A 268)

3. A. "Whenever Moses held up his hand, (Israel prevailed. But whenever he let down his hand, Amalek prevailed)" (Exod. 17:11):[10]

   B. R. Eliezer says, "Did Moses' hands really strengthen Israel or break Amalek?

   C. "Rather, whenever Israel does the will of God and believes in what God commanded Moses, God performs miracles and mighty deeds for them.

   D. "Similar to this, you say: 'They shall take some of the blood and put it on the two doorposts and the lintel of the houses (in which they are to eat it)' (Exod. 12:7).

   E. "Does the blood really benefit the angel, and does the blood really benefit the doorpost?

   F. "Rather, whenever Israel does the will of God and believes in what God commanded Moses to do, God has mercy on them.

[122] G. "Similar to this, you say: 'The Lord said to Moses: "Make a *seraph* figure, etc."' (Num. 21:8).

   H. "Can a snake really kill and resurrect?

   I. "Rather, whenever Israel does the will of God and believes in what God commanded Moses to do, the Holy One, blessed be He, sent them healing."

4. A. R. Akiva says, "Why does Scripture state, 'Israel prevailed,' and why does Scripture state, 'Amalek prevailed' (Exod. 17:11)?

   B. "When Moses would raise his hand, Israel was destined to raise up the words of Torah, which were going to be given by his hands. But when Moses would lower his hands, as if it were possible, Israel was destined to lower the words of Torah, which were going to be given by his hands."

5. A. "'But Moses' hands grew heavy (so they took a stone and put it under him and he sat on it, while Aaron and Hur, one on each side, supported his hands. Thus his hands remained steady until the sun set)' (Exod. 17:12):

### (Textual Source: Midrash ha-Gadol)

   B. "At that moment, Moses' hands grew heavy like a person from whom hung two jugs of water."—Thus are the words of R. Joshua.

   C. R. Eliezer the Modiite says, "Based on this [we learn] that you shouldn't be careless with a divine commandment. For if Moses had immediately said to Joshua, 'Pick some men for me,' he would not have reached that [point of] distress. But he said [to Joshua to pick out the men] tomorrow."

---

[9] Compare XLIV:III:1.A–14.F with *Mekhilta de-Rabbi Ishmael*, Amalek (H/R, 179:16–181:13; Laut., vol. 2, 143:114–147:177; Neus., XLIII:II: 9.A–III:17.B).

[10] Compare 3.A–I with m. Rosh Hashanah 3:8.

| | | |
|---|---|---|
| G | אלו חמשה דברים יש בתורה שאין להם הכרע. ◆ | |
| XLIV:III | | |
| B/A | ויעש יהושע כאשר אמר לו משה ◆ עשה מה | 1 |
| A | שנתפקד ולא עבר על גזירת משה. ◆ ומשה אהרן וחור | 2 |
| A 3 B | עלו ראש הגבעה ◆ לענין שאמרנו ◆ <...> | |
| B | והיה כאשר ירים משה ידו ג' ◆ ר' אליעזר או' וכי | |
| C | ידיו של [משה מגבירות] יש' או שוברות עמלק ◆ אלא | |
| | בזמן שיש' עושין <רצונו> שלמקום ומאמינין במה | |
| | שפקדו המקום למשה המקום עושה להם ניסין | |
| D | וגבורות ◆ כיוצא בו אתה או' ולקחו מן הדם ונתנו על | |
| E | המשקוף ועל שתי המזוזות ג' (שמ' יב ז) ◆ וכי מה הדם | |
| F | מהנה למלאך ומה הדם מהנה למזוזה ◆ אלא כל זמן | |
| | שיש' עושין רצונו שלמקום ומאמינין במה שפקדו | |
| G | <המקום למשה לעשות המקום חס עליהן. ◆ כיוצא בו | |
| | אתה או' ויאמר ה' אל משה עשה לך שרף וג' (במ' כא | |
| I/H | ח) ◆ וכי נחש ממית ומחיה ◆ אלא כל זמן שיש' עושין | |
| | רצונו שלמקום ומאמינים במה שפקדו> המקום | |
| A | למשה לעשות כך הקב"ה שלח להם רפואה ◆ ר' עקיבא | 4 |
| | או' (ו)מה תל' לו' וגבר יש' ומה תל' לו' וגבר עמלק ◆ | |
| B | כשהיה משה מגביה את ידו שעתידין יש' להגביה | |
| | דברי תורה העתידין להינתן על ידיו אף כשהיה משה | |
| | משפיל את ידיו כויכ<ו>ל שעתידין יש' להשפיל דברי | |
| | תורה שעתידין להינתן על ידיו ◆ | |
| B/A | וידי משה כבדים יקרו ידיו של משה ◆ באותה | 5 |
| | שעה כאדם שתלויין בו שני כדי מים כך דברי ר' | |
| C | יהושע. ◆ ר' אלעזר המודעי אומר מכאן שאין מרשלין לדבר | |
| | מצוה שאלו אמר לו משה ליהושע בחר לי אנשים | |
| | מיד לא בא לידי צער ההוא אלא אמר למחר. ◆ | |

(Textual Source: Ms. Firkovich II A 268)

6.   A.   "… so they took a stone and put it, etc." (Exod. 17:12):[11]

     B.   Did they not have there a cushion or a pillow to put under him to sit?

     C.   Rather, he said, "As long as Israel is situated in distress, I too shall be with them in distress!"

     D.   Based on this they said: A person is obligated to suffer with the masses.

7.   A.   "… while Aaron and Hur … supported his hands" (Exod. 17:12):

     B.   This teaches that he was raising and lowering them.

8.   A.   "'Thus his hands remained steady until the sun set' (Exod. 17:12):

     B.   "This teaches that Israel was fasting that entire day."—Thus are the words of R. Joshua.

     C.   R. Eliezer the Modiite says, "'But Moses' hands grew heavy' (Exod. 17:12):

     D.   "The sin weighed heavily on Moses, and he was unable to stand it. What did he do? He turned to the forefathers.

     E.   "As it says in Scripture, '… so they took a stone and put it under him' (Exod. 17:12). This [refers to] the deeds of the forefathers.

     F.   "'… and he sat on it' (Exod. 17:12). This [refers to] the deeds of the Matriarchs."

9.   A.   "… while Aaron and Hur, one on each side, supported his hands" (Exod. 17:12):

     B.   Why does Scripture state "one on each side"?

     C.   This teaches that Aaron would remind [him] about the deed of Levi, and Hur would remind [him] about the deed of Judah.

[123]   D.   Based on this, they said: There are no less than three who go down before the ark on a public fast.

10.   A.   "Thus his hands remained steady" (Exod. 17:12):

     B.   Why does Scripture state "his hands"?

     C.   One [hand], because he took nothing with it from Israel.

     D.   "… steady until the sun set" (Exod. 17:12).

     E.   And with one hand Moses said before the Holy One, blessed be He, "Through my hands You brought them out from Egypt, and through my hands You split the sea for them, and brought down the manna for them, and stirred up the quail for them. And through my hands will You perform miracles for them at this moment!"

11.   A.   Another interpretation:

     B.   "… steady until the sun set" (Exod. 17:12).

     C.   He said, "I have seen all kingdoms, and none of them wages war beyond the sixth hour [of daylight]. This evil kingdom wages war from morning to evening!"

(Textual Source: Midrash ha-Gadol)

12.   A.   "And Joshua overwhelmed Amalek and his people with the sword" (Exod. 17:13):

     B.   R. Joshua says, "In that he came down and cut off the heads of warriors standing at the front of the lines."

---

[11] Compare 6.A–D with b. Ta'anit 11a.

| | | |
|---|---|---|
| [ויקחו] אבן וישימו ג' ◆ וכי לא היה שם כסת אחת או | B/A | 6 |
| גלובקרין א[חד שיניח] תחתיו וישב ◆ אלא אמר כל זמן | C | |
| שיש' שרוין בצרה [אף אני אהא] עמהן בצרה ◆ מיכן אמרו | D | |
| חיב אדם להיצטער ע[ם הציבור]. ◆ ואהרן וחור תמכו | A | 7 |
| בידיו ◆ מלמד (ב) שהיה מעלה בהן ומוריד בהן ◆ ויהי | A 8 | B |
| ידיו אמונה עד בא השמש ◆ מלמד שהיו יש' בתענית כל | B | |
| אותו היום <כך דברי ר' יהושע ◆ ר' אלעזר המודעי | C | |
| אומר וידי משה כבדים> ◆ יקר החטא על משה ולא | D | |
| היה יכול לעמוד בו מה עשה ניפנה לאבות הראשונים ◆ | | |
| שנ' ויקחו אבן ויש<י>מו תחתיו אלו מעשי אבות ◆ וישב | F/E | |
| עליה אלו מעשה אימהות ◆ ואהרן וחור תמכו בידיו | A | 9 |
| מ[זה] אחד ומזה אחד ◆ <מה> ת"ל אחד אחד ◆ מלמד | C/B | |
| שהיה אהרן מזכיר מעשה לוי וחוור מזכיר מעשה | | |
| יהודה ◆ מיכן אמרו אין פחותין משלשה שירדים לפני | D | |
| תיבה בתענית צבור ◆ ויהי ידיו אמ<ו>נה ◆ מה ת"ל ידו ◆ | B/A | 10 |
| אחת שלא נטל בה מיש' ◆ כלום אמונה עד בא | D/C | |
| הש[מש]. ◆ <ובידו אחת> א' משה לפני הק' על ידי | E | |
| הוצאתם ממצ' ועל ידי קרעתה להן את הים | | |
| והורד[ת]ה להן את המן והיגזת <להן> את השליו | | |
| ועל ידי תעשה להן ניסין בשעה זו ◆ [ד"א] ◆ אמונה עד | B/A | 11 |
| בא השמש ◆ אמר ראיתי כל מלכ<י>ות כו[לן אין] | C | |
| עושות מלחמה אלא עד שש שעות מלכות חייבת [זו] | | |
| עושה מלחמה משחרית [ועד ער]בית. ◆ | | |
| ויחלש יהושע את עמלק. ◆ ר' יהושע אומר שירד | B/A | 12 |
| וחתך ראשי גבורים העומדין בראשי שורות. ◆ | | |

C. R. Eliezer the Modiite says, "[The verb 'overwhelmed' is to be interpreted] as an abbreviation [of three verbs]: 'He made [them] sick,' 'he seized [them],' and 'he broke [them].'"

13.    A. "'Amalek' (Exod. 17:13)—[understand it] according to its literal meaning.

B. "'People' (Exod. 17:13)—these are his sons.

C. "'*Et*' (Exod. 17:13)—[the accusative particle refers to] his troops with him."—Thus are the words of R. Joshua.

D. R. Eliezer the Modiite says, "'Amalek' (Exod. 17:13)—[understand it] according to its literal meaning.

E. "'People' (Exod. 17:13)— these are his sons.

F. "'*Et*' (Exod. 17:13)—[the accusative particle refers to] his troops with him.

G. "But since Scripture says 'and *(et)*' (Exod. 17:13)— these are the troops with his sons."

14.    A. "... with the sword" (Exod. 17:13):

B. R. Joshua says, "They didn't disfigure them; rather, they judged them mercifully."

C. R. Eliezer the Modiite says, "'... with the sword' (Exod. 17:13):

D. "We have learned about this war, that it was [commanded] by no one other than the Almighty!"

E. Others say, "'... with the sword' (Exod. 17:13):

F. "What Scripture says later on was upheld for them: 'I will doom you with blood. Blood shall pursue you. For your bloodthirsty hatred, blood shall pursue you' (Ezek. 35:6)."

*Chapter Forty-Five*

(Textual Source: Ms. Firkovich II A 268)

XLV:I[12]

1.    A. "Then the Lord said to Moses, 'Inscribe this in a document as a reminder, (and read it aloud to Joshua: I will utterly blot out the memory of Amalek from under heaven!)'" (Exod. 17:14):

B. The first elders say, "By the very scourge which strikes Israel, [others too] will be struck!

C. "The whole world should learn from Pharaoh, because he came and subjugated Israel.

D. "The Holy One, blessed be He, drowned him in the sea, as it says in Scripture, 'But the Lord hurled the Egyptians (into the sea)' (Exod. 14:27).

E. "And thus you find with Amalek. Because he came, subjugated, and injured Israel, the Holy One, blessed be He, eradicated him from this world and the world to come. As it says in Scripture, 'I will utterly blot out the memory' (Exod. 17:14).

F. "Likewise, any nation or kingdom that should come to injure Israel, by that very same measure will the Holy One, blessed be He, exact punishment from it

G. "Forever they said: 'With what measure a man metes it shall be measured to him again.'"[13]

2.    A. "'Inscribe this in a document as a reminder' (Exod. 17:14):[14]

[124]    B. "'Inscribe'—[this refers to] what is written here.

---

[12] Compare XLV:I:1.A–17.E with *Mekhilta de-Rabbi Ishmael*, Amalek (H/R, 181:15–187:9; Laut., vol. 2, 148:1–161:192; Neus., XLIV:I:1.A–II:11.F).
[13] Compare 1.G with m. Sotah 1:7.

| | | |
|---|---|---|
| ר׳ אלעזר המודעי אומר בו לשון נוטריקון ויחל ויאחז | C | |
| וישבר. ◆ עמלק כמשמעו ◆ עם אלו בניו ◆ את אלו חיילות | C/B/A | 13 |
| שעמו כך דברי ר׳ יהושע. ◆ ר׳ אלעזר המודעי אומר עמלק | D | |
| כמשמעו ◆ עם אלו בניו ◆ את אלו חיילות שעמו. ◆ כשהוא | G/F/E | |
| אומר ואת אלו חיילות שעם בניו. ◆ לפי חרב ◆ ר׳ יהושע | B/A | 14 |
| אומר לא ניוולום אלא היו דנין אותן ברחמים. ◆ ר׳ | C | |
| אלעזר המודעי אומר לפי חרב ◆ למדנו למלחמה זו | D | |
| שלא היית אלא על פי גבורה. ◆ אחרים אומרין לפי | E | |
| חרב ◆ נתקיים בהן מה שנ׳ להלן כי לדם אעשך ודם | F | |
| ירדפך אם לא דם שנאת ודם ירדפך (יחז׳ לה ו). ◆ | | |

| | | |
|---|---|---|
| [ויאמר] ייי [אל] משה כתוב זאת זכרון בספר ◆ | A | 1 |
| זקנים הראשונים אומרים שוט שיש׳ לוקין בו סופו | B | |
| ללקות ◆ ילמוד כל העולם מפרעה שמתוך שבא ושעבד | C | |
| את ישראל ◆ טיבעו הק׳ בים שנ׳ וינער ייי את מצ׳ (שמ׳ | D | |
| יד כז) ◆ וכין [אתה מוצא] בעמלק שמתוך שבא ושעבד | E | |
| והזיק את יש׳ (ארב) אבדו הק׳ מן העולם הזה ומן | | |
| העולם הבא שנ׳ כי מחה אמחה את זכר ◆ וכן כל אומה | F | |
| ומלכות [שתבוא] להזיק את יש׳ בו בדבר הק׳ נפרע | | |
| ממנה ◆ לעולם אמ׳ במדה ש[אדם] מודד בה מודדין לו | G | |
| כתב ‹זאת› זכרון בספר ◆ ‹כתוב משכתוב כאן › ◆ | B/A | 2 |

---

[14] In 2.A–H, each word in the clause from Exod. 17:14 is understood to refer individually to a separate scriptural reference to the war against Amalek. Compare with b. Megillah 7a.

C. "'This'—[this refers to] what is written in Deuteronomy.[15]

D. "'As a reminder'—[this refers to] what is written in the Prophets.[16]

E. "'In a document'—[this refers to] what is written in the Scroll of Esther."[17]—Thus are the words of R. Joshua.

F. R. Eliezer the Modiite says, "'This'—[this refers to] what is written here and in Deuteronomy.

G. "'As a reminder'—[this refers to] what is written in the Scroll of Esther.

H. "'In a document'—[this refers to] what is written in the Prophets."

3.  A. "'... and read it aloud to Joshua' (Exod. 17:14):

    B. "On that very day Joshua was anointed."—Thus are the words of R. Joshua.

    C. R. Eliezer the Modiite says, "This is one of the four [people] who were given a hint. Two took it into consideration and two did not take it into consideration.

    D. "Moses was given a hint, but didn't consider it, [as it says in Scripture,] '... and read it aloud to Joshua' (Exod. 17:14).

    E. "[Thus,] Joshua brought the Israelites into the land, but Moses did not bring the Israelites into the land, and in the end he stood there and made all those pleas,[18] saying, 'Since you've begun to show me a little, show me all of it!'"

4.  A. They told a parable: To what is the matter alike?

    B. It is like a king who decreed that his son should not enter the door of his palace. He entered the first door, and they kept quiet. He entered the second door, and they kept quiet. He came to enter the third door, and they rebuked him, saying to him, "Enough for you right here!"

    C. Likewise, when Moses came and conquered the two nations Sihon and Og and distributed them [to the tribes of Reuven, Gad, and Manasseh], he said, "It appears that the decree has only been decreed conditionally, and we are being judged only conditionally!"

    D. And up to here he [had] requested, saying, "The decree only decreed that I should not enter into it as a king! As it says in Scripture, '... therefore you shall not lead this congregation into the land' (Num. 20:12).

    E. "I will [therefore] enter it as a commoner!"

    F. He[19] said to him, "A king does not enter as a commoner!"

    G. He[20] said before Him, "If the decree has been decreed that I not enter it as either king or commoner, then I shall enter it by the Cave of Caesarion at Paneas!"

    H. He said to him, "(You may view the land from a distance) but you shall not enter it!" (Deut. 32:52).

    I. He said before the Holy One, blessed be He, "If the decree has been decreed that I not enter it as either king or commoner or by the cave, then I shall enter it upon my death!"

[15] See Deut. 25:17–19.
[16] See 1 Sam. 15:8–32.
[17] See Esther 3:1. Haman was an Agagite, i.e., a descendent of Agag, King of the Amalekites.
[18] See Deut. 3:23ff.
[19] I.e., God.
[20] I.e., Moses.

| | | |
|---|---|---|
| זאת משכתוב במשנה תורה. ◆ זכרון משכתוב בנביא ◆ בספר | E/D/C | |
| משכתוב במגלה כך דברי ר' יהושע. ◆ ר' אלעזר המודעי | F | |
| אומ' זאת משכתוב כאן ובמשנה תורה. ◆ זכרון | G | |
| משכתוב במגלה. ◆ בספר משכתוב בנביא> ◆ ושים באזני | A 3 | H |
| יהושע ◆ בו ביום נמש[ח] יהושע <כך דברי ר' יהושע. ◆ ר' | C/B | |
| אלעזר המודעי אומר> זה אחד מארבעה שנתן להם | | |
| רמז שנים חשו ושנים לא חשו ◆ משה נתן לו רמז ולא | D | |
| חש ושים באזני יהושע ◆ יהושע מכניס את יש' לארץ | E | |
| ואן משה מכניס את יש' לארץ לסוף הוא עומד | | |
| ומבקש כל אותן בקשות וא' הואיל והתחלתה תראני | | |
| מקצת הארץ הראיני כולה ◆ משלו <משל> למה דב' דו' ◆ | A | 4 |
| למלך שגזר על בנו שלא יכנס לפתח פלטורין שלו | B | |
| נכנס פתח ראשון ושתקו לו נכנס פתח שיני ושתקו לו | | |
| בא להיכנס לפתח שלישי נזפו בו אמרו לו דיין עד כן ◆ | | |
| כך בשעה שבא משה וכיבש שני עממין סיחון ועוג | C | |
| וחלקם אמר דומה שלא נגזרה גזירה אלא על תנוי | | |
| ואן אנו מנודין אלא על תנוי ◆ ועדאן היה מבקש וא' לא | D | |
| נגזרה גזירה אלא שלא אכנס לה מלך שנ' לכן לא | | |
| תבאו את הקהל הזה (במ' כ יב) ◆ איכנס לה כהדיוט ◆ א' | F/E | |
| לו אין מלך נכנס כהדיוט ◆ א' לפניו אם נגזרה גזירה | G | |
| שלא איכנס לה לא מלך ולא הדיוט איכנס לה | | |
| במחילה של קיסריון פמיוס ◆ אמ' ושמה לא תבוא (דב' | H | |
| לב נב) ◆ או' לפני הק' אם נגזרה גזירה שלא איכנס לה | I | |
| לא מלך ולא הדיוט ולא במחילה איכנס לה במותי ◆ | | |

J.   He said to him, "(Look at it well) for you shall not go across yonder Jordan!" (Deut. 3:27).

K.   And can a dead person really cross [the river Jordan]? Rather, He said to him, "Moses, not even your bones will cross the Jordan!"

5.   A.   And this is what others say:

B.   Moses was sitting and crying, saying to Israel, "'For you are about to cross the Jordan!' (Deut. 11:31). You are going to cross, but not I!"

C.   And up to here would he request: "Let me, please, cross over and see" (Deut. 3:25).

D.   And [the word] "please" is only [a word of] request.

E.   "... and see the good land on the other side (of the Jordan)" (Deut. 3:25)—this is the Land of Israel.

F.   "... that good hill country" (Deut. 3:25)—this is Jerusalem.

G.   "... and the Lebanon" (Deut. 3:25)—this is the Temple.

H.   And thus Scripture states, "And the Lebanon shall fall in majesty" (Isa. 10:34). And Scripture says, "Throw open your gates, O Lebanon, and let fire consume your cedars" (Zech. 11:1).

6.   A.   [And some] say: The view [of the Land of Israel] of Abraham was better than [that of] Moses, because Abraham was not troubled [to see his], but Moses was troubled.

[125]   B.   Concerning Abraham Scripture says, "Raise your eyes and look out from where you are, to the north and south, to the east and west" (Gen. 13:14).

C.   Concerning Moses Scripture says, "Go up to the summit of Pisgah, etc." (Deut. 3:27)—go up [first and then] have a look!

7.   A.   How does one know from Scripture that God granted all the requests that Moses made of the Holy One, blessed be He?

B.   He requested to see the Land of Israel, and He granted it to him. As it says in Scripture, "... and the Lord showed him the whole land, Gilead as far as Dan" (Deut. 34:1).

C.   He requested to see the Temple, and He granted it to him. As it says in Scripture, "... Gilead" (Deut. 34:1).

D.   And "Gilead" refers only to the Temple, as it says in Scripture, "You are as Gilead to Me, as the summit of Lebanon" (Jer. 22:6).

E.   And how does one know from Scripture that He showed him Samson ben Manoaḥ? As it says in Scripture, "... as far as Dan" (Deut. 34:1). And farther on Scripture says, "There was a certain man from Zorah, of the stock of Dan, whose name was Manoaḥ" (Judg. 13:2).

F.   Similar to this, you say, "... and went in pursuit as far as Dan" (Gen. 14:14).

G.   Isn't it the case that the 12 tribes had not yet entered, and the land was not [yet] divided? Rather, this teaches that He said to Abraham, "Your offspring will be 12 tribes, and this will be the portion of one of them!"

H.   And there are those who say: He[21] said to him,[22] "In this place your sons will erect an idol." And his strength was weakened.

I.   And how does one know from Scripture that He showed him Barak ben Abinoam? Ahead Scripture says, "She summoned Barak son of Abinoam (of Kedesh in Naphtali)" (Judg. 4:6).

---

[21] I.e., God.
[22] I.e., Abraham.

| | |
|---|---|
| א׳ לו כי לא תעבור את הירדן הזה (דב׳ ג כז) ◆ וכי מת יכול | K/J |
| לעבור אילא א׳ לו משה אף עצמותיך לא יעברו את | |
| הירדן ◆ הזה אחרים או׳ ◆ היה משה יושב ובוכה וא׳ להן | B/A 5 |
| ליש׳ אתם עברים את הירדן (דב׳ יא לא) אתם | |
| עוברים ולא אני ◆ ועד אן היה מבקש וא׳ אעבר נא | C |
| ואראה (דב׳ ג כה) ◆ אין נא אלא בקשה ◆ ואראה | E/D |
| (ואראה) את הארץ הטובה אשר בעבר זו ארץ ישראל ◆ | |
| ההר הטוב זו ירושלים ◆ והלבנון זה בית המקדש ◆ וכין | H/G/F |
| הוא או׳ הלבנון באדיר יפול (ישע׳ י לד) ואו׳ פתח | |
| לבנון דלתיך ותאכל אש בארזיך (זכ׳ יא א) ◆ וא׳ ח׳ | A 6 |
| חבובה יראתו של אברהם יתיר משל משה שאברהם | |
| <לא> ליבטוהו ומשה ליבטוהו ◆ באב׳ הוא או׳ שא נא | B |
| עיניך וראה מן המקום אשר אתה שם צפונה ונגבה | |
| וקדמה וימה (בר׳ יג יד) ◆ במשה הוא או׳ עלה ראש | C |
| הפסגה וג׳ (דב׳ ג כז) עלה הביט ראה ◆ מנין שכל | A 7 |
| בקשות שביקש משה מלפני הק׳ נתן לו ◆ בקש לראות | B |
| את ארץ יש׳ ונתן לו שנ׳ ויראהו ייי את כל הארץ מן | |
| גלעד ועד דן (דב׳ לד א) ◆ ביקש לראות בית המק׳ ונתן | C |
| לו שנא׳ את הגלעד ◆ ואין גלעד אלא בית המקדש שנא׳ | D |
| גלעד אתה לי ראש הלבנון (ירמ׳ כב ו) ◆ ומנ׳ שהראהו | E |
| שמשון בן מנוח שנ׳ עד דן ולהלן הוא או׳ ויהי איש | |
| [אחד] מצרעה ממשפחת הדני ושמו מנוח (שופ׳ יג ב) ◆ | |
| כיוצא בו אתה או׳ וירדוף עד דן (בר׳ יד יד) ◆ והלוא עד | G/F |
| אן לא באו עשרת השבטים ולא נתחלקה הארץ אלא | |
| מלמד שא׳ לו לאברהם י״ב שבטים מחלציך <יצאו> | |
| [וזהו] חלקו של אחד מהן ◆ ויש אומ׳ כך אמר(ו) לו | H |
| במקום זה עתידין בניך לה[עמי]ד עבדה זרה ותשש | |
| כוחו מעליו ◆ ומנ׳ שהראהו ברק בן אבינועם <...> ולהלן | I |
| הוא או׳ ות[שלח] ותקרא לברק בן אבינעם (שופ׳ ד ו) | |
| ◆ | |

J.  And how does one know from Scripture that He showed him Joshua ben Nun? As it says in Scripture, "From the tribe of Ephraim, Hosea son of Nun" (Num. 13:8).

K.  And how does one know from Scripture that He showed him Gideon ben Joash? As it says in Scripture, "... and Manasseh" (Deut. 34:2). And farther on Scripture says, "Behold, my clan is the humblest in Manasseh, and I am the youngest in my father's household" (Judg. 6:15).

L.  And how does one know from Scripture that He showed him David in his monarchy? As it says in Scripture, "... the whole land of Judah" (Deut. 34:2). And farther on Scripture says, "The Lord God of Israel chose me of all my father's house to be king over Israel forever. For He chose Judah to be ruler, and of the family of Judah, my father's house, and of my father's sons, He preferred to make me king over all Israel" (1 Chron. 28:4).

### (Textual Source: Mekhilta de-Rabbi Ishmael)

M.  And how does one know from Scripture that He showed him the entire west? As it says in Scripture, "... until the Western Sea" (Deut. 34:2).

N.  And how does one know from Scripture that He showed him the graves of the forefathers? As it says in Scripture, "... the Negeb" (Deut. 34:3). And how have we learned from Scripture concerning the graves of the forefathers that they are in the Negeb? As it says in Scripture, "They went into the Negeb, and came to Hebron" (Num. 13:22).

O.  And how does one know from Scripture that He showed him the destruction of Sodom and Gomorrah? As it says in Scripture, "... and the Plain" (Deut. 34:3). And farther on Scripture says, "He annihilated those cities and the entire Plain" (Gen. 19:25).

P.  And how does one know from Scripture that He showed him *Gog* and all his masses? As it says in Scripture, "... the Valley of Jericho" (Deut. 34:3). And we have learned that *Gog* and his masses will rise and fall in the Valley of Jericho.

Q.  Another interpretation: "... the Valley of Jericho" (Deut. 34:3):

R.  Can't anyone see the Valley of Jericho? Rather, just as this valley is settled, with a field full of wheat and a field full of barley, likewise He showed him the entire Land of Israel [settled] like the Valley of Jericho.

S.  And how does one know from Scripture that He showed him Deborah? As it says in Scripture, "... the city of palm trees" (Deut. 34:3). And farther on Scripture says, "She used to sit under the Palm of Deborah" (Judg. 4:5).

T.  And how does one know from Scripture that He showed him the wife of Lot? As it says in Scripture, "... as far as Zoar" (Deut. 34:3). And farther on Scripture says, "... and Lot entered Zoar" (Gen. 19:23).

8.  A.  Jacob was given a hint, but didn't consider it.

B.  As it says in Scripture, "Remember, I am with you. I will protect you" (Gen. 28:15).

C.  But in the end, he was afraid.

[126]  D.  As it says in Scripture, "Jacob was greatly frightened, and in his anxiety ..." (Gen. 32:8).

E.  Is it really possible that one whom God has assured should be afraid? Rather, he said, "Perhaps sin will cause [God to abandon me]!"

9.  A.  David was given a hint, and he considered it.

B.  As it says in Scripture, "Both the lion and bear (your servant has killed)" (1 Sam. 17:36).

C.  He said, "How am I special, that I have killed these three evil beasts? Rather, maybe

ומנ' שהראהו יהושע בן נון שנ' ואת ארץ J

אפרים ואו' למ[טה] אפרים הושע בן נון (במ' יג ח) ◆

ומנ' ש[ה]ר' גדעון בן יואש שנ' ומנשה ו<להלן> הוא K

או' הנה אלפי הדל ב[מנ]שה וא[נ]כי הצעיר ב[בית

אבי] (שופ' ו טו) ◆ ומנ' שהר' דויד במלכותו שנ' ואת כל L

ארץ יהודה ולהלן או' ויבחר ייי אלקי יש' בי מכל בית

אבי להיות למלך על יש' לעולם כי ביהודה בחר לנגיד

ובבית יהודה [בית] אבי ובבית אבי בי רצה להיות

מלך (דה"א כח ד). ◆

◆ ומנין שהראהו את כל המערב שנא' עד הים האחרון ◆ M

ומנין שהראהו קברי אבות שנא' ואת הנגב ומנין N

למדנו על קברי אבות שהם בנגב שנא' ויעלו בנגב

ויבא עד חברון (במ' יג כב) ◆ ומנין שהראהו מהפכת O

סדום ועמורה שנא' ואת הככר ולהלן הוא אומר

ויהפך את הערים האל ואת כל הככר (בר' יט כה) ◆

ומנין שהראהו גוג וכל המונו שנא' בקעת יריחו P

ולמדנו שעתידין גוג וכל המונו לעלות וליפול בבקעת

יריחו. ◆ דבר אחר בקעת יריחו ◆ והלא ההדיוט רואה R/Q

בקעת יריחו אלא מה בקעה זו מיושבת שדה מלאה

חטים כל שהוא שדה מלאה שעורים כל שהוא כך

הראהו את כל ארץ ישראל כבקעת יריחו ◆ ומנין S

שהראהו דברוה שנ' עיר התמרים ולהלן הוא אומר

והיא יושבת תחת תומר דבורה (שופ' ד ה) ◆ ומנין T

שהראהו אשת לוט שנא' עד צוער ולהלן הוא אומר

ולוט בא צוערה (בר' יט כג). ◆ יעקב ניתן לו רמז ולא A 8

חש ◆ שנ' והנה אנכי עמך ושמרתיך (בר' כח טו) ◆ לסוף C/B

היה מתירא ◆ שנא' ויירא יעקב מאד ויצר לו (בר' לב ח) ◆ D

אפשר מי שהבטיחו המקום יהא מתירא אלא אמר E

שמא יגרום החטא. ◆ דוד ניתן לו רמז וחש ◆ שנא' גם את B/A 9

הארי גם הדוב הכה עבדך (ש"א יז לו) ◆ אמר מה אני C

something is about to happen with Israel, and they are destined to be rescued through me!"

D.    Thus it is said, "... and that uncircumcised Philistine shall end up like one of them" (1 Sam. 17:36).

10.    A.    Mordecai was given a hint, and he considered it.

B.    As it says in Scripture, "Every single day Mordecai would walk about in front of the court of the harem" (Esther 2:11).

C.    [He said,] "Is it really possible that this pious woman would marry this uncircumcised one? Rather, maybe something is about to happen with Israel, and they are destined to be rescued through her!"

D.    Immediately: "Mordecai learned of it, and told it to Queen Esther" (Esther 2:22).

11.    A.    "I will utterly blot out" (Exod. 17:14):[23]

B.    "Utterly"—[this refers] to this world.

C.    "Blot out"—[this refers] to the world to come.

12.    A.    "'Utterly (blot out)'—[this refers] to him and his family."—Thus are the words of R. Joshua.

B.    R. Eliezer the Modiite says, "'... Amalek'—this [refers] to Agog. '... the memory of'—this [refers] to Haman. '... utterly (blot out)'—this [refers] to him and his family. '... blot out'—this [refers] to him and all that generation."

13.    A.    "... from under heaven" (Exod. 17:14):

B.    R. Joshua says, "In that Amalek will have neither child nor grandchild, so that they will not say, 'This camel belongs to Amalek. This sheep belongs to Amalek. This tree belongs to Amalek.'"

C.    R. Eliezer the Modiite says,

### (Textual Source: Ms. Firkovich II A 268)

D.    "Because he came to destroy Israel from beneath the wings of heaven, Moses said before the Holy One, blessed be He, 'Master of the World! This evil one has come to destroy Your children from beneath the wings of heaven. Who will read Your Torah scroll?'"

E.    R. Eliezer says, "[Moses said,] '[What will happen to] Your children whom You are destined to scatter to the four winds of the heavens? As it says in Scripture, "... like the four winds of heaven" (Zech. 2:10). Who will read Your Torah scroll?'"

F.    R. Eliezer said, "Moses said, 'May He destroy the name of these [people], and erase their name from the world, and may idolatry and its worshipers be uprooted, and may God be distinct in the world!

G.    "'In accordance with what is said in Scripture, "... they shall march up victorious, etc." (Obad. 1:21). And Scripture says, "And the Lord shall be king over all the earth, etc." (Zech. 14:9).'"

14.    A.    R. Nathan says, "Haman comes only as a reminder for Israel.

B.    "As it says in Scripture, 'And these days of Purim shall never cease, etc.' (Esther 9:28)."

15.    A.    "And Moses built an altar and named it *Adonai-nissi*" (Exod. 17:15):

B.    R. Joshua says, "Moses called it *nissi*.[24]

---

[23] The text interprets here the seemingly doubled verbal form of the infinitive absolute "utterly blot out"—מחה אמחה.
[24] English: my miracle.

|  |  |  |
|---|---|---|
| ספון שהרגתי שלוש בהמות רעות הללו אלא שמא | | |
| דבר עתיד לארע בישראל ועתידין להנצל על ידי ◆ לכך | D | |
| נאמר והיה הפלשתי הערל הזה כאחד מהם (שם). ◆ | | |
| מרדכי ניתן לו רמז וחש ◆ שנא' ובכל יום ויום מרדכי | B/A | 10 |
| מתהלך לפי חצר בית הנשים (אס' ב יא) ◆ אפשר | C | |
| לחסידה זו שתתנשא לערל זה אלא שמא דבר עתיד | | |
| לארע בישראל ועתידין להנצל על ידה ◆ ומיד ויודע | D | |
| הדבר למרדכי ויגד לאסתר המלכה (שם כב). ◆ כי מחה | A | 11 |
| אמחה ◆ מחה בעולם הזה ◆ אמחה לעולם הבא ◆ מחה לו | A 12 | C/B |
| ולכל משפחתו כך דברי ר' יהושע ◆ ר' אלעזר המודעי | B | |
| אומר עמלק זה אגג זכר זה המן מחה לו ולכל | | |
| משפחתו אמחה לו ולכל הדור ההוא. ◆ מתחת השמים ◆ | A | 13 |
| ר' יהושע אומר שלא יהיה לו נין ונכד לעמלק שלא | B | |
| יאמרו גמל זה שלעמלק רחל זו שלעמלק אילן זה | | |
| שלעמלק ◆ ר' אלעזר המודעי אומר ◆ לפי שבא לאבד את | D/C | |
| יש' מתחת כנפי השמים אמר משה לפני הקב"ה | | |
| ריבונו שלעולם רשע זה בא לאבד את בניך מתחת | | |
| כנפי השמים ספר תורה מי יקרא בו ◆ ר' אליעזר או' | E | |
| בניך שעתיד אתה לפזרם בארבע רוחות השמים שנא' | | |
| כי כארבע רוחות השמים ג' (זכ' ב י) ספר תורה מי | | |
| יקרא בו ◆ אמ' ר' אלעזר אמר משה יאבד שמם שלאילו | F | |
| וימחה שמם מן העולם ותיעקר עבודה זרה ועובדיה | | |
| ויהי <ה>מקום יחידי בעולם ◆ כעינין שנ' ועלו מושיעים | G | |
| בהר ציון ג' (עוב' כא) וא' והיה יי' למלך על כל הארץ | | |
| ג' (זכ' יד ט). ◆ ר' נתן או' לא בא המן אלא זכר ליש' | A | 14 |
| שנא' וימי הפורים האלה לא יעבר<ו> ג' (אס' ט כח) ◆ | B | |
| <ויבן משה מזבח ויקרא שמו יי' נסי ◆ ר' יהושע | B/A | 15 |

C.     "He said to them, 'God performed this miracle for you on my behalf!'"

D.     R. Eliezer the Modiite says, "God called it 'My miracle' because whenever the Israelites are situated in a miracle, it is as if it is a miracle before Him. [When] they are situated in distress, it is as if it is distressing before Him. [When] they are situated in joy, it is joyful before Him.

E.     "And thus Scripture says, 'I rejoice in your deliverance' (1 Sam. 2:1)."

16.    A.     "'He said: "It means 'Hand upon the throne of the Lord!' (The Lord will be at war with Amalek from generation to generation)'"' (Exod. 17:16):

       B.     "When He sits on the throne of the Lord, the war of the Lord [will take place].

[127]  C.     "At that moment, 'The Lord will be at war with Amalek from generation to generation' (Exod. 17:16)."—Thus are the words of R. Joshua.

       D.     R. Eliezer the Modiite says, "The Holy One, blessed be He, said, 'Israel should accept all who come from among the nations of the world to convert. But Israel should not accept from among Amalek!'

       E.     "As it says in Scripture, 'David said to the young man who had brought him the news, "Where are you from?" He replied, "I am the son of a resident alien, an Amalekite"' (2 Sam. 1:13).

       F.     "At that moment, David was reminded what had been said to Moses, his master, that Israel should accept all who come from among the nations of the world to convert. But Israel should not accept from among Amalek.

       G.     "[As it says in Scripture,] 'And David said to him, "Your blood be on your own head! Your own mouth, etc."' (2 Sam. 1:16)."

17.    A.     "'... from generation to generation' (Exod. 17:16):

       B.     "'From generation' (Exod. 17:16)—[this refers to] this world. '... to generation' (Exod. 17:16)—[this refers to] the world to come."—Thus are the words of R. Joshua.

       C.     R. Eliezer the Modiite says, "From the generation of Moses to the generation of Samuel."

       D.     R. Eliezer says, "From the generation of Samuel to the generation of the Messiah, which consists of three generations.

       E.     "As it says in Scripture, 'Let them fear You as long as the sun shines, while (the moon lasts, generations on end)' (Ps. 72:5)."

*Chapter Forty-Six*

(Textual Source: Midrash ha-Gadol)

XLVI:I[25]

1.     A.     "Jethro (priest of Midian, Moses' father-in-law,) heard (all that God had done for Moses and for Israel His people, how the Lord had brought Israel out from Egypt)" (Exod. 18:1):[26]

       B.     What did he hear [that motivated him] to come?

       C.     R. Joshua says, "He heard about the war with Amalek, and came.

       D.     "For this is written just next to it,[27] as it says in Scripture, 'And Joshua overwhelmed Amalek' (Exod. 17:13)."

       E.     R. Eliezer the Modiite says, "He heard about the giving of the Torah, and came. For thus

---

[25] Compare XLVI:I:1.A–7.B with *Mekhilta de-Rabbi Ishmael*, Amalek (H/R, 188:1–190:13; Laut., vol. 2, 162:1–167:71; Neus., XLV:I:1.A–15.B).

[26] Compare 1.A–S with parallel at b. Zevaḥim 116a (Neus., XXVIII.C:Tractate Zebahim:14:10:IX.8.A– 9.Z).

[27] I.e., immediately preceding Exod. 18:1 in Scripture.

| | |
|---|---|
| אומר משה קראו נסי ◆ אמר להן נס זה שעשה לכם | C |
| המקום בגני עשאו ◆ ר' אלעזר המודעי אומר המקום | D |
| קראו נסי שכל זמן שיש' שרויין בנס כאלו נס לפניו | |
| שרויין בצרה כאלו צרה היא לפניו שרויין בשמחה | |
| שמחה היא לפניו ◆ וכן הוא אומר כי שמחתי בישועתך | E |
| (ש"א ב א)> ◆ | |

| | | |
|---|---|---|
| ויאמר כי יד על כס(א) יה ג' ◆ משישב על כס יה | B/A | 16 |
| מלחמה [של]יה ◆ באותה שעה מלחמה לייי בעמלק | C | |
| מדור דור כך דברי ר' יהושע ◆ [ר' א]לעזר המודעי או' | D | |
| אמר הקב"ה שאם יבאו מכל האומות להתגייר | | |
| [יק]בלו מהם יש' ומעמלק לא יקבלו מהם יש' ◆ שנ' | E | |
| ויאמר דויד אל [הנער המגי]ד לו אי מזה עם אתה | | |
| ויאמר בן איש גר עמלקי אנכי (ש"ב א יג) ◆ [באותה | F | |
| שעה] נזכר דויד מה נא' לו למשה רבו שאם יבאו מכל | | |
| [אומות העולם להתג]יר יקבלו אתם יש' ומעמלק לא | | |
| יקבלו אתם יש' ◆ [ויאמר אליו דוד דמך] על ראשך כי | G | |
| פיך ג' (שם טז) ◆ מדור דור מדור ◆ [העולם הזה לדור | B/A | 17 |
| העו]לם הבא כך דברי ר' יהושע ◆ ר' אלעזר המודעי [או' | C | |
| מדורו של משה לדורו של] שמואל ◆ <ר' אליעזר או'> | D | |
| מדורו שלשמואל לדורו [של משיח שהם ג' דורות ◆ שנ' | E | |
| ייראוך] עם שמש לפ' ג' (תה' עב ה). ◆ | | |

XLVI:I

| | | |
|---|---|---|
| וישמע יתרו ◆ מה שמועה שמע ובא ◆ ר' יהושע אומר | C/B/A | 1 |
| מלחמת עמלק שמע ובא ◆ שכן היא כתובה בצדה שנ' | D | |
| ויחלש יהושע את עמלק (שמ' יז יג). ◆ ר' אלעזר המודעי | E | |

we find that on the day the Torah was given to Israel, all the kings of the world trembled in their palaces.

F.    "As it says in Scripture, '... while in His temple all say "Glory!"'" (Ps. 29:9).

G.    "One might think they didn't know for what [reason they were praising].

H.    "Scripture states, [however,] '... while in His temple, all say "Glory!" (The Lord sat enthroned at the Flood; the Lord sits enthroned, king forever)' (Ps. 29:9–10).

I.    "All the nations of the world were gathered to Balaam. They said to him, 'It appears that God is destroying His world with water, just as He destroyed the people of the generation of the Flood! In accordance with what is said in Scripture, "The Lord sat enthroned at the Flood" (Ps. 29:10).'

J.    "He said to them, 'Idiots! He already promised that He would not bring [another] flood to the world! As it says in Scripture, "For this to Me is like the waters of Noah. As I swore that the waters of Noah nevermore would flood the earth" (Isa. 54:9).'

K    "They said to him, 'Certainly a flood of water He won't bring. But He will bring a flood of fire!'

L.    "He said to them, 'He will bring neither a flood of water nor a flood of fire. He is giving the Torah to His people, and will pay a reward to those who fear Him!'

M.    "When they heard this from him, each of them returned to his place."

N.    R. Eliezer says, "He heard about the splitting of the Sea of Reeds, and came. For thus we find that on the day that the sea was split for Israel, they heard from one end of the earth to the other.

O.    "As it says in Scripture, 'When all the kings of the Amorites on the western side of the Jordan, and all the kings of the Canaanites near the sea, heard how the Lord had dried up the waters of the Jordan for the sake of the Israelites until they crossed over' (Josh. 5:1).

[128]    P.    "And thus Rahab said to Joshua's messengers, 'For we have heard how the Lord dried up the waters of the Sea of Reeds for you' (Josh. 2:10).

Q.    "They said that she was 10 years old when Israel went out from Egypt. For the entire 40 years that Israel was in the wilderness, she prostituted herself. At 50 years [of age], she converted.

R.    "She said, 'With three things have I sinned. In three ways will He forgive me: with the rope, with the window, and with the sukkah.'

S.    "As it is said in Scripture, 'She let them down by a rope through the window ...' (Josh. 2:15) [and] '... and hidden them under some stalks of flax ...' (Josh. 2:6)."

## (Textual Source: Ms. Cambridge T-S C 4a.5)

2.    A.    "Jethro (priest of Midian, Moses' father-in-law,) heard" (Exod. 18:1):

B.    At first they called him Jether. Once he did good deeds, they added one letter to it, and he was called Jethro.

C.    And thus you find with Abraham. At first they called him Abram. Once he did good deeds, they added one letter to it, and he was called Abraham.

אומר מתן תורה שמע ובא שכן מצינו ביום שניתנה בו
תורה לישראל זעו כל מלכי תבל בהיכליהם ♦ שנ'   F
ובהיכלו כלו אומר כבוד (תה' כט ט). ♦ יכול לא ידעו על   G
מה ♦ ת"ל ובהיכלו כלו אומר כבוד. ♦ נתקבצו כל אומות   I/H
העולם אצל בלעם אמרו לו דומה שהמקום מאבד
את עולמו במים כדרך שאיבדם לאנשי דור המבול
כענין שנ' ה' למבול ישב (תה' כט י). ♦ אמר להן שוטים   J
כבר נשבע שאינו מביא מבול לעולם שנ' כי מי נח זאת
לי אשר נשבעתי מעבר מי נח עוד על הארץ (ישע' נד
ט). ♦ אמרו לו בודאי מבול שלמים אינו מביא אבל   K
מביא הוא מבול שלאש. ♦ אמר להן אינו מביא לא   L
מבול שלמים ולא מבול שלאש. תורה נותן לעמו
ושכר משלם ליראיו. ♦ כיון ששמעו ממנו הדבר הזה פנו   M
כולם איש איש למקומו. ♦ ר' אליעזר אומר קריעת ים   N
סוף שמע ובא שכן מצינו ביום שנקרא ים לישראל
שמעו מסוף העולם ועד סופו ♦ שנ' ויהי כשמעו כל   O
מלכי האמורי אשר בעבר הירדן ימה וכל מלכי
הכנעני אשר על הים את אשר הוביש ה' את מי הירדן
מפני בני ישראל עד עברם (יהו' ה א) ♦ וכן רחב אומרת   P
לשלוחי יהושע כי שמענו את אשר הוביש ה' את מי
ים סוף מפניכם (יהו' ב י). ♦ אמרו בת עשר שנים היתה   Q
בשעה שיצאו ישר' ממצרים. כל ארבעים שנה שהיו
ישראל במדבר זינתה. לחמשים שנה נתגיירה. ♦ אמרה   R
בשלשה דברים חטאתי בשלשה דברים ימחול לי
בחבל ובחלון ובסוכה ♦ שנ' ותורידם בחבל בעד החלון   S
(יהו' ב טו) ותטמנם בפשתי העץ (שם ו). ♦ וישמע [יתרו ♦   A   2
מתחלה היו קורין אותו י]תר כיון שעשה מעשים   B
נאים [הוסיפו לו אות אחת ונקרא ית]רו ♦ שכן את מוצא   C
באברהם מתחלה [היו קורין אותו אברם כיון שעשה
מעש]ים נאים הוסיפו לו אות [אחת ונקרא אברהם
♦

D. And thus you find with Sarah. At first they called her

(Textual Source: Midrash ha-Gadol)

Sarai. Once she did good deeds, they added one letter to it, and she was called Sarah.

E. And thus you find with Joshua. At first they called him Hosea. Once he did good deeds, they added one letter to it, and he was called Joshua.

F. And there are those from whom they subtracted [one letter from their names].

G. You can learn from Ephron. At first they called him Ephron.[28] Once he established [the amount of the] payment with our father Abraham, and said to him, "What is four hundred *shekels* between you and me?" (Gen. 23:15) they subtracted one letter from it, and he was called Ephron.[29]

H. And thus you find with Jehonadab. At first they called him Jehonadab. Once he joined up with Jehu,

(Textual Source: Ms. Cambridge T-S C 4a.5)

they subtracted one letter from it, and he was called Jonadab.

I. Based upon this they said, "One should not join up with an evil person, even to draw him near to Torah."

3.  A. Jethro was called by seven names: Jether, Jethro, Ḥobab, Ben Reuel, Puti, and Keni.

    B. Jether—because he added a chapter in the Torah.

    C. Jethro—because he did good deeds.

    D. Ḥobab—because he was dear to God.

    E. Keni—because he acquired the world to come.

    F. Ben—because he was like a son to God.

    G. Reuel—because he was a friend to God.

    H. Puti—because he despised all who worshiped idols in the world.

4.  A. "(Jethro) priest (of Midian)" (Exod. 18:1):

    B. R. Joshua says, "He was an [idolatrous] priest.

    C. "In accordance with what is said in Scripture, '... and Jonathan son of Gershom, etc.' (Judg. 18:30)."

    D. R. Eliezer the Modiite says, "He was a prince.

[129] E. "In accordance with what is said in Scripture, '... and David's sons were priests' (2 Sam. 8:18). And Scripture says, 'Ira the Jairite also served David as priest' (2 Sam. 20:26)."

5.  A. "... Moses' father-in-law" (Exod. 18:1):

    B. At first, Moses would honor him. As it says in Scripture, "Moses went back to his father-in-law" (Exod. 4:18).

    C. Now his father-in-law began to honor him.

    D. They said to him, "What makes you special?" He said to them, "I am the father-in-law of Moses!"

---

[28] Hebrew: עפרון.
[29] Hebrew: עפרן.

| | | |
|---|---|---|
| D | וכן את מוצא] בשרה מתחלה ה[יו קורין | |
| | אותה] שרי כיון שעשת מעשים נאים הוסיפו לה אות | |
| E | אחת ונקראה שרה. ◆ וכן את מוצא ביהושע מתחלה | |
| | היו קורין אותו הושע וכיון שעשה מעשים נאים | |
| | הוסיפו לו אות אחת ונקרא יהושע. ◆ ויש שמונעין מהן ◆ | |
| F | | |
| G | יש לך ללמוד מעפרון מתחלה היו קורין אותו עפרון | |
| | כיון שפסק דמים עם אבינו אברהם ואמר לו ארבע | |
| | מאות שקל כסף ביני ובינך מה היא (בר' כג טו) מנעו | |
| | ממנו אות אחת ונקרא עפרן. ◆ וכן את מוצא ביהונדב | |
| H | מתחלה היו קורין אותו יהונדב (מ״ב י טו) וכיון | |
| | שנתחבר ליהוא מנעו ממנו אות אחת ונקרא יונדב | |
| | (ירמ' לה ו) ◆ מיכן אמרו אל יתחבר אדם לרשע ואפילו | |
| I | לקרבו לתורה ◆ שבעה שמות נקראו ליתרו יתר ויתרו | |
| A 3 | וחובב בן רעואל פוטי וקיני ◆ יתר שייתר פרשה בתורה | |
| B | יתרו שעשה מעשים נאים ◆ חובב שהיה חביב למקום ◆ | |
| D/C | קיני שקנה העולם הבא ◆ בן שהיה כבן למקום ◆ רעואל | |
| G/F/E | שהיה ריע למקום ◆ פוטי שפט כל עבדי עבדה זרה | |
| H | שבעולם ◆ כהן ◆ ר' יהושע או' כומר היה ◆ כעינין שנ' | |
| C/B/A 4 | ויהונתן בן גרשום ג' (שופ' יח ל) ◆ ר' לעזר המודעי או' | |
| D | שר היה ◆ כעינין שנ' ובני דוד כהנים היו (ש״ב ח יח) ואו' | |
| E | וגם עירא היא<י>רי היה כהן לדוד (שם כ כו) ◆ חתן | |
| A 5 | משה ◆ מתחלה היה משה מכבדו שנ' וילך משה וישב | |
| B | אל יתר חותנו (שמ' ד יח) ◆ עכשיו התחיל חמיו מכבדו ◆ | |
| C | אמרו לו מה טיבך אמר להם חתן משה אנכי ◆ | |
| D | | |

6.   A.   "... all that God had done for Moses and for Israel" (Exod. 18:1):

     B.   Moses is as important as Israel, and Israel is as important as Moses. The master is as important as the disciple, and the disciple [is as important] as the leader.

7.   A.   "... how the Lord had brought Israel out from Egypt" (Exod. 18:1):

     B.   Based on this you learn that the Exodus from Egypt is as important before God as all the miracles and mighty deeds that God performed for Israel.

(Textual Source: Midrash ha-Gadol)

XLVI:II[30]

1.   A.   "Jethro, Moses' father-in-law, took Zipporah, Moses' wife, after she had been sent home" (Exod. 18:2):

     B.   R. Joshua says, "After he divorced her by statement."

     C.   R. Eliezer the Modiite says, "After he divorced her by document.

     D.   "Scripture says here, 'after she had been sent home' (Exod. 18:2), and Scripture says farther on '... and he writes her a bill of divorcement, hands it to her, and sends her away from his house' (Deut. 24:1).

     E.   "Just as 'sending' farther on [involves] a writ of divorce, likewise 'sending' stated here [involves] a writ of divorce."

2.   A.   When was she sent away?

     B.   The moment when God said to Moses, "Go and bring Israel out from Egypt," he took his wife and his children and put them on a donkey.

     C.   God said to Aaron, "Go out and greet your brother in the wilderness!" He went out to greet him, and he began to embrace him and kiss him. He said to him, "Moses, my brother, where have you been all these years?"

     D.   He said to him, "In Midian."

     E.   He said to him, "What is the deal with these people with you?"

     F.   He said to him, "They are my wife and children."

     G.   [He said to him,] "Where are you taking them?"

     H.   He said to him, "To Egypt."

     I.   He said to him, "We are [already] distressed about the first [ones who came down to Egypt]. Now you are bringing the next ones!"

     J.   Immediately he[31] said to her, "Return to your father's house!"

     K.   Immediately, she took her children and returned to her father's house. Thus it is said, "... after she had been sent home, and her two sons" (Exod. 18:2–3).

3.   A.   "... and her two sons—of whom one was named Gershom, because he said, 'I have been a stranger in a foreign land'" (Exod. 18:3):

     B.   R. Joshua says, "It certainly was a foreign land for him!"

     C.   R. Eliezer the Modiite says, "'... in a foreign land'—for all the world practices idolatry, but I worship He who spoke, and the world came into being.

---

[30] Compare XLVI:II:1.A–7.F with *Mekhilta de-Rabbi Ishmael*, Amalek (H/R, 190:14–193:7; Laut., vol. 2, 167:72–173:161; Neus., XLV:I:16.A–II:4.F).
[31] I.e., Moses.

‎6 Λ את כל אשר עשה אלקים למשה (אל למשה) [ולישראל] ✦

‎B שקול משה כיש' ויש' שקולין כמשה שקול הר[ן]ב

‎7 A כתלמיד ותלמיד] כנגיד ✦ כי הוציא יייי את יש' ממצ' ✦

‎B מיכן אתה [למד ששקולה יציאת] מצ' לפני המקום

כנגד כל ניסין וגבורות ש[עשה המקום לישראל] ✦

XLVI:11

‎1 A ויקח יתרו חתן משה את צפרה אשת משה אחר

‎C/B שלוחיה ✦ ר' יהושע אומר אחר שפטרה בדבר. ✦ ר' אלעזר

‎D המודעי אומר אחר שפטרה באגרת ✦ נאמר כאן אחר

שלוחיה ונאמר להלן וכתב לה ספר כריתות ונתן

‎E בידה ושילחה מביתו (דב' כד א) ✦ מה שילוח האמור

‎2 A להלן גט אף שילוח האמור כאן גט. ✦ אימתי שלחה ✦

‎B בשעה שאמר לו המקום למשה לך והוציא את

ישראל ממצרים לקח את אשתו ואת בניו והרכיבם

‎C על החמור ✦ אמר לו המקום לאהרן צא לקראת אחיך

המדברה יצא לקראתו התחיל מגפפו ומנשקו. אמר

‎D לו משה אחי היכן היית כל השנים הללו. ✦ אמר לו

‎F/F במדין. ✦ אמר לו מה טיב אלו בני אדם שעמך ✦ אמר לו

‎H/G אשתי ובני הן. ✦ להיכן אתה מוליכן. ✦ אמר לו למצרים. ✦

‎I אמר לו על הראשונים אנו מצטערין עכשיו אתה

‎J מביא לנו את האחרונים. ✦ מיד אמר לה חזרי לבית

‎K אביך. ✦ מיד נטלה את בניה וחזרה לה לבית אביה לכך

נאמר אחר שלוחיה ואת שני בניה. ✦

‎3 A ואת שני בניה אשר שם האחד גרשום כי אמר גר

‎B הייתי בארץ נכריה. ✦ ר' יהושע אומר ארץ נכריה היא לו

‎C בודאי. ✦ ר' אלעזר המודעי אומר בארץ נכריה שכל העולם

עובדין עבודה זרה ואני עובד את מי שאמר והיה העולם ✦

    D.   "As it says in Scripture, 'God, the Lord God, spoke and summoned the world from east to west' (Ps. 50:1)."

4.    A.   "... and the other was named Eliezer, meaning, 'The God of my father was my help, and He delivered me from the sword of Pharaoh'" (Exod. 18:4):

    B.   When did God deliver him?

    C.   R. Joshua says, "At the time when Dathan said to him, 'Who made you chief and ruler over us?' (Exod. 2:14)."[32]

    D.   R. Eliezer the Modiite says, "They seized Moses and took him up to the platform, bent him over, and placed a sword on his neck. An angel came down from heaven in the image of Moses, [so] they seized the angel and let Moses go."

    E.   R. Eliezer says, "God turned the people who seized Moses into different groups—dumb, deaf, and blind. They said to the dumb ones, 'Where is Moses?' but they could not speak. [They asked] the deaf ones, but they could not hear. [They asked] the blind ones, but they couldn't see.

    F.   "And thus Scripture says, 'Who gives man speech' (Exod. 4:11)."

5.    A.   "Jethro, Moses' father-in-law, brought Moses' sons and wife to Moses" (Exod. 18:5):

    B.   Why is this said?

[130]    C.   Because [when] it says in Scripture, "He sent word to Moses, 'I, your father-in-law Jethro, am coming to you, with your wife and her two sons' (Exod. 18:6)—I don't know if they are Moses' children or her children with someone else.

    D.   Scripture states, [however,] "Jethro, Moses' father-in-law, brought Moses' sons" (Exod. 18:5).

    E.   They are Moses' children, and not her children with someone else.

6.    A.   "... to him in the wilderness" (Exod. 18:5).

    B.   Behold, Scripture is surprised at him. Someone who dwells in a house like his with all the honor of the world now should come to this chaotic wilderness in which there is nothing!

    C.   Thus it is said, "... to him in the wilderness" (Exod. 18:5).

7.    A.   "He sent word to Moses, 'I, your father-in-law Jethro, am coming to you, (with your wife and her two sons)'" (Exod. 18:6):

    B.   R. Joshua says, "He sent [word to him] by means of a messenger."

    C.   R. Eliezer the Modiite says, "He sent [word to him] in a letter, which was sent into the camp, [saying,] 'Do this for me. And if you won't do this for me, do it for your wife. And if you won't do it for your wife, do it for your children.'"

### (Textual Source: Ms. Cambridge T-S C 4a.5)

    D.   R. Eliezer says, "The Holy One, blessed be He, said to Moses, 'It is I who spoke and the world came into being. I draw near and I don't keep distant. As it says in Scripture, 'Am I only a God near at hand' (Jer. 23:23). It is I who drew Jethro near and did not distance him. This person comes to you only to convert; he comes only to enter beneath the wings of God's presence. You, too, should draw him near and not distance him!'

---

[32] Dathan and Abiram, identified as leaders of the revolt against Moses in Numbers 16 and Numbers 26:9–11, are presumed here to be the two fighting Israelites in Exod. 2:11–15 who ultimately caused Moses to flee Egypt. See *Exodus Rabbah* 1:30.

| | |
|---|---|
| D | שנ' אל אלקים ה' דבר ויקרא ארץ ממזרח שמש עד מבואו (תה' נ א, ע''יש). ◆ |
| A 4 | ושם האחד אליעזר כי אלקי אבי בעזרי ויצ' מחרב |
| C/B | פרעה. ◆ אימתי הצילו המקום ◆ ר' יהושע אומר בשעה שאמר לו דתן מי שמך לאיש שר ושפט עלינו (שמ' ב יד). ◆ |
| D | ר' אלעזר המודעי אומר תפסו את משה והעלוהו לבימה כפתוהו והניחו לו סייף על צוארו ירד מלאך מן השמים כדמות משה תפשו את המלאך והניחו את משה. ◆ |
| E | ר' אליעזר אומר בני אדם שתפשו את משה עשאן המקום כתים כתים אלמים חרשים וסומין. אומרין לאלמים היכן הוא משה ואינן יכולים לדבר. לחרשים ואינן שומעין. לסומין ואינן רואין ◆ וכן הוא |
| F | אומ' מי שם פה לאדם וג' (שמ' ד יא). ◆ |
| B/A 5 | ויבא יתרו חתן משה ובניו ואשתו אל משה ◆ למה |
| C | נאמר ◆ לפי שנ' ויאמר אל משה אני חתנך יתרו בא אליך ואשתך ושני בניה איני יודע שלשה או בניה ממקום אחר ◆ |
| E/D | ת''ל ויבא יתרו חתן משה ובניו ◆ בניו שלמשה ולא בניה ממקום אחר. ◆ |
| B/A 6 | אל המדבר ◆ הרי הכת' מתמיה עליו אדם ששרוי בביתו ובכבודו שלעולם עכשו יבוא למדבר תהו הזה שאין בו כלום ◆ לכך נאמר אל המדבר. |
| C | ◆ |
| B/A 7 | ויאמר אל משה אני חתנך יתרו בא אליך ◆ ר' יהושע |
| C | אומר שלח לו ביד שליח. ◆ ר' אלעזר המודעי אומר שלח לו באגרת וירה לתוך מחנה ישראל עשה בגיני |
| D | ואם אי אתה עושה בגיני עשה בגין ◆ אשתך ואם אי אתה עושה בגין אשתך עשה בגין בניך. ר' ליעזר או[ן' אמר לו הקב''ה למשה אני] שאמרתי והיה העולם אני ש[מקר]ב [ואיני מרחק שנ' האלהי] מקרב אני (ירמ' כג כג) אני שקרבתי את [יתרו ולא ריחקתיו אדם זה שבא] אצלך לא בא אלא להתגייר לא [בא אלא להכנס תחת כנפי השכינה] אף אתה קרבהו ואל תרחקהו ◆ |

E. "Based on this they said, 'One should always push away with the left [hand] and draw near with the right.'

F. "Not like Elisha did to Geḥazi, who distanced him forever."

XLVI:III[33]

1.  A. "Moses went out to meet his father-in-law. (He bowed low and kissed him. Each man asked after the other's welfare, and they went into the tent)" (Exod. 18:7):

    B. They said, "Moses and Aaron went out [with] Nadab, Abihu, and 70 of the elders of Israel."

    C. And there are those who say, "Even the Ark went out with them."

### (Textual Source: Midrash ha-Gadol)

2.  A. "He bowed low and kissed him. Each man asked after the other's welfare" (Exod. 18:7):

    B. We don't know who bowed down to whom and who kissed whom.

    C. We hear [in Exod. 18:7 that the person] is called "man." Doesn't this mean Moses?

    D. In accordance with what is said in Scripture, "Now Moses was a very humble man" (Num. 12:3).

    E. Thus, it was only Moses who bowed and kissed Jethro.

    F. Based on this they said, "One should always behave honorably toward his father-in-law."

    G. And thus David says to Saul, "Please, my father, take a close look" (1 Sam. 24:12).

    H. This teaches that he behaved toward him honorably as with his father.

3.  A. "And they went into the tent" (Exod. 18:7):

    B. This is the house of study.

4.  A. "Moses told his father-in-law (everything that the Lord had done to Pharaoh and to the Egyptians for Israel's sake, all the hardships that had befallen them on the way, and how the Lord had delivered them)" (Exod. 18:8):

    B. In order to draw him near to Torah.

    C. "... everything that the Lord had done to Pharaoh and to the Egyptians" (Exod. 18:8):

    D. Pharaoh is equated with Egypt and Egypt is equated with Pharaoh.

    E. "... for Israel's sake" (Exod. 18:8):

    F. So that you should know that Israel is My people.

    G. "... all the hardships" (Exod. 18:8):

    H. In Egypt.

    I. "... that had befallen them" (Exod. 18:8):

    J. At the sea.

    K. "... on the way" (Exod. 18:8):

    L. This is the attack of Amalek.

    M. "... and how the Lord had delivered them" (Exod. 18:8):

    N. From all of them.

---

[33] Compare XLVI:III:1.A–16.K with *Mekhilta de-Rabbi Ishmael*, Amalek (H/R, 193:8–196:4; Laut., vol. 2, 173:162–178:246; Neus., XLV:II:5.A–III:11.C).

[מיכן אמרו לעולם יהא אדם] דוחה בשמאל     E

ומקרב בימי[ן • לא כדרך שעשה אלישע לגיחזי]     F

שרחקו לעולם. •     ◆

XLVI:III

ויצא [משה לקראת חתנו • אמרו יצאו     A     1

משה ואהרן] [נדב ואביהוא ושבע]ים מז[קני     B

ישראל • ויש אומרין אף ארון יצא עמהם]     ◆     C

וישתחו וישק לו וישאלו איש לרעהו לשלום • אין אנו     B/A     2

יודעין מי נשתחוה למי ומי נישק למי • מי שמענו     C

שקרוי איש לא משה • כעניין שנ' והאיש משה עניו מאד     D

(במ' יב ג) • הא לא נשתחוה ולא נישק אלא משה ליתרו •     E

מיכאן אמרו לעולם יהא אדם נוהג כבוד בחמיו. • וכן     G/F

דוד אומר לשאול ואבי ראה גם ראה (ש"ב כד יא) •     ◆

מלמד שהיה נוהג בו כבוד ככבוד אביו. • ויבאו האהלה •     A 3     H

זה בית המדרש. •     B

ויספר משה לחתנו • למשכו ולקרבו לתורה. • את כל     C/B/A     4

אשר עשה ה' לפרעה ולמצרים • שקול פרעה כמצרים     D

ומצרים שקולין כפרעה. • על אודות ישראל • שתדע עמי     F/E

בישראל. • את כל התלאה • במצרים. • אשר מצאתם • על     J/I/H/G

הים. • בדרך • זו ביאת עמלק. • ויצלם ה' • מכולם. •     N/M/L/K

5.    A.    "(And Jethro rejoiced) over all the kindness (that the Lord had shown Israel when He delivered them from the Egyptians)" (Exod. 18:9):

      B.    R. Joshua says, "He told him of the kindness of the manna.

      C.    "He said to him, 'The manna that God gave to us would taste to us like bread, meat, fish, locust—all the good flavors in the world!'

      D.    "As it says in Scripture [not only] 'kindness' [and not only] 'the kindness' [and not only] 'all the kindness,' [but] '... over all the kindness' (Exod. 18:9)."

      E.    R. Eliezer the Modiite says, "He told him of the kindness of the well.

      F.    "He said to him, '[The water from] the well that God gave to us would taste like honey, milk, new wine—all the good flavors in the world!'

      G.    "As it says in Scripture [not only] 'kindness' [and not only] 'the kindness' [and not only] 'all the kindness,' [but] '... over all the kindness' (Exod. 18:9)."

      H.    R. Eliezer says, "He told him of the kindness of the Land of Israel.

      I.    "He said to him, 'God is going to give us the Land of Israel, and the world to come, and a new world, and the kingship of the House of David, and the priesthood and levitical priests.'

[131] J.    "As it says in Scripture [not only] 'kindness' [and not only] 'the kindness' [and not only] 'all the kindness,' [but] '... over all the kindness' (Exod. 18:9)."

6.    A.    "... when He delivered them from the Egyptians" (Exod. 18:9):

      B.    [He delivered them] from beneath that burden of Egypt.

7.    A.    "Jethro said, 'Blessed be the Lord (who delivered you from the hand of the Egyptians and from the hand of Pharaoh, and who delivered the people from under the hand of the Egyptians)'" (Exod. 18:10):[34]

      B.    R. Pappias said, "This is disgraceful of Moses and his followers! For, behold, God brought out 600,000 from Egypt, and not one

### (Textual Source: Ms. Cambridge T-S C 4a.5)

of them opened up and blessed God until Jethro came and blessed God!

      C.    "As it says in Scripture, 'Jethro said, "Blessed be the Lord"' (Exod. 18:10)."

8.    A.    Why does Scripture state "... from the hand of Pharaoh" (Exod. 18:10)?

      B.    [Because elsewhere in Scripture, Pharaoh] is called the mighty monster!

      C.    As it says in Scripture, "I am going to deal with you, O Pharaoh King of Egypt, mighty monster, etc." (Ezek. 29:3).

9.    A.    "... who delivered the people ..." (Exod. 18:10):

      B.    From beneath the burden of Pharaoh.

### (Textual Source: Midrash ha-Gadol)

10.   A.    "Now I know (that the Lord is greater than all gods—yes, by the result of their very schemes against [the people])" (Exod. 18:11):

      B.    Up until now, he had not confessed this.

11.   A.    "... that the Lord is greater than all gods" (Exod. 18:11):

---

[34] Compare 7.A–C with b. Sanhedrin 94a (Neus., XXIIIC:Tractate Sanhedrin:11:1–2:LIII.A–C).

| | | |
|---|---|---|
| על כל הטובה ◆ ר׳ יהושע אומר בטובת המן הגיד | B/A | 5 |
| לו ◆ אמר לו מן שנתן לנו המקום אנו טועמין בו טעם | C | |
| פת טעם בשר טעם דגים טעם חגבים טעם כל | | |
| מטעמים שבעולם ◆ שנ׳ טובה הטובה כל הטובה על | D | |
| כל הטובה. ◆ ר׳ אלעזר המודעי אומר בטובת הבאר | E | |
| הגיד לו ◆ אמר לו באר שנתן לנו המקום אנו טועמין | F | |
| בה טעם דבש טעם חלב טעם יין חדש טעם יין ישן | | |
| טעם כל מטעמים שבעולם ◆ שנ׳ טובה הטובה כל | G | |
| הטובה על כל הטובה. ◆ ר׳ אליעזר אומר בטובת ארץ | H | |
| ישראל הגיד לו ◆ אמר לו עתיד המקום ליתן לנו ארץ | I | |
| ישראל ועולם הבא ועולם חדש ומלכות בית דויד | | |
| וכהונה ולויה ◆ שנ׳ טובה הטובה כל הטובה על כל | J | |
| הטובה. ◆ אשר הצילו מיד מצרים ◆ מתחת סבלון ההוא | B/A | 6 |
| שלמצרים. ◆ | | |
| | | |
| ויאמר יתרו ברוך ה׳ אמר ◆ ר׳ פפיס גנאי למשה | B/A | 7 |
| ולסיעתו שהרי ששים רבוא הוציא המקום ממצרים | | |
| ולא היה מהן אחד שפתח ובירך את המקום עד שבא | | |
| יתרו ובירך את המקום ◆ שנ׳ ויאמר יתרו ברוך ייי ◆ מה | A 8 | C |
| תל׳ לו׳ מיד פרעה ◆ שנקרא התנין הגדול ◆ שנ׳ הנני אליך | C/B | |
| פרעה מלך מצ׳ התנין הגדול ג׳ (יחז׳ כט ג) ◆ אשר הציל | A | 9 |
| את העם ◆ מתחת סבלון שלפרעה. ◆ | B | |
| עתה ידעתי ◆ עד עכשיו לא הודה בדבר. ◆ כי גדול ה׳ | A 11 | B/A 10 |

B.   They said, "At first, no slave was able to flee from Egypt. Now, God has brought out 600,000 people!

C.   "Thus it is said, '... that the Lord is greater than all gods' (Exod. 18:11).

12.   A.   Another interpretation:

B.   "... that the Lord is greater than all gods" (Exod. 18:11):

C.   They said, "There was not an idol in the world that Jethro had not served! Now he confessed this.

D.   "As it says in Scripture [not only] 'gods' [and not only] 'the gods' [and not only] 'all the gods,' [but] '... than all the gods' (Exod. 18:11).

E.   "Naaman confessed this better than he.[35]

F.   "As it says in Scripture, 'Now I know that there is no God in the whole world except in Israel!' (2 Kings 5:15).

G.   "And likewise sang Rahab the prostitute.

H.   "As it says in Scripture, '... for the Lord your God is the only God in heaven above and on earth below' (Josh. 2:11)."

13.   A.   "... yes, by the result of their very schemes against [the people]" (Exod. 18:11):

B.   I have acknowledged Him in the past, but now more so! Because by means of the very scheme that the Egyptians schemed to destroy Israel, God judged them.

C.   [As it says in Scripture], "... yes, by the result of their very schemes against [the people]" (Exod. 18:11).

### (Textual Source: Ms. Cambridge T-S C 4a.5)

14.   A.   "And Jethro, Moses' father-in-law, brought a burnt offering and sacrifices (for God. And Aaron came with all the elders of Israel to partake of the meal before God with Moses' father-in-law)" (Exod. 18:12):

B.   Behold, Scripture is surprised at him. Someone who sacrifices and burns incense to idols every day now should bring a burnt offering and sacrifices to God!

15.   A.   "And Aaron came" (Exod. 18:12):

B.   Where did Moses go? Hadn't he gone out at first to greet him? As it says in Scripture, "Moses went out to meet his father-in-law" (Exod. 18:7).

C.   Rather, this teaches that he stood [there] and served [them].

16.   A.   R. Zadok expounded this matter, "Once Rabban Gamliel stood and served [other Rabbinic authorities at a party].[36]

B.   "They said, 'It's not correct that we recline and Rabban Gamliel stands and serves us.'

C.   "R. Joshua said to them, 'We have found an even greater person than Rabban Gamliel who stood and served!'

D.   "They said to him, 'And who might that be?'

---

[35] I.e., better than Jethro, in that Naaman denied even the existence of other gods.

[36] Compare 16.A–K with *Sifre Deut.*, Piska 38 (Hammer, p. 73; Neus., XXXVIII:I:4.A–H); and b. Kiddushin 32b (Neus., XIX.A:Qiddushin:1:7: II.27.E–28.F).

| | | |
|---|---|---|
| מכל האלהים ◆ אמרו מתחלה לא היה עבד יכול לברוח | | B |
| ממצרים עכשיו הוציא המקום ששים רבוא בני אדם ◆ | | |
| לכך נאמר כי גדול ה' מכל האלהים. ◆ ד"א ◆ כי גדול ה' | B/A 12 | C |
| מכל האלקים ◆ אמרו מתחלה לא הניח יתרו עבודה | | C |
| זרה בעולם שלא עבדה עכשו הודה בדבר ◆ שנ' אלהים | | D |
| האלהים כל האלהים מכל האלהים. ◆ נעמן הודה | | E |
| בדבר יתר ממנו ◆ שנ' הנה נא ידעתי כי אין אלהים בכל | | F |
| הארץ כי אם בישראל (מ"ב ה טו) ◆ וכן רחב הזונה | | G |
| שיירה ◆ שנ' כי ה' אלקיכם הוא אלקים בשמים ממעל | | H |
| ועל הארץ מתחת (יהו' ב יא), ◆ כי בדבר אשר זדו | A 13 | |
| עליהם ◆ מכירו הייתי לשעבר ועכשיו ביותר שבמחשבה | B | |
| שחישבו המצרים לאבד את ישראל בה דן המקום ◆ כי | C | |
| בדבר אשר זדו עליהם. ◆ | | |
| ויקח יתרו חתן משה עלה וזבחים ג' ◆ הרי הכתוב | B/A 14 | |
| (עד) מתמיה עליו אדם שעומד מזבח ומקטר לעבדה | | |
| זרה בכל יום עכשיו יביא עלה וזבחים לאים ◆ ויבא | A 15 | |
| אהרן ◆ משה להיכן הלך והלא מתחלה יצא לקראתו | B | |
| שנ' ויצא משה לקראת חתנו (שמ' יח ז) ◆ אלא מלמד | C | |
| שהיה עומד ומשמש ◆ דבר <זה> דרש ר' צדוק כשהיה | A 16 | |
| רבן גמל' עומד ומשמש ◆ אמרו בדין שאנו מסובין ורבן | B | |
| גמליאל עומד ומשמשנו ◆ אמר להם ר' יהושע מצאנו | C | |
| גדול מרבן גמל' [שעמ]ד ושימש ◆ אמרו לו ואיזה הוא ◆ | D | |

E.   "He said to them, 'Abraham, our father,[37] was the greatest of the generation! As it says in Scripture, "... and he waited on them, etc." (Gen. 18:8).

(Textual Source: Midrash ha-Gadol)

[132]   F.   "'[And Abraham served] not [only] suitable people, but also worshipers of idols who anger God! All the more so should Rabban Gamliel stand and serve suitable people who are engaged in Torah!'"

G.   R. Zadok said to them, "We have found an even greater person than either Abraham or Rabban Gamliel who stands and serves."

H.   They said to him, "Who is this?"

I.   He said to them, "God of the heavens, blessed be He, who gives each and every person his needs and to each and every creature according to its needs.

J.   "As it says in Scripture, 'Who gives food to all flesh' (Ps. 136:25). And Scripture says, '... who gives the beasts their food' (Ps. 147:9).

K.   "[And God provides for] not [only] suitable people, but also worshipers of idols who anger God! All the more so should Rabban Gamliel stand and serve suitable people who are engaged in Torah!"

*Chapter Forty-Seven*

(Textual Source: Midrash ha-Gadol)

XLVII:I[38]

1.   A.   "Next day, (Moses sat as magistrate among the people, while the people stood about Moses from morning until evening)" (Exod. 18:13):

B.   The day after the Day of Atonement.

2.   A.   "Moses sat as magistrate among the people" (Exod. 18:13):

B.   As he was accustomed.

3.   A.   "... from morning until evening" (Exod. 18:13):

B.   Would Moses really sit and judge Israel from morning until evening? Don't judges sit only up to mealtime?

C.   Rather, Scripture attributes to anyone who judges truthfully as if he is a partner in the act of Creation.

D.   Scripture states here "from morning until evening" (Exod. 18:13), and Scripture states above "And there was evening and there was morning" (Gen. 1:5).

4.   A.   "But when Moses' father-in-law saw how much he had to do for the people, (he said, 'What is this thing that you are doing to the people? Why do you sit alone, while all the people stand about you from morning until evening?')" (Exod. 18:14):

B.   He said to him, "[You are] like a king who sits with all his servants standing [around him]. This is what you are doing for Israel! 'Why do you sit alone, while all the people stand about you?' (Exod. 18:14)."

5.   A.   "Moses replied to his father-in-law, 'It is because the people come to me to inquire of God'" (Exod. 18:15):

---

[37] The Cambridge manuscript has the word בפינה immediately following the word "Abraham," a word which is difficult to contextualize in any fashion. I have translated here, instead, the word that appears in the parallel to this tradition in the *Mekhilta de-Rabbi Ishmael*—אבינו.

| | |
|---|---|
| E | אמר להם אברהם בפינה [גדול הדור שנ׳] והוא עומד |
| F | עליהם ג׳ (בר׳ יח ח). ✦ ולא בני אדם כשרים אלא בני |
| | אדם שעובדין ע״ז ומכעיסין לפני המקום. על אחת |
| | כמה וכמה לרבן גמליאל שעומד ומשמש לפני בני |
| G | אדם כשרים ועסיקין בתורה. ✦ אמר להם ר׳ צדוק |
| | מצאנו גדול מאברהם ומרבן גמליאל שעומד ומשמש ✦ |
| I/H | אמרו לו היזה ✦ אמר להן אלוה השמים ברוך הוא |
| | שנותן לכל אחד ואחד צרכיו ולכל גויה וגויה די |
| J | מחסורה ✦ שנ׳ נותן לחם לכל בשר (תה׳ קלו כה) ואומר |
| K | נותן לבהמה לחמה (תה׳ קמז ט) ✦ ולא בני אדם כשרים |
| | אלא בני אדם עובדין ע״ז ומכעיסין לפניו על אחת |
| | כמה וכמה לרבן גמליאל שעומד ומשמש לפני בני |
| | אדם כשרים ועסיקין בתורה. ✦ |

| | | | |
|---|---|---|---|
| | XLVII:I | | |
| B/A 1 | A 2 | ויהי ממחרת ✦ ממחרת יום הכפורים. ✦ וישב משה | |
| B | B/A 3 | לשפט את העם ✦ כמנהגו. ✦ מן הבקר עד הערב ✦ וכי | |
| | | מבקר ועד ערב היה משה יושב ודן את ישר׳ והלא אין | |
| C | | הדיינין יושבין אלא עד זמן סעודה ✦ אלא כל הדן דין | |
| | | אמת לאמתו מעלה עליו הכת׳ כאלו שותף במעשה | |
| D | | בראשית ✦ נאמר כאן מן בקר עד ערב ונאמר להלן ויהי | |
| | | ערב ויהי בקר (בר׳ א ה). ✦ |
| 4 | A | וירא חתן משה את כל אשר הוא עשה לעם וג׳ ✦ |
| | B | אמר לו כמלך שיושב ועבדיו עומדין כך אתה עושה להן |
| | | לישראל מדוע אתה יושב לבדך וכל העם נצב עליך. ✦ |
| 5 | A | ויאמר משה לחתנו כי יבא אלי העם לדרוש אלקים ✦ |

---

[38] Compare XLVII:I:1.A–23.C with *Mekhilta de-Rabbi Ishmael*, Amalek (H/R, 196:5–199:12; Laut., vol. 2, 179:1–185:93; Neus., XLVI:I:1.A–21.C), with the exception of 9.A–F and 22.A–24.C, which are unattested in the *Mekhilta de-Rabbi Ishmael*.

B. Judah ish Kefar Akko asked Rabban Gamliel this: "What prompted Moses to say this: 'It is because the people come to me to inquire of God' (Exod. 18:15)?"

C. He said to him, "If not [this], what might he say?"

D. [He replied,] "[He might have said,] 'It is because the people come to me to inquire.'"

E. [Rabban Gamliel said,] "By saying 'of God' he spoke appropriately."

6. A. "'When they have a dispute, it comes before me, (and I decide between one person and another, and I make known the laws of God and His teachings)'" (Exod. 18:16):

B. [A dispute about deciding] between ritual impurity and purity.

7. A. "'... and I decide between one person'" (Exod. 18:16):

B. This is a judgment without a compromise.

C. "'... and another'" (Exod. 18:16):

D. This is a judgment with a compromise, with [the litigants] going their separate ways as friends.

8. A. "'... and I make known the laws of God' (Exod. 18:16):

B. "These are decrees.

C. "'... and His teachings' (Exod. 18:16):

D. "These are instructions."—Thus are the words of R. Joshua.

E. R. Eliezer the Modiite says, "'... and I make known the laws of God' (Exod. 18:16):

F. "These are the laws of sexual impropriety.

G. "'... and His teachings' (Exod. 18:16):

H. "These are decrees."

9. A. "But Moses' father-in-law said to him, 'The thing you are doing is not right'" (Exod. 18:17):

B. So beloved was Jethro that God allowed him to exalt himself above Him through the appointing of the elders!

C. For wasn't the appointing of the elders a worthwhile thing to the Holy One, blessed be He? So why didn't the Holy One, blessed be He, command it to Moses first?

D. In order to bestow greatness on Jethro in the eyes of Moses and all the Children of Israel to say, "So great was Jethro that the Holy One, blessed be He, agreed with his words!"

E. But Jethro said it only under the condition that the Holy One, blessed be He, agreed with his words!

F. As it says in Scripture, "If you do this—and God so commands you" (Exod. 18:23).

10. A. "'You will surely wear (yourself out, and also these people as well. For the task is too heavy for you. You cannot do it alone)'" (Exod. 18:18):

B. R. Joshua says, "They will degrade you and chide you!"

C. R. Eliezer the Modiite says, "They will wear you out until you drop, like this fig tree with its leaves falling!

D. "And thus Scripture states, 'Like a leaf withering on the vine, or shriveled fruit on a fig tree' (Isa. 34:4)."

11. A. "'... yourself' (Exod. 18:18)—this [refers to] Moses.

| | | |
|---|---|---|
| דבר זה שאל יהודה איש כפר עכו את רבן | B | |
| גמליאל מה ראה משה לומר כך כי יבא אלי העם | | |
| לדרוש אלקים. ◆ אמר לו ואם לאו מה יאמר ◆ כי יבא | D/C | |
| אלי העם לדרוש ◆ כשאמר אלהים יפה אמר. ◆ | E | |
| כי יהיה להם דבר בא אלי ◆ בין טומאה לטהרה. ◆ | B/A | 6 |
| ושפטתי בין איש ◆ זה דין שאין בו פשרה ◆ ובין רעהו ◆ זה | D/C/B/A | 7 |
| דין שיש בו פשרה ונפטרין והולכין כרעים. ◆ והודעתי | A | 8 |
| את חקי האלקים ◆ אלו גזירות ◆ ואת תורותיו ◆ אלו | D/C/B | |
| הוראות כך דברי ר׳ יהושע. ◆ ר׳ אלעזר המודעי אומ׳ | E | |
| והודעתי את חקי האלקים ◆ אלו עריות ◆ ואת תורותיו ◆ | G/F | |
| אלו גזירות. ◆ | H | |
| ויאמר חתן משה אליו לא טוב הדבר אשר אתה | A | 9 |
| עושה ◆ חביב הוא יתרו שניתן לו מקום להתגדר בו זה | B | |
| מנוי זקנים. ◆ והלא מנוי זקנים היה דבר הגון לפני | C | |
| הקב״ה ומפני מה לא צווהו הקב״ה למשה תחלה ◆ אלא | D | |
| כדי ליתן גדולה ליתרו בעיני משה וכל בני ישראל | | |
| לומר גדול היה יתרו שהסכים הקב״ה על דבריו ◆ אף | E | |
| יתרו לא אמרה אלא על תנאי שאם יסכים הקב״ה על | | |
| דבריו ◆ שנ׳ אם את הדבר הזה תעשה וצוך אלקים. ◆ | F | |
| נבל תבל ◆ ר׳ יהושע אומר יחללו אותך ויקנתרו | B/A | 10 |
| אותך. ◆ ר׳ אלעזר המודעי אומ׳ ינבלו אותך וינשרו | C | |
| אותך כתאנה זו שעליה נושרין. ◆ וכן הוא אומ׳ כנבל | D | |
| עלה מגפן וכנבלת מתאנה (ישע׳ לד ד). ◆ אתה זה משה. ◆ | A | 11 |

B.   "'... as well' (Exod. 18:18)—this [refers to] Aaron.

C.   "'... these people' (Exod. 18:18)—these are the 70 elders."—Thus are the words of R. Joshua.

D.   R. Eliezer the Modiite says, "'... yourself' (Exod. 18:18)—this [refers to] Moses.

E.   "'... as well' (Exod. 18:18)—this [refers to] Aaron.

F.   "'... these people' (Exod. 18:18)—these are the 70 elders.

G.   "When Scripture states, '... and also' (Exod. 18:18), this [refers to] Nadab and Abihu."

12.  A.   "'For the task is too heavy for you'" (Exod. 18:18):

B.   He said to him, "Take a look at this beam. When it is still moist [and new], if people get underneath it one at a time, they can't support it. Three or four, [however,] can support it!"

C.   Thus it is said, "'For the task is too heavy for you' (Exod. 18:18)."

D.   [Meaning,] you can't do it alone!

13.  A.   "'Now listen to me. I will give you counsel, (and God be with you! You represent the
[133]     people before God. You bring the disputes before God)'" (Exod. 18:19):

B.   If you listen to me, it will go well for you.

C.   "'I will give you counsel, and God be with you!'" (Exod. 18:19):

D.   If you agree, you will be able to make it. But if not, you will not be able to make it.

E.   "'You represent the people before God'" (Exod. 18:19):

F.   Be like a vessel full of divine speech for them!

G.   "'You bring the disputes before God'" (Exod. 18:19):

H.   Discuss the words that you hear on behalf of the people.

14.  A.   "''Enjoin upon them the laws (and the teachings, and make known to them the way by which they are to go and the practices they are to follow)'" (Exod. 18:20):

B.   "These are decrees.

C.   "''... and the teachings'" (Exod. 18:20):

D.   "These are instructions."—Thus are the words of R. Joshua.

E.   R. Eliezer the Modiite says, "''... the laws'" (Exod. 18:20):

F.   "These are the laws of sexual impropriety. As it says in Scripture, 'You shall keep My charge not to engage in any of the abhorrent practices' (Lev. 18:30).

G.   "''... and the teachings'" (Exod. 18:20):

H.   "These are decrees."

15.  A.   "''... and make known to them the way by which they are to go'" (Exod. 18:20):

B.   "This is a decree. As it says in Scripture, 'Follow only the path that the Lord your God has commanded you' (Deut. 5:30).

C.   "''... and the practices they are to follow'" (Exod. 18:20):

D.   "This is good deed(s)."—Thus are the words of R. Joshua.

E.   R. Eliezer the Modiite says, "''... and make known to them'" (Exod. 18:20):

| | | |
|---|---|---|
| גם זה אהרן. ◆ העם הזה אשר עמך אלו שבעים זקנים | C/B | |
| כך דברי ר׳ יהושע. ◆ ר׳ אלעזר המודעי אומר אתה זה | D | |
| משה ◆ גם זה אהרן ◆ העם הזה אשר עמך אלו שבעים | F/E | |
| זקנים. ◆ כשהוא אומר וגם זה נדב ואביהוא. ◆ כי כבד | A 12 | G |
| ממך הדבר ◆ אמר לו הסתכל בקורה זו כשהיא לחה כל | B | |
| זמן שבני אדם נכנסין תחתיה אחד אחד אין יכולין | | |
| לעמוד בה. שלשה וארבעה יכולין לעמוד בה. ◆ לכך | C | |
| נאמ׳ כי כבד ממך הדר ◆ לא תוכל עשהו לבדך. | D | |
| עתה שמע בקולי איעצך ◆ אם תשמעני ייטב לך. | B/A | 13 |
| איעצך ויהי אלקים עמך ◆ אם מודה לך אתה יכול | D/C | |
| לעמוד ואם לאו אי אתה יכול לעמוד. ◆ היה אתה לעם | E | |
| מול האלקים ◆ היה להם ככלי מלא דברות. ◆ והבאת | G/F | |
| אתה את הדברים אל האלקים ◆ דברים שאתה שומע | II | |
| תבוא תרצה לעם. ◆ | | |
| והזהרתה אתהם את החקים ◆ אלו גזירות ◆ ואת | C/B/A | 14 |
| התורות ◆ אלו הוראות כך דברי ר׳ יהושע. ◆ ר׳ אלעזר | E/D | |
| המודעי אומר את החקים ◆ אלו עריות שנ׳ ושמרתם | F | |
| את משמרתי לבלתי עשות מחוקות התועבות (ויק׳ יח ל) ◆ | | |
| ואת התורות ◆ אלו גזירות. ◆ והודעת להם את הדרך ילכו | A 15 | H/G |
| בה ◆ זו גזירה שנ׳ בכל הדרך אשר צוה ה׳ אלקיכם תלכו | B | |
| (דב׳ ה ל) ◆ ואת המעשה אשר יעשון ◆ זה מעשה הטוב | D/C | |
| כך דברי ר׳ יהושע. ◆ ר׳ אלעזר המודעי אומר והודעת להם ◆ | E | |

F.     "You should make known to them the structure of their lives.

G.     """... the way"' (Exod. 18:20):

H.     "This is acts of loving-kindness.

I.     """... they are to go"' (Exod. 18:20):

J.     "This is visiting the sick.

K.     """... by which"' (Exod. 18:20):

L.     "This is burial of the dead.

M.     """... and the practices"' (Exod. 18:20):

N.     "This is the law.

O.     """... they are to follow"' (Exod. 18:20).

P.     "This is beyond the line of the law."

### (Textual Source: Ms. Cambridge T-S C 4a.5)

16.     A.     """You shall also seek out from among all the people (capable men who fear God, trustworthy men who spurn ill-gotten gains. Set these over them as chiefs of thousands, hundreds, fifties, and tens) "' (Exod. 18:21):

B.     "You shall see them by means of prophecy.

C.     """... capable men"' (Exod. 18:21):

D.     "These are rich people, people of wealth.

E.     """... who fear God"' (Exod. 18:21):

F.     "These are they who fear God in judgment.

G.     """... trustworthy men"' (Exod. 18:21):

H.     "These are people who keep a promise.

I.     """... who spurn ill-gotten gain"' (Exod. 18:21):

J.     "These are people who hate to receive wealth."—Thus are the words of R. Joshua.

K.     R. Eliezer the Modiite says, """You shall also seek out from among all the people"' (Exod. 18:21):

L.     "You shall see them through a speculum, with the glass through which kings look.

M.     """... capable men"' (Exod. 18:21):

N.     "These are people who keep a promise.

O.     """... who fear God"' (Exod. 18:21):

P.     "These are they who make compromises in judgment.

Q.     """... trustworthy men"' (Exod. 18:21):

R.     "Such as R. Ḥananiah ben Dosa and his companions.

S.     """... who spurn ill-gotten gain"' (Exod. 18:21):

T.     "These are they who hate their own wealth. And isn't it a matter of logic? If they hate their own wealth, all the more so the wealth of others!"

17.     A.     "'Set these over them, etc.'" (Exod. 18:21):

| | |
|---|---|
| H/G/F | שתודיע להם בית חייהם. ◆ את הדרך ◆ זו גמילות |
| L/K/J/I | חסדים ◆ ילכו ◆ זה ביקור חולים ◆ בה ◆ זו קבורת |
| P/O/N/M | מתים ◆ ואת המעשה ◆ זה הדין ◆ אשר יעשון ◆ זה לפנים |
| | משורת הדין. ◆ |
| B/A | ואתה תחזה מכל העם ◆ אתה תחזה [להם מנבואה ◆ 16 |
| E/D/C | אנ]שי חיל ◆ אילו עשירים בעלי ממון ◆ יראי אים ◆ |
| H/G/F | אלו [שיראים מן המקום בדין] ◆ אנשי אמת ◆ אלו בעלי |
| J/I | הבטחה ◆ שונאי בצע ◆ אילו [ששונאין לקבל ממון] כך |
| K | דברי ר' יהושע ◆ ר' אלעזר המודעי או' ואתה [תחזה |
| L | מכל העם ◆ תחזה להם באספקלריא] כמחזית זו |
| N/M | שהמלכים חוזים בה ◆ [אנשי חיל ◆ אלו בעלי הבטחה ◆ |
| R/Q/P/O | י]ראי אים ◆ אלו שעושים פשרה בדין ◆ [אנשי אמת ◆ כגון ר' |
| T/S | חנינא רן דוסא וחביריו] ◆ שונאי בצע ◆ אלו ששונאין ממון |
| | עצמן [והלא דברים קל וחומר ומה אם ממון] עצמן הן |
| A | שונאין ממון אחרים [על אחת כמה וכמה ◆ ושמת עליהם ג'] ◆ 17 |

B. The chiefs of thousands were 600. The chiefs of hundreds were 6,000. The chiefs of fifties were 12,000. The chiefs of tens were 60,000.

C. We find that the judges of Israel were 78,600.

(Textual Source: Midrash ha-Gadol)

18. A. "'Let them judge the people at all times. (Have them bring every major dispute to you, but let them decide every minor dispute themselves. Make it easier for yourself by letting them share the burden with you)'" (Exod. 18:22):

B. R. Joshua says, "People who are free from their work should judge Israel at all times."

C. R. Eliezer the Modiite says, "People who are free from their work and are engaged in Torah should judge Israel at all times."

19. A. "'Have them bring every major dispute to you'" (Exod. 18:22):

B. They should bring major disputes to you, and they should judge minor disputes [themselves].

C. Isn't it, instead, they should bring disputes among important people to you, and they should judge [themselves] disputes among unimportant people?

D. Since Scripture says, "... the difficult matters they would bring to Moses" (Exod. 18:26), thus [we know that] "major dispute" is stated only [in regard to] major disputes. Major disputes they should bring to you, and they should judge minor disputes [themselves].

20. A. "'If you do this—and God so commands you—(you will be able to endure, and all these people too will go home in peace)'" (Exod. 18:23):

B. He said to him, "Go, consult with the Almighty! If He agrees with you, you will be able to endure. But if not, you will not be able to endure."

21. A. "'... and all these people too will go home in peace'" (Exod. 18:23):

B. Aaron, Nadab and Abihu, and all the elders of Israel will go home unwearied.

22. A. R. Simai says, "He who adjudicates the law truthfully is like one who removes jealousy
[134] between creatures. And he places only peace among them, as it says in Scripture, 'These are the things you are to do: (Speak the truth to one another,) render true and perfect justice in your gates' (Zech. 8:16).

B. "I only know that the one who has wealth has peace. How does one know from Scripture that even the one who owes money will, in the end, have peace? As it says in Scripture, '... and all these people too will go home in peace' (Exod. 18:23).

C. "I only know that adjudicators [will have peace]. How does one know from Scripture that even all of Israel [will have peace]? Scripture states, '... that he may judge Your people rightly, Your lowly one, justly' (Ps. 72:2).

D. "What is written after it?—'Let the mountains produce peace for the people' (Ps. 72:3).

E. "I only know that people alone [will have peace]. How does one know from Scripture that the judgment of peace [will extend] even to beasts, cattle, and to all living things? Scripture states, 'Thus he shall judge the poor with equity and decide with justice for the lowly of the land ... Justice shall be the girdle of his loins' (Isa. 11:4,5).

| | | |
|---|---|---|
| B | שרי אלפים שש מאות שרי [מאות ששת אלפים שרי | |
| C | חמשי]ם שנים עשר אלף שרי עשרות [ששת ריבוא • נמצאו | |
| | דייני יש'] שבעת ריבוא ו[שמונת אלפים] [ושש מאות] • | |
| B/A | וְשָׁפְטוּ אֶת הָעָם בְּכָל עֵת • ר' יהושע אומ' בני אדם | 18 |
| C | שבטילין ממלאכתן יהיו דנין את ישראל בכל עת. • ר' | |
| | אלעזר המודעי אומ' בני אדם שבטילין ממלאכתן | |
| A | ועסיקין בתורה יהו דנין את ישר' בכל עת. • וְהָיָה כָּל | 19 |
| B | הַדָּבָר הַגָּדֹל יָבִיאוּ אֵלֶיךָ • דברים גדולים יביאו אליך | |
| C | ודברים קטנים ישפטו הם • או אינו אלא דברים שבבני | |
| | אדם גדולים יביאו אליך ודברים שבבני אדם קטנים | |
| D | ישפטו הם • כשהוא אומר את הדבר הקשה יביאון אל | |
| | משה (פסוק כ"ו) הא אין דבר גדול אמור אלא | |
| | בדברים גדולים דברים גדולים יביאו אליך ודברים | |
| | קטנים ישפטו הם. • | |
| B/A | אִם אֶת הַדָּבָר הַזֶּה תַּעֲשֶׂה וְצִוְּךָ אֱלֹקִים • אמר לו | 20 |
| | צא והמלך בגבורה אם מודה לך אתה יכול לעמוד | |
| | ואם לאו אי אתה יכול לעמוד. • וְגַם כָּל הָעָם הַזֶּה עַל | |
| A | מְקֹמוֹ יָבֹא בְשָׁלוֹם • אהרן נדב ואביהוא וכל זקני ישר' | 21 |
| B | על מקומו יבוא בשלום. • ר' סימאי אומר הדן את הדין | |
| A | לאמתו נראה כמטיל קנאה בין הבריות ואינו אלא | 22 |
| | נותן שלום ביניהן שנ' אלה הדברים אשר תעשו וג' | |
| | אמת ומשפט שלום שפטו בשעריכם (זכ' ח טז). • אין | |
| B | לי אלא נוטל ממון שיש לו שלום. מנין שאף המתחייב | |
| | ממון שגם הוא סופו שלום שנ' וגם כל העם הזה על | |
| | מקומו יבא בשלום. • אין לי אלא לבעלי דינין ומנין אף | |
| C | לכל ישראל ת"ל ידין עמך בצדק ועניך במשפט (תה' | |
| | עב ב) • מה כת' אחריו ישאו הרים שלום לעם. • אין לי | |
| E/D | אלא בני אדם בלבד מנין שהמשפט שלום אף לבהמות | |
| | ולחיות ולכל בעלי חיים ת"ל ושפט בצדק דלים | |
| | והוכיח במישור לענוי ארץ וג' והיה צדק אזור מתניו | |
| | • | |

F. "What is written after it?—'The wolf shall dwell with the lamb, the leopard lie down with the kid ... In all of My sacred mount nothing evil or vile shall be done. For the land shall be filled with devotion to the Lord' (Isa. 11:6,9).

G. "This 'devotion' is justice. For thus Scripture states about peace, 'Do you think you are more a king because you compete in cedar? Your father ate and drank and dispensed justice and equity. Then all went well with him. He upheld the rights of the poor and needy. Then all was well. That is the reward for heeding Me, declares the Lord' (Jer. 22:15–16)."

23. A. So great is justice that for all who hate it there is no healing for his wound.

B. As it says in Scripture, "Would one who hates justice govern?"[39] (Job 34:17).

C. And [the word] "govern" means only "healing." As it says in Scripture, "He heals their broken hearts and binds[40] up their wounds" (Ps. 147:3).

## XLVII:II

### (Textual Source: Ms. Cambridge T-S C 4a.5)

1. A. "'Moses heeded his father-in-law' (Exod. 18:24):[41]

B. "Certainly! [or: Literally!].

C. "'... and did just as he had said' (Exod. 18:24):

D. "Whatever

### (Textual Source: Midrash ha-Gadol)

his father-in-law said to him."—Thus are the words of R. Joshua.

E. R. Eliezer the Modiite says, "'Moses heeded his father-in-law' (Exod. 18:24):

F. "Certainly! [or: Literally!].

G. "'... and did just as he had said' (Exod. 18:24):

H. "Whatever God said to him."

2. A. "Moses chose capable men out of all Israel, (and appointed them heads over the people—chiefs of thousands, hundreds, fifties, and tens)" (Exod. 18:25):

B. He appointed judges over them, and commanded the judges to suffer the trouble of the community.

C. In accordance with what is said in Scripture, "I charged your magistrates ... (Hear out your fellow men)" (Deut. 1:16).

D. And he commanded the people to behave honorably with the judges.

E. In accordance with what is said in Scripture, "Thus I instructed you, at that time, about the various things that you should do" (Deut. 1:18).

3. A. "And they judged the people at all times. The difficult matters they would bring to Moses, (and all the minor matters they would decide themselves)" (Exod. 18:26):

B. The Holy One, blessed be He, said to him, "Moses, you [are going to] judge the difficult ones? Behold, the daughters of Zelophehad are coming to seek a judgment for which even the schoolchildren can return [a verdict], but you will not know what verdict to deliver!"

C. Namely, "Moses brought their case before the Lord" (Num. 27:5).

[39] Hebrew: yaḥavosh—יחבוש.
[40] Hebrew: mʾḥabesh—מחבש.
[41] Compare 1.A–C with Mekhilta de-Rabbi Ishmael, Amalek (H/R, 199:13–15; Laut., vol. 2, 185:94–97; Neus., XLVI:II:1.A–D).

<table>
<tr><td align="right">מה כת' אחריו וגר זאב עם כבש ונמר עם גדי</td><td>F</td><td></td></tr>
<tr><td align="right">ירבץ וג' לא ירעו ולא ישחיתו בכל הר קדשי כי מלאה</td><td></td><td></td></tr>
<tr><td align="right">הארץ דעה את ה' (ישע' יא ה - ו, ט) ◆ דעה זו היא</td><td>G</td><td></td></tr>
<tr><td align="right">המשפט שכן הוא אומ' לשלום התמלך כי אתה</td><td></td><td></td></tr>
<tr><td align="right">מתחרה בארז אביך הלא אכל ושתה ועשה משפט</td><td></td><td></td></tr>
<tr><td align="right">וצדקה אז טוב לו דן דין עני ואביון אז טוב הלא היא</td><td></td><td></td></tr>
<tr><td align="right">הדעת אותי נאום ה' (ירמ' כב טז). ◆ גדול המשפט שכל</td><td>A</td><td>23</td></tr>
<tr><td align="right">השונאו אין רפואה למכתו ◆ שנ' האף שונא משפט</td><td>B</td><td></td></tr>
<tr><td align="right">יחבוש (איוב לד יז) ◆ ואין חבישה אלא רפואה שנ'</td><td>C</td><td></td></tr>
<tr><td align="right">הרופא לשבורי לב ומחבש לעצבותם (תה' קמז ג). ◆</td><td></td><td></td></tr>
</table>

XLVII:I

<table>
<tr><td align="right">[וישמע משה ל]קול חותנו ◆ [ודאי ◆ ויעש כל אשר</td><td>C/B/A</td><td>1</td></tr>
<tr><td align="right">אמר ◆ מה שאמר לו] חמיו כך דברי ר' יהושע. ◆ ר' אלעזר</td><td>ח/F</td><td></td></tr>
<tr><td align="right">המודעי אומר וישמע משה לקול חתנו ◆ ודאי ◆ ויעש כל</td><td>G/F</td><td></td></tr>
<tr><td align="right">אשר אמר ◆ מה שאמר לו המקום. ◆</td><td>H</td><td></td></tr>
<tr><td align="right">ויבחר משה אנשי חיל מכל יש' ◆ מינה עליהן דייניין</td><td>B/A</td><td>2</td></tr>
<tr><td align="right">וצוה את הדיינין שיהיו סובלין טורח הצבור ◆ כענין שנ'</td><td>C</td><td></td></tr>
<tr><td align="right">ואצוה את שפטיכם (דב' א טז). ◆ וצוה את העם שיהיו</td><td>D</td><td></td></tr>
<tr><td align="right">נוהגין כבוד בדייניו ◆ כענין שנ' ואצו אתכם בעת ההיא</td><td>E</td><td></td></tr>
<tr><td align="right">את כל הדברים אשר תעשון (שם יח). ◆</td><td></td><td></td></tr>
<tr><td align="right">ושפטו את העם בכל עת את את הדבר ה קשה</td><td>A</td><td>3</td></tr>
<tr><td align="right">יביאון אל משה ◆ אמר לו הקב"ה משה אתה דן את</td><td>B</td><td></td></tr>
<tr><td align="right">הקושיות הרי בנות צלפחד באין לשאל בדין שאפלו</td><td></td><td></td></tr>
<tr><td align="right">תינוקות שלבית רבן משיבין עליו ואין אתה יודע מה</td><td></td><td></td></tr>
<tr><td align="right">להשיב ◆ אלא ויקרב משה את משפטן לפני ה' (במ' כז ה).</td><td></td><td></td></tr>
<tr><td align="right">◆</td><td>C</td><td></td></tr>
</table>

4.     A.     "Then Moses bade his father-in-law farewell, (and he went his way to his own land)" (Exod. 18:27):[42]

        B.     R. Joshua says, "He sent him with worldly honor."

        C.     R. Eliezer the Modiite says, "He gave him many gifts."

5.     A.     He[43] said to him, "I am going to go convert the people of my country."

        B.     And from the response he[44] gave them, you know it.

        C.     What did they say to him?—"Please do not leave us" (Num. 10:31).

        D.     They said to him, "You have given us good advice—great advice—and God has agreed with your words. Please do not leave us!"

        E.     He said to them, "A lamp is only beneficial in a dark place. What does a lamp do among the sun and the moon? You are the sun, and Aaron is the moon! Rather, I am going to go convert the people of my country, and bring them beneath the wings of God's presence!"

6.     A.     One might think that he left, but did not return [to his native land].

        B.     Scripture states, [however,] "The descendants of the Kenite, the father-in-law of Moses, went up with the Judites from the City of Palms to the wilderness of Judah, and they went and settled among the people in the Negeb of Arad" (Judg. 1:16).

        C.     This teaches that there was a large nation with them.

7.     A.     Another interpretation:

        B.     "He said to him, 'I will not go'" (Num. 10:30).

[135]     C.     Why did he return to his native land? This is what Jethro thought, saying, "All these years people gave me deposits, because I was the most trustworthy person in the city. So if I go off and leave them, they will say, 'Jethro has fled and taken all our deposits and given [them] to his son-in-law!' As a result, both you and I will develop a bad reputation! Instead, I'll go and return them all."

8.     A.     Another interpretation:

        B.     "He said to him, 'I will not go'" (Num. 10:31):

        C.     Why did he return?

        D.     He thought, saying, "This year was a year of dearth, and I borrowed money and sustained the poor. If I don't go and pay the debts, the result will be the profanation of the name of heaven! Instead, I'm going to go and pay them."

        E.     And how does one know from Scripture that it was a year of dearth? As it says in Scripture, "Now the flax and barley were ruined" (Exod. 9:31).

        F.     Even though the wheat wasn't struck, the barley was. If there isn't barley, the wheat rises in price.

9.     A.     They went and dwelled with the people of Jabez.[45]

        B.     As it says in Scripture, "The families of the scribes that dwelt at Jabez: the Tirathites, the Shimeathites, the Sucathites. These are the Kenites who came from Hammath, father of the house of Rechab" (1 Chron. 2:55).

---

[42] Compare 4.A–6.C with *Mekhilta de-Rabbi Ishmael*, Amalek (H/R, 199:16–200:5; Laut., vol. 2, 185:98–186:110; Neus., XLVI:II:2.A–3.B).
[43] I.e., Jethro.
[44] I.e., Jethro.
[45] Compare 9.A–17.B with *Mekhilta de-Rabbi Ishmael*, Amalek (H/R, 200:8–202:9; Laut., vol. 2, 186:115–191:182; Neus., XLVI:II:4.A–12.C).

| | | |
|---|---|---|
| וישלח משה את חתנו ♦ ר' יהושע אומר שילחו | B/A | 4 |
| בכבוד שלעולם. ♦ ר' אלעזר המודעי אומ' נתן לו מתנות | C | |
| רבות. ♦ אמר לו הריני הולך ומגייר את בני מדינתי ♦ | A | 5 |
| שמתשובה שאמר להם הוי יודע ♦ מה אמרו לו אל נא | C/B | |
| תעזב אותנו (במ' י לא). ♦ אמרו לו אתה נתת לנו עצה | D | |
| טובה עצה יפה והמקום הודה לדבריך אל נא תעזב | | |
| אותנו ♦ אמר להן כלום הנר מהנה אלא במקום חשך | E | |
| מה יעשה נר בין חמה ללבנה אתה חמה ואהרן לבנה | | |
| אלא הריני הולך ומגייר את בני מדינתי שאביאם | | |
| תחת כנפי שמים. ♦ יכול שהלך ולא חזר ♦ ת"ל ובני קיני | B/A | 6 |
| חתן משה עלו מעיר התמרים את בני יהודה מדבר | | |
| יהודה אשר בנגב ערד וילך וישב את העם (שופ' א | | |
| טז) ♦ [מלמד שהיה עמהן עם רב. ♦ ד"א ♦ ויאמר אליו לא | B/A 7 | C |
| אלך ♦ למה חזר לארצו אלא כך היה יתרו מחשב ואומר | | C |
| כל השנים הללו היו בני אדם מפקידין אצלי פקדונות | | |
| שאני הייתי הנאמן שבעיר ואם אני מניחן והולך לי הן | | |
| אומרין ברח לו יתרו ולקח כל פקדונותי<נ>ו ונתן | | |
| לח(ו)תנו נמצאתי מוצ<י>א שם רע עלי ועליך אלא | | |
| הריני הולך ומחזיר את כולן. ♦ ד"א ♦ ויאמר אליו לא אלך ♦ | B/A | 8 |
| למה חזר ♦ אלא היה מחשב ואומר השנה הזאת שנת | D/C | |
| בצורת היתה ואני לויתי ופרנסתי את העניים ואם אין | | |
| אני הולך ופורע את החובות נמצאתי מחלל שם | | |
| שמים אלא הריני הולך ופורען ♦ ומנין ששנת בצורת | E | |
| היתה שנאמר והפשתה והשעורה נכתה (שמ' ט לא) ♦ | | |
| אף על פי שלא לקו החטים אלא השעורים אם | F | |
| אין שעורים החטים מתיקרים]. ♦ הלכו וישבו להן | A | 9 |
| אצל יושבי יעבץ ♦ שנ' ומשפחות סופרים יושבי | B | |
| יעבץ שמעתים תרעתים שוכתים המה הקנים | | |
| הבאים מחמת אבי בית רכב (דה"א ב נה) ♦ | | |

C. Just as he[46] loved the Torah, likewise his children loved the Torah after him.

D. For thus God says to Jeremiah, "Go to the house of the Rechabites ... and give them wine to drink ... I set bowls full of wine and cups before the men of the house of the Rechabites, and said to them, 'Have some wine'" (Jer. 35:2,5).

E. Jeremiah said to them, "God has said to me that you should drink wine."

F. They said to him, "Our father commanded us not to drink wine all the days that this house is destroyed. And when it had not yet been destroyed, he said to us, 'You will mourn over it, because its fate is to be destroyed.' And he said to us, 'Don't anoint, don't shave, and don't dwell in houses!' and we listened and did all that Jonadab our father commanded us."

G. Thus were they called Tirathites, Shimeathites, and Sucathites.

H. Tirathites—because they didn't want to shave. Sucathites—because they didn't want to anoint. Shimeathites—because they heeded their father.

10. A. Another interpretation:

B. Tirathites—because they heard the blast [of the shofar] from Mount Sinai.

11. A. Another interpretation:

B. [Tirathites]—because they sounded the shofar with their requests, and they were answered.

C. Shimeathites—because they heeded the words of Torah.

12. A. Another interpretation:

B. [Shimeathites]—because their prayer was heard.

C. Sucathites—because they dwelled in booths.

13. A. Another interpretation:

B. [Sucathites]—because they sheltered Israel and defended them.

14. A. It once occurred that someone said, "[Let's offer] an offering today at the house of the Sucathites!"[47]

B. God's divine voice went out from the Holy of Holies and said to them, "He who received the offering of your forefathers in the wilderness will receive your offering at this moment."

C. And who are they? "These are the Kenites who came from Hammath, father of the house of Rechab" (1 Chron. 2:55). And Scripture says, "The descendants of the Kenite, the father-in-law of Moses, went up with the Judites from the City of Palms" (Judg. 1:16).

D. You have to say that the house of Rechab is from Jethro!

15. A. Come and see just how righteous the children of Jethro were!

B. Because Jonadab the son of Rechab heard directly from the prophet that the Temple would be destroyed, and he decreed three decrees over his children:

C. That they should not drink wine.

D. That they should not build houses.

E. That they should not plant vineyards.

---

[46] I.e., Jethro.

[47] This term is problematic as it appears here in *Midrash ha-Gadol* (Hebrew: בית שותי מים), literally translated as something along the lines of "The house of those who drink water." It is unattested, otherwise, in all of the classical Rabbinic corpus. I translate here as if it is a scribal/manuscript corruption of the Hebrew for "the house of the Sucathites" (בית סוכתים).

| | | |
|---|---|---|
| C | | כשם שהיה מחבב את התורה כך בניו חיבבו את |
| D | | התורה מאחריו ♦ שכן המקום אומר לירמיה הלוך אל בית |
| | | הרכבים והשקית אותם יין ואתן לפני בית הרכבים גביעים |
| | | מלאים יין וכוסות ואומר אליהם שתו יין (ירמ׳ לה ה) ♦ |
| F/E | | אמר להם ירמיה המקום אמר לי שתשתו יין ♦ אמרו לו |
| | | אבינו צוה עלינו שלא לשתות יין כל ימים שהבית הזה |
| | | חרב ואדיין היה שלא היה חרב אלא אמר לנו תהו מתאבלין |
| | | עליו שסופו ליחרב ואמר לנו אל תסוכו ואל תספרו |
| | | ואל תשבו בבתים ונשמע ונעש ככל אשר צונו יונדב |
| G | | אבינו. ♦ לכך נקראו תרעתים שמעתים שוכתים. ♦ |
| H | | תרעתים שלא רצו לגלח. סוכתים שלא רצו לסוך. |
| B/A | 10 | שמעתים ששמעו לקול אביהם. ♦ ד״א ♦ תרעתים ששמעו |
| B/A | 11 | תרועה מהר סיני. ♦ ד״א ♦ שהיו מתריעין בבקשתן וענין. ♦ |
| B/A 12 | C | שמעתים ששמעו לקול דברי תורה. ♦ ד״א ♦ שהיתה |
| A 13 | C | תפלתן נשמעת. ♦ סוכתים שהיו יושבין בסכות. ♦ ד״א ♦ |
| A 14 | B | שהיו מסככין על ישראל ומגינין עליהן. ♦ ומעשה באחד |
| | B | שאמר קרבן בית שותי מים היום ♦ יצאת בת קול מבית |
| | | קודש הקדשים ואמרה להן מי שקיבל קרבן |
| C | | אבותיכם במדבר הוא יקבל קרבנכם בשעה זו. ♦ ומי הן |
| | | אלו המה הקינים הבאים מחמת אבי בית רכב. ואומר |
| D | | ובני קיני חתן משה עלו מעיר התמרים (שופ׳ א טז) ♦ הוי |
| A | 15 | אומר בית רכב המה מיתרו. ♦ בוא וראה כמה היה צדקן |
| B | | שלבני יתרו ♦ שהרי יונדב בן רכב שמע מפי הנביא שבית |
| | | המקדש עתיד ליחרב ועמד וגזר על בניו שלש גזירות ♦ |
| E/D/C | | שלא ישתו יין ♦ ושלא יבנו בתים ♦ ושלא יטעו כרמים ♦ |

F.    As it says in Scripture, "They replied, 'We will not drink wine, for our father, Jonadab son of Rechab, commanded us: "You shall not drink wine, either you or your children. Nor shall you build houses or sow fields or plant vineyards, nor shall you own such things. You shall live in tents all your days, so that you may live long upon the land where you sojourn"'" (Jer. 35:6–7).

G.    And how does one learn from Scripture that abstention from wine lengthens [one's] days? Because four people had an obsession for [produce of] the land, and were found unworthy: Cain, Noah, Lot, and Uzziah.

H.    Cain, [as it says in Scripture,] "And Cain became a tiller of the soil" (Gen. 4:2).

I.    Noah, [as it says in Scripture,] "Noah, the tiller of the soil, was the first" (Gen. 9:20).

J.    Lot, [as it says in Scripture,] "Lot looked about him and saw the whole plain of the Jordan" (Gen. 13:10).

K.    Uzziah, [as it says in Scripture,] "... because he loved the soil" (2 Chron. 26:10).

16.   A.    R. Nathan says, "The covenant that the Holy One, blessed be He, made with the children of Jethro is greater than the covenant He made with the children of David.

B.    "For the covenant that was made with David was made only with conditions. As it says in Scripture, 'If your sons keep My covenant and My decrees that I teach them, then their sons also, to the end of time, shall sit upon your throne' (Ps. 132:12).

C.    "But the covenant that was made with Jonadab son of Rechab was made unconditionally. As it says in Scripture, 'Assuredly, thus said the Lord of Hosts, the God of Israel: There shall never cease to be a man of the line of Jonadab son of Rechab standing before Me' (Jer. 35:19)."

[136]   D.    R. Shimon said, "Hadn't the High Priesthood already ceased? How do I justify 'There shall never cease to be a man of the line of Jonadab' (Jer. 35:19)?

E.    "Rather, there will never cease to be members of the Sanhedrin from him.

F.    "And just as with someone from the [other] nations of the land and from the families of the earth—God gave him lovingly because he acted lovingly, how much the more so [will God give lovingly] with these [ones] from Israel!"

17.   A.    R. Ḥananiah ben Gamaliel says, "These things were only said in the second year [of the Exodus], at the time when Moses set up magistrates over Israel.

B.    "And when did he set them up? In the second year. As it says in Scripture, '... each with his standard, under the banners of their ancestral house' (Num. 2:2)."

שנ' ויאמרו לא נשתה יין כי יונדב בן רכב אבינו F
צוה עלינו לאמר לא תשתו יין אתם ובניכם עד
עולם ובית לא תבנו וזרע לא תזרעו וכרם לא תטעו
ולא יהיה לכם כי באהלים תשבו כל ימיכם למען
תחיו ימים רבים על פני האדמה אשר אתם גרים שם
(ירמ' לה ו - ז). ◆ ומנין למד שפרישות היין מארכת G
ימים שהרי ארבעה היו לוהטין אחר האדמה ולא
נמצאו כראוי קין ונוח ולוט ועזיהו. ◆ קין וקין היה עובד H
אדמה (בר' ד ב). ◆ נח ויחל נח איש האדמה (בר' ט כ). ◆ I
ולוט וישא לוט את עיניו וירא את כל ככר הירדן (בר' J
יג י). ◆ עזיהו כי אהב אדמה היה (דה"ב כו י). ◆ ר' נתן K Λ 16
אומר גדול הברית שכרת הקב"ה לבני יתרו יתר מן
הברית שכרת לבני דויד ◆ שהברית שנכרת עם דויד B
אינו כרות אלא על תנאי שנ' אם ישמרו בניך בריתי
ועדותי זו אלמדם גם בניהם עדי עד ישבו לכסא לך
(תה' קלב יב) ◆ אבל הברית שנכרת עם יונדב בן רכב C
לא נכרת על תנאי שנ' לכן כה אמר ה' צבאות אלקי
ישראל לא יכרת איש ליונדב בן רכב עומד לפני כל
הימים (ירמ' לה יט). ◆ אמר ר' שמעון והלא כבר D
נפסקה כהונה גדולה מה אני מקיים לא יכרת איש
ליונדב ◆ אלא שלא יפסקו ממנו יושבי סנהדרין לעולם. ◆ E
מה אם מי שהיה מגויי הארצות וממשפחות האדמה F
על שעשה מאהבה נתן לו המקום מאהבה על אחת
כמה וכמה אלו היה מישראל. ◆ ר' חנינה בן גמליאל A 17
אומר לא נאמרו דברים הללו אלא בשנה שנייה
בשעה שהעמיד משה אכסלטיינות על ישראל ◆ ואימתי B
העמידן בשנה שנייה שנ' איש על דגלו באתת לבית
אבתם (במ' ב ב). ◆

# Tractate Baḥodesh

## Chapter Forty-Eight

(Textual Source: Midrash ha-Gadol)

XLVIII:I

1.
   A. "On the third new moon after the Israelites had gone forth (from the Land of Egypt, on this very day, they entered the wilderness of Sinai)" (Exod. 19:1):[1]

   B. This teaches that they would count months in reference to [the month in which] they left from Egypt.

   C. I only know this to be the case with months. How does one know from Scripture [that this was also the case] with years?

   D. Scripture states, "The Lord spoke to Moses

   (Textual Source: Ms. Cambridge T-S C 4a.5)

   in the wilderness of Sinai ... in the second year (following the Exodus from the Land of Egypt), etc." (Num. 1:1).

   E. I only know this to be the case in that time period. How does one know from Scripture [that this was also the case] in a time period other than that?

   F. Scripture states, "Aaron the priest ascended (Mount Hor ... and died there, in the fortieth year after the Israelites had left the Land of Egypt)" (Num. 33:38).

   G. I only know this to be the case while they had not yet entered the Land of Israel. How does one know from Scripture [that this was also the case] once they had entered the Land of Israel?

   H. Scripture states, "At the end of the four hundred and eightieth year after the Israelites left (the Land of Egypt)" (1 Kings 6:1).

   I. Once the Temple was built, they began to count according to the years of kings[2] and according to the construction [of the two] buildings.

   J. As it says in Scripture, "At the end of the twenty years during which Solomon constructed the two buildings" (1 Kings 9:10). And Scripture says, "In the fourteenth year of King Hezekiah" (Isa. 36:1).

---

[1] Compare 1.A–Q with *Mekhilta de-Rabbi Ishmael*, Baḥodesh (H/R, 203:1–10; Laut., vol. 2, 192:1–193:18; Neus., XLVII:I:1.A–3.B); and y. Rosh Hashanah 56b (Neus., 1:1:8).

# מסכתא דבחודש

בחדש השלישי לצאת בני ישראל ◆ מלמד שהיו    B/A    1

מונים לחדשים ליציאתן ממצרים. ◆ אין לי אלא    C

לחדשים לשנים מנין ◆ ת״ל וידבר ה׳ אל משה במדבר    D

סיני בשנה השנית ג׳ (במ׳ א א) ◆ אין לי אלא באותו    E

הפרק ‹שלא באותו הפרק› מנ׳ ◆ תל׳ לו׳ ויעל אהרן    F

הכהן (במ׳ לג לח) ◆ אין לי אלא עד שלא נכנסו יש׳    G

לארץ משנכנסו יש׳ לארץ ‹מנין› ◆ ת״ל ויהי מקץ    H

שמונים שנה וארבע מאות שנה לצאת בני ישראל

(מ״א ו א) ◆ כיון שנבנה המקדש› התחילו מונים לשני    I

מלכים ולבנין בתים ◆ שנ׳ ויהי מקץ עשרים שנה אשר    J

בנה שלמה את שני הבתים (מ״א ט י) ואו׳ ויהי

בארבע עשרה ‹שנה› למלך חזקיהו (ישע׳ לו א) ◆

---

[2] I.e., in reference to the number of years of a king's reign.

K.  [Once] they no longer merited to count according to their constructions, they counted according to their destructions.

L.  As it says in Scripture, "In the twenty-fifth year of our exile, etc." (Ezek. 40:1).

M.  [Once] they no longer merited to count in reference to themselves, they counted according to other monarchies.

N.  As it says in Scripture, "In the second year of the reign of Nebuchadnezzar, etc." (Dan. 2:1). And Scripture says, "In the second year of King Darius" (Hag. 1:1). And Scripture says, "If you do not know, O fairest of women, etc." (Song 1:8).

O.  And Scripture says, "... because, and because" (Lev. 26:43).

P.  "Because, and because" means only an eye for an eye, measure for measure.

Q.  As it says in Scripture, "Because you would not serve the Lord your God ... you shall have to serve your enemies" (Deut. 28:47–48).

2.  A.  "... on this very day, they entered the wilderness of Sinai" (Exod. 19:1):[3]

B.  This teaches that it was the beginning of the new month.

C.  Scripture says here "on this very day," and before this Scripture says, "This month (shall mark for you the beginning of the months)" (Exod. 12:2).

D.  Just as "this" stated there is the beginning of the new month, likewise "this" stated here is the beginning of the new month.

3.  A.  R. Yosi the son of the Damascene says, "Behold Scripture states, 'God looked upon the
[137]    Israelites, and God took notice of them' (Exod. 2:25).[4]

B.  "He looked upon them because they did repentance, without looking at one another [doing so].

C.  "'God took notice of them'—He took notice of them because they did repentance, and they didn't take notice of each other."

4.  A.  R. Judah ben Lakish says, "Behold Scripture states, 'God looked upon the Israelites' (Exod. 2:25).

B.  "Because they were soon to anger [Him].

C.  "'God took notice of them.'

D.  "Because they were soon to blaspheme [Him]."

5.  A.  R. Yosi says, "Behold Scripture states, 'I did not speak in secret, etc.' (Isa. 45:19):[5]

B.  "[God said,] 'When I gave the Torah to Israel, I didn't give it in secret, nor in a land of darkness.'

C.  "'I did not say to the stock of Jacob' (Isa. 45:19):

D.  "[God didn't say,] 'It's yours!'

E.  "'Seek me out in a wasteland' (Isa. 45:19):

F.  "[God said,] 'I didn't require a pledge for it. Rather, I gave it as a reward!'

G.  "Next to it[6]—'I, the Lord, speak righteousness' (Isa. 45:19):

---

[3] Compare 2.A–D with *Mekhilta de-Rabbi Ishmael*, Baḥodesh (H/R, 204:7–8; Laut., vol. 2, 195:42–44; Neus., XLVII:I:7.A–C).

[4] Compare 3.A–4.D with *Mekhilta de-Rabbi Ishmael*, Baḥodesh (H/R, 205:3–8; Laut., vol. 2, 196:61–197:68; Neus., XLVII:II:5.A–6.D).

[5] Compare 5.A–N with *Mekhilta de-Rabbi Ishmael*, Baḥodesh (H/R, 206:3–9; Laut., vol. 2, 198:90–199:101; Neus., XLVII:II:13.A–14.E).

| | | |
|---|---|---|
| לא זכו למנות לבינינו ומנו לחורבנו ♦ שנ' בעשרים וחמש | L/K | |
| שנה לגלותינו ג' (יחז' מ א) ♦ לא זכו למנות לעצמן ומנו | M | |
| למלכ<י>ות אחרות ♦ שנ' בשנת שתים למלכות | N | |
| נבוכדנצר ג' (דני' ב א) ואו' בשנת שתים לדריוש (חגי | | |
| א א) ואו' אם לא תדעי לך היפה בנשים ג' (שה"ש א | | |
| ח) ♦ <ואו'> יען וביען (ויק' כו מג) ♦ אין יען <ו>ביען אלא | P/O | |
| עין בעין מידה במידה ♦ שנ' תחת אשר לא עבדת את ה' | Q | |
| אלק<י>ך ועבדת את אויבך (דב' כח מח) ♦ ביום הזה | A | 2 |
| באו מדבר סיני ♦ מלמד שהוא ראש חודש ♦ נא' כן ביום | C/B | |
| הזה ונא' להלן החודש הזה (שמ' יב ב) ♦ מה הזה הא' | D | |
| להלן ראש חדש אף הזה <ה>אמור כן ראש חודש ♦ ר' | A | 3 |
| יוסי בן דורמסקית או' הרי הוא או' וירא אלקים את | | |
| בני יש' וידע אלקים (שמ' ב כה) ♦ [ראה בהם שעשו] | B | |
| תשובה והן לא ראו זה את זה ♦ וידע [אלקים ידע בהם | C | |
| שעשו תשובה] והם לא ידעו זה את זה ♦ ר' יהודה בן | A | 4 |
| לקיש א[ו' הרי הוא אומר] וירא אלקים את בני יש' | | |
| שעתידין להכע[י]ס ♦ וידע אלקים ♦ שעתידין ♦ (ו)לנאץ ♦ | D/C/B | |
| ר' יוסי או' הרי הוא [אומר לא בסתר דברתי ג' (ישע' מה | Α | 5 |
| יט) ♦ כשנתתי] תורה ליש' לא נתתיה לא בסתר [ולא | B | |
| בארץ חשך ♦ לא אמרתי] לזרע יעקב (ישע' מה יט) ♦ | C | |
| שלכם הוא ♦ תהו בקש]וני (שם) ♦ לא עשיתיה הפותיקי | F/E/D | |
| אלא נתתי מתן] שכרה ♦ בצדה אני ה' דובר צדק (שם) ♦ | G | |

---

[6] I.e., the next part of the verse says.

H.  "[God said,] 'I speak of the righteousness of Israel!'

I.  "'I announce what is true' (Isa. 45:19):

J.  "[God said,] 'I announce that they act before Me out of love.'

K.  "[Scripture also says,] 'He did not do so for any other nation' (Ps. 147:20):

L.  "What will the

(Textual Source: Midrash ha-Gadol)

nations of the world do? For didn't they learn Torah?

M.  "[Scripture states, rather,] '... of such rules they know nothing' (Ps. 147:20):

N.  "[God said,] 'I gave them the seven [Noahide] commandments, and they couldn't endure [even] them!'"

## XLVIII:II

1.  A.  "They journeyed from Rephidim, and they entered the wilderness of Sinai (and encamped in the wilderness. Israel encamped there in front of the mountain)" (Exod. 19:2):[7]

    B.  Why do I need [this]? Isn't it already explained [in the scriptural portion that discusses] their journeys and their campings in the wilderness of Sinai?[8]

    C.  Why does Scripture state, "They journeyed from Rephidim, and they entered the wilderness of Sinai" (Exod. 19:2)?

    D.  Rather, it equates their journey from Rephidim to their campings in the wilderness of Sinai.

    E.  Just as [with] their journey from Rephidim, the Israelites tested [God] and quarreled, [saying,] "Is the Lord present among us or not?" (Exod. 17:7), likewise [with] their camping in the wilderness, the Israelites tested [God] and quarreled, [saying,] "Is the Lord present among us or not?"

    F.  [This is] to inform you of the power of repentance, because in a very short while after Israel performed repentance they were immediately accepted.

2.  A.  "... and encamped in the wilderness" (Exod. 19:2):[9]

    B.  In a public place in the world.

    C.  This tells that the Torah was given to Israel in a public place in the world.

    D.  For if it was given in the Land of Israel, the Children of Israel would have said, "It is ours!"

    E.  And if it was given in another place, the people of that place would have said, "It is ours!"

    F.  Therefore, it was given to them in a public place in the world, so that whoever wanted to take it could come and take it!

3.  A.  "Israel encamped there in front of the mountain" (Exod. 19:2):

    B.  Elsewhere in Scripture, [when it states] "the Children of Israel journeyed" or "the Children of Israel encamped" [it means that] they journeyed in strife and encamped in strife.

    C.  But here Scripture states, "(Israel) encamped there" (Exod. 19:2).[10]

---

[7] Compare 1.A–F with *Mekhilta de-Rabbi Ishmael,* Baḥodesh (H/R, 204:9–14; Laut., vol. 2, 195:45–196:54; Neus., XLVII:II:1.A–2.B).

[8] See Numbers 33.

[9] Compare 2.A–F with *Mekhilta de-Rabbi Ishmael,* Baḥodesh (H/R, 205:16–18; Laut., vol. 2, 198:80–84; Neus., XLVII:II:8.A–D).

[10] The text here focuses on the singular number of the verb "encamped" (Hebrew: ויחן) in the biblical verse.

| | |
|---|---|
| J/I/H | [דובר אני צדקתן שלישראל • מגיד מיש׳ (שם) • מגיד |
| K | אני שעשו ל[פני מאהבה • ולא עשה כן לכל גוי (תה׳ |
| M/L | קמז כ) • מה יעשו] אומות העולם והלא לא למדו תורה • |
| N | ומשפטים בל ידעום (שם) • שבע מצות נתתי להם ולא |
| | היו יכולין לעמוד בהן. • |

| | | |
|---|---|---|
| | XLVIII:II | |
| B/A | 1 | ויסעו מרפידים ויבאו מדבר סיני • מה אני צריך |
| | | והלא כבר מפורש במסעות נסיעתן מרפידים וחנייתן |
| C | | במדבר סיני • ומה ת״ל ויסעו מרפידים ויבאו מדבר |
| D | | סיני • אלא מקיש נסיעתן מרפידים לחנייתן במדבר |
| E | | סיני • מה נסיעתן מרפידים בני מסה ובני מריבה היש |
| | | ה׳ בקרבנו אם אין (שמ׳ יז ז) אף חנייתן במדבר סיני |
| | | בני מסה ובני מריבה היש ה׳ בקרבנו אם אין. • |
| F | | להודיעך כמה הוא כוחה שלתשובה שבשעה קלה |
| A | 2 | שעשו ישראל תשובה מיד נתקבלו. • ויחנו במדבר • |
| C/B | | בדמסיון שלעולם • מגיד שבדמסיון שלעולם ניתנה |
| D | | להם תורה לישראל. • שאלו נתנה בארץ ישראל היו בני |
| E | | ארץ ישראל אומרין שלנו היא • ואלו ניתנה במקום |
| F | | אחר היו בני אותו מקום אומרין שלנו היא • לפיכך |
| | | ניתנה להם בדמסיון שלעולם כל הרוצה ליטול יבוא |
| B/A | 3 | ויטול. • ויחן שם ישראל נגד ההר • להלן ויסעו |
| | | בני ישראל ויחנו בני ישראל נוסעים במחלוקת |
| C | | וחונים במחלוקת • וכאן הוא אומר ויחן שם • |

D.    One camp, [meaning that] they had devoted their heart in order to love one another and accept the Torah.

4.    A.    Another interpretation:

B.    "Israel encamped there" (Exod. 19:2):

C.    He[11] said to them, "You will tarry there a long time."

D.    And thus we find that in the end, they tarried there 12 months, minus 12 days.

(Textual Source: Yalkut)

5.    A.    "Israel encamped there in front of the mountain" (Exod. 19:2):

B.    He said to them, "Even though you are traveling from north to south and from south to north, you should always turn your face to the east."

C.    And thus Scripture states concerning God's presence, "... and sprinkle it with his finger over the cover on the east side" (Lev. 16:14).

D.    This teaches that the face of God's presence is to the east.

*Chapter Forty-Nine*

(Textual Source: Midrash ha-Gadol)

XLIX:I

1.    A.    "And Moses went up to God. (The Lord called to him from the mountain, saying, 'Thus shall you say to the house of Jacob and declare to the Children of Israel')" (Exod. 19:3):[12]

B.    This was the second day.

2.    A.    One might think that he went up without the permission of the Almighty.

B.    Scripture states, [however,] "Then He said to Moses, 'Come up to the Lord'" (Exod. 24:1). And Scripture says, "The Lord said to Moses, 'Come up to Me on the mountain'" (Exod. 24:12).

C.    This teaches that he only went up with the permission of the Almighty.

[138]    D.    And how does one know from Scripture [that this was also the case] after [God used the command] "call"?

E.    Scripture states, "The Lord called to him from the mountain, saying" (Exod. 19:3).

F.    And how does one know from Scripture [that this was also the case when God used the command] "Moses, Moses"?[13]

G.    Scripture says here "call" and Scripture says "call" at the burning bush. Just as there [God said,] "Moses, Moses," likewise here [God said,] "Moses, Moses. Just as there Moses says, "Here I am!" likewise here Moses says, "Here I am!"

3.    A.    "'Thus'" (Exod. 19:3):[14]

B.    In the holy language.

C.    "'Thus'" (Exod. 19:3):

D.    In this manner.

---

[11] I.e., Moses.

[12] Compare 1.A–B with *Mekhilta de-Rabbi Ishmael*, Baḥodesh (H/R, 207:1; Laut., vol. 2, 201:1–3; Neus., XLVIII:I:1.A–B).

[13] Compare 2.F–G with *Sifra*, Dibura Denedabah 1:10–11 (Neus., I:IV:1.A–2.C).

[14] Compare 3.A–L with *Mekhilta de-Rabbi Ishmael*, Baḥodesh (H/R, 207:2–3; Laut., vol. 2, 201:4–5; Neus., XLVIII:I:3.A–H).

| | | |
|---|---|---|
| D | | חנייה אחת ניתן בלבם כדי שיאהבו זה את זה ויקבלו את |
| C/B/A | 4 | התורה. ♦ ד״א ♦ ויחן שם ♦ אמר להם שהות הרבה אתם |
| D | | שוהין שם ♦ וכן מצינו באחרונה ששהו שנים עשר חדש חסר |
| B/A | 5 | עשרת ימים. ♦ ויחן שם ישראל נגד ההר ♦ אמר להם |
| | | אע״פ שאתם נוסעים מצפון לדרום ומדרום לצפון לעולם |
| C | | תהיו הופכים פנים למזרח ♦ וכן הוא אומר בשכינה |
| D | | והזה באצבעו על פני הכפרת קדמה (ויק׳ טז יד) ♦ לימד |
| | | שפני שכינה למזרח. ♦ |

XLIX:I

| | | |
|---|---|---|
| A/B/A | 2/1 | ומשה עלה אל האלקים ♦ זה היום השני. ♦ יכול עלה |
| B | | שלא על פי גבורה ♦ ת״ל ואל משה אמר עלה אל ה׳ |
| | | (שמ׳ כד א) ואומר ויאמר ה׳ אל משה עלה אלי ההרה |
| D/C | | (שם יב) ♦ מלמד שלא עלה אלא על פי גבורה. ♦ ומניין |
| E | | אף אחר קריאה ♦ ת״ל ויקרא אליו ה׳ מן ההר לאמר. ♦ |
| G/F | | ומניין אף במשה משה ♦ נאמרה כאן קריאה ונאמרה |
| | | קריאה בסנה מה להלן במשה משה אף כאן במשה |
| | | משה מה להלן משה אומר הנני אף כאן משה אומר |
| D/C/B/A | 3 | הנני. ♦ כה ♦ בלשון הקודש ♦ כה ♦ כעניין הזה ♦ |

E.   "'Thus'" (Exod. 19:3):

F.   In this order.

G.   "'Thus'" (Exod. 19:3):

H.   Like these verses.

I.   "'Thus'" (Exod. 19:3):

J.   Like these chapters.

K.   "'Thus'" (Exod. 19:3):

L.   Don't add [to it] or subtract [from it].

4.   A.   "'Thus shall you say to the house of Jacob'" (Exod. 19:3):[15]

     B.   Everything is due to the merit of Jacob.

     C.   "'... and declare to the Children of Israel'" (Exod. 19:3):

     D.   Everything is due to the merit of Israel.

5.   A.   Another interpretation:

     B.   "'Thus shall you say to the house of Jacob'" (Exod. 19:3):

     C.   His name, at first, was Jacob. Now he deserves to take the great name Israel.

     D.   As it says in Scripture, "... for you have striven with God" (Gen. 32:29).

XLIX:II

1.   A.   "'You have seen (what I did to the Egyptians, how I bore you on eagles' wings and brought you to Me)'" (Exod. 19:4):[16]

     B.   [God said,] "I don't talk to you through witnesses, by document, or through tradition."

2.   A.   "'... what I did to the Egyptians,'" (Exod. 19:4):[17]

     B.   [God said,] "Even though the Egyptians were worshipers of

(Textual Source: Ms. Cambridge T-S C 4a.5)

idols, performed sexual improprieties, and were murderers, I didn't exact punishment from them, except on your behalf."

     C.   And thus Scripture states, "Cast away, every one of you, the detestable things of his eyes ... But they defied Me ... But I acted for the sake of My name ..." (Ezek. 20:7–9).

3.   A.   "'... how I bore you on eagles' wings'" (Exod. 19:4):[18]

     B.   R. Eliezer says, "This [refers to] the day [of revelation at] Mount Sinai.

     C.   "'... and brought you to Me' (Exod. 19:4):

     D.   "This [refers to] the Temple."

4.   A.   R. Eliezer the son of R. Yosi ha-Galili says, "Behold Scripture states, 'Like an eagle who rouses his nestlings' (Deut. 32:11).

     B.   "An eagle will hover over its children so that they will not be frightened.

---

[15] Compare 4.A–D with *Mekhilta de-Rabbi Ishmael*, Baḥodesh (H/R, 207:4; Laut., vol. 2, 201:7–9; Neus., XLVIII:I:5.A–D).

[16] Compare 1.A–B with *Mekhilta de-Rabbi Ishmael*, Baḥodesh (H/R, 207:7–8; Laut., vol. 2, 201:12–202:14; Neus., XLVIII:I:7.A–B).

[17] Compare 2.A–C with *Mekhilta de-Rabbi Ishmael*, Baḥodesh (H/R, 207:8–10; Laut., vol. 2, 202:14–18; Neus., XLVIII:I:7.C–D).

[18] Compare 3.A–D with *Mekhilta de-Rabbi Ishmael*, Baḥodesh (H/R, 207:11–15; Laut., vol. 2, 202:18–25; Neus., XLVIII:I:8.A–F).

| | |
|---|---|
| H/G/F/E | כה ◆ כסדר הזה ◆ כה ◆ כפסיקות הללו ◆ |
| L/K/J/I | כה ◆ ••• ◆ כפרשיות הללו ◆ כה ◆ לא לפחות |
| B/A 4 | ולא להוסיף. ◆ כה תאמר לבית יעקב ◆ הכל בזכות יעקב ◆ |
| D/C B/A 5 | ותגד לבני ישראל ◆ הכל בזכות ישראל. ◆ ד״א ◆ כה תאמר |
| C | לבית יעקב ◆ יעקב נקרא שמו מתחלה עכשו זכה ליטול |
| D | שם הגדול ישראל ◆ כי שרית עם אלקים (בר׳ לב כט). ◆ |

XLIX:II

| | |
|---|---|
| B/A 1 | אתם ראיתם ◆ ולא מפי עדים ולא מפי כתב ולא |
| A 2 | מפי מסורת אני אומר לכם. ◆ אשר עשיתי למצרים ◆ |
| B | אע״פ שמצרים עובדי עבודה זרה מגלי עריות ושופכי |
| C | דמים לא נפרעתי מהם אלא בשבילכם ◆ וכן הוא או׳ |
| | ואומר להם איש שיקוצי עיניו השליכו ג׳ וימרו בי ג׳ |
| A 3 | ואעש למען שמי ג׳ (יחז׳ כ ז) ◆ ואשא אתכם על כנפי |
| C/B | נשרים ◆ ר׳ אליעזר ‹אומר› זה יום הר סיני ◆ ואביא |
| A 4 D | אתכם אלי ◆ זה בית העולמים ◆ ר׳ אליעזר בנו של ר׳ יוסי |
| B | הגלילי או׳ ‹הרי הוא או׳› כנשר יעיר קנו (דב׳ לב יא) ◆ דרך |
| | הנשר להיות מסופף על בניו בכנפיו כדי שלא יהיו מתבעתין ◆ |

C. "Likewise, when the Holy One, blessed be He, appeared to give the Torah to Israel, He didn't appear to them from one direction, but from the four directions.

D. "As it says in Scripture, 'The Lord came from Sinai' (Deut. 33:2).

E. "What is the fourth direction [not referred to in Deut. 33:2]?—'God is coming from Teman' (Hab. 3:3)."

(Textual Source: Midrash ha-Gadol)

5. A. "'... on eagles' wings'" (Exod. 19:4):[19]

B. A [small] bird will place its children between its legs, because it is afraid of [birds] stronger than it. But an eagle will place them on its wings, because it is not afraid of [birds] stronger than it. It would place them between its legs, but is afraid of slingshots and of arrows that people shoot at it. Thus, it sets itself as a division between its children and people.

C. Likewise, God set the ministering angels as a division between the Israelites and the Egyptians.

D. As it says in Scripture, "The angel of God moved ..." (Exod. 14:19).

6. A. Another interpretation:

B. ["'... on eagles' wings'" (Exod. 19:4) :]

C. Just as this eagle will spread its wings and retract them for the needs of the moment, likewise the Israelites would walk 12 miles and then retreat 12 miles on each and every command.

D. And thus Scripture states, "You grew more and more beautiful, and became fit for royalty" (Ezek. 16:13).

7. A. Another interpretation:

B. ["'... on eagles' wings'" (Exod. 19:4) :]

C. Just as this eagle rises from below to above in a short amount of time, likewise Israel arose from low to high in a short amount of time.

D. And just as they ascended their ascent in unusual fashion, likewise they descended their descent in unusual fashion.

E. And thus Scripture states, "When they go, I will spread my net over them. I will bring them down like birds of the sky. I will chastise them when I hear their bargaining" (Hosea 7:12).

## XLIX:III

1. A. "'Now then, if you will obey Me faithfully (and keep My covenant, you shall be My treasured possession among all the peoples. Indeed, all the earth is Mine)'" (Exod. 19:5):

B. All this is out of order! For isn't it a matter of logic?

C. [God says,] "If at the time when they hadn't accepted the Torah or kept all the commandments, I performed all these miracles for them, once they have accepted the Torah and kept all the commandments, how much the more so!"

[139]

2. A. Another interpretation:[20]

---

[19] Compare 5.A–D with *Mekhilta de-Rabbi Ishmael*, Baḥodesh (H/R, 207:15–208:6; Laut., vol. 2, 202:25–203:36; Neus., XLVIII:I:9.A–F).
[20] Compare 2.A–D with *Mekhilta de-Rabbi Ishmael*, Baḥodesh (H/R, 208:7–10; Laut., vol. 2, 203:39–42; Neus., XLVIII:I:10.A–11.E).

| | | |
|---|---|---|
| כך כשנגלה הקב״ה ליתן תורה ליש׳ לא נגלה | C | |
| עליהם מרוח אחת אלא מארבע רוחות • שנ׳ ויאמר | D | |
| ה׳ מסיני בא ג׳ (דב׳ לג ב) • איזו היא רוח רביעית | E | |
| אלוה מתימן יבא (חב׳ ג ג) • ד״א • על כנפי נשרים דרך | B/A | 5 |

עוף להיות מניח בניו בין ברכיו מפני שמתירא מפני מי
שחזק ממנו אבל נשר שאין מתירא מפני מי שחזק
ממנו מניחן על כתיפיו. ויניחן בין רגליו מתירא הוא
מאבני קלע ומן החצים שבני אדם מזרקין בו לפיכך

| | | |
|---|---|---|
| עושה עצמו מחיצה בין בניו לבני אדם. • כך עשה | C | |
| המקום מלאכי שרת מחיצה בין ישראל למצרים • שנ׳ | D | |
| ויסע מלאך האלקים וג׳ (שמ׳ יד יט) • <ד״א> • מה נשר | C/B/A | 6 |

זה מפריש בכנפיו ומחזירן לפי שעה כך ישראל היו
הולכין שנים עשר מיל וחוזרין שנים עשר מיל על כל

| | | |
|---|---|---|
| דיבר ודיבר • וכן הוא אומר ותיפי במאד מאד ותצלחי | D | |
| למלוכה (יחז׳ טז יג). • <ד״א> • מה נשר זה עולה ממטה | C/B/A | 7 |

למעלה בשעה קצרה כך ישראל עולין ממטה למעלה

| | | |
|---|---|---|
| בשעה קצרה. • ומה עלייתן עלו שלא כדרך ארץ אף | D | |
| ירידתם ירדו שלא כדרך ארץ • וכן הוא אומ׳ כאשר | E | |

ילכו אפרוש עליהם רשתי כעוף השמים אורידם
איסירם כשמע לעדתם (הושע ז יב). •

| | | |
|---|---|---|
| | | XLIX:III |

| | | |
|---|---|---|
| ועתה אם שמוע תשמעו בקולי • כל אלה למפרע. והלא | B/A | 1 |
| דברים קל וחומר • ומה אם בשעה שלא קיבלו את התורה | C | |

ולא עשו כל המצות עשיתי להן כל הנסים הללו לכשיקבלו

| | | |
|---|---|---|
| את התורה ויעשו כל המצות על אחת כמה וכמה. • ד״א • | A | 2 |

B.   "'Now then, if you will obey Me faithfully'" (Exod. 19:5):

C.   This teaches that all beginnings are difficult. Once one has begun to obey, everything is easy for him.

D.   If one obeys a little, it will cause him to obey a lot. If one obey the words of Torah, they will cause him to obey the words of the Scribes.

3.   A.   "'... and keep My covenant'" (Exod. 19:5):[21]

B.   R. Eliezer says, "This is the covenant of circumcision."

C.   R. Akiva says, "This is the covenant of *Shabbat*."

D.   The Sages say, "This is the covenant [against] idolatry."

4.   A.   "'... you shall be My'" (Exod. 19:5):

B.   [God says,] "You will be special to Me, engaged in My Torah, engaged in My commandments!"

C.   And thus Scripture states, "... and I have set you apart from other peoples to be Mine" (Lev. 20:26).

D.   [God says,] "As long as you are separated from other people, you are Mine. But if not, you are Nebuchadnezzar the wicked's and his companions'!"

5.   A.   "'... treasured possession among all the peoples'" (Exod. 19:5):[22]

B.   [God says,] "Just as a person's treasured possession means the most to him, Israel means the most to Me. Just as a person's treasured possession is dear to him, Israel is dear to Me."

C.   They told a parable: To what is the matter alike?

D.   It is like one who suddenly inherited many fields. He took possession of one of them, and liked that one more than all of them. Why? Because it was his possession.

E.   Likewise, even though the entire world belongs to He who spoke, and the world came into being, He loves only Israel. Why? Because He took them from Egypt, and redeemed them from the house of slaves.

F.   Thus it is said, "'... you shall be My treasured possession among all the peoples'" (Exod. 19:5).

G.   R. Joshua ben Korḥa says, "'... treasured possession' (Exod. 19:5):

H.   "So as not to burst your ear.

I.   "Or, just as the wife is treasured by her husband, and a son is treasured by his father, likewise Israel is treasured [by God] from among the nations of the world.

J.   "Scripture states, 'Indeed, all the earth is Mine' (Exod. 19:5)."

## XLIX:IV

1.   A.   "'But you shall be to Me (a kingdom of priests and a holy nation.' These are the words that you shall speak to the Children of Israel)" (Exod. 19:6):

B.   [God says,] "You will be special to Me, engaged in My Torah, engaged in My commandments!"

2.   A.   "'... a kingdom'" (Exod. 19:6):[23]

B.   R. Eliezer the son of R. Yosi ha-Galili says, "In the time to come, each and every person

---

[21] Compare 3.A–D with *Mekhilta de-Rabbi Ishmael*, Baḥodesh (H/R, 208:10–11; Laut., vol. 2, 204:43–45; Neus., XLVIII:I:12.A–C).

[22] Compare 5.A–J with *Mekhilta de-Rabbi Ishmael*, Baḥodesh (H/R, 208:13–15; Laut., vol. 2, 204:48–53; Neus., XLVIII:I:14.A–15.C).

[23] Compare 2.A–L with *Mekhilta de-Rabbi Ishmael*, Baḥodesh (H/R, 208:17–209:6; Laut., vol. 2, 205:57–68; Neus., XLVIII:I:18.A–19.B).

| | |
|---|---|
| ועתה אם שמע תשמעו בקולי ◆ מלמד שכל | C/B |
| תחלות קשות התחיל אדם לשמוע הכל נוח לו. ◆ | |
| שמע אדם קמעה משמיעין אותו הרבה שמע | D |
| אדם דברי תורה משמיעין אותו דברי סופרים. ◆ | |
| ושמרתם את בריתי ◆ ר' אליעזר אומר זו ברית מילה ◆ ר' | C/B/A 3 |
| עקיבה אומר זו ברית שבת ◆ וחכמים אומ' זו ברית ע"ז. ◆ | D |
| והייתם לי ◆ מיוחדין לי עסיקין בתורתי עסיקין במצותי ◆ | B/A 4 |
| וכן הוא אומ' ואבדיל אתכם מן העמים להיות לי | C |
| (ויק' כ כו) ◆ בזמן שאתם בדילין מן העמים אתם לי | D |
| ואם לאו הרי אתם לנבוכד נצר /לנבוכדנצר/ הרשע | |
| הרשע וחביריו. ◆ סגלה מכל העמים ◆ מה סגולתו של | B/A 5 |
| אדם מרצה עליו כך ישראל מרצין עלי מה סגלתו | |
| שלאדם חביבה עליו כך ישראל חביבין עלי. ◆ מושלין | C |
| אותו משל למה הדבר דומה ◆ לאחד שנפלו לו שדות | D |
| הרבה בירושה ועמד וקנה אחת משלו ואותה היה | |
| מחבב יותר מכולן למה שקנייה משלו. ◆ כך אע"פ שכל | E |
| העולם כולו למי שאמר והיה העולם אינו מחבב אלא | |
| ישראל ולמה שלקחם ממצרים ופדאם מבית עבדים | |
| ◆ לכך נאמר והייתם לי סגלה מכל העמים. ◆ ר' יהושע בן | G/F |
| קרחה אומ' סגולה ◆ שלא להפקיעך אוזן. ◆ או כשם | I/H |
| שהאשה מסתגלת מאחר בעלה ובן מסתגל מאחרי אביו | |
| כך ישראל יסתגלו מאומות העולם ◆ ת"ל כי לי כל הארץ. ◆ | J |

XLIX:IV

| | |
|---|---|
| ואתם תהיו לי ◆ מיוחדין לי עסיקין בתורתי עסיקין | B/A 1 |
| במצותי. ◆ ממלכת ◆ ר' אליעזר בנו שלר' יוסי הגלילי | B/A 2 |

will have [as many] children as those who left Egypt.

C.   "As it says in Scripture, 'Your sons will succeed your ancestors' (Ps. 45:17).

D.   "One might think they will be poor people.

E.   "Scripture states, [however,] 'You will appoint them princes throughout the land' (Ps. 45:17).

F.   "One might think [they will be] princes of trade.

G.   "Scripture states, [however,] '... a kingdom' (Exod. 19:6).

H.   "One might think [they will be] kings of war.

I.   "Scripture states, [however,] '... of priests' (Exod. 19:6).

J.   "If priests—one might think [they will be] unemployed, in accordance with what is said in Scripture, '... and David's sons were priests' (2 Sam. 8:18).

K.   "Scripture states, [however,] '... and a holy nation' (Exod. 19:6).

L.   "Based on this, they said: [All of] Israel was worthy to eat holy food while they had not yet made the Golden Calf. Once they made the Golden Calf, it was taken from them and given to the priests."

3.   A.   "'... nation'" (Exod. 19:6):[24]

B.   This teaches that they were like one body and one soul.

C.   And thus Scripture states, "And who is like Your people Israel, a single nation on earth" (1 Chron. 17:21).

D.   If one of them sins, all of them are punished.

E.   As it says in Scripture, "When Achan son of Zerah violated the proscription, anger struck the whole community of Israel. He was not the only one who perished for that sin" (Josh. 22:20).

F.   If one of them is struck, all of them feel it.

G.   And thus Scripture states, "Israel are a scattered sheep" (Jer. 50:17).

H.   Just as with this sheep, if one of its limbs is struck, all of them feel it, likewise with Israel. If one of them is struck, all of them feel it. But the other nations are happy, each and every one of them.[25]

4.   A.   "'... (but you shall be) ... a holy (nation)'" (Exod. 19:6):

B.   Why does Scripture [need to] state this, because it says in Scripture, "For you *are* a holy people to the Lord" (Deut. 14:2)?

C.   How [do you justify both]?

D.   Such is the holiness of the commandments! For every time the Holy One, blessed be He, adds a commandment to them for Israel, He increases holiness for them!

5.   A.   "These (are the words that you shall speak to the Children of Israel)" (Exod. 19:6):[26]

B.   In the holy language.

C.   "These" (Exod. 19:6):

---

[24] Compare 3.A–H with *Mekhilta de-Rabbi Ishmael*, Baḥodesh (H/R, 209:6–9; Laut., vol. 2, 205:68–206:73; Neus., XLVIII:I:19.D–F).
[25] Compare 3.H with *Leviticus Rabbah* 4:6.
[26] Compare 5.A–L with *Mekhilta de-Rabbi Ishmael*, Baḥodesh (H/R, 209:10–11; Laut., vol. 2, 206:78–79; Neus., XLVIII:I:22.A–23.B).

אומר לעתיד לבוא אין לך כל אחד ואחד שאין הויין

C לו בנים כיוצאי מצרים • שנ' תחת אבותיך יהיו בניך

E/D (תה' מה יז) • יכול יהיו בני אדם עניים • ת"ל תשיתמו

G/F לשרים בכל הארץ. • יכול שרים בעלי פרקמטאות • ת"ל

J/I/H ממלכת. • יכול מלכים בעלי מלחמות • ת"ל כהנים • או

כהנים יכול בטלנים כעניין שנ' ובני דוד כהנים היו

L/K (ש"ב ח יח). • ת"ל וגוי קדוש • מיכאן אמרו ראויין היו

ישראל לאכול בקדשים עד שלא עשו את העגל

B/A 3 ומשעשו את העגל ניטל מהן וניתן לכהנים. • וגוי • מלמד

C שהן כגוף אחד ונפש אחת • וכן הוא אומר ומי כעמך

D ישראל גוי אחד בארץ. • חטא אחד מהן כולן נענשין •

E שנ' הלא עכן בן זרח מעל מעל בחרם ועל כל ישראל

היה קצף והוא איש אחד לא גוע בעונו (יהו' כב כ) •

G/F לקה אחד מהן כולן מרגישין • וכן הוא אומ' שה פזורה

H ישראל (ירמ' נ יז) • מה רחל זו לקה אחד מאבריה כולן

מרגישין כך ישראל לקה אחד מהן כולן מרגישין.

B/A 4 אבל גוים שמחים כולן זה על זה. • קדוש • מה ת"ל

D/C מכלל שנ' כי עם קדוש אתה לה' (דב' יד ב) • הא כיצד • זו

קדושת מצות שכל זמן שהקב"ה מוסיף להם מצוה לישראל

C/B/A 5 הוא מוסיף להם קדושה. • אלה • בלשון הקדש • אלה •

D.   In this manner.

E.   "These" (Exod. 19:6):

F.   In this order.

G.   "These" (Exod. 19:6):

H.   Like these verses.

I.   "These" (Exod. 19:6):

J.   Like these chapters.

K.   "These" (Exod. 19:6):

L.   Don't add [to it] or subtract [from it].

6.   A.   "These are the words that you shall speak to the Children of Israel" (Exod. 19:6):

B.   What are these words?

C.   These are the three crowns with which Israel has been crowned: the crown of Torah; the crown of the Priesthood; and the crown of the monarchy.[27]

D.   R. Nathan says, "The crown of a good name is better than all of them."

XLIX:V

1.   A.   "Moses came (and summoned the elders of the people and put before them all these words that the Lord had commanded him)" (Exod. 19:7):

B.   This teaches that he did not [first] go to his home or turn toward other tasks.

2.   A.   "... the elders of the people" (Exod. 19:7):[28]

B.   This teaches that Moses behaved with honor toward the elders.

C.   This teaches that the elders come before all of Israel.

D.   This teaches that Moses waited upon the elders of his generation.

3.   A.   "... and put before them" (Exod. 19:7):

[140]   B.   He put it in order before them.

4.   A.   "... and put before them" (Exod. 19:7):

B.   He enlightened them with them.

5.   A.   Another interpretation:

B.   "... and put before them" (Exod. 19:7):

C.   Tell them the first part first, and the last part last.

6.   A.   "... all these words that the Lord had commanded him" (Exod. 19:7):

B.   Even to women.

7.   A.   "All the people answered as one, (saying, 'All that the Lord has spoken we will do!' And Moses brought back the people's words to the Lord)" (Exod. 19:8):

B.   They did not answer hypocritically, nor did they take counsel with one another. Rather, they joined together as one.

---

[27] Compare 6.C–D with m. Avot 4:13.

[28] Compare 2.A–7.B with *Mekhilta de-rabbi Ishmael*, Baḥodesh (H/R, 209:12–15; Laut., vol. 2, 206:80–207:87; Neus., XLVIII:II:1.A–5.B).

| | | |
|---|---|---|
| H/G/F/E/D | | כעין הזה ◆ אלה ◆ כסדר הזה ◆ אלה ◆ כפסיקות הללו ◆ |
| L/K/J/I | | אלה ◆ כפרשיות הללו ◆ אלה ◆ לא לפחות ולא להוסיף. ◆ |
| B/A | 6 | אלה הדברים אשר תדבר אל בני ישראל ◆ מה הן |
| C | | הדברים. ◆ אלו שלשה כתרים שנכתרו בהן ישראל כתר |
| D | | תורה וכתר כהונה וכתר מלכות. ◆ ר׳ נתן אומר וכתר |
| | | שם טוב עולה על גביהן. ◆ |

**XLIX:V**

| | | |
|---|---|---|
| B/A | 1 | ויבא משה ◆ מלמד שלא הלך לביתו ולא פנה |
| B/A | 2 | לעסקים אחרים. ◆ ויקרא לזקני העם ◆ מלמד שנהג משה |
| D/C | | כבוד בזקנים. ◆ מלמד שהזקנים קודמין לכל ישראל. ◆ מלמד |
| B/A | 3 | שנשתמש משה בזקנים שבדורו. ◆ וישם לפניהם ◆ מסדירן |
| A 5 | B/A 4 | לפניהם. ◆ וישם לפניהם ◆ מאיר עיניהם בהן. ◆ ד״א ◆ |
| C/B | | וישם לפניהם ◆ אמור על ראשון ראשון ועל אחרון אחרון. ◆ |
| B/A | 6 | את כל הדברים האלה אשר צוהו ה׳. ◆ אף לנשים. ◆ |
| B/A | 7 | ויענו כל העם יחדו ◆ לא בחנופה ענו ולא נטלו עצה |

8. A. "... saying, 'All that the Lord has spoken we will do!'" (Exod. 19:8):

B. [They said,] "We accept [it] upon us!"

9. A. "And Moses brought back the people's words to the Lord" (Exod. 19:8):

B. This is the third day.

10. A. Another interpretation:[29]

B. "And Moses brought back" (Exod. 19:8):

C. This was to give Moses [the opportunity] for a reward for each and every time he went up and for each and every time he went down.

11. A. Another interpretation:

B. "And Moses brought back the people's words to the Lord" (Exod. 19:8):

C. Scripture comes to teach you good manners.

D. Even if someone who sends a messenger hears [the reply] to his commission, he should still require him[30] to bring back his reply.

12. A. "And the Lord said to Moses, 'I will come to you in a thick cloud, (in order that the people may hear when I speak with you and so trust you ever after)'" (Exod. 19:9):[31]

B. The word "cloud" means only a very thick one.

C. As it says in Scripture, "... and a dense cloud upon the mountain" (Exod. 19:17).

13. A. R. Yosi ha-Galili says, "Moses was sanctified in the cloud for seven (days).

B. "As it says in Scripture, '... and the cloud hid him for six days. On the seventh day He called to Moses from the midst of the cloud' (Exod. 24:16).

C. "This was after the divine speech, and the beginning of the 40 days."

14. A. R. Akiva says, "'... and the cloud hid him for six days' (Exod. 24:16):

B. "On the first day of the month, He called Moses to purify him.

C. "'On the seventh day He called to Moses (from the midst of the cloud)' (Exod. 24:16):

D. "This was after the divine speech, and the beginning of the 40 days.

15. A. "'... in order that the people may hear when I speak with you'" (Exod. 19:9):[32]

B. R. Judah says, "The Holy One, blessed be He, said to Moses, 'Behold, I'll say something to you, and you will reply to Me, and then I'll reply and agree with your words.'"

C. Rabbi says, "God didn't agree with his words for the sake of Moses' honor.

D. "Rather, this is what He said to him, 'Behold, I am now changing for you the commandments that I gave to you at Marah.'"

16. A. Scripture does not say, "that the Lord commanded," but "that the Lord had commanded him" (Exod. 19:7).

B. [God said,] "Whoever hears from your mouth is like hearing from the mouth of the Holy One.

C. "And not [only] from your mouth, but also from the mouths of the elders who will come

---

[29] Compare 10.A–C with *Mekhilta de-Rabbi Ishmael*, Baḥodesh (H/R, 210:2–3; Laut., vol. 2, 207:91–92; Neus., XLVIII:II:7.A–B).

[30] I.e., the messenger.

[31] Compare 12.A–C with *Mekhilta de-Rabbi Ishmael*, Baḥodesh (H/R, 210:4–5; Laut., vol. 2, 207:93–95; Neus., XLVIII:II:8.A–C).

[32] Compare 15.A–18.K with *Mekhilta de-Rabbi Ishmael*, Baḥodesh (H/R, 210:5–211:2; Laut., vol. 2, 207:96–209:124; Neus., XLVIII:II:9.A–14.E).

| | | |
|---|---|---|
| A 8 | | זה מזה אלא השוו לב אחד. ❖ ויאמרו כל אשר דבר ה' |
| B | A 9 | נעשה. ❖ מקבלין אנו עלינו. ❖ וישב משה את דברי העם |
| B | C/B/A 10 | אל ה'. ❖ זה יום שלישי. ❖ ד"א ❖ וישב משה ❖ ליתן שכר |
| 11 | A | למשה על כל עלייה ועלייה ועל כל ירידה וירידה. ❖ ד"א ❖ |
| | C/B | וישב משה את דברי העם אל ה'. ❖ בא הכת' ללמדך |
| | D | דרך ארץ ❖ שאע"פ ששמע שולחו של אדם את |
| | | השליחות צריך הוא שיחזיר את שליחותו. ❖ |
| 12 | A | ויאמר ה' אל משה הנה אנכי בא אליך בעב הענן ❖ |
| C/B | A 13 | אין ענן אלא ערפל קשה ❖ שנ' וענן כבד על ההר. ❖ ר' |
| | B | יוסי הגלילי אומר משה נתקדש בענן שבעה ❖ שנ' |
| | | ויכסהו הענן ששת ימים ויקרא אל משה ביום |
| | C | השביעי מתוך הענן (שמ' כד טז) ❖ זה היה אחר דברות |
| 14 | A | והוא תחלת ארבעים יום. ❖ ר' עקיבה אומר ויכסהו |
| | B | הענן ששת ימים ❖ בראש חדש קרא למשה לטהרו ❖ |
| | D/C | ויקרא אל משה ביום השביעי ❖ זה היה אחר דברות |
| 15 | Λ | והוא תחלת ארבעים יום. ❖ בעבור ישמע העם בדברי |
| | B | עמך ❖ ר' יהודה אומר אמר לו הקב"ה למשה הריני |
| | | אומר לך דבר ואתה משיבני והריני חוזר ומודה |
| | C | לדבריך. ❖ ר' אומ' לא מפני כבודו שלמשה הודה |
| | D | המקום לדבריו ❖ אלא כך אמר לו מצות שנתתי לך |
| 16 | A | במרה הריני חוזר ושונה אותן אני לך כאן. ❖ אינו אומר |
| | B | אשר צוה ה' אלא אשר צוהו ה'. ❖ מלמד ששומעין מפיך |
| | C | כשומעין מפי הקודש ❖ ולא מפיך אלא מפי זקנים |

after you, as well as from the mouths of the prophets."

D.   Thus is it said, "'... and so trust you ever after'" (Exod. 19:9).

17.   A.   "'Then Moses reported ...' (Exod. 19:9):

B.   "And just what had the Holy One, blessed be He, said to Moses that he should report to Israel? And what had Israel said to Moses that he should report before God?

C.   "Behold Scripture states, 'You shall set bounds for the people round about, saying ...' (Exod. 19:12)."—The words of R. Yosi b. R. Judah.

D.   Rabbi says, "He [i.e., Moses] told them the rewards [they would receive] if they obeyed [the word of God].

E.   "However, how does one know from Scripture that he told them all the punishments if they didn't obey?

F.   "Scripture states, 'Moses went and repeated to the people all the commands of the Lord and all the rules. And all the people answered with one voice' (Exod. 24:3).

G.   "This teaches that whether it be the voice of an important or unimportant person, they are all equal before God."

18.   A.   Another interpretation:

B.   "Then Moses reported ..." (Exod. 19:9):

C.   And just what had Israel said to Moses that he should report before God? And what had the Holy One, blessed be He, said to Moses that he should report to Israel?

D.   They said, "We want to hear [it] from our king! For it's not the same to hear from the mouth of the governor as it is to hear from the mouth of the king!"

E.   The Holy One, blessed be He, said to him, "I'll give them what they asked for."

F.   [As it says in Scripture,] "'... in order that the people may hear when I speak with you'" (Exod. 19:9).

G.   They said to him, "We want to see our king! For it's not the same to both hear and see as it is to hear but not see!"

H.   The Holy One, blessed be He, said to him, "I'll give them what they requested."

I.   [As it says in Scripture,] "'... for on the third day the Lord will come down, in the sight of all the people'" (Exod. 19:11).

J.   And in the time to come, Israel will see the face of God's presence eye to eye.

K.   As it says in Scripture, "For they will see eye to eye" (Isa. 52:8). And Scripture says, "This is the Lord, in whom we trusted" (Isa. 25:9).

## Chapter Fifty

### (Textual Source: Midrash ha-Gadol)

L:I

1.   A.   "The Lord said to Moses, 'Go to the people and warn them to sanctify themselves today (and tomorrow. Let them wash their clothes)'" (Exod. 19:10):[33]

---

[33] Compare 1.A–N with *Mekhilta de-Rabbi Ishmael,* Baḥodesh (H/R, 211:3–212:2; Laut., vol. 2, 210:1–211:27; Neus., XLIX:I:1.A–5.K).

| | | |
|---|---|---|
| העתידים לבוא אחריך ומפי הנביאים • לכך נאמר וגם | D | |
| בך יאמינו לעולם. • ויגד משה • וכי מה אמר לו הקב"ה | B/A | 17 |
| למשה שיאמר להן לישראל ומה אמרו ישראל למשה | | |
| שיאמר לפני המקום • הרי הוא אומ' והגבלת את העם | C | |
| סביב לאמר וג' דברי ר' יוסי ביר' יהודה. • ר' אומר לפי | D | |
| שאמר להן מתן שכר אם שמעו • ומנין שאם לא ישמעו | E | |
| שאומר להם כל עונשין • ת"ל ויבא משה ויספר לעם | F | |
| את כל דברי ה' ואת כל המשפטים. ויען כל העם קול | | |
| אחד • מלמד שאחד קולו שלגדול ואחד קולו שלקטן | G | |
| שוים לפני המקום. • ד"א • ויגד משה • וכי מה אמרו | C/B/A | 18 |
| ישראל למשה לומר ל<פני ה>מקום ומה אמר | | |
| המקום למשה לומר להן לישראל • אמרו רצונינו | D | |
| לשמוע מן מלכינו שאינו דומה שומע מפי פדגוג | | |
| לשומע מפי המלך. • אמר לו הקב"ה אני אתן להן מה | E | |
| ששאלו • בעבור ישמע העם בדברי עמך. • אמרו לו | G/F | |
| רצונינו לראות מלכינו שאינו דומה שומע ורואה | | |
| לשומע ואינו רואה. • אמר לו הקב"ה אני אתן להם מה | H | |
| שביקשו • ביום השלישי ירד ה' לעיני כל העם. • אף | J/I | |
| לעתיד לבוא עתידין ישראל לראות פני שכינה עין | | |
| בעין • שנ' כי עין בעין יראו (ישע' נב ח) ואומ' זה ה' | K | |
| קוינו לו (ישע' כה ט). • | | |
| | L:I | |
| ויאמר ה' אל משה לך אל העם וקדשתם היום • | A | 1 |

B. This is the fourth day [of the month of Sivan].

C "'... and tomorrow. Let them wash their clothes'" (Exod. 19:10):

D. They should ritually bathe on the fifth day.

E. But is it not the case that if they bathe on the fifth day, then they wait for sundown on the sixth?[34]

F. Why does Scripture state, "'... to sanctify themselves today'" (Exod. 19:10)?

G. [To inform you that] they should bathe on the fourth day.

H. And what did they do on the fifth? Moses wrote all the words like a man who writes them in a codicil.

[141]   I. And concerning the sixth day what does it say?—"Early in the morning, he set up an altar at the foot of the mountain, with twelve pillars" (Exod. 24:4).

J. For whom were these 12 pillars?

K. R. Judah says, "For the 12 tribes of Israel."

L. But the Sages say, "For all Israel.

M. "And thus Scripture states, 'He designated some young men among the Israelites, and they offered burnt offerings' (Exod. 24:5).

N. "All Israel offered them."

2.    A. "'Let them be ready for the third day. (For on the third day the Lord will come down, in the sight of all the people, on Mount Sinai)'" (Exod. 19:11):

B. This teaches that they established for them a meeting place.

3.    A. "'For on the third day the Lord will come down, in the sight of all the people'" (Exod. 19:11):[35]

B. This teaches that there were no blind among them.

4.    A. R. Shimon ben Judah ish Kefar Akkum says, "How does one know from Scripture that if there had been even one missing from those who left Egypt, the Torah would not have been given to them?[36]

B. "Scripture states, 'For on the third day the Lord will come down, in the sight of *all* the people' (Exod. 19:11).

C. "From here [we learn] that no [other] generation arose, and no generation will arise, as worthy to receive the Torah as this.

D. "And Scripture says concerning them, 'He reserves ability for the upright, and is a shield for those who live blamelessly' (Prov. 2:7)."

5.    A. "'You shall set bounds for the people round about saying: (Beware of going up the mountain or touching the border of it. Whoever touches the mountain shall be put to death)'" (Exod. 19:12):

B. This teaches that they set limits for themselves.

6.    A. Because Scripture says, "... neither shall the flocks and the herds graze at the foot of this mountain" (Exod. 34:3), I only know [that this applied] to its east side.[37]

---

[34] The process of personal purification is complete only at sundown, the beginning of the subsequent day. The text here understands it to be problematic for this to occur on the 6th of Sivan—the day of the giving of the Torah at Sinai.

[35] Compare 3.A–B with *Mekhilta de-Rabbi Ishmael,* Baḥodesh (H/R, 212:8; Laut., vol. 2, 212:37–38; Neus., XLIX:I:9.A–B).

[36] Compare 4.A–D with *Mekhilta de-Rabbi Ishmael,* Baḥodesh (H/R, 212:9–12; Laut., vol. 2, 212:40–213:43; Neus., XLIX:I:11.A–D).

| | |
|---|---|
| זה יום הרביעי. ♦ ומחר וכבסו שמלתם ♦ ושיטבלו ביום | D/C/B |
| החמישי. ♦ והלא אם יטבלו ביום החמישי הרי הן עריבי | E |
| שמש לששי ♦ מה ת״ל וקדשתם היום ♦ שיטבלו ביום | G/F |
| הרביעי ♦ ומה היו עושין בחמישי היה משה כותב את | H |
| הדברים כאדם שכותבן בסמפונות. ♦ בששי מהוא | I |
| אומר וישכם (משה) בבקר ויבן מזבח תחת ההר | |
| ושתים עשרה מצבה (שמ׳ כד ד, ע״ש) ♦ למי היו מצבות | J |
| האלו ♦ ר׳ יהודה אומר לשנים עשר שבטי ישראל ♦ | K |
| וחכמים אומרין לכל ישראל ♦ וכן הוא אומר וישלח את | M/L |
| נערי בני ישראל ויעלו עלות (שם ה) ♦ על ידי כל ישראל | N |
| הקריבום. ♦ | |
| | |
| והיו נכונים ליום השלישי ♦ מלמד שקבעו להן בית | B/A 2 |
| ועד. ♦ כי ביום השלישי ירד ה׳ לעיני כל העם ♦ מלמד | B/A 3 |
| שלא היו בהן סומין. ♦ ר׳ שמעון בן יהודה איש כפר | A 4 |
| עיכוס אומר מנין אתה אומ׳ שאם היו יוצאי מצרים | |
| חסירין אפלו אחד לא היתה תורה ניתנת להן ♦ ת״ל כי | B |
| ביום השלישי ירד ה׳ לעיני כל העם ♦ מיכאן שלא עמד | C |
| דור ולא עתיד דור לעמוד הראויין לקבל את התורה | |
| כאלו. ♦ ועליהם הוא אומר יצפן לישרים תושיה מגן | D |
| להולכי תום (מש׳ ב ז). ♦ | |
| | |
| והגבלת את העם סביב לאמר ♦ מלמד שקבעו להן | B/A 5 |
| תחומין ♦ לפי שהוא אומר גם הצאן והבקר אל ירעו אל | A 6 |
| מול ההר ההוא (שמ׳ לד ג) אין לי אלא למזרחו ♦ | |

[37] Compare 6.A–D with *Mekhilta de-Rabbi Ishmael*, Baḥodesh (H/R, 212:13; Laut., vol. 2, 213:44–45; Neus., XLIX:I:12.A–C).

B.   How does one know from Scripture [that this also applied] to its north, south, and west?

C.   Scripture states, "'... round'" (Exod. 19:12).

D.   All the way around.

7.   A.   "'Beware of going up the mountain'" (Exod. 19:12):[38]

B.   Behold, this is the warning.

C.   One might think one should not go up, but it would be permissible to touch [it].

D.   Scripture states, [however,] "'... or touching the border of it'" (Exod. 19:12).

E.   One might think one may go up in a litter.

F.   Scripture states, [however,] "'... going up the mountain'" (Exod. 19:12).

G.   In any instance.

H.   "'Whoever touches the mountain shall be put to death'" (Exod. 19:12):

I.   [This is the] punishment.

8.   A.   "'No hand shall touch him, (but he shall be either stoned or thrown down. Whether beast or man, he shall not live. When the ram's horn sounds a long blast, they may go up on the mountain)'" (Exod. 19:13):[39]

B.   The Temple is not in the category [of things that should not] be touched.[40]

9.   A.   "'No hand shall touch him'" (Exod. 19:13):

B.   And one should not touch him with something else.

10.   A.   "'... but he shall be either stoned'" (Exod. 19:13):[41]

B.   I only know that he may be stoned. How does one know from Scripture that he may even be thrown down?

C.   Scripture states, "'... or thrown down'" (Exod. 19:13).

11.   A.   How does one know from Scripture that if he is stoned, behold, he is [also] thrown down?

B.   Scripture states, "'... thrown down'" (Exod. 19:13).

C.   All who are stoned are thrown down.

D.   How does one know from Scripture that if he dies from being thrown down alone, the obligation is fulfilled?

E.   Scripture states, "'... or thrown down'" (Exod. 19:13).

12.   A.   "'... beast'" (Exod. 19:13):[42]

B.   I only know [this applies to] a domesticated beast. How does one know from Scripture [that this also applies to] a wild animal?

C.    Scripture states, "'... whether beast'" (Exod. 19:13).

---

[38] Compare 7.A–I with *Mekhilta de-Rabbi Ishmael*, Baḥodesh (H/R, 212:14–16; Laut., vol. 2, 213:46–50; Neus., XLIX:I:14.A–15.E).

[39] Compare 8.A–B with *Mekhilta de-Rabbi Ishmael*, Baḥodesh (H/R, 212:17; Laut., vol. 2, 214:52–53; Neus., XLIX:I:17.A–B).

[40] Instead of "him" in Exod. 19:13, the text reads בו as "it."

[41] Compare 10.A–11.E with *Mekhilta de-Rabbi Ishmael*, Baḥodesh (H/R, 212:17–213:1; Laut., vol. 2, 214:54–56; Neus., XLIX:I:18.A–G); y. Sanhedrin 23c (Neus., 6:5:I.A–III.A); and b. Sanhedrin 45a (Neus., XXIIB:Tractate Sanhedrin:6:4A–G:I.A–II.L).

[42] Compare 12.A–13.C with *Mekhilta de-Rabbi Ishmael*, Baḥodesh (H/R, 213:1–2; Laut., vol. 2, 214:57–59; Neus., XLIX:I:19.A–20.C).

| | | |
|---|---|---|
| לצפונו ולדרומו ולמערבו מנין • ת״ל סביב • סביב מכל | D/C/B | |
| מקום. • השמרו לכם עלות בהר • הרי זו אזהרה • יכול לא | C/B/A | 7 |
| יעלה אבל יהא מותר ליגע • ת״ל ונגע בקצהו. • יכול | E/D | |
| יעלה בגלוגתקא • ת״ל עלות בהר • בכל מקום. • כל הנוגע | H/G/F | |
| בהר מות יומת • עונש. • | I | |
| לא תגע בו יד • אין בית עולמים בשום מגע. • לא תגע | A/B/A | 9/8 |
| בו יד • ולא שנגע בו בדבר אחר. • כי סקול יסקל • אין | B/A 10 | B |
| לי אלא נסקל מנין אפלו נדחה • ת״ל או ירה יירה. • מנין | A 11 | C |
| שאם נסקל הרי הוא נדחה • ת״ל או ירה יירה • כל חייבי | C/B | |
| סקילות נדחין. • מנין שאם מת בדחייה אחת יצא • ת״ל או ירה | E/D | |
| יירה. • בהמה • אין לי אלא בהמה חיה מנין • ת״ל אם בהמה. • | C/B/A | 12 |

13. A. "'… man'" (Exod. 19:13):

  B. I only know [this applies to] a man. How does one know from Scripture [that this also applies to] a woman?

  C. Scripture states, "'… or man'" (Exod. 19:13).

14. A. "'… he shall not live'" (Exod. 19:13):

  B. Behold, this is the punishment.

15. A. "'When the ram's horn sounds a long blast, they may go up on the mountain'" (Exod. 19:13):[43]

  B. [Up until] the ram's horn is cut off.

  C. And thus Scripture states, "And when a long blast is sounded on the horn, as soon as you hear that sound of the horn" (Josh. 6:5).

### (Textual Source: Ms. Cambridge T-S C 4a.5)

16. A. R. Yosi says, "It's not the place that brings honor to the person. Rather, it's the person who brings honor to the place.[44]

  B. "For as long as God's presence was on top of Mount Sinai, whoever went up to its peak was culpable of death. Once God's presence went away, [even] people [impure because of] a flux or maimed people were permitted to go up there.

  C. "And as long as the Tent of Meeting was pitched, he who went inside of it was culpable of death. Once the Tent of Meeting was removed [i.e., was no longer used to house God's presence], then impure and maimed people were permitted to enter."

L:II

1. A. "Moses came down from the mountain to the people (and he sanctified the people, and they washed their clothes)" (Exod. 19:14):[45]

  B. This teaches that he did not [first] go to his home or turn toward other tasks.

2. A. How does one know from Scripture that when he would bring back the message, he would only bring it back in the morning?

### (Textual Source: Midrash ha-Gadol)

  B. Scripture states, "So Moses carved two tablets of stone, like the first, and early in the morning" (Exod. 34:4).

  C. This is the general principle to whoever is commanded: Why does Scripture state, "… as the Lord commanded him"? (Exod. 34:4).

  D. This serves to construct a legal category based upon this text.[46]

  E. Whenever Moses would bring back the message, he would only bring it back in the morning.

### (Textual Source: Ms. Cambridge T-S C 4a.5)

3. A. "… and he sanctified the people, and they washed their clothes" (Exod. 19:14).

---

[43] Compare 15.A–16.C with *Mekhilta de-Rabbi Ishmael*, Baḥodesh (H/R, 213:5–8; Laut., vol. 2, 214:63–215:67; Neus., XLIX:I:22A–E).

[44] Compare 16.A–C with parallel at b. Taanit 21b.

[45] Compare 1.A–2.E with *Mekhilta de-Rabbi Ishmael*, Baḥodesh (H/R, 213:9–16; Laut., vol. 2, 215:68–216:83; Neus., XLIX:II:1A–2.D).

[46] The legal category created here is *binyan av* (בנין אב), wherein a global inference is gleaned from the understanding of a single scriptural verse. Thus, the inference here is that whenever Scripture indicates that the Lord commanded Moses to carry His message back, Moses would do so only in the morning. The text understands that the seemingly superfluous clause "… as the Lord commanded him" exists to form this global inference.

| | | |
|---|---|---|
| איש ◆ אין לי אלא איש אשה מנין ◆ ת״ל | C/B/A | 13 |
| אם איש. ◆ לא יחיה ◆ הרי זה עונש. ◆ במשך היובל המה | A/B/A | 15/14 |
| יעלו בהר ◆ כשיפסוק השופר ◆ וכן הוא אומר והיה | C/B | |
| במשך בקרן היובל כשמעכם את קול השופר (יהו׳ ו | | |
| ה). ◆ ר׳ יוסי או׳ לא מקומו שלאדם מכבדו אלא אדם | A | 16 |
| מכבד את מקומו ◆ שכל זמן שהשכינה על גבי הר [סיני | B | |
| העול]ה לראשו חיב מיתה נסתלקה שכינה זבין ובעלי | | |
| [מומין מותרין לעלות] לשם ◆ וכל זמן שאהל מועד | C | |
| נטוי הנכנס [לתוכו חיב מיתה ניסתלק] אהל מועד | | |
| טמאין ובעלי מומין [מותרין ליכנס] ◆ | | |

| | | |
|---|---|---|
| | L:II | |
| וירד משה מן ההר אל העם ◆ מלמד שלא הלך | B/A | 1 |
| [לתוך ביתו ולא פנה לעסיקין] אחרים ◆ מנ׳ שכשהיה | A | 2 |
| מחזיר [את השליחות לא היה מחזירה] אלא בבקר ◆ | | |
| <ת״ל ויפסל שני לוחות אבנים כראשונים וישכם | B | |
| משה בבקר (שמ׳ לד ד) ◆ זה הכלל לכל שנצטוה מה | C | |
| ת״ל כאשר צוה ה׳ אתו (שם) ◆ אלא זה בנין אב ◆ | D | |
| שכשהיה משה מחזיר את השליחות לא היה מחזירה | E | |
| אלא בבקר> ◆ ויקדש את העם [ויכבסו שמלותם ◆ | A | 3 |

[142]     B.   This [mentions] washing of clothes.

    C.   I only know from this [that] washing of clothes [was required]. How does one know from Scripture that they also required ritual bathing?

    D.   It is a matter of logic:

    E.   If in an instance when washing of clothes is not required, ritual bathing is required, then here, when washing of clothes is required, it is logical that ritual bathing would [also] be required.[47]

### (Textual Source: Midrash ha-Gadol)

4.     A.   "And he said to the people, 'Be ready for the third day. (Do not go near a woman)'" (Exod. 19:15):[48]

    B.   One might think that Moses said this of his own accord.[49]

    C.   Scripture states, [however,] "'Let them be ready for the third day'" (Exod. 19:11).

    D.   And here [Scripture states], "'Be ready for the third day'" (Exod. 19:15).

    E.   [Scripture states twice] "Be ready" in order to make a *gezerah shaveh*:[50]

    F.   Just as with "Be ready" stated above—the Holy One said it to Moses, likewise "Be ready" stated here—the Holy One said it to Moses.

    G.   Rabbi says, "It can be proved from its own scriptural context:

    H.   "'... (and the Lord said to Moses, "Go to the people and warn them) to stay pure today (and tomorrow)"' (Exod. 19:10).

    I.   "[Meaning] that they should bathe ritually on the fourth day."[51]

5.     A.   R. Eliezer ben Azariah says, "How does one know from Scripture that a woman who discharged semen (from her vagina) on the third day was impure?

    B.   "As it says in Scripture, '... Be ready for the third day. Do not go near a woman' (Exod. 19:15)."

    C.   R. Ishmael says, "Sometimes [the period of time in which such a discharge would make her impure] is four *onahs*,[52] sometimes five, sometimes six."

    D.   R. Akiva says, "Always five."

### (Textual Source: Ms. Cambridge T-S C 4a.5)

6.     A.   "On the third day, as morning dawned, (there was thunder and lightning, and a dense cloud upon the mountain, and a very loud blast of the horn. All the people who were in the camp trembled)" (Exod. 19:16):

    B.   At the time told to him.

    C.   This teaches that the time and the action assisted the hour in which life[53] was given to all

---

[47] Compare 3.E with parallel at b. Yebamot 46b (Neus., XII.B:Tractate Yebamot:4:12:I.22.E–I).

[48] Compare 4.A–5.D with *Mekhilta de-Rabbi Ishmael*, Baḥodesh (H/R, 213:18–214:5; Laut., vol. 2, 216:86–217:99; Neus., XLIX:II:4.A–5.G).

[49] I.e., Moses added the prohibition against going near a woman.

[50] I.e., the employment of the same word or phrase in separate scriptural contexts, thus facilitating the application of the meaning of the word in one context to the other.

[51] The people were commanded to be pure when receiving the law on the sixth day. Sexual intercourse renders one impure, requiring a ritual bath and the passage of a sunset for purification. Thus, it should have been acceptable to have sexual intercourse with a woman up to the fifth day, allowing enough time for a bath and passage of time for purification. However, since God commands in Exod. 19:10 that the people should purify themselves both "today and tomorrow," the implication is that the people should refrain from all sources of defilement, including sexual intercourse, as early as the third day. According to Rabbi, therefore, all of this can be deduced from Exod. 19:10, without the need for the specificity of Exod. 19:15.

| | | |
|---|---|---|
| זה כיבוס בגד]ים ◆ אין לי אלא כיבוס בגדים [מנ' שהן | C/B | |
| טעונין טבילה ◆ דין הוא ◆ ומה אם ב]שעה שאין טעונין | E/D | |
| כיבוס [בגדים טעונין טבילה כאן ש]טעונין כיבוס | | |
| בגדים דין הוא [שיהו טעונין טבילה] ◆ | | |
| ויאמר אל העם היו נכונים לשלשת ימים ◆ יכול | B/A | 4 |
| משה אמר דבר זה מפי עצמו ◆ ת״ל והיו נכונים ליום | C | |
| השלישי ◆ וכאן היו נכונים לשלשת ימים ◆ נכונים נכונים | E/D | |
| לגזירה שווה ◆ מה והיו נכונים האמור להלן קודש | F | |
| שאמר למשה אף היו נכונים האמור כאן קודש שאמר | | |
| למשה. ◆ ר' אומר <מ>מקומו מוכרע ◆ וקדשתם היו ◆ | H/G | |
| שיטבלו ביום הרביעי. ◆ ר' אלעזר בן עזריה אומר מנין | A 5 | I |
| לפולטת שכבת זרע ביום השלישי שהיא טמאה ◆ שנ' | B | |
| היו נכונים לשלשת ימים אל תגשו אל אשה. ◆ ר' | C | |
| ישמעאל אומר פעמים שהן ארבע עונות פעמים שהן | | |
| חמש פעמים שהן שש. ◆ ר' עקיבה אומר לעולם חמש. | D | |
| [ויהי ביום השלישי] בהיות הבקר ◆ בזמן [שנאמר | B/A | 6 |
| לו ◆ מלמד שהזמן והמעשה מסייעין את] השעה שחיים | C | |

---

[52] An *onah* is one-half of the astronomical day, the portion of daytime or the portion of nighttime.

[53] I.e., the Torah.

the creatures of the world.

(Textual Source: Midrash ha-Gadol)

7.  A.  One might think that [the Torah] was given at night.

    B.  Scripture states, [however,] "(On the third) day" (Exod. 19:16).

    C.  [Meaning,] during the day, and not at night.

8.  A.  One might think it was given in silence.

    B.  Scripture states, [however,] "... there was thunder and lightning" (Exod. 19:16).

    C.  [Meaning,] thunder of thunders, lightning of lightnings—thunder of different types and lightning of different types!

    D.  And thus Scripture states, "The voice of the Lord is over the waters. The God of glory thunders, the Lord over the mighty waters. The voice of the Lord is power. The voice of the Lord is majesty. The voice of the Lord breaks cedars. The Lord shatters the cedars of Lebanon ... The voice of the Lord kindles flames of fire ... The voice of the Lord causes hinds to calve, and strips forests bare. While in His temple all say 'Glory!'" (Ps. 29:3–5,7,9).

9.  A.  Scripture tells that on the day of the giving of Torah, there were clouds and lightning, and rain was coming down.[54]

    B.  And thus Scripture states, "O Lord, when You came forth from Seir, advanced from the country of Edom, the earth trembled. The heavens dripped, yea, the clouds dripped water" (Judg. 5:4). And Scripture says, "Your thunder rumbled like wheels. Lightning lit up the world" (Ps. 77:19).

    C.  All the nations of the world gathered unto Balaam son of Beor, saying to him, "It appears that God is destroying His world with water! In accordance with what is said in Scripture, 'The Lord sat enthroned at the Flood' (Ps. 29:10)."

    D.  He said to them, "Fools of the world! He already promised that He won't [ever again] bring a flood to the world. In accordance with what is said in Scripture, 'For this to Me is like the waters of Noah. As I swore that the waters of Noah nevermore would flood the earth' (Isa. 54:9)."

    E.  They said to him, "Certainly if He is not bringing a flood of water, perhaps He is bringing a flood of fire!"

    F.  He said to them, "He is bringing neither a flood of water nor a flood of fire!"

    G.  They said to him, "Then why all this thunder?"

    H.  He said to them, "He is giving Torah to His people! As it says in Scripture, 'The Lord will grant strength to His people' (Ps. 29:11). And 'strength' means only 'Torah' as it says in Scripture, 'With Him are strength and resourcefulness' (Job 12:16)."

    I.  They said to him, "If this is so, 'May the Lord bless His people with peace' (Ps. 29:11)!"

10. A.  "All the people who were in the camp trembled" (Exod. 19:16):

    B.  They shook from fear.

    C.  And isn't it a matter of logical reasoning?

    D.  If Israel, who was readied before Mount Sinai, shook from fear, how much the more so the nations of the world!

[54] Compare 9.A–I with parallel material above at XLVI:I:1.A–M, and with *Mekhilta de-Rabbi Ishmael,* Amalek (H/R., 188:1–11; Laut., vol. 2, 162:1–163:17; Neus., XLV:I:2.A–G).

נִ[תְּנִין] [בָּהּ לְכָל בָּאֵי הָעוֹלָם]. ◆ יָכוֹל נִיתְּנָה בַלַּיְלָה ◆ תַּ"ל B/A 7

בַּיּוֹם ◆ בַּיּוֹם וְלֹא בַלַּיְלָה. ◆ יָכוֹל נִיתְּנָה בִשְׁתִיקָה ◆ תַּ"ל וַיְהִי B/A 8 C

קוֹלוֹת וּבְרָקִים ◆ קוֹלוֹת וְקוֹלֵי קוֹלוֹת בְּרָקִים וּבִרְקֵי C

בְּרָקִים קוֹלוֹת מְשׁוּנִּין זֶה מִזֶּה וּבְרָקִים מְשׁוּנִּין זֶה מִזֶּה ◆

וְכֵן הוּא אוֹמֵר קוֹל ה' עַל הַמַּיִם אֵל הַכָּבוֹד הִרְעִים ה' D

עַל מַיִם רַבִּים קוֹל ה' בַּכֹּחַ קוֹל ה' בֶּהָדָר קוֹל ה' שׁוֹבֵר

אֲרָזִים קוֹל ה' חוֹצֵב לַהֲבוֹת אֵשׁ קוֹל ה' יְחוֹלֵל אַיָּלוֹת

וַיֶּחֱשֹׂף יְעָרוֹת וּבְהֵיכָלוֹ כֻּלּוֹ אוֹמֵר כָּבוֹד (תה' כט ג - ט) ◆

מַגִּיד הַכְּת' שֶׁבְּיוֹם מַתַּן תּוֹרָה הָיוּ עֲנָנִים וּבְרָקִים A 9

וִירִידַת גְּשָׁמִים ◆ וְכֵן הוּא אוֹמֵר ה' בְּצֵאתְךָ מִשֵּׂעִיר B

בְּצַעְדְּךָ מִשְּׂדֵה אֱדוֹם אֶרֶץ רָעָשָׁה גַּם שָׁמַיִם נָטָפוּ גַּם

עָבִים נָטְפוּ מָיִם (שׁופ' ה ד) וְאוֹמֵר קוֹל רַעַמְךָ בַּגַּלְגַּל

הֵאִירוּ בְרָקִים תֵּבֵל (תה' עז יט) ◆ נִתְקַבְּצוּ כָל אוּמּוֹת C

הָעוֹלָם אֵצֶל בִּלְעָם בֶּן בְּעוֹר אָמְרוּ לוֹ דּוֹמֶה שֶׁהַמָּקוֹם

מְאַבֵּד אֶת עוֹלָמוֹ בַּמַּיִם כָּעִנְיָן שֶׁנֶּ' ה' לַמַּבּוּל יָשָׁב (תה'

כט י) ◆ אָמַר לָהֶן שׁוֹטִים שֶׁבָּעוֹלָם כְּבָר נִשְׁבַּע שֶׁאֵינוֹ D

מֵבִיא מַבּוּל לָעוֹלָם כָּעִנְיָן שֶׁנֶּ' כִּי מֵי נֹחַ זֹאת לִי אֲשֶׁר

נִשְׁבַּעְתִּי מֵעֲבֹר מֵי נֹחַ עוֹד עַל הָאָרֶץ (ישע' נד ט). ◆ אָמְרוּ E

לוֹ וַדַּאי מַבּוּל שֶׁל מַיִם אֵינוּ מֵבִיא אֲבָל מֵבִיא הוּא

מַבּוּל שֶׁלְּאֵשׁ ◆ אָמַר לָהֶם אֵינוּ מֵבִיא לֹא מַבּוּל שֶׁל מַיִם F

וְלֹא מַבּוּל שֶׁלְּאֵשׁ. ◆ אָמְרוּ לוֹ וְהַקּוֹל הַזֶּה לָמָּה ◆ אָמַר H/G

לָהֶם תּוֹרָה הוּא נוֹתֵן לְעַמּוֹ שֶׁנֶּ' ה' עֹז לְעַמּוֹ יִתֵּן (תה'

כט יא) וְאֵין עֹז אֶלָּא תּוֹרָה שֶׁנֶּ' עִמּוֹ עֹז וְתוּשִׁיָּה (איוב

יב טז). ◆ אָמְרוּ לוֹ אִם כֵּן ה' יְבָרֵךְ אֶת עַמּוֹ בַשָּׁלוֹם (תה' I

כט יא). ◆ וַיֶּחֱרַד כָּל הָעָם אֲשֶׁר בַּמַּחֲנֶה ◆ נִזְדַּעְזְעוּ ◆ וַהֲלֹא C/B/A 10

דְבָרִים קַל וָחוֹמֶר ◆ וּמַה יִשְׂרָאֵל שֶׁעֲתִידִין וּמְעוּתָּדִין D

לִפְנֵי הַר סִינַי נִזְדַּעְזְעוּ אוּמּוֹת הָעוֹלָם עַל אַחַת כַּמָּה וְכַמָּה

◆

E. And thus Scripture states, "In heaven You pronounced sentence. The earth was numbed with fright" (Ps. 76:9).

11.  A. "Moses led the people out of the camp toward God, (and they took their places at the foot of the mountain)" (Exod. 19:17):[55]

B. R. Yosi ben Yudan said, "Rabbi would say: "'The Lord came from Sinai' (Deut. 33:2).

[143]  C. "'[Meaning,] "He appeared on Sinai."'

D. "But I[56] say [it means] He came from Sinai to receive His children with joy.

E. "They told a parable: To what is the matter alike?

F. "It is like a groom who went out to greet [his] bride.

G. "From the honor of he who goes out you learn about the honor of he who comes in.

H. "Thus it is said, 'Moses led the people out ... toward God' (Exod. 19:17)."

12.  A. "And they took their places at the foot of the mountain" (Exod. 19:17):

B. They huddled together.

C. And about them it is explained in tradition, "O my dove, in the cranny of the rocks, hidden by the cliff" (Song 2:14).

13.  A. R. Eliezer says, "This verse is said only in reference to the Reed Sea: '... Let me see your face' (Song 2:14).[57]

B. "In accordance with what is said in Scripture, 'Stand by and see the deliverance of the Lord' (Exod. 14:13).

C. "'Let me hear your voice' (Song 2:14):

D. "In accordance with what is said in Scripture, 'As Pharaoh drew near ... the Israelites called out to the Lord' (Exod. 14:10).

E. "'For your voice is sweet' (Song 2:14):

F. "[In accordance with what is said in Scripture,] '... and their cry for help rose up to God' (Exod. 2:23).

G. "'And your face is comely' (Song 2:14):

H. "[In accordance with what is said in Scripture,] 'And the people were convinced' (Exod. 4:31)."

14.  A. R. Akiva says, "This verse is said only in reference to Mount Sinai: '... Let me see your face' (Song 2:14).

(Textual Source: Ms. Cambridge T-S C 4a.5)

B. "In accordance with what is said in Scripture, 'Early in the morning, he set up an altar at the foot of the mountain' (Exod. 24:4).

C. "'Let me hear your voice' (Song 2:14):

D. "In accordance with what is said in Scripture, 'All the people answered as one saying, "All that the Lord has spoken we will do!"' (Exod. 19:8).

E. "'For your voice is sweet' (Song 2:14):

[55] Compare 11.A–H with *Mekhilta de-Rabbi Ishmael*, Baḥodesh (H/R, 214:13–15; Laut., vol. 2, 218:115–219:119; Neus., XLIX:III:7.A–C).
[56] I.e., R. Yosi ben Yudan.
[57] Compare 13.A–H with *Mekhilta de-Rabbi Ishmael*, Baḥodesh (H/R, 215:3–7; Laut., vol. 2, 220:130–36; Neus., XLIX:III:11.A–I).

| | | |
|---:|---:|---:|
| E | | וכן הוא אומר משמים השמעת דין ארץ יראה ושקטה |
| | | (תה׳ עו ט). ◆ |
| B/A | 11 | ויוצא משה את העם לקראת האלקים ◆ <אמר> ר׳ |
| | | יוסי (בן) יודן <ברבי> היה אומר ה׳ מסיני בא (דב׳ לג |
| D/C | | ב) ◆ על סיני נגלה ◆ ואני אומר מסיני בא לקבל בניו |
| F/E | | בשמחה ◆ מושלו משל למה הדבר דומה ◆ לחתן שיצא |
| G | | לקראת כלה ◆ מכבודו שליוצא אתה למד מה כבודו |
| H | | שלנכנס ◆ לכך נאמר ויוצא משה את העם לקראת |
| C/B/A | 12 | האלקים. ◆ ויתיצבו בתחתית ההר ◆ נצפפו ◆ ועליהם |
| | | מפורש בקבלה יונתי בחגוי הסלע בסתר המדרגה |
| A | 13 | (שה״ש ב יד). ◆ ר׳ אליעזר אומ׳ אין דבר זה אמור אלא |
| B | | על הים הראיני את מראיך ◆ כענין שנ׳ התיצבו וראו את |
| D/C | | ישועת ה׳ (שמ׳ יד יג) ◆ השמיעיני את קולך ◆ כענין שנ׳ |
| | | ופרעה הקריב וג׳ ויצעקו בני ישראל אל ה׳ (שם יו״ד) ◆ |
| F/E | | כי קולך ערב ◆ ותעל שועתם אל האלקים (שמ׳ ב כג) ◆ |
| H/G | 14/ | A | ומראך נאוה ◆ ויאמן העם (שמ׳ ד לא). ◆ ר׳ עקיבה אומ׳ |
| | | אין דבר זה אמור אלא לפני הר סיני הראיני את מראיך |
| B | | (שה״ש ב יד) ◆ כענין שנ׳ וישכם בבקר ויבן מזבח |
| D/C | | תחת ההר ◆ [השמיעיני את קולך] ◆ כענין שנ׳ ויענו כל העם |
| E | | יחדיו ויאמרו כל אש[ר דבר ייי] נעשה ג׳ ◆ [כי] קולך ערב ◆ |

F. "[In accordance with what is said in Scripture,] '... they did well to speak thus' (Deut. 5:25).

G. "'And your face is comely' (Song 2:14):

H. "[In accordance with what is said in Scripture,] '... in the Tent of Meeting the whole community came forward and stood before the Lord' (Lev. 9:5)."

15.    A. Rabbi says, "This verse is said only in reference to the coming generations: 'O my dove, in the cranny of the rocks' (Song 2:14).

B. "In accordance with what is said in Scripture, 'It is He who is enthroned above the vault of the earth' (Isa. 40:22).

C. "'Hidden by the cliff' (Song 2:14):

D. "This [refers to] Israel, who dwell in the distress of [other] kingdoms until their time arrives.

E. "'Let me see your face' (Song 2:14):

F. "This is [legal] precedent.

G. "'Let me hear your voice' (Song 2:14):

H. "This is Talmud.

I. "'For your voice is sweet and your face is comely' (Song 2:14):

J. "To inform you how many steps there are between Talmud and precedent."

### (Textual Source: Midrash ha-Gadol)

16.    A. Another interpretation:

B. "... and they took their places at the foot of the mountain" (Exod. 19:17):

C. This teaches that the Holy One, blessed be He, inverted the mountain over them like a roof and said, "If you accept upon yourselves the Torah it will be good, but if not, here will be your graves!"

D. At that moment, all of them cried out and poured out their hearts like water in repentance, and said, "All that the Lord has spoken we will do and obey!" (Exod. 24:7).

E. The Holy One, blessed be He, said, "I need some sureties!"

F. They said, "The heavens and earth will vouch for us!"

G. He said, "They are disqualified!"

H. They said, "Our forefathers will vouch for us!"

I. He said, "They are already taken!"

J. They said, "Our children will vouch for us!"

K. He said, "They are good sureties!"

L. And thus Scripture states, "From the mouths of infants and sucklings You have founded strength" (Ps. 8:3). And Scripture says, "Because you have spurned the teaching of your God, I, in turn, will spurn your children" (Hosea 4:6).

| | | |
|---|---|---|
| הטיבו <כל> אשר דברו (דב' ה כד) • ומראך | G/F | |
| נאוה • באהל מועד ויקרבו כל העדה ויעמדו לפני ה' | H | |
| (ויק' ט ה) • ר' או' אין דבר זה אמור אלא לדורות | A | 15 |
| הבאים יונתי בחגוי הסלע • כעינין שנ' היושב על חוג | B | |
| הארץ (ישע' מ כב) • בסתר המדרגה • אלו יש' שיושבין | D/C | |
| בצד צרתן שלמלכיות עד שיגיע זמנן • הראיני את | E | |
| מראיך • זה מעשה • השמיעיני את קולך • זה תלמוד • כי | I/H/G/F | |
| קולך ע[ר]ב ומראך נאוה • להודיע כמה מעלות בין | J | |
| תלמוד למעשה. • ד"א • ויתיצבו בתחתית ההר • מלמד | C/B/A | 16 |
| שכפה הקב"ה עליהם את ההר כגגית ואמר אם | | |
| מקבלין אתם עליכם את התורה <מוטב> ואם לאו | | |
| כאן תהא קבורתכם • באותה שעה געו כולם ושפכו | D | |
| לבם כמים בתשובה ואמרו כל אשר דבר ה' נעשה | | |
| ונשמע • אמר הקב"ה ערבים אני צריך • אמרו הרי שמים | F/E | |
| וארץ יערבונו • אמר להן בטילין הן. • אמרו אבותינו | H/G | |
| יערבונו • אמר להן עסיקין הן • אמרו בנינו יערבונו • אמר | K/J/I | |
| הרי ערבים טובים • וכן הוא אומר מפי עוללים ויונקים | L | |
| יסדת עוז (תה' ח ג) ואומר ותשכח תורת אלקיך | | |
| אשכח בניך גם אני. (הושע ד ו) • | | |

*Chapter Fifty-One*

(Textual Source: Ms. Cambridge T-S C 4a.5)

LI:I

1.  A. "Now Mount Sinai was all in smoke, (for the Lord had come down upon it in fire. The smoke rose like the smoke of a kiln, and the whole mountain trembled violently)" (Exod. 19:18):[58]

    B. One might think [there was smoke only] in the place of God.

    C. Scripture states, [however,] "... all" (Exod. 19:18).

    D. And not [only] in God's place.

2.  A. "... for the Lord had come down upon it in fire" (Exod. 19:18):

    B. This teaches

(Textual Source: Midrash ha-Gadol)

that the fire lapped the firmament and came down upon Mount Sinai and formed a kind of torch to gesture toward it.

    C. And thus Scripture states, "As when fire kindles brushwood, and fire makes water boil—to make Your name known to Your adversaries" (Isa. 64:1).

3.  A. Concerning fire,

(Textual Source: Ms. Cambridge T-S C 4a.5)

[Scripture] teaches that the words of Torah are compared to fire.[59]

    B. Just as fire [supports] life for the world, likewise the words of Torah [support] life for the world.

    C. Just as with fire, if one draws near he is scalded, if one distances himself from it he is cold, likewise with the words of Torah, if one draws near he is scalded, if one distances himself from it he is cold.

    D. Just as with fire, a small [fire] kindles the large [fire] and the large [fire] is kindled from the small [fire], likewise with the words of Torah, the young one learns from the elder, and the elder learns from the young one.

[144]

    E. Anyone who struggles[60] with fire in this world will gain merit and struggle in the world to come.

    F. And what have we [as Scriptural proof]?—"He who walks in righteousness, speaks uprightly, spurns profit from fraudulent dealings, etc." (Isa. 33:15).

4.  A. Another interpretation:

    B. Anyone who accepts upon himself the yoke of Torah, which is compared to fire, removes from himself the yoke of [foreign] kingdoms, which are compared to fire.

    C. And anyone who removes from himself the yoke of Torah, which is compared to fire, places upon himself the yoke of [foreign] kingdoms, which are compared to fire.

    D. And thus Scripture states, "I will set my face against them. They escaped from fire, but fire shall consume them" (Ezek. 15:7).

---

[58] Compare 1.A–D with *Mekhilta de-Rabbi Ishmael*, Baḥodesh (H/R, 215:8–9; Laut., vol. 2, 220:1–2; Neus., L:I:1.A–C).

[59] Compare 3.A–C with *Mekhilta de-Rabbi Ishmael*, Baḥodesh (H/R, 215:9–11; Laut., vol. 2, 220:3–221:6; Neus., L:I:2.A–D).

[60] The verb that actually appears in the manuscript is מפרפר—to crumble. Instead, I translate the verb מפלפל, assuming a scribal error.

LI:I

| | | |
|---|---|---|
| 1 | C/B/A | והר סיני עשן כולו • יכול מקום הקב"ה • תל' לו' כלו • |
| D | A 2 | ולא מקום ה[קב"ה] • <מפני מה> מ[פני] אשר ירד עליו |
| | B | ה' באש • מלמד <שהאש ליחכה את הרקיע וירדה לה |
| | C | על הר סיני ונעשה כלבת אש לרמוז בו • וכן הוא אומר |
| | | כקדוח אש המסים מים תבעה אש להודיע שמך |
| 3 | A | לצריך (ישע' סד א). • באש מלמד> שנמשלו דברי תורה |
| | B | באש • [מה אש חיים] לעולם אף דברי תורה חיים |
| | C | לעולם • מה אש קרב לה א[דם נכוה רחק] ממנה צנן |
| | | כך דברי תורה <קרב לה אדם נכוה רחק ממנה צנן> • |
| | D | מה אש קטן מדליק א[ת הגדול וגדול מדליק מן |
| | | הקטן כך דברי תורה קטן למד מן [הגדול וגדול למד |
| | E | מן] הקטן • רל המפרפר באש בעולם הזה זוכה |
| | F | ומפרפן]ר לעולם הבא • וכי מה] יש לנו הלך צדקות |
| | | ודבר מישרים [מאס בבצע מעשקות ג' (ישע' לג טו) • |
| 4 | B/A | דבר] אחר • כל המקבל עליו עול תורה [שנמשלה באש |
| | C | פורקין ממנו עול] מלכיות שנמשלו באש • וכל הפ]ורק |
| | | ממנו עול תורה שנמשלה באש] נותנין עליו ע[ו]ל |
| | D | מלכיות שנ]משלו באש • וכן הוא או' ונתתי את פני |
| | | בהם] מהאש יצאו [והאש תאכלם (יחז' טו ז)] • |

(Textual Source: Midrash ha-Gadol)

E.   Just as with fire, all who toil with it are distinguished among the created beings, likewise the disciples of the Sages are distinguished in the market by their speech, their gait, and their garb.

5.   A.   "The smoke rose like the smoke of a kiln" (Exod. 19:18):

B.   Just as this kiln cures the jugs—some of them going for wine, some of them going for oil, and some of them going for beads, likewise the words of Torah cure people.

C.   And thus Scripture states, "The word of the Lord is pure" (Ps. 18:31).

D.   Thus, the commandments were given only to purify [or: refine/smelt] the created beings with them.

6.   A.   "... like the smoke of a kiln" (Exod. 19:18):[61]

B.   One might think, like the smoke of a kiln, literally!

C.   Scripture states, [however,] "The mountain was ablaze with flames" (Deut. 4:11).

D.   Why does Scripture state, "... like the smoke" (Exod. 19:18)?

E.   Scripture speaks metaphorically.[62]

F.   Similar to this, you say: "And there, coming from the east with a roar like the roar of mighty waters, was the Presence of God" (Ezek. 43:2).

G.   Is it possible that His created beings are like Him?

H.   Rather, Scripture speaks metaphorically.

I.   Similar to this, you say: "... the Lord, mighty and valiant, the Lord, valiant in battle" (Ps. 24:8).

J.   Is it possible that His created beings are like Him?

K.   Rather, Scripture speaks metaphorically.

L.   Similar to this, you say: "A lion has roared, who can but fear? My Lord God has spoken" (Amos 3:8).

M.   Is it possible that His created beings are like Him?

N.   Rather, Scripture speaks metaphorically.

O.   Similar to this, you say: "May my discourse come down as the rain" (Deut. 32:2).

P.   Is it possible that the rains are greater than the Torah, to which it is compared?

Q.   Rather, Scripture speaks

(Textual Source: Ms. Cambridge T-S C 4a.5)

metaphorically.

7.   A.   "... and the whole mountain trembled violently" (Exod. 19:18):[63]

B.   It shook from fear.

C.   And thus Scripture states, "... why so hostile, O jagged mountains, etc." (Ps. 68:17).

D.   From where do you distribute your judgment? For you are like one with a defect.

---

[61] Compare 6.A–Q with *Mekhilta de-Rabbi Ishmael*, Baḥodesh (H/R, 215:12–17; Laut., vol. 2, 221:7–16; Neus., L:I:3.A–5.C).
[62] Literally: "Scripture allows the ear to hear what it is able to hear."

| | | |
|---|---|---|
| מה אש בני אדם העמלין בה ניכרין בין הבריות כך תלמידי | E | |
| חכמים ניכרין בדיבורן ובהילוכן ובעטיפתן בשוק. ◆ | | |
| ויעל עשנו כעשן הכבשן ◆ מה כבשן זה בודק את | B/A | 5 |
| החביות מהן יוצאות ליין ומהן יוצאות לשמן ומהן | | |
| יוצאות חרוזות כך דברי תורה בודקין את בני אדם | | |
| ◆ וכן הוא אומר אמרת ה' צרופה (תה' יח לא) ◆ הא לא | D/C | |
| ניתנו מצוות אלא לצרוף בהן את הבריות. ◆ כעשן | A | 6 |
| הכבשן ◆ יכול כעשן הכבשן ודאי ◆ ת"ל [וההר בוער באש | C/B | |
| ומה ת"ל] כעשן ◆ משמיעין את האוזן מה שיכולה | E/D | |
| לשמוע. ◆ כיוצא בו אתה אומר והנה כבוד אלקי ישראל | F | |
| בא מדרך הקדים וקולו כקול מים רבים (יחז' מג ב) ◆ | | |
| אפשר לבריותיו כמותו ◆ אלא משמיעין את האוזן מה | H/G | |
| שיכולה לשמוע. ◆ כיוצא בו אתה אומר ה' עזוז וגבור ה' | I | |
| גבור מלחמה (תה' כד ח) ◆ אפשר לבריותיו כמותו ◆ אלא | K/J | |
| משמיעין את האוזן מה שיכולה לשמוע. ◆ כיוצא בו | L | |
| אתה אומר אריה שאג מי לא יירא ה' אלקים דבר | | |
| (עמוס ג ח) ◆ אפשר לבריותיו כמותו ◆ אלא משמיעין את | N/M | |
| האוזן מה שיכולה לשמוע. ◆ כיוצא בו אתה אומר יערף | O | |
| כמטר לקחי (דב' לב ב) ◆ אפשר שהגשמים גדולים מן | P | |
| התורה שהוא מושלה בהן ◆ אלא משמיעין את [האזן | Q | |
| מה שיכולה] לשמע ◆ ויחרד כל ההר מאד ◆ נזדעזע ◆ וכן | C/B/A | 7 |
| הוא או' למה [תרצד]ון הרים [גב]נונים ג' (תה' סח יז) ◆ | | |
| היכן אתם מרצים דינכם הרי אתם כבעלי מ[ומי]ן ◆ | D | |

---

[63] Compare 7.A–G with *Mekhilta de-Rabbi Ishmael*, Baḥodesh (H/R, 216:1–6; Laut., vol. 2, 221:17–222:25; Neus., L:I:6.A–7.D).

E.  [As it says in Scripture,] "... or who is a hunchback, or a dwarf" (Lev. 21:20).

F.  "... toward the mountain God desired as His dwelling" (Ps. 68:17)—this is Mount Sinai.

G.  "The Lord shall abide there forever" (Ps. 68:17)—this is the Temple.

8.  A.  "The blare of the horn (grew louder and louder. As Moses spoke, God answered him in thunder)" (Exod. 19:19):[64]

B.  Normally, as the blare goes on it weakens.

C.  However, it is not so with He who spoke, and the world came into being. Rather, as the blare goes on it strengthens.

D.  As the children of Torah age, they become more clear-minded.

E.  And thus Scripture states, "Wisdom is in the aged" (Job 12:12).

9.  A.  "As Moses spoke, God answered him in thunder" (Exod. 19:19):

B.  R. Eliezer the Modiite says, "Great was the honor that the Holy One, blessed be He, gave to Moses, for the Holy One, blessed be He, would not speak until Moses said to Him, 'Speak! Your children have already accepted Your words upon themselves!'"

10.  A.  R. Akiva says, "How does one know from Scripture that with the [same] thunder, strength, and tone with which Moses heard Him, he would make Israel hear?

B.  "Scripture states, 'As Moses spoke, God answered him' (Exod. 19:19).

C.  "Literally!

D.  "Why does Scripture state, '... in thunder' (Exod. 19:19)?

E.  "This teaches that with the [same] thunder, strength, and tone with which Moses heard Him, he would make Israel hear."

LI:II

1.  A.  "The Lord came down upon Mount Sinai, on top of the mountain, (and the Lord called Moses to the top of the mountain and Moses went up)" (Exod. 19:20):[65]

B.  One might think that He literally came down!

C.  Scripture states, [however,] "... that I spoke to you from the very heavens" (Exod. 20:19).

D.  One might think that, literally, He did not come down.

E.  Scripture states, [however,] "The Lord came down upon Mount Sinai, on top of the mountain" (Exod. 19:20).

[145]  F.  Say this: The highest heavens were split and permission was given to the fire to illuminate the water.

G.  And thus Scripture states, "As when fire kindles brushwood, and fire makes water boil" (Isa. 64:1).

H.  He came down and spread out the [heavenly] heights and stood on the top [of them on top] of Mount Sinai.

I.  Why does Scripture state, "... that I spoke to you from the very heavens" (Exod. 20:19)?

J.  These are the heavens that were on Mount Sinai.

[64] Compare 8.A–10.E with *Mekhilta de-Rabbi Ishmael*, Baḥodesh (H/R, 216:10–18; Laut., vol. 2, 223:32–44; Neus., L:I:9.A–10.F).

[65] Compare 1.A–2.D with *Mekhilta de-Rabbi Ishmael*, Baḥodesh (H/R, 216:20–217:5; Laut., vol. 2, 224:45–58; Neus., L:I:11.A–13.C).

| | | |
|---|---|---|
| א[ו] ג[ב]ן אב[ן] דק (ויק׳ כא כ) ◆ ההר חמד אים לשבתו | Γ/E | |
| זה הר סיני ◆ אף ייי ישכון לנצח [זה] בית העולמים ◆ | G | |
| ויהי קול השופר ◆ בנוהג שבעולם כל זמן שהקול | B/A | 8 |
| [הוליך הוא ת]ושש ◆ אבל מי שאמר והיה העולם אינו | C | |
| כן אלא כל זמן [שהקול הו]ליך הוא מתגביר ◆ כל זמן | D | |
| שבני תורה הולכין דעתן מתישבת ◆ [וכן ה]וא א[או׳ | E | |
| בי]שישים חכמה (איוב יב יב) ◆ משה ידבר והאים יעננו | A | 9 |
| בקול ◆ ר׳ לעזר [המוד]ע[י אומ׳] [או׳ כבוד] גדול חלק לו | B | |
| הקב״ה למשה שלא היה הקב״ה מדבר [עד] שמ[שה | | |
| אומר לו] דבר כבר קיבלו בניך את דבריך עליהם | | |
| בשמחה ◆ [ר׳ עקיבה או׳ מנ׳ שבקו]ל ובכה ובנעימה | A | 10 |
| שהיה משה שומע <בו> היה משמיע [את יש׳ ◆ תל׳ לו׳ | B | |
| מ]שה ידבר והאים <יעננו> ◆ ודאי ◆ מה תל׳ לו׳ בקול ◆ | E/D/C | |
| מלמד שבקול [ובכה ובנעימה ש]היה משה שומע בו | | |
| היה משמיע את יש׳ ◆ | | |
| | LI:II | |
| [וירד ה׳ על הר סיני א]ל ראש ההר ◆ יכול ירד ודאי ◆ | B/A | 1 |
| תל׳ לו׳ כי מן השמים [דברתי עמכם (שמ׳ כ יט) ◆ יכול] | D/C | |
| לא ירד ודאי ◆ [תל׳] לו׳ וירד ה׳ על הר סיני אל [ראש | E | |
| ההר] אמור מעתה נבקעו ש[מי השמים העליונים ונתנה | F | |
| רשות לאש ללהט את המים ◆ וכן] הוא או׳ כקדוח אש | G | |
| המסים [מים תבעה אש (ישע׳ סד א) ◆ ירד לו היציע העליון | H | |
| ועמד לו על] גבי הר סיני ◆ מה תל׳ לו׳ אתם [ראיתם כי | I | |
| מן השמים ג׳ (שמ׳ כ ט) ◆ אלו שמים שעל גבי הר סיני] ◆ | J | |

2. A. R. Yosi says, "Moses never went up to the [heavenly] heights, and God's presence did not come down onto Mount Sinai.[66]

   B. "And thus Scripture states, 'The heavens belong to the Lord, but the earth He gave over to man' (Ps. 115:16).

   C. "Rather, this teaches that God said to Moses, 'Behold, I shall call out to you from the top of the mountain, and you will come up!'

   D. "As it says in Scripture, '... and the Lord called Moses

   (Textual Source: Midrash ha-Gadol)

   to the top of the mountain and Moses went up' (Exod. 19:20)."

3. A. "The Lord said to Moses, 'Go down, warn the people (not to break through to the Lord to gaze, lest many of them perish)'" (Exod. 19:21):

   B. He admonished the one who went up not to look, and he admonished the one who did not go up not to go up.

4. A. "'... not to break through to the Lord to gaze'" (Exod. 19:21):

   B. So that they won't break through the boundaries.

5. A. "'... lest many of them perish'" (Exod. 19:21):[67]

   B. The word "many" means only "troops."

   C. This tells that if one of them fell to the ground, [God] attributes it to him as if there were troops before Him.

6. A. Another interpretation:

   B. "'... lest many of them perish'" (Exod. 19:21):

   C. The one who impairs, impedes all of it.[68]

7. A. "'The priests also, who come near the Lord, must stay pure, (lest the Lord break out against them)'" (Exod. 19:22):[69]

   B. R. Joshua ben Korḥa says, "These are the first-born."

   C. Rabbi says, "This is Nadab and Abihu. In two instances [in Scripture] 'priests' is stated, but 'Nadab and Abihu' is not stated. And in two instances 'Nadab and Abihu' is stated, but 'priests' is not stated."

8. A. "'... lest the Lord break out against them'" (Exod. 19:22):

   B. So that He won't make a calamity of them!

9. A. Another interpretation:

   B. "'... lest the Lord break out against them'" (Exod. 19:22):

   C. So that they won't break through.

10. A. "But Moses said to the Lord, 'The people cannot come up to Mount Sinai, (for You warned us saying, "Set bounds about the mountain and sanctify it")'" (Exod. 19:23):[70]

    B. This is what R. Judah says, "The Holy One, blessed be He, said to Moses, 'Behold, I'll say something to you, and you will reply to Me, and then I'll reply and agree with your words.'"

---

[66] Compare 2.A–D with parallel at b. Sukkah 5a (Neus., VI.Tractate Sukkah:1:1A–F:X.I–U).

[67] Compare 5.A–6.C with *Mekhilta de-Rabbi Ishmael*, Baḥodesh (H/R, 217:7–9; Laut., vol. 2, 225:61–63; Neus., L:I:17.A–C).

[68] I.e., should even one person break through, many would perish.

| | | |
|---:|---:|---:|
| <ר' יוסי או' מעולם לא עלה משה למרום ולא | A | 2 |
| ירדה שכינה על הר סיני> ♦ וכן הוא או' השמים שמים | B | |
| [לה' והארץ נתן לבני אדם ♦ אלא מלמד שאמר] לו | C | |
| [המק]ום למשה [הריני] <קורא לך מראש ההר ואתה | | |
| עולה ♦ שנ' ויקרא ה' למשה> אל ראש ההר ויעל משה. ♦ | D | |
| ויאמר ה' אל משה רד העד בעם וג' ♦ מי שעלה | B/A | 3 |
| זרזו שלא יראה ומי שלא עלה זרזו שלא יעלה. ♦ פן | A | 4 |
| יהרסו אל ה' לראות ♦ שלא יפגרו את התחומין. ♦ ונפל | A 5 | B |
| ממנו רב ♦ אין רב אלא אכלוסין ♦ מגיד שאם נפל אחד | C/B | |
| מהן לארץ מעלה עליו כאלו אכלוסין לפניו. ♦ ד"א ♦ ונפל | B/A | 6 |
| ממנו רב ♦ ממי שמיעוטו מעכב את רובו. ♦ | C | |
| וגם הכהנים הנגשים אל ה' יתקדשו ♦ ר' יהושע בן | B/A | 7 |
| קרחה אומר אלו בכורות. ♦ ר' אומר זה נדב ואביהוא. | C | |
| (בשני מקומות נאמר כהנים ולא נאמר נדב ואביהוא | | |
| ובשני מקומות נאמר נדב ואביהוא ולא נאמר כהנים). ♦ | | |
| פן יפרץ בהם ה'. ♦ שלא יעשה בהם פרצה. ♦ ד"א ♦ פן יפרץ | B/A/B/A | 9/8 |
| בהם ה' ♦ שלא יפרוצו. ♦ | C | |
| ויאמר משה אל ה' לא יוכל העם לעלות אל הר סיני ♦ | A | 10 |
| זו היא שר' יהודה אומר אמר לו הקב"ה למשה הריני | B | |
| אומר לך דבר ואתה משיבני והריני חוזר ומודה לדבריך ♦ | | |

---

[69] Compare 7.A–C with *Mekhilta de-Rabbi Ishmael,* Baḥodesh (H/R, 217:14–16; Laut., vol. 2, 226:71–74; Neus., L:I:22.A–D); and b. Zevaḥim 115b (Neus., XXVIII.C:Tractate Zebaḥim:14:10:IX.1.I–L).

[70] Compare 10.A–19.B with *Mekhilta de-Rabbi Ishmael,* Baḥodesh (H/R, 217:18–219:5; Laut., vol. 2, 226:77–229:120; Neus., L:I:25.A–II:4.H).

11.  A.  "'… for You warned us saying, "Set bounds about the mountain"'" (Exod. 19:23):

B.  He[71] said to Him, "They have already made boundaries for themselves and have been conscientious [of them]!"

12.  A.  "So the Lord said to him, 'Go down, and come back (together with Aaron. But let not the priests or the people break through to come up to the Lord, lest He break out against them)'" (Exod. 19:24):

B.  One might think that everyone went up with him.

C.  Scripture states, [however,] "'But let not … the people break through to come up'" (Exod. 19:24).

D.  One might think that the priests went up with him.

E.  Scripture states, [however,] "'… and come back together with Aaron'" (Exod. 19:24).

F.  One might think that Aaron was with him in [his] division.

G.  Scripture states, [however,] "'Moses alone shall come near the Lord'" (Exod. 24:2).

H.  Say this from now on: Moses was in a division all to himself, and Aaron was in a division all to himself.

13.  A.  "And Moses went down to the people and spoke to them" (Exod. 19:25):

B.  This teaches that he did not [first] go to his home or turn toward other tasks.

C.  How does one know from Scripture that even with the divine speech [that Moses received in] the Tent of Meeting, he did not [first] go to his home or turn toward other tasks?

D.  Scripture states, "And he came out and told the Israelites what he had been commanded" (Exod. 34:34).

14.  A.  "God spoke all these words, saying" (Exod. 20:1):

B.  He said to them, "I shall apply the law to you in all matters. For if you had not accepted [My law] upon yourselves, I would not exact punishment among you. One who accepts is not the same as one who does not accept!"

C.  R. Judah the Patriarch told a parable: "To what is the matter alike?

D.  "To one who married an important woman. They said to her: 'You married him! Now work with his wool!'

E.  "Likewise [God said], 'You, Israel! You were drawn to Me and pledged to Me, now let's hope that you will do My will!'"

15.  A.  Another interpretation:

B.  "God spoke" (Exod. 20:1):

C.  This teaches that the words that were spoken here [were spoken at the same time as] those that were spoken later. The two of them in one instance. That which is impossible for the mouth to say and impossible for the ear to hear.

[146]  D.  Here Scripture states, "God spoke all these words, saying" (Exod. 20:1), and later Scripture states, "One thing God has spoken. Two things I have heard" (Ps. 62:12).

E.  And Scripture says, "Behold, My word is like fire—declares the Lord" (Jer. 23:29).

F.  Just as this fire is divided into many sparks, likewise one word went out as many verses!

---

[71] I.e., Moses.

11 A ◆ כי אתה העדתה בנו לאמר הגבל את ההר ◆

B ◆ אמר לו כבר עשו להן תחומין ונזדרזו. ◆

12 B/A ◆ ויאמר אליו ה׳ לך רד ועלית ◆ יכול הכל עלו עמו ◆

D/C ◆ ת״ל והעם אל יהרסו לעלות ◆ יכול הכהנים עלו עמו ◆

F/E ◆ ת״ל ועלית אתה ואהרן עמך ואין הכהנים עמך. ◆ יכול

G אהרן היה עמו במחיצה ◆ ת״ל ונגש משה לבדו אל ה׳ ◆

H ◆ אמור מעתה משה מחיצה לעצמו ואהרן מחיצה לעצמו. ◆

13 B/A ◆ וירד משה אל העם ויאמר אליהם ◆ מלמד שלא

C הלך לתוך ביתו ולא פנה לעסיקין אחרים. ◆ אין לי

אלא דברות הר סיני שלא הלך לתוך ביתו ולא פנה

לעסיקין אחרים. מנין אף דברות אהל מועד שלא

D הלך לתוך ביתו ולא פנה לעסיקין אחרים ◆ ת״ל ויצא

ודבר אל בני ישראל את אשר יצוה (שמ׳ לד לד). ◆

14 B/A ◆ וידבר אלקים את כל הדברים האלה לאמר ◆ אמר

להם דין אני נוהג ביניכם ובין כל הדברים שאלו לא

קיבלתם עליכם לא הייתי נפרע מכם אינו דומה

C מקבל לשאינו מקבל. ◆ ר׳ יהודה הנשיא מושלו משל

D למה הדבר דומה ◆ לאחד שנשא אשה ‹חשובה›

E אמרון לה התלקחת ליה פיסי עמריה. ◆ כך אתם

ישראל נמשכתם לי נתמשכנתם לי נקוי שתתעשו לי

15 C/B/A רצוני. ◆ ד״א ◆ וידבר אלקים ◆ מלמד שדברים שנאמרו כאן

הן שנאמרו להלן שניהם לענין אחד מה שאי אפשר

D לו לפה לומר ואי אפשר לה לאוזן לשמוע. ◆ כאן הוא

אומר וידבר אלקים את כל הדברים האלה ולהלן

הוא אומר אחת דבר אלקים שתים זו שמעתי (תה׳

E סב יב) ◆ ואומר הלא כה דברי כאש נאם ה׳ (ירמ׳ כג

F כט) ◆ מה אש זה נחלק לכמה ניצוצות כך דבר אחד

16.  A.  Another interpretation:

B.  "God spoke" (Exod. 20:1):

C.  It is I who exacts punishment Myself like this, and it is I who pays a reward Myself like this.

D.  And thus Scripture states, "Face to face the Lord spoke to you (on the mountain out of the fire)" (Deut. 5:4).

17.  A.  Another interpretation:

B.  "God spoke" (Exod. 20:1):

C.  This teaches that He said the first one to them first and the last one to them last.

18.  A.  "God spoke all [these] words" (Exod. 20:1):

B.  One might think [only after the recitation of the] last [of the Ten Commandments] did they say to him, "We accept [all of them] upon ourselves!"

C.  Scripture states, [however,] "I the Lord am your God" (Exod. 20:2).

D.  "I (the Lord am your God)" was part of the overall commandments, but was singled out specifically in order to teach you about the overall commandments:

E.  Just as "I (the Lord am your God)" was a commandment in and of itself, and was accepted [independently] in and of itself, likewise each and every commandment was a commandment in and of itself and was accepted [independently] in and of itself.

19.  A.  Why does Scripture state "saying" (Exod. 20:1)?

B.  This teaches that He said to them each and every commandment. For each negative commandment [they responded] "No!" and for each positive commandment [they responded] "Yes!"

*Chapter Fifty-Two*

(Textual Source: Midrash ha-Gadol)

LII:I

1.  A.  "'I am the Lord your God (who brought you out of the Land of Egypt, the house of bondage)'" (Exod. 20:2):

B.  [God is saying,] "I am this one, and let he who should have the power come forward and refute it!"

2.  A.  R. Shimon says, "This is said in reference to the destruction of the world.

B.  "[As it says in Scripture,] '... and I will blot out all existence' (Gen. 7:4).

C.  "[God is saying,] 'I am this one, and let he who should have the power come forward and refute it!'

D.  "Similar to this you say: 'I did not speak in secret, at a site in a land of darkness ... I the Lord, speak righteously' (Isa. 45:19).

E.  "[God is saying,] 'I am this one, and let he who should have the power come forward and refute it!'"

3.  A.  Another interpretation:

B.  "'I am the Lord your God'" (Exod. 20:2):

C.  [God is saying,] "I am God over all the creatures of the world!"

| | | |
|---|---|---|
| 16 | C/B/A | יוצא לכמה מקראות. ◆ ד״א ◆ וידבר אלקים ◆ אני שנפרע |
| | D | על ידי כך ואני שמשלם שכר על ידי כך. ◆ וכן הוא |
| 17 | B/A | אומר פנים בפנים דבר ה׳ עמכם (דב׳ ה ד). ◆ ד״א ◆ וידבר |
| | C | אלקים ◆ מלמד שהיה אומר להם על ראשון ראשון ועל |
| 18 | B/A | אחרון אחרון. ◆ ד״א וידבר אלקים את כל הדברים ◆ יכול |
| | C | באחרונה אמרו לו קיבלנו עלינו ◆ ת״ל אנכי ה׳ אלקיך ◆ |
| | D | אנכי היה בכלל ויצא מוצא מן הכלל ללמד על הכלל ◆ |
| | E | מה אנכי היה לו דיבור בפני עצמו וקבלה בפני עצמו |
| | | כך כל דיבר ודבר היה לו דיבור בפני עצמו וקבלה |
| 19 | B/A | בפני עצמו. ◆ מה ת״ל לאמר ◆ מלמד שהיה אומר להן על |
| | | כל דיבר ודיבר על לאו לאו ועל הין הין. ◆ |

LII:I

| | | |
|---|---|---|
| 1 | B/A | אנכי ה׳ אלקיך ◆ אני הוא זה ומי שיש לו רשות |
| 2 | A | יבואו וימחה. ◆ ר׳ שמעון אומר לענין השחתת עולם |
| | C/B | נאמר ◆ ומחיתי את כל היקום (בר׳ ז ד) ◆ אני הוא זה ומי |
| | D | שיש לו רשות יבוא וימחה. ◆ כיוצא בו אתה אומ׳ לא |
| | | בסתר דברתי במקום ארץ חשך ‹וגו׳› אני ה׳ דובר צדק |
| | E | (ישע׳ מה יט) ◆ אני הוא זה ומי שיש לו רשות יבוא וימחה. ◆ |
| 3 | C/B/A | ד״א ◆ אנכי ה׳ אלקיך ◆ אלוה אני על כל באי העולם ◆ |

D. One might think, therefore, that You are, indeed, [God] over [all of] them.

E. Scripture states, [however,] "'... your God'" (Exod. 20:2).

F. One might think, therefore, [He is God] only toward you.

G. Scripture states, [however,] "'I am the Lord'" (Exod. 20:2).

H. [God is saying,] "I am God over all the creatures of the world!"

I. How is it so [that He is both God of all creation and, specifically, your God]?

J. [God is saying,] "I am God over all the creatures of the world, but My name rests [specially] on you!"

4. A. Similar to this, you state: "Three times a year all your males shall appear before the Sovereign Lord (the God of Israel)" (Exod. 34:23).

B. [God is saying,] "I am Sovereign Lord over all the creatures of the world!"

C. One might think, therefore, that You are, indeed, [Sovereign Lord] over [all of] them.

D. Scripture states, [however,] "... the God of Israel" (Exod. 34:23).

E. One might think, therefore, [He is Sovereign Lord] only toward you.

F. Scripture states, [however,] "... before the Sovereign Lord, the God of Israel" (Exod. 34:23).

G. How is it so [that He is both Sovereign Lord over all creation, and, specifically, of Israel]?

H. [God is saying,] "I am Sovereign Lord over all the creatures of the world, but My name rests [specially] on you!"

5. A. Similar to this, you state: "Thus said the Lord of Hosts, the God of Israel ... Behold I am the Lord, the God of all flesh" (Jer. 32:15,27).

B. [God is saying,] "I am God over all the creatures of the world!"

C. One might think, therefore, that You are, indeed, also [God] over [all of] them.

D. Scripture states, [however,] "... the God of Israel" (Jer. 32:15).

E. One might think, therefore, [He is God] only toward you.

F. Scripture states, [however,] "I am the Lord, the God of all flesh" (Jer. 32:27).

G. How is it so?

H. [God is saying,] "I am God over all the creatures of the world, but My name rests [specially] on you!"

6. A. Another interpretation:

B. "'I am the Lord your God'" (Exod. 20:2):

C. Why does Scripture state "your God"?

D. The Holy One, blessed be He, said, "If you do My will, I [will call upon My attribute of loving mercy as] the Lord ...[72]

E. "As it says in Scripture about Me, 'The Lord! The Lord! A God compassionate and gracious ...' (Exod. 34:6).

F. "But if not, [I will call upon My attribute of justice as] your God [and] exact punishment from your enemies.[73]

---

[72] The divine name Lord (YHWH—יהוה) is understood to be indicative of God's attribute of love and mercy.

| | | |
|---|---:|---:|
| יכול אף אתה כיוצא בהן • ת״ל אלקיך • יכול | F/E/D | |
| עליך בפני עצמך • ת״ל אנכי ה׳ • אלוה אני על כל באי | H/G | |
| העולם. • הא כיצד • אלוה אני על כל באי העולם ושמי | J/I | |
| יחול עליך. • כיוצא בדבר אתה אומר שלש פעמים | A | 4 |
| בשנה יראה כל זכורך את פני האדון ה׳ (שמ׳ לד כג) • | | |
| אדון אני על כל באי העולם • יכול אף אתה כיוצא בהן • | C/B | |
| ת״ל ה׳ אלקי ישראל • יכול עליך בפני עצמך • ת״ל את | F/E/D | |
| פני האדון ה׳ אלקי ישראל • הא כיצד • אדון אני על כל | H/G | |
| באי העולם וחל שמי עליך. • כיוצא בדבר אתה אומר | A | 5 |
| כה אמר ה׳ צבאות אלקי ישראל (ירמ׳ לב טו) הנה אני | | |
| ‹ה׳› אלקי כל בשר (שם כז) • אלוה אני על כל באי | B | |
| העולם • יכול אף אתה כיוצא בהן • ת״ל אלקי ישראל • | D/C | |
| יכול עליך בפני עצמך • ת״ל אני ה׳ אלקי כל בשר • הא | G/F/E | |
| כיצד • אלוה אני על כל באי העולם וחל שמי עליך. • ד״א • | A 6 | H |
| ה׳ (אלקיך) • מה ת״ל אלקיך • אמר הקב״ה אם עושין | D/C/B | |
| אתם רצוני הרי אנכי ה׳ • שנ׳ בי ה׳ ה׳ אל רחום וחנון | E | |
| (שמ׳ לד ו) • ואם לאו אלקיך אני נפרע משונאיכם | F | |

---

[73] The divine name God (Elohim—אלהים) is understood to be indicative of God's attribute of justice and divine retribution.

G.   "For Scripture states 'your God' to mean only 'judge.'"

7.   A.   Another interpretation:

B.   "'I am the Lord your God'" (Exod. 20:2):

C.   This teaches that the Holy One, blessed be He, made all the nations of the world read through His Torah, but they did not accept it from Him.

D.   He returned to Israel and said, "'I am the Lord *your* God'" (Exod. 20:2).

8.   A.   "'... who brought you out of the Land of Egypt'" (Exod. 20:2):

B.   [God says,] "I will even require nothing of you. Rather, I brought you deservingly out from the Land of Egypt."

9.   A.   "'... the house of bondage'" (Exod. 20:2):

B.   [God says,] "I will even require nothing of you. Rather, it is enough for Me that I redeemed you from the house of bondage!"

## Chapter Fifty-Three

### (Textual Source: Midrash ha-Gadol)

LIII:I[74]

1.   A.   "'You shall have (no other gods besides Me)'" (Exod. 20:3):[75]

B.   One might think that one should not keep [an idol] for one's self, but may keep one for other people.

C.   Scripture states, [however,] "'There shall not be'" (Exod. 20:3).

D.   Why does Scripture state, "'There shall not be *for you*'" (Exod. 20:3)?

E.   This teaches that whoever keeps an idol for himself transgresses two [commandments]:

F.   "'There shall not be'" and "'For you.'"

2.   A.   "'... gods'" (Exod. 20:3):

B.   One might think that because they are called "gods" there might be some value in them.

C.   Scripture states, [however,] "'... other (gods)'" (Exod. 20:3).

3.   A.   Another interpretation:

B.   Why does Scripture state "'... other gods'" (Exod. 20:3)?

C.   In order that one not fashion a god of silver or a god of gold, saying, "It's not an abomination unless it is [called] a 'god,' and it's not an idol unless it is [called] a 'god.'"

D.   Scripture states, "'... other gods'" (Exod. 20:3).

E.   [Meaning,] even if you don't refer to it by the name "god," you are [still] not permitted to keep it!

4.   A.   Another interpretation:

B.   "'... other'" (Exod. 20:3):

C.   [Which really means] "last."[76]

---

[74] Compare LIII:I:1.A–9.C with *Mekhilta de-Rabbi Ishmael*, Baḥodesh (H/R, 223:3–224:8; Laut., vol. 2, 238:18–241:51; Neus., LII:I:3.A–13.C).

[75] This unit of interpretation is based upon a literal, unidiomatic reading of the biblical verse. The text reads "You shall have no other gods" as "There shall not be for you other gods," by reading literally the possessive preposition לְךָ.

| | | |
|---|---|---|
| G | 7 B/A | שאין ת״ל אלקיך אלא לשון דיין. ◆ ד״א ◆ אנכי ה׳ |
| | C | אלקיך ◆ מלמד שהחזיר הקב״ה תורתו על כל אומות העולם |
| | D | ולא קיבלו הימנו ◆ חזר לו אצל ישראל ואמר אנכי ה׳ |
| | 8 B/A | אלקיך. ◆ אשר הוצאתיך מארץ מצרים ◆ אפילו אין לי |
| | 9 A | עליך אלא שהוצאתיך מארץ מצרים כדאי. ◆ מבית |
| | B | עבדים ◆ אפילו אין לי עליך אלא שפדיתיך מבית |
| | | עבדים דיי. ◆ |

LIII:I

| | | |
|---|---|---|
| | 1 B/A | לא יהיה לך ◆ יכול לא יקיים לעצמו אבל יקיים |
| | F/D/C | לאחרים ◆ ת״ל לא יהיה. ◆ מה ת״ל לא יהיה לך ◆ מלמד |
| | F | שכל המקיים ע״ז לעצמו עובר משום שתים ◆ משום לא |
| | 2 B/A | יהיה ומשום לך. ◆ אלהים ◆ יכול לפי שנקראו אלהים |
| C | 3 B/A | יכול יש בהן צורך לפני ◆ ת״ל אחרים. ◆ ד״א ◆ מה ת״ל |
| C | | אלהים אחרים ◆ שלא יעשה אדם אלוה שלכסף ואלוה |
| | | שלזהב ויאמר לא שיקוץ אלא לאלוה לא גילול אלא לאלוה |
| | E/D | ת״ל אלהים אחרים ◆ אע״פ שאין אתה מחזיק בו לשם |
| | 4 C/B/A | אלוה אי אתה רשאי לקיימו. ◆ ד״א ◆ אחרים ◆ אחרונים |

---

76 Reading the word "other" (Hebrew: aḥerim—אחרים) in Exod. 20:3 instead as "last" (Hebrew: aḥaronim—אחרונים).

D. They are made last.

E. And thus Scripture states, "New ones, who come but lately, who stirred not your fathers' fears" (Deut. 32:17).

F. They didn't work for you, nor did they work for your forefathers! They will never, ever!

5. A. Another interpretation:

B. "'... other'" (Exod. 20:3):

C. In that they delay the good from coming to the world![77]

6. A. Another interpretation:

B. "'... other'" (Exod. 20:3):

C. In that they make those who worship them "other."

7. A. Another interpretation:

B. "'... other'" (Exod. 20:3):

C. In that they are "other" to those who worship them.

D. And thus Scripture states, "If they cry out to it, it does not answer" (Isa. 46:7).

8. A. "'... besides Me'" (Exod. 20:3):

B. Not in My image, nor in the image of My worshipers!

9. A. Another interpretation:

B. "'... besides Me'" (Exod. 20:3):

C. This teaches that they bring anger to the world.

[147]

LIII:II

1. A. "'You shall not make (for yourself a sculptured image, or any likeness of what is in the heavens above, or on the earth below, or in the waters under the earth)'" (Exod. 20:4):

B. Lest you should say, "I'll make [any] image and worship it," Scripture states, "You shall not make" (Exod. 20:4).

C. One might think [it is permissible to make] a human image.

D. Scripture states, [however,] "... the form of a man or a woman" (Deut. 4:16).

E. One might think [it is permissible to make] a stone image.

F. Scripture states, [however,] "... figured stones" (Lev. 26:1).

G. One might think [it is permissible to make] a wooden image.

H. Scripture states, [however,] "You shall not set up a sacred post, any kind of wood" (Deut. 16:21).

I. One might think [it is permissible to make] an image of a fish.

J. Scripture states, [however,] "... the image of any fish" (Deut. 4:18).

K. One might think [it is permissible to make] an image of a bird.

L. Scripture states, [however,] "... that flies in the sky" (Deut. 4:17).

[77] Reading the word "other" (Hebrew: aḥerim—אחרים) in Exod. 20:3 instead as a form of the verb "to delay" (Hebrew: l'aḥer—לאחר).

| | | |
|---|---:|---:|
| E/D | | באחרונה נעשו ◆ <ו>כן הוא אומ׳ חדשים מקרוב |
| F | | באו לא שערום אבותיכם (דב׳ לב יז) ◆ לא |
| | | הועילו לך ולא הועילו לאבותיך ולא הועילו כלום |
| C/B/A | 5 | מימיהן. ◆ ד״א ◆ אחרים ◆ שמאחרין את הטובה מלבוא |
| C/B/A | 6 | לעולם. ◆ ד״א ◆ אחרים ◆ שעושין את עובדיהן אחרים. ◆ |
| D/C/B/A | 7 | ד״א ◆ אחרים ◆ שאחרים הן לעובדיהן ◆ וכן הוא אומר אף |
| B/A | 8 | יצעק אליו ולא יענה (ישע׳ מו ז). ◆ על פני ◆ לא בדמותי |
| C/B/A | 9 | ולא בדמות שמשי. ◆ ד״א ◆ על פני ◆ מלמד שמביאין אף |
| | | לעולם. ◆ |

LIII:II

| | | |
|---|---:|---:|
| B/A | 1 | לא תעשה ◆ שמא תאמר אעשה צורה ואעבוד אותה |
| D/C | | ת״ל לא תעשה ◆ יכול צורת אדם ◆ ת״ל תבנית זכר או |
| F/E | | נקבה ◆ יכול צורת אבן ◆ ת״ל ואבן משכית (ויק׳ כו א) ◆ |
| H/G | | יכול צורת עץ ◆ ת״ל לא תטע לך אשרה כל עץ (דב׳ טז |
| K/J/I | | כא) ◆ יכול צורת דג ◆ ת״ל בנית כל דגה (דב׳ ד יח) ◆ יכול |
| L | | צורת עוף ◆ ת״ל אשר תעוף בשמים (שם יז) ◆ |

M. One might think [it is permissible to make] an image of a beast.

N. Scripture states, [however,] "... the form of any beast" (Deut. 4:17).

O. One might think [it is permissible to make] an image of angels.

P. Scripture states, [however,] "... of what is in the heavens above" (Exod. 20:4).

Q. One might think [it is permissible to make an image of] the depths and darkness.

R. Scripture states, [however,] "... or in the waters under the earth" (Exod. 20:4).

S. One might think [it is permissible to make] a reflected image.

T. Scripture states, [however,] "... or in the waters" (Exod. 20:4).

U. One might think [it is permissible to make an image of] a water snake.

V. Scripture states, [however,] "... or in the waters" (Exod. 20:4).

W. One might think [it is permissible to make] an image of the sun and moon, stars and planets.

X. Scripture states, [however,] "And when you look up to the sky" (Deut. 4:19).

2. A. "'You shall not make for yourself'" (Exod. 20:4):[78]

B. This teaches that whoever keeps an idol for himself transgresses two [commandments]:

C. "'You shall not make'" and "'for yourself.'"

3. A. "'... a sculptured image'" (Exod. 20:4):[79]

B. I only know from this [about the prohibition] of a sculptured image.

C. But when Scripture states, "'... or any likeness'" (Exod. 20:4), it serves to include the sun and moon, stars and planets.

D. "'... of what is in the heavens'" (Exod. 20:4):

E. [This serves] to include [in the prohibition images of] the very heavens themselves.

F. "'... above'" (Exod. 20:4):

G. [This serves] to include [in the prohibition images of] the ministering angels.

H. "'... or on the earth'" (Exod. 20:4):

I. [This serves] to include [in the prohibition images of] the mountains and hills, snakes and scorpions.

J. "'... above'" (Exod. 20:4):

K. [This serves] to include [in the prohibition images of] the depths.

L. "'... or in the waters'" (Exod. 20:4):

M. [This serves] to include [in the prohibition images of] creatures of the sea and the dolphins.

N. "'... below'" (Exod. 20:4):

O. [This serves] to include [in the prohibition images of] the worms.

P. "'... the earth'" (Exod. 20:4):

---

[78] Compare 2.A–C with parallel above at LIII:I:1.A–F and with *Sifra*, Kedoshim 1:12 (Neus., CXCV:I:10.A–H).

[79] Compare 3.A–T with *Mekhilta de-Rabbi Ishmael*, Baḥodesh (H/R, 224:12–225:15; Laut., vol. 2, 241:58–243:86; Neus., LII:II:1.A–2.D); and b. Rosh Hashanah 24b.

| | |
|---|---|
| יכול צורת בהמה • ת״ל תבנית כל בהמה (שם) • יכול צורת | O/N/M |
| מלאכים • ת״ל אשר בשמים ממעל • יכול תהום וחושך • | Q/P |
| ת״ל ואשר במים מתחת לארץ • יכול הבוביא • ת״ל ואשר | T/S/R |
| במים • יכול צורת סרסוירין • ת״ל ואשר במים • יכול | W/V/U |
| צורת חמה ולבנה כוכבים ומזלות • ת״ל ופן תשא עיניך | X |
| השמימה. • לא תעשה • לך מלמד שכל העושה ע״ז | B/A 2 |
| לעצמו עובר משום שתים • משום לא תעשה ומשום | C |
| לך. • פסל • אין לי אלא פסל • כשהוא אומר כל תמונה | C/B/A 3 |
| לרבות חמה ולבנה כוכבים ומזלות. • אשר בשמים • | D |
| לרבות שמים עצמם. • ממעל • לרבות מלאכי שרת • ואשר | H/G/F/E |
| בארץ • לרבות הרים וגבעות נחשים ועקרבים. • מתחת • | J/I |
| לרבות את התהומות. • ואשר במים • לרבות את חיות הים | M/L/K |
| ואת הדולפנין. • מתחת • לרבות את השלשולין. • לארץ • | P/O/N |

Q. [This serves] to include [in the prohibition images of] the earth itself.

R. Since Scripture states, "'... any likeness'" (Exod. 20:4), [it means] not even the likenesses of them, nor their reflected images, nor the images of evil creatures, nor the images of heavenly creatures.

S. If our end result is to include everything [in the prohibition], why does Scripture state [specifically], "'... a sculptured image'" (Exod. 20:4)?

T. [God is saying,] "If you do this, you will end up making the world unfit for Me, and thus I shall make the world unfit for you!"

## LIII:III

1. A. "'You shall not bow down to them (or serve them. For I the Lord your God am an impassioned God, visiting the guilt of the parents upon the children, upon the third and upon the fourth generations of those who reject Me)'" (Exod. 20:5):[80]

B. You may bow down to a person.[81]

C. One might think [one may bow down out of respect to] one who is worshiped like Haman.[82]

D. Scripture states, [however,] "'You shall not bow down to them *or serve them*'" (Exod. 20:5), [meaning, not] as a way of worship.[83]

2. A. "'You shall not bow down to them'" (Exod. 20:5):

B. Bowing down was a part of the general prohibition [against "serving" other gods]. Why was it specifically emphasized?

C. In order to draw an analogy from it:

D. Just as bowing down is specific—a particular action—and one is culpable for it in and of itself, whether or not one [actually] worships it,[84] likewise if any specific form of worship for God is performed for idolatrous purposes, one is culpable for it whether or not one [actually] worships it.

3. A. "'For I the Lord your God'" (Exod. 20:5):

B. This teaches that they saw aspects of God that would be a reward to the righteous in the time to come, about which the prophets declared through various expressions:

C. One verse says, "His garment was like white snow" (Dan. 7:9).

D. And one verse says, "Why is your clothing so red" (Isa. 63:2).

E. And should it occur to you that they only saw this once, it is said in Ezekiel: "... and I saw *visions* of God" (Ezek. 1:1).

F. He[85] said to them, "I saw many visions before I merited to greet [fully] the presence of God."

G. "'... an impassioned God'" (Exod. 20:5):

H. This teaches that they saw aspects of God that would exact punishment from the wicked in the time to come:

---

[80] Compare 1.A–D with b. Sanhedrin 61b (Neus., XXIIIB:Tractate Sanhedrin:7:6:VI.A–F).

[81] One may not bow down to an idol, but presumably it is permissible to bow to a person as a sign of respect.

[82] Presumably, Haman was worshiped by some as a deity. Thus, perhaps it would be permissible to bow down as a sign of worship to a person, but not an idol.

[83] The second clause in Exod. 20:5 ("'... or worship them'") might appear to be redundant. However, the text interprets it to indicate that one should not bow down as a sign of worship to a person.

[84] I.e., the object to which one bows down.

[85] I.e., Ezekiel.

לרבות ארץ עצמה. ◆ כשהוא אומר כל תמונה לא R/Q

בדמותן ולא בדמות בבואה שלהן ולא בדמות חיות

רעות ולא בדמות חיות שלמעלה ◆ אם סופינו לרבות S

כולן מה ת"ל פסל ◆ אלא אם אתה עושה כן נמצאת T

פוסל עולם ממני והריני פוסל עולם ממך. ◆

LIII:III

לא תשתחוה להם ◆ משתחוה אתה לאדם. ◆ יכול C/B/A 1

אפילו נעבד כהמן ◆ ת"ל לא תשתחוה להם ולא D

תעבדם לא תשתחוה דרך עבודה. ◆ לא תשתחוה להם ◆ A 2

השתחויה בכלל היתה למה יצאת ◆ להקיש אליה ◆ מה D/C/B

השתחויה מיוחדת מעשה יחידי וחייבין עליה בפני

עצמה בין שהוא עובדו בין שאינו עובדו כך כל עבודה

המיוחדת לשם אם עשה אותה לע"ז חייבין עליה בין

שהוא עובדו בין שאינו עובדו ◆ כי אנכי ה' אלקיך ◆ A 3

[מלמד שראו פנים שעתידות לשלם שכר לצדיקים B

לעתיד לבא וכלפי שהנביאים משמיעים אותם

בלשונות הרבה ◆ כתוב אחד אומר לבושה כתלג חיור C

(דני' ז ט) ◆ וכתוב אחד אומר מדוע אדום ללבושך (ישע' D

סג ב) ◆ וכי תעלה על דעתך שלפי שעה שהם רואים לכך E

נאמר ביחזקאל ואראה מראות אלהים (יחז' א א) ◆

אמר להם הרבה ראיות ראיתי עד שזכיתי להקביל F

פני השכינה]. ◆ אל קנא ◆ מלמד שראו פנים עתידות H/G

I.   An impassioned God ... A judging God. A harsh God. A merciless God.

4.   A.   Another interpretation:

B.   Is He really jealous! Does He really exact punishment by means of jealousy?

C.   He does not exact punishment by means of a stone, nor by means of an arrow, nor by means of a sling.

D.   As if it were possible, [God is saying,] "You had someone else, so you switched Me for him!"

5.   A.   Agrippas Sabba asked Rabban Gamliel, "Someone is only jealous of others [who are worthy of jealousy]. As it says in Scripture, 'Know therefore this day and keep in mind that the Lord alone is God (in heaven above and on earth below. There is no other)' (Deut. 4:39)."

[148]   B.   He responded to him, "Someone is not jealous of one greater than he, nor of his equal, but rather of one lesser than he.

C.   "And thus Scripture states, 'For My people have done a twofold wrong: They have forsaken Me, the Fount of living waters' (Jer. 2:13).

D.   "[God is saying,] 'If these who have forsaken Me, the Fount of living waters, were insolent, how much the more so [those who] "'... hewed them out cisterns, broken cisterns, which cannot even hold water!'" (Jer. 2:13)'"

6.   A.   "'... visiting'" (Exod. 20:5):

B.   "Visiting" means only to take note.

C.   And thus Scripture states, "The Lord took note of Sarah" (Gen. 21:1). And Scripture says, "I have taken note of them" (Exod. 3:16).

7.   A.   R. Judah says, "[God is saying,] 'I will collect their sins and suspend [their retribution] until the fourth generation like Jehu son of Nimshi!'

B.   "And thus Scripture says, 'Four generations of your descendants shall occupy the throne of Israel' (2 Kings 15:12)—and so it was for him!"

8.   A.   One verse says, "'... visiting the guilt of the parents upon the children'" (Exod. 20:5), and one verse says, "A parent shall not share the burden of a child's guilt, nor shall a child share the burden of a parent's guilt" (Ezek. 18:20).

B.   [This means] if the parents were guiltless, [God] will suspend [retribution] for them.[86] But if not, He will not suspend [retribution] for them.

C.   They told a parable: To what is the matter alike?

D.   It is like one who borrowed from the king 100 *maneh*, and he[87] forgave him of the debt. His[88] son came and borrowed 100 *maneh* from the king, and he forgave him of the debt. Then the son's son came and borrowed 100 *maneh* from the king, and he forgave him of the debt. He didn't lend the fourth [son], because of his forefathers, because they had to be forgiven [of their debts].

E.   And thus Scripture states, "Our fathers sinned and are no more, and we must bear their guilt" (Lam. 5:7).

---

[86] I.e., the children.
[87] I.e., the king.
[88] I.e., the first borrower's son.

| | | |
|---|---|---|
| I | | ליפרע מן הרשעים לעתיד לבוא. ◆ אל קנא אל דיין אל |
| B/A | 4 | קשה אל אכזרי. ◆ ד"א אל קנא ◆ וכי יש לפניו קנאה וכי |
| C | | נפרע על ידי קנאה ◆ הא אין נפרע לא על ידי אבן ולא |
| D | | על ידי חץ ולא על ידי חלקוק ◆ כויכול היה לך אחר |
| A | 5 | חילפתני בו. ◆ שאל אגריפס סבא את רבן גמליאל אין |
| | | מתקנא אלא באחרים שנ' וידעת היום והשבות אל |
| B | | לבביך כי ה' הוא האלקים (דב' ד לט) ◆ אמר לו אין |
| C | | מתקנא לא בגדול ממנו ולא בכיוצא בו אלא בקטן |
| D | | ממנו ◆ וכן הוא אומר כי שתים רעות עשה עמי אותי |
| | | עזבו מקור מים חיים (ירמ' ב יג) ◆ אלו עזבו אותי מקור |
| | | מים חיים עלובין היו על אחת כמה וכמה לחצוב להם |
| | | בארות נשברים אשר לא יכילו המים (שם). ◆ |
| C/B/A | 6 | פקד ◆ אין פוקד אלא מזכיר ◆ וכן הוא אומר וה' פקד את |
| | | שרה (בר' כא א) ואומ' פקד פקדתי אתכם (שמ' ג טז). ◆ |
| A | 7 | ר' יהודה אומר כונס אני עונותיהם לידי ותולה אותן |
| B | | עד ארבעה דורות כיהוא בן נמשי ◆ וכן הוא אומ' בני |
| | | רביעים ישבו לך על כסא ישראל (מ"ב טו יב) והיה לו |
| A | 8 | כן. ◆ כת' אחד אומר פקד עון אבות על בנים וכת' אחד |
| | | אומר אב לא ישא בעון הבן ובן לא ישא בעון האב |
| B | | (יחז' יח כ) ◆ אם היו אבות זכאין תולה להן ואם לאו |
| D/C | | אין תולה להן. ◆ מושלו משל למה הדבר דומה ◆ לאחד |
| | | שלוה מן המלך מאה מנה וכפר בו. בא בנו ולוה מן |
| | | המלך מאה מנה וכפר בו ובא בן בנו ולוה מן המלך |
| | | מאה מנה וכפר בו לרביעי אין מלוין אותו מפני |
| E | | אבותיו שהיו כפרנין ◆ וכן הוא אומ' אבותינו |
| | | חטאו ואינם ואנחנו עונותיהם סבלנו (איכה ה ז) ◆ |

F.     Don't read it as "we must bear their guilt" but rather "we must bear our guilt"!

G.     [The sons say,] "Who caused us to bear the guilt of our souls? Our fathers, who had to be forgiven [of their debts]!"

9.     A.     "'... visiting the guilt of the parents upon the children'" (Exod. 20:5):

B.     One might think [this applies] only to the direct descendants.

C.     Scripture states, [however,] "... and children's children" (Exod. 34:7).

D.     Then let Scripture say only this!

E.     But if so, I might say He suspends the punishment only for them. How does one know from Scripture [also] for the third and fourth generations?

F.     Scripture states, "'... upon the third and upon the fourth generations of those who reject Me'" (Exod. 20:5).

10.     A.     "'... but showing kindness to the thousandth (generation of those who love Me and keep My commandments)'" (Exod. 20:6):

B.     One might think [this applies] only to the direct descendants.

C.     Scripture states, [however,] "... to the thousandth generation" (Deut. 7:9).

D.     Then let Scripture say only this!

E.     But if so, I might say He only does this to the thousandth generation. How does one know from Scripture [also] to the thousandth and thousandth of generations?

F.     Scripture states, "'... to the thousandth generation'" (Exod. 20:6).

11.     A.     "'... of those who love Me'" (Exod. 20:6):

B.     To he who acts before Me out of love.

C.     "'... and keep My commandments'" (Exod. 20:6):

D.     To he who acts before Me out of fear.

E.     This informs you how many degrees of separation there are between he who acts from love and he who acts from fear, and this teaches you that [God's] quality of good is more abundant than [God's] quality of retribution by 500 to 1.

## Chapter Fifty-Four

### (Textual Source: Midrash ha-Gadol)

LIV:I

1.     A.     "'You shall not swear falsely by the name of the Lord your God. (For the Lord will not clear one who swears falsely by His name)'" (Exod. 20:7):

B.     To swear falsely only means [to swear on] something that never happened, isn't happening, and won't happen in the future.

| | | |
|---|---|---|
| G/F | | אל תהי קורא עונותיהם סבלנו אלא עונותינו סבלנו ♦ מי |
| A | 9 | גרם לנו לסבול עונות נפשינו אבותינו שהיו כפרנין. ♦ פקד |
| C/B | | עון אבות על בנים ♦ יכול על יוצאי ירך בלבד ♦ ת״ל ועל |
| E/D | | בני בנים. ♦ יאמר זה ♦ שאלו כן הייתי אומר הא אין תולה |
| F | | אלא להן בלבד מנין לשלשה וארבעה דורות ♦ ת״ל על |
| | | שלשים ועל רבעים לשנאי. ♦ |
| C/B/A | 10 | ועושה חסד לאלפים ♦ יכול ליוצאי ירך בלבד ♦ ת״ל |
| E/D | | לאלף דור. ♦ יאמר זה ♦ שאלו כן הייתי אומר הא אינו |
| | | עושה אלא לאלף דור ומנין לאלפים ולאלפי אלפים ♦ |
| B/A 11 | F | ת״ל ועושה חסד לאלפים. ♦ לאהבי ♦ למי שעושה לפני |
| D/C | | מאהבה. ♦ ולשומרי מצותי ♦ למי שעושה לפני מיראה ♦ |
| E | | להודיעך כמה מעלות יש בין העושה מאהבה לעושה |
| | | מיראה וללמדך שמדת הטוב מרובה יותר ממדת |
| | | הפורענות על אחת חמש מאות. ♦ |

LIV:I

| | | |
|---|---|---|
| B/A | 1 | לא תשא את שם ה׳ אלקיך לשוא ♦ אין לשוא אלא |
| | | דבר שלא היה ולא נהיה ולא עתיד להיות. ♦ |

2.  A.  "'For the Lord will not clear (one who swears falsely by His name)'" (Exod. 20:7):

B.  Since it was said at Horeb that [the act of] repentance[89] will "clear sin,"[90] one might think that [the act of] repentance will [therefore] atone [for swearing falsely by the name of the Lord].

C.  Scripture states, [however,] "'For the Lord will not clear one'"[91] (Exod. 20:7).

D.  Can it be reasoned from this that repentance fails to atone only for a matter for which one is liable for death at the hands of the Lord,[92] or [is it] that repentance fails to atone for every negative commandment[93] in the Torah?

E.  Scripture states, "'For the Lord will not clear one who swears falsely by His name'" (Exod. 20:7), [meaning that] repentance will not atone for this, but it does atone for every [other] negative commandment in the Torah.

F.  Thus, one should [also be able to] reason from this that repentance atones for every positive commandment[94] and for every negative commandment [unto which is joined a commandment] to rise up and do [something]![95]

G.  [However] from this [verse][96] you state that only [transgression of] all [the commandments that come] after "You shall not swear falsely"[97] is a less severe transgression for which repentance atones. But [transgression of] all [the commandments] from "You shall not swear falsely" and above[98] is a more severe transgression, for which repentance does not atone.

H.  One might think that not [even] the Day of Atonement can atone [for them]![99] Scripture states, [however,] "For on this day atonement shall be made for you (to cleanse you of all your sins" (Lev. 16:30).

## LIV:II

1.  A.  ["'Remember the sabbath day and keep it holy'" (Exod. 20:8):][100]

B.  "Remember" (Exod. 20:8) and "Observe" (Deut. 5:12).

C.  The two of them were spoken in one instance. That which is impossible for the mouth to say and impossible for the ear to hear.

D.  Thus Scripture states, "God spoke *all* these words, saying" (Exod. 20:7). And Scripture says, "One thing God has spoken. Two things I have heard" (Ps. 62:12).

2.  A.  Shammai the elder says, "Remember it before it arrives, and observe it once it arrives!"

B.  They said about Shammai the elder that he would not allow the memory of *Shabbat* to vanish from his mouth. He would buy something good and say, "This is for [the sake of] *Shabbat!*" [He would buy] new clothes and say, "This is for the sake of *Shabbat!*"

3.  A.  "'Remember'" (Exod. 20:8):

[149]  B.  R. Judah ben Beteira says, "How does one know from Scripture that when you count [the days of the week] you should count them, 'First after *Shabbat*, Second after *Shabbat*, Third

---

[89] Hebrew: teshuvah—תשובה. It is helpful to note that there are four different methods of expiation that can effect atonement: repentance, the Day of Atonement, correction by suffering, and ultimately, death. See a delineation of these four in the *Mekhilta de-Rabbi Ishmael*, Baḥodesh (H/R, 229:1–9; Laut., vol. 2, 251:45–54; Neus., LIII:I:7.A–G); and t. Yoma 4:6–9. Thus, when our text here speaks of teshuvah it speaks of the first method of expiation.

[90] See Exod. 34:7. However, in order to facilitate its interpretation here, the text reads disjunctively the first verb from the second in the clause "Yet He does not remit all punishment" (Hebrew: v'nakeh lo y'nakeh—ונקה לא ינקה), creating the following meaning for the first clause: "Extending kindness to the thousandth generation, forgiving iniquity and transgression, and clearing sin."

[91] Hebrew: lo y'nakeh—לא ינקה.

[92] I.e., a transgression for which one will be punished eventually by an act of God, either in this world or the world to come.

[93] I.e., a commandment that proscribes an action.

| | | |
|---|---|---|
| כי לא ינקה ה׳ • לתוך שנאמר בחורב תשובה ונקה יכול | B/A | 2 |
| תהא תשובה מכפרת • ת״ל כי לא ינקה ה׳ • אין זה קל | D/C | |
| וחומר מעתה שלא תהא תשובה מכפרת (אלא) על דבר | | |
| שחייבין עליו מיתה לשמים. או על כל לא תעשה | | |
| שבתורה לא תהא תשובה מכפרת • ת״ל כי לא ינקה ה׳ | E | |
| את אשר ישא את שמו לשוא על זה אין תשובה | | |
| מכפרת היא על כל לא תעשה שבתורה • הרי | F | |
| זה קל וחומר מעתה שתהא תשובה מכפרת על מצות | | |
| עשה ועל מצות לא תעשה שיש בה קיום עשה • אמור | G | |
| מעתה כל שהוא מלא תשא ולמטה עבירות קלות | | |
| ותשובה מכפרת. וכל שהוא מלא תשא ולמעלה | | |
| עבירות חמורות ואין תשובה מכפרת. • יכול לא יהא | H | |
| יום הכפורים מכפר ת״ל כי ביום הזה יכפר עליכם. • | | |

LIV:II

| | | |
|---|---|---|
| זכור ושמור • שניהם נאמרו לענין אחד מה שאי | C/B/A | 1 |
| אפשר לפה לדבר ומה שאי אפשר לאוזן לשמוע • כן | D | |
| הוא אומר וידבר אלקים את כל הדברים האלה ואומ׳ | | |
| אחת דבר אלקים שתים זו שמעתי (תה׳ סב יב). • | | |
| שמאי הזקן אומר זכרה עד שלא תבוא ושמרה | A | 2 |
| משתבוא. • אמרו עליו על שמאי הזקן שלא היה זכרון | B | |
| שבת זז מתוך פיו לקח חפץ טוב אמר זה לשבת כלי | | |
| חדש אומ׳ זה לשבת. • זכור • ר׳ יהודה בן בתירה אומר | B/A | 3 |
| מנין שכשאתה מונה הוי מונה אחד בשבת ושני בשבת | | |

---

[94] I.e., a commandment that prescribes an action.

[95] I.e., a negative commandment that is followed immediately thereafter by an associated positive commandment (see, e.g., m. Makkoth 3:7 and m. Hullin 12:4). Transgression of these positive commandments results in a less severe liability than that incurred for transgression of a negative commandment. Since the text has already declared that repentance can atone for all the negative commandments, except for swearing falsely by the name of God, it stands to reason that repentance can atone for these commandments, as well.

[96] I.e., Exod. 20:7.

[97] I.e., commandments four through ten.

[98] I.e., commandments one through three.

[99] See note 89 above.

[100] Compare 1.A–5.D with *Mekhilta de-Rabbi Ishmael*, Baḥodesh (H/R, 229:5–16; Laut., vol. 2, 252:55–253:74; Neus., LIII:II:1.A–8.G).

after *Shabbat*, Fourth after *Shabbat*, Fifth after *Shabbat*, Day before *Shabbat*?

C.   "Scripture says, '"Remember"' (Exod. 20:8).

4.   A.   "'... day'" (Exod. 20:8):

B.   I only know [from this about observance of] the day [of *Shabbat*]. How does one know from Scripture [about] the night?

C.   Scripture states, "'... and keep it holy'" (Exod. 20:8).

D.   If so, why does Scripture state, "'... day'" (Exod. 20:8)?

E.   The honor of the day precedes the honor of the night.

5.   A.   "'... to keep it holy'" (Exod. 20:8):

B.   Make it holy[101] at night.

C.   How does one know from Scripture that if he did not sanctify it at night, he may sanctify it at any point in the day?

D.   Scripture states, "'Remember the sabbath day and keep it holy'" (Exod. 20:8).

6.   A.   Another interpretation:

B.   "'... and keep it holy'" (Exod. 20:8):

C.   With what do you sanctify it?

D.   With food and with drink and with clean clothing.

E.   For your *Shabbat* meal should not be like your weekday meal, and your *Shabbat* garment should not be like your weekday garment.

F.   And how does one know from Scripture that even a poor person's *Shabbat* meal should not be like his weekday meal, and a rich person's *Shabbat* meal should not be like his weekday meal?

G.   Scripture states, "'Remember the sabbath day and keep it holy'" (Exod. 20:8).

7.   A.   "'Six days you shall labor (and do all your work)'" (Exod. 20:9):

B.   Rabbi says, "Behold, this is a different decree! For just as Israel was commanded about the positive commandment[102] of [observance of] *Shabbat*, likewise were they commanded about labor."

C.   R. Eliezer ben Azariah says, "So great is labor that God's presence did not dwell among Israel until they had performed labor.

D.   "As it says in Scripture, 'And let them make Me a sanctuary, and I will dwell among them' (Exod. 25:8)."

E.   R. Yosi ha-Galili says, "So great is labor that God only decrees death over someone on account of cessation of work.

F.   "As it says in Scripture, 'Then he breathed his last and died, and was gathered to his kin' (Gen. 25:17)."

G.   R. Akiva says, "So great is labor that he who enjoys [inappropriately even only] a *perutah* from the consecrated temple property brings [culpability] for unlawful use of sacred

---

[101] I.e., sanctify it.
[102] I.e., a commandment that prescribes an action.

שלישי בשבת רביעי בשבת חמישי בשבת וערב שבת ◆

ת״ל זכור. ◆ את יום ◆ אין לי אלא יום לילה מנין ◆ ת״ל    C/B/A 4   C

לקדשו ◆ ‹אם כן› מה ת״ל יום ◆ כבוד יום קודם לכבוד    E/D

לילה. ◆ לקדשו ◆ בלילה קדשו. ◆ מנין שאם לא קידש    C/B/A 5

בלילה מקדש והולך כל היום ◆ ת״ל זכור את יום השבת    D

לקדשו. ◆ ד״א ◆ לקדשו ◆ במה אתה מקדשו ◆ במאכל    D/C/B/A 6

ובמשקה ובכסות נקייה ◆ שלא תהא סעודתך שלשבת    E

כסעודת החול ולא עטיפתך שלשבת כעטיפתך בחול. ◆

ומנין שאפלו עני לא יהא מאכלו שלשבת כמאכלו    F

שלחול ועשיר לא יהא מאכלו שלשבת כמאכל החול ◆

ת״ל זכור את יום השבת לקדשו. ◆    G

     ששת ימים תעבד ◆ ר׳ אומר הרי זו גזירה אחרת    B/A 7

שכשם שנצטוו ישראל על מצות עשה שלשבת כך

נצטוו על המלאכה. ◆ ר׳ אלעזר בן עזריה אומר גדולה    C

מלאכה שלא שרת שכינה בישראל עד שעשו מלאכה ◆

שנ׳ ועשו לי מקדש ושכנתי בתוכם (שמ׳ כה ח). ◆ ר׳ יוסי    F/D

הגלילי אומר גדולה מלאכה שלא קנס המקום מיתה

על אדם אלא אלא מתוך בטילה ◆ שנ׳ ויגוע וימת ויאסף אל    F

עמיו (בר׳ כה יז). ◆ ר׳ עקיבה אומר גדולה מלאכה שהרי    G

נהנה שווה פרוטה מן ההקדש מביא מעילה וחומשה

property [and must pay the fine of an additional] one-fifth and must offer up a guilt offering of two *sela*. But the laborers, who work with consecrated items, take of their reward from the heave offering of the temple treasury!"

H.    R. Shimon says, "So great is labor that if even the High Priest enters [the Holy of Holies] on the Day of Atonement at an hour not for worship, he is culpable for death. But at an hour for labor, [even] impure and blemished [priests] are permitted to enter."

8.    A.    "'Six days you shall labor and do all your work'" (Exod. 20:9):

B.    This is what the House of Shammai says:

C.    "Ink, dyestuffs, or vetches may not be soaked [on a Friday] unless there is time for them to be [entirely] soaked the same day.[103]

D.    "Nets may not be spread [on a Friday] for wild animals or birds unless there is time for them to be caught the same day.[104]

E.    "Olive-press beams and winepress rollers may not be laid down [on a Friday] unless there is time for them to drip [entirely] the same day.[105]

F.    "Water may not be conducted into a garden [on a Friday] unless it can be filled [entirely] the same day.[106]

G.    "Meat and onions and eggs may not be placed [on a Friday] on top of the fire nor a dish in the oven unless there is time for them to be [entirely] cooked the same day."[107]

H.    But the House of Hillel permits all of them.

I.    But the House of Shammai says, "'Six days you shall labor and do all your work' (Exod. 20:9).

J.    "[Which means] that all of your work should be completed on the eve of *Shabbat*."

K.    But the House of Hillel says, "'Six days you shall labor' (Exod. 20:9):

L.    "[Which means that] you do it all six [days], and the rest of your work can be done by itself on *Shabbat*.

M.    "'... and do all your work' (Exod. 20:9):

N.    "[Which means that] on *Shabbat* you should be like someone who has no work to do."

9.    A.    "'But the seventh day is a sabbath (of the Lord your God. You shall not do any work—you,
[150]       your son or daughter, your male or female slave, or your cattle, or the stranger who is within your settlements)'" (Exod. 20:10):[108]

B.    I only know from this concerning the positive commandment[109] [of *Shabbat* observance]. How does one know from Scripture concerning the negative commandment?[110]

C.    Scripture states, "'... you shall not do any work'" (Exod. 20:10).

D.    I only know from this concerning the positive commandment and the negative commandment [of *Shabbat* observance]. How does one know from Scripture concerning [the culpability] of death [incurred for *Shabbat* transgression]?

E.    Scripture states, "Whoever does work on the sabbath day shall be put to death" (Exod. 31:15).

---

[103] Compare 8.C with m. Shabbat 1:5.
[104] Compare 8.D with m. Shabbat 1:6.
[105] Compare 8.E with m. Shabbat 1:9.
[106] Compare 8.F with t. Shabbat 1:23.
[107] Compare 8.G with m. Shabbat 1:10.
[108] Compare 9.A–L with *Mekhilta de-Rabbi Ishmael*, Baḥodesh (H/R, 230:4–9; Laut., vol. 2, 254:80–89; Neus., LIII:II:11.A–12.E).
[109] I.e., a commandment that prescribes an action.

ומביא אשם בשתי סלעים והפועלין שהיו עושין

H  בהקדש נוטלין שכרן מתרומת הלשכה. ◆ ר' שמעון

אומר גדולה מלאכה שאפלו כהן גדול נכנס ביום

הכפורים שלא בשעת עבודה חייב מיתה ובשעת

A  8  עבודה טמאין ובעלי מומין מותרין להיכנס. ◆ ששת

B  ימים תעבד ועשית כל מלאכתך ◆ זו היא שבית שמאי

C  אומרין ◆ אין שורין דיו וסמנין וכרשינין אלא כדי

D  שישורו מבעוד יום ◆ ואין פורשין מצודות חיות ועופות

E  אלא כדי שיצודו מבעוד יום. ◆ ואין טוענין בקורת בית

F  הבד ובעיגולי הגת אלא כדי שיזובו מבעוד יום. ◆ ואין

פותקין מים לגנות אלא כדי שתתמלא מבעוד יום

G  ואין נותנין בשר בצל וביצה על גבי האש ולא תבשיל

H  לתוך התנור אלא כדי שיצלו מבעוד יום ◆ ובית הלל

I  מתירין בכולן ◆ אלא שבית שמאי אומ' ששת ימים

J  תעבד ועשית כל מלאכתך ◆ שתהא מלאכתך גמורה

L/K  מערב שבת ◆ ובית הלל אומרין ששת ימים תעבד ◆ עושה

אתה כל ששה ושאר מלאכתך היא נעשית מאיליה

N/M  בשבת ◆ ועשית כל מלאכתך ◆ שתהא בשבת כמי שאין

לו מלאכה. ◆

B/A  9  ויום השביעי שבת ◆ אין לי אלא מצות עשה מצות

D/C  לא תעשה מנין ◆ ת"ל לא תעשה כל מלאכה. ◆ אין לי

E  אלא מצות עשה ומצות לא תעשה מיתה מנין ◆ ת"ל כל

העושה מלאכה ביום השבת מות יומת (שמ' לא טו). ◆

---

[110] I.e., a commandment that proscribes an action.

F. We've heard [from Scripture] about the punishment, but we haven't heard the warning.

G. Scripture states, "The Israelite people shall keep the sabbath" (Exod. 31:16).

H. I only know from this concerning the punishment for and warning against work during the day. How does one know from Scripture about the punishment for and warning against work during the night?

I. Scripture states, "... from evening to evening" (Lev. 23:32).

J. If it[111] is not addressing the nights of the Days of Atonement, then let it address the nights of *Shabbatot*.

K. I only know from this concerning the positive commandment and the negative commandment [of *Shabbat* observance]. How does one know from Scripture concerning [the culpability] of death [incurred for *Shabbat* transgression]?

L. Scripture states, "He who profanes it shall be put to death" (Exod. 31:14).

### (Textual Source: Ms. Cambridge T-S C 4a.2)

10. A. "'You shall not do any work'" (Exod. 20:10):

B. One might think he should not clean a vegetable, rinse the dishes, or make the beds!

C. Scripture states, [however,] "'... work'" (Exod. 20:10).

D. Scripture states here "work" and Scripture states "work" concerning the Tent of Meeting (Exod. 35:21).

E. Just as the work stated about the Tent of Meeting is work accompanied by forethought, likewise the work stated about *Shabbat* is work accompanied by forethought.

F. And the rest as written above.[112]

11. A. "'... you, your son or daughter'" (Exod. 20:10):[113]

B. One might think [the prohibition of work on *Shabbat* applies only to] one's adult son and daughter.

C. Since Scripture says, "'... you'" (Exod. 20:10), behold, one's adult son and daughter are [also] said.[114]

D. Why does Scripture state, "'... your son or daughter'" (Exod. 20:9)?

E. These are one's young son or daughter.

F. One should not say to his young son, "Go bring me this vessel from the market. Go bring me this fruit basket from the market!"

G. One might think he should follow after them, so that they don't break vessels or throw pebbles [thus violating *Shabbat*].

H. Scripture states, [however,] "'... you ...'" (Exod. 20:9).

I. Just as you have your own mind [and do] your own work, likewise they have their own mind and do their own work.

12. A. Let Scripture state [only] "'son'" [in Exod. 20:9]! Why does Scripture state [also], "'... daughter'" (Exod. 20:9)?[115]

B. Because there is something about a son that is not so with a daughter, and there is

---
[111] I.e., the prohibition of labor on the Day of Atonement referenced in Lev. 23:32.

[112] See above XI:I:3.A–P.

[113] Compare 11.A–I with *Mekhilta de-Rabbi Ishmael*, Baḥodesh (H/R, 230:10–13; Laut., vol. 2, 254:90–93; Neus., LIII:II:13.A–F).

עונש שמענו אזהרה לא שמענו • ת״ל ושמרו בני ישראל G/F

את השבת (פט״ז). • אין לי אלא עונש ואזהרה למלאכת H

יום עונש ואזהרה למלאכת לילה מנין • ת״ל מערב עד I

ערב (ויק׳ כג לב) • אם אינו ענין לילילי יום הכפורים J

תניהו ענין ללילי שבתות. • אין לי אלא מצות עשה K

ומצות לא תעשה מיתה מנין • ת״ל מחלליה מות יומת L

(שמ׳ לא יד). • לא תעשה כל מלאכה • יכול לא יקנב את B/A 10

הירק ולא ידיח את הכלים ולא יציע את המטות • תל׳ C

לו׳ מלאכה • נאמרה כאן מלאכה ונאמרה מלאכה D

במשכן (שמ׳ לה כא) • מה מלאכה האמורה במשכן E

מלאכה שיש עמה מחשבה אף מלאכה האמורה Γ

בשבת מלאכה שיש עמה מחשבה • וכו׳ כי היכי

דכתיבא לעיל. • אתה ובניך ובתך • יכול בנו ובתו B/A 11

הגדולים • כשהוא אומר אתה הרי בנו ובתו הגדולים C

אמורין • מה תל׳ לו׳ בנך ובתך • אלו בנו ובתו קטנים • E/D

שלא יאמר לבנו קטן הכניס לי כלי זה מן השוק F

הכניס לי כלכלה זו מן השוק. • יכול יחזר אחריהן שלא G

ישברו חרסים שלא ינתזו צרורות • תל׳ לו׳ אתה • מה I/H

אתה מדעת עצמך מלאכת עצמך אף הן מדעת עצמן

מלאכת עצמן. • יאמר בן מה תל׳ לו׳ בת • מפני שיש בבן B/A 12

---

[114] I.e., implied, because the "you" in the verse is an adult.
[115] Compare 12.A–E with *Sifra*, Emor 1:6 (Neus., CCXI:I:10.A–E).

something about a daughter that is not so with a son.

C.    [With] a son—his father is obligated with the commandments to circumcise him, to redeem him, and to teach him Torah and to teach him a trade-skill, and to marry him off to a wife—which is not the case with a daughter.

D.    [With] a daughter—her father has the right of possession of what she finds, what she makes with her hands, and of interference with her vows—which is not the case with a son.

E.    Thus, since there is something about a son that is not so with a daughter, and something about a daughter that is not so with a son, [Scripture] needed to say "son" and needed to say "daughter."

13.    A.    "'... your male or female slave'" (Exod. 20:10):

B.    One might think that Scripture speaks of [any] male and female slave.

C.    Scripture speaks [here] about Hebrew [slaves].

D.    Because Scripture states [elsewhere], "... so that your male and female slave may rest like you" (Deut. 5:14), [it implies that] there is a male and female slave that [should not rest] as you do.

[151]    E.    And which is this? This is the [alien] male and female slave that resides [among you].

14.    A.    "Which type of *Shabbat* rest are you obligated to provide them?[116]

B.    "... [manuscript lacuna] ... are permitted to work.

C.    "Scripture states, "'... or your cattle'" (Exod. 20:10). ... [manuscript lacuna] ...

D.    "One might think that they are forbidden to do work.

E.    "Scripture states, [however,] '... and that your male slave (and the stranger may be refreshed)' (Exod. 23:12). ... [manuscript lacuna] ...

F.    "... the cattle.

G.    "Say from this that the resident stranger and the resident slave may perform [the type of] work on *Shabbat* that the Jew [may perform] on a festival day."—The words of R. Yosi ha-Galili.

H.    R. Akiva says, "'... and that your male slave (and the stranger may be refreshed)' (Exod. 23:12)

I.    "[Scripture] is lenient with them. In accordance with what is said in Scripture, 'Your people are scattered over the hills' (Nah. 3:18).

J.    "Say from this that the resident stranger and the resident slave may perform [the type of] work on *Shabbat* that the Jew [may perform] on the intermediate days of a festival."

K.    R. Yosi says, "One verse states 'your stranger and your cattle' (Exod. 20:10) and one verse states '... that your slave and the stranger may be refreshed' (Exod. 23:12).

L.    "Say from this that the resident stranger may perform [the type of] work on *Shabbat* that the Jew [may perform] on the intermediate days of a festival, and the resident slave may perform [the type of] work on *Shabbat* that the Jew [may perform] on a normal day."

M.    R. Shimon says, "Both resident stranger and resident slave may perform [the type of] work on *Shabbat* that the Jew [may perform] on a normal day."

[116] I.e., to different types of slaves.

| | | |
|---|---|---|
| C | | מה שאין בבת ויש בבת מה שאין בבן. ◆ בן אביו חייב |
| | | בו מצוות למולו ולפדותו וללמדו תורה וללמדו |
| D | | אומנות ולהשיאו אשה מה שאין כן בבת. ◆ בת אביה |
| | | זכאי במציאתה ובמעשה ידיה ובהפר נדריה מה שאין |
| E | | כן בבן. ◆ הא מפני שיש בבן שאין בבת ובבת שאין בן |
| B/A | 13 | צרך לומר בבן וצרך לומר בבת. ◆ ועבדך ואמתך ◆ יכול |
| D/C | | בעבד ואמה ◆ העבריים הכת' מדבר ◆ כשהוא אומר למען |
| | | ינוח עבדך [ואמת]ך כמוך יש עבד ואמה [שאינו כמוך ◆ |
| A 14 | E | ואיזה זה עבד ואמה] התושבים ◆ לאיזו שביתה אתה |
| C/B | | מחייבם...] ◆ מותרין במלאכה ◆ תל' לו' ובהמתך א]... ◆ |
| E/D | | יכול] הן יהו אסורין במלאכה ◆ תל' לו' וינפש בן |
| G/F | | אמתך (שמ' כג יב)...] ◆ הבהמה ◆ [אמ]ור מעתה גר |
| | | ותושב ועבד ו[תושב עושין מלאכה בשבת כיש'] ביום |
| H | | [טוב] דברי ר' יוסי הגלילי ◆ ר' עקיבא או' [וינפש בן |
| I | | אמתך] הרויח [לה]ן כעניין שנ' ונפושו עמך על ההרים |
| J | | (נחום ג יח) ◆ [...אמור] מ[עת]ה גר תושב ועבד תושב |
| K | | עושין מלאכה ב[שבת כיש' בחולו] שלמועד: ◆ ר' יוסי |
| | | או כתוב אחד או' גרך ובהמתך וכתוב אחד או' וינפש |
| L | | בן אמתך והגר הנח לו ◆ אמ[ור] [מ]עתה גר תושב |
| | | עושה מלאכה בשבת כיש' [בחולו שלמועד] עבד תושב |
| M | | עושה מלאכה בשבת כיש' בחול: ◆ ר' שמעון או' אחד גר |
| | | תושב ואחד עבד תושב עושין מלאכה בשבת כיש' בחול. ◆ |

15.    A.    "'... or your cattle'" (Exod. 20:10):

       B.    Why do I need [to hear this]?

       C.    If you teach that [it states this to emphasize that] one may not perform work with it [on *Shabbat*], behold Scripture already has stated "'... you shall not do any work'" (Exod. 20:10)!

       D.    Why does Scripture state, "'... or your cattle'" (Exod. 20:10)?

       E.    [To teach] that one may not rent his cattle to a non-Jew, nor may he lend it—it may not carry a load on *Shabbat*.

       F.    One might think he could push its head down and make it feed, or grab some grass for it so it will eat.

       G.    Scripture states, [however,] "'... you'" (Exod. 20:10).

       H.    One might think he should follow after it, so that it won't tear [something] or uproot [something and eat it, thus violating *Shabbat*].

       I.    Scripture states, [however,] "'... you'" (Exod. 20:10).

       J.    Just as you have your own mind [and do] your own work, likewise they have their own mind and do their own work.

16.    A.    "'... or the stranger who is within your settlements'" (Exod. 20:10):[117]

       B.    If Scripture speaks about the righteous stranger, it has already been stated, "There shall be one law for you—the congregation—and for the stranger who resides" (Num. 15:15).

       C.    So how do I justify "'... or the stranger'" (Exod. 20:10)?

       D.    Scripture speaks about the resident alien.

17.    A.    "'(For in six days the Lord made heaven and earth) and the sea, and all that is in them, (and He rested on the seventh day. Therefore the Lord blessed the sabbath day and hallowed it)'" (Exod. 20:11):

       B.    Wasn't the sea part of the overall act of Creation?

       C.    Rather, this tells that the praiseworthiness of the sea corresponds to [the praiseworthiness of] the entire act of Creation!

       D.    Similar to this, you say: "... and the Leviathan that You formed to sport with" (Ps. 104:26).

       E.    Wasn't the Leviathan part of the overall Creation of [things] in the sea?

       F.    Rather, this tells that the praiseworthiness of the Leviathan corresponds to [the praiseworthiness of] the entire act of Creation!

18.    A.    "'... and He rested on the seventh day'" (Exod. 20:11):

       B.    This teaches that rest wasn't created until the seventh day.

       C.    One might think [God rests on *Shabbat*] even from judgment.

       D.    Scripture states, [however,] "... (and on the seventh day He ceased from work) and was refreshed" (Exod. 31:17).

       E.    This tells that judgment does not ever cease before Him.

       F.    And thus Scripture states, "Righteousness and justice are the base of Your throne" (Ps. 89:15).

---

[117] Compare 16.A–17.F with *Mekhilta de-Rabbi Ishmael,* Baḥodesh (H/R, 230:13–15; Laut., vol. 2, 255:97–102; Neus., LIII:II:15.A–16.B).

| | |
|---|---|
| C/B/A | 15 |
| | ובהמתך ◆ למה אני צריך ◆ אם לימד שלא |
| | יעשה בה מלאכה הרי כבר נאמר לא תעשה כל |
| E/D | מלאכה ◆ מה תל׳ לו׳ ובהמתך ◆ לא ישכיר אדם בהמתו |
| F | לגוי ולא ישאילנו ושלא תצא במשוי בשבת ◆ ‹יכול |
| G | ירכין לה יתר ותאכל ויאחז לה עשבים ותאכל ◆ תל׳ לו׳ |
| H | אתה. ◆ יכול יחזר אחריה שלא תהיה תולשת ועוקרת ◆ |
| J/I | תל׳ לו׳ אתה ◆ מה אתה מדעת עצמך מלאכת עצמך אף |
| A | 16 |
| | היא מדעת עצמה מלאכת עצמה.› ◆ וגרך אשר |
| B | בשעריך ◆ אם בגר צדק הכת׳ מדבר כבר אמור הקהל |
| C | חקה אחת לכם ולגר הגר (במ׳ טו טו) ◆ הא מה אני |
| D | מקיים וגרך ◆ בגר תושב הכת׳ מדבר. |
| B/A | 17 |
| | את הים ואת כל אשר בם ◆ והלא ים בכלל מעשה |
| C | בראשית היה ◆ אלא מגיד שייש שבח בים כנגד כל |
| D | מעשה בראשית. ◆ כיוצא בו אתה אומר לויתן זה יצרת |
| E | לשחק בו (תה׳ קד כו) ◆ והלא לויתן בכלל מעשים |
| F | שבים היה ◆ אלא מגיד שייש שבח בלויתן כנגד כל |
| B/A | 18 |
| | מעשים שבים. ◆ וינח ביום השביעי ◆ מלמד שלא נבראת |
| D/C | הנחה אלא עד יום השביעי. ◆ ‹יכול אף מן הדין ◆ תל׳ |
| F/E | לומ׳ וינפש ◆ מגיד שאין הדין בטל מפניו לעולם ◆ וכן |
| | הוא אומר צדק ומשפט מכון כסאך וגו׳ (תה׳ פט טו).› ◆ |

(Textual Source: Ms. Cambridge T-S C 4a.5)

19.    A.    "'Therefore the Lord blessed the sabbath day and hallowed it'" (Exod. 20:11):[118]

[152]    B.    With what did He bless it?

C.    He blessed it with manna and sanctified it with manna.

D.    Concerning every weekday [in the desert] Scripture says, "… an *omer* to a person" (Exod. 16:16).

E.    But concerning *Shabbat* Scripture says, "… two *omers*" (Exod. 16:22).

F.    Concerning every weekday Scripture says, "… and it stank" (Exod. 16:20).

G.    But concerning *Shabbat* Scripture says, "… and it did not stink, and there were no maggots" (Exod. 16:24).

H.    One part of Scripture states, "… they gathered double the amount of food" (Exod. 16:22), and another part states, "… two *omers*" (Exod. 16:22).

I.    Scripture tells that [on *Shabbat*] it was doubly [appealing] in its taste and in its scent than on the other days.

## Chapter Fifty-Five

(Textual Source: Ms. Cambridge T-S C 4a.5)

LV:I

1.    A.    "'Honor your father and your mother, (that you may long endure on the land that the Lord your God is assigning to you)'" (Exod. 20:12):[119]

B.    I don't know what this honoring is.

C.    Since Scripture says, "Honor the Lord with your wealth" (Prov. 3:9), you say from this [that honoring consists of] food, drink, clothing, shelter, hospitality, and deference.

2.    A.    Scripture says here, "'Honor your father and your mother'" (Exod. 20:12), and Scripture says farther on, "Honor the Lord with your wealth" (Prov. 3:9).

B.    Honor of father and mother is equated with honor of God.

C.    Scripture says, "You shall each fear his mother and father" (Lev. 19:3), and Scripture says,

(Textual Source: Sifra)

"Fear only the Lord" (Deut. 6:13).

D.    Fear of father and mother is equated with fear of God.

E.    Scripture says "He who curses his father and mother shall be put to death" (Lev. 20:9), and Scripture says, "If he pronounces the name Lord, he shall be put to death" (Lev. 24:16).

F.    Cursing of father and mother is equated with cursing of God.

G.    But it's not possible to talk about God and striking.[120]

H.    But it's logical [to make these equations], because the three of them are partners in creating him.[121]

---

[118] Compare 19.A–I with *Mekhilta de-Rabbi Ishmael*, Baḥodesh (H/R, 231:1–5; Laut., vol. 2, 256:112–19; Neus., LIII:II:18.A–G).

[119] Compare 1.A–2.H with *Mekhilta de-Rabbi Ishmael*, Baḥodesh (H/R, 231:6–232:13; Laut., vol. 2, 257:1–259:36; Neus., LIV:I:1–5.F). Compare 1.A–C with b. Kiddushin 31b (Neus., XIX.A:Qiddushin:1:7:II.23.A–E).

[120] See Exod. 21:15.

[121] Compare 2.H with b. Kiddushin 30b (Neus., XIX.A:Qiddushin:1:7:II.3.A–B).

| | | |
|---|---|---|
| על [כן ברך ה' את יום השבת ויקדש]הו ◆ במה | B/A | 19 |
| ברכו ◆ ברכו במן וקידשו במן ◆ [בכל יום הוא או' ע]מר | D/C | |
| לגלגלת (שמ' טז טז) ◆ ובשבת הוא או' שני העמר (שם | E | |
| כב) ◆ [בכל יום הוא או' וי]באש (שם כ) ◆ וביום השבת | G/F | |
| הוא או' ולא הבאיש [ורמה לא היתה] בו (שם כד) ◆ | | |
| כתוב אחד או' לקטו ל[חם] משנה (שם כב) וכתוב | H | |
| [אחד או' שני העמר] ◆ מגיד הכתוב שהיה משונה | I | |
| [בט]עמו [ובריחו משא]ר ימים ◆ | | |

| | | |
|---|---|---|
| כבד את אביך ואת א[מך] ◆ כיבוד [זה איני יודע | B/A | 1 |
| מהוא] ◆ כשהוא או' כבד את יי מהונך (מש' ג ט) אמו]ר | C | |
| מ[עתה [מאכיל ומשקה ומל]ביש ומכסה מכניס | | |
| ומוציא ◆ נא' כן כבד את [אביך ואת אמך] ונא' לחלן | A | ? |
| כבד את יי מהונך ◆ שקול כיבוד אב [ואם ככיבוד] | B | |
| המקום ◆ נא' איש אמו ואביו תיראו (ויק' יט ג) ונא' את | C | |
| ‹ה' אלקיך תירא (דב' ו יג) ◆ שקול מורא אב ואם | D | |
| כמוצא המקום. ◆ נא' מקלל אביו ואמו מות יומת (שמ' | E | |
| כא יז) ונא' ונקב שם ה' מות יומת (ויק' כד טז) ◆ שקולה | F | |
| קללת אב ואם כקללת המקום ◆ אבל אי אפשר לומר מכה | G | |
| כלפי מעלה ◆ וכן בדין מפני ששלשתם שותפים בו›. ◆ | H | |

(Textual Source: Ms. Cambridge T-S C 4a.5)

3.     A.    "'... that you may long endure on the land'" (Exod. 20:12):

       B.    And not in exile and not in [foreign] settlements. ... [manuscript lacuna] ...

## LV:II

1.     A.    "'You shall not murder'" (Exod. 20:13):

       B.    When it says in Scripture, "... the murderer must be put to death" (Num. 35:16), we learn about the punishment. How does one know from Scripture about the [requirement that a] warning [about both the prohibition and the punishment be provided to one who is about to transgress]?

       C.    Scripture states, "'You shall not murder'" (Exod. 20:13).

       D.    How does one know from Scripture that it is permitted [to put the murderer to death without a warning about the punishment] if he said, "Behold, I will murder in order to be put to death"?

       E.    Scripture states, "'You shall not murder'" (Exod. 20:13).

2.     A.    "'You shall not commit adultery'" (Exod. 20:13):

[153]    B.    When it says in Scripture, "... the adulterer and the adulteress must be put to death" (Lev. 20:10), we learn about the punishment. How does one know from Scripture about the [requirement that a] warning [about both the prohibition and the punishment be provided to one about to transgress]?

       C.    Scripture states, "'You shall not commit adultery'" (Exod. 20:13).

       D.    How does one know from Scripture that it is permitted [to put the adulterer to death without a warning about the punishment] if he said, "Behold, I will commit adultery in order to be put to death"?

       E.    Scripture states, "'You shall not commit adultery'" (Exod. 20:13).

       F.    How does one know from Scripture that it is permitted for one to eat from his dish while picturing himself eating from his neighbor's dish, or to drink from his cup while picturing himself drinking from his neighbor's cup?[122]

       G.    Scripture states, "'You shall not commit adultery'" (Exod. 20:13).

3.     A.    "'You shall not steal'" (Exod. 20:13):[123]

       B.    [Not] in order to cause grief, or to repay double restitution, or fourfold or fivefold restitution.

       C.    Ben Bag Bag says, "Don't carry off something [secretly] of yours from another's house, lest you look like a thief. Rather, break his teeth and say to him, 'I'm taking that which is mine!'"

4.     A.    "'You shall not bear false witness against your neighbor'" (Exod. 20:13):

       B.    "Bear false witness" means only to fabricate.

       C.    How so?

       D.    One who deposits something gold with someone should not tell him it's a gem, or [one who deposits] a gem should not tell him it's gold.

---

[122] The text employs here rather transparent sexual euphemisms.
[123] Compare 3.A–C with t. Baba Kamma 10:37–38; *Sifra*, Qedoshim 2:2 (Neus., CXCIX:I:2.A–C); and y. Sanhedrin 26b (Neus., 8:3:I.A–G).

למען יאריכון ימיך על האדמה ◆ ולא בגולה ולא     B/A    3

בתושבות. ◆

LV:II

לא תרצח ◆ מכלל שנ' מות יומת הרוצח (במ' לה     B/A    1

טז) למדנו עונש אזהרה מנין תל' לו' לא תרצח. מנין

אמר הריני רוצח על מנת ליהרג הרי זה מותרה ◆ תל'     C

לו' לא תרצח. ◆ מנין ליוצא ליהרג ואמר הריני רוצח הרי     D

זה מותרה ◆ תל' לו' לא תרצח. ◆ לא תנאף ◆ מכלל שנ' מות     B/A 2    E

יומת הנאף והנאפת (ויק' כ י) למדנו ענש אזהרה מנין ◆

תל' לו' לא תנאף. ◆ מנין אמר הריני נואף על מנת ליהרג     D/C

הרי זה מותרה ◆ תל' לו' לא תנאף. ◆ מנין האוכל בקערו     F/E

ורואה את עצמו כאלו אוכל בקערה שלחבירו והיה

שותה בכוסו ורואה את עצמו כאלו הוא שותה

[ב]כוסו שלח[ברו]בירו הרי זה מותרה ◆ ת"ל לא תנאף] ◆ [לא     A 3    G

תגנוב ◆ על] מנת למיקט לא [תגנוב] על מ[נ]ת לשלם     B

תשלומי כפל ותשלומי ארבעה] וחמש[ה]. ◆ בן בג בג או'     C

אל תטול [את שלך מבית אחרים שמא תראה] גונב אלא

שבור את שניו וא[מור לו שלי אני נוטל. ◆ לא תענה     A    4

ברעך] עד שקר ◆ אין שקר אלא מבדה ◆ כי צד ◆ הפ[ן]קיד     D/C/B

לו זהב לא יאמר לו] מרגלית מרג' לא יאמר לו זהב ◆

5.  A.  Because it says in Scripture, "... you should do to him as he schemed to do to his fellow" (Deut. 19:19).[124]

    B.  [It means, if he schemed with] wealth, [you should gain retribution with] wealth. [If with] blows, [then gain retribution with] blows. [If with] penalties, [then with] penalties.

    C.  We have heard the punishment. How does one know from Scripture about the warning?

    D.  Scripture states, "'You shall not bear false witness against your neighbor'" (Exod. 20:13).

LV:III

1.  A.  [Scripture states here] "'You shall not covet'" (Exod. 20:14), but Scripture states later on "'You shall not crave your neighbor's house'" (Deut. 5:18).

    B.  [This serves to] incur culpability for craving in and of itself and for coveting in and of itself.

    C.  What is craving? He who says to ... [manuscript lacuna] ...

    D.  [What is] coveting? He who hides precious things to take them.

    E.  How does one know from Scripture that the person who craves will eventually covet?

    F.  As it says in Scripture, "You shall not crave" and "You shall not covet."[125]

    G.  How does one know from Scripture that the person who covets will eventually steal?

    H.  As it says in Scripture, "They covet fields, and seize them" (Mic. 2:2).

2.  A.  One might think that if he doesn't crave his daughter, he may take her.

    B.  Scripture states, "'... your neighbor's wife'" (Exod. 20:14, Deut. 5:18).

    C.  Just as with your neighbor's wife—she is prohibited to you, so too with anything that is prohibited to you.

    D.  Perhaps just as with your neighbor's wife one is culpable over her for death by the court, so too might I conclude that only [prohibited is] something for which one is culpable for death by the court?

    E.  Scripture states, [however,] his "house" and "his field" (Deut. 5:18).

    F.  Perhaps just as these are unique, in that they are acquired by means of money, contract, or seizure, so too might I conclude that only [prohibited is] something that is acquired by means of money, contract, or seizure?

    G.  Scripture states, [however,] "... his male or female slave" (Exod. 20:14, Deut. 5:18).

    H.  Perhaps just as these are unique, in that they are like immovable property, so too might I conclude that only [prohibited is] something that is immovable property?

    I.  Scripture states, [however,] "... his ox or his ass" (Exod. 20:14, Deut. 5:18).

    J.  Perhaps just as these are unique, in that guarding them [vigilantly] is incumbent upon you, so too might I conclude that only [prohibited is] something [for] which guarding [vigilantly] is incumbent upon you?

    K.  How does one know from Scripture that one should not crave someone's staff, and one should not crave someone's shoe, and one should not crave someone's wallet?

[154]

---

[124] Compare 5.A–D with *Mekhilta de-Rabbi Ishmael*, Baḥodesh (H/R, 233:7–8; Laut., vol. 2, 261:66–68; Neus., LIV:II:5.A–D).

[125] It appears that the order of these biblical verses does not support the text's interpretation here, i.e., "You shall not crave" (Deut. 5:18) is stated after "You shall not covet" (Exod. 20:14).

| | |
|---|---|
| A 5 | מכלל שנ' [ועשיתם לו כאשר זמם] לעשות לאחיו |
| B | (דב' יט יט) ♦ אם ממון ממון ואם מ[כות מ]כות |
| D/C | [ואם עונשין עונשין] ♦ עונש שמענו אזהרה מנ' ♦ תל' לו' |
| | לא תענה [ברעך עד שקר] ♦ |

LV:III

| | | |
|---|---|---|
| A | 1 | לא תחמד] ולהלן הוא או' ♦ לא תתאוה בית רעך |
| B | | (דב' ה יז) ♦ לחייב ע[ל] תאוה בפני עצמה ועל] חמדה |
| D/C | | בפני עצמה ♦ איזו היא תאוה האומר לו[י' י ש...] ♦ חמדה |
| E | | הכובש כבושין ליטלן ♦ מנ' התאוה אד[ם] סופו לחמוד ♦ |
| G/F | | שנ'] לא תתאוה ולא תחמוד ♦ מנ' חמד אדם סופו |
| H | A 2 | [לגזול ♦ שנ' וחמדו] שדות וגזלו (מיכה ב ב) ♦ יכול לא |
| C/B | | יתאוה על בתו ליטלה ♦ תל' לו' אשת רעך ♦ מה אשת |
| D | | רעך שהיא אסורה לך אף כל דבר שאסור לך. ♦ או מה |
| | | אשת רעך שחייבין עליה מיתת בית דין אף אין לי |
| E | | אלא דבר שחייבין עליו מיתת בית דין ♦ תל' לו' ביתו |
| Γ | | ושדהו. ♦ או מה אלו מיוחדין שנקנין בכסף ובשטר |
| | | ובחזקה אף אין לי אלא דבר שנקנה בכסף ובשטר |
| H/G | | ובחזקה ♦ תל' לו' עבדו ואמתו. ♦ או מה אלו מיוחדין |
| | | דברים שהן כקרקע אף אין לי אלא דבר שהוא כקרקע ♦ |
| J/I | | תל' לו' שורו וחמורו. ♦ או מה אלו מיוחדין ששמירתן |
| K | | עליך אף אין לי אלא דבר ששמירתו עליך ♦ מנין לא |
| | | יתאוה למקלו ולא יתאוה למנעלו ולא יתאוה לפונדתו ♦ |

L. Scripture states, "'... or anything that is your neighbor's'" (Exod. 20:14, Deut. 5:18).

M. One might think one should not say, "If only my eye were like his eye! If only my gate were like his gate!"

N. Scripture states, [however,] "his ox" and "his ass," "his male slave" and "his female slave," "his house" and "his field" (Exod. 20:14, Deut. 5:18).

O. Just as these are unique things, in that they can come into your possession with your companion losing them, likewise I know only [that the prohibition extends] to something that can come into your possession with your companion losing them.

3. A. Another interpretation:

B. "'You shall not covet your neighbor's wife, or his male or female slave, etc.'" (Exod. 20:14):

C. Do you [really] have someone who covets all these things?

D. Rather, when he sleeps with his companion's wife, she bears a son and her husband thinks it is his son. As a result, he bequeaths him his house and his field and his male slave and his female slave and his ox and his ass and all that is his.

4. A. One might think he is not culpable unless he has transgressed all of them.[126]

B. Scripture states, [however,] "You shall not murder. You shall not commit adultery. You shall not steal. You shall not bear false witness. You shall not covet" [in order to stress that one] is culpable for each and every one in and of itself.

C. If so, why does Scripture state [again] later on, "You shall not murder. You shall not commit adultery. You shall not steal. You shall not bear false witness. You shall not covet" (Deut. 5:17)?

D. This tells that all of them effect each other. If someone transgresses one of them, he will ultimately transgress all of them.

E. If someone murders, he will ultimately commit adultery.

F. Scripture states, "My son, if sinners entice you, do not yield. If they say, 'Come with us ... throw in your lot with us, etc.'" (Prov. 1:10–14).

G. And how does one know from Scripture that if someone commits adultery, he will ultimately steal?

H. Scripture states, "When you see a thief, you fall in with him" (Ps. 50:18). What is written [after this]?—"and throw in your lot with adulterers" (Ps. 50:18).

I. How does one know from Scripture that if someone steals, he will ultimately come to give a false oath?

J. As it says in Scripture, "He who shares with a thief is his own enemy. He hears the imprecation and does not tell" (Prov. 29:24).

## Chapter Fifty-Six

### (Textual Source: Ms. Cambridge T-S C 4a.5)

LVI:I

1. A. "All the people witnessed (the thunder and lightning, the blare of the horn and the mountain smoking. And when the people saw it, they fell back and stood at a distance)" (Exod. 20:15):[127]

B. This teaches that there were not any blind people among them.

---

[126] I.e., all the commandments delineated in Exod. 20:13–14.

| | |
|---|---|
| M/L | תל' לו' וכל אשר לרעך. ◆ יכול לא יאמר לאוי |
| N | עיני כעינו לאוי שערי כשערו ◆ תל' לו' שורו וחמורו |
| O | עבדו ואמתו ביתו ושדהו ◆ מה אלו מיוחדין דברים |
| | שאפשר להן לבוא תחת ידיך וחבירך חסירן אף אין |
| | לי אלא דבר שאפשר לו לבוא תחת ידיך וחבירך |
| C/B/A 3 | חסירן. ◆ ד"א ◆ לא תחמד אשת רעך ועבדו ואמתו וגו' ◆ יש |
| D | לך מי שהוא חומד את כל הדברים האלו ◆ אלא מתוך |
| | שהוא בא על אשת חבירו ויולדת בן זכר בעלה סבור |
| | שהוא בנו נמצא מוריש לו ביתו ושדהו ועבדו ואמתו |
| A 4 | ושורו [וחמורו וכל אשר לו]. ◆ יכול לא י[הא חיי]ב עד |
| B | שיעבור [על כולן ◆ תל' לו' ◆ לא תרצח לא] תנאף לא |
| | תגנב לא תענה לא תחמד [לחייב על כל אחד ואחד |
| C | בפני] עצמו ◆ אם כן למה נא' להלן לא תרצח <ו>לא |
| | תנאף [ולא תגנב ולא תענה ולא תחמ]ד (דב' ה יז) ◆ |
| D | מגיד שכולן תפושין זה בזה פרץ אדם באחד [מהן |
| Г/E | סופו לפרוץ בכולן ◆ מנ'] רצח אדם סופו לנאוף ◆ תל' לו' |
| | בני אם יפתוך [חטאים אל תבא א[ם יא]מרו ל]כה |
| G | אתנו ג' גורלך תפיל ג' (מש' א יד) ◆ ומנ' נאף אדם סופו |
| H | [לגנוב ◆ תל' לו' ◆ אם ראית גנב ותירץ עמו (תה' נ יח) מה |
| I | כת' ועם מנאפים חלקך (שם) ◆ מנ' אם [גנב אדם סופו |
| J | לבוא לי]די שבועת שוא ◆ שנ' חולק עם גנב שונא נפשו |
| | אלה [ישמע ולא יגיד (מש' כט כד). ◆ |

LVI:I

| | |
|---|---|
| B/A 1 | וכל העם] ראים ג' ◆ מלמד שלא היה בהן סומין ◆ |

---

[127] Compare 1.A–H with *Mekhilta de-Rabbi Ishmael*, Baḥodesh (H/R, 235:15–19; Laut., vol. 2, 267:14–268:22; Neus., LV:I:6.A–10.B).

C. Because it says in Scripture, "You have been shown, in order to know that the Lord alone is God, etc." (Deut. 4:35), this teaches that there were not any stupid people among them.

D. Because it says in Scripture, "From the heavens He let you hear, etc." (Deut. 4:36), this teaches that there were not any deaf people among them.

E. Because it says in Scripture, "All the people answered as one" (Exod. 19:8), this teaches that there were not any speechless people among them.

F. Because it says in Scripture, "You stand this day (all of you)" (Deut. 29:9), this teaches that there were not any lame people among them.

G. And how does one know from Scripture that none among them worried for his head or worried for his teeth?

H. Scripture states, "... none among their tribes faltered" (Ps. 105:37).

2. A. "... the thunder and lightning" (Exod. 20:15):[128]

B. Normally it is impossible to see thunder, but here "(all the people witnessed) the thunder and the lightning" (Exod. 20:15)!

C. Just as they saw the lightning, so too did they see the thunder!

3. A. "And when (the people) saw" (Exod. 20:15):[129]

B. What did they see? They saw the glory of God.

C. R. Eliezer says, "How does one know from Scripture that a female slave by the sea saw that which the greatest of prophets did not see?

[155] D. "Scripture states, 'And when (the people) saw' (Exod. 20:15).

E. "What did they see? They saw the glory of God."

4. A. "... they fell back" (Exod. 20:15):

B. "Falling back" means only swaying.

C. Thus Scripture says, "The earth is swaying like a drunkard" (Isa. 24:20). And Scripture says, "... their hearts and the hearts of their people trembled as trees of the forest sway before a wind" (Isa. 7:2).

5. A. "They said to Moses, 'You speak to us and we will obey. (But let not God speak to us, lest we die)'" (Exod. 20:16):[130]

B. For this they merited having prophets arise for them.

C. And thus Scripture states, "The Lord your God will raise up for you a prophet from among your own people" (Deut. 18:15).

D. However, once they mocked the messengers of God, the Holy Spirit was cut off from them.

E. Thus Scripture states, "But they mocked the messengers of God ..." (2 Chron. 36:16).

6. A. "'But let not God speak to us, lest we die'" (Exod. 20:16):

B. If one word [from God] was added toward them, they would have died ... [manuscript lacuna] ...

---

[128] Compare 2.A–C with *Mekhilta de-Rabbi Ishmael*, Baḥodesh (H/R, 235:8–10; Laut., vol. 2, 266:1–5; Neus., LV:I:1.A–C).

[129] Compare 3.A–E with parallel above at XXIX:I:8.A–F.

[130] Compare 5.A–E with *Mekhilta de-Rabbi Ishmael*, Baḥodesh (H/R, 237:3–5; Laut., vol. 2, 271:66–70; Neus., LV:I:19.A–E); and *Sifre Deut.*, Piska 176 (Hammer, p. 202; Neus., CLXXVI:I:1.A–C).

מכלל שנ' אתה [הראית לדעת כי ייי] הוא האים ג'    C

(דב' ד לה) מלמד שלא היו בהן טיפשים • כיוצא [בו    D

מכלל שנ' מן ה]שמים השמיעך ג' (שם לו) מלמד

שלא היו בהם חרשים • מכלל שנ' ויענו כל העם יחדו    E

מלמד שלא היו בהן אלמים. • מכלל שנ' אתם נצבים    F

(דב' כט ט) מלמד שלא היו בהן חגרים. • ומנין שלא    G

היו בהן אחד חושש בראשו וחש בשניו • תל' לו' ואין    H

בשבטיו כושל (תה' קה לז). • את הקולות ואת    A    2

הלפידים • בנוהג שבעולם אי אפשר לראות את הקול    B

אבל כן את הקולות ואת הלפידים • כשם שראו את    C

הלפידים כך ראו את הקולות. • וירא העם • מה ראו    B/A    3

כבוד גדול ראו. • ר' אליעזר אומר מנין שראתה שפחה    C

בישראל מה שלא ראה גדול שבנביאים • תל' לו' וירא    D

העם • מה ראו כבוד גדול ראו. • וינועו • אין לשון ניעה    B/A  4  E

אלא טירוף • כן הוא או' נוע תנוע ארץ כשכור (ישע' כד    C

כ). ואו' וינע לבבו ולבב עמו כנוע עצי יער מפני רוח

(ישע' ז ב). • ♦

ויאמרו אל משה דבר אתה עמנו ונשמעה • בזו זכו    B/A    5

שיעמדו להם נביאים • וכן הוא אומר נביא מקרבך    C

מאחיך כמוני יקים לך ה' אלקיך (דב' יח טו) • אבל    D

משהיו מלעיבים במלאכי אלקים (דה"ב לו טז) פסקה

מהם רוח הקדש • כן הוא [או' ויהיו] מלעיבים במלאכי    E

[האלקים (דה"ב לו טז). • ואל ידבר עמנו אלקים פן    A    6

נמות] • אם • [נ]תוספה להם ד[בר] אחד [מתים היו... •    B

C.   Rather, this teaches that they were stooped on their hands ... [manuscript lacuna] ...

The spirit flashed at them ... [manuscript lacuna] ...

7.     A.   R. Eliezer ben Perata says, "How does one know from Scripture that they were stooped ... [manuscript lacuna] ...

8.     A.   "Moses answered the people, 'Be not afraid, (for God has come only in order to test you, and in order that the fear of Him may be ever with you, so that you do not go astray)'" (Exod. 20:17):

B.   He said to them, "He didn't give you the Torah, and He didn't perform miracles and mighty deeds for you to bring you to your death!"

9.     A.   "'... in order to test you'" (Exod. 20:17):[131]

B.   [In order] to raise you above all the nations of the world.

C.   In accordance with what is said in Scripture, "... King Evilmerodach raised the head of (King Jehoiachin of Judah and released him from prison ... and gave him a throne above those of other kings)" (2 Kings 25:27).

10.    A.   Another interpretation:

B.   "'... in order to test you, etc.'" (Exod. 20:17):

C.   To exalt you with commandments.

D.   In accordance with what is said in Scripture, "[They shall be] like crown jewels glittering, etc." (Zech. 9:16). And Scripture says, "Give those who fear You a banner for rallying" (Ps. 60:6).

11.    A.   Another interpretation:

B.   "'... in order to test'" (Exod. 20:17):

C.   In the past you were transgressing inadvertently, but now you will be transgressing consciously! In the past you didn't know the future reward for the righteous and the future blow of the retribution for the wicked, but now you know the future reward for the righteous and the future blow of the retribution for the wicked.

12.    A.   "'... and in order that the fear of Him'" (Exod. 20:17):[132]

B.   Anyone who is bashful will not be quick to sin.

13.    A.   "So the people remained at a distance, while Moses approached the thick cloud (where God was)" (Exod. 20:18):[133]

B.   One might think [Moses approached] the innermost thick cloud or the outermost thick cloud.

C.   Scripture states, [however,] "... where God was" (Exod. 20:18).

D.   Say from this that there were two layers of thick cloud, and Moses walked between them until he arrived at the innermost thick cloud.

E.   And thus Scripture states, "Then Solomon declared: 'The Lord has chosen to abide in a thick cloud, etc.'" (1 Kings 8:12).

---

[131] Compare 9.A–C with *Mekhilta de-Rabbi Ishmael*, Baḥodesh (H/R, 237:15–16; Laut., vol. 2, 272:86–87; Neus., LV:I:24.A–B).
[132] Compare 12.A–B with *Mekhilta de-Rabbi Ishmael*, Baḥodesh (H/R, 237:17–18; Laut., vol. 2, 272:90–92; Neus., LV:I:26.A–C).
[133] Compare 13.A–E with *Mekhilta de-Rabbi Ishmael*, Baḥodesh (H/R, 238:9–11; Laut., vol. 2, 274:114–17; Neus., LV:I:29.A–D).

| | | |
|---|---|---|
| C | | אלא] [מל]מד שהיו שוחיין בידם [...] [שהרו]ח |
| A | 7 | נבזקת בהם מ[... ✦ ר' אלעזר] בן פרטא או' מנין שהיו שוחין עימ... ✦ |
| B/A | 8 | [ויאמר משה] אל העם אל תיראו ✦ אמר להם לא נתן לכם [את התורה ולא עשה לכם נסים] וגבורות |
| A | 9 | אלא) לבוא ולמותכן ✦ כי לבעבור נס]ות אתכם ✦ |
| C/B | | לגדלכם על כל] אומות העולם ✦ כעינין שנ' נשא אויל |
| B/A | 10 | מרודך (מ"ב כה כז) ✦ [דבר אחר ✦ כי לבעבור] נסות אתכם ג' ✦ לגדלכם במצות ✦ כעינין שנ' כי אב]ני נזר |
| D/C | | מתנוססות ג' (זכ' ט טז)] ואו' נתתה ליראיך נס |
| B/A | 11 | להתנוסס ג' (תה' ס ו). ✦ דבר אחר ✦ כ]י ל[בע]בור נסות אתכם ✦ לשעבר] הייתם שוגגין עכשיו אתם מזידין |
| C | | לשעבר לא הייתם [יודעין מתן] שכרן שלצדיקים ומחת פורענותן שלרשעים לעתיד לבוא [עכשיו] אתם יודעין מתן שכרן שלצדיקים ומחת פורענותן של[רשעים] לעתיד לבוא ✦ ובעבור תהיה יראתו ✦ כל מי |
| B/A | 12 | שיש בו בו[שת פנים] לא במהרה הוא חוטא ✦ |
| B/A | 13 | ויעמד העם מרחוק ומשה ני[גש אל ה]ער ✦ <יכול |
| C | | לערפל הפנימי או לערפל החיצון ✦ תל' לו' אשר שם |
| D | | האלקים ✦ אמור מעתה שתי חומות של ערפל היו והיה |
| E | | משה מהלך ביניהן עד שמגיע לערפל הפנימי> ✦ וכן הוא או' בשלמה אז אמר שלמה יי אמר לשכן בע' ג' (מ"א ח יב) ✦ |

*Chapter Fifty-Seven*

(Textual Source: Ms. Cambridge T-S C 4a.2)

LVII:I

1.    A.    ["'Make for Me an altar of earth and sacrifice on it your burnt offerings and your sacrifices of well-being, your sheep and your oxen. In every place where I cause My name to be mentioned I will come to you and bless you'" (Exod. 20:21):]

      B.    Oh happy Moses! Oh happy son of Amram! What does Scripture say about you?

[156]    C.    "'Make for Me an altar of earth'" (Exod. 20:21).

(Textual Source: Midrash ha-Gadol)

2.    A.    "One might think [the altar was] actually made [only] of earth.[134]

      B.    "Scripture states, [however,] 'You must build the altar of the Lord your God of whole stones' (Deut. 27:6).

      C.    "[God is saying,] 'When you enter the Land of Israel, make for Me an altar cemented with earth.'"—The words of R. Judah.

      D.    R. Meir says, "Beneath the enclosures it was hollowed out, and the altar was cemented with earth."

3.    A.    "'... and sacrifice on it'" (Exod. 20:21):[135]

      B.    One might think that a sacrifice should be on top of the altar.

      C.    Scripture states, [however,] "You shall offer your burnt offerings, both the flesh and the blood, on the altar of the Lord your God" (Deut. 12:27).

      D.    And [thus], a sacrifice is not on top of the altar of the Lord your God!

      E.    If so, why does Scripture state, "'... on it'" (Exod. 20:21)?

      F.    [It means] next to it.

      G.    In accordance with what is said, "Next to it the tribe of Manasseh" (Num. 2:20).[136]

4.    A.    How does one know from Scripture that if one was unable to offer incense on top of the altar, he should offer it on the ground?

      B.    Scripture states, "'Make for Me an altar of earth'" (Exod. 20:21).

5.    A.    R. Yosi says, "Behold Scripture states, 'That day the king consecrated the center of the court that was in front of the House ... because the bronze altar that was before the Lord was too small to hold' (1 Kings 8:64).

      B.    "And from just where do we learn that it was small? Has it not already been said, '... on that altar Solomon presented a thousand burnt offerings' (1 Kings 3:4)?

      C.    "When you arrive at the sum of its cubits and its number of burnt offerings, behold, it [actually] was bigger than necessary!

      D.    "If so, why does Scripture state that it was hewn too small?

      E.    "It's like the person who says he is a minor priest."[137]

---

[134] Compare 2.A–D with *Mekhilta de-Rabbi Ishmael,* Baḥodesh (H/R, 242:1–6; Laut., vol. 2, 284:1–10; Neus., LVII:I:1.A–4.F).

[135] Compare 3.A–G with *Mekhilta de-Rabbi Ishmael,* Baḥodesh (H/R, 242:7–22; Laut., vol. 2, 285:11–286:34; Neus., LVII:I:5.A–7.C).

[136] The Hebrew word for "next to it" in Num. 2:20 is the same used for "on it" in Exod. 20:21 (*alav*—עליו), thus substantiating the text's reading of the verse.

[137] Perhaps this means false humility, but the meaning is, admittedly, uncertain.

| | | |
|---|---|---|
| B/A | 1 | ‏[אשריך] משה אשריך בן עמרם מה נא׳ לך ◆ |
| A 2 | C | מזבח אדמה תעשה לי ◆ יכול אדמה ודאי ◆ |
| B | | ת״ל אבנים שלמות תבנה את מזבח ה׳ אלקיך ◆ |
| C | | כשתכנס לארץ עשה לי מזבח המחובר באדמה דברי |
| D | | ר׳ יהודה. ◆ ר׳ מאיר אומר תחת עזרות היה חלול |
| B/A | 3 | והמזבח היה מחובר באדמה. ◆ וזבחת עליו ◆ יכול שתהא |
| C | | זביחה בראשו שלמזבח ◆ ת״ל ועשית עלתיך הבשר |
| | | והדם על מזבח ה׳ אלקיך בשר ודם על מזבח ה׳ |
| E/D | | אלקיך ◆ ואין זביחה על מזבח ה׳ אלקיך ◆ אם כן למה |
| G/F | | נאמר עליו ◆ בסמוך לו ◆ כענין שנאמר ועליו מטה מנשה |
| A 4 | | ‏(במ׳ ב כ) ◆ ‹מנ׳ לא יכולתה להקטיר על גבי המזבח |
| A 5 | B | הקטר על גבי אדמה ◆ תל׳ לו׳ מזבח אדמה תע׳ לי. ◆ ר׳ |
| | | יוסי אומ׳ הרי הוא אומ׳ ביום ההוא קדש המלך את |
| | | תוך החצר כי מזבח הנחושת אשר לפני ה׳ קטן |
| B | | מהכיל ‏(מ״א ח סד) ◆ וכי מיכן אנו למדין שהוא קטן |
| | | והלא כבר נאמר אלף עולות יעלה שלמה על המזבח |
| C | | ההוא ‏(מ״א ג ד) ◆ כשאתה בא לחשבון אמות ולמנין |
| D | | עולות הרי הוא גדול מזה ◆ אם כן למה נאמר |
| E | | קטן נפסל ◆ כאדם שאומר כהן קטן הוא. ◆ |

F.   R. Judah says, "The altar that Solomon made was actually too small, so he would offer sacrifices in the courtyard, because the entire courtyard was suitable to burn the fat offerings."

### (Textual Source: Ms. Cambridge T-S C 4a.2)

6.   A.   How does one know from Scripture that if there were extra portions of sacrifices, extra handfuls of meal offering, and extra libations, one would prepare one burning that would include them all?

 B.   Scripture states, "'... and sacrifice on it your burnt offerings'" (Exod. 20:21).

7.   A.   "'In every place where I cause My name to be mentioned'" (Exod. 20:21):

 B.   Because it says in Scripture, "'... to establish His name there'" (Deut. 12:5), one might think that the Priestly Benediction should be conducted only in the Temple.

 C.   How does one know from Scripture [also] in the border towns?

 D.   Scripture states, "'In every place where I cause My name to be mentioned I will come, etc.'" (Exod. 20:21).

8.   A.   R. Ḥananiah ben Teradion said, "How does one know from Scripture that God's presence dwells among three who sit and engage in Torah?[138]

 B.   "As it says in Scripture, 'God stands in the divine assembly' (Ps. 82:1)."

 C.   R. Ḥalafta ish Kefar Ḥananiah says in his name, "How does one know from Scripture [it is the case] with two?

 D.   "As it says in Scripture, 'In this way have those who revere the Lord been talking, (one to the other. The Lord has heard and noted it)' (Mal. 3:16).

 E.   "How does one know from Scripture [it is the case] with one?

 F.   "As it says in Scripture, 'In every place where I cause My name to be mentioned' (Exod. 20:21)."

## LVII:II

1.   A.   "'(And when you make for Me) an altar of stones, (do not build it of hewn stones. For by wielding your tool upon them you have profaned them)'" (Exod. 20:22):[139]

 B.   One might think it is voluntary [to build an altar of stones].

[157]   C.   Scripture states, "'... (do not) build (it of hewn stones)'" (Exod. 20:22).[140]

 D.   And why does Scripture state, "'And when (you make for Me an altar of stones)'" (Exod. 20:22)?

 E.   This teaches that it[141] was going to stop and start.

 F.   And thus Scripture states, "And even when the Israelites observe the jubilee" (Num. 36:4).

 G.   This teaches that it[142] was going to stop and start.

2.   A.   "'... you make for me'" (Exod. 20:22):

 B.   [God is saying,] "Hewing them, bringing them, and building it [should all be done] in My name!"

3.   A.   "'... do not build it of hewn stones'" (Exod. 20:22):

---

[138] Compare 8.A–F with *Mekhilta de-Rabbi Ishmael,* Baḥodesh (H/R, 243:6–12; Laut., vol. 2, 287:42–52; Neus., LVII:I:10.A–G).
[139] Compare 1.A–G with *Mekhilta de-Rabbi Ishmael,* Baḥodesh (H/R, 243:13–244:3; Laut., vol. 2, 287:53–288:65; Neus., LVII:I:11.A–P).
[140] The text here focuses on the imperative mood of the command "do not build" in the verse.

| | | |
|---|---|---|
| ר׳ יהודה אומר מזבח שעשה שלמה קטן היה | F | |
| ודאי ומקטיר בעזרה היה שכל העזרה כשרה להקטיר | | |
| חלבים> ♦ [ומנין שאם היו אימורין מרובים וקמצי]ן מרובים | A | 6 |
| ונסכים [מרובים] [עושה להם הבערה אחת שתחזיק את | | |
| כול]ם ♦ תל׳ לו׳ וזבחת [עליו את עלתיך ג׳]. ♦ [בכל | A 7 | B |
| המקום אשר אזכיר את שמי ♦ מכלל שנ׳ לשו]ם את | B | |
| שמו שם (דב׳ יב ה) י[כול לא תהא] [ברכת כהנים | | |
| נוהגת אלא בבית ה[מק]דש ♦ [ב]ג[בו]לין מנ׳ ♦ תל׳ לו׳ | D/C | |
| בכל המקום [אשר אזכיר את שמי אבוא ג׳ ♦ אמר ר׳ | A | 8 |
| חנניה] בן תרדיון מנ׳ לשלשה שיושבין [ועוסקין | | |
| בתורה שהשכינה] שורה בהם ♦ שנ׳ אים נצב בעדת אל | B | |
| (תה׳ פב א) ♦ ר׳ חלפתא [איש כפר חנניה אומר משמ]ו | C | |
| מנ׳ לשנים ♦ שנ׳ אז נדברו יראי יי[י] (מלא׳ ג טז) ♦ אחד מנ׳ | E/D | |
| שנ׳ [בכל המקום אשר אזכיר] את שמי ♦ | F | |
| | LVII:II | |
| מזבח אבנים ♦ יכול רשות ♦ תל׳ לו׳ [תבנה ♦ ומה תל׳ | D/C/B/A | 1 |
| לו׳ ואם ♦ מלמד שעתי]ד לפסוק ולחזור ♦ וכן הוא או׳ | F/E | |
| ואם יהיה היובל [לבני יש׳ (במ׳ לו ד) ♦ מלמד שעתיד | G | |
| הי]ובל לפסוק ולחזור ♦ תעשה לי ♦ שתהא חציבתן | B/A | 2 |
| והב(י)אתן [ובניית]ן לשמי ♦ לא תבנה אתהן גזית ♦ | A | 3 |

---

[141] I.e., the building of stone altars.
[142] I.e., jubilee observance.

B. Because Scripture states, "'... for by wielding your sword upon them'" (Exod. 20:22), one might think they[143] would be unsuitable only if hewn with a sword.

C. Scripture states, [however,] "Do not wield an iron tool over them" (Deut. 27:5).

D. Behold, an iron tool is the same as a sword!

E. [But] if we end up making an iron tool the same as a sword, [then] why does Scripture state, "'... your sword'" (Exod. 20:22)?

F. This is what R. Yoḥanan ben Zakkai says: "What [did Scripture] see [here] to disqualify [specifically] iron from all types of metal? Because the sword is made from it, and the sword is a sign of retribution, but the altar is a sign of atonement. One foregoes something that is

### (Textual Source: Midrash ha-Gadol)

a sign of retribution because of something that is a sign of atonement![144]

G. "And isn't it a matter of logical reasoning? If with stones—which don't see and don't hear and don't speak—because they provide [a source of] atonement between Israel and their father who is in heaven, the Holy One, blessed be He, said, "Do not wield an iron tool over them" (Deut. 27:5), then the children of Torah, who are [a source of] atonement for the world, how much the more so should not one of the instruments of injury trouble them!"

4. A. Because it says in Scripture, "Do not wield an iron tool over them" (Deut. 27:5), one might think if he waved iron over them they would be unsuitable.

B. Behold, you should reason: It says "wield" here in Scripture (Exod. 20:22),

### (Textual Source: JTS ENA 3205.8)

and it says "wield" in Scripture farther on (Deut. 27:5).

C. Just as "wield" stated farther on [means actual] touching, so too "wield" stated here [means actual] touching.

D. Just as "wield" stated farther on [causes] an imperfection [in the stone], so too "wield" stated here [causes] an imperfection.

E. From this you say: Iron renders unsuitable by touching. [And anything else renders unsuitable if it makes] a defect. And all other things by an imperfection.[145]

5. A. One might think that the stones of the Temple and [its] courtyards were suitable only if unhewn.

B. For it is a matter of logic: Just as the altar, which is rendered suitable by the stones of the Temple and the courtyards, is suitable only with unhewn stones, then isn't it logical that the stones of the Temple and its courtyards, which render the altar suitable, would be suitable only with unhewn stones?

C. Scripture states, [however,] "'... do not build it of hewn stones'" (Exod. 20:22).

D. [Meaning specifically] it you do not build of hewn stones, [but] you may build the Temple and the courtyards with blemished or razed stones.

6. A. One might think if one stone on the top was blemished, the entire altar would be profaned.

---

[143] I.e., the hewn stones.
[144] Compare 3.F–G with *Mekhilta de-Rabbi Ishmael*, Baḥodesh (H/R, 244:13–19; Laut., vol. 2, 290:80–92; Neus., LVII:I:14.A–15.F); and t. Baba Kamma 7:6.
[145] Meaning of 4.E is uncertain. Compare with parallel at m. Middot 3:4.

| | | |
|---|---|---|
| מכלל שנ' כי חרבך הנפת [יכול ל]א יהו פסולות אלא אם | B | |
| כן נתגזזו בחרב ◆ תל' לו' לא תניף [עליהם בר]זל ◆ הרי | D/C | |
| ברזל כחרב ◆ אם סופינו לעשות ברזל כחרב מה [תל' לו' | E | |
| כי] חרבך ◆ זו היא שרבן יוחנן בן זכאי או' מה ראה ברזל | F | |
| ליפסל [מכל מ]יני מתכות [כולן] מפני שהחרב נעשת | |
| ממנו וחרב [סימן] פורענות ומזבח סימן כפרה | |
| מעבירין דבר שהוא סימן פורענות מפני דבר שהוא | |
| סימן כפרה. ◆ והלא דברים קל וחומר ומה אבנים | G | |
| שאינן לא רואות ולא שומעות ולא מדברות על | |
| שמטילות כפרה בין ישראל לאביהם שבשמים אמר | |
| הקב"ה לא תניף עליהם ברזל בני תורה שהן כפרה | |
| לעולם על אחת כמה וכמה שלא יגע בהם אחד מכל | |
| מזיקין שבעולם. ◆ ‹מכלל שנאמר› לא תניף עליהן | A | 4 |
| ברזל (דב' כז ה) יכול אם הניף עלי' ברזל יהו פסולות ◆ | |
| הרי אתה דן נאמר כאן הנפה ונאמר להלן הנפה ◆ מה | C/B | |
| הנפה האמ' להלן מגע אף הנפה האמ' כאן מגע ◆ מה | D | |
| הנפה האמ' להלן חסרון אף הנפה האמ' כאן חסרון ◆ | |
| מיכן אתה אומר ברזל פוסל בנגיעה ופגימה בכל דבר | E | |
| ושאר כל הדברים בחסרון. ◆ יכול אבני היכל ועזרות | A | 5 |
| לא יהו כשרות אלא אם כן היו שלמות ◆ דין הוא ומה | B | |
| מזבח שאבני היכל ועזרות מכשירות אותו אין כשר | |
| אלא באבנים שלמות אבני היכל ועזרות שמכשירות | |
| את המזבח אינו דין שלא יהו כשרות אלא אם כן היו | |
| שלמות ◆ ת"ל לא תבנה את' גזית ◆ אתהן אי אתה | D/C | |
| בונה גזית בונה אתה (את ההיכל והעזרות) [היכל | |
| ועזרות] באבנים שנפגמו או שנגממו. ◆ יכול אם | A | 6 |
| נפגמה אבן אחת מלמעלה יהא מזבח כולו מחולל ◆ | |

B.    Scripture states, [however,] "'... you have profaned them'" (Exod. 20:22).

C.    [Meaning,] you have profaned [specifically] them, but the altar is not profaned.

(Textual Source: Midrash ha-Gadol)

LVII:III

1.    A.    "'Do not ascend My altar by steps, (that your nakedness may not be exposed upon it)'" (Exod. 20:23):[146]

    B.    One might think he should not ascend [by steps], but it is permissible to descend [by steps].

    C.    Scripture states, [however,] "'... that your nakedness may not be exposed upon it'" (Exod. 20:23).

    D.    So let it say [just] this!

    E.    But if so, I would say that one might think that there could be a small altar, and one could stand on the earth and offer a sacrifice.

    F.    [However] Scripture states, "And the priest shall bring up the burnt offering and the meal offering to the altar" (Lev. 14:20).

    G.    If so, then why does Scripture say, "'Do not ascend (My altar) by steps'" (Exod. 20:23)?

    H.    [To emphasize] that one should not make steps for it.

2.    A.    "'... that your nakedness may not be exposed upon it'" (Exod. 20:23):

    B.    Why do I need [this]?

    C.    For hasn't it already been stated, "You shall also make for them linen breeches to cover their nakedness" (Exod. 28:42)?

    D.    Why does Scripture state, "'... that your nakedness may not be exposed upon it'" (Exod. 20:23)?

    E.    [To emphasize] that when you ascend to the altar, you should not take big steps, but should walk heel touching toe.

3.    A.    I only know [about this prohibition] concerning an altar. How does one know from Scripture [that it is in effect also] in the courtyards?

    B.    Scripture states, "'Do not ascend My altar by steps'" (Exod. 20:23) and then it says, "'... upon it'" (Exod. 20:23).

    C.    "Upon it" means only close by, in accordance with what is said in Scripture, "Next to it: The tribe of Manasseh" (Num. 2:20).

4.    A.    One might think one should not make steps for the Tabernacle and its courtyards.

    B.    Scripture states, [however,] "'Do not ascend My altar by steps'" (Exod. 20:23).

    C.    [God is saying,] "You don't make steps for My altar, but you may make steps for My Tabernacle and its courtyards!"

---

[146] Compare 1.A–2.E with *Mekhilta de-Rabbi Ishmael*, Baḥodesh (H/R, 244:21–245:3; Laut., vol. 2, 290:93–291:100; Neus., LVII:I:16.A–17.G).

| | | |
|---|---|---|
| C/B | ת״ל ותחלליה ◆ היא מחוללת ואין המזבח מחולל. ◆ | |

ולא תעלה במעלות על מזבחי ◆ יכול לא יעלה אבל     B/A  1

מותר לירד ◆ ת״ל אשר לא תגלה ערותך עליו. ◆ יאמר זה ◆     D/C

שאלו כן הייתי אומר יכול יהא מזבח קטן ויעמוד     E

בארץ ויקטיר ◆ ת״ל והעלה הכהן את העולה ואת     F

המנחה המזבחה (ויק׳ יד כ) ◆ אם כן למה נאמר ולא     G

תעלה במעלות ◆ שלא יעשה לו מעלות. ◆ אשר לא תגלה     A 2  H

ערותך עליו ◆ מה אני צריך ◆ והלא כבר נאמר ועשה להם     C/B

מכנסי בד לכסות בשר ערוה (שמ׳ כח מב) ◆ מה ת״ל     D

אשר לא תגלה ערותך עליו ◆ שכשתעלה למזבח לא     E

תהא פוסע פסיעה גסה אלא מהלך עקב בצד גודל. ◆

אין לי אלא למזבח עזרות מנין ◆ ת״ל ולא תעלה     B/A  3

במעלות על מזבחי ונא׳ עליו ◆ אין עליו אלא בסמוך     C

כענין שנ׳ ועליו מטה מנשה ג׳ ◆ יכול לא נעשה מעלות     A 4

[להיכל ולעזרות ◆ תל׳ לו׳ ולא] תעלה במעלות ◆ ‹על     C/B

מזבחי› למזבח אי אתה עושה מ[עלות להיכל ולעזרות]

אתה עושה מעלות ◆

# Tractate Nezikin

*Chapter Fifty-Eight*

(Textual Source: Ms. Cambridge T-S C 4a.2)

LVIII:I

1.  A. "These are the rules that you shall set before them" (Exod. 21:1):

    B. One might think that every rule in the Torah was stated for one subject.

    C. Scripture states, [however,] "These are the rules that you shall set before *them*" (Exod. 21:1).

2.  A. R. Akiva says, "Because the laws are only specified for a man, how does one know from Scripture [that they apply as well to] a woman?

    B. "Scripture states, 'These are the rules (that you shall set before *them*)' (Exod. 21:1)."

    C. R. Ishmael says, "Each and every one was included in its substance."

    D. R. Yosi ha-Galili says, "Behold Scripture states, 'When a man or a woman commits

(Textual Source: Midrash ha-Gadol)

any wrong' (Num. 5:6).

    E. "Scripture equates a woman with a man for all the laws that are in the Torah."

3.  A. "... that you shall set before them" (Exod. 21:1):

    B. "Before the Children of Israel" is not stated here, rather, "before them."

    C. [Meaning,] before the important people among them.[1]

    D. This teaches that one does not teach the laws of property to the ignorant.

4.  A. Another interpretation:

    B. "... that you shall set before them" (Exod. 21:1):

    C. Just as the pearl is not revealed to all human beings, likewise you do not have permission to submerse yourself in the words of Torah, except in the presence of suitable people.

(Textual Source: Babylonian Talmud Tractate Ḥagigah 14b)

5.  A. It once occurred that Rabban Yoḥanan ben Zakkai was riding on his donkey, leaving Jerusalem, with R. Eliezer ben Arach, his disciple, walking behind him.

---

[1] See *Genesis Rabbah* 79:6 on Gen. 33:18 (Theodor-Albeck, p. 940; Neus., LXXIX:VI.1.A–B) for a more elaborate version of this tradition of interpretation that reads the word "before" as "to the important people."

# מסכתא דנזיקין

| | | |
|---|---|---|
| ואלה המשפטים אשר תשים לפניהם ✦ [יכול שכל | B/A | 1 |
| משפט] שבתורה נאמר לעינין אחד ✦ ת"ל לו' ואלה | C | |
| ה[משפטים אשר תשים] לפניהם ✦ ר' עקיבא או' לפי | A | 2 |
| שאין מפורש בד[יני]ן [אלא איש אשה] מנ' ✦ ת"ל ואלה | B | |
| המשפטים ג' ✦ ר' ישמעאל או' כל א[ח]ד [ואחד] | C | |
| מת[רבה] במקומו ✦ ר' יוסי הגלילי או' הרי הוא או' איש | D | |
| או אשה כי יעש[ו]ן [מכל חטאות (במ' ה ו) ✦ השוה | E | |
| הכתוב אשה לאיש לכל דיניין שבתורה] ✦ אשר תשים | A | 3 |
| לפניהם ✦ לפני בני ישראל לא נאמר כן אלא לפניהם ✦ | B | |
| לפנים שבהם ✦ מלמד שאין שונין בדיני ממונות לעם | D/C | |
| הארץ. ✦ ‹ד"א› ✦ אשר תשים לפניהם ✦ מה הפנימה הזאת | C/B/A | 4 |
| אינה נגלית לכל ברייה כך אין לך רשות לשקע עצמך | | |
| על דברי תורה אלא בפני בני אדם כשירין. ✦ ‹ומעשה | A | 5 |
| ברבן יוחנן בן זכאי שהיה רוכב על החמור ויוצא | | |
| מירושלם ור' אלעזר בן ערך תלמידו מהלך אחריו ✦ | | |

B. He[2] said to him, "Rabbi, teach me one portion concerning the Tradition of the Chariot!"[3]

C. He replied to him, "Have I not already taught you that the Chariot [should not be learned] by [only] one person, unless he is wise and can understand it all on his own!"

D. He said to him,

(Textual Source: Cambridge Add 3368)

"If not, then give me permission to talk [about it] before you!"

E. R. Eliezer ben Arach expounded until there was fire glowing on all his sides.

[159] F. When Rabban Yoḥanan ben Zakkai saw that there was fire glowing on all his sides, he got down from his donkey, kissed him, and said to him, "R. Eliezer ben Arach, happy is the one who gave birth to you! Happy is Abraham our father, for this one came from your loins!"

G. He[4] used to say, "If all the wise men of Israel were in one side of the scale, with R. Eliezer ben Arach in the second side, he would outweigh them all!"[5]

## LVIII:II

1. A. "When you acquire a Hebrew slave, (he shall serve six years. In the seventh year he shall go free, without payment)" (Exod. 21:2):[6]

B. How does one know from Scripture that when you acquire [a slave], you should only acquire a Hebrew slave?

C. Scripture states, "When you acquire a Hebrew slave" (Exod. 21:2).

D. And how does one know from Scripture that when he is sold, he should be sold only to you?[7]

E. Scripture states, "... and must be sold over to you" (Lev. 25:39).

F. And how does one know from Scripture that when the court sells him, it should sell him only to you?

G. Scripture states, "If a fellow Hebrew, man or woman, is sold to you" (Deut. 15:12).

2. A. "When you acquire a Hebrew slave" (Exod. 21:2):[8]

B. This is the one who sells himself.

C. And farther on Scripture says, "If a fellow Hebrew, man or woman, is sold to you" (Deut. 15:12).

D. This [refers to] the court selling him to you.

E. Scripture comes to teach you economy of language: "When you acquire a Hebrew slave" (Exod. 21:2) [means] whether he sells himself or the court sells him to you.

3. A. "When you acquire a Hebrew slave" (Exod. 21:2):[9]

(Textual Source: Ms. JTS ENA 1180.41)

B. You may acquire a male Hebrew slave of his own volition, but you may not acquire a female Hebrew slave of her own volition.

C. For isn't it a matter of logic?

---

[2] I.e., R. Eliezer.

[3] The reference here is to Ezekiel's vision of the heavenly creatures, divine throne, and presence of the Lord in Ezekiel 1:1–28, and the mystical secrets it is presumed to contain.

[4] I.e., Rabban Yoḥanan ben Zakkai.

[5] Compare 5.G with m. Avot 2:8.

| | |
|---|---|
| C/B | אמר לו ר′ שנה לי פרק אחד במעשה מרכבה ◆ אמר לו |
| | לא כך שניתי לכם ולא במרכבה ביחיד אלא אם כן |
| D | היה חכם ומבין מדעתו ◆ אמר לו> אם לאו תן לי |
| E | רשות שאומר לפניך. ◆ היה ר′ אלעזר בן ערך דורש עד |
| F | שהייתה האש מלהטת מכל סביביו ◆ כיון שראה רבן |
| | יוחנן בן זכי שהייתה האש מלהטת מכל סביביו ירד |
| | מעל החמור ונשקו ואמר לו ר′ אלעזר בן ערך אשרי |
| G | יולדתך אשריך אברהם אבינו שזה יצא מחלציך. ◆ הוא |
| | היה אומר אם יהיו כל חכמי ישראל בכף מאזנים ור′ |
| | אלעזר בן ערך בכף שנייה מכריע הוא את כולם ◆ פרק |

LVIII:II

| | | |
|---|---|---|
| 1 | B/A | כי תקנה עבד עברי ◆ (ש)מניין כשתהא קונה לא |
| | C | תהא קונה אלא עבד עברי ◆ ת″ל כי תקנה עבד עברי. ◆ |
| | E/D | ומניין כשהא נמכר לא יהא נמכר אלא לך ◆ ת″ל ונמכר |
| | F | לך (ויק′ כה לט) ◆ ומניין כשבית דין מוכרין אותו לא |
| | G | יהוא מוכרין אותו אלא לך ◆ ת″ל כי ימכר לך אחיך |
| 2 | B/A | העברי (דב′ טו יב): ◆ כי תקנה עבד עברי ◆ זה שהוא מוכר |
| | C | את עצמו ◆ ולהלן הוא אומר כי ימכר לך אחיך העברי |
| | E/D | או העבריה ◆ זה שבית דין מוכרים אותו לך ◆ בא הכתוב |
| | | ללמדך לשון קצרה כי תקנה עבד עברי בין שמוכר |
| 3 | A | את עצמו ובין שבית דין מוכרין אותו לך: ◆ כי תקנה |
| | B | עבד עברי ◆ [עבד] [עברי אתה] קו[נ]ה מעצמו |
| | C | ואי אתה קונה עבריה מעצמה ◆ שהיה] בדין ◆ |

[6] Compare 1.A–G with *Sifre Deut.*, Piska 118 (Hammer, p. 164; Neus., CXVIII:III:1.A–G).

[7] I.e., to a Jew.

[8] Compare 2.A–E with *Mekhilta de-Rabbi Ishmael,* Nezikin (H/R, 247:3–6; Laut., vol. 3, 3:23–30; Neus., LVIII:II:1.A–H).

[9] Compare 3.A–J with *Mekhilta de-Rabbi Ishmael,* Nezikin (H/R, 255:5–256:2; Laut., vol. 3, 20:16–21:38; Neus., LX:I:3.A–4.O).

D.   Just as the male Hebrew slave, whose father may not sell him, may sell himself of his own volition, then isn't it logical that the female Hebrew slave, whose father may sell her, should be able to sell herself of her own volition?

E.   Scripture states, [however,] "When you acquire a (male) Hebrew slave" (Exod. 21:2).

F.   [Meaning,] you may acquire a male Hebrew slave of his own volition, but you may not acquire a female Hebrew slave of her own volition.

G.   And isn't it a matter of logical reasoning that the male Hebrew slave's father should be able to sell him?

H.   For just as the father of the female Hebrew slave, who may not sell herself of her own volition, may sell her, then isn't it logical that the father of the male Hebrew slave, who may sell himself of his own volition, may sell him?

I.   Scripture states, [however,] "When a man sells his daughter as a slave" (Exod. 21:7).

J.   [Meaning,] a man may sell his daughter, but a man may not sell his son.

4.   A.   R. Ishmael says, "Scripture speaks [in Exod. 21:2] about the Hebrew[10] slave.[11]

B.   "You say Scripture speaks about the Hebrew slave. Isn't it, rather, about the Canaanite[12] slave?

C.   "Then how do I justify [this verse]: 'You may keep them as a possession for your children after you, etc.' (Lev. 25:46)?

D.   "[It concerns] one who purchases a [non-Jewish] slave from a non-Jew.

E.   "But then might one think that when one purchases a [non-Jewish] slave from a Jew, he must let him go after six years?

F.   "[Rather,] Scripture states [here], 'When you acquire a Hebrew slave, he shall serve six years' (Exod. 21:2), and farther on Scripture says, 'If your fellow Hebrew is sold to you, etc.' (Deut. 15:12).

G.   "That which is said here [is the same as] that which is said farther on.

H.   "'... your fellow' [is stated there]. Likewise here 'your fellow.'"

5.   A.   These commandments are stated in reference to the Hebrew slave by the merit of the past.[13]

B.   Another interpretation: By the merit of Abraham who was from the other side of the river.[14]

[160]   C.   Another interpretation: By the merit of Israel, who spoke the Hebrew language.

D.   As it says in Scripture, "They answered, 'The God of the Hebrews has manifested Himself, etc.'" (Exod. 5:3).

6.   A.   "... he shall serve six years" (Exod. 21:2):[15]

B.   [He shall serve] also the son [of the owner].

C.   One might think [he should serve] also one who inherits [him as a slave].

D.   Scripture states, [however,] "... he shall serve you" (Deut. 15:12).

E.   And not one who inherits.

F.   Just what did you see to include the son and exclude the inheritor?

---

[10] I.e., Jewish.

[11] Compare 4.A–H with *Mekhilta de-Rabbi Ishmael*, Nezikin (H/R, 247:6–14; Laut., vol. 3, 3:31–4:43; Neus., LVIII:II:2.A–K).

[12] I.e., non-Jewish.

[13] This interpretation is based on the affinity between the word for "Hebrew" (*ivri*—עברי) and the word for "past" (*avar*—עבר).

| | | |
|---|---|---|
| ומה עברי שאין אביו מו[כרו הרי הוא מוכר את עצמו] | D | |
| עבריה שאביה מוכרה אינו דין [שתהא מוכרת את עצמה ◆ | | |
| ת״ל] כי תקנה עבד עברי ◆ עברי אתה קונה מע[צמו | F/E | |
| ואי אתה קונה עבריה] מעצמה ◆ קל וחומר לעברי שיהא | G | |
| אביו מו[כרו ◆ ומה עבריה שאין היא] מוכרת את עצמה | H | |
| אביה מוכרה עברי שמו[כר את עצמו אינו דין] שיהא | | |
| אביו מוכרו ◆ ת״ל כי ימכר איש את בתו לאמה (שמ׳ כא | I | |
| ז) ◆ [האיש מוכר] את בתו ואין האיש מוכר את בנו. ◆ ר׳ | A 4 | J |
| ישמעאל אומ׳ אומ׳ בעבד [עברי הכת׳] מדבר ◆ אתה אומ׳ | | B |
| בעבד עברי הכת׳ מדבר או אינו אלא [בעבד] [כנעני ◆ | | |
| ו]מה אני מקיים והתנחלתם אותם לבניכם א[חריכם] | C | |
| [וגומ׳] (ויק׳ כה מו) ◆ בלוקח עבד מן הגוי ◆ אבל לוקח | E/D | |
| עבד מיש׳ יכול יצא בשש ◆ [ת״ל] כי תקנה עבד עברי | F | |
| שש שנים יעבוד ולהלן הוא אומ׳ כי ימ[כר] לך אחיך | | |
| העברי וגומ׳ (דב׳ טו יב) ◆ הוא שנאמר כאן [הוא] שנא׳ | G | |
| להלן ◆ מה להלן אחיך אף כן אחיך ◆ נאמרו מצ[וות] | A 5 | H |
| אלו בעבד [עברי] בזכות<ו> של עבר. ◆ ד״א בזכות | | B |
| אברהם שהיה מעבר הנהר ◆ ד״א בזכות [יש׳] שהיו | | C |
| מדברין בלשון עברי ◆ שנא׳ ויאמרו אלקי העברים נקרא | | D |
| וגומ׳ (שמ׳ ה ג) ◆ שש שנים יעבד ◆ אף את הבן ◆ | B/A | 6 |
| יכול אף את היורש ◆ ת״ל ועבדך (דב׳ טו יב) ◆ ולא את | E/D/C | |
| היורש ◆ מה ראית להביא את הבן ולהוציא את [היורש] ◆ | F | |

[14] This interpretation is based on the affinity between the word for "Hebrew" (*ivri*—עברי) and the word for "other side" (*mei-eiver*—מעבר).

[15] Compare 6.A–H with *Sifre Deut.*, Piska 118 (Hammer, p. 164; Neus., CXVIII:IV:1.A–G).

G.   After Scripture includes expansively, it excludes.

H.   I include the son because he comes after the father in designating [the female Hebrew slave as his wife][16] and in redeeming the ancestral field. But I exclude the inheritor because he does not come after the father in designating [the female Hebrew slave as his wife] and in redeeming the ancestral field.

7.   A.   "… he shall serve six years" (Exod. 21:2):[17]

B.   And not the one who flees[18] [who must make up his lost time].[19]

C.   One might think even if he was ill, but healed [enough to] walk [idly] about the market [he would need, also, to make up his lost time].

D.   Scripture states, [however,] "… he shall serve six years. In the seventh (he shall go free)" (Exod. 21:2).

E.   If this is so,[20] he loses from both sides![21]

F.   [Thus] no! When you speak of the sick slave, it is one who is bedridden, for thus he is unable to work.

8.   A.   "… he shall serve" (Exod. 21:2):[22]

B.   In that he[23] should not hand over his[24] trade to someone else.

C.   For he should not make him a public bath attendant, or a public scribe, or a public baker, or a public banker.[25]

D.   One might think [this would be acceptable] if this was his [original] trade.

E.   Scripture states, [however,] "… he shall serve" (Exod. 21:2).

F.   R. Yosi says, "As long as he[26] doesn't make him develop a new trade."

9.   A.   "In the seventh year he shall go" (Exod. 21:2):[27]

B.   One might think either at the beginning of the year or at its end.

C.   Behold you reason:

D.   The seventh year releases slaves and the jubilee year releases slaves. Just as we have found that [slaves are released] at the beginning of the jubilee year and not at its end, so too this is at its beginning and not its end.

E.   Or you might reason in this manner:

F.   The seventh year nullifies loans [and the seventh year releases slaves]. Just as it has been stated that the nullification of loans in the seventh year is at its end and not its beginning, so here at its end and not its beginning.

---

[16] See Exod. 21:9–10.

[17] Compare 7.A–F with *Mekhilta de-Rabbi Ishmael,* Nezikin (H/R, 251:12–14; Laut., vol. 3, 13:34–36; Neus., LIX:I:8.J–N).

[18] The word here in the Adler manuscript is actually "the sick one" (Hebrew: חולה). I translate, instead, the word בורח based upon its attestation to the parallel to this tradition in *Midrash ha-Gadol.*

[19] I.e., the sick slave, whose illness prohibits him periodically from serving, does not go free at the end of six years, but only once he accumulates a total of six years of provided service.

[20] I.e., the scenario in 7.C–D.

[21] I.e., the owner loses service time when he was sick, and then loses service time when he heals only enough to walk idly in the market.

[22] Compare 8.A–F with *Mekhilta de-Rabbi Ishmael,* Nezikin (H/R, 248:11–17; Laut., vol. 3, 6:64–74; Neus., LVIII:II:6.A–7.G).

[23] I.e., the owner.

[24] I.e., the slave's.

[25] I translate 8.C according to its parallel attestation in Midrash ha-Gadol.

[26] I.e., the slave's master.

[27] Compare 9.A–L with *Sifre Deut.,* Piska 111 (Hammer, p. 158–159; Neus., CXI:II:1.A–4.D).

| | | |
|---|---|---|
| H/G | | [א]חר שריבה הכתוב מיעט ◆ מביא אני את הבן שקם |
| | | תחת האב] [לי]עידה ולשדה אחוזה [ומוציא אני] את |
| | | היו]רש שלא קם] תחת [הא]ב ליעידה ולשדה |
| C/B/A | 7 | אחוזה]. ◆ שש שנ]ים יעבוד ◆ ו]לא [חולה] ◆ יכול [אפילו |
| D | | חלה ונתרפא ו]מטייל בשוק ◆ ת״ל שש שנים [י]עבוד |
| Γ/E | | ובשביעית ◆ נימצא [שאתה בא] על]יו] מיכן ומכאן ◆ לא |
| | | אם אמרת החולה והמוטל למטה [שכן אינו ראוי |
| C/B/A | 8 | ל]עבד ◆ יע]בוד] ◆ שלא ימסור אומ]נו]ת]ו לאח]ר ◆ שאם |
| | | [היה בל]ן] לרבים ספר לרבים נחתום לרבים של[חני] |
| E/D | | [לא יעשה. ◆ יכול אפילו היתה אומנותו כך ◆ ת״ל יעבד ◆] |
| F | | [ר׳ יוסי אומ׳ ובלבד שלא י]חדש לו אומנות שלכוס ◆ |
| C/B/A | 9 | ובשבע׳ [יצא ◆ יכול בתחלת] שנה (ת״ל) או בסופה ◆ הרי |
| D | | אתה [דן ◆ שנת שבע מוציאה ע]בדים ויובל מוציא |
| | | עבדים מה מצינו [ביובל בתחלתו ו]לא בסופו אף זו |
| E | | בתחלתה ולא בסופה ◆ או לך [לכה לדרך זו נאמ׳ כאן]. ◆ |
| F | | שנת שבע בהשמט מלוה מה שנת [שבע האמור בהש]מ]ט |
| | | מלוה בסופה ולא בתחלתה אף כאן בסופה [ולא בתחל]תה ◆ |

G.    Let's see which [case below in H. or J.] it is alike:

H.    You may reason something that depends on[28] the jubilee year from something that depends on the jubilee year. But don't let the nullification of loans serve as an analogy, because it doesn't depend on the jubilee year.

I.    Or you might reason in this manner:

J.    You may reason something that doesn't require sanctification of the court from something that doesn't require sanctification of the court. But don't let the jubilee year serve as an analogy, because it requires sanctification of the court.

K.    [Thus] Scripture states, "... he shall serve six years. In the seventh he shall go" (Exod. 21:20).

L.    Say from this [that it is] in the beginning and not in the end!

10.    A.    "In the seventh year he shall go free, without payment" (Exod. 21:2):

[161]   B.    Because it says in Scripture, "When you set him free from you, etc." (Deut. 15:13), this teaches that it is a commandment to say to him, "Go!"

C    One might think that if he said to him "Go!" behold, he goes, but if not, he doesn't go.

D.    Scripture states, [however,] "In the seventh year he shall go free" (Exod. 21:2).

11.    A.    Scripture states here "free" and Scripture states farther on "free" (Exod. 21:26):

B.    Just as "free" stated farther on [requires] a document, so too "free" stated here [requires] a document.

12.    A.    One might think that if he[29] was sick and bedridden, with his master expending many costs for him, he would have to give [them back] to him [in return before going free].

B.    Scripture states, [however,] "... he shall go free, without payment" (Exod. 21:2).

## LVIII:III

1.    A.    "If he came single, he shall leave single. (If he had a wife, his wife shall leave with him)" (Exod. 21:3):[30]

B.    One might think this is a decree.

C.    Scripture states, [however,] "If" (Exod. 21:3).

D.    This is only voluntary.

2.    A.    R. Eliezer ben Jacob says, "'(If) he came single, he shall leave single' (Exod. 21:3):

B.    "You are due nothing from him except labor."

3.    A.    "If he had a wife" (Exod. 21:3):

B.    Just as he[31] is obligated for his[32] sustenance, likewise is he obligated for his wife and children's sustenance.

C.    Still I might say: His master is obligated for the sustenance of the wife and children who were his[33] when his master had not yet acquired him, for from the outset he acquired him on such a condition. However, his master should not be obligated for the sustenance of the wife and children who became his after his master acquired him, because he had already become obligated for his sustenance.

D.    Or shouldn't one only say this:

---

[28] I.e., occurs in.

[29] I.e., the slave.

[30] Compare 1.A–D with *Mekhilta de-Rabbi Ishmael*, Nezikin (H/R, 249:5–7; Laut., vol. 3, 7:82–85; Neus., LVIII:II:11.A–E).

| | | |
|---|---|---|
| H/G | | נראה למי דומה ◆ דנין דבר שתלוי ביובל מדבר |
| | | [שתלוי ב]יובל ואל יוכח השמט מלוה שאין תלוי |
| J/I | | ביובל ◆ או לך לכה [לד]רך זו ◆ דנין דבר שאין |
| | | צריך קידוש בית דין מדבר דין שאין צריך [קי]דוש בית |
| K | | דין ואל יוכיח יובל שצריך קידוש בית דין ◆ ת״ל [שש] |
| L | | שנים יעבד ובשביעית יצא ◆ אמ׳ מעתה בתחלתה ולא |
| B/A | 10 | בסופה <...> ◆ ◆ ובשביעית יצא לחפשי חנם ◆ מיכלל שנא׳ |
| | | וכי תשלחנו חפשי מעמך וגומ׳ (דב׳ טו יג) [מ]למד |
| C | | שמצוה [לו]מר לו צא ◆ יכול אם אמ׳ לו צא הרי הוא |
| D | | יוצא ואם לאו אינו יוצא ◆ ת״ל ובשביעית יצא לחפשי |
| A | 11 | חנם. ◆ נאמ׳ כאן חפשי ונאמ׳ להלן חפשי (שמ׳ כא כו) ◆ |
| B | | מה חפשי האמ׳ להלן שטר אף חפשי האמ׳ כאן שטר ◆ |
| A | 12 | יכול אם היה חולה ומוטל במטה והוציא עליו רבו |
| B | | הוצאות הרבה (יהא) יהא צריך ליתן לו ◆ ת״ל יצא |
| | | לחפשי חנם. סל׳ פסו׳ ◆ |

LVIII:III

| | | |
|---|---|---|
| D/C/B/A | 1 | [א]ם בגפו יבא בגפו יצא ◆ יכול גזרה ◆ ת״ל [אם] ◆ אינו |
| A | 2 | אל[א] רשות ◆ ר׳ א[לי]עזר בן יעקב אומ׳ בגפו יבא בגפו |
| A 3 | B | יצא ◆ אין לך עליו [אלא עבודה. ◆ אם בעל א]שה הוא ◆ |
| B | | מה הוא חייב במזונותיו אף אשתו ובניו חייב(ין) |
| C | | במזונות<יהן> ◆ עדיין א[נ]י אומר א[שה ובנים [שהיו] לו |
| | | עד שלא לקחו רבו [חיי]ב במזונותיהן [שמתחלה לא |
| | | לקחו] אלא על מנת כן [אבל אשה ובנים ש[היו] לו |
| | | מש[לקחו רבו לא יהא] רבו חייב במזונו[תיהן שכבר |
| D | | נתחייב] במזונותיו ◆ [או אינו אומר כן] אלא אשה ובנים |

---

[31] I.e., the slave's owner.

[32] I.e., the slave's.

[33] I.e., the slave's.

(Textual Source: Midrash ha-Gadol)

His master is obligated for the sustenance of the wife and children who became his after his master acquired him, because he already became obligated for his sustenance. However, his master should not be obligated for the sustenance of the wife and children who were his when his master had not yet acquired him.

E.  Scripture states, "If he had a wife, his wife shall leave with him" (Exod. 21:3).

F.  Two wives [are mentioned] here. One [for the wife who was his] when his master had not yet acquired him, and one [for the wife who became his] after his master acquired him.

G.  One might think [the master must provide for] even the women to whom he is betrothed [but not yet married] and his widowed sister-in-law who is waiting for him to marry her.

H.  Scripture states, [however,] "... his wife shall leave with him" (Exod. 21:3).

I.  [Meaning,] his wife who is with him. Excluded is she who is not with him.

J.  One might think [the master must provide for] his wife even if she was unfit, such as a widow to a High Priest, or a divorcée, or a woman released from levirate marriage to a regular priest.

K.  Scripture states, [however,] "... his wife shall leave with him" (Exod. 21:3).

L.  [Meaning,] his wife who is fit to be maintained with him. Excluded is she who is not fit to be maintained with him.

M.  One might think [the master must provide for] even the woman whom he married unknown to his master.

N.  Scripture states, [however,] "... he" (Exod. 21:3).

O.  Just as his master knew about him, so too [sustenance must be provided only for] his wife whom his master knows.

4.  A.  One might think that the action of his wife and his sons and daughters [is the responsibility] of his master.[34]

    B.  For it is a matter of logic:

    C.  Just as with a Canaanite slave, for whom his master is not responsible for his sustenance, [but] his master is [responsible for] the action of his wife, sons, and daughters, then isn't it logical with this [Hebrew slave], for whom his master is responsible for his sustenance, that his master is [responsible for] the action of his wife, sons, and daughters?

    D.  Scripture states, [however,] "... he" (Exod. 21:3).

[162]  E.  The act of his hands [is the responsibility] of his master, but the act of his sons and daughters is not [the responsibility] of his master.

5.  A.  One might think his[35] found valuable object and his inheritance belong to his master.

    B.  Scripture states, [however,] "... he shall serve you" (Deut. 15:12).

    C.  You are due nothing from him except labor.

    D.  One might think that because he[36] was used [as the basis] to determine a new issue,[37] then he himself does not deserve his wife's found valuable object or her inheritance.

---

[34] Compare 4.A–E with b. Gittin 12a (Neus., XVIII.A:Gittin:1:6A–H:II.1.A–U).
[35] I.e., the slave's.
[36] I.e., the slave.

שהיו לו משלקחו רבו רבו חייב במזונותיהן שכבר

נתחייב במזונותיו אבל אשה ובנים שהיו לו עד שלא

לקחו רבו לא יהא רבו חייב במזונותיהן • ת״ל אם בעל        E

אשה הוא ויצאה אשתו עמו • שתי נשים כאן אחת עד        F

שלא לקחו רבו ואחת משלקחו רבו • יכול אפלו היה לו        G

ארוסה ושומרת יבם • ת״ל ויצאה אשתו עמו • אשתו        I/H

שהיא עמו יצאת זו שאינה עמו. • יכול אפלו היתה        J

אשתו פסולה כגון אלמנה לכהן גדול גרושה וחלוצה

לכהן הדיוט • ת״ל ויצאה אשתו עמו • אשה שהיא ראויה        L/K

להתקיים עמו יצאת זו שאינה ראויה להתקיים עמו. •

יכול אפלו נשא אשה שלא מדעת רבו • ת״ל הוא. • מה        O/N/M

הוא מדעת רבו אף אשתו מדעת רבו. • יכול יהא מעשה        A   4

אשתו ובניו ובנותיו שלרבו • ודין הוא • מה עבד כנעני        C/B

שאין רבו חייב במזונותיו מעשה בניו ובנותיו שלרבו

זה שרבו חייב במזונותיו אינו דין שיהא מעשה בניו

ובנותיו שלרבו • ת״ל הוא. • הוא מעשה ידיו של רבו ואין        E/D

מעשה בניו ובנותיו שלרבו. • (יכול תהא מציאתו        A   5

וירושתו שלרבו • ת״ל ועבדך (דב׳ טו יב) • אין        C/B

לך עליו אלא עבודה. • יכול מפני שיצא לידון        D

בחדש לא יהא זכאי במציאתה ובירושתה שלאשתו •

E. Scripture states, [however,] "... if he had a wife" (Exod. 21:3).

F. Scripture returns him to his general category for interpretation:

G. Behold, he is like [any] husband! Just as a husband deserves his wife's found valuable object and her inheritance, so too this one deserves his wife's found valuable object and her inheritance.

6. A. Another interpretation:

B. "... his wife shall leave with him" (Exod. 21:3).

C. Don't separate him from his wife!

D. And farther on Scripture says, "Then he and his children with him shall be free of your authority" (Lev. 25:41).

E. Don't separate him from his children!

*Chapter Fifty-Nine*

### (Textual Source: Midrash ha-Gadol)

LIX:I

1. A. "(If) his master gave him a wife, (and she has borne him sons or daughters, the wife and her children shall belong to the master, and he shall leave alone)" (Exod. 21:4):[38]

B. One might think this is a decree.

C. Scripture states, [however,] "If" (Exod. 21:4), [which means that] this is only voluntary.

2. A. "... his master gave him a wife" (Exod. 21:4):

B. [Scripture states this, in order] to include the son.[39]

3. A. "... gives him a wife" (Exod. 21:4):

B. Scripture speaks about the Canaanite handmaid.

C. You say that Scripture speaks about the Canaanite handmaid. Doesn't it speak, instead, about the free woman?

D. Scripture states, [however,] "... the wife and her children shall belong to the master" (Exod. 21:4).

E. If [Scripture was speaking] about the free woman, how could the offspring belong to the owner?

4. A. Or one might think that even if he[40] doesn't have an Israelite wife and children, behold, he is permitted [to marry] a Canaanite handmaid.

B. Scripture states, [however,] "... his wife shall leave with him" (Exod. 21:3).

C. As long as he has an [Israelite] wife and children with him, he[41] may give him a [Canaanite] handmaid. But if not, he may not.

5. A. Another interpretation:

B. "... gave him a wife" (Exod. 21:4):

C. He may give him one wife, but he may not give him two wives.

---

[38] Compare 1.A–C with *Mekhilta de-Rabbi Ishmael*, Nezikin (H/R, 250:1–2; Laut., vol. 3, 10:1–3; Neus., LIX:I:1.A–D).

[39] I.e., the same law pertains to the son of the master, who inherits the slave and then gives him over in marriage.

[40] I.e, the Hebrew slave.

[41] I.e., the master.

| | |
|---|---|
| F/E | ת״ל אם בעל אשה הוא ◆ החזירו הכתוב לכללו בפירוש ◆ |
| G | הרי הוא כבעל מה הבעל זכאי במציאתה ובירושתה |
| A 6 | שלאשתו אף זה זכאי במציאתה וירושתה שלאשתו ◆ (ד״א) ◆ |
| D/C/B | ויצאת אשתו עמו ◆ אל תפרישנו מאשתו ◆ ולהלן הוא אומר |
| E | ויצא מעמך הוא ובניו עמו (ויק׳ כה מא) ◆ אל תפרישנו |
| | מבניו. ◆ |

<br>

LIX:I

| | | |
|---|---|---|
| C/B/A | 1 | אדניו יתן לו אשה ◆ יכול גזירה ◆ ת״ל אם אינו אלא |
| A 3 | B/A 2 | רשות. ◆ אדניו יתן לו אשה ◆ לרבות את הבן. ◆ יתן לו אשה ◆ |
| C/B | | בשפחה כנענית הכתוב מדבר ◆ אתה אומר בשפחה |
| | | כנענית הכתוב מדבר או אינו מדבר אלא בבת חורין ◆ |
| E/D | | ת״ל האשה וילדיה תהיה לאדוניה ◆ אם בת חורין היאך |
| A 4 | | ולדות לבעל. ◆ או יכול אפלו אין לו אשה ובנים |
| B | | מישראל הרי הוא מותר בשפחה כנענית ◆ ת״ל ויצאת |
| C | | אשתו עמו ◆ בזמן שעמו אשה ובנים הוא נותן לו שפחה |
| C/B/A | 5 | ואם לאו אינו יכול. ◆ ד״א ◆ יתן לו אשה ◆ אשה אחת נותן |

D.    One might think he[42] should not give two wives to a free man.

E.    Scripture states, [however,] "… his master gave *him* a wife" (Exod. 21:4), [which means that] to him[43] he should not give two wives, but he may give two wives to a free man.

6.    A.    One might think he[44] may give one wife to two [Hebrew slaves], just as he gives one handmaid to his two Canaanite slaves.

B.    Scripture states, [however,] "… his master gave him a wife" (Exod. 21:4), [which means that] he gives him one wife, but he may not give one wife to two.

7.    A.    One might think he[45] should not give one wife to his two Canaanite slaves.

B.    Scripture states, [however,] "… his master gave him a wife" (Exod. 21:4), [which means that] to him[46] he may not give one wife to two, but he may give one wife to his two Canaanite slaves.

8.    A.    "… and she has borne him sons or daughters" (Exod. 21:4):

B.    [Scripture] compares a son to a daughter.

C.    Just as the daughter [of the Hebrew slave] cannot marry a free man, and doesn't need a bill of divorce to leave him, so too the son cannot marry a free woman, and she doesn't need a bill of divorce to leave him.

9.    A.    "… the wife and her children" (Exod. 21:4):

B.    All children to which she gives birth, whether from him or someone else, behold, these are slaves.

10.    A.    "… shall belong to the master" (Exod. 21:4):

B.    This teaches that she[47] leaves him without a bill of divorce.

11.    A.    Another interpretation:

B.    "… the wife and her children shall belong to the master" (Exod. 21:4):

C.    One might think that if his master wanted to sell his wife and children while he was still [serving] him, he could prevent him.

D.    Scripture states, [however,] "… the wife and her children shall belong to the master" (Exod. 21:4).

12.    A.    "… and he shall leave alone" (Exod. 21:4):

B.    [Scripture states this] to include many [moments in time] for him to leave.

## LIX:II

1.    A.    "But if the slave declares, ('I love my master, and my wife and children. I do not wish to go free')" (Exod. 21:5):[48]

B.    Only until he says it a second and third time.

2.    A.    "… the slave" (Exod. 21:5):[49]

B.    But not the handmaid.

C.    Because it says in Scripture, "Do the same with your female slave" (Deut. 15:17), [in

---

[42] I.e., the master.
[43] I.e., a slave.
[44] I.e., the master.
[45] I.e., the master.
[46] I.e., a Hebrew slave.

| | | |
|---|---|---|
| D | | לו ואינו נותן לו שתי נשים. ◆ יכול לא יתן לבן חורין |
| E | | שתי נשים ◆ ת״ל אדניו יתן לו אשה לו אין נותן שתי |
| A | 6 | נשים נותן הוא לבן חורין שתי נשים. ◆ יכול יתן אשה |
| | | אחת לשנים כדרך שנותן לעבדיו הכנעניים שפחה |
| B | | אחת לשנים ◆ ת״ל אדניו יתן לו אשה אשה אחת נותן |
| A | 7 | לו ואין נותן אשה אחת לשנים. ◆ יכול לא יתן לעבדיו |
| B | | הכנעניים שפחה אחת לשנים ◆ ת״ל אדניו יתן לו אשה |
| | | לו אין נותן שפחה אחת לשנים נותן הוא לעבדיו |
| A | 8 | הכנעניים שפחה אחת לשנים. ◆ וילדה לו בנים או בנות ◆ |
| C/B | | מקיש בן לבת ◆ מה הבת אין לה קידושין על בן חורין |
| | | ואינה יוצאת הימנו בגט אף הבן אין לו קידושין על |
| B/A | 9 | בת חורין ואין יוצאה הימנו בגט. ◆ האשה וילדיה ◆ כל |
| | | בנים שיולדת בין ממנו בין ממקום אחר הרי אלו |
| A 11 | B/A 10 | עבדים. ◆ תהיה לאדניה ◆ מלמד שיוצאה בלא גט. ◆ ד״א ◆ |
| C/B | | האשה וילדיה תהיה לאדניה ◆ יכול אם רצה רבו |
| | | למכור אשתו ובניו כשהוא תחתיו יכול הוא לעכב על |
| A 12 | D | ידיו ◆ ת״ל האשה וילדיה תהיה לאדניה. ◆ והוא יצא בגפו ◆ |
| B | | לרבות לו יציאות הרבה. ◆ |
| | LIX:II | |
| A 2 | B/A 1 | ואם אמר יאמר ◆ עד שיאמר וישנה וישלש. ◆ העבד ◆ |
| C/B | | ולא אמה ◆ מכלל שנ׳ ואף לאמתך תעשה כן (דב׳ טו יז) |

---

[47] I.e, the slave's wife.

[48] Compare 1.A–B with *Mekhilta de-Rabbi Ishmael,* Nezikin (H/R, 251:1; Laut., vol. 3, 13:37–38; Neus., LIX:I:9.A–B); Sifre Deut., Piska 121 (Hammer, p. 166; Neus., CXXI:I:1.A–C); y. Qiddushin 59d (Neus., Qiddushin:1:2:XXV.A–G); and b. Qiddushin 22a (Neus., XIX.AQiddushin:1:2: VIII.9.A–C).

[49] Compare 2.A–E with *Sifre Deut.,* Piska 122 (Hammer, p. 168; Neus., CXXII:V:1.A–3.D).

reference] to outfitting the freed slave with gifts, one might think [the situation is the same for male and female slaves] also for ear piercing.

D.   Scripture states, [however,] "... the slave" (Exod. 21:5).

E.   But not the handmaid.

3.   A.   Another interpretation:[50]

B.   "... the slave" (Exod. 21:5):

C.   He must declare it while a slave.

D.   One might think if he declares it before [year] six he may be pierced [at that time].

E.   Scripture states, [however,] "I do not wish to go free" (Exod. 21:5).

F.   He must declare it at the time when he may leave.

G.   If he declares it

### (Textual Source: Ms. Firkovich II A 268)

[163]    before [year] six, he is not pierced.

H.   As it says in Scripture, "But if the slave declares" (Exod. 21:5).

I.   [Which means that] he must declare it while a slave.

4.   A.   "'I love my master, and my wife and children'" (Exod. 21:5):[51]

B.   R. Shimon says, "If not, then what am I to think? For if he doesn't love [them], how can he be pierced?

C.   "Based on this you say: If he loves his master but his master doesn't love him, or if he is loved by his master but he doesn't love his master, behold, this [is a situation in which] he may not be pierced!

D.   "As it says in Scripture, '... for he loves you' (Deut. 15:16).

E.   "[If] he [i.e., the slave] has a wife and children, but his master doesn't have a wife and children, behold, this [is a situation in which] he may not be pierced!

F.   "As it says in Scripture, '... for he loves you and your household' (Deut. 15:16).

G.   "If his master has a wife and children, but he doesn't have a wife and children, behold, this [is a situation in which] he may not be pierced!

H.   "As it says in Scripture, 'I love my master, (and my wife and children)' (Exod. 21:5)."

I.   R. Eliezer ben Azariah says, "If he grew sick of his master, or his master grew sick of him, behold, this [is a situation in which] he may not be pierced!

J.   "As it says in Scripture, '... and is happy with you' (Deut. 15:16)."

---

[50] Compare 3.A–I with *Sifre Deut.*, Piska 121 (Hammer, p. 166; Neus., CXXI:I:1.A–3.C).

[51] Compare 4.A–J with *Mekhilta de-Rabbi Ishmael*, Nezikin (H/R, 252:1–8; Laut., vol. 3, 13:39–14:50; Neus., LIX:I:10.A–13.C); *Sifre Deut.*, Piska 121 (Hammer, p. 166; Neus., CXXI:II:1.A–III:1.B); y. Qiddushin 59d (Neus., Qiddushin:1:2:XXV.F–G); and b. Qiddushin 22a (Neus., XIX.AQiddushin:1:2:VIII.11.E–L).

| E/D | A 3 | ◆ ד״א ◆ ולא אמה. ◆ ת״ל העבד ◆ להעניק יכול אף לרציעה |
|---|---|---|
| | D/C/B | העבד ◆ עד שיאמר כשהוא עבד ◆ יכול אם אמר בתוך |
| | F/E | שש יהא נרצע ◆ ת״ל לא אצא חפשי ◆ עד שיאמר בשעת |
| | H/G | יציאתו ◆ הא אם אמר בתו[ך שש אינו נרצע ◆ שנא׳ אם] |
| I | A 4 | אמ[ור יאמר העבד ◆ עד שיאמר כשה]וא עבד. ◆ אהבתי |
| | B | את אדוני] את אשתי ואת בני ◆ אמ[׳] ר[׳ ש]מעון אם |
| | | לא[ו] מה עלתה על לבי ש[אם אינו אוהב היאך נרצע ◆ |
| | C | מיכן אתה אומ׳ היה הוא אוהב את רבו ורבו אינו |
| | | אוהבו והיה הוא אהוב על רבו והוא אין אוהב את |
| | E/D | רבו הרי זה אין נרצע ◆ שנא׳ כי אהבך (דב׳ טו טז) ◆ לו |
| | | אשה ובנים ולרבו אין אשה ובנים הרי זה אין נרצע ◆ |
| | G/F | שנא׳ כי אהבך ואת ביתך (שם) ◆ לרבו אשה ובנים ולו |
| | H | אין אשה ובנים הרי זה אין נרצה ◆ שנא׳ אהבתי את |
| | I | אדוני וגומ׳. ◆ ר׳ אלעזר בן עזריה אומ׳ חלה אצל רבו |
| | J | <א>ו שחלה רבו אצלו הרי זה אין נרצע ◆ שנא׳ כי טוב |
| | | לו עמך (שם). סל׳ פסו׳ ◆ |

## LIX:III

1.    A.    "... his master shall take him before God. (He shall be brought to the door or the doorpost, and his master shall pierce his ear with an awl. And he shall then remain his slave for life)" (Exod. 21:6):

     B.    He should bring him to [a court] of three people, and he shall make his declaration before them.

2.    A.    "He shall be brought to the door or the doorpost" (Exod. 21:6):[52]

     B.    One might think he may be pierced to the doorpost.

     C.    For it is a matter of logic:

     D.    If a door, which doesn't have the commandment of mezuzah [associated] with it, does have the commandment of piercing [associated] with it, then isn't it logical that a doorpost, which does have the commandment of mezuzah [associated] with it, should have the commandment of piercing [associated] with it?

     E.    Scripture states, [however,] "... and put it through his ear into the door" (Deut. 15:17).

     F.    But not the doorpost.

     G.    One might think [he may be pierced] to a standing door or to a leaning[53] door.

     H.    Scripture states, [however,] "... or the doorpost" (Exod. 21:6).

     I.    Just as the doorpost is standing, so too must the door be standing.

3.    A.    I only know [that the piercing can take place] on a door that has a mezuzah.

     B.    How does one know from Scripture [about] a door that does not have a mezuzah?

     C.    Scripture states, "He shall be brought to the door or the doorpost" (Exod. 21:6).

     D.    The first [word] "door" [in Exod. 21:6 refers to a door] without a mezuzah.

4.    A.    "... and his master shall pierce" (Exod. 21:6):

     B.    Scripture [speaks] expansively.[54]

     C.    And when Scripture has an expansion following an expansion[55] it is only in order to delimit: "his master"—but not his sons; "his master"—but not his servant; "his master"—but not his agent.

5.    A.    "... his ear" (Exod. 21:6):[56]

     B.    "His ear" is stated here, and "his ear" is stated farther on [Lev. 14:14].

     C.    Just as "his ear" stated farther on is the right [ear] high up the ear, so too "his ear" stated here is the right [ear] high up the ear.

     D.    R. Eliezer says, "Judah used to say, 'He should pierce him through the earlobe, lest he be a priest [and if pierced elsewhere on the ear he would] be disqualified from [priestly] labor.'

     E.    "But I say he is not to be pierced."

6.    A.    "'... with an awl' (Exod. 21:6):[57]

---

[52] Compare 2.A–I with *Mekhilta de-Rabbi Ishmael*, Nezikin (H/R, 252:11–17; Laut., vol. 3, 14:55–15:65; Neus., LIX:I:17.A–O); and y. Qiddushin 59d (Neus., Qiddushin:1:2:XXIII.A–G).

[53] I.e., unfixed.

[54] I.e., the morphology of the word for "his master" (אדניו) in Exod. 21:6 allows for the possible translation "his masters."

[55] I.e., the word "his master" appears twice in Exod. 21:6.

| | | |
|---|---|---|
| B/A | 1 | והגישו אדוניו אל האלהים ◆ מוליכו אצל שלשה |
| A | 2 | ואומ׳ דבריו לפניהם. ◆ והגישו אל הדלת או אל המזוזה ◆ |
| D/C/B | | יכול יהא רוצעו במזוזה ◆ דין הוא ◆ <ו>מה דלת שאין |
| | | בה מצות מזוזה יש בה מצות רציעה מזוזה שיש בה |
| E | | מצות מזוזה אינו דין שתהא בה מצות רציעה ◆ ת״ל |
| G/F | | ונתתה באזנו ובדלת ◆ ולא במזוזה ◆ יכול בדלת העומד |
| I/H | | או בדלת העקור ◆ ת״ל או אל המזוזה ◆ מה מזוזה מעומד |
| B/A | 3 | אף דלת מעומד ◆ אין לי אלא דלת שיש בה מזוזה ◆ דלת |
| C | | שאין בה מזוזה מנין ◆ ת״ל והגישו אל הדלת או אל |
| A 4 | D | המזוזה. ◆ ראשונה מה הדלת שאין בה מזוזה. ◆ ורצע |
| C/B | | [אדוניו ◆ ריבה ◆ אין] ריבוי אחר ריבוי בתורה אלא |
| | | למעט. אדוניו ולא [בניו אדוניו ולא עבדו] אדוניו ולא |
| B/A | 5 | שלוחו ◆ את אזנו ◆ נאמ׳ כן אוזנו ונאמר [להלן אוזנו (ויק׳ |
| C | | יד יד) ◆ מה אוזנו הא[מ׳ להלן ימנית בגבוה שבאוזן אף |
| D | | אוזנו האמ׳ [כן ימנית בגבוה שבאוז]ן ◆ ר׳ אלעזר אומ׳ |
| | | יודן היה אומ׳ במילת היה [רוצעו שמה כהן ונמצא |
| A 6 | E | פו]סלו מן העבודה ◆ ואני אומ׳ <אין> כהן נרצע ◆ [מרצע ◆ |

[56] Compare 5.A–E with *Mekhilta de-Rabbi Ishmael,* Nezikin (II/R, 253:2 6; Laut., vol. 3, 15:69 16:76; Neus., LIX:I:19.A–20.G); *Sifre Deut.,* Piska 122 (Hammer, p. 167; Neus., CXXII:II:1.A–III:1.D); y. Qiddushin 59d (Neus., Qiddushin:1:2:XXI.A–H); and b. Qiddushin 15a (Neus., XIX.AQiddushin:1:2:I.3:A–E).

[57] Compare 6.A–E with y. Qiddushin 59d (Neus., Qiddushin:1:2:XXII.A–K) and b. Qiddushin 21b (Neus., XIX.AQiddushin:1:2:VIII.2.A–I).

[164]

B. "I only know about an awl. How does one know from Scripture to include the needle, the stylus, the wood peg, and the thorn?

C. "Scripture states, 'You shall take' (Deut. 15:17)."—The words of R. Yosi b. R. Judah.

D. Rabbi says, "'... with an awl' (Exod. 21:6):

E. "Just as an awl is specifically [made] from metal, so too do I know [that the piercing must be] only [with something made] from metal."

7. A. "... and he shall remain his slave for life" (Exod. 21:6):

B. One might think also the [slave's] son.

C. Scripture states, [however,] "... and *he* shall remain his slave" (Exod. 21:6).

D. And not his son.

E. For one might logically reason:

F. If money, which cannot procure more than six [years of servitude], can procure the son [as a slave], then isn't it logical that piercing, which can procure more than six [years of servitude], should be able to procure the son [as a slave]?

G. Scripture states, [however,] "... and *he* shall become your [slave]" (Deut. 15:17).

H. But not the son.

I. [Then might one not] logically reason that piercing should not be able to procure more than six [years of servitude]?

J. Just as money, which can procure the son [as a slave], but cannot procure more than six [years of servitude], then isn't it logical that piercing, which cannot procure the son [as a slave], should not be able to procure more than six [years of servitude]?

K. Scripture states, [however,] "... and he shall then remain his slave for life" (Exod. 21:6).

8. A. One might think that a pierced [slave] will not go free during the jubilee year.

B. [But isn't it] a matter of logic [otherwise]?

C. If money can procure the son [as a slave], who goes free during the jubilee year, then isn't it logical that piercing, which cannot procure the son [as a slave], should allow one to go free during the jubilee year?

D. No!

E. If you speak of money, which cannot procure more than six [years of servitude], will you say [the same] of piercing, which can procure more than six [years of servitude]?

F. Scripture states, "... each of you shall return to his holding, etc." (Lev. 25:10).

G. This [refers to] the pierced [slave] before the jubilee year, because the jubilee year [does, indeed,] release him.

9. A. "... (and he shall become) your slave forever" (Deut. 15:17):[58]

B. [Meaning,] all the days, forever, for the pierced [slave], even if he was sold 30 years or 40 years before the jubilee.

C. How does one know from Scripture that one should apply [the lesson in B] for the [verse] stated here[59] to [the verse stated] above,[60] and [the same lesson] for the [verse]

---

[58] Compare 9.A–D with *Sifre Deut.*, Piska 122 (Hammer, p. 167–8; Neus., CXXII:V:1.A–2.B).
[59] I.e., Deut. 15:17.
[60] I.e., Exod. 21:6.

| | |
|---|---|
| אין לי אלא מרצע מניין לר[בות את המחט והמכתף | B |
| ואת [הסיל ואת הסירה ♦ ת״ל ולקחת (דב׳ טו יז) דברי | C |
| ר׳ יוסה] ביר׳ יהודה ♦ ר׳ אומ׳ מרצע ♦ מה מרצע [מיוחד | E/D |
| מן המתכת אף אין לי אלא מן ]המתכת. ♦ ועבדו לעולם ♦ | A 7 |
| יכול [אף את הבן ♦ ת״ל ועבדו] ♦ ולא [לבנו ♦ שהיה בדין ♦ | E/D/C/B |
| מה כסף שאין קו]נה יתר ענ]ל ש[ש הרי הוא קונה לבן | F |
| רצ]יעה שהיא קונה יתר על ש[ש אינו דין שתהא קונה | |
| לבן ♦ ת״ל והיה [לך (שם) ♦ ולא לבן ♦ קל וחומר לר]ציעה | I/H/G |
| שלא תהא קונה יתר על שש ♦ מה כסף שהוא קונה לבן | J |
| אינו קונה יתר על שש רציעה <ש>אין קונה לבן אינו | |
| דין שלא תהא קונה יתר על שש ♦ ת״ל ♦ ועבדו לעולם ♦ | K |
| יכול (לעולם) לא תהא רציעה יוצא ביובל ♦ דין הוא ♦ | B/A 8 |
| ומה כסף שהוא קונה לבן הרי הוא יוצא ביובל רציעה | C |
| שאין קונה לבן אינו דין שתהא יוצא ביובל ♦ לא ♦ אם | E/D |
| אמרת כסף שאין קונה יתר על שש תאמר ברציעה | |
| שהיא קונה יתר על שש ♦ ת״ל ♦ ושבתם איש אל אחוזתו | F |
| וגומ׳ (ויק׳ כה י) ♦ זה הנרצע לפני היובל שהיובל מוציאו ♦ | G |
| עבד (ל)עולם (דב׳ טו יז) ♦ כל ימי עולמו של רוצע | B/A 9 |
| אפילו נמכר שלשים שנה וארבעים שנה לפני היובל ♦ | |
| מניין ליתן את האמור כאן להלן ואת האמ׳ להלן | C |

stated above [should be applied to the verse stated] here?

D.  Scripture states, "forever" [in Exod. 21:6] and "forever" [in Deut. 15:17], in order [to support] a *gezerah shaveh*.[61]

## Chapter Sixty

### (Textual Source: Ms. Firkovich II A 268)

LX:I

1.  A.  "When a man sells his daughter as a slave, (she shall not be freed as male slaves are)" (Exod. 21:7):

    B.  Since it says in Scripture, "If he lacks the means, he shall be sold for his theft" (Exod. 22:2), this teaches that the man is sold for his theft.

    C.  One might think the woman also might be sold for her theft.

    D.  Scripture states, [however,] "When a man sells" (Exod. 21:7), [meaning,] the man may be sold for theft, but the woman may not be sold for theft.

    E.  One might think that she may not be sold for her own theft, but may be sold for her father's theft.

    F.  You have said: If she may not be sold for her own theft, may she [nonetheless] be sold for her father's theft? And why can't she be sold for her own theft? Because she cannot sell herself [into slavery]. But she can be sold for her father's theft, because her father can sell her [into slavery, as] Scripture states, "When a man sells" (Exod. 21:7), [meaning,] the man may sell, but the court may not sell.

[165]

    G.  [However,] the [following] reasoning from the minor to the major premise could be refuted, [thus proving that] her father cannot sell her [for his theft]: If with marriage, [the violation] of which results in death and [requires] a writ of divorce for her to terminate [it], her father can marry her off, then all the more so with selling [into slavery for his theft], [the violation] of which does not result in death and does not [require] a writ of divorce to terminate [it], can he sell her [into it]! But why can her father marry her off? Because, likewise, she can marry herself off! But he cannot sell her [for his theft], because she cannot sell herself [into slavery]!

    H.  Thus Scripture states, "When a man sells his daughter as a slave" (Exod. 21:7), to teach that the man may sell his daughter [for his theft], even though she cannot sell herself.

2.  A.  "... as a slave" (Exod. 21:7):[62]

    B.  This teaches that he may sell her to those who are disqualified.[63]

    C.  But isn't it [simply] a matter of logic?

    D.  If he may betroth her to those who are disqualified,[64] may he not [then also] sell her to those who are disqualified?

    E.  [However] what [allows] me [to draw this comparison with the fact] that he may betroth her to those who are disqualified? For he may [also] betroth her while she is a *na'arah*![65] [May we then deduce from this that] he may [also] sell her to those who are disqualified, even though he may not [also] sell her while she is a *na'arah*?

---

[61] I.e., the employment of the same word in separate scriptural contexts, thus facilitating the application of the meaning of the word in one context to the other.

[62] Compare 2.A–F with b. Qiddushin 19b (Neus., XIX.A:Qiddushin:1:2:VI.35.E–I).

[63] I.e., to people who, by virtue of their personal status, are forbidden to marry Jews of untainted descent, such as the *mamzer* (the offspring of illicit relationships punishable by excommunication or death).

[64] Even though marriage may be forbidden between "normal" Jews and Jews of less-than-desirable descent, in many instances, if a marriage such as this should occur, it is considered to be valid in spite of the prohibition.

| | |
|---|---|
| D | כאן ◆ ת״ל עולם עולם לגזירה שוה סל׳ פסו׳ ◆ |

LX:I

| | | |
|---|---|---|
| B/A | 1 | וכי ימכר איש את בתו לאמה. ◆ מכלל שנא׳ אם אין |

לו ונמכר בגנבתו (שמ׳ כב ב) מלמד שה>א<יש נמכר

| D/C | בגנבתו ◆ יכול אף האשה תהא נמכרת בגנבתה ◆ ת״ל כי |

ימכר איש האיש נמכר בגנבה ואין האשה נמכרת

| E | בגנבה ◆ יכול לא תימכר בגנוב עצמה תימכר בגנוב |

| F | אביה ◆ אמרת אם בגנוב עצמה אינה נמכרת ת]ימכר |

בגנוב אביה] מפני מה אין נמכרת בגנוב עצמה שכן

אינה [מוכרת את עצמה] תימכר בגנוב אביה שכן

אביה מוכרה ת]״ל כי ימכר איש האיש] מוכר ואין

| G | בית דין מוכרין ◆ אין זה קל וחו]מר שאין עליו תשובה[?

אביה לא יהא מוכרה ומה קידושי]ן שיש בהן מיתה

חמורה ויוצאה בגט >אביה מקדשה מכירה שאין

בה<] מיתה חמורה ויוצאה שלא בגט א]ינו דין

שמוכרה מפני מה] אביה מקדשה שכן מקדשת [את

| H | עצמה. לא יהא מוכרה שכן אינה] מוכרת עצמה ◆ ת״ל |

כי ימכר [איש את בתו לאמה... מלמד?] ש[האיש

מוכר את בתו ואין היא מוכרת את עצמה?] ה]... ◆

| C/B/A | 2 | לאמה ◆ מלמד שמוכרה לפסולין ◆ והלא דין הוא ◆ |

| E/D | אם מקדשה לפסולין] לא [ימכרנה לפסולין ◆ >מה |

לי מקדשה לפסולין< שכן מקד]שה בנ]עור]יה

ימכרנ]ה לפסולי]ן [שכן אין מוכרה בנ]עוריה ◆

---

[65] A Jewish female has three major stages of maturation. From birth until either the age of 12 or the signs of puberty, whichever comes first, she is considered to be a minor (Hebrew: *ketanah*—קטנה). During this period of her life, her father has the right both to sell her into slavery and to betroth her. From the age of 12 or the first signs of puberty until the following six months she is considered a maiden (Hebrew: *na'arah*—נערה), a period of time in which her father may still betroth her, but may no longer sell her into slavery. Thereafter she is considered to be an adult (Hebrew: *bogeret*—בוגרת), and her father has no rights over her whatsoever.

F.  [Thus] Scripture states, "... as a slave" (Exod. 21:7), [in order] to include [selling her] to those who are disqualified.

3.  A.  R. Eliezer says, "Why do I need [the verse Exod. 21:7]?[66]

B.  "For hasn't it already been stated, 'If she proves to be displeasing to her master (who designated her for himself)' (Exod. 21:8)?

C.  "[Thus, Exod. 21:8] includes [selling her] to those who are disqualified.[67]

D.  "So why does Scripture state, '... as a slave' (Exod. 21:7)?

E.  "[In order] to include [the possibility of selling her to] the relatives.

F.  "For isn't it a matter of logic?

G.  "Since he may sell her to those who are disqualified, may he not [also] sell her to relatives?

H.  "[However] what [allows] me [to draw this comparison with the fact] that he may sell her to those who are disqualified? For he can [also] betroth her to them! [May we then deduce from this that] he may [also] sell her to relatives, to whom he may not [also] betroth her?

I.  "[Thus] Scripture states, '... as a slave' (Exod. 21:7), [in order] to include the relatives."

4.  A.  "'... as a slave' (Exod. 21:7):

B.  "Only as a slave.

C.  "I only know ... [manuscript lacuna] ...[68] You can sell her to him for a fixed sum, even if she is not designated [to him or his son] for marriage."—The words of R. Meir.

D.  But the Sages say, "You cannot sell her to him for a fixed sum [without marriage]."

5.  A.  "'... she shall not be freed as male slaves are' (Exod. 21:7):

B.  "In that she should not carry behind him water buckets and ropes to the bath."—The words of R. Eliezer.[69]

C.  R. Akiva said to him, "Why [would] I need [Exod. 21:7 for this]?

D.  "For hasn't Scripture already stated, '... do not subject him to the treatment of a slave' (Lev. 25:39)?

E.  "[Thus,] why does Scripture state, '... she shall not be freed as male slaves are' (Exod. 21:7)?

F.  "[It means] she should not go free over [the loss of] a tooth or an eye, as males slaves do.

G.  "For isn't it a matter of logic?

H.  "If the Canaanite slave, who does not go free [after six] years, or in the jubilee year, or by a deduction of the purchasing price,[70] does go free over [the loss of] a tooth or an eye, then isn't it logical that this [one in Exod. 21:7], who does go free [after six] years, or in the jubilee year, or by a deduction of the purchasing price, should go free over [the loss of] a tooth or an eye?

---

[66] Compare 3.A–I with b. Qiddushin 19b (Neus., XIX.A:Qiddushin:1:2:VI.35.J–N).

[67] The text does not state overtly how it understands Exod. 21:8 to be indicative of the fact that the father may, indeed, sell his daughter as a slave to one to whom she would be prohibited in marriage, thus rendering Exod. 21:7 as superfluous and unnecessary to make this point. Exod. 21:8 does speak, however, of the owner of a female slave who finds her to be "displeasing" in terms of marriage. It seems that R. Eliezer is presuming that she is displeasing to her owner not physically or emotionally, but rather, because he is disqualified from marrying her in the first place. Given this assumption, Exod. 21:8 serves to prove that a man may sell his daughter to one to whom she would be prohibited in marriage.

[68] There is a possible parallel to this fragmented tradition in y. Qiddushin 59c (Neus., Qiddushin:1:2:XVI.A.–C.).

[69] R. Eliezer's interpretation here is based upon a literal reading of the clause "... she shall not be freed" (Hebrew: לא תצא) in Exod. 21:7 as "she shall not go out."

| | | |
|---|---|---|
| ת"ל לאמה לרבות את הפסולין ◆ ר' אלעזר און[מ' מה | A 3 | F |
| אני] צריך ◆ והלא כבר נאמ' אם רעה בעיני אדוניה ◆ | B | |
| לרבות את הפסולין ◆ מה ת"ל לאמה ◆ לרבות את | E/D/C | |
| הקר‹ו›בים ◆ שהיה בדין ◆ הואיל ומוכרה ‹לפסולין לא | G/F | |
| ימכרנה› לקרובים ◆ מה לי מוכרה לפסולין שכן מקדשה להן | H | |
| ימכרנה לקרובים שכן אין מקדשה להן ◆ ת"ל לאמה | I | |
| לרבות הקרובים ◆ ‹לאמה› ◆ לאמה בלבד ◆ אין לי ‹...› | C/B/A | 4 |
| את קוצץ עמו אף על פי שלא ליעד דברי ר' מאיר ◆ | | |
| וחכמ' אומ' אין יכול לקוץ ◆ לא תצא כצאת העבדים | A 5 | D |
| שלא תהא נוטלת אחריו דלאים ובלוריות למרחץ | B | |
| דברי ר' אל‹י›עזר ◆ אמ' לו ר' עקיב' מה אני צריך ◆ והלא | D/C | |
| כבר נאמר לא תעבד בו עבודת עבד (ויק' כה לט) ◆ מה | E | |
| ת"ל לא תצא רצאת העבדים ◆ שלא תהא יוצאת על | F | |
| השן ועל העין כעבדים ◆ שהיה בדין ◆ ומה עבד כנעני | H/G | |
| שאין יוצא בשנים וביובל ובגירעון כסף הרי הוא יוצא | | |
| על השן ועל העין זו שיוצאה בשנים וביובל ובגירעון | | |
| כסף אינו דין שתהא יוצא על השן ועל העין ◆ | | |

I.   "Scripture states, [however,] '... she shall not be freed as male slaves are' (Exod. 21:7)."

J.   "[Meaning,] she should not go free over [the loss of] a tooth or an eye, as male slaves do."

K.   Based upon this they said: A man may sell his daughter in marriage repeatedly, and into servitude repeatedly, and in marriage after servitude, but not into servitude after marriage.[71]

L.   R. Shimon says, "Just as he may not sell her into servitude after marriage, so too [is it the case that] he should not sell her into servitude after servitude?

M.   "Scripture states, '... she shall not be freed as male slaves are' (Exod. 21:7).

[166]   N.   "[Meaning,] into servitude after marriage, as with male slaves."

LX:II

1.   A.   "If she proves to be displeasing in the eyes of her master, (who designated her for himself, he must let her be redeemed. He shall not have the right to sell her to outsiders, since he broke faith with her)" (Exod. 21:8):

B.   I only know [from this when she is] repulsive.

C.   How does one know from Scripture [when she is] attractive?

D.   Scripture states, "... in the eyes of her master" (Exod. 21:8).

E.   I only know [from this] about the eyes of her master. How does one know from Scripture about the eyes of his son?

F.   Scripture states, "If she proves to be displeasing" (Exod. 21:8).

G.   R. Eliezer ben Jacob says, "'... in the eyes of her master' (Exod. 21:8).

H.   "I can only conclude [that it means] in his eyes."

2.   A.   "... who did not designate her" (Exod. 21:8):[72]

B.   Instead of "not" you should understand it as "did."

C.   Because if he wanted to designate[73] her, behold, he could marry her.

3.   A.   "... designate her" (Exod. 21:8):

B.   He designated her with her consent.

C.   This teaches that he may only marry her with her consent.

4.   A.   "... (who) designated her (for himself), he must let her be redeemed" (Exod. 21:8):[74]

B.   This teaches that the commandment of designation takes precedence over the commandment of redemption.

5.   A.   "... he must let her be redeemed" (Exod. 21:8):

B.   This teaches that she may go free by a deduction of the purchasing price.

6.   A.   "... he must let her be redeemed" (Exod. 21:8):

B.   This teaches that the court may redeem her against his will.

7.   A.   R. Yosi b. R. Judah says, "'... he must let her be redeemed' (Exod. 21:8):[75]

---

[71] Compare 5.K with y. Qiddushin 59c (Neus., Qiddushin:1:2:XVI.O) and b. Qiddushin 18a (Neus., XIX.A:Qiddushin:1:2:VI.24.G).

[72] The text here has translated the word in Exod. 21:8 "for himself" (Hebrew: lo—לו) as its homonym "not" (Hebrew: lo—לא), producing the meaning rendered above.

[73] I.e., designate her for marriage for himself.

| | | |
|---|---|---|
| השן ועל ת״ל לא תצא כצאת העבדים ◆ שלא תהא | J/I | |
| יוצאה על [ה]עין כעבדים ◆ מיכן <אמרו> מוכר אדם את | K | |
| בתו לאישות ושונה ולשפחות [ושונה לאיש]ות אחר | | |
| שפחות אבל לא לשפחות אחר אישות ◆ [ר׳ שמעון אומ׳ | L | |
| כ]שם שאין מוכרה לשפחות אחר אישות כך אין | | |
| [מוכרה לשפחו]ת אחר שפחות ◆ ת״ל לא תצא כצאת | M | |
| העבדים ◆ [ולשפחות אחר [אישות כעבדים. סל׳ פסו׳ ◆ | N | |
| | LX:II | |
| אם רעה [בעיני אדוניה ◆ אין לי] אלא כעורה ◆ נאה | C/B/A | 1 |
| מנין ◆ ת״ל בעיני אדוניה ◆ [אין לי אלא בעיני אדוניה] | E/D | |
| בעיני בנו מנין ◆ ת״ל אם רעה ◆ ר׳ אלי<ע>עזר [בן יעקב | G/F | |
| אומ׳ בעיני אדוניה] ◆ אין לי אלא בע[י]ניו. ◆ אשר לא | A 2 | H |
| יעדה ◆ [מכלל לאו אתה שומע הין ◆ שאם רצה ליעד הרי | C/B | |
| הוא מיעד. ◆ יעדה ◆ יעד]נה [מדעתה ◆ מלמד שאינו | C/B/A | 3 |
| מקדשה אלא מדעתה. ◆ יעדה והפדה ◆ מלמ]ד ש[מצות | B/A | 4 |
| יעידה] קודמת למ[צות פדייה. ◆ והפדה. ◆ מלמד שיוצאה | B/A | 5 |
| ב]גרעון כסף ◆ והפדה ◆ מלמד שבית דין מפדין [אותה | B/A | 6 |
| בעל כורחו. ◆ ר׳ יו[סי בר]׳] יהודה אומ׳ והפדה ◆ | A | 7 |

[74] Compare 4.A–B with *Mekhilta de-Rabbi Ishmael*, Nezikin (H/R, 257:5–6; Laut., vol. 3, 24:80–81; Neus., LX:I:12.A–C).
[75] Compare 7.A–C with y. Qiddushin 59b (Neus., Qiddushin:1:2:XI.A–G) and b. Qiddushin 19a (Neus., XIX:A:Qiddushin:1:2:VI.27.A–D).

B.   "[Which means] as long as there is enough time remaining in the day[76] to be redeemed."

C.   Based upon this they said: If there remains enough [time] for her to do the equivalent of a *perutah*'s work for him, she may be married. But if not, she may not be married.

8.   A.   He may not sell her to outsiders:[77]

B.   One might think he may not sell her, but he may give her as a gift.

C.   Scripture states, [however,] "He shall not have the right ... to outsiders" (Exod. 21:8).

D.   One might think that he may not sell her to outsiders, but he may sell her to relatives.

E.   Scripture states, [however,] "... to the people" (Exod. 21:8) he may not sell [her].[78]

F.   One might think that he may not sell her [to relatives], but he may give her [to them] as a gift.

G.   Scripture states, [however,] "He shall not have the right ... to the people [or] outsiders" (Exod. 21:8).[79]

H.   It says "to others," so why do I need it to say [as well] "to relatives"?

I.   Because if it says "to others" but does not say "to relatives," I would say he may not sell her to others, but may sell her to relatives.

J.   [Thus,] it needs to say "to others" and it needs to say "to relatives."

9.   A.   "... since he broke faith with her" (Exod. 21:8):[80]

B.   Once he[81] has spread his cloak over her,[82] he[83] may not sell her.

C.   R. Shimon says, "The first one who betrayed her[84] doesn't have the right to enslave her!"

D.   Based upon this they said: A man may not sell his daughter into servitude after marriage.[85]

LX:III

1.   A.   "(And if he designated her) for his son, (he shall deal with her as is the practice with free maidens)" (Exod. 21:9):

B.   One might think this is a decree.

[167]   C.   Scripture states, [however,] "And if" (Exod. 21:9), [meaning,] it is only voluntary.

2.   A.   "... he designated her for his son" (Exod. 21:9):

B.   [Scripture says this in order] to ascribe that which is stated about the father to the son, and that which is stated about the son to the father.

3.   A.   ["And if he designated her for his son" (Exod. 21:9)]:[86]

B.   For if he wants to designate [her], behold, he may designate her for his son but not his brother.

---

[76] I.e., in her period of servitude.

[77] Note: This is a paraphrase of Exod. 21:8.

[78] The text reads literally the word לעם in Exod. 21:8 as "to the people," rather than as a part of the term for "outsider," understanding "the people" as indicative of close kin. In what follows, the text understands the term לעם נכרי in Exod. 21:8 to indicate two separate terms and hence peoples—"to the people" and "outsiders."

[79] See note 78.

[80] In the following interpretation, the text reads this clause בבגדו בה in Exod. 21:8 as "with his clothes upon her," understanding the word בבגדו as a form of the noun בגד.

[81] I.e., her owner.

[82] I.e., married her.

[83] I.e., her father may not sell her into slavery once again.

| | | |
|---|---|---|
| עד שיהיה ביום כדי פדייה ◆ מ[י]כן [א]מרו אם שהתה כדי | C/B | |
| שתעשה עמו שווה פרוטה מתקדשת ואם לאו אינה | | |
| מתקדשת. ◆ לנכרי לא ימכר ◆ יכול לא ימכרנה אבל | B/A | 8 |
| יתננה במתנה ◆ ת״ל לנכרי לא ימשול ◆ יכול לא ימכרנה | D/C | |
| לאחרים אבל (לא) ימכרנה לקרובים ◆ ת״ל לעם לא | E | |
| ימכר ◆ יכול לא ימכר אבל יתננה במתנה ◆ ת״ל לעם נכרי | G/F | |
| לא ימשל ◆ יאמ׳ לאחרים מה אני צריך <לומר> | H | |
| לקרובים ◆ שאילו נאמר לאחרים ולא נאמר לקרובים | I | |
| הייתי אומ׳ לא ימכרנה לאחרים אבל ימכרנה | | |
| לקרובים <...> ◆ צריך לומר לאחרין וצריך לומר | J | |
| לקרובים. ◆ בבגדו בה. ◆ כיון שפרס טליתו עליה אין יכול | B/A | 9 |
| למכרה ◆ ר׳ שמע׳ אומ׳ הראשון שבגד בה אין רשאי | C | |
| לשעבדה ◆ מיכן אמרו אין אדם מוכר את בתו לשפחות | D | |
| אחר אישות. סל׳ פסו׳ ◆ | | |

LX:III

| | | |
|---|---|---|
| לבנו ◆ יכול גזירה ◆ ת״ל ואם אינו אלא רשות (ת״ל) ◆ | C/B/A | 1 |
| לבנו ייעדנה ◆ ליתן את האמור באב בבן ואת האמור בבן | B/A | 2 |
| באב ◆ שאם רצה ליעד הרי הוא מיעד לבנו ולא לאחיו ◆ | B/A | 3 |

[84] I.e., her father.
[85] Compare 9.A–D with *Mekhilta de Rabbi Ishmael,* Nezikin (H/R, 257:9–258:3; Laut., vol. 3, 25:88–26:95; Neus., LX:I:17.A–19.E); y. Qiddushin 59c (Neus., Qiddushin:1:2:XVI.T–Y); and b. Qiddushin 18a (Neus., XIX:A:Qiddushin:1:2:VI.24.A–L).
[86] Compare 3.A–E with *Mekhilta de-Rabbi Ishmael,* Nezikin (H/R, 258:4–7; Laut., vol. 3, 26:96–102; Neus., LX:I:20.A–H); and y. Qiddushin 59b (Neus., Qiddushin:1:2:XII.A–O).

C. For one might reason logically:

D. If the son, whom the Torah has not allowed to acquire the levirate wife, may acquire the designated [handmaiden in Exod. 21:9], then isn't it logical that the brother, whom the Torah allows to acquire the levirate wife, should acquire the designated [handmaiden]?

E. Scripture states, [however,] "... for his son" (Exod. 21:9), and not his brother.

4. A. "... he designated her for his son" (Exod. 21:9):

B. While his father is alive he[87] may designate her. But he may not designate her after the death of his father.

5. A. "... he shall deal with her as is the practice with free maidens" (Exod. 21:9):[88]

B. Just as he is obligated [to provide] the sustenance of Israelite daughters, so too with this one is he obligated [to provide] her sustenance.

C. But have we learned anything about the practice of daughters?

D. ... [manuscript lacuna] ... with their sustenance.

E. Just as he may not diminish the clothing or conjugal rights of the Israelite daughter, so too with this one may he not diminish her clothing or conjugal rights.

F. Just as with the Israelite daughter—once her father has married her off, one would be culpable to death at the hands of the court [for adultery with her] and she doesn't go free without a divorce document, so too with this one—once he has designated her, one would be culpable to death at the hands of the court and she doesn't go free without a divorce document. ... [manuscript lacuna] ...

## LX:IV

1. A. "(If) he marries another, (he must not withhold from this one her food, her clothing, or her conjugal rights)" (Exod. 21:10):

B. One might think this is a decree.

C. Scripture states, [however,] "If" (Exod. 21:10), [meaning,] it is only voluntary.

2. A. "... he marries another" (Exod. 21:10):

B. Who is not public property.

3. A. "... he marries another" (Exod. 21:10):

B. Scripture speaks of the free woman.

4. A. "... he marries another" (Exod. 21:10):

B. This teaches that the father has the authority to marry off his youngest daughter.

5. A. "... he marries another" (Exod. 21:10):

B. This teaches that it is permissible to acquire another woman for him for the sake of marriage.

6. A. "... he marries another" (Exod. 21:10):

B. Behold this one is like the other one.

C. Just as the one was acquired by writ, so too is this one acquired by writ.

---

[87] I.e., the son.

[88] Compare 5.A–F with *Mekhilta de-Rabbi Ishmael*, Nezikin (H/R, 258:7–12; Laut., vol. 3, 26:103–27:111; Neus., LX:I:21.A–I).

| | |
|---|---|
| שהיה בדין ◆ מה אם הבן שלא קנתה לו תורה | D/C |
| יבמה קנ[תה] לו יעידה אח שקנתה לו תורה יבמה | |
| אינו דין שת[קנה לו יעידה] ◆ ת״ל לבנו (מכל) ולא | E |
| לאחיו ◆ לבנו ייעדנה ◆ בחיי אביו מ[יעדה ואין מיעדה] | B/A 4 |
| לאחר מיתת אביו. ◆ כמשפט הבנות יעשה לה ◆ [מה בנות | B/A 5 |
| ישראל חייב] במזונותיהן אף זו חייב במזונותיה ◆ וכי | C |
| מה(יר) [למדנו למשפט הבנות...] ◆ במזונותיהן ◆ מה בת | E/D |
| יש׳ כסותה ועונתה [לא יגרע אף זו כסותה] ועונתה | |
| לא יגרע ◆ מה בת <יש׳> משקידשה אב[יה חייבין עליה | F |
| מיתת] בית דין ואינה יוצא אלא בגט אף זו מש[ייעדה | |
| חייבין עליה מיתת] [בית דין ואינה יוצאה אלא בגט...] | |
| [...] [...] ובת [...] משוחררת ובת חו[רי]ן סל׳ פסו׳ ◆ | |

| | |
|---|---|
| אחר[ת יקח לו ◆ יכול] גזירה ◆ ת״ל (ו)אם אינו אלא | C/B/A 1 |
| רשות ◆ אחרת יקח לו ◆ ולא של הפקר ◆ אחרת יקח לו ◆ בבת | B/A/B/A 3/2 |
| חורין הכת׳ מדבר ◆ אחרת יקח לו ◆ מלמד שאב | B/A 4 |
| זכאי בקידושי בתו קטנה ◆ אחרת יקח לו ◆ מלמד | B/A 5 |
| שמותר לקנות לו אשה אחרת לשום אישות ◆ אחרת | A 6 |
| יקח לו ◆ הרי הלז כיוצא בה ◆ מה זו נקנית בשטר אף זו | C/B |

7.  A.  "... her food." (Exod. 21:10):[89]

    B.  This is her maintenance.

    C.  In accordance with what is said in Scripture, "You have devoured My people's flesh,[90] etc." (Mic. 3:3).

    D.  "... her clothing" (Exod. 21:10):

    E.  This is clothing.

    F.  "... or her conjugal rights" (Exod. 21:10):

    G.  This is the marital duty mentioned in the Torah.[91]

8.  A.  Another interpretation:

    B.  "... her flesh" (Exod. 21:10):[92]

    C.  This [refers to] coming near flesh [to uncover nakedness].

[168]  D.  In accordance with what is said in Scripture, "None of you shall come near anyone of his own flesh, etc." (Lev. 18:6).

    E.  "... her clothing" (Exod. 21:10):

    F.  This is clothing.

    G.  "... or her conjugal rights" (Exod. 21:10):

    H.  This is her maintenance.

9.  A.  R. Eliezer ben Jacob says, "'... her flesh, her clothing' (Exod. 21:10):[93]

    B.  "Her clothing should be in accordance with her body, in that he should not dress her with clothing for the elderly in her youth, or clothing for the young in her old age."

10.  A.  "... her flesh, her clothing" (Exod. 21:10):

    B.  Her clothing should be in accordance with her season, in that he should not give her summer clothing in the rainy days, or rain [clothing] in the days of summer.

11.  A.  "... he must not withhold" (Exod. 21:10):

    B.  The father withholds from the son.

LX:V

1.  A.  "If he fails her in these three ways, (she shall go free, without payment)" (Exod. 21:11):

    B.  R. Eliezer says, "This is food, clothing, and conjugal rights."

    C.  R. Akiva said to him, "Why do I need this? For hasn't it already been said in Scripture, '... he must not withhold from this one her food, her clothing, or her conjugal rights' (Exod. 21:10)?

    D.  "Why does Scripture state, 'If (he fails her) in these three ways' (Exod. 21:11)?

    E.  "One might think he should perform for her all the commandments stated in the Torah.

---

[89] Hebrew: *sh'eirah* (שארה). Compare 7.A–8.H with *Mekhilta de-Rabbi Ishmael*, Nezikin (H/R, 258:15–259:1; Laut., vol. 3, 27:116–28:119; Neus., LX:I:23.A–H); y. Ketubot 30b (Neus., Ketubot:5:7:IV.A–VII.A); and b. Ketubot 47b (Neus., XIV.B:Tractate Ketubot:4:4:IX.4.A–I).

[90] Hebrew: *sh'eir* (שאר).

[91] Compare 7.A–G with *Mekhilta de-Rabbi Ishmael*, Nezikin (H/R, 258:15–259:1; Laut., vol. 3, 27:116–28:119; Neus., LX:I:23.A–H).

[92] This rendering of the word *sh'eirah* (שארה) in Exod. 21:8 is required for the following interpretation.

[93] Compare 9.A–10.B with *Mekhilta de-Rabbi Ishmael*, Nezikin (H/R, 259:1–10; Laut., vol. 3, 28:119–29:135; Neus., LX:I:23.I–R); y. Ketubot 30b (Neus., Ketubot:5:7:IV.A–VII.A); and b. Ketubot 47b (Neus., XIV.B:Tractate Ketubot:4:4:IX.4.A–I).

| | | | |
|---|---|---|---|
| C/B/A | 7 | נקנית בשטר. ♦ שארה ♦ זו פרנסתה ♦ כעניך שנא׳ ואשר | |
| E/D | | אכלו שאר עמי וגומ׳ (מיכה ג ג) ♦ כסותה ♦ זו כסות ♦ | |
| C/B/A 8 | G/F | עונתה ♦ זו עונה האמורה בתורה. ♦ ד״א ♦ שארה ♦ זו קרובת | |
| D | | בשר ♦ כעניך שנא׳ איש איש אל כל שאר בשרו וגומ׳ | |
| H/G/F/E | | (ויק׳ יח ו) ♦ כסותה ♦ זו כסות. ♦ עונתה ♦ זו פרנסתה. ♦ | |
| B/A | 9 | ר׳ אליעזר בן יעקב אומ׳ שארה כסותה ♦ לפי שארה | |
| | | תהא כסותה שלא יהא מלבישה כסות זקנה בילדה וכסות | |
| B/A | 10 | ילדה בזקנה. ♦ כסותה ועונתה ♦ לפי עיתה תהא כסותה | |
| | | שלא יתן לה כלים של חמה בימות הגשמים ושלגשמים | |
| B/A | 11 | בימות החמה ♦ לא יגרע ♦ האב גורע לבן. סל׳ פסו׳ ♦ | |
| LX:V | | | |

| | | | |
|---|---|---|---|
| B/A | 1 | ואם שלש אלה לא יעשה לה. ♦ ר׳ אל>י<עזר אומ׳ | |
| C | | זה שאר כסות ועונה אמ׳ לו ♦ ר׳ עקיבה מה אני צריך והלא | |
| D | | כבר נאמר שארה [כסו]תה ועונתה לא יגרע ♦ מה ת״ל ואם | |
| E | | שלש אלה ♦ יכול יעשה לה כל [המצות הא]מורות בתורה ♦ | |

F.   "Scripture states [however, in Exod. 21:11], '... these.'

G.   "One might think he should perform for her everything stated [regarding the] subject [of servitude].

H.   "Scripture states [however, in Exod. 21:11], 'If (he fails her) in these three ways.'

I.   "From this you should say that [it refers to these three things]: If he doesn't designate her for himself, for his son, or if he doesn't redeem her."

2.   A.   "... she shall go free" (Exod. 21:11):[94]

B.   Why do I need this?

C.   If to teach that she should go free at the end of six [years of servitude], behold it already says in Scripture, "If a fellow Hebrew, man or woman, is sold to you, (he shall serve you six years, and in the seventh year you shall set him free)" (Deut. 15:12).

D.   Why does Scripture state, "... she shall go free" (Exod. 21:11)?

E.   Scripture includes for her another [way] of going free.

F.   "... she shall go free" (Exod. 21:11)—this is at the age of adulthood.[95]

G.   "... without payment" (Exod. 21:11)—this is at the age of maidenhood.[96]

3.   A.   Because a man may marry off his daughter and a man can sell his daughter [into servitude, [one may reason that] just as he can marry her off when she has shown the first signs of maidenhood, so too may he sell her when she has shown the first signs of maidenhood.[97]

B.   Then let it[98] [simply] stipulate maidenhood! Why do I need it to stipulate [also] womanhood?

C.   If it stipulated maidenhood but didn't stipulate womanhood, I would say that she may not be enslaved at womanhood, because her father doesn't have authority over her, but she may be enslaved at maidenhood, because her father does have authority over her.

D.   Scripture states [thus], "... she shall go free ..." (Exod. 21:11)—this [refers to] the days of womanhood—[and] "... without payment" (Exod. 21:11)—this [refers to] the days of maidenhood.

E.   Then let it [simply] stipulate womanhood! Why do I need it I need it to stipulate [also] maidenhood!

F.   If it stipulated womanhood but didn't stipulate maidenhood, I would say that she may not be enslaved at womanhood, but may be enslaved at maidenhood.

G.   It needs to stipulate womanhood, and it needs to stipulate maidenhood.

4.   A.   Others say: "There is no payment" (Exod. 21:11) [to act as a ransom for] "he who fatally strikes a man" (Exod. 21:12).[99]

---

[94] Compare 2.A–G with the *Mekhilta de-Rabbi Ishmael,* Nezikin (H/R, 260:1–10; Laut., vol. 3, 30:152–31:166; Neus., LX:I:28.A–32.B); y. Qiddushin 59b (Neus., Qiddushin:1:2:X.A–L); and b. Qiddushin 4a (Neus., XIX:A:Qiddushin:1:1:II.2.A–B).

[95] See note 65 above.

[96] Ibid.

[97] Which would be erroneous. Once the girl becomes a maiden (see note 65 above), the father may no longer sell her into servitude, but he may still marry her off.

[98] I.e., Exod. 21:11.

[99] This puzzling tradition seems to be drawing a connection and mutual implication between the final clause of Exod. 21:11 (אין כסף), which when read out of context would be translated as "there is no payment," and verse Exod. 21:12. It seems to be disconnecting the final clause of Exod. 21:11 from that verse, and reading it, instead, as the initial clause of Exod. 21:12, as translated above. There is a parallel attestation to this tradition in some manuscript traditions of the *Mekhilta de-Rabbi Ishmael* (see H/R, 260:10).

| | | |
|---|---|---|
| G/F | • ת״ל אלה • יכול יעשה לה את כל האמ' בע<נ>ין • | |
| I/H | [ת״ל ואם של]ש אלה • אמור מעתה לא יעדה | |
| B/A | לא הוא ולא בנו ולא פדאה • [ויצאה חנם • מ]ה | 2 |
| C | אני צריך • אם ללמד שתהא יוצא בסוף שש הרי [כבר | |
| | נאמר כי ימ]כר לך אחיך העברי או העברייה (דב' טו | |
| E/D | יב) • מה ת״ל ויצאה [חנם • ריבה לה הכ]ת' (ו)יצאה | |
| G/F | אחרת • ויצאה חנם אלו ימי הבגר • [אין כסף אלו ימי | |
| A | הנעורים] • הואיל ואדם מקדש את בתו ואדם מוכר | 3 |
| | [את בתו מה כשמקדשה מקדשה עד שתביא סימנין | |
| B | אף] [כשמוכרה מוכרה עד שתביא סימנין • יאמר | |
| C | בנעורים מה אני] [צריך לומר בבגר • אילו נאמר | |
| | בנעורים ולא נאמר בבגר הייתי אומ'] לא ישתעבד | |
| | בבג[ר] שאין לא[ב]יה בה רשות אבל ישתעבד | |
| D | בנ[עורים שיש לאביה בה רשות • ת״ל ⟨ויצאה חנם | |
| E | אילו ימי בגר⟩ אין כסף אילו ימ[י] נעורים • יא[מ]ר בבגר | |
| F | מה אני צריך לו⟨מר⟩ בנעורים • שאילו נאמר בבגר | |
| | ולא נאמר בנעורים הייתי אומר לא ישתעבד בבגר | |
| G | ישתעבד בנערים • צריך לומר בבגר וצריך לומר | |
| A | בנערים. • אחרים אומ' אין כסף מכה איש ומת וגומ'. • | 4 |

*Chapter Sixty-One*

(Textual Source: Ms. Firkovich II A 268)

LXI:I

1.  A.  "If one strikes a man (and he dies, he shall surely be put to death)" (Exod. 21:12):[100]

    B.  I only know from this about one who strikes a man.

    C.  How does one know from Scripture concerning one who strikes a woman or child?

    D.  Scripture states, "If a man kills any human being, (he shall surely be put to death)" (Lev. 24:17), [which means] whether man, woman, or child.

    E.  I only know from this[101] concerning a man who strikes a woman.

    F.  How does one know from Scripture concerning a woman who strikes a man?

[169]  G.  Scripture states, "If one strikes" (Exod. 21:12), [which means] whether man or woman.

    H.  I only know concerning a man who strikes a woman or a woman who strikes a man.

    I.  How does one know from Scripture concerning a woman who strikes a woman or a child?

    J.  Scripture states, "... the one who murders will surely die" (Num. 35:16), [which means] in any circumstance.

    K.  If so, why does Scripture state, "If one strikes a man" (Exod. 21:12)?

    L.  For one might think that he would be culpable even if he struck the unviable birth or the child born at eight months.[102]

    M.  Scripture states, [however,] "... a man" (Exod. 21:12).

    N.  Just as a man is unique in that he is viable, the unviable birth and child born at eight months are excluded, because they are not viable.

2.  A.  "... and he dies" (Exod. 21:12):[103]

    B.  This tells that one is not culpable until he[104] has died.

    C.  Based upon this you say: If one struck him [with a blow sufficient to kill] but another came and knocked him senseless [while he was still yet alive], the last person is culpable [for his death].

3.  A.  "... he shall surely be put to death" (Exod. 21:12):

    B.  We do not know by what means this one's death should be.

    C.  Scripture states, [however,] "(If anyone) kills a person, only on the evidence of witnesses (may the manslayer be executed)" (Num. 35:30).

    D.  [Meaning,] by whatever means he murdered shall he be executed.

4.  A.  One might think if he killed him with a knife, he should be killed with a knife [or] if he killed with a reed pole, he should be killed with a reed pole.

    B.  Scripture says here "remove" [the evil from your midst] and Scripture says farther on "remove."[105]

---

[100] Compare 1.A–N with *Mekhilta de-Rabbi Ishmael*, Nezikin (H/R, 261:39; Laut., vol. 3, 32:5–33:15; Neus., LXI:I:2.A–5.D); and *Sifra*, Emor 20:1 (Neus., CCXLIV:I:1.A–I).

[101] I.e., Lev. 24:17.

[102] Neither one of which are considered viable human beings according to Rabbinic law.

[103] Compare 2.A–C with y. Baba Qamma 4c (Neus., Qiddushin:4:6:I.A–IV.J).

[104] I.e., the victim.

LXI:I

| | | |
|---|---|---|
| 1 | B/A | מכה איש ◆ אין לי אלא מכה את האיש ◆ |
| | D/C | מכה את האשה ואת הקטן מנין ◆ ת״ל כי יכה כל נפש |
| | E | אדם (ויק׳ כד יז) בין איש ובין אשה ובין קטן ◆ אין לי |
| | F | אלא איש המכה את האשה ◆ ‹האשה המכה את |
| | H/G | האיש› מנין ◆ ת״ל מכה בין איש ובין אשה ◆ ואין לי אלא |
| | I | איש המכה את האשה ואשה המכה את האיש ◆ אשה |
| | J | ‹ה›מכה את האשה ואת הקטן מנין ◆ ת״ל רוצח מות |
| | K | יומת (במ׳ לה טז) מכל מקום ◆ אם כן מה ת״ל מכה |
| | L | איש ◆ שיכול אפילו הכה את הנפלים ובן שמונה יהא |
| | N/M | חייב ◆ ת״ל איש ◆ מה איש מיוחד שהוא בן קיימה יצאו |
| 2 | B/A | נפלים ובן שמונה שאינן בני קיימה. ◆ ומת ◆ מגיד שאינו |
| | C | חייר עד שעה שימות ◆ מיכן אתה אומ׳ הכהו ובא אחד |
| 3 | B/A | ובלבלו האחרון חייב ◆ מות יומת ◆ אין אנו יודעין במה |
| | C | תהא מיתתו שלזה ◆ ת״ל מכה נפש לפי עדים וגומ׳ |
| 4 | D | (שם ל) ◆ במה שירצח [זה ירצח] זה ◆ יכול המיתו |
| | | בסכין ימיתנו בסכין המיתו בקנה [ימיתנו] בקרימות |
| | B | שלקנה ◆ נאמר כן הבערה ונאמ׳ להלן ה[נ]בערה ◆ |

---

[105] The exact reference of the biblical employments of the term "remove" is unclear. A parallel to this tradition at y. Sanhedrin 24b (Neus., Sanhedrin:7:3:II.A–D) utilizes two scriptural employments of the synonyms for the word "punish" (Exod. 21:20 and Lev. 26:25) to argue for punishment by the sword.

C. Just as the "remove" stated farther on is beheading, so too here beheading.

D. R. Nathan says, "Scripture says here 'vengeance' and Scripture says farther on, 'I will bring a sword against you to wreak vengeance' (Lev. 26:25).

E. "Just as 'vengeance' stated farther on is by the sword, so too here by the sword."

F. R. ... [manuscript lacuna][106] ... says, "Scripture says, 'Love your fellow as yourself' (Lev. 19:18), [meaning,] select for him a quick death!"

## LXI:II

1. A. "If he did not do it by design, (but God imposed it upon him, I will assign you a place to which he can flee)" (Exod. 21:13):

B. [This particular case] was part of the general rule [delineated in Exod. 21:12], but it is singled out [for special consideration] to make another requirement that is a part of the matter.

C. It is singled out to be more lenient and not to be more stringent.

2. A. "If he did not do it by design" (Exod. 21:13):

B. "If he did not do it by design" means only [that] he did not intend it.

C. Thus Scripture states, "... or hurled any object at him unintentionally" (Num. 35:22).

3. A. "... but God imposed it" (Exod. 21:13):

B. "Imposed"[107] means only that He arranged it for him.

C. Thus Scripture states, "Just see for yourselves that he is seeking a pretext[108] against me" (2 Kings 5:7).

D. And thus Scripture states about Samson, "He was seeking a pretext[109] against the Philistines, etc." (Judg. 14:4).

4. A. "If he did not do it by design, but God imposed it upon him" (Exod. 21:13):

B. One heaps merit upon the meritorious and culpability upon the culpable.[110]

C. This is what Trajan asked Lulianus and his brother Papias when he sentenced them to death.[111]

D. He said to them, "I am a descendant of Nebuchadnezzar, and you are descendants of Hananiah, Mishael, and Azariah. Let the one who saved Hananiah, Mishael, and Azariah from Nebuchadnezzar come and save you from me!"

[170]

E. They said to him, "Nebuchadnezzar was privileged enough to have miracles performed on his behalf, and Hananiah, Mishael, and Azariah were privileged enough to have miracles performed on their behalf. Nebuchadnezzar had the authority to not be convicted of spilling innocent blood, and Hananiah, Mishael, and Azariah had the authority to not be condemned to death. But you are not worthy of having miracles performed on your behalf, nor are we worthy of having miracles performed on our behalf! You will be convicted of spilling innocent blood, and we will be condemned to death!

"But if you don't kill us, we won't die ... [manuscript lacuna] ...

---

[106] A parallel to this tradition at t. Sanhedrin 9:11 names R. Judah as the Sage speaking here.
[107] Hebrew: inah—אנה.
[108] Hebrew: mitaneh—מתאנה.
[109] Hebrew: toh'anah—תאנה.
[110] Compare 4.B with y. Sanhedrin 28b (Neus., Sanhedrin:10:2:III.A–C), a different illustrating story.
[111] Compare 4.C–F with Sifra, Emor 9:8 (Neus., CCXXVII:I:5.A–I).

| | |
|---|---|
| C | מה] הבערה האמורה להלן התזת ראש אף כאן התזת |
| D | ר[אש ◆ ר' נתן] אומ' נאמ' כן נקימה ונאמ' להלן והבאתי |
| E | עליכ]ם חרב נוקמת] (ויק' כו כה) ◆ מה נקימה האמ' להלן |
| F | בסייף אף כן בסייף ◆ ר' [... בן...] אומ' ואהבת לרעך |
| | כמוך (שם יט יח) ברור לו מיתה י[פה ◆ |

LXI:II

| | | |
|---|---|---|
| 1 | B/A | ואשר לא צדה] ◆ ה[יה בכלל ויצא לטעון טעון אחר |
| | A 2  C | שהוא כעניינו ◆ יצא להקל ולא להחמיר] ◆ וא[נ]שר לא |
| | C/B | צדה ◆ אין אשר לא צדה אלא שלא נתכוון לו ◆ כן הוא |
| | | אומ' או [השליך עליו כל כלי בלא צדיה (במ' לה כב) ◆ |
| 3 | C/B/A | והאלהים אנה ◆ אין אנה] אל[א שמזדקיף לו ◆ כן הוא |
| | | אומ' כי אך דעו] נא ו[ר]או כ[י מתאנ]ה הוא לי (מ"ב ה |
| | | ז) ◆ וכן הו[א אום' בשמשון כי] תאנה הוא מבקש |
| | D | מפלשתים וגומ' (שופ' יד ד) ◆ ואשר לא צדה |
| 4 | A | ו[האלק]ים אנה לידו ◆ מגלגלין זכות על ידי זכאי |
| | B | וחובה על ידי חייב ◆ זו היא ששאל טריונוס את לולוניס |
| | C | ואת פפיוס אחיו כשגזר עליהן מיתה ◆ אמ' להן אני בנו |
| | D | של נבוכד נצר ואתם בניהם שלחנניה מישאל ועזריה |
| | | יבוא מי שהציל <את> חנניה מישאל ועזריה מיד |
| | | נבוכד נצר ויציל אתכם מידי ◆ אמרו לו נבוכד נצר זכה |
| | E | ליעשות על ידו נסים וחנניה מישאל ועזריה זכו |
| | | שיעשה על ידיהם נסים <נבוכד נצר זכה שלא נתחייב |
| | | לשפוך דם נקי וחנניה מישאל ועזריה זכו> שלא |
| | | נתחייבו מיתה ואתה אי אתה כדאי ליעשות נסים על |
| | | ידיך ואנו אין <אנו> כדאי שיעשו לנו נסים אתה |
| | | נתחייבתה לשפוך דם נקי ואנו נתחייבנו מיתה וכי אם |
| | | אי אתה הורגנו אין אנו מתים <...> כת' בתורתינו |

"It is written in our Torah, 'If he did not do it by design, but God imposed it upon him' (Exod. 21:13) [meaning,] one heaps merit upon the meritorious and culpability upon the culpable! When we die, you will know that we are descendants of Hananiah, Mishael, and Azariah!"

F. They didn't die until he saw them digging out his eyes!

5. A. "... I will assign you" (Exod. 21:13):

B. This teaches that you banish [him] to the wilderness.

6. A. "... a place" (Exod. 21:13):[112]

B. This teaches that you banish him to the camp of the Levites.[113]

C. Scripture says here, "a place," and Scripture says above, "Let everyone remain where he is: let no one leave his place" (Exod. 16:29).

D. Just as the "place" mentioned above is outside [the city by] 2,000 cubits, with the city not taken into account in the measurement, so too is the "place" mentioned here [outside the city by] 2,000 cubits, with the city not taken into account in the measurement.

7. A. "'There. There. There.' Three times [it is stated here in Scripture].[114]

B. "[Meaning,] there[115] will be your dwelling, and there will be your [place of] death, and there will be your grave."—The words of R. Eliezer ben Jacob.

## LXI:III

1. A. "When a man schemes against his neighbor (and kills him treacherously, you shall take him from My very altar to be put to death)" (Exod. 21:14):

B. While others scheme against him at the time of his murderous act.

C. "... and kills him treacherously" (Exod. 21:14):

D. While others were acting treacherously against him.

E. You say the matter is like this. Isn't it, instead ... [manuscript lacuna] ... Scripture states ... [manuscript lacuna] ...

F. Thus, why does Scripture state, "When a man schemes against his neighbor" (Exod. 21:14)?

G. While others scheme against him at the time of his murderous act.

2. A. "... and kills him treacherously ..." (Exod. 21:14):

B. R. ... [manuscript lacuna] ... says, "One might think if he intended to kill one person, but killed another, he would be culpable.

C. "For thus we find that false witnesses are culpable even if they didn't kill, and the one who stalks a man, maiden, or betrothed woman is culpable even if he didn't do anything [other than this to them].

D. "Scripture states, [however,] '... fatally' (Exod. 21:12).

E. "This tells that he isn't culpable until the moment that he dies.

F. "Then why does Scripture state, 'When a man schemes' (Exod. 21:14)?

G. "While others scheme against him at the time of his murderous act.

---

[112] Compare 6.A–D with *Mekhilta de-Rabbi Ishmael*, Nezikin (H/R, 262:16–263:1; Laut., vol. 3, 36:51–57; Neus., LXI:II:3.A–F).
[113] See Num. 35:5.
[114] Compare 7.A–B with m. Makkot 2:7; t. Makkot 3:5; and *Sifre Deut.*, Piska 181 (Hammer, p. 205; Neus., CLXXXI:IV:1.A–B).
[115] I.e., the city of refuge.

ואשר לא צדה והאלהים אנה לידו מגלגלין זכות על

ידי זכאי וחובה על ידי חייב וכשנמות תדע שאנו בניו

של חנניה מישאל ועזריה • לא מתו עד שראו אותן  F

מחטטין את עיניו • ושמתי לך בחייך • מלמד שמגל<י>ן  B/A  5

למדבר • מקום מקומך • מלמד שמגל<י>ן למחנה לויה •  B/A  6

נאמר [כן מקו]ם ונאמר להלן <...> שבו איש תחתיו  C

אל יצא איש ממקומו (שמ׳ טז כט) • מה [מקום  D

האמו]ר להלן חוץ לאלפים אמה ואין העיר עולה מן

המדה [אף כן אלפי]ם אמה ואין העיר עולה מן

המדה • שם שם שם [ג׳ פעמים • ש]ם תהא דירתו ושם  B/A  7

תהא מיתתו ושם תהא [קבורתו דברי ר׳ אליעז]ר בן

יעקב. סל׳ פסר׳ •

LXI:III

וכי יזיד איש על [רעהו • עד שיזיד עליו] אחרין  B/A  1

בשעת הריגתו • להרגו בערמה • [עד שיעריִמו עליו

אחר]ים בשעת הריגתו • אתה אומ׳ בזה הדבר [מדבר  E

או אינו מדבר אלא...] [... ת״ל...] • [הא מה ת״ל כי יזיד  F

איש על רעהו • עד שיזיד עליו אחרי]ם בשעת [הריגתו] •  G

להורגו בע[רמה <...> • ר׳ ... אומ׳ יכול נתכוין להרוג את  B/A  2

ז[ה והרג את זה יהא חייב • שכן מצינו בע[ד]ים זוממין  C

שאף] על פי שלא הרגו חייבין והרודף אחר הזכור

ואחר נערה [המ]אורשה שאף על פי שלא עשה מעשה

(יהא) חייב • ת״ל ומת (שמ׳ כא יב) • מגיד שאינו חייב עד  E/D

שעה שימות • הא מה ת״ל כי יזיד איש • עד שיזיד עליו  G/F

H. "'... and kills him treacherously ...' (Exod. 21:14).

I. "While others were acting treacherously against him."

3. A. "When a *man* schemes" (Exod. 21:14):

B. This excludes the minor.

[171] C. R. Judah says, "Just as the man is unique, in that he can act in premeditated fashion and ejaculate, so too is the minor excluded because he cannot act in premeditated fashion and ejaculate."

4. A. "... against his neighbor" (Exod. 21:14):

B. Which excludes outsiders.

C. "... against his neighbor" (Exod. 21:14):

D. Which excludes the alien resident.

E. Should I exclude outsiders, who do not have the commandments [of the Torah] like Israel [does], but still not exclude the alien resident, who does have the commandments like Israel?

F. Scripture states, "... his neighbor" (Exod. 21:14).

G. Which excludes the resident alien.

5. A. "'... and kills him treacherously' (Exod. 21:14):[116]

B. "Which excludes the person who intended to kill one person, but killed another—he should be exempt."—The words of R. Shimon.

C. R. Judah says, "Even the person who intended to kill one person, but killed another is culpable.

D. "And why does Scripture state, '... and kills him treacherously' (Exod. 21:14)?

E. "To exclude the person who intended to kill the non-Jew, but killed the Jew, or [intended to kill] the child born at eight months, but killed the child born at nine months."

6. A. "... from My very altar" (Exod. 21:14):

B. But not from the beginning of the ramp and not from the head of the altar.

C. But even if the sacrificial service was in his hand, and he was standing and offering incense, you should delay him from it and put him to death.

D. R. Yosi says, "It's a matter of logical reasoning:

E. "If for the sacrificial service, which sets aside [the restrictions] of *Shabbat* [in order to be performed], you should delay him from it in order to put to death a life for a life, then for *Shabbat,* which is set aside [in order to perform] the sacrifical service, is it not only logical that they would put it aside to keep alive one who is doubtfully culpable of death?"[117]

7. A. I only know about the murderer [from Exod. 21:14]. How does one know from Scripture that this includes the others who will be put to death?

B. Scripture states, "... you shall take him ... to be put to death" (Exod. 21:14).

---

[116] Compare 5.A–E with *Mekhilta de-Rabbi Ishmael,* Nezikin (H/R, 274:16–275:4; Laut., vol. 3, 62:1–63:18; Neus., LXV:I:1.A–3.E); m. Sanhedrin 9:2; t. Sanhedrin 12:4; and y. Sanhedrin 27a (Neus., Sanhedrin:9:4:I.A–II.B).

[117] Clearly, 6.D–E is incomplete and somewhat incongruous with what precedes it in 6.A–C. However, compare with much more substantial parallel material in the *Mekhilta de-Rabbi Ishmael,* Nezikin (H/R, 263:12–264:14; Laut., vol. 3, 37:72–40:109; Neus., LXI: II:8.A–13.C).

| | | |
|---|---|---|
| אחרים בשעת הריגתו ♦ להרגו בערמה ♦ עד שיע׳ עליו | I/H | |
| אחרים בשעת הריגתו. ♦ כי יזיד איש ♦ פרט לקטן ♦ ר׳ יהו׳ | C/B/A | 3 |
| אומ׳ מה האיש מיוחד שהוא מיזיד ומזריע יצא קטן | | |
| שאינו מיזיד ומזריע. ♦ על רעהו ♦ פרט לאחרים ♦ רעהו ♦ | C/B/A | 4 |
| פרט לגר תושב ♦ מוציא אני את אחרים שאין להן | E/D | |
| מצות כיש׳ ועדאן לא אוציא את גר תושב שיש לו | | |
| מצות כיש[ר׳] ♦ ת״ל רעהו ♦ פרט לגר תושב ♦ | G/F | |
| להרגו בערמה ♦ פרט למתכוין להרג את זה והרג את | B/A | 5 |
| זה שיפטר דברי ר׳ שמע׳ ♦ ר[׳] יהודה אומ׳ אף המתכוין | C | |
| להרוג את זה והרג את זה חייב ♦ ומה ת״ל להרגו | D | |
| בערמה ♦ פרט למתכוין להמית את הגוי והמית את בן | E | |
| יש׳ את בן שמונה והמית את בן תשעה. ♦ מעם מזבחי ♦ | A | 6 |
| ולא מראש הכבש ולא מראש המזבח ♦ ואפילו עבודה | C/B | |
| בידו ועומד ומקטיר דוחין אותו ממנה ומ[מיתין] | | |
| אותו. ♦ אמ׳ ר׳ יוסי קל וחומר הן הדברים ♦ מה עבדה | E/D | |
| [שהיא דוחה] את השבת דוחין אתו ממנה להמית נפש | | |
| מפני [נפש שבת] שעבדה דוחה את השבת דין הוא | | |
| שידחו אות[ה] בשביל להחיות] ספק נפש ♦ אין לי אלא רוצח | A | 7 |
| בלבד מנין ל[רבות שאר המומתין] ♦ ת״ל תקחנו למות ♦ | B | |

8.    A.    "... to be put to death" (Exod. 21:14):[118]

      B.    But not to be banished [to the city of refuge] to die, or to be given stripes to die, or [to be given] punishments to die, or for other things.

9.    A.    How does one know from Scripture that the Sanhedrin was

(Textual Source: Midrash ha-Gadol)

next to the altar?

      B.    Scripture states, "... you shall take him from My altar to be put to death" (Exod. 21:14).

      C.    And how does one know from Scripture that they only put [people] to death when the Temple is in existence?

      D.    Scripture states, "... you shall take him from My altar to be put to death" (Exod. 21:14).

      E.    [Meaning,] if there is an altar, you may put [people] to death, but if not, you may not put [people] to death.

*Chapter Sixty-Two*

(Textual Source: Midrash ha-Gadol)

LXII:I

1.    A.    "He who strikes his father (or his mother shall surely be put to death)" (Exod. 21:15):[119]

      B.    But not his father's father.

      C.    "... or his mother" (Exod. 21:15):

      D.    But not his mother's mother.

      E.    "... his father" (Exod. 21:15):

      F.    But not if it is doubtful.

      G.    "... his mother" (Exod. 21:15):

      H.    But not if it is doubtful.

2.    A.    "He who strikes his father or his mother shall surely be put to death" (Exod. 21:15):

      B.    One might think he would not be culpable unless he struck both of them together.

      C.    Scripture states, [however,] "... but one who kills a human being shall be put to death" (Lev. 24:21), [meaning,] even [if only] one of them.

      D.    And why does Scripture state, "He who strikes his father or mother" (Exod. 21:15)?

      E.    One might think that the convert[120] whose conception was not in accordance with Jewish sanctity[121] but whose birth was in accordance with Jewish sanctity[122] would be culpable for striking his mother.[123]

      F.    Scripture states, [however,] "He who strikes his father or mother" (Exod. 21:15).

[172]  G.    He who is culpable for striking his father is culpable for striking his mother, but he who

---

[118] Compare 8.A–B with *Mekhilta de-Rabbi Ishmael*, Nezikin (H/R, 264:15–16; Laut., vol. 3, 40:110–11; Neus., LXI:II:14.A–B).

[119] Compare 1.A–H with *Sifra*, Qedoshim 9:8 (Neus., CCVII:I:1.A–2.E).

[120] I.e., the son who was converted along with his mother when she converted. See m. Yebamot 11:2.

[121] I.e., whose father had not converted at the time of the conception of the son.

[122] I.e., the father converted before the time of the birth of the son.

[123] 2.E–G appears to be a confusing, illogical compilation of two separate chains of tradition. 2.E appears to have affinities with m. Yebamot 11:2, whereas 2.F–G appears to have affinities to *Sifra*, Qedoshim 9:8 (Neus., CCVII:I:4.A–C). However, the two chains of tradition

| | | |
|---|---|---|
| למות ◆ <ו>לא לגלות למות ול[א ללקות למות | B/A | 8 |
| ולא] לענשין למות ולא לדברים אחרים ◆ מ[נין שתהא | A | 9 |
| סנהדרין] סמוכה למזבח ◆ ת״ל מעם מזבחי תקחנו | B | |
| למות. ◆ ומנין שאין ממיתין אלא בפני הבית ◆ ת״ל | D/C | |
| מעם מזבחי תקחנו למות ◆ הא אם יש מזבח אתה | E | |
| ממית ואם לאו אי אתה ממית. ◆ | | |

LXII:I

| | | |
|---|---|---|
| ומכה אביו ◆ ולא אבי אביו ◆ אמו ◆ ולא אם אמו. ◆ | D/C/B/A | 1 |
| אביו ◆ ולא הספק. ◆ אמו ◆ ולא הספק. ◆ מכה אביו ואמו | A 2 | H/G/F/E |
| מות יומת ◆ יכול לא יהא חייב עד שיכם שניהם כאחד ◆ | B | |
| ת״ל ומכה אדם יומת (ויק׳ כד כא) ואפלו אחד מהם. ◆ | C | |
| מה ת״ל ומכה אביו ואמו ◆ יכול הגר שהיתה הורתו | E/D | |
| שלא בקדושה ולידתו בקדושה יכול יהא חייב על | | |
| מכת אמו ◆ ת״ל ◆ ומכה אביו ואמו ◆ את שחייב על מכת | G/F | |
| אביו חייב על מכת אמו את שאינו חייב על מכת אביו | | |

are not merged effectively here, and in the case of 2.E, it appears that it is only partially representative of the gist of the pertinent issue as represented in m. Yebamot 11:2. The result here is a confusing merging of tradition.

is not culpable for striking his father is not culpable for striking his mother.

3.  A.  One might think if he strikes them after [their] death he would be culpable.[124]

    B.  For it is a matter of logic:

    C.  If [for] cursing, which doesn't apply to everyone,[125] one is culpable for it after death, then isn't it logical that one would be culpable for smiting, which does apply to everyone, after death?

    D.  Scripture states, [however,] "One who kills a beast ... but one who kills a human being" (Lev. 24:21).

    E.  Just as with smiting a beast, one is not culpable [for doing it to a beast] after [its] death, so too is one not culpable for smiting his father or mother after death.

4.  A.  One might think if he struck them but didn't wound them, he would be culpable.[126]

    B.  Scripture states, [however,] "One who kills a beast ... but one who kills a human being" (Lev. 24:21).

    C.  Just as with smiting a beast, one is not culpable unless he wounds it, so too is one not culpable for smiting his mother or father unless he wounds them.

5.  A.  One might think if he struck them inadvertently, he would be culpable for indemnity payment.

    B.  Scripture states, [however,] "One who kills a beast ... but one who kills a human being" (Lev. 24:21).

    C.  Just as with smiting a beast, there is no distinction in culpability for indemnity payment between one who acts inadvertently or in premeditated fashion, so too is there no distinction in releasing one from indemnity payment for striking his father or his mother.

6.  A.  "... shall surely be put to death" (Exod. 21:15):[127]

    B.  We don't know by what means this person's death should be!

    C.  Scripture states, [however,] "Love your fellow as yourself" (Lev. 19:18).

    D.  [Meaning,] select for him a quick death!

    E.  And which is this? This is execution by strangulation.

    F.  Rabbi says, "It's not [used here] because it is a quick execution. Rather, it's because it is the method of execution used when nothing else is specifically stipulated. And whenever execution is mentioned in the Torah with no specific stipulation, it [means] strangulation."

    G.  How does one know from Scripture that if you cannot execute him by strangulation, you should execute him with any of the methods of execution, whether merciful or harsh?

    H.  Scripture states, "... he shall surely die" (Exod. 21:15).

    I.  By any means.

---

[124] Compare 3.A–E with *Mekhilta de-Rabbi Ishmael*, Nezikin (H/R, 265:3–10; Laut., vol. 3, 41:5–42:18; Neus., LXII:I:2.A–I); *Sifra*, Qedoshim 9:10 (Neus., CCVII:I:5.A–F); and *Sifra*, Qedoshim 20:8 (Neus., CCXLIV:I:11.A–12.C).

[125] I.e., one does not receive the death penalty for cursing everyone, but specifically only for cursing one's parents.

[126] Compare 4.A–C with *Mekhilta de-Rabbi Ishmael*, Nezikin (H/R, 265:3–10; Laut., vol. 3, 41:5–42:18; Neus., LXII:I:2.A–I); *Sifra*, Qedoshim 9:10 (Neus., CCVII:I:5.A–F); and *Sifra*, Qedoshim 20:8 (Neus., CCXLIV:I:11.A–12.C).

[127] Compare 6.A–I with *Mekhilta de-Rabbi Ishmael*, Nezikin (H/R, 265:15–266:8; Laut., vol. 3, 43:25–44:41; Neus., LXII:I:4.A–6.E).

| | | |
|---|---|---|
| אינו חייב על מכת אמו. ◆ יכול אם הכן לאחר מיתה | A | 3 |
| יהא חייב ◆ ודין הוא ◆ ומה קללה שאין נוהגת בכל חייבין | C/B | |
| עליה לאחר מיתה מכה שהיא נוהגת בכל אינו דין | | |
| שיהוא חייבין עליה לאחר מיתה ◆ ת״ל מכה בהמה | D | |
| ומכה אדם ◆ מה מכה בהמה אינו חייב לאחר מיתה אף | E | |
| מכה אביו ואמו לא יהא חייב לאחר מיתה. ◆ יכול אם | A | 4 |
| הכן ולא עשה בהן חבורה יהא חייב ◆ ת״ל מכה בהמה | B | |
| ומכה אדם ◆ מה מכה בהמה אינו חייב עד שיעשה בה | C | |
| חבורה אף מכה אביו ואמו לא יהא חייב עד שיעשה | | |
| בהן חבורה. ◆ יכול אם הכה אותן שוגג יהא חייב | Λ | 5 |
| בתשלומין ◆ ת״ל מכה בהמה ומכה אדם ◆ מה מכה | C/B | |
| בהמה לא חלק בה בין שוגג למזיד לחייבו בתשלומין | | |
| אף מכה אביו ואמו לא חלק בהן בין שוגג למזיד | | |
| לפטרו מן התשלומין. ◆ מות יומת ◆ אין אנו יודעין במה | B/A | 6 |
| תהא מיתתו שלזה ◆ ת״ל ואהבת לרעך כמוך (ויק׳ יט | C | |
| יח) ◆ ברור לו מיתה יפה ◆ והיזה זה זה חנק. ◆ רבי אומר | F/E/D | |
| לא מפני שהיא יפה אלא מפני שהיא מיתה סתם וכל | | |
| מיתה האמורה בתורה סתם היא חנק. ◆ מנין לא יכולת | G | |
| להמיתו בחנק המיתו באחת מכל מיתות בין קלות | | |
| בין חמורות ◆ ת״ל מות יומת ◆ מכל מקום. ◆ | I/H | |

LXII:II

1. A. "He who kidnaps a man, (whether he has sold him or is still holding him, shall surely be put to death)" (Exod. 21:16):[128]

   B. I only know [from this] concerning the one who kidnaps a man. How does one know from Scripture concerning the one who kidnaps the woman or the child?

   C. Scripture states, "If a man is found to have kidnapped a fellow (Israelite)" (Deut. 24:7).

   D. Whether man, woman, or child.

2. A. I only know [from this] concerning the man who kidnaps. How does one know from Scripture concerning the woman who kidnaps?

   B. Scripture states, "The one who kidnaps a man" (Exod. 21:16).[129]

   C. [Meaning,] whether man or woman.

   D. If so, why does Scripture state, "... a man" (Exod. 21:16)?

   E. Because one might think he would be culpable even if he kidnapped an unviable birth or the child born at eight months.

   F. Scripture states, [however,] "... a man" (Exod. 21:16).

   G. Just as a man is unique in that he is a viable, the unviable birth and child born at eight months are excluded, because they are not viable.

3. A. How does one know from Scripture that one is not culpable unless he kidnaps [and is seen] by witnesses?[130]

   B. Scripture states, "If a man is found to have kidnapped" (Deut. 24:7).

   C. And how does one know from Scripture that one is not culpable unless he sold [a kidnapped person in the presence] of witnesses?

   D. Scripture states, "... whether he has sold him or is still holding him" (Exod. 21:16).

4. A. "... or is still (holding him)" (Exod. 21:16):

   B. This excludes when the person was in his power.

   C. Exempt is the father who kidnaps his son.

5. A. One might think if he sold him to one of his relatives he would be culpable.

   B. Scripture states, [however,] "... to have kidnapped a fellow Israelite" (Deut. 24:7), [meaning, he is culpable] only if he separates him from his fellow Israelites.

6. A. One might think that because we have found that one may pay an assessed compensation payment for the [kidnapped] Canaanite slave, then it is also the case here.[131]

   B. Scripture states, [however,] "... whether he has sold him or is still holding him" (Exod. 21:16).

   C. This tells that he is not culpable until he takes him into his possession.

   D. R. Judah says, "Only once he has takes him into his possession and makes use of him.

   E. "As it says in Scripture, '... enslaving him or selling him' (Deut. 24:7). "

7. A. "... shall surely be put to death" (Exod. 21:16):[132]

---

[128] Compare 1.A–4.C with *Mekhilta de-Rabbi Ishmael,* Nezikin (H/R, 266:9–267:10; Laut., vol. 3, 44:42–46:73; Neus., LXII:II:1.A–9.C).

[129] This rendering of the participle "steals" (Hebrew: גונב) is required for the purposes of this interpretation.

[130] Compare 3.A–D with *Sifre Deut.,* Piska 273 (Hammer, p. 268; Neus., CCLXXIII:I:1.A–4.C).

LXII:II

| | | |
|---|---|---|
| וגנב איש ◆ אין לי אלא הגונב את האיש הגונב את | B/A | 1 |
| האשה ואת הקטן מנין ◆ ת״ל כי ימצא איש גנב נפש ◆ בין | D/C | |
| איש בין אשה בין קטן. ◆ אין לי אלא איש הגונב אשה | A | 2 |
| הגונבת מנין ◆ ת״ל גונב איש ◆ בין איש בין אשה ◆ אם כן | D/C/B | |
| למה נאמר איש ◆ שיכול אפלו גנב את הנפלים ובן | E | |
| שמונה יהא חייב ◆ ת״ל איש ◆ מה איש מיוחד שהוא בן | G/F | |
| קיימה יצאו נפלים ובן שמונה שאינן בני קיימה. ◆ מנין | A | 3 |
| שאינו חייב עד שיגנוב בעדים ◆ ת״ל כי ימצא איש גונב. ◆ | B | |
| ומנין שאינו חייב עד שימכור בעדים ◆ ת״ל ומכרו | D/C | |
| ונמצא בידו. ◆ ונמצא ◆ פרט למי שמצויין בידו ◆ יצא האב | C/B/A | 4 |
| שגנב את בנו. ◆ יכול מכרו לאחד מקרוביו יהא חייב ◆ | A | 5 |
| ת״ל גנב נפש מאחיו עד שיפרישנו מאחיו. ◆ (או יכול) | A 6 | B |
| לפי שמצינו בעבד כנעני שכיון שנתן בו דמים קנה | | |
| יכול אף זה כן ◆ ת״ל ומכרו ונמצא בידו ◆ מגיד שאינו | C/B | |
| חייב עד שיכניסנו לרשותו. ◆ ר׳ יהודה אומר משיכניסנו | D | |
| לרשותו וישתמש בו ◆ שנ׳ והתעמר בו ומכרו. ◆ מות יומת ◆ | A 7 | E |

[131] Compare 6.A–E with *Sifre Deut.*, Piska 273 (Hammer, p. 268; Neus., CCLXXIII:II:1.A–C).
[132] Compare 7.A–E with *Sifre Deut.*, Piska 273 (Hammer, p. 268; Neus., CCLXXIII:III:1.A–B).

B.   By the method of execution [used] when [a death is] stipulated in unspecified fashion in the Torah—strangulation.

C.   How does one know from Scripture that if you cannot execute him by strangulation, you should execute him with any of the methods of execution, whether merciful or harsh?

D.   Scripture states, "... he shall surely die" (Exod. 21:16).

E.   By any means.

## LXII:III

1.   A.   "He who insults his father (or his mother shall surely be put to death)" (Exod. 21:17):

B.   But not his father's father.

C.   "... or his mother" (Exod. 21:17):

D.   But not his mother's mother.

E.   "... his father" (Exod. 21:17):

F.   But not if it is doubtful.

G.   "... his mother" (Exod. 21:17):

H.   But not if it is doubtful.

2.   A.   "He who insults his father or his mother shall surely be put to death" (Exod. 21:17):[133]

B.   One might think he would not be culpable unless he curses both of them together.

C.   Scripture states, [however,] "(If anyone) insults his father or his mother" (Lev. 20:9).

[173]   D.   [Even if only] one of them.

E.   And why does Scripture state, "He who insults his father or mother" (Exod. 21:17)?

F.   One might think that the convert whose conception was not in accordance with Jewish sanctity but whose birth was in accordance with Jewish sanctity would be culpable for insulting his mother.[134]

G.   Scripture states, [however,] "He who insults his father or mother" (Exod. 21:17).

H.   He who is culpable for insulting his father is culpable for insulting his mother, but he who is not culpable for insulting his father is not culpable for insulting his mother.

3.   A.   One might think if he insults them after [their] death he would not be culpable.

B.   For it is a matter of logic:

C.   If [for] smiting, which applies to everyone,[135] one is not culpable for it after death, then isn't it logical that one would not be culpable for insulting, which does not apply to everyone, after death?

D.   Scripture states, [however,] "... he has insulted his father and his mother—his bloodguilt (is upon him)" (Lev. 20:9).

E.   Even after death.

4.   A.   One might think he would be guilty even if he insulted them with a euphemism (for God's name).[136]

[133] Compare 2.A–D with *Mekhilta de-Rabbi Ishmael*, Nezikin (H/R, 267:19–21; Laut., vol. 3, 47:89–91; Neus., LXII:III:2.A–C).
[134] Regarding 2.F–H, see notes 120, 121, 122, and 123 above.
[135] I.e., one receives the death penalty for smiting anyone.
[136] Compare 4.A–C with *Mekhilta de-Rabbi Ishmael*, Nezikin (H/R, 268:4–7; Laut., vol. 3, 48:98–49:105; Neus., LXII:III:3.A–H).

| | | |
|---|---|---|
| C/B | | בסתם מיתה האמורה בתורה בחנק ◆ <מנין לא יכולת |
| | | להמיתו בחנק המיתו באחת מכל מיתות בין קלות |
| E/D | | בין חמורות ◆ ת״ל> מות יומת ◆ מכל מקום. ◆ |

<br>

**LXII:III**

| | | | |
|---|---|---|---|
| 1 | D/C/B/A | | ומקלל אביו ◆ ולא אבי אביו. ◆ אמו ◆ ולא אם אמו. ◆ |
| H/G/F/E | A | 2 | אביו ◆ ולא הספק. ◆ אמו ◆ ולא הספק. ◆ ומקלל אביו ואמו |
| | B | | מות יומת ◆ יכול לא יהא חייב עד שיקללם שניהם |
| | C | | כאחת ◆ ת״ל אשר יקלל את אביו ואת אמו (ויק׳ כ ט) ◆ |
| | F/E/D | | אחד מהם. ◆ ומה ת״ל ומקלל אביו ואמו ◆ יכול הגר |
| | | | שהיתה הורתו שלא בקדושה ולידתו בקדושה יהא |
| | H/G | | חייב על קללת אמו ◆ ת״ל מקלל אביו ואמו ◆ את שהוא |
| | | | חייב על קללת אביו חייב על קללת אמו ואת שאינו |
| | A | 3 | חייב על קללת אביו אינו חייב על קללת אמו. ◆ יכול |
| | C/B | | אם קללן לאחר מיתה לא יהא חייב ◆ ודין הוא ◆ ומה |
| | | | מכה שהיא נוהגת בכל אין חייבין עליה לאחר מיתה |
| | | | קללה שאין נוהגת בכל אינו דין שלא יהוא חייבין |
| | E/D | | עליה לאחר מיתה ◆ ת״ל אביו ואמו קלל דמיו בו ◆ אפלו |
| | A | 4 | לאחר מיתה. ◆ יכול אפלו קללם בכנוי יהא חייב ◆ |

B. Scripture states, "He who insults his father or his mother" (Exod. 21:17), and Scripture states, "Anyone who insults his God" (Lev. 24:15).

C. Just as there[137] [culpability for insulting is incurred only] with the Name,[138] so too here [only] with the Name.

5.    A. "... shall surely be put to death" (Exod. 21:17):[139]

B. We don't know by what means

(Textual Source: Ms. Firkovich II A 268)

this person's death should be!

C. Scripture states, [however,] "... his bloodguilt is upon him" (Lev. 20:9), and farther on it says in Scripture, "... their bloodguilt shall be upon them" (Lev. 20:27).

D. Just as "their bloodguilt shall be upon them" stated farther on is stoning, so too "his bloodguilt is upon him" stated here is stoning.

E. How does one know from Scripture that if you cannot execute him by stoning, you should execute him with any of the methods of execution, whether merciful or harsh?

F. Scripture states, "... he shall surely die" (Exod. 21:17).

G. By any means.

*Chapter Sixty-Three*

(Textual Source: Firkovich II A 268)

LXIII:I

1.    A. "When men quarrel (and one man strikes his companion with stone or fist, and he does not die but has to take to his bed)" (Exod. 21:18):[140]

B. Nothing good comes from quarreling.

C. And thus Scripture states, "And there was quarreling between the herdsmen of (Abram's) cattle, etc." (Gen. 13:7).

D. Who caused Lot to separate from that righteous one?[141]

E. You must say it was [the] quarreling.

F. And Scripture says, "When there is a quarrel between men and they go to law, and a decision is rendered" (Deut. 25:1).

G. Who caused this one to be flogged?

H. You must say it was [the] quarreling.

2.    A. "When men quarrel" (Exod. 21:18):

B. At first they will come to the point of the commandments,[142] and afterward to the point of blows, and afterward to the point of punishments.

3.    A. "When men quarrel" (Exod. 21:18):[143]

B. I only know concerning men. How does one know from Scripture to include two men [or] a woman and a man?

---

[137] I.e., Lev. 24:15.

[138] I.e., the Tetragrammaton (YHWH—יהוה).

[139] Compare 5.A–G with *Mekhilta de-Rabbi Ishmael,* Nezikin (H/R, 268:8–10; Laut., vol. 3, 49:106–9; Neus., LXII:III:3.4.A–E).

[140] Compare 1.A–H with *Sifre Deut.,* Piska 286 (Hammer, p. 276; Neus., CCLXXXVI:I:1.A–I) and Piska 292 (Hammer, p. 283; Neus., CCXCII:I:1.A–I).

| | | |
|---|---|---|
| נאמר ומקלל אביו ואמו ונאמר איש איש כי יקלל אלקיו | B | |
| (ויק׳ כד טו) ♦ מה להלן בשם אף כאן בשם. ♦ מות יומת ♦ | A 5 | C |
| אין אנו יודעין במה תהא מיתתו של זה ♦ ת״ל דמיו בו | C/B | |
| (ויק׳ כ ט) ולהלן נאמ׳ דמיהם בם (שם כז) ♦ מה דמיהם | D | |
| בם האמור להלן סקילה אף דמיו בו האמור כאן | | |
| סקילה ♦ מנין לא יכולתה להמיתו בסקילה המיתו | E | |
| באחת מכל מיתות האמורות בין קלות ובין חמורות | | |
| ת״ל מות יומת ♦ מכל מקום ♦ סל׳ פסו׳. ♦ | G/F | |

LXIII:I

| | | |
|---|---|---|
| וכי יריבון אנשים ♦ אין דבר טוב יוצא מתוך מריבה ♦ | B/A | 1 |
| וכן הוא אומ׳ ויהי ריב בין רועה (!) מקנה וגומ׳ (בר׳ יג | C | |
| ז) ♦ מי גרם ללוט לפרוש מן הצדיק ההוא ♦ הוי אומ׳ זו | E/D | |
| מריבה ♦ ואומ׳ כי יהיה ריב בין אנשים ונגשו אל | F | |
| המשפט ושפטום (דב׳ כה א) ♦ מי גרם לזה ללקות ♦ הוי | H/G | |
| אומ׳ זו מריבה ♦ וכי יריבון אנשים ♦ כתחלה הן באין לידי | B/A | 2 |
| מצות ואחר כך לידי מכות ואחר כך באין לידי ענשין. ♦ | | |
| וכי יריבון אנשים. ♦ אין לי אלא אנשים מנין לרבות | B/A | 3 |

[141] I.e., Abram.
[142] I.e., at first they relate cooperatively.
[143] Compare 3.A–J with *Mekhilta de-Rabbi Ishmael,* Nezikin (H/R, 269:7–14; Laut., vol. 3, 51:6–52:16; Neus., LXIII:I:2.A–J); and *Sifre Deut.,* Piska 286 (Hammer, p. 276; Neus., CCLXXXVI:II:1.A–2.B) and Piska 292 (Hammer, p. 283, Neus., CCXCII:II:1.A–D).

C. Scripture states, "... the assailant shall go unpunished" (Exod. 21:19).

D. Whether man or woman.

E. And why does Scripture state, "... men" (Exod. 21:18)?

F. [To stress that this situation applies to] people, and not oxen.

G. For it might be reasoned:

H. If in the instance when one is exempted [from paying] for damages he caused, but is culpable for damages caused by his ox or donkey, then isn't it logical that here, when he is culpable for damages he caused, he would be culpable [also] for his ox or donkey?

I. Scripture states, [however,] "... men" (Exod. 21:18).

J. [Meaning,] people, and not oxen.

4. A. "... and one man strikes" (Exod. 21:18):

B. This excludes the child.

C. "... his companion" (Exod. 21:18):

D. This excludes outsiders.

E. "... his companion" (Exod. 21:18):

F. This excludes the alien resident.

G. Should I exclude outsiders, who do not have the commandments [of the Torah] like Israel [does], but still not exclude the alien resident, who does have the commandments like Israel?

H. Scriptures states, "... his companion" (Exod. 21:18).

[174] I. This excludes outsiders, [and] "... his companion" [also] excludes the alien resident.

5. A. "... with stone or fist" (Exod. 21:18):[144]

B. I only know from this specifically concerning stone and fist. How does one know from Scripture to include anything?

C. Scripture states, "... the assailant shall go unpunished" (Exod. 21:19).

D. [Meaning, an assailant who uses] anything.

E. [Thus,] why does Scripture state, "... with stone or fist" (Exod. 21:18)?

F. Shimon the Yemenite says, "Just as the fist [that serves as a murder weapon] is particular, in that it is brought [for display] to the witnesses and the counsel [of judiciaries], likewise anything [used as a murder weapon] must be brought [for display] to the witnesses and the counsel [of judiciaries]."

G. R. Akiva said to him, "What if we have nothing other than [that] he pushed him off a castle, and he fell and died? Do we say, 'Oh castle, come to the court'?

H. "Rather, it would all depend on witnesses, and [likewise, prosecuting] capital cases depends on witnesses."

6. A. Scripture says here, "... with stone" (Exod. 21:18), and Scripture says farther on, "(If) he struck him with a stone of the hand that could cause death, etc." (Num. 35:17).

B. This tells that one is not culpable unless something else assisted his hand.

[144] Compare 5.A–H with t. Sanhedrin 12:3 and b. Baba Qamma 90b (Neus., XX.C:Tractate Baba Qamma:8:6:I.4.D).

| | | |
|---|---|---|
| D/C | שתי נשים אשה ואיש • ת״ל ונקה המכה • בין איש ובין | |
| G/F/E | אשה • מה ת״ל אנשים • ⟨אנשים⟩ ולא שוורים • שהיה | |
| H | בדין • מה אם במקום שפטר על ניזקי עצמו חייב על | |
| | נזקי שורו וחמורו ⟨כאן שחייב על נזקי עצמו אינו דין | |
| J/I | שיהא חייב על נזקי שורו וחמורו⟩ • ת״ל אנשים • ולא | |
| E/D/C/B/A 4 | שורים. • והכה איש • פרט לקטן • רעהו • פרט לאחרים • את | |
| G/F | רעהו • פרט לגר [תושב • מוציא] אני אחרים שאין להן | |
| | מצות כישראל ועדאן לא יצא [גר] תושב שיש לו | |
| I/H | מצות כיש׳ ת״ל רעהו • פרט לאחרים את ר[עהו] פרט | |
| B/A 5 | לגר תושב. • באבן או באגרוף • אין לי אלא אבן ואגרוף | |
| D/C | המיוחדין מנין לרבות כל דבר • ת״ל ונקה המכה • בכל | |
| F/E | דבר • מה ת״ל באבן או באגרוף • שמע׳ התימני אומ׳ מה | |
| | אגרוף מיוחד שַמסור לעֵדי[ם ולעֵדה כך כל דבר | |
| G | שמסור לעדים ולעדה • אמ׳ לו ר׳ עקיבה [ו]כי אינן | |
| | אלא שדחאו מראש הבירה ונפל ומת אומרין אנו | |
| H | תבוא [בי]רה לבית דין • אלא הכל תלוי בעדים ודיני | |
| A 6 | נפשות תלויין בעדים • [נא׳ כן אבן] נא׳ להלן או (מ׳) | |
| B | באבן יד אשר ימות בה הכהו וגומ׳ (במ׳ לה יז) • מגיד | |
| | ש[אינו חייב] עד שיהא דבר אחר מסייע את ידו • | |

7.      A.   How does one know from Scripture that one would be culpable if he struck him with a needle or a pin?

        B.   Scripture states, "... with stone or fist" (Exod. 21:18).

8.      A.   "... and he does not die" (Exod. 21:18):

        B.   He must give [him] indemnity payment for lost time.

        C.   But if he dies, he is exempt from indemnity payment for lost time.

9.      A.   One might think he must give [him] indemnity payment for lost time and for healing expenses, whether it was a blow strong enough to cause death or a blow not strong enough to cause death.

        B.   Scripture states, [however,] "... the assailant shall go unpunished" (Exod. 21:19), [which means] only if the blow can cause death.

        C.   Say from now on that the blow must be strong enough to cause death.

10.     A.   "... and he does not die but has to take to his bed" (Exod. 21:18):[145]

        B.   And don't we know if he took to his bed that he didn't die?

        C.   [So] why does Scripture state, "... and he does not die but has to take to his bed" (Exod. 21:18)?

        D.   Because since we determined from below [in Exod. 21:19] that he must pay him [indemnity payment] when he arises, one might also think this is the case here [in Exod. 21:18].

        E.   Scripture states, [however,] "... and he does not die but has to take to his bed" (Exod. 21:18).

        F.   [Meaning,] when he takes to his bed he pays him, and not when he arises.

11.     A.   And up to this point Scripture speaks of a blow that can cause death. From this point forward, Scripture speaks of a blow that cannot cause death.

        B.   If they determined [at first] that he might die, but then he got better, they make a second estimation of the indemnity payment.[146]

## LXIII:II

1.      A.   "If he then gets up and walks about (outdoors upon his staff, the assailant shall go unpunished, only he must pay for his idleness and for him to be healed entirely" (Exod. 21:19):[147]

        B.   One might think [this would apply if he walks] from one bed to another bed.

        C.   Scripture states, [however,] "... outdoors" (Exod. 21:19).

        D.   I only know from this concerning outdoors. How does one know from Scripture to include his courtyard and his garden?

        E.   Scripture states, "... and walks about" (Exod. 21:19).

2.      A.   If he cuts off his hand and cuts off his foot, I might assume that this one must [still only be required to] walk about upon his staff [for the assailant to go unpunished].

        B.   Scripture states, [however,] "If he then gets up and walks about" (Exod. 21:19).

        C.   Why does Scripture state, "... upon his staff ..." (Exod. 21:19)?

---

[145] Compare 10.A–F with y. Sanhedrin 27a (Neus., Sanhedrin:9:3:II.A–K).
[146] Compare 11.B with t. Baba Qamma 9:5.
[147] Compare 1.A–E with Mekhilta de-Rabbi Ishmael, Nezikin (H/R, 270:6–7; Laut., vol. 3, 53:37–39; Neus., LXIII:I:8.A–F).

| | | |
|---|---|---|
| מנין הכהו במ[חט ובציגור]ה יהא [ח]ייב • ת״ל באבן או | B/A | 7 |
| באגרוף • ולא ימות • שבת<ו> יתן • הא אם מת פטור | C/B/A | 8 |
| מליתן שבת • יכול אחד מכה שיש בה כדי להמית | A | 9 |
| ואחד מכה שאין בה כדי להמית הוא נותן שבת וריפוי • | | |
| ת״ל ונקה המכה עד שיהא מכה תפס למיתה • אמור | C/B | |
| מעתה מכה שיש בה כדי להמית. • לא ימות ונפל | A | 10 |
| למשכב לפי • וכי אין אנו יודעין שאם נפל למשכב אינו | B | |
| מת • מה ת״ל ולא ימות ונפל למשכב • לפי שמצינו במטן | D/C | |
| שנותן לו בשעת עמידתו יכול אף זה כן • ת״ל לא ימות | E | |
| ונפל למשכב • בשעת נפילתו נותן לו ואין נותן לו | F | |
| בשעת עמידתו • ועד כן הכת׳ מדבר במכה [שי]ש בה | A | 11 |
| כדי (מכה) להמית מיכן ואילך הכת׳ מדבר במכה | | |
| שאין בה כדי להמית • אמדהו ל(ה)מיתה והיקל ממה | B | |
| שהיה אומדין אותו לממון שנייה. סל׳ פסו׳ • | | |

| | | LXIII:II |
|---|---|---|
| אם יקום והתהלך • יכול ממטה זו למטה זו • ת״ל | C/B/A | 1 |
| בחוץ • אין לי אלא חוץ מנין לרבות חצרו וגנת[ו] • ת״ל | E/D | |
| והתהלך • קטע ידו וקטע רגלו שומע אני בזה על | A | 2 |
| משענתו • ת״ל אם יקום והתהלך • מה ת״ל על משענתו • | C/B | |

D. [To mean] if he is fully healthy, [thus, in this case, he will have to pay damages].

3. A. Why does Scripture state, "If he then gets up and walks about" (Exod. 21:19)?

B. Because since we determined above that he pays him [indemnity payment] when he takes to his bed, one might think this is the case here!

C. Scripture states, [however,] "If he then gets up and walks about" (Exod. 21:19).

D. [Meaning,] he pays him at the time when they appraise his injuries, and not when he takes to his bed.

4. A. If they diagnosed that he might die, but then he got somewhat better, and then got somewhat worse, and afterward died, they appraise him: If he died as a result of the original blow, behold, he is culpable. But if not, behold, he is exempt.[148]

B. R. Nehemiah says, "Whether this or that, behold, he is exempt.

C. "As it says in Scripture, 'If he then gets up and walks about outdoors' (Exod. 21:19)."

[175]

D. R. Nehemiah [also] says [regarding Exod. 21:18–19], "If not [as Scripture says here,] what [else] would you [possibly] think? That this one guy should walk about the market and this other guy should be put to death?

E. "Rather, [the verses indicate that] even if [he should die] as a result of the first blow, he is exempt."

5. A. "... the assailant shall go unpunished" (Exod. 21:19):

B. Whether man or woman.

6. A. "... the assailant shall go unpunished" (Exod. 21:19):[149]

B. One might think [he goes unpunished] in any fashion.

C. Scripture states, "... the assailant shall go unpunished, only he must pay for his idleness" (Exod. 21:19).

D. And "his idleness" means only his loss of [work] time.

E. As it says in Scripture, "... and on the seventh day He ceased from work and was refreshed" (Exod. 31:17).

7. A. One might think they should assess him as if he

(Textual Source: Midrash ha-Gadol)

made one *sela* a day or two *sela* a day.

B. Scripture says, "... the assailant shall go unpunished, only he must pay for his idleness" (Exod. 21:19), [meaning,] he must pay only for his final [period] of idleness, but he must not pay for his first [period] of idleness.[150]

8. A. "... and for him to be healed entirely" (Exod. 21:19):[151]

B. [Meaning,] he should pay for him to be healed on an ongoing basis [until he is finally healed].

C. Or might one think he would be responsible [for healing him] even if he[152] went against the advice of the doctor and ate honey and all kinds of sweet things? For honey and sweet things irritate the wound and make it scabby.

D. Scripture states, [however,] "... *only* he must pay ... for him to be entirely healed" (Exod. 21:19).

[148] Compare 4.A–E with t. Baba Qamma 9:6–7.
[149] Compare 6.A–E with *Mekhilta de-Rabbi Ishmael*, Nezikin (H/R, 270:13–15; Laut., vol. 3, 54:50–52; Neus., LXIII:I:13.A–E).
[150] The meaning of 7.B is uncertain. It is unattested elsewhere in the corpus of early Rabbinic literature.

| | | |
|---|---|---|
| D | 3 B/A | על בוריו ❖ מה ת״ל אם יקום והתהלך בחוץ ❖ לפי שמצינו |
| | C | למעלה ש[נותן לו] בשעת נפילתו. יכול אף זה כן ❖ ת״ל |
| | D | אם יקום והתהלך ❖ [בשעת] אמידתו נותן לו <ולא> |
| 4 | A | בשעת נפילתו ❖ אמדוהו למיתה והיק[ל מ]מה שהיה |
| | | הכביד ואחר כך מת אומדין אתו אם מחמת מכה |
| | B | ראשונה מת הרי זה חייב אם לאו הרי זה פטור. ❖ ר׳ |
| | C | נחמיה אומ׳ בין כך ובין כך הרי זה פטור ❖ שנא׳ אם |
| | D | יקום והתהלך ב[חוץ] ❖ אמ׳ ר׳ נחמיה אם לאו מה |
| | | עלתה על לבי שיהא זה מטייל בשוק וזה בא ונהרג ❖ |
| | E | אלא אפילו מחמת מכה ראשונה מ[ת] הרי זה פטור. ❖ |
| 5 B/A | 6 B/A | ונקה המכה ❖ בין איש ובין אשה ❖ ונקה [המכה] ❖ <יכול> |
| | D/C | לכל דבר ❖ <ת״ל> ונקה המכה רק שבתו יתן ❖ אין שבתו |
| | E | אלא [בטילתו] ❖ שנא׳ וביום השביעי שבת וינפש (שמ׳ |
| 7 | A | לא יז) ❖ יכול יהו רו[אין אותו כאלו] הוא עושה סלע |
| | B | ביום וכאלו עושה שתי סלעים ❖ ת״ל ונקה המכה. רק |
| 8 | A | שבתו יתן שבתו אחרונה יתן לא שבתו ראשונה. ❖ ורפא |
| | C/B | ירפא ❖ ירפא וחוזר ומרפא ❖ או יכול אפלו עבר על דברי |
| | | הרופא ואכל דבש ומיני מתיקה שהדבש ומיני מתיקה |
| D | | קשין למכה והעלתה מכתו גרגותני יהא חייב ❖ ת״ל רק |
| | | יתן ורפא ירפא. ❖ |

---

[151] Compare 8.A–D with b. Baba Qamma 85a (Neus., XX.C:Tractate Baba Qamma:8:1A–R:IV.4.A–C).
[152] I.e, the wounded person.

*Chapter Sixty-Four*

(Textual Source: Midrash ha-Gadol)

LXIV:I

1. A. "'When a man strikes his slave, male or female, (with a rod, and he dies under his hand, he must be avenged)' (Exod. 21:20):

   B. "One might think Scripture speaks about the male or female Hebrew slave.

   C. "Scripture states, [however,] '... his slave, male or female' (Exod. 21:20).

   D. "[Which implies] the male or female slave whose religious instruction is comparable to each other.

   E. "The male or female Hebrew slave is excluded, because their religious instruction is not comparable to each other."—The words of R. Judah.

   F. R. Shimon says, "Behold Scripture says, '... since he is the other's property' (Exod. 21:21).

   G. "The male or female Hebrew slave is excluded, because he[153] has no ownership in them."

2. A. "When a man strikes" (Exod. 21:20):

   B. I only know concerning a man. How does one know from Scripture concerning a woman?

   C. Scripture states, [however,] "... he must *certainly*[154] be avenged" (Exod. 21:20).

   D. Whether man or woman.

   E. Why does Scripture state "... a man" (Exod. 21:20?

   F. To exclude the minor.

3. A. "... with a rod" (Exod. 21:20):

   B. I only know concerning a rod. How does one know from Scripture to include anything?

   C. Scripture states, "... he must *certainly*[155] be avenged" (Exod. 21:20).

   D. [Meaning, with] anything.

4. A. "... and he dies under his hand"[156] (Exod. 21:20):[157]

   B. Why do I need this?

   C. Wouldn't he be culpable even if he died 10 hours later?

   D. Why does Scripture state, "... and he dies under his hand" (Exod. 21:20)?

   E. Rather, if it does not pertain to [clarify] the issue [of the slave's] death, then apply it to [clarify] the subject of servitude.[158]

   F. Based on this you say: The one who says to his companion, "This slave is sold to you after 30 days."[159]

   G. R. Eliezer says, "Neither this one [scenario] nor that one is subject to the rule of 'a day or two'[160]—the first one, because [the slave] is not under his [authority], and the second one, because he is not his slave."

---

[153] I.e., the master.

[154] Emphasizing in exaggerated fashion, as does this interpretation, the infinitive absolute ינקם נקם.

[155] Ibid.

[156] "Under his hand" means "there and then."

[157] Compare 4.A–H with b. Baba Qamma 90a (Neus., XX.C:Tractate Baba Qamma:8:5:III.3.E–J).

[158] I.e., understand the clause to mean that the slave died while subjugated as a slave to the master.

[159] I.e., the seller retains the services of the sold slave for 30 days, and then the slave is transferred to the purchaser.

LXIV:I

| | | |
|---|---|---|
| וכי יכה איש את עבדו או את אמתו ◆ יכול בעבד | B/A | 1 |
| ואמה עברים הכתוב מדבר ◆ ת״ל עבד ואמה ◆ עבד | D/C | |
| ואמה שתורתן שווה זו לזו ◆ יצאו עבד ואמה העברים | E | |
| שאין תורתן שווה זו לזו דברי ר׳ יהודה. ◆ ר׳ שמעון | F | |
| אומר הרי הוא אומר כי כספו הוא ◆ יצאו עבד ואמה | G | |
| העברים שאין לו בהן כסף. ◆ וכי יכה איש ◆ אין לי אלא | B/A | 2 |
| איש אשה מניין ◆ ת״ל נקם ינקם ◆ בין איש בין אשה ◆ מה | E/D/C | |
| ת״ל איש ◆ פרט לקטן. ◆ בשבט ◆ אין לי אלא בשבט מניין | B/A 3 | F |
| לרבות כל דבר ◆ ת״ל נקם ינקם ◆ בכל דבר. ◆ ומת תחת ידו ◆ | A 4 | D/C |
| מה אני צריך ◆ והלא אפלו מת לעשר שעות הרי זה | C/B | |
| חייב ◆ מה ת״ל ומת תחת ידו ◆ אלא אם אינו ענין למיתה | E/D | |
| תניהו ענין לשעבוד ◆ מכאן אתה אומר האומר לחברו | F | |
| עבד זה מכור לך לאחר שלשים יום ◆ ר׳ אליעזר אומר | G | |
| זה וזה אינו בדין יום או יומים הראשון מפני שאינו | | |

160 I.e., Exod. 21:20–21.

H.    R. Yosi says, "The two of them are subject to the rule of 'a day or two'—this one, because [the slave] is under his [authority], and this one, because he is his property."[161]

5.    A.    "... he must certainly be avenged" (Exod. 21:20):[162]

B.    Scripture says "vengeance" here, and Scripture says farther on, "I will bring a sword against you to wreak vengeance for the covenant" (Lev. 26:25).

C.    Just as below [is with a sword], so too here with a sword.

6.    A.    One might think you would treat the blow without enough force to kill [the same] as the blow with enough force to kill.[163]

B.    For it is a matter of logic:

C.    One can be culpable [for striking] a slave and culpable [for striking] a free person.

D.    Just as [the culpability] for the free person requires that the blow have enough force to kill, so too [does the culpability] for the slave require that the blow have enough force to kill.

7.    A.    "(But if he survives) a day (or two, he is not to be avenged, since he is the other's property)" (Exod. 21:21):[164]

B.    One might think [this applies only if he survives] one day.

C.    Scripture states, [however,] "... or two" (Exod. 21:21).

D.    One might think [this applies only if he survives] two days.

E.    Scripture states, [however,] "... a day" (Exod. 21:21).

F.    From this you say [that by saying "one day" Scripture means] a day's [length of time][165] that comprises two days.[166]

G.    And you say [that by saying "two days" Scripture means] a [combined] period of 24 hours.

8.    A.    "... the other's property" (Exod. 21:21):

B.    This excludes a jointly-owned [slave].

9.    A.    "... he is" (Exod. 21:21):

B.    This excludes he who is a half-slave and half-free person.

*Chapter Sixty-Five*

## (Textual Source: Midrash ha-Gadol)

[176]

LXV:I

1.    A.    "When men fight, (and one of them pushes a pregnant woman and her children come out, but no other damage ensues, the one responsible shall be fined according as the woman's husband may exact from him, the payment to be based as the judges determine)" (Exod. 21:22):

B.    [Scripture says this] to treat the one who didn't [act] with intention like the one who did [act] with intention.

---

[161] Epstein and Melamed interpolated 4.H into the text here on the basis of its attestation in b. Baba Qamma 90a (see note 157 above).

[162] Compare 5.A–C with *Mekhilta de-Rabbi Ishmael*, Nezikin (H/R, 273:10–13; Laut., vol. 3, 60:58–61:66; Neus., LXIV:I:11.A–I); and b. Sanhedrin 52b (Neus., XXIIIB:Tractate Sanhedrin:7:3A–F:II.A–G).

[163] Compare 6.A–D with *Mekhilta de-Rabbi Ishmael*, Nezikin (H/R, 273:1–6; Laut., vol. 3, 58:37–60:51; Neus., LXIV:I:8.A–F).

[164] Compare 7.A–G with *Mekhilta de-Rabbi Ishmael*, Nezikin (H/R, 274:1–3; Laut., vol. 3, 61:65–69; Neus., LXIV:I:12.A–H).

[165] I.e., a 24-hour period.

[166] I.e., two separate 12-hour periods of daylight.

| | | |
|---|---|---|
| H | | תחתיו והשני מפני שאינו עבדו ♦ ‹ר׳ יוסי אומר שניהם |
| | | ישנן בדין יום או יומים זה מפני שהוא תחתיו וזה |
| B/A | 5 | מפני שהוא כספו› ♦ נקם ינקם ♦ נאמרה כאן נקימה |
| | | ונאמר להלן והבאתי עליכם חרב נקמת נקם ברית |
| C | A 6 | (ויק׳ כו כה) ♦ מה להלן סיף אף כאן בסיף. ♦ יכול יעשה |
| | | בו מכה שאין בה כדי להמית כמכה שיש בה כדי |
| D/C/B | | להמית ♦ ודין הוא ♦ חייב בעבד וחייב בבן חורין ♦ מה בן |
| | | חורין עד שיהא במכה כדי להמית אף בעבד עד שיהא |
| | | במכה כדי להמית. ♦ |
| D/C/B/A | 7 | יום ♦ יכול יום אחד ♦ ת״ל יומים ♦ או יומים יכול שני |
| G/F/E | | ימים ♦ ת״ל יום ♦ אמור מעתה יום שיש בו שני ימים ♦ הוי |
| B/A | 8 | אומר מעת לעת. ♦ כי כספו הוא ♦ יצאו עבד ואמה |
| A | 9 | העברים שאין לו בהם כסף. כספו פרט לשותפין ♦ הוא ♦ |
| B | | פרט למי שחציו עבד וחציו בן חורין. ♦ |
| LXV:I | | |
| B/A | 1 | וכי ינצו אנשים ♦ לעשות את שאין מתכוין כמתכוין. ♦ |

2.     A.    "When men fight, and one of them pushes a pregnant woman" (Exod. 21:22):[167]

       B.    I only know concerning [this instance where Scripture states] "when men fight" that one treats the one who didn't [act] with intention like the one who did [act] with intention.

       C.    How does one know from Scripture also [in the instance in Exod. 21:18 where Scripture states] "when men quarrel" the one who didn't [act] with intention is treated like the one who did [act] with intention?

       D.    Scripture states, "When men fight" (Exod. 21:22) and "When men quarrel" (Exod. 21:18).

       E.    Fighting and quarreling are one and the same commandment.

       F.    Just as [where Scripture states,] "When men fight," the one who didn't [act] with intention is treated like the one who did [act] with intention, so too [where Scripture states,] "When men quarrel," is the one who didn't [act] with intention treated like the one who did [act] with intention.

3.     A.    Here[168] he must pay for damages and pain, and above[169] he must pay for idleness and healing.

       B.    How does one know from Scripture that you apply that which is said here to there, and that which is said there to here?

       C.    Scripture states, "When men fight" (Exod. 21:22) and "When men quarrel" (Exod. 21:18).

       D.    Fighting and quarreling are one and the same commandment!

       E.    Rather, this is to apply that which is said here above and that which is said above here.

4.     A.    "When men fight" (Exod. 21:22):[170]

       B.    I only know concerning men. How does one know from Scripture to include two women [fighting] or a man and a woman [fighting]?

       C.    Scripture states, "... the *one* responsible shall be fined" (Exod. 21:22).

       D.    [Meaning,] whether man or woman.

       E.    Why does Scripture state, "... men" (Exod. 21:22)?

       F.    [To emphasize that this applies to] people, and not oxen.

       G.    Based on this you say: If his ox struck the woman, it is exempt from [responsibility for indemnity payment] for the value of the offspring.[171]

5.     A.    If Scripture had [only] stated [in Exod. 21:22], "And one of them pushes a woman and her children come out, but no other damage ensues," I would say [this is applicable] only if she had two offspring and a husband.[172]

       B.    How does one know from Scripture [this is applicable even] if she has a husband but not [two] offspring, or if she has [two] offspring but not a husband?

       C.    Scripture states, "... and one of them pushes *a pregnant* woman" (Exod. 21:22).

       D.    [Meaning,] in any [of these] situations.

6.     A.    One might think this entire matter speaks only to the [born Jewish and born] free woman.

       B.    How does one know from Scripture to include the convert, the handmaid, and the emancipated handmaid?

---

[167] Compare 2.A–F with y. Sanhedrin 27a (Neus., Sanhedrin:9:3:IV.A–L).
[168] I.e., Exod. 21:21.
[169] I.e., Exod. 21:18.
[170] Compare 4.A–E with y. Baba Qamma 4c (Neus., Baba Qamma:4:5:III.J–W).

| | | |
|---|---|---|
| 2 | B/A | כי ינצו אנשים ונגפו אשה הרה ◆ אין לי אלא |
| | C | בכי ינצו שעשה את שאין מתכוין כמתכוין ◆ מנין אף |
| | D | בכי יריבון נעשה את שאין מתכוין כמתכוין ◆ ת״ל כי |
| | E | ינצו וכי יריבון ◆ מצות היא מריבה ומריבה היא מצות ◆ |
| | F | מה בכי ינצו נעשה את שאין מתכוין כמתכוין אף בכי |
| 3 | A | יריבון נעשה את שאין מתכוין כמתכוין. ◆ כאן הוא נותן |
| | B | נזק וצער ולהלן הוא נותן שבת ורפוי ◆ מנין ליתן את |
| | C | האמור שלזה בזה ואת האמור שלזה בזה ◆ ת״ל כי ינצו |
| | D | אנשים וכי יריבון אנשים ◆ והלא מצות היא מריבה |
| | E | ומריבה היא מצות ◆ אלא ליתן את האמור כאן להלן |
| 4 | B/A | ואת האמור להלן כאן. ◆ כי ינצו אנשים ◆ אין לי אלא |
| | C | אנשים מנין לרבות שתי נשים אשה ואיש ◆ ת״ל ענש |
| | F/E/D | יענש ◆ בין איש בין אשה ◆ מה ת״ל אנשים ◆ אנשים ולא |
| | G | שוורים ◆ מכאן אמרו שורו שנגף את האשה פטור מדמי |
| 5 | A | ולדות. ◆ אלו נאמר ונגפו אשה ויצאו ילדיה ולא יהיה אסון |
| | B | הייתי אומר עד שיהיו לה שני ולדות ובעל ◆ מנין יש לה |
| | C | בעל ואין לה ולדות יש לה ולדות ואין לה בעל ◆ ת״ל ונגפו |
| 6 | A | אשה הרה ◆ מכל מקום. ◆ יכול אין כל העניין מדבר אלא בבת | D |
| | B | חורין ◆ מנין לרבות את הגיורת ואת השפחה המשוחררת ◆ |

---

[171] See m. Baba Kamma 8:2.
[172] Compare 5.A–D with *Mekhilta de-Rabbi Ishmael*, Nezikin (H/R, 275:8–15; Laut., vol. 3, 64:23–65:34; Neus., LXV:I:5.A–6.E).

C.  Scripture states, "… and one of them pushes a pregnant woman" (Exod. 21:22).

D.  [Meaning,] in any [of these] situations.

7.  A.  "… but no other damage ensues" (Exod. 21:22):

B.  I might assume [this means] damage to either the woman or the offspring.

C.  Scripture states, [however,] "He who (fatally) strikes a man" (Exod. 21:12).

D.  This excludes [damage to the unborn] offspring.

E.  So why does Scripture state, "… but no other damage ensues" (Exod. 21:22)?

F.  [To emphasize] damage to the woman, but not the offspring.

8.  A.  "… but no other damage ensues, the one responsible shall be fined" (Exod. 21:22):

B.  But if there is damage there, he is not fined.

9.  A.  "… the one responsible shall be fined" (Exod. 21:22):

B.  Whether man or woman.

10.  A.  "… the one responsible shall be fined" (Exod. 21:22):

B.  By either money or by something of equivalent value.

11.  A.  "… according as the woman's husband may exact from him" (Exod. 21:22):[173]

B.  One might think [this means] if he[174] demands 100 [*shekels*], he must pay 100, or if he demands 10,000, he must pay 10,000.

C.  Scripture states, [however,] "… as the judges determine" (Exod. 21:22).

D.  [Meaning, only the amount determined] by the judges.

E.  If so, then why does Scripture state, "… according as the woman's husband may exact from him" (Exod. 21:22)?

F.  This teaches that the compensation for the offspring belongs to the husband.

12.  A.  "But if other damage ensues, the penalty shall be life (for life, eye for eye, tooth for tooth, hand for hand, foot for foot, burn for burn, wound for wound, bruise for bruise)" (Exod. 21:23–25):[175]

B.  One might think if someone killed a person and beast at the same time, or cut off one person's head and another person's finger at the same time, he would be culpable for both death and indemnity payments.

C.  Scripture states, [however,] "… life for life" (Exod. 21:23).

D.  But not life for a life and a beast, or life for a life and an eye.[176]

E.  But if someone killed a person and afterward killed a beast, or cut off one person's head and afterward cut off another person's finger, he would be liable [for both].

F.  As it says in Scripture, "life for life" along with "a beast" (Lev. 24:17–18) and "life for life" along with "an eye" (Exod. 21:23–24).

G.  This is the general principle: [For] any transgression that merits death and indemnity payments at the same time, one is sentenced to death, but exempt from the indemnity payments.

---

[173] Compare 11.A–F with *Mekhilta de-Rabbi Ishmael*, Nezikin (H/R, 275:11–13; Laut., vol. 3, 66:51–56; Neus., LXV:I:12.A–C).
[174] I.e., the husband.

| | | |
|---|---|---|
| D/C | A 7 | ת״ל ונגפו אשה הרה ◆ מכל מקום. ◆ ולא יהיה |
| | B | אסון ◆ שומע אני אסון באשה או אסון בולדות ◆ |
| | E/D/C | ת״ל מכה איש (פי״ב) ◆ פרט לולדות ◆ הא מה |
| F | A 8 | ת״ל ולא יהיה אסון ◆ באשה ולא בולדות. ◆ ולא יהיה |
| | A 9 | אסון ענוש ◆ הא אם יש שם אסון אין נענש. ◆ ענוש יענש ◆ |
| B | B/A 10 | בין איש בין אשה ◆ ענוש יענש ◆ בכסף ובשווה כסף. ◆ |
| | B/A 11 | כאשר ישית עליו בעל האשה ◆ יכול אם אמר מנה הוא |
| | | נותן מנה ואם אמר מאה מנה הוא נותן מאה מנה ◆ |
| | E/D/C | ת״ל ונתן בפלילים ◆ בדיינים ◆ אם כן למה נאמר כאשר |
| F | | ישית עליו בעל האשה ◆ לימד שדמי ולדות לבעל. ◆ |
| | B/A 12 | ואם אסון יהיה ונתתה נפש ◆ יכול הרג אדם |
| | | ובהמה כאחד וקטע ראשו שלזה ואצבעו שלזה כאחד |
| C | | יכול יהא חייב מיתה ותשלומין ◆ ת״ל נפש תחת נפש |
| D | | (ויק׳ כד יח) ◆ ולא נפש תחת נפש ובהמה ולא נפש תחת |
| E | | נפש ועין. ◆ אבל הרג אדם ואחר כך הרג בהמה קטע |
| F | | ראש שלזה ואחר כך קטע אצבעו שלזה חייב ◆ שנ׳ נפש |
| G | | תחת נפש ובהמה נפש תחת נפש ועין ◆ זה הכלל כל |
| | | שיש בו עון מיתה ותשלומין כאחד נידון במיתה ופטור |
| | | מן התשלומין. ◆ |

---

[175] Compare 12.A–G with t. Baba Qamma 9:17.
[176] I.e., he need not pay the indemnity payment.

13.    A.    Ben Azzai says, "Behold Scripture says, 'bruise for bruise' (Exod. 21:25), and above Scripture says, 'and one strikes the other with stone or fist' (Exod. 21:18).

      B.    "Thus, [we can compare] wound and wound: Just as one must pay for idleness and a complete healing for the wound mentioned above, so too here must he pay for idleness and a complete healing."

14.    A.    One might think [Scripture actually means] "life for life."[177]

      B.    Scripture states, [however,] "You may not accept a ransom for the life of a murderer" (Num. 35:31).

[177]    C.    [Meaning,] for the life of a murderer you may not take a ransom, but you may take a ransom for [the loss] of limbs.

*Chapter Sixty-Six*

(Textual Source: Midrash ha-Gadol)

LXVI:I

1.    A.    "When a man strikes the eye of his slave, (male or female, and destroys it, he shall let him go free on account of his eye)" (Exod. 21:26):[178]

      B.    One might think Scripture speaks about the male or female Hebrew slave.

      C.    Scripture states, [however,] "male or female" (Exod. 21:26).

      D.    [Which implies] the male or female slave whose religious instruction is equivalent to each other.

      E.    The male or female Hebrew slave is excluded, because their religious instruction is not equivalent to each other.

2.    A.    "When a man strikes" (Exod. 21:26):

      B.    I only know concerning a man. How does one know from Scripture concerning a woman?

      C.    Scripture states, "... he shall let him go free" (Exod. 21:26).

      D.    [Meaning,] whether man or woman.

      E.    Why does Scripture state, "... a man" (Exod. 21:26)?

      F.    This excludes the minor.

3.    A.    "... his slave" (Exod. 21:26):

      B.    As long as he intended [to strike and hurt] him.

4.    A.    "... the eye" (Exod. 21:26):

      B.    One might think that [just] because he struck him on his eye, he[179] would go out a free person.

      C.    Scripture states, [however,] "... and destroys it" (Exod. 21:26).

      D.    [Which means that] this one[180] is exempt [from having to let him go free], because he didn't destroy [it, but only struck it].

5.    A.    One might think [he would go free] if he struck him near his eye so that he could not see, or near his ear so that he could not hear.[181]

---

[177] Compare 14.A–C with *Sifra*, Emor 20:7 (Neus., CCXLIV:I:9.A–F); and b. Baba Qama 83b (Neus., XX.C:Tractate Baba Qamma:8:1A–R:I.1.A–C).

[178] See parallel to 1.A–E above at LXIV:I:1.A–G.

[179] I.e., the slave.

| | | |
|---|---|---|
| A | 13 | בן עזאי אומר הרי הוא אומר חבורה תחת |
| | | חבורה ולהלן הוא אומר והכה איש את רעהו באבן |
| B | | או באגרף (פי״ח) ♦ הא חבורה חבורה מה חבורה |
| | | האמורה להלן שבתו יתן ורפא ירפא אף כאן שבתו |
| B/A | 14 | יתן ורפא ירפא. ♦ או יכול אף נפש תחת נפש ת״ל ולא |
| C | | תקחו כפר לנפש רוצח (במ׳ לה לא) ♦ לנפש רוצח אי |
| | | אתה לוקח כפר אבל אתה לוקח כפר לאיברין. ♦ |

LXVI:I

| | | |
|---|---|---|
| B/A | 1 | וכי יכה איש את עין עבדו ♦ יכול בעבד ואמה |
| D/C | | העברים הכתוב מדבר ♦ ת״ל עבד ואמה ♦ עבד ואמה |
| E | | שתורתן שווה זו לזו ♦ יצאו עבד ואמה העברים שאין |
| B/A | 2 | תורתן שווה זו לזו. ♦ וכי יכה איש ♦ אין לי אלא איש |
| E/D/C | | אשה מניין ♦ ת״ל לחפשי ישלחנו ♦ דין איש בין אשה ♦ מה |
| B/A 3 | F | ת״ל איש ♦ פרט לקטן. ♦ את עבדו ♦ עד שיהא מתכוין |
| B/A | 4 | לו. ♦ את עין ♦ יכול כיון שהכהו על עינו יהא יוצא בן |
| A 5 | D/C | חורין ♦ ת״ל ושחתה ♦ יצא זה שלא שחת. ♦ יכול אפלו |
| | | הכהו כנגד עינו ואינו רואה כנגד אזנו ואינו שומע ♦ |

[180] I.e., the owner is this scenario.
[181] Compare 5.A–C with t. Baba Qamma 9:26, b. Baba Qamma 91a (Neus., XX.C:Tractate Baba Qamma:8:6:I.5.D–E), and b. Kiddushin 24b (Neus., XIX.A:Qiddushin:1:3:IV.5.A–B).

B.   Scripture states, [however,] "... the eye" (Exod. 21:26).

C.   Only if he strikes the eye.

6.   A.   "If he knocks out the tooth of his slave, male or female, (he shall send him free on account of his tooth)" (Exod. 21:27):

B.   One might think that [just] because he struck him on his tooth, he would go out a free person.

C.   Scripture states, [however,] "If he knocks out" (Exod. 21:27).

7.   A.   One might think [he only goes free] once he knocks it out and it falls to the ground.

B.   How does one know from Scripture that you say he should go free if he struck his tooth so that it was weakened, and he could not make use of it?

C.   Scripture states "eye" (Exod. 21:26) and "tooth" (Exod. 21:27).

D.   Just as [he goes free because of] the destroyed eye, so too [does he go free because of] the destroyed tooth.

8.   A.   One might think [he goes free] even if he struck his milk tooth.[182]

B.   Scripture states, [however,] "tooth" (Exod. 21:27) and "eye" (Exod. 21:26).

C.   Just as the eye doesn't regenerate, so too must [it be] the tooth that doesn't regenerate.

9.   A.   "If he knocks out" (Exod. 21:27):

B.   As long as he intended [to strike] him.

10.   A.   If his master was a doctor, and he[183] said to him, "Place eye cream on my eye!" but he [accidently] blinded it, or "Clean my tooth," but he [accidently] knocked it out, he[184] has tricked the master

(Textual Source: Ms. Firkovich II A 268)

and gone free.[185]

B.   R. Shimon b. Gamliel says, "He doesn't go free!"

11.   A.   "... he shall send him free" (Exod. 21:27):

B.   This is what we have said: Whether a minor or an adult, whether man or woman.

12.   A.   "... free" (Exod. 21:27):

B.   This is what we have said: Scripture says here "free" and Scripture says "free" farther on [in Lev. 19:20].

C.   Just as "free" stated farther on [requires] a writ, likewise here is a writ [required].

D.   And how does one know from Scripture that "free" mentioned farther on [requires] a writ?

E.   Scripture states, "... or her freedom has not been given to her" (Lev. 19:20), and Scripture states farther on, "... and he writes her (a bill of divorcement)" (Deut. 24:1).

F.   Just as "her" mentioned farther on is a writ, so too is "her" mentioned here a writ.

G.   R. Shimon says, "Scripture says here 'send' and Scripture states farther on [in Deut. 24:1] 'send.'"[186]

---

[182] Compare 8.A–C with *Mekhilta de-Rabbi Ishmael*, Nezikin (H/R, 279:14–15; Laut., vol. 3, 72:40–42; Neus., LXVI:I:9.A–D).
[183] I.e., his slave.
[184] I.e., the slave.

| | | |
|---|---|---|
| ת"ל את עין • עד שיכהו על עינו. • | C/B | |
| ואם שן עבדו או שן אמתו יפיל • יכול כיון שהכהו | B/A | 6 |
| על שנו יהא יוצא בן חורין • ת"ל יפיל • יכול עד שעה | A 7 | C |
| שיפילנה לארץ • מנין אתה אומר הכהו על שנו ונדנדה | B | |
| ואינו יכול להשתמש בה יהא יוצא בן חורין • ת"ל עין | C | |
| ושן • מה עין ששחת אף שן ששחת. • יכול אפלו הפיל | A 8 | D |
| שנו שלחלב • ת"ל שן ועין • מה עין שאינה חוזרת אף שן | C/B | |
| שאינה חוזרת. • יפיל • עד שיתכוין לו • היה רבו רופא | A 10 | B/A 9 |
| אמר לו כחול לי עיני וסימאה חתור לי שני והפילה | | |
| שיחק באדון יוצא בן חורין • רבן שמעון בן גמליאל | B | |
| אומ' לא יצא בן חורין • ישלחנו • זו היא שאמרנו בין | B/A | 11 |
| איש בין אשה • חפשי • זו היא שאמ[רנו] בין קטן ובין | B/Λ | 12 |
| גדול. חפשי [נ]אמ[']  כאן חפשי ונאמר להלן חפשי • מה | C | |
| חפשי האמ' להלן שטר אף כאן שטר • מנין לחפשי | D | |
| האמור להלן שהוא שטר • ת"ל או חפשה לא נתן לה | E | |
| (ויק' יט כ) ונאמ' להלן וכתב לה (דב' כד א) • מה לה | F | |
| האמ' להלן שטר אף לה האמ' כאן שטר • ר' שמעו' | G | |
| אומ' נאמ' כן שלוח ונאמ' להלן שלוח (שם ג) • | | |

---

[185] Compare 10.A–B with t. Baba Qamma 9:15, b. Kiddushin 24b (Neus., XX:C:Tractate Baba Qamma:1:3:IV.9.A–C), and b. Baba Qamma 26b (Neus., XX.A:Tractate Baba Qamma:2:6:I.3.B).

[186] Compare 12.G–H with b. Kiddushin 24b (Neus., XIX.A:Qiddushin:1:3:IV.3.A– 4.D).

H. "Just as 'send' stated farther on [requires] a bill of divorce, so too here is a bill of divorce [required]."

13. A. One might think he should go free with his indemnity payment for damages, [for his master] must pay him the cost of his eye or the cost of his tooth.

B. Scripture states, [however,] "... he shall let him go *free* on account of his eye" (Exod. 21:26).

14. A. "... on account of his eye" (Exod. 21:26):

B. [The master is responsible for] anything that comes about on account of his eye.

C. "... on account of his tooth" (Exod. 21:27):

D. [The master is responsible for] anything that comes about on account of his tooth.

*Chapter Sixty-Seven*

(Textual Source: Ms. Firkovich II A 268)

LXVII:I[187]

1. A. "When (an ox) gores (a man or a woman to death, the ox shall surely be stoned and its flesh shall not be eaten, but the owner of the ox is not to be punished)" (Exod. 21:28):

B. This excludes the one who provokes him to gore.

[178] C. Based on this they said: An ox from the stadium is exempt, because that is all it does.[188]

2. A. "When (an ox) gores" (Exod. 21:28):

B. I only know from this concerning goring. How does one know from Scripture to treat striking, biting, lying on top of, and trampling the same as goring?

C. It is a matter of logic:

D. There is culpability for an ox [goring] an ox, and for an ox [goring] a human being. Just as we have found that [in the case of] an ox [goring] an ox you treat striking, biting, lying on top of, and trampling the same as goring, so too here [in the case of an ox harming a human] is striking, biting, lying on top of, and trampling treated the same as goring.

E. This [reasoning] involves the [ox] that is sentenced [to give up] its life.[189]

F. And there is another way of reasoning:

G. Just as with [the case of] an ox [goring] an ox, which is not sentenced [to give up] its life, you treat striking, biting, lying on top of, and trampling the same as goring, then it is logical that in this case, for which [the ox] is sentenced [to give up] its life, that striking, biting, lying on top of, and trampling are treated the same as goring.

H. No! When you speak of [the case of] the ox [goring] an ox, you treat the unintentional act the same as the intentional one. Will you say the same in this case, where the unintentional act is not treated the same as the intentional one?

I. Scripture states, [however,] "... to death" (Exod. 21:28), [which means you should] treat striking, biting, lying on top of, and trampling the same as goring.

3. A. I only know from this [verse in Scripture] concerning the ox. How does one know from Scripture to treat all cattle, beasts of chase, and birds the same as the ox?

B. It[190] is both the [source of] the question and the answer.

[187] Compare LXVII:I:1.A–8.E with parallel, but often significantly different, material in the *Mekhilta de-Rabbi Ishmael*, Nezikin (H/R, 280:10–281:18; Laut., vol. 3, 74:1–77:40; Neus., LXVII:I:1.A–10.E).

[188] Compare 1.C with m. Baba Kamma 4:4.

מה שלוח האמ' להלן גט אף כן גט ◆ יכול יהא יוצא בניזקו     H    A 13

משלם לו דמי עינו ודמי שינו ◆ תל' לו' לחפשי ישלחנו     B

תחת עינו. ◆ תחת עינו ◆ כל הבא מחמת עינו ◆ (כל) תחת     C/B/A    14

שינו ◆ כל הבא מחמת שינו. סל' פסו'     D

◆ ◆

    LXVII:I

וכי יגח ◆ פרט לשהגיחוהו ◆ מיכן אמרו שור     C/B/A    1

האיצטדין פטור לפי שאינו אלא מעשה. ◆ וכי יגח ◆ אין     B/A    2

לי אלא נגיחה מנין לעשות נגיפה נשיכה רביצה

ובעיטה כיוצא בנגיחה ◆ ודין הוא ◆ חייב שור בשור ושור     D/C

באדם מה מצינו שור בשור עשה בו נגיחה רביצה

נשיכה בעיטה כיוצא בנגיפה אף בזה נעשה בו נגיפה

נשיכה רביצה ובעיטה כיוצא בנגיחה ◆ (זה שנידון     E

בנפשו) ◆ ועוד קל וחומר ◆ מה שור בשור שאין ני[דון]     G/F

בנפשו עש' בו נגיחה נשיכה רביצה בעיטה כיוצא

בנגיפה זה שנידון בנפשו אינו דין שנעשה בו נגיפה

נשיכה רביצה בעיטה כיוצא בנגיחה ◆ לא אם אמרת     H

שור בשור שעשה בו את שאין מתכוין כמתכוין

תאמר בזה שלא עשה בו את שאין מתכוין כמתכוין ◆

ת"ל ומת לעשות נגיפה נשיכה רביצה ובעיטה כיוצא     I

בנגיחה ◆ אין לי אלא שור מנין לעשות שאר בהמה     A    3

חיה ועוף כיוצא בשור ◆ הוא הדין והיא התשובה ◆     B

---

[189] This comment is, most likely, a scribal emendation in the Firkovich manuscript.
[190] I.e., Exod. 21:28.

C. Scripture states, "... the ox shall *surely* be stoned" (Exod. 21:28), [which means that you should] treat all cattle, beasts of chase, and birds the same as the ox.

4. A. "... a man" (Exod. 21:28):

B. As long as it intended [to gore] him.

C. "... or a woman" (Exod. 21:28):

D. As long as it intended [to gore] her.

5. A. Man and woman:[191]

B. I only know concerning the man and woman. How does one know from Scripture to include the male minor, female minor, the one whose sex is unknown, and the hermaphrodite?

C. Scripture states, "... *a* man or *a* woman" (Exod. 21:28).[192]

6. A. "... to death" (Exod. 21:28):

B. This is what we have said: [Scripture states this in order to emphasize that one should] treat striking, biting, lying on top of, and trampling the same as goring.

7. A. "... the ox shall surely be stoned" (Exod. 21:28):

B. This is what we have said: [Scripture states this in order to emphasize that one should] treat all cattle, beasts of chase, and birds the same as the ox.

C. I only know concerning the goring [ox, that it should be stoned]. How does one know from Scripture that the one who sleeps with a beast [also should be stoned]?

D. It is a matter of logic:

E. If the goring ox, where the unintentional act is not treated the same as the intentional one, requires stoning, then isn't it logical that the one who sleeps with a beast, where the intentional act is treated the same as the unintentional one, requires stoning?

F. No! When you speak of [the act of an ox] goring, one may pay the ransom in place of his death.[193] Will you say the same with the one who sleeps with a beast, where one may not pay the ransom in place of his death?

G. Scripture states, [therefore,] "... shall surely be stoned" (Exod. 21:28).

8. A. I only know [that this punishment of being stoned applies] to these [animals mentioned in Exod. 21:28] alone.[194]

B. How does one know from Scripture to include their offspring and their crossbreedings?

C. Scripture states, "... shall surely be stoned" (Exod. 21:28).

D. And they don't stone them immediately. Rather, they keep them in the stockade until they die.

E. R. Eliezer b. R. Shimon says, "All of them are stoned."

## LXVII:II[195]

1. A. "... and its flesh shall not be eaten" (Exod. 21:28):

B. Why do I need [Scripture to say] this? For don't we know that this [ox] is an animal

---

[191] This is a paraphrase of Exod. 21:28.

[192] The text appears to base this interpretation on the fact that the nouns "man" and "woman" in Exod. 21:28 are indefinite objects, but are, nonetheless, preceded by the particle that would identify them as definite objects (*et*—את). The texts understands this as allowing for the possibility for gradations of male and female status.

[193] See Exod. 21:30.

ת״ל סקל יסקל השור לעשות שאר בהמה חיה ועוף כיוצא | C

בשור. ♦ את איש ♦ עד שיהא מתכוין לו ♦ את אשה ♦ עד | D/C/B/A | 4

שיהא מתכוין לה ♦ איש ואשה ♦ אין לי אלא איש ואשה | B/A | 5

מנין לרבות קטן וקטנה טומטום ואנדרגינס ♦ ת״ל את | C

(ה)איש או את (ה)אשה. ♦ ומת ♦ זו היא שאמרנו לעשות | B/A | 6

נגיפה נשיכה רביצה ובעיטה כיוצא בנגיחה ♦ סקול | A | 7

יסקל השור ♦ זו היא שאמרנו לעשות שאר בהמה חיה | B

ועוף כיוצא בשור ♦ ואין לי אלא נוגח רובע מנין ♦ ודין | D/C

הוא ♦ מה נוגח שלא עשה בו את שאינו מתכוין | E

כמתכוין טעון סקילה רובע שעשה בו את שאין | 

מתכוין כמתכוין אינו דין שטעון סקילה ♦ לא אם | F

אמרת בנגיחה שמשלם את הכופר לאחר מיתת נפשו | 

תאמר ברובע שאינו משלם את הכופר לאחר מיתת | 

נפשו ♦ ת״ל סקל יסקל ♦ אין לי אלא אלו בלבד ♦ מנין | B/A 8 | G

לרבות ולדותיהן ועריבתיהן ♦ ת״ל סקל יסקל ♦ ולא יהא | D/C

מסקלו מיד אלא כונסו לכיפה עד שעה שימותו ♦ ור׳ | E

אלעזר בר׳ שמעון אומ׳ בהלהן היו נסקלין. ♦ | 

| | LXVII:II

ולא יאכל את בשרו ♦ מה אני צריך וכי אין אנו | B/A | 1

---

[194] Compare 8.A–E with t. Baba Qamma 5:5

[195] Compare LXVII:II:1.A–4.C with parallel, but often significantly different, material in *Mekhilta de-Rabbi Ishmael*, Nezikin (H/R, 281:19–283:4; Laut., vol. 3, 78:41–80:79; Neus., LXVII:I:6.A–11.C).

that has been inappropriately slaughtered, and inappropriately slaughtered animals are forbidden from being eaten?

C. Why does Scripture state, "... and its flesh shall not be eaten" (Exod. 21:28)?

[179] D. This tells that if they slaughter it [appropriately] once its sentence was rendered, it is [still] forbidden from being eaten.

2. A. One might think if they slaughtered it before its sentence was rendered, its meat would be forbidden from being eaten.

B. Scripture states, [however,] "... the ox shall surely be stoned and its flesh shall not be eaten" (Exod. 21:28).

C. [Meaning,] the meat of that which is in the category [of meriting] stoning is forbidden from being eaten, but the meat of that which is not in the category of stoning may be eaten.

3. A. "... and its flesh shall not be eaten" (Exod. 21:28):

B. I only know concerning its flesh. How does one know from Scripture to include sinew, bones, horns, and hooves like the flesh?

C. It is a matter of logic:

D. This [ox] is prohibited from [being used] for any type of benefit, and the heifer whose neck is broken is prohibited from [being used] for any type of benefit.

E. Just as we have found that one may use the sinew, bones, horns, and hooves, just like the flesh, of the heifer whose neck is broken, so too may one use the sinew, bones, horns, and hooves, just like the flesh, of this ox.

F. No! If you speak of the heifer whose neck has been broken, it comes to atone [for the shedding of blood]. Will you say the same of this [ox], which does not come to atone [for the shedding of blood]?

G. Behold! The one who slaughters a common animal in the courtyard will prove it, for it doesn't come to atone [for the shedding of blood], but one may use its sinew, bones, horns, and hooves, just like the flesh.

H. No! If you speak of the one who slaughters a common animal in the courtyard, one treats the unintentional act like the intentional act. Will you say the same of this [ox], whose unintentional act is not treated the same as its intentional act?

I. Scripture states, [therefore,] "... the ox shall surely be stoned and its flesh shall not be eaten" (Exod. 21:28).

J. Certainly when Scripture says, "its flesh," it is as we have said: to make the sinew, bones, horns, and hooves just like the flesh.

4. A. "... and its flesh shall not be eaten" (Exod. 21:28):

B. Even [eaten] by the dogs.

C. Behold, this serves to prohibit it [from any type] of benefit.

## LXVII:III

1. A. "... but the owner of the ox is not to be punished" (Exod. 21:28):[196]

B. Ben Azzai says, "He is entirely clean of it, like the man who says to his companion, 'So

---

[196] Literally: "... but the owner of the ox is clean." Compare 1.A–B with b. Pesaḥim 22b (Neus., IV.B:Pesaḥim:2:1:DD–GG).

| | | |
|---|---|---|
| יודעין שהיא נבלה ונבלה אסורה באכילה ◆ מה ת״ל | C | |
| ולא יאכל את בשרו (מה אני צריך) ◆ מגיד שאם שחטו | D | |
| משנגמר דינו בשרו אסור באכילה ◆ יכול אם שחטו עד | A | 2 |
| שלא נ[ג]מר דינו יהא בשרו אסור באכילה ◆ ת״ל סקל יסקל | B | |
| השור ולא יאכל את בשרו ◆ את שהוא בכלל סקילה | C | |
| בשרו אסור באכילה ואת שאינו בכלל סקילה בשרו | | |
| מותר באכילה ◆ ולא יאכל את בשרו ◆ אין לי אלא בשרו | B/A | 3 |
| מנין לרבות גידים ועצמות קרנים וטלפים כיוצא בבשר ◆ | | |
| דין הוא ◆ הואיל וזה אסור בהנאה ועגלה ערופה | D/C | |
| אסורה בהנאה ◆ מה מצינו בעגלה ערופה עשה בה | E | |
| גידין ועצמות קרנים וטלפים כיוצא בבשר אף בזה | | |
| נעשה בו גידין [עצמות] קרנים וטלפים כיוצא בבשר ◆ | | |
| לא ‹אח› אמרת בעגלה ערופה שהיא באה לכפר | F | |
| תאמר בזו שאינה באה לכפר ◆ הרי השוחט חולין | G | |
| בעזרה יוכיח שאינו בא לכפר ועשה בו גידין ועצמות | | |
| קרנים וטלפים כיוצא בבשר ◆ לא אם אמרת בשוחט | H | |
| חולין בעזרה שעשה בו את שאינו מתכוין כמתכוין | | |
| תאמר בזה שלא עשה בו את שאין מתכוין כמתכוין ◆ | | |
| ת״ל סקל יסקל השור ולא יאכל את בשרו ◆ ודאי | J/I | |
| כשהוא אום׳ את בשרו זו היא שאמרנו לעשות גידים | | |
| ועצמות קרנים וטלפים כיוצא בבשר. ◆ ולא יאכל את | A | 4 |
| בשרו ◆ אפילו לכלבים ◆ הרי זה בא לאוסרו בהנאה. ◆ | C/B | |

LXVII:III

| | | |
|---|---|---|
| ובעל השור נקי ◆ בן עזאי אום׳ נקי מדמו שלו כולו | B/A | 1 |

and so has been entirely cleaned out of his belongings, so he has no benefit of them whatsoever.'"

2.    A.    R. Eliezer ben Azariah says, "'... but the owner of the ox is not to be punished' (Exod. 21:28):[197]

B.    "He is absolved from any payments for [any aborted] offspring."

C.    R. Akiva said to him, "Why do I need this? For hasn't it already been said in Scripture, '(When) men (fight and one of them pushes a pregnant woman and a miscarriage ensues)' (Exod. 21:22)?[198]

D.    "[Meaning, only] men [must pay damages for an aborted fetus] and not oxen!"

3.    A.    R. Eliezer says, "'... but the owner of the ox is not to be punished' (Exod. 21:28):[199]

B.    "He is exempt from paying half the damages.

C.    "Because I might say: One is obligated [to make payment] when an ox [gores] an ox, [and one is obligated to make payment] when an ox [gores] a person. Just as we have found when a *tam*[200] ox [gores] an ox one pays half damages, and when a *mu'ad*[201] ox [gores an ox] one pays full damages, so too here, when the ox is a *tam* one pays half damages, but if a *mu'ad* one pays full damages."

D.    R. Akiva said to him, "Where did you get this from? For we said that this one only requires stoning if it intended to kill the non-Jew, but killed the Jewish [unborn] eight-month [fetus] or killed [the Jewish, unborn] nine-month [fetus]."[202]

4.    A.    R. Akiva says, "'... but the owner of the ox is not to be punished' (Exod. 21:28):[203]

B.    "He is exempt from paying for the slave.

C.    "Because I might say: One is obligated [to make payment when an ox gores] a slave, and one is obligated [when an ox gores] a free person. Just as in the case of the free person, there is no distinction between the *tam* ox and the *mu'ad* ox concerning a ransom ... [manuscript lacuna] ... slave ... [manuscript lacuna] ... concerning a ransom.

[180]    D.    "And it could also be reasoned: Just as the free person, for whom one must pay the entire ransom, there is no distinction made in the ransom between the *tam* ox and the *mu'ad* ox, then isn't it logical with the slave, for whom one does not pay the entire ransom, that there would be no distinction made in the ransom between the *tam* ox and the *mu'ad* ox?

E.    "Or perhaps I would be more stringent with the slave than the free person. In that if the free person was worth five *sela*s, he would pay five *sela*s, but if the slave was worth five *sela*s, he would pay [nonetheless a fixed amount of] thirty *sela*s.

F.    "So why does Scripture state, '... but the owner of the ox is not to be punished' (Exod. 21:28)?

G.    "[It means that] he is exempt from paying for the slave."

---

[197] Compare 2.A–D with *Mekhilta de-Rabbi Ishmael*, Nezikin (H/R, 283:15–18; Laut., vol. 3, 82:97–104; Neus., LXVII:I:15.A–G).

[198] Compare 2.C with b. Baba Qamma 42b (Neus., XX.B:Tractate Baba Qamma:4:5:II.6.A–D).

[199] Compare 3.A–4.G with *Mekhilta de-Rabbi Ishmael*, Nezikin (H/R, 283:9–15; Laut., vol. 3, 81:87–82:98; Neus., LXVII:I:13.A–14.F).

[200] A *tam* ("innocent") is an animal that has not caused damage three times and whose owner, therefore, has not been informed of this and warned about his liability for future damage.

[201] A *mu'ad* ("forewarned") is an animal that has caused damage three times and whose owner has been informed of this and warned about his liability for future damage. If this animal causes damage again, the owner is fully liable for all indemnification.

[202] 3.D is contextually illogical, and would appear to have thematic affinity to some degree, instead, with 2.A–D immediately above.

[203] Compare 4.A–G with b. Baba Qamma 42b (Neus., XX.B:Tractate Baba Qamma:4:5:II.11.C–G), particularly for material missing in the lacunae above.

כאדם שאומר יצא איש פלו' נקי מנכסיו ואין לו בהן

הנאה של כלום ♦ ר' אלעזר בן עזריה אומ' ובעל השור    A   2

נקי ♦ נקי מדמי ולדות ♦ אמ' לו ר' עקיבה מה אני צריך    C/B

והלא כבר נאמר אנשים ♦ ולא שוורים ♦ ר' אליעזר אומ'    A 3   D

ובעל השור נקי ♦ נקי מחצי נזק ♦ מפני שהייתי אומ' חייב    C/B

שור בשור <ושור> באדם מה מצינו שור בשור בתם

משלם חצי נזק ומועד נזק משלם אף בזה בתם משלם

חצי נזק ומועד נזק שלם ♦ אמ' לו ר' עקיבה וכי מה    D

בפנייך שאמרנו בזה שטעון סקילה אלא במתכוין

להמית את הגוי והמית את בר יש' את בן שמנה

והמית את בן תשעה ♦ ר' עקיבה אומר ובעל השור נקי ♦    A   4

נקי מדמו <שלעבד> ♦ מפני שהייתי אומ' חייב בעבד    C/B

וחייב בבן חורין מה בן חורין (לא) חלק בו בין תם

למועד בכפר <...> עבד <...> בכפר ♦ ועוד קל וחומר    D

ומה בן חורין שמשלם כל כפרו (לא) חלק בו בין תם

למועד בכפר עבד שאין משלם כל כפרו אינו דין

ש(לא) נחלק בו בין תם למועד בכפר ♦ או מחמיר אני    E

בעבד יתר מבן חורין מפני שבן חורין אם היה יפה

חמש סלעים נותן חמש סלעים ועבד אם היה יפה

חמש סלעים נותן של(י)שי<ם> סלע ♦ ומה ת"ל בעל    F

השור נקי ♦ נקי מדמי עבד. סל' פסו' ♦    G

LXVII:IV

1. A. "But if that ox had gored (in times past, and its owner, though warned, has failed to guard it, and it kills a man or a woman—the ox shall surely be stoned and its owner, too, shall be put to death)" (Exod. 21:29):

   B. I only know from this that [the culpability is if] it is a *tam* ox that had gored. How does one know from Scripture that they must also have witnessed it?

   C. Scripture states, "But if *that* ox had gored" (Exod. 21:29).

   D. [Meaning,] with certainty, and no doubt.

2. A. "... in times" (Exod. 21:29):[204]

   B. Behold, this means two.

   C. "... past" (Exod. 21:29):

   D. Behold, this means three.

   E. This teaches that an ox doesn't become a *mu'ad* unless they warn about it for three days, one after the other.

3. A. "... and its owner, though warned" (Exod. 21:29):

   B. I only know from this concerning owners. How does one know from Scripture [that also] the court [must be warned]?

   C. Scripture states, "If it is known" (Exod. 21:36), [which means known] in the court.

   D. Still, I might say: [In the case of the habitually goring ox] below[205] [only] the court [must be warned, but in the case] here[206] [only] the owners [must be warned]. How does one know from Scripture that here the court [also must be warned] and below the owners [also must be warned]?

   E. Scripture states [here], "... in times past" (Exod. 21:29), [and Scripture states below,] "... in times past" (Exod. 21:36), [in order to provide the opportunity to interpret this using] a *gezerah shaveh:*[207]

   F. Just as "in times past" stated here [requires that] the court [be warned], so too does "in times past" stated below [require that] the court [be warned]. And just as "in times past" stated here [requires that] the owners [be warned], so too does "in times past" stated below [require that] the owners [be warned].

4. A. "... and its owner ... has failed to guard it" (Exod. 21:29):[208]

   B. I only know from this concerning its owner. How does one know from Scripture to include the one who guards [it] for free, and the one who borrows [it], the paid guard, and the one who rents [it]?[209]

   C. Scripture states, "... has failed to guard it" (Exod. 21:29).

   D. [Meaning, anyone who fails to guard] something that is his responsibility to guard.

---

[204] Compare 2.A–E with m. Baba Qamma 2:4.

[205] I.e., Exod. 21:36.

[206] I.e., Exod. 21:29.

[207] I.e., the employment of the same word in separate scriptural contexts, thus facilitating the application of the meaning of the word in one context to the other.

[208] Compare 4.A–G with *Mekhilta de-Rabbi Ishmael,* Nezikin (H/R, 284:10–14; Laut., vol. 3, 84:123–30; Neus., LXVII:I:21.A–23.D).

[209] Compare 4.B with m. Baba Metzia 7:8 as standard Rabbinic categories.

| | | |
|---|---|---|
| אם שור נגח הוא • אין לי אלא שנגח והוא תם | B/A | 1 |
| מנין ‹עד› שיעידו בו • ת״ל אם שור נגח הוא • ודאי ולא | D/C | |
| ספק • תמול • הרי שנים • שלשם • הרי שלשה • מלמד שאין | E/D/C/B/A | 2 |
| נעשה מועד עד שיעידו בו שלשה ימים זה אחר זה. • | | |
| והוא עד והועד בבעליו • אין לי אלא בעלים בית דין | B/A | 3 |
| מנין • ת״ל או נודע (שמ׳ כא לו) בבית דין • עדאן אני | D/C | |
| אומ׳ תחתון בבית דין כן ‹ב›בעלים מנין כן בבית | | |
| ‹דין› תחתון בבעלים • ת״ל תמול שלשם תמול שלשם | E | |
| (שם) לגזירה שוה • מה תמול שלשם האמ׳ כן בבית דין | F | |
| אף תמול שלשם האמור למטה בבית דין ומה תמול | | |
| שלשם האמ׳ כן בבעלים אף תמול שלשם האמ׳ | | |
| למטה ררצליח • ולא ישמרנו בעליו • אין לי אלא בעליו | B/A | 4 |
| מנין לרבות שומר חנם והשואל נושא שכר והשוכר • | | |
| ת״ל ולא ישמרנו • את שדרך שמירתו עליו • | D/C | |

E.   This includes the one who guards for free, the one who borrows, the paid guard, and the one who rents.

F.   If so, why does Scripture state, "… and its owner … has failed to guard it" (Exod. 21:29)?

G.   To exclude the one who borrowed [an ox presuming] it to be a *tam,* but it turns out it was a *mu'ad.*[210]

5.   A.   How does one know from Scripture [that] if he was warned when he borrowed it that it was a *mu'ad,* behold, this makes it a *mu'ad*?

B.   Scripture states, "… and its owner … has failed to guard it" (Exod. 21:29).

6.   A.   "… has failed to guard it" (Exod. 21:29):[211]

B.   [Meaning,] he who has the capability to guard.

C.   Excluded are the deaf-mute, madman, and minor, who do not have the capability to guard.

D.   [If] an ox [guarded by] a deaf-mute, madman, or minor gores, they are exempt.

E.   R. Akiva says, "He must pay half-damages."

7.   A.   "[If] an ox broke free from the halter and damaged [someone], whether *tam* or *mu'ad,* [the owner] is culpable."—The words of R. Meir.[212]

B.   But R. Judah says, "[If] *tam* he is culpable, but if *mu'ad* he is exempt."

C.   R. Eliezer ben Jacob says, "Both are exempt."

D.   And R. Eliezer says, "The only way to guard the *mu'ad* ox is with a slaughtering knife!"

8.   A.   "… and it kills a man or a woman" (Exod. 21:29):

[181]   B.   Why do I need this? Hasn't it already been stated in Scripture, "When an ox gores a man or a woman to death" (Exod. 21:28)?

C.   Why does Scripture state, "… and it kills a man or a woman" (Exod. 21:29)?

D.   Because when it says in Scripture, "But if that ox had gored in times past, and its owner, though warned, has failed to guard it" (Exod. 21:29), one might think that if they warn him and it gores, even if it doesn't kill he would be culpable for death.

E.   Scripture states, [therefore,] "… and it kills a man" (Exod. 21:29).

F.   This tells that he is not culpable unless it kills.

9.   A.   "… a man or a woman" (Exod. 21:29):[213]

B.   Just as the man's [uncollected] damage [payments] go to his children, so too the woman's go to her children.

10.   A.   "… the ox shall be stoned" (Exod. 21:29):[214]

B.   Why do I need this? Hasn't it already been stated in Scripture, "… the ox shall surely be stoned" (Exod. 21:28)?

C.   Because when Scripture says, "… and its owner, too, shall be put to death" (Exod. 21:29), one might think that just as the ox is stoned, so too are its owners to be stoned.

[210] Compare 4.G with b. Baba Qamma 40a (Neus., XX.B:Tractate Baba Qamma:4:4:I.9.A–10.Q).
[211] Compare 6.A–E with t. Baba Qamma 4:4.
[212] Compare 7.A–D with t. Baba Qamma 5:7.
[213] Compare 9.A–B with y. Baba Qamma 4c (Neus., 4:6:II.A–C) and b. Baba Qamma 42b (Neus., XX.B:Tractate Baba Qamma:4:5:II.12.A–C).
[214] Compare 10.A–11.J with parallel, but often significantly different, material in *Mekhilta de-Rabbi Ishmael,* Nezikin (H/R, 284:16–285:8; Laut., vol. 3, 84:133–86:151; Neus., LXVII:I:25.A–29.E).

| | | |
|---|---|---|
| לרבות שואל ‹ושומר חנם נושא שכר והשוכר • אם כן מה | F/E | |
| ת״ל ולא ישמרנו בעליו • פרט לשואל› תם ונמצא מועד • | G | |
| מנין הועד בו בפני שואל שהוא מועד הרי זה מועד • ת״ל | B/A | 5 |
| ולא ישמרנו בעליו • לא ישמרנו ולא ישמרנ[ו] • את | B/A | 6 |
| שיש בו דעת לשמר • יצאו חרש שוטה וקטן שאין בהן | C | |
| דעת לשמר • שור חרש שוטה וקטן שנגחו הרי אלו | D | |
| פטורין • ר׳ עקיבה אומ׳ משלם חצי נזק • שור שפסק את | A 7 | E |
| המוסרה ויצא והזיק אחד תם ואחד מועד חייב דברי | | |
| ר׳ מאיר • ור׳ יהודה אומ׳ תם חייב ומועד פטור • ור׳ | C/B | |
| אליעזר בן יעקב אומ׳ זה וזה פטורין • ור׳ אליעזר אומ׳ | D | |
| אין לו שמירה לשור המועד אלא סכין. • והמית איש | A | 8 |
| או אשה • מה אני צריך והלא כבר נאמ׳ וכי יגח שור את | B | |
| איש או ‹את› אשה ומת (שמ׳ כא כח) • מה ת״ל והמית | C | |
| איש או אשה • מכלל שנא׳ ואם שור נגח הוא מתמל | D | |
| שלשם והועד בבעליו ולא ישמרנו יכול כ[יון] שהעידוהו | | |
| ונגח אף על פי שלא המית הרי הוא חייב מיתה • | | |
| ת״ל והמית איש • מגיד שאינו חייב עד שימית • | F/E | |
| ‹איש או אשה› • מה האיש נזק‹י›ו לבניו אף האשה | B/A | 9 |
| נזקיה לבניה. • השור יסקל • מה אני צריך והלא כבר | B/A | 10 |
| נאמר סקול יסקל השור (שם) • לפי שהוא אומ׳ וגם | C | |
| בעליו יומת יכול כשם שהשור נסקל כך בעליו נסקלין • | | |

D.   Scripture states, [however,] "... the ox shall be stoned" (Exod. 21:29).

E.   [Meaning,] the ox is to be stoned, but its owners are not to be stoned.

F.   But still I might say that the owners must die.

G.   Scripture states, [however,] "... he is a murderer—the murderer must be put to death" (Num. 35:16).

H.   [Meaning,] the murderer dies, but the owners do not die.

I.   But still I might say that the owners must die.

J.   Scripture states, [however,] "If anyone kills a person, on the evidence of witnesses the murderer is executed" (Num. 35:30). And Scripture says, "You may not accept a ransom for the life of a murderer, etc." (Num. 35:31).

K.   [Meaning,] a murderer dies, but the owners do not die.

L.   Then why does Scripture state, "... the ox shall be stoned, and its owner, too, shall be put to death" (Exod. 21:29)?

M.   The method of [applying the] death penalty for the owners is like the method of death for the ox. Just as the method of death for the owners would involve pushing [him down], stoning [him], and [a court of] 23 [judges], so too must the death for the ox involve pushing down, stoning, and [a court of] 23.

11.   A.   I only know from this[215] concerning the goring ox. How does one know from Scripture [to include] the one who sleeps with an animal?

B.   Scripture states, "... the ox shall be stoned ..." (Exod. 21:29).

C.   I only know from this concerning goring. How does one know from Scripture to treat striking, biting, lying on top of, and trampling the same as goring?

D.   Scripture states, "... the ox shall be stoned" (Exod. 21:29).

E.   And I also only know from this concerning the *mu'ad*. How does one know from Scripture [the same applies to] the *tam*?

F.   Scripture states, "... the ox shall be stoned" (Exod. 21:29).

G.   And I also only know from this concerning the ox. How does one know from Scripture to treat all cattle, beasts of chase, and birds the same as the ox?[216]

H.   Scripture states, "... the ox shall be stoned" (Exod. 21:29).

I.   And R. Eliezer also says, "The method of [applying the] death penalty for the ox that killed [involves a court of] 23 [judges]. But for all [other] cattle, beasts of chase, and birds that have killed—the first one who kills them has gained merit in heaven!"

J.   R. Judah ben Baba testified that a chicken that killed someone was stoned in Jerusalem.[217]

LXVII:V

1.   A.   "If ransom is laid upon him, (he must pay whatever is laid upon him to redeem his life)" (Exod. 21:30):

B.   One might think if one demands 100 [*shekels*], he must pay 100, or if one demands 10,000, he must pay 10,000.

---

[215] I.e., Exod. 21:29.
[216] Compare 11.G–J with t. Sanhedrin 3:1ff. and b. Sanhedrin 15b (Neus., XXIIIA:Tractate Sanhedrin:LXXI:K–O).
[217] Compare 11.J with m. Eduyot 6:1 and y. Erubin 26a (Neus., 10:1:II.S).

| | | |
|---|---|---|
| ת״ל השור יסקל • השור נסקל ואין בעליו נסקלין • ועד | F/E/D | |
| אן אני אום׳ ימותו בעלין • ת״ל רוצח הוא מות יומת | G | |
| הרצח (במ׳ לה טז) • רוצח מת בעלים אינן מתים • ועד | I/H | |
| אן אני אום׳ ימותו בעלין • ת״ל כל מכה נפש לפי עדים | J | |
| ירוצח את הרוצח (שם ל) ואום׳ ולא תקחו כופר לנפש | | |
| רוצח וגום׳ (שם לא) • רוצח מת ואין בעלין מתין • ומה | L/K | |
| ת״ל השור יסקל וגם בעליו יומת • כמיתת בעלין כך | M | |
| מיתת השור מה מיתת בעלין בדחיה ובסקילה | | |
| ובעשרים ושלשה ‹אף מיתת השור בדחיה ובסקילה | | |
| ובעשרים ושלשה› • אין לי אלא נוגח רובע מנין • ת״ל | B/A | 11 |
| השור יסקל • אין לי אלא נגיחה מנין לעשות נגיפה | C | |
| נשיכה רביצה בעיטה כיוצא בנגיחה • ת״ל השור יסקל • | D | |
| וגם אין לי אלא מועד תם מנין • ‹ת״ל› השור יסקל • | F/E | |
| וגם אין לי אלא שור מנין (לרבות) לעשות שאר בהמה | G | |
| חיה ועוף כיוצא בשור • ת״ל (ו)השור יסקל • וגם ר׳ | I/H | |
| אליעזר אום׳ השור שהמית מיתתו בעשרים ושלשה | | |
| ושאר בהמה חיה ועוף שהמיתו כל הקודם להורגן | | |
| זכה לשמים העיד • [ר׳] יהודה בן בבא שנסקל תרנגול | J | |
| בירושלם שהרג את הנפש. סל[׳] פסו׳ • | | |

| | | |
|---|---|---|
| | LXVII:V | |
| אם כופר יושת עליו • יכול אם אם׳ מנה יהא | B/A | 1 |
| נותן מנה ואם אמר מאה מנה יהא נותן מאה מנה • | | |

C. Scripture says here, [however,] "... laid upon him" (Exod. 21:30), and Scripture says above, "... may exact from him" (Exod. 21:22).

D. Just as the [amount for] "... may exact from him" stated above [is determined by] the court, so too [the amount for] "... laid upon him" stated here [is determined] by the court.

E. Just as "... may exact from him" stated above [refers to the] owners, so too does "... laid upon him" stated here [refer to] the owners.

[182]

2.  A. "... he must pay ... to redeem his life" (Exod. 21:30):[218]

B. One might think [the amount of] the redemption [is based upon the value of] the life of the injured person or [the value of] the life of the one who injures.

C. Scripture states here, "... laid upon him" (Exod. 21:30), and Scripture says above, "... may exact from him" (Exod. 21:22).

D. Just as "... may exact from him" stated above [refers to an amount based upon the value of] the life of the injured person, so too does "... laid upon him" stated here [refer to an amount based upon the value of] the life of the injured person.

E. R. Ishmael b. R. Yoḥanan ben Berukah says, "Since the owners are going to be put to death, and the ransom effects their redemption, you should say from this that the redemption [is based upon the value of] the life of the one who injures."

3.  A. "... is laid upon him" (Exod. 21:30):

B. This includes the son or the daughter.

4.  A. "... whatever is laid upon him" (Exod. 21:30):

B. This includes the one who guards for free, and the one who borrows, the paid guard, and the one who rents.[219]

## Chapter Sixty-Eight

(Textual Source: Ms. Firkovich II A 268)

LXVIII:I

1.  A. "So, too, if it gores a minor male or it gores a minor female, ([the owner] shall be dealt with according to the same rule)" (Exod. 21:31):[220]

B. Why do I need this? Hasn't it already been stated in Scripture, "When an ox gores a man or a woman to death" (Exod. 21:28)?

C. Why does Scripture state, "So, too, if it gores a minor male or it gores a minor female" (Exod. 21:31)?

D. ... [manuscript lacuna] ...

E. It is a matter of logic:

F. A man is culpable [for killing] a man, and an ox is culpable [for killing] a man.

G. Just as we have found that there is no distinction [in the culpability to be put to] death between [the killing of] minors and adults, when a man [kills] a man, so too, here, no distinction is made in [the culpability to be put to] death between [the killing of] minors and adults.

H. Or additionally, one might reason:

---

[218] Compare 2.A–E with *Mekhilta de-Rabbi Ishmael,* Nezikin (H/R, 285:9–12; Laut., vol. 3, 86:152–58; Neus., LXVII:I:30.A–F).

[219] See note 209.

C נאמ' כן יושת עליו ונאמ' להלן ישית עליו (שמ' כא כב) ◆

D מה ישית עליו האמ' להלן בבית דין אף יושת עליו

E האמ' כן בבית דין ◆ מה ישית עליו האמ' להלן בעלין אף

B/A 2 יושת עליו האמ' כן בעלין. ◆ ונתן פדיון נפשו ◆ יכול פדיון

C נפשו של ניזק או פדיון נפשו של מזיק ◆ נאמ' כן יושת

D עליו ונאמ' להלן ישית עליו (שם) ◆ מה ישית עליו האמ'

להלן פדיון נפשו של ניזק אף יושת עליו האמ' כן

E פדיון נפשו של ניזק. ◆ ר' ישמעאל בר' יוחנן בן ברוקה

אומ' הואיל ותפוסת בעלין במיתה ופטירתן בכפר

Λ 3 אמור מעתה פדיון נפשו של מזיק ◆ אשר יושת עליו ◆

B/A 4 B לרבות את הבן ואת הבת ◆ ככל יושת עליו ◆ לרבות

שומר חנם והשואל נושא שכר והשוכר. סל' פסו' ◆

LXVIII:I

B/A 1 או בן יגח או בת יגח ◆ מה אני צריך והלא כבר

נאמר וכי יגח שור את איש או את אשה ומת (שם כח) ◆

F/E/D/C מה ת"ל או בן יגח או בת יגח ◆ <...> ◆ דין הוא ◆ חייב אדם

G באדם ושור באדם ◆ מה מצינו אדם באדם לא חלק

<בו> בין קטנים לגדולים במיתה אף בזה לא נחלק

H בו בין קטנים לגדולים במיתה ◆ ועוד קל וחומר ◆

---

[220] Compare 1.A–K with *Mekhilta de-Rabbi Ishmael,* Nezikin (H/R, 286:15–287:2; Laut., vol. 3, 88:1–8; Neus., LXVIII:I:1.A–4.C); and b. Baba Qamma 43b (Neus., XX.B:Tractate Baba Qamma:4:5:III.1.A–I).

I.  If the minor [who kills] is not culpable like the adult [who kills], but one is equally culpable [for killing] a minor or an adult, then isn't it logical that here, where the minor [ox] is culpable like the adult [ox], that one would be equally culpable [for killing] a minor or adult?

J.  No! When you speak of a man [killing] a man, he is [also] liable for paying indemnity for humiliation. Will you say the same here, where one does not pay for humiliation?

K.  Scripture states, [therefore,] "So, too, if it gores a minor male or it gores a minor female" (Exod. 21:31).

2.  A.  I only know [from Exod. 21:31] concerning the *mu'ad* ox.[221] How does one know from Scripture [that the owner should be dealt with according to the same rule in the case of] the *tam* ox?[222]

B.  It is a matter of logic:

C.  [An ox] is culpable [for killing] a minor, male or female, and [an ox] is culpable [for killing] an adult, male or female.

D.  Just as we have found [when an ox kills] an adult, male or female, there is no distinction [in the ox's culpability to be put to] death between a *tam* and a *mu'ad,* so too [when an ox kills] a minor, male or female, there is no distinction [in the ox's culpability to be put to] death between a *tam* and a *mu'ad.*

E.  Or additionally one might reason:

F.  If a man or woman [who injures or kills] has less advantageous rights regarding damages,[223] but there is no distinction made [in the ox's culpability to be put to] death between a *tam* or a *mu'ad* [ox that kills them], then isn't it logical in the case of a minor, male or female, who has more advantageous rights regarding damages,[224] that there be no distinction made [in the ox's culpability to be put to] death between a *tam* or a *mu'ad* [ox that kills them]?

G.  [No! If you reason this way,] you have judged from [the basis of] a strict case[225] to a lenient case,[226] in order to apply to it a stringency. If it is strict with the *mu'ad,* need it necessarily be strict with a *tam*?

H.  Scripture states, [therefore,] "So, too, if it gores a minor male or it gores a minor female" (Exod. 21:31).

I.  [Scripture states] "goring" twice—one "goring" for the *tam* and one "goring" for the *mu'ad.*[227]

3.  A.  I only know from [Exod. 21:31] concerning the situation when [the ox gores] all of him.[228] How does one know from Scripture to include [the situation where he only gores and damages] his limbs?

B.  It is a matter of logic:

C.  If [in the situation] of one who kidnaps [someone] and who sells [someone into slavery], he is culpable for [damage done to] all of him, but he is not culpable [for damage done only] to his limbs, [then] isn't it logical that in this situation, in which one is not culpable [for damage done to] all of him, one would not be culpable [for damage done] to his limbs?

D.  [The situation of] a man [injuring] a man will prove it, for [in that situation] he is not culpable [for damage done to all of him but] is culpable for [damage done] to his limbs.

---

[221] A *mu'ad* ("forewarned") is an animal that has caused damage three times and whose owner has been informed of this and warned about his liability for future damage. If this animal causes damage again, the owner is fully liable for all indemnification.

[222] A *tam* ("innocent") is an animal that has not caused damage three times and whose owner, therefore, has not been informed of this and warned about his liability for future damage.

[223] I.e., they must pay for damages that they caused.

[224] I.e., as minors they are not responsible to pay for damages that they cause.

מה אם במקום שלא חייב את הקטנים כגדולין חייב     I

על הקטנים כגדולין כאן שחייב את הקטנים כגדולים

אינו דין שנחייב על הקטנים כגדולים ◆ (ו)לא אם     J

אמרת אדם באדם שמשלם את הבושת תאמר בזה שאין

משלם את הבשת ◆ ת״ל או בן יגח או בת יגח ◆     K

אין לי אלא מועד תם מנין ◆ ודין הוא ◆ חייב בבן ובת     C/B/A    2

וחייב באיש ובאשה ◆ מה מצינו באיש ובאשה לא חלק     D

בהן בין תם למועד ‹במיתה› אף בבן ובת לא נחלק(ו)

בהן בין תם למועד במיתה ◆ ועוד קל וחומר ◆ ומה איש     F/E

ואשה שהורע כחן בנזיקין לא חלק בהן בין תם

למועד ‹במיתה› בן ובת שיפה כוחן בנזיקין אינו דין

שלא נחלק בהן בין תם למועד במיתה ◆ אמרתה כך     G

דנין מן החמור לקל להחמיר עליו ואם החמיר במועד

נחמ‹י›ר בתם ◆ ת״ל או בן יגח או בת יגח ◆ שתי נגיחות     I/H

כן נגיחה לתם ונגיחה למועד ◆ אין לי אלא על כולו     A    3

מנין לרבות את אבריו ◆ ודין הוא ◆ מה הגונב והמוכר     C/B

שחייב על כולו אין חייב על אבריו זה שאין חייב על

כולו אינו דין שלא יהא חייב על אבריו ◆ אדם     D

באדם יוכיח שאין חייב על כולו חייב על אבריו ◆

---

[225] I.e., the case of the *mu'ad.*

[226] I.e., the case of the *tam.*

[227] Compare 2.A–I with b. Baba Qamma 44a (Neus., XX.B:Tractate Baba Qamma:4:5:III.1.J–P).

[228] I.e., to the point of death.

[183]    E.    No! If you speak [of the situation of] a man [injuring] a man, he must pay indemnity for humiliation. Will you say [the same] in this case, where he does not pay indemnity for humiliation?

       F.    [The situation of] a man [injuring] a slave will prove it, for [in that situation] he does not pay indemnity for humiliation.

       G.    No! If you speak [of the situation of] a man [injuring] a man, he must pay indemnity for pain, healing, lost time, and humiliation. Will you say the same here, where he does not pay indemnity for pain, healing, lost time, and humiliation?

       H.    Scripture states, [therefore,] "So, too, if it gores a minor male or it gores a minor female" (Exod. 21:31).

       I.    [Scripture states] "goring" twice—[one] "goring" here for [the situation where the person] dies and [one] "goring" for [the situation where there are only] injuries.

4.    A.    One might think whether [the ox is] *tam* or *mu'ad*, one pays full damage indemnity.

       B.    But it is a matter of logic:

       C.    An ox is culpable [for injuring] an ox, and an ox is culpable [for injuring] a human being.

       D.    Just as we have found when a *tam* ox [injures] an ox one pays half-damage indemnity, but if it is a *mu'ad* ox one pays full-damage indemnity, so too here, if *tam* one pays half-damage indemnity, but if *mu'ad* one pays full-damage indemnity.

       E.    Another interpretation:

       F.    One is culpable when [the ox gores] all of him,[229] and one is culpable [if the ox only gores and damages] his limbs.

       G.    Just as we have found [in the situation where the ox gores] all of him, the *tam* is exempt but the *mu'ad* is culpable, so too [where the ox only gores and damages] his limbs, the *tam* is exempt but the *mu'ad* is culpable.

       H.    Let's see which [argument] is most appropriate:

       I.    One may derive [rules] about a [legal] matter that is not sentenced by death from [another legal] matter that is not sentenced by death, but one may not derive [rules] from a [legal] matter that is not sentenced by death from [another legal] matter that is sentenced by death. So don't prove anything [with the case of the ox goring] all of him, because it is sentenced by death.

       J.    Or you could go by this route:[230]

       K.    One may derive [rules from a legal situation involving] one person and another person, but you may not derive [rules from a legal situation involving] a person and an ox.

       L.    [Thus] Scripture states, "... shall be dealt with according to the same rule" (Exod. 21:31).

       M.    [Which means that] the law of the *mu'ad* [injuring] the *mu'ad* [is treated the] same as the law for the *tam* [injuring] the *tam*.

5.    A.    Rabbi Akiva says, "How does one know from Scripture that one pays full damages when a *tam* [injures] a person?

       B.    "Scripture states, '[The owner] shall be dealt with according to the same rule' (Exod. 21:31), [meaning,] the law for the *tam* is like the law for the *mu'ad*.

       C.    "One might think he must pay [restitution] from his best property.[231]

---

[229] Ibid.
[230] I.e., logically reason.

| | |
|---|---|
| לא אם אמרת אדם באדם שמשלם את הבשת תאמר | E |
| בזה שאין משלם את הבשת ◆ אדם בעבד יוכיח שאין | F |
| משלם את הבשת ◆ לא אם אמרת אדם באדם שמשלם | G |
| צער וריפוי ושבת ובשת ‹תאמר בזה שאין משלם | |
| צער וריפוי ושבת ובשת› ◆ ת״ל או בן יגח או בת | H |
| יגח ◆ שתי נגיחות כן נגיחה למיתה ונגיחה לנזיקין ◆ | I |
| יכול אחד תם ואחד מועד משלם נזק שלם ◆ ודין הוא ◆ | B/A | 4 |
| חייב בשור ושור באדם ◆ מה מצינו שור בשור בתם | D/C |
| משלם חצי נזק ומועד משלם נזק שלם אף בזה בתם | |
| משלם חצי נזק במועד משלם נזק שלם. ◆ ד״א ◆ חייב על | F/E |
| כולו וחייב על אבריו ◆ מה מצינו על כולו תם פטור | G |
| ומועד חייב אף על אבריו תם פטור ומועד חייב ◆ נראה | H |
| למי דומה ◆ דנין דבר שאין נידון בנפשו ‹מדבר שאין | I |
| נידון בנפשו ואין דנין דבר שאין נידון בנפשו› מדבר | |
| שנידון בנפשו ואל יוכיח על כולו שנידון בנפשו ◆ או לך | J |
| לך לדרך זו ◆ דנין אדם מאדם ואין דנין אדם משור ◆ | K |
| ת״ל כמשפט הזה יעשה לו ◆ כמשפט ‹ה›מועד במועד | M/L |
| כך משפט התם בתם ◆ ור׳ עקיבה אומ׳ מנין לתם | A | 5 |
| באדם שמשלם נזק שלם ◆ ת״ל כמשפט הזה יעשה לו | B |
| כמשפט מועד כך משפט התם ◆ יכול ישלם מן העליה ◆ | C |

231 Compare 5.C–D with m. Baba Qamma 1:4.

D. "Scripture states, [however,] '... shall be dealt with' (Exod. 21:31), [meaning,] he only pays with its own body."

LXVIII:II

1. A. "But if the ox gores a slave, male or female, (he shall pay thirty *shekels* of silver to the master, and the ox shall be stoned)" (Exod. 21:32):[232]

   B. One might think that Scripture speaks about the male or female Hebrew slave.

   C. [However,] it says here in Scripture, "... slave, male or female" (Exod. 21:32), and it says in Scripture above, "... slave, male or female" (Exod. 21:26).

   D. Just as [with] "slave, male or female" stated above, Scripture speaks of a male or female Canaanite slave, so too with "slave, male or female" here, Scripture speaks of the male or female Canaanite slave.

2. A. "... silver" (Exod. 21:32):[233]

   B. One might think [this means one] *dinar*.

   C. Scripture states, [however,] "... thirty" (Exod. 21:32).

   D. One might think [this means] 30 *dinars*.

   E. Scripture states, [however,] "... *shekels*" (Exod. 21:32).

3. A. "... silver" (Exod. 21:32):[234]

   B. One might think [this means] with Babylonian, Median, and Capadocian [currency].[235]

   C. [However,] it says here in Scripture, "... *shekels*" (Exod. 21:32), and it says below in Scripture, "... *shekels*" (Lev. 27:25).

   D. Just as "*shekels*" stated below [means] holy currency,[236] so too does "*shekels*" stated here [mean] holy currency.

4. A. "... he shall pay ... to the master" (Exod. 21:32):[237]

   B. Whether male or female.

   C. "... he shall pay ... to the master" (Exod. 21:32):

   D. Whether a minor or adult.

   E. "... he shall pay ... to the master" (Exod. 21:32):

   F. One might think with a court of judges, or without a court of judges.

   G. Scripture states, [however,] "... he shall pay ... to the master" (Exod. 22:32).

5. A. "... and the ox shall be stoned" (Exod. 21:32):

   B. Just as its stoning [is done in accordance with the decision] of a court of judges, so too is its donation to the Temple [done in accordance with the decision] of a court of judges.

6. A. "... and the ox shall be stoned" (Exod. 21:32):[238]

[184] B. Why do I need this? Hasn't it already been said, "... the ox shall be stoned" (Exod. 21:28)?

[232] Compare 1.A–D with parallels above at LXIV:I:1.A–G and at LXVI:I:1.A–C.
[233] Compare 2.A–E with *Sifra*, Dibura Dehovah 20:6 (Neus., LXIV:II:5.A–H).
[234] Compare 3.A–D with b. Bekhorot 8:7.
[235] I translate here according to the parallel to this tradition at *Sifra*, Hovah 20:6.
[236] I.e., the currency used at the Temple.
[237] Compare 4.A–B with *Mekhilta de-Rabbi Ishmael*, Nezikin (H/R, 287:10; Laut., vol. 3, 89:20–21; Neus., LXVIII:I:8.A–B).
[238] Compare 6.A–H with y. Baba Qamma 4b (Neus., 4:5:I.A–O).

| | |
|---|---|
| D | ת״ל יעשה לו מלמד שאין משלם אלא מגופו. סל׳ פסו׳ ◆ |

LXVIII:II

| | | |
|---|---|---|
| 1 | B/A | אם עבד יגח השור או אמה ◆ יכול בעבד ואמה |
| | C | העברים הכתוב מדבר ◆ נאמר כן עבד ואמה ונאמ׳ |
| | D | להלן עבד ואמה (שמ׳ כא לב) ◆ מה עבד ואמה האמ׳ |
| | | [לה]לן בעבד ואמה כנע‹נ›ים הכת׳ מדבר אף עבד |
| | | ואמה האמור [כן] בעבד ואמה כנענים הכת׳ מדבר. ◆ |
| 2 | E/D/C/B/A | כסף ◆ יכול דינר ◆ ת״ל שלשים ◆ יכול שלשים דינר ◆ ת״ל |
| 3 | B/A | שקלים. ◆ כסף ◆ יכול בי בבליות ועלמיות וקבודקיות ◆ |
| | D/C | נאמ׳ כן שקלים ונאמ׳ להלן שקלים (ויק׳ כז כה) ◆ מה |
| | | שקלים האמ׳ להלן בשקל הקדש אף שקלים האמ׳ כן |
| | | בשקל הקדש. ◆ יתן לאדוניו ◆ בין איש ובין אשה ◆ יתן |
| 4 | C/B/A | |
| | F/E/D | לאדניו ◆ בין קטן ובין גדול ◆ יתן לאדוניו ◆ יכול בבית דין |
| 5 G | B/A | ושלא בבית דין ◆ ת״ל יתן לאדוניו (.) ◆ והשור יסקל ◆ מה |
| 6 | A | סקילתו בבית דין אף נתינתו בבית דין ◆ ‹ו›השור |
| | B | יסקל ◆ מה אני צריך והלא כבר נאמר סקל יסקל השור |

C.  Why does Scripture state, "and the ox shall be stoned" (Exod. 21:32)?

D.  Since it says in Scripture above, "If, however, that ox has been in the habit of goring" (Exod. 21:29), one might think that [just] because it gored, even if it did not kill, he would be culpable.

E.  Scripture states, [however,] "… the ox shall be stoned" (Exod. 21:28) and "… the ox shall be stoned" (Exod. 21:32), [in order to provide the opportunity to argue] by means of a *gezerah shaveh:*[239]

F.  Just as "… the ox shall be stoned" above [means only if it gored one] to death, so too does "… the ox shall be stoned" here [mean only if it gored one] to death.

G.  And just as "… the ox shall be stoned" here is a *mu'ad* but not a *tam,* so too "… the ox shall be stoned" above [must be] a *mu'ad,* but not a *tam.*

H.  Because it[240] was in the general statement, and was then singled out to make the new judgment, Scripture [repeats it again] to include it [as a part of the] general statement.

7.    A.  Ox, ox—[the word is mentioned] seven times in Exod. 21:28–32.[241]

B.  [This is to inform you to include in the culpability for execution also] the ox belonging to a woman, the ox belonging to a [minor] orphan, the ox belonging [temporarily] to an administrator [of a minor orphan's estate], the wild ox, the ox belonging to the Temple, and the ox belonging to the convert who died [and who left no heirs] so it has no [other] owners. Behold these [also] are culpable [to be put to] death.

C.  R. Judah says, "The wild ox, the ox belonging to the Temple, and the one without owners are exempt from death.

D.  "As it says in Scripture, '… and its owner, though warned' (Exod. 21:29), [meaning,] that [ox] that has owners is culpable [to be put to] death."

E.  In addition to this, R. Judah says, "Even [exempt from culpability to be put to death are] the ox belonging to the commoner that killed, but there was not enough time to bring it to justice before its owner gave it to the Temple, and likewise the ox that killed, but there was not enough time to bring it to justice before its convert [owner] died.

F.  "As it says in Scripture, '… and its owner, though warned, has failed to guard it, and it kills' (Exod. 21:29), [meaning,] that [ox] whose act of killing and whose standing in judgment [before the court] are the same.[242] The [ox] whose act of killing and whose standing in judgment [before the court] are not the same is exempt."

## LXVIII:III

1.    A.  "If a man opens a pit, or digs a pit, (and does not cover it, and an ox or an ass falls into it)" (Exod. 21:33):

B.  Behold this comes to teach you about [the subsequent liability of] the one who digs [a pit] within his own [private property] and it opens up in public property, even though he did not have the right to open it up [as such], he did have the right to dig [on his private property], but the cow [that subsequently falls into it] had the right to walk [on the public property]. [This comes to teach you] as well about the one who digs [a pit] on public property and it opens up within his own [private property], even though he did not have the right to dig it [on public property], he did have the right to open it up [within his own private property], but the cow [that subsequently falls into it] had the right to walk [on the public property].

---

[239] I.e., the employment of the same word in separate scriptural contexts, thus facilitating the application of the meaning of the word in one context to the other.

[240] I.e., the scriptural statement that "it shall be stoned."

| | | |
|---|---|---|
| D/C | | (שמ' כא כח) ♦ מה ת"ל והשור יסקל ♦ מכלל שנא' להלן |
| | | ואם שור נגח הוא (שם כט) יכול כיון שנגח אף על פי |
| E | | שלא המית יהא חייב ♦ ת"ל השור יסקל והשור יסקל |
| F | | לגזירה שוה ♦ מה השור יסקל האמ' להלן למיתה אף |
| G | | השור יסקל האמ' כן למיתה ♦ ומה השור יסקל האמ' |
| | | כן במועד ולא בתם אף השור יסקל האמ' להלן |
| H | | במועד ולא בתם ♦ מפני שהיה בכלל ויצא לידון בחדש |
| B/A | 7 | החזירו הכת' לכללו ♦ שור שור שבע פעמים ♦ שור האשה |
| | | שור היתומים שור האפטרופין שור המדבר שור |
| | | הקודש ושור הגר שמת ושאין לו בעלים הרי אלו |
| C | | חייבין מיתה ♦ ר' יהודה אומ' שור המדבר שור ההקדש |
| D | | ושאין לו בעלים פטורין מן המיתה ♦ שנא' והועד |
| | | בבעליו (שם) את שיש לו בעלים חייב מיתה את שאין |
| E | | לו בעלים פטור מן המיתה ♦ יתר על כן אמ' ר' יהודה |
| | | אפילו שור הדיוט שהמית לא הספיקו לעמד בדין עד |
| | | שהקדישו בעליו וכן שור גר שמת לא הספיקו לעמד |
| F | | בדין עד שמת הגר ♦ שנא' והועד בבעליו ולא ישמרנו |
| | | והמית (שמ' כא כט) את ששות המיתתו להעידתו |
| | | בבית דין חייב ושלא שוות המיתתו להעידתו בבית |
| | | דין פטור. סל' פסו' ♦ |

| | | |
|---|---|---|
| B/A | 1 | וכי יפתח איש בור או כי יכרה איש בור ♦ הרי זה |
| | | בא ללמד על החופר בתוך שלו ופתוח לרשות הרבים |
| | | אף על פי שאין לו רשות לפתוח אבל יש לו רשות |
| | | לחפור ויש לה רשות לבהמה להלך ועל החופר ברש' |
| | | הרב' ופתוח לתוך שלו שאף על פי שאין לו רשות לחפור |
| | | אבל יש לו רשות לפתוח ויש לה רשות לבהמה להלך ♦ |

---

[241] Compare 7.A–F with m. Baba Qamma 4:7, t. Baba Qamma 4:6, and b. Baba Qamma 44b (Neus., XX.B:Baba Qamma:4:7:I.1.A–F).
[242] I.e., the ox must have the same owner at the time it killed as it does at the time it is brought before the court for adjudication.

C. Because we have determined that if a cow causes damage [to something on public property] while walking on public property it is exempt [from liability for such damages], one might think if it[243] is damaged while walking on public property, then [the one causing the damage to it] would be exempt [from liability].

D. Scripture states, [however,] "If a man opens a pit, or digs a pit" (Exod. 21:33).

2. A. I only know concerning the one who [both] opens and digs [a pit]. How does one know from Scripture [about the liability also] of one who opens but does not dig, or digs but does not open?[244]

B. Scripture states, "If a man opens a pit, or digs a pit" (Exod. 21:33).

3. A. One might think [one would be liable] even if he opens or digs [a pit] within his own [private property].

B. Scripture states, [however,] "... to graze in another's land" (Exod. 22:4).

C. Just as this [case] is special in that it [involves land] outside of [the owner of the ox's] responsibility, so too is it for every instance that is outside of his responsibility.

4. A. "If a man opens a pit, or digs a pit" (Exod. 21:33):[245]

B. I only know concerning the one who opens or digs. How does one know from Scripture to include the one who inherits [a pit], purchases [a pit], or receives it as a gift?

C. Scripture states, "... the one responsible for the pit must make restitution" (Exod. 21:34), in order to include the one who inherits, purchases, or receives it as a gift.

D. One might think that [he would be culpable] even if it had not yet come into his possession.

E. Scripture states, [however,] "If a man opens a pit, or digs a pit" (Exod. 21:33).

5. A. I only know concerning the one who opens or digs [a pit]. How does one know from
[185] Scripture to include [as liable] the one who borrows [it], guards [it] for free, the one paid to guard [it], and the one who rents [it]?[246]

B. Scripture states, "... and does not cover it" (Exod. 21:33), [meaning,] he upon whom it is incumbent to cover it, in order to include the one who borrows [it], guards [it] for free, the one paid to guard [it], and the one who rents [it].

6. A. "If a man opens a pit, or digs a pit" (Exod. 21:33):[247]

B. I only know concerning a pit. How does one know from Scripture to include a trench that is 10 handbreadths deep and ditches that are 10 handbreadths deep?

C. Scripture states, "... a pit" (Exod. 21:33).

D. One might think [he would be liable] even if it wasn't 10 handbreadths deep, but was [deep] enough to kill.

E. Scripture states, [however,] "... pit" (Exod. 21:33).

F. Just as a pit is particular, in that it is 10 handbreadths deep and is [deep] enough to kill, so too must [other types of pits] be 10 handbreadths deep and be [deep] enough to kill.

7. A. One might think he would not be liable for [paying reparation for] its damage.[248]

B. For it is a matter of logic:

[243] I.e., the cattle.

[244] Compare 2.A–B with *Mekhilta de-rabbi Ishmael*, Nezikin (H/R, 288:2–5; Laut., vol. 3, 91:41–45; Neus., LXVIII:II:3.A–H).

[245] Compare 4.A–E with y. Baba Qamma 5a (Neus., 5:6:I.G–H).

[246] Compare 5.A with m. Baba Metzia 7:8 as standard Rabbinic categories.

| | | |
|---|---|---|
| לפי שמצינו בבהמה שאם הזיקה כדרך הילוכה | C | |
| ברש׳ הרב׳ פטור עליה יכול אם הוזקה כדרך הילוכה | | |
| ברש׳ הרב׳ יהא פטור עליה ♦ ת״ל כי יפתח איש בור או | D | |
| כי יכרה איש בור ♦ אין לי אלא הפותח והכורה פתח | A | 2 |
| ולא כרה כרה ולא פתח מנין ♦ ת״ל כי יפתח או כי יכרה ♦ | B | |
| יכול אף הפותח והכורה בתוך שלו ♦ ת״ל ובער בשדה | B/A | 3 |
| אחר (שם כב ד) ♦ מה זה מיוחד שהוא חוץ מרשותו כך | C | |
| כל דבר שהוא חוץ מרשותו. ♦ כי יפתח איש בור או כי | A | 4 |
| יכרה איש בור ♦ אין לי אלא הפותח והכורה מנין | B | |
| לרבות את שירש ולקח ושניתן לו במתנה ♦ ת״ל בעל | C | |
| הבור ישלם לרבות את שירש ולקח ושניתן לו | | |
| במתנ[ה] ♦ יכול אף על פי שלא בא לרשות<ו> ♦ ת״ל כי | E/D | |
| יפתח איש בור או כי יכרה איש בור <...> ♦ אין לי אלא | A | 5 |
| הפותח והכורה מנין לרבות שואל ושומר חנם ונושא | | |
| שכר ושוכר ♦ ת״ל <ו>לא יכסנו את שדרך כיסויו עליו | B | |
| לרבות שואל ושומר חנם ונושא שכר ושוכר. ♦ כי יפתח | A | 6 |
| איש בור או כי יכרה איש בור ♦ אין לי אלא בור מנין | B | |
| לרבות חריצין שהן עמוקין י׳ טפ׳ ונעיצין עמוקין י׳ | | |
| טפ׳ ♦ ת״ל בור ♦ יכול אף על פי שאין בו עומק י׳ טפ׳ ויש | D/C | |
| בו להמית ♦ ת״ל בור ♦ מה בור מיוחד שיש בו עומק י׳ | F/E | |
| טפ׳ ויש בו להמית כך כל שיש בו י׳ טפ׳ ויש בו | | |
| להמית ♦ יכול לא יהא חייב בנזקו ♦ ודין הוא ♦ | B/A | 7 |

---

[247] Compare 6.A–F with m. Baba Qamma 5:5.
[248] I.e., in addition to compensation for the death of the ox, the owner of the pit should also have to pay reparations for damages. See m. Baba Qamma 8:1 for the five categories of reparation.

C.   Just as the one who steals and sells [an ox] is responsible [to make restitution] for the full penalty,[249] but is not responsible [to make restitution for damage caused] to its limbs, then in this [case here in Exod. 21:33], where he is not responsible [to make restitution] for the full penalty, is it not logical that he would not be responsible [to make restitution for damage caused] to its limbs?

D.   [The case of ] a man [wounding] a man will [prove the opposite], because [in that case] he is not responsible [to make restitution] for the full penalty, but is responsible [to make restitution for damage caused] to his limbs.

E.   No! When you speak [of the case of] a man [wounding] a man, he must pay [restitution] for indignity. Will you say [the same] here [in the case in Exod. 21:33], where he does not pay [251] [restitution] for indignity?

F.   [The case of] a man [wounding] a slave will [prove it], because [in that case] he does not pay [restitution] for indignity.

G.   No! When you speak [of the case of] a man [wounding] a man, he must pay [restitution] for pain, healing, loss of time, and indignity. Will you say [the same] here [in Exod. 21:33], where he does not pay [restitution] for pain, healing, loss of time, and indignity?

H.   Scripture states, [therefore,] "(The one responsible for the pit must make restitution.) He shall pay money to the owner" (Exod. 21:34), [in order] to include [restitution] for the damages.

8.   A.   "If a man opens a pit, or digs a pit" (Exod. 21:33):

B.   I only know concerning a man. How does one know from Scripture concerning a woman?

C.   Scripture states, "(The owner of the pit) must make restitution" (Exod. 21:34), [meaning,] whether man or woman.

D.   If so, then why does it say in Scripture "man" (Exod. 21:33)? [To] exclude the minor. [And it says] "man" [to] exclude the Most High.[251]

9.   A.   "... man" (Exod. 21:33):[252]

B.   This includes [the pit] belonging to two people.

C.   If a pit belongs to two people, and one of them covers it, and the other one uncovers it, then the one who uncovers it is liable.

D.   If one [of them] covered it, and while watching over [it], it became uncovered, and he saw it but did not cover it, behold, he is liable.

E.   If one [of them] covered it and then left it, if it becomes uncovered afterward, he is exempt [from liability].

10.   A.   "... and an ox or ass falls into it" (Exod. 21:33):[253]

B.   This specifies that one is obligated for the ox that was startled by the sound of the digging and fell into a pit that was in front of it. But [if the pit] was behind it, one is exempt.

11.   A.   If an ox pushes its companion [ox], and it falls into a pit and dies, then the owner of the ox is liable, but the owner of the pit is exempt.[254]

---

[249] I.e., the one who steals and sells an ox must pay four or five times the value of the ox as restitution to the ox's owner. See m. Baba Qamma 7:2–3.

[250] At this point in the Firkovich manuscript there appears to be a scribal error, in the form of a repetition of sentence 7.D directly above. I have omitted it in the translation.

[251] The precise, contextualized meaning of the word here (Hebrew: *gavohah*—גבוה) is difficult to discern. It could mean either "an exalted person" or "the Most High" (i.e., God).

מה הגונב והמוכר שחייב על כולו אין חייב על אבריו זה     C

ש<אין> חייב על כולו דין אינו שלא יהא חייב על

אבריו ◆ אדם באדם יוכיח שאין חייב על כולו וחייב על     D

אבריו ◆ לא אם אמרת אדם באדם שמשלם את הבשת     E

תאמר בזה שאין משלם (שאין חייב על כולו וחייב על

אבריו לא אם אמרת אדם באדם שמשלם את הבשת

תאמר בזה שאין משלם) את הבשת ◆ אדם בעבד יוכיח     F

שאין משלם את הבשת ◆ לא אם אמרת אדם באדם     G

שמשלם צער וריפוי שבת ובשת תאמר בזה שאין

משלם צער וריפוי שבת ובשת ◆ ת״ל כסף ישיב לבעליו     H

לרבות את הנזקין. ◆ כי יפתח איש בור ◆ אין לי אלא     B/A    8

איש אשה מנין ◆ ת״ל ישלם בין איש בין אשה ◆ אם כן     D/C

למה נאמר איש פרט לקטן איש פרט לגבוה ◆ איש ◆     A    9

להביא את השנים ◆ בור שלשנים אחד מכסה ואחד     C/B

מגלה המגלה חייב ◆ כיסהו עד שעמד ונתגלה ראהו     D

ולא כיסהו הרי זה חייב ◆ כיסהו והלך לו אף על פי     E

שנתגלה לאחר כן פטור. ◆ ונפל שמה שור או חמור ◆     A    10

פרט לשור שהרתיע מקול הבירה ונפל לבור שלפניו     B

חייב ושלאחריו פטור ◆ שור שדחף את חבירו ונפל     A    11

לבור ומת בעל השור חייב ובעל הבור פטור ◆

²⁵² Compare 9.A–E with *Mekhilta de-Rabbi Ishmael*, Nezikin (H/R, 288:11–14; Laut., vol. 3, 92:55–60; Neus., LXVIII:II:7.A–8.F); and m. Baba Qamma 8:6.

²⁵³ Compare 10.A–B with *Mekhilta de-Rabbi Ishmael*, Nezikin (H/R, 289:3–5; Laut., vol. 3, 93:68–70; Neus., LXVIII:II:11.A–F); m. Baba Qamma 5:6; and b. Baba Qamma 53a (Neus., XX.B:Tractate Baba Qamma:5:6E–N:III.1.A–K).

²⁵⁴ Compare 11.A–B with t. Baba Qamma 6:1 and b. Baba Qamma 53a (Neus., XX.B:Tractate Baba Qamma:5:6E–N:III.3.C–H).

B.  R. Nathan says, "The owner of the pit pays three-quarters [of the liability], and the owner of the ox pays one-quarter."

12.  A.  "... and an ox or ass falls into it" (Exod. 21:33):[255]

B.  Why do I need [Scripture to state this]?

C.  If to teach that [the owner of the pit] is exempt if a human being [falls into it], behold it already says in Scripture "... but shall keep the dead animal" (Exod. 21:34).

D.  [The owner of the pit is only liable] for that which, when dead, could belong to him. Exempt is the [dead] human being, from which it is prohibited to derive benefit.

E.  Why does Scripture state, "... and an ox or ass falls into it" (Exod. 21:33)?

F.  [To teach that the liability is for] the ox, but not its equipment, and for the ass, but not its equipment.

G.  Based on this you say: If an ox fell into it, and its equipment was broken, or an ass, and its equipment was split, [the owner of the pit] is liable for the damages to the animal, but is exempt from the damages to the equipment. Or if [the ox or ass fell into the pit and] its equipment was dashed against the ground, [the owner of the pit] is liable for the damages to the animal, but is exempt from the damages to the equipment.

13.  A.  "... and an ox or ass falls into it" (Exod. 21:33):[256]

[186]    B.  I only know specifically about the ox and the ass. How does one know from Scripture to treat other domesticated cattle, animals of chase, and birds like the ox?

C.  It is a matter of logic:

D.  Just as with the ox, which is not perpetually *mu'ad*,[257] other domesticated cattle, animals of chase, and birds are treated like the ox [with regard to their status as *mu'ad*], then [with] a pit, which is perpetually *mu'ad*, is it not logical that with regard to it other domesticated cattle, animals of chase, and birds would be treated like the ox?

E.  No! If you speak of the ox, its tendency is to walk and do damage. Will you say the same of the pit, which does not walk and do damage?

F.  [Thus,] Scripture states, "... and an ox or ass falls into it" (Exod. 21:33), [meaning,] to treat other domesticated cattle, animals of chase, and birds like the ox.

G.  R. Yosi says in the name of R. Ishmael, "Scripture states here 'ox and donkey' (Exod. 21:33) and Scripture states in regard to *Shabbat*, 'your ox or your ass' (Deut. 5:14). Just as with 'your ox or your ass' stated in regard to *Shabbat*, other domesticated cattle, animals of chase, and birds are treated like the ox, so too with 'ox and donkey' stated here in regard to damages should other domesticated cattle, animals of chase, and birds be treated like the ox."

14.  A.  Why does Scripture state, "... and an ox or an ass falls in it" (Exod. 21:33)?

B.  [To emphasize that this means] an ox, and not a boy or girl, [as well as to emphasize] an ass, and not a male slave or female slave.

C.  For one might reason: Just as with the ox, which is not perpetually *mu'ad*,[258] behold, [the owner would be liable for damages caused by his ox] to the boy, to the girl, to the male

---

[255] Compare 12.A–G with *Mekhilta de-Rabbi Ishmael*, Nezikin (H/R, 288:15–289:2; Laut., vol. 3, 92:61–93:67; Neus., LXVIII:II:9.A–10.J); y. Baba Qamma 5a (Neus., 5:7:IV.A–VI.I); and b. Baba Qamma 28b (Neus., XX.B:Tractate Baba Qamma:3:1E–I:I.1.D).

[256] Compare 13.A–G with *Mekhilta de-Rabbi Ishmael*, Nezikin (H/R, 280:12–14; Laut., vol. 3, 74:4–8; Neus., LXVII:I:2.A–E); t. Baba Qamma 6:18; and b. Baba Qamma 54b (Neus., XX.B:Tractate Baba Qamma:5:7:VII.1.A–C).

[257] I.e., the ox is not considered intrinsically to be a hazard. Rather, it must first display these tendencies through three damaging actions.

[258] See note 257 above.

| | | |
|---|---|---|
| | B | ר' נתן אומ' <במועד זה נותן מחצה וזה נותן מחצה בתם> |
| 12 | A | בעל הבור משלם שלשה חלקים ובעל השור רביע ♦ ונפל |
| | C/B | שמה שור או חמור ♦ מה אני צריך ♦ אם ללמד על אדם |
| | D | שפטור הרי כבר נאמ' והמת יהיה לו ♦ את שהמת שלו |
| | E | יצא אדם שאסור בהנאה ♦ מה ת״ל ונפל שמה שור או |
| | G/F | חמור ♦ שור ולא כליו חמור ולא כליו ♦ מיכן אתה אומ' |
| | | נפל לתוכו שור וכליו <ו>נשתברו או חמור וכליו |
| | | ונתקרעו חייב על נזקי בהמה ופטור על נזקי כלים או |
| | | הוטחו כלים על קרקע הרי זה חייב על נזקי בהמה |
| | | ופטור על נזקי כלים. ♦ ונפל שמה שור או חמור ♦ אין לי |
| 13 | B/A | אלא שור וחמור המיוחדין מנין לעשות שאר בהמה |
| | | חיה ועוף כיוצא בשור ♦ ודין הוא ♦ מה השור שאין מועד |
| | D/C | לעולם עש' בו שאר בהמה חיה ועוף כיוצא בשור בור |
| | | שמועד לעולם אינו דין שנעשה בו שאר בהמה חיה |
| | | ועוף כיוצא בשור ♦ לא אם אמרת בשור שדרכו לילך |
| | E | ולהזיק תאמר בבור שאין דרכו לילך ולהזיק ♦ ת״ל ונפל |
| | F | שמה שור או חמור לעשות שאר בהמה חיה ועוף |
| | | כיוצא בשור ♦ ר' יוסי אומר מש' ר' ישמעאל נאמ' כן |
| | G | שור חמור ונאמ' לענין שבת שורך וחמורך (דב' ה יג) |
| | | מה שורך וחמורך האמ' לענין שבת (שנא) עש' שאר |
| | | בהמה חיה ועוף כיוצא בשור אף שור וחמור האמ' כן |
| | | לענין נזקין נעשה שאר בהמה חיה ועוף כיוצא בשור ♦ |
| 14 | B/A | מה ת״ל ונפל שמה שור או חמור ♦ שור ולא בן ולא בת |
| | C | חמור ולא עבד ולא אמה ♦ שהיה בדין מה שור שאין |
| | | מועד לעולם הרי הוא חייב על הבן ועל הבת על |

slave, and to the female slave, then [with] a pit, which is perpetually *mu'ad*, is it not logical that [the owner of the pit] would be liable [for damages caused by his pit] to the boy, to the girl, to the male slave, and to the female slave?

D. No! If you speak of the ox, its tendency is to walk and do damage. Will you say the same of the pit, which does not walk and do damage?

E. [Thus,] Scripture states, "… and an ox or ass falls into it" (Exod. 21:33), [to emphasize that this means] an ox, and not a boy or girl, [as well as to emphasize] an ass, and not a male slave or female slave.

15. A. One might think he would not be liable for [paying reparation for] its damage.[259]

B. For it is a matter of logic:

C. Just as the one who steals and sells [an ox] is responsible [to make restitution] for the full penalty,[260] but is not responsible [to make restitution for damage caused] to its limbs, then in this [case here in Exod. 21:33], where he is not responsible [to make restitution] for the full penalty, is it not logical that he would not be responsible [to make restitution for damage caused] to its limbs?

D. [The case of ] a man [wounding] a man will [prove the opposite], because [in that case] he is not responsible [to make restitution] for the full penalty, but is responsible [to make restitution for damage caused] to his limbs.

E. No! When you speak [of the case of] a man [wounding] a man, he must pay [restitution] for indignity. Will you say [the same] here [in the case in Exod. 21:33], where he does not pay [restitution] for indignity?

F. [The case of] a man [wounding] a slave will [prove it], because [in that case] he does not pay [restitution] for indignity.

G. No! When you speak [of the case of] a man [wounding] a man, he must pay [restitution] for pain, healing, loss of time, and indignity. Will you say [the same] here [in Exod. 21:33], where he does not pay [restitution] for pain, healing, loss of time, and indignity?

H. Scripture states, [therefore,] "(The one responsible for the pit must make restitution.) He shall pay money to the owner" (Exod. 21:34), [in order] to include [restitution] for the damages.

16. A. "The one responsible for the pit must make restitution" (Exod. 21:34):

B. This is what we have said: Whether [the owner is] a man or a woman.

C. "The one responsible for the pit must make restitution" (Exod. 21:34):

D. This is what we have said: Whether [the owner is] a minor or an adult.

E. "The one responsible for the pit must make restitution" (Exod. 21:34):

F. This is what we have said: This includes the one who inherited [it], purchased [it], or it was given to him as a gift.

17. A. "He shall pay the price to the owner" (Exod. 21:34):

B. This is what we have said: This includes [payment] for damages.

18. A. "… but shall keep the dead animal" (Exod. 21:34):[261]

B. [Meaning, the carcass belongs] to the one who was damaged.[262]

---

[259] I.e., in addition to compensation for the death of the ox, the owner of the pit should also have to pay reparations for damages. See m. Baba Qamma 8:1 for the five categories of reparation.

[260] I.e., the one who steals and sells an ox must pay four or five times the value of the ox as restitution to the ox's owner. See m. Baba Qamma 7:2–3.

העבד ועל האמה בור שמועד לעולם אינו דין שיהא

D    חייב על הבן ועל הבת ועל העבד ועל האמה ◆ לא אם

אמרת בשור שדרכו לילך ולהזיק תאמר בבור שאין

E    דרכו לילך ולהזיק ◆ ת״ל ונפל שמה שור או חמור שור

A    15    ולא בן ולא בת חמור ולא עבד ולא אמה ◆ יכול לא יהא

C/B    חייב בנזקו ◆ דין הוא ◆ מה הגונב והמוכר שחייב על כולו

אינו חייב על אבריו זה שאין חייב על כולו אינו דין

D    שלא יהא חייב על אבריו ◆ אדם באדם יוכיח שאין חייב

E    על כולו וחייב על איבריו ◆ לא אם אמרת אדם באדם

שמשלם את הבשת תאמר בזה שאן משלם את

G/F    הבושת ◆ אדם בעבד יוכיח שאין משלם את הבושת ◆ לא

אם אמרת אדם באדם שמשלם צער וריפוי שבת

ובושת תאמר בזה שאין משלם ‹צער וריפוי שבת

H    ו‹בושת ◆ ת״ל כסף ישיב לבעליו לרבות את הנזקין.

סל׳ פסו׳ ◆

B/A    16    בעל הבור ישלם ◆ זו היא שאמרנו בין איש ובין

D/C    אשה ◆ בעל הבור ישלם ◆ זו היא שאמרנו בין קטן ובין

F/E    גדול ◆ בעל הבור ישלם ◆ זו היא שאמרנו לרבות את

B/A    17    שירש ולקח וניתן לו במתנה. ◆ כסף ישיב לבעליו ◆ זו

B/A    18    היא שאמרנו לרבות הנזקין. ◆ והמת יהיה לו ◆ לניזק ◆

---

[261] Compare 18.A–G with *Mekhilta de-Rabbi Ishmael*, Nezikin (H/R, 289:9–10; Laut., vol. 3, 93:76–94:79; Neus., LXVIII:II:14.A–G); and b. Baba Qamma 10b (Neus., XX.A:Tractate Baba Qamma:1:2:III.1.A–3.B).

[262] I.e., the owner of the dead ox.

C.   One might think [it belongs] also to the one who caused the damage. But you must say that it can't be this way, for why [then] does Scripture [need to] state it?[263]

D.   [Scripture states twice,] "... but shall keep the dead animal" (Exod. 21:34) [and] "... but shall keep the dead animal" (Exod. 21:36), [in order to provide the opportunity to argue] by means of a *gezerah shaveh*:[264]

E.   Just as "but shall keep the dead animal" stated here [means] he must pay [to him] only a compensatory price, so too does "but shall keep the dead animal" mentioned there [mean] that he must pay [to him] only a compensatory price.

F.   And just as "but shall keep the dead animal" stated there [means] the owners take care of the carcass, so too does "but shall keep the dead animal" stated here [mean] that the owners take care of the carcass.

[187]   G.   Just as "but shall keep the dead animal" stated there [means that one pays as recompense the price of the] ox for the ox, but not [the price of both the] ox and the carcass for the ox, so too does "but shall keep the dead animal" stated here [mean that one pays as recompense the price of the] ox for the ox, but not [the price of both the] ox and the carcass for the ox.[265]

19.   A.   Others say, "How does one know from Scripture that the owner of the pit needs to [be the one who] raises his [dead] ox from the pit?[266]

B.   "Scripture states, '... he shall pay the price to the owner, and the carcass' (Exod. 21:34).[267]

C.   "[Which means] he must return both the [dead] ox and the [damage] payment to its owner."

*Chapter Sixty-Nine*

(Textual Source: Ms. Firkovich II A 268)

LXIX:I

1.   A.   "If a man's ox (injures his neighbor's ox and it dies, they shall sell the live ox and divide its price)" (Exod. 21:35):[268]

B.   I only know from this concerning goring. How does one know from Scripture to treat striking, biting, lying on top of, and trampling the same as goring?

C.   It is a matter of logic:

D.   There is culpability for an ox [goring] a person, and for an ox [goring] an ox. Just as we have found that [in the case of] an ox [goring] a person you treat striking, biting, lying on top of, and trampling the same as goring, so too here [in the case of an ox goring an ox] is striking, biting, lying on top of, and trampling treated the same as goring.

E.   And there is another way of reasoning:

F.   Just as with [the case of] an ox [goring] a person, where the unintentional act is not treated the same as the intentional act, you treat striking, biting, lying on top of, and trampling the same as goring, then isn't it logical that in this case, where the unintentional act is treated the same as the intentional one, that striking, biting, lying on top of, and trampling are treated the same as goring.

---

[263] I.e., it would be obvious that the person who paid the full price of the ox as recompense would, then, own the carcass.

[264] I.e., the employment of the same word in separate scriptural contexts, thus facilitating the application of the meaning of the word in one context to the other.

[265] This most likely means that the owner of the ox does not receive as recompense both the price of his ox and his ox's carcass; rather, the responsible party need only pay as recompense the price of the ox minus the value of the carcass. See parallels in note 261 above.

[266] Compare 19.A–C with b. Baba Qamma 11a (Neus., XX.A:Tractate Baba Qamma:1:2:III.4.B).

[267] This interpretation reads literally the clause in Exod. 21:34 as, "... he shall return the price to the owner and the carcass."

[268] Compare 1.A–H with parallel above at LXVII:I.2.A–I.

| | |
|---|---|
| יכול אף למזיק אמרת לא כך היה הא מה ת״ל ◆ והמת | D/C |
| יהיה לו המת יהיה לו לגזירה שוה ◆ מה המת יהיה לו | E |
| האמור כן אין משלם אלא דמים אף המת יהיה לו האמ׳ | |
| להלן (שמ׳ כא לו) אין משלם אלא דמים ◆ ומה אף | F |
| המת יהיה לו האמ׳ להלן בעלין מיטפלין בנבלה אף | |
| המת יהיה לו האמ׳ כן בעלים מיטפלין בנבלה. ◆ מה | G |
| המת יהיה לו האמ׳ להלן שור תחת השור ולא שור | |
| ונבלה תחת השור אף המת יהיה לו האמ׳ כן שור | |
| תחת השור ולא שור ונבלה תחת השור. ◆ אחרים אומ׳ | A |
| מנין לבעל הבור שצריך להעלות שורו מן הבור ◆ ת״ל | B |
| כסף ישיב לבעליו ‹והמת› ◆ גם את השור וגם את | C |
| הכסף ישיב לבעליו. סל׳ פסו׳ ◆ | |

| | |
|---|---|
| | LXIX:I |
| וכי יגף ◆ אין לי אלא נגיפה מנין לעשות נגיחה | B/A |
| נשיכה רביצה ובעיטה כיוצא בנגיפה ◆ ודין הוא ◆ חייב | D/C |
| שור באדם ושור בשור מה מצינו שור באדם עשה בו | |
| נגיפה נשיכה רביצה ‹ו›בעיטה כיוצא בנגיחה אף זה | |
| נעשה בו נגיחה נשיכה רביצה ובעיטה כיוצא בנגיפה ◆ | |
| ועוד קל וחומר ◆ מה שור באדם שלא עשה בו את שאין | F/E |
| מתכוין כמתכוין עשה בו נגיפה [נ]שיכה רביצה ובעיטה | |
| כיוצא בנגיחה זה שעשה בו את שאין מתכוין כמתכוין אינו | |
| דין שנעשה בו נגיחה נשיכה רבי׳ ובעי׳ כיוצא בנגיפה ◆ | |

Numbers in right margin: 19 (next to A), 1 (next to B/A)

G. No! When you speak of [the case of] the ox [goring] a person, [the owner of the ox] can be judged [liable] for his life. Will you say the same in this case, where [the owner of the ox] cannot be judged [liable] for his life?

H. Scripture states, [however,] "... and it dies" (Exod. 21:28), [which means you should] treat striking, biting, lying on top of, and trampling the same as goring.

2.   A. I only know concerning the ox. How does one know from Scripture to treat other domesticated cattle, animals of chase, and birds like the ox?

B. [The verse is actually the source] of the question and the answer.

C. Scripture states, "... they shall sell the *live* ox" (Exod. 21:35), [in order] to include all living creatures.

3.   A. "... man's" (Exod. 21:35):[269]

B. This excludes [the goring ox belonging to] the minor.[270]

C. One might think [these reparations] should not be paid to the minor,[271] as the minor does not pay [these reparations] to someone else.

D. Scripture states, [however,] "... he must restore"[272] (Exod. 21:36), [in order] to include [the ox] belonging to the deaf and dumb person, the madman, and the minor.

4.   A. "... man's" (Exod. 21:35):

B. This excludes [the goring ox belonging to] God.[273]

C. One might think [these reparations] should not be paid to the Temple [by someone else], because the Temple does not pay [these reparations] to someone else, because the Temple takes priority.[274]

D. Scripture states, [however,] "... man's" (Exod. 21:35), which excludes [from paying these reparations only] God [but not someone else].

5.   A. "... his neighbor's" (Exod. 21:35):[275]

B. This excludes [the ox belonging] to others.[276]

C. "... his neighbor's" (Exod. 21:35):

D. This excludes the [ox belonging to the] alien resident.

E. One might think [these reparations] should not be paid to the non-Jew, as the non-Jew does not pay [these reparations] to someone else.

F. Scripture states, [however,] "... he must restore"[277] (Exod. 21:36), [in order] to include [the ox] belonging to the non-Jew and the alien resident.

G. One might think that one should [in all instances] pay half-reparations for [injury caused by] the *tam*[278] and full reparations for [injury caused by] the *mu'ad*.[279]

---

[269] Units LXIX:I:3.A–D, I:5.A–I, and II:5.A–D share very similar halakhic concerns and rhetorical language. However, the precise meaning of each unit, particularly in comparison with each other, is elusive and difficult to discern precisely. It is possible that portions of these units (particularly 3.A–D and 5.A–D), through both transmission and the process of considerable reconstruction, have either been confusingly combined, or simply misunderstood. I have attempted to translate these units consistently, even if this has resulted in contradictory halakhic meaning. An in-depth discussion of the complicated nature of these particular units of tradition can be referenced in A. Burgansky, "Edited Portions of the Mekhilta of Rabbi Shimon b. Yohai: Interconnected Interpretations," (Hebrew) in *Sidra* 17:5–22.

[270] I.e., if an ox belonging to a minor gores another ox, the minor is not responsible for reparation payment for the damages caused by his ox.

[271] I.e., if an ox belonging to a minor is gored by an ox belonging to someone else, one might think that the owner of the goring ox would be exempt from paying reparations to the minor.

[272] The text here interprets the apparently doubled form שלם ישלם as indicative of an extension of the parameters of liability.

[273] I.e., if an ox belonging to the Temple gores another ox, the Temple is not responsible for reparation payment for the damages caused by its ox.

| | |
|---|---|
| G | לא אם אמרת בשור (ו)באדם שנידו בנפשו תאמרן |
| H | בזה שאין נידון בנפשו ♦ ת״ל ומת לעשות נגי׳ נשי׳ |
| A 2 | רבי׳ ובעי׳ כיוצא בנגיפה ♦ אין לי אלא שור מנין |
| B | לעשות שאר בהמה חיה ועוף כיוצא בשור ♦ הוא הדין |
| C | והוא התשובה ♦ ת״ל ומכרו את השור החי לרבות כל |
| C/B/A 3 | בעלי חיין ♦ איש ♦ פרט לקטן ♦ יכול לא ישלם על ידי קטן |
| D | ולא יהא קטן משלם על ידיו ♦ ת״ל שלם ישלם לרבות |
| C/B/A 4 | של חרש ושל שוטה ושל קטן. ♦ איש ♦ פרט לגבוה ♦ יכול |
| | (לא) ישלם על ידי הקדש ולא יהא הקדש משלם על ידיו |
| D | שכן מצינו שיד ההקדש על העליונה ♦ ת״ל איש פרט |
| D/C/B/A 5 | לגבוה ♦ רעהו ♦ פרט לאחרין ♦ רעהו ♦ פרט לגר תושב ♦ |
| E | יכול לא ישלם על ידי הגוי ולא יהא הגוי משלם על |
| F | ידיו ♦ ת״ל שלם ישלם לרבות שלגוים של גר תושב. |
| G | יכול יהו משלמין בתם חצי נזק במועד נזק שלם ♦ |

[274] The ox dedicated to the Temple is considered ownerless, or more specifically, to be the property of God. As such, damages paid by the ox itself would, in reality, be paid by the Temple and its priests.

[275] See note 269 above.

[276] I.e., non-Jews.

[277] The text here interprets the apparently doubled form שלם ישלם as indicative of an extension of the parameters of liability.

[278] A *tam* ("innocent") is an animal that has not caused damage three times and whose owner, therefore, has not been informed of this and warned about his liability for future damage.

[279] A *mu'ad* ("forewarned") is an animal that has caused damage three times and whose owner has been informed of this and warned about his liability for future damage. If this animal causes damage again, the owner is fully liable for all indemnification.

H.  Scripture states, [however,] "... his neighbor's ox" (Exod. 21:35), [meaning,] that his neighbor's ox[280] is resolved in this manner, but others' oxen[281] are not resolved in this manner.

I.  And concerning them Scripture says, "He appeared from Mount Paran" (Deut. 33:2), [which means] He revealed aspects [of law] corresponding to all the people of the world.

6.   A.  "... and it dies" (Exod. 21:35):

B.  This is what we have said: [Scripture says this, in order to indicate that] one treats striking, biting, lying on top of, and trampling the same as goring.

C.  "... they shall sell the live ox" (Exod. 21:35):

D.  This is what we have said: [Scripture says this, in order to indicate that] this includes all living creatures.

7.   A.  "'... they shall sell the live ox and divide its price' (Exod. 21:35):[282]

[188]   B.  "[If] an ox worth 200 [zuz] gored an ox worth 200 [zuz], and the carcass was worth 50 zuz, [then] the one takes half [the value] of the living [ox] and half [the value] of the dead one, and the other takes half [the value] of the living [ox] and half [the value] of the dead one.

C.  "As it says in Scripture, '... they shall sell the live ox and divide its price, etc.'"—The words of R. Judah.

D.  R. Meir says, "The Torah did not speak of [a case] such as this; rather, [of a case] when there isn't a carcass worth anything.

E.  "And why does Scripture state, '... they shall also divide the dead animal' (Exod. 21:35)?

F.  "[It means] they should divide [into the split value of the live ox] the depreciated value [of the dead ox, which must be paid to the owner of the dead ox]."[283]

8.   A.  [If] an ox worth 100 zuz gored an ox worth five sela,[284] and the corpse was worth nothing, the one takes half [the value] of the living [ox] and half [the value] of the dead one, and the other takes half [the value] of the living [ox] and half [the value] of the dead one.[285]

B.  Why [does Scripture in Exod. 21:36] single out the mu'ad—to be more stringent about it or to be more lenient about it? You have to say it is to be more stringent about it! So just as with the mu'ad, which was singled out to be more stringent about it, [the owner of it] does not pay [in reparation] more than [the value] of that which [his ox] damaged, then is it not logical that with the tam, which was singled out to be more lenient about it, [the owner of it] should not pay [in reparation] more than [the value] of that which [his ox] damaged?

C.  [Therefore,] the Torah only speaks about the situation in which the two of them are equal in value.

9.   A.  [If] an ox worth five sela gored an ox worth 100 zuz, and the corpse was worth 50 zuz, the one takes half [the value] of the living [ox] and half [the value] of the dead one, and the other takes half [the value] of the living [ox] and half [the value] of the dead one. Do we find that the damager who [might] profit [from the damage he causes] in any situation should [actually] profit?[286]

---

[280] I.e., the ox belonging to a fellow Jew.

[281] I.e., oxen belonging to non-Jews.

[282] Compare 7.A–F with t. Baba Qamma 3:3 and b. Baba Qamma 34a (Neus., XX.A:Tractate Baba Qamma:3:9D–I:I.1.A–I.5.F).

[283] I.e., the owner of the gored ox must also be reimbursed for half of the difference between the depreciated value of his ox when alive and when dead.

[284] Five selas equal 20 zuz.

[285] At issue in this situation is the fact that, according to the rules for reparations dictated in Exod. 21:35, the owner of the gored ox would receive more in reparation than the value of his ox when it was alive. Note, as well, the odd fact that this scenario is one in which

| | | |
|---|---|---|
| ת"ל שור רעהו שור רעהו יוצא כסדר הזה ולא שלאחרין | H | |
| יוצא כסדר הזה ◆ ועליהן הוא אומ' הופיע מהר פארן | I | |
| (דב' לג ב) הופיע פנים כנגד כל באי העולם ◆ ומת ◆ זו | B/A | 6 |
| היא שמרנו לעשות נגי' נשי' רבי' בעי' כיוצא בנגיפה. ◆ | | |
| ומכרו את השור החי ◆ זו היא שאמ' לרבות כל בעלי | D/C | |
| חיין. ◆ [ו]מכרו את השור החי וחצו את כספו ◆ שור יפה | B/A | 7 |
| מאתים שנגח שור יפה מאתים והנבלה יפה חמשים | | |
| זוז זה נוטל חצי החי וחצי המת וזה נוטל חצי החי | | |
| וחצי המת ◆ שנא' ומכרו את השור החי וחצו את כספו | C | |
| וגומ'. דברי ר' יהודה ◆ אמ' לו ר' מאיר לא בזה דברה | D | |
| תורה לא דברה אלא בשאין נבלה יפה כלום ◆ והא מה | E | |
| ת"ל וגם את המת יחצון ◆ <אף> את הפחות יחצון שור | F | |
| יפה מנה שנגח שור יפה חמש סלעים ואין הנבלה | A | 8 |
| שווה כלום יהא זה זה נוטל חצי החי וחצי המת ויהא זה | | |
| נוטל חצי החי וחצי המת ◆ <וכי> למה יצא מועד | B | |
| להחמ[י]ר עליו או להקל עליו הוי אומ' להחמיר עליו | | |
| ומה מועד ש[י]צא לה[ח]מיר עליו אין משלם יתיר על | | |
| מה שהזיק תם שיצא להקל עליו דין אינו שלא ישלם | | |
| יתר על מה שהזיק ◆ לא דברה תורה אלא בזמן | C | |
| ששניהם שוין ◆ שור יפה חמש סלעים שנגח שור יפה | A | 9 |
| מנה [והנבל]ה יפה חמשים זוז יהא זה זה נוטל חצי החי | | |
| וחצי המת וזה נוטל חצי החי וחצי המת היכן | | |
| מצינו שהמזיק נשכר בכל מקום שיהא נשכר ◆ | | |

the carcass is deemed to have no value, but nonetheless determines that the two owners would split its value. In fact, the parallel to this tradition at b. Baba Qamma 34b (Neus., XX.A:Tractate Baba Qamma:3:9D–I:I.2.C) declares the carcass to have a value of one *sela*.

[286] As opposed to 8.A–C above, in this scenario the owner of the goring ox would receive more in reparation than the value of his ox when it gored the other ox. Compare 9.A–B with b. Baba Qamma 34b (Neus., XX.A:Tractate Baba Qamma:3:9D–I:I.3.A–I.4.B).

B. Therefore, Scripture says, "... he must pay" (Exod. 21:36),[287] [in order to emphasize that] owners [of the goring ox] pay, and owners [of the goring ox] do not make a profit.

10. A. [If] an ox worth 100 *zuz* gored an ox worth 200 [*zuz*], and the corpse was worth 50 *zuz*, the one takes half [the value] of the living [ox] and half [the value] of the dead one, and the other takes half [the value] of the living [ox] and half [the value] of the dead one.

B. As it says in Scripture, "... they shall sell the live ox and divide its price" (Exod. 21:35).

C. This is [all] certain:

D. Why does Scripture state, "... they shall also divide the dead animal" (Exod. 21:35)?

E. [It means] they divide among themselves whatever [value] the dead animal brings. If 200 *zuz*, then the one takes 100 and the other takes 100.

F. "... and divide its price" (Exod. 21:35) [means] they estimate the cash value of the damaged [ox] and the cash value of the damaging [ox] and divide it between them.

11. A. I only know [from Exod. 21:35] concerning the situation when [the ox gores] all of it.[288] How does one know from Scripture to include [the situation where it only gores and damages] his limbs?

B. It is a matter of logic:

C. If [in the situation] of one who kidnaps [someone] and who sells [him into slavery], he is culpable for [damage done to] all of him, but he is not culpable [for damage done only] to his limbs, [then] isn't it logical that in this situation, in which one is not culpable [for damage done to] all of him, one would not be culpable [for damage done] to his limbs?

D. [The situation of] a man [injuring] a man will prove it, for [in that situation] he is not culpable [for damage done to all of him but] is culpable for [damage done] to his limbs.

### (Textual Source: Reconstructed from Parallel Material Above)[289]

E. No! If you speak [of the situation of] a man [injuring] a man, he must pay indemnity for humiliation. Will you say [the same] in this case, where he does not pay indemnity for humiliation?

F. [The situation of] a man [injuring] a slave will prove it, for [in that situation] he does not pay indemnity for humiliation.

G. No! If you speak [of the situation of] a man [injuring] a man, he must pay indemnity for pain, healing, lost time, and humiliation. Will you say the same here, where he does not pay indemnity for pain, healing, lost time, and humiliation?

H. Scripture states, [therefore,] "(The one responsible for the pit must make restitution.) He shall pay money to the owner" (Exod. 21:34), [in order] to include [restitution] for the damages.

### (Textual Source: m. Baba Qamma 4:1)[290]

[189] I. Based on this they said: If an ox gored four or five oxen, one after the other, the very last one profits. How so? If an ox worth 200 [*zuz*] gored an ox worth 200 [*zuz*], and then gored another ox worth 200 [*zuz*], the one takes 100 *zuz* and the other one takes 100 *zuz*. If he gored another ox worth 200 [*zuz*], the [owner of] the last one takes 100 *zuz* and the one before takes 100 *zuz*, and [the owner of] the first one loses out.

---

[287] The text here interprets the apparently doubled form שלם ישלם as indicative of an extension of the parameters of liability.

[288] I.e., gores the other ox to the point of death.

[289] See above LXVIII:I:3.A–I, III:7.A–H, and III:15.A–H.

[290] The editors have reconstructed this section based upon m. Baba Qamma 4:1, but not exactly as it appears in the Mishnah. Their

B    כן ת״ל שלמישלם בעלין משלמין ואין הבעלין נשכרין ◆

10 A    שור יפה מנה שנגח שור יפה מאתים והנבלה יפה חמשים

זוז זה נוטל חצי החי וחצי המת וזה נוטל חצי החי וחצי

C/B    המת ◆ שנא׳ ומכרו את השור החי וחצו את כספו ◆ ודאי ◆

E/D    מה ת״ל וגם את המת יחצון ◆ מחצצין את המיתה

ביניהן כמה נטלה (מיתד) מיתה מאתים זוז זה נוטל

F    מנה וזה נוטל מנה ◆ וחצו את כספו מלמד ששמין

11 A    לניזק בכסף ולמזיק בכסף משמנין ביניהן ◆ אין לי אלא

C/B    על כולו מנין לרבות את אבריו ◆ ודין הוא ◆ מה הגונב

והמוכר שחייב על כולו אין חייב על איבריו זה שאין

D    חייב על כולו אינו דין שלא יהא חייב על אבריו ◆ אדם

E    באדם יוכיח שאין חייב על כולו וחייב על אבריו ◆ [לא

אם אמרת אדם באדם שמשלם את הבושת תאמר

F    בזה שאין משלם] [את הבושת ◆ אדם בעבד יוכיח שאין

G    משלם את הבושת ◆ לא אם אמרת] [אדם באדם

שמשלם צער וריפוי שבת ובושת תאמר בזה שאין

H    משלם] [צער וריפוי שבת ובושת ◆ ת״ל ◆ כסף ישיב

I    לבעליו לרבות את הנזקין]. ◆ [מיכן אמרו שור שנגח

ארבעה וחמשים שוורים זה אחר זה האחרון] [אחרון

נשכר כיצד שור יפה מאתים שנגח שור יפה מאתים

וחזר] [ונגח שור אחר יפה מאתים זה נוטל מנה וזה

נוטל מנה חזר] [ונגח שור אחר יפה מאתים האחרון

נוטל מנה ושלפניו נוטל] [מנה] והראשון מפסיד ר׳

changes seem unwarranted, given the fact that the continuation of this tradition, incorporated here from the JTS manuscript, is also a part of this mishnaic quotation. Moreover, the addition of the initial clause here—"Based on this they said"—is puzzling, because it creates the impression that this unit is inherently a continuation of the unit prior, which it does not appear to be.

(Textual Source: JTS ENA 1180)

R. Shimon says, "Everyone takes something. Rather, what is the meaning of '... and divide its price' (Exod. 21:35)? If an ox worth 200 [zuz] gored an ox worth 200 [zuz], and then gored another ox worth 200 [zuz], the [owner of] the last one takes 100 zuz, and [as for the owners of the oxen gored] before him—this one takes 50 [zuz] and this one takes 50 [zuz]. If it gored yet another ox worth 200 [zuz], the [owner of] the last one takes 100 zuz, and [as for the owners of the oxen gored] before him—[the owner of the ox gored immediately before the last one] takes 50 [zuz], and [as for the owners of] the first two—this one takes a golden dinar[291] and this one takes a golden dinar."

## LXIX:II

1. A. "If, however, it is known (that the ox was in the habit of goring, and its owner has failed to guard it, he must restore ox for ox, but shall keep the dead animal)" (Exod. 21:36):[292]

   B. [It is known] to a court of judges.

   C. How does one know from Scripture [that it must also be known] to the owners?

   D. Scripture states, "... and its owner, though warned" (Exod. 21:29).

   E. Still, I might say: [In the case of the habitually goring ox here[293] [only] the court [must be warned, but in the case] above[294] [only] the owners [must be warned]. How does one know from Scripture that above the court [also must be warned] and here the owners [must also be warned]?

   F. Scripture states [here], "... in times past" (Exod. 21:36), [and Scripture states above,] "... in times past" (Exod. 21:29):

   G. Just as "in times past" stated here [requires that] the court [be warned], so too does "in times past" stated above [require that] the court [be warned]. And just as "in times past" stated above [requires that] the owners [be warned], so too does "in times past" here [require that] the owners [be warned].

2. A. "... and its owner has failed to guard it" (Exod. 21:36):[295]

   B. I only know [from this] concerning its owner. How does one know from Scripture to include [as liable] the one who borrows [it], [the one who] guards [it] for free, the one paid to guard [it], and the one who rents [it]?

   C. Scripture states, "... has failed to guard it" (Exod. 21:36), [meaning,] he upon whom it is incumbent to cover it, in order to include the one who borrows [it], [the one who] guards [it] for free, the one paid to guard [it], and the one who rents [it].

   D. Why does Scripture state, "... and its owner has failed to guard it" (Exod. 21:36)?

   E. To exclude the one who borrowed [an ox presuming] it to be a tam, but it turns out it was a mu'ad.

3. A. How does one know from Scripture that if a warning was made about it in the presence of the borrower, this [ox is then considered] a mu'ad?

   B. Scripture states "... and its owner has failed to guard it" (Exod. 21:36).

4. A. [Scripture states,] "... its owner" (Exod. 21:29) and "... its owner" (Exod. 21:36), twice, [in order to emphasize that] he who has the capability to guard [it is liable].[296]

---

[291] Which has a value of 25 zuz.
[292] Compare 1.A–G with parallel above at LXVII:I:2.A–I.
[293] I.e., Exod. 21:36.
[294] I.e., Exod. 21:29.

שמ[ע]' אומ' כולן היו נוטלין אלא [מהו וחצו] [את

כספו] שור יפה מאתים שנגח שור יפה מאתים וחזר

ו[נגח] [שור א]חר יפה מאתים האחרון נוטל מנה

ושלפניו זה נוטל חמשים [זוז וז]ה נוטל חמשים זוז

וחזר ונגח שור אחר יפה מאתים האחרון [נוטל] מנה

ושלפניו חמשים זוז ושנים הראשונים זה נוטל דינר

זהב [וזה] נוטל דינר זהב לפיהן משלמין סל' פסו' ◆

LXIX:II

| | | |
|---|---|---|
| D/C/B/A | 1 | או נודע ◆ בבית דין ◆ [בבע]ל[י]ם מ[נין ◆ ת'[ל] |
| E | | והועד בבעליו (שמ' כא כט) ◆ עדי[ין] אני אומ' כן בבית |
| F | | דין עליון בעלין [מנין עליון ב]ית דין כן בעלים ◆ ת'ל |
| G | | תמול שלשם תמול שלשם [למעלן] (שם) ◆ [מ]ה תמול |

שלשום האמור כאן בבית דין אף תמול שלשום האמ'

[למעלן בבי]ת דין ומה תמ' של' האמ' למעלן בעלים

| A | 2 | אף תמ' של' האמ' [כאן בעלים] ◆ ולא ישמרנו בעליו ◆ |
| B | | אין לי אלא בעליו מנין לרבות שואל ושומר [חנם שוכר] |
| C | | ונושא שכר ◆ ת'ל ולא ישמרנו את שדרך שמירתו עליו |
| D | | [להביא] שואל ושומר חנם שוכר ונושא שכר ◆ מה ת'ל |
| E | | ולא ישמרנו בעליו ◆ [פרט ל]שואל ששאלו בחזקת |
| A | 3 | שהוא תם ונמצא מועד ◆ מנין הועד בו בפני שואל [הרי |
| A 4 | B | ז]ה מועד ◆ ת'ל לא ישמרנו בעליו ◆ לא ישמרנו ולא |

ישמרנו שני פעמים [א]ת שיש בו דעת לשמ[ר] ◆

---

[295] Compare 2.A–E with m. Baba Qamma 4:9, t. Baba Qamma 5:4, y. Baba Qamma 4b (Neus., 4:4:I.F–M), and b. Baba Qamma 40a (Neus., XX.B:Tractate Baba Qamma:4:4:I.9.A–10.Q).
[296] Compare 4.A B with m. Baba Qamma 4:4.

B. Excluded are the deaf and dumb person, the madman, and the minor, who are not capable to guard [it].

5. A. "... he must restore" (Exod. 21:36):[297]

B. This is what we have said: [Scripture says this] to include [liability for an ox that gores an ox] belonging to a deaf and dumb person, a madman, and a minor.

(Textual Source: Midrash ha-Gadol and m. Baba Qamma 4:4)

C. How is it so [also that a deaf and dumb person, a madman, and a minor would be liable if their ox gores another ox]?

D. If the ox of a deaf and dumb person, or a madman, or a minor gored, the court appoints guardians over them and they testify about them[298] in the presence of the guardians, and if they [thereafter] cause damage, they[299] are liable to pay.

(Textual Source: Midrash ha-Gadol)

6. A. "... ox for ox" (Exod. 21:36):

B. This teaches that one pays full-damage reparation.

7. A. "... but shall keep the dead animal" (Exod. 21:36):

B. [It belongs to the one whose ox] was damaged.

8. A. One might think it could [be resolved like this]: This one would say to him, "Give me 100 zuz [in cash] for [the damages your ox caused] my ox." But the other one would say, "Take, [instead,] an ox worth 50 sela.[300]

B. [However,] Scripture says here, "... for" (Exod. 21:36), and Scripture says above, "... for" (Exod. 21:24). Just as "for" stated above means one may only make damage payments with money, so too does "for" stated here mean that one may only make damage payments with money.

9. A. "... but shall keep the dead animal" (Exod. 21:36):

B. He must take care of the carcass as long as it is his.

LXIX:III

1. A. "When a man steals (an ox or a sheep, and slaughters it or sells it, he shall pay five oxen for the ox, and four sheep for the sheep)" (Exod. 21:37):

B. I only know concerning a man.

(Textual Source: JTS ENA 1180)

[190]     How does one know from Scripture [to include] a woman?

C. Scripture states, "... shall pay" (Exod. 21:37), [meaning,] whether man or woman.

D. If so, why does Scripture state, "... man" (Exod. 21:37)?

E. For the purpose of the matter below concerning how a man is sold [into slavery] on account of [liability] for his act of thievery, but a woman is not sold on account of her act of thievery.

2. A. "... ox or sheep" (Exod. 21:37):[301]

B. I only know specifically concerning an ox and a sheep. How does one know from Scripture

---

[297] See note 269 above.

[298] I.e., about the oxen—they testify before the guardians about the tendency of these oxen to gore.

[299] I.e., the owners of the oxen.

| | | |
|---|---|---|
| יצאו חרש שוטה וקטן שאין בהן דעת [לשמר ◆ שלם | A 5 | B |
| י]שלם ◆ זו היא שאמרנו לרבות שלחרש ש[וטה] [וקטן ◆ | | B |
| הא כיצד ◆ <שור שלחרש שוטה וקטן שנגח בית דין> | D/C | |
| מעמידין] [להן אפוטרופין ומעידין <להן> בפני | | |
| אפוטרופין ואם הזיקו יהו] [חייבין לשלם. ◆ שור תחת | A | 6 |
| השור ◆ מלמד שמשלם נזק שלם ◆ והמת יהיה] [לו ◆ | A 7 | B |
| לניזק ◆ יכול יהא <זה> אומר לו תן לי מאה <מנה> תחת | A 8 | B |
| שורי] [והלז אומר טול שור יפה חמש סלעים תחת | | |
| שורך ◆ נאמר כן] [תחת ונאמר להלן תחת (פכ"ד) מה | | B |
| תחת האמור להלן אין משלם אלא דמים] [אף <תחת | | |
| האמור> כן אין משלם אלא דמים ◆ והמת יהיה לו ◆ | A | 9 |
| מיטפל] [בנבלה עד שימציא]ה לו סל' פ[סו' ◆ | | B |
| | LXIX:III | |
| כי יגנב איש ◆ אין לי אלא איש] [אשה] מנין ◆ ת"ל | C/B/A | 1 |
| ישלם בין איש ובי]ן אשה ◆ א[ם כן [למה נאמ' איש] ◆ | | D |
| [לעניין] שלמטה האיש נמכר בגניבו ואין האשה | | E |
| נמכרת [בגניבה] ◆ שור או ש ה ◆ אין לי אלא שור ושה | B/A | 2 |

[300] Compare 8.A–B with *Mekhilta de-Rabbi Ishmael,* Nezikin (H/R, 289:9–10; Laut., vol. 3, 93:76–94:79; Neus., LXVIII:II:14.A–G) and with LXVIII:III:18.A–G above.

[301] Compare 2.A–E with t. Baba Qamma 7:15 and b. Baba Qamma 77b (Neus., XX.B:Tractate Baba Qamma:7:4:III.2.A–O).

to include the hybrid [ox-sheep]?

C.  Scripture states "... or sheep" (Exod. 21:37).

D.  One might think that I should include the *koy*.[302]

E.  Scripture states, [however,] "... he shall pay five oxen for the ox, etc." (Exod. 21:36), [meaning, included is only] something that is entirely [a breed] of sheep. Excluded is this one, which is not entirely a [breed of] sheep.

3.  A.  "... and slaughters it" (Exod. 21:37):[303]

B.  Because we have found that the [punishment of] the double payment [paid as a fine upon returning stolen goods][304] is applied to the [stolen] impure cattle like [it is applied] to the pure [stolen cattle], one might think that is also the case here [that the law is applied the same way to both pure and impure oxen or sheep].

C.  Scripture states, [however,] "... and slaughters it" (Exod. 21:37).

D.  Excluded are impure cattle, which cannot be [ritually] slaughtered.

E.  By implication, [therefore,] I should exclude [here] the impure cattle, which cannot be [ritually] slaughtered, but should include the pure cattle, which may be [ritually] slaughtered.

### (Textual Source: Midrash ha-Gadol)

F.  Scripture states, [however,] "... ox" (Exod. 21:37), and not an animal of chase.

G.  For one might logically reason: If cattle, which are not [subject] to the commandment of covering [its blood with ashes],[305] are [subject] to the four- or five-fold [reparation] payment [in Exod. 21:37], then is it not logical that an animal of chase, which is [subject] to the commandment of covering [its blood with ashes], should be [subject] to the four- or five-fold payment?

H.  Scripture states, [however,] "... ox" (Exod. 21:37), and not an animal of chase.

4.  A.  "... a sheep" (Exod. 21:37):

B.  But not birds.

C.  For one might logically reason: If cattle, which are not [subject] to [the law against taking] the mother together with her young,[306] are [subject] to the four- or five-fold [reparation] payment [in Exod. 21:37], then is it not logical that a bird, which is [subject] to [the law against taking] the mother together with her young, should be [subject] to the four- or five-fold payment?

D.  Scripture states, [however,]

### (Textual Source: JTS ENA 1180)

"... a sheep" (Exod. 21:37). But not birds.

5.  A.  "... and slaughters it or sells it" (Exod. 21:37):

B.  I only know concerning his slaughtering of it and his selling it.

C.  How does one know from Scripture [to include liability for four- or five-fold payment] even if he said to others that they should slaughter it, and even if he said to others that they should sell it?

---

[302] See m. Bikkurim 2:8—"The *koy* is in some ways like a wild animal, in some ways like wild animals and cattle, and in some ways not like wild animals or cattle." The precise identification or characteristics of the *koy* is unclear in early Rabbinic literature.
[303] Compare 3.A–H with *Mekhilta de-Rabbi Ishmael*, Nezikin (H/R, 292:3–11; Laut., vol. 3, 99:73–100:89; Neus., LXIX:II:10.A–J).

| | | |
|---|---|---|
| המיוחדין מנין לרבות את ה[כלאים] ◆ ת״ל או שה ◆ יכול | D/C | |
| שני מרבה את הכוי ◆ ת״ל חמשה בקר ישלם ת[חת] | E | |
| השור וגומ׳ את שכולו שה יצא זה שאין כולו שה. ◆ | | |
| וטבחו (לפני) ◆ [לפי] ש[מצינו] בתשלומי כפל שעשה | B/A | 3 |
| בהן בהמה טמאה כטהורה יכול אף זה כ[ן] ◆ ת״ל | C | |
| וטבחו ◆ יצאת בהמה טמאה שאין לה טביחה ◆ מ[שמ]ע | E/D | |
| [מוציא את] בהמה טמאה שאין לה טביחה ומביא | | |
| את הבהמ[ה הטהורה] שיש לה טביחה ◆ ת״ל שור ולא | F | |
| חיה ◆ שהיה בדין מה בהמה [שאינה] [ב]מצות כיסוי | G | |
| הרי היא בתשלומי ד׳ וה׳ חיה שהיא במצ[ות כיסוי] | | |
| אינו דין שתהא בתשלומי ד׳ וחמשה ◆ ת״ל ‹שור ולא | H | |
| חיה. ◆ שה ◆ ולא עופות ◆ שהיה בדין מה בהמה שאינה | C/B/A | 4 |
| באם על הבנים הרי היא בתשלומי ארבעה וחמשה | | |
| עוף שהוא באם על הבנים אינו דין שיהא בתשלומי | | |
| ארבעה וחמשה ת״ל› ◆ שה ולא עופות. ◆ וט[בחו] או | A 5 | D |
| מכרו ◆ אין לי אלא טבחו ומכרו ◆ מנין אפילו אמ׳ | C/B | |
| לאחרים [לטובחו] ואפילו אמ׳ לאחרים למוכרו ◆ | | |

304 See Exod. 22:3.
305 See Lev. 17:13.
306 See Deut. 22:6–7.

D.  Scripture states, "... and slaughters it or sells it" (Exod. 21:37).

6.  A.  One might think [there would be liability for four- or five-fold payment] even if others slaughtered it without knowing [it was stolen] or if others sold it without knowing [it was stolen].

B.  Scripture states, [however,] "When a man steals an ox or a sheep, and slaughters it" (Exod. 21:37).

7.  A.  The one who steals [it is liable for four- or five-fold payment] as long as he [is the one] who slaughters.

B.  One might think the one who steals [it] and gives it as a gift, or the one who steals [it] and sends it as a present to his father-in-law's home would [not be liable][307] to pay the four- or five-fold payment.

C.  Scripture states, [however,] "... and slaughters it or sells it" (Exod. 21:37), [meaning, there is liability for] any form of exchange.

8.  A.  One might think

(Textual Source: Midrash ha-Gadol)

[he would] even [be liable] if he stole [it] and sold it on terms, or stole [it] and bartered it away, or stole [it] and paid his debt [with it], or stole [it] and paid his loan [with it].

B.  Scripture states, [however,] "... or sold it" (Exod. 21:37).

9.  A.  One might think if one stole [it from one's father, who then died so he subsequently] inherited it and afterward slaughtered it, or if he stole it, then dedicated it, and afterward slaughtered it,[308] he would [be liable] to pay the four- or five-fold payment.[309]

B.  Scripture states, [however,] "When a man steals an ox or a sheep, and slaughters it or sells it" (Exod. 21:37).

[191]  C.  Just as [liability for] stealing [is incurred only for] something that is not his, so too [is liability for] slaughtering or selling [incurred only for] something that is not his. This is excluded [from liability], because it is his.

10. A.  One might think if one sold [a stolen ox or sheep] except for its foreleg, except for its hind leg, except for its horn, or except for its fleece, he should pay the four- or five-fold payment.[310]

B.  Scripture states, [however,] "... and slaughters it or sells it" (Exod. 21:37).

C.  Just as slaughtering [an animal involves] all of it, so too does selling [involve] all of it.

(Textual Source: JTS ENA 1180)

11. A.  One might think if one steals objects consecrated for the Temple and sells them he should pay the four- or five-fold payment.

B.  Scripture states, [however,] "... and slaughters it or sells it" (Exod. 21:37).

C.  Just as with slaughtering, one does not become liable for excommunication for slaughtering it, so too with selling, one does not become liable for excommunication for selling it.

D.  Excluded [therefore from the payment] are objects consecrated for the Temple.

---

[307] For contextual meaning, I have added the word "not."
[308] There is no liability for four- or five-fold payment for dedicated animals. See m. Baba Metzia 4:9.
[309] Compare 9.A–C with m. Baba Qamma 7:4.
[310] Compare 10.A–C with t. Baba Qamma 7:18.

| | | |
|---|---|---|
| D | A 6 | ת״ל וטבחו או מ(ו)כרו ♦ יכול אפי[לו טב]חוהו [א]חרין |
| | B | שלא מדעתו ואפי׳ מכרוהו אחרין שלא מדעתו ♦ ת״ל כי |
| 7 | A | יגנב [אי]ש שור או שה וטבחו או מכרו ♦ הגונב עד |
| | B | שיהא טובה ♦ ומוכר יכול (יכול) הגונב ונותן במתנה |
| | | הגונב ו(ה)שולח סיבלונות לבית חמיו יהא [מש]לם תשלומי |
| C | A 8 | ד׳ וה׳ ♦ ת״ל וטבחו או מכרו כל שדרך מכירה ♦ יכול |
| | | [אפילו גנב והקיף גנב והחליף גנב ופרע בחובו גנב |
| B | A 9 | ופרע בהיקפו] ♦ [ת״ל או מכרו. ♦ יכול גנב וירש ואחר כך |
| | | טבח גנב והקדיש ואחר כך] [טבח יהא משלם |
| B | | תשלומי ארבעה וחמשה ♦ ת״ל כי יגנב איש שור או שה] |
| C | | [וטבחו או מכרו ♦ מה גניבה שאינה שלו אף טביחה |
| 10 | A | ומכירה שאינה שלו] [יצא זה שהוא שלו. ♦ יכול מכרה |
| | | חוץ מידה וחוץ מרגלה <חוץ מקרנה> [<וחוץ |
| B | | מגיזותיה> יהא משלם תשלומי ארבעה וחמשה ♦ ת״ל |
| C | | וטבחו או] [מכרו ♦ מה טביחה כולה אף מכירה כולה. ♦ |
| 11 | A | יכול הגונב את הקדשים] [ומוכרן יהא משלם |
| C/B | | תשלומי ד׳ וה׳] ♦ ת״ל וטבחו או מכרו ♦ [מה טביחה |
| | | [שאין חייבין] כרת על טביחתה אף מכירה שאין |
| D | | חייבין כרת [על] [מכיר]תה ♦ יצאו קדשים ♦ |

E. Or just as with slaughtering, it is not permissible to eat it, likewise with selling, it is not permissible to eat it.

F. Excluded [therefore] are nonconsecrated objects.

G. When you reason one way, you only include consecrated objects, and when you reason the other way, you only include nonconsecrated objects!

H. Scripture says here, [however,] "... for" (Exod. 21:37), and Scripture says above "... for" (Exod. 21:36). Just as "for" said above excludes [objects belonging] to God, so too does "for" said here exclude [objects belonging] to God.

12. A. One might think if one steals an animal that is *treifah*[311] and slaughters it he should pay the four- or five-fold payment.[312]

B. Scripture states, [however,] "... and slaughters it or sells it" (Exod. 21:37), [meaning,] selling something that can be eaten. Excluded is *treifah,* which cannot be slaughtered [for the purposes] of being eaten.

13. A. One might think the one who steals an ox condemned to death by stoning and the one who slaughters [an animal] in [the temple court intending to eat it] as common food[313] should pay the four- or five-fold payment.[314]

B. Scripture states, [however,] "... and slaughters it or sells it" (Exod. 21:37), [meaning,] a slaughtering [that would render the animal suitable] for selling. These are excluded, because their slaughtering does not [render the animal suitable] for selling.

14. A. "... he shall pay five oxen for the ox, and four sheep for the sheep" (Exod. 21:37):

B. This is a royal declaration.

C. One might think [the liability could be resolved like this]: This one would say to him, "Give me 100 zuz [in cash] for [the liability for] my ox." But the other one would say, "Take, [instead,] five five-year-old oxen, [each worth] five *selas,* for your ox."

D. [However,] Scripture says here, "... for" (Exod. 21:37), and Scripture says above "... for" (Exod. 21:24). Just as "for" stated above means one may only make damage payments with money, so too does "for" stated here means that one may only make damage payments with money.

*Chapter Seventy*

(Textual Source: JTS ENA 1180)

LXX:I

1. A. "(If the thief is seized) while tunneling under a wall[315] (and he is beaten to death, there is no bloodguilt[316] in his case)" (Exod. 22:1):[317]

B. I only know concerning tunneling under a wall [into a house]. How does one know from Scripture to include his courtyard and his garden?

C. Scripture says, "If the thief is seized" (Exod. 22:1), [meaning, tunneling] in any manner.

---

[311] This term can refer to an animal that has been injured or killed by another animal, an animal that has been inappropriately slaughtered, or simply an animal that, under no circumstances, would be suitable for Jewish consumption. In all instances, it refers to an animal that cannot be consumed by a Jew.

[312] Compare 12.A–B with m. Baba Qamma 7:2.

[313] Slaughtering it inside the Temple, but intending to eat it as unconsecrated, common food, would render it unsuitable for consumption or any other use.

[314] Compare 13.A–B with m. Baba Qamma 7:2.

[315] The text assumes that Exod. 22:1 speaks specifically of one who tunnels under a wall to break into a house.

| | | |
|---|---|---|
| E | | או מה טביחה שאין לה התר אכילה אף מכירה שאין |
| G/F | | לה התר אכילה • ויצאו חולין • כשאתה בא לדרך זו אין |
| | | כן אלא קדשים וכשאתה בא לדרך זו אין כן אלא חולין • |
| H | | נאמ' כן תחת [ו]נאמ' להלן תחת (שמ' כא לו) מה |
| | | תחת האמ' להלן פרט לגבוה אף תחת האמ' [כן] פרט |
| A | 12 | לגבוה • יכול הגונב טרפה וטבחה יהא משלם תשלומי |
| B | | ד' וה' • [ת"ל] • וטבחו או מכרו מכירה שיש לה אכילה |
| A | 13 | יצאת טרפה שאין לטביחתה אכילה • יכול הגונב שור |
| | | הנסקל והשוחט בני חולין בפנים יהא משלם תשלומי |
| B | | ד' וה' • ת"ל • וטבחו או מכרו טביחה שיש לה מכירה |
| A | 14 | יצאו אלו [שאין ל]טביחתן מכירה. • חמשה בקר ישלם |
| B | | תחת השור וארב' צאן [תחת הש]ה. • גזרת מלך היא • |
| C | | יכול יהא זה אומ' לו תן לי <מאה> מנה תחת שורי |
| | | והל[ז אומ'] לו טול חמשה שוורין בני חמשה חמשה |
| D | | סלעין תחת שורך • נאמ' כן תחת ונאמ' להלן תחת |
| | | (שמ' כא כד) מה תחת האמ' להלן אין אין משלם אלא |
| | | דמים אף כן אין משלם אלא דמים. סל' פסו' • |

LXX:I

| | | |
|---|---|---|
| B/A | 1 | אם במחתרת • אין לי אלא במחתרת מנין לרבות |
| C | | את חצרו וגנתו • ת"ל ימצא הגנב מכל מקום • |

---

[316] To say that the thief has no bloodguilt means, essentially, it is permissible to kill the thief in this scenario with no concern for culpability for his death. To say that the thief has bloodguilt (as in the next verse) means it is not permissible to kill the thief, and there is possible culpability for his death.

[317] Compare 1.A–E with y. Sanhedrin 26c (Neus., 8:8:II.A–III.E) and b. Sanhedrin 72b (Neus., XXIIIB:Tractate Sanhedrin:8:6:VI.A–L).

D.     If so, why does Scripture say, "while tunneling under a wall [into a house]"?

E.     [It means to emphasize] that while tunneling under a wall [into a house] he is seized and beaten to death. Excluded [is the situation where he is seized and beaten to death] when not tunneling under a wall, where there is bloodguilt.

2.     A.     I only know concerning tunneling under a wall. How does one know from Scripture to include

(Textual Source: Midrash ha-Gadol)

anything else?

[192]     B.     Scripture states, "... while tunneling under a wall" (Exod. 22:1), [meaning,] anything that is like a wall.

3.     A.     One might think that there need to be witnesses.

B.     Scripture states, [however,] "... while tunneling under a wall" (Exod. 22:1). It is a wall; it is his witness.

C.     If so, why does Scripture state, "is seized" (Exod. 22:1)?

D.     For the subject [addressed] above [about] the five oxen, etc.

4.     A.     One might think he should pay [reparations] on his own.[318]

B.     Scripture states, [however,] "... is seized" (Exod. 22:1). There is no seizing without witnesses.

5.     A.     "... and is beaten" (Exod. 22:1): By anyone.[319]

B.     "... to death" (Exod. 22:1): In any manner.

6.     A.     "... there is no bloodguilt" (Exod. 22:1):[320]

B.     Whether on a weekday or on *Shabbat.*

C.     Ahead Scripture states, "... there is bloodguilt" (Exod. 22:2).

D.     There is bloodguilt whether on a weekday or on *Shabbat.*

## LXX:II

1.     A.     "If the sun has risen on him, (there is bloodguilt in that case. He must make restitution. If he lacks the means, he shall be sold for his theft)" (Exod. 22:2):[321]

B.     And does the sun shine on him alone? Doesn't it shine on the entire world?

C.     Rather, [it says this to make the point that] just as the shining sun is obvious, so too in any event where [the robber's intention not to cause harm] is obvious.

D.     Just as when the sun, which is peaceful to him, shines on him, there is bloodguilt whether on a weekday or on *Shabbat,* so too in any instance where [it is obvious] that he[322] is peaceful to him,[323] there is bloodguilt whether on a weekday or on *Shabbat.*

---

[318] I.e., without any witnesses to bring charges.

[319] Compare 5.A–B with b. Sanhedrin 72b (Neus., XXIIIB:Tractate Sanhedrin:8:6:V.A–N).

[320] Compare 6.A–D with b. Sanhedrin 72b (Neus., XXIIIB:Tractate Sanhedrin:8:6:IV.A–H).

[321] 1.A–F is a difficult unit, with apparent problems in the manuscript. The basic gist of the unit, however, is clear, particularly when compared with the parallels: If the thief obviously has no intentions of causing harm, and the owner murders him, there will be bloodguilt. If the owner is unable to discern clearly the intentions of the robber, he may kill him in self-defense without concern for bloodguilt. Compare parallel material in *Mekhilta de-Rabbi Ishmael,* Nezikin (H/R, 292:12–293:12; Laut., vol. 3, 101:1–103:28; Neus., LXX:I:1.A–5.I.); *Sifre Deut.,* Piska 237; y. Ketubot 28c (Neus., 4:4:III.D–E); and b. Sanhedrin 72a (Neus., XXIIIB:Tractate Sanhedrin:8:6:II.A–K).

[322] I.e., the thief.

[323] I.e., the thief obviously does not have harmful intentions toward the owner of the house he is robbing.

| | |
|---|---|
| E/D | אם כן למה נאמ' במחתרת • במחתרת והכה ומת יצא חוץ |
| A 2 | למחתרת דמים לו • אין לי אלא במחתרת מנין לרבות |
| B | כל [דבר • ת"ל במחתרת כל דבר שהוא כמחתרת • |
| B/A 3 | יכול יהא צריך עדים] • [ת"ל במחתרת היא מחתרת היא |
| D/C | עדותו • אם כן למה נאמר ימצא • לעינין] [שלמעלה |
| B/A 4 | חמשה בקר וג' • יכול ישלם על פי עצמו • ת"ל ימצא אין |
| B/A 5 | ימצא] [בכל מקום אלא בעדים • והכה בכל אדם • ומת |
| B/A 6 | בכל דבר. • אין לו דם] [אין לו דמים • בין בחול בין |
| D/C | בשבת • ולהלן הוא אומר דם לו • דמים לו] [בין בחול |
| | בין בשבת. ‹סל' פסו'› • |

| | | |
|---|---|---|
| | LXX:II | |
| B/A 1 | אם זרחה השמש עליו • וכי עליו • [בלבד חמה |
| C | זורחת והלא על כל העולם כולו היא זורחת • אלא מה] |
| | [זריחת השמ]ש שהיא ב‹ג›לוי כך כל דבר שהוא בגלוי • |
| D | מה [זריחת השמש] [שהוא שלם לו] (שהוא שלום לו) |
| | דם לו דמין לו בין בחול ובין בשב]ת כך] [כל דבר |
| | ש]הוא שלם לו ‹דם לו דמים לו› בין בחול (ו)בין בשבת • |

E. And thus Scripture says, "... that of a man attacking another, etc." (Deut. 22:26).

F. Behold this case [in Exod. 22:2] is like that case [in Deut. 22:26]: Just as the one [case] has a doubt about [his intention] to kill, so too does the other [case] have a doubt about [his intention] to kill. Just as [in] the one [case] he tried to prevent killing him first, and then killed him, so too [in] the other [case] he tried to prevent killing him first, and then killed him.

2.    A. "... there is bloodguilt in that case. He must make restitution" (Exod. 22:2):

B. Thus, if there is not bloodguilt, he need not make restitution.

C. Just as this is specific, [in that] it treats the unintentional act like the intentional one, and when one pays with one's life, one is exempt from [paying restitution] for property, so too in any matter should the unintentional act be treated like the intentional one, and when one pays with one's life, one should be exempt from [paying restitution] for property.

3.    A. "If he lacks the means" (Exod. 22:2): This teaches that you don't determine the value of what might [one day] be added to an estate as with what is already in possession.

B. "If he lacks the means" (Exod. 22:2): This teaches that you don't determine the value by means of movable chattel.

C. "If he lacks the means" (Exod. 22:2): You don't delay [selling him into slavery for his theft] until his father dies [and he inherits and can pay it off] or until his ship comes in.

4.    A. "... he shall be sold for his theft" (Exod. 22:2):[324]

B. He is sold on account of the object he stole, but not on account of his false testimony.

C. He is sold on account of the object he stole, but not on account of [his liability to pay] double [the value of the stolen goods found in his possession].

[193]  D. He is sold [once] on account of the object he stole, but is not sold twice on account of the object he stole. You have nothing on him more than the amount of the object he stole.

E. R. Eliezer says, "He can be sold on account of the object he stole, as long as he is worth the object he stole [when sold into slavery]."

5.    A. "... for his theft" (Exod. 22:2):

B. The man is sold on account of the object he stole, but the woman is not sold on account of the object she stole.

## LXX:III

1.    A. "But if what he stole is found in his possession (alive, whether ox or ass or sheep, he shall pay double)" (Exod. 22:3):

B. [If] they saw him as he entered, but they didn't find the object he stole in his possession, [or if] they found the object he stole in his possession, but didn't see him as he entered, he is exempt [from liability. He is only liable] as long as they saw him entering and they found the object he stole in his possession.

2.    A. Since it says above in Scripture, "... and they are stolen from the man's house" (Exod. 22:6), Scripture informs that one is not liable unless he takes them[325] from the private domain of the owner of the house.

---

[324] Compare 4.A–E with y. Sotah 19b (Neus., 3:8:VII.A–K) and b. Qiddushin 18a (XIX.A:Qiddushin:1:2:VI.21.A–22.C).
[325] I.e., the stolen objects.

| | | |
|---|---|---|
| E | וכן הוא אומ' כי כ[אשר יקום] איש על רעהו | |
| F | וגומ' (דב' כב כו) ◆ הרי זה כזה מה זה ספק | |
| | נפשות אף זה ספק נפשות מה זה אם מיחה בידו | |
| | להורגו קודם והורגו אף זה אם מיחה בידו להורגו | |
| | קודם והורגו. ◆ דמים לו <שלם> ישלם ◆ הא אם א[י]ן לו | B/A | 2 |
| C | דמים אין משלם ◆ מה זה מיוחד עשה את שאין מתכוין | |
| | כמ[תכוין] ונידון בנפשו פטור מן הממון כך כל דבר | |
| | שנעשה את ש[אין מתכוין] כמתכוין ונידון בנפשו | |
| | פטור מן הממון. ◆ אם אין לו מלמד שא[י]ן [שמ]ין לו | A | 3 |
| B | בראוי כבמוחזק. ◆ אם אין לו מלמד שאין שמין לו [מן] | |
| C | [המ]יטלטלין ◆ אם אין לו אין ממתינין לו עד שימות | |
| A | אביו או עד [שתבוא] [ספינתו מ]מדינת הים ◆ ונמכר | 4 |
| C/B | בגניבתו ◆ נמכר בגנבו ואין [נמכר] [בזממו] ◆ נמכר בגניבו | |
| D | ואין נמכר בכפילו. ◆ נמכר בגניבו ואין נ[מכר] [ונשנה | |
| E | בגנ]בו אין לך עליו מעתה אלא כדי גניבו ◆ ור' אליעזר | |
| A | אומ' [עד] [שיה]א שקול כנגד גניבו ◆ נמכר בגניבו ◆ | 5 |
| B | האיש נמכר בגניבו ואין האשה [נמכ]רת בגניבה סל' פסו' ◆ | |

LXX:III

| | | |
|---|---|---|
| B/A | אם המצא תמצא בידו הגניבה. ◆ ראו [אותו] שנכנס | 1 |
| | ולא מצאו בידו גניבה מצאו בידו גניבה ולא ראו אותו | |
| | [שנכנס] פטור עד שיראו אותו <שנכנס וימצאו בידו גניבה. ◆ | |
| A | בידו מכלל שנאמר להלן וגנב מבית האיש (שמ' כב ו) | 2 |
| | מגיד הכתוב שאינו חייב עד שיוציאו> מרשות בעל הבית ◆ | |

B.   One might think this would even be the case here [in Exod. 22:3]

(Textual Source: Ms. Firkovich II A 268)

C.   How do you say from Scripture that he will be liable if he lifted it up within the private domain of the owner of the house?[326]

D.   Scripture states, "But if what he stole is found[327] in his possession" (Exod. 22:3).

3.   A.   "... whether ox" (Exod. 22:3):[328]

B.   Since we have found that the one who steals in partnership or the one who steals from his partner is exempt from the four- or five-fold payment, one might think this is also the case here [in Exod. 22:3].

C.   Scripture states, [however,] "... whether ox" (Exod. 22:3), [which means] even [if one's part constitutes] only part of the ox.

4.   A.   "... or sheep" (Exod. 22:3):

B.   Since we have found that the one who sold [a stolen animal] except for its foreleg or except for its hind leg is exempt from the four- or five-fold payment,[329] one might think this is also the case here [in Exod. 22:3].

C.   Scripture states, [however,] "... or sheep" (Exod. 22:3), [which means] even part of a sheep.

5.   A.   "... whether ox or ass or sheep" (Exod. 22:3):[330]

B.   Let Scripture state [only] "ox" and "what he stole," and everything else could be included in the general principle![331]

C.   If so, I might say that just as this [ox] is special, in that its first-born is [consecrated and offered up] on the altar, so too, as I extend [the general principle], I should only include an animal whose first-born is [consecrated and offered up] on the altar.

D.   [Now, just] which [other animal might I think] this [possibly could] be? A sheep!

E.   [But] Scripture states, "... or sheep" (Exod. 22:3). A sheep is already [specifically] mentioned!

F.   Why does Scripture state, "... what he stole" (Exod. 22:3)? [In order] to include [any] other item.

G.   [Then] let Scripture state "ox" and "sheep" and "stolen item," and everything else could be included in the general principle!

H.   If so, I might say that just as these [animals] are special, in that their first-born [are given] to the priests, so too, as I extend [the general principle], I should only include an animal whose first-born is [given] to the priests.

I.   [Now, just] which [other animal might I think] this [possibly could] be? An ass!

J.   [But] Scripture states, "... or ass" (Exod. 22:3). An ass is already [specifically] mentioned!

K.   Why does Scripture state, "... what he stole" (Exod. 22:3)? [In order] to include [any] other item.

L.   [Then] let Scripture state "ox" and "sheep" and "ass" and "stolen item," and everything else could be included in the general principle.

---

[326] Compare 2.C with m. Baba Qamma 7:6.

[327] This interpretation justifies this special emphasis on the basis of the apparently doubled form of the infinitive absolute "is found" (Hebrew: הִמָּצֵא תִמָּצֵא).

[328] Compare 3.A–C with b. Baba Qamma 78b (Neus., XX.B:Tractate Baba Qamma:7:5A–F:I.3.A–F).

[329] See LXIX:III:10.A–C above.

יכול אף זה כן • מנין [מנ]ין אתה אומ' הגביהו — C/B

ברשות בעל הבית הרי זה חייב • ת"ל אם ‹המצא› תמצא — D

בידו הגנבה • משור • לפי שמ[צ]אנו בו ב[ת]שלומי — B/A  3

ד' וה' שהגונב בשותפות ושותף שג[נ]ב מח[ברו שהו

פטור [יכו]ל אף זה כן • ת"ל משור אפילו מקצת — C

שור • ‹עד שה› • לפי שמצאנו בתשלומי ד' וה' שאם — B/A  4

מכרו חוץ מידו וחוץ מרגלו שהוא פטור יכול אף

זה [כ]ן • ת"ל עד שה אפי' מקצת שה • משור עד חמור — A 5  C

עד שה • יאמר שור וגניבה והכל בכלל • אילו כן הייתי — C/B

אומ' מה זה מיוחד שיש בו בכורה ל[מז]בח אף כשאני

מרבה איני מרבה אלא דבר שיש בו בכורה למזבח •

ואיזה זה זה שה • ת"ל שה כבר שה אמור • מה ת"ל — F/E/D

גניבה לרבות דבר אחר • יאמר שור ושה וגניבה — G

‹ו›הכל בכלל • אילו כן הייתי אומ'] מה זה מיוחד — H

ש[י]ש בו בכורה לכה[ני]ם אף כשאני מרבה איני מרבה

אלא דבר שיש בו בכורה לכהנים • ואי זה זה. זה חמור — I

ת"ל חמור כבר חמור אמור • מה ת"ל גניבה לרבות — K/J

דבר אחר • יאמר שור ושה וחמור וגניבה והכל בכלל • — L

---

[330] Compare 5.A–O with b. Baba Qamma 63b (Neus., XX.B:Tractate Baba Qamma:7:1:II.4.CC–5.S).

[331] I.e., why did Scripture state specifically an ox, ass, and sheep, when it could have simply established the general principle by mentioning "what he stole" and "an ox"?

[194]     M.   If so, I might say that just as these [animals] are special, in that they are alive, so too, as I extend [the general principle], I should only include something that is alive.

        N.   [But] Scripture states, "... alive" (Exod. 22:3). Alive is already [specifically] mentioned!

        O.   Why does Scripture states, "... what he stole" (Exod. 22:3)? [In order] to include [any] other item.

6.       A.   "... he shall pay double" (Exod. 22:3):[332]

        B.   One might think that the one who steals his son and sells him should pay the doubled payment.

        C.   For it is a matter of logic:

        D.   If these [people in Exod. 22:3], who are not liable for the death penalty for their thievery, pay the doubled payment, then isn't it logical that [the one who steals] his son, for which he is liable for the death penalty, should pay the doubled payment?

        E.   Scripture states, [however,] "... whether ox or ass or sheep" (Exod. 22:3). Just as these are special, in that they [are things that in a different scenario] he could have the authority to sell, his son is excluded [from liability for the doubled payment], because he could not have the authority to sell him.

        F.   Perhaps I should exclude his son, whom he could not have the authority to sell, but still I should not exclude his daughter [from liability for the doubled payment], whom he could have the authority to sell.

        G.   Scripture states, [however,] "... whether ox or ass or sheep" (Exod. 22:3). Just as these are special, in that [their owner] always has the authority to sell them, his daughter is excluded, because he does not always have the authority to sell her.

        H.   Perhaps I should exclude his daughter, whom he does not always have the authority to sell, but still I should not exclude land [from liability for the double payment], which he does always have the authority to sell.

        I.   Scripture states, [however,] "... whether ox or ass or sheep" (Exod. 22:3). Just as these are special, in that they can be injured, captured, and can die, land is excluded, because it can't be injured, captured, and [can't] die.

        J.   Perhaps I should exclude land, which cannot be injured, captured, and cannot die, but still I should not exclude the slaves [from liability for the doubled payment], which can be injured, captured, and can die.

        K.   Scripture states, [however,] "... whether ox or ass or sheep" (Exod. 22:3). Just as these are special, in that guarding them is your [responsibility], slaves are excluded, because guarding them is not your [responsibility].

        L.   Perhaps I should exclude slaves, because guarding them is not your [responsibility], but still I should not exclude bonds [from liability for the doubled payment], because guarding them is your [responsibility].

        M.   Scripture states, [however,] "... whether ox or ass or sheep" (Exod. 22:3). Just as these are special, in that giving them away is final, bonds are excluded, because you have nothing in them except proof [of ownership].[333]

7.       A.   "... alive ... he shall pay double" (Exod. 22:3):

        B.   Even without an oath.

---

[332] Compare 6.A–M with t. Shebuot 37b (Neus., 6:6:II.A–W).

[333] I.e., when you give away an ox, ass, or sheep, you relinquish possession of the actual object, whereas a bond is only representative of ownership of an object, and one can give it away while maintaining possession of the object itself.

| | |
|---|---|
| M | אילו כן הייתי אומ׳ <מה> אלו מיוחדין שיש בהן |
| | רוח חיין אף <כשאני מרבה> איני מרבה אלא דבר |
| N | [שי]ש בו רוח חיים • ת״ל חיים כבר חיים אמור • |
| O 6 B/A | ומה ת״ל גניבה לרבות דבר אחר • שנים ישלם • יכול |
| C | הגונב את בנו ומכרו יה[א] משלם תשלומ[י] כפ[ל • ודין |
| D | הוא • מה אם אלו <שאין> חייב על מכירתן <מיתה> |
| | משלם תשלומי כפל בנו שחייב על מכירתו מיתה אינו |
| E | דין שישלם תשלומי כפל • ת״ל משור עד חמ[ו]ר עד |
| | שה מה אלו מיוחדין שזכאי במכירתן יצא בנו שאין |
| F | זכאי במכירתו • מוציא אני את בנו שאין זכאי במכירתו |
| G | ועדאן לא אוציא את בתו שזכאי במכירתה • ת״ל משור |
| | עד חמור עד שה מה אלו מיוחדין שזכאי במכירתן |
| H | לעולם יצאת בתו שאין זכאי במכירתה לעולם • מוציא |
| | אני את בתו שאין זכאי במכירתה לעולם ועד אן לא |
| I | אוציא את הקרקעות שזכי במכירתן לעולם • ת״ל |
| | משור עד חמור עד שה מה אלו מיוחדין שיש בהן |
| | שבר ושביה ומיתה יצאו קרקעות שאין בהן שבר |
| J | <ו>שביה ומיתה • מוציא אני את הקרקעות שאין בהן |
| | שבר <ו>שביה ומיתה ועדאן לא אוציא את העבדים |
| K | שיש בהן שבר ושביה ומיתה • ת״ל משור עד חמור עד |
| | שה מה אלו מיוחדין ששמירתן עליך יצאו עבדים |
| L | שאין שמירתן עליך • מוציא אני את העבדים שאין |
| | שמירתן עליך ועדאן לא אוציא את השטרות ששמירתן |
| M | עליך • ת״ל משור עד חמור עד שה מה אלו מיוחדין |
| | שמתנתן גמורות לך יצאו שטרות שאין לך בהן אלא |
| 7 B/A | ראיה. • חיים שנים ישלם • אף על פי שלא בשבועה • |

C.   For it is a matter of logic:

D.   He is liable here, and the owner of the house is liable [for misappropriating items entrusted in his care].[334] Just as we have found that the owner of the house only pays [reparations] after an oath, so too here he should only pay after an oath!

E.   And an additional reasoning: Just as the owner of the house, who must pay an additional fifth [of the value of the item] and a guilt offering, only pays after an oath, then isn't it logical that this one, who doesn't pay an additional fifth and a guilt offering, should only pay after an oath?

F.   Scripture states, [however,] "... alive ... he shall pay double" (Exod. 22:2), [meaning,] even without an oath.

G.   One might think he should pay on his own word [alone].[335]

H.   For it is a matter of logic:

I.   He is liable here, and the owner of the house is liable. Just as we have found that the owner of the house does not pay on his own word [alone], so too here he should not pay on his own word [alone].

J.   And an additional reasoning: Just as the owner of the house, who must pay an additional fifth and a guilt offering, does not pay on his own word [alone], then isn't it logical that this one, who doesn't pay an additional fifth and a guilt offering, should not pay on his own word [alone].

[195]   K.   No! When you speak of the owner of the house, he pays only after an oath. Will you say the same of this one, who pays [both] before an oath and after an oath? Because he pays [both] before an oath and after an oath, he should pay on his word [alone]!

L.   Scripture states, [however,] "... is found" (Exod. 22:3), [and] "is found" in all events [means] with witnesses.

*Chapter Seventy-One*

(Textual Source: Ms. Firkovich II A 268)

LXXI:I

1.   A.   "When a man causes (a field or vineyard) to be grazed bare, (or sends out his livestock to graze in another's land, he must make restitution for the excellence of that field or vineyard)" (Exod. 22:4):[336]

B.   The one who [knowingly] causes [the field or vineyard] to be grazed is liable.

C.   Based on this you say: If thieves [as a part of their robbery] opened the stable or opened the storage space in the shed, and [as a result] the cattle went out and did damage, the thieves are exempt from liability and the owner of the farm is exempt from liability.

D.   As it says in Scripture, "... or sends out his livestock" (Exod. 22:4).

E.   Each is exempt, because he didn't [knowingly] send out [the cattle].

F.   If the thieves let it loose [knowingly as a part of their robbery], the thieves are liable, but the owner of the farm is exempt from liability.

G.   As it says in Scripture, "When a man causes (a field or vineyard) to be grazed" (Exod. 22:4).

2.   A.   "... he must make restitution" (Exod. 22:4):

---

[334] See Exod. 22:6–12.
[335] I.e., by admitting guilt, but without the testimony of additional witnesses.

| | |
|---|---|
| D/C | והלא דין הוא ♦ חייב כן וחייב בבעל הבית מה |
| | מצינו בבעל הבית אין משלם אלא לאחר שבועה אף |
| E | זה לא ישלם אלא לאחר שבועה ♦ ועוד קל וחומר ומה |
| | בעל הבית שמשלם חומש ואשם אין משלם אלא |
| | לאחר שבועה זה שאין משלם חומש ואשם אינו דין |
| F | שלא ישלם אלא לאחר שבועה ♦ ת״ל חיים שנים ישלם |
| H/G | ואף על פי שלא בשבועה ♦ יכול ישלם על פי עצמו ♦ ודין |
| I | הוא ♦ חייב כן וחייב בבעל הבית מה מצינו בבעל הבית |
| | אין משלם על פי עצמו [אף זה לא ישלם על פי עצמו] ♦ |
| J | ועוד קל וחומר <ו>מה בעל הבית שמשלם חומש |
| | ואשם אין משלם על פי עצמו זה שאין משלם [חו]מש |
| K | ואשם אינו דין שלא ישלם על פי עצמו ♦ לא אם אמרת |
| | בבעל הבית שאין משלם אלא לאחר שבועה תאמר |
| | בזה שמשלם לפני שבועה ולאחר שבועה הואיל |
| | ומשלם לפני שבועה ולאחר שבועה ישלם על פי עצמו ♦ |
| L | ת״ל ימצא אין ימצא בכל מקום אלא בעדים. סל׳ פסקא׳ ♦ |

<br>

| | | |
|---|---|---|
| | | LXXI:I |
| 1 | C/B/A | כי יבער ♦ המבעיר חייב ♦ מיכן אתה אומ׳ הגנבין |
| | | שפתחו את הדיר ופתחו את המוקצה ויצאה בהמה |
| D | | והזיקה הגנבין פטורין ובעל הבית פטור ♦ שנאמר |
| F/E | | ושלח את בעירו ♦ יצא זה שלא שילח ♦ הוציאוה הגנבין |
| G | A 2 | הגנבין חייבין ובעל הבית פטור ♦ שנא׳ כי יבער ♦ ישלם ♦ |

<br>

---

[336] Compare 1.A–2.H with *Mekhilta de-Rabbi Ishmael*, Nezikin (H/R, 296:6–14; Laut., vol. 3, 108:1–109:16; Neus., LXXI:I:1.A–4.D); m. Baba Qamma 6:1; and t. Baba Qamma 6:19.

B.   The one who causes the grazing is liable to pay.

C.   If he[337] locked [the gate] as normal, and tied up [the gate] as normal, and made a fence for it that was 10 handbreadths high, and then handed over [supervision] of it to someone who was ill or old, but [nonetheless] had the capability [to watch over it], and then cattle got out and caused damage, he is exempt from liability.

D.   As it says in Scripture, "... or sends out his livestock" (Exod. 22:4).

(Textual Source: Midrash ha-Gadol)

E.   This one is exempt from liability, because he didn't send out (livestock).

F.   If one locked [the stable] abnormally, and tied up [the gate] abnormally, and made a fence for it that was less than 10 handbreadths high, and then handed over [supervision] of it to a deaf-mute, idiot, or minor, who did not have the capability [to watch over it], and then cattle got out and caused damage, he is liable.

G.   As it says in Scripture, "When a man causes (a field or vineyard) to be grazed ... he must make restitution" (Exod. 22:4).

H.   The one who causes the grazing

(Textual Source: Ms. Firkovich II A 268)

is liable to pay.

3.   A.   "... a field or vineyard" (Exod. 22:4):

B.   I only know from this specifically about a field or vineyard. How does one know from Scripture to include any [type of field]?

C.   Scripture states, "... vineyard" (Exod. 22:4).

4.   A.   I might think I should include [in the liability of Exod. 22:4 the ox] that damaged clothing or ate utensils.[338]

B.   Scripture states, [however,] "... vineyard" (Exod. 22:4).

C.   Just as a vineyard is special in that [it comprises] fruit, so too [included in the liability of Exod. 22:4] is [only the field that comprises] fruit.

D.   Or, just as a vineyard [comprises] ripened fruit, so too do I only know about ripened fruit. How does one know from Scripture that if [the ox] saw seeds and ate them, they [also] estimate that [for reparation].

E.   Scripture states, "... a field" (Exod. 22:4).

F.   But R. Shimon says, "'... vineyard' (Exod. 22:4):

G.   "Wasn't a vineyard included in the general category of a 'field'? Why does Scripture state, '... a field or vineyard' (Exod. 22:4)?

H.   "This teaches that if it ate unripened fruit or half-ripened fruit they regard them as if they were ripened fruit."

5.   A.   "... or sends out his livestock" (Exod. 22:4):

B.   If a cow was walking in its normal way in public property and fell into a garden and enjoyed [some of the produce in the garden], if he[339] [knowingly] sent it out, he must pay for what it enjoyed, and if [he sent it] out, he must pay for what it damaged.

---

[337] I.e., the owner of the stable.

[338] Compare 4.A–H with *Mekhilta de-Rabbi Ishmael*, Nezikin (H/R, 296:12; Laut., vol. 3, 109:12–13; Neus., LXXI:I:3.A–B); m. Baba Qamma 2:2; and t. Baba Qamma 6:2.

המבעיר את הבערה חייב לשלם ◆ נעל כראוי וקשר C/B

כראוי ועשה לה מחיצה גבוהה עשרה טפחים ומסרה

לחולה ולזקן שיש בהן דעת ‹ו›יצאה בהמה והזיקה

פטור ◆ שנא׳ ושלח את בעירו ◆ ‹יצא זה שלא ישלח ◆ נעל F/E/D

שלא כראוי וקשר שלא כראוי ועשה מחיצה שאינה

גבוהה עשרה טפחים ומסרה לחרש שוטה וקטן

שאין בהן דעת ויצתה בהמה והזיקה חייב ◆ שנא׳ כי G

יבער ישלם ◆ המבעיר› חייב לשלם. ◆ שדה או כרם ◆ אין B/A 3 H

לי אלא שדה וכרם המיוחדין מנין לרבות כל דבר ◆ ת״ל C

כרם ◆ יכול שני מביא את [שק]רעה כסות ושאכלה את A 4

הכלים ◆ ת״ל כרם ◆ מה כרם ‹מיוחד› שהוא פירות כך C/B

כל דבר שהוא פרות ◆ או מה כרם פירות גמורין אף אין D

לי אלא פירות גמורין מנין ראתה זרעין ואכלתן הרי

אלו שמין לו ◆ ת״ל שדה ◆ ור׳ שמע׳ אומ׳ כרם ◆ והלא G/F/E

כרם בכלל שדה היה מה ת״ל שדה או כרם ◆ מלמד שאם H

אכלה פגין או בוסר רואין אותן כאילו הן פירות

גמורין. ◆ ושלח את בעירה ◆ בהמה שהיתה מהלכת B/A 5

כדרכה ברש׳ הרב׳ ונפלה לגינה ונהנת אם שילחה מאליו

משלם מה שנהנת. ואם מאליה משלם מה שהזיקה ◆

[196]   C.   But they do not estimate [the value of the damage] neither in terms of a *kab*'s measurement,[340] because this would increase [unjustly the value of the damaged property], nor in terms of a *kor*'s measurement,[341] because this would decrease [it unjustly]. Rather, they estimate [the value] of a *se'ah*[342] in that field in terms of how much it was worth [before the damage], and how much it is now worth.[343]

6.   A.   "… or sends out his livestock" (Exod. 22:4):[344]

### (Textual Source: Ms. Oxford Heb. D 63.43)

   B.   I only know [from this verse] concerning [the liability for damage caused by an ox's] tooth eating what it is fit to eat. How does one know from Scripture [to include as liable the damage caused by an ox's] leg breaking [what it tramples upon] as it walks along its normal way?

   C.   Scripture states, "… or sends out his livestock" (Exod. 22:4).

### (Textual Source: Ms. Firkovich II A 268)

   D.   But wasn't the tooth a part of the general category of the leg? As it says in Scripture, "I will remove its hedge, that it may be ravaged, etc." (Isa. 5:5).

   E.   I only know [from this verse] concerning this [general principle of liability] alone. How does one know from Scripture [that the liability here is the same as when livestock] causes damage while walking along its normal way [or when] a donkey [causes damage] with its load along its normal way?

   F.   Just as these [cases] are special, in that when they cause damage along their [normal] way, in ways fit for them, one pays full restitution, so too with any [animal] that causes damage along its [normal] way in a way fit for it one pays full restitution.

7.   A.   "… or sends out his livestock" (Exod. 22:4):

   B.   I only know [from this verse] concerning [the liability for damage caused by an ox's] tooth eating what it is fit to eat and [its] leg breaking [what it tramples upon] as it walks along its normal way. How does one know from Scripture [to include as liable the damage caused by] the tooth eating what it is not fit to eat and the leg breaking as it walks along in an abnormal way?

   C.   Scripture states, "… to graze in another's land" (Exod. 22:4), in order to include other things.

8.   A.   One might think in every [situation] one pays full restitution.

   B.   For it is a matter of logic:

   C.   Wasn't the ox that damages its companion [ox] a part of the general category [of the ox that causes damage]? Why did it [receive] separate [emphasis]? In order to draw an analogy from it: Just as the ox is special, in that when it causes damage in an abnormal way, if it is a *tam*[345] [the owner] pays half-damage restitution, but if it is a *mu'ad*[346] he pays full-damage restitution, so too in any situation where [any animal] damages in an abnormal way, if it is a *tam* [the owner] pays half-damage restitution, but if it is a *mu'ad* he pays full-damage restitution.

9.   A.   "… to graze in another's land" (Exod. 22:4):[347]

   B.   But not in the land belonging to the owner [of the livestock].

---

[340] A *kab* is a measurement of area equaling 75,000 square cubits.

[341] A *kor* is a measurement of area equaling approximately 417 square cubits.

[342] A *se'ah* is a measurement of area equaling 2,500 square cubits.

[343] Compare 5.C with m. Baba Qamma 6:21, t. Baba Qamma 6:21, and y. Baba Qamma 5b (Neus., 6:2:III.A–M).

[344] Compare 6.A–F with t. Baba Qamma 1:8, where these situations are stipulated specifically as causing liability for full restitution.

| | | |
|---|---|---|
| אין שמין בית קב מפני שהוא משביח ולא בית | C | |
| כור מפני שהוא פוגם אלא שמין בית סאה באותה | | |
| שדה כמה היתה יפה וכמה היא יפה. ◆ ושלח את | A | 6 |
| בעירו ◆ <אין לי אלא שן לאכול את הראוי לה מנין | B | |
| לרגל לשבר בדרך הילוכה ◆ ת״ל ושלח את בעירו> ◆ | C | |
| והלא השן בכלל הרגל היתה שנא׳ הסר מסוכתו והיה | D | |
| לבער וגומ׳ (ישע׳ ה ה) ◆ אין לי אלא זו בלבד מנין | E | |
| הזיקה כדרכה כדרך הילוכה חמור במשאוי שעליו | | |
| כדרך הילוכו ◆ מה אלו מיוחדין שהזיקו כדרכן ובראוי | F | |
| להן משלמין נזק שלם כך כל המזיק כדרכו ובראוי לו | | |
| משלם נזק שלם. ◆ ושלח את בעירה ◆ אין לי אלא שן | B/A | 7 |
| לאכל את הראוי לה ולרגל לשבר כדרך הילוכה מנין | | |
| לשן לאכל את שאין ראוי לה. ולרגל לשבר שלא | | |
| כדרך הילוכה ◆ ת״ל ובער בשדה אחר לרבות דברים | C | |
| אחרים ◆ יכול על הכל משלם נזק שלם ◆ ודין הוא ◆ והלא | C/B/A | 8 |
| שור שהזיק את חבירו בכלל היה ולמה יצא להקיש | | |
| אליו מה שור מיוחד שהזיק כדרכו בשאין ראוי לו | | |
| בתם משלם חצי נזק ובמועד נזק שלם כך כל דבר | | |
| שהזיק כדרכו בשאין ראוי לו בתם משלם חצי נזק ובמועד | | |
| נזק שלם. ◆ ובער בשדה אחר ◆ ולא בשדה בעל הבית ◆ | B/A | 9 |

---

[345] A *tam* ("innocent") is an animal that has not caused damage three times and whose owner, therefore, has not been informed of this and warned about his liability for future damage.

[346] A *mu'ad* ("forewarned") is an animal that has caused damage three times and whose owner has been informed of this and warned about his liability for future damage. If this animal causes damage again, the owner is fully liable for all indemnification.

[347] Compare 9.A–D with *Mekhilta de-Rabbi Ishmael*, Nezikin (H/R, 296:14–16; Laut., vol. 3, 109:17–21; Neus., LXXI:I:5.A–C).

C.  One might think [the owner would be liable if his livestock did damage to stacks of grain on his land that belong to another person] if the owner [of both the land and the damaging animal] gave him permission to stack [them there].

D.  Scripture states, [however,] "... to graze in another's land" (Exod. 22:4), [meaning,] in any event.

10.  A.  "... he must make restitution for the excellence of that field or vineyard" (Exod. 22:4):

B.  This teaches that one only estimates [and collects the value of the damage] from choice land.

C.  One might think if it damaged the worst-quality land, one would estimate [and collect the value of the damage] from the choice land.

D.  Scriptures states, [however,] "... *that* field" (Exod. 22:4), [meaning,] the field stated above.[348]

11.  A.  "... he must make restitution for the excellence of that field or vineyard" (Exod. 22:4):

B.  This teaches that one only estimates [and collects the value of the damage] from choice land.

C.  I only know [that this pertains] to this [situation] alone. How does one know from Scripture that whenever one pays a fine one only estimates [and collects the value of the damage] from the choice land?

D.  Scripture states, "... he must make restitution for the excellence of that field or vineyard" (Exod. 22:4)—this [serves as] a case precedent [requiring that] whenever one pays a fine, one only estimates [and collects the value of the damage] from the choice land.

12.  A.  "... he must make restitution for the excellence of that field or vineyard" (Exod. 22:4):

B.  This teaches that one only estimates [and collects the value of the damage] from the movable chattel.

[197]
C.  I only know [that this pertains] to this [situation] alone. How does one know from Scripture that whenever one pays a fine, one only estimates [and collects the value of the damage] from the movable chattel?

D.  Scripture states, "... he must make restitution for the excellence of that field or vineyard" (Exod. 22:4)—this [serves as] a case precedent [requiring that] whenever one pays a fine, one only estimates [and collects the value of the damage] from the movable chattel.

13.  A.  "... he must make restitution for the excellence of that field or vineyard" (Exod. 22:4):

B.  This teaches that one does not estimate [the value of the damages] using [that portion of] his vineyard that is destined to accrue, specifically, mortgaged property.

14.  A.  "... he must make restitution for the excellence of that field or vineyard" (Exod. 22:4):

B.  This teaches that one does not estimate [the value of the damage] using [that portion of] his vineyard that is destined to accrue, specifically, [that portion of the property devoted] to the Most High.

15.  A.  "... he must make restitution" (Exod. 22:4):

B.  In any event.

C.  As it says in Scripture, "... he must make restitution" (Exod. 22:4), [meaning,] he must make full restitution.

---

[348] I.e., from the worst-quality land.

| | | |
|---|---|---|
| יכול אף על פי שנתן לו רשות בעל הבית לגדוש ◆ | C | |
| ת״ל ובער בשדה אחר מכל מקום. ◆ מיטב שדהו | A 10 | D |
| <ו>מיטב כרמו ישלם. ◆ מלמד שאין שמין לו אלא מן | B | |
| העידית ◆ יכול אם הזיקה בזיבורית יהו שמין לו מן | C | |
| העידית ◆ ת״ל שדהו שדה האמ׳ למעלה (.) ◆ מיטב שדהו | A 11 | D |
| ומיטב כרמו ישלם ◆ מלמד שאין שמין <לו> אלא מן | B | |
| העידית ◆ אין לי אלא זה בלבד מנין לכל שמשלם קנס | C | |
| שאין שמין לו אלא מן העידית ◆ ת״ל מיטב שדהו | D | |
| ומיטב כרמו ישלם. זה בנין אב לכל המשלם קנס | | |
| שאין שמין לו אלא מן העידית ◆ מיטב שדהו ומיטב | A 12 | |
| כרמו ישלם ◆ מלמד שאין שמין לו אלא מן המטלטלין ◆ | B | |
| אין לי אלא זה בלבד מנין לכל המשלם קנס שאין | C | |
| שמין לו אלא מן המטלטלין ◆ ת״ל מיטב שדהו ומיטב | D | |
| כרמו ישלם זה בנין אב לכל המשלם קנס שאין שמין | | |
| לו אלא מן המטלטלין ◆ מיטב שדהו ומיטב כרמו | A 13 | |
| ישלם ◆ מלמד שאין שמין לו הראוי כבמוחזק כרמו | B | |
| פרט למשועבדין ◆ מיטב שדהו ומיטב כרמו ישלם ◆ | A 14 | |
| מלמד שאין שמין לו הראוי כמוחזק כרמו פרט לגבוה ◆ | B | |
| ישלם ◆ כל מקום ◆ שנא׳ ישלם משלם נזק שלם. סל׳ | C/B/A 15 | |

◆ פסו׳

LXXI:II

1. A. "When a fire is started (and spreads to thorns, so that stacked, standing, or a field of grain is consumed, he who started the fire must make restitution for the fire)" (Exod. 22:5):[349]

   B. [Scripture says this] to treat the unintentional [act] like the intentional.

   C. If one lights a fire within his [property] and the fire goes out and consumes [something] within [the property] of his neighbor, behold, he is liable.

   D. Just as this [situation] is special, in that it makes the unintentional [act] like the intentional, so too in any matter we treat the unintentional [act] like the intentional.

2. A. One might think if it passed over a river or a pond, by way of private [property] or by way of public [property], a distance of 16 cubits, or [over] a fence that is 4 cubits [high], he would be liable.[350]

   B. Scripture states, [however,] "... and spreads" (Exod. 22:5), [meaning, only if] it is [readily] accessible to it.

   C. One might think [he would be liable] only if it went along a pathway before it.

   D. Scripture states, [however,] "... thorns" (Exod. 22:5).

   E. Or perhaps [the significance of thorns] is that just as thorns grew on their own, I might think that I only know about [liability] for something [consumed] that grew on its own.

   F. Scripture states, [however,] "... stacked grain" (Exod. 22:5).

   G. Or perhaps [the significance of stacked grain] is that just as stacked grain is special, in that it is detached from the ground, I might think that I only know about [liability] for something [consumed] that is detached from the ground.

   H. Scripture states, [however,] "... standing grain" (Exod. 22:5).

   I. Or perhaps [the significance of all] these is that they are special in that they are apt to be burnt. I might think that I only know about [liability] for something [consumed] that is apt to be burnt. How does one know from Scripture [to include liability] if candles lapped[351] and scorched marble stones, or a heap of flax, or stones used to build furnaces?

   J. Scripture states, "... a field" (Exod. 22:5).

   K. I only know concerning things that were not kindled. How does one know from Scripture [to include liability] for something kindled, [for example,] if it consumed plaster furnaces or potter's furnaces?

   L. Scripture states, "... he who started the fire" (Exod. 22:5).

   M. I only know concerning something kindled. How does one know from Scripture [to include liability] for something extinguished, [for example,] if one had extinguished plaster furnaces or potter's furnaces?

   N. Scripture states, "... for the fire" (Exod. 22:5).

3. A. One might think [one must pay restitution for damage caused by his fire] even when someone stacks grain in his neighbor's field without his permission.[352]

   B. Scripture states, [however,] "... stacked, standing" (Exod. 22:5).

---

[349] Compare 1.A–D with *Mekhilta de-Rabbi Ishmael*, Nezikin (H/R, 297:1–4; Laut., vol. 3, 110:26–31; Neus., LXXI:II:1.A–H).

[350] Compare 2.A–N with m. Baba Qamma 6:4, y. Baba Qamma 5c (Neus., 6:4:I.A–III.D), b. Baba Qamma 60a (Neus., XX.B:Tractate Baba Qamma:6:4A–F:II.1.A–6:4:G–H:I.1.O), and b. Baba Qamma 61a (Neus., XX.B:Tractate Baba Qamma:6:4I:I.1.A–III.1.I).

[351] I translate here the word (Hebrew: ליחכה) that appears in the parallel to this tradition in y. Baba Qamma, as opposed to the word that appears here in the Firkovich manuscript, which makes no contextual sense.

LXXI:II

| | | |
|---|---|---|
| B/A | 1 | כי תצא אש ◆ לעשות את שאין מתכוין כמתכוין ◆ |
| C | | המדליק בתוך שלו יצאת אש ואכלה בתוך של חבירו |
| D | | הרי זה חייב ◆ מה זה מיוחד עשה את שאין מתכוין |
| | | כמתכוין כך כל דבר נעשה את שאין מתכוין כמתכוין ◆ |
| A | 2 | יכול עיברה נחל או שלולית דרך היחיד ודרך הרבים |
| B | | שש עשרה אמה וגדר שהוא גבוה ד' אמות יהא חייב ◆ |
| C | | ת״ל ומצאה עד שיהא מצוי לה ◆ יכול עד שיהא מכבש |
| E/D | | לפניה והולך ◆ ת״ל קוצים ◆ או מה קוצים שגדלו מחמת |
| F | | עצמן יכול אין לי אלא דבר שגדל מחמת עצמו ◆ ת״ל |
| G | | גדיש ◆ או מה גדיש מיוחד שהוא תלוש מן הקרקע |
| H | | יכול אין לי אלא דבר שתלוש מן הקרקע ◆ ת״ל קמה ◆ |
| I | | או מה אלו מיוחדין שהן ראויין לידלק יכול אין לי |
| | | אלא דבר שראוי לידלק מנין סיפספה נירות |
| | | וסיפספה מציב>ו<ת של[שיש] ומצבת שלפשתן |
| K/J | | ואבנים שמותקנות לו לכיבשנות ◆ ת״ל שדה ◆ אין לי |
| | | אלא דבר שלא הובער דבר שהובער מנין אכלה |
| L | | כיבשנות שלסיד כיבשנות של יוצרים ◆ ת״ל המבעיר ◆ |
| M | | אין לי אלא המבעיר המכבה מנין כיבת כיבשנות |
| N | A 3 | שלסיד כיבשנות של יוצרים ◆ ת״ל הבערה ◆ יכול אף |
| B | | המגדיש בתוך שדה חברו שלא ברשו' ◆ ת״ל גדיש וקמה ◆ |

[352] I.e., if one starts a fire that consumes stacks of grain in someone else's field, he might think he is liable to pay restitution for both stacks of grain that belong to the owner of the field and for stacks of grain that were placed in the field by the owner's neighbor without the owner's knowledge or permission. Compare 3.A–C with t. Baba Qamma 6:24.

C.   Just as standing [grain, for which he is liable] is [knowingly] a part of his[353] [property], so too [must] the stacked grain be [knowingly] a part of his [property].

4.    A.   "If one lights a fire within his own [property], and the fire goes out and consumes his stack
[198]       of grain and the stack of grain of his neighbor [placed there unknowingly and without the owner of the field's permission], behold, he is liable. If there were utensils in it and they caught fire, he is liable for the stack of grain, and he is liable for the utensils."—The words of R. Judah.[354]

B.   But the Sages say, "They view the space of the utensils as if it was filled with grain, and one pays him only for the price of the stack."

C.   R. Judah agrees with the Sages [that in the case where] one lends space [in his field] to his neighbor to stack grain, and he hides in it utensils, and they caught on fire, he pays only for the price of the stack.

### (Textual Source: Ms. Oxford Heb. D.)

D.   If it was a stack of wheat covered with barley or a stack of barley covered with wheat, one pays him only for the price of the barley.

### (Textual Source: Ms. Firkovich II A 268)

5.    A.   If, tied to a stack of wheat, there was an ox that caught on fire along with it [the wheat], or a donkey tied to a stack of wheat that caught on fire along with it, he is liable [for restitution payment for the ox or donkey, as well].[355]

B.   [But] if they were permitted [to be there by the owner of the field], he is exempt, as it says in Scripture, "... stacked, standing grain" (Exod. 22:5). Just as these are special, in that they cannot flee, these are exempt [from liability for restitution], because they are able to flee.

6.    A.   Because we have found[356] if an ox is delivered into the care of a deaf-mute, idiot, or minor, [the owner] is liable [for the damage the ox causes in their care], one might think even the one who causes the fire by means of a deaf-mute, idiot, or minor would be liable [for the damage it causes].[357]

B.   Scripture states, [however,] "When a man causes ... he must make restitution" (Exod. 22:4), [meaning,] the one who causes the damage must pay.

7.    A.   If one lights a fire within his [property] and the fire goes out and consumes [something] within [the property] of his neighbor, behold, he is liable, for it is normal for a courtyard to gather everything within it.[358]

B.   I only know about these [scenarios] alone. How does one know from Scripture to include [as liable] the one who strikes [something] with a hammer [causing sparks to fly out] and causes damage, whether in the public domain or in the private domain, or the one who blows a spark onto iron, which flies out and causes damage, whether in the private domain or in the public domain?

C.   Just as this [scenario in Exod. 22:5] is special, in that it holds liable the one who acts within his own [property] but causes damage in [property] that is not his, so too would anyone be liable who acts within his own [property] and causes damage in [property] that is not his.

---

[353] I.e., the owner of the field.
[354] Compare 4.A–D with m. Baba Qamma 6:5 and t. Baba Qamma 6:24.
[355] Compare 5.A–B with m. Baba Qamma 6:5.
[356] See m. Baba Qamma 6:1.
[357] Compare 6.A–B with m. Baba Qamma 6:2 and 6:4.
[358] Compare 7.A–G with m. Baba Qamma 6:6 and t. Baba Qamma 6:22.

◆ מה קמה בתוך שלו אף גדיש בתוך שלו C

המדליק בתוך שלו יצאת אש ואכלה גדישו וגדיש A 4
ש<לחברו הרי זה חייב היה בו כלים ודלקו חייב על

הגדיש וחייב על הכלים דברי ר' יהודה ◆ וחכמים אומ' B
רואין את מקום הכלים כאילו מלא תבואה ואין

משלמין לו אלא דמי גדיש בלבד ◆ מודה ר' יהודה C
לחכמ' במשאיל מקום לחבירו להגדיש והטמין (והיו)

בו כלים ודלקו ואין משלם אלא דמי גדיש בלבד ◆

<היה גדיש חיטין ומחופה שעורין או שעורין ומחופה D

חיטין אין משלם לו אלא דמי שעורין בלבד> ◆ היה Λ 5
שור קשור בגדיש ודלק(ו) עמו או חמור קשור בגדיש

ודלק עמו חייב ◆ אם היו מותרין פטור שנא' גדיש B
וקמה מה אלו מיוחדין שאינן יכולין לברח יצאו אלו

שהן יכולין לברוח ◆ לפי שמצינו בשור שאם מסרו A 6
לחרש שוטה וקטן חייב יכול אף השולח את הבעירה

ביד חרש שוטה וקטן יהא חייב ◆ ת"ל כי יבער ישלם B
המבעיר חייב לשלם. ◆ המדליק בתוך שלו יצאת אש A 7

ואכלה בתוך של חבירו הרי זה חייב שכן דרך חצר

להיות מכנס את הכל לתוכה ◆ אין לי אלא אלו בלבד B
מנין המכה בפטיש והזיק בין ברשות הרבים ובין

ברשות היחיד ונופח שהניח גץ על גבי ברזל יצא והזיק

בין ברש' היה' בין ברשות הרב' ◆ מה זה מיוחד שע<ו>שה C
בתוך שלו ומזיק בתוך שאינו שלו הרי זה חייב כך

כל העושה בתוך שלו ומזיק בתוך שאינו שלו יהא חייב ◆

D.    I only know about these [scenarios] alone. How does one know from Scripture that when one [person] brings the flame and one [other person] brings the wood, or when one [person] brings the wood and one [other person] brings the flame, the last [person to act] is liable?

E.    Scripture states, "When a man causes ... he must make restitution" (Exod. 22:4), [meaning,] the one who causes the damage is liable to pay.

F.    I only know about these [scenarios] alone. How does one know from Scripture that when one [person] brings the wood and one [other person] brings the flame, or when one [person] brings the flame and one [other person] brings the wood, and someone else comes along and, there being enough to blow ablaze, blows it ablaze, he is the one liable?

G.    Scripture states, "When a man causes ... he must make restitution" (Exod. 22:4), [meaning,] the one who causes the damage is liable to pay.

8.    A.    How does one know from Scripture that [included as liable for damage restitution is]
[199]    the [damage-causing quality] of the ox that is not like that of the grazing animal, as well as the [damage-causing quality] of the grazing animal that is not like that of the ox? And [even though the damage-causing quality] of each of these, which are alive, is not like that of fire, which is not alive [it too is included as liable for damage restitution]? And [even though the damage-causing quality] of each of these [three], which tend to do damage while moving along, is like the pit, whose nature is not to do damage while moving along [it too is included as liable for damage restitution]?[359]

B.    Scripture states, "When a man causes ... he must make restitution" (Exod. 22:4), [meaning,] the one who causes the damage is liable to pay.

C.    Based on this they said: There are four primary categories of damages—the ox, the pit, the grazing animal, and fire.

*Chapter Seventy-Two*

(Textual Source: Ms. Firkovich II A 268)

LXXII:I

1.    A.    "When a man gives (money or utensils to his companion for safekeeping, and they are stolen from the man's house, if the thief is caught, he shall pay double)" (Exod. 22:6):[360]

B.    When a child gives, it amounts to nothing.

C.    I only know [this] concerning the instance when as a child he gives [something for safekeeping] and brings charges. How does one know from Scripture [that it also amounts to nothing] in the instance when as a child he gives [something for safekeeping] but as an adult brings charges?

D.    As it says in Scripture, "... the case of the two parties shall come before God" (Exod. 22:8), [meaning,] only when [the situation] is the same at the time of the charges as at the time of the giving [of the item for safekeeping].

2.    A.    "... a man" (Exod. 22:6):

B.    This excludes [items dedicated to] God.[361]

C.    I only know [this] concerning the instance when one gives something that is dedicated to the Temple. How does one know from Scripture [to exclude as well] the instance when one gives something to him [for safekeeping] that is dedicated to the Temple?

---

[359] Compare 8.A–C with *Mekhilta de-Rabbi Ishmael*, Nezikin (H/R, 297:16–298:10; Laut., vol. 3, 112:52–113:70; Neus., LXXI:II:6.A–8.E); and m. Baba Kamma 6:1.
[360] Compare 1.A–D with y. Shebuot 37a (Neus., 6:5:I.A–F) and b. Baba Qamma 102b (Neus., XX.C:Tractate Baba Qamma:9:7A–F:IV.11.B).
[361] I.e., something dedicated to the Temple.

אין לי אלא אלו בלבד מנין אחד הביא את האור     D

ואחד הביא את העצים אחד הביא את העצים ואחד

הביא את האור מנין שאחרון ‹אחרון חיב • ת״ל› כי     E

יבער ישלם המבעיר חייב לשלם • אין לי אלא     F

אלו בלבד מנין אחד הביא את העצים ואחד הביא

את האור ואחד הביא את האור ואחד הביא את

העצים ‹ובא› אחר וניבח ויש בו כדי לנבח הרי הוא

חייב • ת״ל כי יבער ישלם המבעיר חייב לשלם •     G

מנין לא השור כהרי המבעה ולא המבעה כהרי השור ולא     A   8

זה וזה שיש בהן רוח חיים [כהרי האש שאין בה רוח

חיים] ולא זה וזה שדרכן לילך ולהזיק כהרי הבור

שאין דרכו לילך ולהזיק • ת״ל כי יבער ישלם המבעיר     B

חייב לשלם • מיכן אמרו ארבעה הן אבות נזיקים השור     C

והבור המבעה וההבער. סל׳ פסו׳ •

                                                                      LXXII:I

כי יתן איש. • אין מתנת קטן כלום • אין לי אלא בזמן     C/B/A   1

שנתן קטן ותבע קטן נתן קטן ותבע גדול מנין • שנאמ׳     D

עד האלהים יבא דבר שניהם (שמ׳ כב ח) עד שתהא

שעת תביעה כשעת נתינה שוין. • איש • פרט לגבוה • אין     C/B/A   2

לי אלא בזמן שנתן להקדש נתן לו הקדש מנין •

D.  Scripture states, "… he has not laid hands on the other's property" (Exod. 22:7).

E.  I only know [this] concerning the instance when one gives something to him that is dedicated to God or when he gives [for safekeeping] something that is dedicated to the Temple? How does one know from Scripture [to exclude as well when] he gives something devoted to the Temple to the temple treasurer, who then redeemed it, or ordinary objects that he then sanctified to the Temple?

F.  Scripture states, "… the two of them shall be brought before God" (Exod. 22:8), [meaning,] when [the situation] is the same at the time of the charges as at the time of the giving [of the item for safekeeping].

3.  A.  "… to his companion" (Exod. 22:6):

B.  This excludes others.

C.  "… to his companion" (Exod. 22:6):

D.  This excludes the resident alien.

E.  I only know [this] concerning the instance when one gives [something for safekeeping] to a non-Jew. How does one know from Scripture [to exclude as well when] the non-Jew gives [something for safekeeping] to him?

F.  Scripture states, "… that he has not laid hands on the other's property" (Exod. 22:7).

G.  I only know [this] concerning the instance when one gives [something for safekeeping] to a non-Jew or when a non-Jew gives him [something for safekeeping]. How does one know from Scripture [to exclude as well when] one gives [something for safekeeping] to a non-Jew who [afterward] converted or [when] a non-Jew gives him [something for safekeeping] and afterward converted.

H.  Scripture states, "… (the two of them shall be brought) before God" (Exod. 22:8), [meaning,] only when [the situation] is the same at the time of the charges as at the time of the giving [of the item for safekeeping].

4.  A.  "'… money' (Exod. 22:6):

B.  "Just as money [is made] from [materials] that are formed in the earth, I might think I should exclude utensils [made] from [materials] found in the sea.

C.  "Scripture states, [however,] '… or utensils' (Exod. 22:6)."—The words of R. Judah.

5.  A.  "Because we have found that one [can be determined to be] liable through a legal claim or through a confession of guilt, [then one might think that] just as [the case is litigated for] a confession [for something worth] a *perutah*, so too [is the case litigated for] a legal claim [for something worth] a *perutah*.[362]

B.  "Scripture states, [however,] '… money' (Exod. 22:6), [meaning, at least] a *ma'ah* of silver."—The words of the House of Shammai.

C.  But Beit Hillel says, "[At least] two [*ma'ahs*] of silver."

6.  A.  Since it says in Scripture, "… his companion" (Exod. 22:6), this excludes [items dedicated to] God.

[200]  B.  I might think I should exclude tithe money.

C.  Scripture states, [however,] "… money (or utensils) to keep" (Exod. 22:6), [meaning, items]

---

[362] Compare 5.A–C with m. Shebuot 6:1 and y. Shebuot 36d (Neus., 6:1:I.A–II.C).

| | | |
|---|---|---|
| ת״ל אם לא שלח ידו במלאכת רעהו (שם ז) ◆ אין לי אלא | E/D | |
| בזמן שנתן לו הקדש ונתן להקדש נתן לגיזבר הקדש | | |
| ופדאו וחולין והקדישן מנין ◆ ת״ל עד האלהים יבא דבר | F | |
| שניהם כשתהא שעת תביעה לשעת נתינה שווה. ◆ רעהו ◆ | A | 3 |
| פרט לאחרין. ◆ רעהו. ◆ פרט לגר תושב ◆ אין לי אלא | E/D/C/B | |
| בזמן שנתן לגוי נתן לו ‹ה›גוי מנין ◆ ת״ל אם לא שלח | F | |
| ידו במלאכת רעהו ◆ אין לי אלא בזמן שנתן לגוי ונתן | G | |
| לו הגוי מנין נתן לגוי ונתגייר או שנתן לו הגוי ואחר | | |
| כך נתגייר ◆ ת״ל עד האלהים עד שתהא שעת תביעה | H | |
| כשעת נתינה שוין. ◆ כסף ◆ מה כסף מן הגדול בארץ יכול | B/A | 4 |
| שני מוצ‹י›א את כלי הים שאינן מן הגדול בארץ ◆ ת״ל | C | |
| או כלים דברי ר׳ יהודה ◆ לפי שמצינו שחייב בטענה | A | 5 |
| חייב בהודאה מה הודאה בשוה פרוטה ת״ל כסף אף | | |
| הטענה בשוה פרוטה ◆ ת״ל כסף מעה כסף דברי בית | B | |
| שמאי ◆ ובית הלל אומ׳ שתי כסף ◆ מכלל שנא׳ רעהו | A 6 | C |
| פרט לגבוה ◆ יכול שני מוצ‹י›א כסף מעשר ◆ ת״ל | C/B | |
| כסף לשמר ולא לאבד לשמר ולא לחלק לשמר ולא | | |

not to destroy, "to keep" [meaning, items] not to distribute, " to keep" [meaning, items] not to throw away, "to keep" [meaning, items] not to give as a gift.[363]

7. A. "... and they are stolen from the man's

(Textual Source: Midrash ha-Gadol)

house" (Exod. 22:6):[364]

  B. And not from the top of his roof. This tells [you] that [even] if he did not guard [it] the way one normally guards [it], he is [still] liable.

8. A. "... and they are stolen from the man's

(Textual Source: Ms. Firkovich II A 268)

house" (Exod. 22:6):[365]

  B. And not from the thief's house, [meaning,] the one who steals [something] after it was stolen does not pay the double payment, and the one who slaughters and sells [an animal] after it was stolen does not pay the four- or five-fold payment.

9. A. "... if the thief is caught" (Exod. 22:6):[366]

  B. Why do I need [Scripture to state this]? Has it not already been said, "But if what he stole ... is found (alive) in his possession, (he shall pay double)" (Exod. 22:3)?

  C. Why does Scripture state, "... if the thief is caught" (Exod. 22:6)? This tells [you] that if the person charged with guarding [it] paid [the owner for its theft], and afterward the thief is found, he[367] must pay the double and four- or five-fold payments to the second [person].[368]

10. A. R. Ishmael says, "'... if the thief is caught' (Exod. 22:6):

  B. "Why do I need [Scripture to state this]? Has it not already been said, 'But if what he stole ... is found (alive) in his possession' (Exod. 22:3)?

  C. "Why does Scripture state, '... if the thief is caught' (Exod. 22:6)?

  D. "[This pertains] if they find witnesses against the owner of the house, who [falsely] made the claim of thievery.[369]

  E. "One might think he[370] should pay [restitution] based on his own [confession]. For it is a matter of logic: One is liable [in the situation described] here, and one is liable as a thief [in the situation described in Exod. 22:3]. Just as we have found with that thief does not pay based on his own [confession], so too this one should not pay based on his own [confession].

  F. "No! If you speak of the thief, he pays the double-restitution payment. Will you say the same with this one, who does not pay the double-restitution payment?

  G. "So since he does not pay the double-restitution payment, let him pay on his own [testimony]!

  H. "Scripture states, [however,] '... (if the thief) is caught' (Exod. 22:6), and 'caught' always means by means of witnesses.

---

[363] Compare 6.C with y. Baba Qamma 38b (Neus., 8:1:II.A) and b. Baba Qamma 93a (Neus., XX.C:Tractate Baba Qamma:8:7:III.1.A–G).

[364] Compare 7.A–B with y. Baba Qamma 38b (Neus., 8:1:II.C).

[365] Compare 8.A–B with *Mekhilta de-Rabbi Ishmael*, Nezikin (H/R, 299:4–8; Laut., vol. 3, 114:11–18; Neus., LXXII:I:4.A–I); and b. Baba Qamma 69b (Neus., XX.B:Tractate Baba Qamma:7:1:IV.5.H).

[366] Compare 9.A–C with m. Baba Metzia 3:1.

[367] I.e., the thief.

[368] I.e., the person entrusted with guarding the items.

[369] The text here appears to read the clause "if the thief is caught" in Exod. 22:6 as "if he is found to be the thief."

[370] I.e., the custodian of an item who claims falsely that the item was stolen.

| | |
|---|---|
| ◆ ‹האיש | להשליך לשמר ולא ליתן במתנה. ◆ וגנב מבית ‹האיש ◆ |
| B | ולא מראש גגו מגיד שאם לא שימר כדרך שומרין |
| B/A | חייב. ◆ וגנב מבית› האיש ◆ ולא מבית הגנב אין שגונב |
| | אחר גונב משלם תשלומי כפל ולא הטובח ומוכר |
| B/A | אחר הגנ]ב[ משלם תשלומי ד׳ וה׳. ◆ אם ימצא הגנב ◆ מה |
| | אני צריך והלא כ]בר[ נאמר אם המצא תמצא בידו |
| C | הגנבה (שמ׳ כב ג) ◆ מה ת״ל אם ימצא הגנב מגיד שאם |
| | שלם לבעל הפקדון ואחר כך נמצא גנב משלם |
| A | תשלומי כפל וד׳ וה׳ לשני ◆ ר׳ ישמעאל אומ׳ אם ימצא |
| B | הגנב ◆ מה אני צריך והלא כבר נאמר אם המצא תמצא |
| D/C | בידו הגנבה (שם) ◆ מה ת״ל אם ימצא הגנב ◆ אם |
| E | ימצא‹ו› לו עדים לבעל הבית שטענו טענת גנב ◆ יכול |
| | ישלם על פי עצמו ודין הוא חייב כן וחייב בגנב מה |
| | מצינו בגנב אין משלם על פי עצמו אף זה לא ישלם |
| F | על פי עצמו ◆ לא אם אמרת בגנב שמשלם תשלומי |
| G | כפל תאמר בזה שאין משלם תשלומי כפל ◆ הואיל |
| | ואין משלים תשלומי כפל ישלם על פי עצמו ◆ |
| H | ת״ל ימצא אין ימצא בכל מקום אלא עדים ◆ |

I.  "One might think he should pay [either] before [taking] an oath [that he didn't steal it] or after [taking] an oath [that he didn't steal it].

J.  "For it is a matter of logic: One is liable [in the situation described] here and one is liable as a thief [in the situation described in Exod. 22:3]. Just as we have found that the thief pays [either] before [taking] an oath or after [taking] an oath, so too this one should pay [either] before [taking] an oath or after [taking] an oath.

K.  "Or [one could reason using] an additional *kal va-ḥomer:* If the thief, who does not pay the one-fifth [surcharge] or [bring] the guilt offering,[371] pays [either] before an oath or after an oath, then isn't it logical that this one, who does pay the one-fifth [surcharge] and [brings] the guilt offering, should pay [either] before an oath or after an oath?

L.  "Scripture states, [however,] 'But if what he stole is found in his possession' (Exod. 22:3). When is something designated as stolen? After an oath."

11.  A.  Another interpretation:

B.  "He whom God declares guilty" (Exod. 22:8):

C.  When is one declared guilty [for the double-restitution payment]? One should say after [taking] an oath [that he didn't *steal* the object entrusted in his care].

D.  One might think one would be liable [for the double-restitution payment] on account of making a [false] claim [that an item entrusted in his care] was *lost.*

[201]  E.  But it is a matter of logic: One is liable here [as an unpaid guardian] and one is liable, as a paid guardian. Just as we have found that the paid guardian is not liable [for the double-restitution payment] on account of making a [false] claim [that an item entrusted in his care] was lost, so too this one should not be liable on account of making a [false] claim [that an item entrusted in his care] was lost.

F.  Or [one could reason using] an additional *kal va-ḥomer:* If the paid guardian, who must pay [restitution for an item entrusted in his care] that was stolen or lost, is not liable [for the double-restitution payment] on account of making a [false] claim [that an item entrusted in his care] was lost, then isn't it logical that this one, who does not pay [restitution for an item entrusted in his care] that was stolen or lost, should not be liable [for the double-restitution payment] on account of making a [false] claim [that an item entrusted in his care] was lost?

G.  No! If you speak of the paid guardian, who [never] pays the double payment, will you say [the same] with this one, who does pay the double payment?

H.  [Thus] Scripture states, "... if the thief is caught" (Exod. 22:6), [meaning,] he is liable [for the double-restitution payment] on account of making a [false] claim [that an item entrusted in his care] was stolen, but he is not liable [for it] on account of making a [false] claim [that an item entrusted in his care] was lost.

I.  One might think if [the object was actually] lost or stolen from him he would be liable [for the double payment].

J.  For it is a matter of logic: One is liable here [as an unpaid guardian], and one is liable as a paid guardian. Just as we have found that the paid guardian pays for loss and thievery, so too this one should pay for loss and thievery.

K.  Or [one could reason using] an additional *kal va-ḥomer:* If the paid guardian, who does not pay the double-restitution payment, pays for loss and thievery, then isn't it logical

יכול ישלם לפני שבועה ולאחר שבועה ◆ ודין הוא חייב כן J/I

וחייב בגנב מה מצינו בגנב משלם לפני שבועה ולאחר

שבועה אף זה ישלם לפני שבועה ולאחר שבועה ◆ ועוד K

קל וחומר ומה גנב שאין משלם חומש ואשם משלם

לפני שבועה ולאחר שבועה זה שמשלם חומש ואשם

אינו דין שישלם לפני שבועה ולאחר שבועה ◆ ת״ל אם L

המצא תמצא בידו הגנבה (שם) אמתי גניבה מתיחדת

לאחר שבועה. ◆ ד״א ◆ אשר ירשיעון אלהים (שם ח) ◆ B/A    11

אימתי נקרא רשע הוי אומ׳ לאחר שבועה ◆ יכול יהא D/C

חייב על טענת אבד ◆ ודין הוא חייב כאן וחייב בנושא E

שכר מה מצינו בנושא שכר אינו חייב על טענת אבד

אף זה לא יהא חייב על טענת אבד. ◆ ועוד קל וחומר F

ומה נושא שכר שמשלם אבדה וגנבה אינו חייב על

טענת אבד זה שאין משלם אבדה וגנבה אינו דין

שלא יהא חייב על טענת אבד ◆ לא אם אמרת בנושא G

שכר שאין משלם תשלומי כפל תאמר בזה שמשלם

תשלומי כפל ◆ ת״ל אם ימצא הגנב על טענת גניבה H

הוא חייב ואינו חייב על טענת אבד ◆ יכול אם איבדו או I

שנגנבו אצלו יהא חייב ◆ ודין הוא חייב כן וחייב בנושא J

שכר מה מצינו בנושא שכר משלם אבדה וגניבה אף

זה ישלם אבדה וגניבה ◆ ועוד קל וחומר מה נושא שכר K

שאין משלם תשלומי כפל משלם גניבה ואבדה זה

that this one, who does pay the double-restitution payment, should pay for loss and thievery?

L.  Scripture states, [however,] "... that he has not laid hands on the other's property" (Exod. 22:7).

M.  One might think that he should pay the double-restitution payment for laying [his] hand [on the property].

N.  But it is a matter of logic: One is liable here [as an unpaid guardian], and one is liable as a paid guardian. Just as we have found that the paid guardian does not pay the double-restitution payment for laying [his] hand [on the property], so too this one should not pay the double-restitution payment for laying [his] hand [on the property].

O.  Or [one could reason using] an additional *kal va-ḥomer*: If the paid guardian, who pays for loss and thievery, does not pay the double-restitution payment for laying [his] hand [on the property], then isn't it logical that this one, who does not pay for loss and thievery, should not pay the double-restitution payment for laying [his] hand [on the property]?

P.  No! If you speak of the paid guardian, who [never] pays the double payment, will you say [the same] with this one, who does pay the double payment?

Q.  Scripture states, [however,] "But if what he stole is found in his possession" (Exod. 22:3), [meaning,] for the thievery he pays the double-restitution payment, but he does not pay the double-restitution payment for laying [his] hand [on the property].

## LXXII:II

1.  A.  "If the thief is not caught, (the owner of the house shall draw near and depose before God that he has not laid hands on the other's property)" (Exod. 22:7):

    B.  [Meaning,] if they do not find witnesses [who can testify] about the owner of the house that he made a [false] claim [that an item entrusted in his care] was stolen.

2.  A.  "... the owner of the house shall draw near and depose before God" (Exod. 22:7):

    B.  By an oath.

    C.  Or one might think by means of payment.

    D.  Scripture states, [however,] "... that he has not laid hands on the other's property" (Exod. 22:7).

3.  A.  Another interpretation:[372]

    B.  Scripture states here, "draw near," and Scripture states elsewhere, "draw near."[373] Just as "draw near" stated elsewhere [means by] an oath, so too does "draw near" stated here [mean by] an oath.

4.  A.  "... that he has not laid hands on the other's property" (Exod. 22:7):

    B.  [If] he removed utensils from the cattle feed basket and removed cattle and rode upon it, he would be liable.

    C.  As it says in Scripture, "... that he has not laid hands on the other's property" (Exod. 22:7).

    D.  "Laid" [means] in any manner.

5.  A.  If he intended to lay [his] hand on his companion's item in his care, Beit Shammai holds
[202]    him liable, but Beit Hillel releases him from liability.[374]

---

[372] Compare 3.A–B with *Mekhilta de-Rabbi Ishmael*, Nezikin (H/R, 300:6–12; Laut., vol. 3, 116:41–117:48; Neus., LXXII:I:8.A–J).

[373] The precise scriptural reference here is uncertain. Epstein suggests Mal. 3:5.

שמשלם תשלומי כפל אינו דין שישלם אבידה וגניבה ◆

◆ ת״ל אם לא שלח ידו במלאכת רעהו (שמ׳ כב ז) ◆ יכול | M/L

ישלם תשלומי כפל על שליחות יד ◆ ודין הוא חייב כן | N

וחייב בנושא שכר מה מצינו בנושא שכר אין משלם

תשלומי כפל על שליחות יד אף זה לא ישלם תשלומי

כפל על שליחות יד. ◆ ועוד קל וחומר ומה נושא שכר | O

שמשלם אבדה וגניבה אין משלם תשלו׳ כפל על

שליחות יד זה שאין משלם אבדה וגניבה אינו דין

שלא ישלם תשלומי כפל על שליחות יד ◆ לא אם | P

אמרתה בנושא שכר שאין משלם (אבדה וגנבה אינו

דין שמשלם) תשלומי כפל תאמר בזה שמשלם

תשלומי כפל ◆ ת״ל אם המצא תמצא בידו הגנבה (שם | Q

ג) על הגנבה משלם תשלומי כפל ואין משלם תשלומי

כפל על שליחות יד. סל׳ פסו׳ ◆

LXXII:II

ואם לא ימצא הגנב ◆ אם לא ימצאו לו עדים לבעל | B/A | 1

הבית שטענו טענת גנב(ו) ◆ ונקרב בעל הבית אל | A | 2

האלהים ◆ לשבועה ◆ או יכול לתשלומין ◆ ת״ל אם לא | D/C/B

שלח ידו במלאכת רעה<ו> ◆ ד״א> ◆ נאמ׳ כן קריבה ונאמ׳ | B/A | 3

להלן קריבה מה קריבה האמ׳ להלן שבועה אף

קריבה האמ׳ כן שבועה. ◆ אם לא שלח ידו במלאכת | A | 4

רעהו. ◆ מה אני צריך והלא בידו היית מה ת״ל אם לא | B

שלח ידו במלאכת רעהו הוציא כלים מתחת קלצטר

והוציא בהמה ורכב עליה חייב ◆ שנא׳ אם לא שלח ידו | C

במלאכת רעהו ◆ שלח זה מכל מקום ◆ חישב לשלוח יד | A 5 | D

בפקדונו שלחברו בית שמאי מחייבין ובית הלל פוטרין ◆

---

[374] Compare 5.A–E with *Mekhilta de-Rabbi Ishmael*, Nezikin (H/R, 300:12–15; Laut., vol. 3, 117:49–55; Neus., LXXII:I:9.A–H); y. Baba Metzia 9b (3:9:II.A–D); and b. Baba Metzia 44a (Neus., XXIIB:Tractate Baba Mesia:3:12:I.1.A–H).

B.  Beit Shammai says, "'In all charges of misappropriation' (Exod. 22:8), [which] makes intention like action."

C.  But Beit Hillel says, "'... that he has not laid hands on the other's property' (Exod. 22:7), [which] tells that he is not liable unless he lays his hand [on the property]."

D.  If so, why does Scripture state, "In all charges of misappropriation" (Exod. 22:8)? Because one might think that one only knows [from Exod. 22:7 that the liability is incurred] if he [is the one who lays his hand on his companion's property]. How does one know from Scripture to include [liability for such an action by] his servant or his agent?

E.  Scripture states, "In all charges of misappropriation" (Exod. 22:8).

6.    A.  If one tilted the jar and took from it a quarter *log* [of the wine it contained], and it broke, he only pays for the quarter *log*.[375]

B.  As it says in Scripture, "In all charges of misappropriation" (Exod. 22:8), [meaning,] for that which he [intentionally] misappropriated.

C.  If he moved it from place to place for his own sake and it broke in his hand, he is liable. [If he moved it] for its sake [and it broke in his hand], he is exempt. [If it broke] when he placed it down, whether [moving it] for his sake or for its sake, he is exempt. As it says in Scripture, "... misappropriation" (Exod. 22:8). This [last example] is exempt [from liability] because it is not misappropriation.

## LXXII:III

1.    A.  "In all charges of misappropriation—pertaining to an ox, an ass, a sheep, a garment, (or any other loss, whereof one party alleges, 'This is it'—the case of the two of them shall come before God. He whom God declares guilty shall pay double to the other)" (Exod. 22:8):

B.  Let Scripture state [only] "an ox" and "misappropriation," and everything else could be included in the general principle![376]

C.  If so, I might say that just as this [ox] is special, in that its first-born is [consecrated and offered up] on the altar, so too, as I extend [the general principle], I should only include an animal whose first-born is [consecrated and offered up] on the altar.

D.  [Now, just] which [other animal might I think] this [possibly could] be? A sheep!

E.  [But] Scripture states, "... a sheep" (Exod. 22:8). A sheep is already [specifically] mentioned!

F.  Why does Scripture state, "... misappropriation" (Exod. 22:8)? [In order] to include [any] other item.

G.  [Then] let Scripture state "ox" and "sheep" and "ass" and "misappropriation," and everything else could be included in the general principle!

H.  If so, I might say that just as these [animals] are special, in that their first-born [are given] to the priests, so too, as I extend [the general principle], I should only include an animal whose first-born is [given] to the priests.

I.  [Now, just] which [other animal might I think] this [possibly could] be? An ass!

J.  [But] Scripture states, "... an ass" (Exod. 22:8). An ass is already [specifically] mentioned!

K.  Why does Scripture state, "... misappropriation" (Exod. 22:3)? [In order] to include [any] other item.

---

[375] Compare 6.A–C with m. Baba Metzia 3:9 and 3:12.

[376] I.e., why did Scripture state specifically an ox, an ass, a sheep, and a garment when it could have simply established the general principle by mentioning "an ox" and "misappropriation"?

בית שמאי אומ' על כל דבר פשע (שמ' כב ח)        B

לעשות מחשבה כמעשה ◆ ובית הלל אומ' אם לא שלח        C

ידו במלאכת רעהו מגיד שאינו חייב עד שישלח ידו ◆

אם כן למה נאמ' על כל דבר פשע שיכול אין לי אלא        D

הוא מנין לרבות עבדו ושלוחו ◆ ת"ל על כל דבר פשע ◆        E

חיטא את החבית נטל ממנה רביעית ונשברה אין        A        6

משלם אלא רביעית ◆ שנא' על פשע על מה <ש<פשע

עקרה משלם דמי כולה שנא' על כל דבר פשע על כל

מה שפשע ◆ עקרה ממקום למקום ונשברה בתוך ידו        C

לצורכו חייב לצורכה פטור ואם משהניחה בין לצורכו

בין לצורכה פטור שנא' פשע יצא זה שלא פשע. סל'

פסו' ◆

LXXII:III

על כל דבר פשע על שור על חמור על שלמה ◆        A        1

יאמר שור ופשע והכל בכלל ◆ אילו כן הייתי אומ' מה        C/B

זה מיוחד שיש בו בכורה למזבח ואף כשאני מרבה לא

ארבה אלא דבר שיש בו בכורה למזבח ◆ ואי זה זה        D

שה ◆ ת"ל ת"ל שה כבר שה אמור ◆ מה ת"ל פשע לרבות        F/E

דבר אחר ◆ יאמר שור ושה (וחמור) ופשע והכל בכלל ◆        G

אילו כן הייתי אומ' מה <זה> מיוחד שיש בו בכורה        H

לכהנים אף כשאני מרבה איני מרבה אלא דבר שיש בו

בכורה לכהנים (ושה וחמור ופשע). ◆ ואי זה זה חמור        I

ת"ל חמור כבר חמור אמר ◆ מה ת"ל פשע לרבות דבר אחר. ◆        K/J

L.   [Then] let Scripture state "ox" and "sheep" and "ass" and "misappropriation," and everything else could be included in the general principle.

M.   If so, I might say that just as these [animals] are special, in that they are alive, so too, as I extend [the general principle], I should only include something that is alive.

N.   [But] Scripture states, "… a garment" (Exod. 22:8).

2.   A.   One might think [one should include in the general principle of items in Exod. 22:8] even the immovable property.

B.   Scripture states, [however,] "… an ox, an ass, a sheep" (Exod. 22:8). Just as these are special, in that they have bone fractures, [can be held in] captivity, and [will experience] death, I should exclude the immovable property, which cannot have bone fractures, [cannot be held in] captivity, and [will not experience] death.

C.   But still, I should not exclude the servants, which have bone fractures, [can be held in] captivity, and [will experience] death!

[203]   D.   Scripture states, [however,] "… an ox, an ass, a sheep" (Exod. 22:8). Just as these are special, in that [the responsibility] for watching over them [naturally] is your responsibility,[377] I should exclude the servants, for whom [the responsibility] for watching over them is not [naturally] your responsibility.

E.   But still, I should not exclude the legal documents, for which [the responsibility] for watching over them is your responsibility!

F.   Scripture states, [however,] "… an ox, an ass, a sheep" (Exod. 22:8). Just as these are special, in that [the responsibility] for watching over them is your responsibility [and they are] entirely yours [in actual substance], excluded are the legal documents, in which you have only proof [of ownership].

3.   A.   One might think one would be liable [over an item] worth less than a *perutah*.

B.   Scripture states, [however,] "… a garment" (Exod. 22:8). Just as a garment is special, in that it is worth a *perutah* and one must announce [it as a lost item], so too is one liable [only] for anything that has the value of a *perutah* and that one must announce [as a lost item].

4.   A.   If one should make a claim against another for an ox and an ass and a sheep, and he[378] admitted [only to misappropriating] one of them, behold, he is liable.

B.   As it says in Scripture, "… an ox … or any other loss whereof one party alleges 'This is it,'" [and it says,] "… an ass … or any other loss whereof one party alleges 'This is it,'" [and it says,] "… a sheep … or any other loss whereof one party alleges 'This is it'" (Exod. 22:8).

C.   [But] if one should make a claim against another for an ox, and he admitted to [misappropriating] a sheep, [or he sued him] for a sheep, and he admitted to an ox, he is exempt.

D.   What reason have you to include this [first example in 4.A–B in liability] but to exclude this [second example in 4.C]?

E.   I include this [first example] because he admitted [to misappropriating at least] part of the claim [against him], and I exclude this [second example] because he did not admit to part of the claim [against him].

5.   A.   [If one should make a claim against another saying,] "You have a *maneh* of mine in your possession," [but the person replies,] "I have nothing of yours in my possession," [or he replies,] "I had a *maneh* of yours in my possession, but I gave it [back] to you," [or if one should

---

[377] I.e., as animals, they require, by their very nature, to be cared for, watched over, etc.
[378] I.e., the one being sued.

| | | |
|---|---|---|
| M/L | | יאמר [שור ו]שה וחמור ופשע והכל בכלל ◆ אילו |
| | | כן (כן) הייתי אומ' מה אלו מיוחדין שיש בהן רוח |
| | | חיים אף כשאני מרבה איני מרבה אלא דבר שיש בו |
| N | B/A 2 | רוח חיים ת"ל שלמה ◆ יכול אף הקרקעות ◆ ת"ל על |
| | | שור על חמור על שה מה אלו מיוחדין שיש בהן שבר |
| | | שביה ומיתה מוציא אני את הקרקעות שאין בהן |
| C | | שבר שביה ומיתה ◆ ועדאן לא אוציא את העבדים שיש |
| D | | בהן שבר שביה ומיתה ◆ ת"ל על שור על חמור על שה |
| | | מה אלו מיוחדין שישמירתן עליך יצאו עבדים שאין |
| | | שמירתן עליך מוציא אני את העבדים שאין שמירתן |
| E | | עליך ◆ ועד אין לא אוציא את השטרות ששמירתן עליך ◆ |
| F | | ת"ל על שור על חמור על שה מה אלו מיוחדין |
| | | ששמירתן עליך וגמורה לך יצאו שטרות שאין <לך> |
| A 3 | | בהן אלא ראיה ◆ יכול יהא חייב על פחות משוה פרוטה ◆ |
| B | | ת"ל שלמה מה שלמה מיוחדת שיש בה שוה פרוטה |
| | | וחייב להכריז כך כל דבר שיש בו שוה פרוטה וחייב |
| A 4 | | להכריז ◆ טענו שור וחמור ושה והודה באחד מהן הרי |
| B | | זה חייב ◆ שנא' על שור ועל כל אבידה אשר יאמר כי |
| | | הוא זה ועל חמור ועל כל אבדה אשר יאמר כי הוא זה |
| | | ועל שה (ועל חמור) ועל <כל> אבדה אשר יאמר כי |
| C | | הוא זה ◆ טענו בשור והודה בשה בשה והודה בשור |
| E/D | | פטור ◆ מה ראית להביא את זה ולהוציא את זה ◆ מביא |
| | | אני את זה שהודה במקצת טענה ומוציא אני את זה |
| A 5 | | שלא הודה במקצת טענה ◆ מנה לי בידך אין לך בידי |

make a claim against another saying,] "You have a *maneh*'s [worth] of my clothing in your possession," [or,] "You have a *maneh*'s [worth] of my cattle in your possession," [the one being sued] is exempt [from having to take an oath swearing he does not have the claimed item].[379]

B. [But if the one being sued should reply,] "[Yes,] but I gave you back 50 *dinars* [of what you are claiming against me], he is liable [to take an oath].

C. What reason have you to include this [second example in 5.B in liability] but to exclude this [first example in 5.A]?

D. I include this [second example] because he admitted to part of the claim [against him], and I exclude this [first example] because he did not admit to part of the claim [against him].

6. A. [If one should make a claim against another saying,] "You found two oxen of mine," [but the person replies,] "I only found one," [the one being sued] is exempt.

B. [But if the one being sued should reply,] "I found two oxen of yours, but I gave you back one of them," he is liable.

C. What reason have you to include this [second example in 6.B in liability] but to exclude this [first example in 6.A]?

D. I include this [second example] because he swore on his own about the claim, and I exclude this [first example] because he did not swear on his own about the claim.

7. A. Because one can be liable for claiming [falsely that an item entrusted in his care was misappropriated] and for admitting [that an item entrusted in his care was misappropriated], [I might think that] just as a claim [must be for at least] two pieces of silver, so too an admission [must be for at least] two pieces of silver.

B. Scripture states, [however,] "... 'This is it'" (Exod. 22:8), [meaning,] even if [only for] the equivalent of a *perutah*.

8. A. ["... the case of the two of them shall come before God" (Exod. 22:8):]

B. If he made a claim against him outside [of the court,] and he admitted [to the claim], and the matter [then] came before the court, and he renounced [his admission], if he[380] has witnesses in whose presence he admitted, he is liable. But if not, he is exempt.

C. As it says in Scripture, "... the case of the two of them[381] shall come before God" (Exod. 22:8), [meaning, you bring before the court] what the two of them said outside [the court].

D. One might think even a woman and a minor [could serve as the two required witnesses].[382]

E. [However,] it says here in Scripture "case" (Exod. 22:8), and it says farther on in Scripture "case" (Deut. 19:15). Just as the "case" stated farther on requires the testimony of two [competent] witnesses, so too here is the testimony of two [competent] witnesses required.

9. A. ["... the case of the two of them shall come before God" (Exod. 22:8) and "An oath before the Lord shall decide between the two of them" (Exod. 22:10):]

B. [Twice stated— ]"the two of them, the two of them"—[in order to provide the opportunity to interpret this using] a *gezerah shaveh*:[383]

[204] C. Just as "the two of them" stated there [requires] an oath, so too here is an oath [required].

---

[379] Compare 5.A–B with t. Shebuot 5:5.

[380] I.e., the one making the claim.

[381] Hebrew: *d'var sh'neihem*—דבר־שניהם. More literally, "the statement of the two of them."

[382] Women and minors are not competent to testify as witnesses in some aspects of Jewish law. There is no discussion of competency of witnesses in the Hebrew Bible, however, Josephus claims that women were not allowed to act as witnesses (see Ant. 4:219). Compare 8.D–E with b. Gittin 90a (Neus., XVIII.C:Gittin:9:10:I.1.A– 2.H).

|  |  |  |
|---|---|---|
| | | היה לך בידי ונתתי לך יֵש לי בידך מנה כסות ומנה |
| C/B | | בהמה פטור ♦ ונתתי לך מהן חמשים דינר חייב ♦ מה |
| D | | ראית להביא את זה ולהוציא את זה ♦ מביא אני את זה |
| | | שהודה ממין הטענה ומוציא אני את זה שלא הודה |
| A | 6 | ממין הטענה ♦ שני שוורין מצאתה לי ולא מצאתי אלא |
| B | | אחד פטור ♦ שני שוורים מצאתי לך ונתתי לך אחד מהן |
| C | | חייב ♦ מה ראית להביא את זה ולהוציא את זה – ♦ |
| D | | מביא<ני> זה שנשבע על טענת עצמו ומוציא אני זה |
| A | 7 | שלא נשבע על טענת עצמו ♦ לפי שחייב בטע' וחייב |
| | | בהודאה מה טענה שתי כסף אף הודאה שתי כסף ♦ |
| B/A 8 | B | ת"ל כי הוא זה אפילו בשוה פרוטה ♦ טענו בחוץ והודה |
| | | ובא דבר לפני בית דין וכפר אם יש לו עדים שהודה |
| C | | בפניהם חייב ואם לאו פטור ♦ שנא' עד האלהים יבא |
| D | | דבר שניהם מה שדיברו שניהם בחוץ ♦ יכול אפי' אשה |
| E | | ואפילו קטן ♦ נאמ' כאן דבר ונאמ' להלן דבר מה |
| | | דבר האמ' להלן על פי שנים עדים אף כאן על |
| C/B/A | 9 | פי שנים ♦ עדים שניהם שניהם לגזרה שוה ♦ מה |
| | | שניהם האמ' להלן (שמ' כב י) שבועה אף כאן שבועה ♦ |

<hr>

[383] I.e., the employment of the same word in separate scriptural contexts, thus facilitating the application of the meaning of the word in one context to the other.

D. Just as "the two of them" stated there is if there is an admission, and the admission is about part of the claim,[384] so too here must there be an admission, and the admission must be about part of the claim.[385]

10. A. How does one know from Scripture they may not reach a verdict of conviction based either upon [multiple] witnesses or one witness?[386]

B. Scripture states, "He whom God declares guilty" (Exod. 22:8).

C. How does one know from Scripture that noncapital cases are decided by three [judges]?

D. Scripture states, "He whom God declares guilty" (Exod. 22:8).

E. [Scripture states here[387] "God"] three [times] to teach you that noncapital cases are decided by three [judges].

F. Rabbi Nathan says, "Three [times is the word] 'God' written in the scriptural section, to teach you that noncapital cases are decided by [three] judges."

G. R. Shimon says, "If not [determined by a court of three], what fault is it of the one who gave the item to be kept? For if he[388] admitted on his own, shouldn't he pay the double-restitution payment [anyway] based on his own [admission]?

H. "Scripture states, [however,] 'He whom God declares guilty' (Exod. 22:8), [meaning,] one pays the double payment on the basis of a court, and one does not pay the double-restitution payment on one's own.

11. A. "... shall pay double to the other" (Exod. 22:8): And not to the Temple.[389]

B. "... to the other" (Exod. 22:8): Which excludes [paying] other people.

C. "... to the other" (Exod. 22:8): Which excludes [paying] the alien resident.

## Chapter Seventy-Three

### (Textual Source: Ms. Firkovich II A 268)

LXXIII:I

1. A. "When a man gives (his companion an ass, an ox, a sheep or any other animal to guard, and it dies or is injured or is carried off, with no one seeing it)" (Exod. 22:9):

B. I only know about a man. How does one know from Scripture about a woman?

C. Scripture states, "... shall pay" (Exod. 22:8), [meaning,] whether man or woman.

D. If so, why is it said in Scripture, "... a man" (Exod. 22:9)?

E. In order to exclude the minor.

2. A. "... his companion" (Exod. 22:9)—this excludes other people.

B. "... his companion" (Exod. 22:9)—this excludes the alien resident.

C. Should I exclude other people, who do not have the [same] commandments as Israel, but yet not exclude the alien resident, who has the [same] commandments as Israel?

D. Scripture states, "... his companion" (Exod. 22:9)—this excludes other people.

E. "... his companion" (Exod. 22:9)—this excludes the alien resident.

---

[384] See parallel at m. Shebuot 6:1.

[385] Compare 9.D with *Mekhilta de-Rabbi Ishmael*, Nezikin (H/R, 301:9–10; Laut., vol. 3, 119:71–73; Neus., LXXII:I:12.A–D).

[386] Compare 10.A–H with *Mekhilta de-Rabbi Ishmael*, Nezikin (H/R, 302:1–9; Laut., vol. 3, 119:73–120:88; Neus., LXXII:I:12.A–13.P); and m. Sanhedrin 4:1

[387] I.e., in Exod. 22:7–8.

| | | |
|---|---|---|
| מה שניהם האמ' להלן עד שתהא שם הודאה והודאה ממין | D | |
| הטענה אף כאן עד שתהא שם הודאה והודאה ממין | | |
| הטענה ◆ מנין שאין מטין על פי עדים או על פי (עד) | A | 10 |
| אחד לחובה ◆ ת"ל אשר ירשיעון אלהים. ◆ מנין שדיני | C/B | |
| ממונות בשלשה ◆ ת"ל אשר ירשיעון אלהים ◆ שלשה | E/D | |
| ללמדך (שאני) [שדיני] ממונות בשלשה ◆ ר' נתן אומ' | Γ | |
| שלשה אלהים הכתובים בפרשה ללמדך שדיני | | |
| ממונות בשלשה ◆ ר' שמע' אומ' אם לאו מה חטא | G | |
| מפקיד שאם הודה מפי עצמו יכול יהא משלם | | |
| תשלומי כפל על פי עצמו ◆ ת"ל אשר ירשיעון אלהים | H | |
| על פי בית דין משלם תשלומי כפל ואין משלם | | |
| תשלומי כפל על פי עצמו ◆ ישלם שנים לרעהו ולא | A | 11 |
| להקדש ◆ לרעהו פרט לאחרים ◆ לרעהו פרט לגר תושב. | C/B | |
| סל' פסו' ◆ | | |

| | | |
|---|---|---|
| | LXXIII:I | |
| כי יתן איש ◆ אין לי אלא איש אשה מנין ◆ ת"ל ישלם | C/B/A | 1 |
| (שם) בין איש ובין אשה ◆ אם כן למה נאמר איש ◆ פרט | E/D | |
| לקטן ◆ רעהו פרט לאחרים ◆ רעהו פרט לגר תושב ◆ | B/A | 2 |
| מוצי<י>א אני את אחרין שאין להן מצות כיש' ועד אן | C | |
| לא אוציא את הגר תושב שיש לו מצות כיש' ◆ ת"ל | D | |
| רעהו פרט לאחרים ◆ רעהו פרט לגר תושב. ◆ | E | |

[388] I.e., the one entrusted with keeping the item.

[389] Compare 11.A–C with *Mekhilta de-Rabbi Ishmael,* Nezikin (H/R, 302:13; Laut., vol. 3, 120:96–97; Neus., LXXII:I:15.A–16.B).

3.    A.    "... an ass, an ox, a sheep" (Exod. 22:9):[390]

        B.    I only know specifically about an ass, an ox, or a sheep. How does one know from Scripture to include the remaining [other] animals?

        C.    Scripture states, "... or any other animal" (Exod. 22:9).

        D.    How does one know from Scripture to include the other movable chattel?

        E.    Scripture states, "... to guard ... and the owner must acquiesce, and no restitution shall be made" (Exod. 22:9–10), [meaning,] concerning that for which owners typically receive [restitution].

        F.    From this you state [that] these [include] the movable chattel!

        G.    I might think that I should include servants, documents, and immovable property.

        H.    Scripture states, [however,] "... an ass, an ox, a sheep or any other animal" (Exod. 22:9).

4.    A.    "... and it dies or is injured or is carried off" (Exod. 22:9):

        B.    Let Scripture [only] speak of death! Why do I need it to speak of injury and carrying off?

        C.    If so, I might say that just as death is unique, in that it doesn't have the spirit of life, injury and carrying off are excluded, because they have[391] the spirit of life. Thus, Scripture needs to speak of death, injury, and carrying off.

        D.    Let Scripture [only] speak of injury! Why do I need it to speak of carrying off and death?

        E.    If so, I might say that just as injury is unique, in that it is in your presence, carrying off and death are excluded, because they are not in your presence. Thus, Scripture needs to speak of death, injury, and carrying off.

        F.    Let Scripture [only] speak of carrying off! Why do I need it to speak of injury and death?

[205]    G.    If so, I might say that just as carrying off is unique, in that it has the spirit of life, injury and death are excluded, because they do not have the spirit of life. Thus, Scripture needs to speak of death, injury, and carrying off.

        H.    How does one know from Scripture to include other [types of] injury?

        I.    Scripture states, "... and it dies or is injured or is carried off" (Exod. 22:9).

5.    A.    "... with no one seeing it, an oath before the Lord (shall decide between the two of them)" (Exod. 22:9–10):[392]

        B.    Thus, if there are people who saw, he is exempt from having to swear.

        C.    One might think even a woman and even a minor [could serve here as witnesses].[393]

        D.    [However,] Scripture states here, "seeing," and Scripture states farther on, "seeing"—"... also able to testify as one who has either seen or learned of the matter" (Lev. 5:1). Just as "seeing" stated farther on requires the testimony of two [competent] witnesses, so too "seeing" stated here requires the testimony of two [competent] witnesses.

---

[390] Compare 3.A–H with *Mekhilta de-Rabbi Ishmael*, Nezikin (H/R, 302:17–303:3; Laut., vol. 3, 121:5–12; Neus., LXXIII:I:2.A–J).

[391] The text here reads "because they don't" (Hebrew: שאין), which contextually is counterintuitive. I translate here, instead, the opposite.

[392] Compare 5.A–D with *Mekhilta de-Rabbi Ishmael*, Nezikin (H/R, 303:12–16; Laut., vol. 3, 122:25–123:32; Neus., LXXIII:I:5.A–7.E).

[393] Women and minors are not competent to testify as witnesses in some aspects of Jewish law. There is no discussion of competency of witnesses in the Hebrew Bible, however, Josephus claims that women were not allowed to act as witnesses (see Ant. 4:219).

| | | |
|---|---|---|
| חמור או שור או שה. ◆ אין לי אלא חמור שור ושה | B/A | 3 |
| המ[ן]יוחדין מנין לרבות שאר בהמה ◆ ת״ל <ו>כל בהמה ◆ | C | |
| מנין לרבות שאר המטלטלין ◆ ת״ל לשמור ולקח בעליו | E/D | |
| ולא ישלם (שם) את שדרך בעלים לקבל אותו ◆ אמור | F | |
| מעתה אלו המטלטלין ◆ יכול שני מרבה עבדים | G | |
| ושטרות וקרקעות ◆ ת״ל חמור או שור או שה וכל | H | |
| בהמה <...> ◆ ומת או נשבר או נשבה ◆ יאמר מתה מה | B/A | 4 |
| אני צריך לומר שבורה ושבויה ◆ אילו כן הייתי אומ׳ מה | C | |
| מיתה מיוחדת שאין בה רוח חיים יצאת שבורה | | |
| ושבויה שאין בהן רוח חיים צריך הכת׳ לומר מיתה | | |
| שבורה ושבויה ◆ יאמר שבורה מה אני צריך לומר | D | |
| שבויה ומתה ◆ אילו כן הייתי אומ׳ מה שבורה מיוחדת | E | |
| שהיא בפניך יצאת שבורה (שבויה) ומתה שאינן | | |
| בפניך צריך הכת׳ לומר מיתה שבורה ושבויה ◆ (ו)יאמר | F | |
| שבויה מה אני צריך <לומר> שבורה ומתה ◆ אילו כן | G | |
| הייתי אומ׳ מה שבויה מיוחדת שיש בה רוח חיים | | |
| יצאו שבורה ומתה שאין בהן רוח חיים צריך הכת׳ | | |
| לומ׳ מיתה שבורה ושבויה ◆ מנין לרבות שאר האנסין ◆ | H | |
| ת״ל ומת או נשבר או נשבה ◆ אין רואה שבועת יי׳ ◆ הא | B/A 5 | I |
| אם יש לו ראויין פטור מלישבע ◆ יכול אפי׳ אשה ואפי׳ | C | |
| קטן ◆ נאמ׳ כן ראיה ונאמ׳ להלן ראיה והוא עד או ראה | D | |
| או ידע (ויק׳ ה א) מה ראיה האמ׳ להלן על פי שני | | |
| עדים אף ראיה האמ׳ כן על פי שנים עדים. סל׳ פסו׳ ◆ | | |

LXXIII:II

1. A. "An oath before the Lord shall decide between the two (of them that the one has not laid hands on the property of the other. The owner must acquiesce, and no restitution shall be made)" (Exod. 22:10):

   B. We don't know which one should give the oath and relinquish [the claim] and which one should take the oath and take [the claim].

   C. Scripture states, [however,] "The owner must acquiesce, and no restitution shall be made" (Exod. 22:10), [meaning,] once the owner has accepted the oath, the other one is exempt from having to pay.

   D. One might think this is also the case [when there is a similar claim involving] a hired person, one who has been robbed, or one who has been wounded.[394]

   E. Scripture states "the two of them" (Exod. 22:10), [meaning] that sometimes the one should take the oath and sometimes the other one should take the oath.

   F. And how does one know from Scripture that when the [one litigant] is not to be trusted, even when taking an oath, the other one takes an oath and takes [his claim]?

   G. Scripture states "the two of them" (Exod. 22:10), [meaning] that sometimes the one should take the oath and sometimes the other one should take the oath.

   H. How does one know from Scripture that just as the oath can come to rest upon the one taking the oath, so too the oath can come to rest on the one administering the oath.

   I. Scripture states, "An oath before the Lord shall decide between the two of them" (Exod. 22:10), [in order to provide the opportunity to interpret this using] a *gezerah shaveh*:[395]

   J. Just as "the two of them" stated there (Exod. 22:8) is if there is an admission, and the admission is about part of the claim,[396] so too here must there be an admission, and the admission must be about part of the claim.[397]

2. A. "... that the one has not laid hands on the property of the other" (Exod. 22:10):

   B. Why do I need [Scripture to state this]? Wasn't it in his hand? Why does Scripture state, "... that the one has not laid hands on the property of the other" (Exod. 22:10)?

   C. [In order to teach that] if he was grazing [the animal] in front of the door to his house, and a robber came and took it, he is exempt. If he was riding on it, and a robber came and took it, he is liable for it.

   D. As it says in Scripture, "... that the one has not laid hands on the property of the other" (Exod. 22:10).

   E. "... laid" (Exod. 22:10)—this [means] in any method.

3. A. If he lent him an ox, and it violated someone or gored someone [while in his possession]— if he gave it back to its owner while its litigation was not complete, he is exempt. But if he gave it back to its owner after its litigation was complete, he is liable.[398]

   B. As it says in Scripture, "The owner must acquiesce, and no restitution shall be made" (Exod. 22:10), [meaning, in situations that represent how] owners would normally accept it [back]. This [case] is excluded, because it is not how owners would normally accept it [back].

4. A. Another interpretation:

[394] Compare 1.D–G with m. Shebuot 7:1.

[395] I.e., the employment of the same word in separate scriptural contexts, thus facilitating the application of the meaning of the word in one context to the other.

| | | |
|---|---|---|
| שבועת ייי תהיה וגומ' ♦ אין אנו יודעין אי זה ישבע | B/A | 1 |
| ויטול אי זה ישבע ויתן ♦ ת"ל ולקח בעליו ולא ישלם | C | |
| כיון שקיבלו בעלים שבועה הלז פטור מלשלם ♦ יכול | D | |
| אף השכיר והנגזל והנחבל ♦ ת"ל בין שניהם פעמים | E | |
| שזה נשבע ופעמים שזה נשבע ♦ ומנין שכנגדו חשוד על | F | |
| השבועה הרי זה נשבע ונוטל ♦ ת"ל בין שניהם פעמים | G | |
| שזה נשבע ופעמים שזה נשבע ♦ מנין שכשם שהשבועה | H | |
| חלה על הנשבע כך שבועה חלה על המשביע ♦ ת"ל | I | |
| שבועת ייי תהיה בין שניהם לגזרה שוה ♦ מה שניהם | J | |
| האמ' להלן עד שתהא שם הודאה והודאה ממין | | |
| הטענה אף שניהן האמ' כן עד שתהא שם הודאה | | |
| ‹והודאה› ממין הטענה. ♦ אם לא שלח ידו במלאכת | A | 2 |
| רעהו ♦ מה אני צריך והלא בידו היית מה ת"ל אם לא | B | |
| שלח ידו במלאכת רעהו ♦ היתה רועה לפניו על פתח | C | |
| הבית בא גייס ונטלה פטור רכב עליה ובא גייס | | |
| ונטלה חייב עליה ♦ שנא' אם לא שלח ידו ♦ שלח זה | E/D | |
| מכל מקום ♦ השאילו שור ורבע את האדם ושור | A | 3 |
| ונגח את האדם אם עד שלא נגמר די[נו] מסרו לבעליו | | |
| פטור ואם משנגמר דינו מסרו לבעליו חייב ♦ שנא' | B | |
| ולקח בעליו ולא ישלם את שדרך בעלים לקבל | | |
| אותו יצא זה שאין דרך בעלים לקבל אותו. ♦ ד"א ♦ | A | 4 |

---

396 See parallel at m. Shebuot 6:1.
397 Compare 1.J with *Mekhilta de-Rabbi Ishmael*, Nezikin (H/R, 301:9–10; Laut., vol. 3, 119:71–73; Neus., LXXII:I:12.A–D).
398 Compare 3.A–B with t. Baba Qamma 5:4.

B. "… and it dies or is injured or is carried off" (Exod. 22:9):

C. Just as death [is an act of God], and a court did not put it to death, so too should the injury [be an act of God], and not an injury administered by the court.

5. A. If he lent him an ox, and he[399] saw a band of robbers coming, he shouldn't [then] say to him,[400] "Take the ox, and then you swear to me!"

B. As it says in Scripture, "… the owner must acquiesce, and no restitution shall be made" (Exod. 22:10), [meaning,] once the owner has accepted the oath, the other one is exempt from having to pay.

C. If he lent him an ox, and he saw a band of robbers coming, and he gave it back to him, as they come upon them, he shouldn't say to him, "Give me the ox, and I'll swear to you!"

D. As it says in Scripture, "… the owner must acquiesce, and no restitution shall be made" (Exod. 22:10), [meaning,] once the owner has accepted [it back], the other one is exempt from having to pay.

[206]

6. A. "The owner must acquiesce, and no restitution shall be made" (Exod. 22:10):

B. This is what we have said [above]: once the owner has accepted [it back], the other one is exempt from having to pay.

## LXXIII:III

1. A. "But if [the animal] was stolen from him, he shall make restitution to its owner" (Exod. 22:11):[401]

B. I only know about stealing. How does one know from Scripture [to include] losing [it]?

C. It is a matter of logic: One is liable here, and one is liable [above in the case involving] the owner of the house.[402] Just as we have found that the owner of the house does not pay for loss, so too this one does not pay for loss.

D. [Or one could reason using] an additional *kal va-ḥomer:* If the owner of the house, who pays the one-fifth [surcharge] and [brings] the guilt offering,[403] does not pay for loss, then isn't it logical that this one, who does not pay the one-fifth [surcharge] or [bring] the guilt offering, should not pay for loss?

E. Scripture states, [however,] "But if [the animal] was stolen, etc." (Exod. 22:11).[404]

2. A. "(If it was torn by beasts), he shall bring it as evidence. (He need not replace what has been torn by beasts)" (Exod. 22:12):[405]

B. [If] he brings witnesses that it was torn by beasts, he is exempt from paying.

C. Abba Shaul says, "'… he shall bring it as evidence' (Exod. 22:11). As it says in Scripture, 'Thus said the Lord: As a shepherd rescues, etc.' (Amos 3:12)."

## LXXIII:IV

1. A. "When a man borrows ([an animal] from his companion and it dies or is injured, its owner not being with it, he must make restitution)" (Exod. 22:13):

B. I only know about a man. How does one know from Scripture about a woman?

---

[399] I.e., the owner/lender of the ox.

[400] I.e., the borrower.

[401] Compare 1.A–E with *Mekhilta de-Rabbi Ishmael,* Nezikin (H/R, 305:3–5; Laut., vol. 3, 124:56–125:61; Neus., LXXII:II:2.A–3.B); y. Shebuot 38b (Neus., 8:1:III.J–S); and b. Baba Metzia 94b (Neus., XXID:Tractate Baba Mesia:8:1:I.3.A–J).

[402] I.e., Exod. 22:6–8. See above LXXII:I:1.A–III:11.C

| | | |
|---|---|---|
| C/B | | ומת או נשבר או נשבה ◆ מה מיתה שאין בית דין ממיתין |
| A | 5 | אותו אף שבורה שאין בית דין שוברין אותו. ◆ ד״א ולקח |
| B | | בעליו ולא ישלם. השאילו שור וראה גדודי ליסטים באין |
| | | לא יאמר לו טול את השור ואתה נשבע לי ◆ שנא׳ ולקח |
| C | | בעליו ולא ישלם כיון שקיבלו בעלים שבועה הלז |
| | | פטור מלשלם. ◆ השאילו שור וראה גדודי ליסטין |
| D | | באים נתנו לו והלכו להן לא יאמר לו תן לי את השור |
| | | ואני נשבע לך ◆ שנא׳ ולקח בעליו ולא ישלם כיון |
| A | 6 | שקיבלו בעלים שלהן הלז פטור מלשלם. ◆ ולקח בעליו |
| B | | ולא ישלם ◆ זו היא שאמרנו כיון שקיבלו בעלים <שלהן> |
| | | הלז פטור מלישבע. סל׳ פסו׳ ◆ |

LXXIII:III

| | | |
|---|---|---|
| B/A | 1 | ואם גנב יגנב. ◆ אין לי אלא גניבה (ל)אבדה מנין ◆ |
| C | | ודין הוא חייב כאן וחייב בבעל הבית מה מצינו בבעל |
| | | הבית אין משלם את האבדה אף זה לא ישלם את |
| D | | האבדה. ◆ ועוד קל וחומר מה בעל הבית שמשלם |
| | | חומש ואשם אין משלם את האבדה זה שאין משלם |
| E | | חומש ואשם אינו דין שלא ישלם את האבדה ◆ ת״ל אם |
| | | גנב יגנב וגומ׳ ◆ |
| B/A | 2 | יביאהו ◆ עד יביא עדים שנטרפה והלז פטור מלשלם ◆ |
| C | | אבא שאול אומ׳ יביא עדידה (כה) שנא׳ כה אמר ייי |
| | | כאשר יציל (.) הרועה וגומ׳ (עמ׳ ג יב). סל׳ פסו׳ ◆ |

LXXIII:IV

| | | |
|---|---|---|
| B/A | 1 | כי ישאל איש ◆ אין לי אלא איש אשה מנין ◆ |

---

[403] See Lev. 5:20–26.

[404] The text here seems to interpret the apparently doubled form of the infinitive absolute in Exod. 22:11 (Hebrew: גנב יגנב—"But if [the animal] was stolen") as enlarging the scope of liability beyond stealing.

[405] Compare 2.A–C with *Mekhilta de-Rabbi Ishmael,* Nezikin (H/R, 305:6–306:8; Laut., vol. 3, 125:63–126:83; Neus., LXXII:II:6.A–8.J); and b. Baba Kamma 10b (Neus., XX.A:Tractate Baba Qamma:1:2:III.2.A–D).

C. Scripture states, "... must make restitution" (Exod. 22:13), [meaning,] whether man or woman.

D. If so, why does Scripture state, "... man" (Exod. 22:13)? [In order] to exclude the minor.

2.   A. "... from his companion" (Exod. 22:13)—this excludes other people.

B. "... from his companion" (Exod. 22:13)—this excludes the alien resident.

C. Should I exclude other people, who do not have the [same] commandments as Israel, but yet not exclude the alien resident, who has the [same] commandments as Israel?

D. Scripture states, "... from his companion" (Exod. 22:9)—this excludes other people.

E. "... his companion" (Exod. 22:9)—this excludes the alien resident.

3.   A. "... and it dies or is injured" (Exod. 22:13):[406]

B. I only know about injury and death. How does one know from Scripture [to include ] loss and theft?

C. It is a matter of logic: One is liable here, and one is liable as a paid guardian. Just as we have found that the paid guardian pays for loss and theft, so too this one should pay for loss and theft.

D. [Or one could reason using] an additional *kal va-ḥomer*: If the paid guardian, who does not pay for unavoidable accidents, pays for loss and theft, then isn't it logical that this one, who does pay for unavoidable accidents, should pay for loss and theft?

E. This is a *kal va-ḥomer* for which you have no response!

4.   A. "... and it dies or is injured" (Exod. 22:13):[407]

B. I only know about injury and death. How does one know from Scripture [to include] carrying off?

C. It is a matter of logic: Scripture states here injury and death, and Scripture states above[408] injury and death. Just as the injury and death stated above [includes] carrying off with them, so too [here] is carrying off [included] with them. Just as the carrying off and death stated above excludes slaves, documents, and immovable property, so too here are slaves, documents, and immovable property excluded.

5.   A. "... its owner not being with it, he must make restitution. If its owner was with it, he does not make restitution" (Exod. 22:13–14):

B. One might think if its owner was with it, he should not pay. For don't we know that if its owner was not with it, he must pay? Or if its owner was with it, he does not pay?

C. Rather, sometimes its owner is with it, and he is liable [to pay], and [sometimes] its owner is not with it, and he is exempt [from paying].

D. How so? If one borrowed a cow and borrowed [the services of] its owner with it, or if one rented a cow and rented [the services of] its owner with it, or borrowed it and rented [the services of] its owner, or rented it and borrowed [the services of] its owner, even if the owner is present but is plowing in some other place, and it falls and dies, he is exempt [from paying].[409]

E. As it says in Scripture, "If its owner was with it, he does not make restitution" (Exod. 22:14).

---

[406] Compare 3.A–E with *Mekhilta de-Rabbi Ishmael*, Nezikin (H/R, 306:11–14; Laut., vol. 3, 127:88–95; Neus., LXXII:II:11.A–J); y. Shebuot 38b (Neus., 8:1:J–S); and b. Baba Metzia 95a (Neus., XXID:Tractate Baba Mesia:8:1:I.5.A–J).

[407] Compare 4.A–C with *Mekhilta de-Rabbi Ishmael*, Nezikin (H/R, 306:11–14; Laut., vol. 3, 127:88–95; Neus., LXXII:II:11.A–J); and y. Shebuot 38c (Neus., 8:1:T–Y).

[408] I.e., Exod. 22:9.

| | |
|---|---|
| ת״ל ישלם בין איש ובין אשה • אם כן למה נאמ׳ איש | D/C |
| פרט לקטן • מעם רעהו פרט לאחרים • מעם רעהו פרט | B/A 2 |
| לגר תושב • מוציא אני את האחרים שאין להן מצות כיש׳ | C |
| ועדאין לא אוציא את גר תושב שיש לו מצות כיש׳ • | |
| ת״ל מעם רעהו פרט לאחרים • מעם רעהו פרט לגר | E/D |
| תושב. • ונשבר או מת • אין לי אלא שבירה ומיתה אבדה | B/A 3 |
| וגנבה מנין • ודין הוא חייב כן וחייב בנושא שכר מה | C |
| מצינו בנושא שכר משלם אבדה וגנבה אף זה ישלם | |
| אבדה וגנבה • ועוד קל וחומר ומה נושא שכר (.) שאין | D |
| משלם את האונסין משלם אבדה וגנבה זה שמשלם | |
| את האונסין אינו דין שישלם אבדה וגנבה • זה הוא קל | E |
| וחומר שאין לך עליו תשובה. • ונשבר או מת • אין לי | B/A 4 |
| אלא שבירה ומיתה שבויה מנין • ודין הוא נא׳ כן | C |
| שבירה ומיתה ונא׳ להלן שבירה ומיתה (שמ׳ כב ט) | |
| מה שבירה ומיתה האמ׳ להלן ש>ב<ויה עמהן אף כן | |
| שבויה עמהן מה שבו׳ ומיתה האמ׳ להלן פרט לעבדים | |
| ולשטרות ולקרקעות אף כן פרט לע׳ ולש׳ ולק׳. • | |
| בעליו אין אמו שלם ישלם • יכול ואם בעליו עמו | B/A 5 |
| לא ישלם (שם יד) וכי אין אנו יודעין שבעליו אין עמו | |
| שלם ישלם ואם בעליו עמו לא ישלם • אלא פעמים | C |
| שבעליו עמו חייב ואין בעליו עמו פטור. • כיצד השואל | D |
| את הפרה ושאל בעליה עמה השוכר פרה ושכר בעלה | |
| עמה שאלה ושכר בעלה או שכרה ושאל בעלה אף | |
| על פי שהבעלים עומדין וחורשין במקום אחר נפלה | |
| ומיתה פטור • שנא׳ אם בעליו עמו לא ישלם • | E |

[207]    F.    But if he borrowed it, then afterward borrowed [the services of] its owner, or rented it, then afterward rented [the services of] its owner, or rented it, then afterward borrowed [the services of] its owner, or borrowed it, then afterward rented [the services of] its owner, even if the owner is present and plowing on its back, and it falls and dies, he is liable [to pay].

G.    As it says in Scripture, "... its owner not being with it, he must make restitution" (Exod. 22:13).

6.    A.    One might think that [since] damage and death, for which the paid guardian is exempt—[that is,] if its owner was with it, he is exempt, but if its owner was not with it, he is liable—[then concerning] loss and theft, for which the paid guardian is liable, whether the owner was with it or whether the owner was not with it, he is liable.[410]

B.    But how did we learn about loss and thievery, except for damage and death?—Just as with damage and death, when the owners are with it, one is exempt, [and when] the owners are not with it, one is liable, so too with loss and thievery, when the owners are with it, one is exempt, [and when] the owners are not with it, one is liable.

C.    I only know this [however] for one who borrows. How does one know from Scripture [that this is also the case] for the paid guardian?

D.    It is a matter of logic: Just as this [one who borrows] pays for the unavoidable accidents—when its owners are with it, he is exempt, [and] when its owners are not with it, he is liable—then [with] the paid guardian, who does not pay for the unavoidable accidents, it is logical [that] when its owners are with it, he is exempt, [but] when its owners are not with it, he is liable.

7.    A.    "But if it was hired, he is entitled to the hire" (Exod. 22:14):

B.    Behold, this one is like the paid guardian: Just as the paid guardian takes an oath about the unavoidable accidents and pays for loss and theft, so too this one takes an oath about the unavoidable accidents and pays for loss and theft.

8.    A.    The first [scriptural unit here[411] pertains to] the one who guards for free. The second[412] [pertains to] the paid guardian. The third[413] [pertains to] the one who borrows.[414]

B.    Why [did Scripture] exempt [the one who guards for free] from everything? Because he derived no benefit from everything.

C.    And the third one pays everything, because he derived benefit from it.

D.    And the one in the middle takes an oath [of exemption] on part and pays for part, because he took benefit and paid benefit. You must say that this one is the paid guardian!

E.    Based on this they said: There are 13 types of damages: The ox, the pit, the destroying animal, the fire, the one who borrows, the one who guards for free, the one who rents, the paid guardian, injury, pain, healing, loss of work income, and humiliation.[415]

---

[410] Compare 6.A–D with y. Shebuot 38c (Neus., 8:1:IV.A–V).

[411] I.e., Exod. 22:6–8.

[412] I.e., Exod. 22:9–12.

[413] I.e., Exod. 22:13–14.

[414] Compare 8.A–D with y. Shebuot 38b (Neus., 8:1:III.A–D) and b. Baba Metzia 94b (Neus., XXIID:Tractate Baba Mesia:8:1:I.2.A–X).

[415] Compare 8.E with t. Baba Qamma 9:1, y. Baba Qamma 2a (Neus., 1:1:II.A–H), and Baba Qamma 4b (Neus., XX.A:Tractate Baba Qamma:1:1ff.).

F אבל שאלה ואחר כך שאל בעלה או שכרה ואחר כך שכר
בעלה שכרה ואחר כך שאל בעלה שאלה ואחר כך
שכר בעלה אף על פי שהבעלין עומדין וחורשין על

G גבה נפלה ומיתה חייב ◆ שנאמ' בעליו אין עמו שלם

A 6 ישלם ◆ יכול שבורה ומיתה שפטר בנושא שכר בזמן
שבעליו עמו פטור אין בעליו עמו חייב. אבדה וגניבה
שחייב בנושא שכר בין שבעליו עמו ובין שאין בעליו

B עמו הוא חייב ◆ וכי מהיכן למדנו לאבדה וגניבה אלא
משבורה ומיתה מה שבורה ומיתה בזמן שבעלים עמו
פטור אין בעלים <עמו חייב אף אבידה וגניבה בזמן
שבעלים עמו פטור אין בעלים> עמו חייב ◆ אין לי אלא

C
D שואל נושא שכר מנין ◆ ודין הוא (בזמן שבעלין עמו
פטור אין בעלין עמו חייב אין לי אלא שואל נושא
שכר מנין ודין הוא) מה אם זה שמשלם את האנסין
בזמן שבעליו עמו פטור אין בעליו עמו חייב נושא
שכר שאין משלם את האנסין דין הוא בזמן שבעליו
עמו פטור אין בעליו עמו חייב. ◆ אם שכיר הוא בא

A 7 בשכרו ◆ הרי הוא כנושא שכר מה נושא שכר נשבע על

B האנסין משלם אבדה וגניבה אף זה נשבע על האונסין
משלם אבדה וגנבה ◆ פרשה עליונה בשומר חנם שנייה

A 8 בנושא שכר שלישית בשואל ◆ מפני מה פטר בה

B מכלום מפני שאין לו בה הנאה של כולום ◆ ושלישית

C משלם את הכל מפני שכל הנאה שלו ◆ והאמצעית

D נשבע מקצת ומשלם מקצת מפני שנהנה ומהנה הוי

E אומ' זה נושא שכר ◆ מיכן אמרו שלשה עשר הן אבות
נזיקין השור והבור והמבעה וההבער שואל ושומר
חנם שכיר ונושא שכר נזק וצער וריפוי ושבת ובושת.
◆ סל' פסקא' ◆

*Chapter Seventy-Four*

(Textual Source: Ms. Firkovich II A 268)

LXXIV:I[416]

1.    A.    "If a man seduces a virgin for whom the bride-price has not been paid, (and lies with her, he must make her his wife by payment of a bride-price)" (Exod. 22:15):

      B.    This excludes [the woman] who had been betrothed and divorced.

      C.    Let Scripture state [simply that the man] rapes [her]! Why do I need [Scripture] to speak of seduction? [Needn't one only reason that] just as with rape, the more significant [transgression of the two], one is not liable if [the woman] had been betrothed and divorced, then isn't it logical with seduction, the less significant [transgression of the two], that one would not be liable if [the woman] had been betrothed and divorced?

      D.    Scripture needs to state it, [for otherwise one might reason that] just as with seduction, the less significant [transgression of the two], one is liable if [the woman] had been betrothed and divorced, then isn't it logical with rape, the more significant [transgression of the two], that one would be liable if [the woman] had been betrothed and divorced?

      E.    Scripture states, [therefore,] "If a man seduces a virgin for whom the bride-price has not been paid" (Exod. 22:15), [in order] to exclude [the woman] who had been betrothed and divorced.

2.    A.    "... a virgin" (Exod. 22:15):

      B.    And not a woman who is not a virgin.

      C.    Let Scripture state [simply] that the man rapes [her]! Why do I need [Scripture] to speak of seduction? [Needn't one only reason that] just as with rape, the more significant [transgression of the two], one is only liable if the woman is a virgin, then isn't it logical with seduction, the less significant [transgression of the two], that one would only be liable if the woman is a virgin?

[208] D.    Scripture needs to state it, [for otherwise one might reason that] just as with seduction, the less significant [transgression of the two], one is liable either if the woman is or is not a virgin, then isn't it logical with rape, the more significant [transgression of the two], that one would be liable either if the woman is or is not a virgin?

      E.    Scripture states, [therefore,] "... a virgin" (Exod. 22:15), [in order] to exclude a woman who is not a virgin.

3.    A.    I only know about the woman who is not a virgin because of sexual intercourse. How does one know from Scripture to include [the woman who loses her virginity by means of] a blow of a stick?

      B.    Scripture states, "... a virgin" (Exod. 22:15), [in order] to exclude [the woman who loses her virginity by means of] a blow of a stick.

4.    A.    Since Scripture does not speak concerning seduction of a maiden,[417] ... [manuscript lacuna] ...

      B.    From a *kal va-ḥomer:* Just as with rape, the more significant [transgression of the two], one is only liable with a maiden, then isn't it logical with seduction, the less significant [transgression of the two], that one would only be liable if the woman is a maiden?

      C.    Scripture needs to state it, [for otherwise one might reason that] just as with seduction, the less significant [transgression of the two], one is liable either if the woman is or is not

---

[416] Compare LXXIV:I:1.A–4.F with *Sifre Deut.,* Piska 244 (Hammer, p. 249; Neus., CCXLIV:I:1.A–III:3.A).

[417] A maiden is a girl between the age of 12 years and a day and 12 years 6 months and a day.

LXXIV:I

| | |
|---:|:---|
| B/A 1 | פרט • וכי יפתה איש בתולה אשר לא אורסה |
| C | לשנתארסה ונתגרשה • יאמר באונס מה אני צריך |
| | לומר במפותה מה אונס חמור אינו חייב ⟨על |
| | שנתארסה ונתגרשה מפתה הקל אינו דין שלא יהא |
| D | חייב⟩ על שנתארסה ונתגרשה • צריך לאומרו מה |
| | מפתה הקל חייב על שנתארסה ונתגרשה אונס חמור |
| E | אינו דין שיהא חייב על שנתארסה ונתגרשה • ת״ל וכי |
| | יפתה איש בתולה אשר לא אורסה פרט לשנתארסה |
| C/B/A 2 | ונתגרשה. • בתולה • ולא בעולה • יאמר באונס מה אני |
| | צריך לומר במפתה מה אונס חמור אינו חייב אלא על |
| | הבתולה מפתה הקל אינו דין שלא יהא חייב ⟨אלא⟩ |
| D | על הבתולה • צריך לאומרו מה מפתה הקל חייב על |
| | בתולה ועל שאינה בתולה אונס חמור אינו דין שיהא |
| E | חייב על הבתולה ועל שאינה בתולה • ת״ל בתולה פרט |
| A 3 | לבעולה • (אין לי) (אלא) ואין לי אלא בעולה מוכת עץ |
| A 4 B | מנין • ת״ל בתולה פרט למוכת עץ • לפי שלא נאמר |
| B | במפתה נערה ⟨...⟩ • מקל וחומר ומה אונס חמור אינו |
| | חייב אלא על הנערה מפתה הקל אינו דין שלא יהא |
| C | חייב אלא על הנערה • צריך לאמרו מה מפתה הקל |

a maiden, then isn't it logical with rape, the more significant [transgression of the two], that one would be liable either if the woman is or is not a maiden?

D.  Scripture states, "(The man who lay with her) shall pay the maiden's father" (Deut. 22:29), [in order to stress] not [paying] the father of an adult woman.

E.  But isn't it [also possible to reason with] a *kal va-ḥomer*—just as with rape, the more significant [transgression of the two], one is not liable if the woman is an adult, then isn't it logical that with seduction, the less significant [transgression of the two], that one would not be liable if the woman is an adult?

F.  You cannot change the reasoning [like this], because Scripture has already stated "maiden" two times.

LXXIV:II

1.    A.  "If a man seduces" (Exod. 22:15):

      B.  The woman is seduced, but the man is not seduced.

      C.  "... and lies with her" (Exod. 22:15):

      D.  Any manner of lying.

      E.  One might think she would be acquired to him as a wife through seduction.

      F.  Scripture states, [however,] "... he must make her (his wife)" (Exod. 22:15). This teaches that she requires [a valid method of achieving] *kiddushin*[418] from him.

      G.  One might think [she could be his wife] even if she was not suitable to him for matrimony.

      H.  Scripture states, [however,] "... he must make her his wife" (Exod. 22:15), [meaning,] she who is suitable to him for matrimony.

      I.  Should I exclude [women prohibited due to] the forbidden relationships for which one is liable to death at the hands of the court, but yet should I not exclude [women prohibited due to] the forbidden relationships for which one is liable to excommunication at the hands of heaven?

      J.  Scripture states, "... he must make her his wife" (Exod. 22:15), [meaning,] she who is suitable to him for matrimony.

      K.  Should I exclude [women prohibited due to] the forbidden relationships for which one is liable to excommunication at the hands of heaven, but yet should I not exclude [women prohibited due to being proscribed] by a negative commandment?

      L.  Scripture states, "... he must make her his wife" (Exod. 22:15), [meaning,] she who is suitable to him for matrimony.

      M.  One might think that if she is suitable to him for matrimony, he is not liable for the fine.

      N.  Scripture states, [however,] "If her father refuses to give her to him, (he must still weigh out silver in accordance with the bride-price for virgins)" (Exod. 22:14), [meaning,] he is liable for the fine for she to whom he is refused valid marriage.

      O.  Should I include [women prohibited due to being proscribed] by a negative commandment that [forbids] one of the forbidden relationships, but yet should I not include [women prohibited due to] the forbidden relationships for which one is liable to excommunication at the hands of heaven?

      P.  Scripture states, "If her father refuses to give her to him" (Exod. 22:14), [meaning,] he is

---

[418] I.e., in order to establish *kiddushin* (i.e., Jewish marriage) with her, he must utilize one of the valid methods of doing so (see m. Kiddushin 1:1ff.).

חייב על נערה ועל שאינה נערה אונס חמור אינו דין

שיהא חייב על נערה ועל שאינה נערה ◆ ת"ל ונתן לאבי   D

הנערה (דב' כב כט) ולא לאבי הבוגרת ◆ והלא דברים   E

קל וחומר ומה אונס חמור אינו חייב על הבוגרת

מפתה הקל אינו דין שלא יהא חייב על הבוגרת ◆ לחלף   F

את הדין אי אתה יכול שכבר נאמר נערה שתי פעמים ◆

וכי יפתה איש ◆ האשה מתפתה ואין האיש   B/A   1

מתפתה. ◆ ושכב עמה ◆ כל שכיבה ◆ יכול תהא נקנית לו   E/D/C

בפתוי ◆ ת"ל מהר ימהרנה לו מלמד ש<צ>ריכה הימנו   F

קידושין ◆ יכול אף על פי שאינה ראויה לו לאישות ◆ ת"ל   H/G

מהר ימהרנה לו לאשה את שראויה לו לאישות ◆

מוציא אני העריות שחייבין עליהן מיתות בית דין ועד   I

אן לא אוציא את העריות שחייבין עליהן כרת בידי

שמים ◆ ת"ל מהר ימהרנה לו לאשה את שרא' לו   J

לאישות ◆ מוציא אני את העריות שחייבין עליהן כרת   K

בידי שמים ועדאן לא אוציא <את העריות> שהן בלא

תעשה ◆ ת"ל מהר ימהרנה לו לאשה את שראויה לו   L

לאישות ◆ יכול הואיל ואינה ראויה לו לאישות לא יהא   M

חייב בקנסה ◆ ת"ל אם מאן ימאן אביה לתתה לו את   N

שמאן בה קדשה הרי הוא חייב בקנסה ◆ מביא אני את   O

העריות שהן בלא תעשה ועדאן לא אביא את העריות

שחייבין עליהן כרת בידי שמים ◆ ת"ל ואם מאן ימאן   P

liable for the fine for she to whom he is refused valid marriage ... [manuscript lacuna] ...

Q.   I should exclude [women prohibited due to] the forbidden relationships for which one is liable to excommunication at the hands of heaven and [women prohibited due to] the forbidden relationships for which one is liable to death at the hands of the court. I exclude them based upon one [scriptural] conclusion: "He must make restitution" (Exod. 22:2).

## LXXIV:III

1.   A.   "If her father refuses (to give her to him, he must still weigh out silver in accordance with the bride-price for virgins)" (Exod. 22:16):

B.   This teaches that the authority to refuse is in the hands of her father.

C.   I only know about [the authority to refuse being] in the hands of her father. How does one know from Scripture [about it being as well] in her hands?

D.   Scripture states, "If her father refuses" (Exod. 22:16).[419]

E.   But he[420] cannot refuse, as it says in Scripture, "... and she shall be his wife" (Deut. 22:29).

2.   A.   "... to give her to him" (Exod. 22:16):

B.   If one man married one woman, behold, she is [validly] married. If two [men] married one woman, she is not [validly] married.

[209]   C.   One might think she cannot be [validly] married to the two of them, but she would [still] be [validly] married to one of them.

D.   Scripture states, [however,] "... to give her to him" (Exod. 22:16), [meaning, if] one man married one woman, she is [validly] married. If two married one woman, she is not [validly] married.

3.   A.   "... to give her to him" (Exod. 22:16):[421]

B.   This teaches that a father has control over the betrothal of his minor daughter.

4.   A.   "... to give her to him" (Exod. 22:16):[422]

B.   Because we have found that the one who rapes pays the fine immediately, one might think this is also the case here.[423]

C.   Scripture states, [however,] "... to give her to him" (Exod. 22:16), which tells that he is only liable at the time that he excludes [her to him as a wife].

D.   One might think this [payment] also [serves as the reparation payment] for her shame and for her blemish.

E.   Scripture states, [however,] "... the bride-price for virgins" (Exod. 22:16), [meaning,] he fulfills his obligation [with this payment] for this matter, but he does not fulfill his obligation for another matter.

5.   A.   One might think [he could pay the bride-price] with a *dinar*.

B.   Scripture states, [however,] "... he must still weigh out (silver)" (Exod. 22:16).

C.   One might think [he could pay the bride price with] copper.

---

[419] The text here interprets the seemingly doubled form of the infinitive absolute (מאן ימאן) as indicative of this extension of meaning.
[420] I.e., the man who seduced and raped her.
[421] Compare 3.A–B with m. Ketubot 4:4.
[422] Compare 4.A–E with m. Ketubot 3:4.
[423] I.e., that he must weigh out immediately the silver in accordance with the bride-price for virgins, as stipulated in Exod. 22:16.

אביה לתתה לו את שמאן בה קדשה הרי הוא חייב

בקנסה <...> ◆ מוציא אני את העריות שחייבין עליהן

כרת בידי שמים ועריות שחייבין עליהן מיתת בית דין

משמע אחד מוציאן שנא' דמים לו שלם ישלם (שמ'

כב ב). סל' פסו' ◆

LXXIV:III

| | | |
|---|---|---|
| ואם מאן ימאן אביה ◆ מלמד שהרשות ביד אביה | B/A | 1 |
| למאן ◆ אין לי אלא ביד אביה בידה מנין ◆ ת״ל אם מאן | D/C | |
| ימאן ◆ אבל הוא אין יכול למאן שנא' ולו תהיה לאשה | E | |
| וגומ' (דב' כב כט) ◆ לתתה לו ◆ איש אחד שקידש אשה | B/A | 2 |
| אחת הרי זו מקודשת שנים שקידשו אשה אחת אינה | | |
| מקודשת ◆ יכו<ל> לא תהא מקודשת לשניהן אבל | C | |
| תהא מקודשת לאחד מהן ◆ ת״ל לתתה לו איש אחד | D | |
| שקידש אשה אחת מקודשת שנים שקידש[ו] אשה | | |
| אחת אינה מקודשת. ◆ לתתה לו ◆ מלמד שאב זכאי | B/A | 3 |
| בקידושי בתו קטנה ◆ לתתה לו ◆ לפי שמצינו באונס | B/A | 4 |
| שנותן קנסה מיד יכול אף זה כן ◆ ת״ל לתתה לו מגיד | C | |
| שאינו חייב עד שעה שיוציא ◆ יכול אף בשתה ופגמה כן | D | |
| ת״ל כמוהר הבתולות לדבר זה יצא ולא יצא לדבר | E | |
| אחר כסף ◆ יכול דינר ◆ ת״ל ישקל ◆ יכול שקלי נחושת ◆ | C/B/A | 5 |

D. Scripture states, [however,] "... silver" (Exod. 22:16).

E. One might think [he could pay the bride price with] Babylonian, Elamite, and Cappadocian [currency].

F. Scripture says here, [however,] "... he must ... weigh out" (Exod. 22:16), and Scripture says farther on, "... (in silver by the sanctuary) weight" (Lev. 5:15). Just as "weight" stated farther on [requires] sanctuary currency, so too "weigh" stated here [requires] sanctuary currency.

G. But you don't know [from Scripture here] how much silver. Behold I can reason: Scripture states here, "silver," and Scripture states concerning rape [in Deut. 22:28], "silver." Just as "silver" stated concerning rape is 50 [shekels of] silver, so too "silver" stated here is 50 [shekels] of silver.[424]

H. Or you can take your [reasoning] in this manner: Scripture says here, "silver," and Scripture says concerning [the issue of a man making up charges against a woman and] defaming [her], "silver" (Deut. 22:19). Just as "silver" stated concerning defaming [her] is 100 [shekels] of silver, so too "silver" stated here is 100 [shekels] of silver.

I. Let's see how they compare: One may reason a matter in which one may be judged [culpable] for his life from a matter in which one may be judged [culpable] for his life. So one may not prove [this using the issue of false] defamation, for which one may not be judged [culpable] for his life.

J. Or you can take your [reasoning] in this manner: One may reason [a matter involving] a virgin [from a matter involving] a virgin, but one may not reason [a matter involving] a woman who is not a virgin.

K. Scripture states, [therefore,] "... in accordance with the bride-price for virgins" (Exod. 22:16), [meaning,] not in accordance with the fine for virgins.

6. A. "... in accordance with the bride-price for virgins" (Exod. 22:16):

B. Behold, all virgins [are compensated] like this one: Just as this one [is compensated] with silver, so too are all virgins [compensated] with silver. Just as this one [is compensated with 50 [shekels] of silver, so too are all virgins [compensated] with 50 [shekels] of silver.

C. Rabban Shimon ben Gamliel says, "A woman's settlement is not a value fixed by the Torah."

## LXXIV:IV

1. A. "(You shall not let) a sorceress (live)" (Exod. 22:17):

B. By implication this means the male sorcerer and the female sorcerer.

C. And why are sorcerers [typically] called by the feminine form [sorceress]? Because most sorcerers are women.

2. A. "You shall not let ... live" (Exod. 22:17):[425]

B. R. Yosi ha-Galili says, "Scripture says here, 'You shall not let ... live,' and Scripture states farther on, '... you shall not let a soul live' (Deut. 20:16). Just as 'you shall not let a soul live' stated farther on [involves death] by the sword, so too does 'you shall not let ... live' stated here [involve death] by the sword."

C. But R. Akiva says, "Scripture says here, 'You shall not let ... live,' and Scripture states farther on, '... beast or man, he shall not live' (Exod. 19:13). Just as 'he shall not let' stated

---

[424] Compare 5.G with *Mekhilta de-Rabbi Ishmael*, Nezikin (H/R, 309:4–6; Laut., vol. 3., 132:47–133:49; Neus., LXIV:I:7.A–D).
[425] Compare 2.A–G with b. Sanhedrin 67a (Neus., XXIIB:Tractate Sanhedrin:7:11:I.A–M).

| | |
|---|---|
| ת״ל כסף ◆ יכול בבליות עלמיות וקפוטקיות ◆ נאמ׳ כן | F/E/D |
| ישקל ונא׳ להלן שקלים מה שקלים האמ׳ להלן בשקל | |
| הקדש אף שקלים האמ׳ כאן בשקל הקדש ◆ אבל אי | G |
| אתה יודע כמה הוא כסף הרי אני דן נאמ׳ כאן כסף | |
| ונאמ׳ באונס כסף (שם) מה כסף האמ׳ באונס חמשים | |
| כסף אף כסף האמ׳ כן חמשים כסף ◆ או לך לך לדרך זו | H |
| נאמ׳ כאן כסף ונאמ׳ במוציא שם רע כסף (שם יט) | |
| מה כסף האמ׳ במוציא שם רע מאה כסף אף כסף | |
| האמ׳ כאן מאה כסף ◆ נראה למי דומה דנין דבר | I |
| שנידון בנפשו ממי שנידון בנפשו ואל יוכיח מוציא | |
| שם רע שאין נידון בנפשו ◆ או לך לך לדרך זו דנין | J |
| בתולה מבתולה ואין דנין בתולה מבעולה ◆ ת״ל כמהר | K |
| הבתולות ולא כקונס הבתולות ◆ כמהר הבתולות ◆ הרי | B/A | 6 |
| כל הבתולות כזו מה זו בכסף אף כל הבתולות בכסף | |
| (או) מה זו בחמשים כסף אף כל הבתולות בחמשים | |
| כסף ◆ רבן שמע׳ בן גמליאל אומ׳ כתובת אשה אין לה | C |
| קיצבה מן התורה. סל׳ פסו׳ ◆ | |

| | |
|---|---|
| מכשף מכשפה ◆ משמע תפס את הזכר ו(לא) תפס | B/A | 1 |
| את הנקבה ◆ ומפני מה נקראו כשפים על שום נשים | C |
| לפי שרוב כשפים בנשים. ◆ לא תחיה ◆ ר׳ יוסי הגלילי | B/A | 2 |
| אומר נאמ׳ כאן לא תחיה ונאמ׳ להלן לא תחיה כל | |
| נשמה (שם כ טז) מה לא תחיה האמ׳ להלן בסיף אף | |
| כאן בסיף ◆ ור׳ עקיבה אומ׳ נאמ׳ כן לא תחיה ונאמ׳ | C |
| להלן אם בהמה אם איש לא יחיה (שמ׳ יט יג) מה לא | |

farther on [involves death] by stoning, so too does 'you shall not let ... live' stated here [involve death] by stoning."

D.    R. Yosi ha-Galili said to him, "Akiva, I reason 'You shall not let ... live' from [another example of] 'You shall not let live.' But you reason 'You shall not let ... live' from [an example of] 'He shall not live!'" He said [in reply] to him, "You reason from [an example of] the non-Jewish nations, which only [are put to] death by the sword. But I reason from Israel, which has many [methods] of [putting to] death!"

E.    Ben Azzai says, "'Whoever lies with a beast shall be put to death' (Exod. 22:18): It [i.e., Exod. 22:18] is given in relation to it [i.e., Exod. 22:17]—just as this [beast is put to death] by stoning, so too [in this case is the sorceress put to death] by stoning."

F.    R. Judah ben Beteira says, "Behold Scripture states, 'A man or a woman who has a ghost or a familiar spirit (shall be put to death. They shall be pelted with stones)' (Lev. 20:27).

G.    "Wasn't this [case included] in the general [case of the] sorcerer? Why was it singled out? In order to draw an analogy from it: Just as this [case involves death] by stoning, so too this [case in Exod. 22:17 involves death] by stoning. Just as [in] this [case] he is not designated [as possessed and worthy of death] until he does something [to indicate this], so too [with] this [case in Exod. 22:17] he is not liable until he does something."

## LXXIV:V[426]

1.    A.    "Whoever lies with a beast (shall be put to death)" (Exod. 22:18):

B.    Why do I need (Scripture to state this), if (Scripture) already discusses (elsewhere) the man who has intercourse with a beast, and if (Scripture) already discusses (elsewhere) the woman who allows a beast to have intercourse with her?[427]

C.    Why does Scripture state, "Whoever lies with a beast shall be put to death" (Exod. 22:18)?

D.    This [refers to] the male who allows a beast to have intercourse with him.

2.    A.    I only know about domesticated cattle.[428] How does one know from Scripture (to include in the prohibition) beasts of chase?

B.    Scripture states, "Whoever lies with a beast" (Exod. 22:18).

3.    A.    "... shall be put to death" (Exod. 22:18):

B.    By stoning.

## LXXIV:VI

1.    A.    "Whoever sacrifices to a god, (other than the Lord alone,) shall be proscribed" (Exod. 22:19):

B.    One might think that Scripture speaks of the one who slaughters consecrated animals outside of the Temple.[429]

C.    Scripture states, [however,] "... other than the Lord alone" (Exod. 22:19), [which means it speaks of] the one who sacrifices to an idol.

D.    I only know about the one who sacrifices. How does one know from Scripture [to include in the prohibition] the one who sprinkles [sacrificial blood] and the one who offers a libation?

---

[426] Compare LXXIV:V:1.A–3.B with *Mekhilta de-Rabbi Ishmael*, Nezikin (H/R, 310:3–11; Laut., vol. 3., 134:71–135:84; Neus., LXXIV:III: 1.A–4.B).

[427] See, e.g., Lev. 18:23.

[428] Exod. 22:18 states בהמה, which at its most specific means domesticated cattle.

[429] The initial clause in Exod. 22:19 can be read, "Whoever sacrifices to God shall be proscribed." The text, therefore, states that one might think the text speaks of one who sacrifices to God in a manner that would merit being proscribed, i.e., outside of the temple confines.

D יחיה האמ' להלן סקילה אף כן סקילה ◆ אמ' לו ר' יוסי

הגלילי עקיבה אני דן לא תחיה מלא תחיה ואתה דן

לא תחיה מלא יחיה אמ' לו אתה דנו מן הגוים שאין

להן מיתה אלא בסיף ואני דנו מיש[ר]אל שיש להן

E מיתות הרבה ◆ בן עזאי אומ' כל שוכב עם בהמה מות

יומת (שם כב יח) נתנו ענין לו מה זה בסקילה אף זה

F בסקילה ◆ ר' יהודה בן בתירה אומ' הרי הוא אומ' איש

או אשה כי יהיה בהם אוב או ידעוני (ויק' כ כז) ◆

G ו[ה]לא אף זה בכלל מכשף היה ולמה יצא להקיש

אליו מה זה בסקילה אף זה בסקילה מה זה אינו

מיוחד עד שיעשה מעשה אף זה לא יהא חייב עד

שיעשה מעשה. סל' פסו' ◆

LXXIV:V

B/A 1 כל שוכב עם בהמה ◆ מה אני צריך אם הבא על

הבהמה כבר אמור ואם מביאה את הבהמה כבר

D/C אמורה ◆ מה ת"ל כל שוכב עם בהמה מות יומת ◆ זה

A 2 הזכור המביא את הבהמה ◆ אין לי אלא בהמה חיה

B/A 3 B מנין ◆ ת"ל כל שוכב עם בהמה ◆ מות יומת ◆ בסקילה.

סל' פסו' ◆

LXXIV:VI

B/A 1 זבח לאלהים יחרם. ◆ יכול בשוחט קדשים בחוץ

C הכת' מדבר ◆ ת"ל בלתי ליי' לבדו זה הזובח לעבודה

D זרה עצמה ◆ אין לי אלא זובח זורק ומנסך מנין ◆

E.   Scripture states, "... other than the Lord alone" (Exod. 22:19), [meaning,] this includes[430] any [forms of] sacrificial worship [that should only be directed] to the special Name.[431]

F.   One might think [this includes] even the one who embraces [an idol], and kisses [an idol], and honors [an idol], and lies down with [an idol], and washes [an idol].

G.   Scripture states, [however,] "Whoever sacrifices to a god ... shall be proscribed" (Exod. 22:19). Just as slaughtering is specific, in that it is a form of sacrificial worship, these are excluded, because they are not forms of sacrificial worship.

H.   Because we have found with slaughtering that one is liable for slaughtering consecrated animals outside of the Temple, I might think that I should exclude [from liability] the one who bowed down [to an idol].

I.   Scripture states, [however,] "You shall not bow down to them or serve them" (Exod. 20:5). Bowing down is specified [here in order] to teach about it [being prohibited], and [Scripture states in Exod. 22:19,] "slaughtering," in order to teach about all other [methods of worship].

2.   A.   One might think that one would be prohibited from deriving benefit from the property of one who worships idols.

B.   Scripture states, [however,] "Whoever sacrifices to a god ... shall be proscribed" (Exod. 22:19), [but] his property is not prohibited from [being used] to derive benefit.

C.   One might think that an idol would not be prohibited from [being used] to derive benefit.

D.   Scripture states, [however,] "You must reject it as abominable and abhorrent, etc." (Deut. 7:26), [meaning,] an idol in and of itself is prohibited from [being used] to derive benefit, but one may derive benefit from the one who worships idols.

3.   A.   "... other than the Lord" (Exod. 22:19):

B.   This includes the one who associates [the Lord's name with another idol].

*Chapter Seventy-Five*

(Textual Source: Ms. Firkovich II A 268)

LXXV:I

1.   A.   "You shall not wrong a stranger (or oppress him, for you were strangers in the Land of Egypt)" (Exod. 22:20):[432]

B.   Two [forms of] wronging [a person are implied here] in one word: Wronging with financial matters and wronging with words.

C.   "... or oppress him" (Exod. 22:20):

D.   Two [forms of] oppression [of a person are implied here] in one word: Oppression with financial matters and oppression with words.

E.   "... for you were strangers in the Land of Egypt" (Exod. 22:20):

F.   If you harass him for being a convert,[433] I[434] will harass you for being strangers in the Land of Egypt.

G.   And thus Scripture states, "Else I will strip her naked, etc." (Hosea 2:5).

---

[430] The Firkovich manuscript here has the word חזקה, which makes no contextual sense. I translate here, instead, what is attested in the Schocken manuscript of the parallel to this tradition in Midrash ha-Gadol—ריבה.

[431] I.e., the tetragrammaton—YHWH.

ת״ל בלתי לייי לבדו חזקה על כל העבודות לשם המיוחד ◆    E

יכול אף המגפף והמנשק והמכבד והמרביץ והמרחיץ ◆    F

ת״ל זבח לאלהים יחרם מה זביחה מיוחדת שהיא    G

משום עבדה יצאו אלו שאינן משום עבודה ◆ לפי    H

שמצינו בזביחה שחייבין עליה משום השוחט קדשין

בחוץ יכול שאני מוציא את השתחואה ◆ ת״ל לא    I

תשתחוה להם ולא תעבדם (שמ' כ ד) יצאת

השתחואה ללמד על עצמה וזביחה ללמד על כולן ◆

יכול העובד עבו' זרה נכסיו אסורין בהנאה ◆ ת״ל זבח    B/A    2

לאלהים יחרם אין נכסיו אסורין בהנאה ◆ יכול עבו'    C

זרה לא תהא אסורה בהנאה ◆ ת״ל שקץ תשקצנו ותעב    D

תתעבנו וגומ' (דב' ז כו). עבו' זרה עצמה אסורה

בהנאה ואין העובד עבודה זרה אסור בהנאה. ◆ בלתי    A    3

לייי לבדו ◆ להביא את המשתף. סל' פסו' ◆    B

                                              LXXV:I

וגר לא תונה. ◆ שתי אונאות בדבר אחת אונאת    B/A    1

ממון ואחת אונאת דברים. ◆ ולא תלחצנו ◆ שתי לחיצות    D/C

בדבר אחת לחיצת ממון ואחת לחיצת דברים. ◆ כי    E

גרים הייתם בארץ מצ' ◆ אמ' להן אם תופסין אתם    F

אותו לשום גר תופס אני אתכם על שום כי גרים

הייתם בארץ מצ' ◆ וכן הוא אומ' פן אפשיטנה ערומ[ה    G

ו]גומ' (הושע ב ה). ◆

---

[432] Compare 1.A–G with *Mekhilta de-Rabbi Ishmael*, Nezikin (H/R, 311:3–11; Laut., vol. 3, 137:1–138:8; Neus., LXXV:I:1.A–4.D).

[433] The text here understands the term "stranger" (Hebrew: גר) in Exod. 22:20 to refer to a convert to Judaism.

[434] I.e., God.

2.  A.  "(You shall not ill-treat) any widow or orphan" (Exod. 22:21):[435]

    B.  I only know about the widow and orphan. How does one know from Scripture to include any person?

    C.  Scripture states, "You shall not ill-treat ... *any*" (Exod. 22:21).

    D.  If so, why does Scripture state, "... widow or orphan" (Exod. 22:21)?

[211]   E.  [God is saying,] "I will be quick to exact punishment on behalf of the widow and orphan more than for any person! For the wife receives [support] from her husband, and the child receives [support] from his father. But these have no one who will support them, except for Me alone!"

3.  A.  "You shall not ill-treat" (Exod. 22:21):[436]

    B.  Since it says in Scripture, "If you do mistreat them" (Exod. 22:22), one might think he would not be liable unless he oppressed [them once] and then oppressed [them again].[437]

    C.  Scripture states, [however,] "You shall not ill-treat" (Exod. 22:21), [meaning,] even one act of oppression.

    D.  If so, why does Scripture state, "If you do mistreat them" (Exod. 22:22)? To [emphasize individual] liability for each and every act of oppression.

4.  A.  "(If you do mistreat him, I will heed his outcry,) as soon as he cries out to Me" (Exod. 22:22):

    B.  One might think one would not be liable unless [the person] cried out [once] and then cried out [again].[438]

    C.  Scripture states, [however,] "... his outcry" (Exod. 22:22), [meaning,] even one outcry.

    D.  If so, why does Scripture state, "... as soon as he cries out to me" (Exod. 22:22)? To [emphasize individual] liability for each and every outcry.

5.  A.  "... I will heed his outcry" (Exod. 22:22):[439]

    B.  I don't hear [the outcry] of this one the same as [the outcry] of this one.

6.  A.  "My anger shall blaze forth (and I will put you to the sword, and your own wives shall become widows and your children orphans)" (Exod. 22:23):[440]

    B.  Scripture says [here], "anger blaze forth," and Scripture says farther on, "anger blaze forth" (Deut. 11:17). Just as "anger blaze forth" here [is expressed through] a sword, so too farther on [it is expressed through] a sword. Just as "anger blaze forth" said farther on [is expressed through] stopping the rains and exile, so too "anger blaze forth" said here [is expressed through] stopping the rains and exile.

7.  A.  "... and I will put you to the sword" (Exod. 22:23):

    B.  Would God [actually be the one] who kills them? Rather, He brings someone upon them who kills them by the sword!

8.  A.  "... and your own wives shall become widows and your children orphans" (Exod. 22:23):[441]

    B.  And don't we know that once He kills them by the sword their wives will become widows and their children orphans? Rather, they will be captive [in widowhood], and won't be

---

[435] Compare 2.A–E with *Mekhilta de-Rabbi Ishmael*, Nezikin (H/R, 313:1–3; Laut., vol. 3, 141:49–52; Neus., LXXV:I:8.A–D).

[436] Compare 3.A–D with *Mekhilta de-Rabbi Ishmael*, Nezikin (H/R, 313:4–5; Laut., vol. 3, 141:53–55; Neus., LXXV:I:10.A–B).

[437] Reading literally the seemingly doubled infinitive absolute verbal form in Exod. 22:21—ענה תענה.

[438] Reading literally the seemingly doubled infinitive absolute verbal form in Exod. 22:22—צעק יצעק.

[439] For a possible understanding of 5.A–B compare with *Mekhilta de-Rabbi Ishmael*, Nezikin (H/R, 313:16–314:5; Laut., vol. 3, 143:74–84; Neus., LXXV:I:13.A–J).

| | |
|---|---|
| B/A | 2 אלמנה ויתום ◆ אין לי אלא אלמנה ויתום מנין |
| D/C | לרבות כל אדם ◆ ת״ל כל [לא תענו]ן ◆ אם כן למה נאמ׳ |
| E | אלמנה ויתום ◆ ממהר אני ליפרע על ידי אלמנה ויתום |
| | יתר מכל אדם שהאשה קובלת לבעלה בין קובל |
| | לאביו אבל אלו אין להן מי שיקבלו לו אלא לי בלבד ◆ |
| B/A | 3 לא תענון ◆ מכלל שנא׳ אם ענה תענה אותו יכול לא |
| C | יהא חייב עד שיענה ויענה ◆ ת״ל לא תענון אפילו עינוי |
| D | אחד ◆ אם כן למה נאמ׳ אם ענה תענה אותו לחיב אותו על |
| | כל עינוי ‹ועינוי›. ◆ |
| B/Λ | 4 כי אם צעק יצעק אלי ◆ יכול לא יהא חייב עד |
| D/C | שיצעק ויצעק ◆ ת״ל צעקתו אפילו צעקה אחת ◆ אם |
| | כן למה נאמ׳ כי אם צעק יצעק לחייב על כל צעקה |
| B/A | 5 וצעקה ◆ שמוע אשמע צעקתו ◆ לא כשם שאני שומע |
| | מ‹ז›ה אני שומע מזה. סל׳ פסו׳ ◆ |
| B/A | 6 וחרה אפי ◆ נאמ׳ כאן חרון אף ונאמ׳ להלן חרון אף |
| | (דב׳ יא יז) מה חרון אף האמ׳ כן חרב אף להלן חרב |
| | מה חרון אף האמ׳ להלן עצירת גשמים וגלות אף |
| A | 7 חרון אף האמ׳ כן עצירת גשמים וגלות. ◆ והרגתי אתכם |
| B | בחרב. ◆ וכי המק׳ הורג אותן אלא מביא עליהן מי |
| A | 8 שהורג אותם בחרב. ◆ והיו נשיכם אלמנות ובניכם |
| B | יתומים ◆ וכי אין אנו יודעין שכשיהרגם בחרב נשיהן |
| | אלמנות ובניהם יתומים אלא נשיהן יושבות |
| | ומשמרות בשביין ואינן יכולין להינשא ובניהם |

[440] Compare 6.A–B with *Mekhilta de-Rabbi Ishmael,* Nezikin (H/R, 314:6–8; Laut., vol. 3, 144:85–89; Neus., LXXV:I:14.A–E).

[441] Compare 8.A–B with *Mekhilta de-Rabbi Ishmael,* Nezikin (II/R, 314:9–315:4; Laut., vol. 3, 144:90–146:118; Neus., LXXV:I:15.A–K).

able to marry [again], and their sons will be orphans, in that they will be captive [as orphans], and they won't be able to take [their] inheritance.[442]

9.    A.    Another interpretation:

       B.    [God is saying,] "If you delay the execution, in the end their wives will suffer in another court and their sons will suffer in another court!"

10.    A.    Abba Yudan of Zidon says in the name of Rabban Gamliel, "How does one know from Scripture that one should not say, 'It's enough if I pray for the Temple and for the Land of Israel'?

       B.    "Scripture says, 'I will heed their outcry' (Exod. 22:22).

       C.    "And which divine attribute is more abundant, [God's] attribute toward good or [God's] attribute toward exacting punishment? You have to say [God's] attribute toward good is more abundant!

       D.    And if with [God's] attribute toward exacting punishment—the lesser [of the two]—an individual prays and God heeds his prayer, then it is only logical with [God's] attribute toward good—the more abundant [of the two]—[that when] an individual prays, God heeds his prayer![443]

---

[442] I.e., these husband/fathers, however, will be like those killed with no evidence of their death. Without evidence of death, wives cannot remarry and sons cannot inherit.

[443] I.e., since God will heed the prayer of the individual when he prays for God to act upon His attribute of divine punishment, it only follows that God will heed the prayer of the individual when He prays for God to act upon His attribute toward doing good. Therefore, the individual should not limit his prayer to requesting God to rebuild the Temple and restore the Land of Israel (both actions based upon God's attribute of good), but also should pray and request of God other acts of beneficence.

יתומים שהיו יושבין ומשמרין בשבי[ן] ואינ[ן] יכולין

לירד [ל]נחלה. ◆ ד״א ◆ אם [מ]ענים אתם [את] [הדי]ן     B/A   9

[לסוף נ]שיהם מתענות [בבתי דינין אח]רים [וב]ניהם

מת[ענין] בבתי דינין א[חרים. ◆ אב[ה יו[דן] א[יש צי[דן     A   10

אומ׳ משום רבן גמליאל מנין שלא יאמר [אדם] איני

כ[דאי] שאתפלל על בית המק[דש ועל ארץ] ישראל ◆

ת״ל שמ[ע א[שמ[ע צעקתו ◆ וכי אי זו מדה מרובה     C/B

מדת הטוב] או מדת פורענות הוי א[ום׳ מד[ת הטוב

מרובה ◆ ומה <מדת פור[ענות] מועטת היחיד מתפלל     D

והמק[ום] שומע ת[פ]לתו מדת הט[וב] מרובה דין

הוא שה[יחיד] מתפלל והמקום [שומ]ע את תפילת[ו].

סל׳ פסקא׳ ◆

# Tractate Kaspa

*Chapter Seventy-Six*

(Textual Source: Ms. Firkovich II A 268)

**LXXVI:I**

1.  A.  "If you lend money (to My people, to the poor among you, do not act toward them as a creditor. Exact no interest from them)" (Exod. 22:24):

    B.  I only know about money. How does one know from Scripture to include cattle, fruit, and utensils?

    C.  Scripture states, "... you lend" (Exod. 22:24).

    D.  I only know about the loan. How does one know from Scripture to include damage payments, half-damage payments, double-damage payments, and four- or five-fold damage payments?

    E.  Scripture states, "If ... money" (Exod. 22:24).

[212]  F.  If so, then why does Scripture state, "... you lend" (Exod. 22:24)? Based on this you say that one may increase the charge for rent, but one may not increase the sale price. How is this so? If one rents someone his house or rents someone his field, and says to him, "If you pay me now it is 100 *shekel*s, but if [you pay me] later, it is 150," this is exempt from [being considered] interest. But if he sells him his house or sells him his field, and says to him, "If you pay me now it is 100 *shekel*s, but if later, it is 150," this is prohibited as interest.[1]

    G.  As it says in Scripture, "If you lend money to My people" (Exod. 22:24).

2.  A.  "... to the poor among you" (Exod. 22:24):[2]

    B.  Just as the one who borrows is unique, in that you don't [necessarily] collect [payment] from him from what you lent him,[3] this one is excluded, in that you [must] collect [payment] from him from what you lent him.

3.  A.  "... to the poor among you" (Exod. 22:24):

    B.  I only know about the poor. How does one know from Scripture [that this is also the rule] for a rich person?

    C.  Scripture states, "... among you" (Exod. 22:24).

---

[1] Compare 1.F with m. Baba Metzia 5:2.
[2] Compare 2.A–B with *Mekhilta de-Rabbi Ishmael*, Kaspa (H/R, 315:13–14; Laut., vol. 3, 148:11–14; Neus., LXXVI:I:2.A–3.B).
[3] I.e., you might lend him money, but receive payment in goods.

# מסכתא דכספא

אם כסף תלוה • [אין לי] אלא כסף מנין לרבות     B/A   1

בהמ[ה] פירות וכל[י]ם • ת״ל תל[וה] • אין לי אל[א]     D/C

הל[וא]ה מנין לרבות נזק וח[צי] נזק ותשלומי כפל

ותשלומי ד׳ וה׳ • ת[נ]״ל אם כסף • אם כן למה נאמ[׳]     F/F.

תלוה מיכן אתה אומ׳ מרבין על השכר ואין מרבין על

המכר הא כיצד השכיר לו ביתו והשכיר [לו ש]דהו

אמ׳ לו (ביתי) אם ‹מ›עכשיו אתה נותן לי במנה ואם

לאח[ר] זמן במ[א]ה וחמשים מותר משום רבית מכר

לו ביתו ומכר לו שדה[ו] א[מ׳] לו אם מעכשיו אתה

נותן לי במנה ולאחר זמן במאה וחמשים אסור מש׳

ריבית • שנא׳ אם כסף תלוה את עמי • את העני עמך • מה     B/A 2   G

הלואה מיוחדת לא ממה שאתה נותן לו אתה נוטל

ממנו יצא זה שממה שאתה נותן לו אתה נוטל ממנו •

את העני עמך • אין לי אלא עני עשיר מנין • ת״ל עמך •     C/B/A   3

D. How does one know from Scripture [that this is also the rule] for a woman?

E. Scripture states, "... My people" (Exod. 22:24).

F. If so, why does Scripture state, "... to the poor" (Exod. 22:24)?

G. [God is saying,] "I will be quicker to exact punishment on behalf of the poor than the rich."

4. A. "... do not act toward them as a creditor" (Exod. 22:24):

B. If he wouldn't normally inquire about his welfare, he shouldn't inquire about his welfare. [If he wouldn't normally] send him a present, he shouldn't send him a present.

5. A. "Exact no interest from them" (Exod. 22:24):

B. What is interest?

C. [Charging] a *se'ah* for a *kor*[4] or a *sela* for a *maneh*.[5]

6. A. [If] one says to another, "That which I am going to inherit today is [already] sold to you. That which will turn up in my net today is [already] sold to you," how does one know from Scripture that all his words are valid?[6]

B. As it says in Scripture, "*If* you lend money to My people, to the poor *among you*" (Exod. 22:24).[7]

## (Textual Source: Midrash ha-Gadol)

## LXXVI:II

1. A. "If you take (your neighbor's garment) in pledge, (you must return it to him before the sun sets)" (Exod. 22:25):[8]

B. One might think that he[9] has the authority on his own to take [the item] as a pledge.

C. Scripture states, [however,] "... you must not enter his house to seize his pledge" (Deut. 24:10).

D. If so, why does Scripture state, "If you take (your neighbor's garment) in pledge" (Exod. 22:25)? Scripture is speaking about he who has the authority as the agent of the court to seize [the item].

2. A. "If you take" (Exod. 22:25):

B. [Scripture says this to emphasize] liability for each and every [act of] taking.[10]

3. A. "... before the sun sets" (Exod. 22:25):[11]

B. You can't say, "before," because it already says in Scripture, "... at sunset" (Deut. 24:13), and you can't say, "at sunset," because it already says in Scripture, "... before the sun sets" (Exod. 22:25)!

C. Why does Scripture state, "... before the sun sets," and why does Scripture state "... at

---

[4] As a liquid or dry measurement, 30 *se'ah* equal 1 *kor*.

[5] As a measurement of weight, 1 *maneh* equals 100 *shekels*, and 1 *sela* equals 2 *shekels*.

[6] Compare 6.A-B with t. Baba Metzia 4:10.

[7] The text here reads specifically in the verse the words "if" and "among you," which can also be understood as "with you." Thus, this interpretation understands the verse to say, in effect, that "if" one lends [or in this case, sells] an object that is "with you," i.e., already in your possession, it is a valid act of lending. In these scenarios, therefore, the emphasis is on the fact that one promises to sell an object that will be in his possession *today*, i.e., with certainty, and as such is considered to be in his possession at the time he promises to sell it.

[8] Compare 1.A-D with *Sifre Deut.*, Piska 276 (Hammer, p. 269; Neus., CCLXXVI:I:1.A-4.A); and b. Baba Metzia 113b (Neus., XXIID:Tractate Baba Mesia:9:13A-H:I.1.H.-O).

[9] I.e., the creditor.

[10] Reading literally the seemingly doubled infinitive absolute verbal form in Exod. 22:25—חבל תחבל.

| | | |
|---|---|---|
| G/F/E/D | | אשה מנין ◆ ת״ל את עמי ◆ אם כן למה נאמ׳ עני ◆ ממהר |
| A | 4 | אני ליפרע על ידי עני יתר מן העשיר. ◆ לא תהיה לו |
| B | | כנשה ◆ לא יהא למד לשאול בשלומ[ו] לא ישאל |
| A | 5 | בשלומו לשלוח לו דורון לא ישלח לו דורון. ◆ לא |
| C/B | | תשימון עליו נשך ◆ איזה הוא נשך ◆ סאה מכור וסלע |
| A | 6 | ממנה ◆ אמ׳ לו מה שאירש מאבא היום מכור לך מה |
| | | שתעלה היום מצודתי מכור לך מנין כל דבריו קיימין ◆ |
| B | | שנא׳ אם כס[ף] תלוה את עמי את העני עמך ◆ |

LXXVI:II

| | | |
|---|---|---|
| C/B/A | 1 | אם חבל תחבל ◆ יכול שהרשות בידו לחבול ◆ ת״ל |
| D | | לא תבוא אל ביתו לעבוט עבטו (דב׳ כד י) ◆ אם כן |
| | | למה נאמר אם חבל תחבל מי שיש לו רשות לחבול |
| | | בשלוח בית דין הכתוב מדבר. ◆ חבל תחבל ◆ לחייב על |
| B/A | 2 | כל חבול וחבול. ◆ עד בוא השמש ◆ אי אפשר לומר עד |
| B/A | 3 | בוא שכבר נאמר כבוא השמש (דב׳ כד יג) ואי אפשר |
| C | | לומר כבוא שכבר נאמר עד בוא ◆ מה ת״ל עד בוא ומה |

---

[11] Compare 3.A–C with *Mekhilta de-Rabbi Ishmael*, Kaspa (H/R, 316:14–317:4; Laut., vol. 3, 150:44–50; Neus., LXXVI:I:10.A–G); m. Baba Metzia 9:13; and *Sifre Deut.*, Piska 277 (Hammer, p. 269; Neus., CCLXXVII:III:1.A–C).

sunset"? This teaches that one must return to him an item used during the day by the daytime and an item used at night by nighttime, [e.g.,] one returns to him the blanket by nighttime and the plow by daytime, but one needn't return to him the blanket by daytime nor the plow by nighttime.

4.    A.    "... you must return it to him" (Exod. 22:25):[12]

      B.    You must return it to him, and you must not return it to his heirs.

5.    A.    "... clothing" (Exod. 22:26): This refers to his shirt.[13]

      B.    "... covering" (Exod. 22:26): This refers to his cloak.

      C.    "... for his skin" (Exod. 22:26): This refers to his leather spread.

      D.    "In what else shall he sleep?" (Exod. 22:26): This includes the mattress, the cushion, and the sheet.

      E.    I only know about these alone. How does one know from Scripture to include other items?

      F.    Scripture states, "It is his [only] clothing, the [sole] covering for his skin. In what else shall he sleep?" (Exod. 22:26).

      G.    One might think [this would be the case] even if he had two [of the same] items, and he didn't require one of them.

      H.    Scripture states, [however,] "It is his [only] clothing, the [sole] covering for his skin. In what else shall he sleep?" (Exod. 22:26).

6.    A.    Ben Azzai says, "'... for his skin' (Exod. 22:26):

      B.    "Something which he uses for his skin. This excludes the folded [garment] placed in the chest."

7.    A.    "Therefore, if (he cries out to Me, I will pay heed, for I am compassionate)" (Exod. 22:26):

      B.    "If"[14] means only "immediately."

      C.    "... he cries out to Me, I will pay heed, for I am compassionate" (Exod. 22:26):

      D.    [God says,] "Even though I exact punishment Myself, I am also He who gives reward."

[213]    E.    R. Shimon says, "[God says,] 'Those who love wealth love one another, and thieves love one another, and extortioners love one another, and those who charge interest love one another. For whom is it most becoming for Me to punish among all of these—I, who lacks even one of these qualities!'"

## LXXVI:III

1.    A.    "You shall not insult God, (nor put a curse upon a chieftain among your people)" (Exod. 22:27):

      B.    One might think if someone said to him, "You are cursed," he would be guilty.

      C.    Scripture states, [however,] "You shall not revile God" (Exod. 22:27). This tells that one is not liable unless he specifies the name [of God] or a euphemism [for God].

2.    A.    R. Eliezer ben Jacob says, "'You shall not insult God' (Exod. 22:27):[15]

      B.    "This is a warning about [the need to] bless the name [of God]."

---

[12] Compare 4.A–B with m. Baba Metzia 9:13.

[13] Compare 5.A–H with *Mekhilta de-Rabbi Ishmael*, Kaspa (H/R, 317:5–6; Laut., vol. 3, 151:51–52; Neus., LXXVI:I:11.A–F); m. Baba Metzia 9:13; and t. Baba Metzia 10:9.

[14] The text here finds special meaning in the word היה in Exod. 22:26.

[15] Compare 2.A–B with b. Sanhedrin 66a (Neus., XXIIIB:Tractate Sanhedrin:7:8B–E:III.A–F).

ת״ל כבוא מלמד שמחזיר לו כלי יום ביום וכלי לילה
בלילה מחזיר לו את הסגוס בלילה ואת המחרישה
ביום אבל אין מחזיר לו את הסגוס ביום ולא את
המחרישה בלילה. ✦ תשיבנו לו ✦ לו אתה מחזיר ואי אתה	B/A	4
מחזיר ליורשיו. ✦

כסותה זו חלוקו ✦ שמלתו זו טליתו ✦ לעורו זה עור	C/B/A	5
קטבוליה שלו ✦ במה ישכב לרבות את הכר ואת הכסת	D
ואת הסדין ✦ אין לי אלא אלו בלבד מנין לרבות שאר	E
הכלים ✦ ת״ל כסותה שמלתו לעורו במה ישכב. ✦ יכול	G/F
אפלו היו לו שני כלים ואין צריך לאחד מהן ✦ ת״ל היא	H
כסותה היא שמלתו והיא לעורו במה ישכב. ✦ בן עזאי	A	6
אומר לעורו ✦ את שעורו משתמש בה פרט למקופלת	B
ומונחת בתיבה. ✦ והיה ✦ אין והיה אלא מיד. ✦ כי יצעק אלי	C/B/A	7
ושמעתי כי חנון אני ✦ אע״פ שאני נפרע על ידי כך אני	D
הוא שנותן שכר על ידי כך. ✦ היה ר׳ שמעון אומר	E
אוהבי ממון אוהבין זה את זה והגזלנין אוהבין זה את
זה והחמסנין אוהבין זה את זה ומלוי רבית אוהבין זה
את זה למי נאה ליפרע מכל אלו אני הוא שאין בי
אחת מכל המדות הללו. ✦

LXXVI:III

אלהים לא תקלל ✦ יכול אם אמר לו ארור אתה	B/A	1
יהא חייב ✦ ת״ל אלהים לא תקלל מגיד שאינו חייב עד	C
שיפרש בשם או בכנוי. ✦ ר׳ אליעזר בן יעקב אומר	A	2
אלהים לא תקלל ✦ ליתן אזהרה על ברכת השם. ✦	B

3.      A.      One might think if one cursed [someone] after [his] death he would be liable.

     B.      For it is a matter of logic: If one is liable for committing a punishable sin—the lesser [type of sin]—[toward someone after his] death, then it is only logical that he would be liable for committing a "You shall not ..." sin—the more significant [type of sin]—[toward someone after his] death.

     C.      Scripture states, [however,] "You shall not insult the deaf" (Lev. 19:14), [meaning,] just as the deaf person is special, in that he is alive, so too [is one only guilty for cursing] anyone who is alive.

## LXXVI:IV

1.      A.      "(You shall not delay to offer up) from the first yields of your vats" (Exod. 22:28):[16]

     B.      "The first yields" (Exod. 22:28)—these are the first fruits that are taken from the full harvest.

     C.      "... of your vats"[17] (Exod. 22:28)—this is the heave offering, which is called *dema*.[18]

     D.      "You shall not delay to offer up" (Exod. 22:28)—do not delay [to offer up] something that should precede something else. This teaches that whoever [offers up] the heave offering before the first fruits, [or offers up] the first tithe before the heave offering, [or offers up] the second tithe before the first transgresses a negative commandment.[19]

2.      A.      R. Eliezer ben Jacob says, "'You shall not delay to offer up' (Exod. 22:28):

     B.      "In that you should not delay [after] the time of the threshing floor giving it to its owners."[20]

3.      A.      "You shall give Me the first-born among your sons" (Exod. 22:28):

     B.      One might think one should actually give them to Him!

     C.      Scripture states, [however,] "And gave the redemption money to Aaron and his sons (at the Lord's bidding, as the Lord had commanded Moses)" (Num. 3:51).

     D.      I only know this was the case during that time. How does one know from Scripture [that it was also the case for the following] generations?

     E.      Scripture states, "... at the Lord's bidding, as the Lord had commanded Moses" (Num. 3:51).

     F.      If so, why does Scripture state, "You shall give Me the first-born among your sons" (Exod. 22:28)? [God is saying,] "Whenever you give it[21] as commanded, I attribute it to you as if you [actually] gave him[22] to Me. Whenever you don't give it as commanded, I attribute it to you as if you [actually] slapped Me!"

4.      A.      "You shall give Me the first-born among your sons. You shall do the same with your cattle and your flocks" (Exod. 22:28–29):

     B.      Just as the human first-born [is given] in the provinces, so too is the first-born of cattle [given] in the provinces.

5.      A.      Since Scripture says, "... on the eighth day you shall give it to Me" (Exod. 22:29), one might think that Jews should give the first-born of cattle to the priest when it is eight days old.

---

[16] Compare 1.A–D with *Mekhilta de-Rabbi Ishmael,* Kaspa (H/R, 318:9–319:4; Laut., vol. 3, 153:80–154:94; Neus., LXXVI:III:1.A–M).

[17] Hebrew: *dima'kha*—דמעך.

[18] Hebrew: דמע.

[19] I.e., a commandment that proscribes an action.

[20] I.e., do not delay giving the required tithe of the threshed harvest to the priests and to God.

[21] I.e., the redemption money for the first-born.

[22] I.e., the first-born son.

| | |
|---|---|
| B/A | 3 |
| | |
| C | |

יכול אם קללן לאחר מיתה יהא חייב ♦ ודין הוא ומה
עונש מועט חייבין עליו לאחר מיתה אזהרה מרובה אינו
דין שיהו חייבין עליו לאחר מיתה ♦ ת״ל לא תקלל חרש
(ויק׳ יט יד) מה חרש מיוחד שהוא בחיים אף כל
שהוא בחיים. ♦

| | |
|---|---|
| B/A | 1 |
| D/C | |

מלאתך ודמעך ♦ מלאתך אלו בכורים שהן ניטלין
מן המליא ♦ ודמעך זו תרומה שהיא נקראת דמע. ♦ לא
תאחר לא תאחר דבר שראוי להקדימו מלמד שכל
המקדים תרומה לבכורים מעשר ראשון לתרומה
מעשר שני לראשון עובר בלא תעשה. ♦

| | |
|---|---|
| A | 2 |
| B | |

ר׳ אליעזר בן
יעקב אומר לא תאחר ♦ שלא תאחרם בשעת הגורן
מליתנם לבעלים. ♦

| | |
|---|---|
| B/A | 3 |
| C | |
| E/D | |
| F | |

בכור בניך תתן לי ♦ יכול יתנם לו
ודאי ♦ ת״ל ויתן משה את כסף הפדיום לאהרן ולבניו
(במ׳ ג נא) ♦ אי לי אלא בזמן ההוא לדורות מנין ♦ ת״ל על
פי ה׳ כאשר צוה ה׳ את משה (שם) ♦ אם כן למה נאמר
בכור בניך תתן לי כל זמן שאתה נותנו כמצותו מעלה
אני עליך כאלו לי נתתו ובזמן שאין אתה נותנו
כמצותו מעלה אני עליך כאלו אותי קפחת. ♦

| | |
|---|---|
| B/A | 4 |
| A | 5 |

בכור בניך תתן לי כן תעשה לשורך לצאנך ♦ מה
בכור אדם בגבולין כך בכור בהמה בגבולין. ♦ לפי
שהוא אומ׳ ביום השמיני תתנו לי יכול יהו ישראל
נותנין בכור בהמה לכהן כשהוא בן שמונה ♦

B. Scripture states, [however,] "You shall give Me the first-born among your sons. You shall do the same with your cattle and your flocks" (Exod. 22:28–29), [meaning,] just as the human first-born is redeemed only at the age of 30 days, so too the first-born of cattle [is only redeemed] at the age of 30 days.

C. Based on this you say: How long must a Jew care for the first-born of small cattle? Thirty days.

D. One might think even large cattle [are redeemed] at the age of 30 days.

E. Scripture states, [however,] "You shall do the same with your cattle" (Exod. 22:29). Scripture added to it another additional [statement] of "doing."[23]

F. How long must a Jew care for cattle? Small [cattle] for 30 days and large [cattle] for 50 days.

6.    A. "Seven days it shall remain with its mother. On the eighth day (you shall give it to Me)" (Exod. 22:29):[24]

B. One might think that fit [cattle are given only] on the eighth day, but defective [cattle may be given] from the eighth day forward.

C. Scripture states, [however,] of [cattle] consecrated [to be sacrificed to God], "... from the eighth day on it shall be acceptable" (Lev. 22:27).

D. One might think that fit [cattle are given] on the eighth day forward, but defective [cattle are given only] on the eighth day.

E. Scripture states, [however,] "On the eighth day you shall give it to Me" (Exod. 22:29).

F. How does one know from Scripture to apply that which is said about this one to that one and that which is said about that one to this one?

G. Scripture states "its mother" [in Exod. 22:29] and "its mother" [in Lev. 22:27], [in order to provide the opportunity to interpret them using] a *gezerah shaveh:*[25]

H. Just as with "its mother" stated farther on, the consecrated [animal] nurses from the unconsecrated [animal], so too with "its mother" stated here does the consecrated [animal] nurse from the unconsecrated [animal].

I. Based on this they said: One does not nurse consecrated animals with each other.

7.    A. "... you shall give it to Me" (Exod. 22:29):

B. This teaches that all the offerings are suitable from the eighth day.

## Chapter Seventy-Seven

### (Textual Source: Midrash ha-Gadol)

### LXXVII:I

1.    A. "(You shall be holy) people (to Me. You must not eat flesh torn by beasts in the field. You shall cast it to the dogs)" (Exod. 22:30):

B. I only know about men. How does one know from Scripture about women?

C. Scripture states, "You shall be ... to Me" (Exod. 22:30).

---

[23] I.e., after saying "You shall give Me the first-born among your sons" the biblical text continues with "You shall *do* the same with your cattle and your flocks."

[24] Compare 6.A–I with *Mekhilta de-Rabbi Ishmael,* Kaspa (H/R, 319:12–320:8; Laut., vol. 3, 155:118–156:135; Neus., LXXVI:III:7.A–9.B); and *Sifra,* Emor 8:5 (Neus., CCXXV:I:4.A–7.D).

[25] I.e., the employment of the same word in separate scriptural contexts, thus facilitating the application of the meaning of the word in one context to the other.

| | | |
|---|---|---|
| ת״ל בכור בניך תתן לי כן תעשה לשורך לצאנך מה בכור | B | |
| אדם אינו נפדה אלא לשלשים יום אף בכור בהמה | | |
| לשלשים יום ✦ מכאן אתה אומר עד כמה חייבין ישראל | C | |
| ליטפל בבכור בבהמה דקה שלשים יום ✦ יכול אף | D | |
| בגסה שלשים יום ✦ ת״ל כן תעשה לשורך ריבה לו | E | |
| הכתוב עשייה אחרת ✦ עד כמה ישראל חייבין ליטפל | F | |
| בבכור בדקה שלשים יום ובגסה חמשים יום. ✦ שבעת | A | 6 |
| ימים יהיה עם אמו ביום השמיני ✦ יכול בכור כשר ביום | B | |
| השמיני ופסול מיום השמיני ולהלן ✦ ת״ל במוקדשין | C | |
| מיום השמיני והלאה ירצה (ויק׳ כב כז) ✦ יכול יהו | D | |
| כשרין משמיני ואילך ופסולין ביום השמיני ✦ ת״ל ביום | E | |
| השמיני תתנו לי ✦ מנין ליתן את האמור שלזה בזה ואת | F | |
| האמור שלזה בזה ✦ ת״ל אמו אמו לגזירה שוה ✦ מה אמו | H/G | |
| האמור להלן קדש יונק מן החול אף אמו האמור כאן | | |
| קדש יונק מן החול ✦ מכאן אמרו לא יניקו קדשים זה | I | |
| את זה. ✦ תתנו לי ✦ מלמד שכל הקרבנות כשרין מיום | B/A | 7 |
| השמיני. ✦ | | |

| | | |
|---|---|---|
| ואנשי ✦ אין לי אלא אנשים נשים מנין ✦ ת״ל תהיון לי. ✦ | C/B/A | 1 |

2.  A.  "... flesh ... in the field" (Exod. 22:30):[26]

    B.  I only know about [flesh] torn in the field.

[214]   C.  How does one know from Scripture [to include flesh torn] on a roof, in a courtyard, or in a deserted building?

    D.  Scripture states, "You must not eat ... torn" (Exod. 22:30).

    E.  One might think it would be [entirely] prohibited if it was torn on its ear or on its leg.

    F.  Scripture states, [however,] "You shall cast it to the dogs." (Exod. 22:30).

3.  A.  R. Eliezer ben Jacob says, "'You must not eat flesh torn' (Exod. 22:30):[27]

    B.  "[Scripture says this] to provide a warning against torn flesh.

    C.  "I only know about [flesh] that was torn. How does one know from Scripture to include in the prohibition flesh that was separated [otherwise] from the cattle?

    D.  "Scripture states, 'You must not eat flesh ... by beasts in the field' (Exod. 22:30).

    E.  "How does one know from Scripture if a limb of an embryo came out [of the cow's vagina], and then its mother was slaughtered, it [would be prohibited] as a negative commandment?

    F.  "Scripture states, '... flesh torn ... in the field' (Exod. 22:30).

    G.  "How does one know from Scripture that [higher] consecrated meat that went outside the curtains of the Temple, and [lesser] consecrated meat that went outside the walls of Jerusalem, and meat of the paschal sacrifice that went outside a group formed to share a paschal lamb [would be prohibited] as a negative commandment?

    H.  "Scripture states, '... flesh ... in the field' (Exod. 22:30)."

4.  A.  "You must not eat" (Exod. 22:30):

    B.  Nothing less than an olive's amount constitutes "eating."

5.  A.  "You shall cast it to the dogs" (Exod. 22:30):

    B.  This teaches that it is permitted [to be used otherwise] to gain benefit.

6.  A.  "... it" (Exod. 22:30):

    B.  You cast it to the dogs, but you do not cast consecrated cattle that die to the dogs.

## LXXVII:II

1.  A.  "You must not carry false rumors" (Exod. 23:1):[28]

    B.  In that they should not have advocates speak before them [in court in place of the actual parties themselves].

    C.  How does one know from Scripture that a judge should not listen to the charge of one of the litigants until his fellow [litigant] arrives?

    D.  Scripture states, "You must not carry false rumors" (Exod. 23:1).

    E.  And how does one know from Scripture that a person should not make a false charge?

    F.  Scripture states, "You must not carry[29] false rumors" (Exod. 23:1), [which you should also

---

[26] Compare 2.A–F with *Mekhilta de-Rabbi Ishmael,* Kaspa (H/R, 320:14–321:8; Laut., vol. 3, 157:8–158:22; Neus., LXXVII:I:4.A–9.C).
[27] Compare 3.A–H with b. Ḥullin 73b (Neus., XXX.B:Tractate Ḥullin:IV.1.A–V.2.D).
[28] Compare 1.A–J with *Mekhilta de-Rabbi Ishmael,* Kaspa (H/R, 321:19–322:5; Laut., vol. 3, 160:40–48; Neus., LXXVII:II:1.A–4.D).
[29] Hebrew: *tisah*—תשא.

| | | |
|---|---|---|
| 2 | C/B/A | ובשר בשדה ◆ אין לי אלא שנטרפה בשדה ◆ בגג ובחצר |
| | E/D | ובחרבה מנין ◆ ת״ל טרפה לא תאכלו ◆ יכול נטרפה |
| | F | באזנה וברגלה תהא אסורה ◆ ת״ל לכלב תשליכון |
| 3 | A | אותו. ◆ ר׳ אליעזר בן יעקב אומר טרפה לא תאכלו ◆ |
| | C/B | ליתן אזהרה על הטרפה. ◆ אין לי אלא שנטרפה מנין |
| | D | לבשר שפירש מן הבהמה שהוא באזהרה ◆ ת״ל ובשר |
| | E | בשדה לא תאכלו. ◆ מנין לאבר עובר שיצא ואחר כך |
| | F | נשחטה אמו שהוא בלא תעשה ◆ ת״ל ובשר בשדה |
| | G | טרפה. ◆ מנין לבשר קדשים שיצא חוץ לקלעים ובשר |
| | | קדשים קלים שיצא חוץ לחומת ירושלם ובשר פסח |
| | H | שיצא חוץ לחבורה שהן בלא תעשה ◆ ת״ל ובשר בשדה. ◆ |
| 4 B/A | 5 A | לא תאכלו ◆ אין אכילה פחותה מכזית. ◆ לכלב תשליכון |
| | B/A 6 | מלמד שהיא מותרת בהנאה. ◆ אותו ◆ אותו אתה משליך |
| | | לכלב ואין אתה משליך בהמת קדשים שמתה לכלב. ◆ |

LXXVII:II

| | | |
|---|---|---|
| 1 | B/A | לא תשא שמע שוא ◆ שלא ידברו סניגורין לפניהן. ◆ |
| | C | מנין לדיין שלא ישמע טענת אחד מבעלי דינין עד |
| | E/D | שלא יבוא חבירו ◆ ת״ל לא תשא שמע שוא. ◆ ומנין שלא |
| | F | יטעון אדם טענת שקר ◆ ת״ל לא תשא שמע שוא לא |

read as] "You must not incite[30] false rumors."

G. And how does one know from Scripture that it is prohibited to tell false rumors and to accept false rumors?

H. Scripture states, "You must not carry" (Exod. 23:1), [which you should also read as] "You must not incite."

I. And how does one know from Scripture that if a witness knows that his companion is wicked, he should not testify on his behalf?

J. Scripture states, "You must not join hands with the guilty (to act as a malicious witness)" (Exod. 23:1), [meaning,] don't join up with him in testimony.

## LXXVII:III

1. A. "You should not side with the majority to do wrong. (You shall not give perverse testimony in a dispute so as to pervert it in favor of the majority)" (Exod. 23:2):[31]

   B. How does one know from Scripture that capital cases [are tried] in front of 23 judges?

   C. Scripture states, "(In such cases) the assembly shall decide (between the slayer and the blood-avenger). The assembly shall protect (the manslayer from the blood-avenger)" (Num. 35:24–25).

   D. One assembly decides and one assembly protects, [that is,] 10 [judges] declare innocent and 10 declare guilty. How does one know from Scripture [that there are] three [more judges]?

   E. By implication from what it says in Scripture, "You should not side with the majority to do wrong" (Exod. 23:3), meaning, you should not side with them to do wrong, but you may side with them to do good.

   F. Might one think you should not side with them to do evil under any circumstance?

   G. Scripture states, "... in favor of the majority" (Exod. 23:2).

   H. From this you say: Since the Torah said to give the death penalty on the basis of witnesses and to give the death penalty on the basis of a majority, just as witnesses means no less than two, so too must the majority be no less than two. Since there cannot be a court with an even number [of judges], you add another one to them, and behold—23 [judges]!

2. A. Rabbi says, "By implication from what it says in Scripture—'You should not side with the majority to do wrong' (Exod. 23:2)—I assume he should side with them to do good.

   B. "If so, why is it said in Scripture, '... in favor of the majority' (Exod. 23:2)? So that [you know that] your siding [with the majority] to do good is not like your siding [with the majority] to do wrong. Your siding [with the majority] to do good [can be] with [a majority of only] one. [Your siding with the majority] to do wrong [can be] with [a majority of only] two."

3. A. "You shall not give perverse testimony so as to pervert" (Exod. 23:2):

   B. You should not say at the time of the verdict, "It's sufficient that I [vote] as my Master So and So [votes]!" Rather, speak [based upon] what is before you!

4. A. "You shall not show deference to a poor man (in his dispute)" (Exod. 23:3):[32]

   B. One might think he should not show deference to him with his wealth.

   C. Scripture states, [however,] "... in his dispute" (Exod. 23:3), [meaning,] he should not

---

[30] Hebrew: tasi—תשיא.

[31] Compare 1.A–3.B with m. Sanhedrin 1:6 and t. Sanhedrin 3:7–8.

[32] Compare 4.A–D with Sifre Deut., Piska 17 (Hammer, p. 40; Neus., XVII:II:1.A–C).

תשיא שמע שוא. ◆ ומנין שלא יטעים אדם דבריו לדיין G

תחלה ת״ל לא תשא שמא שוא לא תשיא שמע שוא.

ומנין אזהרה למספר לשון הרע ולמקבל לשון הרע ◆

ת״ל לא תשא לא תשיא. ◆ ומנין לעד אחד שיודע I/H

בחבירו שהוא רשע אל יעיד עמו ◆ ת״ל אל תשת ידך J

עם רשע אל תצטרף עמו לעדות. ◆

LXXVII:III

לא תהיה אחרי רבים לרעות ◆ מנין שדיני נפשות B/A 1

בעשרים ושלשה ◆ ת״ל ושפטו העדה והצילו העדה C

(במ׳ לה כד - כה) ◆ עדה שופטת ועדה מצלת עשרה D

מזכין ועשרה מחייבין שלשה מנין ◆ ממשמע שנאמר E

לא תהיה אחרי רבים לרעות מכלל שאי אתה הווה

עמהן לרעה את הווה עמהן לטובה ◆ יכול שאי אתה F

הווה עמהן לרעה כל עיקר ◆ ות״ל אחרי רבים להטות ◆ G

אמור מעתה הואיל ואמרה תורה הרוג על פי עדים H

הרוג על פי מה עדים אין פחות משנים אף מטין

אין פחות משנים אין בית דין שקול מוסיפין עליהן

עוד אחד הרי שלשה ועשרים. ◆ ר׳ אומר ממשמע A 2

שנאמר לא תהיה אחרי רבים לרעות שומע אני היה

עמהן לטובה ◆ אם כן למה נאמר אחרי רבים להטות B

שלא תהא הטותך לטובה כהטותך לרעה הטותך

לטובה על פי אחד ולרעה על פי שנים. ◆ ולא תענה על A 3

רב לנטות ◆ שלא תאמר (בשעת מנין) דיי שאהיה B

כ‹רבי› פלוני אלא אמור מה שלפניך. [יכול אף דיני

ממונות כן ת״ל אחרי רבים להטות]. ◆

ודל לא תהדר ◆ יכול לא יהדרנו בממון ◆ ת״ל בריבו. C/B/A 4

[215]   show deference to him in law, in that you should not say, "This one is poor, the son of good [parents]. I will acquit him so that he may be sustained [through charity] with honor."

D.   Scripture states, "You shall not show deference to a poor man in his dispute" (Exod. 23:3). And farther ahead Scripture says, "Do not favor the poor" (Lev. 19:15).

LXXVII:IV

1.   A.   "When you encounter (your enemy's ox or ass wandering, you must take it back to him)" (Exod. 23:4):[33]

B.   I only know about a positive commandment.[34] How does one know from Scripture about [the corresponding] negative commandment?[35]

C.   Scripture states, "Do not look (at your fellow's ox or sheep gone astray) and ignore it" (Deut. 22:1).

D.   "… your fellow's ox" (Deut. 22:1): I only know about your fellow's. How does one know from Scripture about your enemy's?

E.   Scripture states, "… your enemy's ox" (Exod. 23:4), [meaning,] in any event.

F.   One might think [this is also the case for the ox] belonging to other people [than these].

G.   Scripture states, "… your fellow's" (Deut. 22:1). Just as your brother is of your people, so too [is this the case only] with anyone who is of your people.

H.   [God says,] "If you conquer your inclination to make your enemy your friend, I promise you that I will make your enemy your friend."

2.   A.   "When you encounter" (Exod. 23:4):[36]

B.   One might think [this means] actually encounter.

C.   Scripture states, [however,] "When you see" (Exod. 23:5).

D.   One might think [this applies even] when one sees it from a distance.

E.   Scripture states, [however,] "When you encounter" (Exod. 23:4).

F.   How is this so? Seeing is like meeting [when the distance is] two-fifteenths of a mile—the measure of a *ris*.

3.   A.   "… wandering" (Exod. 23:4):[37]

B.   Anything lost along its way.

C.   Based on this you say: If an ass was grazing along its way with its gear placed as it normally would be, they are not obligated [to return it]. If a donkey was wandering through a vineyard with its gear spread out in the middle of the way, they are obligated [to return it].

4.   A.   "You must take it back to him" (Exod. 23:4):[38]

B.   Since it says in Scripture, "Honor your father and your mother" (Exod. 20:12), one might think if his father and his mother said to him, "Don't return [it]," he should listen to them.

C.   Scripture states, [however,] "You *must* take it back to him" (Exod. 23:4).[39]

---

[33] Compare 1.A–H with *Sifre Deut.*, Piska 222 (Hammer, p. 233; Neus., CCXXII:I:1.A–2.F).

[34] I.e., a commandment that prescribes an action or behavior.

[35] I.e., a commandment that proscribes an action or behavior.

[36] Compare 2.A–F with *Mekhilta de-Rabbi Ishmael*, Kaspa (H/R, 323:10–324:2; Laut., vol. 3, 163:80–85; Neus., LXXVII:III:1.A–H); and *Sifre Deut.*, Piska 222 (Hammer, p. 233; absent in Neus.).

[37] Compare 3.A–C with m. Baba Metzia 2:9.

[38] Compare 4.A–E with m. Baba Metzia 2:10.

[39] The text here interprets in this fashion the seemingly doubled verbal form of the infinitive absolute (השב תשיבנו).

שלא יהדרנו בדין שלא תאמר עני הוא זה בן טובים
הוא אזכנו בדין ונמצא מתפרנס בנקיות ◆ ת״ל ודל לא
תהדר בריבו ולהלן הוא אומר לא תשא פני דל (ויק׳
יט טו). ◆

כי תפגע ◆ אין לי אלא מצות עשה מצות לא תעשה     B/A    1
מנין ◆ ת״ל לא תראה (דב׳ כב א). ◆ את שור אחיך אין לי     D/C
אלא אחיך אויבך מנין ◆ ת״ל שור אויבך מכל מקום. ◆     E
יכול אף שלאחרים כן ◆ ת״ל אחיך מה אחיך שהוא     G/F
עמות עמך כך כל אדם שהוא עמות עמך ◆ אם כפת     H
את יצרך לעשות שונאך אוהבך מבטיחך אני שאני
עושה שונאך אוהבך. ◆ כי תפגע ◆ יכול פגיעה ממש ◆ ת״ל     C/B/A    2
כי תראה ◆ יכול משיראנו מרחוק ◆ ת״ל כי תפגע ◆ הא     F/E/D
כאיזה צד ראייה שהיא כפגיעה אחד משבעה ומחצה
במיל שיעור רוס. ◆ תעה ◆ כל שדרך תעיתו ◆ מכאן אתה     C/B/A    3
אומר היה חמור רועה כדרכו וכלים מונחין כדרכן אין
נזקק להן. חמור מפסיג בין הכרמים כלים מונחין באמצע
דרך הרי זה יזקק להן. ◆ השב תשיבנו ◆ מכלל שנא׳     B/A    4
כבד את אביך ואת אמך (שמ׳ כ יא) יכול אפלו אמרו לו
אביו ואמו אל תחזיר ישמע להם ◆ ת״ל השב תשיבנו. ◆     C

D. If he returned it and it fled [again], and he returned it [again] and it fled [again], how does one know from Scripture that he is obligated to return it [even again]?

E. Scripture states, "You *must* take it back to him" (Exod. 23:4)—even 100 times.[40]

## LXXVII:V

1. A. "When you see (the ass of your enemy lying under its burden and would refrain from helping it, you must nevertheless help him with it)" (Exod. 23:5):[41]

   B. I only know about a positive commandment.[42] How does one know from Scripture about [the corresponding] negative commandment?[43]

   C. Scripture states, "Do not look (at your fellow's ass or ox fallen on the road and ignore it)" (Deut. 22:4).

2. A. "When you see" (Exod. 23:5):

   B. One might think [this applies even] when one sees it from a distance.

   C. Scripture states, [however,] "When you encounter" (Exod. 23:4).

   D. One might think [this means] actually encounter.

   E. Scripture states, [however,] "When you see" (Exod. 23:5).

   F. How is this so? Seeing can constitute meeting. And when does seeing constitute meeting? The Sages calculated two-fifteenths of a mile—the measure of a *ris*.

3. A. "... lying" (Exod. 23:5):

   B. And not standing.

   C. "... under its burden" (Exod. 23:5):

   D. And not unloaded.

   E. "... and would refrain from helping it" (Exod. 23:5):

   F. How can you say from Scripture that if one was an important person or was a priest and it[44] was in the graveyard, or it was nightfall on the eve of *Shabbat,* he would not be permitted to be engaged with it?[45]

   G. Scripture states, "... and would refrain" (Exod. 23:5), [meaning,] sometimes you refrain and sometimes you don't refrain.

4. A. "... you must nevertheless help him with it" (Exod. 23:5):

   B. This is the commandment of relieving an overburdened animal.

   C. And farther on Scripture says, "... you must help him raise it" (Deut. 22:4).

   D. This is the commandment of assisting in loading an animal.

   E. Relieving an overburdened animal is for free, but assisting in loading an animal is for hire. The commandment of relieving an overburdened animal takes precedence over the commandment of assisting in loading an animal.

---

[40] Ibid.

[41] Compare 1.A–C with *Mekhilta de-Rabbi Ishmael,* Kaspa (H/R, 325:7–8; Laut., vol. 3, 165:116–118; Neus., LXXVII:III:13.A–B); and *Sifre Deut.,* Piska 225 (Hammer, p. 235; Neus., CCXXV:I:1.A–D).

[42] I.e., a commandment that prescribes an action or behavior.

[43] I.e., a commandment that proscribes an action or behavior.

[44] I.e., the burdened animal.

[45] Compare 3.F–G with *Sifre Deut.,* Piska 225 (Hammer, p. 235; Neus., CCXXV:II:1.A–G).

| | | |
|---:|---:|---:|
| E/D | | החזירה וברחה החזירה החזירה וברחה מנין שחייב להחזיר ✦ ת״ל |
| | | השב תשיבנו אפלו מאה פעמים. ✦ |

| | | |
|---:|---:|---:|
| B/A | 1 | כי תראה ✦ אין לי אלא מצות עשה מצות לא תעשה |
| B/A 2 | C | מנין ✦ ת״ל לא תראה (דב׳ כב ד). ✦ [כי תראה ✦ יכול אפי׳ |
| D/C | | מרחוק ✦ ת״ל כי תפגע ✦ אי כי תפגע יכול פגיעה ממש ✦ |
| F/E | | ת״ל כי תראה ✦ הא כיצד ראיה שיש בה פגיעה ‹ואיזו |
| | | היא ראיה שיש בה פגיעה› שיערו חכמים אחד |
| B/A | 3 | משבעה ומחצה במיל וזה הוא ריס]. ✦ רבץ ✦ ולא עומד. ✦ |
| F/E/D/C | | תחת משאו ✦ ולא פרוק. ✦ וחדלת מעזב לו ✦ מנין אתה |
| | | אומר היה אדם גדול או שהיה כהן והיא בבית |
| | | הקברות או שחשיכה לילי שבת שאין רשאי ליזקק |
| G | | לה ✦ ת״ל וחדלת פעמים שאתה חודל פעמים שאי |
| C/B/A | 4 | אתה חודל. ✦ עזב תעזב עמו ✦ זו מצות פריקה ✦ ולהלן הוא |
| E/D | | אומר הקם תקים עמו (דב׳ כב ד) ✦ זו מצות טעינה ✦ פריקה |
| | | בחנם וטעינה בשכר. מצות פריקה קודמת למצות טעינה. ✦ |

5.    A.    "... you must nevertheless help him with it" (Exod. 23:5):[46]

      B.    If he[47] sits there[48] and says to him, "Since you are commanded, if you want to unload, then unload or don't unload," he would be exempt (if he didn't help him).

      C.    As it says in Scripture, "... help him" (Exod. 23:5).

      D.    One might think [this would be the case] even [if the owner of the animal] was old or sick.

      E.    Scripture states, [however,] "... you must nevertheless help" (Exod. 23:5).

6.    A.    "... him with it" (Exod. 23:5):

      B.    This includes the load that is on his shoulders.

## Chapter Seventy-Eight

### (Textual Source: Midrash ha-Gadol)

### LXXVIII:I

1.    A.    "You shall not subvert the rights of your needy (in their disputes)" (Exod. 23:6):[49]

      B.    Why do I need Scripture to say this? Has it not already been said, "You shall not judge unfairly" (Deut. 16:18), [meaning,] whether poor or rich?

      C.    Why does Scripture say, "You shall not subvert the rights of your needy" (Exod. 23:6)? This [refers] to the one needy [in performance of] the commandments, in that you should not say, "This one is wicked, so whether it is ascertained that he is lying or ascertained that he isn't lying, I'll treat him too severely."

      D.    Scripture states, "You shall not subvert the rights of your needy" (Exod. 23:6).

2.    A.    ["Keep far from a false charge. Do not bring death on those who are innocent and in the right, for I will not acquit the wrongdoer" (Exod. 23:7) :][50]

      B.    How does one know from Scripture that if three people claim a debt against one person, that one should not become the litigant and two the witnesses and then collect it from him and divide it?

[216]    C.    Scripture states, "Keep far from a false charge" (Exod. 23:7).

3.    A.    "Do not bring death on those who are innocent and in the right" (Exod. 23:7):[51]

      B.    How do you say from Scripture if one has a witness [against him] but doesn't have the legal warning[52] [against him, or] has the legal warning but doesn't have the witnesses, he is exempt? Or if two testify against one that he violated *Shabbat,* one testifying that he picked figs and one testifying that he picked grapes [or] one testifying that he picked black figs and one testifying that he picked white figs,[53] one might think that since, in any event, he did violate *Shabbat* he should be put to death.

      C.    Scripture states, [however,] "Do not bring death on those who are innocent and in the right" (Exod. 23:7).

4.    A.    "Do not bring death on those who are innocent and in the right" (Exod. 23:7):[54]

---

[46] Compare 5.A–E with m. Baba Metzia 2:10 and *Sifre Deut.,* Piska 225 (Hammer, p. 235; Neus., CCXXV:II:3.A–4.B).

[47] I.e., the owner of the animal.

[48] I.e., unwilling to help.

[49] Compare 1.A–D with *Mekhilta de-Rabbi Ishmael,* Kaspa (H/R, 326:11–15; Laut., vol. 3, 168:1–8; Neus., LXXVIII:I:1.A–3.D).

[50] Compare 2.A–C with b. Shebuot 31a (Neus., XXVII.B:Tractate Shebuot:4:2:I.20.V–W).

[51] Compare 3.A–C with *Mekhilta de-Rabbi Ishmael,* Kaspa (H/R, 327:5–11; Laut., vol. 3, 169:22–170:31; Neus., LXXVIII:I:9.A–10.F).

[52] I.e., the legal warning given to an offender just before he commits his crime.

[53] He cannot officially be proven guilty of violating *Shabbat,* because he lacks two corroborating witnesses on either count.

5 B/A עזב תעזב עמו • הלך וישב לו ואמר לו הואיל

ועליך מצוה אם רצית לפרוק פרוק או לא תפרוק

E/D/C פטור • שנא' עמו • יכול אפלו זקן וחולה • ת״ל עזב

6 B/A תעזב. עמו • לרבות משוי שעל כתיפו. •

LXXVIII:I

1 B/A לא תטה משפט אבינך • מה אני צריך והלא כבר

נאמר לא תטה משפט (דב' טז יט) אחד עני ואחד

C עשיר • מה ת״ל לא תטה משפט אבינך זה אביון

במצות שלא תאמר רשע הוא חזקתו שהוא משקר

D וחזקת זה שאינו משקר אעבר עליו את הדין • ת״ל לא

תטה משפט אבינך. •

2 B/A [מנין לשלשה שנושין באחד מנה שלא יהא אחד

C בעל דין ושנים עדים ויוציאו ממנו ויחלוקו • תלמוד

3 B/A לומר מדבר שקר תרחק]. • ונקי וצדיק אל תהרג • מנין

אתה אומר יש לו עדים ואין לו התראה יש לו התראה

ואין לו עדים פטור שנים מעידין בו שחילל את

השבת אחד מעיד שליקט תינין ואחד מעיד שליקט

ענבים אחד מעיד שליקט שחורות ואחד מעיד שליקט

לבנות יכול הואיל וחלל זה שבת מכל מקום יבוא

A 4 C ויהרג • ת״ל ונקי וצדיק אל תהרג. • ונקי וצדיק אל תהרג •

---

[54] Compare 4.A–L with *Mekhilta de-Rabbi Ishmael,* Kaspa (H/R, 327:18–328:6; Laut., vol. 3, 171:42–172:52; Neus., LXXVIII:I:13.A–14.H); y. Sanhedrin 22a (Neus., 4:3:I.A–II.C); and b. Sanhedrin 33b (Neus., XXIIIB:Tractate Sanhedrin:4:2:VIII.A–Q).

B.  This teaches that you can grant one a new trial in order to find him innocent.

C.  One might think you can grant one a new trial in order to find him guilty.

D.  Scripture states, [however,] "Do not bring death on those who are innocent and in the right" (Exod. 23:7).

E.  I only know about [the one sentenced] to death. How does one know from Scripture about [the one sentenced] to exile?

F.  Scripture states here, "... charge" (Exod. 23:7), and Scripture states farther on, "... charge" (Deut. 19:4). Just as "charge" stated farther on [involves a sentence of] exile, so too does "charge" stated here [involve a sentence of] exile.

G.  I only know about [the one sentenced] to exile. How does one know from Scripture about [the one sentenced] to stripes?

H.  Scripture states here, "... wrongdoer" (Exod. 23:7), and Scripture states farther on, "... wrong-doer" (Deut. 25:2). Just as "wrongdoer" stated farther on [involves a sentence of] stripes, so too does "wrongdoer" stated here [involve a sentence of] stripes.

I.  One might think even in property cases you cannot grant him a new trial in order to find him guilty.

J.  Scripture states, [however,] "Do not bring death on those who are innocent and in the right" (Exod. 23:7), [meaning,] you may not grant him a new trial for death, but you may grant him a new trial for property [cases].

K.  One might think that just as [the wicked] might go out acquitted by you, so too will they go out acquitted by Me.[55]

L.  Scripture states, [however,] "... for I will not acquit the wrongdoer" (Exod. 23:7).

5.  A.  "... for I will not acquit the wrongdoer" (Exod. 23:7):

B.  [God says,] "But I will acquit him through repentence."

## LXXVIII:II[56]

1.  A.  "Do not take bribes, (for bribes blind the clear-sighted and upset the pleas of those who are in the right)" (Exod. 23:8):

B.  Scripture doesn't need to speak of bribes of money, rather, even [i.e., only] of bribes of words.

C.  "For bribes blind the wise" (Deut. 16:19): All the more so fools.

D.  "... and they upset the pleas of those who are in the right" (Deut. 16:19): All the more so those who are in the wrong.

2.  A.  Another interpretation:

B.  "For bribes blind the wise" (Deut. 16:19): [Those who] say that an impure person is pure.

C.  "... and they upset the pleas of those who are in the right" (Deut. 16:19): [Those who] say that something prohibited is allowed, or that something allowed is prohibited.

---

[55] I.e., God.

[56] Compare LXXVIII:II:1.A–2.C with *Mekhilta de-Rabbi Ishmael*, Kaspa (H/R, 328:7–14; Laut., vol. 3, 172:53–173:66; Neus., LXXVIII:I:15. A–16.I); and b. Ketubot 105a (XIV.C:Tractate Ketubot:13:1:I.4.A–5.A).

| | |
|---|---|
| מלמד שמחזירין אותו לזכות ◆ יכול יהו מחזירין אותו | C/B |
| לחובה ◆ ת״ל ונקי וצדיק אל תהרג. ◆ ואין לי אלא | E/D |
| למיתה לגלות מנין ◆ נאמר כאן דבר ונאמר להלן דבר | F |
| (דב׳ יט ד) מה דבר האמור להלן גלות אף דבר | |
| האמור כאן גלות. ◆ ואין לי אלא לגלות למכות מנין ◆ | G |
| נאמר כאן רשע ונאמר להלן רשע (דב׳ כה ב) מה רשע | H |
| האמור להלן מכות אף רשע האמור כאן מכות. ◆ יכול | I |
| אף בדיני ממונות לא יהו מחזירין אותו לחובה ◆ ת״ל | J |
| נקי וצדיק אל תהרג למיתה אי אתה מחזירו מחזירו | |
| אתה לממון. ◆ יכול כשם שיצאו ידך כך יצאו ידי ◆ ת״ל כי | L/K |
| לא אצדיק רשע. ◆ כי לא אצדיק רשע ◆ מצדיקו אני | B/A 5 |
| בתשובה. ◆ | |

LXXVIII:II

| | |
|---|---|
| ושחד לא תקח ◆ אינו צריך לומר שוחד ממון אלא | B/A 1 |
| אפלו שוחד דברים ◆ כי השחד יעור עיני חכמים וקל | C |
| וחומר לטיפשים ◆ ויסלף דברי צדיקים וקל וחומר | D |
| לרשעים. ◆ ד״א ◆ כי השחד יעור עיני חכמים אומרין על | B/A 2 |
| טמא טהור ועל טהור טמא ◆ ויסלף דברי צדיקים אומ׳ | C |
| על אסור מותר ועל מותר אסור. ◆ | |

## LXXVIII:III

1. A. "Six years you shall sow your land and gather in its yield" (Exod. 23:10):[57]

   B. How does one know from Scripture that one gathers in the seventh year rice, millet, sprouts, and sesame grain that took root before the beginning of the year [i.e., of the seventh year]?

   C. Scripture states, "... and gather in its yield" (Exod. 23:10), [meaning,] in the seventh [year].

   D. One might think [one gathers these in the seventh year] even if they didn't take root [before the beginning of the seventh year].

   E. Scripture states, [however,] "Six years you shall sow and gather" (Exod. 23:10), [meaning,] six seedings and six gatherings, not six seedings and seven gatherings.

2. A. R. Nathan ben Joseph says, "One verse says, 'Six years you may sow your field' (Lev. 25:3), and one verse says, 'Six years you shall sow your land' (Exod. 23:10).

   B. "How are these verses fulfilled? One was when Israel entered the Land of Israel, and one was when they returned from the exile."

3. A. "But in the seventh you shall let it rest" (Exod. 23:11)—from gathering.[58]

   B. "And lie fallow" (Exod. 23:11)—from clearing stones.

   C. One might think he could set bailees over it until the time of removal of the produce arrived, and then he could give it to them.

   D. Scripture states, [however,] "... and lie fallow" (Exod. 23:11).

4. A. "Let the needy among your people eat of it, (and what they leave let the wild beasts eat)" (Exod. 23:11):[59]

   B. I only know from this about the poor person. How does one know from Scripture about the rich person?

   C. Scripture states, "But you may eat whatever the land during its sabbath will produce" (Lev. 25:6).

   D. If so, why does Scripture state, "... the needy among your people" (Exod. 23:11)?

   E. [To emphasize that] most of it is for the poor.

5. A. "... and what they leave let the wild beasts eat" (Exod. 23:11):[60]

   B. Would one really think that the wild beast could not eat [the produce in the field] that is of no good to you?

   C. Why does Scripture state "... and what they leave let the wild beasts eat" (Exod. 23:11)?

[217] D. [In order to teach that] as long as the wild beast eats from the field, you may eat [seventh-year produce collected] inside the house. Once it ceases [to eat] from the field, you must cease [eating it] inside the house.

   E. Based on this they said: He who preserves five types of preserves in one jar.[61]

---

[57] Compare 1.A–E with Sifra, Behar 1:7–8 (Neus., CCXLV:I:8.A–9.C).

[58] Compare 3.A–D with b. Sukkah 44b (Neus., VI.Tractate Sukkah:4:4:XI.A–V).

[59] Compare 4.A–E with Mekhilta de-Rabbi Ishmael, Kaspa (H/R, 330:3–7; Laut., vol. 3, 175:100–176:109; Neus., LXXVIII:II:6.A–7.D); m. Shebiit 9:8; and t. Shebiit 8:1.

[60] Compare 5.A–K with b. Pesaḥim 52b (Neus., IV.C:Pesaḥim:4:2:IV.2.A–C).

[61] Compare 5.E with m. Shebiit 9:5.

LXXVIII:III

| | | |
|---|---|---|
| B/A | 1 | ושש שנים תזרע את ארצך ◆ מנין לאורז ולדוחן |
| | | ולפרגין ולשומשמין שהשרישו לפני ראש השנה |
| C | | שכונסם אתה בשביעית ◆ ת״ל ואספת את תבואתה |
| E/D | | בשביעית. ◆ יכול אע״פ שלא השרישו ◆ ת״ל שש שנים |
| | | תזרע ואספת ששה זריעים ששה אסיפים לא ששה |
| A | 2 | זריעים ושבעה אסיפים. ◆ ר׳ נתן בן יוסף אומר כתוב |
| | | אחד אומר שש שנים תזרע שדך וכתוב אחד אומר |
| B | | שש שנים תזרע את ארצך ◆ כאיזה צד יתקיימו שני |
| | | כתובים אחד כשנכנסו ישראל לארץ ואחד כשעלו מן |
| | | הגולה. ◆ |

| | | |
|---|---|---|
| B/A | 3 | ‹וה›שביעית תשמטנה מלקשש ◆ ונטשתה מלסקל. ◆ |
| C | | יכול יהא מושיב עליה שומרין עד שתגיע שעת |
| A 4 | D | הביעור ויתננה להן ◆ ת״ל ונטשתה. ◆ ואכלו אביני |
| C/B | | עמך ◆ אין לי אלא עני עשיר מנין ◆ ת״ל והיתה שבת |
| D | | הארץ לכם לאכלה ◆ אם כן למה נאמר אביני עמך ◆ |
| B/A 5 | E | רובה לעניים. ◆ ויתרם תאכל חית השדה ◆ וכי שלא |
| C | | בטובתך אין חית השדה אוכלת ◆ מה ת״ל ויתרם תאכל |
| D | | חית השדה ◆ כל זמן שחיה אוכלת מן השדה אתה |
| E | | אוכל מתוך הבית כלה מן השדה כלה מן הבית ◆ מכאן |
| | | אמרו הכובש חמשת מיני כבשין בחבית אחת ◆ |

F.    Rabban Gamliel says, "He who has ceased [eating] his species from the field must destroy it and its money equivalent from the house."

G.    One might think everything should be destroyed together. Scripture states, [however,] "... with your vineyard" (Exod. 23:11).

H.    One might think all the [seventh-year produce of all] the countries should be destroyed together. Scripture states, [however,] "... and your olive groves" (Exod. 23:11).

I.    Just as we have found with [the produce of these] two types of trees, the one has its own destruction and the other has its own destruction, so too each and every thing has its own destruction.

J.    One might think each and every field should be destroyed on its own. Scripture states, [however,] "... in the land" (Lev. 25:10), [meaning, God says,] "I speak about the land, but I don't speak about each and every field."

K.    Based on this they said: Three countries [are to be distinguished regarding] destruction: Judah, beyond Jordan, and the Galilee.[62]

6.    A.    "You shall do the same with your vineyards and your olive groves" (Exod. 23:11):

    B.    And weren't vineyards and olive groves part of the general classification? Why were they specified?

    C.    In order to draw an analogy with them: Just as the vineyard is unique, in that it is [included in the] positive commandment[63] [of declaring its produce during the seventh year free for the taking] but one [also] transgresses with it the negative commandment[64] [against gathering together its grapes[65]], so too with any [produce] that is [included in the] positive commandment [of declaring its produce during the seventh year free for the taking] one [also] transgresses with it the negative commandment [against gathering together its produce].

7.    A.    How does one know from Scripture that owners [of land] may not spread manure, strip off leaves, pluck, fumigate, trim branches, or arrange soil?[66]

    B.    Scripture states, "... your vineyards" (Exod. 23:10).

    C.    And how does one know from Scripture that owners [of land] may not trim trees, nip shoots, chip stones, arrange stones, or tap for sap?

    D.    Scripture states, "... and your olive groves" (Exod. 23:10).

## LXXVIII:IV

1.    A.    "Six days you shall do your work, (but on the seventh day you shall cease from labor, in order that your ox and your ass may rest, and that your bondman and the stranger may be refreshed)" (Exod. 23:12):

    B.    Since it says in Scripture, "Six days you shall labor and do all your work, but the seventh day is a sabbath" (Exod. 20:9), one might think that you only observe *Shabbat* at a time when you have done all [your] work. How does one know from Scripture [even] at a time when you have not done all [your] work?

---

[62] Compare 5.K with m. Shebiit 9:2.

[63] I.e., a commandment that prescribes behavior.

[64] I.e., a commandment that proscribes behavior.

[65] See Lev. 25:6. Thus, one may randomly pick and eat the grapes of a vineyard during the seventh year, but one may not gather them together and then eat them.

[66] Compare 7.A–D with *Sifra*, Behar 1:5 (Neus., CCXLV:I:3.A–6.G).

רבן גמליאל אומר מי שכלה מינו מן השדה מבעיר אותו | F

ואת דמיו מן הבית. ◆ יכול יהו כולן מתבערין כאחת | G

ת״ל כרמך. ◆ יכול יהו כל הארצות מתבערין כאחת ת״ל | H

זיתך ◆ מה מצינו בשני מינין שבאילן לזה ביעור בפני | I

עצמו ולזה ביעור בפני עצמו כך כל אחד ואחד יש לו

ביעור בפני עצמו. ◆ יכול תהא כל שדה ושדה מתבערת | J

בפני עצמה ת״ל בארץ בארץ דברתי ולא דברתי בכל

שדה ושדה ◆ מכאן אתה אומר שלוש ארצות לביעור | K

יהודה ועבר הירדן והגליל. ◆ כן תעשה לכרמך לזיתך ◆ | A | 6

והלא הכרם והזית בכלל היו ולמה יצאו ◆ להקיש | C/B

אליהם מה כרם מיוחד שהוא בעשה ועוברין עליו

בלא תעשה כך כל שהוא בעשה עוברין עליו בלא

תעשה. ◆ מנין אין מזבלין ואין מפרקין אין מעפקין אין | A | 7

מעשנין אין מגזמין ואין מצדדין בעלין ◆ ת״ל כרמך ◆ | B

ומנין אין מקרסמין ואין מזרדין ואין מפסלין ואין | C

מצדדין ואין מגזמין בעלין ◆ ת״ל זיתך. ◆ | D

שׁשׁת ימים תעשה מעשיך ◆ מכלל שנא׳ ששת ימים | B/A | 1

תעבד ועשית כל מלאכתך ויום השביעי שבת (שמ׳ כ

ט) יכול אין אתה שובת אלא בשעה שאתה עושה כל

מלאכה בשעה שאין אתה עושה כל מלאכה מנין ◆

C.    Scripture states, "... but on the seventh day you shall cease from labor" (Exod. 23:12), [meaning,] in any event.

2.    A.    Scripture draws a comparison [here] between *Shabbat* and the sabbatical year: Just as the sabbatical year, for which one does not receive death [for its transgression], one begins to observe its rest in the sixth year 30 days before the seventh year, then isn't it only logical that for *Shabbat,* for which one does receive death [for its transgression], one needs to add mundane time onto the holy?[67]

3.    A.    "... that your ox and your ass may rest, etc." (Exod. 23:12):[68]

B.    One might think one cannot allow it to pluck [food to eat] and one cannot allow it to uproot [food to eat].

C.    Scripture states, [however,] "... that ... may rest" (Exod. 23:12), and [to disallow] this would not be rest, but rather suffering!

4.    A.    "... and that your bondman ... may be refreshed" (Exod. 23:12):

B.    R. Yosi ha-Galili says, "Remit him."

C.    But R. Akiva says, "Give him relief!"

*Chapter Seventy-Nine*

### (Textual Source: Midrash ha-Gadol)

**LXXIX:I**

1.    A.    "Be on guard concerning all that I have told you. (Make no mention of the names of other gods. They shall not be heard on your lips)" (Exod. 23:13):[69]

B.    R. Eliezer ben Jacob says, "[Scripture says this in order] to give a negative commandment[70] to correspond with every positive commandment[71] said in the scriptural portion."[72]

2.    A.    "Make no mention of the names of other gods" (Exod. 23:13):

B.    This is a warning to the prophet who prophesies in the name of idolatry.

C    Because Scripture says, "... that prophet shall die" (Deut. 18:20), we have heard the punishment. How does one know from Scripture about the warning?

D.    Scripture states, "Make no mention of the names of other gods" (Exod. 23:13).

3.    A.    "They shall not be heard on your lips" (Exod. 23:13):[73]

B.    This is a warning against the one who leads people subtly to idolatry as well as the one who stirs people up to idolatry.

**LXXIX:II**

1.    A.    "Three festivals (you shall celebrate for Me in the year)" (Exod. 23:14):

B.    But not those on crutches.[74]

2.    A.    "Three festivals"[75] (Exod. 23:14):

---

[67] I.e., begin observance of *Shabbat* early, before the actual beginning of the seventh day of the week.

[68] Compare 3.A–C with *Mekhilta de-Rabbi Ishmael,* Kaspa (H/R, 331:2–5; Laut., vol. 3, 177:129–178:134; Neus., LXXVIII:III:2.A–F).

[69] Compare 1.A–B with *Mekhilta de-Rabbi Ishmael,* Kaspa (H/R, 331:14–332:1; Laut., vol. 3, 179:1–8; Neus., LXXIX:I:1.A–2.E).

[70] I.e., a commandment that proscribes behavior.

[71] I.e., a commandment that prescribes behavior.

[72] Hence, the negative commandment to refrain from mentioning the names of other gods corresponds to the positive commandment to be on guard.

[73] Compare 3.A–B with b. Sanhedrin 63b (Neus., XXIIIB:Tractate Sanhedrin:7:6:X.A–N).

[74] This interpretation is based on the Hebrew word for foot (*regel*—רגל), which is also the word for "festival."

| | | |
|---|---|---|
| ת״ל וביום השביעי תשבת מכל מקום ◆ מקיש שבת לשביעית ומה שביעית שאין בה עון מיתה שובת הוא מערב שביעית לשביעית בשלשים יום שבת שיש בה עון מיתה אינו דין שצריך להוסיף מחול על קודש. ◆ | A 2 | C |
| [למען ינוח שורך וחמורך וגו׳ ◆ יכול לא יניחנו תולש לא | B/A | 3 |
| יניחנו עוקר ◆ ת״ל למען ינוח ואין זה נייח אלא צער]. ◆ | C | |
| וינפש בן אמתך ◆ ר׳ יוסי הגלילי אומר הנח לו ◆ ור׳ עקיבה אומר הרויח לו. ◆ | C/B/A | 4 |

| | | |
|---|---|---|
| ובכל אשר אמרתי אליכם תשמרו ◆ ר׳ אליעזר בן יעקב אומר ליתן לא תעשה על כל עשה האמור בפרשה. ◆ | B/A | 1 |
| ושם אלהים אחרים לא תזכירו ◆ זו אזהרה לנביא המתנבא בשם ע״ז ◆ לפי שהוא אומר ומת הנביא | B/A | 2 |
| ההוא (דב׳ יח כ) עונש שמענו אזהרה מנין ◆ ת״ל ושם | C | |
| אלהים אחרים לא תזכירו. ◆ לא ישמע על פיך ◆ (זו) אזהרה למדיח (ולמסית). ◆ | D | |
| | B/A | 3 |

| | | |
|---|---|---|
| שלש רגלים ◆ ולא בעלי קבין. ◆ שלש רגלים ◆ | A/B/A | 2/1 |

---

[75] Hebrew: *r'galim*—רגלים.

B.   Everything depends on the legs[76] of the man. The one who comes from Beit Pagay[77] is not the same as the one who comes from Persia!

[218]

3.   A.   "... you shall celebrate *for Me*" (Exod. 23:14):

B.   A person fulfills his obligation through a festival sacrifice [intentionally] offered for that purpose. A person does not fulfill his obligation through a festival sacrifice [that is not intentionally] offered for that purpose.

C.   If so, why does Scripture state, "... *you shall celebrate* for Me" (Exod. 23:14)?

D.   [God is saying,] "Whenever you offer the festival sacrifice in accordance with how it is commanded, I attribute it to you as if you brought it as a freewill offering. Whenever you do not offer the festival sacrifice appropriately, I attribute it to you as if you committed sacrilege to the Temple and its courtyards."

E.   Thus Scripture says, "That you come to appear before Me—who asked that you trample My courts?" (Isa. 1:12).

## LXXIX:III

1.   A.   "You shall observe the Feast of Unleavened Bread, (eating unleavened bread for seven days as I have commanded you, at the set time in the month of Abib, for in it you went forth from Egypt. And none shall appear before Me empty-handed)" (Exod. 23:15):

B.   Since it says in Scripture, "Observe the month of Abib and offer a paschal sacrifice" (Deut. 16:1), one might think you only offer a paschal sacrifice when you have a spring crop.[78] How does one know from Scripture [you must also offer a paschal sacrifice] when you don't have a spring crop.[79]

C.   Scripture states, [however,] "You shall observe the Feast of Unleavened Bread" (Exod. 23:15).

2.   A.   Another interpretation:

B.   Just as with [the generations of] the Exodus from Egypt, even though you didn't have a spring crop, but only unleavened bread [you offered a paschal sacrifice], so too here, even if you don't have a spring crop, but only unleavened bread, [you should offer a paschal sacrifice].

3.   A.   How does one know from Scripture to apply that which is said about the paschal sacrifice of [the generation departing from] Egypt to the paschal sacrifice of the subsequent generations, and that which is said about the paschal sacrifice of the subsequent generations to the paschal sacrifice of [the generation departing from] Egypt?

B.   Scripture states, "... eating unleavened bread for seven days as I have commanded you (at the set time in the month of Abib)" (Exod. 23:15).

C.   This teaches that the year in which Israel exited from Egypt was like the set rule.

4.   A.   "And none shall appear before Me empty-handed" (Exod. 23:15):[80]

B.   Even if only with what [little] one is able.

C.   But the Sages say, "It is not appropriate to give less than a *ma'ah* of silver for a burnt offering, and two [*ma'ah*] of silver for a festival offering."

---

[76] Hebrew: *r'galim*—רגלים.
[77] A suburb of Jerusalem.
[78] The name of the month Abib (Hebrew: אביב) literally means the early ripening stage of the spring harvest.
[79] E.g., in a sabbatical year.
[80] Compare 4.A–C with *Sifre Deut.*, Piska 143 (Hammer, p. 182; Neus., CXLIII:V:1.A–F).

| | | |
|---|---|---|
| B | | הכל לפי רגליו שלאדם אין דומה הבא מבית פוגי להבא |
| B/A | 3 | מבית פרס. ◆ תחג לי ◆ בחגיגה הבאה לשמה אדם יוצא |
| | | ידי חובתו אין אדם יוצא ידי חובתו בחגיגה שאין באה |
| D/C | | לשמה ◆ אם כן למה נאמר תחג לי ◆ כל זמן שאתה חוגג |
| | | כמצותו מעלה אני עליך כאלו נדבה הבאתו ובזמן |
| | | שאי אתה חוגג כראוי מעלה אני עליך כאלו אתה |
| E | | מועל בהר הבית ובעזרות ◆ כן הוא אומר כי תבואו |
| | | לראות פני מי בקש זאת מידכם רמוס חצרי (ישע׳ א |
| | | יב). ◆ |

LXXIX:III

| | | |
|---|---|---|
| B/A | 1 | את חג המצות תשמר ◆ מכלל שנאמר שמור את |
| | | חדש האביב ועשית פסח (דב׳ טז א) יכול אין אתה |
| | | עושה פסח אלא בשעה שיש לך אביב בשעה שאין לך |
| | | אביב מנין ◆ ת״ל את חג המצות תשמר. ◆ ד״א ◆ מה יציאת |
| B/A 2 | C | מצרים אע״פ שאין לך אביב אלא מצה אף כאן אע״פ |
| A | 3 | שאין לך אביב אלא מצה ◆ מנין ליתן את האמור בפסח |
| | | מצרים בפסח דורות ואת האמור בפסח דורות בפסח |
| B | | מצרים ◆ ת״ל שבעת ימים תאכל מצות כאשר צויתיך ◆ |
| C | | מלמד שהשנה שיצאו בה ישראל ממצרים היתה |
| C/B/A | 4 | כתקנה. ◆ ולא יראו פני ריקם ◆ אפלו כל שהוא ◆ וחכמים |
| | | אומרין אין פחות לעולת ראיה ממעה כסף ולחגיגה |
| | | שתי כסף. ◆ |

LXXIX:IV

1. A. "And the Feast of the Harvest, (of the first fruits of your work, of what you sow in the field. And the Feast of Ingathering at the end of the year, when you gather in the results of your work from the field)" (Exod. 23:16):[81]

   B. R. Ishmael says, "Whenever the Feast of Pentecost occurs on *Shabbat*, the day of the slaughtering [of the festival sacrifice] is after [*Shabbat*], and [then] you slaughter and harvest."

2. A. "... the first fruits of your works" (Exod. 23:16):[82]

   B. Since it says in Scripture, "... first fruits of the wheat harvest" (Exod. 34:22), I only know about the [the first fruits] of wheat. How does one know from Scripture about [the first fruits] of barley?

   C. Scripture states "... of what you sow in the field" (Exod. 23:16).

   D. I only know about that which was sown. How does one know from Scripture about that which grew on its own?

   E. Scripture states, "... of what ... in the field" (Exod. 23:16).

   F. I only know about that which is in the field. How does one know from Scripture about [that which is grown] on the roof, in the courtyard, or in a deserted building?

   G. Scripture states, "The first fruits of everything in their land" (Num. 18:13).

3. A. "... and the Feast of Ingathering at the end of the year" (Exod. 23:16):

   B. Since it says in Scripture, "You shall set aside every year a tenth part of all the yield of your sowing that is brought from the field" (Deut. 14:22), I don't know when the year is.

   C. Scripture states, [therefore,] "... and the Feast of Ingathering at the end of the year" (Exod. 23:16), and farther ahead it says, "... at the turn of the year" (Exod. 34:22).

   D. When does the year end? You must say at the solstice!

   E. One might think this is the winter solstice.

   F. Scripture states, [however,] "... and the Feast" (Exod. 23:16). The winter solstice is eliminated, because it is not a feast.

   G. One might think this is the spring equinox, because it is a feast!

   H. Scripture states, [however,] "... and the Feast of Ingathering" (Exod. 23:16), [meaning, a feast] that has an ingathering. The spring equinox is eliminated, because it does not have an ingathering.

   I. One might think this is the summer solstice, which is an ingathering.

   J. Scripture states, [however,] "... and the Feast of Ingathering at the end of the year" (Exod. 23:16) and farther ahead it says, "... at the turn of the year" (Exod. 34:22), [meaning,] a solstice that is a feast, an ingathering, and the year ends on it.

   K. And which is this? This is the autumnal equinox!

4. A. "... when you gather in[83] the results of your work" (Exod. 23:16):

---

[81] Compare 1.A–B with m. Ḥagigah 2:4 and b. Ḥagigah 18a (Neus., XII:Ḥagigah:2:4:I.5.A–B).
[82] Compare 2.A–G with *Sifra,* Dibbura Denaba 12:7–8 (Neus., XXIV:IV:2.A–J).
[83] Hebrew: באספך.

| | | |
|---|---|---|
| B/A | 1 | וחג הקציר ❖ ר׳ ישמעאל אומר כל זמן שעצרת |
| A | 2 | בשבת יום טבוח אחר שבת חוגג וקוצר. ❖ בכורי מעשיך ❖ |
| B | | מכלל שנא׳ בכורי קציר חטים (שמ׳ לד כב) אין לי |
| C | | אלא חלטים שלשעורים מנין ❖ ת״ל אשר תזרע בשדה ❖ |
| E/D | | אין לי אלא שזרע שעלה מאיליו מנין ❖ ת״ל אשר בשדה ❖ |
| F | | אין לי אלא שבשדה שבגג ושבחצר ושבחרבה מנין |
| A 3 | G | ת״ל בכורי כל אשר בארצם (במ׳ יח יג). ❖ וחג האסיף |
| B | | בצאת השנה ❖ מכלל שנא׳ עשר תעשר את כל תבואת |
| | | זרעך היוצא השדה שנה שנה (דב׳ יד כב) איני יודע |
| C | | אימתי היא שנה ❖ ת״ל וחג האסיף בצאת השנה ולהלן |
| D | | הוא אומר תקופת השנה (שמ׳ לד כב) ❖ אימתי שנה |
| F/E | | יוצאה הוי אומר בתקופה. ❖ יכול תקופת טבת ❖ ת״ל חג |
| G | | יצאת תקופת טבת שאין בה חג ❖ יכול תקופת ניסן |
| H | | שהרי יש בו חג ❖ ת״ל חג האסיף שיש בה אסיף יצאת |
| I | | תקופת ניסן שאין בה אסיף ❖ יכול תקופת תמוז שהרי |
| J | | יש בה אסיף ❖ ת״ל חג האסיף בצאת השנה ולהלן הוא |
| | | אומר תקופת השנה תקופה שיש בה חג ואסיף ושנה |
| A 4 | K | יוצאה בה ❖ והיזו זו זו תקופת תשרי. ❖ באספך את מעשיך ❖ |

B. You have nothing in them but a harvest.[84]

C. How does one know from Scripture that each and every person should have his own harvest?

D. Scripture states, "... when you gather in the results of your work" (Exod. 23:16), [meaning,] each and every one at the time of his [own] harvest.

5. A. One might think that [the festival of] the New Year should serve as the beginning of the year for all the fruits of the tree.[85]

B. Scripture states, [however,] "... when you gather in the results of your work" (Exod. 23:16), [meaning,] each and every one has its own harvest.

C. Based on this they said: The 1st of Shevat is the beginning of the year [for the reckoning of the age of fruit] trees, according to the House of Shammai. But the House of Hillel says the 15th of the month. Any tree whose fruits ripened before the 15th of Shevat, that [tree's year begins] on the previous [15th of Shevat. Any tree whose fruits ripened after the 15th of Shevat], that [tree's year begins] on the forthcoming [15th of Shevat].

## LXXIX:V[86]

1. A. "Three times (a year all your males shall appear before the Sovereign, the Lord)" (Exod. 23:17):

B. One might think [one should appear before the Lord three times] for each and every festival.

C. Scripture states, [however,] "... a year" (Exod. 23:17).

D. One might think [one may appear] whenever he wants.

E. Scripture states, [however,] "... times" (Exod. 23:17), [and] "times" means only [set] times, as it says in Scripture, "To be trampled underfoot, by the feet of the needy, by the soles of the needy."[87]

2. A. "... shall appear" (Exod. 23:17):

B. This excludes the blind person, who cannot see.[88]

3. A. "... your males" (Exod. 23:17):

B. [Scripture says this in order] to exclude the women.

C. "... all your males" (Exod. 23:17):

D. [Scripture says this in order] to include the minors.

E. This is what the House of Hillel says: "Any child who can hold the hand of his father and go up from Jerusalem to the Temple Mount is obligated to appear."[89]

4. A. "... before the Sovereign, the Lord" (Exod. 23:17):

B. [God is saying,] "If you do everything said in this matter, behold, I will turn aside from all My work and will only work with you!"

[219]

## LXXIX:VI

1. A. "You shall not slaughter (the blood of My sacrifice) with anything leavened" (Exod. 23:18):

B. I only know about slaughtering. How does one know from Scripture about sprinkling and pouring [the blood]?

---

[84] Hebrew: אָסִיף.

[85] Compare 5.A–C with m. Rosh Hashanah 1:1 and t. Shebiit 4:20.

[86] Compare LXXIX:V:1.A–4.B with *Sifre Deut.*, Piska 143 (Hammer, p. 182; Neus., CXLIII:I:1.A—V:1.F ).

[87] The Hebrew word for foot is *regel* (רגל), which is also the word for "festival." The Hebrew for "sole" is *pa'am* (פעם), which is also the

| | | |
|---|---|---|
| אין לך בהן אלא אסיף. ◆ מנין לכל אחד ואחד | C/B | |
| שיהא לו אסיף בפני עצמו ◆ ת״ל באספך מעשיך כל | D | |
| אחד ואחד בשעת אסיפו. ◆ יכול תהא ראש שנה ראש | A | 5 |
| לכל פירות האילן ◆ ת״ל באספך מעשיך כל אחד ואחד | B | |
| יש לו אסיף בפני עצמו ◆ מיכן אמרו באחד בשבט ראש | C | |

שנה לאילן דברי בית שמאי ובית הלל אומ׳ בחמשה
עשר בו. כל אילן שחנטו פירותיו לפני חמשה עשר
בשבט הרי הוא לשעבר לאחר חמשה עשר בשבט
הרי הוא לעתיד לבא. ◆

LXXIX:V

| | | |
|---|---|---|
| שלש פעמים ◆ יכול בכל רגל ורגל ◆ ת״ל בשנה | C/B/A | 1 |
| יכול בכל זמן שירצה ◆ ת״ל פעמים אין פעמים אלא זמנים | E/D | |

שנא׳ תרמסנה רגל רגלי עני פעמי דלים (ישע׳ כו ו).
◆

| | | |
|---|---|---|
| יראה ◆ פרט לסומה שאין יכול לראות ◆ זכורך ◆ להוציא | B/A 3 | B/A /2 |
| את הנשים ◆ כל זכורך ◆ לרבות את הקטנים ◆ זו היא | E/D/C | |

שבית הלל אומרין כל קטן שיכול לאחוז בידו
שלאביו ולעלות מירושלם להר הבית חייב בראייה.
◆

| | | |
|---|---|---|
| את פני האדון ◆ אם עושה אתה את כל האמור בענין | B/A | 4 |

הריני פונה מכל עסקאי ואיני עוסק אלא בך. ◆

LXXIX:VI

| | | |
|---|---|---|
| לא תזבח על חמץ ◆ אין לי אלא זובח זורק ומנסך מנין ◆ | B/A | 1 |

word for "time." Thus, a strong association is drawn between the notion of appearing before God during a festival and at a set time.

[88] A semantic connection is drawn here between the shared Hebrew root (ראה) for "to appear" and "to see."

[89] Compare 3.E with parallel at m. Ḥagigah 1:1.

C.    Scripture states, "... the blood of My sacrifice" (Exod. 23:18).

D.    And thus Scripture says, "You shall say: It is the passover sacrifice to the Lord" (Exod. 12:27).

2.    A.    "And the fat of My festal offering shall not be left lying until morning" (Exod. 23:18):

B.    Based on this they said: The duty to offer up the fat lasts all night.[90]

3.    A.    "And the fat of My festal offering shall not be left lying until morning" (Exod. 23:18):

B.    Because we have found that the time of the eating of the most holy offerings is the time of the offering, one might think this is also the case with the minor holy offerings.

C.    Scripture states, [however,] "And the fat of My festal offering shall not be left lying until morning" (Exod. 23:18).

D.    I only know about the fat of the festal offering. How does one know about the fat of the paschal offering?

E.    Scripture states, "... and the sacrifice of the Feast of Passover shall not be left lying until morning" (Exod. 34:25).

## Chapter Eighty

### (Textual Source: Midrash ha-Gadol)

### LXXX:I

1.    A.    "The first (of the fruits of your soil you shall bring to the house of the Lord your God)" (Exod. 23:19):[91]

B.    Scripture says here, "first" (Exod. 23:19), and Scripture says farther ahead, "first" (Deut. 18:4). One might think just as "first" stated farther ahead [means] as long as he keeps back a part, so too does "first" stated here [mean] as long as he keeps back a part. How does one know from Scripture that if one wants to he may designate his entire field as first fruits?

C.    Scripture states, "The first fruits of your soil" (Exod. 23:19).

D.    If so, why does Scripture state, "first" (Exod. 23:19)? In order to give them the power [of being] first, in that they should precede the heave offering.

2.    A.    "... of your soil" (Exod. 23:19): This excludes the arbor.[92]

B.    "... of your soil" (Exod. 23:19): This excludes the robber.

3.    A.    "... you shall bring to the house of the Lord" (Exod. 23:19):[93]

B.    This teaches that he is liable for attending to bringing them until he brings them to the Temple.

4.    A.    "You shall not boil a kid (in its mother's milk)" (Exod. 23:19):[94]

B.    R. Akiva says, "[The inclusion of an] animal of chase and a bird [in this prohibition] is not from the Torah. As it says in Scripture, 'You shall not boil a kid in its mother's milk' (Exod. 34:26), [and] 'You shall not boil a kid in its mother's milk' (Deut. 14:21), [for a total of] three times.

C.    "In order to exclude the animal of chase, bird, and impure cattle."

D.    R. Yosi ha-Galili says, "Scripture says, 'You shall not eat anything that has died a natural

[90] Compare 2.B with m. Berachot 1:1.

[91] Compare 1.A–D with b. Ḥullin 136b (Neus., XXX.C:Tractate Ḥullin:11:1:I.24.A–H).

[92] Compare 2.A–B with m. Bikkurin 1:2.

[93] Compare 3.A–B with m. Bikkurin 1:9.

| | | |
|---|---|---|
| D/C | | ת״ל דם זבחי. זבחי זה הפסח ◆ וכן הוא אומר |
| A | 2 | ואמרתם זבח פסח הוא לה׳ (שמ׳ יב כז). ◆ לא ילין חלב |
| B | 3 A | חגי עד בקר ◆ מכאן אמרו הקטר חלבים כל הלילה. ◆ לא |
| B | | ילין חלב חגי עד בקר ◆ לפי שמצינו בקדשי קדשים |
| | | שבזמן אכילתן הקטרתן יכול אף קדשים קלים כן ◆ |
| D/C | | ת״ל לא ילין חלב חגי עד בקר ◆ אין לי אלא חלבי חגיגה |
| E | | חלבי פסח מנין ◆ ת״ל ולא ילין לבקר זבח חג הפסח. ◆ |

| | | |
|---|---|---|
| LXXX:I | | |
| B/A | 1 | ראשית ◆ נאמר כאן ראשית ונאמר להלן ראשית |
| | | (דב׳ יח ד) יכול מה ראשית האמור להלן עד שישייר |
| | | מקצת אף ראשית האמור כאן עד שישייר מקצת מנין |
| | | שאם רוצה אדם לעשות כל שדהו בכורים עושה ◆ ת״ל |
| C | | בכורי אדמתך ◆ אם כן למה נאמר ראשית ליתן בהן |
| D | | כוח ראשית שיהו קודמין לתרומה. ◆ אדמתך פרט |
| A | 2 | לערים ◆ אדמתך פרט לגזלן. ◆ תביא בית ה׳ אלקיך ◆ |
| B | 3 A | מלמד שהוא חייב בטיפול הבאתן עד שיביאם לבית |
| B | | הבחירה. ◆ לא תבשל גדי ◆ ר׳ עקיבה אומר חיה ועוף אינן |
| B/A | 4 | מן התורה שנא׳ לא תבשל גדי בחלב אמו לא תבשל |
| C | | גדי בחלב אמו שלשה פעמים ◆ פרט לחיה ועוף |
| D | | ולבהמה טמאה. ◆ ר׳ יוסי הגלילי אומר נאמר לא |

[94] Compare 4.A–5.C with *Mekhilta de-Rabbi Ishmael*, Kaspa (H/R, 337:1–339:7; Laut., vol. 3, 187:1–196:127; Neus., LXX:II:1.A–17.F); m. Ḥullin 8:4; and *Sifre Deut.*, Piska 104 (Hammer, p. 149; Neus., CIV:I:1.A–III:1.G).

death' (Deut. 14:21), and Scripture says, 'You shall not boil a kid in its mother's milk' (Exod. 23:19).

E.    "That which is prohibited when it dies a natural death is prohibited to boil in milk. One might think that a bird, which is prohibited when it dies a natural death, would be prohibited to boil in milk.

F.    "Scripture states, [however,] '... in its mother's milk' (Exod. 23:19). A bird is excluded, because it doesn't have mother's milk."

5.    A.    "You shall not boil a kid in its mother's milk" (Exod. 23:19):

B.    I only know about a kid in its mother's milk. How does one know from Scripture about the cow in its mother's milk?

C.    Scripture states, "... milk" (Exod. 23:19), [meaning,] in any event.

*Chapter Eighty-One*

## (Textual Source: Midrash ha-Gadol)

### LXXXI:I

1.    A.    "I am sending an angel before you (to guard you on the way and to bring you to the place that I have made ready)" (Exod. 23:20):

B.    This [refers to] a prophet. And thus Scripture says, "An angel of the Lord came up from Gilgal to Bochim" (Judg. 2:1).

C.    "... before you" (Exod. 23:20): [God says,] "He should illuminate before you like a candle that lights up the whole house!"

D.    "... to guard you on the way" (Exod. 23:20): [God says,] "In order to warn you about the words of Torah! For thus Scripture says, 'Follow only the path that the Lord your God has enjoined upon you' (Deut. 5:30)."

E.    "... and to bring you" (Exod. 23:20): [This refers to] the Land of Israel.

F.    "... to the place" (Exod. 23:20): This is Shiloh.

G.    "... that I have made ready" (Exod. 23:20): This is the Temple. And thus Scripture says, "Gad came to David the same day and said to him, 'Go and set up an altar to the Lord on the threshing floor of Araunah the Jebusite'" (2 Sam. 24:18). What does Scripture [then] say there?—"David said, 'Here will be the House of the Lord and here the altar of burnt offerings for Israel'" (1 Chron. 22:1). And Scripture says, "This is my resting-place for all time" (Ps. 132:14).

2.    A.    "(Pay heed to him and obey him. Do not defy him) for he will not pardon your offenses (since My Name is in him)" (Exod. 23:21):

B.    [God says, "Just as] I don't forgive sin or pardon transgression, neither does he. For you don't sin before him, but rather before Me!

C.    "And thus Scripture says, 'Your grumbling is not against us, but against the Lord!' (Exod. 16:8)."

3.    A.    "But if you obey him (and do all that I say, I will be an enemy to your enemies and a foe to your foes)" (Exod. 23:22):

B.    Whenever Israel does the will of God, He acts on their behalf as an adversary against their enemies.

C.    As it says in Scripture, "... I will be an enemy to your enemies and a foe to your foes" (Exod. 23:22).

תאכלו כל נבלה (דב׳ יד כא) ונאמר לא תבשל גדי
בחלב אמו ♦ את שאסור משום נבלה אסור לבשל    E
בחלב עוף שאסור משום נבלה יכול אסור לבשלו
בחלב ♦ ת״ל בחלב אמו יצא עוף שאין לו חלב אם. ♦ לא    A 5   F
תבשל גדי בחלב אמו ♦ אין לי אלא גדי בחלב אמו    B
פרה בחלב אמה מנין ♦ ת״ל בחלב מכל מקום. ♦    C

LXXXI:I

הנה אנכי שלח מלאך לפניך ♦ זה נביא וכן הוא    B/A   1
אומר ויעל מלאך ה׳ מן הגלגל אל הבוכים (שופ׳ ב א).
♦ ♦ לפניך שיהא מאיר לפניך כנר שהוא מאיר לכל הבית.    C
♦ לשמרך בדרך להזהירך על דברי תורה וכן הוא אומר    D
בכל הדרך אשר צוה ה׳ אלקיכם אתכם תלכו (דב׳ ה
ל). ♦ ולהביאך לארץ ישראל ♦ אל המקום זה שילה.    F/E
♦ אשר הכינתי זה בית עולמים וכן הוא אומר ויבא גד    G
אל דוד ‹ביום ההוא› ויאמר ‹לו› עלה הקם לה׳
מזבח בגרן ארונה היבוסי (ש״ב כד יח) מהוא אומ׳
שם ויאמר דויד זה הוא בית ה׳ ‹ה›אלקים וזה מזבח
לעלה לישראל (דה״א כב א) ואומר זאת מנוחתי עדי
עד (תה׳ קלב יד). ♦

כי לא ישא לפשעכם ♦ לא כשם שאני נושא עון    B/A   2
ועובר על פשע כך הוא שלא לפניו אתם חוטאין אלא
לפני ♦ שנ׳ כי שמי בקרבו. וכן הוא אומר לא עלינו    C
תלנתיכם כי על ה׳ (שמ׳ טז ח). ♦

כי אם שמע תשמע ♦ כל זמן שישראל עושין רצונו    B/A   3
שלמקום הוא נעשה להן אנטדיקוס כנגד אויביהם ♦
שנא׳ ועשית כל אשר אדבר ואיבתי את איביך.    C

D. [God says,] "You have done what I commanded you. So too will I do what I promised you. And thus Scripture says, '... for the Lord, the God of Israel, fought for Israel' (Josh. 10:42)."

[220]

4.  A. "You shall serve the Lord your God, (and He will bless your bread and your water. And I will remove sickness from your midst)" (Exod. 23:25):

    B. This is prayer. And thus Scripture says, "... serving Him with all your heart" (Deut. 11:13).

    C. Which service is of the heart? You must say this is prayer! And thus Scripture says of Daniel, "Your God, whom you serve so regularly, will deliver you" (Dan. 6:17).

    D. And was there really sacrificial service in Babylonia? Rather, this [verse in Daniel refers to] prayer! And thus Scripture says, "... three times a days he knelt down, prayed" (Dan. 6:11).

5.  A. Another interpretation:

    B. "You shall serve the Lord your God" (Exod. 23:25):

    C. Serve him with His Torah. Serve Him in His sanctuary!

6.  A. "No woman (in your land) shall miscarry" (Exod. 23:26):

    B. In accordance with what is said in Scripture, "All of them bear twins, and not one loses her young" (Song 4:2).

    C. "... or be barren" (Exod. 23:26):

    D. In accordance with what is said in Scripture, "There shall be not sterile male or female among you or among your livestock" (Deut. 7:14).

    E. "... I will let you enjoy the full count of your days" (Exod. 23:26):

    F. In accordance with what is said in Scripture, "No more shall there be an infant or graybeard who does not live out his days" (Isa. 65:20).

    G. "... I will let you enjoy the full count of your days" (Exod. 23:26):

    H. Not in accordance with what is said in Scripture, "... those murderous, treacherous men; they shall not live out half their days" (Ps. 55:24).

7.  A. "I will send forth My terror before you" (Exod. 23:27):

    B. This is dread of You.

    C. And thus Scripture says, "When we heard about it, we lost heart" (Josh. 2:11).

    D. "... and I will throw into panic all the people" (Exod. 23:27):

    E. This is plague.

    F. "... and I will make all your enemies turn back before you" (Exod. 23:27):

    G. In accordance with what is said in Scripture, "Made my enemies turn back before me" (2 Sam. 22:41).

8.  A. "I will not drive them out before you in a single year, (lest the land become desolate and the wild beasts multiply to your hurt)" (Exod. 23:29):

    B. [God says,] "Little by little will I drive them out!"

    C. Based on this [you know] that the wicked were created to obey the righteous.

    D. And thus Scripture says, "The Lord made everything for a purpose" (Prov. 16:4).

    E. One might think this will also be the case in the time to come.

| | | |
|---|---|---|
| D | | אתם עשיתם מה שגזרתי עליכם אף אני אעשה מה שהבטחתי אתכם וכן הוא אומר כי ה׳ אלקי ישראל נלחם לישראל (יהו׳ י מב). ◆ |
| B/A | 4 | ועבדתם את ה׳ אלקיכם ◆ זו תפלה וכן הוא אומר |
| C | | ולעבדו בכל לבבכם (דב׳ יא יג) ◆ איזו היא עבודה שבלב הוי אומר זו תפלה וכן הוא אומר בדניאל אלהך די אנת פלח ליה בתדירא הוא ישיזבינך (דני׳ ו יז) ◆ וכי יש עבודה בבבל אלא זו תפלה וכן הוא אומר |
| D | | וזמנין תלתה ביומא הוא בריך על ברכוהי (דני׳ ו יא). ◆ |
| C/B/A | 5 | ד״א ◆ ועבדתם את ה׳ אלקיכם ◆ עבדהו בתורתו עבדהו במקדשו. ◆ |
| B/A | 6 | לא תהיה משכלה ◆ בענין שנא׳ שכלם מתאימות |
| D/C | | ושכולה אין בהם (שה״ש ד ב). ◆ ועקרה ◆ כענין שנא׳ לא יהיה בך עקר ועקרה ובבהמתך (דב׳ ז יד). ◆ את מספר |
| E | | ימיך אמלא ◆ כענין שנא׳ לא יהיה שם זקן ועול ימים |
| F | | אשר לא ימלא את ימיו (ישע׳ סה כ). ◆ את מספר ימיך |
| G | | אמלא ◆ לא כענין שנא׳ אנשי דמים ומרמה לא יחצו |
| H | | ימיהם (תה׳ נה כד). ◆ |
| C/B/A | 7 | את אימתי אשלח לפניך ◆ זה המורך ◆ וכן הוא אומר |
| E/D | | ונשמע וימס לבבנו (יהו׳ ב יא). ◆ והמתי את כל העם ◆ זו |
| G/F | | מגפה. ◆ ונתתי את כל איביך אליך ערף ◆ כענין שנא׳ ואיבי תתה לי ערף (ש״ב כב מא). ◆ |
| B/A | 8 | לא אגרשנו מפניך בשנה. ◆ מעט מעט אגרשנו ◆ |
| D/C | | מכאן שהרשעים נבראו לצוות לצדיקים ◆ וכן הוא אומר כל |
| E | | פעל ה׳ למענהו (מש׳ טז ד) ◆ יכול אף לעתיד לבוא ◆ |

F.     Scripture states, [however,] "Even the wicked for an evil day" (Prov. 16:4).

9.     A.     "You shall make no covenant with them and their gods" (Exod. 23:32):

       B.     Behold, this is a warning not to make a covenant with the seven nations!

       C.     And thus Joshua says, "But perhaps you live among us. How then can we make a pact with you?" (Josh. 9:7). What else does Scripture say at the end?—"Therefore, be accursed!" (Josh. 9:23).

10.     A.     "They shall not remain in your land, (lest they cause you to sin against Me. For you will serve their gods, and it will prove a snare to you)" (Exod. 23:33):

       B.     Behold, this is a warning that they should not settle amongst themselves a non-Jewish idol worshiper.

       C.     One might think [they could do this randomly] for no reason.

       D.     Scripture states, [however,] "... lest they cause you to sin against Me" (Exod. 23:33).

       E.     [God says,] "I already promised you that 'the angel of the Lord camps around those who fear Him and rescues them' (Ps. 34:8). He will rescue them from sin! How can I place them[95] among you, lest you will sin against Me? They intend to cause you to rebel against Me! And what will be in your hands [to do] when you are so close to them that you become doomed to destruction? Therefore, I warn you, 'They shall not remain in your land' (Exod. 23:33)!"

*Chapter Eighty-Two*

## (Textual Source: Midrash ha-Gadol)

### LXXXII:I

1.     A.     "Then He said to Moses: Come up to the Lord, (you with Aaron, Nadab and Abihu, and seventy elders of Israel, and bow low from afar)" (Exod. 24:1):

       B.     This is what we have said [elsewhere]: "... and Moses went up to God" (Exod. 19:3).

       C.     One might think [he went up on his own].

       D.     Scripture states, [however,] "Then He said to Moses: Come up to the Lord" (Exod. 24:1). This teaches that he only went up by command of the *Shekhinah*.

       E.     One might think this instance is separate in and of itself and above [at Exod. 19:24] is separate in and of itself.

       F.     Scripture states [here, however], "Come up to the Lord, you with Aaron" (Exod. 24:1), and above Scripture says, "... and come back together with Aaron" (Exod. 19:24).

       G.     "... and bow low from afar" (Exod. 24:1):

       H.     And above [Scripture says], "So the people stood at a distance" (Exod. 20:18).

       I.     "Moses alone shall come near" (Exod. 24:2):

       J.     And above [Scripture says], "... while Moses approached the thick cloud" (Exod. 20:18).

       K.     You have to say that these two [instances] are one! Why is it repeated? In order to complete our instance [here]!

2.     A.     "Moses went and repeated to the people all the commands of the Lord and all the rules" (Exod. 24:3):

       B.     [Scripture] draws an analogy between laws and divine speech: Just as divine speech is

---

[95] I.e., non-Jewish idol worshipers.

| | | |
|---|---|---|
| F | | ת״ל וגם רשע ליום רעה (שם). ◆ |
| 9 | B/A | לא תכרת להם ולאלהיהם ברית ◆ הרי זו אזהרה |
| | C | שלא לכרות ברית לשבעה עממין ◆ וכן יהושע אומר |
| | | אולי בקרבי אתה יושב ואיך אכרות לך ברית (יהושע |
| | | ט ז) מהוא אומר בסוף ועתה ארורים הם (שם כג). ◆ |
| 10 | B/A | לא ישבו בארצך ◆ ‹הרי› זו אזהרה שלא יושיבו |
| | D/C | גוי עובד ע״ז ביניהם. ◆ יכול על חנם ◆ ת״ל פן יחטיאו |
| | E | אותך לי ◆ כבר הבטחתיך חנה מלאך ה׳ סביב ליראיו |
| | | ויחלצם (תה׳ לד ח) יחלצם מלחטוא היאך אניחם |
| | | ביניכם פן יחטיאו אותך לי הן מתכוונין להמרידכם |
| | | בי ומה תעלה יש בידכם ואתם נוקשין בהן ומתחייבין |
| | | לי כלייה לכך אני מזהירך לא ישבו בארצך. ◆ |

LXXXII:I

| | | |
|---|---|---|
| 1 | B/A | ואל משה אמר עלה אל ה׳ ◆ זו היא שאמרנו ומשה |
| | D/C | עלה אל האלקים (שמ׳ יט ג) ◆ יכול מעצמו ◆ ת״ל ואל |
| | | משה אמר עלה אל ה׳ ◆ מלמד שלא עלה אלא על פי |
| | E | שכינה ◆ יכול זה ענין בפני עצמו ולהלן ענין בפני עצמו |
| | F | ת״ל עלה אל ה׳ ◆ אתה ואהרן ולהלן הוא אומר ועלית |
| | H/G | אתה ואהרן עמך. ◆ והשתחויתם מרחוק ◆ ולהלן ויעמד |
| | J/I | העם מרחוק (שמ׳ כ יח). ◆ ונגש משה לבדו ◆ ולהלן ומשה |
| | K | נגש אל הערפל (שם) ◆ הוי אומר שניהם ענין אחד למה |
| | | נשנה להשלים ענינו. ◆ |
| 2 | A | ויבא משה ויספר לעם את כל דברי ה׳ ואת כל |
| | B | המשפטים ◆ מקיש דינין לדיברות מה דיברות מסיני |

from Sinai, so too are the laws from Sinai.

C.  "And all the people answered with one voice" (Exod. 24:3):

D.  In that they did not confer among themselves.

E.  "All the things that the Lord has commanded we will do!" (Exod. 24:3):

F.  In that they preceded [acceptance for] doing [the commandments] before hearing [them]! In that if anyone should hear [them] and not be inclined to do [them], it would be better for him that he not have been created!

3.  A.  "Moses then wrote down all the commands of the Lord" (Exod. 24:4): These are the words that preceded the giving of the Torah.

B.  "He arose early in the morning" (Exod. 24:4): This is the 6th [day of the month of Sivan].

C.  Scripture says here, "morning," and Scripture says above, "as morning dawned" (Exod. 19:16). I don't know if divine speech preceded the sacrificial offerings or if the sacrificial offerings preceded the divine speech.

D.  Scripture states, [however,] "He arose early in the morning and set up an altar" (Exod. 24:4), and above Scripture says, "as morning dawned" (Exod. 19:16). This teaches that the sacrificial offerings preceded the divine speech.

E.  "... and set up an altar" (Exod. 24:4): For the sacrificial service.

F.  "... with twelve pillars" (Exod. 24:4): Corresponding to the 12 tribes.

4.  A.  "He designated some young men among the Israelites" (Exod. 24:5): This [refers to] the first fruits.

B.  "... and they offered burnt offerings" (Exod. 24:5): They offered them on behalf of all Israel.

5.  A.  "Moses took one part of the blood" (Exod. 24:6): This teaches that the blood was divided up.

B.  "... and put it in basins" (Exod. 24:6): This teaches that the burnt offering required utensils.

C.  I only know this concerning the burnt offering at Sinai. How does one know from Scripture [the same was the case for the burnt offerings of the subsequent] generations?

D.  Scripture states, "... the regular burnt offerings instituted at Mount Sinai" (Num. 28:6). [Scripture] draws an analogy between the regular burnt offering and the burnt offering at Sinai: Just as the burnt offering at Sinai required utensils, so too did the burnt offering of the [subsequent] generations require utensils.

E.  I only know this concerning the burnt offering. How does one know from Scripture [the same was the case for the] sin offering, guilt offering, and peace offering?

[221]  F.  Scripture states, "Such are the rituals of the burnt offering, the meal offering, the sin offering, the guilt offering, the offering of ordination and the sacrifice of well-being" (Lev. 7:37), [meaning,] one ritual for all of them.

## LXXXII:II

1.  A.  "Then he took the record of the covenant and read it aloud to the people" (Exod. 24:7):

B.  [He read] from the beginning of the book until here.

C.  "And they said: All that the Lord has spoken we will do and we will hear!" (Exod. 24:7):

D.  Because they put doing [the commandments] first, Moses said to them, "Is it possible to do something without hearing [about it]? Hearing [about it] allows one to do [it]! They repeated, saying, "We will do and we will hear" (Exod. 24:7), [meaning,] we will do what

| | |
|---|---|
| D/C | כך הדינין מסיני. ♦ ויען כל העם קול אחד ♦ שלא נטלו |
| E | עצה זה מזה. ♦ כל הדברים אשר דבר ה' נעשה ♦ |
| F | שהקדימו עשייה לשמיעה שכל השומע ואין בדעתו |
| | לעשות נוח לו שלא נברא. ♦ |

| | | |
|---|---|---|
| A | 3 | ויכתב משה את כל דברי ה' אלו דברים שקדמו |
| C/B | | למתן תורה. ♦ וישכם בבקר זה יום הששי ♦ נאמר כן |
| | | בבקר ונאמר להלן בהיות הבקר (שמ' יט טז) איני |
| | | יודע אם דיברות קדמו לקרבנות או קרבנות קדמו |
| D | | לדיברות ♦ ת"ל וישכם בבקר ויבן מזבח ולהלן הוא |
| | | אומר בהיות הבקר (שמ' יט טז) מלמד שקדמו |
| | | קרבנות לדיברות. ♦ ויבן מזבח לעבודה. ♦ ושתים עשרה |
| F/E | | מצבה כנגד שנים עשר שבטים. ♦ |

| | | |
|---|---|---|
| B/A | 4 | וישלח את נערי בני ישראל אלו הבכורים. ♦ ויעלו |
| | | עלות על ידי כל ישראל הקריבום. ♦ |

| | | |
|---|---|---|
| A | 5 | ויקח משה חצי הדם מלמד שנחלק הדם מאיליו. ♦ |
| C/B | | וישם באגנות מלמד שהעולה טעונה כלי ♦ אין לי אלא |
| D | | עולת סיני. לדורות מנין ♦ ת"ל עלת תמיד העשויה בהר |
| | | סיני (במ' כח ו) מקיש עולת תמיד לעולת סיני מה |
| | | עולת סיני טעונה כלי אף עולת דורות טעונה כלי. ♦ אין |
| E | | לי אלא עולה חטאת ואשם ושלמים מנין ♦ ת"ל זאת |
| F | | התורה לעולה למנחה ולחטאת ולאשם ולמלואים ולזבח |
| | | השלמים (ויק' ז לז) תורה אחת לכולן. ♦ |

LXXXII:II

| | | |
|---|---|---|
| B/A | 1 | ויקח ספר הברית ויקרא באזני העם ♦ מתחלת |
| C | | הספר ועד כאן. ♦ ויאמרו כל אשר דבר ה' נעשה ונשמע ♦ |
| D | | לפי שהקדימו בתחלה עשייה אמ' להן משה וכי |
| | | אפשר לעשייה בלא שמיעה שמיעה מביאה לידי |

we will [soon] hear! This teaches that they accepted upon themselves both doing and hearing [the commandments] before the [actual] giving of the Torah.

E.  And thus Scripture says, "You devoted your ears to Me. You do not ask for burnt offering and sin offering. Then I said: 'See, I will bring a scroll written by Me!'" (Ps. 40:7–8).

2.  A.  "Then Moses ascended" (Exod. 24:9): Moses was a group in himself.

B.  "... and Aaron" (Exod. 24:9): Aaron was a group in himself.

C.  "... Nadab and Abihu, and seventy elders of Israel" (Exod. 24:9): Each one was a group in itself.

D.  One might think that even Nadab, Abihu, and the 70 elders ascended.

E.  Scripture states, [however,] "... Nadab, Abihu, and seventy elders of Israel, and they saw" (Exod. 24:9–10), [meaning,] they saw, but they did not ascend.

F.  Scripture says here, "and they saw" (Exod. 24:10), and Scripture says above, "... and he saw the place from afar" (Gen. 22:4).

3.  A.  "And they saw the God of Israel" (Exod. 24:10):

B.  This teaches that their eyes feasted on the splendor of the *Shekhinah*.

C.  "... under His feet" (Exod. 24:10): This teaches that they became emboldened, and likened the heavenly beings to the earthly beings.

D.  "... the likeness of a pavement of sapphire" (Exod. 24:10): And [Scripture says] farther on, "... they gleamed like sapphire" (Ezek. 1:16). Just as farther on [it refers to] a wheel, so too here [does it refer to] a wheel.

E.  One might think this was actually a pavement of sapphire.

F.  Scripture states, [however,] "... the likeness" (Exod. 24:10), and farther ahead Scripture says, "... for the rims of all four were covered all over with eyes" (Ezek. 1:18).

G.  "... like the very sky for purity" (Exod. 24:10):

H.  One might think it was actually the purity of the heavenly firmament.

I.  Scripture states, [however,] "... like" (Exod. 24:10). This teaches that [Scripture] speaks in a way that the ear is able to comprehend.

*Chapter Eighty-Three*

(Textual Source: Midrash ha-Gadol)

LXXXIII:I

1.  A.  "When they enter the Tent of Meeting (they shall wash with water, that they may not die. Or when they approach the altar to serve, to turn into smoke an offering by fire to the Lord, they shall wash their hands and feet, that they may not die)" (Exod. 30:20–21):

B.  Why does Scripture state, "Or when they approach the altar" (Exod. 30:20)?

C.  If Scripture [only said, "When they enter the Tent of Meeting,"] I would say one would be liable whether he enters [unwashed] for the purpose of sacrificial worship or whether not for the sake of sacrificial worship.

D.  Scripture states, [therefore,] "Or when they approach the altar to serve" (Exod. 30:20), [meaning,] just as below [it is for the sake of] sacrificial worship, so too here [it is for the sake of] sacrificial worship.

E.  Then let it [only] say, "Or when they approach" (Exod. 30:20)! Why does Scripture state,

עשייה חזרו ואמרו נעשה ונשמע נעשה מה שנשמע E
מלמד שקיבלו עליהם עשייה ושמיעה קודם מתן
תורה ♦ וכן הוא אומר אזנים כרית לי עולה וחטאה לא
שאלת אז אמרת<י> הנה באתי במגלת ספר כתוב
עלי (תה' מ ז - ח). ♦

ויעל משה מחצה בפני עצמו. ♦ ואהרן אהרן מחצה B/A 2
בפני עצמו. ♦ נדב ואביהוא ושבעים מזקני ישראל כל C
אחד מחצה בפני עצמו. ♦ יכול אף נדב ואביהוא ושבעים D
זקנים עלו ♦ ת"ל נדב ואביהוא ושבעים מזקני ישראל E
ויראו ראו ולא עלו. ♦ ויראו נאמר כן ויראו ולהלן הוא F
אומר וירא את המקום מרחוק (בר' כב ד) מה להלן
מרחוק אף כאן מרחוק. ♦

ויראו את אלקי ישראל ♦ מלמד שניזונו עיניהן מזיו B/A 3
השכינה. ♦ ותחת רגליו מלמד שהגיסו דעתן והשו C
עליונים לתחתונים. ♦ לבנת הספיר ולהלן כעין תרשיש D
(יחז' א טז) מה להלן אופן אף כאן אופן. ♦ יכול לבנת E
ספיר ממש ♦ ת"ל כמעשה ולהלן הוא אומר מלאות F
עינים סביב לארבעתן (יחז' א יח). ♦ וכעצם השמים G
לטהר ♦ כטהרו שלרקיע יכול ממש ♦ ת"ל וכעצם מלמד I/H
שמשמיעין את האוזן מה שיכולה לשמוע. ♦

LXXXIII:I

יאמר בבואם אל אהל מועד ♦ מה ת"ל או בגשתם B/A 1
אל המזבח ♦ אלו כן הייתי אומר בין נכנס לעבודה בין C
שלא לעבודה חייב ♦ ת"ל או בגשתם אל המזבח לשרת D
מה להלן עבודה אף כאן עבודה ♦ אלא מעתה יאמר E

"When they enter" (Exod. 30:20)?

F. If [Scripture only said, "Or when they approach the altar,"] I would say [entering] for the sake of turning an offering into smoke requires sanctification, but all other [forms of] sacrificial worship do not require sanctification.

G. Thus, Scripture says [both] "When they enter" and "When they approach" (Exod. 30:20).

2.  A. "It shall be a law for all time for them, (for him and his offspring, throughout the ages)" (Exod. 30:21):

B. It is a law from He who spoke, and the world came into being!

C. Scripture says here, "a law for all time" (Exod. 30:21), and Scripture says above, "a law for all time for him and for his offspring to come" (Exod. 28:43). Just as above profanes the sacrificial service, so too here profanes the sacrificial service.

D. "... for him and his offspring" (Exod. 28:43):

E. The matter [in Exod. 28:43] is related to Aaron and his offspring, for which they would be liable for death. Excluded is consecration of the High Priest on the Day of Atonement, which does not apply to Aaron and his offspring.

3.  A. "With it anoint the Tent of Meeting" (Exod. 30:26):

B. This teaches that all of the [sacrificial] utensils are only consecrated through anointing.

C. And thus Scripture states, "... he anointed and consecrated them" (Num. 7:1).

D. Or one might think that all utensils of [the subsequent] generations require anointing.

E. Scripture states, [however,] "(They shall take all the service vessels) with which the service in the sanctuary is performed" (Num. 4:12).

F. For [sacrificial] service alone are they consecrated.

4.  A. "... and you must not make anything like it" (Exod. 30:32):

B. Behold, this is the warning! How does one know from Scripture about the punishment?

C. Scripture states, "Whoever compounds its like ... shall be cut off" (Exod. 30:33):

D. But one might think one would be liable even if one [made it] for practice.

E. When it states in Scripture, [however,] "Whoever makes any like it, to smell of it, shall be cut off" (Exod. 30:37), [this means that] just as below [in Exod. 30:37 one is liable] only if he intends to smell of it, so too here [in Exod. 30:32 is one liable] only if he intends to smell of it.

F. Excluded is the one who makes [it] for practice or to sell to others.

5.  A. "... shall be cut off from his kin" (Exod. 30:32):

B. But his kin remain in peace.

ובגשתם מה ת״ל בבואם • אלו כן הייתי אומר F

להקטרה טעון קידוש לשאר עבודות אינו טעון

קידוש • לכך נאמר בבאם ובגשתם. • G

והיתה להם חק עולם • חק הוא ממי שאמר והיה B/A 2

העולם. • נאמר כן חק עולם ונאמר להלן חקת עולם לו C

ולזרעו אחריו (שמ׳ כח מג) מה להלן מחלל עבודה אף

כאן מחלל עבודה. • לו ולזרעו • דבר השווה באהרן E/D

ובזרעו חייבין עליו מיתה יצא קידוש כהן גדול ביום

הכפורים שאינו נוהג באהרן ובזרעו. •

ומשחת בו את אהל מועד • מלמד שאין כל הכלים B/A 3

מתקדשין אלא במשיחה • וכן הוא אומר וימשחם C

ויקדש אותם (במ׳ ז א). • או יכול יהוא כל הכלים D

טעונין משיחה לדורות • ת״ל אשר ישרתו בם בקדש E

(במ׳ ד יב) • בשירות בלבד הן מתקדשין. • F

לא תעשו כמוהו • הרי זה באזהרה עונש מנין • ת״ל C/B/A 4

איש אשר ירקח כמוהו ונכרת • או יכול אפלו עשה D

להתלמד יהא חייב • כשהוא אומר בקטרת איש אשר E

יעשה כמוה להריח בה ונכרת (פל״ח) מה להלן עד

שיתכוין להריח אף כאן עד שיתכוין להריח • יצא F

העושה להתלמד או למכור לאחרים. • ונכרת מעמיו A 5

ועמיו בשלום. • B

# Tractate Shabbata

*Chapter Eighty-Four*

(Textual Source: Midrash ha-Gadol)

LXXXIV:I

1.    A.    "And the Lord said to Moses: Speak to the Israelite people (and say: Nevertheless, you must keep My sabbaths, for this is a sign between Me and you throughout the ages, that you may know that I the Lord have consecrated you)" (Exod. 31:12–13):[1]

        B.    [Meaning,] you [should speak], and not through a messenger or agent!

2.    A.    "Whoever does work on it (shall be put to death)" (Exod. 31:14):[2]

        B.    As long as he does a complete task.

        C.    For I might assume that he who wrote one letter in the morning [on *Shabbat*] and one letter at dusk, or who wove one thread in the morning and wove one at dusk, would be liable.

        D.    Scripture states, [however,] "Whoever does work on it" (Exod. 31:15), [meaning,] as long as he does a complete task.

[222]

3.    A.    "... shall be cut off" (Exod. 31:14):

        B.    Why is this said? Because when Scripture says, "He who profanes it shall be put to death" (Exod. 31:14), I only know about the one who transgresses on purpose with the advance warning [against doing so] of witnesses. How does one know from Scripture about the one who transgresses on purpose alone?

        C.    Scripture says, "... shall be cut off" (Exod. 31:14), in order to include the one who transgresses on purpose alone.

4.    A.    "... shall be cut off" (Exod. 31:14):

        B.    Cutting off only means separation.

5.    A.    "'... that person' (Exod. 31:14):

        B.    "The one who transgresses on purpose."—The words of R. Akiva.

6.    A.    "... from among his kin" (Exod. 31:14):

        B.    But his kin remain in peace.

---

[1] Compare 1.A–B with *Mekhilta de-Rabbi Ishmael*, Shabbata (H/R, 340:1; Laut., vol. 3, 197:1–2; Neus., LXXXI:I:1.A–C).

[2] Compare 2.A–D with *Mekhilta de-Rabbi Ishmael*, Shabbata (H/R, 342:7–11; Laut., vol. 3, 201:65–70; Neus., LXXXI:I:10.A–H).

# מסכתא דשבתא

7.  A.  "(Six days may work be done), but on the seventh day there shall be a sabbath of complete rest, holy to the Lord" (Exod. 31:15):[3]

    B.  Why is this said? Because when Scripture says, "These are the set times of the Lord ... which you shall declare at its appointed times"[4] (Lev. 23:4), one might think that just as [the responsibility to declare the beginning] of festivals is transmitted to the court,[5] so too should [the responsibility to declare the beginning] of *Shabbat* be transmitted to the court.

    C.  Scripture states, [however,] "... but on the seventh day there shall be a sabbath of complete rest, holy to the Lord" (Exod. 31:15), [meaning, the beginning of] *Shabbat* is transmitted to God, and [the beginning of] *Shabbat* is not transmitted to the court.

    D.  And thus Scripture says, "... it shall be a sabbath of the Lord throughout your settlements" (Lev. 23:3).

8.  A.  "... whoever does work on the sabbath day (shall be put to death)" (Exod. 31:15):

    B.  Even the work of the Tabernacle.

9.  A.  "... shall be put to death" (Exod. 31:15):

    B.  I might assume by any [means] of death.

    C.  Scripture states, [however,] "Then the Lord said to Moses: The man shall be put to death. (The whole community) shall pelt him with stones (outside the camp)" (Num. 16:35).

    D.  You should say it is by stoning!

*Chapter Eighty-Five*

(Textual Source: Midrash ha-Gadol)

LXXXV:I

1.  A.  "Beware of making a covenant with the inhabitants of the land (against which you are advancing, lest they be a snare in your midst)" (Exod. 34:12):

    B.  Behold this is a warning not to make a covenant with idolaters.

    C.  "You must tear down their altars" (Exod. 34:13):

    D.  Behold, this is a positive commandment[6] to destroy idolatry, anyone who serves it, and anything done on its behalf.

2.  A.  "For you must not worship[7] any other god, (because the Lord, whose name is Impassioned, is an impassioned God)" (Exod. 34:14):

    B.  This assigns liability for bowing down to it, even if this is not the [normal] way of worshiping it.

3.  A.  "You shall not make molten gods for yourselves" (Exod. 34:17):

    B.  Thus, if one eats of their sacrifices, he will marry from among their daughters, and they will lead him astray so that he will worship idols.

4.  A.  "You shall not make ... for yourselves" (Exod. 34:17):

    B.  Even if only for adornment.

---

[3] Compare 7.A–D with *Mekhilta de-Rabbi Ishmael*, Shabbata (H/R, 343:4–7; Laut., vol. 3, 203:90–96; Neus., LXXXI:I:18.A–G).

[4] *Midrash ha-Gadol* here differs slightly from the biblical text: "These are the set times of the Lord ... which you shall declare *as sacred occasions.*"

| | | |
|---|---|---|
| וביום השביעי שבת שבתון קדש לה׳ ♦ למה נאמר | B/A | 7 |
| לפי שהוא אומר אלה מועדי ה׳ אשר תקראו אותם | | |
| מקראי קדש (ויק׳ כג ד) ‹יכול› כשם שמועדות | | |
| מסורין לבית דין כך תהא שבת מסורה לבית דין ♦ ת״ל | C | |
| ביום השביעי שבת שבתון קדש לה׳ לשם שבת | | |
| מסורה ואין שבת מסורה לבית דין ♦ כך הוא אומר | D | |
| שבת הוא לה׳ בכל מושבותיכם. ♦ כל העושה מלאכה | A | 8 |
| ביום השבת ♦ אפילו מלאכת המשכן. ♦ מות יומת ♦ שומע | B/A 9 | B |
| אני בכל מיתה ♦ ת״ל ויאמר ה׳ אל משה מות יומת | C | |
| האיש רגום אותו באבנים (במ׳ טו לה) ♦ הוי אומר | D | |
| בסקילה. ♦ | | |

| | | |
|---|---|---|
| | | LXXXV:I |
| השמר לך פן תכרת ברית ליושב הארץ ♦ ‹הרי› זו | B/A | 1 |
| אזהרה שלא לכרות ברית לעובדי ע״ז. ♦ כי את | C | |
| מזבחותם תתצון ♦ הרי זו מצות עשה לאבד ע״ז וכל | D | |
| משמשיה וכל הנעשה בשבילה. ♦ | | |
| כי לא תשתחוה לאל אחר ♦ לחייב על ההשתחוייה | B/A | 2 |
| אפילו שלא דרך עבודתה בכך. ♦ אלהי מסכה לא תעשה | A | 3 |
| לך ♦ הא אם אכל מזבחם הוא נושא מבנותם והן | B | |
| מטעין אותו והוא עושה ע״ז. ♦ לא תעשה לך ♦ ואפלו | B/A | 4 |
| לנואי. ♦ | | |

---

5 See m. Rosh Hashanah 2:7–9 and 3:1.
6 I.e., a commandment that prescribes behavior.
7 Or: "bow down to."

LXXXV:II

1.    A.    "(You shall observe the Feast of Unleavened Bread—eating unleavened bread for seven days, as I have commanded you)—at the set time of the month of Abib, (for in the month of Abib you went forth from Egypt)" (Exod. 34:18):

      B.    One might think that whenever there is spring[8] you must observe Passover, but if not, you do not observe Passover.

      C.    Scripture states, [however,] "You shall observe the Feast of Unleavened Bread" (Exod. 34:18), [meaning,] whether you have spring or if you don't have spring.

      D.    If so, why does Scripture state, "... at the set time of the month of Abib" (Exod. 34:18)?

      E.    Scripture marks it as a sign for it.

2.    A.    "Every first issue of the womb is Mine, (from all your livestock that drop a male as firstling, whether cattle or sheep)" (Exod. 34:19):

      B.    One might think even the female.

      C.    Scripture states, [however,] "... from all your livestock that drop a male as firstling" (Exod. 34:19).

      D.    Just as the first-born of the cattle [that is God's] is male, so too the human first-born is male, and not female.

3.    A.    R. Joshua ben Korḥa says, "'Every first issue of the womb is Mine' (Exod. 34:19):

      B.    "Behold, this is the general principle. One might think [this is even the case of cattle that] belong to others.

      C.    "Scripture states, [however,] '... your livestock' (Exod. 34:19).

      D.    "One might think even the female [offspring].

      E.    "Scripture states, [however,] '... drop a male' (Exod. 34:19).

      F.    "One might think even [the firstling] of a beast of chase.

      G.    "Scripture states, [however,] '... as firstling, whether cattle or sheep' (Exod. 34:19).

      H.    "This is a general principle that needs specification."

4.    A.    "But the firstling of an ass you shall redeem (with a sheep. If you do not redeem it, you must break its neck)" (Exod. 34:20):

      B.    [Scripture states] "the firstling of an ass" two times,[9] [meaning that the law applies] only if the mother is an ass and the offspring is an ass.[10]

5.    A.    "... you shall redeem with a sheep" (Exod. 34:20):

      B.    A sheep in any instance—whether male or female, whether unblemished or blemished, whether minor or adult.

6.    A.    "... with a sheep" (Exod. 34:20):[11]

[223]    B.    Not with a calf, not with a beast of chase, not with a fatally ill animal, and not with a mixed breed, and not with a *koy*.[12]

---

[8] The word "Abib" means spring.

[9] Exod. 13:13 and 30:20.

[10] Compare 4.B with m. Bekhorot 1:2.

[11] Compare 6.A–B with m. Bekhorot 1:5.

[12] An unspecified type of wild, crossbred species referred to frequently in Rabbinic literature.

| | | |
|---:|---:|---:|
| B/A | 1 | למועד חדש האביב ◆ יכול בזמן שיש אביב אתה |
| C | | עושה פסח ואם לאו אין אתה עושה פסח ◆ ת״ל את חג |
| | | המצות תשמר בין שיש לך אביב בין שאין לך אביב ◆ |
| E/D | | אם כן מה ת״ל למועד חדש האביב ◆ עשאו הכתוב |
| | | סימן לו. ◆ |
| C/B/A | 2 | כל פטר רחם לי ◆ יכול אפלו נקבה ת״ל ◆ וכל מקנך |
| D | | תזכר ◆ מה בכור בהמה זכר ולא נקבה אף בכור אדם |
| A | 3 | זכר ולא נקבה. ◆ ר׳ יהושע בן קרחה אומר כל פטר |
| C/B | | רחם לי ◆ הרי זה כלל יכול אף שלאחרים ◆ ת״ל מקנך ◆ |
| G/F/E/D | | יכול אף שלנקבה ◆ ת״ל תזכר ◆ יכול אף שלחיה ◆ ת״ל פטר |
| H | | שור ושה ◆ זה הוא כלל שצריך לפרט. ◆ |
| B/A | 4 | ופטר חמור תפדה ◆ בשה ופטר חמור שני פעמים |
| B/A | 5 | עד שיהיה היולד חמור והנולד חמור. ◆ תפדה בשה ◆ שה |
| | | מכל מקום בין זכרים בין נקבות בין תמימים בין |
| B/A | 6 | בעלי מומין בין קטנים בין גדולים. ◆ ד״א בשה ◆ לא |
| | | בעגל ולא בחיה ולא בטריפה ולא בכלאים ולא בכוי ◆ |

C.    And not with animals that should be consecrated [as firstlings] but are unsuitable.[13] For Scripture speaks of them along with the gazelle and ram,[14] [meaning that] just as one does not redeem with them, so too does one not redeem with animals that should be consecrated but are unsuitable.

7.    A.    "... you shall redeem with a sheep. If you do not redeem it, you must break its neck" (Exod. 34:20):

B.    The commandment of redemption precedes the commandment of breaking the neck.

8.    A.    "... you must break its neck" (Exod. 34:20):

B.    Scripture speaks here of breaking the neck, and Scripture speaks farther ahead of breaking the neck (Deut. 21:4). Just as ahead is with a hatchet and from behind, and [the corpse] is prohibited [from being used] for benefit, so too here is with a hatchet and from behind, and [the corpse] is prohibited [from being used] for benefit.

9.    A.    "And you must redeem every first-born among your sons. None shall appear before Me empty-handed" (Exod. 34:20):

B.    Should it be that one has before him [the obligation to fulfill both] the redemption of his son and the pilgrimage burnt offering, but he doesn't have enough [money] for both, the redemption of his son precedes.

C.    As it says in Scripture, "And you must redeem every first-born among your sons" and then "None shall appear before Me empty-handed" (Exod. 34:20).

10.    A.    "(Six days you shall work, but on the seventh day you shall cease from labor.) You shall cease from labor even at plowing time and harvest time" (Exod. 34:21):[15]

B.    R. Shimon ben Eliezer says, "Since Scripture says, 'You shall cease from labor even at plowing time and harvest time' (Exod. 34:21), you have a commanded harvest that overrides [the prohibition against harvesting] on *Shabbat*.

C.    "And which is this? This is the harvest of the *omer*."[16]

D.    R. Ishmael says, "One might think that the plowing of the *omer* should [also] override *Shabbat*.

E.    "Scripture states, [however,] '... at plowing time and harvest time' (Exod. 34:21). Harvest time [overrides *Shabbat*], because its time is fixed. Plowing time is excluded, because its time is not fixed."

F.    R. Judah says, "'You shall cease from labor even at plowing time and harvest time' (Exod. 34:21): [This refers to] a plowing time whose harvest time is prohibited—this is the plowing time of the sixth year that extends into the sabbatical year—and a harvest time whose plowing time is prohibited—this is the harvest time of the sabbatical year that extends into the following year."

G.    R. Shimon says, "You rest from the plowing time at the time of harvesting, and you rest from harvest time at the time of plowing."

11.    A.    "You shall observe the Feast of Weeks" (Exod. 34:22):[17]

B.    This is the Feast of Pentecost.

---

[13] Because of a blemish. See Deut. 15:19–23.

[14] See Deut. 15:22.

[15] Compare 10.A–G with m. Shebiit 1:4.

[16] The *omer* refers to the flour offering made from the initial barley harvest, as commanded in Lev. 23:10. Only upon offering the *omer* could the harvest be used. The harvesting of the *omer* superseded the prohibition against such work on *Shabbat*. See m. Menahot 10:1ff.

[17] Compare 11.A–E with parallel above at LXXIX:IV:3.A–K.

| | | |
|---|---|---|
| ולא בפסולי המוקדשין שהרי נאמר בהן כצבי וכאיל | C | |
| מה צבי ואיל אין פודין בהן אף פסולי המוקדשין אין | | |
| פודין בהן. ◆ תפדה בשה ואם לא תפדה וערפתו ◆ מצות | B/A | 7 |
| פדייה קודמת למצות עריפה. ◆ וערפתו ◆ נאמ' כאן | B/A | 8 |
| עריפה ונאמ' להלן עריפה (דב' כא ד) מה להלן | | |
| בקפיס ומאחוריו ואסור בהנאה אף כאן בקפיס | | |
| ומאחוריו ואסור בהנאה. ◆ כל בכור בניך תפדה ולא | A | 9 |
| יראו פני ריקם ◆ הרי שהיה לפניו פדיון בנו ועולת | B | |
| ראייה ואין לו כדי לזה וכדי לזה פדיון בנו קודם ◆ שנא' | C | |
| כל בכור בניך תפדה ואחר כך ולא יראו פני ריקם. ◆ | | |
| בחריש ובקציר תשבת ◆ ר' שמעון בן אלעזר אומר | B/A | 10 |
| מכלל שנא' בחריש ובקציר תשבת יש לך קציר מצוה | | |
| שהוא דוחה את השבת ◆ והיזה זה זה קציר העומר. ◆ ר' | D/C | |
| ישמעאל אומר יכול תהא חרישת העומר דוחה את | | |
| השבת ◆ ת"ל בחריש ובקציר קציר שזמנו קבוע יצא | E | |
| חריש שאין לו זמן קבוע. ◆ ר' יהודה אומר בחריש | F | |
| ובקציר תשבת חריש שקצירו אסור זה חריש שלערב | | |
| שביעית וקציר שחרישו אסור זה קציר שלמוצאי | | |
| שביעית. ◆ ור' שמעון אומר שבות מן החריש בשעת | G | |
| קציר ושבות מן הקציר בשעת חריש. ◆ | | |
| וחג שבועות תעשה לך ◆ זה חג העצרת. ◆ | B/A | 11 |

C. "... and the Feast of Ingathering at the turn of the year" (Exod. 34:22):

D. And above Scripture says, "... (and the Feast of Ingathering) at the end of the year" (Exod. 23:16).

E. Which is the festival that has an ingathering, a solstice, and the year ends on it? This is the autumnal equinox!

12.  A. "Three times a year" (Exod. 34:23):[18]

B. "Times" only means [set] times.

C. "... all your males shall appear" (Exod. 34:23):

D. [Scripture says this in order] to include the minor.

E. Based on this you say: Any child who can hold the hand of his father and go up from Jerusalem to the Temple Mount is obligated to go up.[19]

F. "... before the Sovereign Lord" (Exod. 34:23): [God says,] "I am Lord over all the creatures of the world."[20]

G. One might think, therefore, that You are, indeed, also [God] over [all of] them. Scripture states, [however,] "... the God of Israel" (Exod. 34:23).

H. One might think [He is God] only over you. Scripture states, [however,] "... before the Sovereign Lord" (Exod. 34:23).

I. How is it so?

J. [God is saying,] "I am God over all the creatures of the world, but My name rests [specially] on you!"

13.  A. "I will drive out nations from your path (and enlarge your territory). No one will covet your land (when you go up to appear before the Lord your God three times a year)" (Exod. 34:24):

B. The Torah speaks against the [evil] inclination, lest Israel should say, "How can we leave our land, and our houses, and our fields, and our vineyards, and go up for a festival, lest others come and dwell in our places?"

C. Therefore the Holy One, blessed be He, pledges to them: "No one will covet your land when you go up to appear" (Exod. 34:24).

D. And not only this, but also that no one of those who would injure you has authority.

E. It once occurred that someone left his lamb, and came [back] and found lions arranged [dead] around it. And it once occurred that someone left his henhouse, and came [back] and found cats lying torn in front of it. This upholds [this meaning of the verse] "No one will covet your land" (Exod. 34:24).

14.  A. "The choice first fruits of your soil (you shall bring to the house of the Lord your God)" (Exod. 34:26):[21]

[224]  B. Scripture states here, "first," and Scripture states farther ahead, "first" (Deut. 26:2). Just as ahead [means] the seven species so too, here, the seven species.

C. "... of your soil" (Exod. 34:26): This excludes the arbor and the robber.[22]

---

[18] Compare 12.A–E with parallel above at LXXIX:V:3.A–E.
[19] Compare 12.E with Ḥagigah 1:1.
[20] Compare 12.F–J with parallel above at LII:I:5.A–H.
[21] Compare 14.A–E with parallel above at LXXX:I:2.A–3.B.
[22] Compare 14.C with m. Bikkurin 1:2.

| | |
|---|---|
| D/C | וחג האסיף תקופת השנה ◆ ולהלן הוא אומר בצאת השנה |
| E | (שמ׳ כג טז) ◆ איזה הוא חג שיש בו אסיף ותקופה ושנה |
| | יוצאה בו הוי אומר זה תשרי. ◆ |
| 12 C/B/A | שלש פעמים בשנה. ◆ אין פעמים אלא זמנים. ◆ יראה |
| E/D | כל זכורך ◆ לרבות את הקטן ◆ מכאן אמרו כל קטן |
| | שיכול לאחוז בידו שלאביו ולעלות מירושלים להר |
| | הבית אביו חייב להעלותו. ◆ את פני האדון ה׳ אדון אני |
| F | על כל באי העולם ◆ יכול אף אתה כיוצא בהן ת״ל |
| G | אלקי ישראל. ◆ יכול עליך בלבד ת״ל את פני האדון ה׳ ◆ |
| H | הא כיצד ◆ אלוה אני על כל באי העולם ושמי יחול |
| J/I | עליך. ◆ |
| 13 A | כי אוריש גוים מפניך ולא יחמד איש את ארצך ◆ |
| B | דברה תורה כנגד היצר שלא יאמרו ישראל היאך אנו |
| | מניחין ארצינו ובתינו ושדותינו וכרמינו ועולין לרגל |
| C | שמא יבואו אחרים וישבו במקומותינו ◆ לפיכך ערב |
| | להן הקב״ה ולא יחמד איש את ארצך בעלותך לראות. ◆ |
| D | ולא עוד אלא שאין רשות לאחד מן המזיקין להזיק |
| E | אתכם ◆ ומעשה באחד שהניח את כריו ובא ומצא |
| | אריות סובבין אותו ומעשה באחד שהניח בית |
| | תורנגלין ובא ומצא חתולות מקורעות בפניהם לקיים |
| | ולא יחמד איש את ארצך. ◆ |
| 14 B/A | ראשית בכורי אדמתך ◆ נאמר כאן ראשית ונאמר |
| | להלן ראשית (דב׳ כו ב) מה להלן שבעת מינים אף |
| C | כאן שבעת מינים. ◆ אדמתך פרט לעריס ולגזלן. ◆ |

D.   "... you shall bring to the house of the Lord your God" (Exod. 34:26):

E.   This teaches that he is liable for attending to bringing them until he brings them to the Temple.

15.   A.   "You shall not boil a kid in its mother's milk" (Exod. 34:26):

B.   Behold, this is brought [here] to prohibit boiling it; all the more so, eating it!

C.   I only know about a kid in its mother's milk. How does one know from Scripture about the meat of an ox in its mother's milk?

D.   Scripture states, "You shall not boil ... in milk" (Exod. 34:26).

*Chapter Eighty-Six*

(Textual Source: Midrash ha-Gadol)

LXXXVI:I

1.   A.   "(On six days work may be done, but on the seventh day you shall have a) sabbath of complete rest, (holy) to the Lord" (Exod. 35:2):[23]

B.   For [the responsibility for declaring the beginning of *Shabbat*] is transmitted to God, and not to the court.

2.   A.   "Whoever does any work *on it* shall be put to death" (Exod. 35:2):[24]

B.   But not [for work done] on it and on its neighboring day.

C.   Thus, if one wrote two letters [of the alphabet]—one on *Shabbat* and one on the Day of Atonement—or if one sewed two threads—one on *Shabbat* and one on the Day of Atonement, I might assume he would be liable for each [letter] in and of itself.

D.   Scripture states, [however,] "Whoever does any work *on it* shall be put to death" (Exod. 35:2), [meaning, not for work done] on it and its neighboring day.

E.   Similar to this: If [the Day] of Atonement [was on the day] before *Shabbat,* and one did work at twilight [between the two], one might think he would be liable.

F.   Scripture states, [however,] "Whoever does any work *on it*" (Exod. 35:2), [meaning,] as long as the day is appointed.

3.   A.   I only know [from Exod. 35:2] about the prohibition of primary work and secondary work. How does one know from Scripture about the prohibition of actions unbecoming to the tone of the day?

B.   Scripture states, "... any work" (Exod. 35:2).

C.   One might think that he would be liable for a sin offering for violating the prohibition of actions unbecoming to the tone of the day.

D.   Scripture states, [however,] "... work" (Exod. 35:2), [meaning,] one is liable for specific [types] of work, and one is not liable for the prohibition of actions unbecoming to the tone of the day.

E.   How does one know from Scripture that buying and selling and loaning and placing things in deposit are labeled as work?

F.   Scripture states, "... that the one has not laid hands on the property[25] of the other" (Exod. 22:10).

[23] Compare 1.A–B with parallel above at LXXXIV:I:7.A–D.
[24] Compare 2.A–F with *Mekhilta de-Rabbi Ishmael,* Shabbata (H/R, 346:4–6; Laut., vol. 3, 207:29–33; Neus., LXXXII:I:4.A–E).

| | | |
|---|---|---|
| E/D | | תביא בית ה׳ אלקיך • מלמד שהוא חייב להטפל בהן עד |
| B/A | 15 | שיביאם לבית הבחירה. • לא תבשל גדי בחלב אמו • הרי |
| C | | זה בא לאיסור בישולו קל וחומר אכילתו. • אין לי אלא |
| D | | גדי וחלב אם בשר שור בחלב מנין • ת״ל לא תבשל |
| | | בחלב. • |

| | | |
|---|---|---|
| B/A | 1 | שבת שבתון לה׳ • שהיא אסורה לשם לא לבית |
| C/B/A | 2 | דין. • כל העושה בו מלאכה יומת • לא בו ובחבירו. • הרי |
| | | שכתב שתי אותות אחת בשבת ואחת ביום הכפורים |
| | | וארג שני חוטין אחד בשבת ואחד ביום הכפורים |
| | | שומע אני יהא חייב (על זה בפני עצמו ועל זה בפני |
| D | | עצמו) • ת״ל כל העושה בו מלאכה יומת לא בו ובחבירו. • |
| E | | כיוצא בו שבת וכפור לפניו ועשה מלאכה בין |
| F | | השמשות יכול יהא חייב • ת״ל כל העושה בו עד |
| A | 3 | שיקבע היום. • אין לי אלא מלאכות ותולדות שהן |
| C/B | | אסורין מנין לאיסור שבות • ת״ל כל מלאכה • יכול יהוא |
| D | | חייבין חטאת על איסור שבות • ת״ל מלאכה מלאכה |
| | | המיוחדת חייבין עליה ואין חייבין על איסור שבות. • |
| E | | מנין למקח וממכר והלואה ופקדונות שנקראו מלאכה |
| F | | ת״ל אם לא שלח ידו במלאכת רעהו (שמ׳ כב י). • |

---

[25] Hebrew: m'lekhet—מלאכת, derived from the same word for work in Exod. 35:2, melakhah —מלאכה.

G. How does one know from Scripture that legal judgments, legal claims and appeals, and all work of a court, are labeled as work?

H. Scripture states, "Chenaniah and his sons were over Israel as clerks and magistrates for affairs outside [the sanctuary]" (1 Chron. 26:29).

I. How does one know from Scripture that marriages and divorces are labeled as work?

J. Scripture states, "However, many people are involved, and it is the rainy season ... nor is this the work of a day or two" (Ezra 10:13).

K. How does one know from Scripture that accounting is labeled as work?

L. Scripture states, "... he came into the house to do his work" (Gen. 39:11).

G מנין לדינין ולטענות ולערעורין ולכל מעשה בית

H דין שנקראו מלאכה ◆ ת״ל כנניהו ובניו למלאכה

החיצונה על ישראל לשוטרים ולשופטים (דה״א כו

J/I כט). ◆ מנין לקידושין ולגטין שנקראו מלאכה ◆ ת״ל אבל

העם רב והעת גשמים והמלאכה לא ליום אחד ולא

L/K לשנים (עז׳ י יג). ◆ מנין לחשבונות שנקראו מלאכה ◆ ת״ל

ויבא הביתה לעשות מלאכתו (בר׳ לט יא). ◆

# Index of Scriptural Passages

# Index of Names

## A

Abba, 160
Abba Shaul, 130, 341
Abba Yudan of Zidon, 351
Abraham ha-Laḥmi, 2, 6, 8, 9
Agrippas Sabba, 241
Aḥa, 103
Akiva, 8, 18, 19, 21, 23, 34, 35,
    36, 41, 42, 44, 54, 68, 69, 73,
    74, 85, 101, 115, 116, 117,
    122, 130, 188, 218, 221, 226,
    228, 232, 244, 247, 259, 271,
    275, 286, 298, 300, 304, 347,
    348, 365, 369, 376
Avtalion, 102
Avtilas the Elder, 101

## B

Banyah, 101
Beit Hillel, 70, 331, 335
Beit Shammai, 19, 70, 334, 335
Ben Azzai, 76, 293, 297, 348, 354
Ben Bag Bag, 16, 17, 250

## E

Eliezer, 3, 5, 11, 22, 28, 42, 48,
    54, 58, 68, 69, 73, 100, 117,
    129, 160, 162, 167, 168, 176,
    177, 178, 180, 184, 185, 188,
    194, 195, 196, 199, 201, 216,
    218, 228, 253, 268, 271, 275,
    289, 298, 300, 301, 321
Eliezer b. Jacob, 72
Eliezer b. Judah ish Bartotha, 9
Eliezer ben Arach, 4, 259, 260
Eliezer ben Azariah, 21, 25, 102,
    226, 244, 267, 298
Eliezer ben Jacob, 263, 272, 275,
    279, 300, 354, 355, 357, 365

Eliezer ben Judah ish Bartotha,
    102
Eliezer ben Perata, 254
Eliezer ben Taddai, 122
Eliezer Ḥisma, 177, 183
Eliezer the Modiite, 8, 102, 159,
    161, 162, 163, 164, 165, 166,
    167, 169, 170, 172, 173, 174,
    176, 177, 178, 179, 180, 183,
    187, 188, 189, 190, 191, 194,
    195, 197, 198, 199, 201, 204,
    205, 206, 207, 208, 209, 232
Eliezer the son of R. Yosi ha-
    Galili, 171, 216, 218

## G

Gamliel, 124, 202, 203, 204, 241,
    351, 364

## H

Ḥalafta ish Kefar Ḥananiah, 256
Ḥananiah, 185
Ḥananiah ben Dosa, 206
Ḥananiah ben Gamliel, 211
Ḥananiah ben Nekhusa, 102
Ḥananiah ben Teradion, 256
Ḥananyah ben Ḥachinai, 19
Hillel the Elder, 22
Ḥiyya, 3
House of Hillel, 245, 368
House of Shammai, 245, 331, 368

## I

Ilai, 22
Isaac, 165
Ishmael, 23, 42, 61, 100, 130, 226,
    259, 261, 309, 332, 367, 379
Ishmael b. R. Yoḥanan, 302
Ishmael b. R. Yoḥanan ben
    Berukah, 162

Isi ben Akiva, 174
Isi ben Judah, 187
Isi ben Shammai, 128

## J

Jacob, 24
Jeremiah, 176
Joshua, 3, 6, 58, 100, 159, 161,
    162, 163, 164, 165, 166, 167,
    168, 169, 170, 172, 174, 176,
    177, 178, 179, 180, 183, 184,
    187, 188, 189, 190, 191, 194,
    195, 197, 198, 199, 201, 202,
    204, 205, 206, 207, 208, 209
Joshua b. Korḥa, 7, 76
Joshua ben Korḥa, 218, 233, 378
Josiah, 171, 178, 179, 182, 183
Judah, 3, 7, 10, 14, 16, 17, 22,
    24, 30, 32, 36, 64, 66, 71, 78,
    104, 107, 108, 111, 114, 132,
    179, 182, 221, 223, 233, 241,
    255, 256, 280, 283, 289, 300,
    306, 313, 329, 331, 379
Judah b. Ilai, 160
Judah ben Baba, 35, 301
Judah ben Beteira, 101, 243, 348
Judah ben Lakish, 213
Judah ish Kefar Akko, 204
Judah the Patriarch, 125, 234

## M

Meir, 10, 77, 87, 100, 102, 107,
    255, 271, 300, 313

## N

Nathan, 49, 83, 84, 102, 104, 107,
    113, 194, 211, 220, 278, 309,
    338
Nathan ben Joseph, 162, 184,
    363

# Index of Places